McDougal Littell

Pre-Algebra

$(x+3)^2$

$2x - 8 \leq 4x$

$V = \frac{1}{3}\pi r^2 h$

Larson   **Boswell**   **Kanold**   **Stiff**

McDougal Littell

A DIVISION OF HOUGHTON MIFFLIN COMPANY

Evanston, Illinois • Boston • Dallas

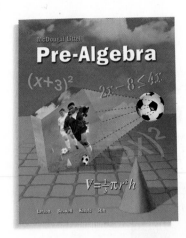

About Pre-Algebra

McDougal Littell Pre-Algebra will give you a strong foundation in algebra while also preparing you for future study of geometry, probability, and data analysis. The clearly written lessons make even difficult math concepts and methods understandable by providing numerous stepped-out examples. Each lesson's exercise set includes a wide variety of exercises, ranging from basic exercises that help you develop and practice skills to challenging exercises that involve logical reasoning and problem solving.

This book will also help you become better at taking notes and taking tests. Look for a notetaking strategy at the beginning of each chapter as well as helpful marginal notes throughout each chapter. The marginal notes give you support in keeping a notebook, studying math, reading algebra and geometry, doing homework, using technology, and reviewing for tests. Also look for instruction and practice that prepare you for taking standardized tests with questions in multiple choice, short response, and extended response formats. In all these ways—and many more—*McDougal Littell Pre-Algebra* puts you on the road to success in mathematics.

ISBN-13: 978-0-618-80076-6
ISBN-10: 0-618-80076-X   23456789–DJM–13 12 11 10 09 08

Internet Web Site: http://www.mcdougallittell.com

Ron Larson

Ron Larson is a professor of mathematics at Penn State University at Erie, where he has taught since receiving his Ph.D. in mathematics from the University of Colorado. Dr. Larson is well known as the author of a comprehensive program for mathematics that spans middle school, high school, and college courses. Dr. Larson's numerous professional activities keep him in constant touch with the needs of teachers and supervisors. He closely follows developments in mathematics standards and assessment.

Laurie Boswell

Laurie Boswell is the mathematics department chair at Profile Junior-Senior High School in Bethlehem, New Hampshire. A recipient of the Presidential Award for Excellence in Mathematics Teaching, she has also been a Tandy Technology Scholar. She serves on the National Council of Teachers of Mathematics Board of Directors. She speaks frequently on topics related to instructional strategies and course content.

Timothy Kanold

Timothy Kanold is the superintendent of Adlai E. Stevenson High School District 125 in Lincolnshire, Illinois, where he served as a teacher and the Director of Mathematics for 16 years. He has a Ph.D. from Loyola University Chicago. Dr. Kanold is a recipient of the Presidential Award for Excellence in Mathematics and Science Teaching and served on The Academy Services Committee for NCTM. He is a frequent speaker at mathematics meetings where he shares his in-depth knowledge of teaching and curriculum.

Lee Stiff

Lee Stiff is a professor of mathematics education in the College of Education of North Carolina State University at Raleigh. His extensive experience in mathematics education includes teaching at the middle school and high school levels. He has received the W. W. Rankin Award for Excellence in Mathematics Education, and was Fulbright Scholar to the Department of Mathematics of the University of Ghana. He served as President of the National Council of Teachers of Mathematics (2000–2002).

Advisers and Reviewers

Curriculum Advisers and Reviewers

Donna Foley
Curriculum Specialist for Math
Chelmsford Middle School
Chelmsford, MA

Barbara Nunn
Secondary Mathematics Specialist
Broward County Schools
Fort Lauderdale, FL

Wendy Loeb
Mathematics Teacher
Twin Groves Junior High School
Buffalo Grove, IL

Tom Scott
Resource Teacher
Duval County Public Schools
Jacksonville, FL

Teacher Panels

Florida Panel

Kathy Adams
Mathematics Teacher
Allapattah Middle School
Miami, FL

Micki Hawn
Mathematics Teacher
Pompano Beach Middle School
Pompano Beach, FL

Barbara Schober
Mathematics Department Chair
Okeeheelee Middle School
West Palm Beach, FL

Sue Carrico-Beddow
Mathematics Teacher
Bayonet Point Middle School
New Port Richey, FL

Pat Powell
Mathematics Department Chair
Stewart Middle School
Tampa, FL

Laurie St. Julien
Mathematics Teacher
Oak Grove Middle School
Clearwater, FL

Melissa Grabowski
Mathematics Teacher
Stone Middle School
Melbourne, FL

Kansas and Missouri Panel

Linda Cordes
Department Chair
Paul Robeson Middle School
Kansas City, MO

Rhonda Foote
Mathematics Department Chair
Maple Park Middle School
North Kansas City, MO

Jan Rase
Mathematics Teacher
Moreland Ridge Middle School
Blue Springs, MO

Linda Dodd
Mathematics Department Chair
Argentine Middle School
Kansas City, KS

Cas Kyle
District Math Curriculum Coordinator
Richard A. Warren Middle School
Leavenworth, KS

Dan Schoenemann
Mathematics Teacher
Raytown Middle School
Kansas City, MO

Melanie Dowell
Mathematics Teacher
Raytown South Middle School
Raytown, MO

Texas Panel

Judy Carlin
Mathematics Teacher
Brown Middle School
McAllen, TX

Judith Cody
Mathematics Teacher
Deady Middle School
Houston, TX

Lisa Hiracheta
Mathematics Teacher
Irons Junior High School
Lubbock, TX

Kay Neuse
Mathematics Teacher
Wilson Middle School
Plano, TX

Louise Nutzman
Mathematics Teacher
Sugar Land Middle School
Sugar Land, TX

Clarice Orise
Mathematics Teacher
Tafolla Middle School
San Antonio, TX

Wonda Webb
Mathematics Teacher
William H. Atwell Middle School and Law Academy
Dallas, TX

Karen Young
Mathematics Teacher
Murchison Elementary School
Pflugerville, TX

Teacher Reviewers

Debra Dean
Oberon Middle School
Arvada, CO

Linda Gojak
John Carroll University
University Heights, OH

Stephen Goodly
McDonough 35 Senior High School
New Orleans, LA

Debbie Gray
Carter G. Woodson Learning Academy
New Orleans, LA

Chris Kelly
Adlai Stevenson High School
Lincolnshire, IL

Donna Simpson Leak
Revere Elementary Accelerated School
Chicago, IL

Wendy Loeb
Twin Groves Junior High School
Buffalo Grove, IL

Nina McGibney
Jefferson County School District R-1
Golden, CO

Rick Nelson
Eastmont Junior High School
East Wenatchee, WA

Karen Tripoli
Lexington Public Schools
Lexington, MA

Variables, Expressions, *and* Integers

Internet Resources
CLASSZONE.COM
eEdition Plus Online
eWorkbook Plus Online
eTutorial Plus Online
State Test Practice
More Examples

Reading, Writing, and Notetaking

Student Help

Problem Solving

Pre-Course Assessment

Add integers to find a diver's position, pp. 29–30

Solving Equations

Use algebra to find dimensions of a llama pen, p. 75

Multi-Step Equations *and* Inequalities

Internet Resources
CLASSZONE.COM
eEdition Plus Online
eWorkbook Plus Online
eTutorial Plus Online
State Test Practice
More Examples

Reading, Writing, and Notetaking
Vocabulary, 118, 122, 127, 133, 140, 146, 151, 154
Reading Algebra, 121, 139
Writing, 119, 130, 135, 141, 153
Notetaking, 118, 132, 150

Student Help
Study Strategy, 131, 133, 139, 145
Homework Help, 123, 127, 134, 141, 146, 151
Tech Help, 136

Problem Solving
Guided Problem Solving, 122, 127, 140, 146, 151
Extended Problem Solving, 123, 147, 153
Challenge, 124, 129, 135, 142, 148, 152

UNIT 1 Assessment

Building Test-Taking Skills:
Multiple Choice Questions, 160
Practicing Test-Taking Skills, 162
Cumulative Practice, 164

Use an equation to find rafting costs, p. 123

CHAPTER

4

Factors, Fractions, *and* Exponents

Internet Resources
CLASSZONE.COM
eEdition Plus Online
eWorkbook Plus Online
eTutorial Plus Online
State Test Practice
More Examples

Reading, Writing, and Notetaking
Vocabulary, 170, 174, 179, 184, 189, 196, 201, 206, 210
Reading Algebra, 199, 204, 205
Writing, 171, 175, 181, 190, 197, 202, 207
Notetaking, 170, 173, 178, 195

Student Help
Study Strategy, 173, 175, 182, 188
Homework Help, 175, 179, 185, 190, 197, 202, 207
Tech Help, 209

Problem Solving
Guided Problem Solving, 179, 184, 201
Extended Problem Solving, 176, 180, 203, 208
Challenge, 176, 181, 186, 191, 198, 203, 208

Use fractions to compare snowboarding data, p. 188

Rational Numbers *and* Equations

Reading, Writing, and Notetaking
Vocabulary, 218, 222, 227, 233, 239, 245, 249, 255, 258
Reading Algebra, 220, 254
Writing, 223, 234, 241, 250, 257
Notetaking, 218, 221, 235

Student Help
Study Strategy, 221, 226, 232, 237, 243, 247
Homework Help, 222, 228, 234, 240, 245, 249, 256
Tech Help, 252

Problem Solving
Guided Problem Solving, 227, 233, 249
Extended Problem Solving, 223, 234, 240, 246
Challenge, 224, 229, 235, 241, 246, 251, 257
Focus on Problem Solving: Making a Plan, 264

Assessment

Multiply fractions to extend a recipe, p. 241

Ratio, Proportion, *and* Probability

Internet Resources
CLASSZONE.COM
eEdition Plus Online
eWorkbook Plus Online
eTutorial Plus Online
State Test Practice
More Examples

Reading, Writing, and Notetaking
Vocabulary, 268, 272, 277, 282, 290, 295, 302, 309, 315, 318
Reading Algebra, 275, 281, 300, 306, 308, 310
Reading Geometry, 288
Writing, 278, 283, 292, 310, 316
Notetaking, 268, 282, 290

Student Help
Study Strategy, 289, 294, 307, 314
Homework Help, 272, 278, 283, 291, 295, 302, 309, 315
Tech Help, 312
Student Reference: Basic Geometry Concepts, 285

Problem Solving
Guided Problem Solving, 272, 282, 295, 302, 309, 315
Extended Problem Solving, 273, 284, 292, 310
Challenge, 274, 279, 284, 292, 297, 304, 311, 317

Use a proportion to find how much an elephant eats, pp. 275, 277

Percents

Apply percents to chess, p. 332

Linear Functions

Reading, Writing, and Notetaking
Vocabulary, 384, 387, 394, 400, 407, 415, 422, 428, 433, 439, 442
Reading Algebra, 389, 412, 414, 436
Writing, 389, 395, 403, 407, 408, 417, 424, 430, 440, 441
Notetaking, 384, 404, 432

Student Help
Study Strategy, 385, 387, 392, 393, 399, 413, 414, 427, 437
Homework Help, 388, 394, 400, 407, 415, 422, 429, 434, 439
Tech Help, 397, 425, 433, 435
Student Reference: Parallel, Perpendicular, and Skew Lines, 410

Problem Solving
Guided Problem Solving, 394, 415, 422, 439
Extended Problem Solving, 389, 395, 401, 408, 416, 423, 429, 435, 440
Challenge, 390, 396, 402, 409, 417, 424, 430, 435, 441
Focus on Problem Solving: Solving the Problem, 448

Use a graph to find the speed of a wakeboarder, p. 406

Real Numbers *and* Right Triangles

Apply square roots to determine film speeds, p. 456

Internet Resources
CLASSZONE.COM
eEdition Plus Online
eWorkbook Plus Online
eTutorial Plus Online
State Test Practice
More Examples

Reading, Writing, and Notetaking
Vocabulary, 452, 455, 460, 467, 472, 479, 485, 491, 496, 500
Reading Algebra, 458, 466, 476, 492
Reading Geometry, 489
Writing, 457, 461, 464, 468, 473, 482, 486, 488, 492, 497
Notetaking, 452, 454, 484

Student Help
Study Strategy, 453, 466, 470, 471, 477, 484
Homework Help, 456, 460, 467, 473, 479, 486, 491, 497
Tech Help, 454, 490, 499
Student Reference: Triangles, 462

Problem Solving
Guided Problem Solving, 455, 467, 496
Extended Problem Solving, 457, 461, 469, 474, 481, 486, 493, 498
Challenge, 457, 461, 469, 474, 481, 487, 493, 498

Measurement, Area, *and* Volume

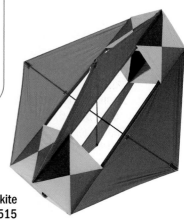

Use geometry to find kite dimensions, p. 515

Data Analysis *and* Probability

Internet Resources
CLASSZONE.COM
eEdition Plus Online
eWorkbook Plus Online
eTutorial Plus Online
State Test Practice
More Examples

Reading, Writing, and Notetaking

Student Help

Problem Solving

Assessment

Apply combinations to count basketball matchups, p. 620

CHAPTER

12

Polynomials *and* Nonlinear Functions

Reading, Writing, and Notetaking
Vocabulary, 650, 653, 659, 664, 670, 676, 682, 689, 695, 698
Reading Algebra, 652, 687
Writing, 654, 660, 665, 667, 671, 677, 683, 689, 695
Notetaking, 650, 669, 687

Student Help
Study Strategy, 651, 680, 681, 686, 693, 694
Homework Help, 654, 660, 664, 670, 677, 682, 689, 695
Tech Help, 685

Problem Solving
Guided Problem Solving, 664, 682, 689
Extended Problem Solving, 655, 660, 665, 672, 678, 684, 690, 696
Challenge, 655, 661, 666, 672, 678, 684, 691, 697
Focus on Problem Solving: Looking Back, 704

Assessment

Use polynomials to find the height of a golf ball, p. 654

Angle Relationships *and* Transformations

Analyze angles in chair design, p. 719

Contents *of* Student Resources

Student Handbook

Help with Taking Notes

One of the most important tools for success in mathematics is organizing what you have learned. Writing down important information in a notebook helps you remember key concepts and skills. You can use your notebook as a reference when you do your homework or when you study for a test.

Vocabulary
Your notebook is a good place to include definitions for vocabulary terms that appear at the beginning of each chapter and each lesson.

Notetaking Strategies
You'll find a different notetaking strategy at the beginning of each chapter.

Note Worthy
Look for notes in each chapter that provide helpful hints about notetaking.

Taking Notes
Your textbook displays important ideas and definitions on a notebook. You'll want to include this information in your notes.

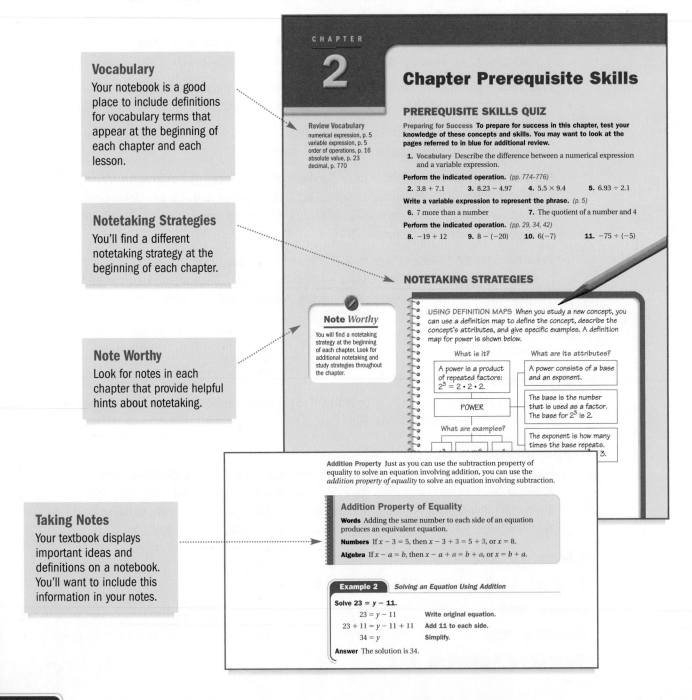

CHAPTER

2

Chapter Prerequisite Skills

Review Vocabulary
numerical expression, p. 5
variable expression, p. 5
order of operations, p. 16
absolute value, p. 23
decimal, p. 770

PREREQUISITE SKILLS QUIZ

Preparing for Success To prepare for success in this chapter, test your knowledge of these concepts and skills. You may want to look at the pages referred to in blue for additional review.

1. Vocabulary Describe the difference between a numerical expression and a variable expression.

Perform the indicated operation. *(pp. 774–776)*

2. $3.8 + 7.1$ **3.** $8.23 - 4.97$ **4.** 5.5×9.4 **5.** $6.93 \div 2.1$

Write a variable expression to represent the phrase. *(p. 5)*

6. 7 more than a number   **7.** The quotient of a number and 4

Perform the indicated operation. *(pp. 29, 34, 42)*

8. $-19 + 12$ **9.** $8 - (-20)$ **10.** $6(-7)$ **11.** $-75 \div (-5)$

NOTETAKING STRATEGIES

Note *Worthy*
You will find a notetaking strategy at the beginning of each chapter. Look for additional notetaking and study strategies throughout the chapter.

USING DEFINITION MAPS When you study a new concept, you can use a definition map to define the concept, describe the concept's attributes, and give specific examples. A definition map for power is shown below.

What is it?

A power is a product of repeated factors: $2^3 = 2 \cdot 2 \cdot 2$.

POWER

What are examples?

What are its attributes?

A power consists of a base and an exponent.

The base is the number that is used as a factor. The base for 2^3 is 2.

The exponent is how many times the base repeats.

Addition Property Just as you can use the subtraction property of equality to solve an equation involving addition, you can use the *addition property of equality* to solve an equation involving subtraction.

Addition Property of Equality

Words Adding the same number to each side of an equation produces an equivalent equation.

Numbers If $x - 3 = 5$, then $x - 3 + 3 = 5 + 3$, or $x = 8$.

Algebra If $x - a = b$, then $x - a + a = b + a$, or $x = b + a$.

Example 2 *Solving an Equation Using Addition*

Solve $23 = y - 11$.

$23 = y - 11$	Write original equation.
$23 + 11 = y - 11 + 11$	Add **11** to each side.
$34 = y$	Simplify.

Answer The solution is 34.

Help with Learning Mathematics

Your textbook helps you succeed in mathematics. Keep your eye out for notes that help you with understanding important concepts, reading algebra and geometry, and doing your homework. Some examples of the types of notes you'll see are shown below.

Study Strategy

These notes help you understand and apply new skills and concepts. They also suggest alternative methods for solving problems and ways to check the reasonableness of answers.

Study *Strategy*

Another Way You can also evaluate the expression $4(-7)(25)$ in Example 2 simply by multiplying from left to right:

$$4(-7)(25) = -28(25)$$
$$= -700$$

However, this calculation is more difficult to do mentally.

Example 2   *Using Properties of Multiplication*

Evaluate $4xy$ when $x = -7$ and $y = 25$.

$$4xy = 4(-7)(25) \qquad \text{Substitute } -7 \text{ for } x \text{ and } 25 \text{ for } y.$$
$$= [4(-7)](25) \qquad \text{Use order of operations.}$$
$$= [-7(4)](25) \qquad \text{Commutative property of multiplication}$$
$$= -7[(4)(25)] \qquad \text{Associative property of multiplication}$$
$$= -7(100) \qquad \text{Multiply 4 and 25.}$$
$$= -700 \qquad \text{Multiply } -7 \text{ and 100.}$$

✓ **Checkpoint**

In Exercises 1–3, evaluate the expression. Justify each of your steps.

1. $(17 + 36) + 13$ **2.** $8(-3)(5)$ **3.** $3.4 + 9.7 + 7.6$

4. Evaluate $5x^2y$ when $x = -6$ and $y = 20$.

Reading Algebra

It's important that you read your textbook carefully. *Reading Algebra* notes help you understand and use the language of algebra. You'll also find *Reading Geometry* notes that help you understand the language of geometry.

Reading *Algebra*

In an expression like $16x^{-6}y$, the exponent is associated only with the variable that comes directly before it, not with the coefficient of the variable.

Example 1   *Powers with Negative and Zero Exponents*

Write the expression using only positive exponents.

a. $3^{-5} = \dfrac{1}{3^5}$ Definition of negative exponent

b. $m^0 n^{-4} = 1 \cdot n^{-4}$ Definition of zero exponent

$\qquad\quad = \dfrac{1}{n^4}$ Definition of negative exponent

c. $16x^{-6}y = \dfrac{16y}{x^6}$ Definition of negative exponent

✓ **Checkpoint**

Write the expression using only positive exponents.

1. 5^{-2} **2.** $1,000,000^0$ **3.** $3y^{-2}$ **4.** $a^{-7}b^3$

Help with Homework

These notes tell you which textbook examples may help you with homework exercises, and let you know where to find extra help on the Internet.

Practice and Problem Solving

Homework *Help*

Example	Exercises
1	13–21, 40
2	22–31, 41
3	32–39
4	32–39

Online Resources
CLASSZONE.COM
• More Examples
• eTutorial Plus

Solve the equation by first clearing the fractions.

13. $\frac{1}{2}t + \frac{1}{4} = \frac{5}{16}$ **14.** $\frac{5}{6}s + \frac{2}{9} = -\frac{7}{12}$ **15.** $\frac{3}{4} = \frac{5}{6}a + \frac{2}{9}$

16. $\frac{5}{8} = \frac{1}{10} + \frac{5}{14}m$ **17.** $-\frac{41}{60} + \frac{17}{20}p = \frac{29}{30}$ **18.** $\frac{3}{8} = -\frac{1}{4}x - \frac{3}{5}$

19. $-\frac{3}{2}t - \frac{5}{6} = -\frac{4}{9}$ **20.** $-\frac{3}{5}z - 4 = -\frac{77}{20}$ **21.** $4w + \frac{2}{7} = -\frac{4}{5}$

Solve the equation by first clearing the decimals.

22. $6.2x + 3.7 = 22.3$ **23.** $7.8y + 6 = 23.16$ **24.** $10.7w + 4 = 47.87$

25. $2 = -6.4z + 10$ **26.** $-3.3x + 6.5 = 1.55$ **27.** $1.6b - 3 = -9.4$

28. $-1.7w - 4 = 2.63$ **29.** $2.875y + 9 = 12.45$ **30.** $4.125c + 5 = -9.85$

31. Saving Money You want to save $400 for a camping trip. You have $64.96 in your savings account. Each week you deposit your paycheck from your part-time job. Each paycheck is for $69.80. How many paychecks must you deposit to reach your goal of $400?

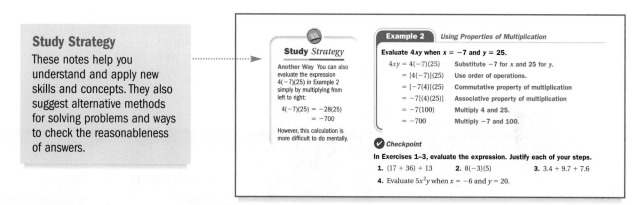

Continued ➡

Reading Your Textbook

You need special skills to read a math textbook. These skills include identifying the main idea, learning new vocabulary, and focusing on the important concepts in a lesson. Most important, you need to be an active reader.

Identify the Main Idea

Even before you begin reading a lesson, check to see what the lesson is about. Then you'll know what to focus on in the lesson. You can also assess how well you understand the lesson content when you finish reading the lesson.

Lesson Opener
Look at the lesson opener for information about the main idea of the lesson.

Example Heads
Use other clues, such as the heads that appear above examples, to identify the main idea.

Understand the Vocabulary

Reading mathematics involves using new vocabulary terms. Refer to diagrams and examples to clarify your understanding of new terms. If you forget what a term means, look back at previous lessons or use the Glossary, which starts on page 824.

Vocabulary
New vocabulary terms are highlighted within a lesson. In addition, the Vocabulary list at the beginning of the lesson lists the important vocabulary terms in the lesson.

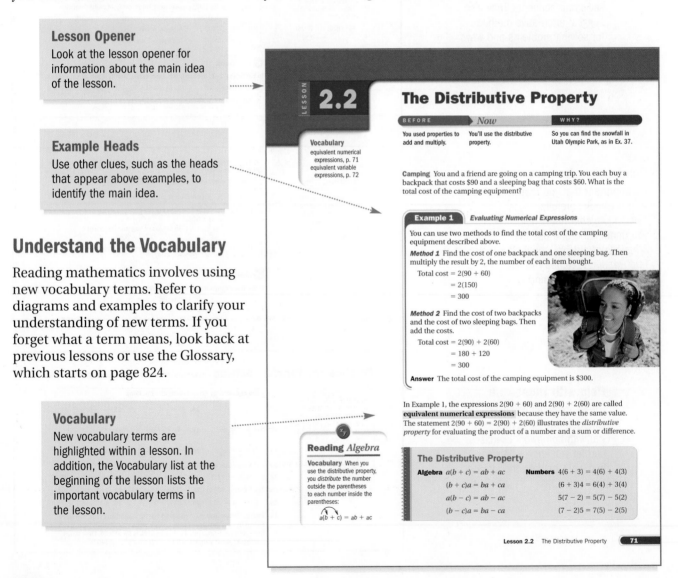

LESSON

2.2 The Distributive Property

BEFORE	*Now*	WHY?
You used properties to add and multiply.	You'll use the distributive property.	So you can find the snowfall in Utah Olympic Park, as in Ex. 37.

Vocabulary
equivalent numerical expressions, p. 71
equivalent variable expressions, p. 72

Camping You and a friend are going on a camping trip. You each buy a backpack that costs $90 and a sleeping bag that costs $60. What is the total cost of the camping equipment?

Example 1 *Evaluating Numerical Expressions*

You can use two methods to find the total cost of the camping equipment described above.

Method 1 Find the cost of one backpack and one sleeping bag. Then multiply the result by 2, the number of each item bought.

$$\text{Total cost} = 2(90 + 60)$$
$$= 2(150)$$
$$= 300$$

Method 2 Find the cost of two backpacks and the cost of two sleeping bags. Then add the costs.

$$\text{Total cost} = 2(90) + 2(60)$$
$$= 180 + 120$$
$$= 300$$

Answer The total cost of the camping equipment is $300.

In Example 1, the expressions $2(90 + 60)$ and $2(90) + 2(60)$ are called **equivalent numerical expressions** because they have the same value. The statement $2(90 + 60) = 2(90) + 2(60)$ illustrates the *distributive property* for evaluating the product of a number and a sum or difference.

Reading *Algebra*

Vocabulary When you use the distributive property, you *distribute* the number outside the parentheses to each number inside the parentheses:

$$a(b + c) = ab + ac$$

The Distributive Property

Algebra	$a(b + c) = ab + ac$	**Numbers**	$4(6 + 3) = 4(6) + 4(3)$
	$(b + c)a = ba + ca$		$(6 + 3)4 = 6(4) + 3(4)$
	$a(b - c) = ab - ac$		$5(7 - 2) = 5(7) - 5(2)$
	$(b - c)a = ba - ca$		$(7 - 2)5 = 7(5) - 2(5)$

Lesson 2.2 The Distributive Property **71**

Know What's Important

Focus on the important information in a lesson. Pay attention to highlighted vocabulary terms. Be on the lookout for definitions, properties, formulas, and other information displayed on a notebook. Make sure that you understand the worked-out examples.

Notebook
Focus on key ideas that are displayed on a notebook.

Worked-Out Examples
Do the worked-out examples to make sure you know how to apply new concepts.

Be an Active Reader

As you read, keep a pencil in your hand and your notebook ready so that you can write down important information, practice new skills, and jot down questions to ask in class.

Checkpoint
Solve the Checkpoint exercises to make sure you understand new material.

Use Your Notebook
As you solve the examples yourself, you may find it helpful to describe the steps you follow. Write down any questions you have so you can ask them in class.

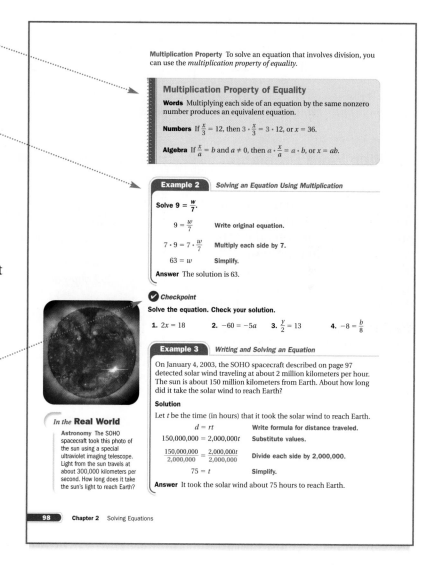

Multiplication Property To solve an equation that involves division, you can use the *multiplication property of equality*.

Multiplication Property of Equality

Words Multiplying each side of an equation by the same nonzero number produces an equivalent equation.

Numbers If $\frac{x}{3} = 12$, then $3 \cdot \frac{x}{3} = 3 \cdot 12$, or $x = 36$.

Algebra If $\frac{x}{a} = b$ and $a \neq 0$, then $a \cdot \frac{x}{a} = a \cdot b$, or $x = ab$.

Example 2   *Solving an Equation Using Multiplication*

Solve $9 = \frac{w}{7}$.

$9 = \frac{w}{7}$ Write original equation.

$7 \cdot 9 = 7 \cdot \frac{w}{7}$ Multiply each side by 7.

$63 = w$ Simplify.

Answer The solution is 63.

✓ *Checkpoint*

Solve the equation. Check your solution.

1. $2x = 18$ **2.** $-60 = -5a$ **3.** $\frac{y}{2} = 13$ **4.** $-8 = \frac{b}{8}$

Example 3   *Writing and Solving an Equation*

On January 4, 2003, the SOHO spacecraft described on page 97 detected solar wind traveling at about 2 million kilometers per hour. The sun is about 150 million kilometers from Earth. About how long did it take the solar wind to reach Earth?

Solution

Let t be the time (in hours) that it took the solar wind to reach Earth.

$d = rt$ Write formula for distance traveled.

$150{,}000{,}000 = 2{,}000{,}000t$ Substitute values.

$\frac{150{,}000{,}000}{2{,}000{,}000} = \frac{2{,}000{,}000t}{2{,}000{,}000}$ Divide each side by 2,000,000.

$75 = t$ Simplify.

Answer It took the solar wind about 75 hours to reach Earth.

In the **Real World**

Astronomy The SOHO spacecraft took this photo of the sun using a special ultraviolet imaging telescope. Light from the sun travels at about 300,000 kilometers per second. How long does it take the sun's light to reach Earth?

Continued

Reading and Problem Solving

The language in your math textbook is precise. When you do your homework, be sure to read carefully. For example, the direction line below from Chapter 8 asks you to do two things for each of the exercises: find the slope and y-intercept of a line, and then use the slope and y-intercept to graph an equation.

Identify the slope and y-intercept of the line with the given equation. Use the slope and y-intercept to graph the equation.

14. $y = -2x + 3$ **15.** $y = \frac{1}{4}x + 1$ **16.** $y = -2$

17. $3x + y = -1$ **18.** $2x - 3y = 0$ **19.** $5x - 2y = -4$

Reading Word Problems

Before you can solve a word problem, you need to read and understand it. You may find it useful to copy a word problem into your notebook. Then you can highlight important information, cross out irrelevant information, and organize your thinking. You can use these strategies to solve problems throughout your study of pre-algebra.

To make dough for two pizzas, you need 4 cups of flour, 2 tablespoons of olive oil, $1\frac{1}{2}$ teaspoons of salt, $2\frac{1}{4}$ teaspoons of yeast, and $1\frac{1}{2}$ cups of water. What is the greatest number of pizzas you can make if you have 20 cups of flour and 6 teaspoons of yeast?

Ingredient	Needed (for 2 pizzas)	Already have
Flour	4 c	20 c
Yeast	$2\frac{1}{4}$ tsp	6 tsp

Make sure that you've solved a word problem completely. For example, to solve the word problem at the right, you need to find the mean of each rider's distances. But to answer the question, you need to compare the means to see which is greater.

Over a period of 4 days, you rode these distances on your bike: 10 mi, 12 mi, 11 mi, 8 mi. Over a period of 5 days, your friend rode these distances: 11 mi, 14 mi, 8 mi, 8 mi, 8 mi. On average, which of you rode farther each day?

You: $\dfrac{10 + 12 + 11 + 8}{4} = 10.25$ miles each day

Your friend: $\dfrac{11 + 14 + 8 + 8 + 8}{5} = 9.8$ miles each day

On average, you rode farther than your friend each day.

Additional Resources in Your Textbook

Your textbook contains many resources that you can use for reference when you are studying or doing your homework.

Skills Review Handbook Use the Skills Review Handbook on pages 770–802 to review material learned in previous courses.

Student Reference Pages Use the Student Reference pages that appear throughout the book to review key material for use in upcoming lessons.

Tables Refer to the tables on pages 816–823 if you need information about mathematical symbols, measures, formulas, and properties.

English and Spanish Glossaries Use the glossaries on pages 840–865 and 866–893 to look up the meanings of math vocabulary terms. Each glossary entry also tells where in your book a term is covered in more detail.

Index Use the Index on pages 894–922 as a quick guide for finding out where a particular math topic is covered in the book.

Selected Answers Use the Selected Answers starting on page SA1 to check your work or to see whether you are on the right track in solving a problem.

TEXTBOOK *Scavenger Hunt*

Get some practice using your textbook. Use the additional resources described above to answer each question. Give page numbers to show where you found the answer to the question.

1. What is a rational number?

2. On what page of the book can you find selected answers for Lesson 1.1?

3. What formula can you use to find the surface area of a cone?

4. Tell what each of these symbols means: $m\angle B$, $|a|$, $\leq$.

5. Where can you find a statement of the associative property of multiplication?

6. What is a scatter plot?

7. How many pounds are there in one ton?

8. On what page can you review the skill of classifying angles?

9. What is the freezing point of water in degrees Fahrenheit? in degrees Celsius?

10. On what pages can you review the topics *mean*, *median*, *mode*, and *range*?

Assessing Progress

Strategies for Success on Tests

Your book will help you succeed on tests. At the end of each unit, a *Building Test-Taking Skills* section guides you, step by step, through strategies for solving common types of test questions, including multiple choice, short response, context-based multiple choice, and extended response questions. You'll also learn how to evaluate your work using a scoring rubric. You can practice test-taking skills in every lesson, in every chapter, and in every unit.

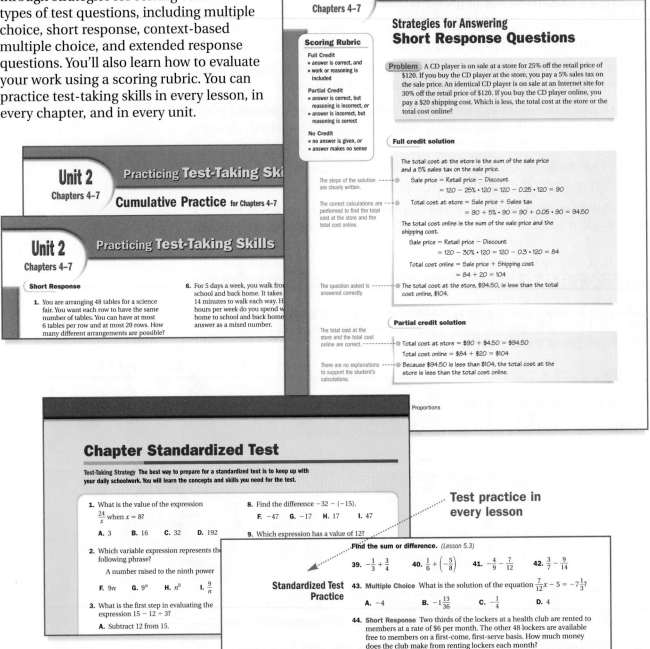

Unit 2
Chapters 4–7

Building Test-Taking Skills

Strategies for Answering
Short Response Questions

Scoring Rubric

Full Credit
- answer is correct, *and*
- work or reasoning is included

Partial Credit
- answer is correct, but reasoning is incorrect, *or*
- answer is incorrect, but reasoning is correct

No Credit
- no answer is given, *or*
- answer makes no sense

Problem A CD player is on sale at a store for 25% off the retail price of $120. If you buy the CD player at the store, you pay a 5% sales tax on the sale price. An identical CD player is on sale at an Internet site for 30% off the retail price of $120. If you buy the CD player online, you pay a $20 shipping cost. Which is less, the total cost at the store or the total cost online?

Full credit solution

The total cost at the store is the sum of the sale price and a 5% sales tax on the sale price.

The steps of the solution are clearly written. → Sale price = Retail price − Discount
$$= 120 − 25\% \cdot 120 = 120 − 0.25 \cdot 120 = 90$$

The correct calculations are performed to find the total cost at the store and the total cost online. → Total cost at store = Sale price + Sales tax
$$= 90 + 5\% \cdot 90 = 90 + 0.05 \cdot 90 = 94.50$$

The total cost online is the sum of the sale price and the shipping cost.

Sale price = Retail price − Discount
$$= 120 − 30\% \cdot 120 = 120 − 0.3 \cdot 120 = 84$$

Total cost online = Sale price + Shipping cost
$$= 84 + 20 = 104$$

The question asked is answered correctly. → The total cost at the store, $94.50, is less than the total cost online, $104.

Partial credit solution

The total cost at the store and the total cost online are correct. → Total cost at store = $90 + $4.50 = $94.50
Total cost online = $84 + $20 = $104

There are no explanations to support the student's calculations. → Because $94.50 is less than $104, the total cost at the store is less than the total cost online.

Proportions

Unit 2
Chapters 4–7

Practicing Test-Taking Ski

Cumulative Practice for Chapters 4–7

Unit 2
Chapters 4–7

Practicing Test-Taking Skills

Short Response

1. You are arranging 48 tables for a science fair. You want each row to have the same number of tables. You can have at most 6 tables per row and at most 20 rows. How many different arrangements are possible?

6. For 5 days a week, you walk from school and back home. It takes 14 minutes to walk each way. H hours per week do you spend w home to school and back home answer as a mixed number.

Chapter Standardized Test

Test-Taking Strategy The best way to prepare for a standardized test is to keep up with your daily schoolwork. You will learn the concepts and skills you need for the test.

1. What is the value of the expression $\frac{24}{x}$ when $x = 8$?

    A. 3   **B.** 16   **C.** 32   **D.** 192

2. Which variable expression represents the following phrase?

    A number raised to the ninth power

    F. $9n$ **G.** 9^n **H.** n^9 **I.** $\frac{9}{n}$

3. What is the first step in evaluating the expression $15 − 12 \div 3$?

    A. Subtract 12 from 15.

8. Find the difference $−32 − (−15)$.

    F. $−47$ **G.** $−17$ **H.** 17   **I.** 47

9. Which expression has a value of 12?

Test practice in every lesson

Find the sum or difference. *(Lesson 5.3)*

39. $−\frac{1}{3} + \frac{3}{4}$ **40.** $\frac{1}{6} + \left(−\frac{5}{8}\right)$ **41.** $−\frac{4}{9} − \frac{7}{12}$ **42.** $\frac{3}{7} − \frac{9}{14}$

Standardized Test Practice   **43. Multiple Choice** What is the solution of the equation $\frac{7}{12}x − 5 = −7\frac{1}{3}$?

    A. $−4$ **B.** $−1\frac{13}{36}$ **C.** $−\frac{1}{4}$ **D.** 4

44. Short Response Two thirds of the lockers at a health club are rented to members at a rate of $6 per month. The other 48 lockers are available free to members on a first-come, first-serve basis. How much money does the club make from renting lockers each month?

Pre-Course Test

▶ Estimation

Place Value and Rounding *(Skills Review, p. 770)*

Give the place and value of the red digit. Then round the number to that place.

1. 49.21

2. 1097.253

3. 352,453.349

4. 7482.9154

Estimating *(Skills Review, pp. 771–772)*

Estimate the sum or difference by rounding each number to the place of its leading digit.

5. $93,120 + 28,643$

6. $87,302 - 32,218$

7. $59,265 - 14,794$

8. $78,942 + 41,678$

Find a low and high estimate for the product or quotient.

9. 823×26

10. 4897×872

11. $7231 \div 82$

12. $5461 \div 64$

▶ Decimals

Comparing and Ordering Decimals *(Skills Review, p. 773)*

13. Order the numbers 0.2, 0.25, 0.02, and 0.252 from least to greatest.

Decimal Operations *(Skills Review, pp. 774–776)*

Perform the indicated operation.

14. $5.6 + 9.2$

15. $12.87 + 4.58$

16. $5.1 - 2.67$

17. $4.21 - 3.78$

18. 0.86×0.3

19. $61.95 \div 3.5$

20. $455.7 \div 9.8$

21. 0.04×9.8

▶ Fractions

Fractions, Mixed Numbers, and Improper Fractions *(Skills Review, pp. 777–778)*

Write the mixed number as an improper fraction or the improper fraction as a mixed number.

22. $4\frac{1}{8}$

23. $5\frac{4}{9}$

24. $\frac{23}{3}$

25. $\frac{61}{7}$

Fraction Operations *(Skills Review, pp. 779–780)*

Perform the indicated operation.

26. $\frac{2}{5} + \frac{1}{5}$

27. $\frac{5}{9} + \frac{2}{9}$

28. $\frac{3}{17} + \frac{11}{17}$

29. $\frac{14}{15} - \frac{1}{15}$

30. $\frac{14}{19} - \frac{10}{19}$

31. $\frac{3}{8} \times 24$

32. $12 \times \frac{5}{6}$

33. $\frac{3}{10} \times 20$

Data Analysis

Reading Graphs *(Skills Review, pp. 781–783)*

In Exercises 34 and 35, use the bar graph, which shows the results of a survey of 120 people asked about their favorite summer activity.

34. How many people said camping is their favorite summer activity?

35. What summer activity did the greatest number of people say is their favorite?

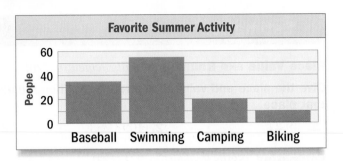

In Exercises 36 and 37, use the circle graph, which shows the results of a survey of 300 people asked about their favorite fruit.

36. What type of fruit did the greatest number of people say is their favorite?

37. How many more people chose oranges as their favorite fruit than chose grapes as their favorite fruit?

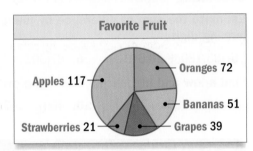

Venn Diagrams and Logical Reasoning *(Skills Review, p. 784)*

38. Using the whole numbers less than 22, draw a Venn diagram showing set *A*, which consists of even numbers less than 15, and set *B*, which consists of numbers that are factors of 5.

Geometry and Measurement

Basic Geometric Figures *(Skills Review, p. 785)*

39. What is the perimeter of a rectangle with a length of 7 centimeters and a width of 4 centimeters?

Measurement *(Skills Review, pp. 786–791)*

In Exercises 40–42, copy and complete the statement.

40. 15 yards = _?_ feet

41. 25 kilograms = _?_ grams

42. 32 ounces = _?_ pounds

43. Find the area of the square.

44. Find the volume of the cube.

9 in.

9 in.

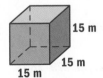

15 m

15 m

15 m

Using a Protractor and Compass *(Skills Review, pp. 792–794)*

45. Use a protractor to draw an angle with a measure of 86°. Classify the angle as *acute*, *right*, *obtuse*, or *straight*.

46. Use a compass to draw a circle with a radius of 4 centimeters.

Pre-Course Practice

▶ Estimation

Place Value and Rounding *(Skills Review, p. 770)*

Give the place and value of the red digit. Then round the number to that place.

1. 0.598

2. 63.9721

3. 356,418

4. 12,590.6

5. 15,213.04

6. 312,145,203

7. 213.392

8. 214,986.32

Estimating *(Skills Review, pp. 771–772)*

Estimate the sum or difference by rounding each number to the place of its leading digit.

9. $781 + 615$

10. $58,498 + 34,215$

11. $23,619 + 78,278$

12. $815 - 478$

13. $81,592 - 79,902$

14. $324,981 - 142,243$

Find a low and high estimate for the product or quotient.

15. 467×47

16. 758×312

17. 9738×852

18. $823 \div 32$

19. $4516 \div 77$

20. $62,491 \div 16$

▶ Decimals

Comparing and Ordering Decimals *(Skills Review, p. 773)*

Copy and complete the statement using <, >, or =.

21. 0.32 _?_ 0.3

22. 5.0 _?_ 5

23. 6.02 _?_ 6.2

24. 78.3 _?_ 77.8

25. 0.54 _?_ 0.45

26. 2.323 _?_ 2.3230

Order the numbers from least to greatest.

27. 1.2, 2.1, 2.15, 1.9

28. 7.7, 7.77, 6.77, 7.71

29. 0.5, 0, 0.25, 0.51

30. 9.4, 9.43, 9.5, 9.3

31. 3.4, 3.04, 3.41, 3.14

32. 10.01, 1.01, 10.1, 11

Decimal Operations *(Skills Review, pp. 774–776)*

Perform the indicated operation.

33. $4.3 + 9.2$

34. $6.5 + 7.6$

35. $5.04 + 9.27$

36. $8.98 + 1.76$

37. $8.4 + 3.15$

38. $4.8 - 2.3$

39. $18.954 - 13.785$

40. $24.6 - 19.83$

41. $54.1 - 39.806$

42. 9.2×0.4

43. 5.3×9.8

44. 2.12×4.65

45. $8.343 \div 2.7$

46. $62.685 \div 3.5$

47. $11.7 \div 1.3$

Fractions, Mixed Numbers, and Improper Fractions
(Skills Review, pp. 777–778)

Write a fraction or mixed number to represent the shaded region.

48.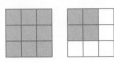

49.

Write the mixed number as an improper fraction.

50. $1\frac{5}{9}$

51. $4\frac{3}{4}$

52. $9\frac{7}{12}$

53. $15\frac{2}{3}$

Write the improper fraction as a mixed number.

54. $\frac{23}{6}$

55. $\frac{83}{8}$

56. $\frac{59}{6}$

57. $\frac{53}{2}$

Fraction Operations *(Skills Review, pp. 779–780)*

Find the sum or difference.

58. $\frac{4}{7} + \frac{2}{7}$

59. $\frac{9}{13} + \frac{3}{13}$

60. $\frac{7}{11} + \frac{2}{11}$

61. $\frac{10}{21} + \frac{1}{21}$

62. $\frac{2}{3} - \frac{1}{3}$

63. $\frac{7}{17} - \frac{3}{17}$

64. $\frac{11}{23} - \frac{5}{23}$

65. $\frac{12}{25} - \frac{4}{25}$

Find the product.

66. $6 \times \frac{2}{3}$

67. $\frac{5}{11} \times 22$

68. $\frac{2}{7} \times 7$

69. $12 \times \frac{1}{4}$

▶ **Data Analysis**

Reading Graphs *(Skills Review, pp. 781–783)*

In Exercises 70–72, use the bar graph, which shows the most popular boys' names given to babies in 2001.

70. What was the most popular boys' name in 2001?

71. What two names were given to about the same number of boys?

72. About how many more boys were given the name Michael than were given the name Christopher?

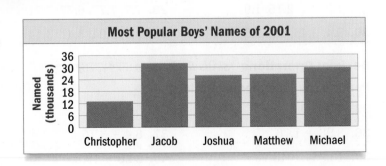

In Exercises 73–75, use the line graph, which shows the first year sales at a store.

73. Between what two months did sales increase the most?

74. Between what two months did sales decrease the most?

75. Between what two months did sales stay the same?

First Year Sales

In Exercises 76–78, use the circle graph, which shows the results of a survey of 200 people asked about favorite places to vacation.

76. What is the most favorite place to vacation?

77. What is the least favorite place to vacation?

78. How many more people prefer visiting a lake than prefer visiting a city?

Favorite Vacation Place

Ocean 80
Lake 54
Mountains 36
City 30

Venn Diagrams and Logical Reasoning (*Skills Review, p. 784*)

Draw a Venn diagram of the sets described.

79. Of the whole numbers less than 20, set *A* consists of numbers less than 15 and greater than 8, and set *B* consists of even numbers.

80. Of the odd whole numbers less than 50, set *A* consists of multiples of 3, and set *B* consists of multiples of 5.

Use the Venn diagram you drew in Exercise 80 to tell whether the statement is *true* or *false*. Explain your reasoning.

81. More than one odd whole number less than 50 is a multiple of 3 and 5.

82. All odd whole numbers less than 50 are multiples of 3.

▶ Geometry and Measurement

Basic Geometric Figures (*Skills Review, p. 785*)

Find the perimeter of the figure described.

83. A square with sides 2 in. long

84. A triangle with sides 3 cm, 5 cm, and 6 cm long

Measurement (*Skills Review, pp. 786–791*)

Copy and complete the statement.

85. 48 inches = _?_ feet   86. 24 ounces = _?_ pounds   87. 5 kilograms = _?_ grams

Use a ruler to draw a segment with the given length.

88. $4\frac{3}{8}$ inches   89. $\frac{1}{2}$ inch   90. 3.2 centimeters   91. 4.8 centimeters

Use a ruler to find the length of the segment in inches and in centimeters.

92. _____

93. _____

Find the area of the square.

94. 6 ft / 6 ft

95. 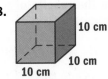 3 yd / 3 yd

96. 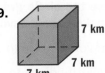 8 m / 8 m

Find the volume of the cube.

97. 2 ft / 2 ft / 2 ft

98. 10 cm / 10 cm / 10 cm

99. 7 km / 7 km / 7 km

In Exercises 100–102, copy and complete the statement using <, >, or =.

100. 3.5 tons _?_ 7500 lb

101. 14 lb _?_ 220 oz

102. 437 g _?_ 4.3 kg

103. Find the weight of the cheese.

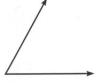

104. Find the amount of liquid in the measuring cup.

Using a Protractor and Compass *(Skills Review, pp. 792–794)*

Use a protractor to draw an angle with the given measure.

105. 45°

106. 175°

107. 180°

108. 93°

Find the measure of the angle. Classify the angle as *acute*, *right*, *obtuse*, or *straight*.

109.

110.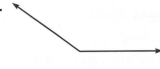

Use a compass to draw a circle with the given radius.

111. 3 inches

112. 5 centimeters

113. 2 centimeters

114. 2.5 inches

115. Use a straightedge and a compass to draw a segment whose length is the *sum* of the lengths of the two given segments.

Integers, Equations, *and* Inequalities

Chapter 1 Variables, Expressions, and Integers

- Write and evaluate variable expressions.
- Perform operations with integers.
- Plot points in a coordinate plane.

Chapter 2 Solving Equations

- Use mathematical properties to simplify variable expressions.
- Write and solve one-step equations.
- Perform operations with positive and negative decimals.

Chapter 3 Multi-Step Equations and Inequalities

- Write and solve multi-step equations.
- Write and solve inequalities.

From Chapter 2, p. 100
How long does it take a gray whale to migrate?

Variables, Expressions, *and* Integers

How tall is an iceberg?

CHAPTER 1

INTERNET Preview

CLASSZONE.COM

- eEdition Plus Online
- eWorkbook Plus Online
- eTutorial Plus Online
- State Test Practice
- More Examples

M A T H) *In the* **Real World**

Icebergs Icebergs like this one in LeConte Bay, Alaska, typically float with most of their mass below sea level. In this chapter, you will use *integers* to describe distances above and below sea level.

What do you think? Suppose the highest point on an iceberg is 45 feet above the water's surface. The lowest point is 357 feet below the surface. Find the vertical distance between these two points.

Chapter Prerequisite Skills

PREREQUISITE SKILLS QUIZ

Review Vocabulary

sum, p. 771
difference, p. 771
product, p. 772
quotient, p. 772
factor, p. 772

Preparing for Success To prepare for success in this chapter, test your knowledge of these concepts and skills. You may want to look at the pages referred to in blue for additional review.

Vocabulary Copy and complete the statement using a review word.

1. In the multiplication equation $12 \cdot 5 = 60$, 12 and 5 are called __?__ and 60 is called the __?__.

2. When you divide one number by another, the result is called the __?__.

Find the sum or difference. *(p. 774)*

3. $7.2 + 13.7$ **4.** $2.41 + 34.6$ **5.** $10.5 - 7.3$ **6.** $27.1 - 18.6$

Find the product or quotient. *(pp. 775, 776)*

7. 3.2×1.4 **8.** 0.5×27 **9.** $27.88 \div 8.2$ **10.** $11.9 \div 1.7$

NOTETAKING STRATEGIES

Note *Worthy*

You will find a notetaking strategy at the beginning of each chapter. Look for additional notetaking and study strategies throughout the chapter.

KEEPING A NOTEBOOK Some useful items to put in your notebook include the following.

- assignments
- vocabulary
- formulas
- symbols
- rules and properties
- worked-out examples

When you copy examples into your notebook, you may find it helpful to draw a diagram. Include comments that make the solution process clear. For example, a diagram can help you to order the numbers 3.2, 3.09, 3, 3.15, 3.12, and 3.02 from least to greatest.

Draw a number line and graph the numbers:

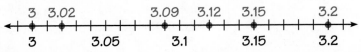

Write the numbers in the order in which they appear from left to right: 3, 3.02, 3.09, 3.12, 3.15, 3.2.

In Lesson 1.8, you may want to include a diagram of a coordinate plane in your notebook.

Expressions *and* Variables

BEFORE	Now	WHY?
You evaluated numerical expressions.	You'll evaluate and write variable expressions.	So you can find the amount left on a gift card, as in Ex. 39.

Vocabulary

numerical expression,
  p. 5
variable, p. 5
variable expression,
  p. 5
evaluate, p. 5
verbal model, p. 6

Blue Whales During its summer feeding season, a blue whale eats about 4 tons of food every day. To find about how many tons of food a blue whale eats in a given number of days, you can multiply the number of days by 4, as shown in the table.

Days	Tons of food eaten
1	4 · 1
2	4 · 2
10	4 · 10
d	4 · d

A **numerical expression** consists of numbers and operations. In the table, the expression 4 · 10 is a numerical expression. It can also be written as 4×10 or 4(10).

A **variable** is a letter used to represent one or more numbers. A **variable expression** consists of numbers, variables, and operations.

One way you can use a variable expression is to generalize a pattern, as in the table. The variable expression 4 · d represents the amount of food a blue whale can eat in d days. You can also write 4 · d as 4d.

To **evaluate** a variable expression, substitute a number for each variable and evaluate the resulting numerical expression.

Study *Strategy*

When you write a variable expression involving multiplication, avoid using the symbol $\times$. It may be confused with the variable x.

Example 1 | *Evaluating a Variable Expression*

Evaluate the expression 4 · d when $d = 120$ to find about how many tons of food a blue whale eats in a feeding season of 120 days.

Solution

$$4 \cdot d = 4 \cdot 120 \qquad \text{Substitute 120 for } d.$$
$$= 480 \qquad \text{Multiply.}$$

Answer A blue whale eats about 480 tons of food in 120 days.

Example 2 Evaluating Expressions with Two Variables

Evaluate the expression when $x = 10$ and $y = 4$.

   a. $x + y = 10 + 4$ Substitute 10 for x and 4 for y.

               $= 14$ Add.

   b. $xy = 10(4)$ Substitute 10 for x and 4 for y.

             $= 40$ Multiply.

 **Checkpoint**

Evaluate the expression when $x = 6$ and $y = 12$.

1. $y + 8$ **2.** $9 - x$ **3.** $y - x$ **4.** xy

Writing Variable Expressions You can solve a real-world problem by creating a *verbal model* and using it to write a variable expression. A **verbal model** describes a problem using words as labels and using math symbols to relate the words. The table shows common words and phrases that indicate mathematical operations.

Common Words and Phrases that Indicate Operations			
Addition	**Subtraction**	**Multiplication**	**Division**
plus	minus	times	divided by
the sum of	the difference of	the product of	divided into
increased by	decreased by	multiplied by	the quotient of
total	fewer than	of	
more than	less than		
added to	subtracted from		

Watch Out

Order is important in subtraction and division expressions. "The difference of a number and 7" means $n - 7$, *not* $7 - n$. "The quotient of a number and 5" means $\frac{n}{5}$, *not* $\frac{5}{n}$.

Example 3 Writing a Variable Expression

Baseball You plan to divide the 120 players in a baseball league into teams with the same number of players. Use a verbal model to write a variable expression for the number of teams if you know the number of players on each team.

Solution

Let p represent the number of players on each team. The word *divide* indicates division.

Number of teams	=	Number of players in league	÷	Number of players on each team

              $= 120 \div p$

Answer The number of teams is $120 \div p$, or $\dfrac{120}{p}$.

Reading Algebra

When you write a variable expression involving division, use a fraction bar instead of the division symbol ÷. For example, write "the quotient of n and 12" as $\frac{n}{12}$.

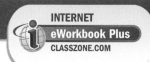

Guided Practice

Vocabulary Check
1. Identify the variable in the expression $21 + d$.

2. Compare and contrast the expressions $2 + x$ and $2 + 3$.

Skill Check **Evaluate the expression when $x = 4$.**

3. $10 - x$ 4. $x + 7$ 5. $2x$ 6. $\dfrac{32}{x}$

Evaluate the expression when $m = 5$ and $n = 6$.

7. $\dfrac{n}{2}$ 8. $m + n$ 9. $n - m$ 10. mn

Guided Problem Solving
11. **Astronauts** In 2002, astronauts Carl Walz and Dan Bursch spent 196 days in orbit. How many sunrises did they see?

  1 An astronaut in orbit circles Earth every 90 minutes and sees 16 sunrises each day. Let d be the number of days an astronaut is in orbit. Write a variable expression for the number of sunrises seen in d days.

  2 Identify the value of d for Walz's and Bursch's 2002 space flight.

  3 Find the number of sunrises Walz and Bursch saw.

Practice and Problem Solving

Homework *Help*

Example	Exercises
1	12–19, 39
2	20–31, 40
3	32–38, 40

Online Resources
CLASSZONE.COM
• More Examples
• eTutorial Plus

Evaluate the expression when $x = 6$.

12. $x + 3$ 13. $15 - x$ 14. $2x$ 15. $\dfrac{x}{3}$

16. $20x$ 17. $\dfrac{24}{x}$ 18. $30 - x$ 19. $15 + x$

Evaluate the expression when $a = 4$, $b = 2$, and $c = 16$.

20. $a + b$ 21. $c - a$ 22. ab 23. $\dfrac{a}{b}$

24. bc 25. $\dfrac{c}{a}$ 26. $a - b$ 27. $\dfrac{c}{b}$

28. $b + c$ 29. $c - b$ 30. ac 31. $a + c$

Write a variable expression to represent the phrase.

32. The product of 72 and a number

33. The difference of a number and 1

34. 13 more than a number

35. The sum of a number and 9.4

36. The quotient of a number and 3

37. A number divided by 41

38. Error Analysis Describe and correct the error in writing a variable expression for the difference of a number and 31.

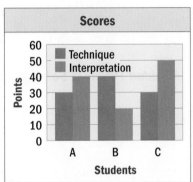

39. Gift Card You can evaluate the expression $50 - d$ to find the amount you have left on a $50 gift card after you have spent d dollars. Find the amount left after you have spent $18.

40. Music Competition The double bar graph shows three students' scores in a music competition. A student's final score is the sum of the points for technique t and for interpretation i.

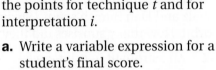

a. Write a variable expression for a student's final score.

b. Find each student's final score.

c. Interpret You earn 35 points for technique. At least how many points must you earn for interpretation to have a higher score than students A, B, and C?

Evaluate the expression when $a = 2.5$, $b = 15$, and $c = 3.5$.

41. $a + b$

42. $b - c$

43. bc

44. $a + c$

45. $\dfrac{b}{a}$

46. $c - a$

47. $\dfrac{c}{a}$

48. ac

Write a variable expression to represent the phrase.

49. The number of inches in x feet

50. The number of pounds in y ounces

Review *Help*

For help with units of length, see p. 786. For help with units of weight and mass, see p. 790.

51. DVD Rentals You belong to an online DVD rental service. Your yearly rental budget is $200. Each rental costs $4.

a. Copy and complete the table.

b. Write a variable expression for the cost of r rentals.

c. Write a variable expression for the amount of your budget left after r rentals.

DVDs	Cost (dollars)	Amount left (dollars)
1	4	196
2	8	192
3	?	?
4	?	?

d. *Writing* How many DVDs will you be able to rent before the $200 is spent? Explain how you found your answer.

52. Extended Problem Solving
In football, each field goal (FG) is worth 3 points. Each kicked point after touchdown (PAT) is worth 1 point. The table shows career totals for three leading kickers.

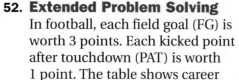

Player	FGs	PATs
George Blanda	335	943
Nick Lowery	383	562
Norm Johnson	366	638

  a. Let p be the number of points after touchdown that a kicker scored, and let f be the number of field goals. Write a variable expression for the total number of points.

  b. Evaluate Find the total number of points for each kicker.

  c. Compare List the players in order from least total number of points to greatest.

53. Critical Thinking Are there any values of the variable a for which the expressions $2 + a$ and $2a$ have the same value? Explain.

Logical Reasoning Describe the pattern shown in the table. Then write a variable expression involving *n* to complete the table. In the table, the three dots indicate that the pattern continues.

54.

Cost of item (dollars)	1.00	2.00	3.00	4.00	...	n
Cost with tax (dollars)	1.05	2.10	3.15	4.20	...	?

55.

Cost of item (dollars)	1.00	1.50	2.00	2.50	...	n
Cost with coupon (dollars)	0.50	1.00	1.50	2.00	...	?

56. Challenge The plastic tips on the ends of a shoelace are called aglets. Suppose a sneaker factory produces p pairs of shoes each hour and is in operation for h hours each day. Write a variable expression for the number of single aglets the factory uses each day. Evaluate the expression when $p = 200$ and $h = 24$. Explain what your answer means.

Review *Help*

For help with looking for a pattern, see p. 796.

Mixed Review

Find the sum or difference. *(p. 774)*

57. $3.2 + 4.7$ **58.** $5.1 + 6.8$ **59.** $7.3 - 2.1$ **60.** $9.9 - 5.4$

Find the product or quotient. *(pp. 775, 776)*

61. $8(13.2)$ **62.** $\dfrac{12.5}{5}$ **63.** $\dfrac{24.32}{3.2}$ **64.** $(6.5)(4.3)$

65. Order the decimals from least to greatest: 8.9, 8.79, 7.98, 9.87, 7.8, 9.78. *(p. 773)*

Standardized Test Practice

66. Multiple Choice Write a variable expression for a length of time in minutes if you know the number s of seconds.

  A. $s + 60$ **B.** $\dfrac{s}{60}$ **C.** $60s$ **D.** $\dfrac{60}{s}$

67. Multiple Choice Evaluate the expression $x - y$ when $x = 12.8$ and $y = 4$.

  F. 3.2 **G.** 8.8 **H.** 12.4 **I.** 13.2

Powers *and* Exponents

BEFORE	Now	WHY?
You multiplied whole numbers and decimals.	You'll use powers to describe repeated multiplication.	So you can find the total number of e-mails sent, as in Ex. 29.

Vocabulary

power, p. 10
base, p. 10
exponent, p. 10

A **power** is the result of a repeated multiplication of the same factor. For example, the number 125 is a power because $125 = 5 \cdot 5 \cdot 5$. A power can be written in a form that has two parts: a number called the **base** and a number called the **exponent**. The exponent shows the number of times the base is used as a factor.

$$\underset{\text{base}}{\underbrace{5}}{}^{\overset{\text{exponent}}{\downarrow}{}^{3}} = \underset{\text{factors}}{\underbrace{5 \cdot 5 \cdot 5}}$$

The base 5 is used as a factor 3 times.

The table shows how to read and write powers. Numbers raised to the first power, such as 12^1, are usually written without the exponent.

Power	In words	Value
12^1	12 to the first power	$12^1 = 12$
$(0.5)^2$	0.5 to the second power, or 0.5 squared	$(0.5)(0.5) = 0.25$
4^3	4 to the third power, or 4 cubed	$4 \cdot 4 \cdot 4 = 64$
8^4	8 to the fourth power	$8 \cdot 8 \cdot 8 \cdot 8 = 4096$

Note *Worthy*

Write additional examples of your own in your notebook. For each product, identify the base and the exponent, then write the product using an exponent.

Example 1   *Using Exponents*

Write the product using an exponent.

  a. $13 \cdot 13 \cdot 13 \cdot 13 = 13^4$ **The base 13 is used as a factor 4 times.**

  b. $(0.2)(0.2)(0.2) = (0.2)^3$ **The base 0.2 is used as a factor 3 times.**

  c. $n \cdot n \cdot n \cdot n \cdot n \cdot n = n^6$ **The base n is used as a factor 6 times.**

  d. $t \cdot t \cdot t \cdot t \cdot t = t^5$ **The base t is used as a factor 5 times.**

✔ *Checkpoint*

Write the product using an exponent.

  1. $10 \cdot 10 \cdot 10$ **2.** $(4.3)(4.3)$ **3.** $x \cdot x \cdot x \cdot x$

  4. Critical Thinking Evaluate each power: $0^2, 0^3, 0^4$. Use your results to write a rule for the value of 0 raised to any nonzero whole number exponent.

Example 2 | *Evaluating Powers with Variables*

Evaluate the expression x^4 when $x = 0.5$.

$$x^4 = (0.5)^4 \qquad \text{Substitute 0.5 for } x.$$
$$= (0.5)(0.5)(0.5)(0.5) \qquad \text{Use 0.5 as a factor 4 times.}$$
$$= 0.0625 \qquad \text{Multiply.}$$

✔ **Checkpoint**

Evaluate the expression when $m = 3$.

5. m^2 **6.** m^3 **7.** m^4 **8.** m^5

Review *Help*

For help with area and volume, see p. 789.

Using Formulas A formula describes a relationship between quantities. Some formulas involve powers. For example, you can use a formula to find the area of a square or the volume of a cube.

Area *A* of a square | **Volume *V* of a cube**
$A = s^2$ | $V = s^3$

Area is measured in square units, such as square feet (ft^2) or square centimeters (cm^2). Volume is measured in cubic units, such as cubic inches ($in.^3$) or cubic meters (m^3).

Example 3 | *Using Powers in Formulas*

Ice Sculpture An artist uses a cube-shaped block of ice to make an ice sculpture for a competition. Find the volume of the block of ice.

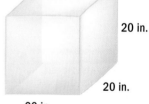
20 in. / 20 in. / 20 in.

Solution

Use the formula for the volume of a cube.

$$V = s^3 \qquad \text{Write the formula.}$$
$$= (20)^3 \qquad \text{Substitute 20 for } s.$$
$$= 8000 \qquad \text{Evaluate power.}$$

Answer The volume of the block of ice is 8000 cubic inches.

In the **Real World**

Ice Sculpture A cubic inch of ice weighs about 0.03 pound. If the artist carves away about 2000 cubic inches from the block in Example 3, about how much does the resulting sculpture weigh?

✔ **Checkpoint**

Find the area of a square with the given side length.

9. 9 meters **10.** 11 inches **11.** 1.5 centimeters

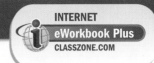

Guided Practice

Vocabulary Check
1. Identify the base and the exponent in the expression 13^5.

2. How are the expressions 3^4 and 4^3 different?

Skill Check **Write the power in words and as a repeated multiplication. Then evaluate the power.**

3. 12^2 4. $(0.3)^3$ 5. $(1.2)^3$ 6. 5^4

Evaluate the expression when $k = 6$.

7. k^2 8. k^3 9. k^4 10. k^5

11. **Gift Box** A gift box has the shape of a cube with an edge length of 14 inches. Find the volume of the box.

12. **Error Analysis** Describe and correct the error in writing 2^3 as a repeated multiplication.

$$\times \quad 2^3 = 3 \cdot 3$$

Practice and Problem Solving

Homework *Help*

Example	Exercises
1	13–29
2	30–33
3	36

Online Resources
CLASSZONE.COM
• More Examples
• eTutorial Plus

Write the product using an exponent.

13. $32 \cdot 32$ 14. $11 \cdot 11 \cdot 11$ 15. $6 \cdot 6 \cdot 6 \cdot 6 \cdot 6$ 16. $2 \cdot 2 \cdot 2 \cdot 2$

17. $(5.6)(5.6)(5.6)$ 18. $(1.7)(1.7)$ 19. $z \cdot z \cdot z$ 20. $n \cdot n \cdot n \cdot n$

Write the power in words and as a repeated multiplication. Then evaluate the power.

21. 8^3 22. 2^5 23. 10^6 24. 12^3

25. 9^3 26. 4^4 27. $(0.2)^2$ 28. $(0.6)^4$

29. **Extended Problem Solving** You send an e-mail to 4 friends. Each friend sends the e-mail to 4 more friends. Each of those friends sends it to 4 friends, and so on.

   a. Copy and complete the table.

   b. **Calculate** Find the number of e-mails sent at stage 9.

   c. **Estimate** Estimate the stage at which more than 1,000,000 e-mails will be sent. Use a calculator to check your estimate.

Stage	E-mails sent, as a power	Value of power
1	4^1	4
2	4^2	16
3	?	?
4	?	?

Evaluate the expression when $n = 7$ and when $n = 0.4$.

30. n^2 **31.** n^3 **32.** n^4 **33.** n^5

34. *Writing* The *square* of a number is the second power of the number. The *cube* of a number is the third power of the number. Explain why these names are reasonable.

35. Critical Thinking Explain why 1 raised to any power is equal to 1.

36. Aquariums An aquarium has a square base with a side length of 15 inches. You fill the aquarium with water to a height of 15 inches.

 a. Find the volume of the water in the aquarium.

 b. A cubic inch of water weighs approximately 0.036 pound. Find the approximate weight of the water in the aquarium.

37. Patterns The table shows sums of odd numbers.

 a. Copy and complete the table. Identify any pattern that you see.

 b. Write a variable expression for the sum of the first n odd numbers.

 c. Use your expression from part (b) to find the sum of the first 100 odd numbers.

n	Sum of first n odd numbers
1	1
2	$1 + 3 = 4$
3	$1 + 3 + 5 = ?$
4	$1 + 3 + 5 + 7 = ?$
5	?

38. Challenge Find values of x, y, and z so that each of the expressions x^2, y^3, and z^6 has a value of 64.

Mixed Review

Find the product or quotient. *(pp. 775, 776)*

39. $(2.5)(7.1)$ **40.** $(2.3)(8.4)$ **41.** $1.2 \div 2.4$ **42.** $5.2 \div 1.25$

43. Olympics The bar graph shows the number of gold medals won by the four countries with the most gold medals in the 2000 Olympic Summer Games. How many gold medals did the four countries win in all? *(p. 781)*

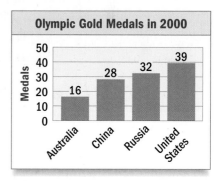

Evaluate the expression when $x = 15$. *(Lesson 1.1)*

44. $x + 4$ **45.** $200 - x$ **46.** $x - 11$ **47.** $3x$

Standardized Test Practice

48. Multiple Choice Which expression has a value of 81?

 A. 4^3 **B.** 3^4 **C.** 2^8 **D.** 27^3

49. Short Response Compare each number in the top row of the table with the number below it. Describe any pattern you see. Complete the table with a variable expression involving n.

1	2	3	4	...	n
1	8	27	64	...	?

A Problem Solving Plan

▶ **Review** this topic in preparation for solving problems in Lesson 1.3. For a review of problem solving strategies, see pp. 795–802.

A Problem Solving Plan

You can use the following 4-step plan to solve a problem.

1 *Read and Understand* Read the problem carefully. Identify the question and any important information.

2 *Make a Plan* Decide on a problem solving strategy.

3 *Solve the Problem* Use the problem solving strategy to answer the question.

4 *Look Back* Check that your answer is reasonable.

Reading and Planning

Example You plan to ship 5 books to a friend. The table shows the masses of the books. Is it possible to ship the books in 2 boxes, each with a mass of 6 kilograms or less? Explain.

Book	A	B	C	D	E
Mass (kg)	1.4	2.1	3.8	1.9	2.5

Read and Understand

What do you know?

The mass of each box must be 6 kilograms or less.
The table gives the mass of each book.

What do you want to find out?

Is it possible to put the books in 2 boxes so that each box has a mass of 6 kilograms or less?

Make a Plan

How can you relate what you know to what you want to find out?

Check that the total mass of the books doesn't exceed 12 kilograms. If it does, you can't divide the books as you want.
Use the strategy *guess, check, and revise* to choose books for each box.

Solving and Looking Back

To solve the problem from page 14 about shipping books, carry out the plan. Then check the answer.

Solve the Problem

The total mass of the books is $1.4 + 2.1 + 3.8 + 1.9 + 2.5 = 11.7$ kg, so it may be possible to ship the books as you want.

Now use the strategy *guess, check, and revise.* Put the 3 lightest books in one box and the 2 heaviest in the other. The mass of the second box is more than 6 kg.

Books	Total mass (kg)
A, D, B	$1.4 + 1.9 + 2.1 = 5.4$
C, E	$3.8 + 2.5 = 6.3$

Try switching books B and E. The mass of each box is less than 6 kg.

Books	Total mass (kg)
A, D, E	$1.4 + 1.9 + 2.5 = 5.8$
C, B	$3.8 + 2.1 = 5.9$

Answer It is possible to ship the books in 2 boxes, each with a mass of 6 kg or less. Put books A, D, and E in one box and books C and B in the other.

Look Back

It makes sense that the box with 3 books contains the 2 lightest books and the box with 2 books contains the heaviest book. So, the answer is reasonable.

✔ Checkpoint

▶ **Test** your knowledge of the problem solving plan by solving these problems.

1. **Pool Schedules** A community pool offers 3 swim sessions each Saturday morning. Each session lasts 35 minutes, with 10 minutes between sessions. The final session ends at 11:05 A.M. At what time does the first session begin?

2. **Theater Seating** The center section of a theater has 10 rows. There are 41 seats in row 10, 38 seats in row 9, 35 seats in row 8, and so on. How many seats are in row 1?

3. **Movie Marathon** You have invited friends over to watch movies. You have rented 4 movies: one action, one science fiction, one comedy, and one animated. In how many different orders can you watch the movies?

Order *of* Operations

BEFORE	Now	WHY?
You performed basic operations.	You'll use order of operations to evaluate expressions.	So you can find the height of a boojum, as in Ex. 28.

Vocabulary

order of operations, p. 16

Flower Flag There are about 2000 plants in each of the 50 stars of this flower flag. There are about 64,100 plants in each of the 7 short stripes and 106,700 plants in each of the 6 long stripes. The blue region contains about 198,900 plants. You can approximate the total number of plants by evaluating the expression

$$50 \cdot 2000 + 7 \cdot 64{,}100 + 6 \cdot 106{,}700 + 198{,}900.$$

To evaluate expressions involving more than one operation, mathematicians have agreed on a set of rules called the **order of operations**.

Note *Worthy*

You should include material that appears on a notebook like the one shown in your own notebook.

Order of Operations

1. Evaluate expressions inside grouping symbols.

2. Evaluate powers.

3. Multiply and divide from left to right.

4. Add and subtract from left to right.

Example 1   *Using Order of Operations*

To approximate the total number of plants in the flower flag described above, use the order of operations to evaluate the expression $50 \cdot 2000 + 7 \cdot 64{,}100 + 6 \cdot 106{,}700 + 198{,}900$.

$50 \cdot 2000 + 7 \cdot 64{,}100 + 6 \cdot 106{,}700 + 198{,}900$	**Write expression.**
$= 100{,}000 + 448{,}700 + 640{,}200 + 198{,}900$	**Multiply.**
$= 1{,}387{,}800$	**Add.**

Answer There are approximately 1,387,800 plants in the flower flag.

Grouping Symbols Parentheses ( ), brackets [ ], and fraction bars are common grouping symbols. Grouping symbols indicate operations that should be performed first. For example, compare the expressions $3 \cdot 2 + 5$ and $3(2 + 5)$. To evaluate $3 \cdot 2 + 5$, you multiply first, then add. To evaluate $3(2 + 5)$, you add first, then multiply.

Example 2 Using Grouping Symbols

Evaluate the expression.

a. $8(17 - 2.3) = 8(14.7)$ Subtract within parentheses.

$\qquad\qquad\qquad = 117.6$ Multiply.

b. $\dfrac{14 + 6}{12 - 7} = (14 + 6) \div (12 - 7)$ Rewrite fraction as division.

$\qquad\qquad = 20 \div 5$ Evaluate within parentheses.

$\qquad\qquad = 4$ Divide.

c. $5 \cdot [36 - (13 + 9)] = 5 \cdot [36 - 22]$ Add within parentheses.

$\qquad\qquad\qquad\qquad = 5 \cdot 14$ Subtract within brackets.

$\qquad\qquad\qquad\qquad = 70$ Multiply.

 Checkpoint

Evaluate the expression.

1. $28 - 63 \div 7$ **2.** $52 + 12.5 \cdot 4$ **3.** $9 \cdot 6 + 27 \div 3$

4. $10(1.5 + 0.6)$ **5.** $\dfrac{70 - 9.2}{3 + 5}$ **6.** $72 \div [(11 - 7) \cdot 2]$

Example 3 Evaluating Variable Expressions

Evaluate the expression when $x = 2$ and $y = 5$.

a. $4(x + y) = 4(2 + 5)$ Substitute 2 for x and 5 for y.

$\qquad\quad = 4(7)$ Add within parentheses.

$\qquad\quad = 28$ Multiply.

b. $3(x + y)^2 = 3(2 + 5)^2$ Substitute 2 for x and 5 for y.

$\qquad\qquad = 3(7)^2$ Add within parentheses.

$\qquad\qquad = 3(49)$ Evaluate power.

$\qquad\qquad = 147$ Multiply.

 Checkpoint

Evaluate the expression when $x = 4$ and $y = 2$.

7. $1.2(x + 3)$ **8.** $1.2x + 3$ **9.** $3x - 2y$

10. $0.5[y - (x - 2)]$ **11.** $x^2 - y$ **12.** $2(x - y)^2$

Watch *Out*

When grouping symbols appear inside other grouping symbols, as in part (c) of Example 2, work from the innermost grouping symbols out.

Study *Strategy*

You can use the first letters of the words of the sentence *Please Excuse My Dear Aunt Sally* to help you remember the order of operations.

P parentheses
E exponents
M ⎫ multiplication and
D ⎭ division
A ⎫ addition and
S ⎭ subtraction

Example 4 *Using a Problem Solving Plan*

Sewing You buy a pattern and enough material to make two pillows. The pattern costs $5. Each pillow requires $3.95 worth of fabric and a button that costs $.75. Find the total cost.

Solution

Read and Understand You buy one pattern plus fabric and buttons for two pillows. You are asked to find the total cost.

Make a Plan Write a verbal model.

| Total cost | = | Cost of pattern | + | Number of pillows | • | Cost of each pillow |

Solve the Problem Write and evaluate an expression.

$$\text{Total cost} = 5 + 2(3.95 + 0.75) \qquad \text{Substitute values into verbal model.}$$
$$= 5 + 2(4.70) \qquad \text{Add within parentheses.}$$
$$= 5 + 9.40 \qquad \text{Multiply.}$$
$$= 14.40 \qquad \text{Add.}$$

Answer The total cost is $14.40.

Look Back Use estimation to check that the answer is reasonable. The cost of materials for each pillow is about $4 + $1 = $5. The total cost is about $5 + 2($5) = $15. The answer is reasonable.

1.3 Exercises

More Practice, p. 803

INTERNET
eWorkbook Plus
CLASSZONE.COM

Guided Practice

Vocabulary Check

1. Give three examples of grouping symbols.

2. Describe in order the steps you would take to evaluate the expression $12(x - 3)^2$ when $x = 5$.

Skill Check **Evaluate the expression.**

3. $15 - 3 \cdot 4$

4. $48 \div 6 + 2$

5. $3 \cdot 8 + 5 \cdot 4$

6. $\dfrac{18 + 12}{7 - 2}$

7. $17 - (3^2 - 2)$

8. $4[15 - (2 + 5)]$

9. Twin Convention The table shows the numbers of sets of twins, triplets, quadruplets, and quintuplets registered at a twin convention. Write and evaluate an expression for the total number of people who registered at the convention.

Type	Sets
Twins	2697
Triplets	29
Quadruplets	2
Quintuplets	1

Practice and Problem Solving

Homework *Help*

Example	Exercises
1	10–13
2	14–18
3	19–27
4	28–31

Online Resources
CLASSZONE.COM

• More Examples
• eTutorial Plus

Evaluate the expression.

10. $47.7 - 12 \cdot 3$

11. $11 \cdot 7 - 9 \cdot 5$

12. $14 \div 7 + 36 \div 4$

13. $5.8(3) + 3(1.1)$

14. $\dfrac{36 - 12}{2 + 6}$

15. $\dfrac{9.8 + 2.2}{7 - 5}$

16. $5(21 - 3^2)$

17. $7[2.5 + 3(12 - 7)]$

18. $84 \div [(18 - 16) \cdot 3]$

Evaluate the expression when $x = 3$, $y = 4$, and $z = 5$.

19. $0.25y + x$

20. $0.25(y + x)$

21. $4(z - x)$

22. $\dfrac{6.5y}{x - 1}$

23. $x + \dfrac{24.4}{y}$

24. $7z - x^2$

25. $x + 2[z - (y - 1)]$

26. $(x + y)^2 - 3.6$

27. $y + (z - 1)^2$

28. Plants A boojum is a very slow-growing cactus. One fifty-year-old boojum is 1.5 meters tall and has been growing about 0.03 meter each year. Assume the growth pattern continues.

  a. Write an expression for the height in meters of the boojum y years from now.

  b. Apply How tall will the boojum be in 50 years?

29. Craft Fair Your school is setting up a row of 5 tables for a craft fair. Each table is 72 inches long. The space between each pair of neighboring tables must be 48 inches. Write and evaluate an expression to find the length of the space needed for the tables from the beginning of the first table to the end of the last table.

30. Basketball In basketball, players score points by making free throws worth 1 point each, field goals worth 2 points each, and field goals worth 3 points each. A player scores 4 free throws, 7 two-point field goals, and 2 three-point field goals. Write and evaluate an expression for the total number of points the player scores.

31. Movies You buy 4 videotapes for $14.99 each and 3 DVDs for $19.99 each. Find the total cost of the movies.

Evaluate the expression when $x = 4$ and $y = 3$.

32. $5x^2 + 2y$

33. $7(x^2 - 5y)$

34. $\dfrac{x^2 + 9}{y + 2}$

35. $\dfrac{6.5y + 2}{x + 1}$

36. Cell Phone You and your sister share cell phone service. You divide the bill equally, including the monthly fee of $39 plus $.30 for each additional minute beyond your free minutes.

  a. Write an expression for your share of the bill in a month when you are charged for m extra minutes.

  b. Apply One month, you are charged for 125 additional minutes. Find your share of the bill.

37. Extended Problem Solving Digital cameras capture images in rows and columns of *pixels*, which are small rectangular colored dots. The more pixels in a given space, the greater the detail of the image.

   a. Calculate The total number of pixels in an image is the product of the number of pixels in a row and the number of pixels in a column. Your camera produces an image that has 1280 pixels in a row and 1024 pixels in a column. Find the total number of pixels.

   b. A megapixel is 1,000,000 pixels. Find, to the nearest tenth, the number of megapixels in the image in part (a).

   c. Apply Let m be the number of megapixels in an image, and let l and w be the length and width in inches of a printed photo. A print is clear if the value of the expression $\dfrac{m}{lw}$ is 0.017 or greater. Can you make a clear 8 inch by 10 inch print of the image in part (a)? Explain.

38. Museum Cost A group of 20 members and 5 nonmembers visited a museum. The admission cost was $6 for members and $10 for nonmembers. The group decided to divide the total cost evenly among all 25 people. What did each person pay?

39. Challenge You are decorating a square mouse pad. You place a colored sticker at each corner. If you have r different colors available, the number of possible patterns is the value of the expression $\dfrac{r^4 + 2r^3 + 3r^2 + 2r}{8}$. Two patterns are different if you cannot produce either pattern by turning the other around.

   a. *Writing* Tell whether the patterns shown are the same. Explain.

   b. You decide to use two colors. Find the number of possible patterns.

   c. Sketch all the possible patterns for two different colors.

Mixed Review

Copy and complete the statement using <, >, or =. *(p. 773)*

40. 1.99 <u>?</u> 1.98   **41.** 0.56 <u>?</u> 0.65   **42.** 0.32 <u>?</u> 0.23

43. Color Monitor The *bit depth* of a color monitor is the number of colors it can display and is expressed as a power of 2. A 32 bit monitor can display 2^{32} colors. Write and evaluate an expression for the number of colors an 8 bit monitor can display. *(Lesson 1.2)*

Standardized Test Practice

44. Extended Response The number of calories in a serving of food is the sum of the calories from carbohydrate, protein, and fat. A cup of whole milk has 11 g of carbohydrate, 8 g of protein, and 8 g of fat.

Component	Calories in 1 gram
Carbohydrate	4
Protein	4
Fat	9

   a. How many calories are there in a cup of whole milk?

   b. If you drank enough whole milk to get 20 g of protein, how many calories would it provide? Explain how you found your answer.

1.3 Using Order of Operations

Goal Use a calculator to evaluate expressions using the order of operations.

Example

Baseball **Alex Rodriguez played for the Texas Rangers during the 2002 baseball season. Use the following information to calculate his batting average for that season.**

To find a baseball player's batting average, you divide the number of hits he made by the number of times he was at bat and round the quotient to the nearest thousandth. The table gives Alex Rodriguez's 2002 batting statistics.

2002 season	Hits	At bats
Before All-Star Game	100	328
After All-Star Game	87	296

Solution

Divide the total number of hits by the total number of times at bat. Use parentheses around each sum.

> The arrow indicates that the display does not show the entire entry.

Keystrokes

```
(100+87)÷(328→
       0.299679487
```

Answer Alex Rodriguez's batting average for the entire season was 0.300, which is usually written as .300.

Draw Conclusions

Use a calculator to evaluate the expression.

1. $50 + 21 \div 3$ 2. $15 \times (24 + 8)$ 3. $(8 + 10) \div 2$ 4. $(5 + 2)^2 - 3^2$

5. $(24 - 16) \div 2$ 6. $(12 - 7)^2 - 1$ 7. $38 \div (2 + 17)$ 8. $(8 + 3)^2 + 2$

9. **Critical Thinking** What result would you get in the example above if you didn't use parentheses when entering the expression? Why?

10. **Baseball** Barry Bonds played for the San Francisco Giants during the 2002 season. Use the information in the table to calculate his batting average for the entire 2002 season.

2002 season	Hits	At bats
Before All-Star Game	80	232
After All-Star Game	69	171

Tech *Help*

The keystrokes shown may not be the same as on your calculator. See your calculator's instruction manual for alternative keystrokes. For additional keystroke help, visit the website below.

 **Online Resources**
CLASSZONE.COM

• Keystroke Help

Comparing *and* Ordering Integers

Vocabulary

integer, p. 22
negative integer, p. 22
positive integer, p. 22
absolute value, p. 23
opposite, p. 23

Supercooled Insects Water freezes at 0°C, but some animals can resist freezing by producing a chemical that lowers the temperature at which the water in their bodies freezes. This temperature is called the supercooling point. Which of the insects listed in the table has the lowest supercooling point?

Insect	Supercooling point (°C)
Arctic beetle	−54
Gall beetle	−35
Goldenrod gallfly	−9
Snow flea	−19
Wooly bear caterpillar	−70

The numbers in the table are *negative integers*. The **integers** are the numbers . . . , −3, −2, −1, 0, 1, 2, 3, ... (The dots indicate that the numbers continue without end in both the positive and negative directions). **Negative integers** are integers that are less than 0. **Positive integers** are integers that are greater than 0.

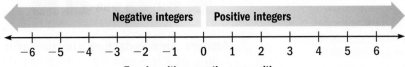

Zero is neither negative nor positive.

Example 1 *Graphing and Ordering Integers*

To determine which insect in the table above has the lowest supercooling point, graph the integers on a number line.

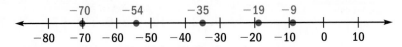

Read the numbers from left to right: −70, −54, −35, −19, −9.

Answer At −70°C , the wooly bear caterpillar has the lowest supercooling point.

Wooly bear caterpillar

✔ *Checkpoint*

1. Use a number line to order these integers from least to greatest: −8, 5, −4, 2, 0, 6.

Absolute Value The **absolute value** of a number is its distance from 0 on a number line. The absolute value of a number a is written as $|a|$. You can use a number line to find the absolute value of a number.

Example 2 | *Finding Absolute Value*

State the absolute value of the number.

a. 5   **b.** -7

Solution

a.

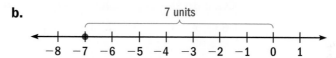

5 units

The distance between 5 and 0 is 5. So, $|5| = 5$.

b.

7 units

The distance between -7 and 0 is 7. So, $|-7| = 7$.

Reading *Algebra*

The expression $-a$ is always read as "the opposite of a" and *not* as "negative a." If a is a positive number, then $-a$ is a negative number. If a is a negative number, then $-a$ is a positive number.

Opposites Two numbers are **opposites** if they have the same absolute value but different signs. For example, -10 and 10 are opposites. The expression -10 can be read as "the opposite of 10" or as "negative 10." The expression "$-a$" is read as "the opposite of a."

Example 3 | *Finding Opposites*

State the opposite of the number.

a. 6   **b.** -15

Solution

a.

6 units   6 units

The opposite of 6 is -6.

b.

15 units   15 units

The opposite of -15 is 15.

 Checkpoint

State the absolute value and the opposite of the number.

2. 3   **3.** -1 **4.** 10   **5.** -11

Example 4 *Evaluating Variable Expressions*

Evaluate the expression when $y = -5$.

  a. $-y$ **b.** $17 - |y|$

Solution

  a. $-y = -(-5)$ Substitute -5 for y.

         $= 5$ The opposite of -5 is 5.

  b. $17 - |y| = 17 - |-5|$ Substitute -5 for y.

               $= 17 - 5$ The absolute value of -5 is 5.

               $= 12$ Subtract.

 **Checkpoint**

Evaluate the expression when $x = -4$.

  6. $-x$ **7.** $12 - |x|$ **8.** $|x| + 9$ **9.** $|x| - 1$

1.4 Exercises

More Practice, p. 803

INTERNET
eWorkbook Plus
CLASSZONE.COM

Guided Practice

Vocabulary Check

1. Which of these numbers is *not* an integer: $-31, 74, 22.5, -7,$ or 19?

2. Explain why the absolute value of a number is never negative.

Skill Check

3. Write the integers in order from least to greatest: $-9, 12, 6, -3, 0, -5$.

State the absolute value of the number.

  4. 1 **5.** -9 **6.** 15 **7.** -12

State the opposite of the number.

  8. 14 **9.** -33 **10.** -24 **11.** 81

Evaluate the expression when $x = -3$.

  12. $|x| + 8$ **13.** $|x| + |-1|$ **14.** $20 - |x|$ **15.** $|50| - |x|$

16. Error Analysis Describe and correct the error in evaluating the expression $|-17|$.

$|-17| = -17$

17. Volcanoes The elevation of the top of a volcano relative to sea level is called the summit elevation. The summit elevation of Kilauea in Hawaii is 1222 meters. The summit elevation of the underwater volcano Loihi in the Pacific Ocean is -980 meters. Which is farther from sea level, the top of Kilauea or the top of Loihi?

Practice and Problem Solving

Homework *Help*

Example	Exercises
1	18-25, 38, 42, 51
2	26-33, 52
3	34-41, 52
4	43-50

Online Resources
CLASSZONE.COM
• More Examples
• eTutorial Plus

Copy and complete the statement using < or >.

18. -8 ? 3   **19.** -9 ? -12 **20.** 0 ? -4 **21.** -15 ? -7

Graph the integers on a number line. Then write the integers in order from least to greatest.

22. $-12, 4, -6, 0, -1$ **23.** $15, -8, -4, 7, -5$

24. $35, 60, -10, -5, 40$ **25.** $-22, -30, -25, -16$

State the absolute value of the number.

26. -22 **27.** 7   **28.** 21   **29.** -40

30. 38   **31.** -42 **32.** -73 **33.** 105

State the opposite of the number.

34. 6   **35.** 9   **36.** -2 **37.** -11

38. -31 **39.** -67 **40.** 81   **41.** 100

42. Neptune's Moons In 1989, data collected by the Voyager spacecraft showed the surface temperature of Triton, Neptune's largest moon, to be about $-392°F$. Eight years later, data from the Hubble telescope showed the temperature to be about $-389°F$. Did the Hubble data indicate a temperature *less than* or *greater than* the one based on the Voyager data?

Neptune and Triton

Evaluate the expression when $x = -8$.

43. $-x$ **44.** $|x| - 1$ **45.** $32 - |x|$ **46.** $-x - 2$

47. $5|x|$ **48.** $-x - 3$ **49.** $5 + (-x)$ **50.** $|x| + 10$

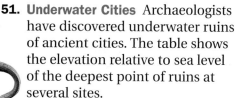

51. Underwater Cities Archaeologists have discovered underwater ruins of ancient cities. The table shows the elevation relative to sea level of the deepest point of ruins at several sites.

Site	Elevation relative to sea level
Helike, Greece	3 meters below
Heraklion, Egypt	8 meters below
Port Royal, Jamaica	12 meters below
Unnamed city, Bay of Bengal	37 meters below

a. Write an integer to represent each elevation in the table.

b. Graph the integers on a number line.

c. Identify the site whose deepest point is farthest from sea level.

d. Compare The elevation of the modern-day Greek city of Polónia is 1 meter above sea level. Is Polónia *closer to* or *farther from* sea level than the deepest point of the ruins of Helike?

Stoneware cups found at Port Royal, Jamaica

52. *Writing* Explain why the absolute value of 0 is 0.

53. Extended Problem Solving The table shows the daily high temperature at Alaska's Barrow Observatory over a seven-day period.

Day	Temperature
Sunday	$-19°C$
Monday	$-17°C$
Tuesday	$-14°C$
Wednesday	$-9°C$
Thursday	$-13°C$
Friday	$-18°C$
Saturday	$-21°C$

a. Did the temperature *increase* or *decrease* from Sunday to Monday?

b. Did the temperature *increase* or *decrease* from Friday to Saturday?

c. Compare Which day's high temperature was highest for the week? Which was lowest?

d. Interpret and Apply Describe any periods of two or more days during the week when the daily high temperature consistently increased or decreased.

Evaluate the expression when $a = -2$ and $b = -13$.

54. $|a| + |b|$ **55.** $-a + (-b)$ **56.** $-a + |b|$

57. $|b| - |a|$ **58.** $-|b|$ **59.** $|-a|$

60. Critical Thinking Are there values of x for which $-x$ is less than x? Are there values of x for which $-x$ is greater than x? Explain.

Evaluate the expression when $x = -7$.

61. $|-x|$ **62.** $|x| + |-x|$ **63.** $|x| - |-x|$ **64.** $-|-x|$

65. Challenge Copy and complete using x or $-x$: If $x > 0$, then $|x| = \underline{?}$. If $x < 0$, then $|x| = \underline{?}$.

Mixed Review

Estimation Estimate the sum or difference by rounding each number to the place of its leading digit. *(p. 771)*

66. $278 + 119 + 602$ **67.** $588 - 131$ **68.** $112 + 193 + 583$

Find a low and high estimate for the product or quotient. *(p. 772)*

69. 62×708 **70.** $31{,}217 \div 218$ **71.** 371×47

Evaluate the expression when $x = 2$ and $y = 8$. *(Lesson 1.3)*

72. $6(x + y)$ **73.** $xy + 1$ **74.** $\dfrac{x + 22}{y}$

Standardized Test Practice

75. Multiple Choice Which list of integers is in order from least to greatest?

A. $2, 16, -17, 21, -35$ **B.** $2, -16, -17, -21, -35$

C. $-35, -17, 2, 16, 21$ **D.** $21, 16, 2, -17, -35$

76. Multiple Choice Which of the following is the value of the expression $|x| + |-5|$ when $x = 5$?

F. -5 **G.** 0 **H.** 5 **I.** 10

Mid-Chapter Quiz

Evaluate the expression when $x = 2$ and $y = 14$.

1. $x + 5$ **2.** $y - 2$ **3.** $x + y$ **4.** $\dfrac{y}{x}$

5. Word Processing Your computer's word-processing program fits about 250 words on one page. Let p represent the number of pages in a report. Write a variable expression for the approximate number of words in the report.

Write the product using an exponent.

6. $11 \cdot 11 \cdot 11 \cdot 11$ **7.** $(2.6)(2.6)(2.6)$ **8.** $s \cdot s \cdot s \cdot s$ **9.** $y \cdot y \cdot y \cdot y \cdot y$

Evaluate the expression.

10. $18 - 3 \cdot 2$ **11.** $27 \div 3 + 6$ **12.** $\dfrac{20 + 12}{11 - 3}$ **13.** $4(20 - 3^2)$

Evaluate the expression when $x = 20$ and $y = 5$.

14. $0.5x + y$ **15.** $\dfrac{x + 5}{y}$ **16.** $3(x - y)$ **17.** $y^2 - x$

18. Graph the integers -18, 4, -20, -2, -6, 0 on a number line. Then write the integers in order from least to greatest.

State the absolute value and the opposite of the number.

19. -24 **20.** 8 **21.** 31 **22.** -17

23. Evaluate the expression $44 - |x|$ when $x = -10$.

Take 5

Use each of the digits 1, 2, 3, 4, and 5 exactly once in each statement to make a true statement.

$(? + ? - ? \times ?) \div ? = 1$

$(? + ? \times ?) \div ? - ? = 0$

$(? \div ? + ? - ?) \times ? = 8$

1.5 Adding Integers on a Number Line

Goal
Add integers
on a number line.

Materials
- paper
- pencil

Investigate

Use a number line to find the sum of two integers.

① Add $-3 + 7$.

Draw a number line. Place a pencil at 0 and move 3 units to the left to reach -3. Then move 7 units to the right to show addition of 7. Find your final position on the number line.

Copy and complete the statement:

$$-3 + 7 = \underline{\ ?\ }.$$

② Add $-1 + (-7)$.

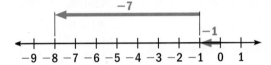

Draw a number line. Place a pencil at 0 and move 1 unit to the left to reach -1. Then move 7 units to the left to show addition of -7. Find your final position on the number line.

Copy and complete the statement:

$$-1 + (-7) = \underline{\ ?\ }.$$

Draw Conclusions

Use a number line to find the sum.

1. $-6 + 13$ **2.** $-5 + 10$ **3.** $-8 + 4$ **4.** $-1 + 6$

5. $10 + (-6)$ **6.** $10 + (-12)$ **7.** $9 + (-3)$ **8.** $-9 + (-3)$

9. $10 + (-7)$ **10.** $8 + (-11)$ **11.** $-7 + (-8)$ **12.** $4 + (-8)$

13. *Writing* Suppose you are adding a positive integer and a negative integer. Explain how you can tell without actually adding whether the sum of the integers is *positive*, *negative*, or *zero* by considering the lengths of the arrows that represent the integers.

14. **Critical Thinking** Another way to add integers on a number line is to start at the first number in the sum and to move a distance and direction determined by the second integer. Identify the addition expression represented in the diagram and find the sum.

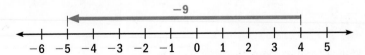

Adding Integers

BEFORE	Now	WHY?
You added decimals.	You'll add integers.	So you can find a hockey player's plus-minus rating, as in Ex. 40.

Vocabulary

additive inverse, p. 30

Scuba Diver A scuba diver studying marine life is 4 feet below sea level. From that depth, the diver descends 72 feet to the ocean floor and then rises 61 feet. The diver rests there to avoid decompression illness. Where is the diver relative to sea level? In Example 3, you will see how to answer this question by adding integers.

One way to add integers is to use a number line.

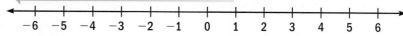

To add a positive integer, move to the right.

To add a negative integer, move to the left.

$-6 \quad -5 \quad -4 \quad -3 \quad -2 \quad -1 \quad 0 \quad 1 \quad 2 \quad 3 \quad 4 \quad 5 \quad 6$

Example 1   Adding Integers Using a Number Line

Study *Strategy*

In the activity on page 28, you used two arrows to add two integers on a number line. The first arrow started at 0 and ended at the first number in the sum. In Example 1, you see that you can draw only one arrow if you start at the first number in the sum.

Use a number line to find the sum.

a. $3 + (-9)$

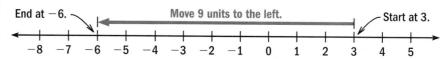

End at -6.   Move 9 units to the left.   Start at 3.

$-8 \quad -7 \quad -6 \quad -5 \quad -4 \quad -3 \quad -2 \quad -1 \quad 0 \quad 1 \quad 2 \quad 3 \quad 4 \quad 5$

Answer The final position is -6. So, $3 + (-9) = -6$.

b. $-5 + 3$

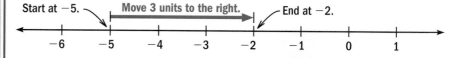

Start at -5.   Move 3 units to the right.   End at -2.

$-6 \quad -5 \quad -4 \quad -3 \quad -2 \quad -1 \quad 0 \quad 1$

Answer The final position is -2. So, $-5 + 3 = -2$.

 Checkpoint

Use a number line to find the sum.

1. $-11 + 6$ **2.** $-1 + (-8)$ **3.** $10 + (-5)$

Absolute Values You can use absolute values to find the sum of two or more integers.

> ## Adding Integers
>
> | **Words** | **Numbers** |
> |---|---|
> | **1. Same Sign** Add the absolute values and use the common sign. | $8 + 12 = 20$
$-6 + (-4) = -10$ |
> | **2. Different Signs** Subtract the lesser absolute value from the greater absolute value and use the sign of the number with greater absolute value. | $5 + (-8) = -3$
$-11 + 13 = 2$ |
> | **3. Opposites** The sum of a number and its opposite is 0. | $7 + (-7) = 0$ |

Additive Inverse Property The opposite of a number is also called its **additive inverse** . Item 3 in the notebook can be written algebraically as $a + (-a) = 0$ and is called the *additive inverse property*.

Example 2 Adding Two Integers

a. Find the sum $-54 + (-28)$.

$$-54 + (-28) = -82$$

— Same sign: Add $|-54|$ and $|-28|$.

— Both integers are negative, so the sum is negative.

b. Find the sum $38 + (-17)$.

$$38 + (-17) = 21$$

— Different signs: Subtract $|-17|$ from $|38|$.

— $|38| > |-17|$, so the sum has the same sign as 38.

Example 3 Adding More Than Two Integers

To answer the question about the position of the scuba diver at the top of page 29, you can find the sum $-4 + (-72) + 61$.

$$-4 + (-72) + 61 = -76 + 61 \qquad \text{Add } -4 \text{ and } -72.$$
$$= -15 \qquad \text{Add } -76 \text{ and } 61.$$

Answer The sum is -15, so the diver is 15 feet below sea level.

 Checkpoint

Find the sum.

4. $-41 + 26$ **5.** $-19 + (-11)$ **6.** $52 + (-30) + (-46)$

Watch *Out*

When you substitute a negative number for a variable, you may have to enclose the number in parentheses, as in part (b) of Example 4, to avoid confusion with an operation sign.

Example 4 **Evaluating Variable Expressions**

Evaluate the expression when $x = -22$ and $y = -12$.

   a. $x + (-9)$ **b.** $x + 17 + y$

Solution

  a. $x + (-9) = -22 + (-9)$ Substitute -22 for x.
                $= -31$ Add.

  b. $x + 17 + y = -22 + 17 + (-12)$ Substitute for x and for y.
                   $= -5 + (-12)$ Add -22 and 17.
                   $= -17$ Add -5 and -12.

 Checkpoint

Evaluate the expression when $a = -18$ and $b = -3$.

  7. $a + (-8)$ **8.** $32 + a$ **9.** $a + b + 30$

1.5 Exercises

More Practice, p. 803

Guided Practice

Vocabulary Check
1. Copy and complete: To add two integers without using a number line, you need to use the ? of each number.

2. How can you tell whether the sum of -71 and 43 is positive or negative without actually finding the sum?

Skill Check **Use a number line to find the sum.**

  3. $-9 + 11$ **4.** $-2 + (-13)$ **5.** $15 + (-7)$

Find the sum.

  6. $24 + (-16)$ **7.** $-15 + 3$ **8.** $-11 + (-2)$

Evaluate the expression when $x = -9$.

  9. $x + 3$ **10.** $-6 + x$ **11.** $x + (-3)$

12. Food Science Food scientists tested the effects that freezing and thawing have on the texture of a cheese filling for ravioli. The filling was frozen to a temperature of $-18°C$. The temperature was then raised $108°C$. What was the final temperature of the filling?

13. Error Analysis
Describe and correct the error in using a number line to find the sum of -2 and 5.

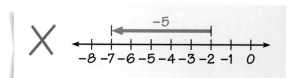

Practice and Problem Solving

Homework *Help*

Example	Exercises
1	14–23, 39
2	24–29, 40
3	30–32, 41
4	33–38

Online Resources
CLASSZONE.COM
• More Examples
• eTutorial Plus

14. Match the correct sum with the addition shown on the number line.

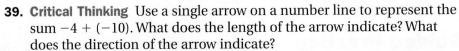

A. $-6 + 8$ **B.** $6 + (-8)$ **C.** $-6 + (-8)$

Use a number line to find the sum.

15. $1 + (-17)$ **16.** $-4 + 13$ **17.** $-7 + (-3)$

18. $13 + (-3)$ **19.** $-9 + (-5)$ **20.** $-6 + (-7)$

21. $8 + (-2)$ **22.** $-3 + 6$ **23.** $-5 + (-4)$

Find the sum.

24. $-54 + 40$ **25.** $-20 + (-32)$ **26.** $66 + (-16)$

27. $19 + (-45)$ **28.** $-32 + 17$ **29.** $-72 + (-30)$

30. $7 + (-9) + 15$ **31.** $-40 + 33 + 12$ **32.** $55 + (-28) + (-6)$

Evaluate the expression when $x = -8$, $y = 4$, and $z = -5$.

33. $x + 15$ **34.** $y + (-75)$ **35.** $-19 + z$

36. $x + y$ **37.** $x + z$ **38.** $y + z$

39. Critical Thinking Use a single arrow on a number line to represent the sum $-4 + (-10)$. What does the length of the arrow indicate? What does the direction of the arrow indicate?

40. Hockey In the National Hockey League, a player is assigned a positive point each time his team scores while he is on the ice. He is assigned a negative point each time the opposing team scores while he is on the ice. (No points are assigned if the scoring team has more players on the ice than the other team.) The sum of the positive and negative points is called the player's plus-minus rating. The table shows the points awarded to a player in two games.

a. Find the player's plus-minus rating for game 1.

b. Find the player's plus-minus rating for game 2.

Game	Positive points	Negative points
1	3	-1
2	2	-5

c. Find the total plus-minus rating for the two games.

d. Interpret and Apply Did the player have a better plus-minus rating in game 1 or in game 2? Explain.

41. Overdraft Your checking account shows an *overdraft*, or a negative balance. Your present balance is $-\$25$. You deposit \$100, then write a check for \$12. What is your new balance?

Tech *Help*

To enter a negative number on a calculator, use (−), not −.

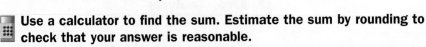 **Use a calculator to find the sum. Estimate the sum by rounding to check that your answer is reasonable.**

42. $-345 + (-978)$ **43.** $2172 + (-4087)$ **44.** $-1117 + 539$

45. Lake Vostok Lake Vostok, an unfrozen lake buried under Antarctic ice, is about 1200 meters deep. Scientists drilled down 3623 meters into the ice to test for signs of life, but stopped 120 meters above the top of the lake to avoid contaminating it.

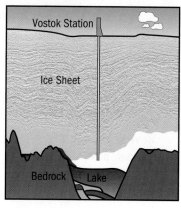

    a. Find the position of the top of the lake relative to the ice surface.

    b. Find the position of the bottom of the lake relative to the ice surface.

46. *Writing* Write three different pairs of integers, each of which has a sum of -24. Explain how you chose the integers.

Find the sum.

47. $-35 + 16 + (-12) + 7$ **48.** $-2 + 10 + (-3) + 5$

49. $90 + (-24) + (-6) + 5$ **50.** $-9 + 16 + (-12) + 3$

Evaluate the expression when $a = -14$, $b = 5$, and $c = -8$.

51. $a + b + c$ **52.** $-15 + b + c$ **53.** $8 + a + (-4) + c$

Critical Thinking Using the given information and the fact that x and y are integers, tell whether the sum $x + y$ is *even* or *odd*. Explain your reasoning.

54. x and y are even.   **55.** x and y are odd.   **56.** x is even; y is odd.

57. For what values of x is $|x| + x = 0$? Explain.

58. Absolute value bars are grouping symbols. Use the order of operations to evaluate the expression $-3 + |-x + 2|$ when $x = 12$.

Challenge Find values of a and b for which the statement is true.

59. $|a + b| = |a| + |b|$ **60.** $|a + b| < |a| + |b|$

Mixed Review   Write a variable expression to represent the phrase. *(Lesson 1.1)*

61. The sum of a number and 14.5

62. The difference of a number and 2.75

63. Area You are building a house on a square-shaped lot. The side length of the lot is 70 yards. Find the area of the lot. *(Lesson 1.2)*

Copy and complete the statement using <, >, or =. *(Lesson 1.4)*

64. $|15| \underline{\ ?\ } 15$ **65.** $-12 \underline{\ ?\ } |12|$ **66.** $|-2| \underline{\ ?\ } -2$

Standardized Test Practice   **67. Multiple Choice** What is the value of the expression $x + |y|$ when $x = -3$ and $y = 12$?

    A. -15 **B.** -9 **C.** 9 **D.** 15

68. Short Response For what integer value(s) of x is the value of the expression $-10 + |x|$ greater than 0? Explain your reasoning.

1.6

Subtracting Integers

BEFORE	Now	WHY?
You subtracted decimals.	You'll subtract integers.	So you can find the difference in road elevations, as in Ex. 11.

Review Vocabulary

opposite, p. 23
difference, p. 771

Earth Science Kick-'em-Jenny is an underwater volcano in the Caribbean Sea.

Eruptions have caused the volcano to grow. In 1962, the summit elevation of Kick-'em-Jenny was −235 meters. In 2002, the summit elevation was −182 meters. By how many meters did the elevation of the volcano change? Example 3 uses integer subtraction to answer this question.

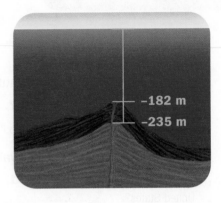

−182 m
−235 m

Reading *Algebra*

Check to see that other pairs of expressions, such as 8 − 3 and 8 + (−3), also have the same value. The process of looking at specific examples and drawing a general conclusion is called *inductive reasoning*.

As you can see from the number lines below, the expressions $5 - 4$ and $5 + (-4)$ have the same value, 1.

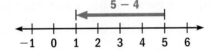

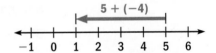

These equivalent expressions suggest the following rule for subtracting integers.

Subtracting Integers

Words To subtract an integer, add its opposite.

Numbers $3 - 7 = 3 + (-7) = -4$ **Algebra** $a - b = a + (-b)$

Example 1	*Subtracting Integers*

a. $4 - 10 = 4 + (-10)$ To subtract 10, add its opposite, −10.

$\quad\quad = -6$ Add 4 and −10.

b. $7 - (-5) = 7 + 5$ To subtract −5, add its opposite, 5.

$\quad\quad = 12$ Add 7 and 5.

c. $-2 - (-9) = -2 + 9$ To subtract −9, add its opposite, 9.

$\quad\quad = 7$ Add −2 and 9.

Example 2   *Evaluating Variable Expressions*

Evaluate the expression when $x = -9$.

a. $x - (-40)$ 　　　　　　　　　　　　**b.** $7 - x$

Solution

a. $x - (-40) = -9 - (-40)$ 　　**Substitute -9 for x.**

$ = -9 + 40$ 　　　　　**To subtract -40, add 40.**

$ = 31$ 　　　　　　　　**Add -9 and 40.**

b. $7 - x = 7 - (-9)$ 　　**Substitute -9 for x.**

$ = 7 + 9$ 　　　**To subtract -9, add 9.**

$ = 16$ 　　　　　**Add 7 and 9.**

 **Checkpoint**

Find the difference.

1. $2 - 6$ 　　　　**2.** $3 - (-8)$ 　　　　**3.** $-7 - 4$ 　　　　**4.** $-1 - (-13)$

Evaluate the expression when $y = -14$.

5. $y - 3$ 　　　　**6.** $25 - y$ 　　　　**7.** $y - 10$ 　　　　**8.** $-9 - y$

Evaluating Change You can use subtraction to find the change in a variable quantity such as elevation or temperature. Subtract the original value of the quantity from the value after the change.

Example 3   *Evaluating Change*

To answer the question on page 34 about the change in elevation of the volcano Kick-'em-Jenny, you can subtract the elevation in 1962 from the elevation in 2002. Write a verbal model.

Change in elevation	=	Elevation in 2002	−	Elevation in 1962

$ = -182 - (-235)$ 　　**Substitute values.**

$ = -182 + 235$ 　　　　**To subtract -235, add 235.**

$ = 53$ 　　　　　　　　**Add -182 and 235.**

Answer The difference is 53, so the summit elevation of Kick-'em-Jenny increased by 53 meters from 1962 to 2002.

In the **Real World**

Earth Science After four years of eruptions, an underwater volcano off the coast of Iceland broke through the ocean's surface. The eruptions began 130 meters below sea level. The volcano became the island of Surtsey, with an elevation of 174 meters. What was the change in elevation?

 **Checkpoint**

Find the change in temperature.

9. From $32°F$ to $-10°F$ 　　　　　　　**10.** From $-45°F$ to $-80°F$

11. From $8°C$ to $-3°C$ 　　　　　　　**12.** From $-2°C$ to $15°C$

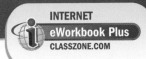

Guided Practice

Vocabulary Check

1. Write the phrase as a variable expression: the difference of -15 and a number x.

2. Explain how you would find the difference of -45 and -60.

Skill Check

Find the difference.

3. $3 - 8$ **4.** $6 - (-2)$ **5.** $-9 - 4$ **6.** $-5 - (-1)$

Evaluate the expression when $m = -6$.

7. $m - 4$ **8.** $m - 16$ **9.** $7 - m$ **10.** $-7 - m$

Guided Problem Solving

11. The Big Dig Boston's Central Artery Project, called "The Big Dig," is one of the most complex highway projects in American history. The project includes an underground highway and a tunnel. The lowest point of the highway is 110 feet below sea level. The lowest point of the tunnel is 90 feet below sea level. What is the difference in these two elevations?

    1 Write an integer to represent the elevation of the lowest point of the highway.

    2 Write an integer to represent the elevation of the lowest point of the tunnel.

    3 Find the difference of the elevations in Steps 1 and 2.

Practice and Problem Solving

Homework *Help*

Example	Exercises
1	12-23, 32
2	24-31
3	33-38

Online Resources
CLASSZONE.COM
- More Examples
- eTutorial Plus

Find the difference.

12. $8 - 9$ **13.** $1 - (-8)$ **14.** $-10 - 6$ **15.** $-5 - (-17)$

16. $0 - 15$ **17.** $2 - (-37)$ **18.** $-20 - 4$ **19.** $-1 - (-53)$

20. $24 - 41$ **21.** $-39 - 32$ **22.** $79 - (-98)$ **23.** $-86 - (-34)$

Evaluate the expression when $m = -6$.

24. $17 - m$ **25.** $4 - m$ **26.** $m - 7$ **27.** $-16 - m$

28. $m - 19$ **29.** $m - 3 - 10$ **30.** $20 - m - 5$ **31.** $14 - 30 - m$

32. Error Analysis Describe and correct the error in finding the difference of -2 and -5.

$$\begin{aligned} -2 - (-5) &= -2 + (-5) \\ &= -7 \end{aligned}$$

33. Temperatures The most extreme temperature change in Canadian history occurred when the temperature in Pincher Creek, Alberta, rose from $-19°C$ to $22°C$ in one hour. Find the change in temperature.

34. Extended Problem Solving There are four stages in the production of ice cream. First, the mix is pasteurized to destroy bacteria. Next, the temperature of the mix is lowered for aging. Flavors are added and the temperature is lowered even more to harden the ice cream. Finally, the ice cream is stored in a freezer. The graph shows the temperature at each stage.

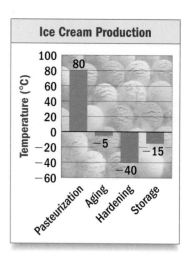

a. Calculate Find the change in temperature between each two consecutive stages. Then find the absolute value of each change.

b. Compare Between which two consecutive stages is the absolute value of the temperature change the greatest?

c. Estimate You can use the formula $C = \frac{5(F - 32)}{9}$ to convert a temperature F in degrees Fahrenheit to a temperature C in degrees Celsius. Suppose the temperature in your mouth is about 99°F. Use mental math to estimate the temperature in your mouth in degrees Celsius. About how much greater is the temperature in your mouth than the temperature of ice cream just out of a freezer?

Find the change in temperature or elevation.

35. From $-15°C$ to $10°C$

36. From $-5°F$ to $-13°F$

37. From -120 feet to -90 feet

38. From 30 meters to -70 meters

Find the value of the expression.

39. $-15 - 75 - 100$

40. $-402 + 74 - 281$

41. $-10 - (-525) - 280$

42. $118 - (-2) - 315$

Evaluate the expression when $x = -5$, $y = 14$, and $z = -7$.

43. $-3 - y - x$ **44.** $y - (-9) - z$ **45.** $z - y - x$ **46.** $x - y - z$

47. Chemistry Ethylene glycol is a chemical that can be added to water to lower its freezing point, the temperature at which it freezes. The freezing point of solution A, which is one part ethylene glycol and three parts water, is $-12°C$. The freezing point of solution B, which is two parts ethylene glycol and two parts water, is $-36°C$. Which solution has a lower freezing point? How much lower is it?

48. Avalanches An avalanche may occur when the temperature keeps snow crystals from sticking together. The room temperature in an avalanche research lab is $-30°C$. Scientists study changes in snow crystals by melting snow on a hot plate that heats to only $-1°C$. In a regular lab, the room temperature is about 18°C and a hot plate heats to about 300°C. How many degrees warmer is the hot plate than the room temperature in each lab? Which difference is greater? How much greater?

49. Critical Thinking Let a and b be integers. Is the value of the expression $a + b$ always greater than the value of the expression $a - b$? Explain.

Evaluate the expression $3 - (-x) + 8 - 10$ for the given value of x.

50. 18   **51.** 5   **52.** -2 **53.** -3

54. Challenge If a is a negative integer and b is a positive integer, tell whether the expression represents a *positive* or a *negative* integer. Explain your thinking.

     a. $a - b$ **b.** $b - a$ **c.** $|a| + |b|$ **d.** $-|a| - |b|$

Mixed Review   **55. Work Backward** You want to arrive at school at 7:45 A.M. It takes you half an hour to shower and get dressed, 15 minutes to eat breakfast, and 20 minutes to walk to school. What is the latest you can get up and still arrive at school on time? *(p. 801)*

Evaluate the expression when $x = 6$ and $y = 12$. *(Lesson 1.3)*

56. $5x - y$ **57.** $3x + y$ **58.** $3(x + y)$

59. $\dfrac{x + y}{3}$ **60.** $x + \dfrac{y}{3}$ **61.** $7x - (y + 1)$

Find the sum. *(Lesson 1.5)*

62. $89 + (-14)$ **63.** $-104 + 53$ **64.** $-67 + (-303)$

Standardized Test Practice   **65. Multiple Choice** Which expression has a value closest to 0?

     A. $23 - 25$ **B.** $23 - (-22)$ **C.** $-23 - 23$ **D.** $23 - (-25)$

66. Multiple Choice The top of a cliff overlooking the ocean is 1250 feet above sea level. The sea floor at the foot of the cliff is 40 feet below sea level. A rock falls off the cliff and drops to the sea floor. Which expression represents the change in elevation of the rock?

     F. $-40 - 1250$ **G.** $40 - 1250$ **H.** $1250 - 40$ **I.** $1250 - (-40)$

Brain GAME — -10 and Counting

In the expression $-1 + (-2) + (-3) + (-4)$, each of the integers -1, -2, -3, and -4 appears exactly once. The value of the expression is -10.

Use each of the integers -1, -2, -3, and -4 exactly once to write an expression that involves addition or subtraction or both and has a value of -8. You may use grouping symbols as needed.

Use the same rules to write four more expressions with values of -6, -4, -2, and 0.

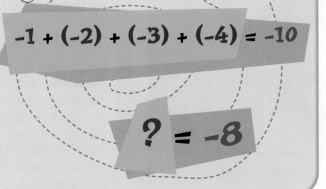

Mean, Median, Mode, *and* Range

▶ **Review** these topics in preparation for solving problems that involve mean, median, mode, and range in Lesson 1.7.

Mean

Data are numbers or facts. The **mean** of a data set is the sum of the values divided by the number of values. The mean is a *measure of central tendency,* that is, an average.

Example **The numbers of trails at ten Colorado ski resorts are listed below. Find the mean of the data.**

$$76, 61, 112, 146, 65, 139, 43, 125, 85, 28$$

First, add the ten values. Then divide by 10, the number of values.

$$\text{Mean} = \frac{76 + 61 + 112 + 146 + 65 + 139 + 43 + 125 + 85 + 28}{10}$$

$$= \frac{880}{10} = 88$$

Answer The mean of the data is 88.

Median

The *median* is another measure of central tendency. The **median** of a data set is the middle value when the values are written in numerical order. If a data set has an even number of values, the median is the mean of the two middle values.

Example **The numbers of ski lifts at ten Colorado ski resorts are listed below. Find the median of the data.**

$$8, 5, 4, 13, 2, 25, 7, 23, 14, 5$$

First, write the values in order from least to greatest.

| 2 | 4 | 5 | 5 | 7 | 8 | 13 | 14 | 23 | 25 |

The data set has an even number of values, so the median is the mean of the two middle values, 7 and 8.

$$\text{Median} = \frac{7 + 8}{2} = \frac{15}{2} = 7.5$$

Answer The median of the data is 7.5.

Continued ➡

Mode

The *mode* is another measure of central tendency. The **mode** of a data set is the value that occurs most often. A data set can have no mode, one mode, or more than one mode.

Example Ten Colorado ski resorts have scheduled openings in the following months. Find the mode of the data.

November, November, December, November, October,
October, December, November, November, December

The month that occurs most often is November.

Answer The mode of the data is November.

Range

The *range* of a data set is a *measure of dispersion*, that is, an indicator of how spread out the data are. The **range** of a data set is the difference of the greatest value and the least value.

Example The average annual snowfall amounts (in inches) for ten Colorado ski resorts are listed below. Find the range of the data.

300, 367, 300, 307, 410, 300, 200, 280, 300, 240

Range = Greatest value − Least value = 410 − 200 = 210

Answer The range of the data is 210 inches.

✔ Checkpoint

▶ **Test** your knowledge of mean, median, mode, and range by solving these problems.

Find the mean, median, mode(s), and range of the data.

1. 85, 96, 72, 88, 95, 80, 86

2. 7, 11, 13, 9, 7, 8, 9, 12

3. 0.8, 0.5, 0.5, 0.7, 0.3, 0.9, 0.5

4. 90, 112, 105, 118, 96, 128, 110, 133

5. Birds The table shows the numbers of bird species observed in five national parks. Find the mean, median, mode(s), and range of the data.

National Park	Species
Joshua Tree	239
Mesa Verde	216
North Cascades	178
Yosemite	147
Nez Perce	135

1.7 Multiplying Integers

Goal
Use patterns to multiply integers.

Materials
• paper
• pencil

Investigate

Use patterns to multiply integers.

Expression	Product
3(3)	9
3(2)	6
3(1)	3
3(0)	?
3(−1)	?
3(−2)	?

Identify a pattern in the second column of the table. Copy the table and use the pattern to complete the table. Then copy and complete the following statement:

The product of a positive integer and a negative integer is _?_ .

Expression	Product
2(−3)	?
1(−3)	?
0(−3)	?
−1(−3)	?
−2(−3)	?
−3(−3)	?

Copy the table. Apply your results from Step 1 to complete rows 1–3. Identify a pattern in the second column. Use that pattern to complete the table. Then copy and complete the following statement:

The product of two negative integers is _?_ .

Draw Conclusions

Find the product.

1. 3(−3) **2.** 3(−4) **3.** −3(5) **4.** −5(6)

5. 10(−2) **6.** 4(−7) **7.** −8(−5) **8.** −3(−12)

9. When one factor in a product is a positive integer, you can think of multiplication as repeated addition. For example, the product 3(−1) is equal to the sum −1 + (−1) + (−1). Use this idea to justify the statements 4(−2) = −8 and −3(5) = −15.

10. **Critical Thinking** Suppose that a and b are positive integers. Exercise 9 showed that if you multiply a by the opposite of b, or b by the opposite of a, the result is the opposite of ab. That is, if a and b are positive integers, then $(-a)b = -ab$ and $a(-b) = -ab$. Suppose you apply this rule to the product $(-a)(-b)$ twice:

$$(-a)(-b) = -[(-a)b] = -(-ab).$$

What is the opposite of the opposite of ab? Use your answer to copy and complete this statement: $(-a)(-b) = $ _?_ .

Multiplying *and* Dividing Integers

Review Vocabulary
mean, p. 39

BEFORE	*Now*	WHY?
You multiplied and divided decimals.	You'll multiply and divide integers.	So you can find the position of a submarine, as in Ex. 27.

Stock Market You own shares of stock in a computer company and in a utility. The value of the shares changes over time. The table shows the number of shares of each type of stock you own and the change in the value of each share over a one-year period. What was the total change in the value of your shares of stock? In Example 2, you will see how to multiply integers to answer this question.

Stock Portfolio		
Stock	**Shares**	**Change in value of one share**
Computer	200	Decreased $3
Utility	150	Increased $2

In the activity on page 41, you may have recognized patterns in the products of integers. These patterns suggest the following rules.

Multiplying Integers

Words	**Numbers**	
The product of two integers with the same sign is positive.	$2(4) = 8$	$-2(-4) = 8$
The product of two integers with different signs is negative.	$2(-4) = -8$	$-2(4) = -8$
The product of any integer and 0 is 0.	$2(0) = 0$	$-2(0) = 0$

Example 1 *Multiplying Integers*

a. $-3(-12) = 36$ Same sign: Product is positive.

b. $-7(9) = -63$ Different signs: Product is negative.

c. $-24(0) = 0$ The product of any integer and 0 is 0.

Watch Out

You cannot divide a number by 0.

Example 2 *Multiplying Integers*

To find the total change in the value of the shares of stock described on page 42, first multiply the number of shares of each type of stock by the change in the price of each share. Then add the results.

Total change	=	Computer shares	·	Change in 1 share	+	Utility shares	·	Change in 1 share

$$= 200(-3) + 150(2) \quad \text{Substitute values.}$$
$$= -600 + 300 \quad \text{Multiply.}$$
$$= -300 \quad \text{Add.}$$

Answer The total change in value was -300. The value of the stocks decreased by $300.

Dividing Integers Because $3(-4) = -12$, you know that $-12 \div 3 = -4$ and $-12 \div (-4) = 3$. This relationship between products and quotients suggests that the rules for dividing integers are like the rules for multiplying integers.

Dividing Integers

Words	**Numbers**
The quotient of two integers with the same sign is positive.	$8 \div 4 = 2 \qquad -8 \div (-4) = 2$
The quotient of two integers with different signs is negative.	$-8 \div 4 = -2 \qquad 8 \div (-4) = -2$
The quotient of 0 and any nonzero integer is 0.	$0 \div 4 = 0 \qquad 0 \div (-4) = 0$

Example 3 *Dividing Integers*

a. $-48 \div (-6) = 8$ Same sign: Quotient is positive.

b. $56 \div (-8) = -7$ Different signs: Quotient is negative.

c. $0 \div 9 = 0$ The quotient of 0 and any nonzero integer is 0.

 **Checkpoint**

Find the product or quotient.

1. $9(-11)$ **2.** $-6(-8)$ **3.** $0(-100)$ **4.** $-4(-8)$

5. $-24 \div 3$ **6.** $0 \div (-25)$ **7.** $-35 \div (-7)$ **8.** $24 \div (-6)$

Antarctic Temperatures The table shows record low monthly temperatures from June to November at McMurdo Station in Antarctica. Find the mean of the temperatures.

Month	June	July	Aug.	Sept.	Oct.	Nov.
Temperature (°F)	−42	−59	−57	−47	−40	−19

Solution

To find the mean of the temperatures, first add the temperatures. Then divide by 6, the number of temperatures.

$$\text{Mean} = \frac{-42 + (-59) + (-57) + (-47) + (-40) + (-19)}{6}$$

$$= \frac{-264}{6} = -44$$

Answer The mean of the temperatures is −44°F.

1.7 Exercises

More Practice, p. 803

INTERNET
eWorkbook Plus
CLASSZONE.COM

Guided Practice

Vocabulary Check
1. Explain what the mean of a data set is.

2. If a and b are integers and the expression ab is positive, what do you know about the signs of a and b?

Skill Check **Tell whether the product or quotient is *positive* or *negative*.**

3. $-238(-17)$ 4. $\dfrac{920}{-23}$ 5. $465(-147)$ 6. $\dfrac{-256}{-32}$

7. $-1209 \div 31$ 8. $-65(219)$ 9. $-98 \div (-2)$ 10. $-99(-716)$

Guided Problem Solving
11. **Electronics** An electronic device is tested to determine how it reacts to changes in temperature. The device is placed in a test chamber at 22°C. After each minute, the temperature in the chamber is lowered 3°C. What is the temperature in the chamber after 9 minutes?

   1) Write an integer that represents the change in temperature in the chamber in one minute.

   2) Write a product of integers that represents the total change in temperature in 9 minutes. Then evaluate the product.

   3) Find the temperature in the chamber after 9 minutes.

Practice and Problem Solving

Homework *Help*

Example	Exercises
1	12-26, 29-34
2	27
3	12-25, 29-34
4	28

Online Resources
CLASSZONE.COM
• More Examples
• eTutorial Plus

Find the product or quotient.

12. $12(5)$　　　**13.** $28 \div 14$　　　**14.** $65 \div (-5)$　　　**15.** $6(-22)$

16. $-7(50)$　　　**17.** $-26 \div 13$　　　**18.** $-72 \div (-36)$　　　**19.** $12(-30)$

20. $\dfrac{175}{-25}$　　　**21.** $\dfrac{-51}{-3}$　　　**22.** $-17(-20)$　　　**23.** $\dfrac{-840}{7}$

24. Error Analysis Describe and correct the error in multiplying -5 and -12, then dividing by -4.

$$\times \qquad \frac{-5(-12)}{-4} = \frac{-60}{-4} = 15$$

25. Compare and Contrast Tell how the rules for multiplying and dividing integers are alike and how they are different.

26. Critical Thinking The table below gives expressions involving the multiplication of integers.

Expression	Number of integers	Product	Sign of product
$-1(-2)$	?	?	?
$-1(-2)(-3)$	?	?	?
$-1(-2)(-3)(-4)$	?	?	?
$-1(-2)(-3)(-4)(-5)$	?	?	?

a. Copy and complete the table.

b. *Writing* Write a rule for the sign of the product of more than two negative integers.

c. Number Sense Suppose that in part (b) the product included positive integer factors as well. Would your rule change? Explain.

27. MIR Submersible A MIR submersible is a type of submarine. As a MIR dives, its elevation changes by -100 feet each minute.

a. From the surface, a MIR takes about 200 minutes to reach the lowest point to which it can dive. What is its elevation at that point?

b. How long would a MIR take to dive to 1000 feet below sea level?

MIR submersible being launched

28. Free Diving *Free diving* means diving without breathing equipment. The graph shows the position with respect to sea level for five record free dives.

a. Find the mean of the positions.

b. Find the median of the positions.

c. Compare Does the mean or the median represent a lower position?

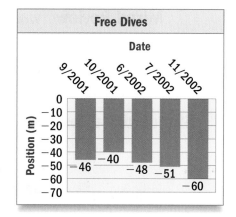

Simplify.

29. $-5(-10)(-25)$ **30.** $16(-4)(-8)$

31. $360 \div (-36) \div (-2)$ **32.** $-72 \div 12 \div 3$

33. $-2(-14) \div (-7)$ **34.** $20(-45) \div (-9)$

Number Sense **Without performing the indicated divisions, copy and complete the statement using >, <, or =.**

35. $-738 \div 82 \; \underline{?} \; -192 \div (-32)$ **36.** $288 \div (-36) \; \underline{?} \; 756 \div 18$

37. Sports A batter hits a baseball. The ball's height h (in feet) above the ground t seconds after it is hit is given by the equation $h = -16t^2 + 80t + 3$. Find the height of the ball 4 seconds after it is hit.

In Exercises 38–41, evaluate the variable expression when $x = -4$.

Example *Evaluating Variable Expressions*

$$-7x^2 = -7(-4)^2 \quad \text{Substitute } -4 \text{ for } x.$$
$$= -7(16) \quad \text{Evaluate power.}$$
$$= -112 \quad \text{Multiply.}$$

Answer When $x = -4$, $-7x^2 = -112$.

38. $-10x^2$ **39.** $\dfrac{72}{x^2}$ **40.** $-6x^2$ **41.** $\dfrac{4x^2}{-10}$

42. For what value of n is $\dfrac{-4 + (-3) + 5 + 4 + (-3) + n}{-7} = 0$ true?

43. Explain You know that for any positive integer n, $1^n = 1$. Is the statement $(-1)^n = -1$ true for any positive integer n? Explain.

44. Challenge Tell whether the statement is *always, sometimes,* or *never* true. Explain your answer.

     a. If k is any integer and n is less than 0, then nk is less than n.

     b. If k is any integer and n is greater than 1, then nk is greater than n.

Mixed Review **Write the integers in order from least to greatest.** *(Lesson 1.4)*

45. $-12, -21, 31, 0, -5, 13$ **46.** $-45, -54, -22, -16, -70$

Find the sum or difference. *(Lessons 1.5, 1.6)*

47. $-27 + 51$ **48.** $-17 + (-12)$ **49.** $-18 - 33$ **50.** $-41 - (-9)$

Standardized Test Practice **51. Multiple Choice** Which expression has a positive value?

     A. $\dfrac{-16(-5)}{4(-9)}$ **B.** $-7^2 - 2$ **C.** $5 - 4(-6)$ **D.** $19 - 6(7)$

52. Short Response Find the mean of these temperatures: $-12°F$, $7°F$, $-22°F$, $-11°F$, $20°F$, $-6°F$. Describe the steps you used.

The Coordinate Plane

BEFORE	Now	WHY?
You used number lines.	You'll identify and plot points in a coordinate plane.	So you can compare the fuel economy of cars, as in Ex. 27.

Vocabulary

coordinate plane, p. 47
ordered pair, p. 47
scatter plot, p. 48

A **coordinate plane** is formed by the intersection of a horizontal number line called the **x-axis** and a vertical number line called the **y-axis**. The axes meet at a point called the **origin** and divide the coordinate plane into four **quadrants**.

Each point in a coordinate plane is represented by an **ordered pair**. The first number is the **x-coordinate**, and the second number is the **y-coordinate**.

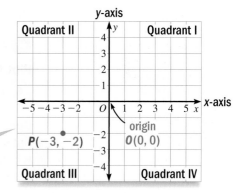

Point P is represented by the ordered pair $(-3, -2)$.
Point P is in Quadrant III.

Note *Worthy*

You may find it helpful to draw a coordinate plane in your notebook. Label the origin and the axes. Use colored arrows as in Example 1 to illustrate how to find the coordinates of a point.

Example 1 Naming Points in a Coordinate Plane

Give the coordinates of the point.

a. A **b.** B

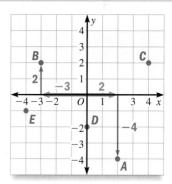

Solution

a. Point A is 2 units to the right of the origin and 4 units down. The x-coordinate is 2, and the y-coordinate is -4. The coordinates are $(2, -4)$.

b. Point B is 3 units to the left of the origin and 2 units up. The x-coordinate is -3, and the y-coordinate is 2. The coordinates are $(-3, 2)$.

 Checkpoint

Use the coordinate plane in Example 1. Give the coordinates of the point.

1. C **2.** D **3.** E

Example 2 — Plotting Points in a Coordinate Plane

Plot the point in a coordinate plane. Describe the location of the point.

a. $A(4, 1)$ **b.** $B(0, -3)$ **c.** $C(-2, -5)$

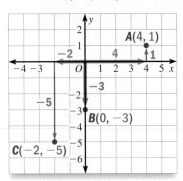

Solution

a. Begin at the origin and move 4 units to the right, then 1 unit up. Point A is in Quadrant I.

b. Begin at the origin and move 3 units down. Point B is on the y-axis.

c. Begin at the origin and move 2 units to the left, then 5 units down. Point C is in Quadrant III.

✔ Checkpoint

Plot the point in a coordinate plane. Describe the location of the point.

4. $P(-1, 1)$ **5.** $Q(4, -5)$ **6.** $R(0, 0)$ **7.** $S(-2, 0)$

Scatter Plots A **scatter plot** uses a coordinate plane to display paired data. Each data pair is plotted as a point. A scatter plot may suggest whether a relationship exists between two sets of data.

Example 3 — Making a Scatter Plot

Fish A biologist measured the lengths and masses of eight rainbow trout. Make a scatter plot of the data shown in the table and describe any relationship you see.

Length (millimeters)	405	360	413	395	247	280	265	351
Mass (grams)	715	557	754	584	184	248	223	506

Solution

1 Write the data as ordered pairs. Let the x-coordinate represent the length, and let the y-coordinate represent the mass: (405, 715), (360, 557), (413, 754), (395, 584), (247, 184), (280, 248), (265, 223), (351, 506)

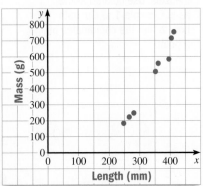

2 Plot the ordered pairs in a coordinate plane. You need only the first quadrant.

Notice that the points rise from left to right. You can conclude that as the lengths of the rainbow trout increase, their masses tend to increase.

Reading *Algebra*

Points on the x-axis or on the y-axis are not in any quadrant.

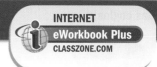

Guided Practice

Vocabulary Check

1. What is the *x*-coordinate of the point $(-12, 7)$? What is the *y*-coordinate?

2. A point has one positive coordinate and one negative coordinate. Can you determine in which quadrant the point lies? Explain.

Skill Check   **Plot the point in a coordinate plane. Describe the location of the point.**

3. $J(2, 3)$ 4. $K(-5, -1)$ 5. $L(0, -3)$ 6. $M(4, -4)$

Guided Problem Solving

7. **Earth Science** Scientists studying the Columbia River in Washington measured the speed of the water at one location in the river, but at different depths. The table shows the results. Is there any relationship between the depth of the water and its speed?

Depth (inches)	8	24	31	71	88	103	119	127	134
Speed (inches per second)	19	13	17	14	11	7	7	5	3

1. Write the data as ordered pairs. Let the *x*-coordinate represent depth, and let the *y*-coordinate represent speed.

2. Make a scatter plot of the data.

3. Does the scatter plot suggest any relationship between the depth of the water and its speed? Explain.

Practice and Problem Solving

Homework *Help*

Example	Exercises
1	8–15
2	16–26
3	27

Online Resources
CLASSZONE.COM

• More Examples
• eTutorial Plus

Give the coordinates of the point.

8. *A*   9. *B*

10. *C*   11. *D*

12. *E*   13. *F*

14. *G*   15. *H*

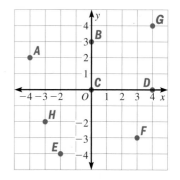

16. *Writing* Explain how to plot the point $(6, -3)$ in a coordinate plane.

Plot the point in a coordinate plane. Describe the location of the point.

17. $P(5, 5)$ 18. $Q(-1, 0)$ 19. $R(8, -4)$ 20. $S(2, -4)$

21. $T(-3, -6)$ 22. $U(0, -5)$ 23. $V(-4, -1)$ 24. $W(6, -5)$

Gas engine

Electric motor

In the **Real World**

Fuel Economy The hybrid car powered by the combined gas engine and electric motor shown has a fuel economy of 46 miles to the gallon in city driving and 51 miles to the gallon on the highway. Suppose you drive the hybrid car about 10,000 miles in the city each year. If you pay $1.75 for one gallon of gas, how much do you pay for gas in a year?

25. Error Analysis
Describe and correct the error in locating the point $(2, -8)$.

 The point $(2, -8)$ is 8 units to the left of the origin and 2 units up.

26. Critical Thinking How can you tell by looking at the coordinates of a point whether the point is on the *x*-axis? on the *y*-axis?

27. Fuel Economy The table shows the engine sizes of several cars and the average highway mileage for each car.

Engine size (liters)	3	6	2	4	1	4	5
Mileage (miles per gallon)	28	19	33	25	47	24	22

  a. Make a scatter plot of the data.

  b. **Interpret** Does the scatter plot suggest any relationship between the size of the engine in a car and the car's average highway mileage? Explain.

28. Geometry Use a coordinate plane.

  a. Plot the points $(-3, -2)$, $(-3, 6)$, $(5, 6)$, and $(5, -2)$. Connect the points in order. Connect the last point to the first.

  b. Identify the figure. Explain your reasoning.

29. Geometry Use the variable expression $2x + 1$.

  a. Evaluate the expression when $x = -3, -2, -1, 0, 1, 2,$ and 3.

  b. Use your results from part (a) to write a list of ordered pairs in the form $(x, 2x + 1)$.

  c. Plot the order pairs $(x, 2x + 1)$ from part (b) in a coordinate plane.

  d. *Writing* Describe what you notice about the points.

30. Extended Problem Solving In the game *Go*, each player begins with a supply of black or white stones. Each player in turn places a stone on a grid at the intersection of two grid lines. A player captures another player's stone by surrounding it on four sides with his or her own stones. (Diagonals do not count.) For example, the diagram shows that a black stone has been captured. In the diagram, coordinate axes have been superimposed on part of a *Go* board.

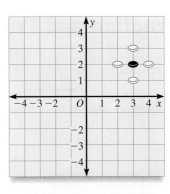

  a. **Identify** Give the coordinates of each of the stones shown in the diagram.

  b. **Apply** A white stone is placed at $(-3, 2)$. Give the coordinates of the points that a player must cover with black stones to capture the white stone.

31. Geometry Point O is the origin of a coordinate plane. Choose points P, Q, and R so that O, P, Q, and R are the corners of a square with a side length of 5 units. Identify the coordinates of P, Q, and R. Explain your reasoning.

Challenge The point (a, b) is in Quadrant II of a coordinate plane. Describe the location of the point with the given coordinates.

32. (b, a) **33.** (a, a) **34.** (b, b)

Mixed Review

35. Movie Tickets Let c represent the cost in dollars of a ticket at the local movie theater. You use a \$20 bill to pay for two tickets. Write a variable expression for the amount of change you receive. *(Lesson 1.1)*

Tell whether the sum is *always*, *sometimes*, or *never* negative. *(Lesson 1.5)*

36. The sum of two negative integers

37. The sum of two positive integers

38. The sum of a negative integer and a positive integer

Find the product or quotient. *(Lesson 1.7)*

39. $-15(3)$ **40.** $-252 \div 12$ **41.** $-63 \div (-3)$ **42.** $9(-17)$

Standardized Test Practice

43. Multiple Choice In which quadrant is the point $(-22, 35)$ located?

   A. Quadrant I   **B.** Quadrant II   **C.** Quadrant III   **D.** Quadrant IV

44. Multiple Choice What are the coordinates of point A?

   F. $(-3, 1)$ **G.** $(1, -3)$

   H. $(3, -1)$ **I.** $(-1, 3)$

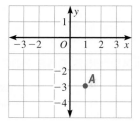

What Is It?

Plot each pair of points on a coordinate grid and connect the two points to solve the riddle:

What force and strength cannot get through, it with a gentle touch can do. And many in the street would stand, were it not a friend at hand. What is it?

- $(-1, 3)$ and $(-1, -1)$
- $(3, 1)$ and $(4, 3)$
- $(-4, 1)$ and $(-2, -1)$
- $(-8, 3)$ and $(-6, -1)$
- $(-1, 3)$ and $(1, 3)$

- $(3, -1)$ and $(3, 1)$
- $(2, 3)$ and $(3, 1)$
- $(-1, 1)$ and $(1, 1)$
- $(-1, -1)$ and $(1, -1)$
- $(-4, 3)$ and $(-4, -1)$

- $(-9, 1)$ and $(-7, 1)$
- $(-4, 1)$ and $(-2, 3)$
- $(-10, -1)$ and $(-8, 3)$

Chapter Review

Vocabulary Review

numerical expression, p. 5	base, p. 10	absolute value, p. 23	origin, p. 47
variable, p. 5	exponent, p. 10	opposite, p. 23	quadrant, p. 47
variable expression, p. 5	order of operations, p. 16	additive inverse, p. 30	ordered pair, p. 47
evaluate, p. 5	integer, p. 22	coordinate plane, p. 47	x-coordinate, p. 47
verbal model, p. 6	negative integer, p. 22	x-axis, p. 47	y-coordinate, p. 47
power, p. 10	positive integer, p. 22	y-axis, p. 47	scatter plot, p. 48

1. Draw a coordinate plane. Label the x-axis, the y-axis, the origin, and the quadrants.

2. Explain how these vocabulary terms are related: power, base, exponent.

3. Describe how to find the opposite of an integer.

4. What is a variable expression?

1.1 Expressions and Variables

Examples on pp. 5–6

▶ **Goal**

Evaluate variable expressions.

Example Evaluate the expression xy when $x = 12$ and $y = 3$.

$$xy = 12(3) \quad \text{Substitute 12 for } x \text{ and 3 for } y.$$
$$= 36 \quad \text{Multiply.}$$

✔ Evaluate the expression when $p = 12$ and $q = 1.5$.

5. $35 - p$ **6.** $q + 2$ **7.** $\dfrac{60}{p}$ **8.** $16q$

9. $p + q$ **10.** $p - q$ **11.** $\dfrac{p}{q}$ **12.** pq

1.2 Powers and Exponents

Examples on pp. 10–11

▶ **Goal**

Evaluate powers.

Example Evaluate the power $(0.4)^3$.

$$(0.4)^3 = (0.4)(0.4)(0.4) \quad \text{Use 0.4 as a factor 3 times.}$$
$$= 0.064 \quad \text{Multiply.}$$

✓ **Evaluate the power.**

13. 10^4 **14.** $(0.3)^3$ **15.** $(12.5)^2$ **16.** 3^5

17. 5^5 **18.** 15^2 **19.** $(1.2)^3$ **20.** $(0.8)^4$

1.3 Order of Operations

Examples on pp. 16–18

▶ *Goal*

Use the order of operations to evaluate expressions.

Example   Evaluate the expression $800 - 7(2 + 3)^2$.

$$800 - 7(2 + 3)^2 = 800 - 7(5)^2 \quad \text{Add within parentheses.}$$
$$= 800 - 7(25) \quad \text{Evaluate power.}$$
$$= 800 - 175 \quad \text{Multiply.}$$
$$= 625 \quad \text{Subtract.}$$

✓ **Evaluate the expression.**

21. $20 \cdot 5 + 7 \cdot 3$ **22.** $\dfrac{5 + 4}{3} - 2$ **23.** $28 \div (5 - 1) \cdot 3$

1.4 Comparing and Ordering Integers

Examples on pp. 22–24

▶ *Goal*

Compare and order integers.

Example   **Graph the integers $-2, 3, 0, 2, -3$ on a number line. Then write the integers in order from least to greatest.**

Write the integers from left to right: $-3, -2, 0, 2, 3$.

Example   **State the absolute value and the opposite of -2.**

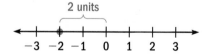

The absolute value of -2 is 2.   The opposite of -2 is 2.

✓ **Graph the integers on a number line. Then write the integers in order from least to greatest.**

24. $4, 0, -3, 7, -6$ **25.** $2, -4, -3, 6, 5, -6$ **26.** $-8, -12, 4, -7, 1$

✓ **State the absolute value and the opposite of the number.**

27. 18   **28.** -9 **29.** 4   **30.** -100

1.5 Adding Integers

Examples on pp. 29–31

▶ **Goal**

Add Integers.

Example Find the sum.

a. $-42 + (-17)$

These integers have the same sign.

$$-42 + (-17) = -59$$

— Add $|-42|$ and $|-17|$.

Both integers are negative, so the sum is negative.

b. $-51 + 63$

These integers have different signs.

$$-51 + 63 = 12$$

— Subtract $|-51|$ from $|63|$.

$|63| > |-51|$, so the sum is positive.

✔ **Find the sum.**

31. $12 + (-18)$ **32.** $-8 + (-7)$ **33.** $-27 + 38$ **34.** $-11 + (-18)$

35. $61 + (-44)$ **36.** $-13 + (-21)$ **37.** $-21 + 9$ **38.** $-22 + (-7)$

39. At 6:00 A.M., the temperature was $-5°$F. By 2:00 P.M., the temperature had risen $22°$F. What was the temperature at 2:00 P.M.?

1.6 Subtracting Integers

Examples on pp. 34–35

▶ **Goal**

Subtract Integers.

Example Find the difference.

a. $7 - 15 = 7 + (-15)$ To subtract 15, add its opposite, -15.

          $= -8$ Add 7 and -15.

b. $-9 - (-11) = -9 + 11$ To subtract -11, add its opposite, 11.

            $= 2$ Add -9 and 11.

✔ **Find the difference.**

40. $0 - 8$ **41.** $-2 - (-2)$ **42.** $-46 - 29$ **43.** $6 - (-13)$

44. $-15 - (-17)$ **45.** $31 - 40$ **46.** $-16 - 9$ **47.** $20 - (-11)$

48. Find the difference of an elevation of 30 feet below sea level and an elevation of 118 feet above sea level.

1.7 Multiplying and Dividing Integers

Examples on pp. 42–44

▶ *Goal*

Multiply and divide integers.

Example **Find the product or quotient.**

a. $-4(-15) = 60$ **Same sign: Product is positive.**

b. $-6(14) = -84$ **Different signs: Product is negative.**

c. $-42 \div (-7) = 6$ **Same sign: Quotient is positive.**

d. $20 \div (-5) = -4$ **Different signs: Quotient is negative.**

✔ **Find the product or quotient.**

49. $-9(-12)$ **50.** $52 \div (-4)$ **51.** $-17(3)$ **52.** $90 \div (-15)$

53. $\dfrac{-80}{-16}$ **54.** $20(-12)$ **55.** $\dfrac{48}{-16}$ **56.** $-33(-3)$

1.8 The Coordinate Plane

Examples on pp. 47–48

▶ *Goal*

Identify and plot points in a coordinate plane.

Example **Give the coordinates of point *P*.**

Point *P* is 4 units to the left of the origin and 1 unit up. The *x*-coordinate is -4, and the *y*-coordinate is 1. The coordinates of point *P* are $(-4, 1)$.

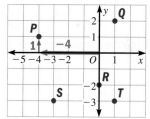

✔ **Use the coordinate plane shown in the example. Give the coordinates of the point.**

57. Q **58.** R **59.** S **60.** T

Example **Plot the point *A*(1, −3) in a coordinate plane. Describe the location of the point.**

Begin at the origin and move 1 unit to the right, then 3 units down. Point *A* is in Quadrant IV.

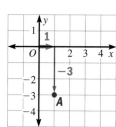

✔ **Plot the point in a coordinate plane. Describe the location of the point.**

61. $B(-2, 5)$ **62.** $C(0, 4)$

63. $D(-3, -1)$ **64.** $E(4, -2)$

Evaluate the expression when $y = 16$ and $z = 4$.

1. $y + 9$ **2.** $11 - z$ **3.** $\dfrac{y}{z}$ **4.** yz

Write the power in words and as a repeated multiplication. Then evaluate the power.

5. 8^2 **6.** 2^7 **7.** $(0.2)^5$ **8.** $(0.7)^4$

9. Sewing You are making a beanbag footstool in the shape of a cube with an edge length of 50 centimeters. In order to fill the footstool with plastic beads, you need to know its volume. Find the volume of the footstool.

Evaluate the expression.

10. $70.2 + 4(3.5)$ **11.** $\dfrac{75 - 39}{4 \cdot 3}$ **12.** $90 \div 5 + 4$ **13.** $18 + 30 \div 6$

Evaluate the expression when $r = 4$ and $s = 6$.

14. $3.5s + r$ **15.** $(r + 1)^2 - s$ **16.** $4r + s^2$ **17.** $2(r^2 - 15)$

State the absolute value and the opposite of the number.

18. -78 **19.** 121 **20.** -33 **21.** 19

Find the sum or difference.

22. $35 + (-11)$ **23.** $-28 + (-40)$ **24.** $-38 + (-8)$ **25.** $43 + (-22)$

26. $5 - (-16)$ **27.** $-60 - 7$ **28.** $-19 - 35$ **29.** $-48 - (-72)$

Find the product or quotient.

30. $-20(32)$ **31.** $\dfrac{-76}{4}$ **32.** $-25(-30)$ **33.** $840 \div (-24)$

34. $18(-4)$ **35.** $700 \div (-35)$ **36.** $-12(-16)$ **37.** $\dfrac{-270}{-18}$

38. Investments The integers below represent the monthly gains and losses in the value of an investment over one year. Find the mean of the integers.

$-\$190, \$75, -\$65, \$100, \$72, -\$54, -\$62, -\$87, \$92, \$81, -\$73, \$63$

39. Geometry Plot the points listed below in the same coordinate plane. Describe any pattern you see in the graph.

$(-3, -6), (-2, -5), (-1, -4), (0, -3), (1, -2), (2, -1)$

Chapter Standardized Test

Test-Taking Strategy The best way to prepare for a standardized test is to keep up with your daily schoolwork. You will learn the concepts and skills you need for the test.

1. What is the value of the expression $\frac{24}{x}$ when $x = 8$?

   A. 3   **B.** 16   **C.** 32   **D.** 192

2. Which variable expression represents the following phrase?

   A number raised to the ninth power

   F. $9n$ **G.** 9^n **H.** n^9 **I.** $\frac{9}{n}$

3. What is the first step in evaluating the expression $15 - 12 \div 3$?

   A. Subtract 12 from 15.

   B. Divide 12 by 3.

   C. Subtract 3 from 15.

   D. Divide 15 by 3.

4. What is the value of the expression $x + y^2$ when $x = 3$ and $y = 5$?

   F. 64   **G.** 34   **H.** 28   **I.** 13

5. Which expression has a value of -4?

   A. $-(-4)$ **B.** $|-4|$ **C.** $|4|$ **D.** $-|4|$

6. Which list of integers is in order from least to greatest?

   F. $-4, -7, 0, 2$ **G.** $0, 2, -4, -7$

   H. $-7, -4, 0, 2$ **I.** $2, 0, -7, -4$

7. What is the value of the expression $-11 + 24 + (-32)$?

   A. -67 **B.** -19 **C.** 19   **D.** 67

8. Find the difference $-32 - (-15)$.

   F. -47 **G.** -17 **H.** 17   **I.** 47

9. Which expression has a value of 12?

   A. $\frac{-144}{-12}$ **B.** $\frac{36}{-3}$

   C. $2(-6)$ **D.** $-3(4)$

10. In a coordinate plane, point P is 8 units to the left of the origin and 6 units up. What are the coordinates of point P?

   F. $(6, -8)$ **G.** $(-6, 8)$

   H. $(8, -6)$ **I.** $(-8, 6)$

11. Short Response The integers -6, 12, -2, and -16 represent yards gained or lost by a football team on 4 plays. Describe the steps you would use to find the mean of the integers. Then find the mean.

12. Extended Response The table lists the thicknesses of the trunks of 6 loblolly pine trees and their heights.

   a. Make a scatter plot of the data.

   b. Describe any relationship the scatter plot suggests. Explain your thinking.

Thickness (inches)	Height (feet)
6	36
9	44
10	46
12	52
15	61
16	67

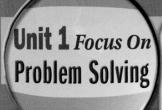
Reading *the* Problem

Recognizing Relevant, Irrelevant, and Missing Information

When you read a problem, you should decide what information you need to solve the problem.

Problem In football, the turnover margin for a team is given by the expression $t - g$, where t is the number of times the team takes the ball away from an opposing team through an interception or a fumble and g is the number of times the team gives the ball to an opposing team through an interception or a fumble. Information about a team is given in the table below. Did this team improve its turnover margin from 2000 to 2001? from 2001 to 2002?

Season	Games played	Takes ball		Gives ball	
		Intercep.	Fumbles	Intercep.	Fumbles
2000	16	11	8	20	13
2001	16	13	15	26	11

1 What information is relevant?

To solve the problem, you need all the information given in the table except for the number of games played. That information is irrelevant for finding turnover margins.

2 Is any information missing?

The table gives you enough information to find the turnover margins for 2000 and 2001 but not for 2002. So, you can determine whether the team improved its turnover margin from 2000 to 2001 but not whether it improved its turnover margin from 2001 to 2002.

3 How is the problem solved?

Find the turnover margins for 2000 and 2001 by evaluating the expression $t - g$. To find t, add the number of interceptions and the number of fumbles for "Takes ball." Likewise, to find g, add the number of interceptions and the number of fumbles for "Gives ball."

2000 season: $t - g = (11 + 8) - (20 + 13)$
$$= 19 - 33$$
$$= -14$$

2001 season: $t - g = (13 + 15) - (26 + 11)$
$$= 28 - 37$$
$$= -9$$

Answer Because $-9 > -14$, you can conclude that the team improved its turnover margin from 2000 to 2001. You need information about the team's turnovers for 2002 to determine whether the team improved its turnover margin from 2001 to 2002.

Problem Solving Practice

1. **Apples** You buy 10 apples that weigh a total of 4 pounds for $3.92. What is the cost of a pound of apples? How much would 6 pounds of apples cost?

2. **Baking** You are baking cookies that require 6 cups of cereal for each batch. Use the nutrition facts below to find the number of boxes of cereal you will need to make 3 batches of cookies. Then determine how many cookies you can make.

Nutrition Facts

Serving size: $1\frac{1}{2}$ cups (40 g)

Servings per package: 10

---

3. **Lemonade** You are making lemonade that requires 2 quarts of water. If you have already added 3 cups of water, how much more do you need to add? (If you do not know how many cups are in a quart, where can you find this information?)

4. **Vacation** Your family is going on a vacation. Your destination is 880 miles away. Your family is driving there at an average speed of 55 miles per hour for 8 hours a day. The car gets 28 miles per gallon of gas, and the car's gas tank holds 10 gallons of gas. If you start your vacation with a full tank of gas, how many times will your family have to stop to fill the gas tank on your way to your destination?

5. **Roller Coaster** A roller coaster takes a group of 24 people every 5 minutes. The ride lasts 3 minutes. There are 52 people in front of you. It takes 10 minutes to walk from the roller coaster to the concert stage, where you have reservations for the 2:00 show. If it is 1:30 now, can you ride the roller coaster and still make it to the show on time?

6. **Football** Use the information on the previous page along with the 2002 information below to determine if the team improved its turnover margin from 2001 to 2002. What was the team's average points scored per game in 2002?

Games played	Takes ball		Gives ball	
	Intercep.	Fumbles	Intercep.	Fumbles
18	7	12	25	12

7. **Temperature** To find the departure from normal temperature, you can use the expression $a - n$, where a is the actual average temperature for the day and n is the normal, or average, temperature historically. Use the table below to find the departure from normal temperature for each day. Then find the mean departure from normal temperature for the week.

Day	Normal temp.	Actual temp.	Precipitation
Sunday	39°F	33°F	0.0 in.
Monday	38°F	42°F	0.1 in.
Tuesday	38°F	25°F	0.5 in.
Wednesday	37°F	24°F	0.0 in.
Thursday	37°F	38°F	0.0 in.
Friday	37°F	29°F	1.6 in.
Saturday	36°F	36°F	0.3 in.

Solving Equations

How far can an athlete run in 10 seconds?

CHAPTER 2

INTERNET Preview
CLASSZONE.COM

- eEdition Plus Online
- eWorkbook Plus Online
- eTutorial Plus Online
- State Test Practice
- More Examples

M A T H *In the* **Real World**

Track Race The world's fastest athletes can run 100 meters in under 10 seconds. In this chapter, you will use equations to solve problems like finding the average rate at which an athlete runs a race.

What do you think? Suppose an athlete runs at an average rate of 10.5 meters per second for 10 seconds. Use the formula *distance = rate × time* to find the distance the athlete runs.

Chapter Prerequisite Skills

Review Vocabulary

numerical expression, p. 5
variable expression, p. 5
order of operations, p. 16
absolute value, p. 23
decimal, p. 770

PREREQUISITE SKILLS QUIZ

Preparing for Success **To prepare for success in this chapter, test your knowledge of these concepts and skills. You may want to look at the pages referred to in blue for additional review.**

1. **Vocabulary** Describe the difference between a numerical expression and a variable expression.

Perform the indicated operation. *(pp. 774–776)*

   2. $3.8 + 7.1$ 3. $8.23 - 4.97$ 4. 5.5×9.4 5. $6.93 \div 2.1$

Write a variable expression to represent the phrase. *(p. 5)*

   6. 7 more than a number   7. The quotient of a number and 4

Perform the indicated operation. *(pp. 29, 34, 42)*

   8. $-19 + 12$ 9. $8 - (-20)$ 10. $6(-7)$ 11. $-75 \div (-5)$

NOTETAKING STRATEGIES

Note *Worthy*

You will find a notetaking strategy at the beginning of each chapter. Look for additional notetaking and study strategies throughout the chapter.

USING DEFINITION MAPS When you study a new concept, you can use a definition map to define the concept, describe the concept's attributes, and give specific examples. A definition map for power is shown below.

What is it?

A power is a product of repeated factors: $2^3 = 2 \cdot 2 \cdot 2$.

POWER

What are examples?

2^3 $(0.5)^6$ n^4

What are its attributes?

A power consists of a base and an exponent.

The base is the number that is used as a factor. The base for 2^3 is 2.

The exponent is how many times the base repeats. The exponent for 2^3 is 3.

A definition map will be helpful in Lesson 2.3.

Properties *and* Operations

BEFORE	Now	WHY?
You found sums and products of numbers.	You'll use properties of addition and multiplication.	So you can compare the lengths of two fish, as in Ex. 48.

Vocabulary

additive identity,
   p. 64
multiplicative identity,
   p. 64

In English, *commute* means to change locations, and *associate* means to group together. These words have similar meanings in mathematics. *Commutative* properties let you change the positions of numbers in a sum or product. *Associative* properties let you group numbers in a sum or product together.

Commutative and Associative Properties	
Commutative Property of Addition	**Commutative Property of Multiplication**
Words In a sum, you can add the numbers in any order.	**Words** In a product, you can multiply the numbers in any order.
Numbers $4 + (-7) = -7 + 4$	**Numbers** $8(-5) = -5(8)$
Algebra $a + b = b + a$	**Algebra** $ab = ba$
Associative Property of Addition	**Associative Property of Multiplication**
Words Changing the grouping of the numbers in a sum does not change the sum.	**Words** Changing the grouping of the numbers in a product does not change the product.
Numbers $(9 + 6) + 2 = 9 + (6 + 2)$	**Numbers** $(3 \cdot 10) \cdot 4 = 3 \cdot (10 \cdot 4)$
Algebra $(a + b) + c = a + (b + c)$	**Algebra** $(ab)c = a(bc)$

Example 1	*Using Properties of Addition*

Music You buy a portable CD player for $48, rechargeable batteries with charger for $25, and a CD case for $12. Find the total cost.

Solution

The total cost is the sum of the three prices. Use properties of addition to group together prices that are easy to add mentally.

$$48 + 25 + 12 = (48 + 25) + 12 \qquad \text{Use order of operations.}$$
$$= (25 + 48) + 12 \qquad \text{Commutative property of addition}$$
$$= 25 + (48 + 12) \qquad \text{Associative property of addition}$$
$$= 25 + 60 \qquad \text{Add 48 and 12.}$$
$$= 85 \qquad \text{Add 25 and 60.}$$

Answer The total cost is $85.

Example 2	*Using Properties of Multiplication*

Evaluate 4xy when x = −7 and y = 25.

$4xy = 4(-7)(25)$	Substitute −7 for x and 25 for y.
$= [4(-7)](25)$	Use order of operations.
$= [-7(4)](25)$	Commutative property of multiplication
$= -7[(4)(25)]$	Associative property of multiplication
$= -7(100)$	Multiply 4 and 25.
$= -700$	Multiply −7 and 100.

✔ *Checkpoint*

In Exercises 1–3, evaluate the expression. Justify each of your steps.

1. $(17 + 36) + 13$ **2.** $8(-3)(5)$ **3.** $3.4 + 9.7 + 7.6$

4. Evaluate $5x^2y$ when $x = -6$ and $y = 20$.

Example 3	*Using Properties to Simplify Variable Expressions*

Simplify the expression.

a.
$x + 3 + 6 = (x + 3) + 6$	Use order of operations.
$= x + (3 + 6)$	Associative property of addition
$= x + 9$	Add 3 and 6.

b.
$4(8y) = (4 \cdot 8)y$	Associative property of multiplication
$= 32y$	Multiply 4 and 8.

✔ *Checkpoint*

Simplify the expression.

5. $m + 5 + 9$ **6.** $6(3k)$ **7.** $4 + x + (-1)$ **8.** $(2r)(-5)$

Identity Properties When 0 is added to any number, or when any number is multiplied by 1, the result is *identical* to the original number. These properties of 0 and 1 are called *identity properties*, and the numbers 0 and 1 are called *identities*.

Identity Properties	
Identity Property of Addition	**Identity Property of Multiplication**
Words The sum of a number and the additive identity , 0, is the number.	**Words** The product of a number and the multiplicative identity , 1, is the number.
Numbers $-6 + 0 = -6$	**Numbers** $4 \cdot 1 = 4$
Algebra $a + 0 = a$	**Algebra** $a \cdot 1 = a$

Example 4 — Identifying Properties

Statement	Property Illustrated
a. $(-5)(1) = -5$	Identity property of multiplication
b. $2 + (-9) = -9 + 2$	Commutative property of addition
c. $y^2 + 0 = y^2$	Identity property of addition
d. $2(pq) = (2p)q$	Associative property of multiplication

Review *Help*

To write the conversion factor $\frac{1 \text{ foot}}{12 \text{ inches}}$, you need to know that 1 foot = 12 inches. To help you convert measures, see the Table of Measures on p. 817.

Unit Analysis You can use *unit analysis* to find a *conversion factor* that converts a given measurement to different units. A conversion factor, such as $\frac{1 \text{ foot}}{12 \text{ inches}}$, is equal to 1:

$$\frac{1 \text{ foot}}{12 \text{ inches}} = \frac{12 \text{ inches}}{12 \text{ inches}} = 1$$

So, the identity property of multiplication tells you that multiplying a measurement by a conversion factor does not change the measurement.

Example 5 — Multiplying by a Conversion Factor

Roller Coasters The Steel Dragon 2000 is the world's longest roller coaster. Its length is 2711 yards. How long is the roller coaster in feet?

Solution

1. Find a conversion factor that converts yards to feet. The statement 1 yard = 3 feet gives you two conversion factors.

Factor 1: $\frac{1 \text{ yard}}{3 \text{ feet}}$ **Factor 2:** $\frac{3 \text{ feet}}{1 \text{ yard}}$

Unit analysis shows that a conversion factor that converts yards to feet has feet in the numerator and yards in the denominator:

$$\text{yards} \cdot \frac{\text{feet}}{\text{yards}} = \text{feet}$$

So, factor 2 is the desired conversion factor.

2. Multiply the roller coaster's length by factor 2 from Step 1.

$2711 \text{ yards} = 2711 \text{ yards} \cdot \frac{3 \text{ feet}}{1 \text{ yard}}$ **Use the conversion factor. Divide out common unit.**

$= 8133 \text{ feet}$ **Multiply.**

Answer The roller coaster is 8133 feet long.

The Steel Dragon 2000, located in Nagashima, Japan

✔ *Checkpoint*

9. Identify the property illustrated by the statement $z^4 \cdot 1 = z^4$.

10. Use a conversion factor to convert 400 centimeters to meters.

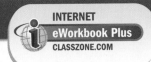

More Practice, p. 804

Guided Practice

Vocabulary Check

1. Which property allows you to write $4 + (3 + 9) = (4 + 3) + 9$?

2. Explain how the commutative and associative properties of multiplication can help you evaluate the product $5 \cdot 17 \cdot 2$ mentally.

Skill Check **Mental Math Evaluate the expression. Justify each of your steps.**

3. $(26 + 18) + 34$ **4.** $-4(9)(-5)$ **5.** $(3.45)(6.26)(0)$

Evaluate the expression when $x = 5$ and $y = -2$.

6. $33xy$ **7.** $x \cdot 11 \cdot y^2$ **8.** $x^2 + y^3 + 15$

Simplify the expression.

9. $x + 6 + 11$ **10.** $9(-5a)$ **11.** $-2 + y + 8$

Identify the property that the statement illustrates.

12. $n + q = q + n$ **13.** $-4ab = -4ba$ **14.** $(3 \cdot 8) \cdot 2 = 3 \cdot (8 \cdot 2)$

15. Error Analysis Describe and correct the error in converting 80 ounces to pounds.

$$80 \text{ ounces} = 80 \text{ ounces} \cdot \frac{16 \text{ ounces}}{1 \text{ pound}} = 1280 \text{ pounds} \quad \times$$

Practice and Problem Solving

Mental Math Evaluate the expression. Justify each of your steps.

Homework *Help*

Example	Exercises
1	16–23, 36, 41–47
2	16–23, 37, 41–46, 48
3	24–27
4	28–31
5	32–35, 38, 39, 48

Online Resources
CLASSZONE.COM

• More Examples
• eTutorial Plus

16. $32 + 16 + 8$ **17.** $15(-9)(2)$ **18.** $7 \cdot 1 + 0$ **19.** $45 + 29 + 55$

Evaluate the expression when $a = 9$ and $b = -4$.

20. $5ab$ **21.** $b(25a^2)$ **22.** $11 + 4b + a$ **23.** $3a + b^2 + 13$

Simplify the expression.

24. $x + 17 + 12$ **25.** $3 + j + (-9)$ **26.** $-8(6c)$ **27.** $(5y)(26)$

Identify the property that the statement illustrates.

28. $mn + 0 = mn$ **29.** $19 \cdot 5^3 = 5^3 \cdot 19$

30. $(2x + 3y) + z = 2x + (3y + z)$ **31.** $(-7u)(1) = -7u$

Use a conversion factor to perform the indicated conversion.

32. 4 miles to feet   **33.** 7.5 kilograms to grams

34. 360 seconds to minutes   **35.** 432 square inches to square feet

36. Nutrition The calories in a breakfast sandwich come from three sources: 144 Calories are from carbohydrates, 108 Calories are from fat, and 56 Calories are from protein. Use properties of addition to find the total number of calories in the sandwich.

37. Summer Job During the summer, you work 4 hours each day as a cashier and earn $7 each hour. Use properties of multiplication to find how much money you earn during a 5 day work week.

38. Dinosaurs Scientists believe that the heaviest dinosaur was *Argentinosaurus*, which weighed about 110 tons. Use a conversion factor to find the weight of *Argentinosaurus* in pounds.

39. Tennis The area of a regulation tennis court is 2808 square feet. Use a conversion factor to find the area of a tennis court in square yards.

40. *Writing* Are putting on your socks and putting on your shoes commutative activities? Explain.

Mental Math **Evaluate the expression. Justify each of your steps.**

41. $1.25 + 1.38 + 0.75$ **42.** $44 + 19 + 16 + 31$ **43.** $4(20)(25)(-5)$

Evaluate the expression when $x = -5$, $y = 3$, and $z = 2$.

44. x^2yz^2 **45.** $15yxz$ **46.** $2x + 9y + 5z$

47. Surveying A surveyor measures the depth of a river at three different points and obtains depths of 4.7 meters, 8.5 meters, and 6.3 meters.

  a. Use properties of addition to find the sum of the surveyor's measurements.

  b. Analyze What is the mean depth?

48. Extended Problem Solving One type of fish eaten by swordfish is the mackerel. A swordfish can grow to a length of about 5 yards, while the length of an adult mackerel is about 18 inches.

  a. Copy and complete:

  $$5 \text{ yards} = 5 \text{ yards} \cdot \frac{? \text{ feet}}{1 \text{ yard}} \cdot \frac{? \text{ inches}}{1 \text{ foot}}$$

  b. Evaluate Use properties of multiplication to evaluate the product in part (a). What is the length of a swordfish in inches?

  c. Compare A swordfish is how many times as long as a mackerel?

49. Logical Reasoning Copy and complete the table. Use the results in each row to decide whether subtraction and division are commutative or associative operations. Explain your reasoning.

Expression	Result	Expression	Result
$8 - 3$	?	$3 - 8$	?
$10 \div 5$	?	$5 \div 10$	?
$(15 - 9) - 4$	?	$15 - (9 - 4)$	?
$(48 \div 6) \div 2$	?	$48 \div (6 \div 2)$	?

50. Critical Thinking When you divide any number a by 1, what is the result? Write an algebraic statement that expresses this property.

In the **Real World**

Dinosaurs A replica of an *Argentinosaurus* skeleton was built in the Fernbank Museum of Natural History in Atlanta, Georgia. The skeleton is 42 yards long. What is the skeleton's length in feet?

51. Fundraising To raise money for a charitable organization, 10 members each sell x boxes of greeting cards for $12 a box. Each box costs the organization $4.

    a. The profit on each box of cards sold is the difference of the selling price and the organization's cost. What is the profit on each box?

    b. Use properties of multiplication to write a simplified variable expression for the organization's total profit from card sales.

    c. Apply What is the total profit if each member sells 25 boxes of cards?

52. Challenge When mathematician Carl Friedrich Gauss was a child, his teacher is said to have asked Gauss and his classmates to add up the integers 1 through 100. Gauss found the answer almost immediately. He first wrote the sum forwards and backwards, as shown.

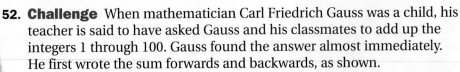

    a. You can pair each number in the top sum with the number below it in the bottom sum. What is the sum of the numbers in each pair?

    b. How many pairs of numbers are there?

    c. Use your answers from parts (a) and (b) to complete this statement: If S is the sum of the integers 1 through 100, then $2S = \underline{\ ?\ }$.

    d. Interpret What is the sum of the integers 1 through 100? Explain.

Stamp from 1977 honoring Carl Friedrich Gauss

Mixed Review   **Evaluate the expression.** *(Lessons 1.2, 1.3)*

53. 3^4 **54.** 2^5 **55.** 10^3

56. $2 + 3 \cdot 8$ **57.** $7 + 6^2 \div 9$ **58.** $19 + 5 \cdot 11 - 4$

59. Groceries At a grocery store, you buy 3 boxes of spaghetti for $1.19 each and 4 jars of spaghetti sauce for $2.39 each. What is the total cost of your items? *(Lesson 1.3)*

Plot the point in a coordinate plane. Describe the location of the point. *(Lesson 1.8)*

60. $P(4, 3)$ **61.** $Q(2, -2)$ **62.** $R(-5, 0)$ **63.** $S(-1, -4)$

Standardized Test Practice   **64. Multiple Choice** Which conversion factor would you use to find the number of pints in 3 quarts?

    A. $\dfrac{1 \text{ quart}}{2 \text{ pints}}$ **B.** $\dfrac{2 \text{ pints}}{1 \text{ quart}}$ **C.** $\dfrac{2 \text{ quarts}}{1 \text{ pint}}$ **D.** $\dfrac{1 \text{ pint}}{2 \text{ quarts}}$

65. Multiple Choice Identify the property illustrated by this statement:

$$2 \cdot (9 \cdot 17) = (2 \cdot 9) \cdot 17$$

    F. Identity property of multiplication

    G. Commutative property of multiplication

    H. Associative property of multiplication

    I. Associative property of addition

Perimeter *and* Area

Perimeter

Below are formulas for the perimeter of several basic geometric figures.

Triangle	Square	Rectangle
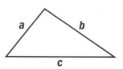		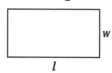
$P = a + b + c$	$P = 4s$	$P = 2l + 2w$

Example Find the perimeter of the square.

$P = 4s$ Write formula for perimeter.

$\quad = 4(7)$ Substitute 7 for *s*.

$\quad = 28$ cm   Multiply.

7 cm

7 cm

Area of a Square or Rectangle

Below are formulas for the area of a square and a rectangle.

Square	Rectangle
	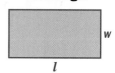
Area = (Side length)^2	**Area = Length × Width**
$A = s^2$	$A = lw$

Example Find the area of the rectangle.

$A = lw$ Write formula for area.

$\quad = 9(5)$ Substitute 9 for *l* and 5 for *w*.

$\quad = 45$ in.^{2} Multiply.

5 in.

9 in.

Continued ▶

Area of a Triangle

You can find a triangle's area if you know its base and its height.

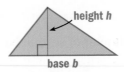

height *h*

base *b*

Area = $\frac{1}{2}$ × Base × Height

$$A = \frac{1}{2} bh$$

Example Find the area of the triangle.

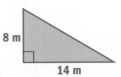

8 m

14 m

$A = \frac{1}{2}bh$ **Write formula for area.**

$= \frac{1}{2}(14)(8)$ **Substitute 14 for *b* and 8 for *h*.**

$= 56 \text{ m}^2$ **Multiply.**

✔ Checkpoint

▶ **Test** your knowledge of perimeter and area by solving these problems.

Find the perimeter of the triangle, square, or rectangle.

1.

7 ft

11 ft

2.

8.5 m

8.5 m

3.

22 in.

27 in.

24 in.

Find the area of the triangle, square, or rectangle.

4.

18 in.

18 in.

5.

20 cm

30 cm

6.

6 m

10 m

7. Basketball A regulation high school basketball court is a rectangle 84 feet long and 50 feet wide. Find the perimeter and the area of the basketball court.

8. Critical Thinking The sides of square B are twice as long as the sides of square A, as shown.

Square A

3 ft

3 ft

Square B

6 ft

6 ft

    a. Find the perimeter of each square.

    b. Find the area of each square.

    c. Compare How are the perimeters of the squares related? How are the areas of the squares related?

2.2

The Distributive Property

Vocabulary

equivalent numerical
expressions, p. 71
equivalent variable
expressions, p. 72

Camping You and a friend are going on a camping trip. You each buy a backpack that costs $90 and a sleeping bag that costs $60. What is the total cost of the camping equipment?

Example 1 | Evaluating Numerical Expressions

You can use two methods to find the total cost of the camping equipment described above.

Method 1 Find the cost of one backpack and one sleeping bag. Then multiply the result by 2, the number of each item bought.

$$\text{Total cost} = 2(90 + 60)$$
$$= 2(150)$$
$$= 300$$

Method 2 Find the cost of two backpacks and the cost of two sleeping bags. Then add the costs.

$$\text{Total cost} = 2(90) + 2(60)$$
$$= 180 + 120$$
$$= 300$$

Answer The total cost of the camping equipment is $300.

In Example 1, the expressions $2(90 + 60)$ and $2(90) + 2(60)$ are called **equivalent numerical expressions** because they have the same value. The statement $2(90 + 60) = 2(90) + 2(60)$ illustrates the *distributive property* for evaluating the product of a number and a sum or difference.

Reading *Algebra*

Vocabulary When you use the distributive property, you *distribute* the number outside the parentheses to each number inside the parentheses:

$$a(b + c) = ab + ac$$

The Distributive Property

Algebra $a(b + c) = ab + ac$ **Numbers** $4(6 + 3) = 4(6) + 4(3)$

$(b + c)a = ba + ca$ $(6 + 3)4 = 6(4) + 3(4)$

$a(b - c) = ab - ac$ $5(7 - 2) = 5(7) - 5(2)$

$(b - c)a = ba - ca$ $(7 - 2)5 = 7(5) - 2(5)$

Example 2   *Using the Distributive Property*

Geodes After touring a cave, you visit the gift shop and buy 3 geodes. Each geode costs \$5.95. Use the distributive property and mental math to find the total cost of the geodes.

Solution

Total cost = $3(5.95)$	Write expression for total cost.
$= 3(6 - 0.05)$	Rewrite 5.95 as $6 - 0.05$.
$= 3(6) - 3(0.05)$	Distributive property
$= 18 - 0.15$	Multiply using mental math.
$= 17.85$	Subtract using mental math.

Answer The total cost of the geodes is \$17.85.

✔ **Checkpoint**

Use the distributive property to evaluate the expression.

1. $3(8 + 5)$ **2.** $(2 + 9)2$ **3.** $6(11 - 4)$ **4.** $(3 - 14)(-5)$

Evaluate the expression using the distributive property and mental math.

5. $4(105)$ **6.** $3(97)$ **7.** $5(2.9)$ **8.** $8(7.02)$

Two variable expressions that have the same value for all values of the variable(s) are called **equivalent variable expressions** . You can use the distributive property to write equivalent variable expressions.

Example 3   *Writing Equivalent Variable Expressions*

Use the distributive property to write an equivalent variable expression.

a.	$3(x + 7) = 3(x) + 3(7)$	Distributive property
	$= 3x + 21$	Multiply.
b.	$(n + 4)(-2) = n(-2) + 4(-2)$	Distributive property
	$= -2n + (-8)$	Multiply.
	$= -2n - 8$	Definition of subtraction
c.	$-5(2y - 3) = -5(2y) - (-5)(3)$	Distributive property
	$= -10y - (-15)$	Multiply.
	$= -10y + 15$	Definition of subtraction

✔ **Checkpoint**

Use the distributive property to write an equivalent variable expression.

9. $8(x + 2)$ **10.** $(7 - t)(-4)$ **11.** $9(3m + 5)$ **12.** $-2(6y - 4)$

In the **Real World**

Geodes A geode is a hollow rock whose interior is lined with crystals. Many geodes are small enough to fit in your hand, but a giant geode in Spain is 26 feet long and can hold 10 people inside. How does this geode's length compare with the length of your hand?

Example 4 *Finding Areas of Geometric Figures*

Find the area of the rectangle or triangle.

a.

7

2x + 5

b.
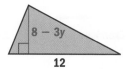
8 − 3y

12

Solution

a. Use the formula for the area of a rectangle.

$$A = lw$$
$$= (2x + 5)(7)$$
$$= 2x(7) + 5(7)$$
$$= 14x + 35$$

Answer The area is $(14x + 35)$ square units.

b. Use the formula for the area of a triangle.

$$A = \frac{1}{2}bh = \frac{1}{2}(12)(8 − 3y)$$
$$= 6(8 − 3y)$$
$$= 6(8) − 6(3y)$$
$$= 48 − 18y$$

Answer The area is $(48 − 18y)$ square units.

Guided Practice

Vocabulary Check

1. What property is illustrated by the statement $3(4 − 9) = 3(4) − 3(9)$?

2. Are $2(x + 1)$ and $2x + 1$ equivalent variable expressions? Explain.

Skill Check **Evaluate the expression using the distributive property and mental math.**

3. $3(96)$ **4.** $6(103)$ **5.** $2(8.95)$ **6.** $4(7.09)$

Use the distributive property to write an equivalent variable expression.

7. $2(x − 6)$ **8.** $(y + 11)(−3)$ **9.** $5(4k + 9)$ **10.** $−4(2n − 7)$

11. Game Room You are building a game room adjacent to your living room. The widths of the two rooms must be the same. There are no restrictions on the game room's length l.

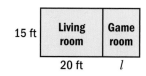
15 ft | Living room | Game room
20 ft | l

a. Write an expression for the total area of both rooms by multiplying their common width by their combined length.

b. Write a second expression for the total area by finding the area of each room separately and then adding the two areas.

c. Show that the expressions from parts (a) and (b) are equivalent.

Practice and Problem Solving

Homework *Help*

Example	Exercises
1	12–19, 36, 41–43
2	20–27, 37
3	28–35, 44, 45
4	38–40

Online Resources
CLASSZONE.COM

- More Examples
- eTutorial Plus

Use the distributive property to evaluate the expression.

12. $2(5 + 3)$ **13.** $5(9 - 3)$ **14.** $(4 - 10)7$ **15.** $(7.2 + 1.9)2$

16. $-10(18 + 8)$ **17.** $(6 + 21)(-3)$ **18.** $(12 - 7)(-4)$ **19.** $6(-2.3 + 3.8)$

Evaluate the expression using the distributive property and mental math.

20. $4(98)$ **21.** $7(109)$ **22.** $(211)(-3)$ **23.** $-5(396)$

24. $8(3.1)$ **25.** $2(1.99)$ **26.** $-6(10.95)$ **27.** $(4.02)(-9)$

Use the distributive property to write an equivalent variable expression.

28. $4(x - 2)$ **29.** $3(y + 9)$ **30.** $-2(3 - r)$ **31.** $(s + 20)(-7)$

32. $6(2p + 1)$ **33.** $-5(5q - 4)$ **34.** $9(11 - 6m)$ **35.** $(-2n - 3)(-8)$

36. Basketball There are 29 teams in the National Basketball Association (NBA). Each team can have a maximum of 12 healthy players plus 3 players on injured reserve. Use the distributive property to find the maximum number of players who can be in the NBA.

37. Snowfall Utah Olympic Park, site of the 2002 Olympic Winter Games, gets an average of 295 inches of snow each year. Use estimation to predict the total snowfall in Utah Olympic Park over a 5 year period. Justify your answer using the distributive property and mental math.

Geometry Find the area of the rectangle or triangle.

38.

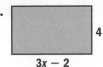

4

$3x - 2$

39.

$5a + 7$

18

40.

13

$6 - 2y$

Study *Strategy*

In Exercises 41–44, you can use an extended version of the distributive property. For example, an expression of the form

$a(b + c + d)$

can be written as

$ab + ac + ad$.

Use the distributive property to evaluate the expression.

41. $5(7 + 2 + 4)$ **42.** $-3(9 - 1 + 6)$ **43.** $(21 - 11 - 3)4$

44. Giant Pumpkins A giant pumpkin can be difficult to weigh directly on a scale. To estimate the weight, you can first measure the distances a, b, and c (in inches) as shown below. The weight W (in pounds) can then be approximated using the formula $W = 1.9(a + b + c)$.

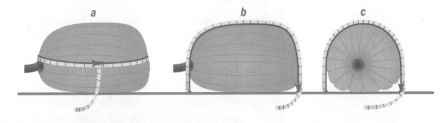

a   b   c

a. Use the distributive property to write the given formula without parentheses.

b. For a certain pumpkin, $a = 132$ inches, $b = 91$ inches, and $c = 85$ inches. Approximate the weight of the pumpkin to the nearest pound.

45. Extended Problem Solving For a cylindrical corn silo with the dimensions shown, the weight W (in pounds) of the corn silage inside is typically given by $W = 4400(40 - d)$, where d is the distance (in feet) from the top of the corn to the top of the silo.

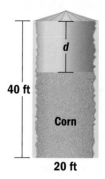

40 ft

d

Corn

20 ft

a. Use the distributive property to write the given formula without parentheses.

b. Calculate Suppose $d = 15$ feet. What is the weight of the corn in the silo?

c. Interpret and Apply How many days will the amount of corn from part (b) last if it is used to feed a herd of 100 cows and each cow eats 10 pounds of corn a day?

Use the distributive property to write an equivalent variable expression.

46. $x(x + 9)$ **47.** $m(5 - m)$ **48.** $(2u - 7)u$ **49.** $-3y(y + 8)$

50. Challenge Llamas are often raised as pets or to carry supplies in mountainous areas. Suppose you are building a rectangular pen for a herd of llamas. You use 500 feet of fencing for the pen. Let x represent the pen's length (in feet).

a. *Writing* Write an expression for the width of the pen. Explain the steps you used to find the expression.

b. Use the distributive property to write an expression without parentheses for the area of the pen.

c. Find the width and the area of the pen if the length is 160 feet.

Mixed Review

Find the sum or difference. *(Lessons 1.5, 1.6)*

51. $20 + (-9)$ **52.** $-34 + 16$ **53.** $-81 - 58$ **54.** $65 - (-27)$

55. Temperature Find the mean of the following temperatures: $-15°F$, $-7°F$, $8°F$, $3°F$, $-9°F$. *(Lesson 1.7)*

Identify the property that the statement illustrates. *(Lesson 2.1)*

56. $(x + 5y) + 2 = x + (5y + 2)$ **57.** $3m + 2n = 2n + 3m$

58. $r^2s = sr^2$ **59.** $c^7 \cdot 1 = c^7$

Standardized Test Practice

60. Multiple Choice Which expression is equivalent to $-3(-7 + 2x)$?

A. $21 - 6x$ **B.** $21 + 2x$ **C.** $21 + 6x$ **D.** $-21 - 6x$

61. Multiple Choice What is the area (in square units) of the rectangle shown?

5

4y + 8

F. $4y + 13$ **G.** $8y + 26$

H. $20y + 8$ **I.** $20y + 40$

62. Short Response You and a friend go to the movies. You each buy a ticket for $9.00 and a popcorn-and-drink combo for $5.25. Describe two methods you can use to find the total amount of money you and your friend spend. What is the total amount spent?

Rates *and* Unit Analysis

▶ **Review** these topics in preparation for solving problems that involve rates and unit analysis in Lesson 2.3. You will learn more about these topics in Lesson 6.1.

Writing Unit Rates

A **rate** is a comparison, using division, of quantities measured in different units. Rates are often expressed as fractions. A **unit rate** has a denominator of 1 unit when the rate is written as a fraction. When a unit rate is expressed as a verbal phrase, it often contains the word *per*, which means "for every."

Example   **Unit rate as a phrase**   **Unit rate as a fraction**

   a. 45 miles per hour $\dfrac{45 \text{ mi}}{1 \text{ h}}$

   b. $3 per square foot $\dfrac{\$3}{1 \text{ ft}^2}$

Rates and Unit Analysis

You can include unit analysis in a calculation so that you know the units in the answer.

Example At a grocery store, the price of bananas is $1.19 per pound. What is the cost of 3 pounds of bananas?

   Total cost = Price per pound × Number of pounds

   $\qquad = \dfrac{\$1.19}{1 \text{ lb}} \times 3 \text{ lb}$ **Substitute. Divide out common unit.**

   $\qquad = \$3.57$ **Multiply.**

Answer The cost of the bananas is $3.57.

Rates and Variable Expressions

You can use a rate to write a variable expression.

Example You fill a pool with water at a rate of 20 gallons per minute. Write an expression for the volume of water in the pool after *t* minutes.

   Volume = Gallons per minute × Number of minutes

   $\qquad = 20t$

Answer The volume of water in the pool is $20t$ gallons.

Using a Formula

Many rate problems involve units of distance and time. The formula below relates distance traveled to the rate of travel and the travel time.

$$\text{Distance} = \text{Rate} \times \text{Time}$$
$$d = rt$$

In problems about distance, rate, and time, the word *speed* means the same thing as *rate*.

Example **An ocean liner travels at a constant speed of 36 miles per hour. How far does the ocean liner travel in 4.5 hours?**

$d = rt$	Write formula for distance traveled.
$= \dfrac{36 \text{ mi}}{1 \text{ h}} \times 4.5 \text{ h}$	Substitute. Divide out common unit.
$= 162 \text{ mi}$	Multiply.

Answer The ocean liner travels 162 miles.

✅ *Checkpoint*

▶ **Test** your knowledge of rates and unit analysis by solving these problems.

Write the rate as a fraction.

1. 17 meters per second

2. $360 per ounce

3. 1.5 inches per hour

4. 0.75 pound per square foot

5. **Cows** A milk cow grazing in a field eats about 30 pounds of grass per day. How many pounds does the cow eat in 5 days?

6. **Snails** A snail travels at a speed of about 23 inches per hour. How far can a snail travel in 4 hours?

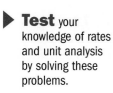

7. **Carpeting** You want to carpet a rectangular bedroom that is 5 yards long and 4 yards wide. You buy the carpet for $11.50 per square yard. What is the total cost of the carpet?

8. **Space Probe** In 1989, the space probe *Magellan* was launched. It traveled toward the planet Venus at a speed of about 25,000 miles per hour. How far did *Magellan* travel in one day?

9. **Nutrition** A certain brand of salsa contains 15 Calories per ounce. Write an expression for the number of calories in *x* ounces.

10. **Skiing** You ski down a hill at a speed of 70 feet per second. Write an expression for the distance you travel in *t* seconds.

Simplifying Variable Expressions

Vocabulary

term, p. 78
coefficient, p. 78
constant term, p. 78
like terms, p. 78

BEFORE	*Now*	WHY?
You wrote variable expressions.	You'll simplify variable expressions.	So you can find the weight of a freight train's cargo, as in Ex. 32.

Fitness You work out each day after school by jogging around a track and swimming laps in a pool. In Example 4, you'll see how to write and simplify a variable expression that describes the number of calories you burn.

The parts of an expression that are added together are called **terms** . In the expression below, the terms are $5x$, $4x$, and 7. The **coefficient** of a term with a variable is the number part of the term.

Terms

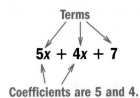

$$5x + 4x + 7$$

Coefficients are 5 and 4.

A **constant term** , such as 7, has a number but no variable. **Like terms** are terms that have identical variable parts. In the expression above, $5x$ and $4x$ are like terms. Two or more constant terms are also considered like terms.

Note *Worthy*

In your notebook, make a definition map for *variable expression*, a concept you first studied in Lesson 1.1. Your definition map should discuss terms, coefficients, constant terms, and like terms.

Example 1	*Identifying Parts of an Expression*

Identify the terms, like terms, coefficients, and constant terms of the expression $y + 8 - 5y - 3$.

Solution

① Write the expression as a sum: $y + 8 + (-5y) + (-3)$.

② Identify the parts of the expression. Note that because $y = 1y$, the coefficient of y is 1.

Terms: $y, 8, -5y, -3$ **Like terms:** y and $-5y$; 8 and -3

Coefficients: $1, -5$ **Constant terms:** $8, -3$

Simplifying Expressions You can use the distributive property to write an expression such as $7x + 4x$ as a single term:

$$7x + 4x = (7 + 4)x = 11x$$

The like terms $7x$ and $4x$ have been *combined*, and the expression $7x + 4x$ has been *simplified*. A variable expression is simplified if it contains no grouping symbols and all like terms are combined.

Example 2 *Simplifying an Expression*

$4n - 7 - n + 9 = 4n + (-7) + (-n) + 9$	Write as a sum.
$= 4n + (-n) + (-7) + 9$	Commutative property
$= 4n + (-1n) + (-7) + 9$	Coefficient of $-n$ is -1.
$= [4 + (-1)]n + (-7) + 9$	Distributive property
$= 3n + 2$	Simplify.

 Checkpoint

For the given expression, identify the terms, like terms, coefficients, and constant terms. Then simplify the expression.

1. $3x + 2 + 5x$ **2.** $-7b + 3 + b - 10$ **3.** $5 + 8w - 6 - w$

A quick way to combine like terms containing variables is to add their coefficients mentally. In Example 2, for instance, $4n + (-n) = 3n$ because $4 + (-1) = 3$. This shortcut will be used from now on in this book.

Study *Strategy*

When you use the distributive property in part (b) of Example 3, you can think of $3k - 8(k + 2)$ as $3k + (-8)(k + 2)$ and then distribute -8 through the parentheses. You can use a similar method in part (c).

Example 3 *Simplifying Expressions with Parentheses*

a. $2(x - 4) + 9x + 1 = 2x - 8 + 9x + 1$	Distributive property
$= 2x + 9x - 8 + 1$	Group like terms.
$= 11x - 7$	Combine like terms.
b. $3k - 8(k + 2) = 3k - 8k - 16$	Distributive property
$= -5k - 16$	Combine like terms.
c. $4a - (4a - 3) = 4a - 1(4a - 3)$	Identity property
$= 4a - 4a + 3$	Distributive property
$= 0 + 3$	Combine like terms.
$= 3$	Simplify.

 Checkpoint

Simplify the expression.

4. $4(x + 1) + 2x + 5$ **5.** $10y - 3(6 - y)$ **6.** $8c + 2 - (c + 2)$

Reading *Algebra*

An expression written *in terms of* a variable contains that variable and no others.

Example 4 | *Writing and Simplifying an Expression*

During your workout described on page 78, you spend a total of 45 minutes jogging and swimming. You burn 14 Calories per minute when jogging and 8 Calories per minute when swimming.

a. Let j be the time you jog (in minutes). Write an expression in terms of j for the total calories you burn during your workout.

b. Find the total number of calories burned if you jog for 20 minutes.

Solution

a. Write a verbal model for the total number of calories burned.

| Calories per minute jogging | · | Jogging time | + | Calories per minute swimming | · | Swimming time |

Use the verbal model to write a variable expression, then simplify it. Note that because your entire workout lasts 45 minutes and your jogging time is j, your swimming time must be $45 - j$.

$$14j + 8(45 - j) = 14j + 360 - 8j \qquad \text{**Distributive property**}$$
$$= 14j - 8j + 360 \qquad \text{**Group like terms.**}$$
$$= 6j + 360 \qquad \text{**Combine like terms.**}$$

b. Evaluate the expression in part (a) when $j = 20$.

$$6j + 360 = 6(20) + 360 = 480 \text{ Calories}$$

2.3 Exercises

More Practice, p. 804

INTERNET
eWorkbook Plus
CLASSZONE.COM

Guided Practice

Vocabulary Check

1. What are terms that have a number but no variable called?

2. What is the coefficient of y in the expression $8 - 3y + 1$?

Skill Check **For the given expression, identify the terms, like terms, coefficients, and constant terms. Then simplify the expression.**

3. $6x + x + 2 + 4$ **4.** $-4k - 12 + 3k$ **5.** $5n + 1 - n - 8$

Simplify the expression.

6. $5x + 2 + 3(x - 1)$ **7.** $-7(2r + 3) + 11r$ **8.** $p + 6 - 6(p - 2)$

9. Error Analysis Describe and correct the error in simplifying $5a - (3a - 7)$.

$$\begin{aligned} 5a - (3a - 7) &= 5a - 3a - 7 \\ &= 2a - 7 \end{aligned}$$

Practice and Problem Solving

Homework *Help*

Example	Exercises
1	10-15
2	10-20
3	21-30
4	31-36

Online Resources
CLASSZONE.COM
• More Examples
• eTutorial Plus

For the given expression, identify the terms, like terms, coefficients, and constant terms. Then simplify the expression.

10. $10x + 7 + 3x$

11. $4y + 23 - y - 6$

12. $-19 - 11a + a + 16$

13. $2b - 8 + 4b - 6b$

14. $9 + n - 1 - 7n$

15. $8p - 5p + 5 - p - 2$

Simplify the expression.

16. $4x + 2x$

17. $10a - 3a$

18. $b - 9b$

19. $x + 2x + 3x$

20. $9c^2 - 4c^2 + 2c^2$

21. $3(2y + 5y)$

22. $4(d + 3) + 7d$

23. $5(k - 7) - k + 7$

24. $-2(2m - 1) + 4m$

25. $8n - (n - 3)$

26. $20u - 6(u + 5)$

27. $-w + 4 - (3w - 13)$

28. $p - 5(2 - 3p) + 1$

29. $3(q + 4) + 4q + 1$

30. $-7(r^2 + 2) + 3r^2$

31. Fitness Look back at Example 4 on page 80. Let *s* represent the time (in minutes) that you spend swimming. Write and simplify an expression in terms of *s* for the total number of calories you burn during your workout.

32. Trains A freight train with 80 cars transports coal and iron ore. Each car carries either 100 tons of coal or 90 tons of iron ore.

a. Let *c* represent the number of cars carrying coal. Write and simplify an expression in terms of *c* for the total weight of the freight transported by the train.

b. Suppose 28 of the train's cars carry coal. What is the total weight of all the freight?

Geometry Write and simplify an expression for the perimeter of the triangle or rectangle.

33.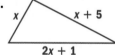

34.

35.

36. Extended Problem Solving You are making a rectangular rug. You want the rug to be twice as long as it is wide. Let *w* represent the width (in feet) of the rug.

a. Write an expression in terms of *w* for the perimeter of the rug.

b. Write an expression in terms of *w* for the area of the rug.

c. Calculate Copy and complete the table.

Width (feet)	1	2	4	8	16
Perimeter (feet)	?	?	?	?	?
Area (square feet)	?	?	?	?	?

d. *Writing* Explain how doubling the width of the rug affects the perimeter and the area.

37. Agriculture A farmer grows tomatoes and cucumbers in the field shown. The annual cost of growing tomatoes is $.27 per square foot. The annual cost of growing cucumbers is $.10 per square foot. Let x represent the width (in feet) of the tomato portion of the field.

a. In terms of x, what is the area of the tomato portion? of the cucumber portion?

b. Write and simplify an expression in terms of x for the annual cost of growing both crops.

c. Find the annual cost of growing both crops if the width of the tomato portion is 350 feet.

38. Challenge You want to stock your aquarium with three types of fish: angelfish, swordtails, and tetras. Each angelfish costs $5, each swordtail costs $2, and each tetra costs $3. You plan to buy 20 fish.

a. Let a be the number of angelfish and s be the number of swordtails you buy. In terms of a and s, how many tetras do you buy?

b. Write and simplify an expression in terms of a and s for the total cost of your fish.

c. Of the 20 fish you buy, 4 are angelfish and 10 are swordtails. Use your expression from part (b) to find your total cost.

Mixed Review

39. Cubing a Number When a number x is cubed, the result is 2744. Use the problem solving strategy *guess, check, and revise* to find the value of x. *(p. 797)*

Write a variable expression to represent the phrase. *(Lesson 1.1)*

40. The product of 8 and a number   **41.** 3 less than a number

42. A number increased by 10   **43.** The quotient of a number and 6

Use the distributive property to write an equivalent variable expression. *(Lesson 2.2)*

44. $4(a + 2)$ **45.** $-2(x + 3)$ **46.** $7(p - 4)$ **47.** $(m - 5)(-6)$

48. $5(2q + 11)$ **49.** $8(3t - 7)$ **50.** $-4(1 - 5u)$ **51.** $(8w + 9)(-3)$

Standardized Test Practice

52. Multiple Choice Which terms are *not* like terms?

A. $8y$ and $-4y$ **B.** 2 and 3.14   **C.** x^2 and x^5 **D.** x^2 and $5x^2$

53. Multiple Choice Which expression is equivalent to $8t - 6(2t - 1)$?

F. $4t + 6$ **G.** $-4t - 6$ **H.** $-4t - 1$ **I.** $-4t + 6$

54. Short Response You have a canteen that holds 32 fluid ounces and weighs 0.25 pound when empty. Water weighs 0.065 pound per fluid ounce. You begin a hike with a full canteen of water. Write and simplify an expression for the weight of the canteen and water after you drink x fluid ounces. Show and justify each step of your solution.

2.3 Simplifying Expressions

Goal Use a graphing calculator to check simplified variable expressions.

Example

Simplify the expression $5x - 2(x - 4)$. Use a graphing calculator to check the result.

1 Simplify the given expression.

$$5x - 2(x - 4) = 5x - 2x + 8 \qquad \text{Distributive property}$$
$$= 3x + 8 \qquad \text{Combine like terms.}$$

2 To check the result from Step 1, first enter the original expression and the simplified expression into the calculator.

Keystrokes

$\boxed{Y=}$ **5** $\boxed{x}$ $\boxed{-}$ **2**

$\boxed{(}$ $\boxed{x}$ $\boxed{-}$ **4** $\boxed{)}$

$\boxed{ENTER}$ **3** $\boxed{x}$ $\boxed{+}$ **8**

```
Y1 ▆5X-2(X-4)
Y2 ▆3X+8
Y3=
Y4=
```

3 Use the calculator's *table* feature to evaluate the original and simplified expressions for different values of x. Press $\boxed{\text{2nd}}$ **[TBLSET]** and enter the settings shown in the first screen below. Then press $\boxed{\text{2nd}}$ **[TABLE]** to display the table shown in the second screen.

```
TABLE SETUP
 TblStart=0
 ΔTbl=1
Indpnt: Auto Ask
Depend: Auto Ask
```

```
 X   │ Y1 │ Y2
 0   │ 8  │ 8
 1   │ 11 │ 11
 2   │ 14 │ 14
 3   │ 17 │ 17
 4   │ 20 │ 20
 5   │ 23 │ 23
X=0
```

4 Compare the values of the original expression in the column for Y1 with the values of the simplified expression in the column for Y2. The values are the same, so the simplification is correct.

Tech *Help*

In the TABLE SETUP screen, TblStart is the first value of x in the table, and ΔTbl is the amount by which x increases from one value to the next.

Online Resources
CLASSZONE.COM
• Keystroke Help

Draw Conclusions

Simplify. Use a graphing calculator to check the result.

1. $7(x + 2)$ **2.** $2x + 4x + 6x$ **3.** $3x - 9 - 8x + 5$

4. $-6(x - 3) + 5x$ **5.** $11x - 3(x + 5)$ **6.** $2(3x + 4) - 6x$

7. Critical Thinking Show that $2(x - 1) + x$ and $4x - 2$ are equal when $x = 0$. Are the expressions equivalent? Explain.

Mid-Chapter Quiz

Evaluate the expression. Justify each of your steps.

1. $29 + 18 + 21$

2. $1.3 + 6.8 + 2.7$

3. $4(9)(-25)$

4. $5(-7)(-12)$

5. Swimming In 1998, Susie Maroney set a record for the longest ocean swim without flippers. She swam 122 miles from Mexico to Cuba. Use a conversion factor to find this distance in feet.

Use the distributive property to evaluate the expression.

6. $-3(8 + 5)$

7. $(11 - 4)6$

8. $5(98)$

9. $7(4.03)$

Use the distributive property to write an equivalent variable expression.

10. $2(x - 3)$

11. $-5(y + 4)$

12. $4(9p + 7)$

13. $(6 - 2m)(-3)$

14. Geometry Find the area of the triangle shown.

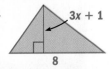

$3x + 1$

8

For the given expression, identify the terms, like terms, coefficients, and constant terms. Then simplify the expression.

15. $12x + 5 + 3x$

16. $9 + a - 2 - 7a$

17. $-8c + 3 - c + 1$

18. $6n - 4n - 2n$

Simplify the expression.

19. $3(x + 7) + 2x$

20. $y - 2(y - 6)$

21. $4(r - 1) + 5r + 3$

22. $8s - 4(2s + 3)$

Brain GAME

Word Scramble

For each statement in the table, identify the type of property the statement illustrates and write the corresponding letter. Unscramble the letters to solve this riddle:

What word has six letters, but when you subtract one, twelve remain?

Statement	Associative	Commutative	Identity
$8 \cdot 1 = 8$	R	T	E
$3 \cdot 9 = 9 \cdot 3$	A	D	L
$(2 + 5) + 3 = 2 + (5 + 3)$	N	Y	B
$4x + y = y + 4x$	H	S	U
$5(7c) = (5 \cdot 7)c$	O	P	C
$xy + 0 = xy$	M	I	Z

2.4 Variables *and* Equations

BEFORE	Now	WHY?
You evaluated variable expressions.	You'll solve equations with variables.	So you can find worldwide sales of computers, as in Ex. 33.

Vocabulary

equation, p. 85
solution of an
   equation, p. 85
solving an equation,
   p. 86

Biology Lotus flowers like the one shown can be grown from seeds hundreds of years old. In Example 4, you'll see how an *equation* can be used to estimate the year when an ancient lotus seed was formed.

An **equation** is a mathematical sentence formed by placing an equal sign, =, between two expressions. A **solution** of an equation with a variable is a number that produces a true statement when it is substituted for the variable.

Example 1 *Writing Verbal Sentences as Equations*

Verbal Sentence	**Equation**
a. The sum of x and 6 is 9.	$x + 6 = 9$
b. The difference of 12 and y is 15.	$12 - y = 15$
c. The product of -4 and p is 32.	$-4p = 32$
d. The quotient of n and 2 is 9.	$\dfrac{n}{2} = 9$

Reading *Algebra*

Symbol	Meaning
$=$	is equal to
$\stackrel{?}{=}$	is equal to?
$\neq$	is not equal to

In general, when you see a question mark above a relation symbol (such as $=$), a question is being asked. A relation symbol with a slash through it has the opposite meaning of the same symbol without the slash.

Example 2 *Checking Possible Solutions*

Tell whether 9 or 7 is a solution of $x - 5 = 2$.

a. Substitute 9 for x.

$$x - 5 = 2$$
$$9 - 5 \stackrel{?}{=} 2$$
$$4 \neq 2$$

Answer 9 is not a solution.

b. Substitute 7 for x.

$$x - 5 = 2$$
$$7 - 5 \stackrel{?}{=} 2$$
$$2 = 2 \checkmark$$

Answer 7 is a solution.

✔ Checkpoint

In Exercises 1 and 2, write the verbal sentence as an equation.

1. The sum of 3 and z is -10.

2. The quotient of m and 6 is 4.

3. Tell whether -5 or 5 is a solution of $-8y = 40$.

Solving Equations Finding all solutions of an equation is called **solving the equation**. You can use mental math to solve a simple equation by thinking of the equation as a question.

Example 3 **Solving Equations Using Mental Math**

	Equation	Question	Solution	Check
a.	$x + 3 = 11$	What number plus 3 equals 11?	8	$8 + 3 = 11$ ✓
b.	$16 - m = 9$	16 minus what number equals 9?	7	$16 - 7 = 9$ ✓
c.	$20 = 5t$	20 equals 5 times what number?	4	$20 = 5(4)$ ✓
d.	$\dfrac{y}{6} = -3$	What number divided by 6 equals -3?	-18	$\dfrac{-18}{6} = -3$ ✓

 Checkpoint

Solve the equation using mental math.

4. $x - 10 = 7$ **5.** $2 + n = -6$ **6.** $3w = -15$ **7.** $4 = \dfrac{36}{s}$

Example 4 **Writing and Solving an Equation**

From 1998 to 2002, biologist Jane Shen-Miller grew several lotus plants from ancient seeds she found in China. The oldest seed was about 500 years old. Estimate the year when this seed was formed.

Solution

First write a verbal model for this situation.

Year seed was formed	+	Age of seed when it sprouted	=	Year seed sprouted

Let x represent the year when the seed was formed. Because you are only trying to estimate x (rather than determine x precisely), you can use 2000 for the year when the seed sprouted. This year simplifies mental calculations and lies within the given time period, 1998–2002.

$$x + 500 = 2000 \qquad \text{Substitute for quantities in verbal model.}$$
$$1500 + 500 = 2000 \qquad \text{Use mental math to solve for } x.$$

Answer Because $x = 1500$, the seed was formed around the year 1500.

Jane Shen-Miller with lotus plants

 Checkpoint

8. Go-cart rides cost $5 each at a county fair. During the first day of the fair, the go-cart operator takes in a total of $1000. How many times did people ride the go-carts that day? Write and solve an equation to find the answer.

Guided Practice

Vocabulary Check

1. Copy and complete: A(n) _?_ of an equation is a number that produces a true statement when it is substituted for the variable.

2. What question would you ask yourself if you want to solve the equation $-4t = 28$ mentally?

Skill Check **Write the verbal sentence as an equation. Then tell whether 5 is a solution of the equation.**

3. The sum of x and 10 is 15.

4. The difference of 3 and x is 2.

5. The product of -6 and x is 54.

6. The quotient of -40 and x is -8.

Guided Problem Solving

7. Appetizers You are having a party and are serving quesadillas as appetizers. There will be 12 people at the party. Each quesadilla will be cut into 4 wedges, and you expect each person to eat 3 wedges. How many quesadillas do you need to make?

1 Let x represent the number of quesadillas you need. Write an expression for the number of wedges in x quesadillas.

2 How many quesadilla wedges do you need to feed 12 people?

3 Use your answers from Steps 1 and 2 to write an equation that you can use to find the number of quesadillas needed.

4 Solve your equation to find how many quesadillas you need.

Practice and Problem Solving

Homework *Help*

Example	Exercises
1	8–11
2	12–15
3	16–31
4	32–36, 38

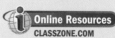
Online Resources
CLASSZONE.COM
• More Examples
• eTutorial Plus

Write the verbal sentence as an equation.

8. The difference of x and 8 is -4.

9. The sum of 26 and y is 43.

10. The quotient of p and 7 is 16.

11. The product of 14 and m is 56.

Tell whether the given value of the variable is a solution of the equation.

12. $x + 9 = 12; x = -3$

13. $21 - z = -4; z = 25$

14. $91 = 7c; c = 13$

15. $\frac{y}{4} = -8; y = 32$

Match the equation with the corresponding question. Then solve.

16. $n + 3 = 12$

A. 3 times what number equals 12?

17. $3n = 12$

B. What number divided by 3 equals 12?

18. $3 = n + 12$

C. What number plus 3 equals 12?

19. $\frac{n}{3} = 12$

D. 3 equals what number plus 12?

Mental Math Solve the equation using mental math.

20. $x + 6 = 13$ **21.** $x - 8 = 20$ **22.** $0 = t + 79$ **23.** $-4 + y = -9$

24. $11 - p = 19$ **25.** $-2 = r - 7$ **26.** $7x = 63$ **27.** $-10a = 130$

28. $-54 = -9g$ **29.** $\dfrac{x}{5} = 6$ **30.** $\dfrac{48}{u} = -3$ **31.** $1 = \dfrac{n}{231}$

In Exercises 32–34, use an equation to solve the problem.

32. Insects The dragonfly is the fastest flying insect. It can move at a speed of about 50 feet per second. Find the approximate time it takes a dragonfly to travel 400 feet.

33. Computers From 2000 to 2001, annual worldwide sales of personal computers declined by about 6 million. In 2001, about 128 million personal computers were sold. Find the approximate number of personal computers sold in 2000.

34. Snacks You divide a bag of trail mix into 8 portions for you and your friends to have as snacks on a bike ride. Each portion weighs 3 ounces. Find the total weight of the trail mix originally in the bag.

35. Geometry The perimeter of the figure shown is 35 centimeters.

   a. Write an equation that you can use to find x.

   b. Solve your equation. What is the value of x?

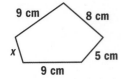

36. Extended Problem Solving Scientists often use the Kelvin scale to measure temperature. The temperature K in kelvins (K) is related to the temperature C in degrees Celsius (°C) by this formula:

$$K = C + 273$$

   a. *Writing* Explain in words how to find the Kelvin temperature that is equivalent to a given Celsius temperature.

   b. The lowest possible temperature a substance can have is 0 K, which is called absolute zero. What is absolute zero in degrees Celsius?

   c. The table shows the melting points of several chemical elements in kelvins. Find each melting point in degrees Celsius.

Element	Nitrogen	Chlorine	Gallium	Radium
Melting point (K)	63	172	303	973
Melting point (°C)	?	?	?	?

   d. Interpret and Apply Based on your results from parts (b) and (c), explain in words how to find the Celsius temperature C that is equivalent to a given Kelvin temperature K. Then write a formula that gives C in terms of K.

37. Compare and Contrast Describe the difference between an equation and an expression. Give an example of each.

38. Crafts You make a decorative paper chain with n links by cutting a 9 inch by 12 inch sheet of construction paper into n strips.

12 in.

n strips   9 in. →

n links

a. Write an expression in terms of n for the width of each paper strip.

b. Suppose you want each strip to be 0.75 inch wide. Use the problem solving strategy *guess, check, and revise* to find the number of links your paper chain will have.

39. Aviation The Thunderbirds are a United States Air Force team of pilots who fly in air shows around the world. The type of plane they fly, the F-16 Falcon, can climb at a rate of about 800 feet per second.

a. Suppose the Thunderbirds perform a straight-up climb from an altitude of 200 feet to an altitude of 13,000 feet. Let x represent the time (in seconds) that it takes to complete this maneuver. Use the verbal model below to write an equation you can use to find x.

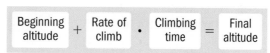

| Beginning altitude | + | Rate of climb | · | Climbing time | = | Final altitude |

b. Use the *table* feature on a graphing calculator to evaluate the left side of your equation for different values of x. What is the solution of the equation? How long does it take the Thunderbirds to complete the climb?

40. Challenge Solve the equation $2x + 3 = 11$ using mental math. Explain the reasoning you used to find the solution.

Thunderbirds

Mixed Review

Evaluate the expression when $x = -5$ and $y = -3$. *(Lessons 1.5, 1.6)*

41. $x + y$ **42.** $x - y + 6$ **43.** $-x + 2 + 3y$

Evaluate the expression using the distributive property and mental math. *(Lesson 2.2)*

44. $8(104)$ **45.** $5(197)$ **46.** $4(2.8)$

Simplify the expression. *(Lesson 2.3)*

47. $5c + 2 + 7c$ **48.** $13k - 8k - k$ **49.** $6x - 3 + 4x + 1$

50. $3(y + 7) + 11y$ **51.** $p - 6 - (4 + p)$ **52.** $2n - 7(n - 8)$

Standardized Test Practice

53. Multiple Choice Two more than a number is 8. Which equation can you solve to find the number?

A. $2x = 8$ **B.** $x + 2 = 8$ **C.** $x + 8 = 2$ **D.** $2 + 8 = x$

54. Multiple Choice What is the solution of the equation $12p = 60$?

F. 3   **G.** 4   **H.** 5   **I.** 6

2.5 Modeling Addition Equations

Goal
Model and solve
addition equations.

Materials
• algebra tiles

You can use algebra tiles to model and solve simple addition equations.

x-tile

An x-tile represents the variable x.

1-tile

A 1-tile represents the number 1.

Investigate

Use algebra tiles to solve x + 3 = 5.

1 Model $x + 3 = 5$ with algebra tiles.

2 Get the x-tile by itself on one side of the equation by removing three 1-tiles from each side.

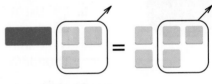

3 The x-tile is equal to two 1-tiles. So, the solution of $x + 3 = 5$ is 2.

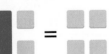

Draw Conclusions

1. Which model would you use to represent the equation $x + 2 = 4$?

A. 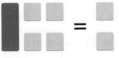   **B.**

Use algebra tiles to model and solve the equation.

2. $x + 1 = 4$ **3.** $x + 2 = 6$ **4.** $x + 5 = 7$ **5.** $x + 4 = 10$

6. $3 + x = 8$ **7.** $2 + x = 11$ **8.** $8 = x + 7$ **9.** $16 = 9 + x$

10. *Writing* In Step 2, why is it necessary to subtract three 1-tiles from *each* side of the equation, rather than from just the left side?

11. **Critical Thinking** Describe how you can use algebra tiles to solve the equation $2 + x + 4 = 9$. Then solve.

2.5

Solving Equations Using Addition *or* Subtraction

BEFORE	Now	WHY?
You solved equations using mental math.	You'll solve equations using addition or subtraction.	So you can determine the size of a star, as in Ex. 30.

Vocabulary

inverse operations, p. 91
equivalent equations, p. 91

Horses One method for weighing a horse is to put it in a trailer of known weight and weigh the horse and trailer together on a truck scale. As you'll see in Example 3, the horse's weight can then be found by using an *inverse operation* to solve an equation.

Inverse operations are two operations that undo each other, such as addition and subtraction. When you perform the same inverse operation on each side of an equation, you obtain an *equivalent equation*. **Equivalent equations** have the same solution.

> ## Subtraction Property of Equality
>
> **Words** Subtracting the same number from each side of an equation produces an equivalent equation.
>
> **Numbers** If $x + 3 = 5$, then $x + 3 - 3 = 5 - 3$, or $x = 2$.
>
> **Algebra** If $x + a = b$, then $x + a - a = b - a$, or $x = b - a$.

Reading *Algebra*

Vocabulary When you solve an equation, your goal is to write an equivalent equation that has the variable by itself on one side. This process is called *solving for the variable.*

Example 1   *Solving an Equation Using Subtraction*

Solve $x + 9 = -3$.

$x + 9 = -3$	Write original equation.
$x + 9 - 9 = -3 - 9$	Subtract 9 from each side.
$x = -12$	Simplify.

Answer The solution is -12.

✓ **Check**

$x + 9 = -3$	Write original equation.
$-12 + 9 \stackrel{?}{=} -3$	Substitute -12 for x.
$-3 = -3$ ✓	Solution checks.

Addition Property Just as you can use the subtraction property of equality to solve an equation involving addition, you can use the *addition property of equality* to solve an equation involving subtraction.

> ### Addition Property of Equality
>
> **Words** Adding the same number to each side of an equation produces an equivalent equation.
>
> **Numbers** If $x - 3 = 5$, then $x - 3 + 3 = 5 + 3$, or $x = 8$.
>
> **Algebra** If $x - a = b$, then $x - a + a = b + a$, or $x = b + a$.

Example 2   *Solving an Equation Using Addition*

Solve $23 = y - 11$.

$23 = y - 11$	Write original equation.
$23 + 11 = y - 11 + 11$	Add **11** to each side.
$34 = y$	Simplify.

Answer The solution is 34.

Example 3   *Writing and Solving an Equation*

You weigh a horse using the method described on page 91. The weight of the trailer alone is 2150 pounds. The combined weight of the horse and trailer is 3375 pounds. What is the weight of the horse?

Solution

Let w represent the horse's weight (in pounds). Write a verbal model. Then use the verbal model to write an equation.

Weight of horse	+	Weight of trailer	=	Combined weight

$w + 2150 = 3375$	Substitute.
$w + 2150 - 2150 = 3375 - 2150$	Subtract **2150** from each side.
$w = 1225$	Simplify.

Answer The weight of the horse is 1225 pounds.

 Checkpoint

Solve the equation. Check your solution.

1. $x + 8 = 19$ **2.** $-7 = y + 13$ **3.** $n - 4 = -11$ **4.** $26 = p - 61$

5. While holding his cat, Ben steps on a scale. The scale reads 161 pounds. Ben weighs 148 pounds. What is the weight of the cat?

In the **Real World**

Horses One of the smallest horses is the Shetland pony. If a typical Shetland pony is weighed using the trailer in Example 3, the combined weight of the pony and trailer would be about 2550 pounds. About how much does a Shetland pony weigh?

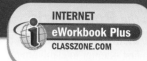

Guided Practice

Vocabulary Check

1. Copy and complete: Addition and subtraction are _?_ operations.

2. Which property of equality would you use to solve $x - 5 = 7$? Explain.

Skill Check Solve the equation. Check your solution.

3. $x + 4 = 10$
4. $t + 9 = -5$
5. $u - 3 = 6$

6. $y - 7 = -2$
7. $16 = a + 25$
8. $-70 = b - 30$

9. **Error Analysis** Describe and correct the error in solving $x + 8 = 10$.

$$x + 8 = 10$$
✗ $$x + 8 - 8 = 10 + 8$$
$$x = 18$$

10. **Population** From 1990 to 2000, the population of Cresco, Iowa, increased by 236. The population in 2000 was 3905. Use an equation to find the population in 1990.

Practice and Problem Solving

Homework *Help*

Example	Exercises
1	11–25, 32–37
2	11–25, 32–37
3	26–30, 38–42

Online Resources
CLASSZONE.COM
• More Examples
• eTutorial Plus

Solve the equation. Check your solution.

11. $x + 7 = 12$
12. $y + 9 = 0$
13. $-2 = z + 6$

14. $a - 5 = 8$
15. $b - 14 = -3$
16. $37 = c - 29$

17. $21 + m = 4$
18. $n - 72 = 72$
19. $p - 24 = -53$

20. $q + 8 = 57$
21. $r - 23 = -6$
22. $28 = g + 28$

23. $-13 + t = 10$
24. $216 = u - 129$
25. $177 = 403 + w$

26. **Rebates** The advertised price of a DVD player is $185 after a $30 mail-in rebate. Using the verbal model below, write and solve an equation to find the price of the DVD player before the rebate is applied.

$$\boxed{\text{Price before rebate}} - \boxed{\text{Rebate amount}} = \boxed{\text{Price after rebate}}$$

27. **Biology** When attacked by a giant hornet, Japanese honeybees cluster together to form a ball around the hornet and then generate heat by buzzing. The honeybees can endure temperatures of up to 48°C, which is 3°C greater than the hornet can tolerate. Find the maximum temperature tolerated by a Japanese giant hornet.

28. **Archaeology** The Great Pyramid in Egypt was built around 2560 B.C. Over the years, it has lost 30 feet of height off its top and is now 451 feet tall. Find the original height of the Great Pyramid.

29. Mountain Climbing In 1988, Stacy Allison became the first woman from the United States to reach the summit of Mount Everest, which is 29,035 feet high. One year earlier, she and a team of Americans had attempted to climb Mount Everest but were forced to turn back at an altitude of 26,000 feet due to severe storms. How close to the summit did Stacy Allison get on her first attempt?

30. Astronomy Cepheid stars appear to pulsate because they expand and contract in size. In its contracted phase, the Cepheid star Zeta Geminorum is 51 million miles across. This is 5 million miles less than the star's distance across in its expanded phase. Find the distance across Zeta Geminorum in its expanded phase.

31. *Writing* In Example 1 on page 91, the subtraction property of equality is used to solve $x + 9 = -3$. Explain how you can also solve this equation using the addition property of equality.

Solve the equation. Check your solution.

32. $a + 5 + 8 = 20$ **33.** $3 + c + 6 = -9$ **34.** $9 + x - 4 = 2$

35. $n - 6 - 1 = 5$ **36.** $0 = r + 7 - 32$ **37.** $-5 = -17 + y + 8$

Geometry Find the value of *x* for the given triangle or rectangle.

38. Perimeter = 34 in.   **39.** Perimeter = 59 cm   **40.** Perimeter = 352 ft

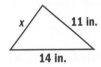

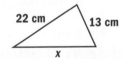

41. Extended Problem Solving Doctors measure the cholesterol in your blood to see if you are at risk for heart disease. The formula below gives your total cholesterol level in terms of your LDL (or "bad") cholesterol, your HDL (or "good") cholesterol, and your triglycerides.

$$\text{Total cholesterol} = \text{LDL} + \text{HDL} + \frac{\text{Triglycerides}}{5}$$

All values are measured in milligrams per deciliter (mg/dL) of blood.

a. When your cholesterol is checked by a doctor, the total cholesterol, HDL cholesterol, and triglycerides are measured directly. The LDL cholesterol is then calculated from these values. Write an equation that you can use to find the LDL level for the patient whose lab results are shown.

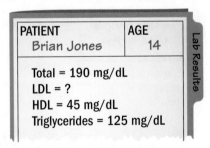

PATIENT	AGE
Brian Jones	14

Total = 190 mg/dL
LDL = ?
HDL = 45 mg/dL
Triglycerides = 125 mg/dL

Lab Results

b. Solve Find the patient's LDL level by solving your equation from part (a).

c. Interpret For teenagers, LDL levels below 110 mg/dL are considered acceptable. Levels from 110 mg/dL to 129 mg/dL are borderline, and levels of 130 mg/dL or greater are too high. Classify the LDL level of the given patient as *acceptable*, *borderline*, or *too high*.

Vasa Museum in Stockholm, Sweden

42. History In 1628, the Swedish ship *Vasa* sank in Stockholm Harbor in 105 feet of water. In 1959, salvagers used pontoons and cables to move the *Vasa* to a shallower depth of 50 feet. Underwater repairs were then made to strengthen the ship, and in 1961 the *Vasa* was lifted to the surface.

   a. Find the change in the *Vasa*'s position with respect to sea level as a result of the salvage work done in 1959.

   b. Find the number of years the *Vasa* remained underwater.

43. Critical Thinking In Example 2 on page 92, you saw that the equation $34 = y$ is equivalent to $23 = y - 11$. Write an equation that has $y + 5$ as its right side and is also equivalent to $23 = y - 11$.

44. Quilting You are making a quilt and have $150 to spend on materials. To make the main body of the quilt, you buy 5 yards of solid-color fabric for $4 per yard and 12 yards of printed fabric for $8 per yard. You also buy 2 yards of batting (material used to stuff the quilt) for $11 per yard. How much can you spend on fabric for a decorative border?

45. Challenge In the United States, annual sales of tennis shoes increased by $4 million from 1996 to 1997, decreased by $30 million from 1997 to 1998, decreased by $10 million from 1998 to 1999, and increased by $15 million from 1999 to 2000. In 2000, sales of tennis shoes were $520 million. Find the sales of tennis shoes in 1996.

Mixed Review

Write the product using an exponent. *(Lesson 1.2)*

46. $6 \cdot 6 \cdot 6 \cdot 6$ **47.** $(0.3)(0.3)$ **48.** $x \cdot x \cdot x$ **49.** $t \cdot t \cdot t \cdot t \cdot t \cdot t$

Evaluate the power. *(Lesson 1.2)*

50. 2^6 **51.** 7^4 **52.** $(0.8)^2$ **53.** $(2.5)^3$

State the opposite of the number. *(Lesson 1.4)*

54. 8 **55.** -27 **56.** 0 **57.** 144

Evaluate the expression when $x = 4$ and $y = -7$. *(Lesson 1.4)*

58. $|x|$ **59.** $|y|$ **60.** $|y| + |-y|$ **61.** $|y| - |-x|$

62. Dolphins A dolphin can swim at a constant speed of 20 miles per hour for long periods of time. How long does it take a dolphin to swim 60 miles? *(Lesson 2.4)*

Standardized Test Practice

63. Multiple Choice What is the solution of $x + 18 = -13$?

   A. -31 **B.** -5 **C.** 5 **D.** 31

64. Multiple Choice What is the solution of $-21 = a - 47$?

   F. -68 **G.** -26 **H.** 26 **I.** 68

65. Short Response A company hired 140 employees during a year in which 93 employees retired or left the company for other reasons. At the end of the year, the company had 816 employees. Find the number of employees the company had at the beginning of the year. Show and justify each step of your solution.

2.6 Modeling Multiplication Equations

Goal
Model and solve
multiplication equations.

Materials
• algebra tiles

You can use algebra tiles to model and solve simple multiplication
equations. For a description of algebra tiles, see page 90.

Investigate

Use algebra tiles to solve $3x = 12$.

1 Model $3x = 12$ with algebra tiles.

2 There are three x-tiles, so divide
the x-tiles and 1-tiles into three
equal groups.

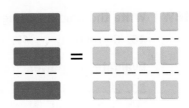

3 One x-tile is equal to four 1-tiles.
So, the solution of $3x = 12$ is 4.

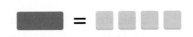

Draw Conclusions

Use algebra tiles to model and solve the equation.

1. $2x = 4$ **2.** $2x = 10$ **3.** $3x = 18$ **4.** $4x = 12$

5. $6x = 6$ **6.** $5x = 20$ **7.** $21 = 7x$ **8.** $21 = 3x$

9. *Writing* For each algebra-tile equation in the example shown
above, write a corresponding algebraic equation. Based on your
results, describe an algebraic method that you can use to solve
$8x = 56$. Then use your method to find the equation's solution.

10. Critical Thinking Describe how you can use algebra tiles to
solve the equation $2x + 3x = 15$. Then solve.

Solving Equations Using Multiplication *or* Division

Review Vocabulary

solving an equation,
  p. 86
inverse operations,
  p. 91
equivalent equations,
  p. 91

BEFORE	*Now*	WHY?
You solved addition and subtraction equations.	You'll solve equations using multiplication or division.	So you can find how long it takes whales to migrate, as in Ex. 35.

Astronomy In 1995, the Solar and Heliospheric Observatory (SOHO) was launched into space. SOHO studies the sun, including high-speed gas called solar wind that is ejected from the sun and travels throughout the solar system.

In Example 3, you'll see how to use a multiplication equation to find how long it takes solar wind to reach Earth. You can use division to solve such an equation, because multiplication and division are inverse operations.

Watch *Out*

Remember that you cannot divide a number or an expression by 0.

Division Property of Equality

Words Dividing each side of an equation by the same nonzero number produces an equivalent equation.

Numbers If $3x = 12$, then $\frac{3x}{3} = \frac{12}{3}$, or $x = 4$.

Algebra If $ax = b$ and $a \neq 0$, then $\frac{ax}{a} = \frac{b}{a}$, or $x = \frac{b}{a}$.

Example 1   Solving an Equation Using Division

Solve $-6x = 48$.

$$-6x = 48 \qquad \text{Write original equation.}$$

$$\frac{-6x}{-6} = \frac{48}{-6} \qquad \text{Divide each side by } -6.$$

$$x = -8 \qquad \text{Simplify.}$$

Answer The solution is -8.

✓**Check** $\quad -6x = 48 \qquad$ Write original equation.

$$-6(-8) \overset{?}{=} 48 \qquad \text{Substitute } -8 \text{ for } x.$$

$$48 = 48 \checkmark \qquad \text{Solution checks.}$$

Multiplication Property To solve an equation that involves division, you can use the *multiplication property of equality*.

> ## Multiplication Property of Equality
>
> **Words** Multiplying each side of an equation by the same nonzero number produces an equivalent equation.
>
> **Numbers** If $\frac{x}{3} = 12$, then $3 \cdot \frac{x}{3} = 3 \cdot 12$, or $x = 36$.
>
> **Algebra** If $\frac{x}{a} = b$ and $a \neq 0$, then $a \cdot \frac{x}{a} = a \cdot b$, or $x = ab$.

Example 2   Solving an Equation Using Multiplication

Solve $9 = \frac{w}{7}$.

$$9 = \frac{w}{7} \qquad \text{Write original equation.}$$

$$7 \cdot 9 = 7 \cdot \frac{w}{7} \qquad \text{Multiply each side by 7.}$$

$$63 = w \qquad \text{Simplify.}$$

Answer The solution is 63.

 Checkpoint

Solve the equation. Check your solution.

1. $2x = 18$ **2.** $-60 = -5a$ **3.** $\frac{y}{2} = 13$ **4.** $-8 = \frac{b}{8}$

Example 3   Writing and Solving an Equation

On January 4, 2003, the SOHO spacecraft described on page 97 detected solar wind traveling at about 2 million kilometers per hour. The sun is about 150 million kilometers from Earth. About how long did it take the solar wind to reach Earth?

Solution

Let t be the time (in hours) that it took the solar wind to reach Earth.

$$d = rt \qquad \text{Write formula for distance traveled.}$$

$$150,000,000 = 2,000,000t \qquad \text{Substitute values.}$$

$$\frac{150,000,000}{2,000,000} = \frac{2,000,000t}{2,000,000} \qquad \text{Divide each side by 2,000,000.}$$

$$75 = t \qquad \text{Simplify.}$$

Answer It took the solar wind about 75 hours to reach Earth.

In the **Real World**

Astronomy The SOHO spacecraft took this photo of the sun using a special ultraviolet imaging telescope. Light from the sun travels at about 300,000 kilometers per second. How long does it take the sun's light to reach Earth?

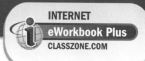

Guided Practice

Vocabulary Check

1. Copy and complete: Multiplication and ? are inverse operations.

2. Which property of equality would you use to solve $\frac{x}{5} = 12$? Explain.

Skill Check

Solve the equation. Check your solution.

3. $5c = -15$ 4. $54 = 9x$ 5. $6 = \frac{u}{4}$ 6. $\frac{y}{-10} = 7$

Guided Problem Solving

7. **Printers** You buy the inkjet printer shown in the advertisement. You use it to print a 40 page document in black and white and a 20 page document in color. How long does it take to print both documents?

   1 Write and solve an equation to find the time it takes to print the black and white document.

   2 Write and solve an equation to find the time it takes to print the color document.

   3 Find the time it takes to print both documents.

SALE! Inkjet Printers

• 8 pages/min in black and white
• 5 pages/min in color

Practice and Problem Solving

Homework *Help*

Example	Exercises
1	8–23, 28–33
2	8–23, 28–33
3	24–27, 34, 36

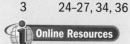
Online Resources
CLASSZONE.COM

• More Examples
• eTutorial Plus

Solve the equation. Check your solution.

8. $3x = 27$ 9. $4y = 52$ 10. $-65 = 13u$ 11. $84 = -21v$

12. $\frac{x}{7} = 5$ 13. $\frac{y}{-3} = 8$ 14. $16 = \frac{p}{6}$ 15. $-7 = \frac{q}{11}$

16. $-23a = 0$ 17. $-95 = -5b$ 18. $-r = 38$ 19. $301 = 43s$

20. $\frac{c}{-2} = -91$ 21. $17 = \frac{d}{17}$ 22. $9 = \frac{m}{-36}$ 23. $\frac{n}{62} = -54$

24. **Football** During the 2002 regular season of the National Football League, running back Michael Bennett played in 16 games and averaged 81 rushing yards per game. Find his total rushing yards by using the verbal model below to write and solve an equation.

$$\text{Average rushing yards per game} = \frac{\text{Total rushing yards}}{\text{Number of games played}}$$

25. Drilling One type of thermal ice drill can drill through ice at a rate of 15 feet per minute by using heat to melt the ice. Find the time it takes the drill to melt through a sheet of ice 75 feet thick.

26. Reforestation In 1998, fire destroyed 100 acres of the Oakwood National Wildlife Refuge in Arkansas. The U.S. Fish and Wildlife Service reforested this area by planting tree seedlings at a density of 300 seedlings per acre. Find the total number of seedlings planted.

27. Computers Your favorite rock band distributes one of its songs for free on its website. The size of the song file is 3584 kilobytes (KB). The table shows the maximum speed at which files can be downloaded using each type of Internet service offered in your town.

Type of service	Dial-up	DSL	Cable
Download speed (KB/sec)	7	96	188

In the **Real World**

Computers A kilobyte is a unit of data storage capacity in computer science. It takes about 16 kilobytes to store 1 second of CD-quality music on a computer. If the song file in Ex. 27 is CD-quality, about how long is the song?

To the nearest second, how long does it take to download the song file using dial-up service? using DSL service? using cable service?

Solve the equation. Check your solution.

28. $7x - 3x = 24$ **29.** $-110 = 12y + 10y$ **30.** $-4(9g) = 252$

31. $150 = 6(5h)$ **32.** $-3 = \dfrac{z}{6 + 11}$ **33.** $\dfrac{w}{8} = 9 - (-4)$

34. Geometry The figure shown is composed of a triangle and a rectangle.

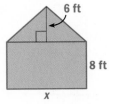

6 ft

8 ft

x

  a. Write and simplify an expression in terms of x for the area of the figure.

  b. What is the value of x if the area of the figure is 154 square feet?

35. Extended Problem Solving Each year gray whales migrate about 5000 miles from the Baja Peninsula of Mexico to their feeding grounds near Alaska. The whales travel about 100 miles per day.

  a. Write an expression for the distance the whales travel in x days.

  b. Copy and complete the table using your expression from part (a).

Travel time (days)	0	5	10	15	20	25
Distance traveled (miles)	?	?	?	?	?	?

  c. Make a scatter plot of the data in the table. Show travel time on the x-axis and distance traveled on the y-axis. Describe the pattern formed by the points in the scatter plot.

  d. **Apply** Extend the pattern you described in part (c) by plotting points for $x = 30, 35$, and so on until you plot a point whose y-coordinate is 5000. How many days does it take the whales to migrate from the Baja Peninsula to Alaska?

  e. **Reasonableness** Justify your solution to part (d) by solving the equation $100x = 5000$.

36. Watches A wristwatch has a built-in digital camera with a rectangular viewfinder. An image shown by the viewfinder consists of 6240 tiny rectangular dots called pixels arranged in rows and columns. The viewfinder has 80 rows of pixels. How many columns does it have?

37. *Writing* Describe a real-life problem that can be solved using the equation $50x = 400$. Then solve the problem.

38. Lightning On July 1, 2001, a Pennsylvania weather station detected an average of 80 lightning strikes per minute over a 24 hour period. Find the total number of lightning strikes detected during that time.

39. Challenge The problem below is a variation of one that appears in the ancient Chinese text *Nine Chapters on the Mathematical Art*. (In the problem, a *tou* is a Chinese unit of measure.)

> A goat, a horse, and a cow mistakenly enter a farmer's wheat field and eat some stalks of wheat. The horse eats twice as many stalks as the goat, and the cow eats twice as many stalks as the horse. The farmer demands 5 tou of wheat from the owners of the animals to replace what was eaten. How much wheat should be replaced by the goat's owner? by the horse's owner? by the cow's owner?

a. Let x be the amount of wheat (in *tou*) that should be replaced by the goat's owner. What is an expression in terms of x for the amount that should be replaced by the horse's owner? by the cow's owner?

b. Write and solve an equation to find x. To the nearest tenth of a *tou*, how much wheat should be replaced by each animal's owner?

Mixed Review **Perform the indicated operation.** *(pp. 774–776)*

40. $2.9 + 8.4$ **41.** $7.63 + 5.18$ **42.** $13.8 - 9.3$ **43.** $3.239 - 1.74$

44. 4.6×2.3 **45.** 6.51×9.22 **46.** $53.6 \div 6.7$ **47.** $8.16 \div 3.4$

Perform the indicated operation. *(Lessons 1.5–1.7)*

48. $-19 + 40$ **49.** $-26 + (-7)$ **50.** $3 - 18$ **51.** $-12 - (-10)$

52. $5(-14)$ **53.** $-23(-8)$ **54.** $-90 \div 15$ **55.** $-36 \div (-4)$

56. Plants From 1994 to 2001, the number of plant species classified as endangered increased by 177. There were 593 endangered plant species in 2001. Find the number of endangered plant species in 1994. *(Lesson 2.5)*

Standardized Test Practice **57. Multiple Choice** What is the solution of $\frac{x}{-2} = -8$?

   A. -16 **B.** -4 **C.** 4 **D.** 16

58. Multiple Choice Starting with a full tank of gas, your family's car is driven 420 miles and then refueled. It takes 12 gallons of gas to fill the car's tank. How many miles per gallon did the car get?

   F. 25 mi/gal   **G.** 30 mi/gal   **H.** 35 mi/gal   **I.** 40 mi/gal

Decimal Operations *and* Equations *with* Decimals

Review Vocabulary
absolute value, p. 23
solving an equation,
  p. 86
decimal, p. 770

BEFORE	*Now*	WHY?
You solved equations involving integers.	You'll solve equations involving decimals.	So you can find the speed of an airplane, as in Ex. 47.

Hibernation When a chipmunk hibernates, its heart rate decreases, its body temperature drops, and the chipmunk loses weight as its stored body fat is converted to energy. In Example 5, you'll see how to use an equation with decimals to describe a chipmunk's weight loss during hibernation.

You already know how to perform operations with positive decimals. However, just as there are negative integers, such as −2, there are also negative decimals, such as −2.5. The number line below shows several positive and negative decimals.

$$-2.5 \quad -1.3 \qquad 0.5 \quad 1.75$$
$$-3 \quad -2 \quad -1 \quad 0 \quad 1 \quad 2 \quad 3$$

The rules for performing operations with decimals are the same as those you learned for integers in Chapter 1.

Review *Help*

For help with decimal operations, see pp. 774–776.

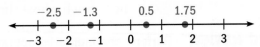

Example 1	*Adding and Subtracting Decimals*

a. Find the sum −2.9 + (−6.5).

Use the rule for adding numbers with the same sign.

$$-2.9 + (-6.5) = -9.4$$

Add $|-2.9|$ and $|-6.5|$.

Both decimals are negative, so the sum is negative.

b. Find the difference −25.38 − (−42.734).

First rewrite the difference as a sum: −25.38 + 42.734. Then use the rule for adding numbers with different signs.

$$-25.38 + 42.734 = 17.354$$

Subtract $|-25.38|$ from $|42.734|$.

$|42.734| > |-25.38|$, so the sum has the same sign as 42.734.

Find the sum or difference.

1. $-1.3 + (-4.2)$ **2.** $10.57 + (-6.89)$ **3.** $9.817 - (-1.49)$

Example 2   *Multiplying and Dividing Decimals*

Perform the indicated operation.

a. $-0.7(18.4)$ **b.** $-4.5(-9.25)$

c. $-29.07 \div (-1.9)$ **d.** $16.83 \div (-3.3)$

Solution

a. $-0.7(18.4) = -12.88$ **Different signs: Product is negative.**

b. $-4.5(-9.25) = 41.625$ **Same sign: Product is positive.**

c. $-29.07 \div (-1.9) = 15.3$ **Same sign: Quotient is positive.**

d. $16.83 \div (-3.3) = -5.1$ **Different signs: Quotient is negative.**

Study *Strategy*

Reasonableness You can use estimation to check the results of operations with decimals. In part (c) of Example 2, for instance, notice that $-29.07 \div (-1.9)$ is about $-30 \div (-2)$, or 15. So, an answer of 15.3 is reasonable.

 **Checkpoint**

Find the product or quotient.

4. $3.1(-6.8)$ **5.** $-11.41 \div (-0.7)$ **6.** $-15.841 \div 2.17$

7. Critical Thinking Explain how you can use estimation to check that your answer to Exercise 4 is reasonable.

Solving Equations You can use what you know about decimal operations to solve equations involving decimals.

Example 3   *Solving Addition and Subtraction Equations*

Solve the equation.

a. $x + 4.7 = 3.5$ **b.** $y - 6.91 = -2.26$

Solution

a. $x + 4.7 = 3.5$ **Write original equation.**

     $x + 4.7 - 4.7 = 3.5 - 4.7$ **Subtract 4.7 from each side.**

             $x = -1.2$ **Simplify.**

b. $y - 6.91 = -2.26$ **Write original equation.**

     $y - 6.91 + 6.91 = -2.26 + 6.91$ **Add 6.91 to each side.**

             $y = 4.65$ **Simplify.**

Study *Strategy*

Always check your solution when solving an equation. To check the solution in part (a) of Example 3, for instance, substitute -1.2 for x in the original equation.

$x + 4.7 = 3.5$

$-1.2 + 4.7 \stackrel{?}{=} 3.5$

$3.5 = 3.5 \checkmark$

 **Checkpoint**

Solve the equation. Check your solution.

8. $x + 3.8 = 5.2$ **9.** $a + 10.4 = -1.17$ **10.** $6.29 + c = 4.01$

11. $y - 7.8 = 22.3$ **12.** $r - 0.88 = -0.56$ **13.** $-9.34 = t - 2.75$

Example 4   Solving Multiplication and Division Equations

Solve the equation.

a. $-0.6m = -5.1$

b. $\dfrac{n}{-8} = 1.75$

Solution

a. $-0.6m = -5.1$ Write original equation.

$\dfrac{-0.6m}{-0.6} = \dfrac{-5.1}{-0.6}$ Divide each side by -0.6.

$m = 8.5$ Simplify.

b. $\dfrac{n}{-8} = 1.75$ Write original equation.

$-8\left(\dfrac{n}{-8}\right) = -8(1.75)$ Multiply each side by -8.

$n = -14$ Simplify.

 Checkpoint

Solve the equation. Check your solution.

14. $7x = 40.6$ **15.** $-1.8u = 6.3$ **16.** $\dfrac{y}{11.5} = 0.4$ **17.** $-9.1 = \dfrac{v}{-5.9}$

Example 5   Writing and Solving an Equation

When a chipmunk hibernates, its weight decreases by about 0.31 pound. After hibernation, a chipmunk weighs about 0.35 pound. Find the weight of a chipmunk before hibernation.

Solution

Let w represent a chipmunk's weight (in pounds) before hibernation. Write a verbal model. Then use the verbal model to write an equation.

Weight before hibernation	−	Weight loss	=	Weight after hibernation

$w - 0.31 = 0.35$ Substitute.

$w - 0.31 + 0.31 = 0.35 + 0.31$ Add 0.31 to each side.

$w = 0.66$ Simplify.

Answer A chipmunk weighs about 0.66 pound before hibernation.

 Checkpoint

18. You use an automated teller machine (ATM) to deposit a check for $122.94 into your savings account. Your receipt from the ATM shows a balance of $286.59 after the deposit. Find the balance of your savings account before the deposit.

In the **Real World**

Hibernation During hibernation, a chipmunk's body temperature drops to 37.4°F, which is 61.2°F below the normal body temperature for a chipmunk. What is a chipmunk's normal body temperature?

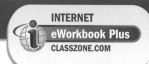

Guided Practice

Vocabulary Check

1. Copy and complete: The sum of a positive decimal and a negative decimal has the same sign as the decimal with the greater __?__ .

2. Describe how you would solve the equation $-7.9x = 86.9$.

Skill Check

Perform the indicated operation.

3. $-6.2 + 4.5$ **4.** $1.9 - (-9.1)$ **5.** $-0.4(-8.3)$ **6.** $7.35 \div (-2.1)$

Solve the equation. Check your solution.

7. $x - 2.2 = 3.2$ **8.** $y + 0.6 = -1$ **9.** $\dfrac{n}{-7.1} = 5.8$ **10.** $-5.2a = -1.3$

Guided Problem Solving

11. Earth Science The table shows the year-to-year changes in the mean January water level of Lake Superior during the period 1997–2001. Positive changes represent increases in the water level, while negative changes represent decreases. In 2001, the water level was 182.98 meters. What was the water level in 1997?

Time period	1997 to 1998	1998 to 1999	1999 to 2000	2000 to 2001
Change (meters)	-0.19	-0.28	0.04	-0.18

1 Find the overall change in the water level from 1997 to 2001 by adding the changes in the table.

2 Write an equation that you can use to find the water level in 1997.

3 Solve your equation. What was Lake Superior's water level in 1997?

Practice and Problem Solving

Homework *Help*

Example	Exercises
1	12–17, 45
2	18–23, 45
3	24–29
4	30–35
5	37, 38, 42–44

Online Resources
CLASSZONE.COM
• More Examples
• eTutorial Plus

Perform the indicated operation.

12. $7.8 + (-9.3)$ **13.** $-1.25 + 14.4$ **14.** $-2.583 + (-5.399)$

15. $6.1 - 18.7$ **16.** $-3.72 - 4.58$ **17.** $-0.62 - (-0.741)$

18. $-4.8(0.1)$ **19.** $-11.7(-6.82)$ **20.** $2.03(-1.66)$

21. $34.1 \div (-5.5)$ **22.** $-0.63 \div 0.7$ **23.** $-7.532 \div (-2.69)$

Solve the equation. Check your solution.

24. $x + 8.5 = 13.7$ **25.** $a + 4.8 = 2.29$ **26.** $-3.36 = b + 5.12$

27. $y - 1.3 = -7.4$ **28.** $g - 6.27 = 10.63$ **29.** $-0.504 + h = -0.18$

30. $8w = 75.2$ **31.** $-0.96j = -0.72$ **32.** $3.498 = -0.53k$

33. $\dfrac{z}{6.9} = -3$ **34.** $\dfrac{r}{0.4} = 0.8$ **35.** $-9.1 = \dfrac{s}{-7.12}$

36. 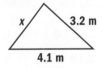 Use the *table* feature on a graphing calculator to evaluate $3.7x$ for different values of x. Set TblStart to 0 and ΔTbl to 0.1. Scroll through the table to find the solution of $3.7x = 4.81$.

37. Telescopes The W.M. Keck Observatory, located on top of the dormant volcano Mauna Kea in Hawaii, has two telescopes. Each telescope has a mirror composed of 36 identical sections that are fitted together. The total area of the mirror is about 75.8 square meters. Find the area of each section of the mirror to the nearest tenth of a square meter.

38. Baseball A baseball player's batting average is defined by the verbal model below. During the 2001 Major League Baseball season, Ichiro Suzuki of the Seattle Mariners batted 692 times and had a batting average of .350. How many hits did Suzuki have?

$$\text{Batting average} = \frac{\text{Number of hits}}{\text{Number of times at bat}}$$

W.M. Keck Observatory

Simplify the expression.

39. $2.6x - 7.1x$ **40.** $-3.5(4a + 1.9)$ **41.** $0.8(3 - 11n) + 1.4n$

Geometry Find the value of x for the given triangle or rectangle.

42. Perimeter = 10 m   **43.** Area = 75.52 ft²   **44.** Area = 15.75 cm²

x 3.2 m
4.1 m

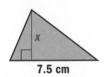

x
11.8 ft

x
7.5 cm

45. Extended Problem Solving The table shows the difference between the amount of money the U.S. government received and the amount it spent for the years 1995–2000. Positive amounts, called surpluses, mean that the government received more than it spent. Negative amounts, called deficits, mean that it received less than it spent.

Year	1995	1996	1997	1998	1999	2000
Surplus or deficit (billions of dollars)	−164.0	−107.5	−22.0	69.2	124.6	236.4

a. *Writing* Without performing any calculations, tell whether the U.S. government received *more money* or *less money* than it spent over the entire period 1995–2000. Explain how you got your answer.

b. Check your answer from part (a) by calculating the overall surplus or deficit for 1995–2000.

c. To the nearest tenth of a billion dollars, what was the mean annual surplus or deficit for 1995–2000?

d. **Compare** Find the median annual surplus or deficit for 1995–2000. Compare the median with the mean.

Review *Help*

For help with mean and median, see p. 39.

46. Challenge Solve the equations $0.1x = 1$, $0.01x = 1$, $0.001x = 1$, and $0.0001x = 1$. What happens to the solutions as the coefficients of x get closer to 0?

47. Aviation The Mach number for an airplane is the speed of the airplane divided by the speed of sound. The speed of sound depends on altitude. The table shows the typical Mach numbers of several airplanes and the speed of sound at each airplane's cruising altitude.

Airplane	Mach number at cruising altitude	Speed of sound at cruising altitude (mi/h)
Cessna Skyhawk	0.19	740
Boeing 747	0.86	663
Concorde	2.04	660

a. Find each airplane's speed at its cruising altitude by solving an equation. Round your answers to the nearest mile per hour.

b. To the nearest tenth of an hour, how long does it take each airplane to fly 550 miles?

Mixed Review

For the given expression, identify the terms, like terms, coefficients, and constant terms. Then simplify the expression. *(Lesson 2.3)*

48. $5x + 11 + 8x$

49. $-3p + 2 + p - 4$

50. $7w - w + 9 - 6w$

51. $8 + 2y - 1 - 9y + 3$

Solve the equation. Check your solution. *(Lessons 2.5, 2.6)*

52. $x + 12 = 5$ **53.** $y - 9 = -4$ **54.** $32c = 192$ **55.** $\dfrac{d}{19} = -8$

Standardized Test Practice

56. Extended Response When you watch waves pass an anchored boat or other stationary point, the elapsed time between waves is called the period. In deep water, the period T (in seconds) and the wave speed s (in miles per hour) are related by the formula $s = 3.49T$.

a. Suppose a storm near Antarctica generates a series of waves with a period of 11 seconds. Find the speed of the waves.

b. Waves from Antarctic storms can reach the coast of Alaska, 8000 miles away. How many hours does it take the waves from part (a) to reach the Alaskan coast? How many days does it take?

Brain GAME   **Runoff**

How long is a marathon?

To find the answer, first solve equation 1. Then substitute the solution of equation 1 for a in equation 2, and solve equation 2. Finally, substitute the solution of equation 2 for b in equation 3, and solve equation 3. The solution of equation 3 is a marathon's length in miles.

Equation 1: $12.7 + a = 65.6$

Equation 2: $b - a = 38.8$

Equation 3: $3.5x = b$

Chapter Review

Vocabulary Review

additive identity, p. 64
multiplicative identity, p. 64
equivalent numerical
  expressions, p. 71

equivalent variable
  expressions, p. 72
term, p. 78
coefficient, p. 78
constant term, p. 78

like terms, p. 78
equation, p. 85
solution of an equation,
  p. 85

solving an equation, p. 86
inverse operations, p. 91
equivalent equations, p. 91

1. What number is the additive identity? What number is the multiplicative identity?

2. Describe how you would solve an equation of the form $ax = b$ where $a \neq 0$.

3. Copy and complete: The expressions $2(8 + 3)$ and $2(8) + 2(3)$ are _?_.

4. In the expression $5 - 9n$, what is the coefficient of n? What is the constant term?

2.1 Properties and Operations

Examples on pp. 63–65

▶ *Goal*

Use properties of addition and multiplication.

Example **Evaluate the expression.**

$$
\begin{aligned}
\textbf{a. } 57 + 28 + 13 &= (57 + 28) + 13 && \text{Use order of operations.} \\
&= (28 + 57) + 13 && \text{Commutative property of addition} \\
&= 28 + (57 + 13) && \text{Associative property of addition} \\
&= 28 + 70 && \text{Add 57 and 13.} \\
&= 98 && \text{Add 28 and 70.}
\end{aligned}
$$

$$
\begin{aligned}
\textbf{b. } -5(19)(20) &= [-5(19)](20) && \text{Use order of operations.} \\
&= [19(-5)](20) && \text{Commutative property of multiplication} \\
&= 19[-5(20)] && \text{Associative property of multiplication} \\
&= 19(-100) && \text{Multiply } -5 \text{ and 20.} \\
&= -1900 && \text{Multiply 19 and } -100.
\end{aligned}
$$

✔ **Evaluate the expression. Justify each of your steps.**

5. $16 + 18 + 14$

6. $38 + 23 + (-8)$

7. $4.7 + 2.5 + 2.3$

8. $4(11)(25)$

9. $5(-3)(12)$

10. $6(13)(0.5)$

2.2 The Distributive Property

Examples on pp. 71–73

▶ *Goal*

Use the distributive property.

Example Use the distributive property to evaluate 5(204).

$$5(204) = 5(200 + 4) \qquad \text{Rewrite 204 as 200 + 4.}$$
$$= 5(200) + 5(4) \qquad \text{Distributive property}$$
$$= 1000 + 20 \qquad \text{Multiply.}$$
$$= 1020 \qquad \text{Add.}$$

Example Write an expression equivalent to 4(3*x* − 2).

$$4(3x - 2) = 4(3x) - 4(2) \qquad \text{Distributive property}$$
$$= 12x - 8 \qquad \text{Multiply.}$$

✔ **Use the distributive property to evaluate the expression.**

11. 3(106)   **12.** 6(99)   **13.** 8(5.2)   **14.** (7.95)4

Write an equivalent variable expression.

15. $-2(x + 4)$ **16.** $5(y - 8)$ **17.** $4(7a + 2)$ **18.** $(6 - 11c)(-3)$

2.3 Simplifying Variable Expressions

Examples on pp. 78–80

▶ *Goal*

Simplify variable expressions.

Example Identify the terms, like terms, coefficients, and constant terms of the expression 7*n* − 5 − 3*n* + 2.

Terms: $7n, -5, -3n, 2$ **Like terms:** $7n$ and $-3n$; -5 and 2

Coefficients: $7, -3$ **Constant terms:** $-5, 2$

Example Simplify the expression 3*p* + 5 − 8(*p* + 2).

$$3p + 5 - 8(p + 2) = 3p + 5 - 8p - 16 \qquad \text{Distributive property}$$
$$= 3p - 8p + 5 - 16 \qquad \text{Group like terms.}$$
$$= -5p - 11 \qquad \text{Combine like terms.}$$

✔ **Identify the terms, like terms, coefficients, and constant terms.**

19. $4t + 13t + 2$ **20.** $x + 5 - 3x - 1$ **21.** $12 - 7k + 9 - k$

Simplify the expression.

22. $5x - 9 - x + 2$ **23.** $3(u + 1) + 4u + 1$ **24.** $8a - 2(7a - 3)$

2.4 Variables and Equations

Examples on pp. 85–86

▶ **Goal**

Use mental math to solve equations.

Example Solve the equation using mental math.

Equation	Question	Solution	Check
a. $x + 7 = 11$	What number plus 7 equals 11?	4	$4 + 7 = 11$ ✓
b. $y - 9 = 5$	What number minus 9 equals 5?	14	$14 - 9 = 5$ ✓
c. $3n = 21$	3 times what number equals 21?	7	$3(7) = 21$ ✓
d. $-6 = \dfrac{30}{w}$	-6 equals 30 divided by what number?	-5	$-6 = \dfrac{30}{-5}$ ✓

✔ **Solve the equation using mental math.**

25. $x + 10 = 23$ **26.** $7 - y = -1$ **27.** $36 = -4a$ **28.** $\dfrac{b}{5} = 8$

29. Trip Your family drives 150 miles to an amusement park at an average speed of 50 miles per hour. How long does the trip take?

2.5 Solving Equations Using Addition or Subtraction

Examples on pp. 91–92

▶ **Goal**

Use addition or subtraction to solve equations.

Example Solve $x + 19 = 6$.

$$x + 19 = 6 \qquad \text{Write original equation.}$$
$$x + 19 - 19 = 6 - 19 \qquad \text{Subtract 19 from each side.}$$
$$x = -13 \qquad \text{Simplify.}$$

Example Solve $m - 42 = -15$.

$$m - 42 = -15 \qquad \text{Write original equation.}$$
$$m - 42 + 42 = -15 + 42 \qquad \text{Add 42 to each side.}$$
$$m = 27 \qquad \text{Simplify.}$$

✔ **Solve the equation. Check your solution.**

30. $x + 8 = 21$ **31.** $-9 = t + 16$ **32.** $p - 7 = -8$ **33.** $29 = r - 64$

34. Salary An engineer receives a promotion that includes a raise of $4500 in her annual salary. Her new salary is $50,750. What was the engineer's salary before the promotion?

2.6 Solving Equations Using Multiplication or Division

Examples on pp. 97–98

▶ **Goal**

Use multiplication or division to solve equations.

Example Solve $\dfrac{r}{-13} = -5$.

$$\dfrac{r}{-13} = -5 \qquad \text{Write original equation.}$$

$$-13\left(\dfrac{r}{-13}\right) = -13(-5) \qquad \text{Multiply each side by } -13.$$

$$r = 65 \qquad \text{Simplify.}$$

✔ **Solve the equation. Check your solution.**

35. $-5x = 45$ **36.** $-54 = -3y$ **37.** $\dfrac{a}{8} = 4$ **38.** $9 = \dfrac{c}{-9}$

39. Craft Fair You divide a stack of fliers for a craft fair into 6 smaller stacks for volunteers to distribute. Each smaller stack contains 15 fliers. What is the total number of fliers distributed?

2.7 Decimal Operations and Equations with Decimals

Examples on pp. 102–104

▶ **Goal**

Use positive and negative decimals.

Example Perform the indicated operation.

a. $9.74 + (-3.31) = 6.43$ Add using rule for different signs.

b. $-4.2 - 7.9 = -4.2 + (-7.9)$ Rewrite as a sum.

$ = -12.1$ Add using rule for same signs.

c. $-2.6(8.4) = -21.84$ Different signs: Product is negative.

d. $-17.67 \div (-3.1) = 5.7$ Same sign: Quotient is positive.

Example Solve $-1.9k = 0.76$.

$$-1.9k = 0.76 \qquad \text{Write original equation.}$$

$$\dfrac{-1.9k}{-1.9} = \dfrac{0.76}{-1.9} \qquad \text{Divide each side by } -1.9.$$

$$k = -0.4 \qquad \text{Simplify.}$$

✔ **Perform the indicated operation.**

40. $-6.6 + 1.4$ **41.** $2.8 - (-4.7)$ **42.** $-9.4(-5.31)$ **43.** $7 \div (-2.5)$

Solve the equation. Check your solution.

44. $x + 6 = 1.8$ **45.** $2.4h = -8.4$ **46.** $\dfrac{n}{-5} = -7.3$ **47.** $u - 4.6 = 3.7$

Chapter Review   **111**

Evaluate the expression. Justify each of your steps.

1. $48 + 25 + 22$ **2.** $15(-7)(4)$ **3.** $5.9 + 10.4 + 2.1$ **4.** $36 \cdot 1 + 0$

Identify the property that the statement illustrates.

5. $-8(5) = 5(-8)$ **6.** $4 + 0 = 4$ **7.** $x^2 + y = y + x^2$ **8.** $7(xy^2) = (7x)y^2$

9. Waves The highest ocean wave ever reliably measured was sighted by the U.S.S. *Ramapo* during a typhoon in 1933. The wave was about 37 yards high. Use a conversion factor to find this height in feet.

Use the distributive property to evaluate the expression.

10. $7(8 - 3)$ **11.** $(4 + 6)(-6)$ **12.** $5(309)$ **13.** $8(4.95)$

Geometry Find the area of the rectangle or triangle.

14. 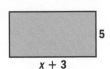   **15.**   **16.**   **17.**

For the given expression, identify the terms, like terms, coefficients, and constant terms. Then simplify the expression.

18. $4x + 2 + 5x$ **19.** $-a + 3a + 7 - 4$ **20.** $8k - 5 - 2k + 1$ **21.** $y + 7y - 9 - 3y$

Simplify the expression.

22. $2(x - 7) - 3x$ **23.** $-4(n + 1) + 15n$ **24.** $8p + 4 - (p + 4)$ **25.** $9t - 3(3t - 2)$

Write the verbal sentence as an equation. Tell whether 12 is a solution.

26. The difference of 17 and x is 4.   **27.** The quotient of a and 4 is 3.

Solve the equation.

28. $x + 12 = 9$ **29.** $-4 = h - 20$ **30.** $-3r = 87$ **31.** $\frac{s}{7} = 13$

32. Books You buy a book that is 540 pages long. You can read about 30 pages per hour. How long does it take you to read the book?

Perform the indicated operation.

33. $-3.1 + (-7.3)$ **34.** $5.85 - 9.47$ **35.** $-6.2(-0.9)$ **36.** $7.15 \div (-1.3)$

Solve the equation.

37. $x + 6.5 = -4.5$ **38.** $c - 2.59 = 1.48$ **39.** $-9.12 = -2.4y$ **40.** $\frac{m}{-3.4} = 8.3$

Chapter Standardized Test

Test-Taking Strategy For difficult questions, first try eliminating answer choices that you know are *not* correct.

1. Which equation illustrates the identity property of multiplication?

   A. $(xy)z = x(yz)$ **B.** $x \cdot 0 = 0$

   C. $x \cdot 1 = x$ **D.** $x + 0 = x$

2. The average height of a male giraffe is 17 feet. What is this height in inches?

   F. 29 inches   **G.** 51 inches

   H. 170 inches   **I.** 204 inches

3. Which expression represents the area (in square units) of the triangle shown?

   8
   $4x + 6$

   A. $32x + 48$ **B.** $16x + 24$

   C. $4x + 14$ **D.** $32x + 6$

4. Which number is *not* a coefficient of n in the expression $3n + 8 - n + 4n$?

   F. -1 **G.** 1   **H.** 3   **I.** 4

5. Which expression is equivalent to $5a + 8 - 2(a + 4)$?

   A. $3a$ **B.** $3a + 4$

   C. $3a + 12$ **D.** $3a + 16$

6. Which equation represents the sentence "The difference of 9 and x is 5."?

   F. $9 = x - 5$ **G.** $9 = 5 - x$

   H. $9 - x = 5$ **I.** $x - 9 = 5$

7. Which equation does *not* have 6 as a solution?

   A. $t + 5 = 11$ **B.** $3 - t = -3$

   C. $7t = 42$ **D.** $\frac{24}{t} = 3$

8. What is the solution of $y + 31 = 19$?

   F. -50 **G.** -12 **H.** 12   **I.** 50

9. What is the solution of $-20 = g - 4$?

   A. -24 **B.** -16 **C.** 5   **D.** 80

10. What is the solution of $\frac{x}{-3} = -18$?

    F. -54 **G.** -6 **H.** 6   **I.** 54

11. What is the value of $-4.85 - (-6.32)$?

    A. -11.17 **B.** -1.47

    C. 1.47   **D.** 11.17

12. What is the solution of $5.2w = -2.08$?

    F. -2.5 **G.** -0.4 **H.** 0.4   **I.** 2.5

13. **Short Response** Once a week, you either rent a movie for $4 or see a movie in a theater for $9. Let r represent the number of movies you rent in a year (52 weeks). Write and simplify an expression in terms of r for the total amount you spend on movies during the year.

14. **Extended Response** You have been hired to mow a rectangular lawn that is 300 feet long and 150 feet wide. You want to earn $12 per hour of work, and you can mow about 20,000 square feet per hour.

    a. What is the area of the lawn?

    b. About how long will it take you to mow the lawn?

    c. How much money should you charge for mowing the lawn?

Measuring Indirectly

Goal
Find the height of a stack of coins that is too high to be measured directly.

Key Skill
Indirect measurement

Materials
- at least ten pennies
- ruler
- calculator

One penny doesn't amount to much. But suppose you could save one million pennies. Students in the Los Angeles area did just that during a school year and used the money to buy new computers for their school. Suppose you made a stack of one million pennies. How tall would the stack be? Would it be taller than the Empire State Building? taller than Mount Everest?

You cannot find the height of the stack with a ruler or any other common measuring tool. However, you can use *indirect measurement* to find the height.

Investigate

1 Stack at least ten pennies and use a ruler to measure the height of the stack in millimeters.

2 Use the following verbal model to write an equation.

Height of your stack	=	Number of pennies in your stack	·	Height of one penny

3 Solve the equation that you wrote in Step 2 to find the height of one penny.

4 To find the height of a stack of one million pennies, multiply the height of one penny by 1,000,000.

Consider and Decide

Compare the height of a stack of one million pennies with the heights of the Empire State Building and Mount Everest. Consider the following:

- The Empire State Building is 381 meters tall. Mount Everest is 8850 meters tall.

- What unit of measurement did you use to write the height of a stack of one million pennies? Is this unit appropriate? Convert the unit if necessary.

Present Your Results

Write a short explanation of how you found the height of a stack of one million pennies. Include your measurements and equations. Describe how the height of the stack compares with the height of the Empire State Building and the height of Mount Everest.

Project Extensions

Research CLASSZONE.COM The U.S. Mint produces coins. Use the Internet to find out how many pennies, nickels, dimes, and quarters were produced by the U.S. Mint last year. Find the total value (in dollars) of each coin type produced. Then find the combined value. Explain how you found your answers.

Experiment Every day about 17 million $1 bills are printed, most of which are used to replace bills already in circulation. Use indirect measurement to find the thickness of a $1 bill. Suppose you made a stack of all the $1 bills printed in one day. How tall would this stack be? Explain the steps you took to find your answers.

Career The U.S. Mint has facilities in Washington, D.C., San Francisco, Fort Knox, and other locations. Employees of the U.S. Mint work to produce and protect American currency. Find out more about careers at the U.S. Mint.

Multi-Step Equations *and* Inequalities

At what wind speeds do wind turbines produce power?

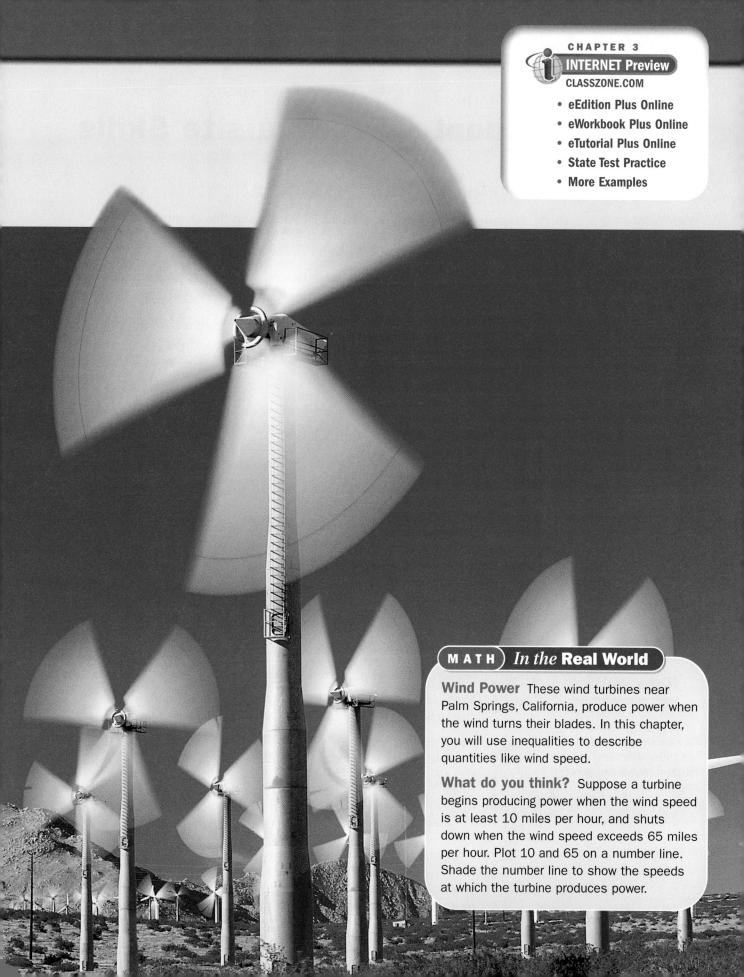

CHAPTER 3

INTERNET Preview
CLASSZONE.COM

- eEdition Plus Online
- eWorkbook Plus Online
- eTutorial Plus Online
- State Test Practice
- More Examples

MATH *In the* **Real World**

Wind Power These wind turbines near Palm Springs, California, produce power when the wind turns their blades. In this chapter, you will use inequalities to describe quantities like wind speed.

What do you think? Suppose a turbine begins producing power when the wind speed is at least 10 miles per hour, and shuts down when the wind speed exceeds 65 miles per hour. Plot 10 and 65 on a number line. Shade the number line to show the speeds at which the turbine produces power.

Chapter Prerequisite Skills

PREREQUISITE SKILLS QUIZ

Review Vocabulary

like terms, p. 78
equation, p. 85
solution of an equation, p. 85
inverse operations, p. 91
equivalent equations, p. 91

Preparing for Success **To prepare for success in this chapter, test your knowledge of these concepts and skills. You may want to look at the pages referred to in blue for additional review.**

1. **Vocabulary** Explain what an equation is. Then give an example of an equation with a variable in it.

Use the distributive property to write an equivalent variable expression.
(p. 71)

2. $9(x - 4)$ 3. $8(z - 7)$ 4. $-6(-m + 12)$ 5. $-10(n - 5)$

Simplify the expression. (p. 78)

6. $c + 4 - c$ 7. $9b - 12b + 3$ 8. $4(a + 2) + a$ 9. $2(2d + 5 + d)$

Solve the equation. Check your solution. (pp. 91, 97, and 102)

10. $x + 13 = 7$ 11. $\dfrac{h}{6} = -8$ 12. $q - 9.6 = 2$ 13. $65 = -13b$

NOTETAKING STRATEGIES

Note _Worthy_

You will find a notetaking strategy at the beginning of each chapter. Look for additional notetaking and study strategies throughout the chapter.

SUMMARIZING At the end of each lesson, summarize the main idea of the lesson in your notes. Include important details.

Lesson 2.6 Solving Equations Using Multiplication or Division

Main Idea: Multiplying or dividing each side of an equation by the same nonzero number results in an equivalent equation.

Use division to solve multiplication equations.

$$2x = 6$$

$$\frac{2x}{2} = \frac{6}{2}$$

$$x = 3$$

Use multiplication to solve division equations.

$$\frac{x}{5} = 10$$

$$5\left(\frac{x}{5}\right) = 5(10)$$

$$x = 50$$

You may find this strategy helpful in Lesson 3.6 when you solve multi-step inequalities.

Concept Activity

3.1 Modeling Two-Step Equations

Goal
Model and solve two-step equations.

Materials
• algebra tiles

Investigate

Use algebra tiles to solve $3x + 6 = 12$.

1 Model $3x + 6 = 12$ using algebra tiles.

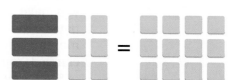

2 Remove six 1-tiles from each side.

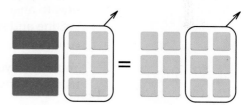

3 Divide the remaining tiles into three equal groups. Each x-tile is equal to two 1-tiles. So, the solution is 2.

Draw Conclusions

Use algebra tiles to model and solve the equation.

1. $1 + 2x = 9$ **2.** $4x + 1 = 5$ **3.** $2x + 2 = 8$

4. $9 = 2x + 5$ **5.** $11 = 2 + 3x$ **6.** $5x + 3 = 8$

7. Critical Thinking What property of equality is used in Step 2? in Step 3?

8. *Writing* For each algebra-tile model shown above, write a corresponding algebraic equation.

9. Interpret Describe the steps you would take to solve $2x + 1 = 5$ without using algebra tiles.

Solving Two-Step Equations

BEFORE	Now	WHY?
You solved one-step equations.	You'll solve two-step equations.	So you can find the cost of a rafting trip, as in Ex. 21.

Review Vocabulary

verbal model, p. 6
equation, p. 85
inverse operations, p. 91

Drum Set You are buying a drum set that costs $495. The music store lets you make a down payment. You can pay the remaining cost in three equal monthly payments with no interest charged. You make a down payment of $150. How much is each monthly payment? In Example 4, you will see how to answer this question by writing and solving a *two-step equation*.

You can solve a two-step equation by using two inverse operations.

Example 1   *Using Subtraction and Division to Solve*

Solve $3x + 7 = -5$. Check your solution.

$3x + 7 = -5$	Write original equation.
$3x + 7 - 7 = -5 - 7$	Subtract 7 from each side.
$3x = -12$	Simplify.
$\dfrac{3x}{3} = \dfrac{-12}{3}$	Divide each side by 3.
$x = -4$	Simplify.

Answer The solution is -4.

✓**Check** $3x + 7 = -5$	Write original equation.
$3(-4) + 7 \stackrel{?}{=} -5$	Substitute -4 for x.
$-5 = -5$ ✓	Solution checks.

✔ *Checkpoint*

Solve the equation. Check your solution.

  1. $4x + 1 = 5$ **2.** $3n + 8 = 2$ **3.** $1 = 2r + 9$ **4.** $2 = 6h + 20$

  5. Critical Thinking How is solving $3x - 7 = -5$ different from solving $3x + 7 = -5$?

Example 2   *Using Addition and Multiplication to Solve*

Solve $\frac{x}{2} - 3 = 1$. Check your solution.

$\frac{x}{2} - 3 = 1$	Write original equation.
$\frac{x}{2} - 3 + 3 = 1 + 3$	Add 3 to each side.
$\frac{x}{2} = 4$	Simplify.
$2\left(\frac{x}{2}\right) = 2(4)$	Multiply each side by 2.
$x = 8$	Simplify.

Answer The solution is 8.

✓**Check** $\frac{x}{2} - 3 = 1$	Write original equation.
$\frac{8}{2} - 3 \overset{?}{=} 1$	Substitute 8 for *x*.
$1 = 1$ ✓	Solution checks.

✔ *Checkpoint*

Solve the equation. Check your solution.

6. $\frac{b}{4} - 8 = 1$ **7.** $\frac{c}{6} - 2 = 6$ **8.** $2 = \frac{d}{5} - 1$ **9.** $12 = \frac{f}{2} - 8$

Example 3   *Solving an Equation with Negative Coefficients*

Solve $7 - 4y = 19$. Check your solution.

$7 - 4y = 19$	Write original equation.
$7 - 4y - 7 = 19 - 7$	Subtract 7 from each side.
$-4y = 12$	Simplify.
$\frac{-4y}{-4} = \frac{12}{-4}$	Divide each side by −4.
$y = -3$	Simplify.

Answer The solution is −3.

✓**Check** $7 - 4y = 19$	Write original equation.
$7 - 4(-3) \overset{?}{=} 19$	Substitute −3 for *y*.
$19 = 19$ ✓	Solution checks.

Reading *Algebra*

When you subtract 7 from the left side of the equation in Example 3, you are left with the equation $0 - 4y = 12$. This equation is equivalent to $0 + (-4y) = 12$, or $-4y = 12$.

✔ *Checkpoint*

Solve the equation. Check your solution.

10. $12 - 4s = -12$ **11.** $6 - 2m = 8$ **12.** $-2 = 5 - n$

| Example 4 | Writing and Solving a Two-Step Equation |

Find the monthly payment for the drum set described on page 120.

Solution

Let p represent the monthly payment. Write a verbal model.

| Total cost of drum set | = | Amount of down payment | + | Number of months | · | Monthly payment |

$$495 = 150 + 3p \qquad \text{Substitute.}$$
$$495 - 150 = 150 + 3p - 150 \qquad \text{Subtract 150 from each side.}$$
$$345 = 3p \qquad \text{Simplify.}$$
$$\frac{345}{3} = \frac{3p}{3} \qquad \text{Divide each side by 3.}$$
$$115 = p \qquad \text{Simplify.}$$

Answer The monthly payment is $115.

3.1 Exercises

More Practice, p. 805

INTERNET
eWorkbook Plus
CLASSZONE.COM

Guided Practice

Vocabulary Check

1. Copy and complete: You can use two ? operations to solve a two-step equation.

2. Describe the steps you would use to solve the equation $9 + 2s = 15$.

Skill Check Solve the equation. Check your solution.

3. $5c + 6 = 31$ **4.** $-2 = \frac{t}{3} - 11$ **5.** $-9z + 4 = -5$ **6.** $-8 - 8d = 64$

Guided Problem Solving

7. Car Repair The total cost of repairing a car is the sum of the amount paid for parts and the amount paid for labor. You paid $78 for parts and $45 for each hour of labor. The total cost to repair the car was $168. How many hours did it take to repair the car?

1 Copy and complete the verbal model.

| Total cost for repairs | = | ? | + | Cost for each hour of labor | · | ? |

2 Let h represent the number of hours spent on labor. Write an equation based on your verbal model.

3 Solve the equation to find how many hours it took to repair the car.

Practice and Problem Solving

Homework *Help*

Example	Exercises
1	8–19
2	8–19
3	8–19
4	20–22

Online Resources
CLASSZONE.COM
• More Examples
• eTutorial Plus

Solve the equation. Check your solution.

8. $12k + 7 = 31$

9. $13n + 42 = 81$

10. $56 = 17p - 29$

11. $\dfrac{w}{4} - 21 = -3$

12. $\dfrac{h}{9} - 19 = -10$

13. $\dfrac{d}{12} + 25 = 29$

14. $12 = \dfrac{a}{36} + 17$

15. $18 - r = 42$

16. $80 = 23 - 3v$

17. $-2q - 63 = 47$

18. $-\dfrac{x}{2} + 4 = 12$

19. $-5 = -19 - \dfrac{x}{7}$

20. Driving Your family is taking a long-distance car trip. You begin with 16 gallons of gasoline in the fuel tank. Your car uses 3 gallons of gasoline per hour of driving. You will stop to refuel when there is exactly 1 gallon of gasoline remaining in the tank.

    a. Analyze List the information you are given and the information you need to find.

    b. Write a verbal model. Then write an equation based on your verbal model.

    c. After how many hours will you need to stop to refuel? Justify your solution by making a table.

21. Rafting A group of 9 friends takes a white-water rafting trip. The total price of the trip before any discounts is $810. Each person in the group receives a student discount. The total price with the discount is $729. How much is the discount per person?

22. Trains A train consisting of 50 cars and one locomotive weighs a total of 4725 tons. The locomotive weighs 125 tons. All of the cars have the same weight. Find the weight (in tons) of one car.

Write the verbal sentence as an equation. Then solve the equation.

23. Five minus the product of 2 and a number is 7.

24. Thirty-two minus the product of 9 and a number is 140.

25. Thirteen plus the product of 6 and a number is 67.

26. Negative 8 minus the product of 3 and a number is 19.

27. Extended Problem Solving Your class has raised $755 for a hunger relief organization. The organization provides farm animals that people can use to produce food. Your class plans to buy animals for a family recovering from an earthquake.

    a. Calculate One heifer (a young cow) costs $500, and each flock of chicks costs $20. If your class buys one heifer, how many flocks of chicks can your class buy?

    b. Calculate Your class can also buy pigs for $120 each. If your class buys a heifer for $500, how many pigs can your class buy?

    c. Interpret and Apply If your class decides to buy the heifer and pigs as described in part (b), does your class have enough money to also buy a flock of chicks? Explain your reasoning.

Solve the equation. Check your solution.

28. $54.7 = -9.3n + 8.2$

29. $-5.7 + 2.6d = -14.02$

30. $3.2r + 14.7 = -6.74$

31. $9.1 = \dfrac{k}{3.7} + 4.1$

32. $11.3 - \dfrac{p}{2.8} = 1.5$

33. $-6.8 - \dfrac{c}{1.2} = -2.9$

34. Compare and Contrast Your friend solved the equation $18 - 2x = -36$ by first adding $2x$ to each side of the equation. You solved the equation by subtracting 18 from each side as the first step. Compare and contrast the two methods. What do you notice?

35. Class Trip You are saving money for a class trip to Washington, D.C. You need $850 for the trip. You have saved $278. You can save an additional $50 each month.

Number of months from now	Amount of money saved
0	$278
1	?
2	?
3	?
4	?

  a. Write a variable expression to represent the total amount of money you have saved after m months. Evaluate your expression for whole-number values of m. Record your results in a table like the one shown.

  b. Analyze Use the data in your table to make a scatter plot. Put months on the horizontal axis and savings on the vertical axis. What pattern do you notice in your graph? How can you use the graph to find the number of months it will take you to save enough money for the trip?

  c. Write and solve an equation to find the number of months it will take you to save enough money for the trip.

  d. Compare List some advantages and disadvantages of the methods you used in parts (a), (b), and (c).

36. Challenge Solve $\dfrac{x+2}{4} = 2$. Explain how you solved the equation and how you know your solution is correct.

Mixed Review **Use the distributive property to write an equivalent variable expression.** *(Lesson 2.2)*

37. $11(6z + 14)$ **38.** $-9(2x + 12)$ **39.** $12(3 - 5y)$ **40.** $8(4 - 7w)$

Algebra Basics Solve the equation. Check your solution. *(Lesson 2.5)*

41. $c + 12 = 23$ **42.** $b + 14 = 91$ **43.** $x - 17 = -45$ **44.** $d - 22 = -43$

Standardized Test Practice **45. Multiple Choice** What is the solution of the equation $15y - 63 = 57$?

  A. -8 **B.** 8 **C.** 9 **D.** 10

46. Short Response You purchase a video game system for $150. You make a down payment of $25. You pay the rest of the money you owe in 5 equal monthly payments with no interest. How much is each monthly payment? Show how you found your answer.

3.2

Solving Equations Having Like Terms *and* Parentheses

Review Vocabulary
like terms, p. 78

BEFORE	Now	WHY?
You used the distributive property.	You'll solve equations using the distributive property.	So you can budget for fishing rods, as in Ex. 20.

School Spirit Your school's basketball team is playing in the championship game. For the game, the cheerleaders want to buy a banner that costs $47. They also want to buy small items to give to students in the stands. Pompoms cost $5.20 each. Noisemakers cost $.80 each. The cheerleaders have a total budget of $377 for the game. If they buy equal numbers of pompoms and noisemakers, how many can they afford to buy?

Example 1 | *Writing and Solving an Equation*

Find how many pompoms and noisemakers the cheerleaders can afford to buy, as described above.

Solution

Let n represent the number of pompoms and the number of noisemakers. Then $5.20n$ represents the cost of n pompoms, and $0.80n$ represents the cost of n noisemakers. Write a verbal model.

Cost of n pompoms	+	Cost of n noisemakers	+	Cost of banner	=	Total budget

$5.20n + 0.80n + 47 = 377$ **Substitute.**

$6.00n + 47 = 377$ **Combine like terms.**

$6n + 47 - 47 = 377 - 47$ **Subtract 47 from each side.**

$6n = 330$ **Simplify.**

$\dfrac{6n}{6} = \dfrac{330}{6}$ **Divide each side by 6.**

$n = 55$ **Simplify.**

Answer The cheerleaders can afford to buy 55 pompoms and 55 noisemakers.

Distributive Property You can use the distributive property to solve equations involving parentheses.

Review *Help*

For help with using the distributive property, see p. 71.

Example 2 *Solving Equations Using the Distributive Property*

Solve the equation.

a. $-21 = 7(3 - x)$

b. $-3(8 - 4x) = 12$

Solution

a.
$-21 = 7(3 - x)$	Write original equation.
$-21 = 21 - 7x$	Distributive property
$-21 - 21 = 21 - 7x - 21$	Subtract 21 from each side.
$-42 = -7x$	Simplify.
$\dfrac{-42}{-7} = \dfrac{-7x}{-7}$	Divide each side by -7.
$6 = x$	Simplify.

Answer The solution is 6.

b.
$-3(8 - 4x) = 12$	Write original equation.
$-24 + 12x = 12$	Distributive property
$-24 + 12x + 24 = 12 + 24$	Add 24 to each side.
$12x = 36$	Simplify.
$\dfrac{12x}{12} = \dfrac{36}{12}$	Divide each side by 12.
$x = 3$	Simplify.

Answer The solution is 3.

Example 3 *Combining Like Terms After Distributing*

Solve $5x - 2(x - 1) = 8$.

$5x - 2(x - 1) = 8$	Write original equation.
$5x - 2x + 2 = 8$	Distributive property
$3x + 2 = 8$	Combine like terms.
$3x + 2 - 2 = 8 - 2$	Subtract 2 from each side.
$3x = 6$	Simplify.
$\dfrac{3x}{3} = \dfrac{6}{3}$	Divide each side by 3.
$x = 2$	Simplify.

 Checkpoint

Solve the equation. Check your solution.

1. $3n - 40 + 2n = 15$ 2. $2(s - 1) = 6$ 3. $13 = 2y - 3(y + 4)$

3.2 Exercises

More Practice, p. 805

Guided Practice

Vocabulary Check

1. What property do you use when you rewrite the equation $6(x + 1) = 12$ as $6x + 6 = 12$?

2. Identify the like terms you would combine to solve the equation $-3x + 5 - 2x + 8 = 12$.

Skill Check

Solve the equation. Check your solution.

3. $4 + x + 7 = 10$ **4.** $3x + 2x = 25$ **5.** $21 = 4x - 9 - x$

6. $3(x + 1) = 6$ **7.** $16 = 8(x - 1)$ **8.** $5 + 2(x - 2) = 19$

Guided Problem Solving

9. Geometry The perimeter of the rectangle shown is 28 units. The length is 10 units. What is the width of the rectangle?

$x + 2$

10

① Write an equation for the perimeter of the rectangle in terms of x.

② Solve the equation to find the value of x.

③ Find the width of the rectangle using the value of x.

④ Check your answer.

Practice and Problem Solving

Homework *Help*

Example	Exercises
1	11–13, 20, 21
2	14–19
3	22–31

Online Resources
CLASSZONE.COM

• More Examples
• eTutorial Plus

10. Error Analysis Describe and correct the error in solving the equation $-2(5 - n) = 2$.

$$-2(5 - n) = 2$$
$$-10 - 2n = 2$$
$$-10 - 2n + 10 = 2 + 10$$
$$-2n = 12$$
$$n = -6$$

Solve the equation. Check your solution.

11. $13t - 7 - 10t = 2$ **12.** $22 + 4y - 14 = 0$ **13.** $2d + 24 + 3d = 84$

14. $4(x + 5) = 16$ **15.** $3(7 - 2y) = 9$ **16.** $-2(z + 11) = 6$

17. $-5(3n + 5) = 20$ **18.** $-30 = 6(f - 5)$ **19.** $12 = 3(m - 17)$

20. Fishing A family of five people has $200 to spend on fishing rods and fishing licenses. They spend a total of $20 on licenses. Assuming they buy 5 identical rods, what is the maximum amount they can spend on each rod?

21. Karaoke You want to organize a group of friends to go to a karaoke studio this Friday night. You must pay $30 to reserve a private karaoke room plus $5 for each person in the group. You also want to have snacks for the group at a cost of $2 per person. How many people can be in the group in order for the total cost to be $65?

Solve the equation. Check your solution.

22. $-5(2w + 1) = 25$

23. $4(5 - p) = 8$

24. $-40 - (2x + 5) = -61$

25. $2 = 4(3k - 8) - 11k$

26. $42 = 18t + 4(t + 5)$

27. $-3(2z - 8) + 10z = 16$

28. $-5g - (8 - g) = 12$

29. $-5 = 0.25(4 + 20r) - 8r$

30. $2m + 0.5(m - 4) = 9$

31. $-12 = -2h + 0.2(20 - 6h)$

32. Photograph The perimeter of a rectangular photograph is 22 inches. The length of the photograph is 1 inch more than the width. What are the dimensions of the photograph?

Geometry Find the value of *x* for the given triangle, rectangle, or square.

33. Perimeter = 40 units

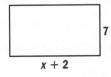

7

x + 2

34. Perimeter = 22 units

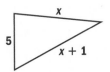

x

5

x + 1

35. Perimeter = 104 units

x + 11

x + 11

36. Perimeter = 32 units

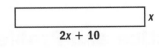

x

2*x* + 10

37. Cell Phones Your cell phone provider charges a monthly fee of $19.50 for 200 minutes. You are also charged $.25 per minute for each minute over 200 minutes. Last month, your bill was $29.50.

a. Let *m* represent the total number of minutes you used last month. Use the verbal model below to write an equation.

Total phone bill	=	Monthly fee	+	Charge for each additional minute	•	Number of minutes over 200

b. Solve the equation you wrote in part (a).

c. How many additional minutes did you use last month?

38. Critical Thinking Solve each equation by first dividing each side of the equation by the number outside the parentheses. Then solve each equation by first using the distributive property. What do you notice? When would you recommend using each method? Explain.

a. $3(x + 7) = 42$

b. $4(6x - 8) = 14$

39. Challenge The figure shown is composed of a triangle and a rectangle. The figure has a total area of 1258 square units. Find the value of x.

24

25

$3x + 1$

Mixed Review

Plot the point in a coordinate plane. Describe the location of the point. *(Lesson 1.8)*

40. $J(-3, 8)$ **41.** $K(8, -3)$ **42.** $L(4, -4)$ **43.** $M(-1, -1)$

44. $N(0, 2)$ **45.** $P(5, 1)$ **46.** $Q(-9, 0)$ **47.** $R(-5, -8)$

Simplify the expression. *(Lesson 2.3)*

48. $a - 2 - (3 + a)$

49. $3b + 8 + 2(b - 4)$

50. $-2x + 5 - 7(x + 1)$

51. $2y - 4 + 3(y + 1)$

52. $-(2x + 3) + 4(x + 2)$

53. $3(2x - 7) + 8(4 - x)$

54. Family Party A family wants to hold a dinner party at a restaurant. The restaurant charges $150 to rent space for the party. The food cost for each person at the party is $18. How many people can come to the party if the family has $600 to spend? *(Lesson 3.1)*

Standardized Test Practice

55. Multiple Choice What is the solution of the equation $-3(2x - 1) = -21$?

A. -4 **B.** -3 **C.** 3 **D.** 4

56. Short Response The length of a rectangle is 5 feet less than twice its width. The perimeter of the rectangle is 38 feet. Let w represent the width. Write an equation for the perimeter of the rectangle in terms of w. Then solve the equation to find the length and width of the rectangle.

Brain GAME

Patent Puzzle

Solve each equation. In each group, there are two equations that have the same solution. Write the value of this solution in the corresponding letter's blank to find the year blue jeans were patented.

$\dfrac{?}{A}$ $\dfrac{?}{B}$ $\dfrac{?}{C}$ $\dfrac{?}{D}$

A. $10x + 7 = 17$

$2(7x + 6) = 40$

$-(x - 11) = 10$

B. $8x - 15 = -47$

$6(2x - 1) = 90$

$-7x + 4x = -24$

C. $-5x + 4x = -6$

$7x - (-12) = 61$

$7(x + 2) = 63$

D. $2(6x + 7) = 50$

$-5x - 3x = -56$

$-11x - 9 = -42$

Lesson 3.2   Solving Equations Having Like Terms and Parentheses   **129**

3.3 Modeling Equations with Variables on Both Sides

Goal
Solve equations using algebra tiles.

Materials
• algebra tiles

Investigate

Use algebra tiles to solve $4x + 6 = 10 + 2x$.

1 Model $4x + 6 = 10 + 2x$ using algebra tiles.

2 Remove two x-tiles from each side.

3 Remove six 1-tiles from each side.

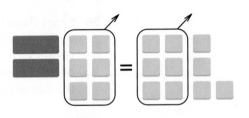

4 Divide the remaining tiles into two equal groups. Each x-tile is equal to two 1-tiles. So, the solution is 2.

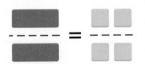

Draw Conclusions

Use algebra tiles to model and solve the equation.

1. $9 + 2x = 1 + 3x$ **2.** $3x + 4 = 8 + x$ **3.** $5x + 2 = 3x + 14$

4. Critical Thinking In the activity above, would you find the correct solution if you performed Step 3 before Step 2? Explain.

5. *Writing* Explain how solving an equation with variables on both sides of the equal sign is different than solving an equation with the variable on one side.

Solving Equations *with* Variables *on* Both Sides

Review Vocabulary
equation, p. 85
solution of an
    equation, p. 85
inverse operations,
    p. 91

BEFORE	*Now*	WHY?
You solved two-step equations.	You'll solve equations with variables on both sides.	So you can find the price of a DVD, as in Ex. 10.

Spanish Club The Spanish club is arranging a trip to a Mexican restaurant in a nearby city. Those who go must share the $60 cost of using a school bus for the trip. The restaurant's buffet costs $5 per person. How many students must sign up for this trip in order to limit the cost to $10 per student? In Example 2, you will see how to use an equation to answer this question.

Every equation in this lesson has variables on both sides of the equation. You can solve such an equation by getting the variable terms on one side of the equation and the constant terms on the other side.

Study *Strategy*

Another Way To solve the equation in Example 1, you might choose to first subtract $10n$ from each side to obtain the equation $-3n - 5 = 13$. When you solve this equation for n, you get the same solution as in the example, -6.

Example 1　　*Solving an Equation with the Variable on Both Sides*

Solve $7n - 5 = 10n + 13$.

$7n - 5 = 10n + 13$	Write original equation.
$7n - 5 - 7n = 10n + 13 - 7n$	Subtract $7n$ from each side.
$-5 = 3n + 13$	Simplify.
$-5 - 13 = 3n + 13 - 13$	Subtract 13 from each side.
$-18 = 3n$	Simplify.
$\dfrac{-18}{3} = \dfrac{3n}{3}$	Divide each side by 3.
$-6 = n$	Simplify.

Answer The solution is -6.

 Checkpoint

Solve the equation. Check your solution.

　1. $5n - 2 = 3n + 6$　　**2.** $8y + 4 = 11y - 17$　　**3.** $m - 1 = 9m + 15$

Flautas are fried tacos, a Mexican specialty.

Example 2 — *Writing and Solving an Equation*

How many students must go on the Spanish club trip to the Mexican restaurant, as described on page 131, in order for the cost per student to be $10?

Solution

Let s represent the number of students. Write a verbal model.

Cost per student	•	Number of students	=	Cost of buffet	•	Number of students	+	Cost of school bus

$$10s = 5s + 60 \qquad \text{Substitute.}$$

$$10s - 5s = 5s - 5s + 60 \qquad \text{Subtract 5s from each side.}$$

$$5s = 60 \qquad \text{Simplify.}$$

$$\frac{5s}{5} = \frac{60}{5} \qquad \text{Divide each side by 5.}$$

$$s = 12 \qquad \text{Simplify.}$$

Answer The club needs 12 students to go on the trip.

Number of Solutions When you solve an equation, you may find that it has no solution or that every number is a solution.

Example 3 — *An Equation with No Solution*

Solve $5(2x + 1) = 10x$.

$$5(2x + 1) = 10x \qquad \text{Write original equation.}$$

$$10x + 5 = 10x \qquad \text{Distributive property}$$

Notice that $10x + 5 = 10x$ is not true because the number $10x$ cannot be equal to 5 more than itself. The equation has no solution. As a check, you can continue solving the equation.

$$10x + 5 - 10x = 10x - 10x \qquad \text{Subtract 10x from each side.}$$

$$5 = 0 \; ✗ \qquad \text{Simplify.}$$

The statement $5 = 0$ is not true, so the equation has no solution.

Note *Worthy*

You should summarize what you have learned in Chapter 2 and Chapter 3 about solving equations in your notes.

Example 4 — *Solving an Equation with All Numbers as Solutions*

Solve $6x + 2 = 2(3x + 1)$.

$$6x + 2 = 2(3x + 1) \qquad \text{Write original equation.}$$

$$6x + 2 = 6x + 2 \qquad \text{Distributive property}$$

Notice that for all values of x, the statement $6x + 2 = 6x + 2$ is true. The equation has every number as a solution.

Example 5 | *Solving an Equation to Find a Perimeter*

Geometry Find the perimeter of the square.

1 A square has four sides of equal length. Write an equation and solve for x.

$$2x = x + 4 \qquad \text{Write equation.}$$
$$2x - x = x + 4 - x \qquad \text{Subtract } x \text{ from each side.}$$
$$x = 4 \qquad \text{Simplify.}$$

2 Find the length of one side by substituting 4 for x in either expression.

$$2x = 2(4) = 8 \qquad \text{Substitute 4 for } x \text{ and multiply.}$$

3 To find the perimeter, multiply the length of one side by 4.

$$4 \cdot 8 = 32$$

Answer The perimeter of the square is 32 units.

Study *Strategy*

Make sure you understand what you are being asked to find in a problem. In Example 5, you first solve for x, but the problem asks you to find the perimeter of the square.

3.3   Exercises

More Practice, p. 805

INTERNET
eWorkbook Plus
CLASSZONE.COM

Guided Practice

Vocabulary Check

1. Describe what steps you would take to solve $8x + 5 = 2x - 7$.

2. Explain why the equation $5z + 2 = 5z$ has no solution.

Skill Check   **Solve the equation. Check your solution.**

3. $13m - 22 = 9m - 6$

4. $19c + 26 = 41 + 14c$

5. $15 - 4x = 42 - 7x$

6. $14 + 5y = 50 - 4y$

7. $18w - 2 = 10w + 14$

8. $-5a + 6 = 6a - 38$

9. Error Analysis Describe and correct the error in solving the equation $4x + 7 = x - 2$.

$$4x + 7 = x - 2$$
$$4x + 7 - 4x = x - 2 - 4x$$
$$7 = 3x - 2$$
$$7 + 2 = 3x - 2 + 2$$
$$9 = 3x$$
$$3 = x$$

10. Shopping You spend $60 on clothes and buy 3 DVD movies. Your friend spends nothing on clothes and buys 8 DVD movies. You both spend the same amount of money. All the DVDs cost the same amount. How much does each DVD cost?

Practice and Problem Solving

Homework *Help*

Example	Exercises
1	11-22
2	27, 32
3	11-22
4	11-22
5	28-30

Online Resources
CLASSZONE.COM
• More Examples
• eTutorial Plus

Solve the equation. Check your solution.

11. $25u + 74 = 23u + 92$

12. $-5k - 19 = 5 - 13k$

13. $-11y + 32 = 104 - 5y$

14. $-15n + 16 = 86 - 29n$

15. $25t = 5(5t + 1)$

16. $13 - 3p = -5(3 + 2p)$

17. $-24s - 53 = 39 - s$

18. $14a - 93 = 49 - 57a$

19. $7(2p + 1) = 14p + 7$

20. $8v = 2(4v + 2)$

21. $3x + 6 = 3(2 + x)$

22. $2(-4h - 13) = 37 + 13h$

Write the verbal sentence as an equation. Then solve the equation.

23. Nine plus 2 times a number is equal to 2 less than 3 times the number.

24. Three less than 11 times a number is equal to 9 plus 5 times the number.

25. Four minus 7 times a number is equal to 12 minus 3 times the number.

26. Twelve less than -9 times a number is equal to 8 minus 4 times the number.

27. Toll Booth You lose your electronic tag that you use to pay tolls on the highway in your city. It costs you $24 to replace the tag. The cost of one toll when you don't use the tag is $3. The cost of the same toll when you do use the tag is $1.50. How many times will you have to use the tag to pay for the tolls in order for the total cost to be the same as not using the tag?

Find the perimeter of the square.

28. $36 - 5x$

$4x$

29. $12x$

$7x + 30$

30. 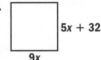 $5x + 32$

$9x$

Houston, Texas

31. Driving Your family is driving to Houston, Texas. A sign indicates that you are 700 miles from Houston. Your car's trip odometer indicates that you are 400 miles from home. You are traveling at an average speed of 60 miles per hour.

a. Write an expression for the distance (in miles) you will be from Houston in x hours.

b. Write an expression for the distance (in miles) you will be from home in x hours.

c. Use the expressions from parts (a) and (b) to write and solve an equation to find the number of hours you will drive until you are exactly halfway between Houston and your home.

d. Suppose you travel by local roads instead of the highway. You travel the 700 miles at a speed of 45 miles per hour. How long will you drive before you are exactly halfway between Houston and your home?

32. Pasta Machine A pasta machine costs $33. The ingredients to make one batch of pasta cost $.33. The same amount of pasta purchased at a store costs $.99. How many batches of pasta will you have to make for the cost of the machine and ingredients to equal the cost of buying the same amount of pasta at the store?

33. *Writing* Describe a real-life situation that can be modeled by the equation $11x + 5 = 8x + 23$. Then solve the equation and interpret your solution.

Solve the equation. Check your solution.

34. $3x - 7 = 8 + 6(x + 2)$

35. $13y + 19 = 6(9 + y) + 14$

36. $8(z + 4) = 5(13 + z)$

37. $8a - 2(a + 5) = 2(a - 1)$

38. Geometry The perimeter of the square is equal to the perimeter of the triangle. The sides of the triangle are equal in length.

3x

2x + 3

5x − 3

a. Estimate Without doing any calculations, estimate which figure has the greater side length. Explain your choice.

b. What is the side length of each figure?

c. What is the perimeter of each figure?

Use a calculator to solve the equation. Check your solution.

39. $0.75m + 14 = 1.87m - 10.3936$

40. $19.5 + 0.5t = 10.6206 - 0.4t$

41. $-9.39 - 3.4d = -1.1d + 11.08$

42. $-130.5 - 9b = -55.104 + 3.2b$

43. Challenge Consider the equation $ax + 6 = 2(x + 3)$.

a. For what value(s) of a does the equation have all numbers as a solution?

b. For what value(s) of a does the equation have just one solution?

Mixed Review

Algebra Basics Solve the equation. Check your solution. *(Lesson 2.5)*

44. $c - 20 = 14$ **45.** $d + 9 = -12$ **46.** $x - 3 = 17$ **47.** $y - 21 = -15$

48. Gym Membership To join a gym, your friend pays a one-time fee of $75 and $45 per month for the duration of the membership. Your friend has paid a total of $345. How long has your friend been a member of the gym? *(Lesson 3.1)*

49. The perimeter of the square shown is 32 units. Find the value of x. *(Lesson 3.2)*

x + 3

Standardized Test Practice

50. Multiple Choice What is the solution of the equation $2(3x + 4) = 6x + 5$?

A. 1   **B.** 3   **C.** All numbers   **D.** No solution

51. Multiple Choice For which equation is 6 a solution?

F. $-2y - 7 = 11 - 5y$

G. $11y - 32 = 7y - 12$

H. $18y - 16 = 13y + 19$

I. $-7y - 24 = -8 - 9y$

3.3 Solving Equations

Goal Use a table to solve an equation with the variable on both sides.

Example

Use a table to solve $5x - 1 = 4x + 3$.

1 Enter the expressions on each side of the equal sign into a graphing calculator. The expression on the left is called Y1, and the expression on the right is Y2.

Keystrokes

```
Y1=5X-1
Y2=4X+3
Y3=
Y4=
```

2 Use the calculator's *table* feature to find the value of each expression for different values of *x*. Press **2nd** **[TBLSET]** and enter the settings shown on the first screen below. ($\triangle$Tbl represents the increment the calculator uses to go from one *x*-value to the next in the table.) Then, press **2nd** **[TABLE]** to display the table shown on the second screen.

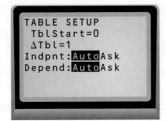

```
TABLE SETUP
 TblStart=0
 ΔTbl=1
Indpnt:Auto Ask
Depend:Auto Ask
```

X	Y1	Y2
0	-1	3
1	4	7
2	9	11
3	14	15
4	19	19
5	24	23

X=4

3 Compare the values of the expression in the Y1 column with the values of the expression in the Y2 column. The values are the same when $x = 4$. So, the solution of the equation $5x - 1 = 4x + 3$ is 4.

Tech *Help*

If you do not see the value of *x* that makes the values of both expressions equal, try using the up or down arrow keys to see additional values of *x*.

Online Resources
CLASSZONE.COM

• Keystroke Help

Draw Conclusions

Use a table to solve the equation.

1. $x - 2 = 2x - 6$ **2.** $3x + 1 = x + 7$ **3.** $12 - x = x - 4$

4. $7x = 16 - x$ **5.** $5x + 2 = 8x - 1$ **6.** $4x - 6 = 2x + 4$

7. Critical Thinking Solve the equation $3x + 6 = 13x + 2$ using paper and a pencil. Explain how you would change the settings in the TABLE SETUP menu so that you could solve the equation using a calculator.

Mid-Chapter Quiz

Write the verbal sentence as an equation. Then solve the equation.

1. Twice a number plus 5 is equal to 27.

2. Seven times the sum of 4 and a number is -14.

3. Three more than 4 times a number is equal to 9 less than twice the number.

Solve the equation. Check your solution.

4. $11k + 9 = 42$

5. $\frac{a}{3} + 11 = -5$

6. $\frac{w}{2} - 18 = -7$

7. $2 + 5t - 3 = 34$

8. $-3y + 15 - y = 39$

9. $5(n + 2) = 10$

10. $2 - 5(h + 3) = -28$

11. $5s = 7s + 1 - 2s$

12. $4d - 5 = -d$

13. $17 - 5m = 50 + 6m$

14. $3f - 12 = 3(f - 12)$

15. $8(4p + 1) = 32p + 8$

16. Income Your friend works as a waitress at a local restaurant. Her income consists of an hourly wage plus tips. On Wednesday, your friend earned $25 in tips over a 5 hour period. On Friday, your friend earned $30.76 in tips over a 3 hour period. How much is your friend's hourly wage if your friend earned the same amount of money on Wednesday as on Friday?

17. All three sides of the triangle shown are equal in length. Find the perimeter of the triangle.

$2x + 5$ $4x - 3$

Brain GAME

All *Boxed* In

Two people are packing equal numbers of small boxes into large boxes. One person has 3 large boxes that are full of smaller boxes and 24 small boxes that are not yet packed. The other person has 5 large boxes that are full of smaller boxes and 10 small boxes that are not yet packed. Each large box holds the same number of small boxes. How many small boxes can each large box hold? What is the total number of small boxes each person will pack? How many large boxes will each person need in order to pack all of his or her small boxes?

Solving Inequalities Using Addition *or* Subtraction

Vocabulary

inequality, p. 138
solution of an inequality, p. 138
equivalent inequalities, p. 139

BEFORE	*Now*	WHY?
You solved one-step equations.	You'll solve inequalities using addition or subtraction.	So you can find the weight a truck can tow, as in Ex. 14.

An **inequality** is a statement formed by placing an inequality symbol between two expressions. For example, $y + 5 \leq -6$ is an inequality.

The **solution of an inequality** with a variable is the set of all numbers that produce true statements when substituted for the variable. You can show the solution of an inequality by graphing the inequality on a number line. When you graph an inequality of the form $x > a$ or $x < a$, use an open circle at a. When you graph an inequality of the form $x \geq a$ or $x \leq a$, use a closed circle at a.

Inequality	Words	Graph
$x < 3$	All numbers less than 3	
$y > 2$	All numbers greater than 2	
$z \leq 4$	All numbers less than or equal to 4	
$n \geq 2$	All numbers greater than or equal to 2	

Example 1 *Writing and Graphing an Inequality*

Science The freezing point of water is 0°C. At temperatures at or below the freezing point, water is a solid (ice). Write an inequality that gives the temperatures at which water is a solid. Then graph the inequality.

Solution

Let t represent the temperature of water. Water is a solid at temperatures less than or equal to 0°C.

Answer The inequality is $t \leq 0$. The graph is shown below.

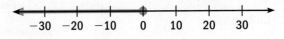

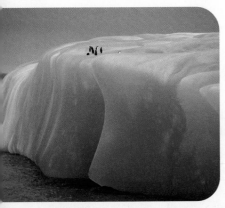

Penguins on a glacier

Solving Inequalities You can use the following properties to find the solutions of inequalities involving addition and subtraction. Using these properties, you can write *equivalent inequalities*. **Equivalent inequalities** are inequalities that have the same solution.

Addition and Subtraction Properties of Inequality

Words Adding or subtracting the same number on each side of an inequality produces an equivalent inequality.

Algebra If $a < b$, then $a + c < b + c$ and $a - c < b - c$.

If $a > b$, then $a + c > b + c$ and $a - c > b - c$.

Example 2   *Solving an Inequality Using Subtraction*

Solve $m + 5 \geq 10$. Graph and check your solution.

$$m + 5 \geq 10 \qquad \text{Write original inequality.}$$
$$m + 5 - 5 \geq 10 - 5 \qquad \text{Subtract 5 from each side.}$$
$$m \geq 5 \qquad \text{Simplify.}$$

Answer The solution is $m \geq 5$.

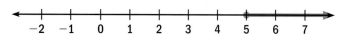

✓ **Check** Choose any number greater than or equal to 5. Substitute the number into the original inequality.

$$m + 5 \geq 10 \qquad \text{Write original inequality.}$$
$$8 + 5 \overset{?}{\geq} 10 \qquad \text{Substitute 8 for } m.$$
$$13 \geq 10 \checkmark \qquad \text{Solution checks.}$$

Example 3   *Solving an Inequality Using Addition*

Solve $-10 > x - 12$. Graph your solution.

$$-10 > x - 12 \qquad \text{Write original inequality.}$$
$$-10 + 12 > x - 12 + 12 \qquad \text{Add 12 to each side.}$$
$$2 > x \qquad \text{Simplify.}$$

Answer The solution is $2 > x$, or $x < 2$.

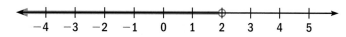

 Checkpoint

Solve the inequality. Graph and check your solution.

1. $n + 7 > 3$ **2.** $10 \geq y + 4$ **3.** $-6 \leq x - 9$ **4.** $z - 5 < 1$

Ironman Triathlon in Roth, Germany

| **Example 4** | *Writing and Solving an Inequality* |

Triathlon You are competing in a triathlon, a sports competition with three events. Last year, you finished the triathlon in 85 minutes. The table shows your times for this year's first two events. What possible times can you post in the running event and still beat last year's finishing time?

Triathlon Times	
Event	**Time (min)**
Swimming	17
Biking	45
Running	?

Solution

Let t represent this year's running time. Write a verbal model.

| Swimming time | + | Biking time | + | Running time | < | Last year's finishing time |

$$17 + 45 + t < 85 \qquad \text{Substitute.}$$
$$62 + t < 85 \qquad \text{Simplify.}$$
$$62 + t - 62 < 85 - 62 \qquad \text{Subtract 62 from each side.}$$
$$t < 23 \qquad \text{Simplify.}$$

Answer To beat last year's finishing time, you must post a time in the running event that is less than 23 minutes.

3.4 Exercises

More Practice, p. 805

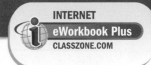

INTERNET
eWorkbook Plus
CLASSZONE.COM

Guided Practice

Vocabulary Check　**1.** What are equivalent inequalities?

2. Explain how the graph of $x > 5$ is different from the graph of $x \geq 5$.

Skill Check　**Tell whether the given number is a solution of $-5 < n$.**

3. 8　　　　　**4.** -8　　　　　**5.** -4　　　　　**6.** 4

Solve the inequality. Graph and check your solution.

7. $x + 2 > -3$　　**8.** $1 \geq x - 9$　　**9.** $x + 4 < 3$　　**10.** $x + 3 > 7$

Guided Problem Solving　**11. Astronauts** To become a NASA pilot astronaut, a NASA pilot must log at least 1000 hours as pilot-in-command of a jet aircraft. A NASA pilot has completed all other qualifications and has 250 hours logged. How many more hours must the pilot log to become a pilot astronaut?

　① Write an inequality to represent the situation.

　② Solve the inequality. Then graph and check the solution.

　③ Interpret the solution in terms of the real-life situation.

Practice and Problem Solving

Homework *Help*

Example	Exercises
1	12–16, 33, 38
2	21–32, 34–37
3	21–32, 34–37
4	40

Online Resources
CLASSZONE.COM

- More Examples
- eTutorial Plus

Write an inequality to represent the situation.

12. The greatest weight that a forklift can raise is 2500 pounds.

13. The speed limit is 55 miles per hour.

14. A truck can tow a maximum weight of 7700 pounds.

15. You must be at least 48 inches tall to ride the roller coaster.

16. You can save up to $50 on DVD players this week.

Write an inequality represented by the graph.

17.
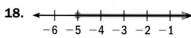

18.

19.

20.

Solve the inequality. Graph your solution.

21. $x + 4 < 5$ **22.** $m + 8 \geq 12$ **23.** $-11 < y + 5$ **24.** $-8 \geq d - 7$

25. $-45 > g - 16$ **26.** $z - 15 > 72$ **27.** $f + 1 \geq -8$ **28.** $h + 19 \leq 15$

29. $18.1 \leq p - 7$ **30.** $t - 7 < 3.4$ **31.** $b + 2.5 \leq 2.5$ **32.** $a - 10.2 > 5.3$

33. Neon The lowest temperature at which neon is a gas, called its boiling point, is $-411°F$. Write and graph an inequality to show the temperatures at which neon is a gas.

Solve the inequality. Graph your solution.

34. $5 + m + 8 \geq 14$ **35.** $13 + n - 26 < 38$

36. $2.35 + p + 14.9 > 49.25$ **37.** $q + 4 + 16 \geq 30$

38. Bacteria In 1969, Apollo 12 astronauts found a small colony of *Streptococcus* bacteria that had apparently traveled unprotected to the moon on the Surveyor 3 spacecraft's TV camera about three years earlier. The bacteria survived at temperatures as low as $-280°F$. Write and graph an inequality to show the temperatures at which the bacteria survived.

39. *Writing* Is it possible to check *all* the numbers that are solutions of an inequality? Explain. Does checking just *one* number guarantee that a solution is correct?

40. Train Travel You are traveling by train. You are allowed two carryon bags, each with a maximum weight of 50 pounds. You have two bags: one that weighs 14 pounds and one that weighs 21 pounds.

   a. Write and solve an inequality that represents the weight w (in pounds) of personal belongings you can add to the first bag without exceeding the weight limit.

   b. Write and solve an inequality that represents the weight w (in pounds) of personal belongings you can add to the second bag without exceeding the weight limit.

In the **Real World**

Neon Neon is used for signs because it glows when an electric current passes through a glass tube containing the gas. Neon is a liquid if the temperature is between its freezing point and its boiling point. The freezing point of neon is about 5°F lower than its boiling point. Between what temperatures is neon a liquid?

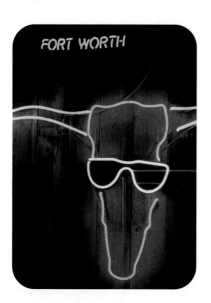

FORT WORTH

In Exercises 41 and 42, graph the *compound inequality*. A compound inequality consists of two inequalities joined by the word *and* or *or*.

Example *Graphing Compound Inequalities*

Graph the compound inequality $x > 3$ *and* $x < 10$.

Include numbers that are both greater than 3 and less than 10.

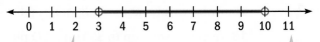

Numbers to the left of 3 are not included because they are not greater than 3.

Numbers to the right of 10 are not included because they are not less than 10.

41. $x \geq -1$ and $x \leq 4$ **42.** $x < 3$ and $x \geq 0$

43. Skiing The ski wax you use keeps your skis performing well at temperatures from $-6°C$ to $15°C$. Express the lower limit of the ski wax as an inequality, and express the upper limit as an inequality. Then write the inequalities as a compound inequality and graph it.

44. Challenge Explain how you can graph the compound inequality $x \leq 8$ or $x \geq 10$. How does this graph look different from the graph of $x \geq 8$ and $x \leq 10$?

Mixed Review

45. Geometry Find the length of a side of a square with a perimeter of 36.6 meters. *(Lesson 2.7)*

46. Fundraising A basketball team is raising money for uniforms and equipment. So far, the team has raised $1275. The team plans to spend $450 on equipment and buy as many uniforms as possible. Each uniform costs $55. How many uniforms can the team buy with the money it has raised? *(Lesson 3.1)*

Write the verbal sentence as an equation. Then solve the equation.
(Lesson 3.3)

47. Five plus 4 times a number is equal to the sum of 7 times the number and 11.

48. Eight less than 3 times a number is equal to -3 plus twice the number.

Standardized Test Practice

49. Multiple Choice Which inequality is represented by the graph shown?

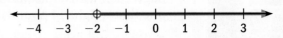

A. $y < -2$ **B.** $y > -2$ **C.** $y \leq -2$ **D.** $y \geq -2$

50. Multiple Choice Which number is a solution of the inequality $b + 2 > 2$?

F. 4   **G.** 0   **H.** -1 **I.** -2

Concept Activity

3.5 Multiplication and Division Properties of Inequality

Goal
Perform multiplications and divisions on inequality statements.

Materials
• pencil
• paper

Investigate

Determine how multiplication or division affects an inequality.

1 Choose two different integers and insert an inequality symbol between them to make a true statement.

$$-2 < 4$$

2 Multiply each number in the original inequality by 2. Is the new inequality a true statement?

$$2 \cdot (-2) \overset{?}{<} 2 \cdot 4$$
$$-4 < 8 \checkmark$$
Yes, -4 is less than 8.

3 Multiply each number in the original inequality by -2. Is the new inequality a true statement?

$$-2 \cdot (-2) \overset{?}{<} -2 \cdot 4$$
$$4 < -8 \ \boldsymbol{\times}$$
No, 4 is not less than -8.

4 Divide each number in the original inequality by 2. Is the new inequality a true statement?

$$\frac{-2}{2} \overset{?}{<} \frac{4}{2}$$
$$-1 < 2 \checkmark$$
Yes, -1 is less than 2.

5 Divide each number in the original inequality by -2. Is the new inequality a true statement?

$$\frac{-2}{-2} \overset{?}{<} \frac{4}{-2}$$
$$1 < -2 \ \boldsymbol{\times}$$
No, 1 is not less than -2.

Draw Conclusions

1. Critical Thinking Repeat the steps above with a new pair of integers. In Steps 3 and 5, what could you do to the inequality symbols to make the statements true?

Given that $a > b$, copy and complete using $<$ or $>$ to make a true statement.

2. $\dfrac{a}{2} \ \underline{\overset{?}{}} \ \dfrac{b}{2}$ **3.** $\dfrac{a}{-2} \ \underline{\overset{?}{}} \ \dfrac{b}{-2}$ **4.** $-a \ \underline{\overset{?}{}} \ -b$ **5.** $3a \ \underline{\overset{?}{}} \ 3b$

Solving Inequalities Using Multiplication *or* Division

Review Vocabulary

inequality, p. 138
equivalent inequalities, p. 139

BEFORE	*Now*	**WHY?**
You solved two-step equations.	You'll solve inequalities using multiplication or division.	So you can find how fast you should bike, as in Ex. 38.

Geese Migration Some flocks of Canada geese can fly nonstop for up to 16 hours. In this time, a flock can migrate as far as 848 miles. At what average speeds can such a flock fly during migration? In Example 3, you will see how to answer this question by solving an inequality.

As shown below, when each side of the inequality $2 < 8$ is multiplied by a positive number, the inequality remains true. When each side is multiplied by a negative number, the inequality sign must be reversed.

$$2 < 8 \qquad\qquad\qquad 2 < 8$$
$$4 \cdot 2 \overset{?}{<} 4 \cdot 8 \qquad\qquad -4 \cdot 2 \overset{?}{<} -4 \cdot 8$$
$$8 < 32 \qquad\qquad\qquad -8 > -32 \qquad \textbf{Reverse inequality sign.}$$

These examples suggest the following rules for solving inequalities.

Multiplication Property of Inequality

Words Multiplying each side of an inequality by a *positive* number produces an equivalent inequality.

Multiplying each side of an inequality by a *negative* number and *reversing the direction of the inequality symbol* produces an equivalent inequality.

Algebra If $a < b$ and $c > 0$, then $ac < bc$.

If $a < b$ and $c < 0$, then $ac > bc$.

Example 1	*Solving an Inequality Using Multiplication*

$$\frac{m}{-3} > 3 \qquad \textbf{Original inequality}$$

$$-3 \cdot \frac{m}{-3} < -3 \cdot 3 \qquad \textbf{Multiply each side by −3.}$$
$$\textbf{Reverse inequality symbol.}$$

$$m < -9 \qquad \textbf{Simplify.}$$

Division The rules for solving an inequality using division are like the rules for solving an inequality using multiplication.

> ## Division Property of Inequality
>
> **Words** Dividing each side of an inequality by a *positive* number produces an equivalent inequality.
>
> Dividing each side of an inequality by a *negative* number and *reversing the direction of the inequality symbol* produces an equivalent inequality.
>
> **Algebra** If $a < b$ and $c > 0$, then $\dfrac{a}{c} < \dfrac{b}{c}$.
>
> If $a < b$ and $c < 0$, then $\dfrac{a}{c} > \dfrac{b}{c}$.

Study *Strategy*

The multiplication and division properties of inequality are also true for inequalities involving $>$, $\leq$, and $\geq$.

Example 2 *Solving an Inequality Using Division*

$$-10t \geq 34 \qquad \text{Original inequality}$$

$$\frac{-10t}{-10} \leq \frac{34}{-10} \qquad \begin{array}{l}\text{Divide each side by } -10.\\ \text{Reverse inequality symbol.}\end{array}$$

$$t \leq -3.4 \qquad \text{Simplify.}$$

 Checkpoint

Solve the inequality. Graph your solution.

1. $\dfrac{n}{6} > 7$ **2.** $\dfrac{t}{-4} \leq 8$ **3.** $2x > -8$ **4.** $-7s \leq 14$

Example 3 *Writing and Solving an Inequality*

Find the average speeds at which the flock of Canada geese described on page 144 can fly during migration.

Solution

Let s represent the average flight speeds. Write a verbal model.

Flight time	•	Average flight speeds	≤	Maximum flight distance

$$16s \leq 848 \qquad \text{Substitute.}$$

$$\frac{16s}{16} \leq \frac{848}{16} \qquad \text{Divide each side by 16.}$$

$$s \leq 53 \qquad \text{Simplify.}$$

Answer The flock of Canada geese can fly at average speeds of 53 miles per hour or less during migration.

In the **Real World**

Geese Migration In North America, not all Canada geese migrate. About 3.6 million "resident" geese live in urban and suburban areas, such as parks, throughout the year. Resident Canada geese outnumber migrating Canada geese. Write an inequality that compares the numbers of migrating geese and resident geese.

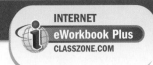
Guided Practice

Vocabulary Check
1. Which property would you use to solve the inequality $-7y \leq 49$?

2. Explain how solving $2x > -14$ is different from solving $-2x > 14$.

Skill Check **Solve the inequality. Graph and check your solution.**

3. $\dfrac{v}{-2} < -8$
4. $8b > 32$
5. $\dfrac{u}{6} \geq 3$
6. $-6s \leq 54$

7. $5a < -35$
8. $\dfrac{p}{7} > 6$
9. $3r \geq 21$
10. $\dfrac{t}{4} \leq -9$

Guided Problem Solving
11. **Training** While training for a marathon, you try to consume at least 2400 Calories each day. For one meal, you like to eat at least 500 Calories. You choose to eat pasta that has 200 Calories per cup. How many cups of pasta should you eat?

1 Let c represent the number of cups of pasta. Write an inequality based on the verbal model given below.

| Calories per cup | · | Number of cups | ≥ | Total calories for meal |

2 Solve the inequality.

3 Explain what the solution tells you about the situation.

Practice and Problem Solving

Homework *Help*

Example	Exercises
1	12–27
2	12–27
3	29, 36–38

Online Resources
CLASSZONE.COM
• More Examples
• eTutorial Plus

Solve the inequality. Graph your solution.

12. $\dfrac{a}{2} < -9$
13. $\dfrac{b}{7} > 7$
14. $\dfrac{c}{8} \geq 3$
15. $-16y > 48$

16. $5z < 65$
17. $\dfrac{d}{-11} \leq 6$
18. $12x \geq -60$
19. $4w \leq 68$

20. $\dfrac{t}{9} < -12$
21. $\dfrac{h}{-6} \leq 13$
22. $-16k \geq 96$
23. $6q > -84$

24. $-7s \geq -84$
25. $4m < -60$
26. $\dfrac{v}{5} > -2$
27. $\dfrac{n}{-3} \geq -5$

28. **Error Analysis** Describe and correct the error in solving the inequality $9x > -45$.

$$9x > -45$$

$$\dfrac{9x}{9} < \dfrac{-45}{9}$$

$$x < -5$$

29. In-Line Skates You want to use in-line skates. You can either rent in-line skates for $12 per day or purchase them for $60. How many times will you have to use the in-line skates in order for the cost of purchasing them to be less than the total cost of renting them?

Write the verbal sentence as an inequality. Then solve the inequality.

30. Five times a number is at least 45.

31. A number divided by 4 is at most 8.

32. A number divided by -3 is less than 6.

33. Seven times a number is greater than -35.

34. A number divided by 2 is no more than 5.

35. Three times a number is more than -18.

36. Extended Problem Solving The weight limit for freight loaded onto a freight elevator is 7500 pounds. The elevator is being used to move 50 heavy crates. Each crate weighs 375 pounds.

    a. Interpret Write and solve an inequality to determine how many crates you can move in one trip on the elevator. Assume that weight is the only factor affecting how many crates you can move at one time.

    b. Apply How many times will you need to load the elevator to move all of the crates? Explain.

37. Reading You need to read at least 105 pages of a book for your English class in the next 7 days. How many pages should you read each day?

38. Biking You want to bike at least 45 miles as part of a training program. If you bike for 5 hours, what average speeds will allow you to meet your goal?

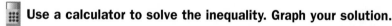

Use a calculator to solve the inequality. Graph your solution.

39. $-8.9b \geq 40.94$ **40.** $\dfrac{x}{2.4} \geq 8.5$ **41.** $\dfrac{z}{7.2} < -3.4$

42. $6.3a > 10.71$ **43.** $-3.9c \leq 43.68$ **44.** $\dfrac{y}{-9.1} \leq 6.5$

45. Water Filling the bathtub uses 60 gallons of water. Taking a shower uses 2 gallons per minute. How many minutes can you be in the shower and still use less water than you would by filling the bathtub?

46. Caribou A herd of caribou can migrate as far as 36 miles in 24 hours.

    a. Write and solve an inequality to find the average speeds (in miles per hour) at which caribou can migrate.

    b. A caribou herd has been moving for three days. On a number line, graph the distances (in miles) the herd could have traveled.

47. Carpeting Your parents have decided to install new carpeting in your room, which is rectangular and measures 10 feet by 12 feet. They want to spend at most $200 on the carpeting. At the flooring store, carpeting is sold by the square foot. How much money will your parents spend per square foot for carpeting?

48. Critical Thinking The inequalities $2x < 3$ and $4x < 6$ are equivalent inequalities. Write a third inequality equivalent to $2x < 3$ and $4x < 6$.

49. Challenge An underwater camera can withstand pressures up to 1500 pounds per square inch. The formula $P = 14.7 + 0.45d$ can be used to find the water pressure P (in pounds per square inch) at depth d (in feet) underwater. Find the depths at which the camera can be used.

Mixed Review **Algebra Basics Solve the equation. Check your solution.** *(Lesson 2.7)*

50. $x + 3.5 = 9.2$ **51.** $x - 6.7 = 5.8$ **52.** $44.72 = 5.2x$ **53.** $\dfrac{x}{7.6} = 9.5$

54. Find the perimeter of the square. *(Lesson 3.3)*

$3x - 5$
$2x$

Solve the inequality. Graph your solution. *(Lesson 3.4)*

55. $x + 12 > 96$ **56.** $x + 17 \geq 44$ **57.** $x - 26 \leq 33$ **58.** $x - 14 < 29$

Standardized Test Practice

59. Multiple Choice Which number is *not* a solution of $\dfrac{t}{-9} \geq 3$?

   A. -35　　　**B.** -30　　　**C.** -27　　　**D.** -25

60. Multiple Choice Which number is a solution of $\dfrac{x}{-7} < 6$?

   F. -100　　　**G.** -56　　　**H.** -42　　　**I.** -14

61. Multiple Choice Which inequality is equivalent to $-18 \leq 3p$?

   A. $p \geq -54$　　　**B.** $-54 \geq p$　　　**C.** $p \geq -6$　　　**D.** $-6 \geq p$

Brain GAME

Youngest to Oldest

Use the given information to list the six cousins in order from least to greatest age and give their ages. No two cousins are the same age.

Erika is 4 years old.
Charlie's age is greater than 4 times Dawn's age.
All the girls' ages are greater than Anthony's age.
All the cousins' ages are less than or equal to 13.
Matthew is older than exactly three cousins.
Stephanie is 6 years older than Erika.
All the cousins' ages are greater than or equal to 2.
Erika is 1 year older than Dawn.
One boy is 6 years old.

3.6 Solving Multi-Step Inequalities

Review Vocabulary
inequality, p. 138

Soccer Your school's soccer team is trying to break the school record for goals scored in one season. Your team has already scored 88 goals this season. The record is 138 goals. With 10 games remaining on the schedule, how many goals, on average, does your team need to score per game to break the record?

To solve a multi-step inequality like $2x + 1 > 5$, you should use the properties of inequality from Lessons 3.4 and 3.5 to get the variable terms on one side of the inequality and the constant terms on the other side.

Example 1 *Writing and Solving a Multi-Step Inequality*

Find the average number of goals your team needs to score per game to break the school record, as described above.

Solution

Let *g* represent the average number of goals scored per game. Write a verbal model.

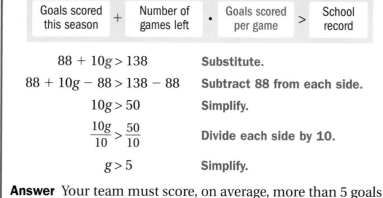

| Goals scored this season | $+$ | Number of games left | $\cdot$ | Goals scored per game | $>$ | School record |

$$88 + 10g > 138 \qquad \text{Substitute.}$$
$$88 + 10g - 88 > 138 - 88 \qquad \text{Subtract 88 from each side.}$$
$$10g > 50 \qquad \text{Simplify.}$$
$$\frac{10g}{10} > \frac{50}{10} \qquad \text{Divide each side by 10.}$$
$$g > 5 \qquad \text{Simplify.}$$

Answer Your team must score, on average, more than 5 goals per game.

 Checkpoint

1. Look back at Example 1. Suppose the season goal record is 124 goals and your team has already scored 52 goals. With 12 games remaining on the schedule, how many goals, on average, does your team need to score per game to break the record?

Note *Worthy*

You may find it helpful to summarize the process used to solve a multi-step inequality in your notes.

Example 2 *Solving a Multi-Step Inequality*

$$\frac{x}{-4} - 6 \geq -5 \qquad \text{Original inequality}$$

$$\frac{x}{-4} - 6 + 6 \geq -5 + 6 \qquad \text{Add 6 to each side.}$$

$$\frac{x}{-4} \geq 1 \qquad \text{Simplify.}$$

$$-4 \cdot \frac{x}{-4} \leq -4 \cdot 1 \qquad \begin{array}{l}\text{Multiply each side by } -4. \\ \text{Reverse inequality symbol.}\end{array}$$

$$x \leq -4 \qquad \text{Simplify.}$$

Example 3 *Combining like Terms in a Multi-Step Inequality*

Ice Skating You plan to go ice skating often this winter. The skating rink charges $4 for admission. You can either rent ice skates at the skating rink for $5 per day or buy your own pair for $45. How many times do you have to use the ice skates in order for the cost of buying them to be less than the total cost of renting them?

Solution

You have two options: buying skates or renting skates. Let v represent the number of visits to the skating rink. Write a variable expression for the cost of each option.

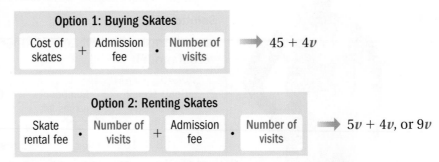

To find the values of v for which the cost of option 1 is less than the cost of option 2, write and solve an inequality.

Cost of option 1	<	Cost of option 2

$$45 + 4v < 9v \qquad \text{Substitute.}$$

$$45 + 4v - 4v < 9v - 4v \qquad \text{Subtract 4v from each side.}$$

$$45 < 5v \qquad \text{Simplify.}$$

$$\frac{45}{5} < \frac{5v}{5} \qquad \text{Divide each side by 5.}$$

$$9 < v \qquad \text{Simplify.}$$

Answer If you buy skates, the cost will be less after more than 9 visits.

Guided Practice

Vocabulary Check
1. Write and solve an inequality for the following verbal sentence: Five plus 2 times a number is less than 20.

2. List the steps you would take to solve the inequality $-5x + 12 < -8$.

Skill Check
Solve the inequality. Graph and check your solution.

3. $4x + 1 > 1$ **4.** $7 \geq 5x - 3$ **5.** $\dfrac{x}{-2} + 6 < -14$

6. $10 > 6 + \dfrac{y}{5}$ **7.** $5y + 2 \leq y + 34$ **8.** $6 + y \geq 2y - 3$

Guided Problem Solving
9. Amusement Parks You are trying to decide whether to pay $120 for a season pass to an amusement park. If you buy the pass, you get an unlimited number of visits to the park and reduced parking for $8. If you do not buy the pass, you pay $23 admission and $10 for parking each time you visit the park. After how many visits to the park will the cost of the season pass be less than the cost of visiting without the season pass?

   1) Write a variable expression for the cost of making v visits to the park if you don't buy a season pass.

   2) Write an inequality in terms of v showing that the cost of visiting the park with a season pass is less than the cost of visiting the park without a season pass.

   3) Solve the inequality.

Practice and Problem Solving

Homework *Help*

Example	Exercises
1	23
2	14–21
3	22, 31

Online Resources
CLASSZONE.COM
• More Examples
• eTutorial Plus

Tell whether the given number is a solution of $5x - 10 > 2x + 4$.

10. 8 **11.** 5 **12.** 4 **13.** -2

Solve the inequality. Graph your solution.

14. $2y + 7 > 11$ **15.** $6n - 3 \leq -9$

16. $11 - 4z < -1$ **17.** $3m - 8 > -30 + 5m$

18. $19 \geq \dfrac{x}{90} - 25$ **19.** $3 + \dfrac{b}{3} < 7$

20. $14p - 5 \geq -3p + 114$ **21.** $-3x - 3 < 2x - 83$

22. Movie Rental At a video store, you have two options for renting movies. You can pay $4 per movie, or you can pay a one-time membership fee of $10 and then pay only $1.50 per movie. After how many movie rentals will the cost of the membership be less than the cost of renting movies without the membership?

23. Advertising A small company has an advertising budget of $15,000. The company plans to produce and air a television commercial. It will cost $500 to produce the commercial and an additional $50 each time the commercial is aired. How many days can the company afford to run the commercial if it is aired once a day?

24. Error Analysis Describe and correct the error in solving the inequality $4x > 6x + 3$.

$$4x > 6x + 3$$
$$4x - 6x > 6x + 3 - 6x$$
$$-2x > 3$$
$$\frac{-2x}{-2} > \frac{3}{-2}$$
$$x > -\frac{3}{2}$$

Television crew filming a commercial

Solve the inequality. Graph your solution.

25. $4(5 - 3b) > 4b + 4$ **26.** $\dfrac{x - 2}{3} > 4$ **27.** $3y - 5 < 2(17 - 5y)$

28. $\dfrac{x + 5}{3} \le 2$ **29.** $\dfrac{-5s - 8}{4} \ge -22$ **30.** $-3 \le \dfrac{2x + 4}{4}$

31. Fundraising You are designing greeting cards on your computer to raise money for a charity. You buy card stock at a cost of $.50 per card and rent a table at the fundraiser for $20. You will sell the cards in sets of 12 for $10.20. How many sets of cards do you have to sell in order to make more than what you spend?

32. Long-Distance Calls The table gives information about three long-distance telephone companies. For each company, the table gives the monthly fee and the charge per minute for making long-distance calls.

Long-Distance Rates by Company		
Company	Monthly fee	Per-minute charge
A	$2.00	$.039
B	No fee	$.049
C	$1.95	$.044

a. After how many minutes of long-distance calls is the cost of using company A for one month less than the cost of using company B for one month?

b. After how many minutes of long-distance calls is the cost of using company C for one month less than the cost of using company B for one month?

c. Interpret and Apply If you spend 150 minutes each month making long-distance calls, which company should you use? Explain why.

33. Challenge Find all the values of x that make both of the following inequalities true: $2x + 4 < 10$ and $5 - 3x \le 17$. Show how you found your answer.

34. Extended Problem Solving You and a friend join different health clubs. You pay a one-time membership fee of $150 and a monthly fee of $35. Your friend pays a one-time membership fee of $100 and a monthly fee of $40.

a. Analyze Let m be the number of months that you and your friend have been health club members. Make a table with a column for the number m of months, a column for the amount you have paid after m months, and a column for the amount your friend has paid after m months. Complete the table for whole-number values of m from 1 to 12 to represent one year of membership at each health club.

b. Make a scatter plot of the data from part (a). Show months on the x-axis and the amount paid on the y-axis. Plot points representing the amount you have paid in blue and the amount your friend has paid in red.

c. *Writing* Using the scatter plot, determine the number of months you and your friend need to be members of your health clubs before you have paid less than your friend. Explain your reasoning.

d. Check your answer to part (c) by writing and solving an inequality.

Mixed Review

Give the coordinates of the point. *(Lesson 1.8)*

35. A **36.** B

37. C **38.** D

39. E **40.** F

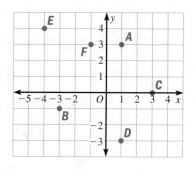

Simplify the expression. *(Lesson 2.3)*

41. $13(2a + 1)$ **42.** $12 + c + 8$ **43.** $5a + a$

Algebra Basics Solve the equation. Check your solution. *(Lesson 3.2)*

44. $3(x + 4) = 9$ **45.** $4(2d + 1) = 28$ **46.** $-10 = 2(7 - 2x)$

47. Write and solve an equation for the following verbal sentence: Nine more than 3 times a number is equal to 7 less than twice the number. *(Lesson 3.3)*

Standardized Test Practice

48. Multiple Choice Which graph shows the solution of the inequality $7 - 6x \geq 13$?

A.

B.

C.

D.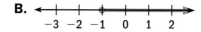

49. Multiple Choice Which number is a solution of the inequality $-7x + 3 < -7.5$?

F. -3 **G.** -1 **H.** 1 **I.** 3

Chapter Review

Vocabulary Review

inequality, p. 138   solution of an inequality, p. 138   equivalent inequalities, p. 139

1. Copy and complete: The value of a variable that, when substituted into an inequality, makes a true statement is a(n) ? .

2. Give an example of an inequality.

3. Copy and complete: The inequalities $2x < 2$ and $x < 1$ are ? inequalities.

4. Are $-2x > 6$ and $x > -3$ equivalent inequalities? Why or why not?

3.1 Solving Two-Step Equations

Examples on pp. 120–122

▶ **Goal**

Solve two-step equations.

> **Example** Solve the following problem.

A one-year membership in a video rental club costs $10. Members pay $1.25 per video rental. You spend $45 in one year. How many videos did you rent?

Solution

Let v represent the number of videos you rented. Write a verbal model.

Total amount	=	Club fee	+	Charge per video rental	·	Number of video rentals

$$45 = 10 + 1.25v \qquad \text{Substitute.}$$

$$45 - 10 = 10 + 1.25v - 10 \qquad \text{Subtract 10 from each side.}$$

$$35 = 1.25v \qquad \text{Simplify.}$$

$$\frac{35}{1.25} = \frac{1.25v}{1.25} \qquad \text{Divide each side by 1.25.}$$

$$28 = v \qquad \text{Simplify.}$$

Answer You rented 28 videos.

 5. Spaghetti Your friend bought a box of spaghetti for $1.59 and 2 jars of spaghetti sauce. The total cost was $6.49. Find the cost of one jar of sauce.

3.2 Solving Equations Having Like Terms and Parentheses

Examples on pp. 125–126

▶ *Goal*

Solve equations having like terms and parentheses.

Example Solve $2x - x + 1 = 5$ and $4(3r - 9) = 36$.

a.
$$2x - x + 1 = 5 \qquad \text{Write original equation.}$$
$$x + 1 = 5 \qquad \text{Combine like terms.}$$
$$x + 1 - 1 = 5 - 1 \qquad \text{Subtract 1 from each side.}$$
$$x = 4 \qquad \text{Simplify.}$$

b.
$$4(3r - 9) = 36 \qquad \text{Write original equation.}$$
$$12r - 36 = 36 \qquad \text{Distributive property}$$
$$12r - 36 + 36 = 36 + 36 \qquad \text{Add 36 to each side.}$$
$$12r = 72 \qquad \text{Simplify.}$$
$$\frac{12r}{12} = \frac{72}{12} \qquad \text{Divide each side by 12.}$$
$$r = 6 \qquad \text{Simplify.}$$

✔ **Solve the equation. Check your solution.**

6. $17h - 47 + 6h = 160$ **7.** $2(4p + 8) = 128$ **8.** $6(w - 4) + 18 = 30$

3.3 Solving Equations with Variables on Both Sides

Examples on pp. 131–133

▶ *Goal*

Solve equations with variables on both sides.

Example Solve $13n - 45 = 36 + 4n$.

$$13n - 45 = 36 + 4n \qquad \text{Write original equation.}$$
$$13n - 45 - 4n = 36 + 4n - 4n \qquad \text{Subtract 4n from each side.}$$
$$9n - 45 = 36 \qquad \text{Simplify.}$$
$$9n - 45 + 45 = 36 + 45 \qquad \text{Add 45 to each side.}$$
$$9n = 81 \qquad \text{Simplify.}$$
$$\frac{9n}{9} = \frac{81}{9} \qquad \text{Divide each side by 9.}$$
$$n = 9 \qquad \text{Simplify.}$$

✔ **Solve the equation. Check your solution.**

9. $11t + 14 = 95 - 16t$ **10.** $9n + 64 = -144 - 17n$

11. $3 + 2x = 2(2 + x)$ **12.** $3(2 + 6b) = 18b$

3.4 Solving Inequalities Using Addition or Subtraction

Examples on pp. 138–140

▶ **Goal**

Solve inequalities using addition or subtraction.

Example Solve $x + 13 \leq 20$. Graph your solution.

$x + 13 \leq 20$ Write original inequality.

$x + 13 - 13 \leq 20 - 13$ Subtract 13 from each side.

$x \leq 7$ Simplify.

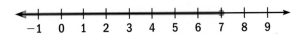

✓ **Solve the inequality. Graph your solution.**

13. $y + 11 < 23$ **14.** $15 \geq z + 9$ **15.** $x - 5 \leq 14$ **16.** $m - 8 < 26$

3.5 Solving Inequalities Using Multiplication or Division

Examples on pp. 144–145

▶ **Goal**

Solve inequalities using multiplication and division.

Example Solve $5x > 30$ and $\dfrac{t}{-8} \leq 5$. Graph your solutions.

a. $5x > 30$ Write original inequality.

$\dfrac{5x}{5} > \dfrac{30}{5}$ Divide each side by 5.

$x > 6$ Simplify.

b. $\dfrac{t}{-8} \leq 5$ Write original inequality.

$-8 \cdot \dfrac{t}{-8} \geq -8 \cdot 5$ Multiply each side by -8. Reverse inequality symbol.

$t \geq -40$ Simplify.

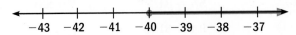

✓ **Solve the inequality. Graph your solution.**

17. $3 > \dfrac{a}{-9}$ **18.** $\dfrac{b}{7} \geq 13$ **19.** $12c \leq 96$ **20.** $-68 < -17d$

21. $-2 > \dfrac{r}{-6}$ **22.** $196 \leq 14z$ **23.** $7h < -56$ **24.** $\dfrac{p}{5} > -6$

3.6 Solving Multi-Step Inequalities

Examples on pp. 149–150

▶ **Goal**

Solve multi-step inequalities.

Example Solve $-8y + 5 \leq 29$ and $3x - 5 > 6x + 13$. Graph your solutions.

a.
$-8y + 5 \leq 29$	Write original inequality.
$-8y + 5 - 5 \leq 29 - 5$	Subtract 5 from each side.
$-8y \leq 24$	Simplify.
$\dfrac{-8y}{-8} \geq \dfrac{24}{-8}$	Divide both sides by -8. Reverse inequality symbol.
$y \geq -3$	Simplify.

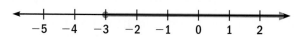

b.
$3x - 5 > 6x + 13$	Write original inequality.
$3x - 5 - 3x > 6x + 13 - 3x$	Subtract $3x$ from each side.
$-5 > 3x + 13$	Simplify.
$-5 - 13 > 3x + 13 - 13$	Subtract 13 from each side.
$-18 > 3x$	Simplify.
$\dfrac{-18}{3} > \dfrac{3x}{3}$	Divide each side by 3.
$-6 > x$	Simplify.

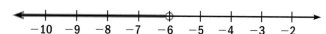

✔ **Solve the inequality. Graph your solution.**

25. $-8m - 6 < 10$ **26.** $8p + 1 \geq 17$ **27.** $24 \geq 5z - 6$

28. $8 > 2 + \dfrac{b}{3}$ **29.** $\dfrac{p}{28} + 3 \leq 9$ **30.** $\dfrac{n}{3} + 4 > 5$

31. $12 - 4q \geq 6q + 2$ **32.** $6x - 5 > 12x + 1$ **33.** $6(3 - a) \leq 8a - 10$

34. Snowboarding A ski resort charges $45 for an all-day lift pass and $40 per day for renting boots and a snowboard. At a store, you can buy boots and a snowboard for $360. How many times must you go snowboarding at the ski resort for the cost of buying your own boots and snowboard to be less than renting them?

Chapter Test

Solve the equation. Check your solution.

1. $7f + 5 = 68$

2. $14 - 3g = 32$

3. $\dfrac{h}{3} - 14 = -11$

4. $\dfrac{z}{-2} + 5 = 7$

5. $12 - 2m + 5 = -1$

6. $-6y + 4 + 11y = -16$

7. $3(8 - a) = 12$

8. $-6(3x + 15) = 18$

9. $5t + 5 = 5t - 4$

10. $2n - 6 = -8n + 14$

11. $8b + 4 = 4(b - 7)$

12. $16p + 8 = 2(8p + 4)$

13. Movie Tickets A family of four goes to a movie theater and spends $26.50. They buy 2 tickets for children at $3.50 per ticket, 2 tickets for adults, and 3 boxes of popcorn at $2.50 per box. What is the cost of one adult movie ticket?

14. Ocean Water The more salt that ocean water contains, the lower the temperature at which it freezes. Some ocean water freezes at temperatures of $-1.9°C$ or less. Write and graph an inequality to show the temperatures at which this ocean water freezes.

Solve the inequality. Graph your solution.

15. $x + 75 > -125$

16. $w - 18 < -10$

17. $\dfrac{t}{12} \geq 3$

18. $-3a - 6 \leq -9$

19. $4(2 - d) \geq -12$

20. $2c - 5 < -21 - 2c$

21. School Supplies You go to the store to buy supplies for class. You want to buy 5 identical folders. The most you can spend is $5.75. What are the individual folder prices that you can afford?

Write the verbal sentence as an inequality. Then solve the inequality.

22. Nine is greater than or equal to 15 minus a number.

23. Eight times the sum of 5 and a number is less than 56.

24. Fifteen is greater than 3 times the difference of a number and 4.

25. Seven times a number minus 5 is less than or equal to 16.

26. Making Bread A bread-making machine costs $99. The ingredients to make a one pound loaf of bread cost $.45. At a store, you pay $2.19 for the same size loaf of bread. How many whole loaves of bread will you have to make in order for the cost of the machine and ingredients to be less than the cost of buying an equivalent amount of bread at the store?

Chapter Standardized Test

Test-Taking Strategy Start working as soon as the testing time begins and try to stay focused on the test.

1. What is the solution of the equation
   $\frac{t}{5} - 12 = 10$?

   A. -14 **B.** 10 **C.** 38 **D.** 110

2. What is the solution of the equation
   $-4(n + 5) = -32$?

   F. -13 **G.** -12 **H.** 3 **I.** 13

3. The perimeter of the triangle shown is 15 units. What is the value of x?

   A. 1 **B.** 2 **C.** 3 **D.** 4

4. Which equation has no solution?

   F. $4t - 8 = 4(t - 2)$

   G. $3(r - 1) = -2(2 + r)$

   H. $6p + 2 = 9p - 4$

   I. $7(s + 1) = -3 + 7s$

5. Giants Stadium in New Jersey can seat up to 80,242 people. Which inequality represents the number n of people that the stadium can seat?

   A. $n < 80{,}242$ **B.** $n > 80{,}242$

   C. $n \le 80{,}242$ **D.** $n \ge 80{,}242$

6. What is the solution of the inequality
   $\frac{z}{-4} + 3 < 15$?

   F. $z < -48$ **G.** $z > -48$

   H. $z < -3$ **I.** $z > -3$

7. What is the solution of the inequality
   $-12 > y + 6$?

   A. $y < -18$ **B.** $y < -6$

   C. $y > -18$ **D.** $y > -6$

8. Which value is *not* a solution of the inequality $-5y - 2 \ge 30.5$?

   F. -162.5 **G.** -10 **H.** -6.5 **I.** -3

9. **Short Response** Two of your friends go bowling. One friend rents a pair of bowling shoes for $3 and bowls 3 games. The other friend brings his own bowling shoes, bowls 4 games, and buys a soda for $.50. Both friends spend the same amount of money. Show how you can write and solve an equation to find the cost of one game.

10. **Extended Response** The table below shows the cost of renting a moving van for 1 day from two companies. The daily charge and the charge per mile are given.

Company	Daily charge	Charge per mile
A	$80	$.35
B	$75	$.39

   a. How many miles m will you have to drive before the cost of renting a van for one day from company A is less than the cost of renting a van for one day from company B? Express your answer as an inequality.

   b. Graph your inequality from part (a).

   c. Which company is less expensive if you drive 100 miles in one day? Explain.

Strategies for Answering
Multiple Choice Questions

You can use the problem solving plan on page 14 to solve a problem. If you have difficulty solving a problem in multiple choice format, you may be able to use one of the strategies below to choose the correct answer. You may also be able to use these strategies and others to check whether your answer to a multiple choice question is reasonable.

Strategy: Use Estimation

Problem 1 You and a friend share the cost of a pizza and a salad. The pizza costs $8.98. The salad costs $3.98. How much do each of

To solve this problem, you need to add the cost of the two items and divide by 2.

you pay?

A. $6.48   **B.** $8.47   **C.** $10.97   **D.** $12.96

Estimate: $\dfrac{9 + 4}{2} = \dfrac{13}{2} = 6.5$, so the correct answer is A.

Strategy: Use Visual Clues

Problem 2 The line graph shows the number of people (in millions) who participated in snowboarding in the United States from 1991 to 2001. What was the greatest increase in participation in

To solve this problem, you need to identify the period with the greatest increase, then find the amount of increase for that period.

any two-year period?

F. About 0.5 million

G. About 1 million

H. About 1.5 million

I. About 2 million

Snowboarding Participation

The greatest change occurred between 1999 and 2001. The vertical distance between the points for 1999 and 2001 is about 2 units. Each unit represents 1 million people. So, the correct answer is I.

Strategy: Use Number Sense

Problem 3 The temperature in a freezer is $-12°C$. During one 8 minute period, the temperature drops about 0.5°C each minute. What is the temperature after those 8 minutes?

To solve this problem, you need to find the total change in temperature and add it to the original temperature.

A. $-16°C$ ------ The product $-0.5(8)$ is a negative integer. The sum of a negative integer and -12 is a negative integer less than -12. So, the correct answer is A.

B. $-12.5°C$

C. $-11.5°C$

D. $-8°C$

Eliminating Unreasonable Choices The strategies used to find the correct answers for Problems 1–3 can also be used to eliminate answer choices that are unreasonable or obviously incorrect.

Problem 4 The length of a rectangle is 5 meters less than twice the width. The perimeter is 26 meters. What is the width of the rectangle?

To solve this problem, you need to use the perimeter formula $P = 2l + 2w$ and the given information to write and solve an equation.

A. 2 m ------ Not correct; if $w = 2$, then $l = 2(2) - 5 = -1$, but length is never negative.

B. 6 m

C. $10.\overline{3}$ m --- Not correct; if $w \approx 10$, then $l \approx 2(10) - 5 = 15$, and $P \approx 50$.

D. 42 m^2 ---- Not correct; width is *not* measured in square units.

Checkpoint

Explain why the highlighted answer choice is unreasonable.

1. You and 4 friends share the $29.95 cost of a lunch. How much does each person pay?

   A. $5.99   **B.** $7.49   ✗ **C.** $24.95   **D.** $34.95

2. What is the solution of the equation $5x + 3 = -15$?

   F. -3.6 **G.** -2.4 **H.** 2.4 ✗ **I.** 3.6

3. At 9 P.M., the temperature is $0°F$. It drops $3°F$ each hour for 4 hours. What is the temperature at 1 A.M.?

   A. $-12°F$ **B.** $-7°F$ **C.** $7°F$ ✗ **D.** $12°F$

Watch *Out*

Some answers may appear correct at first glance, but they may be incorrect answers you would get by making common errors.

Unit 1
Chapters 1–3

Practicing Test-Taking Skills

Multiple Choice

1. Which variable expression represents the number of inches in y yards?

A. $36y$ **B.** $\dfrac{y}{36}$ **C.** $\dfrac{36}{y}$ **D.** $36 - y$

2. What is the value of the expression $15 - 14 \div 2 + 5$?

F. $\dfrac{1}{7}$ **G.** $5\dfrac{1}{2}$ **H.** 8 **I.** 13

3. During the month of January, the average high temperature in Montreal, Canada, is $-6°C$, and the average low temperature is $-15°C$. How much greater is the average high temperature than the average low temperature?

A. $-21°C$ **B.** $-9°C$

C. $9°C$ **D.** $21°C$

4. Which point has coordinates $(1, -2)$?

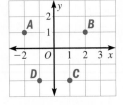

F. A

G. B

H. C

I. D

5. Which expression is equivalent to $3(0.9 + 7)$?

A. $3(0.9) + 7$ **B.** $0.27 + 21$

C. $3(0.9) + 3(7)$ **D.** $2.7 + 7$

6. Which terms of the expression $4x + 9 + 9x - 4$ are like terms?

F. $4x$ and -4 **G.** $4x$ and 4

H. $4x$ and $9x$ **I.** $9x$ and 9

7. What is the solution of $10 + x = -19$?

A. -29 **B.** -9 **C.** 9 **D.** 29

8. Which expression is equivalent to $8(x + 2) - 5(x - 3)$?

F. $3x + 31$ **G.** $3x + 1$

H. $3x - 1$ **I.** $13x + 31$

9. What is the solution of $3 - 8x = -141$?

A. -18 **B.** -12 **C.** $\dfrac{1}{18}$ **D.** 18

10. What is the solution of $7(x + 5) - 10 = 2x$?

F. -5 **G.** -1 **H.** 5 **I.** 7

11. Which of the inequalities has the solution whose graph is shown?

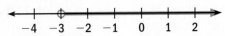

A. $2x + 10 < 16$ **B.** $-4x - 5 < 7$

C. $-3x + 8 < -1$ **D.** $4 - 2x > 10$

12. A soccer goalie has made 175 saves so far this season. The school record is 236 saves in a season. There are 6 games left to play. Which inequality could you solve to find the average number of saves the goalie must make in each of the remaining games to break the school record?

F. $175 + 6x < 236$ **G.** $175 + 6x > 236$

H. $236 + 6x > 175$ **I.** $236 + 6x < 175$

13. What is the solution of the inequality $-3x + 14 > 2x - 11$?

A. $x > -5$ **B.** $x > 5$

C. $x < -5$ **D.** $x < 5$

Short Response

14. Tell whether the statement $|a - b| = |a| - |b|$ is *always*, *sometimes*, or *never* true for integers a and b. Give examples to explain your reasoning.

15. While waiting in the checkout line at the grocery store, you add the prices of the 3 items you are buying to make sure you have enough money. Explain how to use mental math and the properties of addition to find the total cost if the prices of the 3 items are $1.85, $2.74, and $4.15. Find the total cost.

16. Profit is the difference of income and expenses. The table shows one store's profit for each of its first 4 months. Find the mean profit. Explain your method.

Month	Profit
March	−$670
April	−$340
May	$320
June	$400

17. You have at most 3 hours to do homework. You spend 45 minutes on math. You want to divide the time remaining equally among 4 other subjects. Write and solve an inequality to find the number of minutes you can spend on each one. Explain your method.

Extended Response

18. You are painting a room that is 16 feet long, 14 feet wide, and 8 feet high. The room has two identical windows and two identical doors. One door leads to a closet 4 feet long, 4 feet wide, and 8 feet high. You do not plan to paint the closet.

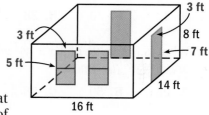

a. The paint you choose is available in both 1 gallon cans that cover about 400 square feet each and 1 quart cans that cover about 100 square feet each. You plan to put 2 coats of paint on each wall, not including the doors or windows. How much paint should you buy?

b. A 1 gallon can of paint costs $13.90, and a 1 quart can of paint costs $8.90. How much will it cost to put 2 coats of paint on each wall?

c. You've budgeted $40 for paint. Can you afford to paint the inside walls of the closet, excluding the door, with 1 coat of paint?

19. The table shows the annual fee at two gyms and the fee each time members take an aerobics class.

a. In a year's time, which gym is less expensive if you plan to take 4 aerobics classes each month?

b. Write and solve an inequality to determine the number of aerobics classes for which the total cost for 1 year at gym A is less than that at gym B.

c. How many aerobics classes should you average each month so that the total cost for 1 year at gym B is less than that at gym A?

Gym Costs		
Gym	Annual fee	Class fee
A	$540	$3
B	$360	$5

Cumulative Practice for Chapters 1–3

Chapter 1

Multiple Choice In Exercises 1–11, choose the letter of the correct answer.

1. What is the value of $9 - x$ when $x = 5$? *(Lesson 1.1)*

   A. 1   **B.** 4   **C.** 14   **D.** 45

2. How can you write $7 \times 7 \times 7$ as a power? *(Lesson 1.2)*

   F. 7×3 **G.** 3×7 **H.** 7^3 **I.** 3^7

3. What is the value of 6^4? *(Lesson 1.2)*

   A. 24   **B.** 216   **C.** 1296   **D.** 4096

4. What is the value of $28 \div 7 + 16$? *(Lesson 1.3)*

   F. 4   **G.** 20   **H.** 28   **I.** 212

5. What is the value of $2(x + y)^2$ when $x = 3$ and $y = 4$? *(Lesson 1.3)*

   A. 28   **B.** 50   **C.** 98   **D.** 2401

6. Which list of integers is in order from least to greatest? *(Lesson 1.4)*

   F. $-3, -5, -7, -9$ **G.** $-5, -3, 0, 4$

   H. $-2, 4, -5, 9$ **I.** $-8, 7, -6, 3$

7. What is the value of $-15 + 9$? *(Lesson 1.5)*

   A. -24 **B.** -6 **C.** 6   **D.** 24

8. What is the value of $-27 - x$ when $x = -8$? *(Lesson 1.6)*

   F. -35 **G.** -19 **H.** 19   **I.** 35

9. In 24 hours, the temperature went from $-8°C$ to $12°C$. What was the change in temperature? *(Lesson 1.6)*

   A. $-20°C$ **B.** $-4°C$ **C.** $4°C$ **D.** $20°C$

10. What is the value of $\dfrac{x^2}{y}$ when $x = -4$ and $y = -2$? *(Lesson 1.7)*

    F. -8 **G.** $-\dfrac{1}{8}$ **H.** $\dfrac{1}{8}$ **I.** 8

11. In which quadrant is the point $(-2, -3)$ located? *(Lesson 1.8)*

    A. Quadrant I   **B.** Quadrant II

    C. Quadrant III   **D.** Quadrant IV

12. **Short Response** You have $500 in a savings account. You make deposits of $30, $125, $10, $20, and $65, and you make withdrawals of $75, $89, $143, $15, and $20. Write a positive integer to represent each deposit and a negative integer to represent each withdrawal. Find the final balance in your savings account. *(Lessons 1.5, 1.6)*

13. **Extended Response** The table shows the number of cell phone subscribers (in millions) in the United States from 1996 to 2001. *(Lesson 1.8)*

Years since 1996	Subscribers (millions)
0	44
1	55
2	69
3	86
4	109
5	128

   a. Explain how to make a scatter plot of the data.

   b. Make a scatter plot.

   c. Does the scatter plot suggest any relationship between the number of years since 1996 and the number of cell phone subscribers? Explain.

Chapter 2

Multiple Choice In Exercises 14–24, choose the letter of the correct answer.

14. Which property is illustrated by the statement $2x + (y + 1) = (2x + y) + 1$? *(Lesson 2.1)*

    A. Identity property of addition

    B. Commutative property of addition

    C. Associative property of addition

    D. Associative property of multiplication

15. Use a conversion factor to convert 1.5 miles to feet. *(Lesson 2.1)*

    F. $\frac{1}{7290}$ foot   **G.** $\frac{1}{7290}$ mile

    H. 7920 feet   **I.** 7920 miles

16. Which variable expression is equivalent to $4x - 6$? *(Lesson 2.2)*

    A. $2(2x - 6)$ **B.** $4(x - 6)$

    C. $2(2x + 3)$ **D.** $2(2x - 3)$

17. What is the value of $x(y - z)$ when $x = -2.5$, $y = 4$, and $z = 0.1$? *(Lesson 2.2)*

    F. -10.25 **G.** -9.75

    H. 9.75   **I.** 10.25

18. Which terms of the expression $-6k - 6 + 4 + 4k$ are like terms? *(Lesson 2.3)*

    A. $-6k$ and -6 **B.** $-6k$ and $4k$

    C. $6k$ and $4k$ **D.** 4 and $4k$

19. Which expression is equivalent to $15y - 2(y + 3)$? *(Lesson 2.3)*

    F. $13y - 6$ **G.** $13y + 3$

    H. $13y + 6$ **I.** $16y + 1$

20. Whippets are among the fastest running dogs. Suppose a whippet can run at a rate of 52 feet per second for a short period of time. How long would it take the whippet to run 156 feet? *(Lesson 2.4)*

    A. 1 second   **B.** 2 seconds

    C. 3 seconds   **D.** 4 seconds

21. What is the solution of $x + 11 = 20 - 7$? *(Lesson 2.5)*

    F. 2   **G.** 13   **H.** 16   **I.** 24

22. What is the solution of $\frac{z}{-12} = 24$? *(Lesson 2.6)*

    A. -288 **B.** -2 **C.** 2   **D.** 288

23. You went shopping with $42.60 and came home with $3.33. How much money did you spend? *(Lesson 2.7)*

    F. $3.33   **G.** $38.70   **H.** $39.27   **I.** $45.93

24. What is the solution of $-3y = 14.7$? *(Lesson 2.7)*

    A. -44.1 **B.** -4.9 **C.** 4.9   **D.** 17.7

25. **Short Response** A square has a perimeter of 84 meters. Explain how to write an equation to find the side length of the square. Then find the side length. *(Lesson 2.6)*

26. **Extended Response** At store A, a wide-screen TV sells for $1500 after a $250 mail-in rebate. Store A charges $50 for delivery and setup. Store B promises to sell any TV for $75 less than any competitor's original price and to include free delivery and setup. *(Lesson 2.5)*

    a. What is the original price of the TV at store A?

    b. Which store offers a better deal? Explain your reasoning.

Chapter 3

Multiple Choice In Exercises 27–36, choose the letter of the correct answer.

27. What is the solution of $-2x + 7 = 25$? *(Lesson 3.1)*

A. -16 **B.** -9 **C.** 9 **D.** 16

28. You pay $12.99 for a small pizza and two orders of breadsticks. The pizza costs $7.99. How much does one order of breadsticks cost? *(Lesson 3.1)*

F. $1.99   **G.** $2.50   **H.** $3.00   **I.** $5.00

29. What is the solution of the equation $15 - 2(w + 5) = 11$? *(Lesson 3.2)*

A. -7 **B.** -3 **C.** 8 **D.** 12

30. The area of the rectangle is 28 square units. What is the value of x? *(Lesson 3.2)*

$3x + 4$

4

F. 1 **G.** 2

H. 7 **I.** 8

31. Which statement about the equation $2(x - 1) = 3x - (x + 2)$ is true? *(Lesson 3.3)*

A. The equation has no solution.

B. The solution is -0.5.

C. The solution is -1.

D. The equation has every number as a solution.

32. At temperatures less than $-458°$F, helium is a solid. Which inequality describes the temperatures t (in degrees Fahrenheit) at which helium is a solid? *(Lesson 3.4)*

F. $t > -458$ **G.** $t < -458$

H. $t \geq -458$ **I.** $t \leq -458$

33. You and a friend have $25 to pay for your dinners at a restaurant. Your friend's dinner costs $13.35. How much can you spend on your dinner? *(Lesson 3.4)*

A. Less than $11.65   **B.** More than $11.65

C. At most $11.65   **D.** At least $11.65

34. What is the solution of $\dfrac{h}{-7} \geq 14$? *(Lesson 3.5)*

F. $h \leq -2$ **G.** $h \geq -2$

H. $h \leq -98$ **I.** $h \geq -98$

35. Which number is *not* a solution of $-4s < 42$? *(Lesson 3.5)*

A. -11 **B.** -10 **C.** 10 **D.** 11

36. What is the solution of $4 + 6x \geq -8 + 4x$? *(Lesson 3.6)*

F. $x \geq -6$ **G.** $x \leq -6$

H. $x \geq -1$ **I.** $x \leq -1$

37. Short Response Describe the steps you would take to solve the equation $15z - 12 = 3(14 + 3z) - 12$. Then find the solution. *(Lesson 3.3)*

38. Extended Response Your school is having a fundraising dance. Your costs include $125 for a DJ and $47.50 for decorations. You plan to charge $4.50 for each ticket. *(Lesson 3.6)*

a. How many tickets must you sell before you start making a profit?

b. How many tickets must you sell to make a profit of at least $300?

c. How would raising the ticket price to $5.00 affect your answers to parts (a) and (b)? Explain.

Rational Numbers *and* Proportions

Chapter 4 Factors, Fractions, and Exponents

- Find greatest common factors and least common multiples.
- Identify equivalent fractions and write fractions in simplest form.
- Use rules of exponents and scientific notation.

Chapter 5 Rational Numbers and Equations

- Write fractions as decimals and decimals as fractions.
- Perform operations with fractions and mixed numbers.
- Solve equations and inequalities with rational numbers.

Chapter 6 Ratio, Proportion, and Probability

- Write and compare ratios and rates.
- Write and solve proportions.
- Find theoretical and experimental probabilities.

Chapter 7 Percents

- Find and use equivalent decimals, fractions, and percents.
- Use proportions and the percent equation to solve percent problems.
- Solve problems involving percent of change.

From Chapter 7, p. 338

How many solar cars competed in a race?

Factors, Fractions, *and* Exponents

BEFORE

In previous chapters you've . . .

- Evaluated powers
- Compared and ordered integers
- Written and evaluated variable expressions

Now

In Chapter 4 you'll study . . .

- Factoring numbers and monomials
- Finding common factors and common multiples
- Simplifying and comparing fractions
- Multiplying and dividing powers
- Writing numbers in scientific notation

WHY?

So you can solve real-world problems about . . .

How far away is this giant cloud of gas and dust?

CHAPTER 4

INTERNET Preview
CLASSZONE.COM
- eEdition Plus Online
- eWorkbook Plus Online
- eTutorial Plus Online
- State Test Practice
- More Examples

MATH *In the* **Real World**

Astronomy New stars are forming in the Orion Nebula, a vast cloud of gas and dust nearly 15,100,000,000,000,000 kilometers from Earth. In this chapter, you will learn to use scientific notation to express large numbers like this one.

What do you think? The distance from Earth to the Orion Nebula can be read as 15.1 *quadrillion* kilometers. How many zeros are there in 1 quadrillion?

Chapter Prerequisite Skills

PREREQUISITE SKILLS QUIZ

Review Vocabulary

power, p. 10
base, p. 10
exponent, p. 10
positive integer, p. 22
negative integer, p. 22
numerator, p. 777
denominator, p. 777

Preparing for Success **To prepare for success in this chapter, test your knowledge of these concepts and skills. You may want to look at the pages referred to in blue for additional review.**

1. Vocabulary Label the power, the base, and the exponent in the expression 9^3.

Write the mixed number as an improper fraction. *(p. 778)*

2. $5\frac{1}{3}$ **3.** $6\frac{2}{5}$ **4.** $3\frac{7}{9}$ **5.** $8\frac{5}{6}$

Find the product. *(p. 780)*

6. $20 \times \frac{3}{5}$ **7.** $32 \times \frac{7}{8}$ **8.** $\frac{2}{3} \times 27$ **9.** $\frac{9}{10} \times 50$

Write the power in words and as a repeated multiplication. Then evaluate the power. *(p. 10)*

10. 5^4 **11.** 12^3 **12.** $(1.3)^3$ **13.** $(0.2)^2$

NOTETAKING STRATEGIES

Note *Worthy*

You will find a notetaking strategy at the beginning of each chapter. Look for additional notetaking and study strategies throughout the chapter.

RECORDING THE PROCESS When copying examples in class, be sure to write a verbal description next to each step in a calculation. Then you can refer to the example when solving similar exercises.

Calculation step:

$$-5x - 8 = -23$$
$$-5x - 8 + 8 = -23 + 8$$
$$-5x = -15$$
$$\frac{-5x}{-5} = \frac{-15}{-5}$$
$$x = 3$$

Verbal description:

Write original equation.

Add 8 to each side.

Simplify.

Divide each side by -5.

Simplify.

The strategy above will be helpful in Lesson 4.5 when you are simplifying variable expressions with powers.

4.1 Finding Prime Numbers

Goal
Investigate prime and composite numbers using multiples.

Materials
• pencil
• paper

A *prime number* is a whole number that is greater than 1 and has exactly two whole number factors, 1 and itself. A *composite number* is a whole number that is greater than 1 and has more than two whole number factors. A *multiple* of a number is the product of the number and any nonzero whole number.

Investigate

Use patterns to determine if a number is prime or composite.

1 Write the whole numbers from 2 to 60 in rows of 6 as shown.

2 Start with the number 2. Circle it and cross out every multiple of 2 after 2. (The first few multiples of 2 have been crossed out for you.)

3 Move to the next number that is not crossed out. Circle it and cross out all other multiples of that number.

4 Repeat Step 3 until every number is either crossed out or circled.

②	3	4̸	5	6̸	
7	8̸	9	10	11	12
13	14	15	16	17	18
19	20	21	22	23	24
25	26	27	28	29	30
31	32	33	34	35	36
37	38	39	40	41	42
43	44	45	46	47	48
49	50	51	52	53	54
55	56	57	58	59	60

Draw Conclusions

1. *Writing* What can you say about the numbers that have been crossed out? What can you say about the numbers that have been circled? Use the words *prime* and *composite* in your answers.

2. **Critical Thinking** All the numbers in the sixth column are crossed out because they are all multiples of 6. Explain why all the numbers in the second column (except for 2), in the third column (except for 3), and in the fourth column are crossed out.

3. **Predict** Suppose you repeated the activity but arranged the numbers in rows of 10 instead of 6. Predict which columns would contain only crossed-out numbers. Then check your prediction.

Factors *and* Prime Factorization

Vocabulary

prime number, p. 173
composite number, p. 173
prime factorization, p. 173
factor tree, p. 173
monomial, p. 174

BEFORE	*Now*	WHY?
You found the product of two or more numbers.	You'll write the prime factorization of a number.	So you can count ways to display a firefly collection, as in Ex. 56.

Yearbook You are working on your school yearbook. Each page will have 24 student photos. The photos will be arranged in a rectangular display with the same number of photos in each row. How many ways can you arrange the photos so that there are no more than 10 photos in any row or column?

You can use factors to determine the number of possible displays. In this chapter, finding the factors of a given whole number means finding whole numbers that divide the given number without a remainder. For example, two factors of 50 are 5 and 10.

Example 1 Writing Factors

For the yearbook described above, each possible display will consist of 24 photos. Because there will be the same number of photos in each row, the number of photos in each row will be a factor of 24.

1 Write 24 as a product of two whole numbers in all possible ways.

$$1 \cdot 24 \qquad 2 \cdot 12 \qquad 3 \cdot 8 \qquad 4 \cdot 6$$

The factors of 24 are 1, 2, 3, 4, 6, 8, 12, and 24.

2 Use the factors to find all the rectangular displays with no more than 10 photos in any row or column.

3 rows of 8 photos	6 rows of 4 photos
8 rows of 3 photos	4 rows of 6 photos

Answer There are 4 possible displays.

 Checkpoint

Write all the factors of the number.

1. 30 **2.** 31 **3.** 45 **4.** 87

Prime and Composite Numbers A **prime number** is a whole number that is greater than 1 and has exactly two whole number factors, 1 and itself. A **composite number** is a whole number that is greater than 1 and has more than two whole number factors. The number 1 is neither prime nor composite.

Examples of Prime and Composite Numbers		
Number	**Factors**	**Prime or composite?**
24	1, 2, 3, 4, 6, 8, 12, 24	Composite
41	1, 41	Prime
51	1, 3, 17, 51	Composite
89	1, 89	Prime
121	1, 11, 121	Composite

Prime Factorization When you write a number as a product of prime numbers, you are writing its **prime factorization**. You can use a diagram called a **factor tree** to write the prime factorization of a number.

Note *Worthy*

It is helpful to include diagrams in your notes. Include a different factor tree for the number 630 in your notes.

Example 2 *Writing a Prime Factorization*

Write the prime factorization of 630.

One possible factor tree:

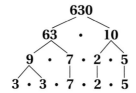

630   Write original number.

30 · 21   Write 630 as 30 · 21.

6 · 5 · 3 · 7   Write 30 as 6 · 5. Write 21 as 3 · 7.

2 · 3 · 5 · 3 · 7   Write 6 as 2 · 3.

Another possible factor tree:

630   Write original number.

63 · 10   Write 630 as 63 · 10.

9 · 7 · 2 · 5   Write 63 as 9 · 7. Write 10 as 2 · 5.

3 · 3 · 7 · 2 · 5   Write 9 as 3 · 3.

Both trees give the same result: $630 = 2 \cdot 3 \cdot 3 \cdot 5 \cdot 7 = 2 \cdot 3^2 \cdot 5 \cdot 7$.

Answer The prime factorization of 630 is $2 \cdot 3^2 \cdot 5 \cdot 7$.

✔ *Checkpoint*

Tell whether the number is *prime* or *composite*. If it is composite, write its prime factorization.

5. 32   **6.** 56   **7.** 59   **8.** 83

9. 101   **10.** 175   **11.** 180   **12.** 420

Factoring Monomials A **monomial** is a number, a variable, or the product of a number and one or more variables raised to whole number powers.

Monomials	Not monomials
$7x$	$7 + x$
$25mn^2$	$25m - n^2$
$24y^3z^2$	$24 + y^3 + z^2$

To *factor* a monomial, write the monomial as a product of prime numbers and variables with exponents of 1.

Example 3   *Factoring a Monomial*

Factor the monomial $28xy^3$.

$$28xy^3 = 2 \cdot 2 \cdot 7 \cdot x \cdot y^3 \qquad \text{Write 28 as } 2 \cdot 2 \cdot 7.$$
$$= 2 \cdot 2 \cdot 7 \cdot x \cdot y \cdot y \cdot y \qquad \text{Write } y^3 \text{ as } y \cdot y \cdot y.$$

✓ *Checkpoint*

Factor the monomial.

13. $6ab$ **14.** $15n^3$ **15.** $3x^3y^2$ **16.** $36s^4t$

4.1   Exercises

More Practice, p. 806

INTERNET
eWorkbook Plus
CLASSZONE.COM

Guided Practice

Vocabulary Check   **1.** Describe how to write the prime factorization of a number.

2. Explain why 34 is a composite number.

Skill Check   **Write all the factors of the number.**

3. 16   **4.** 32   **5.** 29   **6.** 55

Tell whether the number is *prime* or *composite*.

7. 9   **8.** 15   **9.** 17   **10.** 23

Write the prime factorization of the number.

11. 10   **12.** 18   **13.** 25   **14.** 39

15. Error Analysis Describe and correct the error in writing the prime factorization of 60.

$$\times \quad 60 = 3 \cdot 4 \cdot 5$$

Practice and Problem Solving

Homework *Help*

Example	Exercises
1	16–23, 46, 56
2	24–45
3	48–55

Online Resources
CLASSZONE.COM
- More Examples
- eTutorial Plus

Write all the factors of the number.

16. 8   **17.** 53   **18.** 12   **19.** 33

20. 36   **21.** 60   **22.** 71   **23.** 144

Tell whether the number is *prime* or *composite*.

24. 7   **25.** 16   **26.** 21   **27.** 19

28. 121   **29.** 51   **30.** 84   **31.** 141

Copy and complete the factor tree. Then write the prime factorization of the number.

32.
$$104$$
$$8 \cdot \, ?$$
$$2 \cdot \, ? \cdot \, ?$$
$$2 \cdot 2 \cdot \, ? \cdot 13$$

33.
$$180$$
$$9 \cdot \, ?$$
$$3 \cdot \, ? \cdot 5 \cdot \, ?$$
$$3 \cdot \, ? \cdot \, ? \cdot 2 \cdot 2$$

Write the prime factorization of the number.

34. 26   **35.** 58   **36.** 63   **37.** 85

38. 120   **39.** 160   **40.** 154   **41.** 195

42. 202   **43.** 210   **44.** 217 *not 1 + 7 it's 17*   **45.** 225

46. Coin Collecting The U.S. Mint began issuing state quarters in 1999. There will be one state quarter for each of the 50 states. You are collecting the state quarters and want to design a rectangular display with the same number of quarters in each row. How many ways can you arrange your display?

47. *Writing* Give an expression that is a monomial and tell why it is an example of a monomial. Then give an expression that is *not* a monomial and tell why it is not an example of a monomial.

Factor the monomial.

48. $11cd$ **49.** $19m^3$ **50.** $3f^6$ **51.** $21ab$

52. $5xy^2$ **53.** $35rs^5$ **54.** $2y^4z^3$ **55.** $40m^2n$

56. Fireflies There are 69 species of flashing fireflies, also known as lightning bugs, in the United States. A museum is designing a rectangular display of these 69 species with the same number of fireflies in each row. How many displays are possible?

57. Critical Thinking Explain why all two-digit whole numbers with 5 as the ones' digit are composite.

Study *Strategy*

In Exercises 58–61, to list all the factors of a number, first list all the prime factors. Then list all products of two prime factors. Then list all products of three prime factors, and so on.

Use the prime factorization of the number to list all of its factors.

58. 240   **59.** 335   **60.** 500   **61.** 201

List all the factors of the monomial.

62. $6ab^2$ **63.** $52w$ **64.** $2r^3s$ **65.** $7xyz$

66. Extended Problem Solving A geologist has collected 102 different types of silicate minerals. The geologist has taken a photograph of each mineral and wants to make a display of the photographs.

    a. Calculate How many rectangular arrangements of the photographs are possible?

    b. The geologist wants no more than 15 photographs in any row or column. How many rectangular arrangements satisfying this requirement are possible?

    c. Analyze The geologist decreases the number of photographs in the display to 96. How many rectangular arrangements, with no more than 15 photographs in any row or column, are now possible?

67. Conjecture The square of an integer is called a *perfect square*. Write the prime factorizations, with exponents, for these perfect squares: 4, 9, 16, 25, 36, and 64. Make a conjecture about the exponents in the prime factorization of a perfect square.

68. Perfect Numbers A *perfect number* is a number that is the sum of all its factors except for itself. The smallest perfect number is 6, because $6 = 1 + 2 + 3$. The next perfect number is between 20 and 30. Find the next perfect number.

69. Critical Thinking If 18 is a factor of a number, what other numbers must also be factors of that number? Give examples to support your answer.

70. Challenge What is the least whole number that has exactly 7 factors, including 1 and itself? Explain your answer.

Mixed Review

Algebra Basics Solve the equation. Check your solution. *(Lessons 2.5, 2.6)*

71. $a + 24 = 16$ **72.** $33 + b = 58$ **73.** $c - 14 = 18$ **74.** $d - 10 = 10$

75. $6r = 48$ **76.** $-10s = 50$ **77.** $\frac{t}{9} = -7$ **78.** $\frac{u}{-2} = -14$

Write the verbal sentence as an equation. Then solve the equation.
(Lesson 3.3)

79. Fifteen plus a number is equal to 21 minus the number.

80. Two times the sum of 3 and a number is equal to 5 plus the number.

81. Eight plus a number is equal to -3 times the number.

Standardized Test Practice

82. Multiple Choice For which value of x is the value of the expression $7x + 1$ a prime number?

    A. 0   **B.** 1   **C.** 3   **D.** 4

83. Multiple Choice Which expression is the prime factorization of 252?

    F. $2^2 \cdot 3^2 \cdot 7^2$ **G.** $2^2 \cdot 3^2 \cdot 7$ **H.** $2 \cdot 3^2 \cdot 7$ **I.** $2 \cdot 3^2 \cdot 7^2$

84. Short Response The area of a rectangle is 54 square inches. The length and width are whole numbers of inches. Find all possible dimensions of the rectangle. Which dimensions result in the rectangle having the greatest perimeter?

Greatest Common Factor

BEFORE	*Now*	WHY?
You found all the factors of a whole number.	You'll find the GCF of two or more whole numbers.	So you can organize bands at a music camp, as in Ex. 32.

Vocabulary

common factor, p. 177
greatest common
 factor (GCF), p. 177
relatively prime, p. 178

Music Choir A choir director wants to divide a choir into smaller groups. The choir has 24 sopranos, 60 altos, and 36 tenors. Each group will have the same number of each type of voice. What is the greatest number of groups that can be formed? How many sopranos, altos, and tenors will be in each group?

A **common factor** is a whole number that is a factor of two or more nonzero whole numbers. The greatest of the common factors is the **greatest common factor (GCF)**.

Example 1 *Finding the Greatest Common Factor*

For the choir described above, the greatest number of groups that can be formed is given by the GCF of 24, 60, and 36. You can use one of two methods to find the GCF.

Method 1 List the factors of each number. Identify the greatest number that is on every list.

Factors of 24: 1, 2, 3, 4, 6, 8, ⑫, 24
Factors of 60: 1, 2, 3, 4, 5, 6, 10, ⑫, 15, 20, 30, 60
Factors of 36: 1, 2, 3, 4, 6, 9, ⑫, 18, 36

} The common factors are 1, 2, 3, 4, 6, and 12. The GCF is 12.

Method 2 Write the prime factorization of each number. The GCF is the product of the common prime factors.

$$24 = 2 \cdot 2 \cdot 2 \cdot 3$$
$$60 = 2 \cdot 2 \cdot 3 \cdot 5$$
$$36 = 2 \cdot 2 \cdot 3 \cdot 3$$

The common prime factors are 2, 2, and 3. The GCF is the product $2 \cdot 2 \cdot 3 = 12$.

Answer The greatest number of groups that can be formed is 12. Each group will have $24 \div 12 = 2$ sopranos, $60 \div 12 = 5$ altos, and $36 \div 12 = 3$ tenors.

Watch *Out*

In Method 2 of Example 1, the number 2 appears at least twice in the prime factorization of each number. So, include 2 twice when finding the GCF.

✔ *Checkpoint*

Find the greatest common factor of the numbers.

1. 12, 30   **2.** 21, 42   **3.** 16, 32, 40   **4.** 27, 45, 90

Relatively Prime Two or more numbers are **relatively prime** if their greatest common factor is 1.

Note *Worthy*

To clarify the meaning of a vocabulary term like *relatively prime*, include both examples and nonexamples of the term in your notebook.

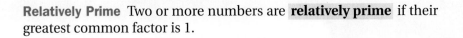

Example 2 *Identifying Relatively Prime Numbers*

Find the greatest common factor of the numbers. Then tell whether the numbers are relatively prime.

a. 24, 45   **b.** 35, 54

Solution

a. List the factors of each number. Identify the greatest number that the lists have in common.

    Factors of 24: 1, 2, ③, 4, 6, 8, 12, 24

    Factors of 45: 1, ③, 5, 9, 15, 45

The GCF is 3. So, the numbers are not relatively prime.

b. Write the prime factorization of each number.

    $35 = 5 \cdot 7$ $54 = 2 \cdot 3 \cdot 3 \cdot 3$

There are no common prime factors. However, two numbers always have 1 as a common factor. So, the GCF is 1, and the numbers are relatively prime.

 Checkpoint

Find the greatest common factor of the numbers. Then tell whether the numbers are relatively prime.

5. 18, 33   **6.** 39, 50   **7.** 110, 77   **8.** 21, 160

9. Critical Thinking Suppose you divide two numbers by their greatest common factor. What is the relationship between the resulting quotients?

Monomials and the GCF You can find the greatest common factor of two or more monomials by factoring each monomial.

Example 3 *Finding the GCF of Monomials*

Find the greatest common factor of $18xy^2$ and $28x^2y^2$.

Factor the monomials. The GCF is the product of the common factors.

$$18xy^2 = 2 \cdot 3 \cdot 3 \cdot x \cdot y \cdot y$$
$$28x^2y^2 = 2 \cdot 2 \cdot 7 \cdot x \cdot x \cdot y \cdot y$$

Answer The GCF is $2xy^2$.

 Checkpoint

Find the greatest common factor of the monomials.

10. $6x, 15x$ **11.** $20x^2, 36x$ **12.** $32y^2, 6x^2y$ **13.** $7xy^3, 28xy^2$

Guided Practice

Vocabulary Check

1. What does it mean for a number to be a common factor of two numbers?

2. Find two pairs of relatively prime numbers from 5, 10, 16, and 25.

Skill Check

Find the greatest common factor of the numbers. Then tell whether the numbers are relatively prime.

3. 7, 28   **4.** 34, 38   **5.** 11, 51   **6.** 32, 81

Find the greatest common factor of the monomials.

7. $18c, 4c$ **8.** r, r^4 **9.** $5m, 20m^3$ **10.** $3x^2, 15x^3$

Guided Problem Solving

11. **Art Supplies** To celebrate a grand opening, the owner of an art supplies store is making free gift bags for customers. The owner has 225 pastel crayons, 75 paintbrushes, and 120 tubes of oil paint. Each gift bag must be identical. What is the greatest number of gift bags the owner can make?

1 Write the prime factorization of each number.

2 What are the common prime factors of the numbers? What is the GCF of the numbers?

3 What does the GCF represent in this situation?

Practice and Problem Solving

Homework *Help*

Example	Exercises
1	12–19, 32–33
2	20–27, 34–36
3	28–31, 37–45

Online Resources
CLASSZONE.COM
• More Examples
• eTutorial Plus

Find the greatest common factor of the numbers.

12. 28, 42   **13.** 21, 99   **14.** 34, 85   **15.** 12, 36

16. 32, 55   **17.** 54, 89   **18.** 76, 86   **19.** 120, 960

Find the greatest common factor of the numbers. Then tell whether the numbers are relatively prime.

20. 9, 26   **21.** 11, 55   **22.** 12, 33   **23.** 77, 51

24. 58, 60   **25.** 121, 280   **26.** 64, 144   **27.** 28, 84

Find the greatest common factor of the monomials.

28. $16x, 36x$ **29.** $18m^2, 7m$ **30.** $18k, 15k^3$ **31.** $2x, 8x^2, 6x^3$

32. Music Camp A summer music camp has 88 participants. The camp has 32 vocalists, 16 drummers, 24 guitarists, and 16 bassists. What is the greatest number of identical bands that can be formed using all the participants? How many vocalists will be in each band?

33. Flower Bouquets The science club is selling flowers for a fundraiser. The club wants to make bouquets from 4 types of flowers. The circle graph shows how many flowers of each type the club has. What is the greatest number of identical bouquets that can be made? What will each bouquet contain?

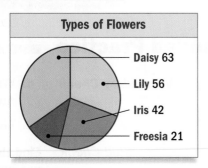

Types of Flowers

Daisy 63
Lily 56
Iris 42
Freesia 21

Review *Help*

For help with reading circle graphs, see p. 783.

Tell whether the numbers are relatively prime.

34. 115, 207   **35.** 224, 243   **36.** 152, 171

Find the greatest common factor of the monomials.

37. $12m^2n^3, 70m^3n$ **38.** $72a^3b^2, 86a$ **39.** $44m^2n, 48mn^2$

40. a^2b^3, ab^3 **41.** $3x, 7xy^2$ **42.** $4rs^2, 27st^3$

43. $18wx^2, 45wx$ **44.** $12y^2, 15y^3, 5y$ **45.** rs^3, s^3t, r^2st^2

46. Community Garden You want to cover the walkway of a community garden with square clay tiles. The space you want to cover is a rectangle 42 inches wide by 72 inches long. Assuming you want to cover the space exactly without cutting any tiles, what is the greatest side length you can use for the tiles?

47. Bracelets You want to make woven plastic bracelets. You have 3 pieces of plastic lacing with lengths 45 cm, 75 cm, and 60 cm. You need to cut the lacing into pieces of the same length. What is the greatest possible length each piece can be, without any lacing being wasted?

48. Critical Thinking The greatest common factor of 30 and a number n is 6. Find a possible value for n. Are there other possible values for n? Explain.

49. Extended Problem Solving In the future, scientists may want to make a unit of time that is convenient for people living on both Earth and Mars. The new unit of time, called the space-hour, should divide evenly into the number of minutes in each planet's day. Under the current Earth definition of minutes, Earth has 1440 minutes per day, and Mars has approximately 1480 minutes per day.

a. Analyze What is the greatest number of minutes that could be in a space-hour?

b. Apply How many space-hours would there be each day on Earth? on Mars?

c. A spacecraft that uses current technology can take 210 days to travel from Earth to Mars. Use a calculator to find how long this trip would be in space-hours.

In the **Real World**

Mars Shown above is an illustration of what a base on Mars might look like. On Mars, there are about 669 solar days in one year. Assuming each day has 1480 minutes, about how many minutes are there in one year on Mars?

50. *Writing* If a and b are nonzero whole numbers and a is a factor of b, what is the GCF of a and b? Explain your thinking and give three numerical examples to support your answer.

51. Critical Thinking If a and b are relatively prime numbers and b and c are relatively prime numbers, are a and c relatively prime numbers? Give examples to support your answer.

52. Challenge Consider the pattern $2x$, $6x^2$, $18x^3$, $54x^4$, ... What are the next two monomials in the pattern? What is the GCF of all the monomials in the pattern? What is the GCF of all the monomials in the pattern excluding the first monomial?

Mixed Review

Find the sum or difference. *(p. 779)*

53. $\frac{2}{9} + \frac{5}{9}$ **54.** $\frac{3}{7} + \frac{3}{7}$ **55.** $\frac{14}{15} - \frac{8}{15}$ **56.** $\frac{11}{20} - \frac{3}{20}$

Find the product. *(p. 780)*

57. $60 \times \frac{3}{10}$ **58.** $28 \times \frac{1}{4}$ **59.** $\frac{5}{12} \times 36$ **60.** $\frac{3}{7} \times 49$

Write the prime factorization of the number. *(Lesson 4.1)*

61. 125   **62.** 70   **63.** 52   **64.** 200

Standardized Test Practice

65. Multiple Choice Which numbers are *not* relatively prime?

    A. 32, 65   **B.** 34, 69   **C.** 63, 91   **D.** 26, 85

66. Short Response You are making first-aid kits to go camping. You have 48 bandages, 15 squares of gauze, 6 tubes of antibiotic ointment, and 6 ice packs. What is the greatest number of identical first-aid kits that you can make? How many of each item will each first-aid kit contain?

Brain GAME

Common Factor Commotion

Each number in the third column of the table is the greatest common factor of the numbers in the same row. Each number in the first two columns has exactly one digit that is different from the number above it and exactly one digit that is different from the number below it.

Copy the table and fill in each of the blanks with a number that satisfies the conditions.

First number	Second number	GCF
945	?	105
?	435	15
648	432	?
?	532	14

Equivalent Fractions

BEFORE	Now	WHY?
You wrote fractions and mixed numbers.	You'll write equivalent fractions.	So you can compare the life stages of butterflies, as in Ex. 48.

Vocabulary

equivalent fractions, p. 182

simplest form, p. 183

A *fraction* is a number of the form $\frac{a}{b}$, where a is the *numerator* and b is the *denominator*. The value of b cannot be 0.

The number lines show the graphs of two fractions, $\frac{1}{3}$ and $\frac{2}{6}$. From the number lines, you can see that these fractions represent the same number. Two fractions that represent the same number are called **equivalent fractions**. You can use the following rule to write equivalent fractions.

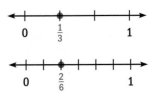

Equivalent Fractions

Words To write equivalent fractions, multiply or divide the numerator and the denominator by the same nonzero number.

Algebra For all numbers a, b, and c, where $b \neq 0$ and $c \neq 0$,

$$\frac{a}{b} = \frac{a \cdot c}{b \cdot c} \text{ and } \frac{a}{b} = \frac{a \div c}{b \div c}.$$

Numbers $\dfrac{1}{3} = \dfrac{1 \cdot 2}{3 \cdot 2} = \dfrac{2}{6}$ $\qquad\qquad$ $\dfrac{2}{6} = \dfrac{2 \div 2}{6 \div 2} = \dfrac{1}{3}$

Study *Strategy*

In Example 1, there are many fractions that are equivalent to $\frac{8}{12}$ because you can multiply the numerator and the denominator by *any* nonzero number.

Example 1   *Writing Equivalent Fractions*

Write two fractions that are equivalent to $\dfrac{8}{12}$.

Multiply or divide the numerator and the denominator by the same nonzero number.

$$\frac{8}{12} = \frac{8 \cdot 3}{12 \cdot 3} = \frac{24}{36} \qquad \textbf{Multiply numerator and denominator by 3.}$$

$$\frac{8}{12} = \frac{8 \div 4}{12 \div 4} = \frac{2}{3} \qquad \textbf{Divide numerator and denominator by 4.}$$

Answer The fractions $\dfrac{24}{36}$ and $\dfrac{2}{3}$ are equivalent to $\dfrac{8}{12}$.

Review *Help*

For help with modeling fractions, see p. 777.

For help with modeling fractions, see p. 777.

 Checkpoint

Write two fractions that are equivalent to the given fraction.

1. $\frac{5}{10}$ **2.** $\frac{6}{9}$ **3.** $\frac{12}{20}$ **4.** $\frac{18}{24}$

Simplest Form A fraction is in **simplest form** when its numerator and its denominator are relatively prime. To write a fraction in simplest form, divide the numerator and the denominator by their GCF.

| **Example 2** | *Writing a Fraction in Simplest Form* |

Write $\frac{12}{30}$ in simplest form.

Write the prime factorizations of the numerator and denominator.

$12 = 2^2 \cdot 3$ $30 = 2 \cdot 3 \cdot 5$

The GCF of 12 and 30 is $2 \cdot 3 = 6$.

$\frac{12}{30} = \frac{12 \div 6}{30 \div 6}$ **Divide numerator and denominator by GCF.**

$= \frac{2}{5}$ **Simplify.**

| **Example 3** | *Simplifying a Fraction* |

Geography The map at the left shows the 48 contiguous states in the United States. (The word *contiguous* means "connected without a break.") Of the 48 contiguous states, 21 are coastal states. These states border the Pacific Ocean, the Atlantic Ocean, or the Gulf of Mexico. Write the fraction, in simplest form, of the contiguous states that are coastal states.

Solution

$\dfrac{\text{Number of coastal states}}{\text{Number of contiguous states}} = \dfrac{21}{48}$ **Write fraction.**

$= \dfrac{21 \div 3}{48 \div 3}$ **Divide numerator and denominator by GCF, 3.**

$= \dfrac{7}{16}$ **Simplify.**

Answer Of the contiguous states, $\frac{7}{16}$ are coastal states.

 Checkpoint

Write the fraction in simplest form.

5. $\frac{4}{14}$ **6.** $\frac{8}{36}$ **7.** $\frac{27}{42}$ **8.** $\frac{28}{49}$

Variable Expressions To simplify fractions that contain variables, factor the numerator and the denominator. Then divide out common factors. In this book, you should assume that any variable in the denominator of a fraction is not equal to zero.

Example 4   *Simplifying a Variable Expression*

Write $\dfrac{10xy}{15y^2}$ in simplest form.

$$\dfrac{10xy}{15y^2} = \dfrac{2 \cdot 5 \cdot x \cdot y}{3 \cdot 5 \cdot y \cdot y}$$ Factor numerator and denominator.

$$= \dfrac{2 \cdot \overset{1}{\cancel{5}} \cdot x \cdot \overset{1}{\cancel{y}}}{3 \cdot \underset{1}{\cancel{5}} \cdot \underset{1}{\cancel{y}} \cdot y}$$ Divide out common factors.

$$= \dfrac{2x}{3y}$$ Simplify.

4.3   Exercises

More Practice, p. 806

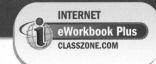

INTERNET
eWorkbook Plus
CLASSZONE.COM

Guided Practice

Vocabulary Check

1. What does it mean for a fraction to be in simplest form?

2. Explain how to find fractions that are equivalent to $\dfrac{3}{7}$.

Write two fractions that are equivalent to the given fraction.

3. $\dfrac{12}{16}$ **4.** $\dfrac{15}{18}$ **5.** $\dfrac{8}{14}$ **6.** $\dfrac{10}{25}$

Write the fraction in simplest form.

7. $\dfrac{16}{38}$ **8.** $\dfrac{35}{40}$ **9.** $\dfrac{21a^3}{11a}$ **10.** $\dfrac{6b}{24b^2}$

Guided Problem Solving

11. Film Ratings The table shows the number of rated films that are owned by a film library. What fraction of the films were rated G?

Rating	G	PG	PG-13
Number of films	30	55	163

1) Find the total number of films owned by the library.

2) Write a fraction for the number of films that were rated G.

3) Simplify the fraction from Step 2.

Practice and Problem Solving

Homework *Help*

Example	Exercises
1	12–19
2	20–27, 41–46
3	28, 37
4	29–36

Online Resources
CLASSZONE.COM
• More Examples
• eTutorial Plus

Write two fractions that are equivalent to the given fraction.

12. $\dfrac{6}{12}$ **13.** $\dfrac{5}{15}$ **14.** $\dfrac{14}{16}$ **15.** $\dfrac{18}{21}$

16. $\dfrac{16}{20}$ **17.** $\dfrac{3}{27}$ **18.** $\dfrac{7}{10}$ **19.** $\dfrac{5}{8}$

Write the fraction in simplest form.

20. $\dfrac{32}{36}$ **21.** $\dfrac{25}{35}$ **22.** $\dfrac{46}{72}$ **23.** $\dfrac{8}{30}$

24. $\dfrac{54}{60}$ **25.** $\dfrac{36}{45}$ **26.** $\dfrac{39}{42}$ **27.** $\dfrac{48}{76}$

28. Anatomy The human skeleton can be divided into two systems. The axial system has 80 bones. It consists of the skull, spine, and ribs. The appendicular system has 126 bones. It consists of the shoulders, pelvis, and limbs.

    a. What fraction of the body's bones are in the axial system? Give your answer in simplest form.

    b. What fraction of the body's bones are in the appendicular system? Give your answer in simplest form.

Write the fraction in simplest form.

29. $\dfrac{6a}{6a^2}$ **30.** $\dfrac{4mn^3}{10n^2}$ **31.** $\dfrac{27bcd}{12b}$ **32.** $\dfrac{5s^2t^2}{40st}$

33. $\dfrac{36w}{60w^2}$ **34.** $\dfrac{42r^3}{56r^2}$ **35.** $\dfrac{77x^3}{6x}$ **36.** $\dfrac{49t^2}{7t^3}$

37. Checkers Checkers is a game for two players. A checkerboard has 64 squares. Each player begins with 12 pieces. Players capture each other's pieces.

    a. What fraction of the squares hold pieces at the start of the game?

    b. Later in the game, one player has 5 pieces on the board. The other player has 3 pieces on the board. Now what fraction of the squares hold pieces?

Use a number line to determine whether the fractions are equivalent.

38. $\dfrac{1}{4}, \dfrac{2}{10}$ **39.** $\dfrac{3}{4}, \dfrac{14}{16}$ **40.** $\dfrac{5}{8}, \dfrac{10}{16}$

Write the fractions in simplest form. Tell whether they are equivalent.

41. $\dfrac{12}{15}, \dfrac{26}{30}$ **42.** $\dfrac{18}{20}, \dfrac{45}{50}$ **43.** $\dfrac{9}{24}, \dfrac{15}{48}$

44. $\dfrac{63}{84}, \dfrac{45}{60}$ **45.** $\dfrac{49}{63}, \dfrac{21}{27}$ **46.** $\dfrac{30}{36}, \dfrac{57}{72}$

47. Critical Thinking Consider the fractions $\dfrac{-12}{27}, \dfrac{25}{-35}$, and $\dfrac{-33}{-55}$. Explain how to simplify each of the fractions.

48. Monarch Butterflies Monarch butterflies go through four stages of life: egg, caterpillar, pupa, and butterfly. A regular monarch lives as a butterfly for about 5 weeks. However, migrating monarchs (born in early fall) live as butterflies for up to 30 weeks.

Length of Monarch's Life Stages in Weeks				
Monarch type	Egg	Caterpillar	Pupa	Butterfly
Regular	1	2	1	5
Migrating	1	2	1	30

a. What fraction of a regular monarch's life is spent as a butterfly?

b. What fraction of a migrating monarch's life is spent as a butterfly?

In the **Real World**

Monarch Butterflies Some monarchs migrate as far as 2000 miles. If a 2000 mile migration were to last for 3.5 months, what is the average distance the monarchs would fly in 1 day? (Assume there are 30 days in a month.)

Tell what value of x makes the fractions equivalent.

49. $\dfrac{5}{6}, \dfrac{x}{24}$ **50.** $\dfrac{7}{9}, \dfrac{28}{x}$ **51.** $\dfrac{x}{12}, \dfrac{80}{192}$ **52.** $\dfrac{3}{8}, \dfrac{2+x}{32}$

53. Critical Thinking Consider the expression $\dfrac{8x^2y}{6x^2y^2}$.

a. First evaluate the expression when $x = 2$ and $y = 3$. Then simplify.

b. Now return to the original expression. First simplify the expression. Then evaluate it when $x = 2$ and $y = 3$.

c. Analyze Compare your results from parts (a) and (b). Which method requires less work? Explain your answer.

d. Analyze Now repeat parts (a) and (b) with the values $x = 3$ and $y = 4$. Compare your results.

54. Challenge Does *adding* the same nonzero number to the numerator and denominator of a fraction produce an equivalent fraction? If so, explain why. If not, tell whether it *ever* produces an equivalent fraction.

Mixed Review   **Evaluate the expression when $x = 4$ and $y = -9$.** *(Lesson 1.4)*

55. $|x| + |y|$ **56.** $|-19| + |y|$ **57.** $x + |-14|$

Identify the property that the statement illustrates. *(Lesson 2.1)*

58. $n + p = p + n$ **59.** $1 \cdot \dfrac{5}{6} = \dfrac{5}{6}$ **60.** $16 + 0 = 16$

Find the greatest common factor of the monomials. *(Lesson 4.2)*

61. $2x, 8x^2$ **62.** $9m^2, 27m^3$ **63.** $10r, 25r^4$

Standardized Test Practice   **64. Multiple Choice** Which fraction is *not* equivalent to $\dfrac{39}{52}$?

A. $\dfrac{36}{48}$ **B.** $\dfrac{3}{4}$ **C.** $\dfrac{78}{104}$ **D.** $\dfrac{31}{42}$

65. Multiple Choice Which fraction is *not* in simplest form?

F. $\dfrac{13}{65}$ **G.** $\dfrac{8}{17}$ **H.** $\dfrac{9}{16}$ **I.** $\dfrac{15}{37}$

4.4

Least Common Multiple

You found the GCF of two numbers.

You'll find the least common multiple of two numbers.

So you can design a fitness schedule, as in Ex. 38.

Vocabulary

multiple, p. 187
common multiple, p. 187
least common multiple (LCM), p. 187
least common denominator (LCD), p. 188

Agriculture Crop rotation is a system in which farmers vary the crops they plant in their fields each year. Suppose a farmer grows alfalfa in a certain field every 6 years. In another field, the farmer grows alfalfa every 10 years. This year, the farmer is growing alfalfa in both fields. In how many years will the farmer grow alfalfa in both fields again?

A **multiple** of a whole number is the product of the number and any nonzero whole number. A multiple that is shared by two or more numbers is a **common multiple**. Some of the common multiples of 8 and 12 are shown in blue below.

Multiples of 8: 8, 16, **24**, 32, 40, **48**, 56, 64, **72**, 80, . . .

Multiples of 12: 12, **24**, 36, **48**, 60, **72**, 84, 96, . . .

The least of the common multiples of two or more numbers is the **least common multiple (LCM)**. The LCM of 8 and 12 is 24.

Example 1 *Finding the Least Common Multiple*

For the crop rotation system described above, the number of years until the farmer grows alfalfa in both fields again is given by the LCM of 6 and 10. You can use one of two methods to find the LCM.

Method 1 List the multiples of each number. Identify the least number that is on both lists.

Multiples of 6: 6, 12, 18, 24, (30), 36, 42, 48, 54, **60**
Multiples of 10: 10, 20, (30), 40, 50, **60**

The LCM of 6 and 10 is 30.

Method 2 Find the common factors of the numbers.

$$6 = 2 \cdot 3$$
$$10 = 2 \cdot 5$$

The common factor is 2.

Multiply all of the factors, using each common factor only once.

$$LCM = 2 \cdot 3 \cdot 5 = 30$$

Answer The farmer will grow alfalfa in both fields again in 30 years.

 Checkpoint

Find the least common multiple of the numbers.

1. 16, 24   **2.** 20, 25   **3.** 6, 8, 20   **4.** 15, 30, 50

Find the least common multiple of $9xy^2$ and $15x^2y$.

$$9xy^2 = \boxed{3} \cdot 3 \cdot \boxed{x} \cdot \boxed{y} \cdot y$$
$$15x^2y = \boxed{3} \cdot 5 \cdot \boxed{x} \cdot x \cdot \boxed{y}$$
$$\text{LCM} = 3 \cdot x \cdot y \cdot 3 \cdot 5 \cdot x \cdot y = 45x^2y^2$$

Common factors are circled and used only once in the LCM.

Answer The least common multiple of $9xy^2$ and $15x^2y$ is $45x^2y^2$.

Study *Strategy*

In Example 2, notice that the LCM of the two monomials includes the higher power of each variable, as well as the higher power of each prime number factor.

Least Common Denominator The **least common denominator (LCD)** of two or more fractions is the least common multiple of the denominators. You can use the LCD to compare and order fractions.

Winter Sports Last year, a winter resort had 144,000 visitors, including 45,000 snowboarders. This year, the resort had 160,000 visitors, including 56,000 snowboarders. In which year was the fraction of snowboarders greater?

Solution

① Write the fractions and simplify.

Last year: $\dfrac{\text{Number of snowboarders}}{\text{Total number of visitors}} = \dfrac{45,000}{144,000} = \dfrac{5}{16}$

This year: $\dfrac{\text{Number of snowboarders}}{\text{Total number of visitors}} = \dfrac{56,000}{160,000} = \dfrac{7}{20}$

② Find the LCD of $\dfrac{5}{16}$ and $\dfrac{7}{20}$.

The LCM of 16 and 20 is 80. So, the LCD of the fractions is 80.

③ Write equivalent fractions using the LCD.

Last year: $\dfrac{5}{16} = \dfrac{5 \cdot 5}{16 \cdot 5} = \dfrac{25}{80}$ **This year:** $\dfrac{7}{20} = \dfrac{7 \cdot 4}{20 \cdot 4} = \dfrac{28}{80}$

④ Compare the numerators: $\dfrac{25}{80} < \dfrac{28}{80}$, so $\dfrac{5}{16} < \dfrac{7}{20}$.

Answer The fraction of snowboarders was greater this year.

✔ *Checkpoint*

Find the least common multiple of the monomials.

5. $15x^2, 27x$ **6.** $6m^2, 10m^3$ **7.** $14ab, 21bc$ **8.** $r^2, 5rst$

Use the LCD to determine which fraction is greater.

9. $\dfrac{5}{6}, \dfrac{7}{9}$ **10.** $\dfrac{5}{8}, \dfrac{13}{20}$ **11.** $\dfrac{7}{12}, \dfrac{11}{15}$ **12.** $\dfrac{5}{16}, \dfrac{3}{10}$

Review *Help*

For help with writing mixed numbers as improper fractions, see p. 778.

| **Example 4** | *Ordering Fractions and Mixed Numbers* |

Order the numbers $3\frac{4}{15}$, $\frac{33}{10}$, **and** $\frac{19}{6}$ **from least to greatest.**

(1) Write the mixed number as an improper fraction.

$$3\frac{4}{15} = \frac{3 \cdot 15 + 4}{15} = \frac{49}{15}$$

(2) Find the LCD of $\frac{49}{15}$, $\frac{33}{10}$, and $\frac{19}{6}$.

The LCM of 15, 10, and 6 is 30. So, the LCD is 30.

(3) Write equivalent fractions using the LCD.

$$\frac{49}{15} = \frac{49 \cdot 2}{15 \cdot 2} = \frac{98}{30} \qquad \frac{33}{10} = \frac{33 \cdot 3}{10 \cdot 3} = \frac{99}{30} \qquad \frac{19}{6} = \frac{19 \cdot 5}{6 \cdot 5} = \frac{95}{30}$$

(4) Compare the numerators.

$$\frac{95}{30} < \frac{98}{30} \text{ and } \frac{98}{30} < \frac{99}{30}, \text{ so } \frac{19}{6} < \frac{49}{15} \text{ and } \frac{49}{15} < \frac{33}{10}.$$

Answer From least to greatest, the numbers are $\frac{19}{6}$, $3\frac{4}{15}$, and $\frac{33}{10}$.

4.4 Exercises

More Practice, p. 806

INTERNET
eWorkbook Plus
CLASSZONE.COM

Guided Practice

Vocabulary Check

1. How are the terms *least common multiple* and *least common denominator* related?

2. Describe how you would use the LCD to compare $\frac{4}{7}$ and $\frac{7}{12}$.

Skill Check

Find the least common multiple of the numbers.

3. 3, 4   **4.** 4, 8   **5.** 18, 24   **6.** 10, 16

Find the least common multiple of the monomials.

7. $3s, s^2$ **8.** x^4, x^2 **9.** $15m^2, 9m$ **10.** $8b, 20b^2$

Use the LCD to determine which fraction is greater.

11. $\frac{3}{4}, \frac{5}{8}$ **12.** $\frac{2}{3}, \frac{13}{16}$ **13.** $\frac{2}{5}, \frac{3}{8}$ **14.** $\frac{3}{4}, \frac{7}{10}$

15. Error Analysis Describe and correct the error in finding the LCM of 16 and 30.

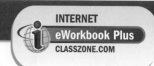

$$16 = 2^4 \qquad 30 = 2 \cdot 3 \cdot 5$$
$$\text{LCM} = 2^5 \cdot 3 \cdot 5 = 480$$

Practice and Problem Solving

Homework *Help*

Example	Exercises
1	16–27, 36, 38
2	28–35
3	39–46
4	47–54

Online Resources
CLASSZONE.COM

- More Examples
- eTutorial Plus

Find the least common multiple of the numbers.

16. 9, 12   **17.** 3, 8   **18.** 4, 16   **19.** 10, 15

20. 21, 14   **21.** 30, 36   **22.** 55, 15   **23.** 42, 66

24. 3, 6, 12   **25.** 8, 11, 36   **26.** 10, 12, 14   **27.** 16, 20, 30

Find the least common multiple of the monomials.

28. $5a^2, 16a^3$ **29.** $21w, 9w^2$ **30.** $17b^2, 3b^3$ **31.** $14x^4, 21x^2$

32. $60s^4, 24s^3$ **33.** $2n^3, 8n^2$ **34.** $25a, 40a^2$ **35.** $11s, 33s^2$

36. Visual Patterns In the first pattern shown below, the green star repeats every 6 figures. In the second pattern, the green star repeats every 8 figures. How many figures after the first figure will both patterns have a green star?

37. *Writing* Could you find the *greatest* common multiple of two numbers? Explain your thinking.

38. Fitness You lift weights every third day and take karate class every Monday. Today you have karate and are lifting weights. In how many days will you next lift weights and have karate on the same day?

Use the LCD to determine which fraction is greater.

39. $\frac{1}{4}, \frac{2}{7}$ **40.** $\frac{2}{3}, \frac{5}{8}$ **41.** $\frac{7}{10}, \frac{11}{15}$ **42.** $\frac{3}{5}, \frac{6}{11}$

43. $\frac{5}{12}, \frac{4}{15}$ **44.** $\frac{7}{20}, \frac{9}{25}$ **45.** $\frac{5}{18}, \frac{8}{21}$ **46.** $\frac{11}{42}, \frac{20}{63}$

Order the numbers from least to greatest.

47. $\frac{7}{6}, \frac{11}{9}, 1\frac{1}{3}$ **48.** $\frac{13}{4}, 3\frac{1}{2}, \frac{27}{8}$ **49.** $\frac{8}{15}, \frac{1}{5}, \frac{3}{10}$ **50.** $\frac{5}{11}, \frac{14}{33}, \frac{9}{22}$

51. $\frac{3}{4}, \frac{4}{9}, \frac{7}{15}$ **52.** $\frac{5}{6}, \frac{7}{10}, \frac{11}{15}$ **53.** $\frac{12}{5}, 2\frac{5}{12}, \frac{43}{18}$ **54.** $1\frac{1}{3}, \frac{10}{7}, 1\frac{13}{33}$

55. Critical Thinking What is the least number for which the LCM of the number and 12 is 300? Explain your thinking.

Find the least common multiple of the monomials.

56. $24de^2, 36d^3e$ **57.** $x^3y, 15xy^5$ **58.** $10a^2b^2, 20ab$ **59.** $45gh^3, 33g^4h$

60. xyz^3, x^2yz^2 **61.** $26ab^2, 28ac^3$ **62.** $11rst, 15r^3t^2$ **63.** $30df^2, 40d^3ef$

64. Vice Presidents During the period 1800–1900, 6 out of 23 U.S. Vice Presidents later became U.S. Presidents. During the period 1901–2000, 7 out of 21 Vice Presidents later became Presidents. During which period did a greater fraction of Vice Presidents become Presidents?

In Exercises 65–68, rewrite the variable expressions with a common denominator.

Example *Rewriting Variable Expressions*

To rewrite $\dfrac{2a}{5b}$ and $\dfrac{3}{4ab^2}$ with a common denominator, first find the LCD of the fractions.

The LCM of $5b$ and $4ab^2$ is $20ab^2$. So, the LCD is $20ab^2$.

Then write equivalent fractions using the LCD.

$$\frac{2a}{5b} = \frac{2a \cdot 4ab}{5b \cdot 4ab} = \frac{8a^2b}{20ab^2} \qquad \frac{3}{4ab^2} = \frac{3 \cdot 5}{4ab^2 \cdot 5} = \frac{15}{20ab^2}$$

65. $\dfrac{x}{3}, \dfrac{x}{4}$ **66.** $\dfrac{x}{6y}, \dfrac{y}{8x}$ **67.** $\dfrac{3x}{4y^2}, \dfrac{2}{5xy}$ **68.** $\dfrac{3x}{2yz}, \dfrac{5y}{4xz}$

69. Critical Thinking Let a and b represent nonzero whole numbers. Find a fraction $\dfrac{a}{b}$ such that $\dfrac{1}{6} < \dfrac{a}{b}$, $\dfrac{a}{b} < \dfrac{2}{7}$, and $b < 30$.

70. Challenge Copy and complete the table for the given values of a and b. Describe any relationships you notice between the product of the LCM and the GCF and the product of a and b.

Given numbers	Prime factorizations	LCM	GCF	LCM · GCF	a · b
$a = 6, b = 18$	?	?	?	?	?
$a = 15, b = 35$	?	?	?	?	?
$a = 6, b = 20$	?	?	?	?	?
$a = 12, b = 60$	?	?	?	?	?

Mixed Review

Evaluate the expression when $n = 5$. *(Lesson 1.2)*

71. n^2 **72.** n^3 **73.** n^4 **74.** n^5

Write the prime factorization of the number. *(Lesson 4.1)*

75. 28 **76.** 39 **77.** 81 **78.** 165

79. Cookies You are making gift boxes filled with cookies to give to friends. You have 64 peanut butter cookies, 80 chocolate chip cookies, and 56 sugar cookies. What is the greatest number of identical gift boxes that you can make? *(Lesson 4.2)*

Standardized Test Practice

80. Multiple Choice Which expression is the least common multiple of the monomials $27w^4z$ and $75w^2z^2$?

A. $3w^2z$ **B.** $75w^4z^2$ **C.** $675w^2z$ **D.** $675w^4z^2$

81. Multiple Choice Which list shows the fractions in order from least to greatest?

F. $\dfrac{2}{9}, \dfrac{1}{6}, \dfrac{4}{25}$ **G.** $\dfrac{3}{7}, \dfrac{11}{24}, \dfrac{9}{21}$ **H.** $\dfrac{7}{20}, \dfrac{3}{8}, \dfrac{5}{12}$ **I.** $\dfrac{2}{5}, \dfrac{19}{40}, \dfrac{21}{45}$

Mid-Chapter Quiz

Tell whether the number is *prime* or *composite*. If it is composite, write its prime factorization using exponents.

1. 46　　　　　　**2.** 57　　　　　　**3.** 61　　　　　　**4.** 89

Factor the monomial.

5. $25m^3$　　　　**6.** $14n^4$　　　　**7.** $19a^2b$　　　　**8.** $64f^2g^2$

Find the greatest common factor of the numbers. Then tell whether the numbers are relatively prime.

9. 9, 16　　　　**10.** 12, 51　　　　**11.** 18, 49　　　　**12.** 56, 75

13. Soccer A soccer league has 180 members. The league consists of 24 eight-year-olds, 96 nine-year-olds, and 60 ten-year-olds. You want to divide the members into teams that have the same number of eight-year-olds, nine-year-olds, and ten-year-olds. What is the greatest number of teams that can be formed? How many ten-year-olds will be on each team?

Write the fraction in simplest form.

14. $\dfrac{18}{48}$　　　**15.** $\dfrac{42}{81}$　　　**16.** $\dfrac{32a}{8a^2}$　　　**17.** $\dfrac{15b}{39b^4}$

Find the least common multiple of the numbers.

18. 4, 11　　　**19.** 10, 24　　　**20.** 15, 45　　　**21.** 30, 54

Use the LCD to determine which fraction is greater.

22. $\dfrac{3}{8}, \dfrac{4}{9}$　　**23.** $\dfrac{7}{10}, \dfrac{18}{25}$　　**24.** $\dfrac{5}{12}, \dfrac{9}{20}$　　**25.** $\dfrac{11}{18}, \dfrac{13}{24}$

Brain GAME

Fraction Scramble

Rearrange the numerators and denominators in the five fractions shown to create five new fractions that are all equivalent to each other. Numerators can become denominators and vice versa. The question mark can be any positive integer.

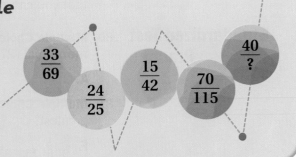

$\dfrac{33}{69}$　$\dfrac{24}{25}$　$\dfrac{15}{42}$　$\dfrac{70}{115}$　$\dfrac{40}{?}$

4.5 Finding Rules of Exponents

Goal

Use patterns to discover rules for multiplying and dividing powers.

Materials
- pencil
- paper

Investigate

Use patterns to discover rules for multiplying and dividing powers.

Copy and complete each table.

Products			
Expression	**Expression written as repeated multiplication**	**Number of factors**	**Product as a power**
$2^4 \cdot 2^3$	$(2 \cdot 2 \cdot 2 \cdot 2) \cdot (2 \cdot 2 \cdot 2)$	7	2^7
$3^1 \cdot 3^4$	$(3) \cdot (3 \cdot 3 \cdot 3 \cdot 3)$	?	$3^?$
$5^2 \cdot 5^4$	?	?	?

Quotients				
Expression	**Expression written as repeated multiplication**	**Simplified expression**	**Number of factors**	**Quotient as a power**
$\dfrac{2^8}{2^3}$	$\dfrac{2 \cdot 2 \cdot 2 \cdot 2 \cdot 2 \cdot \overset{1}{\cancel{2}} \cdot \overset{1}{\cancel{2}} \cdot \overset{1}{\cancel{2}}}{\underset{1}{\cancel{2}} \cdot \underset{1}{\cancel{2}} \cdot \underset{1}{\cancel{2}}}$	$2 \cdot 2 \cdot 2 \cdot 2 \cdot 2$	5	2^5
$\dfrac{3^5}{3^3}$	?	?	?	$3^?$
$\dfrac{5^7}{5^6}$	?	?	?	?

Draw Conclusions

1. **Critical Thinking** In the *Products* table, how are the exponents in the first and last columns related?

2. Use your answer to Exercise 1 to write the product $10^7 \cdot 10^4$ as a power.

3. **Critical Thinking** In the *Quotients* table, how are the exponents in the first and last columns related?

4. Use your answer to Exercise 3 to write the quotient $\dfrac{6^9}{6^7}$ as a power.

4.5 Rules *of* Exponents

BEFORE	Now	WHY?
You evaluated powers.	You'll multiply and divide powers.	So you can estimate the number of stars, as in Ex. 58.

Review Vocabulary

power, p. 10
exponent, p. 10
base, p. 10

Notice what happens when you multiply two powers with the same base.

$$\overbrace{a^4 \cdot a^3}= \underbrace{(\overbrace{a \cdot a \cdot a \cdot a}^{\text{4 factors}}) \cdot (\overbrace{a \cdot a \cdot a}^{\text{3 factors}})}_{\text{7 factors}} = a^{4 + 3} = a^7$$

This example suggests a rule for multiplying powers with the same base.

Product of Powers Property

Words To multiply powers with the same base, add their exponents.

Algebra $a^m \cdot a^n = a^{m + n}$ **Numbers** $4^3 \cdot 4^2 = 4^{3 + 2} = 4^5$

Example 1   *Using the Product of Powers Property*

Lake Powell Lake Powell, the reservoir behind the Glen Canyon Dam in Arizona, can hold about 10^{12} cubic feet of water when full. There are about 10^{27} water molecules in 1 cubic foot of water. About how many water molecules can the reservoir hold?

Solution

Number of water molecules in reservoir	=	Cubic feet of water in reservoir	·	Number of water molecules in a cubic foot

$$= 10^{12} \cdot 10^{27} \quad \textbf{Substitute values.}$$
$$= 10^{12 + 27} \quad \textbf{Product of powers property}$$
$$= 10^{39} \quad \textbf{Add exponents.}$$

Answer Lake Powell can hold about 10^{39} molecules of water.

✔ *Checkpoint*

Find the product. Write your answer using exponents.

1. $2^3 \cdot 2^2$ **2.** $8^7 \cdot 8^5$ **3.** $5 \cdot 5^2$ **4.** $4^6 \cdot 4^4 \cdot 4^3$

Example 2 — Using the Product of Powers Property

a. $x^6 \cdot x^9 = x^{6+9}$ Product of powers property

      $= x^{15}$ Add exponents.

b. $3x \cdot 5x^5 = 3 \cdot 5 \cdot x^1 \cdot x^5$ Commutative property of multiplication

      $= 3 \cdot 5 \cdot x^{1+5}$ Product of powers property

      $= 3 \cdot 5 \cdot x^6$ Add exponents.

      $= 15x^6$ Multiply.

Note *Worthy*

When taking notes about Example 2, be sure to write a verbal description next to each step in the calculation.

Quotients of Powers There is a related rule you can use for dividing powers with the same base. The following example suggests this rule.

$$\frac{a^5}{a^2} = \frac{\overbrace{a \cdot a \cdot a \cdot a \cdot a}^{5 \text{ factors}}}{\underbrace{a \cdot a}_{2 \text{ factors}}} = \frac{a \cdot a \cdot a \cdot \overset{1}{\cancel{a}} \cdot \overset{1}{\cancel{a}}}{\underset{1}{\cancel{a}} \cdot \underset{1}{\cancel{a}}} = \underbrace{a \cdot a \cdot a}_{3 \text{ factors}} = a^{5-2} = a^3$$

Quotient of Powers Property

Words To divide powers with the same base, subtract the exponent of the denominator from the exponent of the numerator.

Algebra $\dfrac{a^m}{a^n} = a^{m-n}$, where $a \neq 0$ **Numbers** $\dfrac{6^8}{6^5} = 6^{8-5} = 6^3$

Example 3 — Using the Quotient of Powers Property

a. $\dfrac{7^6}{7^2} = 7^{6-2}$ Quotient of powers property

      $= 7^4$ Subtract exponents.

b. $\dfrac{4x^8}{10x^2} = \dfrac{4x^{8-2}}{10}$ Quotient of powers property

      $= \dfrac{4x^6}{10}$ Subtract exponents.

      $= \dfrac{2x^6}{5}$ Divide numerator and denominator by 2.

 Checkpoint

Find the product or quotient. Write your answer using exponents.

5. $b^7 \cdot b^2$ **6.** $a \cdot a^5 \cdot a^2$ **7.** $2n^{11} \cdot 6n^8$ **8.** $2m^4 \cdot 7m^5$

9. $\dfrac{6^9}{6^4}$ **10.** $\dfrac{10^{11}}{10^7}$ **11.** $\dfrac{z^8}{z^3}$ **12.** $\dfrac{12n^5}{8n^2}$

Example 4   *Using Both Properties of Powers*

Simplify $\dfrac{3m^5 \cdot m^2}{6m^3}$.

$$\dfrac{3m^5 \cdot m^2}{6m^3} = \dfrac{3m^{5+2}}{6m^3}$$ **Product of powers property**

$$= \dfrac{3m^7}{6m^3}$$ **Add exponents.**

$$= \dfrac{3m^{7-3}}{6}$$ **Quotient of powers property**

$$= \dfrac{3m^4}{6}$$ **Subtract exponents.**

$$= \dfrac{m^4}{2}$$ **Divide numerator and denominator by 3.**

✔ *Checkpoint*

Simplify.

13. $\dfrac{a^4 \cdot 10a^3}{a^2}$ **14.** $\dfrac{13b^4 \cdot b^4}{b}$ **15.** $\dfrac{x \cdot 7x^5}{10x^4}$ **16.** $\dfrac{12y^2 \cdot y^8}{16y^5}$

4.5   Exercises

More Practice, p. 806

INTERNET
eWorkbook Plus
CLASSZONE.COM

Guided Practice

Vocabulary Check

1. Copy and complete: To multiply two powers with the same base, __?__ their exponents.

2. Give an example of an expression you could simplify using the quotient of powers property.

Skill Check   **Find the product or quotient. Write your answer using exponents.**

3. $4^2 \cdot 4^9$ **4.** $5^3 \cdot 5^8$ **5.** $6^7 \cdot 6$ **6.** $7^3 \cdot 7^4 \cdot 7^2$

7. $\dfrac{2^{12}}{2^7}$ **8.** $\dfrac{5^{14}}{5^2}$ **9.** $\dfrac{3^5}{3^2}$ **10.** $\dfrac{10^9}{10^7}$

Simplify.

11. $m^4 \cdot m^3$ **12.** $2x^7 \cdot 5x^2$ **13.** $\dfrac{x^{10}}{x^4}$ **14.** $\dfrac{15y^7}{5y^3}$

15. Error Analysis Describe and correct the error in simplifying $2x^5 \cdot 2x^4$.

$$\times \quad 2x^5 \cdot 2x^4 = 2x^{5+4}$$
$$= 2x^9$$

Practice and Problem Solving

Homework *Help*

Example	Exercises
1	16–19, 36, 37–39
2	24–31, 43–44
3	20–23, 32–35, 40, 42, 45
4	46–57

Online Resources
CLASSZONE.COM
• More Examples
• eTutorial Plus

Find the product or quotient. Write your answer using exponents.

16. $10^6 \cdot 10^7$ **17.** $9^2 \cdot 9^3$ **18.** $11^4 \cdot 11^4$ **19.** $8 \cdot 8^5 \cdot 8^2$

20. $\dfrac{6^3}{6^2}$ **21.** $\dfrac{8^{12}}{8^6}$ **22.** $\dfrac{7^{20}}{7^4}$ **23.** $\dfrac{9^{11}}{9}$

Simplify.

24. $a^4 \cdot a^8$ **25.** $b^9 \cdot b^6$ **26.** $3w^3 \cdot w^2$ **27.** $z^7 \cdot 8z^4$

28. $3n^4 \cdot 6n^9$ **29.** $4r^5 \cdot 2r$ **30.** $x^2 \cdot x^2 \cdot x$ **31.** $z^5 \cdot z^2 \cdot z^7$

32. $\dfrac{x^9}{x^4}$ **33.** $\dfrac{7y^8}{y^5}$ **34.** $\dfrac{24m^{11}}{18m^3}$ **35.** $\dfrac{28s^{15}}{42s^{12}}$

36. The Great Pyramid The Great Pyramid in Egypt is composed of about 2^{21} limestone and granite blocks. The average mass of one of these blocks is about 2^{11} kilograms. Use the product of powers property to approximate the total mass in kilograms of the Great Pyramid.

Copy and complete the statement using <, >, or =.

37. $3^8 \underline{\ ?\ } 3^6 \cdot 3^2$ **38.** $2^7 \underline{\ ?\ } 2 \cdot 2^5$ **39.** $6^5 \underline{\ ?\ } 6^2 \cdot 6^2$

40. Computers Computer memory is measured in bytes. The table shows related units used to measure computer memory.

Number of bytes	10^3	10^6	10^9	10^{12}	10^{15}
Name of unit	Kilobyte	Megabyte	Gigabyte	Terabyte	Petabyte

a. How many kilobytes are in a megabyte?

b. How many gigabytes are in a petabyte?

c. How many megabytes are in a petabyte?

41. *Writing* Explain why the product of powers property cannot be used to simplify $a^7 \cdot b^7$.

Find the missing exponent.

42. $\dfrac{a^?}{a^3} = a^5$ **43.** $y^5 \cdot y^? = y^7$ **44.** $b^? \cdot b^6 = b^7$ **45.** $\dfrac{z^7}{z^?} = z^4$

Simplify.

46. $x^2 \cdot y^4 \cdot x^3$ **47.** $4m^4(n^7 m)$ **48.** $(4ab)(5a^2b^3)$ **49.** $(p^3q^2)(p^4q^2)$

50. $\dfrac{14a^3b^4}{4ab}$ **51.** $\dfrac{63m^5n^6}{27mn}$ **52.** $\dfrac{24w^4z^9}{15w^2z^3}$ **53.** $\dfrac{28c^{10}d^{13}}{24c^6d^8}$

54. $\dfrac{2x^6 \cdot 4x^3}{24x^5}$ **55.** $\dfrac{3a \cdot 4a^4}{28a^2}$ **56.** $\dfrac{6z^9 \cdot 8z^3}{27z^2}$ **57.** $\dfrac{2w^6 \cdot 36w^8}{18w^4}$

58. Astronomy There are over 100 billion stars in our galaxy, the Milky Way. Scientists estimate there are about 100 billion galaxies in the universe. Recall that 1 billion $= 10^9$. If every galaxy has about 100 billion stars, about how many stars are in the universe?

In the **Real World**

Astronomy The galaxy shown below, called M33, is a spiral galaxy like our own Milky Way galaxy. The Milky Way and M33 are about 2.3 million light-years apart. What is this distance in kilometers? Use the fact that 1 light-year is approximately equal to 10 trillion kilometers.

59. Logical Reasoning Consider the equation $\dfrac{5^m}{5^n} = 5$.

    a. Rewrite the left side of the equation using the quotient of powers property.

    b. Find a pair of integers m and n for which the equation is true.

    c. Are there other pairs of integers m and n for which the equation is true? Explain your reasoning.

60. Write $2 \cdot 2^n$ as a power of 2.

61. Critical Thinking Write three products of powers that are equal to 2^6. Then write three quotients of powers that are equal to 2^6.

62. Simplify the expression $\dfrac{a^{m+n}}{a^n}$.

63. Challenge Find a value of n that makes $3^{4n} \cdot 3^{n+4} = 3^{14}$ a true statement. Explain how you found your answer.

Mixed Review

Find the sum or difference. *(Lessons 1.5, 1.6)*

64. $-14 + 98$ **65.** $26 + (-19)$ **66.** $-89 - 23$ **67.** $78 - (-34)$

Find the greatest common factor. *(Lesson 4.2)*

68. $44x^3, 24x^2$ **69.** $21xy, 25x^2$ **70.** $42x^3y, 70xy^2$ **71.** $100x^3, 75y^3$

Find the least common multiple. *(Lesson 4.4)*

72. $6x^2, 12xy^3$ **73.** $3y, 5x^2y^2$ **74.** $4x^3, 7xy^2$ **75.** $9x^2y^3, 8xy$

Standardized Test Practice

76. Multiple Choice Which expression is equivalent to $\dfrac{24m^{18}}{36m^6}$?

   A. $\dfrac{24m^3}{36}$ **B.** $\dfrac{2m^6}{3}$ **C.** $\dfrac{24}{36m^{12}}$ **D.** $\dfrac{2m^{12}}{3}$

77. Multiple Choice Which expression is equivalent to $36x^3 \cdot 9x^2$?

   F. $4x$ **G.** $4x^5$ **H.** $324x$ **I.** $324x^5$

Brain GAME

Ones' Digit Wonder

For powers of 3, the digits in the ones' place follow a certain pattern. What is the pattern? What is the digit in the ones' place for 3^{100}?

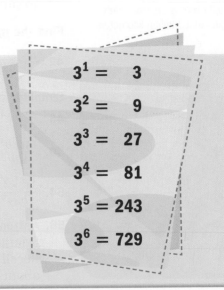

$3^1 = 3$

$3^2 = 9$

$3^3 = 27$

$3^4 = 81$

$3^5 = 243$

$3^6 = 729$

Negative *and* Zero Exponents

BEFORE | *Now* | **WHY?**

You worked with positive exponents. | You'll work with negative and zero exponents. | So you can compare nanoseconds to milliseconds, as in Ex. 15.

Review Vocabulary
power, p. 10
exponent, p. 10
base, p. 10

Consider the following pattern of powers of 2.

$$2^3 = 8$$
$$2^2 = 4$$
$$2^1 = 2$$
$$2^0 = ?$$
$$2^{-1} = ?$$
$$2^{-2} = ?$$

As exponents decrease by 1 . . .   the values of the powers are halved.

By extending the pattern, you can conclude that $2^0 = 1$, $2^{-1} = \frac{1}{2}$, and $2^{-2} = \frac{1}{4}$. Because $\frac{1}{2} = \frac{1}{2^1}$ and $\frac{1}{4} = \frac{1}{2^2}$, the pattern suggests the following definitions for negative and zero exponents.

Negative and Zero Exponents

For any nonzero number a, $a^0 = 1$.

For any nonzero number a and any integer n, $a^{-n} = \frac{1}{a^n}$.

Reading *Algebra*

In an expression like $16x^{-6}y$, the exponent is associated only with the variable that comes directly before it, not with the coefficient of the variable.

Example 1   *Powers with Negative and Zero Exponents*

Write the expression using only positive exponents.

a. $3^{-5} = \dfrac{1}{3^5}$ Definition of negative exponent

b. $m^0 n^{-4} = 1 \cdot n^{-4}$ Definition of zero exponent

$\phantom{m^0 n^{-4}} = \dfrac{1}{n^4}$ Definition of negative exponent

c. $16x^{-6}y = \dfrac{16y}{x^6}$ Definition of negative exponent

✔ **Checkpoint**

Write the expression using only positive exponents.

1. 5^{-2} **2.** $1{,}000{,}000^0$ **3.** $3y^{-2}$ **4.** $a^{-7}b^3$

Rewriting Fractions You can use the prime factorization of a number to write a fraction as an expression involving negative exponents.

Example 2 **Rewriting Fractions**

Write the expression without using a fraction bar.

a. $\dfrac{1}{16}$

b. $\dfrac{a^2}{c^3}$

Solution

a. $\dfrac{1}{16} = \dfrac{1}{2^4}$ Write prime factorization of 16.

$\phantom{\dfrac{1}{16}} = 2^{-4}$ Definition of negative exponent

b. $\dfrac{a^2}{c^3} = a^2 c^{-3}$ Definition of negative exponent

---

Products and Quotients of Powers You can use the product of powers property and the quotient of powers property to find products and quotients that involve negative exponents.

Example 3 *Using Powers Properties with Negative Exponents*

Find the product or quotient. Write your answer using only positive exponents.

a. $5^{10} \cdot 5^{-6}$

b. $\dfrac{8n^{-3}}{n^2}$

Solution

a. $5^{10} \cdot 5^{-6} = 5^{10 + (-6)}$ Product of powers property

$\phantom{5^{10} \cdot 5^{-6}} = 5^4$ Add exponents.

b. $\dfrac{8n^{-3}}{n^2} = 8n^{-3-2}$ Quotient of powers property

$\phantom{\dfrac{8n^{-3}}{n^2}} = 8n^{-5}$ Subtract exponents.

$\phantom{\dfrac{8n^{-3}}{n^2}} = \dfrac{8}{n^5}$ Definition of negative exponent

---

 Checkpoint

Write the expression without using a fraction bar.

5. $\dfrac{1}{25}$

6. $\dfrac{1}{1000}$

7. $\dfrac{2}{a^8}$

8. $\dfrac{x^7}{z^2}$

Find the product or quotient. Write your answer using only positive exponents.

9. $3^{-7} \cdot 3^{11}$

10. $5^{-8} \cdot 5^{-7}$

11. $m^{-3} \cdot m^{-1}$

12. $a^{-2} \cdot a^{10}$

13. $\dfrac{2^{-3}}{2^4}$

14. $\dfrac{7^2}{7^{-8}}$

15. $\dfrac{5k^3}{k^{-9}}$

16. $\dfrac{b^{-4}}{b^{-6}}$

Example 4 | *Solving Problems Involving Negative Exponents*

Geckos Geckos can easily climb smooth vertical surfaces. Biologists have discovered that tiny hairs are the reason that the feet of a gecko are so sticky. Each hair is about 100 micrometers long. A micrometer is 10^{-6} meter. What is the length of one hair in meters?

Solution

To find the length of one hair in meters, multiply the length of the hair in micrometers by the number of micrometers in one meter.

$$100 \cdot 10^{-6} = 10^2 \cdot 10^{-6} \qquad \text{Rewrite 100 as } 10^2.$$
$$= 10^{2 + (-6)} \qquad \text{Product of powers property}$$
$$= 10^{-4} \qquad \text{Add exponents.}$$
$$= \frac{1}{10^4} \qquad \text{Definition of negative exponent}$$
$$= \frac{1}{10,000} \qquad \text{Evaluate power.}$$

Answer The length of one hair is about $\frac{1}{10,000}$ meter.

4.6 Exercises

More Practice, p. 806

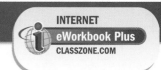

INTERNET
eWorkbook Plus
CLASSZONE.COM

Guided Practice

Vocabulary Check

1. Write 7^{-2} using a positive exponent.

2. If a is nonzero, does the value of a^0 depend of the value of a? Explain.

Skill Check **Write the expression using only positive exponents.**

3. 5^{-3} **4.** 3^{-5} **5.** $4a^{-6}$ **6.** $b^{-3}c^0$

Write the expression without using a fraction bar.

7. $\frac{1}{27}$ **8.** $\frac{1}{10^8}$ **9.** $\frac{4}{x^3}$ **10.** $\frac{11}{c^5}$

Find the product. Write your answer using only positive exponents.

11. $6^{-4} \cdot 6^7$ **12.** $3^{-2} \cdot 3^{-8}$ **13.** $x^{11} \cdot x^{-3}$ **14.** $z^{-5} \cdot z^{-1}$

Guided Problem Solving

15. How many nanoseconds are in a millisecond?

   ① Write the quotient of the duration of a millisecond and the duration of a nanosecond.

   ② Use the quotient of powers property to simplify the quotient in Step 1.

Name of unit	Duration
Millisecond	10^{-3} sec
Microsecond	10^{-6} sec
Nanosecond	10^{-9} sec

Practice and Problem Solving

Homework *Help*

Example	Exercises
1	16–23
2	24–31
3	32–39, 43–50
4	40, 55

ⓘ Online Resources
CLASSZONE.COM

• More Examples
• eTutorial Plus

Write the expression using only positive exponents.

16. 13^{-6} **17.** 121^0 **18.** 8^{-9} **19.** 20^{-4}

20. xy^0 **21.** $18f^{-1}$ **22.** $6g^{-5}$ **23.** c^3d^{-1}

Write the expression without using a fraction bar.

24. $\dfrac{1}{25}$ **25.** $\dfrac{1}{19}$ **26.** $\dfrac{1}{10,000}$ **27.** $\dfrac{1}{64}$

28. $\dfrac{8}{c^5}$ **29.** $\dfrac{4}{d}$ **30.** $\dfrac{4y}{x^3}$ **31.** $\dfrac{9a^2}{b^6}$

Find the product. Write your answer using only positive exponents.

32. $3^4 \cdot 3^{-7}$ **33.** $5 \cdot 5^{-5}$ **34.** $10^{-2} \cdot 10^{-8}$ **35.** $13^0 \cdot 13^6$

36. $2s^{-5} \cdot s^3$ **37.** $5t^{-3} \cdot 3t^{-8}$ **38.** $4a^0 \cdot 7a^{-4}$ **39.** $b^{-5} \cdot b^{-9}$

40. Historical Documents Scientists have discovered that nanoparticles of a substance called slaked lime can help preserve historical documents. The diameters of these nanoparticles are less than $\dfrac{1}{100,000,000,000}$ meter. Write this number using a negative exponent.

41. Critical Thinking Explain how 6^{-2} is different from 6^2.

42. *Writing* Explain why the rule $a^{-n} = \dfrac{1}{a^n}$ does not apply to $a = 0$.

Find the quotient. Write your answer using only positive exponents.

43. $\dfrac{2^5}{2^8}$ **44.** $\dfrac{4^{-2}}{4^6}$ **45.** $\dfrac{16^{-9}}{16^{-8}}$ **46.** $\dfrac{15^3}{15^{-4}}$

47. $\dfrac{17a^3}{a^7}$ **48.** $\dfrac{15b^{-5}}{3b^4}$ **49.** $\dfrac{26w^{-4}}{13w^{-12}}$ **50.** $\dfrac{11g^2}{g^{-4}}$

▦ Use a calculator to evaluate the expression. If necessary, round the result to the nearest thousandth.

51. $(4.5)^{-3}$ **52.** $(8.1)^{-2}$ **53.** $(3.2)^{-4}$ **54.** $(7.5)^{-3}$

55. Brittle Stars The brittle star is a type of starfish. A certain species of brittle star has a skeleton that is covered in microscopic crystals. Scientists have discovered that these crystals act as lenses that allow the brittle star to sense light.

a. The surface of each crystal has an area of $\dfrac{1}{1,000,000,000}$ square meter. Write this number using a negative exponent.

b. Approximately 10^4 crystals cover the skeleton of a brittle star. What is the total area of all the crystals on a single brittle star? Write your answer using a negative exponent.

Find the quotient. Write your answer using only positive exponents.

56. $\dfrac{a^6b^4}{a^3b^7}$ **57.** $\dfrac{c^2d^{11}}{c^8d^5}$ **58.** $\dfrac{m^8n^4}{m^2n^9}$ **59.** $\dfrac{x^2y}{x^{10}y^7}$

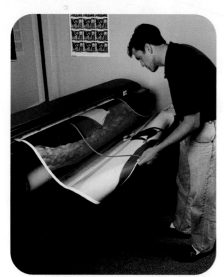

This printer can print pages several feet wide.

60. Extended Problem Solving Inkjet printers spray droplets of ink onto paper. The volume of a single droplet is about 10 picoliters. Some printers spray as many as 10^6 droplets to completely cover a square inch of paper.

a. Find the volume of ink in picoliters needed to completely cover a square inch of paper.

b. There are 10^{12} picoliters in a liter. Find the volume of ink in liters needed to completely cover a square inch of paper.

c. Estimate Find the area of a 8.5 inch by 11 inch piece of paper and round this number to the nearest power of 10. Then estimate the volume of ink (in liters) needed to completely cover an entire piece of paper.

d. Apply Suppose an inkjet cartridge contains 60 milliliters of ink. About how many pages can this cartridge print if each page is 8.5 inches by 11 inches and is covered completely in ink?

61. Challenge One way to develop the definitions of zero and negative exponents is to use the quotient of powers property.

a. Consider $\dfrac{a^n}{a^n}$. First, simplify using the quotient of powers property.

b. Then simplify the expression in part (a) in a different way: Write the numerator and denominator as a product of a's and divide out common factors. Which definition of exponents have you developed?

c. Now consider $\dfrac{a^0}{a^n}$. First, simplify using the quotient of powers property.

d. Then simplify the expression in part (c) by using the definition of a zero exponent. Which definition of exponents have you developed?

Mixed Review

Algebra Basics **Solve the equation using mental math.** *(Lesson 2.4)*

62. $9 + x = 17$ **63.** $8 - x = 3$ **64.** $-3x = 36$ **65.** $\dfrac{x}{-8} = 6$

66. Amusement Parks You must be at least 46 inches tall to ride the bumper cars at an amusement park. Write and graph an inequality to show the heights for which you can ride the bumper cars. *(Lesson 3.4)*

Find the product or quotient. Write your answer using exponents. *(Lesson 4.5)*

67. $3^2 \cdot 3^2$ **68.** $5^4 \cdot 5$ **69.** $\dfrac{2^9}{2^4}$ **70.** $\dfrac{10^8}{10^5}$

Standardized Test Practice

71. Multiple Choice Which expression is *not* equivalent to $x^2 \cdot x^{-6}$?

A. x^{-4} **B.** $x^{-2} \cdot x^6$ **C.** $\dfrac{1}{x^4}$ **D.** $\dfrac{x^2}{x^6}$

72. Multiple Choice Which expression is equivalent to $\dfrac{24a^6}{3b^2}$?

F. $24a^{-6}b^2$ **G.** $24a^6b^{-2}$ **H.** $8a^6b^{-2}$ **I.** $8a^{-6}b^2$

Scientific Notation

BEFORE ▶ *Now* WHY?

You used properties of exponents.

You'll write numbers using scientific notation.

So you can calculate how much a whale eats, as in Ex. 53.

Vocabulary

scientific notation, p. 204

Anatomy The retina is a layer of the eyeball that contains rods and cones. Rods and cones are cells that absorb light and change it to electric signals that are sent to the brain. The human retina is about 0.00012 meter thick and contains about 120,000,000 rods and about 6,000,000 cones.

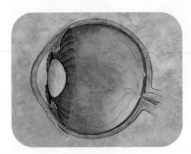

You can use *scientific notation* to write these numbers. Scientific notation is a shorthand way of writing numbers using powers of 10.

Reading *Algebra*

The inequality $1 \le c < 10$ is read as "1 is less than or equal to c, and c is less than 10."

Using Scientific Notation

A number is written in **scientific notation** if it has the form $c \times 10^n$ where $1 \le c < 10$ and n is an integer.

Standard form	Product form	Scientific notation
725,000	$7.25 \times 100,000$	7.25×10^5
0.006	6×0.001	6×10^{-3}

Example 1 | *Writing Numbers in Scientific Notation*

a. The retina has 120,000,000 rods. Write this number in scientific notation.

Standard form	Product form	Scientific notation
120,000,000	$1.2 \times 100,000,000$	1.2×10^8
Move decimal point 8 places to the left.		Exponent is 8.

b. The thickness of the human retina is 0.00012 meter. Write this number in scientific notation.

Standard form	Product form	Scientific notation
0.00012	1.2×0.0001	1.2×10^{-4}
Move decimal point 4 places to the right.		Exponent is −4.

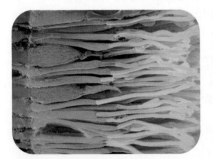

Color-enhanced image of rods and cones in the human retina

Reading *Algebra*

For a positive number written in scientific notation, a positive exponent means the number is greater than 1, and a negative exponent means the number is between 0 and 1.

Example 2 | **Writing Numbers in Standard Form**

a. Write 3.2×10^7 in standard form.

Scientific notation	**Product form**	**Standard form**
3.2×10^7	$3.2 \times 10{,}000{,}000$	32,000,000
Exponent is 7.		Move decimal point 7 places to the right.

b. Write 8.69×10^{-5} in standard form.

Scientific notation	**Product form**	**Standard form**
8.69×10^{-5}	8.69×0.00001	0.0000869
Exponent is −5.		Move decimal point 5 places to the left.

✔ *Checkpoint*

Write the number in scientific notation.

1. 4100   **2.** 0.000067   **3.** 34,600,000   **4.** 0.0000145

Write the number in standard form.

5. 7.1×10^4 **6.** 1.93×10^{-3} **7.** 3.641×10^{-6} **8.** 5.59×10^8

Comparing Numbers To compare numbers written in scientific notation, first compare the powers of 10, then compare the decimal parts.

Example 3 | **Ordering Numbers Using Scientific Notation**

Order 3.9×10^6, 3,800,000, and 4.2×10^5 from least to greatest.

1 Write each number in scientific notation if necessary.

$$3{,}800{,}000 = 3.8 \times 10^6$$

2 Order the numbers with different powers of 10.

Because $10^5 < 10^6$, $4.2 \times 10^5 < 3.9 \times 10^6$ and $4.2 \times 10^5 < 3.8 \times 10^6$.

3 Order the numbers with the same power of 10.

Because $3.8 < 3.9$, $3.8 \times 10^6 < 3.9 \times 10^6$.

4 Write the original numbers in order from least to greatest.

$$4.2 \times 10^5; \; 3{,}800{,}000; \; 3.9 \times 10^6$$

✔ *Checkpoint*

Order the numbers from least to greatest.

9. 2.4×10^5; 3.3×10^4; 49,000   **10.** 8.16×10^6; 635,000; 4.08×10^5

11. 0.00017; 1.9×10^{-4}; 2.8×10^{-3} **12.** 7.8×10^{-3}; 7.9×10^{-3}; 0.00056

Example 4 **Multiplying Numbers in Scientific Notation**

Plants A wolffia plant is the smallest flowering plant in the world. One wolffia plant has a mass of about 1.5×10^{-4} gram. At least 5×10^3 wolffia plants could fit in a thimble. What is the mass of 5×10^3 wolffia plants?

Solution

Total mass	=	Mass of one plant	$\times$	Number of plants

$$= (1.5 \times 10^{-4})(5 \times 10^3)$$ Substitute values.

$$= (1.5 \times 5) \times (10^{-4} \times 10^3)$$ Commutative and associative properties of multiplication

$$= 7.5 \times (10^{-4} \times 10^3)$$ Multiply 1.5 and 5.

$$= 7.5 \times 10^{-4+3}$$ Product of powers property

$$= 7.5 \times 10^{-1}$$ Add exponents.

Answer The mass of 5×10^3 wolffia plants is 7.5×10^{-1} gram, or 0.75 gram.

This thimble is filled with wolffia plants.

4.7 Exercises

More Practice, p. 806

INTERNET
eWorkbook Plus
CLASSZONE.COM

Guided Practice

Vocabulary Check

1. Give an example of a number that is between 0 and 1 and is written in scientific notation.

2. Explain why 12.5×10^7 is *not* written in scientific notation.

Skill Check **Write the number in scientific notation.**

3. 9,180,000   **4.** 0.000062   **5.** 723,000   **6.** 0.00000002

Write the number in standard form.

7. 2.78×10^7 **8.** 5.67×10^{-3} **9.** 4.15×10^{-5} **10.** 1.96×10^5

11. Bicycle Chain Scientists have made a tiny bicycle chain out of silicon links that are thinner than a human hair. The centers of the links are 0.00005 meter apart. Write this distance in scientific notation.

12. Error Analysis Describe and correct the error in comparing 6.5×10^3 and 6.4×10^4.

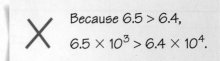
Because $6.5 > 6.4$,
$6.5 \times 10^3 > 6.4 \times 10^4$.

Practice and Problem Solving

Homework *Help*

Example	Exercises
1	13–21, 31–33, 39
2	22–30, 34–36
3	40–43, 48–51
4	44–47, 52

Online Resources
CLASSZONE.COM
• More Examples
• eTutorial Plus

Write the number in scientific notation.

13. 46,200,000   **14.** 9,750,000   **15.** 1700

16. 8,910,000,000   **17.** 104,000   **18.** 0.00000062

19. 0.000023   **20.** 0.00095   **21.** 0.0000106

Write the number in standard form.

22. 4.18×10^4 **23.** 5.617×10^6 **24.** 7.894×10^8

25. 3.8×10^{-9} **26.** 9.83×10^{-2} **27.** 6×10^{-7}

28. 1.03×10^{-5} **29.** 2.28×10^9 **30.** 8.391×10^4

In Exercises 31–33, write the number in scientific notation.

31. Population of Asia in 2001: 3,721,000,000

32. Distance (in meters) to the star Vega: 239,000,000,000,000,000

33. Time (in seconds) required for light to travel 1 meter: 0.000000000334

In Exercises 34–36, write the number in standard form.

34. Distance (in centimeters) that the North Pacific plate slides along the San Andreas fault in 1 hour: 5.71×10^{-4}

35. Diameter (in meters) of a xylem cell in a redwood tree: 3.0×10^{-5}

36. Cruising speed (in miles per hour) of a supersonic jet: 1.336×10^3

37. Critical Thinking Your friend thinks that 4×10^3 is twice as great as 2×10^2. What error is your friend making? Explain your reasoning.

38. *Writing* When a number between 0 and 1 is written in scientific notation, what can you say about the exponent? When a number greater than 1 is written in scientific notation, what can you say about the exponent?

39. Dust Mites Dust mites are microscopic organisms that can be found in most natural and synthetic fibers. Dust mites are 0.00042 meter in length and 0.00028 meter in width. An average mattress contains 2,000,000 dust mites. Write these numbers in scientific notation.

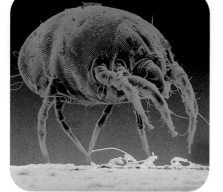

Color-enhanced image of a dust mite

Copy and complete the statement using <, >, or =.

40. 3.21×10^3 ? 321,000   **41.** 91,600 ? 9.61×10^4

42. 2.3×10^{-6} ? 1.3×10^{-2} **43.** 0.00875 ? 8.75×10^{-4}

Find the product. Write your answer in scientific notation.

44. $(2.5 \times 10^4)(3 \times 10^2)$ **45.** $(6 \times 10^7)(9 \times 10^5)$

46. $(5 \times 10^{-3})(7.5 \times 10^8)$ **47.** $(8.5 \times 10^{-2})(7 \times 10^{-7})$

Order the numbers from least to greatest.

48. 2.6×10^4; 3500; 9.2×10^4 **49.** 8700; 1.97×10^3; 3.98×10^4

50. 9.1×10^{-4}; 5.2×10^{-2}; 0.0013   **51.** 7.61×10^{-3}; 0.00009 ; 8.4×10^{-6}

Enlarged image of the pits and lands on a compact disc

52. Compact Discs The information stored on a compact disc is encoded in a series of pits. The spaces between the pits are called lands. Each land is about 0.000003 meter long, and the average pit length is 0.0000022 meter.

   a. Write each of these lengths in scientific notation. Then write the combined length of a pit and a land in scientific notation.

   b. Suppose a compact disc contains 2,000,000,000 pits and 2,000,000,000 lands. How long would this series of pits and lands be if laid out in a straight line? Give your answer in scientific notation.

53. Extended Problem Solving Plankton are microscopic organisms that drift in water. A right whale feeds by swimming through masses of plankton with its mouth open. Answer the following questions using scientific notation.

   a. Analyze When a right whale feeds, about 2.3 cubic meters of water pass through its mouth each second. Right whales feed in areas with about 9000 plankton per cubic meter. How many plankton does a right whale ingest each second?

   b. How many plankton does a right whale ingest in 1 hour of feeding?

   c. A right whale may feed for up to 15 hours a day. Use a calculator to find how many plankton a right whale ingests in a day.

   d. Estimate Suppose a right whale consumes 500,000 Calories per day. About how many calories does a single plankton contain?

54. Challenge Let n be any positive integer. Consider the expressions $n \times 10^{n+1}$ and $(n+1) \times 10^n$.

   a. Make a table of values for each expression when $n = 1, 2, 3,$ and 4.

   b. Is the value of $n \times 10^{n+1}$ *always, sometimes,* or *never* greater than the value of $(n+1) \times 10^n$? Explain.

Mixed Review

Order the integers from least to greatest. *(Lesson 1.4)*

55. $-16, 13, 11, -17$ **56.** $-23, 24, -27, 25$ **57.** $-119, 99, -114, -98$

Algebra Basics Solve the equation. *(Lesson 2.7)*

58. $x + 3.6 = -10.8$ **59.** $y - 9.5 = 11.2$ **60.** $2.5m = -5.1$

Solve the inequality. Graph and check your solution. *(Lesson 3.6)*

61. $3x - 7 > 8$ **62.** $-4y + 16 < 36$ **63.** $2 - 5x > 27$

Standardized Test Practice

64. Extended Response The table shows the 2001 populations of several countries.

   a. Which country has the greatest population?

   b. Which country has the least population?

   c. How many times greater is the population of the country in part (a) than the population of the country in part (b)? Explain.

Country	Population
China	1.273×10^9
Fiji	844,000
Iceland	2.78×10^5
Russia	142,300,000

4.7 Using Scientific Notation

Goal Use a scientific calculator to perform operations on numbers written in scientific notation.

Example

Use a calculator to solve the following problem.

Scientists have discovered over 100 exoplanets (planets outside of our solar system). One of these exoplanets orbits the star Epsilon Eridani. The mass of this exoplanet is about 2.3×10^{27} kilograms. The star and the exoplanet are about 10.5 light-years from the Sun.

How many times more massive is the exoplanet than Earth, which has a mass of 6×10^{24} kilograms? Given that 1 light-year is equal to 9.5×10^{12} kilometers, what is the distance (in kilometers) from the Sun to the exoplanet?

Solution

1 To find how many times more massive the exoplanet is than Earth, divide the mass of the exoplanet by the mass of Earth.

Keystrokes

2.3 **EE** 27 **÷** 6 **EE** 24 **=**

The exoplanet is about 383 times more massive than Earth.

2 To find the distance (in kilometers) of the exoplanet from the Sun, multiply the distance in light-years by the number of kilometers in a light-year.

Keystrokes

9.5 **EE** 12 **×** 10.5 **=**

The exoplanet is about 9.98×10^{13} kilometers from the Sun.

Tech *Help*

Use the exponent key **EE** on a calculator to enter numbers written in scientific notation.

Draw Conclusions

Use a calculator to find the product or quotient.

1. $(6.13 \times 10^{17}) \times (8.92 \times 10^{-11})$ **2.** $(4.09 \times 10^{-9}) \div (5.31 \times 10^{23})$

3. Tau Boo The star Tau Boo has an exoplanet that is about 2.5×10^3 times as massive as Earth. What is the mass (in kilograms) of the Tau Boo exoplanet?

CHAPTER 4

Chapter Review

Vocabulary Review

prime number, p. 173
composite number, p. 173
prime factorization, p. 173
factor tree, p. 173
monomial, p. 174

common factor, p. 177
greatest common factor
  (GCF), p. 177
relatively prime, p. 178
equivalent fractions, p. 182

simplest form, p. 183
multiple, p. 187
common multiple, p. 187
least common multiple
  (LCM), p. 187

least common denominator
  (LCD), p. 188
scientific notation, p. 204

1. Give an example of a prime number and an example of a composite number.

2. What does it mean for two nonzero whole numbers to be relatively prime?

3. Write two equivalent fractions and explain why they are equivalent.

4. Is the number 0.32×10^{-4} written in scientific notation? Why or why not?

4.1 Factors and Prime Factorization

Examples on pp. 172–174

▶ **Goal**

Factor numbers and monomials.

Example Write the prime factorization of 240.

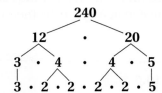

240   Write original number.

12 · 20   Write 240 as 12 · 20.

3 · 4 · 4 · 5   Write 12 as 3 · 4 and 20 as 4 · 5.

3 · 2 · 2 · 2 · 2 · 5   Write 4 as 2 · 2, twice.

The prime factorization of 240 is $2^4 \cdot 3 \cdot 5$.

Example Factor the monomial $42x^4y$.

$$42x^4y = 2 \cdot 3 \cdot 7 \cdot x^4 \cdot y \qquad \text{Write 42 as 2 · 3 · 7.}$$

$$= 2 \cdot 3 \cdot 7 \cdot x \cdot x \cdot x \cdot x \cdot y \qquad \text{Write } x^4 \text{ as } x \cdot x \cdot x \cdot x.$$

✔ **Write the prime factorization of the number.**

5. 75   **6.** 104   **7.** 129   **8.** 138

Factor the monomial.

9. $36a^4b^3$ **10.** $98x^3y^2$ **11.** $72w^6z$ **12.** $15r^2s^2$

4.2 Greatest Common Factor

Examples on pp. 177–178

▶ **Goal**

Find the GCF of numbers and monomials.

Example Find the greatest common factor of 45, 18, and 90.

Write the prime factorization of each number.

$$45 = 3 \cdot 3 \cdot 5$$
$$18 = 2 \cdot 3 \cdot 3$$
$$90 = 2 \cdot 3 \cdot 3 \cdot 5$$

The common prime factors are 3 and 3. The GCF is the product $3 \cdot 3 = 9$.

✔ **Find the greatest common factor of the numbers.**

13. 26, 74 **14.** 32, 64 **15.** 12, 40, 68 **16.** 15, 42, 63

4.3 Equivalent Fractions

Examples on pp. 182–184

▶ **Goal**

Write fractions in simplest form.

Example Write $\frac{60}{75}$ in simplest form.

Write the prime factorization of the numerator and the denominator.

$$60 = 2^2 \cdot 3 \cdot 5 \qquad\qquad 75 = 3 \cdot 5 \cdot 5$$

The GCF of 60 and 75 is $3 \cdot 5 = 15$.

$$\frac{60}{75} = \frac{60 \div 15}{75 \div 15} \qquad \text{Divide numerator and denominator by GCF.}$$

$$= \frac{4}{5} \qquad \text{Simplify.}$$

Example Write $\frac{21a^2}{49ab}$ in simplest form.

$$\frac{21a^2}{49ab} = \frac{3 \cdot 7 \cdot a \cdot a}{7 \cdot 7 \cdot a \cdot b} \qquad \text{Factor numerator and denominator.}$$

$$= \frac{3 \cdot \overset{1}{\cancel{7}} \cdot \overset{1}{\cancel{a}} \cdot a}{7 \cdot \underset{1}{\cancel{7}} \cdot \underset{1}{\cancel{a}} \cdot b} \qquad \text{Divide out common factors.}$$

$$= \frac{3a}{7b} \qquad \text{Simplify.}$$

✔ **Write the fraction in simplest form.**

17. $\frac{4}{18}$ **18.** $\frac{12}{21}$ **19.** $\frac{17}{68}$ **20.** $\frac{30}{72}$

21. $\frac{6ab}{4b^2}$ **22.** $\frac{5cd}{2d}$ **23.** $\frac{8xy}{2x^2y}$ **24.** $\frac{22m^2n}{11mn^2}$

4.4 Least Common Multiple

Examples on pp. 187–189

▶ *Goal*

Use the LCD to compare fractions.

Example Use the LCD to compare $\frac{5}{36}$ and $\frac{17}{90}$.

① Find the least common multiple of the denominators.

$$36 = 2 \cdot 2 \cdot 3 \cdot 3$$
$$90 = 2 \cdot 3 \cdot 3 \cdot 5$$

The common factors are 2, 3, and 3.

Multiply all of the factors, using the common factors only once.

LCM = $2 \cdot 3 \cdot 3 \cdot 2 \cdot 5 = 180$, so the LCD = 180.

② Write equivalent fractions using the LCD.

$$\frac{5}{36} = \frac{5 \cdot 5}{36 \cdot 5} = \frac{25}{180} \qquad \frac{17}{90} = \frac{17 \cdot 2}{90 \cdot 2} = \frac{34}{180}$$

③ Compare the numerators: $\frac{25}{180} < \frac{34}{180}$, so $\frac{5}{36} < \frac{17}{90}$.

✔ Use the LCD to determine which fraction is greater.

25. $\frac{1}{12}, \frac{3}{40}$ **26.** $\frac{4}{15}, \frac{7}{27}$ **27.** $\frac{7}{30}, \frac{11}{36}$ **28.** $\frac{4}{45}, \frac{13}{60}$

29. Soccer You and your friend are on different soccer teams. This season, your team won 14 out of 20 games. Your friend's team won 18 out of 24 games. Which team won a greater fraction of its games?

4.5 Rules of Exponents

Examples on pp. 194–196

▶ *Goal*

Use rules of exponents to simplify products and quotients.

Example Find the product. Write your answer using exponents.

a. $5^8 \cdot 5^6 = 5^{8+6}$ Product of powers property

$= 5^{14}$ Add exponents.

b. $7a^2 \cdot a^6 = 7 \cdot (a^2 \cdot a^6)$ Associative property of multiplication

$= 7 \cdot a^{2+6}$ Product of powers property

$= 7a^8$ Add exponents.

✔ Find the product. Write your answer using exponents.

30. $2^{11} \cdot 2^3$ **31.** $3^5 \cdot 3^7$ **32.** $7^8 \cdot 7^9$ **33.** $10^4 \cdot 10^4$

34. $16b^4 \cdot b^2$ **35.** $c^9 \cdot 8c^2$ **36.** $5x \cdot 4x^9$ **37.** $y^4 \cdot y^3 \cdot y^2$

4.6 Negative and Zero Exponents

Examples on pp. 199–201

▶ **Goal**

Rewrite expressions containing negative or zero exponents.

Example Write $8^0 b^{-5}$ using only positive exponents.

$$8^0 b^{-5} = 1 \cdot b^{-5} \qquad \text{Definition of zero exponent}$$

$$= \frac{1}{b^5} \qquad \text{Definition of negative exponent}$$

✔ **Write the expression using only positive exponents.**

38. 12^{-4} **39.** 6^0 **40.** $7c^{-3}$ **41.** $15d^{-9}$

4.7 Scientific Notation

Examples on pp. 204–206

▶ **Goal**

Write numbers in scientific notation.

Example Write the number in scientific notation.

	Standard form	Product form	Scientific notation
a.	41,800,000	$4.18 \times 10,000,000$	4.18×10^7
b.	0.0000037	3.7×0.000001	3.7×10^{-6}

Example Order 4.7×10^{-5}, 0.000056, and 3.2×10^{-6} from least to greatest.

① Write each number in scientific notation if necessary.

$$0.000056 = 5.6 \times 10^{-5}$$

② Order the numbers with different powers of 10.

Because $10^{-6} < 10^{-5}$, $3.2 \times 10^{-6} < 4.7 \times 10^{-5}$ and $3.2 \times 10^{-6} < 5.6 \times 10^{-5}$.

③ Then order the numbers with the same power of 10.

Because $4.7 < 5.6$, $4.7 \times 10^{-5} < 5.6 \times 10^{-5}$.

④ Write the original numbers in order from least to greatest.

$$3.2 \times 10^{-6}; \ 4.7 \times 10^{-5}; \ 0.000056$$

✔ **Write the number in scientific notation.**

42. 0.000000745   **43.** 67,000,000   **44.** 0.000000881   **45.** 4,280,000,000

Copy and complete the statement using <, >, or =.

46. 4.8×10^{-5} ___?___ 4.8×10^{-8} **47.** 1.08×10^6 ___?___ 1.09×10^7

Chapter Test

Write the prime factorization of the number.

1. 27   **2.** 60   **3.** 84   **4.** 260

Find the greatest common factor of the numbers. Then tell whether they are relatively prime.

5. 25, 75   **6.** 30, 49   **7.** 32, 90   **8.** 42, 108

Write the fraction in simplest form.

9. $\dfrac{27}{90}$ **10.** $\dfrac{46}{60}$ **11.** $\dfrac{8xy}{16y}$ **12.** $\dfrac{12a^2}{2ab}$

Use the LCD to determine which fraction is greater.

13. $\dfrac{3}{5}, \dfrac{8}{15}$ **14.** $\dfrac{11}{12}, \dfrac{11}{20}$ **15.** $\dfrac{3}{35}, \dfrac{7}{45}$ **16.** $\dfrac{29}{50}, \dfrac{61}{100}$

17. Basketball The table shows the points you scored and the total points your team scored for each game in the season playoff.

Game	You	Your team
1	12	42
2	19	57
3	15	65
4	4	52
5	16	60

    a. For each game, write the fraction of your team's points that you scored. Give your answers in simplest form.

    b. In which game did you score the greatest fraction of points?

Find the product or quotient. Write your answer using exponents.

18. $13^6 \cdot 13^4$ **19.** $4m^7 \cdot 5m^6$ **20.** $\dfrac{7^6}{7^9}$ **21.** $\dfrac{4w^{15}}{24w^3}$

Write the expression using only positive exponents.

22. 15^{-4} **23.** $16h^{-7}$ **24.** $12x^0$ **25.** $m^{-4}n^5$

Write the number in scientific notation.

26. 5,100,000,000   **27.** 6,450,000,000,000   **28.** 0.00000000897   **29.** 0.00000093

Copy and complete the statement using <, >, or =.

30. $9.0 \times 10^{17} \underline{\ ?\ } 5.2 \times 10^{18}$ **31.** $7.31 \times 10^{-2} \underline{\ ?\ } 7.31 \times 10^{-3}$

32. $1.25 \times 10^{-9} \underline{\ ?\ } 1.05 \times 10^{-9}$ **33.** $8.12 \times 10^5 \underline{\ ?\ } 8.18 \times 10^4$

Chapter Standardized Test

Test-Taking Strategy Be sure to completely read the question and all answer choices before choosing an answer.

1. Which number is *not* prime?

   A. 7   **B.** 37   **C.** 53   **D.** 57

2. Which expression is the prime factorization of 168?

   F. $2^2 \cdot 3^2 \cdot 7$ **G.** $2 \cdot 3 \cdot 7^2$

   H. $2^3 \cdot 3 \cdot 7$ **I.** $2^3 \cdot 3 \cdot 7^2$

3. What is the greatest common factor of $14x^2$ and $38x^3$?

   A. $2x^3$ **B.** $2x^2$ **C.** $266x^3$ **D.** $532x^2$

4. Which numbers are relatively prime?

   F. 25, 36   **G.** 12, 20

   H. 24, 28   **I.** 45, 84

5. Which fraction is *not* in simplest form?

   A. $\frac{1}{2}$ **B.** $\frac{21}{32}$ **C.** $\frac{35}{54}$ **D.** $\frac{54}{72}$

6. In a florist's window, 30 of 36 plants are flowering. Write the fraction of flowering plants in simplest form.

   F. $\frac{5}{6}$ **G.** $\frac{10}{12}$ **H.** $\frac{15}{18}$ **I.** $\frac{30}{36}$

7. What is the LCM of 16 and 80?

   A. 8   **B.** 80   **C.** 160   **D.** 320

8. Which fraction is greater than $\frac{17}{60}$?

   F. $\frac{4}{15}$ **G.** $\frac{7}{30}$ **H.** $\frac{19}{45}$ **I.** $\frac{29}{120}$

9. Which expression is equivalent to $8x^4 \cdot 5x^3$?

   A. $20x^7$ **B.** $40x^7$ **C.** $20x^{12}$ **D.** $40x^{12}$

10. Which expression is equivalent to $\frac{15b^9}{25b^3}$?

    F. $\frac{3b^3}{5}$ **G.** $\frac{3}{5b^3}$ **H.** $\frac{3b^6}{5}$ **I.** $\frac{3}{5b^6}$

11. Which expression is *not* equivalent to $\frac{1}{64}$?

    A. 2^{-6} **B.** 4^{-4} **C.** 8^{-2} **D.** 64^{-1}

12. Which expression is equivalent to $3^{-4}x^0$?

    F. $\frac{1}{81}$ **G.** 3^4 **H.** $\frac{1}{81x}$ **I.** $\frac{x}{81}$

13. Which list of numbers is in order from least to greatest?

    A. 1.4×10^6, 3.28×10^3, 6.3×10^2, 8.2×10^3

    B. 6.3×10^2, 8.2×10^3, 3.28×10^3, 1.4×10^6

    C. 1.4×10^6, 6.3×10^2, 3.28×10^3, 8.2×10^3

    D. 6.3×10^2, 3.28×10^3, 8.2×10^3, 1.4×10^6

14. **Short Response** A certain type of bacteria has been found in lengths 0.000018 meter, 7.5×10^{-6} meter, and 2.5×10^{-6} meter. Order these lengths from least to greatest.

15. **Extended Response** You have a wooden board that measures 54 centimeters by 90 centimeters. You want to cut the board into identical square pieces with integer side lengths and use all of the wood.

    a. Make a sketch of the board. Find three possible side lengths for the squares.

    b. What is the largest side length you can choose? Explain.

    c. How many square pieces will you have?

Rational Numbers *and* Equations

How can you compare bison populations?

CHAPTER 5

INTERNET Preview

CLASSZONE.COM

- eEdition Plus Online
- eWorkbook Plus Online
- eTutorial Plus Online
- State Test Practice
- More Examples

M A T H *In the* **Real World**

Bison To monitor bison populations, biologists make yearly counts of the adult bison and calves in a herd. In this chapter, you will use fractions to work with quantities like animal populations.

What do you think? Suppose that in one year there were 6 calves and 32 adult bison in a herd of bison. The next year there were 9 calves and 36 adult bison in the herd. In which year was the fraction of calves in the herd greater?

Chapter Prerequisite Skills

PREREQUISITE SKILLS QUIZ

Review Vocabulary

equation, p. 85
inequality, p. 138
least common multiple (LCM),
  p. 187
least common denominator
  (LCD), p. 188

Preparing for Success **To prepare for success in this chapter, test your knowledge of these concepts and skills. You may want to look at the pages referred to in blue for additional review.**

1. **Vocabulary** Describe how to find the least common denominator of two fractions.

Solve the equation. Check your solution. *(p. 97)*

2. $4q = 48$　　　3. $-9p = 81$　　　4. $\dfrac{n}{4} = 8$　　　5. $\dfrac{m}{-5} = 3$

Solve the inequality. Graph your solution. *(p. 144)*

6. $3s > -27$　　　7. $-7r > 49$　　　8. $\dfrac{x}{-4} \le -6$　　　9. $\dfrac{y}{3} < -12$

Use the LCD to determine which fraction is greater. *(p. 187)*

10. $\dfrac{3}{4}, \dfrac{7}{9}$　　　11. $\dfrac{2}{7}, \dfrac{3}{5}$　　　12. $\dfrac{7}{8}, \dfrac{5}{6}$　　　13. $\dfrac{13}{15}, \dfrac{11}{18}$

Simplify. *(p. 194)*

14. $\dfrac{18x^2}{24x}$　　　15. $\dfrac{16a^3}{22a}$　　　16. $\dfrac{15z^3}{63z}$　　　17. $\dfrac{27m^4}{45m^2}$

NOTETAKING STRATEGIES

Note *Worthy*

You will find a notetaking strategy at the beginning of each chapter. Look for additional notetaking and study strategies throughout the chapter.

USING YOUR HOMEWORK When you are doing your homework and come to an exercise you don't understand, write a question for your teacher. Ask the question the next time you have class.

Write the prime factorization of 324.

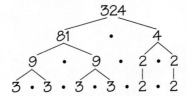

324

Does it matter in what order I write the factors? Ask in class tomorrow.

The prime factorization is $3^4 \cdot 2^2$.

As you do your homework in Chapter 5, write down questions you have about performing operations on fractions and mixed numbers.

5.1

Rational Numbers

BEFORE

You wrote decimals and fractions.

Now

You'll write fractions as decimals and vice versa.

WHY?

So you can assess a recycling plan, as in Ex. 45.

Vocabulary

rational number, p. 219
terminating decimal, p. 219
repeating decimal, p. 219

A **rational number** is a number that can be written as a quotient of two integers. Whole numbers and integers are part of the set of rational numbers, as shown in the Venn diagram.

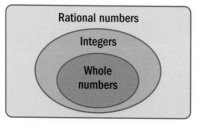

Rational numbers

Integers

Whole numbers

Example 1 *Identifying Rational Numbers*

Show that the number is rational by writing it as a quotient of two integers.

  a. 7 　　**b.** -10 　　**c.** $5\frac{3}{4}$ 　　**d.** $-3\frac{1}{2}$

Solution

  a. Write the integer 7 as $\frac{7}{1}$.

  b. Write the integer -10 as $\frac{-10}{1}$ or $\frac{10}{-1}$. These fractions are equivalent.

  c. Write the mixed number $5\frac{3}{4}$ as the improper fraction $\frac{23}{4}$.

  d. Think of $-3\frac{1}{2}$ as the opposite of $3\frac{1}{2}$. First write $3\frac{1}{2}$ as $\frac{7}{2}$. Then you can write $-3\frac{1}{2}$ as $-\frac{7}{2}$. To write $-\frac{7}{2}$ as a quotient of two integers, you can assign the negative sign to either the numerator or the denominator. You can write $\frac{-7}{2}$ or $\frac{7}{-2}$.

Review *Help*

For help with writing mixed numbers as improper fractions, see p. 778.

Terminating and Repeating Decimals If you take a rational number in the form $\frac{a}{b}$ and carry out the division of a by b, the quotient will be either a *terminating decimal* or a *repeating decimal*. In a **terminating decimal**, the division ends because you obtain a final remainder of zero. In a **repeating decimal**, a digit or block of digits in the quotient repeats without end. Example 2 on page 220 shows how to write both a terminating decimal and a repeating decimal.

When you use a bar to show which digit or digits repeat in a decimal, be sure to put the bar over only the repeating digits. For example,

$$0.45555\ldots = 0.4\overline{5}$$
$$3.26767\ldots = 3.2\overline{67}$$

Example 2	*Writing Fractions as Decimals*

a. Write $\frac{3}{8}$ as a decimal.   **b.** Write $\frac{5}{11}$ as a decimal.

a.
```
   0.375
8)3.000
   24
   ──
   60
   56
   ──
   40
   40
   ──
    0
```

b.
```
    0.4545...
11)5.0000
   44
   ──
   60
   55
   ──
   50
   44
   ──
   60
   55
```

Answer The remainder is 0, so the decimal is a terminating decimal: $\frac{3}{8} = 0.375$.

Answer Use a bar to show the repeating digits in the repeating decimal: $\frac{5}{11} = 0.\overline{45}$.

✔ **Checkpoint**

Write the fraction or mixed number as a decimal.

1. $\frac{3}{10}$ **2.** $-\frac{2}{3}$ **3.** $1\frac{9}{20}$ **4.** $\frac{29}{80}$

In the **Real World**

Biology The yellow-bellied marmot belongs to the order Rodentia. Yellow-bellied marmots typically live at elevations from 6500 feet to 13,500 feet. Find the difference of these two elevations.

Example 3	*Using Decimals to Compare Fractions*

Biology Of the 50 mammal species found in Canyonlands National Park, 20 species belong to the order Rodentia. Of the 54 mammal species found in Badlands National Park, 24 belong to Rodentia. In which park is the fraction of mammal species belonging to Rodentia greater?

Solution

① Write a fraction for each park. Then write each fraction as a decimal by dividing the numerator by the denominator.

Canyonlands National Park	$\dfrac{\text{Rodentia species}}{\text{Mammal species}} = \dfrac{20}{50}$	Write fraction.
	$= 0.4$	Divide.
Badlands National Park	$\dfrac{\text{Rodentia species}}{\text{Mammal species}} = \dfrac{24}{54}$	Write fraction.
	$= 0.444\ldots$	Divide.
	$= 0.\overline{4}$	Repeating digit

② Compare the decimals. By writing 0.4 as 0.400, you can see that 0.444... is greater than 0.400. So $0.\overline{4} > 0.4$, and $\frac{24}{54} > \frac{20}{50}$.

Answer The fraction in Badlands National Park is greater.

Writing Decimals as Fractions To write a terminating decimal as a fraction or a mixed number, use the place of the last digit to determine the denominator of the fraction, as shown in Example 4. Example 5 shows a method for writing a repeating decimal as a fraction.

Note *Worthy*

In your notebook, you may want to include a list of common fraction-decimal equivalents. You can refer to the list when solving problems, or you may want to memorize the list. Here are some examples you might include:

$\frac{1}{2} = 0.5, \frac{1}{3} = 0.\overline{3},$

$\frac{1}{4} = 0.25, \frac{1}{8} = 0.125$

Example 4   *Writing Terminating Decimals as Fractions*

a. $0.7 = \frac{7}{10}$ 7 is in tenths' place, so denominator is 10.

b. $-3.05 = -3\frac{5}{100}$ 5 is in hundredths' place, so denominator is 100.

        $= -3\frac{1}{20}$ Simplify fraction.

Example 5   *Writing a Repeating Decimal as a Fraction*

To write $0.\overline{93}$ as a fraction, let $x = 0.\overline{93}$.

1) Because $0.\overline{93}$ has 2 repeating digits, multiply each side of $x = 0.\overline{93}$ by 10^2, or 100. Then $100x = 93.\overline{93}$.

2) Subtract x from $100x$.

$$\begin{array}{r} 100x = 93.\overline{93} \\ -\ (x = 0.\overline{93}) \\ \hline 99x = 93 \end{array}$$

3) Solve for x and simplify. $\frac{99x}{99} = \frac{93}{99}$

                         $x = \frac{31}{33}$

Answer The decimal $0.\overline{93}$ is equivalent to the fraction $\frac{31}{33}$.

✔ *Checkpoint*

5. Critical Thinking Compare writing 0.3 as a fraction with writing $0.\overline{3}$ as a fraction.

Example 6   *Ordering Rational Numbers*

Order the numbers $-\frac{5}{4}$, -0.2, 4.31, -3, $\frac{5}{2}$, $-\frac{13}{3}$ from least to greatest.

Graph the numbers on a number line. You may want to write improper fractions as mixed numbers.

Study *Strategy*

Another Way To order the numbers in Example 6, you can instead write the fractions as decimals. Then order the decimals.

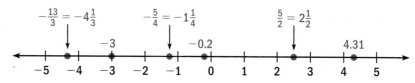

Read the numbers from left to right: $-\frac{13}{3}$, -3, $-\frac{5}{4}$, -0.2, $\frac{5}{2}$, 4.31.

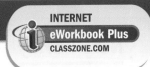

INTERNET
eWorkbook Plus
CLASSZONE.COM

Guided Practice

Vocabulary Check   **Tell whether the number is a *terminating decimal* or a *repeating decimal*.**

1. 0.667   **2.** 0.4747. . .   **3.** 35.35   **4.** $2.4\overline{3}$

5. How can you tell whether a number is a rational number?

Skill Check   **Show that the number is rational by writing it as a quotient of two integers.**

6. 15   **7.** -2 **8.** $5\frac{4}{7}$ **9.** $-1\frac{1}{3}$

Write the fraction or mixed number as a decimal.

10. $\frac{2}{9}$ **11.** $1\frac{4}{5}$ **12.** $-\frac{13}{15}$ **13.** $-9\frac{5}{8}$

Write the decimal as a fraction or mixed number.

14. 0.4   **15.** 0.324   **16.** $0.\overline{78}$ **17.** $2.\overline{6}$

18. Swim Teams Of the 20 students on the girls' swim team, 9 are seniors. Of the 24 students on the boys' swim team, 10 are seniors. On which team is the fraction of students who are seniors greater?

19. Error Analysis Describe and correct the error in writing the repeating decimal 5.07878. . . using a bar.

$5.07878\ldots = 5.\overline{078}$

Practice and Problem Solving

Homework *Help*

Example	Exercises
1	20–27
2	28–35
3	44–45
4	36–43
5	49–56
6	45, 57–60

Online Resources
CLASSZONE.COM
• More Examples
• eTutorial Plus

Show that the number is rational by writing it as a quotient of two integers.

20. 24   **21.** -29 **22.** $5\frac{7}{18}$ **23.** $-\frac{1}{8}$

24. 1   **25.** $-2\frac{3}{7}$ **26.** 0.3   **27.** 0.87

Write the fraction or mixed number as a decimal.

28. $\frac{1}{5}$ **29.** $-\frac{7}{8}$ **30.** $-\frac{5}{3}$ **31.** $\frac{19}{6}$

32. $3\frac{4}{25}$ **33.** $-\frac{13}{11}$ **34.** $8\frac{5}{44}$ **35.** $-13\frac{7}{10}$

Write the decimal as a fraction or mixed number.

36. 0.54   **37.** 0.63   **38.** 7.6   **39.** 2.093

40. -0.85 **41.** 0.019   **42.** -5.895 **43.** -1.102

44. Leaves You and a friend are collecting leaves. In your collection of 45 leaves, 4 are oak leaves. In your friend's collection of 36 leaves, 3 are oak leaves. Whose collection has a greater fraction of oak leaves?

45. Recycling The table shows monthly amounts of trash and recycled trash at a school.

Month	Total trash (lb)	Recycled trash (lb)
Nov.	350	112
Dec.	315	119
Jan.	270	189
Feb.	330	234
Mar.	300	214

  a. For each month, find the fraction of trash that was recycled.

  b. **Compare** Use a calculator to write the fractions in part (a) as decimals. Order the decimals from least to greatest. In which month was the fraction of trash that was recycled the greatest?

  c. *Writing* As of January 1, a new recycling plan was introduced at the school. What effect do you think the plan had on recycling efforts in January and the months that followed? Explain.

Copy and complete the statement using *always*, *sometimes*, or *never*.

46. An integer is _?_ a rational number.

47. A fraction can _?_ be written as a terminating decimal.

48. A repeating decimal is _?_ a rational number.

Write the decimal as a fraction or mixed number.

49. $0.\overline{8}$ **50.** $0.\overline{7}$ **51.** $-0.\overline{4}$ **52.** $-9.\overline{6}$

53. $0.\overline{12}$ **54.** $-1.\overline{36}$ **55.** $0.8\overline{97}$ **56.** $2.\overline{707}$

Order the numbers from least to greatest.

57. $-2, \dfrac{7}{8}, 0.8, 2.1, 1\dfrac{1}{3}$ **58.** $0.7, -1, -\dfrac{5}{4}, \dfrac{4}{3}, -2.3, -\dfrac{9}{2}$

59. $0.21, 2.3, \dfrac{8}{3}, -0.1, -\dfrac{1}{5}, 0.\overline{2}$ **60.** $0.3, 0.\overline{3}, 0.\overline{30}, -0.3, -0.\overline{3}$

61. Extended Problem Solving The table shows the number of at bats and hits that players on a softball team had in three games.

Player	Game 1		Game 2		Game 3	
Maria	4 at bats	2 hits	5 at bats	2 hits	4 at bats	1 hit
Laura	4 at bats	1 hit	5 at bats	1 hit	4 at bats	1 hit
Jenny	4 at bats	3 hits	4 at bats	2 hits	4 at bats	1 hit

  a. Find the total number of at bats and the total number of hits for each player for the three games.

  b. **Analyze** A player's batting average is the total number of hits divided by the total number of at bats. The batting average is usually expressed as a decimal rounded to the nearest thousandth. Find each player's batting average for the three games.

  c. **Apply** Rank the players based on batting averages. Explain.

62. Measurement You have a rope that is $4\frac{1}{3}$ feet long. Your friend has a rope that is $1\frac{1}{2}$ yards long. Who has the longer rope?

63.  **Critical Thinking** Try using a calculator to find a decimal value for $\frac{1}{17}$. What do you notice? Then use long division to write $\frac{1}{17}$ as a terminating or repeating decimal. Explain the calculator result you obtained.

64. Critical Thinking Let a and b represent nonzero integers. Find a rational number in the form $\frac{a}{b}$ so that $-1.7 < \frac{a}{b}$ and $\frac{a}{b} < -\frac{5}{3}$. Explain how you found the number.

65. Challenge Write the decimal $0.3\overline{21}$ as a fraction.

Mixed Review

Simplify the expression. (Lesson 2.3)

66. $k - 9 - (2 + k)$ **67.** $m + 5 - 2(m + 7)$

Find the least common multiple of the numbers. (Lesson 4.4)

68. $240, 340$ **69.** $18, 60$ **70.** $55, 77$ **71.** $27, 189$

72. Chemistry A common number used for calculations in chemistry is Avogadro's number, which is approximately equal to 6.02×10^{23}. Write this number in standard form. (Lesson 4.7)

Standardized Test Practice

73. Multiple Choice Which number is *not* equivalent to $\frac{40}{66}$?

A. $\frac{20}{33}$ **B.** $\frac{60}{99}$ **C.** $0.\overline{6}$ **D.** $0.\overline{60}$

74. Multiple Choice Which number is greater than -1.5?

F. $-1.\overline{5}$ **G.** $-\frac{3}{2}$ **H.** $-1.\overline{45}$ **I.** $-\frac{7}{2}$

75. Short Response Write $0.\overline{475}$ as a fraction. Describe the steps you take to write the fraction.

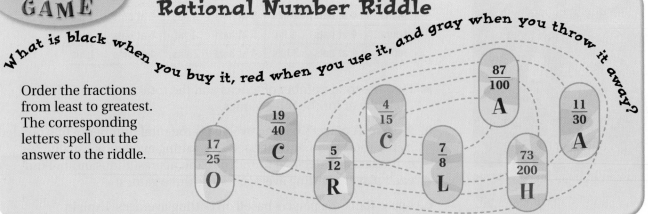

Brain GAME

Rational Number Riddle

What is black when you buy it, red when you use it, and gray when you throw it away?

Order the fractions from least to greatest. The corresponding letters spell out the answer to the riddle.

$\frac{17}{25}$ **O** $\frac{19}{40}$ **C** $\frac{5}{12}$ **R** $\frac{4}{15}$ **C** $\frac{7}{8}$ **L** $\frac{87}{100}$ **A** $\frac{73}{200}$ **H** $\frac{11}{30}$ **A**

5.2

Adding *and* Subtracting Like Fractions

Review Vocabulary
variable expression,
p. 5

BEFORE	Now	WHY?
You added and subtracted decimals.	You'll add and subtract like fractions.	So you can analyze a lobster's growth, as in Ex. 52.

Astronomy One night, $\frac{77}{100}$ of the moon's visible surface is illuminated. The next night, an additional $\frac{9}{100}$ is illuminated. What fraction of the moon's visible surface is illuminated on the second night?

Adding and Subtracting Like Fractions

Words To add or subtract fractions with the same denominator, write the sum or difference of the numerators over the denominator.

Numbers $\frac{4}{9} + \frac{1}{9} = \frac{5}{9}$ $\qquad$ $\frac{9}{11} - \frac{2}{11} = \frac{7}{11}$

Algebra $\frac{a}{c} + \frac{b}{c} = \frac{a+b}{c}, c \neq 0$ $\qquad$ $\frac{a}{c} - \frac{b}{c} = \frac{a-b}{c}, c \neq 0$

Review *Help*

For help with adding and subtracting fractions, see p. 779.

Example 1 *Adding Like Fractions*

To find the fraction of the moon's visible surface that is illuminated on the second night, as described above, find the sum of $\frac{77}{100}$ and $\frac{9}{100}$.

$$\frac{77}{100} + \frac{9}{100} = \frac{77 + 9}{100}$$ **Write sum of numerators over denominator.**

$$= \frac{86}{100} = \frac{43}{50}$$ **Add. Then simplify.**

Answer On the second night, $\frac{43}{50}$ of the visible surface is illuminated.

Study *Strategy*

When you perform operations with negative fractions, be sure to assign a negative sign in front of a fraction to the numerator of the fraction. For instance, in part (a) of Example 2, $-\dfrac{4}{7}$ is written as $\dfrac{-4}{7}$.

Example 2   *Subtracting Like Fractions*

a. $-\dfrac{4}{7} - \dfrac{2}{7} = \dfrac{-4-2}{7}$ Write difference of numerators over denominator.

$\qquad = \dfrac{-6}{7} = -\dfrac{6}{7}$ Subtract.

b. $\dfrac{1}{10} - \left(-\dfrac{3}{10}\right) = \dfrac{1}{10} + \dfrac{3}{10}$ To subtract $-\dfrac{3}{10}$, add $\dfrac{3}{10}$.

$\qquad = \dfrac{1+3}{10}$ Write sum of numerators over denominator.

$\qquad = \dfrac{4}{10} = \dfrac{2}{5}$ Add. Then simplify.

✔ **Checkpoint**

Find the sum or difference.

1. $\dfrac{3}{8} + \dfrac{2}{8}$ **2.** $-\dfrac{1}{6} + \dfrac{5}{6}$ **3.** $\dfrac{2}{15} - \dfrac{7}{15}$ **4.** $\dfrac{1}{12} - \left(-\dfrac{7}{12}\right)$

Mixed Numbers To add or subtract mixed numbers, you can first write the mixed numbers as improper fractions.

Example 3   *Adding and Subtracting Mixed Numbers*

a. $5\dfrac{5}{9} + 2\dfrac{7}{9} = \dfrac{50}{9} + \dfrac{25}{9}$ Write mixed numbers as improper fractions.

$\qquad = \dfrac{50 + 25}{9}$ Write sum of numerators over denominator.

$\qquad = \dfrac{75}{9}$ Add.

$\qquad = \dfrac{25}{3} = 8\dfrac{1}{3}$ Simplify. Then write fraction as a mixed number.

b. $-10\dfrac{6}{13} - 6\dfrac{8}{13} = \dfrac{-136}{13} - \dfrac{86}{13}$ Write mixed numbers as improper fractions.

$\qquad = \dfrac{-136 - 86}{13}$ Write difference of numerators over denominator.

$\qquad = \dfrac{-222}{13} = -17\dfrac{1}{13}$ Subtract. Then write fraction as a mixed number.

✔ **Checkpoint**

Find the sum or difference.

5. $2\dfrac{3}{4} + 1\dfrac{3}{4}$ **6.** $-6\dfrac{2}{3} + 3\dfrac{1}{3}$ **7.** $4\dfrac{1}{5} - 2\dfrac{3}{5}$ **8.** $-3\dfrac{2}{7} - 6\dfrac{3}{7}$

For help with simplifying fractions that include variables, see p. 184.

Example 4 Simplifying Variable Expressions

a. $\dfrac{3a}{20} + \dfrac{5a}{20} = \dfrac{3a + 5a}{20}$ Write sum of numerators over denominator.

$= \dfrac{\overset{2}{\cancel{8a}}}{\underset{5}{\cancel{20}}}$ Add. Divide out common factor.

$= \dfrac{2a}{5}$ Simplify.

b. $-\dfrac{8}{3b} - \left(-\dfrac{2}{3b}\right) = -\dfrac{8}{3b} + \dfrac{2}{3b}$ To subtract $-\dfrac{2}{3b}$, add $\dfrac{2}{3b}$.

$= \dfrac{-8 + 2}{3b}$ Write sum of numerators over denominator.

$= \dfrac{\overset{-2}{\cancel{-6}}}{\underset{1}{\cancel{3b}}}$ Add. Divide out common factor.

$= \dfrac{-2}{b} = -\dfrac{2}{b}$ Simplify.

5.2 Exercises

More Practice, p. 807

Guided Practice

Vocabulary Check

1. Copy and complete: To find the sum of two fractions with the same denominator, write the sum of the __?__ over the denominator.

2. Explain how to simplify the expression $\dfrac{5m}{3} + \left(-\dfrac{2m}{3}\right)$.

Skill Check **Find the sum or difference.**

3. $\dfrac{7}{9} + \dfrac{1}{9}$

4. $-\dfrac{2}{7} + \dfrac{5}{7}$

5. $\dfrac{3}{8} - \dfrac{5}{8}$

6. $5\dfrac{9}{13} + 9\dfrac{8}{13}$

7. $-3\dfrac{7}{16} - 8\dfrac{11}{16}$

8. $1\dfrac{3}{14} - 10\dfrac{5}{14}$

Guided Problem Solving

9. **Crafts** You have $5\dfrac{1}{4}$ feet of ribbon. You want to cut one piece that is $3\dfrac{3}{4}$ feet long and one that is $1\dfrac{3}{4}$ feet long. Do you have enough ribbon?

① Write $3\dfrac{3}{4}$ and $1\dfrac{3}{4}$ as improper fractions.

② Find the sum of the improper fractions.

③ Compare the sum in Step 2 with $5\dfrac{1}{4}$ to determine whether you have enough ribbon.

Practice and Problem Solving

Homework Help

Example	Exercises
1	10-17, 27
2	10-17
3	18-25, 28, 37, 44
4	29-36

Online Resources
CLASSZONE.COM
• More Examples
• eTutorial Plus

Find the sum or difference.

10. $\dfrac{3}{5} + \dfrac{4}{5}$
11. $\dfrac{12}{19} + \dfrac{8}{19}$
12. $-\dfrac{17}{27} - \dfrac{13}{27}$
13. $\dfrac{3}{7} - \left(-\dfrac{6}{7}\right)$

14. $\dfrac{13}{15} + \left(-\dfrac{8}{15}\right)$
15. $-\dfrac{21}{26} + \dfrac{15}{26}$
16. $\dfrac{9}{22} - \dfrac{19}{22}$
17. $-\dfrac{6}{17} - \dfrac{12}{17}$

18. $4\dfrac{1}{4} - 5\dfrac{3}{4}$
19. $3\dfrac{4}{5} + \left(-8\dfrac{4}{5}\right)$
20. $6\dfrac{3}{10} + 7\dfrac{9}{10}$
21. $\dfrac{1}{3} - \left(-2\dfrac{2}{3}\right)$

22. $8\dfrac{9}{11} - 3\dfrac{6}{11}$
23. $-5\dfrac{5}{18} - \dfrac{17}{18}$
24. $3\dfrac{7}{16} - 8\dfrac{11}{16}$
25. $2\dfrac{1}{14} - 11\dfrac{3}{14}$

26. Error Analysis Describe and correct the error in adding $-\dfrac{3}{7}$ and $\dfrac{2}{7}$.

$$-\dfrac{3}{7} + \dfrac{2}{7} = \dfrac{-3 + 2}{7 + 7}$$

$$\times \qquad = -\dfrac{1}{14}$$

27. Homework One day, you studied math for $\dfrac{3}{4}$ hour and English for $\dfrac{3}{4}$ hour. What was the total time that you studied both subjects?

28. Baking A blueberry muffin recipe calls for $1\dfrac{2}{3}$ cups of flour. A banana muffin recipe calls for $2\dfrac{2}{3}$ cups of flour. How much flour do you need to make both recipes?

Simplify the expression.

29. $\dfrac{5x}{8} + \dfrac{x}{8}$
30. $\dfrac{t}{13} + \dfrac{12t}{13}$
31. $-\dfrac{11}{6p} + \dfrac{17}{6p}$
32. $\dfrac{29}{12s} + \dfrac{19}{12s}$

33. $\dfrac{2n}{15} - \dfrac{7n}{15}$
34. $\dfrac{m}{21} - \dfrac{5m}{21}$
35. $-\dfrac{5}{18a} - \dfrac{23}{18a}$
36. $-\dfrac{15}{4d} - \dfrac{21}{4d}$

37. Carpentry You are making a shelf from a board that is $12\dfrac{3}{4}$ inches long. You want to cut the board so that it is $10\dfrac{1}{4}$ inches long. What length should you cut from the board?

Evaluate the expression.

38. $\dfrac{3}{9} + \dfrac{7}{9} + \dfrac{4}{9}$
39. $\dfrac{3}{10} + \dfrac{5}{10} + \left(-\dfrac{7}{10}\right)$
40. $-\dfrac{7}{9} + \dfrac{2}{9} + \left(-\dfrac{4}{9}\right)$

41. $\dfrac{1}{5} - \left(-\dfrac{3}{5}\right) + \dfrac{2}{5}$
42. $-\dfrac{17}{31} - \dfrac{21}{31} - \dfrac{27}{31}$
43. $-\dfrac{13}{14} - \dfrac{11}{14} - \dfrac{9}{14}$

44. Shot Put The school record for the shot put is 45 feet, $3\dfrac{3}{8}$ inches. Your personal record is 42 feet, $6\dfrac{7}{8}$ inches. How much farther must you throw the shot put to match the school record?

45. Critical Thinking Find two fractions, one positive and one negative, having the same denominator and a sum of $\frac{1}{2}$.

Solve the equation. Check your solution.

46. $x + \frac{3}{7} = \frac{5}{7}$

47. $y + \frac{8}{11} = \frac{2}{11}$

48. $-\frac{7}{12} + z = -\frac{5}{12}$

49. $m + 2\frac{4}{9} = 5\frac{2}{9}$

50. $7\frac{3}{8} = n + 6\frac{5}{8}$

51. $-1\frac{5}{13} + t = 4\frac{10}{13}$

52. Lobsters A lobster periodically sheds its shell and grows a new shell. During this process, which is called molting, the weight of the lobster increases, as shown in the table.

a. How many pounds did the lobster gain after each molting?

b. How many pounds in all did the lobster gain after four moltings?

c. Suppose the lobster gains $2\frac{1}{4}$ pounds after molting one more time. How much does it weigh then?

Lobster Weights (lb)	
Before molting	$1\frac{1}{4}$
After 1 molting	$1\frac{3}{4}$
After 2 moltings	$2\frac{2}{4}$
After 3 moltings	$3\frac{3}{4}$
After 4 moltings	$5\frac{1}{4}$

53. Challenge Solve the equation $\frac{5}{8} + \frac{7x}{3} = \frac{8x}{3}$. Explain how you found the solution.

Mixed Review

54. Watch You buy a watch and a battery for $57.99. The battery costs $2.99. Write and solve an equation to find the cost of the watch. *(Lesson 2.5)*

Write the fraction in simplest form. *(Lesson 4.3)*

55. $\frac{15s^3}{5s^2}$

56. $\frac{120t^2}{140t^5}$

57. $\frac{65m^4}{80m^2}$

58. $\frac{54a^5}{78a^2}$

Find the least common multiple of the monomials. *(Lesson 4.4)*

59. $18m, 3mn$

60. $5t, 20s^2t$

61. $12a^3b, 6a$

62. $9vw, 36v^2w^2$

Standardized Test Practice

63. Multiple Choice Find the difference $\frac{13}{16} - \left(-\frac{7}{16}\right)$.

A. $-1\frac{1}{4}$

B. $-\frac{3}{8}$

C. $\frac{3}{8}$

D. $1\frac{1}{4}$

64. Multiple Choice Simplify the expression $\frac{16}{3y} - \frac{28}{3y}$.

F. $-\frac{12}{3y}$

G. $-\frac{4}{y}$

H. 0

I. $\frac{44}{3y}$

65. Short Response A rectangular picture frame is made of wooden strips that are $\frac{3}{4}$ inch wide. The outside edge of the frame is $8\frac{1}{4}$ inches long and $6\frac{3}{4}$ inches wide. Can a rectangular picture that is 7 inches long and $5\frac{1}{2}$ inches wide fit inside the frame? Explain your answer.

5.3 Combining Fractions with Different Denominators

Goal
Use area models to add and subtract fractions with different denominators.

Materials
• paper
• colored pencils

Investigate

Use area models to add and subtract fractions.

To model finding the sum $\frac{1}{4} + \frac{2}{3}$, follow the steps below.

1 Draw area models for $\frac{1}{4}$ and $\frac{2}{3}$, as shown.

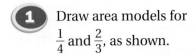

2 Redraw the models so they have the same number of equal parts.

3 Combine the shaded parts to find the sum.

$$\frac{1}{4} + \frac{2}{3} = \frac{11}{12}$$

To model finding the difference $\frac{3}{5} - \frac{1}{2}$, follow the steps below.

1 Draw area models for $\frac{3}{5}$ and $\frac{1}{2}$, as shown.

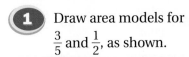

2 Redraw the models so they have the same number of equal parts.

3 Find the difference of the numbers of shaded parts in the two models.

$$\frac{3}{5} - \frac{1}{2} = \frac{1}{10}$$

Draw Conclusions

Use area models to find the sum or difference.

1. $\frac{3}{4} + \frac{1}{6}$ **2.** $\frac{1}{2} + \frac{2}{7}$ **3.** $\frac{2}{3} - \frac{1}{4}$ **4.** $\frac{5}{6} - \frac{2}{5}$

5. Critical Thinking Show how you can use an area model to find the difference $2 - \frac{2}{5}$.

Adding *and* Subtracting Unlike Fractions

Review Vocabulary

least common
denominator (LCD),
p. 188

BEFORE	Now	WHY?
You worked with like fractions.	You'll add and subtract unlike fractions.	So you can find the range of salamander lengths, as in Ex. 34.

Hiking You are hiking between two campsites in the Chesapeake and Ohio Canal National Historic Park. The distance between the campsites is $10\frac{1}{5}$ miles. You have already hiked $5\frac{3}{4}$ miles. How many more miles do you have to hike? Example 3 answers this question by finding the difference of two mixed numbers.

To add or subtract fractions with different denominators, begin by using the LCD of the fractions to write equivalent fractions that have the same denominator.

Review *Help*

For help with finding the least common denominator (LCD) of two or more fractions, see p. 188.

Example 1	*Adding and Subtracting Fractions*

a. $\dfrac{5}{12} + \dfrac{1}{3} = \dfrac{5}{12} + \dfrac{4}{12}$ Write $\dfrac{1}{3}$ using LCD.

$\qquad = \dfrac{5+4}{12}$ Write sum of numerators over denominator.

$\qquad = \dfrac{9}{12}$ Add.

$\qquad = \dfrac{3}{4}$ Simplify.

b. $-\dfrac{5}{6} - \dfrac{7}{9} = \dfrac{-15}{18} - \dfrac{14}{18}$ Write fractions using LCD.

$\qquad = \dfrac{-15-14}{18}$ Write difference of numerators over denominator.

$\qquad = \dfrac{-29}{18}$ Subtract.

$\qquad = -1\dfrac{11}{18}$ Write fraction as a mixed number.

Study *Strategy*

Reasonableness You can use estimation to check the reasonableness of an answer. In Example 2, you can estimate the result by adding $-4\frac{1}{2}$ and $-2\frac{1}{2}$. Because the sum, -7, is close to $-6\frac{52}{55}$, the answer is reasonable.

Example 2   *Adding Mixed Numbers*

$$-4\frac{2}{5} + \left(-2\frac{6}{11}\right) = \frac{-22}{5} + \left(\frac{-28}{11}\right)$$ Write mixed numbers as improper fractions.

$$= \frac{-242}{55} + \left(\frac{-140}{55}\right)$$ Write fractions using LCD.

$$= \frac{-242 + (-140)}{55}$$ Write sum of numerators over denominator.

$$= \frac{-382}{55} = -6\frac{52}{55}$$ Add. Then write fraction as a mixed number.

 Checkpoint

Find the sum or difference.

1. $-\frac{2}{3} + \frac{1}{4}$ **2.** $\frac{3}{10} - \frac{4}{5}$ **3.** $-\frac{4}{15} - \frac{9}{10}$

4. $3\frac{5}{9} + 2\frac{1}{6}$ **5.** $6\frac{7}{10} + \left(-1\frac{1}{5}\right)$ **6.** $-2\frac{1}{3} + 6\frac{3}{5}$

Example 3   *Subtracting Mixed Numbers*

How many more miles do you need to hike before you reach the next campsite in the Chesapeake and Ohio Canal National Historic Park, as described on page 231?

Solution

Your total hiking distance is $10\frac{1}{5}$ miles. You have already hiked $5\frac{3}{4}$ miles. To find the remaining distance, subtract.

$$10\frac{1}{5} - 5\frac{3}{4} = \frac{51}{5} - \frac{23}{4}$$ Write mixed numbers as improper fractions.

$$= \frac{204}{20} - \frac{115}{20}$$ Write fractions using LCD.

$$= \frac{204 - 115}{20}$$ Write difference of numerators over denominator.

$$= \frac{89}{20} = 4\frac{9}{20}$$ Subtract. Then write fraction as a mixed number.

Answer You need to hike $4\frac{9}{20}$ miles, or about $4\frac{1}{2}$ miles.

 Checkpoint

Find the difference.

7. $5\frac{4}{11} - 2\frac{2}{3}$ **8.** $-1\frac{3}{7} - 2\frac{3}{14}$ **9.** $4\frac{3}{8} - \left(-1\frac{2}{3}\right)$

Example 4   *Simplifying an Expression*

Simplify the expression $\dfrac{a}{2} - \dfrac{a}{6}$.

$$\dfrac{a}{2} - \dfrac{a}{6} = \left(\dfrac{a}{2} \cdot \dfrac{3}{3}\right) - \dfrac{a}{6}$$ Write $\dfrac{a}{2}$ using LCD.

$$= \dfrac{3a}{6} - \dfrac{a}{6}$$ Multiply.

$$= \dfrac{3a - a}{6}$$ Write difference of numerators over denominator.

$$= \dfrac{2a}{6}$$ Subtract.

$$= \dfrac{\overset{1}{\cancel{2}}a}{\underset{3}{\cancel{6}}}$$ Divide out common factor.

$$= \dfrac{a}{3}$$ Simplify.

5.3 Exercises

More Practice, p. 807

INTERNET
eWorkbook Plus
CLASSZONE.COM

Guided Practice

Vocabulary Check

1. What is the LCD of $\dfrac{2}{3}$ and $\dfrac{1}{2}$?

2. Explain how to add two fractions with different denominators.

Skill Check   **Find the sum or difference.**

3. $-\dfrac{1}{4} + \dfrac{1}{8}$ **4.** $-\dfrac{3}{4} - \dfrac{1}{3}$ **5.** $-4\dfrac{3}{5} + 7\dfrac{4}{15}$ **6.** $2\dfrac{7}{12} - 9\dfrac{2}{3}$

Simplify the expression.

7. $\dfrac{a}{15} + \dfrac{a}{6}$ **8.** $\dfrac{b}{8} + \dfrac{b}{12}$ **9.** $\dfrac{5a}{3} - \dfrac{a}{6}$ **10.** $-\dfrac{d}{5} - \dfrac{5d}{6}$

Guided Problem Solving

11. Lumber Newly cut lumber contains a lot of moisture. Before the wood is used for carpentry or construction, it is usually dried. Suppose a freshly cut board weighs $10\dfrac{1}{2}$ pounds. After drying, the board weighs $4\dfrac{2}{3}$ pounds. What was the weight of the water that evaporated?

   1 Write $10\dfrac{1}{2}$ and $4\dfrac{2}{3}$ as improper fractions.

   2 Rewrite the improper fractions using the LCD of the fractions.

   3 Find the difference of the improper fractions from Step 2.

Practice and Problem Solving

Homework *Help*

Example	Exercises
1	12–23
2	24–33, 45–50
3	24–31, 34, 45–50
4	36–43

Online Resources
CLASSZONE.COM

• More Examples
• eTutorial Plus

Find the sum or difference.

12. $\dfrac{1}{12} + \dfrac{3}{16}$ **13.** $\dfrac{5}{6} + \left(-\dfrac{2}{3}\right)$ **14.** $-\dfrac{7}{10} + \dfrac{7}{20}$ **15.** $-\dfrac{1}{9} - \dfrac{5}{18}$

16. $-\dfrac{4}{15} - \dfrac{7}{25}$ **17.** $\dfrac{5}{8} - \dfrac{11}{14}$ **18.** $-\dfrac{6}{7} + \left(-\dfrac{16}{21}\right)$ **19.** $-\dfrac{1}{5} - \left(-\dfrac{2}{11}\right)$

Evaluate the expression when $m = -\dfrac{5}{12}$ and $n = \dfrac{7}{9}$.

20. $m + n$ **21.** $m - n$ **22.** $n - m$ **23.** $-m - n$

Find the sum or difference.

24. $5\dfrac{1}{4} + 1\dfrac{2}{5}$ **25.** $-3\dfrac{3}{4} + 10\dfrac{7}{8}$ **26.** $6\dfrac{7}{18} - 8\dfrac{21}{54}$ **27.** $2\dfrac{5}{13} - \left(-1\dfrac{1}{2}\right)$

28. $-4\dfrac{7}{10} - 9\dfrac{7}{15}$ **29.** $3\dfrac{1}{2} - \left(-2\dfrac{1}{3}\right)$ **30.** $-1\dfrac{5}{12} + 4\dfrac{5}{14}$ **31.** $15\dfrac{1}{6} - 7\dfrac{3}{10}$

32. Snow On one day it snows $2\dfrac{1}{2}$ inches. On the next day it snows $2\dfrac{1}{4}$ inches, and on the third day it snows $4\dfrac{1}{8}$ inches. What was the total amount of snowfall over the three-day period?

33. Geometry The width of a rectangle is $2\dfrac{3}{8}$ inches. The rectangle is $1\dfrac{3}{4}$ inches longer than it is wide. Find the length of the rectangle and the perimeter of the rectangle.

34. Salamanders Texas blind salamanders have been found in lengths varying from $3\dfrac{1}{4}$ inches to $5\dfrac{3}{8}$ inches. Find the range of these lengths.

35. Extended Problem Solving A catalog gives the information below about hats. Head size is the distance around a person's head.

Hat size	Small		Medium		Large		Extra Large	
Head size (in.)	$21\dfrac{1}{8}$	$21\dfrac{1}{2}$	$21\dfrac{7}{8}$	$22\dfrac{1}{4}$	$22\dfrac{5}{8}$	23	$23\dfrac{1}{2}$	$23\dfrac{7}{8}$

a. Analyze For each hat size, find the range in head sizes.

b. Apply The catalog says that if your head size is between two hat sizes, you should buy the larger hat size. You are ordering hats for friends whose head sizes (in inches) are $22\dfrac{1}{2}$, $21\dfrac{3}{4}$, $21\dfrac{5}{8}$, $23\dfrac{3}{4}$, $22\dfrac{1}{8}$, and $22\dfrac{3}{8}$. How many hats of each size should you buy?

c. *Writing* If you assume that customers always measure head size to the nearest $\dfrac{1}{8}$ inch, how would you revise the table to include all possible head sizes between 21 inches and 24 inches?

In the **Real World**

Salamanders The Texas blind salamander inhabits underground streams whose average temperature is about 21°C. Use the formula $F = 1.8C + 32$, where F is the temperature in degrees Fahrenheit, and C is the temperature in degrees Celsius, to convert the average stream temperature to degrees Fahrenheit.

Simplify the expression.

36. $\dfrac{d}{6} + \dfrac{2d}{9}$ **37.** $-\dfrac{y}{5} + \dfrac{y}{7}$ **38.** $\dfrac{3a}{2} - \dfrac{a}{6}$ **39.** $-\dfrac{9r}{11} - \dfrac{r}{8}$

40. $\dfrac{4z}{7} - \dfrac{7z}{4}$ **41.** $-\dfrac{x}{8} + \dfrac{x}{12}$ **42.** $-\dfrac{5c}{3} - \dfrac{4c}{15}$ **43.** $-\dfrac{5w}{12} + \dfrac{7w}{9}$

44. Horses Of the three different types of horses on a ranch, $\dfrac{1}{4}$ are Arabians, $\dfrac{2}{5}$ are Thoroughbreds, and the rest are Morgans. What fraction of the horses are Morgans?

Evaluate the expression.

45. $5\dfrac{1}{2} + 1\dfrac{1}{4} + 2\dfrac{1}{2}$ **46.** $-\dfrac{2}{3} + 1\dfrac{5}{6} - \dfrac{3}{4}$ **47.** $\dfrac{3}{4} + \dfrac{11}{12} - 1\dfrac{3}{8}$

48. $1\dfrac{1}{2} - \dfrac{3}{8} + 3\dfrac{4}{5}$ **49.** $-\dfrac{3}{5} - 1\dfrac{2}{15} - \dfrac{7}{10}$ **50.** $5\dfrac{13}{64} - \left(-\dfrac{3}{16}\right) + 1\dfrac{1}{8}$

51. Critical Thinking Can you use 48 as a common denominator when you find the sum of $\dfrac{7}{8}$ and $\dfrac{5}{12}$? Will you get the same answer that you do if you use the least common denominator of the fractions? Compare the steps you would use to find the sum using each common denominator.

52. Challenge Find a value of x so that the sum $\dfrac{1}{x} + \dfrac{3}{2x}$ is equal to 1. Explain how you found your answer.

Mixed Review **Find the product.** *(p. 780)*

53. $8 \times \dfrac{3}{4}$ **54.** $\dfrac{5}{8} \times 16$ **55.** $\dfrac{6}{7} \times 21$ **56.** $20 \times \dfrac{3}{5}$

Find the product or quotient. Write your answer using exponents.
(Lesson 4.5)

57. $b^3 \cdot b^8$ **58.** $c^2 \cdot c^5$ **59.** $\dfrac{d^5}{d^7}$ **60.** $\dfrac{3a^6}{a^2}$

61. Track and Field The school record for the javelin throw is 186 feet, $2\dfrac{1}{4}$ inches. Your personal record for the javelin throw is 172 feet, $\dfrac{3}{4}$ inch. Suppose you want to match the school record. By how much do you need to increase the distance you can throw the javelin? *(Lesson 5.2)*

Standardized Test Practice

62. Multiple Choice Find the sum $-6\dfrac{1}{2} + \dfrac{5}{8}$.

A. $-7\dfrac{1}{16}$ **B.** $-7\dfrac{1}{8}$ **C.** $-5\dfrac{7}{8}$ **D.** $-5\dfrac{7}{16}$

63. Multiple Choice Simplify the expression $\dfrac{x}{4} - \dfrac{5x}{6}$.

F. $-\dfrac{4x}{12}$ **G.** $-\dfrac{7x}{12}$ **H.** $\dfrac{4x}{12}$ **I.** $\dfrac{7x}{12}$

Note *Worthy*

You should write down any questions you have about performing operations on fractions in your notebook.

Mid-Chapter Quiz

Write the fraction or mixed number as a decimal.

1. $\dfrac{1}{12}$ **2.** $-\dfrac{42}{56}$ **3.** $-\dfrac{7}{4}$ **4.** $1\dfrac{6}{11}$

Write the decimal as a fraction or mixed number.

5. 0.55 **6.** -4.22 **7.** $0.\overline{8}$ **8.** $0.\overline{54}$

Find the sum or difference.

9. $\dfrac{2}{15} + \dfrac{7}{15}$ **10.** $-\dfrac{1}{6} + \dfrac{5}{6}$ **11.** $\dfrac{11}{12} - \dfrac{7}{12}$ **12.** $-\dfrac{13}{30} + \dfrac{17}{30}$

13. $-\dfrac{1}{4} + \dfrac{2}{9}$ **14.** $\dfrac{2}{3} - \dfrac{9}{14}$ **15.** $\dfrac{11}{28} - \dfrac{25}{42}$ **16.** $-\dfrac{3}{4} + \left(-\dfrac{17}{25}\right)$

17. $-4\dfrac{9}{10} - 2\dfrac{3}{10}$ **18.** $3\dfrac{1}{4} + 5\dfrac{3}{4}$ **19.** $-1\dfrac{1}{4} + \dfrac{11}{18}$ **20.** $-10\dfrac{1}{2} - 14\dfrac{3}{5}$

Simplify the expression.

21. $\dfrac{9d}{12} - \dfrac{d}{12}$ **22.** $\dfrac{7}{3a} + \dfrac{5}{3a}$ **23.** $-\dfrac{7c}{9} + \dfrac{c}{6}$ **24.** $\dfrac{b}{14} - \dfrac{b}{22}$

25. Jogging You are jogging on a trail around a pond. The distance around the pond is $1\dfrac{5}{16}$ miles. So far, you have jogged $\dfrac{3}{8}$ mile. How much farther do you need to jog before you have gone exactly once around the pond?

Brain GAME *Magic Square*

Arrange the fractions $\dfrac{1}{10}, \dfrac{3}{20}, \dfrac{1}{5}, \dfrac{1}{4}, \dfrac{3}{10}, \dfrac{7}{20}, \dfrac{2}{5},$ and $\dfrac{9}{20}$ in the square so that the sum of the numbers in each row, column, and diagonal is $\dfrac{3}{4}$.

5.4 Multiplying Fractions

Review Vocabulary
numerator, p. 777
denominator, p. 777

BEFORE	Now	WHY?
You added and subtracted fractions.	You'll multiply fractions and mixed numbers.	So you can adjust ingredients in a recipe, as in Ex. 36.

You can use an area model to find the product of two fractions, such as $\frac{3}{5} \cdot \frac{1}{4}$.

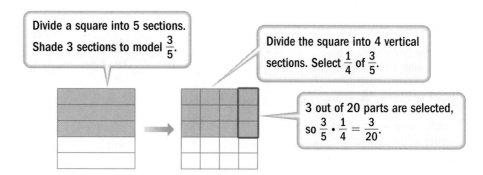

Divide a square into 5 sections. Shade 3 sections to model $\frac{3}{5}$.

Divide the square into 4 vertical sections. Select $\frac{1}{4}$ of $\frac{3}{5}$.

3 out of 20 parts are selected, so $\frac{3}{5} \cdot \frac{1}{4} = \frac{3}{20}$.

The area model suggests the following rule for multiplying fractions.

Multiplying Fractions

Words The product of two or more fractions is equal to the product of the numerators over the product of the denominators.

Numbers $\frac{3}{5} \cdot \frac{4}{7} = \frac{3 \cdot 4}{5 \cdot 7} = \frac{12}{35}$

Algebra $\frac{a}{b} \cdot \frac{c}{d} = \frac{ac}{bd}$, where $b \neq 0$ and $d \neq 0$

Study *Strategy*

Another Way In Example 1, you can also multiply the fractions without first dividing out common factors. You must simplify the resulting fraction.

$\frac{7 \cdot (-4)}{10 \cdot 21} = \frac{-28}{210}$

$= -\frac{2}{15}$

Example 1 | *Multiplying Fractions*

$\frac{7}{10} \cdot \left(-\frac{4}{21}\right) = \frac{7}{10} \cdot \left(\frac{-4}{21}\right)$ **Assign negative sign to numerator.**

$= \frac{7 \cdot (-4)}{10 \cdot 21}$ **Use rule for multiplying fractions.**

$= \frac{\overset{1}{7} \cdot (\overset{-2}{-4})}{\underset{5}{10} \cdot \underset{3}{21}}$ **Divide out common factors.**

$= \frac{-2}{15} = -\frac{2}{15}$ **Multiply.**

Example 2 — Multiplying a Mixed Number and an Integer

Emmys Each year, the Academy of Television Arts and Sciences presents gold-plated Emmy awards for programs and individuals in the television industry. Each Emmy statue weighs $4\frac{3}{4}$ pounds.

In 2002, 63 statues were awarded. What was the combined weight of all the statues?

Solution

$$\text{Combined weight} = \text{Statue weight} \cdot \text{Number of statues}$$

$$= 4\frac{3}{4} \cdot 63 \qquad \text{Substitute values.}$$

$$= \frac{19}{4} \cdot \frac{63}{1} \qquad \text{Write numbers as improper fractions.}$$

$$= \frac{19 \cdot 63}{4 \cdot 1} \qquad \text{Use rule for multiplying fractions.}$$

$$= \frac{1197}{4} \qquad \text{Multiply.}$$

$$= 299\frac{1}{4} \qquad \text{Write fraction as a mixed number.}$$

Answer The combined weight of the statues was $299\frac{1}{4}$ pounds.

 Checkpoint

Find the product.

1. $\dfrac{2}{3} \cdot \dfrac{7}{8}$ **2.** $\left(-\dfrac{5}{12}\right)\left(\dfrac{3}{10}\right)$ **3.** $10 \cdot \left(-2\dfrac{3}{11}\right)$ **4.** $\left(\dfrac{3}{4}\right)(-12)$

Example 3 — Multiplying Mixed Numbers

$$-2\frac{3}{4} \cdot 3\frac{1}{5} = \frac{-11}{4} \cdot \frac{16}{5} \qquad \text{Write mixed numbers as improper fractions.}$$

$$= \frac{-11 \cdot \overset{4}{\cancel{16}}}{\underset{1}{\cancel{4}} \cdot 5} \qquad \begin{array}{l}\text{Use rule for multiplying fractions.}\\\text{Divide out common factor.}\end{array}$$

$$= \frac{-44}{5} \qquad \text{Multiply.}$$

$$= -8\frac{4}{5} \qquad \text{Write fraction as a mixed number.}$$

 **Checkpoint**

Find the product.

5. $4\dfrac{7}{8} \cdot 5\dfrac{2}{3}$ **6.** $-3\dfrac{2}{7} \cdot 1\dfrac{1}{2}$ **7.** $-3\dfrac{3}{5} \cdot \left(-1\dfrac{5}{9}\right)$ **8.** $4\dfrac{1}{8} \cdot \left(-1\dfrac{2}{3}\right)$

Example 4 **Simplifying Expressions**

Simplify the expression.

a. $\dfrac{m}{3} \cdot \left(-\dfrac{12}{5}\right)$

b. $\dfrac{n^2}{10} \cdot \dfrac{5n^3}{9}$

Solution

a. $\dfrac{m}{3} \cdot \left(-\dfrac{12}{5}\right) = \dfrac{m \cdot (-\overset{-4}{\cancel{12}})}{\underset{1}{\cancel{3}} \cdot 5}$ Use rule for multiplying fractions.
Divide out common factor.

$= \dfrac{-4m}{5} = -\dfrac{4m}{5}$ Multiply.

b. $\dfrac{n^2}{10} \cdot \dfrac{5n^3}{9} = \dfrac{n^2 \cdot \overset{1}{\cancel{5}}n^3}{\underset{2}{\cancel{10}} \cdot 9}$ Use rule for multiplying fractions.
Divide out common factor.

$= \dfrac{n^{2+3}}{18}$ Product of powers property

$= \dfrac{n^5}{18}$ Add exponents.

 Checkpoint

Simplify the expression.

9. $\dfrac{3y}{4} \cdot \dfrac{y^5}{9}$ **10.** $\dfrac{x^4}{6} \cdot \left(-\dfrac{16x}{3}\right)$ **11.** $\dfrac{3z^5}{25} \cdot \dfrac{2z^4}{15}$ **12.** $-\dfrac{4v^2}{21} \cdot \dfrac{7v^3}{16}$

Review *Help*

For help with using the product of powers property, see p. 194.

5.4   Exercises

More Practice, p. 807

INTERNET
eWorkbook Plus
CLASSZONE.COM

Guided Practice

Vocabulary Check   **1.** Copy and complete: The product of two or more fractions is equal to the product of the __?__ over the product of the __?__.

2. Show how to simplify the expression $\dfrac{a^2}{7} \cdot \dfrac{7a}{2}$.

Skill Check   **Find the product.**

3. $\dfrac{3}{4} \cdot \dfrac{5}{8}$ **4.** $\left(-\dfrac{7}{12}\right)\left(-\dfrac{4}{21}\right)$ **5.** $\dfrac{5}{6} \cdot (-8)$ **6.** $-2\dfrac{1}{2} \cdot 1\dfrac{3}{4}$

7. Error Analysis Describe and correct the error in simplifying the expression $\dfrac{c^2}{7} \cdot \dfrac{4c^4}{5}$.

$$\dfrac{c^2}{7} \cdot \dfrac{4c^4}{5} = \dfrac{c^2 \cdot 4c^4}{7 \cdot 5}$$
$$= \dfrac{4c^8}{35}$$

Practice and Problem Solving

Homework *Help*

Example	Exercises
1	8–11
2	12–15, 22
3	16–21
4	23–28

Online Resources
CLASSZONE.COM
- More Examples
- eTutorial Plus

Find the product.

8. $\dfrac{5}{6} \cdot \dfrac{3}{8}$

9. $\dfrac{3}{10}\left(-\dfrac{5}{12}\right)$

10. $-\dfrac{9}{28} \cdot \dfrac{49}{54}$

11. $-\dfrac{35}{38} \cdot \left(-\dfrac{19}{40}\right)$

12. $32 \cdot \dfrac{17}{24}$

13. $-18\left(\dfrac{8}{9}\right)$

14. $\dfrac{5}{16} \cdot (-36)$

15. $-\dfrac{25}{28} \cdot (-21)$

16. $4\dfrac{14}{15} \cdot 1\dfrac{7}{38}$

17. $6\dfrac{1}{14} \cdot 6\dfrac{37}{51}$

18. $-7\dfrac{1}{11} \cdot 5\dfrac{1}{24}$

19. $-3\dfrac{3}{20} \cdot \left(-2\dfrac{14}{23}\right)$

20. Pineapples About $\dfrac{4}{5}$ of the weight of a pineapple is water. About how much water would you expect to find in $2\dfrac{1}{2}$ pounds of pineapple?

21. Painting You want to paint a wall that is $8\dfrac{3}{4}$ feet high and $11\dfrac{1}{4}$ feet long. You have a can of paint that will cover 200 square feet with one coat.

    a. Find the area of the wall.

    b. Interpret If you want to apply two coats of paint, do you have enough paint? Explain.

22. Sewing You are making 20 fleece jackets for a craft fair. For each jacket, you need $1\dfrac{7}{8}$ yards of fleece. If fleece costs \$9 per yard, how much money will you spend?

Simplify the expression.

23. $\dfrac{a}{5} \cdot \dfrac{3a}{11}$

24. $\dfrac{16b}{7} \cdot \dfrac{35b^3}{4}$

25. $-\dfrac{11c^2}{6} \cdot \dfrac{8c^7}{3}$

26. $-\dfrac{d^5}{13} \cdot \left(-\dfrac{3d^7}{4}\right)$

27. $-\dfrac{4x}{7} \cdot \left(-\dfrac{2x}{5}\right)$

28. $\dfrac{ab}{4} \cdot \dfrac{2a^5b}{9}$

29. Extended Problem Solving The tread depth of the tires on your family's new car is $\dfrac{3}{8}$ inch. You predict that, as a result of driving the car, the change in tire tread depth will be about $-\dfrac{3}{64}$ inch per year.

    a. Analyze Write a variable expression for the tire tread depth after y years of driving. Use your expression to make a table showing the tire tread depth after 1, 2, and 3 years.

    b. Apply Tires should be replaced when the tread depth is $\dfrac{1}{16}$ inch.

    Extend your table from part (a) to find the approximate number of years the car can be driven before the tires need to be replaced.

Evaluate the expression.

30. $\dfrac{2}{3} \cdot \left(-\dfrac{9}{10}\right) \cdot \dfrac{7}{12}$

31. $-\dfrac{3}{4} \cdot \left(-\dfrac{8}{15}\right) - \dfrac{2}{5}$

32. $\dfrac{99}{8} \cdot \dfrac{2}{17} + \dfrac{27}{34}$

33. $3 + \dfrac{5}{6} \cdot \left(-\dfrac{3}{20}\right)$

34. $-2 \cdot \dfrac{7}{8} + \left(-\dfrac{5}{28}\right)$

35. $\dfrac{5}{11} + \dfrac{5}{22} \cdot \left(-\dfrac{8}{33}\right)$

36. Recipe The recipe shown makes 60 sugar cookies. You want to bake 90 cookies.

a. Write a fraction comparing the number of cookies you want to bake with the number of cookies the recipe makes.

b. *Writing* How much of each ingredient will you need to make 90 cookies? Explain how you got your answer.

Ingredients	
$2\frac{1}{2}$ cups flour	1 tsp baking soda
$\frac{1}{2}$ tsp salt	1 cup butter
$\frac{3}{4}$ cup white sugar	$\frac{3}{4}$ cup brown sugar
1 tsp vanilla	2 eggs

In Exercises 37–40, use the following example to find a quotient of two numbers that are written in scientific notation.

Example *Finding a Quotient of Numbers in Scientific Notation*

$$\frac{6.6 \times 10^3}{1.5 \times 10^4} = \frac{6.6}{1.5} \times \frac{10^3}{10^4}$$ Write quotient as a product of two fractions.

$$= 4.4 \times 10^{3-4}$$ Divide. Use quotient of powers rule.

$$= 4.4 \times 10^{-1}$$ Subtract exponents.

37. $\dfrac{7.2 \times 10^5}{3.6 \times 10^3}$ **38.** $\dfrac{8.4 \times 10^5}{3.0 \times 10^8}$ **39.** $\dfrac{2.4 \times 10^2}{1.2 \times 10^6}$ **40.** $\dfrac{5.4 \times 10}{1.2 \times 10^7}$

41. Challenge Find the next three numbers in the following pattern:
$\dfrac{2}{3}, \dfrac{2}{5}, \dfrac{6}{25}, \dfrac{18}{125}, \ldots$. Explain your reasoning.

Mixed Review

Evaluate the expression. *(Lesson 1.3)*

42. $72 \div [6 - 14 - 1]$ **43.** $3 \cdot [22 - (16 + 4)]$ **44.** $5 \cdot [49 \div 7 + 2]$

Solve the equation. Check your solution. *(Lessons 2.6, 2.7)*

45. $-14y = 42$ **46.** $33w = 39.6$ **47.** $-37.7 = -5.8z$

Solve the inequality. Graph your solution. *(Lesson 3.5)*

48. $\dfrac{a}{-10} < -7$ **49.** $\dfrac{b}{2} > -1$ **50.** $13 \geq \dfrac{c}{-7}$

Standardized Test Practice

51. Multiple Choice Find the product $2\dfrac{13}{36} \cdot \left(-1\dfrac{1}{5}\right)$.

A. $-2\dfrac{5}{6}$ **B.** $-2\dfrac{13}{180}$ **C.** $-1\dfrac{209}{216}$ **D.** $2\dfrac{5}{6}$

52. Multiple Choice Which product is greater than 1?

F. $-\dfrac{4}{5} \cdot 5\dfrac{2}{3}$ **G.** $-\dfrac{3}{8} \cdot \left(-\dfrac{6}{7}\right)$ **H.** $\dfrac{1}{4} \cdot 2\dfrac{1}{2}$ **I.** $1\dfrac{1}{7} \cdot 1\dfrac{1}{3}$

5.5 Dividing Rational Numbers

Goal
Divide rational numbers.

Materials
- paper
- pencil

Investigate

Apply patterns observed in dividing whole numbers to dividing rational numbers.

1 Copy and complete the table. How are the dividend and the divisor of each expression related to the dividend and divisor of the expression $1000 \div 8$? What do you notice about the quotients?

Expression	Simplified expression	Quotient
$1000 \div 8$	$1000 \div 8$	?
$\frac{1}{2}(1000) \div \frac{1}{2}(8)$	$? \div ?$	?
$\frac{1}{4}(1000) \div \frac{1}{4}(8)$	$? \div ?$	?
$\frac{1}{8}(1000) \div \frac{1}{8}(8)$	$? \div ?$	?

2 Use the pattern you observed in Step 1 to find the quotient $\frac{3}{4} \div \frac{2}{3}$. Copy and complete the table by following the arrow. Begin by finding a fraction to replace the red fraction in the table. That is, find a fraction that makes the following statement true.

$$\frac{?}{?} \cdot \frac{2}{3} = 1$$

Expression	Simplified expression	Quotient
$\frac{3}{4} \div \frac{2}{3}$	$\frac{3}{4} \div \frac{2}{3}$	?
$\frac{?}{?}\left(\frac{3}{4}\right) \div \frac{?}{?}\left(\frac{2}{3}\right)$	$\frac{?}{?} \div 1$	?

Draw Conclusions

In Exercises 1–8, find the quotient using the method shown above.

1. $\frac{3}{5} \div \frac{1}{2}$ 2. $\frac{4}{5} \div \frac{1}{3}$ 3. $\frac{7}{9} \div \frac{3}{10}$ 4. $\frac{11}{12} \div \frac{5}{6}$

5. $\frac{5}{9} \div \frac{2}{7}$ 6. $\frac{4}{13} \div \frac{5}{8}$ 7. $\frac{6}{11} \div \frac{1}{5}$ 8. $\frac{3}{16} \div \frac{2}{5}$

9. Copy and complete: For all integers a and all nonzero integers b, c, and d, $\frac{a}{b} \div \frac{c}{d} = \frac{a}{b} \cdot \frac{?}{?}$.

10. **Critical Thinking** Show how you could find the quotient $2\frac{3}{5} \div \frac{7}{8}$ by multiplying the dividend and the divisor by a number that makes the divisor equal to 1.

Dividing Fractions

BEFORE	Now	WHY?
You multiplied fractions and mixed numbers.	You'll divide fractions and mixed numbers.	So you can find how many book covers you can print, as in Ex. 36.

Vocabulary
reciprocals, p. 243

Two nonzero numbers whose product is 1 are **reciprocals** . The pairs of numbers below are examples of reciprocals.

Number	Reciprocal	Justification
5	$\frac{1}{5}$	$5 \cdot \frac{1}{5} = 1$
$\frac{2}{7}$	$\frac{7}{2}$	$\frac{2}{7} \cdot \frac{7}{2} = 1$
$-\frac{5}{8}$	$-\frac{8}{5}$	$-\frac{5}{8}\left(-\frac{8}{5}\right) = 1$
0.1	10	$0.1(10) = 1$

Study Strategy

To find the reciprocal of a decimal, you can write the decimal as a fraction. For example, because $0.1 = \frac{1}{10}$, the reciprocal of 0.1 is $\frac{10}{1}$, or 10.

As you may have seen in the activity on page 242, you can use reciprocals when dividing rational numbers.

Using Reciprocals to Divide

Words To divide by any nonzero number, multiply by its reciprocal.

Numbers $\frac{2}{9} \div \frac{3}{7} = \frac{2}{9} \cdot \frac{7}{3} = \frac{14}{27}$

Algebra $\frac{a}{b} \div \frac{c}{d} = \frac{a}{b} \cdot \frac{d}{c} = \frac{ad}{bc}$, where $b \neq 0$, $c \neq 0$, and $d \neq 0$

Example 1   *Dividing a Fraction by a Fraction*

$$-\frac{2}{5} \div \frac{4}{7} = \frac{-2}{5} \cdot \frac{7}{4}$$ **Multiply by reciprocal.**

$$= \frac{\overset{-1}{\cancel{-2}} \cdot 7}{5 \cdot \underset{2}{\cancel{4}}}$$ **Use rule for multiplying fractions. Divide out common factor.**

$$= \frac{-7}{10} = -\frac{7}{10}$$ **Multiply.**

✓**Check** To check, multiply the quotient by the divisor:

$$-\frac{7}{10} \cdot \frac{4}{7} = -\frac{2}{5} \checkmark$$ **Solution checks.**

Example 2   *Dividing a Mixed Number by a Mixed Number*

$$4\frac{1}{6} \div \left(-1\frac{2}{3}\right) = \frac{25}{6} \div \left(-\frac{5}{3}\right)$$ Write mixed numbers as improper fractions.

$$= \frac{25}{6} \cdot \left(-\frac{3}{5}\right)$$ Multiply by reciprocal.

$$= \frac{\overset{5}{25} \cdot (\overset{-1}{-3})}{\underset{2}{6} \cdot \underset{1}{5}}$$ Use rule for multiplying fractions. Divide out common factors.

$$= \frac{-5}{2} = -2\frac{1}{2}$$ Multiply. Then write fraction as a mixed number.

✔ **Checkpoint**

Find the quotient.

1. $\dfrac{7}{12} \div \dfrac{2}{3}$ **2.** $-\dfrac{4}{9} \div \left(-\dfrac{8}{11}\right)$ **3.** $\dfrac{3}{8} \div 9\dfrac{1}{6}$ **4.** $-5\dfrac{1}{4} \div 2\dfrac{2}{5}$

Example 3   *Dividing a Whole Number by a Mixed Number*

Woodworking You want to join strips of wood that are 15 inches long and $1\frac{5}{8}$ inches wide to make a cutting board that is at least 12 inches wide. How many strips are needed?

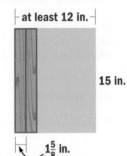

Solution

Divide to find how many strips are needed.

Number of strips = **Cutting board width ÷ Strip width**

$$= 12 \div 1\frac{5}{8}$$ Substitute values.

$$= \frac{12}{1} \div \frac{13}{8}$$ Write numbers as improper fractions.

$$= \frac{12}{1} \cdot \frac{8}{13}$$ Multiply by reciprocal.

$$= \frac{12 \cdot 8}{1 \cdot 13}$$ Use rule for multiplying fractions.

$$= \frac{96}{13}$$ Multiply.

$$= 7\frac{5}{13}$$ Write fraction as a mixed number.

Answer Because a whole number of strips is needed, you should use 8 strips to make sure that the cutting board is at least 12 inches wide.

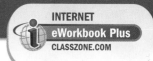

Guided Practice

Vocabulary Check

1. Explain why 0.25 and 4 are reciprocals.

2. Describe the steps you would take to find the quotient $\frac{2}{5} \div 1\frac{2}{3}$.

State the reciprocal of the number.

3. 8

4. $-\frac{2}{3}$

5. 0.75

6. 2.5

Skill Check **Find the quotient.**

7. $\frac{8}{11} \div \frac{33}{40}$

8. $\frac{2}{15} \div \left(-\frac{8}{25}\right)$

9. $-\frac{4}{9} \div \frac{16}{11}$

10. $6\frac{1}{3} \div \left(-3\frac{8}{9}\right)$

11. $1\frac{13}{14} \div 13$

12. $12 \div \left(-\frac{5}{12}\right)$

13. $\frac{3}{13} \div 15$

14. $7\frac{1}{5} \div \left(-1\frac{3}{10}\right)$

15. Error Analysis Describe and correct the error in finding the quotient $6\frac{1}{4} \div \frac{1}{2}$.

$$6\frac{1}{4} \div \frac{1}{2} = \frac{25}{4} \cdot \frac{1}{2}$$
$$= \frac{25}{8} = 3\frac{1}{8}$$

Practice and Problem Solving

Homework *Help*

Example	Exercises
1	16–19
2	20–23, 29
3	24–28

Online Resources
CLASSZONE.COM

• More Examples
• eTutorial Plus

Find the quotient.

16. $\frac{13}{18} \div \frac{20}{27}$

17. $\frac{15}{16} \div \left(-\frac{25}{36}\right)$

18. $-\frac{32}{45} \div \frac{48}{35}$

19. $-\frac{18}{19} \div \left(-\frac{9}{17}\right)$

20. $7\frac{7}{9} \div 1\frac{11}{45}$

21. $6\frac{6}{13} \div 2\frac{28}{39}$

22. $8\frac{4}{15} \div \left(-\frac{2}{5}\right)$

23. $-1\frac{17}{55} \div 1\frac{11}{70}$

24. $34 \div \left(-\frac{4}{5}\right)$

25. $27 \div \left(-\frac{3}{11}\right)$

26. $-\frac{40}{77} \div (-44)$

27. $-\frac{16}{21} \div 18$

28. Bookmarks You want to cut bookmarks that are 6 inches long and $2\frac{3}{8}$ inches wide from a sheet of decorative paper that is 13 inches long and 6 inches wide. If you cut the bookmarks as shown, what is the maximum number of bookmarks that you can cut from the paper?

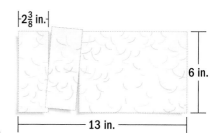

29. School Fair At a school fair, the field for a three-legged race is $31\frac{1}{2}$ feet across. Each lane is $5\frac{1}{4}$ feet across. How many lanes are there?

Evaluate the expression.

30. $\dfrac{6}{7} \div \dfrac{2}{3} - \dfrac{3}{7}$

31. $\dfrac{5}{9} \div \left(\dfrac{4}{9} - \dfrac{3}{18}\right)$

32. $-\dfrac{8}{15} \div \left(\dfrac{7}{25} + \dfrac{9}{15}\right)$

33. $5\dfrac{1}{17} \div 1\dfrac{9}{34} - \dfrac{19}{30}$

34. $1\dfrac{29}{35} \div 1\dfrac{11}{21} + \dfrac{7}{15}$

35. $\dfrac{70}{61} \div \dfrac{21}{122} - \dfrac{55}{13}$

36. Extended Problem Solving Book covers are printed on large sheets of paper. A cover is printed multiple times on a sheet. In parts (a)–(c), assume that a sheet measures $21\frac{1}{2}$ inches by 36 inches.

   a. Analyze A particular book cover is $7\frac{1}{2}$ inches high and $11\frac{1}{8}$ inches wide. What is the greatest number of covers that can be printed on a sheet? Show how the covers should be arranged.

   b. Analyze Another book cover is 8 inches high and $9\frac{1}{2}$ inches wide. What is the greatest number of these covers that can be printed on a sheet? Show how the covers should be arranged.

   c. Apply Suppose you need to print 12,000 covers of each of the books in parts (a) and (b). How many sheets do you need for each book?

37. Challenge Solve the equation $\dfrac{6}{11}x = 12$. Explain how you solved it.

Mixed Review

Solve the equation. Check your solution. *(Lesson 3.1)*

38. $9m + 5 = 4$ **39.** $1 - n = -5$ **40.** $0 = \dfrac{m}{-5} + 3$ **41.** $1 = 2 + \dfrac{n}{-7}$

Use the LCD to determine which fraction is greater. *(Lesson 4.4)*

42. $\dfrac{3}{13}, \dfrac{1}{4}$ **43.** $\dfrac{7}{15}, \dfrac{9}{20}$ **44.** $\dfrac{9}{17}, \dfrac{25}{51}$ **45.** $\dfrac{3}{8}, \dfrac{29}{84}$

Simplify the expression. *(Lessons 5.2, 5.3)*

46. $\dfrac{a}{13} + \left(-\dfrac{6a}{65}\right)$ **47.** $\dfrac{3b}{22} - \dfrac{7b}{22}$ **48.** $-\dfrac{c}{11} - \dfrac{10c}{11}$ **49.** $\dfrac{5d}{18} + \dfrac{7d}{9}$

Standardized Test Practice

50. Extended Response After reading that the average women's shoe size is $8\frac{1}{2}$, a shoe store owner records the sizes of women's shoes sold in one morning. The sizes sold were $6\frac{1}{2}$, $9\frac{1}{2}$, $5\frac{1}{2}$, 10, 11, $8\frac{1}{2}$, 9, and 8.

   a. For each shoe size, find the deviation from the average stated above by subtracting the average from the shoe size. What does a positive deviation from the average indicate? What does a negative deviation from the average indicate?

   b. Find the mean of the deviations from part (a). What might the store owner conclude? Explain your thinking.

5.6

Using Multiplicative Inverses *to* Solve Equations

Vocabulary

multiplicative inverse,
  p. 247

BEFORE	Now	WHY?
You used reciprocals to divide fractions.	You'll use multiplicative inverses to solve equations.	So you can find the width of a U.S. flag, as in Ex. 19.

Caves Stalactites are icicle-shaped stone formations found on cave ceilings. They form from minerals deposited by dripping water. Suppose a stalactite is 10 inches long and is growing at a rate of about $\frac{1}{8}$ inch per decade. How long will it take for the stalactite to reach a length of 1 foot? In Example 3, you'll see how to answer this question by writing and solving an equation.

To solve an equation that has a fractional coefficient, you can multiply each side of the equation by the fraction's *multiplicative inverse*. The **multiplicative inverse** of a nonzero number is the number's reciprocal.

Multiplicative Inverse Property

Words The product of a number and its multiplicative inverse is 1.

Numbers $\frac{3}{5} \cdot \frac{5}{3} = 1$

Algebra $\frac{a}{b} \cdot \frac{b}{a} = 1$, where $a \neq 0, b \neq 0$

Study *Strategy*

When you solve an equation with fractional coefficients, remember to check your solution by substituting the value of the variable in the original equation.

Example 1   *Solving a One-Step Equation*

$$\frac{4}{7}x = -12 \qquad \text{Original equation}$$

$$\frac{7}{4}\left(\frac{4}{7}\right)x = \frac{7}{4}(-12) \qquad \text{Multiply each side by multiplicative inverse of } \frac{4}{7}.$$

$$1x = \frac{7}{4}(-12) \qquad \text{Multiplicative inverse property}$$

$$x = -21 \qquad \text{Multiply.}$$

Answer The solution is -21.

Example 2   *Solving a Two-Step Equation*

$$-\frac{11}{15}x + \frac{4}{5} = \frac{1}{3}$$ **Original equation**

$$-\frac{11}{15}x + \frac{4}{5} - \frac{4}{5} = \frac{1}{3} - \frac{4}{5}$$ **Subtract $\frac{4}{5}$ from each side.**

$$-\frac{11}{15}x = \frac{1}{3} - \frac{4}{5}$$ **Simplify.**

$$-\frac{11}{15}x = \frac{5}{15} - \frac{12}{15}$$ **Write fractions using LCD.**

$$-\frac{11}{15}x = -\frac{7}{15}$$ **Subtract.**

$$-\frac{15}{11}\left(-\frac{11}{15}\right)x = -\frac{15}{11}\left(-\frac{7}{15}\right)$$ **Multiply each side by multiplicative inverse of $-\frac{11}{15}$.**

$$x = \frac{7}{11}$$ **Multiply.**

✔ *Checkpoint*

Solve the equation. Check your solution.

1. $\frac{5}{6}m = 20$ **2.** $-16 = \frac{3}{4}n - 20$ **3.** $-\frac{2}{3}p + \frac{1}{2} = \frac{5}{6}$

Example 3   *Writing and Solving a Two-Step Equation*

Find how long it will take the stalactite described on page 247 to reach a length of 1 foot.

Solution

Write a verbal model. Let x represent the number of decades it will take the stalactite to reach a length of 1 foot.

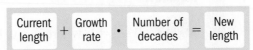

| Current length | + | Growth rate | • | Number of decades | = | New length |

$$10 + \frac{1}{8}x = 12$$ **Write equation. Write 1 foot as 12 inches.**

$$10 + \frac{1}{8}x - 10 = 12 - 10$$ **Subtract 10 from each side.**

$$\frac{1}{8}x = 2$$ **Simplify.**

$$8\left(\frac{1}{8}x\right) = 8(2)$$ **Multiply each side by multiplicative inverse of $\frac{1}{8}$.**

$$x = 16$$ **Multiply.**

Answer The stalactite will be 1 foot long after 16 decades, or 160 years.

In the **Real World**

Caves The photo above was taken in La Grotte de Gournier, a cave in France. Cave explorers have found that the deepest point in this cave is 680 meters beneath Earth's surface. Give the depth of the cave in kilometers. Then use the fact that 1 km ≈ 0.62 mi to find the depth of the cave in miles. Is the cave more than or less than half a mile deep?

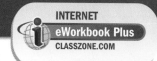

Guided Practice

Vocabulary Check
1. What is the multiplicative inverse of a nonzero number?

2. Describe how to solve the equation $\frac{5}{6}x = \frac{2}{7}$.

Skill Check **Solve the equation. Check your solution.**

3. $\frac{4}{9}x = -16$

4. $-\frac{7}{12}x = 28$

5. $-\frac{2}{3}x = \frac{6}{7}$

6. $\frac{1}{3}x + 5 = 11$

7. $\frac{7}{8}x - 9 = 5$

8. $-\frac{3}{4}x + \frac{3}{8} = \frac{27}{32}$

Guided Problem Solving
9. **Ants** The diagram shows the distances of two ants from the edge of a picnic table. Ant A travels in a straight line at a speed of $\frac{3}{4}$ inch per second. Ant B travels in a straight line at a speed of $\frac{7}{8}$ inch per second. Which ant will reach the edge first?

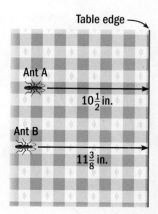

① Use the formula *distance = rate × time* to write an equation for each ant.

② Solve each equation from Step 1.

③ Compare your solutions to determine which ant will reach the edge first.

Practice and Problem Solving

Homework Help

Example	Exercises
1	11–20
2	21–29
3	30–31

Online Resources
CLASSZONE.COM
• More Examples
• eTutorial Plus

10. **Error Analysis** Describe and correct the error in solving the equation $-\frac{1}{6}x = \frac{2}{3}$.

$$-\frac{1}{6}x = \frac{2}{3}$$

$$\times \quad 6\left(-\frac{1}{6}x\right) = 6\left(\frac{2}{3}\right)$$

$$x = 4$$

Solve the equation. Check your solution.

11. $\frac{2}{9}x = 12$

12. $\frac{3}{8}x = 15$

13. $-\frac{5}{12}x = 25$

14. $-\frac{1}{6}x = 8$

15. $\frac{5}{7}x = -\frac{9}{14}$

16. $\frac{2}{5}x = -\frac{8}{15}$

17. $-\frac{17}{22}x = \frac{4}{11}$

18. $-\frac{10}{21}x = \frac{2}{3}$

19. United States Flag The length of the United States flag is $1\frac{9}{10}$ times the width of the flag. A particular U.S. flag is 5 feet long. Write and solve an equation to find the width of the flag.

20. *Writing* Solve the equation $\frac{3}{7}x = 5$ by using a multiplicative inverse. Then solve the equation by dividing each side of the equation by $\frac{3}{7}$.

Compare these two methods of solving the equation. How are they alike? How are they different?

Solve the equation. Check your solution.

21. $\frac{4}{9}x + 7 = 31$ **22.** $\frac{7}{11}x + (-17) = 4$ **23.** $4 + \left(-\frac{3}{5}\right)x = 16$

24. $\frac{2}{13} = \frac{8}{13}x + \frac{4}{13}$ **25.** $-\frac{8}{17} = \frac{11}{17} - \frac{5}{17}x$ **26.** $\frac{13}{15}x - \frac{7}{9} = -\frac{1}{5}$

27. $\frac{5}{14} + \frac{2}{7}x = 1\frac{5}{42}$ **28.** $\frac{7}{8}x - \frac{9}{10} = -\frac{1}{8}$ **29.** $-\frac{5}{48} = -\frac{5}{6} + \frac{5}{16}x$

30. Geometry The figure shown is composed of two rectangles. The area of the figure is 1 square inch.

a. Find the area of the red rectangle.

b. Write an expression for the area of the blue rectangle.

c. Write an equation relating the sum of the areas in parts (a) and (b) to the total area of the figure. Solve the equation to find the value of x.

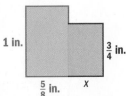

1 in.

$\frac{3}{4}$ in.

$\frac{5}{8}$ in. x

31. Panama Canal Locks on the Panama Canal are used to move a ship from a higher elevation to a lower elevation. When a ship enters a lock chamber on the canal, water is allowed to spill out of the lock chamber into the next lock chamber until the water levels in the two chambers are equal. Suppose the water level in one lock chamber is 72 feet. As water spills out of the chamber, the depth changes at a rate of about $-3\frac{1}{2}$ feet per minute until the water level is 41 feet. How many minutes does it take for the depth to change from 72 feet to 41 feet?

32. Baseball Game At a college baseball game, $\frac{4}{5}$ of the spectators are home team fans. The rest of the spectators are opposing team fans. There are 750 opposing team fans.

a. Find the fraction of spectators who are opposing team fans.

b. Find the total number of spectators at the game.

c. One third of the home team fans at the game attend the college. How many home team fans attend the college?

33. Critical Thinking Suppose you want to solve the equation $\left(-2\frac{1}{2}\right)x = \frac{8}{15}$ by using the multiplicative inverse of $-2\frac{1}{2}$. What is the multiplicative inverse of $-2\frac{1}{2}$?

In the **Real World**

Panama Canal In the year 2002, 390 general cargo ships traveled through the Panama Canal from the Atlantic Ocean to the Pacific Ocean. The number of general cargo ships was 6 less than 3 times the number of passenger ships. How many passenger ships passed from the Atlantic to the Pacific?

34. Challenge The following is based on a famous problem about Diophantus, a Greek mathematician from the third century.

Let x be the number of years Diophantus lived. Find how long he lived by using the following facts about him to write and solve an equation.

> ONE SIXTH OF HIS LIFE WAS SPENT IN BOYHOOD.
>
> ONE TWELFTH OF HIS LIFE WAS SPENT AS A YOUTH.
>
> AFTER $\frac{1}{7}$ MORE OF HIS LIFE PASSED, HE GOT MARRIED.
>
> FIVE YEARS AFTER GETTING MARRIED, HE HAD A SON.
>
> HIS SON LIVED $\frac{1}{2}$ AS LONG AS DIOPHANTUS LIVED.
>
> THE SON DIED FOUR YEARS BEFORE DIOPHANTUS DIED.

Mixed Review

Algebra Basics Solve the inequality. Graph your solution. *(Lesson 3.6)*

35. $-17 + 2y > 11$ **36.** $5x - 23 < 12$ **37.** $-6z + 13 \leq 31$

38. Commuting Of the 1458 students at school A, 324 students take the bus. Of the 2123 students at school B, 242 take the bus. At which school is the fraction of students who take the bus greater? *(Lesson 5.1)*

Find the sum or difference. *(Lesson 5.3)*

39. $-\dfrac{1}{3} + \dfrac{3}{4}$ **40.** $\dfrac{1}{6} + \left(-\dfrac{5}{8}\right)$ **41.** $-\dfrac{4}{9} - \dfrac{7}{12}$ **42.** $\dfrac{3}{7} - \dfrac{9}{14}$

Standardized Test Practice

43. Multiple Choice What is the solution of the equation $\dfrac{7}{12}x - 5 = -7\dfrac{1}{3}$?

A. -4 **B.** $-1\dfrac{13}{36}$ **C.** $-\dfrac{1}{4}$ **D.** 4

44. Short Response Two thirds of the lockers at a health club are rented to members at a rate of $6 per month. The other 48 lockers are available free to members on a first-come, first-serve basis. How much money does the club make from renting lockers each month?

CD Sort

Your friend has a collection of CDs: $\frac{2}{3}$ of the CDs have booklets, $\frac{1}{2}$ of the CDs are singles, and $\frac{1}{4}$ are singles with booklets. All but two of the CDs are either singles or have booklets or both. How many CDs does your friend have?

5.6 Solving Equations with Fractions

Goal Use a calculator to solve an equation with a fractional coefficient.

Example

Use a calculator to solve the following problem.

Your horses eat about $\frac{2}{3}$ of a bale of hay every day. You have 33 bales of hay. After how many days will you need to buy more hay?

1 To represent the situation, use the equation $\frac{2}{3}d = 33$, where d is the number of days. To solve this equation, you can multiply each side by the multiplicative inverse of $\frac{2}{3}$. To obtain this multiplicative inverse on a calculator, use these keystrokes:

Keystrokes

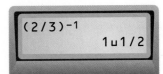

2 Now find the product of the multiplicative inverse and 33.

Keystrokes

$\boxed{\times}$ 33 $\boxed{=}$

Ans refers to the answer, or result, from the previous calculation.

Answer You will run out of hay in $49\frac{1}{2}$ days. To be sure your horses have enough hay, you need to buy more after 49 days.

Tech *Help*

The symbol ⊔ on the calculator display indicates that the number is a mixed number. For example $1⊔1/2$ means $1\frac{1}{2}$.

Draw Conclusions

Use a calculator to solve the equation.

1. $\frac{3}{4}x = 27$ **2.** $\frac{5}{16}x = -55$ **3.** $\frac{2}{7}x = -26$ **4.** $-\frac{9}{11}x = 39$

5. Sewing Use a calculator to solve the following problem:

The stitches made by a sewing machine are each $\frac{3}{16}$ inch long and lie end to end in a line. How many stitches are there in a line of stitches that is 21 inches long?

5.7

Equations *and* Inequalities *with* Rational Numbers

Review Vocabulary
inequality, p. 138
solution of an
 inequality, p. 138

BEFORE	*Now*	WHY?
You used reciprocals to solve equations.	You'll use the LCD to solve equations and inequalities.	So you can find the original price of a sale item, as in Ex. 39.

So far you have followed these steps to solve equations with fractions:

- Undo any addition or subtraction in order to get the variable term alone on one side of the equation.

- Multiply both sides of the equation by the multiplicative inverse of the coefficient of the variable term.

Another way to solve an equation with fractions is to clear fractions by multiplying each side of the equation by the LCD of the fractions. The resulting equation is equivalent to the original equation.

Example 1 *Solving an Equation by Clearing Fractions*

$$-\frac{5}{6}x + \frac{1}{2} = \frac{3}{4}$$ **Original equation**

$$12\left(-\frac{5}{6}x + \frac{1}{2}\right) = 12\left(\frac{3}{4}\right)$$ **Multiply each side by LCD of fractions.**

$$12\left(-\frac{5}{6}x\right) + 12\left(\frac{1}{2}\right) = 12\left(\frac{3}{4}\right)$$ **Use distributive property.**

$$-10x + 6 = 9$$ **Simplify.**

$$-10x + 6 - 6 = 9 - 6$$ **Subtract 6 from each side.**

$$-10x = 3$$ **Simplify.**

$$\frac{-10x}{-10} = \frac{3}{-10}$$ **Divide each side by −10.**

$$x = -\frac{3}{10}$$ **Simplify.**

! **Watch** *Out*

In Example 1, notice that each term in the equation is multiplied by the LCD of the fractions in the equation.

 Checkpoint

Solve the equation by first clearing the fractions.

1. $\frac{1}{2}x + \frac{7}{10} = \frac{4}{5}$ **2.** $\frac{3}{8}x - \frac{2}{3} = \frac{7}{12}$ **3.** $-\frac{2}{9} = \frac{3}{4}x - \frac{1}{6}$

Solving Equations with Decimals As shown in Example 2 on page 254, you can clear decimals from an equation.

Reading *Algebra*

Multiplying each side of the equation in Example 2 by 100 produces an equivalent equation. The new equation, $230 = 514 + 80m$, has the same solution as the equation $2.3 = 5.14 + 0.8m$.

Example 2 | *Solving an Equation by Clearing Decimals*

Solve the equation 2.3 = 5.14 + 0.8m.

Because the greatest number of decimal places in any of the terms with decimals is 2, multiply each side of the equation by 10^2, or 100.

$2.3 = 5.14 + 0.8m$	Write original equation.
$100(2.3) = 100(5.14 + 0.8m)$	Multiply each side by 100.
$230 = 514 + 80m$	Use distributive property. Simplify.
$230 - 514 = 514 + 80m - 514$	Subtract 514 from each side.
$-284 = 80m$	Simplify.
$\dfrac{-284}{80} = \dfrac{80m}{80}$	Divide each side by 80.
$-3.55 = m$	Simplify.

Solving Inequalities You can use the methods you have learned for solving equations with fractional coefficients to solve inequalities.

Example 3 | *Solving an Inequality with Fractions*

Shopping A sign in a clothing store says to take $\frac{1}{3}$ off the marked price of a shirt. You have \$20 in cash and a \$5 gift certificate. What are the original prices of the shirts you can afford to buy?

Solution

Write a verbal model. Let x represent the original prices of the shirts you can afford to buy.

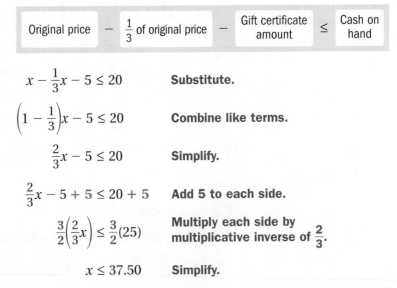

$x - \dfrac{1}{3}x - 5 \le 20$	Substitute.
$\left(1 - \dfrac{1}{3}\right)x - 5 \le 20$	Combine like terms.
$\dfrac{2}{3}x - 5 \le 20$	Simplify.
$\dfrac{2}{3}x - 5 + 5 \le 20 + 5$	Add 5 to each side.
$\dfrac{3}{2}\left(\dfrac{2}{3}x\right) \le \dfrac{3}{2}(25)$	Multiply each side by multiplicative inverse of $\dfrac{2}{3}$.
$x \le 37.50$	Simplify.

Answer You can afford a shirt whose original price is \$37.50 or less.

More Practice, p. 807

Example 4 — Solving an Inequality by Clearing Fractions

$$-\frac{3}{4}m - \frac{1}{8} \le -\frac{1}{4}$$ Original inequality

$$8\left(-\frac{3}{4}m - \frac{1}{8}\right) \le 8\left(-\frac{1}{4}\right)$$ Multiply each side by LCD of fractions.

$$8\left(-\frac{3}{4}m\right) - 8\left(\frac{1}{8}\right) \le 8\left(-\frac{1}{4}\right)$$ Distributive property

$$-6m - 1 \le -2$$ Simplify.

$$-6m - 1 + 1 \le -2 + 1$$ Add 1 to each side.

$$-6m \le -1$$ Simplify.

$$\frac{-6m}{-6} \ge \frac{-1}{-6}$$ Divide each side by −6. Reverse inequality symbol.

$$m \ge \frac{1}{6}$$ Simplify.

5.7 Exercises

Guided Practice

Vocabulary Check

1. Copy and complete: To clear the fractions in an equation, multiply each side of the equation by the _?_ of the fractions.

2. To clear the decimals in an equation, how do you determine what power of 10 to multiply each side of the equation by?

Skill Check   **Solve the equation by first clearing the fractions or the decimals.**

3. $\frac{2}{3}n + 17 = \frac{5}{6}$ **4.** $\frac{2}{5} = \frac{5}{8}n - 4$ **5.** $\frac{3}{4}n - \frac{1}{2} = \frac{7}{4}$

6. $2.3m - 11 = -29.4$ **7.** $5.3m - 6 = -27.2$ **8.** $-1.2m + 1.25 = 0.77$

Solve the inequality by first clearing the fractions.

9. $\frac{7}{13}x - 1 > \frac{1}{2}$ **10.** $\frac{4}{5} \ge \frac{2}{3} - \frac{2}{7}x$ **11.** $\frac{8}{15}x - \frac{17}{30} < \frac{7}{10}$

12. Error Analysis Describe and correct the error in clearing the fractions in the equation $\frac{2}{3}x + 5 = \frac{5}{2}$.

$$\frac{2}{3}x + 5 = \frac{5}{2}$$

$$6\left(\frac{2}{3}x\right) + 5 = 6\left(\frac{5}{2}\right)$$

$$4x + 5 = 15$$

Practice and Problem Solving

Homework *Help*

Example	Exercises
1	13–21, 40
2	22–31, 41
3	32–39
4	32–39

Online Resources
CLASSZONE.COM
- More Examples
- eTutorial Plus

Solve the equation by first clearing the fractions.

13. $\frac{1}{2}t + \frac{1}{4} = \frac{5}{16}$

14. $\frac{5}{6}s + \frac{2}{9} = -\frac{7}{12}$

15. $\frac{3}{4} = \frac{5}{6}a + \frac{2}{9}$

16. $\frac{5}{8} = \frac{1}{10} + \frac{5}{14}m$

17. $-\frac{41}{60} + \frac{17}{20}p = \frac{29}{30}$

18. $\frac{3}{8} = -\frac{1}{4}x - \frac{3}{5}$

19. $-\frac{3}{2}t - \frac{5}{6} = -\frac{4}{9}$

20. $-\frac{3}{5}z - 4 = -\frac{77}{20}$

21. $4w + \frac{2}{7} = -\frac{4}{5}$

Solve the equation by first clearing the decimals.

22. $6.2x + 3.7 = 22.3$

23. $7.8y + 6 = 23.16$

24. $10.7w + 4 = 47.87$

25. $2 = -6.4z + 10$

26. $-3.3x + 6.5 = 1.55$

27. $1.6b - 3 = -9.4$

28. $-1.7w - 4 = 2.63$

29. $2.875y + 9 = 12.45$

30. $4.125c + 5 = -9.85$

31. Saving Money You want to save $400 for a camping trip. You have $64.96 in your savings account. Each week you deposit your paycheck from your part-time job. Each paycheck is for $69.80. How many paychecks must you deposit to reach your goal of $400?

Solve the inequality.

32. $-\frac{4}{11}z - 1 > -\frac{8}{11}$

33. $\frac{1}{5}k + 14 \le \frac{2}{9}$

34. $-\frac{31}{4} < -13 + \frac{7}{8}f$

35. $\frac{1}{7}r + \frac{53}{56} > \frac{6}{7}$

36. $\frac{5}{6}n - \frac{1}{5} < -\frac{8}{15}$

37. $\frac{1}{3} + \frac{1}{13}d \ge \frac{17}{39}$

38. Fundraiser Your class is selling gift wrap for a school fundraiser. One fourth of the money collected will be used to pay for the gift wrap. Your class wants to raise at least $675 after paying for the gift wrap. How much money does your class need to collect?

39. Sale Price A store displays the sign shown. You want to buy a belt that costs $8 and a pair of jeans. You have $18. Write and solve an inequality to find the original prices of the jeans you can afford to buy.

> **CLEARANCE SALE!**
> Take $\frac{2}{3}$ off the price of all jeans!

40. Pets Each morning you feed your dog $\frac{3}{4}$ cup of dry dog food. At night you feed him $\frac{1}{3}$ cup of dry dog food. You buy a bag of dog food that contains 40 cups. How many days will the bag last?

41. Physics The speed of sound in air depends on temperature. The relationship between the speed of sound and the air temperature is given by the equation $v = 331.4 + 0.6T$, where v is the speed of sound in meters per second and T is the air temperature in degrees Celsius. During a storm, the speed of sound was measured at 343.37 meters per second. What was the air temperature?

42. *Writing* Compare and contrast the method of using multiplicative inverses with the method of clearing fractions when solving an equation like $\frac{2}{3}x - 1 = \frac{5}{6}$.

43. Costumes You buy $12\frac{1}{2}$ yards of material to make costumes for a school play. Each costume consists of a matching hat and cape. You need $1\frac{1}{4}$ feet of the material for each hat. You need $3\frac{1}{2}$ feet of material for each cape. How many costumes can you make?

44. Critical Thinking Can you clear fractions in an equation by multiplying each side of the equation by a common denominator other than the LCD? Give an example to explain your reasoning.

45. Money You are visiting Canada. You have $21.25 in Canadian currency, and the rest of your money is in U.S. currency. You want to exchange your U.S. currency for Canadian currency. For every dollar you have in U.S. currency, you can get $1.557 in Canadian currency. You want to buy a souvenir that costs $25.50 in Canadian currency. How much money in U.S. currency do you need to exchange to have enough to buy the souvenir?

46. Challenge Solve the equation $\frac{4}{9}\left(\frac{1}{3}x + 6\right) = \frac{5}{18}x + \frac{1}{3}$. Show the steps you take.

Mixed Review

Find the product or quotient. *(Lesson 1.7)*

47. $-3(-40)$ **48.** $-5(11)$ **49.** $-180 \div 5$ **50.** $90 \div (-6)$

Simplify the expression. *(Lesson 5.3)*

51. $\frac{r}{5} + \frac{7r}{9}$ **52.** $\frac{s}{7} - \frac{s}{3}$ **53.** $\frac{5t}{2} - \frac{t}{6}$ **54.** $-\frac{3d}{10} - \frac{8d}{15}$

55. Rain Gauge The water level in a rain gauge is $2\frac{3}{4}$ inches. A steady rain raises the water level by $\frac{1}{8}$ inch each hour. When the rain stops, the gauge reads 4 inches. How many hours did the rain last? *(Lesson 5.6)*

Standardized Test Practice

56. Multiple Choice Which graph represents the solution of the inequality $-\frac{3}{8}x > -9$?

A.
```
←—+——+——⊕——+——+—→
  22   23   24   25   26
```

B.
```
←—+——+——⊕——+——+—→
  22   23   24   25   26
```

C.
```
←—+——+——⊕——+——+—→
 -26 -25 -24 -23 -22
```

D.
```
←—+——+——⊕——+——+—→
 -26 -25 -24 -23 -22
```

57. Multiple Choice Which number is *not* a solution of the inequality $2 - \frac{5}{7}m \geq -3$?

F. -9 **G.** -7 **H.** 7 **I.** 9

Vocabulary Review

rational number, p. 219   repeating decimal, p. 219   multiplicative inverse, p. 247
terminating decimal, p. 219   reciprocals, p. 243

1. Give an example of a number that is an integer but not a whole number.

2. Give an example of a number that is a rational number but not a whole number.

3. Give an example of a rational number that is a whole number and an integer.

4. Which number is greater, the repeating decimal $0.\overline{7}$ or the decimal 0.77? Why?

5. Give an example of two numbers that are reciprocals.

6. How is the term *multiplicative inverse* related to the term *reciprocal*?

5.1 Rational Numbers

Examples on
pp. 219–221

▶ *Goal*

Write, compare, and order rational numbers.

Example Write the fraction as a decimal.

a. $-\dfrac{39}{1000} = -0.039$

b. $\dfrac{3}{11} = 0.272727\ldots = 0.\overline{27}$

Example Order $1\dfrac{19}{20}$, -3.06, -0.8, $\dfrac{9}{20}$, and $-\dfrac{54}{25}$ from least to greatest.

Graph the numbers on a number line. Write improper fractions as mixed numbers.

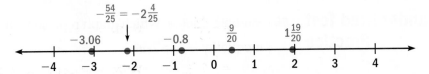

From least to greatest, the numbers are -3.06, $-\dfrac{54}{25}$, -0.8, $\dfrac{9}{20}$, $1\dfrac{19}{20}$.

✔ **Write the fraction or mixed number as a decimal.**

7. $\dfrac{7}{11}$

8. $-\dfrac{7}{80}$

9. $-2\dfrac{3}{5}$

10. $4\dfrac{2}{90}$

11. Order $-5.2\overline{3}$, $5.\overline{3}$, $\dfrac{134}{25}$, $-\dfrac{263}{25}$, and $5\dfrac{9}{20}$ from least to greatest.

5.2 Adding and Subtracting Like Fractions

Examples on pp. 225–227

▶ **Goal**

Add and subtract fractions and mixed numbers with the same denominator.

Example Find the sum $-6\frac{5}{8} + \left(-4\frac{1}{8}\right)$.

$-6\frac{5}{8} + \left(-4\frac{1}{8}\right) = \frac{-53}{8} + \left(\frac{-33}{8}\right)$ Write mixed numbers as improper fractions.

$= \frac{-53 + (-33)}{8}$ Write sum of numerators over denominator.

$= \frac{-86}{8}$ Add.

$= \frac{-43}{4} = -10\frac{3}{4}$ Simplify. Then write improper fraction as a mixed number.

✔ **Find the sum or difference.**

12. $\frac{1}{12} + \left(-\frac{5}{12}\right)$ **13.** $-\frac{4}{7} - \frac{5}{7}$ **14.** $7\frac{2}{9} - 3\frac{8}{9}$ **15.** $9\frac{7}{10} + 5\frac{3}{10}$

5.3 Adding and Subtracting Unlike Fractions

Examples on pp. 231–233

▶ **Goal**

Add and subtract fractions and mixed numbers with different denominators.

Example Find the difference $4\frac{5}{18} - 6\frac{8}{9}$.

$4\frac{5}{18} - 6\frac{8}{9} = \frac{77}{18} - \frac{62}{9}$ Write mixed numbers as improper fractions.

$= \frac{77}{18} - \frac{124}{18}$ Write $\frac{62}{9}$ using LCD.

$= \frac{77 - 124}{18}$ Write difference of numerators over denominator.

$= \frac{-47}{18}$ Subtract.

$= -2\frac{11}{18}$ Write improper fraction as a mixed number.

✔ **Find the sum or difference.**

16. $\frac{7}{12} - \frac{5}{24}$ **17.** $-\frac{8}{21} + \frac{9}{14}$ **18.** $\frac{3}{17} - \frac{15}{34}$

19. $2\frac{3}{4} + 2\frac{5}{6}$ **20.** $-13\frac{9}{14} + 21\frac{17}{28}$ **21.** $9\frac{14}{15} - 18\frac{5}{21}$

5.4 Multiplying Fractions

▶ **Goal**

Multiply fractions and mixed numbers.

Example Find the product $-\dfrac{4}{5}\left(\dfrac{25}{42}\right)$.

$$-\frac{4}{5}\left(\frac{25}{42}\right) = \frac{\overset{-2}{\cancel{4}} \cdot \overset{5}{25}}{\underset{1}{\cancel{5}} \cdot \underset{21}{\cancel{42}}}$$ Use rule for multiplying fractions.
Divide out common factors.

$$= -\frac{10}{21}$$ Multiply.

Example Simplify the expression.

$$\frac{m^3}{8} \cdot \frac{2m}{5} = \frac{m^3 \cdot \overset{1}{\cancel{2}}m}{\underset{4}{\cancel{8}} \cdot 5}$$ Use rule for multiplying fractions.
Divide out common factor.

$$= \frac{m^{3+1}}{20}$$ Product of powers property

$$= \frac{m^4}{20}$$ Add exponents.

✔ **Find the product.**

22. $\dfrac{18}{19}\left(-\dfrac{38}{27}\right)$ **23.** $-\dfrac{2}{15} \cdot \dfrac{5}{8}$ **24.** $-3\dfrac{1}{17} \cdot \left(-\dfrac{3}{4}\right)$ **25.** $6\dfrac{3}{4} \cdot \left(-7\dfrac{1}{9}\right)$

Simplify the expression.

26. $\dfrac{a^3}{2} \cdot \dfrac{2a}{9}$ **27.** $\dfrac{3b^2}{4} \cdot \dfrac{16b}{21}$ **28.** $-\dfrac{12n^3}{5} \cdot \dfrac{n^4}{3}$ **29.** $-\dfrac{5s}{4} \cdot \dfrac{12s^4}{25}$

5.5 Dividing Fractions

▶ **Goal**

Divide fractions and mixed numbers.

Example Find the quotient $\dfrac{2}{3} \div \left(-\dfrac{6}{7}\right)$.

$$\frac{2}{3} \div \left(-\frac{6}{7}\right) = \frac{2}{3} \cdot \left(-\frac{7}{6}\right)$$ Multiply by reciprocal.

$$= \frac{\overset{1}{\cancel{2}} \cdot (-7)}{3 \cdot \underset{3}{\cancel{6}}}$$ Use rule for multiplying fractions.
Divide out common factor.

$$= -\frac{7}{9}$$ Multiply.

✔ **Find the quotient.**

30. $-\dfrac{6}{7} \div \dfrac{36}{77}$ **31.** $-\dfrac{21}{58} \div \dfrac{3}{16}$ **32.** $16\dfrac{2}{3} \div 2$ **33.** $-3\dfrac{3}{11} \div 1\dfrac{17}{55}$

5.6 Using Multiplicative Inverses to Solve Equations

Examples on
pp. 247–248

▶ **Goal**

Use multiplicative inverses to solve equations with fractional coefficients.

Example Solve the equation $\frac{4}{5}t = -\frac{8}{11}$.

$$\frac{4}{5}t = -\frac{8}{11} \qquad \text{Write original equation.}$$

$$\frac{5}{4}\left(\frac{4}{5}t\right) = \frac{5}{4}\left(-\frac{8}{11}\right) \qquad \text{Multiply each side by multiplicative inverse of } \frac{4}{5}.$$

$$1t = \frac{5}{4}\left(-\frac{8}{11}\right) \qquad \text{Multiplicative inverse property}$$

$$t = -\frac{10}{11} \qquad \text{Multiply.}$$

✔ **Solve the equation.**

34. $\frac{14}{27}x = -\frac{7}{12}$ **35.** $-\frac{5}{8}x = \frac{10}{17}$ **36.** $1\frac{3}{8} = \frac{3}{4}x + 1$ **37.** $\frac{5}{6}x - \frac{1}{4} = -\frac{11}{24}$

5.7 Equations and Inequalities with Rational Numbers

Examples on
pp. 253–255

▶ **Goal**

Solve equations and inequalities with rational numbers.

Example Solve the equation $-\frac{8}{9}x + \frac{1}{6} = \frac{49}{54}$ by first clearing the fractions.

$$-\frac{8}{9}x + \frac{1}{6} = \frac{49}{54} \qquad \text{Write original equation.}$$

$$54\left(-\frac{8}{9}x + \frac{1}{6}\right) = 54\left(\frac{49}{54}\right) \qquad \text{Multiply each side by LCD of fractions.}$$

$$54\left(-\frac{8}{9}x\right) + 54\left(\frac{1}{6}\right) = 54\left(\frac{49}{54}\right) \qquad \text{Distributive property}$$

$$-48x + 9 = 49 \qquad \text{Simplify.}$$

$$-48x + 9 - 9 = 49 - 9 \qquad \text{Subtract 9 from each side.}$$

$$-48x = 40 \qquad \text{Simplify.}$$

$$\frac{-48x}{-48} = \frac{40}{-48} \qquad \text{Divide each side by } -48.$$

$$x = -\frac{5}{6} \qquad \text{Simplify.}$$

✔ **Solve the equation by first clearing the fractions.**

38. $\frac{3}{7}x + \frac{5}{14} = \frac{19}{42}$ **39.** $\frac{5}{16} = -\frac{3}{32} + \frac{7}{8}n$ **40.** $-\frac{3}{4}x - \frac{5}{8} = -\frac{1}{56}$

Chapter Test

Write the fraction or mixed number as a decimal.

1. $-\dfrac{7}{125}$ **2.** $10\dfrac{4}{9}$ **3.** $-\dfrac{2}{27}$ **4.** $\dfrac{37}{10{,}000}$

Write the decimal as a fraction or mixed number.

5. 11.85 **6.** -7.52 **7.** $0.\overline{7}$ **8.** $0.\overline{63}$

Find the sum or difference.

9. $-\dfrac{15}{24} + \dfrac{19}{24}$ **10.** $-4\dfrac{1}{3} - 8\dfrac{1}{3}$ **11.** $\dfrac{4}{5} - \dfrac{11}{15}$ **12.** $-3\dfrac{5}{7} + 1\dfrac{2}{9}$

13. Birds The Northern junco, a bird found in Alaska and Canada, varies in length from $5\dfrac{1}{2}$ inches to $6\dfrac{3}{4}$ inches. Find the range of the lengths of the Northern junco.

Simplify the expression.

14. $\dfrac{4m}{21} + \dfrac{17m}{21}$ **15.** $-\dfrac{3t}{22} - \dfrac{5t}{44}$ **16.** $-\dfrac{7n}{18} - \dfrac{11n}{30}$ **17.** $-\dfrac{4z}{35} - \dfrac{8z}{25}$

18. Geometry The side lengths of a triangle are $3\dfrac{5}{8}$ inches, $4\dfrac{5}{16}$ inches, and 2 inches. What is the perimeter of the triangle?

Find the product or quotient.

19. $\dfrac{8}{9} \cdot \left(-\dfrac{3}{10}\right)$ **20.** $4 \div \left(-2\dfrac{4}{15}\right)$ **21.** $-\dfrac{9}{20} \cdot 2\dfrac{2}{3}$ **22.** $14\dfrac{5}{6} \div 2\dfrac{1}{8}$

Simplify the expression.

23. $\dfrac{4r^3}{15} \cdot \dfrac{5r^3}{12}$ **24.** $-\dfrac{7n^2}{12} \cdot \left(-\dfrac{18n}{49}\right)$ **25.** $-\dfrac{9t^2}{13} \cdot \dfrac{t}{12}$ **26.** $-\dfrac{25w^3}{42} \cdot \left(-\dfrac{3w}{10}\right)$

27. Encyclopedia An encyclopedia has 30 volumes. The total weight of these volumes is $71\dfrac{1}{4}$ pounds. Find the average weight of a volume.

Solve the equation. Check your solution.

28. $\dfrac{7}{8}m = -8$ **29.** $\dfrac{9}{25} = \dfrac{3}{5}t$ **30.** $-\dfrac{13}{20} = \dfrac{1}{4} + \dfrac{3}{5}t$ **31.** $\dfrac{1}{7}g + 8 = 2$

Solve the equation or inequality by first clearing the fractions or decimals.

32. $9.2m + 1.4 = 12.9$ **33.** $10 = 8.22w - 3.152$ **34.** $\dfrac{2}{15}b - \dfrac{4}{5} < \dfrac{2}{3}$ **35.** $\dfrac{1}{3}m - \dfrac{7}{18} = \dfrac{4}{9}$

Chapter Standardized Test

Test-Taking Strategy Mark test questions that you can't answer on the first try. Move on to new questions and return later to the marked questions.

1. Which fraction is equivalent to $0.\overline{52}$?

   A. $\frac{4}{9}$　　**B.** $\frac{51}{99}$　　**C.** $\frac{52}{99}$　　**D.** $\frac{5}{9}$

2. Which list of numbers is in order from least to greatest?

   F. $-\frac{33}{10}, -3.2, \frac{7}{8}, 0.9, 0.\overline{9}$

   G. $-3.2, -\frac{33}{10}, \frac{7}{8}, 0.9, 0.\overline{9}$

   H. $-3.2, -\frac{33}{10}, \frac{7}{8}, 0.\overline{9}, 0.9$

   I. $-\frac{33}{10}, -3.2, 0.\overline{9}, 0.9, \frac{7}{8}$

3. Simplify the expression $-\frac{12n}{35} - \frac{13n}{35}$.

   A. $-\frac{25n}{35}$　　**B.** $-\frac{5n}{7}$　　**C.** $-\frac{n}{35}$　　**D.** $\frac{25n}{35}$

4. Find the sum $3\frac{1}{4} + \left(-2\frac{3}{8}\right)$.

   F. $-5\frac{5}{8}$　　**G.** $-\frac{7}{8}$　　**H.** $\frac{7}{8}$　　**I.** $5\frac{5}{8}$

5. Find the product $-2\frac{5}{8} \cdot \left(-5\frac{3}{7}\right)$.

   A. $-14\frac{1}{4}$　　**B.** $-2\frac{19}{28}$　　**C.** $2\frac{19}{28}$　　**D.** $14\frac{1}{4}$

6. Find the quotient $1\frac{1}{12} \div 2\frac{7}{16}$.

   F. $\frac{2}{21}$　　**G.** $\frac{4}{9}$　　**H.** $2\frac{7}{192}$　　**I.** $2\frac{41}{64}$

7. What is the solution of the equation $\frac{4}{5} - 12 = \frac{3}{10}x$?

   A. $-37\frac{1}{3}$　**B.** $-9\frac{1}{3}$　**C.** $9\frac{1}{3}$　**D.** $37\frac{1}{3}$

8. Half the books you own are mysteries. One third are historical fiction. The other four books are science fiction. How many of your books are mysteries?

   F. 4　　**G.** 8　　**H.** 12　　**I.** 24

9. Which number is *not* a solution of $\frac{2}{3}x + \frac{1}{6} \geq 1\frac{17}{18}$?

   A. 2　　**B.** 3　　**C.** 4　　**D.** 5

10. **Short Response** You have a length of cloth that is $2\frac{3}{4}$ yards long and $1\frac{1}{4}$ yards wide. You want to cut the cloth into 20 squares that are $1\frac{1}{4}$ feet long on each side. Do you have enough cloth to cut all the squares? Explain why or why not.

11. **Extended Response** A recipe for making 24 pretzels calls for using $1\frac{1}{2}$ cups of milk. A baker wants to use the recipe to make pretzels to sell. He wants to buy enough milk to make 100 pretzels each day over the next 5 days.

    a. How many cups of milk does the baker need for all the pretzels?

    b. How many gallons of milk should he buy? Use the fact that 1 gallon = 16 cups. Explain your answer.

Making *a* Plan

Using Multiple Strategies

When you make a plan to solve a problem, be aware that there is often more than one strategy you can use to find the solution.

Problem You and your younger brother have volunteered to paint a wall of a community center as part of a community service project. You could paint the wall by yourself in 3 hours. Your brother (who has less experience painting) could paint the wall by himself in 6 hours. How long will it take to paint the wall if you and your brother work together?

1 Use estimation.

An upper limit on the time you and your brother take to paint the wall is the time it would take the faster painter to do the job working alone. Because you are the faster painter and can do the job in 3 hours, you can estimate that you and your brother will paint the wall in less than 3 hours.

2 Draw a diagram.

Your work rate when painting is $\frac{1}{3}$ of the wall per hour. Your brother's work rate is $\frac{1}{6}$ of the wall per hour. Use these rates to draw a diagram showing how much of the wall is painted after each hour. The diagram below shows that you and your brother will take 2 hours to paint the wall.

After 1 hour:

You   Brother

After 2 hours:

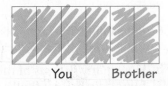

You   Brother

3 Solve an equation.

A third way to solve the problem is to use an equation. Let t represent the time (in hours) that you and your brother take to paint the wall. Make a table to find how much work each person does in t hours.

	Work rate	× Time	= Work done
You	$\frac{1}{3}$	t	$\frac{t}{3}$
Brother	$\frac{1}{6}$	t	$\frac{t}{6}$

The sum of your work and your brother's work equals 1 whole wall painted. Use this fact to write and solve an equation.

$$\frac{t}{3} + \frac{t}{6} = 1$$

$$6\left(\frac{t}{3} + \frac{t}{6}\right) = 6(1)$$

$$6\left(\frac{t}{3}\right) + 6\left(\frac{t}{6}\right) = 6$$

$$2t + t = 6$$

$$3t = 6$$

$$t = 2$$

So, you and your brother will take 2 hours to paint the wall.

Problem Solving Practice

1. **Wallpapering** You and your sister are wallpapering a wall of your family's living room. The diagram below shows how much of the wall each of you finished in 1 hour. What is the total time you and your sister spend wallpapering the wall?

You   Sister

In Exercises 2–5, use at least two strategies to solve the problem.

2. **Shingling a Roof** A contractor estimates that either she or her assistant could shingle the roof of a certain building in 8 days working alone. How long would the contractor and her assistant take to shingle the roof if they work together?

3. **Splitting Wood** Paul can split a cord of wood in 12 hours. His father can split a cord of wood in 4 hours. How long do Paul and his father take to split a cord of wood if they work together?

4. **Shoveling Snow** Sara can shovel the snow off her family's driveway in 30 minutes. Her sister can shovel the driveway in 20 minutes. How long do Sara and her sister take to shovel the driveway if they work together?

5. **Mowing a Lawn** You and a friend run a lawn mowing service. You can mow your next-door neighbor's lawn in 45 minutes. Your friend can mow the lawn in 1 hour. How long do you and your friend take to mow the lawn when working together?

6. **Filling a Sink** The faucet of a sink can fill the sink with water in 2 minutes. The drain can empty the sink in 3 minutes. If the faucet is turned on and the drain is left open, does the sink ever fill up with water? Justify your answer in two different ways.

7. **Painting** Look back at the painting problem on page 264. Suppose your sister helps you and your brother paint the wall. She can paint the wall by herself in 2 hours. Use a diagram and an equation to find how long the three of you take to paint the wall when working together.

8. **Biking** Heidi is riding her bike from her house to a park. After Heidi has traveled 400 feet, her brother Josh leaves the house on his bike to catch up to her. Heidi's speed is 22 feet per second, while Josh's speed is 27 feet per second. In parts (a) and (b), use the specified strategy to find how long Josh takes to catch up to Heidi.

   a. Copy and complete the table below. Continue adding rows to the table until you know the solution to the problem.

Time (sec)	Heidi's distance traveled (ft)	Josh's distance traveled (ft)
0	400	0
10	?	?
20	?	?

   b. Write and solve an equation.

9. **Car Wash** A science club holds a car wash to raise money. Two groups of students wash the cars. One group can wash 6 cars per hour. The other group can wash 4 cars per hour. How long do both groups take to wash a total of 30 cars? Use a diagram and an equation to find the answer.

Ratio, Proportion, *and* Probability

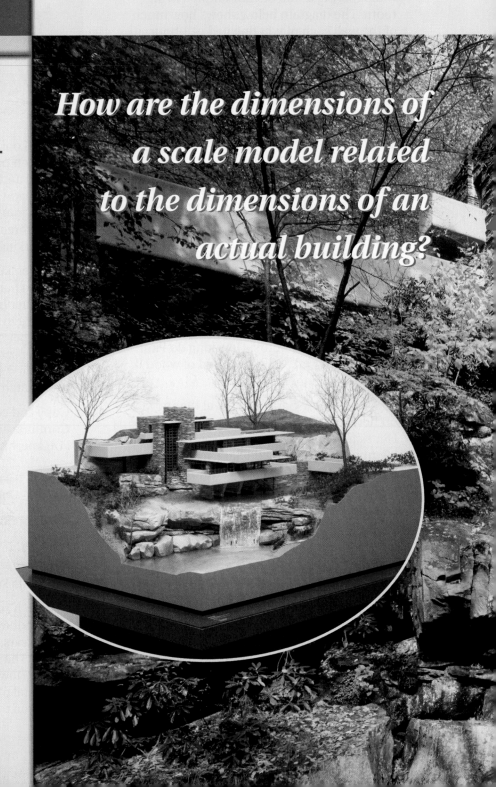

How are the dimensions of a scale model related to the dimensions of an actual building?

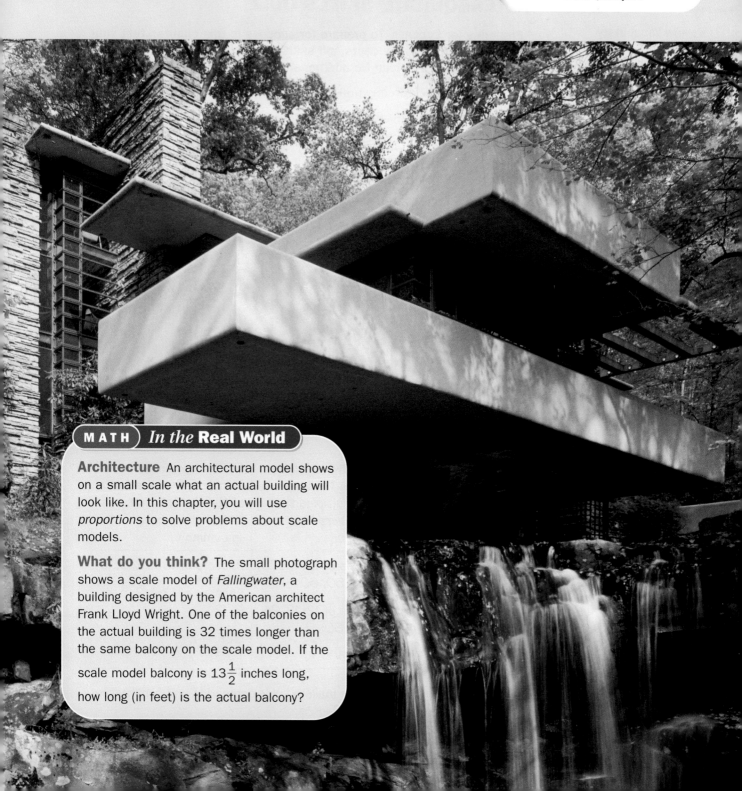

CHAPTER 6

INTERNET Preview
CLASSZONE.COM

- eEdition Plus Online
- eWorkbook Plus Online
- eTutorial Plus Online
- State Test Practice
- More Examples

M A T H *In the* **Real World**

Architecture An architectural model shows on a small scale what an actual building will look like. In this chapter, you will use *proportions* to solve problems about scale models.

What do you think? The small photograph shows a scale model of *Fallingwater*, a building designed by the American architect Frank Lloyd Wright. One of the balconies on the actual building is 32 times longer than the same balcony on the scale model. If the scale model balcony is $13\frac{1}{2}$ inches long, how long (in feet) is the actual balcony?

Chapter Prerequisite Skills

PREREQUISITE SKILLS QUIZ

Preparing for Success **To prepare for success in this chapter, test your knowledge of these concepts and skills. You may want to look at the pages referred to in blue for additional review.**

1. Vocabulary How can you tell whether two fractions are equivalent?

Solve the equation. *(p. 97)*

2. $-45 = 5x$ **3.** $4y = -32$ **4.** $-12 = \dfrac{n}{4}$ **5.** $\dfrac{x}{6} = 7$

Write the fraction in simplest form. *(p. 182)*

6. $\dfrac{24}{40}$ **7.** $\dfrac{42}{144}$ **8.** $\dfrac{14x^2y^3}{35xy^2}$ **9.** $\dfrac{a^3b^2c^2}{bc^2}$

Solve the equation. *(p. 247)*

10. $\dfrac{2}{9}x + \dfrac{5}{9} = 3$ **11.** $-\dfrac{3}{8}x - 5 = 7$ **12.** $\dfrac{1}{4}x - \dfrac{3}{8} = 9$ **13.** $\dfrac{3}{5}x - \dfrac{2}{5} = 2$

NOTETAKING STRATEGIES

COMPARING AND CONTRASTING When you learn related vocabulary words or ideas, it may be helpful to make a table comparing and contrasting the ideas.

Definition	LCM of two or more numbers: The least of the multiples that the numbers have in common	GCF of two or more numbers: The greatest of the factors that the numbers have in common
Example	Multiples of 10: 10, 20, 30, 40, 50, ⑥⓪ Multiples of 12: 12, 24, 36, 48, ⑥⓪ LCM = 60	Factors of 10: 1, ②, 5, 10 Factors of 12: 1, ②, 3, 4, 6, 12 GCF = 2

In Lesson 6.4, you can make a table comparing and contrasting similar and congruent figures.

6.1

Ratios *and* Rates

BEFORE	Now	WHY?
You wrote equivalent fractions.	You'll find ratios and unit rates.	So you can see if you'll have enough for a guitar, as in Ex. 38.

Vocabulary
ratio, p. 269
equivalent ratios, p. 270

Archery An archer shoots 60 arrows at a target, with 44 arrows hitting the scoring area and 16 missing the scoring area. How can you evaluate the archer's performance? You can compare the archer's number of hits to the archer's number of misses using a *ratio*. A **ratio** uses division to compare two quantities.

Writing Ratios

You can write the ratio of two quantities, a and b, where b is not equal to 0, in three ways.

$$a \text{ to } b \qquad a:b \qquad \frac{a}{b}$$

Each ratio is read "the ratio of a to b." You should write the ratio in simplest form, as shown in Example 1 below.

Review *Help*

For help with simplifying fractions, see p. 182.

Example 1 *Writing Ratios*

Use the archery information given above. Write the ratio in three ways.

  a. The number of hits to the number of misses

  b. The number of hits to the number of shots

Solution

  a. $\dfrac{\text{Number of hits}}{\text{Number of misses}} = \dfrac{44}{16} = \dfrac{11}{4}$

  Three ways to write the ratio are $\dfrac{11}{4}$, 11 to 4, and $11:4$.

  b. $\dfrac{\text{Number of hits}}{\text{Number of shots}} = \dfrac{44}{60} = \dfrac{11}{15}$

  Three ways to write the ratio are $\dfrac{11}{15}$, 11 to 15, and $11:15$.

✔ *Checkpoint*

1. Using the archery information above, compare the number of misses to the number of shots using a ratio. Write the ratio in three ways.

Comparing Ratios To compare two ratios, you can write both ratios as fractions or as decimals. Two ratios are called **equivalent ratios** when they have the same value.

Example 2 *Comparing and Ordering Ratios*

Biology The ratio comparing the length of a bird's wings to the average width of the bird's wings is the bird's *aspect ratio*. Order the birds in the table from the greatest aspect ratio to the least.

Bird	Wing length (cm)	Average wing width (cm)
White-tailed eagle	209	30
European jay	47	12
Black-headed gull	83	8

Solution

Write each ratio as a fraction. Then use a calculator to write each fraction as a decimal. Round to the nearest hundredth and compare the decimals.

White-tailed eagle: $\dfrac{\text{Wing length}}{\text{Wing width}} = \dfrac{209}{30} \approx 6.97$

European jay: $\dfrac{\text{Wing length}}{\text{Wing width}} = \dfrac{47}{12} \approx 3.92$

Black-headed gull: $\dfrac{\text{Wing length}}{\text{Wing width}} = \dfrac{83}{8} \approx 10.38$

Answer The gull's aspect ratio of 10.38 is the greatest. The eagle's aspect ratio of 6.97 is the next greatest. The jay's aspect ratio of 3.92 is the least.

In the **Real World**

Biology Birds with high aspect ratios are better suited for gliding over long distances, while birds with low aspect ratios have adapted for rapid takeoffs and maneuverability. Which bird in Example 2 is best suited for gliding over long distances?

Rates A rate is a ratio of two quantities measured in different units. A *unit rate* is a rate that has a denominator of 1 when expressed in fraction form. Unit rates are often expressed using the word *per*, which means "for every."

Example 3 *Finding a Unit Rate*

Party You host a party for 12 people. The food and drinks for the party cost $66. What is the cost per person?

Solution

First, write a rate comparing the total cost of the party to the number of people at the party. Then rewrite the rate so the denominator is 1.

$\dfrac{\$66}{12 \text{ people}} = \dfrac{\$66 \div 12}{12 \text{ people} \div 12}$ **Divide numerator and denominator by 12.**

$= \dfrac{\$5.50}{1 \text{ person}}$ **Simplify.**

Answer The cost of food and drinks is $5.50 per person.

Review *Help*

For help with using conversion factors, see p. 65.

Example 4 *Writing an Equivalent Rate*

Jet A jet flies 540 miles per hour. Write its rate in miles per minute.

Solution

To convert from miles per hour to miles per minute, multiply the rate by a conversion factor. There are 60 minutes in 1 hour, so $\dfrac{1\text{ h}}{60\text{ min}} = 1$.

$$\frac{540\text{ mi}}{1\text{ h}} = \frac{540\text{ mi}}{1\text{ h}} \cdot \frac{1\text{ h}}{60\text{ min}} \qquad \textbf{Multiply rate by conversion factor.}$$

$$= \frac{\overset{9}{540}\text{ mi}}{1\text{ h}} \cdot \frac{1\text{ h}}{\underset{1}{60}\text{ min}} \qquad \textbf{Divide out common factor and unit.}$$

$$= \frac{9\text{ mi}}{1\text{ min}} \qquad \textbf{Simplify.}$$

Answer The jet travels at a rate of 9 miles per minute.

Example 5 *Using Equivalent Rates*

Robots Engineers designed a miniature robot that can crawl through pipes and vents that humans can't access. The robot travels 1 inch in 3 seconds. How many feet does the robot travel in 4 minutes?

Solution

1 Express the robot's rate in inches per minute.

$$\frac{1\text{ in.}}{3\text{ sec}} = \frac{1\text{ in.}}{\underset{1}{3}\text{ sec}} \cdot \frac{\overset{20}{60}\text{ sec}}{1\text{ min}} \qquad \begin{array}{l}\textbf{Multiply by conversion factor.}\\ \textbf{Divide out common factor and unit.}\end{array}$$

$$= \frac{20\text{ in.}}{\text{min}} \qquad \textbf{Simplify.}$$

2 Find the distance (in feet) that the robot can travel in 4 minutes.

$$\text{Distance} = \text{Rate} \cdot \text{Time} \qquad \textbf{Write formula for distance.}$$

$$= \frac{20\text{ in.}}{\text{min}} \cdot 4\text{ min} \qquad \begin{array}{l}\textbf{Substitute values.}\\ \textbf{Divide out common unit.}\end{array}$$

$$= 80\text{ in.} \qquad \textbf{Multiply.}$$

$$= \overset{20}{80}\text{ in.} \cdot \frac{1\text{ ft}}{\underset{3}{12}\text{ in.}} \qquad \begin{array}{l}\textbf{Multiply by conversion factor.}\\ \textbf{Divide out common factor and unit.}\end{array}$$

$$= 6\frac{2}{3}\text{ ft} \qquad \textbf{Simplify.}$$

Answer The robot travels $6\frac{2}{3}$ feet in 4 minutes.

The miniature robot is 0.25 cubic inch in volume and weighs less than 1 ounce.

✔ *Checkpoint*

Write the equivalent rate.

2. $\dfrac{5\text{ cm}}{1\text{ min}} = \dfrac{?\text{ cm}}{1\text{ h}}$

3. $\dfrac{5\text{ m}}{1\text{ sec}} = \dfrac{?\text{ m}}{1\text{ h}}$

4. $\dfrac{3\text{ lb}}{\$1} = \dfrac{?\text{ oz}}{\$1}$

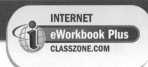

Guided Practice

Vocabulary Check

1. What is a unit rate? Give an example.

2. Write the ratio 8 to 5 in two other ways.

Skill Check **Tell whether the ratio is in simplest form. If not, write it in simplest form. Then write the ratio in two other ways.**

3. 8 to 6   **4.** 7 to 26   **5.** $39 : 13$ **6.** $120 : 64$

Order the ratios from least to greatest.

7. 2 to 9, $1 : 7$, $\frac{7}{28}$, 2 to 6, $\frac{3}{10}$ **8.** 1 to 3, $\frac{2}{8}$, $5 : 18$, 7 to 20, $\frac{9}{25}$

Guided Problem Solving

9. Roses Three decorators purchased bouquets of roses. Decorator A paid $120 for 5 bouquets that contained 25 roses each. Decorator B paid $204 for 20 bouquets that contained 12 roses each. Decorator C paid $180 for 40 bouquets that contained 6 roses each. Which decorator paid the least amount per rose?

1 Find the total number of roses each decorator bought.

2 Find the price per rose for each decorator.

3 Compare the unit prices to determine which decorator paid the least per rose.

Practice and Problem Solving

Homework *Help*

Example	Exercises
1	10–17, 36, 41
2	18–21, 40
3	22–29, 37, 39, 45
4	30–35, 45
5	38, 39, 46

Online Resources
CLASSZONE.COM

- More Examples
- eTutorial Plus

Tell whether the ratio is in simplest form. If not, write it in simplest form. Then write the ratio in two other ways.

10. 9 to 12   **11.** $4 : 5$ **12.** $\frac{15}{3}$ **13.** $\frac{50}{6}$

14. $63 : 18$ **15.** $24 : 8$ **16.** 64 to 3   **17.** 28 to 10

Order the ratios from least to greatest.

18. $\frac{4}{2}$, 11 to 2, $22 : 3$, $\frac{30}{4}$, $36 : 5$ **19.** $\frac{15}{4}$, 19 to 5, $\frac{53}{15}$, $4 : 1$, 18 to 6

20. $7 : 11$, $8 : 12$, $6 : 10$, $\frac{1}{2}$, $7 : 4$ **21.** $\frac{22}{4}$, $65 : 12$, $9 : 2$, $\frac{100}{19}$, $5 : 1$

Find the unit rate.

22. $\dfrac{140 \text{ words}}{4 \text{ min}}$ **23.** $\dfrac{\$161}{7 \text{ shares}}$ **24.** $\dfrac{80 \text{ oz}}{2.5 \text{ servings}}$ **25.** $\dfrac{70 \text{ mi}}{5 \text{ h}}$

26. $\dfrac{\$320}{4 \text{ people}}$ **27.** $\dfrac{26 \text{ points}}{3 \text{ quarters}}$ **28.** $\dfrac{24 \text{ muffins}}{\$15}$ **29.** $\dfrac{25 \text{ wins}}{40 \text{ games}}$

Write the equivalent rate.

30. $\dfrac{15 \text{ mi}}{1 \text{ h}} = \dfrac{? \text{ ft}}{1 \text{ h}}$

31. $\dfrac{300 \text{ mi}}{20 \text{ sec}} = \dfrac{? \text{ mi}}{1 \text{ min}}$

32. $\dfrac{390 \text{ m}}{1 \text{ min}} = \dfrac{? \text{ m}}{1 \text{ h}}$

33. $\dfrac{\$33,000}{1 \text{ year}} = \dfrac{? \text{ dollars}}{1 \text{ month}}$

34. $\dfrac{\$43}{1 \text{ day}} = \dfrac{? \text{ dollars}}{1 \text{ week}}$

35. $\dfrac{45 \text{ min}}{2 \text{ mi}} = \dfrac{? \text{ h}}{1 \text{ mi}}$

36. Nature As a tadpole, the paradoxical frog is 24 centimeters long. As an adult, the frog is 6 centimeters long.

   a. Write the ratio of the tadpole's length to the adult frog's length.

   b. Something is called *paradoxical* if it seems impossible. What is paradoxical about the frog? Explain using your answer to part (a).

37. Estimate A store sells 16 cookies for $11.88. Estimate the cost per cookie. Explain how you made your estimate.

38. Guitar You want to save all the money you earn to buy a guitar that costs $400. You earn $9 per hour and plan to work 15 hours each week for the next 3 weeks. Will you earn enough money in that time to buy the guitar?

39. Extended Problem Solving Your family used two full tanks of gasoline on a road trip. Your car drives about 25 miles per gallon, and the tank holds 12 gallons of gasoline.

   a. Find the approximate number of gallons of gasoline used on the trip.

   b. Find the approximate number of miles you drove on the trip.

   c. Calculate Assume gasoline costs $1.50 per gallon. How much did you spend per mile on gasoline?

   d. Apply You have $20 to spend on gasoline for another trip. The trip is 350 miles. You spend the same amount per mile on gasoline as on the first trip. Do you have enough money for gasoline? Explain.

40. Drinks A restaurant sells drinks in 3 sizes of cups: small, medium, and large. The small cup costs $.89 and holds 9 ounces. The medium cup costs $1.29 and holds 12 ounces. The large cup costs $1.59 and holds 15 ounces. Which size cup costs the least per ounce?

41. Aquarium An aquarium has twice as many angelfish as goldfish. The aquarium contains only angelfish and goldfish. Write a ratio for the number of goldfish to the total number of fish.

42. Geometry For each rectangle below, the measure of the longer side is the length, and the measure of the shorter side is the width.

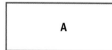

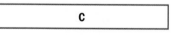

   a. Which rectangle has the greatest ratio of length to width?

   b. For which rectangle is the ratio of length to width closest to 1 : 1?

   c. Critical Thinking The ratio of another rectangle's length to its width is 1 : 1. What type of rectangle is it?

Find the ratio of the area of the shaded region to the area of the unshaded region. The figures are composed of squares and triangles.

43.

44.

45. Running In 2002, Khalid Khannouchi set the world record for a marathon when he ran 26.2 miles in 2 hours, 5 minutes, and 38 seconds. Round your answers to the nearest tenth.

  a. Find Khannouchi's rate in miles per hour.

  b. Find Khannouchi's rate in miles per minute.

  c. Find Khannouchi's rate in feet per minute.

46. **Earth Science** Due to the movement of Earth's landmasses, Los Angeles and other portions of coastal Southern California are moving northwest toward San Francisco at an average rate of 46 millimeters per year.

  a. How many meters per year does Los Angeles move?

  b. How many meters per century does Los Angeles move?

  c. In 2000, San Francisco was 554,000 meters from Los Angeles. In about how many years will Los Angeles be where San Francisco was in 2000?

47. Challenge If you travel 55 miles per hour, how many minutes will it take you to travel 1 mile?

Mixed Review

Find the product. *(Lesson 5.4)*

48. $\frac{3}{8} \cdot \left(\frac{6}{15}\right)$　　**49.** $-\frac{6}{21} \cdot \left(\frac{14}{54}\right)$　　**50.** $-2\frac{3}{4} \cdot \left(-3\frac{5}{9}\right)$

51. Stamps You have 15 stamps from Canada in your stamp collection. These stamps make up $\frac{3}{11}$ of your entire collection. The rest of the stamps are from the U.S. How many stamps are in your collection? How many stamps from the U.S. do you have? *(Lesson 5.6)*

Solve the inequality. *(Lesson 5.7)*

52. $\frac{2}{3}x + 9 \le \frac{17}{2}$　　**53.** $\frac{1}{5}y + 14 \le \frac{13}{5}$　　**54.** $-\frac{5}{9}x + 1 > \frac{22}{27}$

Standardized Test Practice

55. Multiple Choice Which of the following ratios is greater than $5 : 12$?

  A. $25 : 99$　　**B.** $12 : 36$　　**C.** $4 : 8$　　**D.** $5 : 13$

56. Short Response One afternoon, you read 24 pages of a novel in 30 minutes. Another afternoon, you read 33 pages in 45 minutes. How can you decide whether you read at the same rate or at different rates on the two afternoons? On which afternoon did you read at a faster rate? Explain.

Writing *and* Solving Proportions

BEFORE	*Now*	WHY?
You wrote and compared ratios.	You'll write and solve proportions.	So you can find the salinity of saltwater, as in Ex. 31.

Vocabulary
proportion, p. 275

Elephants Each day, an elephant eats 5 pounds of food for every 100 pounds of its body weight. How much does a 9300 pound elephant eat per day?

In Example 3, you'll see how to use a *proportion* to answer this question.

Reading *Algebra*

The proportion $\frac{2}{3} = \frac{8}{12}$ is read "2 is to 3 as 8 is to 12."

Proportions

Words A **proportion** is an equation that states that two ratios are equal.

Numbers $\frac{2}{3} = \frac{8}{12}$

Algebra $\frac{a}{b} = \frac{c}{d}$, where $b \neq 0$ and $d \neq 0$

Equivalent Ratios If one of the numbers in a proportion is unknown, you can solve the proportion to find the unknown number. One way to solve a proportion is to use mental math to find an equivalent ratio.

Example 1   *Solving a Proportion Using Equivalent Ratios*

Solve the proportion $\frac{5}{6} = \frac{x}{18}$.

1 Compare denominators.

$$\frac{5}{6} \xrightarrow{\times 3} \frac{x}{18}$$

2 Find x.

$$\frac{5}{6} \xrightarrow{\times 3} \frac{x}{18}$$

Answer Because $5 \times 3 = 15$, $x = 15$.

✔ *Checkpoint*

Use equivalent ratios to solve the proportion.

1. $\frac{2}{7} = \frac{x}{21}$ **2.** $\frac{3}{8} = \frac{x}{32}$ **3.** $\frac{x}{2} = \frac{20}{10}$ **4.** $\frac{x}{48} = \frac{6}{12}$

Using Algebra You can use the same methods you used to solve equations to solve proportions that have a variable in the numerator.

| **Example 2** | *Solving a Proportion Using Algebra* |

Solve the proportion $\frac{x}{12} = \frac{2}{8}$. **Check your answer.**

$$\frac{x}{12} = \frac{2}{8}$$ Write original proportion.

$$12 \cdot \frac{x}{12} = 12 \cdot \frac{2}{8}$$ Multiply each side by 12.

$$x = \frac{24}{8}$$ Simplify.

$$x = 3$$ Divide.

✓**Check** $\frac{x}{12} = \frac{2}{8}$ Write original proportion.

$$\frac{3}{12} \overset{?}{=} \frac{2}{8}$$ Substitute 3 for x.

$$\frac{1}{4} = \frac{1}{4} \checkmark$$ Simplify. Solution checks.

✔ *Checkpoint*

Use algebra to solve the proportion.

5. $\frac{2}{5} = \frac{x}{25}$ **6.** $\frac{3}{10} = \frac{x}{100}$ **7.** $\frac{x}{9} = \frac{42}{54}$ **8.** $\frac{x}{4} = \frac{13}{2}$

Setting up a Proportion There are different ways to set up a proportion. Consider the following problem.

Yesterday you rode your bike 18 miles in 2.5 hours. Today you plan to ride for 3.5 hours. If you ride at the same rate as yesterday, how far will you ride?

The tables below show two ways of arranging the information from the problem. In each table, x represents the number of miles that you can ride in 3.5 hours. The proportions follow from the tables.

	Today	Yesterday
Miles	x	18
Hours	3.5	2.5

	Miles	Hours
Today	x	3.5
Yesterday	18	2.5

Proportion: $\frac{x}{3.5} = \frac{18}{2.5}$ **Proportion:** $\frac{x}{18} = \frac{3.5}{2.5}$

When writing a proportion, make sure you use comparable ratios. For example, you cannot write a proportion to compare $\frac{\text{miles}}{\text{hours}}$ and $\frac{\text{hours}}{\text{miles}}$.

Example 3 **Writing and Solving a Proportion**

Use the information on page 275 to write and solve a proportion to determine how much food an elephant that weighs 9300 pounds eats per day.

Solution

First, write a proportion involving two ratios that compare the weight of the food with the weight of the elephant.

$$\frac{5}{100} = \frac{x}{9300} \quad \longleftarrow \text{ Weight of food}$$
$$\qquad\qquad\qquad \longleftarrow \text{ Weight of elephant}$$

Then, solve the proportion.

$$9300 \cdot \frac{5}{100} = 9300 \cdot \frac{x}{9300} \qquad \textbf{Multiply each side by 9300.}$$

$$\frac{46{,}500}{100} = x \qquad\qquad\qquad \textbf{Simplify.}$$

$$465 = x \qquad\qquad\qquad\quad \textbf{Divide.}$$

Answer A 9300 pound elephant eats about 465 pounds of food per day.

✔ *Checkpoint*

9. Use the information given on page 275 to determine how much food a 12,500 pound elephant eats per day.

6.2 Exercises

More Practice, p. 808

Guided Practice

Vocabulary Check

1. Give an example of a proportion that uses the numbers 2, 3, 4, and 6.

2. Explain how to use equivalent ratios to solve the proportion $\frac{3}{2} = \frac{x}{12}$.

Skill Check **Solve the proportion.**

3. $\frac{1}{2} = \frac{x}{50}$ **4.** $\frac{3}{4} = \frac{y}{24}$ **5.** $\frac{a}{9} = \frac{21}{27}$ **6.** $\frac{b}{5} = \frac{28}{35}$

7. Error Analysis Describe and correct the error in writing a proportion to find the cost of 30 pencils if 12 pencils cost $2.00.

$$\frac{12}{2.00} = \frac{x}{30}$$

8. Pizza You know that 3 pizzas are enough to feed 12 people. Write and solve a proportion to find the number of pizzas that will feed 28 people.

Practice and Problem Solving

Homework Help

Example	Exercises
1	9–16
2	17–24
3	25–28, 30–34

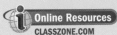

Online Resources
CLASSZONE.COM

• More Examples
• eTutorial Plus

Use equivalent ratios to solve the proportion.

9. $\dfrac{5}{6} = \dfrac{x}{30}$ **10.** $\dfrac{6}{7} = \dfrac{y}{49}$ **11.** $\dfrac{a}{12} = \dfrac{33}{36}$ **12.** $\dfrac{b}{14} = \dfrac{27}{42}$

13. $\dfrac{14}{3} = \dfrac{a}{15}$ **14.** $\dfrac{11}{9} = \dfrac{y}{81}$ **15.** $\dfrac{x}{5} = \dfrac{200}{25}$ **16.** $\dfrac{b}{15} = \dfrac{26}{30}$

Use algebra to solve the proportion.

17. $\dfrac{x}{8} = \dfrac{35}{56}$ **18.** $\dfrac{y}{4} = \dfrac{42}{28}$ **19.** $\dfrac{a}{32} = \dfrac{9}{16}$ **20.** $\dfrac{b}{45} = \dfrac{8}{9}$

21. $\dfrac{25}{60} = \dfrac{c}{12}$ **22.** $\dfrac{39}{54} = \dfrac{d}{18}$ **23.** $\dfrac{17}{26} = \dfrac{w}{52}$ **24.** $\dfrac{3}{7} = \dfrac{z}{63}$

25. School Supplies At a store, 5 erasers cost $2.50. How many erasers can you buy for $7.50?

26. Driving You are driving 2760 miles across the country. During the first 3 days of your trip, you drive 1380 miles. If you continue to drive at the same rate each day, how many days will the entire trip take?

27. Lacrosse Last season, a lacrosse player scored 41 goals in 15 games. So far this season, the player has scored 24 goals in 9 games.

    a. Does the player have a greater number of goals per game this season compared with last season?

    b. Suppose the player plays in as many games this season as last season and continues to score at this season's rate. Write and solve a proportion to find the number of goals the player will score this season.

28. Exchange Rates In 2003, the exchange rate between the United States and Canada was about 3 Canadian dollars to 2 U.S. dollars. Cindy had 78 U.S. dollars to exchange when she visited Canada. How many Canadian dollars could she get in exchange?

29. *Writing* Write a proportion without using any variables. In how many different ways can you rearrange the four numbers so that ratios are still equivalent? Explain your answer.

30. 📟 **Population Density** A region's population density is the number of people per square mile. The tiny country of Monaco has the highest population density in the world, with 33,000 people living in an area of 0.75 square mile. The state of New York has a population of about 19,000,000 people living in an area of about 47,000 square miles. Use a calculator to complete the following. Round your answers to the nearest whole number.

    a. Write and solve a proportion to find how many people would live in Monaco if Monaco had the population density of New York.

    b. Write and solve a proportion to find how many people would live in New York if New York had the population density of Monaco.

31. Saltwater The salinity of saltwater is the ratio of the mass of the salt in the water to the mass of the salt and fresh water mixed together.

   a. A sample of saltwater is made by mixing 3 grams of salt with 75 grams of water. Find the salinity of the sample.

   b. A sample of saltwater has a salinity of 3 : 45. The sample has a mass of 30 kilograms. How much salt is in the sample?

32. Jewel Cases Store A sells 10 CD jewel cases for $9. Store B sells 15 CD jewel cases for $12. How much money will you save if you buy 30 CD jewel cases at the store with the lower unit price?

33. Knitting You are knitting an afghan with red, green, and blue stripes. There are equal numbers of red and blue stripes. There are twice as many green stripes as there are red stripes. The afghan has 20 stripes.

   a. Find the ratio of the number of red stripes to the total number of stripes on the afghan.

   b. How many red stripes are there on the afghan?

34. Election In an election, the winning candidate received 3 votes for every vote the opponent received. Altogether, 1000 votes were cast. How many votes did the winner receive?

35. Critical Thinking In the proportion $\dfrac{10}{x} = \dfrac{y}{6}$, how does the value of y change as the value of x increases?

36. Challenge A painter is making a specific shade of green that requires 3 parts of yellow paint for every 4 parts of blue paint. To make the mixture, the painter uses 9 ounces of yellow paint and 2 tubes of blue paint. How many ounces are in each tube of blue paint?

Mixed Review

Simplify the expression. *(Lesson 4.5)*

37. $\dfrac{8m^3 \cdot 9m^4}{3m^5}$ **38.** $\dfrac{7n^3 \cdot n^2}{n^4}$ **39.** $\dfrac{5a^2 \cdot 2a^2}{10a^4}$ **40.** $\dfrac{2x^4 \cdot x^3}{6x^6}$

Find the quotient. *(Lesson 5.5)*

41. $-\dfrac{3}{20} \div \dfrac{4}{5}$ **42.** $\dfrac{15}{16} \div \left(-\dfrac{5}{8}\right)$ **43.** $\dfrac{11}{42} \div \dfrac{4}{7}$ **44.** $\dfrac{25}{36} \div \dfrac{8}{9}$

Solve the inequality. *(Lesson 5.7)*

45. $\dfrac{3}{8}z - \dfrac{4}{5} > \dfrac{9}{10}$ **46.** $\dfrac{1}{3} < \dfrac{6}{7}y - \dfrac{7}{15}$ **47.** $\dfrac{1}{3} \geq \dfrac{7}{12}x - \dfrac{11}{15}$ **48.** $-\dfrac{2}{5}x + \dfrac{6}{5} \geq \dfrac{1}{10}$

Standardized Test Practice

49. Multiple Choice Solve the proportion $\dfrac{48}{28} = \dfrac{x}{63}$.

   A. $5\dfrac{1}{3}$ **B.** 96   **C.** 108   **D.** 432

50. Short Response A 12 ounce box of pasta costs $.99. A 2 pound box costs $2.09. Which box has the lower price per ounce? You buy 6 pounds of pasta. How much money do you save if you buy pasta in the box with the lower price per ounce? Explain.

Solving Proportions Using Cross Products

Vocabulary

cross product, p. 280

BEFORE	*Now*	WHY?
You solved simple proportions.	You'll solve proportions using cross products.	So you can find the mass of gold in a ring, as in Ex. 35.

Every pair of ratios has two *cross products*. A **cross product** of two ratios is the product of the numerator of one ratio and the denominator of the other ratio.

Ratios: $\dfrac{3}{5}, \dfrac{6}{10}$ $\qquad\qquad$ $\dfrac{2}{3}, \dfrac{6}{11}$

Cross products: $\qquad$ $3 \cdot 10 \qquad 5 \cdot 6$ $\qquad$ $2 \cdot 11 \qquad 3 \cdot 6$

Notice that for the ratios $\dfrac{3}{5}$ and $\dfrac{6}{10}$, the ratios are equal and their cross products are also equal. For the ratios $\dfrac{2}{3}$ and $\dfrac{6}{11}$, the ratios are not equal, and neither are their cross products.

You can use cross products to tell whether two ratios form a proportion. If the cross products are equal, then the ratios form a proportion.

Example 1 Determining if Ratios Form a Proportion

Tell whether the ratios form a proportion.

a. $\dfrac{9}{51}, \dfrac{6}{34}$ $\qquad\qquad\qquad$ **b.** $\dfrac{12}{20}, \dfrac{32}{50}$

Solution

a. $\qquad \dfrac{9}{51} \overset{?}{=} \dfrac{6}{34}$ $\qquad$ Write proportion.

$\qquad 9 \cdot 34 \overset{?}{=} 51 \cdot 6$ $\qquad$ Form cross products.

$\qquad\quad 306 = 306$ $\qquad$ Multiply.

Answer The ratios form a proportion.

b. $\qquad \dfrac{12}{20} \overset{?}{=} \dfrac{32}{50}$ $\qquad$ Write proportion.

$\qquad 12 \cdot 50 \overset{?}{=} 20 \cdot 32$ $\qquad$ Form cross products.

$\qquad\quad 600 \neq 640$ $\qquad$ Multiply.

Answer The ratios do not form a proportion.

Tell whether the ratios form a proportion.

1. $\frac{6}{14}, \frac{3}{7}$ **2.** $\frac{14}{35}, \frac{8}{20}$ **3.** $\frac{6}{11}, \frac{9}{16}$ **4.** $\frac{15}{24}, \frac{10}{16}$

You can use the multiplication property of equality to demonstrate an important property about the cross products of a proportion.

Reading *Algebra*

The sequence of steps shown at the right constitutes a *proof*, or convincing argument, for the cross products property. The process of starting with one or more given facts, such as $\frac{a}{b} = \frac{c}{d}$, and using rules, definitions, or properties to reach a conclusion, such as $ad = cb$, is called *deductive reasoning*.

$$\frac{a}{b} = \frac{c}{d} \qquad \text{Given}$$

$$\frac{a}{\cancel{b}_1} \cdot \frac{\cancel{b}^1 d}{1} = \frac{c}{\cancel{d}_1} \cdot \frac{b \cancel{d}^1}{1} \qquad \begin{array}{l}\text{Multiply each side by } bd.\\ \text{Divide out common factors.}\end{array}$$

$$ad = cb \qquad \text{Simplify.}$$

This result proves the following property.

Cross Products Property

Words The cross products of a proportion are equal.

Numbers Given that $\frac{2}{5} = \frac{6}{15}$, you know that $2 \cdot 15 = 5 \cdot 6$.

Algebra If $\frac{a}{b} = \frac{c}{d}$, where $b \neq 0$ and $d \neq 0$, then $ad = bc$.

You can use the cross products property to solve proportions.

In the **Real World**

Hair The average adult human head has an area of about 120 square inches and contains about 100,000 hairs. How many hairs per square inch does the average adult human have?

Example 2   *Writing and Solving a Proportion*

Hair Growth Human hair grows about 0.7 centimeter in 2 weeks. How long does hair take to grow 14 centimeters?

Solution

$$\frac{0.7}{2} = \frac{14}{x} \leftarrow \begin{array}{l}\text{Length of hair grown}\\ \leftarrow \text{Number of weeks}\end{array}$$

$$0.7 \cdot x = 2 \cdot 14 \qquad \text{Cross products property}$$

$$0.7x = 28 \qquad \text{Multiply.}$$

$$\frac{0.7x}{0.7} = \frac{28}{0.7} \qquad \text{Divide each side by 0.7.}$$

$$x = 40 \qquad \text{Simplify.}$$

Answer Hair takes about 40 weeks to grow 14 centimeters.

 Checkpoint

Use the cross products property to solve the proportion.

5. $\frac{18}{42} = \frac{3}{t}$ **6.** $\frac{16}{p} = \frac{10}{45}$ **7.** $\frac{9}{b} = \frac{1.5}{7}$ **8.** $\frac{0.4}{6} = \frac{18}{z}$

Note *Worthy*

The main ideas from Lessons 6.2 and 6.3 are summarized at the right. You may want to include a summary like this one in your notes.

SUMMARY Methods for Solving a Proportion

To solve the proportion $\frac{5}{12} = \frac{x}{36}$, use one of the following:

Equivalent ratios

$$\frac{5}{12} \xrightarrow{\times 3} \frac{x}{36} \qquad \frac{5}{12} \xrightarrow{\times 3} \frac{15}{36}$$

Algebra

$$36 \cdot \frac{5}{12} = 36 \cdot \frac{x}{36} \qquad \text{Multiply each side by 36.}$$

$$15 = x \qquad \text{Simplify.}$$

Cross products

$$5 \cdot 36 = 12x \qquad \text{Cross products property}$$

$$15 = x \qquad \text{Divide each side by 12.}$$

6.3 Exercises

More Practice, p. 808

INTERNET
eWorkbook Plus
CLASSZONE.COM

Guided Practice

Vocabulary Check   1. Find the cross products of the proportion $\frac{3}{4} = \frac{9}{12}$.

2. Explain how to use cross products to determine if two ratios are equal.

Skill Check   **Tell whether the ratios form a proportion.**

3. $\frac{5}{8}, \frac{10}{16}$ 4. $\frac{9}{32}, \frac{3}{8}$ 5. $\frac{40}{125}, \frac{8}{25}$ 6. $\frac{6}{9}, \frac{12}{16}$

Use the cross products property to solve the proportion.

7. $\frac{24}{36} = \frac{2}{x}$ 8. $\frac{60}{15} = \frac{12}{y}$ 9. $\frac{0.8}{a} = \frac{3.2}{8}$ 10. $\frac{1.6}{b} = \frac{8}{25}$

Guided Problem Solving   11. **Long Distance** You made a 12 minute phone call using a calling card. The call cost $.66. There is $1.21 left on your calling card. The cost per minute of long distance calls is constant. How many more minutes can you talk long distance using your calling card?

① Write a ratio of the form $\dfrac{\text{Cost of phone call}}{\text{Minutes of phone call}}$ for the phone call.

② Let m represent the number of minutes you can talk for $1.21. Write a ratio of the same form as the one in Step 1.

③ Use the two ratios to write a proportion. Solve the proportion.

Practice and Problem Solving

Homework *Help*

Example	Exercises
1	12–19, 32
2	20–31, 33–35, 42

Online Resources
CLASSZONE.COM
- More Examples
- eTutorial Plus

Tell whether the ratios form a proportion.

12. $\frac{12}{30}, \frac{18}{45}$ **13.** $\frac{42}{20}, \frac{63}{60}$ **14.** $\frac{28}{8}, \frac{42}{6}$ **15.** $\frac{45}{35}, \frac{9}{21}$

16. $\frac{40}{210}, \frac{60}{630}$ **17.** $\frac{588}{105}, \frac{84}{20}$ **18.** $\frac{70}{147}, \frac{50}{105}$ **19.** $\frac{75}{40}, \frac{15}{8}$

Solve the proportion.

20. $\frac{16}{36} = \frac{4}{d}$ **21.** $\frac{3}{21} = \frac{c}{35}$ **22.** $\frac{30}{w} = \frac{24}{12}$ **23.** $\frac{35}{z} = \frac{7}{5}$

24. $\frac{144}{40} = \frac{x}{5}$ **25.** $\frac{9}{105} = \frac{15}{y}$ **26.** $\frac{t}{12} = \frac{20}{8}$ **27.** $\frac{s}{21} = \frac{16}{12}$

28. $\frac{7}{m} = \frac{0.6}{3}$ **29.** $\frac{26}{p} = \frac{13}{0.4}$ **30.** $\frac{51}{3.4} = \frac{n}{4}$ **31.** $\frac{1.4}{1.05} = \frac{4}{r}$

32. Drink Mix A store is selling powdered drink mix in two different sizes. You can buy 10 ounces for $2.25, or you can buy 35 ounces for $7. Are the two rates equivalent? Explain.

33. Gasoline You paid $5 at a gas station for 3 gallons of gasoline.

   a. How much would 12 gallons of gasoline cost?

   b. How much gasoline can you buy for $30?

34. Biking You travel 24 miles in 2 hours while biking.

   a. At this rate, how far can you bike in 5 hours?

   b. At this rate, how long will it take to bike 30 miles? Write your answer in hours and minutes.

35. Gold Jewelers often mix gold with other metals. A *karat* is a unit of measure that compares the mass of the gold in an object with the mass of the object. Karats are expressed as a number that is understood to be the numerator of a ratio whose denominator is 24. For example, 24 karat gold means an object is pure gold, and 18 karat gold means that $\frac{18}{24}$, or $\frac{3}{4}$, of the object's mass is gold.

   a. A 15 karat gold ring has a mass of 200 grams. How much gold is in the ring?

   b. An 18 karat gold bracelet contains 27 grams of gold. What is the mass of the bracelet?

36. *Writing* Describe three ways you could solve the proportion $\frac{6}{10} = \frac{x}{40}$.

Find the value of x.

37. $\frac{36}{54} = \frac{18}{x+5}$ **38.** $\frac{39}{x+7} = \frac{21}{7}$ **39.** $\frac{15-x}{45} = \frac{15}{75}$ **40.** $\frac{28}{16} = \frac{x-8}{20}$

41. Critical Thinking Use the cross products property to show that if $\frac{a}{b} = \frac{c}{d}$, then $\frac{d}{c} = \frac{b}{a}$.

In the **Real World**

Gold Gold is heated in a crucible and poured into a mold to form gold bars. Suppose a gold bar weighs 400 ounces and the price of gold on a given day is $322 per ounce. How much is the bar of gold worth?

42. Extended Problem Solving The tables show ingredients needed to make colored glass. Use the numbers in the *Parts* columns to form ratios comparing the masses of ingredients. For example, if you use 65 grams of sand to make yellow glass, you need 3 grams of chalk.

Saffron and Red Tower is a glass sculpture by Dale Chihuly.

Red Glass	
Ingredients	**Parts**
Sand	50
Red lead	100
Copper oxide	3
Ferric oxide	3

Yellow Glass	
Ingredients	**Parts**
Sand	65
Soda ash	25
Chalk	3
Wood charcoal	1

a. Calculate A piece of red glass contains 60 grams of sand. How much ferric oxide does it contain?

b. Calculate A piece of yellow glass contains 31 kilograms of soda ash. How much chalk does it contain?

c. Compare Which has more sand: red glass with 200 grams of red lead, or yellow glass with 4 grams of wood charcoal? Explain.

43. Critical Thinking The ratio $\frac{a}{b}$ is equivalent to $\frac{3}{4}$. The ratio $\frac{b}{c}$ is equivalent to $\frac{4}{5}$. What is the ratio $\frac{a}{c}$ equivalent to? Explain.

44. Challenge For a half circle like the one shown below, if you know lengths a and b, then length x can be found by solving $\frac{a}{x} = \frac{x}{b}$.

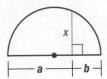

a. Let $a = 9$ and $b = 4$. What is the value of x?

b. Let $a = 18$ and $b = 8$. What is the value of x?

c. In terms of x, what does ab equal?

Mixed Review

Use a ruler to draw a segment with the given length. (p. 787)

45. 1.2 centimeters   **46.** 3.5 centimeters   **47.** 0.2 centimeters

Write the number in scientific notation. (Lesson 4.7)

48. 34,000,000,000   **49.** 5,001,000   **50.** 0.000000000672

Write the ratio in simplest form. (Lesson 6.1)

51. 8 to 18   **52.** 6 : 22   **53.** $\frac{14}{24}$

Standardized Test Practice

54. Multiple Choice Solve the proportion $\frac{90}{y} = \frac{27}{12}$.

A. 3.6   **B.** 40   **C.** 90   **D.** 1080

55. Multiple Choice Last week you saved $24. At this rate, how many weeks will it take you to save $600?

F. 24 days   **G.** 14,400 weeks   **H.** 25 weeks   **I.** 15 weeks

Basic Geometry Concepts

▶ **Review** these topics in preparation for solving problems that involve basic geometry concepts in Lessons 6.4 and 6.5.

Points, Lines, and Planes

Word	Notation	Diagram
point	point A	• A
line	$\overleftrightarrow{BC}$	B C
plane	M	M

Example Use the diagram to name three points, two lines, and a plane.

Three points are point J, point K, and point L.

Two lines are $\overleftrightarrow{KL}$ and $\overleftrightarrow{JL}$.

The plane is plane P.

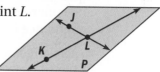

Segments, Rays, and Angles

Word	Notation	Diagram
line segment, or segment length of a line segment	$\overline{AB}$ AB	endpoints A B
ray	$\overrightarrow{CD}$	endpoint C D
angle measure of an angle	$\angle EFG$ or $\angle F$ $m\angle EFG$ or $m\angle F$	E 23° F G vertex

Example Use the diagram to name two segments and their lengths, two rays, and an angle and its measure.

A segment is $\overline{MP}$, and $MP = 4$ centimeters.

Another segment is $\overline{NP}$, and $NP = 6$ centimeters.

Two rays are $\overrightarrow{PM}$ and $\overrightarrow{PN}$.

An angle is $\angle P$, and $m\angle P = 80°$.

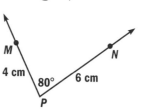

Continued ➡

Triangles, Quadrilaterals, and Congruent Parts

Word	Notation	Diagram
triangle	$\triangle ABC$	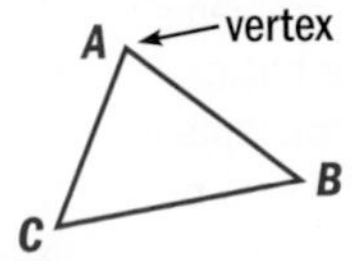 A ←vertex B C
A **quadrilateral** is made of four segments that intersect only at their endpoints.	quadrilateral $PQRS$	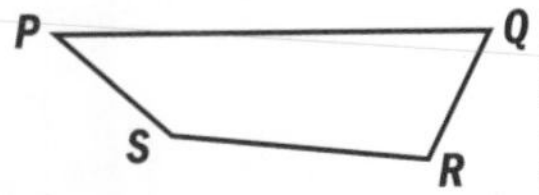 P Q S R

Congruent segments have equal lengths, and **congruent angles** have equal measures. Congruent sides of a figure are marked using tick marks, and congruent angles of a figure are marked using arcs. The symbol for congruence is $\cong$.

Example **Identify the angles, sides, congruent angles, and congruent sides of the triangle.**

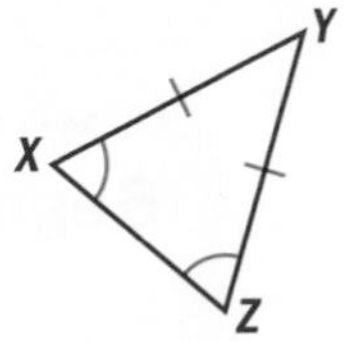

The angles of the triangle are $\angle X$, $\angle Y$, and $\angle Z$.

The sides of the triangle are $\overline{XY}$, $\overline{YZ}$, and $\overline{XZ}$.

Congruent angles: $\angle X \cong \angle Z$

Congruent sides: $\overline{XY} \cong \overline{YZ}$

✔ Checkpoint

Test your knowledge of basic geometry concepts by solving these problems.

In Exercises 1–6, use figure 1.

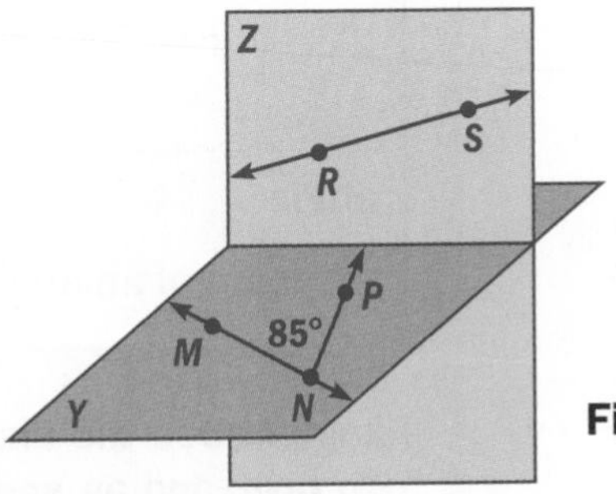

1. Name three points.

2. Name two lines.

3. Name two planes.

4. Name two rays.

5. Name a segment.

6. Name an angle and give its measure.

Figure 1

In Exercises 7–10, use figure 2.

7. Name the quadrilateral.

8. Name the sides.

9. Name the angles.

10. Identify the congruent angles and congruent sides.

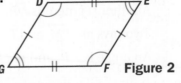

Figure 2

6.4 Investigating Similar Figures

Goal

Investigate corresponding sides and angles of similar figures.

Materials

- graph paper
- metric ruler
- protractor

Two figures are *similar* if they have the same shape but not necessarily the same size. For example, when a figure is enlarged, the enlarged figure is similar to the original figure.

Investigate

Compare corresponding parts of a figure and its enlargement.

1 Draw △*ABC* so that $m\angle A = 90°$, $AB = 1.5$ cm, and $AC = 2$ cm. Find *BC* to the nearest 0.1 cm.

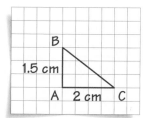

2 Draw △*DEF* so that $m\angle D = 90°$, $DE = 2 \cdot AB$, and $DF = 2 \cdot AC$. Find the side lengths of △*DEF*.

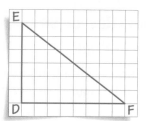

3 Use a protractor to find the measures of the angles of both triangles to the nearest degree.

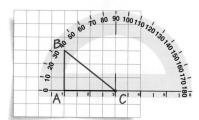

Draw Conclusions

1. Copy and complete the tables.

Side of △*ABC*	Corresponding side of △*DEF*
AB = 1.5 cm	*DE* = ?
AC = 2 cm	*DF* = ?
BC = ?	*EF* = ?

Angle of △*ABC*	Corresponding angle of △*DEF*
$m\angle A = 90°$	$m\angle D = 90°$
$m\angle B = ?$	$m\angle E = ?$
$m\angle C = ?$	$m\angle F = ?$

2. For each pair of corresponding sides, find the ratio of the length of a side of △*ABC* to the length of the corresponding side of △*DEF*. What do you notice about these ratios?

3. What do you notice about the measures of the corresponding angles?

4. **Conjecture** Use your answers to Exercises 2 and 3 to write two conjectures about similar figures.

Similar *and* Congruent Figures

BEFORE **Now** **WHY?**

You worked with basic geometric figures.

You'll identify similar and congruent figures.

So you can compare TV screens to computer screens, as in Ex. 20.

Vocabulary

similar figures, p. 288
corresponding parts, p. 288
congruent figures, p. 290

Two figures are **similar figures** if they have the same shape but not necessarily the same size. The symbol ~ indicates that two figures are similar. When working with similar figures, you should identify the *corresponding parts* of the figures. **Corresponding parts** of figures are sides or angles that have the same relative position.

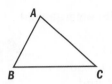 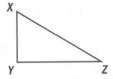

$\triangle ABC \sim \triangle DEF$ $\triangle XYZ$ is not similar to $\triangle UVW$

Reading *Geometry*

When naming similar figures, list the letters of the corresponding vertices in the same order. For the diagram at the right, it is *not* correct to say $\triangle CBA \sim \triangle EFD$, because $\angle C$ and $\angle E$ are not corresponding angles.

Properties of Similar Figures

$\triangle ABC \sim \triangle DEF$

1. Corresponding angles of similar figures are congruent.

   $\angle A \cong \angle D, \angle B \cong \angle E, \angle C \cong \angle F$

2. The ratios of the lengths of corresponding sides of similar figures are equal.

   $\dfrac{AB}{DE} = \dfrac{BC}{EF} = \dfrac{AC}{DF} = \dfrac{1}{2}$

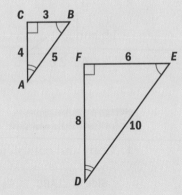

Example 1   *Identifying Corresponding Parts of Similar Figures*

Given $\triangle LMN \sim \triangle PQR$, name the corresponding angles and the corresponding sides.

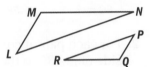

Solution

Corresponding angles: $\angle L$ and $\angle P$, $\angle M$ and $\angle Q$, $\angle N$ and $\angle R$

Corresponding sides: $\overline{LM}$ and $\overline{PQ}$, $\overline{MN}$ and $\overline{QR}$, $\overline{LN}$ and $\overline{PR}$

1. Given $ABCD \sim WXYZ$, name the corresponding angles and the corresponding sides.

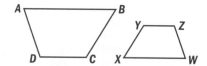

Study *Strategy*

Because all the ratios of the lengths of corresponding sides of the figures in Example 2 are equal, you can use any pair of lengths of corresponding sides to write the ratio. To check the solution, choose another pair of lengths of corresponding sides.

Example 2 *Finding the Ratio of Corresponding Side Lengths*

Given ***ABCD*** ∼ ***JKLM***, find the ratio of the lengths of corresponding sides of ***ABCD*** to ***JKLM***.

Write a ratio comparing the lengths of a pair of corresponding sides. Then substitute the lengths of the sides and simplify.

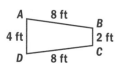

$$\frac{AB}{JK} = \frac{8}{12} = \frac{2}{3}$$

Answer The ratio of the lengths of the corresponding sides is $\frac{2}{3}$.

Example 3 *Checking for Similarity*

Soccer A soccer field is a rectangle that is 70 yards long and 40 yards wide. The penalty area of the soccer field is a rectangle that is 35 yards long and 14 yards wide. Is the penalty area similar to the field?

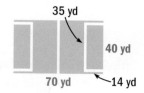

Solution

Because all rectangles have four right angles, the corresponding angles are congruent. To decide if the rectangles are similar, determine whether the ratios of the lengths of corresponding sides are equal.

$$\frac{\text{Length of field}}{\text{Length of penalty area}} \stackrel{?}{=} \frac{\text{Width of field}}{\text{Width of penalty area}} \qquad \textbf{Write proportion.}$$

$$\frac{70}{35} \stackrel{?}{=} \frac{40}{14} \qquad \textbf{Substitute values.}$$

$$70 \cdot 14 \stackrel{?}{=} 35 \cdot 40 \qquad \textbf{Form cross products.}$$

$$980 \neq 1400 \qquad \textbf{Multiply.}$$

Answer The ratios of the lengths of corresponding sides are not equal, so the penalty area is not similar to the field.

✔ **Checkpoint**

2. Inside the penalty area of the soccer field in Example 3 is a smaller rectangle known as the goal area. The goal area of a soccer field is 19 yards long and 6 yards wide. Is the goal area similar to the penalty area? Explain.

Congruent Figures Two figures are **congruent** if they have the same shape *and* the same size. If two figures are congruent, then the corresponding angles are congruent and the corresponding sides are congruent. Congruent figures are also similar.

In the diagram, $\triangle JKL \cong \triangle PQR$ because:

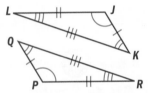

1. $\angle J \cong \angle P$, $\angle K \cong \angle Q$, and $\angle L \cong \angle R$.
2. $\overline{JK} \cong \overline{PQ}$, $\overline{KL} \cong \overline{QR}$, and $\overline{JL} \cong \overline{PR}$.

Example 4   *Finding Measures of Congruent Figures*

Given $ABCD \cong WXYZ$, find the indicated measure.

   a. WZ **b.** $m\angle W$

Solution

Because the quadrilaterals are congruent, the corresponding angles are congruent and the corresponding sides are congruent.

   a. $\overline{WZ} \cong \overline{AD}$. So, $WZ = AD = 12$ m.
   b. $\angle W \cong \angle A$. So, $m\angle W = m\angle A = 105°$.

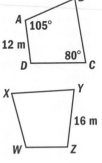

6.4   Exercises

More Practice, p. 808

Guided Practice

Vocabulary Check

1. What do you know about the corresponding angles and corresponding sides of two figures that are congruent?

2. Given $\triangle JKL \sim \triangle PQR$, identify all pairs of corresponding sides and corresponding angles.

Skill Check   **In Exercises 3–6, $\triangle ABC \sim \triangle DEF$.**

3. Identify all corresponding sides and corresponding angles.

4. Find the ratio of the lengths of corresponding sides of $\triangle ABC$ to $\triangle DEF$.

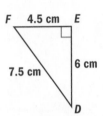

5. Find $m\angle B$.

6. **Error Analysis** Describe and correct the error in writing another similarity statement for the triangles.

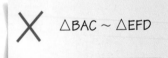

$\triangle BAC \sim \triangle EFD$

Practice and Problem Solving

Homework *Help*

Example	Exercises
1	7, 8
2	9–12
3	9–12, 20
4	13–15

Online Resources
CLASSZONE.COM
• More Examples
• eTutorial Plus

Name the corresponding angles and the corresponding sides.

7. △ABC ~ △DEF

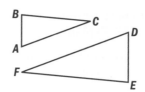

8. JKLMN ≅ XWVZY

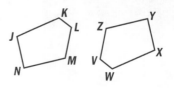

The figures are similar. Find the ratio of the lengths of corresponding sides of figure A to figure B.

9.

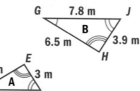

10.

11.

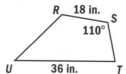

12.

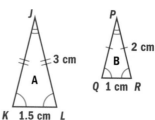

Given RSTU ≅ ABCD, find the indicated measure.

13. m∠R

14. m∠B

15. AB

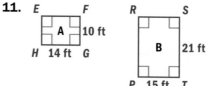

Critical Thinking Copy and complete the statement using *always*, *sometimes*, or *never*. Explain your answer.

16. Congruent figures are _?_ similar. **17.** Similar figures are _?_ congruent.

18. Two squares are _?_ similar. **19.** Two rectangles are _?_ congruent.

20. Screens The table shows the heights and widths of various rectangular viewing screens. Use the table to complete the following.

a. Are the two computer screens similar? Explain.

b. Is the television screen similar to either computer screen? Explain.

c. Compare Compare the height to width ratios of the high definition TV and movie screen.

Item	Height	Width
Television	18 in.	24 in.
Computer 1	9 in.	12 in.
Computer 2	12 in.	15 in.
High definition TV	48 in.	27 in.
Movie screen	32 ft	18 ft

Giant TV screen at the Olympic Stadium in Barcelona, Spain

21. Money It is illegal to reproduce a genuine U.S. bill except according to the following rule: Every side length of the reproduction must be less than $\frac{3}{4}$ times, or greater than $1\frac{1}{2}$ times, the corresponding side length of a genuine bill. Genuine bills are 6.14 inches long and 2.61 inches wide.

   a. Is it legal to make a reproduction that is 9.41 inches long and 4.00 inches wide? Explain.

   b. Is it legal to make a reproduction that is 4.00 inches long and 1.70 inches wide? Explain.

   c. If a reproduction is 2 feet long and 9 inches wide, is it similar to a genuine U.S. bill?

22. Extended Problem Solving Use the similar rectangles to complete the following.

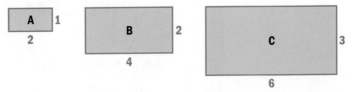

   a. Copy and complete the table.

   b. *Writing* Explain how the ratio of the areas of similar rectangles is related to the ratio of the lengths of corresponding sides.

Figures	Ratio of side lengths	Ratio of areas
A to B	?	?
A to C	?	?
B to C	?	?

   c. Predict Rectangle D is similar to rectangle A. The ratio of a side length of rectangle D to a corresponding side length of rectangle A is 10 : 1. Predict the area of rectangle D. Explain your thinking.

23. Challenge Draw $\triangle ABC$ and $\triangle DEF$ so that $\triangle ABC$ is congruent to both $\triangle DEF$ and $\triangle DFE$.

Mixed Review **Write the fraction in simplest form.** *(Lesson 4.3)*

24. $\frac{48}{64}$ **25.** $\frac{90}{108}$ **26.** $\frac{7ab^5}{21a^2}$ **27.** $\frac{24x}{60x^2y^3}$

28. A bird flies 266 miles in 19 hours. Find the bird's speed in miles per hour. *(Lesson 6.1)*

29. You can hike 6.5 miles in 2 hours. At this rate, how long will it take you to hike 19.5 miles? *(Lesson 6.3)*

Standardized Test Practice **30. Multiple Choice** If quadrilateral $ABCD \cong$ quadrilateral $GHEF$, which angle must be congruent to $\angle C$?

   A. $\angle E$ **B.** $\angle F$ **C.** $\angle G$ **D.** $\angle H$

31. Short Response A tablecloth is spread over a 5 foot by 3 foot rectangular table. The tablecloth extends 1 foot beyond the table's surface on each side. Is the tablecloth similar to the surface of the table? Explain.

6.5

Similarity *and* Measurement

Review Vocabulary
ratio, p. 269
proportion, p. 275
similar figures, p. 288

BEFORE	Now	WHY?
You identified similar figures.	You'll find unknown side lengths of similar figures.	So you can find the height of a palm tree, as in Ex. 5.

Cactus A man who is 6 feet tall is standing near a saguaro cactus. The length of the man's shadow is 2 feet. The cactus casts a shadow 5 feet long. How tall is the cactus?

In Example 2, you will see how to use similar triangles to measure the cactus's height indirectly.

Example 1 | *Finding an Unknown Side Length in Similar Figures*

Given *ABCD ~ EFGH*, find *EH*.

Solution

Use the ratios of the lengths of corresponding sides to write a proportion involving the unknown length, *EH*.

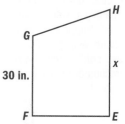

$\dfrac{BC}{FG} = \dfrac{AD}{EH}$ Write proportion involving *EH*.

$\dfrac{12}{30} = \dfrac{16}{x}$ Substitute.

$12x = 30 \cdot 16$ Cross products property

$12x = 480$ Multiply.

$x = 40$ Divide each side by 12.

Answer The length of $\overline{EH}$ is 40 inches.

✔ *Checkpoint*

1. Given $\triangle STU \sim \triangle DEF$, find *DF*.

2. Given *JKLM ~ PQRS*, find *PQ*.

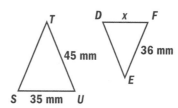

Indirect Measurement You can use similar figures to find lengths that are difficult to measure directly.

In the **Real World**

Cactus To live in the desert, a cactus contains an enormous quantity of water inside its trunk. Suppose a saguaro cactus weighs 8000 pounds and holds 1 ton of water. What fraction of the cactus's weight is water?

Example 2   *Using Indirect Measurement*

Use indirect measurement to find the height of the cactus described on page 293. The cactus and the man are perpendicular to the ground. The sun's rays strike the cactus and the man at the same angle, forming two similar triangles.

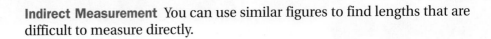

Solution

Write and solve a proportion to find the height h (in feet) of the cactus.

$$\frac{\text{Height of cactus}}{\text{Height of man}} = \frac{\text{Length of cactus's shadow}}{\text{Length of man's shadow}}$$

$$\frac{h}{6} = \frac{5}{2} \qquad \textbf{Substitute.}$$

$$2h = 6 \cdot 5 \qquad \textbf{Cross products property}$$

$$2h = 30 \qquad \textbf{Multiply.}$$

$$h = 15 \qquad \textbf{Divide each side by 2.}$$

Answer The cactus has a height of 15 feet.

✔ *Checkpoint*

3. A cactus is 5 feet tall and casts a shadow that is 1.5 feet long. How tall is a nearby cactus that casts a shadow that is 8 feet long?

Example 3   *Using Algebra and Similar Triangles*

Given $\triangle ABC \sim \triangle DEC$**, find** BE**.**

To find BE, write and solve a proportion.

$$\frac{AB}{DE} = \frac{BC}{EC} \qquad \textbf{Write proportion.}$$

$$\frac{AB}{DE} = \frac{BE + EC}{EC} \qquad \textbf{Use the fact that } \boldsymbol{BC = BE + EC.}$$

$$\frac{20}{15} = \frac{x + 36}{36} \qquad \textbf{Substitute.}$$

$$20 \cdot 36 = 15(x + 36) \qquad \textbf{Cross products property}$$

$$720 = 15x + 540 \qquad \textbf{Multiply.}$$

$$180 = 15x \qquad \textbf{Subtract 540 from each side.}$$

$$12 = x \qquad \textbf{Divide each side by 15.}$$

Answer The length of $\overline{BE}$ is 12 inches.

Study *Strategy*

To solve a problem like the one in Example 3, you may find it helpful to redraw the two triangles so they don't overlap.

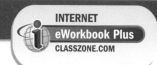
Guided Practice

Vocabulary Check
1. $EFGH \sim JKLM$. Which side of $EFGH$ corresponds with $\overline{JM}$?
2. Describe how similar triangles are useful for indirect measurement.

In Exercises 3 and 4, $\triangle ABC \sim \triangle DEF$.

Skill Check
3. Find EF.

4. Find FD.

Guided Problem Solving
5. **Palm Tree** A man who is 74 inches tall stands beside a palm tree. The length of the man's shadow is 26 inches. The palm tree's shadow is 80 inches long. How tall is the palm tree?

  ① The rays of the sun create similar triangles for the man and the palm tree. Write a proportion using the triangles.

  ② Find the height of the palm tree to the nearest inch.

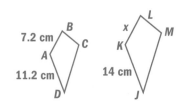

Practice and Problem Solving

Homework *Help*

Example	Exercises
1	6–9, 13
2	12, 14
3	10, 11, 15

Online Resources
CLASSZONE.COM
• More Examples
• eTutorial Plus

6. Given $\triangle ABC \sim \triangle LMN$, find LN.

7. Given $LMNP \sim QRST$, find RS.

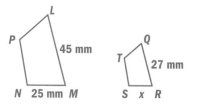

8. Given $ABCD \sim KLMJ$, find KL.

9. Given $ABCD \sim RSTU$, find UR.

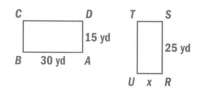

Find the length of $\overline{DE}$.

10. $\triangle ABC \sim \triangle ADE$

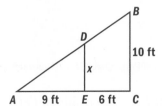

11. $ABCD \sim AGFE$

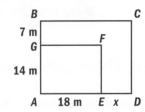

12. Bryce Canyon Bryce Canyon National Park in Utah is known for its unusual rock formations. One rock casts a shadow 21 feet long. A girl standing near this rock is 5 feet 3 inches tall and casts a shadow 7 feet long.

Hikers in Bryce Canyon National Park, Utah

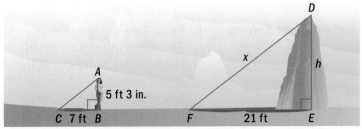

a. Convert Write the girl's height in inches.

b. Write and solve a proportion to find the height of the rock in feet and inches.

13. Poster You are enlarging a photograph to make a poster. The poster will be similar to the original photograph. The photograph is 6 inches tall and 4 inches wide. The poster will be 2.5 feet wide. How tall will the poster be? Find the poster's perimeter.

Review *Help*

You may find it helpful to draw a diagram when solving problems about similar figures. For help with drawing a diagram, see p. 795.

14. Surveying You can use indirect measurement to find the distance across a river by following these steps.

1. Start at a point A directly across the river from a landmark, such as a tree, at point B.

2. Walk 30 feet along the river to point C and place a stake.

3. Walk 20 feet farther along the river to point D.

4. Turn and walk directly away from the river. Stop at point E, where the stake you planted lines up with the landmark. $\triangle ABC \sim \triangle DEC$.

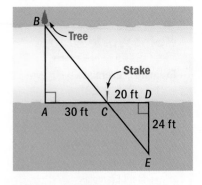

Suppose you walk 24 feet away from the river along $\overline{DE}$ before the stake lines up with the landmark. Write and solve a proportion to find the distance AB across the river.

15. In the figure, $\triangle ABC$, $\triangle ADE$, and $\triangle AFG$ are all similar.

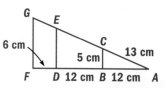

    a. Find DE and FG.

    b. Find AE and AG.

16. Critical Thinking Given $\triangle ABC \sim \triangle DEF$, tell whether the given information is enough to find the specified measurements. Explain your thinking.

    a. You know AB, BC, CA, and DE. You want to find EF and FD.

    b. You know AB, BC, and FD. You want to find CA.

    c. You know $m\angle B$. You want to find $m\angle E$.

17. Challenge A rectangular box has a length of 3 inches, a width of 2 inches, and a height of 4 inches. Find the dimensions of three similar boxes: one that has a length of 6 inches, one that has a width of 6 inches, and one that has a height of 6 inches.

Mixed Review

Solve the equation. *(Lesson 5.6)*

18. $\frac{5}{7}x = 16$ **19.** $-\frac{4}{9}x = 12$ **20.** $\frac{3}{4}x + \frac{5}{8} = 1$ **21.** $-\frac{1}{2}x + 6 = 5\frac{4}{5}$

Order the ratios from least to greatest. *(Lesson 6.1)*

22. $5:3, 6:4, \frac{11}{3}, 3 \text{ to } 1, 33:100$ **23.** $15 \text{ to } 9, 35:25, \frac{44}{33}, \frac{22}{20}, 8:3$

Standardized Test Practice

In Exercises 24 and 25, $\triangle RST \sim \triangle VUT$.

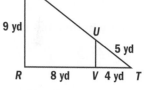

24. Multiple Choice Find UV.

    A. 3 yards   **B.** 4 yards

    C. 4.5 yards   **D.** 5 yards

25. Multiple Choice Find ST.

    F. 8 yards   **G.** 10 yards   **H.** 12 yards   **I.** 15 yards

Putting the Pieces Together

Arrange the four congruent triangles to create a larger similar triangle. Arrange the four congruent rectangles to create a larger similar rectangle. Sketch your answers.

Can you arrange the four congruent quadrilaterals in the bottom row to create a larger similar quadrilateral?

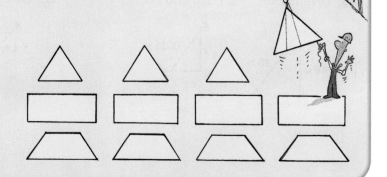

Mid-Chapter Quiz

1. **Activities** The table gives the number of hours Chad spends doing various activities on a school day. Write the following ratios in simplest form.

   a. The hours he is at school or traveling to and from school to the hours in a day

   b. The hours he is asleep to the hours in a day

   c. The hours he is awake to the hours he is asleep

Daily activities	Time
School	7 hours
Relaxing or doing homework at home	5 hours
Football practice	2 hours
Traveling to and from school	1 hour
Sleeping	9 hours

2. **Car** A car travels at a speed of 44 feet per second. What is this speed in miles per hour?

Solve the proportion.

3. $\dfrac{w}{7} = \dfrac{36}{42}$

4. $\dfrac{x}{10} = \dfrac{35}{50}$

5. $\dfrac{3}{4} = \dfrac{y}{52}$

6. $\dfrac{7}{12} = \dfrac{z}{105}$

7. $\dfrac{5}{8} = \dfrac{25}{a}$

8. $\dfrac{8}{b} = \dfrac{60}{75}$

9. $\dfrac{0.4}{c} = \dfrac{1.2}{21}$

10. $\dfrac{5.2}{3} = \dfrac{78}{d}$

Tell whether the ratios form a proportion.

11. $\dfrac{25}{36}, \dfrac{5}{6}$

12. $\dfrac{8}{9}, \dfrac{36}{32}$

13. $\dfrac{8}{18}, \dfrac{12}{27}$

14. $\dfrac{6}{31.2}, \dfrac{2.5}{13}$

15. **American Flag** The blue portion of the American flag is known as the union. Using the measurements in the diagram, determine if the rectangle enclosing the union is similar to the rectangle enclosing the entire flag.

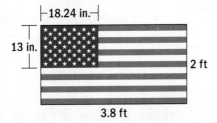

18.24 in.

13 in.

2 ft

3.8 ft

16. Given $\triangle ABC \sim \triangle FGH$, find FG.

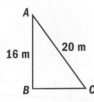

16 m   20 m x 11.25 m

17. Given $PQRS \sim JKLM$, find KL.

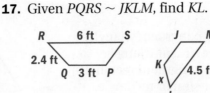

6 ft   2.4 ft   3 ft   4.5 ft x

6.6 Making a Scale Drawing

Goal
Make a scale drawing of an object.

Materials
• metric ruler

A *scale drawing* is a drawing that is similar to the object it represents. You are making a scale drawing of a rectangular stage so that you can plan the arrangement of props for a school play. The stage is 12 meters long and 9 meters wide. In your drawing, 1 centimeter represents 3 meters on the stage. What dimensions should you use for the stage in the drawing?

Investigate

Use proportions to make a scale drawing.

 1 Use a proportion to find the length l (in centimeters) of the stage in the drawing.

$$\frac{1 \text{ cm}}{3 \text{ m}} = \frac{l}{12 \text{ m}}$$

$$1 \cdot 12 = 3 \cdot l$$

$$4 = l$$

2 Use a proportion to find the width w (in centimeters) of the stage in the drawing.

$$\frac{1 \text{ cm}}{3 \text{ m}} = \frac{w}{9 \text{ m}}$$

$$1 \cdot 9 = 3 \cdot w$$

$$3 = w$$

3 Use a ruler to draw a 4 cm by 3 cm rectangle. This rectangle represents the stage.

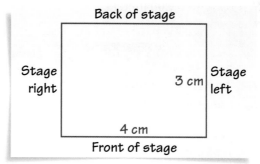

Draw Conclusions

1. The table shows the dimensions of rectangular pieces of furniture to be placed on the stage. Find the length and width you should use for each piece of furniture in the scale drawing.

Item	Length	Width
Sofa	1.8 m	0.9 m
Table	1.2 m	0.9 m
Upright piano	1.5 m	0.6 m

2. Make a scale drawing of the stage. Include scale drawings of the sofa, the table, and the piano so that the sofa is near the back of the stage, the table is stage left near the front, and the piano is stage right near the front.

Scale Drawings

You solved proportions. | You'll use proportions with scale drawings. | So you can find the height of a roller coaster, as in Ex. 40.

Vocabulary

scale drawing, p. 300
scale model, p. 300
scale, p. 300

Reading *Algebra*

In this course, all scales are written as
scale measure : actual measure.

Scale Drawings The map shows a portion of Teotihuacan, a large city built over 2000 years ago. The ruins of the city still exist in central Mexico.

The map is an example of a *scale drawing*. A **scale drawing** is a two-dimensional drawing that is similar to the object it represents. A **scale model** is a three-dimensional model that is similar to the object it represents.

The **scale** of a scale drawing or scale model gives the relationship between the drawing or model's dimensions and the actual dimensions. For example, in the map shown, the scale 1 cm : 200 m means that 1 centimeter in the scale drawing represents an actual distance of 200 meters.

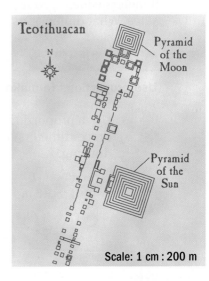

Teotihuacan

N

Pyramid of the Moon

Pyramid of the Sun

Scale: 1 cm : 200 m

Example 1   *Using a Scale Drawing*

Teotihuacan On the map, the center of the Pyramid of the Sun is 4 centimeters from the center of the Pyramid of the Moon. What is the actual distance from the center of the Pyramid of the Sun to the center of the Pyramid of the Moon?

Solution

Let x represent the actual distance (in meters) between the two pyramids. The ratio of the map distance between the two pyramids to the actual distance x is equal to the scale of the map. Write and solve a proportion using this relationship.

$$\frac{1 \text{ cm}}{200 \text{ m}} = \frac{4 \text{ cm}}{x \text{ m}} \quad \leftarrow \text{ Map distance} \\ \leftarrow \text{ Actual distance}$$

$$1x = 200 \cdot 4 \quad \text{Cross products property}$$

$$x = 800 \quad \text{Multiply.}$$

Answer The actual distance is 800 meters.

View of the Pyramid of the Sun from the Pyramid of the Moon

✓ **Checkpoint**

1. On the map on page 300, the Pyramid of the Sun has a length and a width of 1.1 centimeters. Find the actual dimensions of the Pyramid of the Sun.

The floral carpet in 2002 was made of 800,000 begonias.

Example 2	Finding the Scale of a Drawing

Floral Carpet Every few years, the Grand Place in Brussels, Belgium, is decorated with a large floral carpet made of begonias. Before making the carpet, designers make detailed scale drawings. Suppose the floral carpet is to be 40 meters wide. A designer creates a scale drawing of the carpet that is 20 centimeters wide. Find the drawing's scale.

Solution

Write a ratio using corresponding side lengths of the scale drawing and the actual carpet. Then simplify the ratio so that the numerator is 1.

$$\frac{20 \text{ cm}}{40 \text{ m}} \longleftarrow \text{ Width of scale drawing}$$
$$\longleftarrow \text{ Width of carpet}$$

$$\frac{20 \text{ cm}}{40 \text{ m}} = \frac{1 \text{ cm}}{2 \text{ m}} \qquad \textbf{Simplify.}$$

Answer The drawing's scale is 1 cm : 2 m.

The scale of a scale drawing or scale model can be written without units if the measurements have the same unit. To write the scale from Example 2 without units, write 2 meters as 200 centimeters, as shown.

Scale with units   **Scale without units**

$$1 \text{ cm} : 2 \text{ m} \implies \frac{1 \text{ cm}}{2 \text{ m}} \implies \frac{1 \text{ cm}}{200 \text{ cm}} \implies 1 : 200$$

Example 3	Finding a Dimension of a Scale Model

Space Shuttle A model of a space shuttle has a scale of 1 : 52. The space shuttle has a wingspan of 78 feet. Find the model's wingspan.

Solution

Write a proportion using the scale.

$$\frac{1}{52} = \frac{x}{78} \quad \longleftarrow \text{ Dimension of model}$$
$$\longleftarrow \text{ Dimension of space shuttle}$$

$$78 = 52x \qquad \textbf{Cross products property}$$

$$1.5 = x \qquad \textbf{Divide each side by 52.}$$

Answer The wingspan of the model is 1.5 ft.

✓ **Checkpoint**

2. The length of a space shuttle is a 122 feet. Find the length of the scale model in Example 3 to the nearest tenth of a foot.

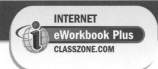
Guided Practice

Vocabulary Check

1. What is a scale drawing?

2. Write the scale 1 inch : 1 foot without units.

Skill Check **A map has a scale of 1 inch : 40 miles. Use the given map distance to find the actual distance.**

3. 5 inches   4. 12 inches   5. 32 inches   6. 1 foot

Write the scale without units.

7. 1 in. : 28 yd   8. 1 in. : 4 ft   9. 1 cm : 12 m   10. 1 mm : 2 m

Guided Problem Solving

11. **Bedroom** Shown below is a scale drawing of a student's bedroom. Use the scale drawing to determine the dimensions of the student's desk.

    1 The student's bed is 2 meters long. In the scale drawing, the bed is 2.5 centimeters long. Find the scale of the drawing.

    2 Write the scale from Step 1 without units.

    3 In the drawing, the desk is 1.5 centimeters long and 0.5 centimeter wide. Write and solve a proportion to find the dimensions of the student's actual desk.

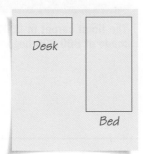

Practice and Problem Solving

A map has a scale of 1 centimeter : 5 kilometers. Use the given map distance to find the actual distance.

12. 6 cm   13. 11 cm   14. 26 cm   15. 37 cm

16. 0.6 cm   17. 1.5 cm   18. 20 cm   19. 9 cm

A map has a scale of 1 inch : 3 kilometers. Use the given actual distance to find the distance on the map.

20. 18 km   21. 90 km   22. 76 km   23. 14 km

24. 0.9 km   25. 1.5 km   26. 0.3 km   27. 0.5 km

Write the scale without units.

28. 1 in. : 10 yd   29. 1 in. : 20 ft   30. 1 cm : 1 m   31. 1 mm : 36 cm

32. 1 cm : 3 km   33. 1 cm : 5 km   34. 1 cm : 2 m   35. 1 mm : 34 cm

36. **Architecture** In a scale drawing, a wall is 8 centimeters long. The actual wall is 20 meters long. Find the scale of the drawing.

37. **Interior Design** A sofa is 8 feet long. In a scale drawing, the sofa is 3 inches long. Find the scale of the drawing.

38. **Basketball Court** A scale drawing of a basketball court has a scale of 1 inch : 9 feet.

   a. The basketball court is 94 feet by 50 feet. Find the dimensions of the court in the drawing.

   b. The free throw line is 15 feet from the backboard. How far is the free throw line from the backboard in the drawing?

39. **Carpentry** A carpenter is building a house from an architect's blueprint. The blueprint has a scale of 1 : 42.

   a. Find the actual length of a wall that is 3 inches long in the blueprint.

   b. A door on the blueprint is 2 inches high. Find the height of the actual door.

   c. A window on the house is drawn as a rectangle that is $\frac{1}{2}$ inch by $\frac{3}{4}$ inch. Find the actual dimensions of the window.

40. **Model Roller Coaster** You are building a model of the Viper roller coaster in California using a scale of 1 : 47. The model is 4 feet high. How many feet high is the Viper?

41. **Banner** You want to make a banner that says WELCOME HOME. You want the letters to be 2 feet high. You make a sketch in which the letters are 2 inches high. The entire phrase in your sketch is 20 inches long. What length of paper should you buy?

42. **Lincoln** A mask of Abraham Lincoln's head was made when he was alive. The mask has a height of $9\frac{3}{4}$ inches.

   a. The profile of Lincoln's head on a penny has a height of $\frac{11}{32}$ inch. Write the scale of the penny to the mask without units.

   b. The carving of Lincoln's face on Mount Rushmore is 60 feet high. Write the scale of the mask to the carving without units.

   c. Write the scale of the penny to the carving without units.

   d. Lincoln's nose on the penny is about $\frac{1}{16}$ inch long. Find the length of Lincoln's nose on the carving and on the mask. Round your answers to the nearest inch.

43. **Critical Thinking** The ratio of the length of an object to its width is 3 : 2. A scale drawing of the object has a scale of 1 inch : 3 feet. In the scale drawing, what is the ratio of the object's length to its width?

44. **Critical Thinking** Write a scale for a scale model whose dimensions are 20 times the dimensions of the actual object. Explain your reasoning.

Review *Help*

For help with using a ruler to measure lengths, see p. 788.

45. Ant At the right is a scale drawing of a carpenter ant. The scale of the drawing is 1 cm : 2.5 mm. Find the actual length of the ant's head, thorax, and abdomen. Round your answers to the nearest hundredth of a millimeter.

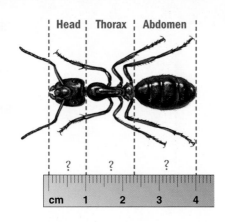

46. Challenge You made a scale model of Earth and the moon. The Earth's diameter is about 1.3×10^4 kilometers. In the model, Earth's diameter is 50 centimeters. The moon's diameter is about 3.5×10^3 kilometers. Find the diameter of the moon in your model. Round your answer to the nearest tenth of a centimeter.

Mixed Review

Find the sum or difference. *(Lesson 5.2)*

47. $9\frac{8}{11} + 7\frac{6}{11}$ **48.** $7\frac{5}{6} - 1\frac{5}{6}$ **49.** $-6\frac{7}{12} - 8\frac{11}{12}$

50. Baseball A square tarp is spread over a 90 foot by 90 foot baseball infield. The tarp extends 15 feet beyond each edge of the infield. Is the tarp similar to the infield? *(Lesson 6.4)*

Standardized Test Practice

51. Extended Response An architect builds a scale model of a house. The model has a scale of 1 inch : 1 yard.

a. The scale model is 1 foot high. How high is the actual house?

b. The house's deck is a 15 foot by 12 foot rectangle. Explain how to find the area of the deck in the model.

Brain GAME

Rolling out the Carpet

Sierpinski's carpet is a pattern that involves repeatedly dividing a square into 9 smaller squares of equal size and removing the center square. The first and second stages of this pattern are shown below.

How many new white squares are in the third stage?

Write a ratio that compares the side lengths of the white square in the first stage to one small white square in the second stage. Explain how you found this ratio.

First Stage

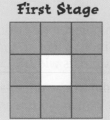

Second Stage

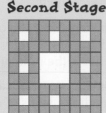

Third Stage

?

6.7 Performing an Experiment

Goal
Use an experiment to estimate the likelihood that an event will occur.

Materials
• paper cup

Investigate

Perform an experiment to find the position in which a tossed paper cup will land most often.

1 Toss a small paper cup 30 times. Note whether the cup lands on its side, lands rim side up, or lands bottom side up.

2 For each toss, record the result in the *Tally* column of a frequency table like the one shown below. After 30 tosses, record the frequencies.

Position of cup	Tally	Frequency
On its side	ЖΓ I	?
Rim side up	I	?
Bottom side up	I	?

Draw Conclusions

1. **Analyze** For what fraction of the tosses did the cup land on its side? rim side up? bottom side up?

2. **Critical Thinking** In which position do you think the paper cup is most likely to land on your next toss? Explain your choice.

3. **Predict** Find the ratio of the number of times the cup landed on its side to the total number of times the cup was tossed. Use the ratio to predict the number of times the cup will land on its side if it is tossed 1000 times.

4. **Compare** Cut the paper cup so that it is only half as tall. Repeat the experiment. Then compare your results with the results of the first experiment.

5. **Predict** Use the results from Exercise 4 to predict the number of times the cut cup will land on its side if it is tossed 1000 times.

Probability *and* Odds

BEFORE   ▶ *Now*   WHY?

You wrote ratios.   You'll find probabilities.   So you can describe the accuracy of a weather forecast, as in Ex. 6.

Vocabulary

outcomes, p. 306
event, p. 306
favorable outcomes, p. 306
probability, p. 306
theoretical probability, p. 307
experimental probability, p. 307
odds in favor, p. 308
odds against, p. 308

You are rolling a number cube and want to know how likely you are to roll a certain number. Each time you roll the number cube there are six possible results.

Rolling a number cube is an example of an experiment. The possible results of an experiment are **outcomes**. When you roll a number cube, there are 6 possible outcomes: rolling a 1, 2, 3, 4, 5, or 6. An **event** is an outcome or a collection of outcomes, such as rolling a 1 or rolling an odd number. Once you specify an event, the outcomes for that event are called **favorable outcomes**. The favorable outcomes for rolling an odd number are rolling a 1, rolling a 3, and rolling a 5.

The **probability** that an event occurs is a measure of the likelihood that the event will occur.

Reading *Algebra*

Vocabulary The set of all possible outcomes for an experiment is sometimes called the *sample space*.

Probability of an Event

The probability of an event when all the outcomes are equally likely is:

$$P(\text{event}) = \frac{\text{Number of favorable outcomes}}{\text{Number of possible outcomes}}$$

Example 1   *Finding a Probability*

Suppose you roll a number cube. What is the probability that you roll an even number?

Solution

Rolls of 2, 4, and 6 are even, so there are 3 favorable outcomes. There are 6 possible outcomes.

$$P(\text{rolling an even number}) = \frac{\text{Number of favorable outcomes}}{\text{Number of possible outcomes}}$$

$$= \frac{3}{6} = \frac{1}{2}$$

Answer The probability that you roll an even number is $\frac{1}{2}$.

✔ **Checkpoint**

1. Suppose you roll a number cube. What is the probability that you roll a number greater than 1?

Experimental Probability The probability found in Example 1 is an example of a *theoretical probability*. A **theoretical probability** is based on knowing all of the equally likely outcomes of an experiment. A probability that is based on repeated *trials* of an experiment is called an **experimental probability**. Each trial in which the event occurs is a *success*.

Experimental Probability

The experimental probability of an event is:

$$P(\text{event}) = \frac{\text{Number of successes}}{\text{Number of trials}}$$

Example 2   *Finding Experimental Probability*

Miniature Golf A miniature golf course offers a free game to golfers who make a hole-in-one on the last hole. Last week, 44 out of 256 golfers made a hole-in-one on the last hole. Find the experimental probability that a golfer makes a hole-in-one on the last hole.

Solution

$$P(\text{hole-in-one}) = \frac{44}{256} \quad \leftarrow \text{Number of successes} \atop \leftarrow \text{Number of trials}$$

$$= \frac{11}{64} \quad \text{Simplify.}$$

Answer The experimental probability that a golfer makes a hole-in-one on the last hole is $\frac{11}{64}$, or about 0.17.

✔ **Checkpoint**

2. You interviewed 45 randomly chosen students for the newspaper. Of the students you interviewed, 15 play sports. Find the experimental probability that the next randomly chosen student will play sports.

Interpreting Probabilities Probabilities can range from 0 to 1. The closer the probability of an event is to 1, the more likely the event will occur.

$P = 0$	$P = 0.25$	$P = 0.50$	$P = 0.75$	$P = 1$
Impossible	Unlikely	Occurs half the time	Likely	Certain

You can use probabilities to make predictions about uncertain occurrences.

Study *Strategy*

Probabilities can be written as fractions or decimals.

Example 3   *Using Probability to Make a Prediction*

Basketball Today, you attempted 50 free throws and made 32 of them. Use experimental probability to predict how many free throws you will make tomorrow if you attempt 75 free throws.

Solution

1 Find the experimental probability that you make a free throw.

$$P(\text{make a free throw}) = \frac{32}{50} = 0.64$$

2 Multiply the experimental probability by the number of free throws you will attempt tomorrow.

$$0.64 \cdot 75 = 48$$

Answer If you continue to make free throws at the same rate, you will make 48 free throws in 75 attempts tomorrow.

 Checkpoint

3. Use the information in Example 3 to predict how many free throws you would make if you attempt 150 free throws.

Odds When all outcomes are equally likely, the ratio of the number of favorable outcomes to the number of unfavorable outcomes is called the **odds in favor** of an event. The ratio of the number of unfavorable outcomes to the number of favorable outcomes is called the **odds against** an event.

$$\text{Odds in favor} = \frac{\text{Number of favorable outcomes}}{\text{Number of unfavorable outcomes}}$$

$$\text{Odds against} = \frac{\text{Number of unfavorable outcomes}}{\text{Number of favorable outcomes}}$$

Example 4   *Finding the Odds*

Suppose you randomly choose a number between 1 and 20.

a. What are the odds in favor of choosing a prime number?

b. What are the odds against choosing a prime number?

Solution

a. There are 8 favorable outcomes (2, 3, 5, 7, 11, 13, 17, and 19) and $20 - 8 = 12$ unfavorable outcomes.

$$\text{Odds in favor} = \frac{\text{Number of favorable outcomes}}{\text{Number of unfavorable outcomes}} = \frac{8}{12} = \frac{2}{3}$$

The odds are $\frac{2}{3}$, or 2 to 3, that you choose a prime number.

b. The odds against choosing a prime number are $\frac{3}{2}$, or 3 to 2.

Reading *Algebra*

While probabilities are often expressed in $\frac{a}{b}$ form, odds are often expressed in *a* to *b* form.

Guided Practice

Vocabulary Check

1. Copy and complete: When a coin is flipped 20 times and lands heads up 11 times, the _?_ probability that the coin lands heads up is $\frac{11}{20}$.

2. The odds in favor of event A are 2 to 1. The odds against event B are 2 to 1. Which event is more likely to occur, event A or event B?

Skill Check

In Exercises 3–5, suppose you roll a number cube. Find the probability of the event.

3. A prime number   **4.** A multiple of 2   **5.** A number less than 5

Guided Problem Solving

6. **Forecast** Over the course of a month, you keep track of how many times the next day's weather forecast is accurate. The forecast is correct 22 times in a month of 30 days. Predict how many days over the course of a year the forecast will be correct.

  1 Find the experimental probability that the forecast is correct.

  2 Multiply your answer from Step 1 by 365 to predict how many days the forecast will be correct over the course of a year.

Practice and Problem Solving

Homework *Help*

Example	Exercises
1	7, 11–12
2	12, 14
3	10, 13, 14, 19
4	8–9, 11

Online Resources
CLASSZONE.COM
• More Examples
• eTutorial Plus

In Exercises 7–10, use the spinner to find the probability. The spinner is divided into equal parts.

7. What is the probability that the spinner stops on a multiple of 3?

8. What are the odds in favor of stopping on a multiple of 4?

9. What are the odds against stopping on a 1 or a 2?

10. If you spin the spinner 100 times, how many times do you expect it to stop on 8?

11. Each letter in the word THEORETICAL is written on a separate slip of paper and placed in a hat. A letter is chosen at random from the hat.

  a. What is the probability that the letter chosen is an E?

  b. What is the probability that the letter chosen is a vowel?

  c. What are the odds in favor of choosing a consonant?

  d. **Critical Thinking** Find a word for which the probability that you choose an R when you randomly choose a letter from the word is $\frac{2}{5}$.

Review *Help*

When finding an experimental probability, you may find it helpful to use the *act it out* strategy for problem solving. For help with this strategy, see p. 798.

12. Experiment Use a coin to complete the following.

   a. What is the theoretical probability that the coin lands heads up when tossed?

   b. Flip the coin 20 times. Record whether it lands heads up or tails up for each flip. Then find the experimental probability that the coin lands heads up when tossed.

   c. *Writing* Compare the theoretical probability with the experimental probability. What do you think would happen if you tossed the coin 100 times? Explain.

13. Flowers You plant 30 African violet seeds and 9 of them sprout. Use an experimental probability to predict how many African violet seeds will sprout if you plant 20 more seeds.

14. Extended Problem Solving In normal English texts, letters appear with regular frequency. The table gives the probability that a letter, chosen at random from a page of English text, will be a certain letter.

Letter	Probability
e	0.131
t	0.104
a	0.081
s	0.061
x	0.002
z	0.001

   a. Predict A page contains 300 letters. Predict how many *e*'s are on the page and how many *a*'s.

   b. Predict An essay contains 1000 letters. How many *z*'s would you predict are in the essay? How many *x*'s?

   c. Compare The three sentences in part (b) contain 68 letters. Find the experimental probability that a letter randomly chosen from these sentences is a *t* and the probability that it is an *s*. How do these probabilities compare with the probabilities given in the table?

15. Critical Thinking If you know the probability of an event, explain how to find the odds in favor of and the odds against the event.

16. *Writing* Describe a situation where you would use experimental probability and a situation where you would use theoretical probability.

In Exercises 17 and 18, use *geometric probability* to solve the problem. If a point in a region is chosen at random, the geometric probability that the point is located in a specified part of the region is given by

$$P(\text{point in part}) = \frac{\text{Area of specified part}}{\text{Area of entire region}}$$

Reading *Algebra*

The probability of an event is often called the *chance* that the event will occur.

17. Ring You lost a ring in a rectangular field that is 110 yards by 65 yards. You search a rectangular section of the field that is 25 yards by 32 yards. What is the probability that the ring is in the section you search?

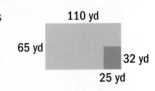

18. Treasure Chest A treasure chest is buried somewhere in a rectangular field. The field is 100 feet by 60 feet. You search 25 square feet of the field. What is the chance that the chest is in the region you search?

19. **Websites** Many websites have ads whose appearance is based on probability. Advertisers pay the website based on the number of times the ad appears.

   a. The probability that an ad appears when a particular website is loaded is 0.2. The website gets 2000 hits a day. About how many times does the ad appear?

   b. The probability that an ad appears when a particular website is loaded is 0.05. About how many hits must the website have for the ad to appear 1000 times?

20. **Critical Thinking** An event has *even odds* when the odds in favor of (or against) the event are 1 : 1. What is the probability of an event with even odds?

21. **Critical Thinking** The probability of rolling a 1 on a number cube is $\frac{1}{6}$. What is the probability of *not* rolling a 1? In general, if the probability of an event is $\frac{1}{n}$, what is the probability that the event does *not* occur? Explain your thinking.

22. **Challenge** A train runs every 15 minutes. You arrive at the train station without consulting the train's time schedule. What is the probability that you will wait more than 10 minutes for the train?

Mixed Review   **Algebra Basics Evaluate the expression when $x = 3$, $y = -3$, and $z = 4$.** *(Lesson 1.7)*

23. $2xy$ 24. $5yz$ 25. $7xyz$ 26. $6xz$

Order the numbers from least to greatest. *(Lesson 5.1)*

27. $1\frac{5}{9}, -\frac{3}{5}, \frac{13}{5}, -1.5, -2.7$ 28. $-0.625, -\frac{3}{8}, 1\frac{5}{8}, \frac{21}{8}, -1.6$

29. Given $ABCD \sim EFGH$, find EH. *(Lesson 6.5)*

30. Given $\triangle LMN \sim \triangle PQR$, find LN. *(Lesson 6.5)*

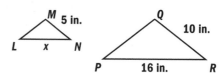

Standardized Test Practice

31. **Multiple Choice** You have a bag filled with 12 red marbles, 9 blue marbles, and 14 green marbles. You randomly select a marble from the bag. What is the probability that you select a blue marble?

   A. $\frac{1}{9}$ **B.** $\frac{1}{35}$ **C.** $\frac{9}{35}$ **D.** $\frac{9}{26}$

32. **Short Response** A traffic light is green for 17 seconds, yellow for 3 seconds, and red for 20 seconds. Suppose your approach to the light is not affected by traffic or other factors. What is the probability that the light will be green when you first see the light? Explain.

6.7 Generating Random Numbers

Goal Use a calculator to generate random integers.

Example

Use a calculator to solve the following problem.

On average, how many people do you need to assemble in a group for two members of the group to have the same birth month?

Although months have different numbers of days, you can make a good prediction by assuming that the 12 months of the year are equally likely to be a person's birth month. Assign the integers 1 through 12 to the months of the year and use a calculator's random number generator to generate numbers as described below.

1 To generate a random integer from 1 through 12, use the random integer generator on a calculator. Note that your calculator may generate a different number than the one in the display below.

Keystrokes

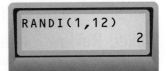

2 Continue to generate random numbers until one of the numbers repeats. A repeated number means that two members of the group have the same birth month. Record how many random numbers you generate until a number repeats.

3 Perform the experiment described in Steps 1 and 2 a total of 10 times. Keep a tally of your results in a table like the one below.

Trial	1	2	3	4	5	6	7	8	9	10
Number of people in group	3	6	7	7	6	6	5	5	5	4

Tech *Help*

To tell the calculator that you want random integers from 1 to 12, you should enter 1 and 12 after RANDI(.

Online Resources
CLASSZONE.COM
• Keystroke Help

Draw Conclusions

1. **Analyze** The number of random numbers generated in each trial represents the size of the group you need to assemble for two people to have the same birth month. What is the average (mean) size of such a group?

2. **Left-handed** About 10% of people are left-handed. Choose a number from 1 to 10 to represent a left-handed person. Then use your calculator to perform an experiment to determine how many people you need to assemble before 2 of them are left-handed. Perform the experiment 10 times and find the average (mean) of your results.

6.8

The Counting Principle

BEFORE	*Now*	WHY?
You counted outcomes to find probabilities.	You'll use the counting principle to find probabilities.	So you can count possible NBA finals matchups, as in Ex. 9.

Vocabulary

tree diagram, p. 313
counting principle, p. 314

Eyeglasses You are buying new eyeglasses and must choose the frame material and shape. The frame material can be plastic or metal. The frame shape can be rectangular, oval, cat's eye, or round. How many different frames are possible?

One way to count the number of possibilities is to use a **tree diagram**. A tree diagram uses branching to list choices.

Example 1 *Making a Tree Diagram*

To count the number of possible choices for frames, as described above, make a tree diagram.

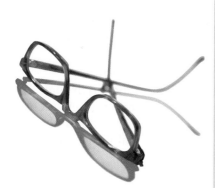

List the frame materials.	List the frame shapes for each frame material.	List the possibilities.
plastic	rectangular	plastic rectangular
	oval	plastic oval
	cat's eye	plastic cat's eye
	round	plastic round
metal	rectangular	metal rectangular
	oval	metal oval
	cat's eye	metal cat's eye
	round	metal round

Answer Eight different frames are possible.

✔ *Checkpoint*

1. Suppose each of the different eyeglasses in Example 1 also comes in two colors, black and red. Copy the tree diagram above and add the new choices. How many possible choices for frames are there?

Counting Principle A quick way to count the number of possibilities displayed in a tree diagram is to use the *counting principle*. The **counting principle** uses multiplication to find the number of possible ways two or more events can occur.

The Counting Principle

If one event can occur in *m* ways, and for each of these ways a second event can occur in *n* ways, then the number of ways that the two events can occur together is *m* · *n*.

The counting principle can be extended to three or more events.

Study Strategy

Another Way In Example 2, you can make a table to list the 36 possible outcomes. The beginning of such a table is shown below.

	1	2	3
1	1, 1	1, 2	1, 3
2	2, 1	2, 2	2, 3
3	3, 1	3, 2	3, 3

Example 2   *Using the Counting Principle*

You roll a blue and a red number cube. Use the counting principle to find the number of different outcomes that are possible.

Number of outcomes for the red cube	Number of outcomes for the blue cube	Total number of possible outcomes
6	• 6	= 36

Answer There are 36 different possible outcomes.

✓ *Checkpoint*

2. How many different outcomes are possible when you flip a coin and roll a number cube?

Example 3   *Finding a Probability*

Combination Lock A combination lock has 40 numbers on its dial. To open the lock, you must turn the dial right to the first number, left to the second number, then right to the third number. You randomly choose three numbers on the lock. What is the probability that you choose the correct combination?

Solution

First find the number of different combinations.

  40 · 40 · 40 = 64,000   **Use the counting principle.**

Then find the probability that you choose the correct combination.

$$P(\text{correct combination}) = \frac{1}{64,000} \longleftarrow \textbf{There is only one correct combination.}$$

Answer The probability that you choose the correct combination is $\frac{1}{64,000}$.

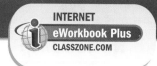
Guided Practice

Vocabulary Check

1. Draw a tree diagram to show the possible outcomes when you flip two coins.

2. Explain how to use the counting principle to determine how many outcomes are possible if you roll 3 number cubes.

Skill Check

In Exercises 3–5, use the counting principle to determine the number of possible outfits that can be made using 1 of each type of item from the articles of clothing listed.

3. 4 shirts and 3 pairs of pants

4. 5 shirts, 3 pairs of pants, and 5 pairs of socks

5. 8 shirts, 4 pairs of pants, 4 pairs of socks, and 2 belts

Guided Problem Solving

6. **Coins** You flip three coins. What is the probability that all three coins show heads or all three coins show tails?

   1. Make a tree diagram to show all the different possible outcomes.

   2. How many different possible outcomes are there?

   3. How many favorable outcomes are there?

   4. Find the probability that all three coins show heads or all three coins show tails.

Practice and Problem Solving

Homework *Help*

Example	Exercises
1	7, 8, 16, 17
2	8, 9, 11–14
3	11–17

Online Resources
CLASSZONE.COM
• More Examples
• eTutorial Plus

7. **Computers** You are ordering a computer and must choose a multimedia drive, a hard drive, and a monitor. Using the choices listed in the tables, make a tree diagram of the different computers you can order. How many different computers can you order?

Multimedia Drive
CD-ROM
DVD-ROM
CD-RW

Hard Drive
40 GB
60 GB

Type of Monitor
CRT
Flat panel

8. **Music Store** A music store manager wants to arrange the store's merchandise into different sections. The manager wants to put CDs, tapes, and singles in different sections. Each section will be divided into different genres: rock, R & B, rap, classical, international music, and country. How many different divisions will the store have?

Review *Help*

Sometimes solving a simpler problem can help you to solve a problem that seems complicated. For help with this strategy, see p. 800.

9. **Playoffs** In the National Basketball Association (NBA), there are 15 teams in the Eastern Conference and 14 teams in the Western Conference. One team from each conference advances to the finals.

   a. How many different team matchups could there be in the finals?

   b. Eight teams from the Eastern Conference and eight teams from the Western Conference make the NBA playoffs. How many different matchups of the playoff teams could meet in the finals?

   c. *Writing* Can you use the result from part (b) to determine the probability that two teams in the NBA playoffs meet in the finals? Explain why or why not.

10. **Critical Thinking** A student claims that because he has 3 sweaters and 3 pairs of pants, he has 6 different possible combinations of sweaters and pants. Describe and correct the student's error.

In Exercises 11–14, use the counting principle to find the total number of possible outcomes. Then determine the probability of the specified event. Each spinner is divided into equal parts.

11. You spin spinner A two times. Find the probability that the spinner stops on 1, then 2.

12. You spin spinner B two times. Find the probability that the spinner stops on 1, then 2.

13. You spin each spinner once. Find the probability that both spinners stop on the same number.

14. You spin spinners A and B two times each. Find the probability that the spinner stops on the same number in all four spins.

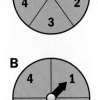

15. 📱 **Password** Your computer password has 4 capital letters followed by 4 digits. Your friend randomly chooses 4 capital letters and 4 digits. Use a calculator to find the probability that your friend chooses your password.

16. **Art Classes** You want to take two art classes after school. You may take only one painting and one sculpture class per week. The table gives the days that the classes are offered. The classes are offered at 3:00 each day, so you cannot take both classes on the same day.

Class	Days offered
Painting	M, T, W, Th
Sculpture	T, W

   a. Make a tree diagram of all the possible schedules for the two classes you could take. Be sure to eliminate the possibilities where you have both classes on the same day.

   b. How many different possible schedules for the two classes are there?

   c. You sign up for the two classes and are randomly assigned a schedule. What is the probability that your sculpture class is on Tuesday?

   d. *Writing* Explain why, for a situation like this one, it is better to make a tree diagram than to use the counting principle.

17. Multiple Choice Tests A multiple choice test contains four answer choices (A, B, C, and D) for each question. You guess randomly on two questions on the test.

   a. Make a tree diagram of the possible answers for the two questions.

   b. What is the probability that you answer both questions correctly?

   c. Analyze Suppose the answer to both questions is A. Use the tree diagram to count how many outcomes there are in which you answer at least one of the two questions correctly. What is the probability that you answer at least one question correctly?

18. Challenge You roll an 8-sided number octahedron, and your friend rolls a 4-sided number pyramid.

   a. How many different possible outcomes are there for the pairs of numbers rolled?

   b. Find the probability that you and your friend roll the same number.

   c. Find the odds in favor of rolling a number greater than the number your friend rolls.

19. Phone Numbers You remember part of your friend's 7-digit phone number, but you cannot remember the rest.

   a. Your friend's number begins with 79 and ends with five other digits. How many different phone numbers can begin with 79?

   b. You remember that the next digit after 79 is 8. How many possible phone numbers can begin with 798?

   c. How many digits of a 7-digit phone number do you have to know before the probability that you randomly guess the number correctly on the first try is $\frac{1}{100}$?

Mixed Review   **Find the quotient.** *(Lesson 5.5)*

20. $-\dfrac{4}{9} \div \dfrac{2}{3}$ **21.** $\dfrac{5}{6} \div \left(-\dfrac{2}{3}\right)$ **22.** $\dfrac{11}{24} \div \dfrac{3}{8}$ **23.** $\dfrac{25}{63} \div \dfrac{8}{9}$

Solve the proportion. *(Lesson 6.3)*

24. $\dfrac{y}{20} = \dfrac{15}{4}$ **25.** $\dfrac{15}{6} = \dfrac{p}{8}$ **26.** $\dfrac{5}{g} = \dfrac{2}{14}$ **27.** $\dfrac{8}{9} = \dfrac{12}{b}$

28. Cash You have four $1 bills, two $5 bills, and one $20 bill in your wallet. You choose one of the bills at random. Find the odds in favor of and the odds against choosing a bill greater than $1. *(Lesson 6.7)*

Standardized Test Practice

29. Multiple Choice A car comes in two different styles. Each style comes in four colors. How many different versions of the car are available?

   A. 2   **B.** 4   **C.** 6   **D.** 8

30. Multiple Choice A hot dog stand sells 2 sizes of hot dog, 6 kinds of soda, and 3 sizes of soda. How many different combinations of a hot dog and soda could you order?

   F. 12   **G.** 24   **H.** 36   **I.** 11

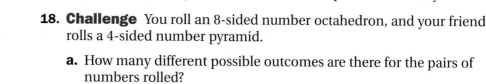

CHAPTER 6

Chapter Review

Vocabulary Review

ratio, p. 269	congruent figures, p. 290	favorable outcomes, p. 306	odds against, p. 308
equivalent ratios, p. 270	scale drawing, p. 300	probability, p. 306	tree diagram, p. 313
proportion, p. 275	scale model, p. 300	theoretical probability, p. 307	counting principle, p. 314
cross product, p. 280	scale, p. 300	experimental probability,	
similar figures, p. 288	outcomes, p. 306	p. 307	
corresponding parts, p. 288	event, p. 306	odds in favor, p. 308	

1. Explain how to tell if two ratios are equivalent.

2. What is a proportion?

3. How are similar figures different from congruent figures?

4. What is the difference between an outcome and a favorable outcome?

5. Describe the difference between the probability that an event occurs and the odds in favor of an event.

6. What is the counting principle?

6.1 Ratios and Rates

Examples on pp. 269–271

▶ *Goal*

Find and interpret a unit rate.

Example **You worked 15 hours and earned $195. How much did you earn per hour?**

$$\frac{\$195}{15 \text{ hours}} = \frac{\$195 \div 15}{15 \text{ hours} \div 15}$$ Divide numerator and denominator by 15.

$$= \frac{\$13}{1 \text{ hour}}$$ Simplify.

Answer You earned $13 per hour.

 **Find the unit rate.**

7. $\dfrac{330 \text{ miles}}{6 \text{ hours}}$ **8.** $\dfrac{60 \text{ minutes}}{4 \text{ games}}$ **9.** $\dfrac{5 \text{ laps}}{20 \text{ minutes}}$ **10.** $\dfrac{24 \text{ ounces}}{4 \text{ servings}}$

11. Tickets The drama club pays $144.50 to buy 17 movie tickets. What is the cost per ticket?

12. Cereal One brand of cereal contains 18 ounces and costs $3.20. Another brand contains 1 pound and costs $3.00. Which brand has a lower price per ounce?

6.2 Writing and Solving Proportions

Examples on pp. 275–277

▶ **Goal**

Solve proportions using algebra.

Example Solve the proportion $\frac{x}{9} = \frac{15}{27}$.

$\frac{x}{9} = \frac{15}{27}$ **Write original proportion.**

$9 \cdot \frac{x}{9} = 9 \cdot \frac{15}{27}$ **Multiply each side by 9.**

$x = \frac{15}{3}$ **Simplify.**

$x = 5$ **Divide.**

✔ **Use algebra to solve the proportion.**

13. $\frac{10}{25} = \frac{a}{5}$ **14.** $\frac{18}{24} = \frac{x}{4}$ **15.** $\frac{z}{6} = \frac{35}{42}$ **16.** $\frac{b}{54} = \frac{8}{9}$

17. Lions Lions sleep 5 out of every 6 hours. Write and solve a proportion to find how many hours per day lions sleep.

6.3 Solving Proportions Using Cross Products

Examples on pp. 280–282

▶ **Goal**

Solve proportions using the cross products property.

Example Solve the proportion $\frac{8}{20} = \frac{38}{y}$ using the cross products property.

$\frac{8}{20} = \frac{38}{y}$ **Write original proportion.**

$8 \cdot y = 20 \cdot 38$ **Cross products property**

$8y = 760$ **Multiply.**

$\frac{8y}{8} = \frac{760}{8}$ **Divide each side by 8.**

$y = 95$ **Simplify.**

✔ **Use the cross products property to solve the proportion.**

18. $\frac{6}{2.7} = \frac{40}{z}$ **19.** $\frac{6}{17} = \frac{3}{x}$ **20.** $\frac{17}{c} = \frac{34}{46}$ **21.** $\frac{50}{a} = \frac{25}{7}$

22. Field Trip Your school is going on a field trip. It takes 2 buses to carry 64 people. Write and solve a proportion to find the number of buses needed to carry 150 people.

6.4 Similar and Congruent Figures

Examples on
pp. 288–290

▶ **Goal**

Find the ratio of corresponding side lengths of similar figures.

Example Given △*ABC* ~ △*MNP*, find the ratio of the lengths of corresponding sides of △*ABC* to △*MNP*.

Two corresponding sides are $\overline{AB}$ and $\overline{MN}$.

The ratio of the length of these sides is $\frac{AB}{MN}$.

Substitute the lengths of the sides and simplify.

$$\frac{AB}{MN} = \frac{40}{48} = \frac{5}{6}$$

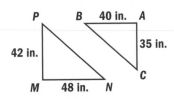

Answer The ratio of the lengths of the corresponding sides is $\frac{5}{6}$.

✔ **Find the ratio of the lengths of corresponding sides of figure A to figure B.**

23. *GHJK* ~ *PQRS*

24. *KLMN* ~ *WXYZ*

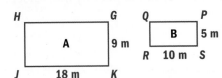

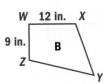

6.5 Similarity and Measurement

Examples on
pp. 293–294

▶ **Goal**

Find unknown side lengths of similar figures.

Example Given *DEFG* ~ *JKLM*, find *KL*.

$\dfrac{EF}{KL} = \dfrac{FG}{LM}$ Write proportion involving *KL*.

$\dfrac{6}{x} = \dfrac{14}{21}$ Substitute.

$6 \cdot 21 = 14x$ Cross products property

$126 = 14x$ Multiply.

$9 = x$ Divide each side by 14.

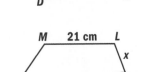

Answer The length of $\overline{KL}$ is 9 centimeters.

✔ **In Exercises 25 and 26, use the similar figures above.**

25. Find *JM*.

26. Find *DE*.

6.6 Scale Drawings

Examples on pp. 300–301

▶ **Goal**

Find distances using scales and scale drawings.

Example The distance between two cities on a map is 7 centimeters. The map has a scale of 1 cm : 20 km. Find the actual distance between the two cities.

$$\frac{1 \text{ cm}}{20 \text{ km}} = \frac{7 \text{ cm}}{x \text{ km}} \qquad \text{Write proportion.}$$

$$1x = 20 \cdot 7 \qquad \text{Cross products property}$$

$$x = 140 \qquad \text{Multiply.}$$

Answer The actual distance is 140 kilometers.

✔ A scale drawing has a scale of 1 inch : 3 yards. Use the given distance from the drawing to find the actual distance.

27. 7 inches **28.** 14 inches **29.** 18 inches **30.** 22 inches

6.7 Probability and Odds

Examples on pp. 306–308

▶ **Goal**

Find the probability of an event.

Example The spinner shown is divided into equal parts. Find the probability that the spinner stops on a 5.

$$P(\text{stopping on a 5}) = \frac{\text{Number of favorable outcomes}}{\text{Number of outcomes}} = \frac{3}{8}$$

✔ Find the probability that the spinner above stops on the number.

31. 4 **32.** 3 **33.** 2 **34.** 1

6.8 The Counting Principle

Examples on pp. 313–314

▶ **Goal**

Use the counting principle to count possibilities.

Example In a game, you are to choose a 2 letter code from the 26 capital letters of the alphabet. Find the number of possible codes.

Number of possibilities for first letter		Number of possibilities for second letter		Total number of possibilities
26	•	26	=	676

✔ **35. Clothing** You have 6 shirts and 3 pairs of pants. How many outfits are possible using one of each item?

Chapter Test

Order the ratios from least to greatest.

1. 51 to 25, $\dfrac{5}{4}$, 13 : 10, $\dfrac{33}{20}$, 17 to 20

2. $\dfrac{64}{25}$, 9 to 40, 59 : 20, $\dfrac{53}{25}$, 37 : 20

Write the equivalent rate.

3. $\dfrac{18 \text{ ft}}{1 \text{ sec}} = \dfrac{? \text{ ft}}{1 \text{ min}}$

4. $\dfrac{\$5.60}{1 \text{ lb}} = \dfrac{?}{1 \text{ oz}}$

5. $\dfrac{1296 \text{ cars}}{1 \text{ day}} = \dfrac{? \text{ cars}}{1 \text{ hour}}$

6. $\dfrac{8.5 \text{ km}}{1 \text{ h}} = \dfrac{? \text{ m}}{1 \text{ h}}$

7. Cashews Cashews cost $.40 per ounce. You have $6. Can you buy one pound of cashews? Explain.

Solve the proportion.

8. $\dfrac{5}{12} = \dfrac{x}{36}$

9. $\dfrac{4}{7} = \dfrac{a}{35}$

10. $\dfrac{b}{54} = \dfrac{12}{18}$

11. $\dfrac{7}{8} = \dfrac{z}{12}$

12. $\dfrac{9}{t} = \dfrac{3}{8}$

13. $\dfrac{21}{7} = \dfrac{9}{p}$

14. $\dfrac{6}{14} = \dfrac{15}{c}$

15. $\dfrac{8}{w} = \dfrac{1.2}{3}$

16. Given $\triangle ABC \cong \triangle EFG$, name the corresponding angles and the corresponding side lengths. Then find the unknown side lengths.

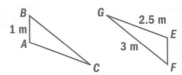

17. Football The shadow of a goalpost on a football field is 20 feet long. A football player who is 6 feet tall stands next to the goalpost and casts a shadow 32 inches long. How tall is the goalpost?

A scale drawing has a scale of 1 inch : 10 feet. Use the given actual length to find the length of the object in the scale drawing.

18. 8 feet

19. 7 feet

20. 6 feet

21. 4 feet

22. Marbles A bag contains 8 blue marbles, 6 red marbles, 15 green marbles, and 16 orange marbles. A marble is chosen at random from the bag. What is the probability that the marble is red? What are the odds in favor of choosing a green marble?

23. Wildlife A wildlife preserve identifies each animal in the preserve with a one-digit number and a capital letter. How many animals can the preserve identify? How many animals can the preserve identify using a two-digit number and a capital letter?

Chapter Standardized Test

Test-Taking Strategy Work at a comfortable pace. Do not pay attention to how fast other students are working.

1. Which rate is equivalent to $\frac{15 \text{ mi}}{1 \text{ h}}$?

   A. $\frac{22 \text{ ft}}{1 \text{ min}}$ **B.** $\frac{1320 \text{ ft}}{1 \text{ min}}$

   C. $\frac{79{,}200 \text{ ft}}{1 \text{ min}}$ **D.** $\frac{4{,}752{,}000 \text{ ft}}{1 \text{ min}}$

2. What is the solution of the proportion $\frac{x}{5} = \frac{16}{20}$?

   F. 2   **G.** 4   **H.** 6   **I.** 8

3. What is the solution of the proportion $\frac{2.4}{4} = \frac{3}{y}$?

   A. 0.2   **B.** 0.5   **C.** 2   **D.** 5

4. Which statement is *not* necessarily true?

   F. Corresponding angles of similar figures are congruent.

   G. Corresponding sides of similar figures are congruent.

   H. Two squares with different side lengths are similar figures.

   I. Corresponding sides of congruent figures are congruent.

5. A woman is standing next to a tree. She is 64 inches tall and casts a shadow 24 inches long. The tree's shadow is 67.5 inches long. How tall is the tree?

   A. 10 feet   **B.** 15 feet

   C. 22.75 feet   **D.** 180 feet

6. A bag holds 8 slips of paper numbered 1 through 8. You randomly choose one slip of paper. What is the probability that the number on the slip of paper is greater than 5?

   F. $\frac{1}{8}$ **G.** $\frac{3}{8}$ **H.** $\frac{1}{2}$ **I.** $\frac{5}{8}$

7. An identification system assigns each item a code using 3 capital letters. How many different codes are possible?

   A. 78   **B.** 7800

   C. 15,600   **D.** 17,576

8. **Short Response** You make a pattern by drawing three similar rectangles. The width of the smallest rectangle is $\frac{4}{5}$ of the width of the medium-sized rectangle. The width of the medium-sized rectangle is $\frac{4}{5}$ of the width of the largest rectangle. The largest rectangle is 12 inches long and 8 inches wide. Find the dimensions of the smallest rectangle. Explain your reasoning.

9. **Extended Response** You are making a scale drawing of a room using a scale of 1 inch : 4 feet.

   a. The room is 14 feet by 18 feet. Find its dimensions in the drawing.

   b. A sofa in the room has a length of 6 feet. Find the length of the sofa in the drawing.

   c. You want to enlarge the scale drawing. How would you change the scale to double the dimensions of the drawing? Explain.

Making a **Business Decision**

Goal
Decide what the prices of ads in the school yearbook will be.

Key Skill
Solving proportions

Materials
• graph paper

To help pay for the cost of publishing a school yearbook, some yearbook staffs sell ads in the yearbook. Suppose you want to raise $1800 for your school's yearbook. What prices should you set for the ads in order to reach your goal?

Here are the guidelines:

• You have 10 pages of ads to sell.

• The ad pages are divided into 9 sections.

• A single ad can cover 1, 2, 4, or 9 sections, as shown.

  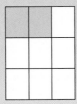 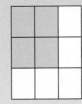 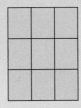

| 1 section | 2 sections | 2 sections | 4 sections | 9 sections |

A reasonable way to set the prices for ads of different sizes is to let the price of an ad be proportional to its area.

Investigate

1 In order to raise $1800, how much must you raise from each page of ads?

2 Let the amount you calculated in Step 1 be the cost of a 9-section (full-page) ad. Write and solve a proportion to calculate the cost of a 4-section ad.

3 Write and solve proportions to calculate the cost of a 2-section ad and a 1-section ad.

4 On graph paper, sketch a few different ways that an ad page can be filled with the ad sizes shown above.

Consider and Decide

Decide on the prices for the ads. Consider the following:

- When designing the layout of a page with ads, you may have some ads that include photos and text and others that include only text. You may want to charge more for ads that include photos.

- You may want to slightly discount the price of larger ads in order to encourage customers to buy larger ads. For example, you may want to make the price of a 4-section ad slightly less than 4 times the cost of a 1-section ad.

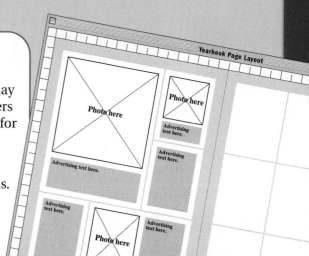

Present Your Results

Make a poster that shows the sizes of the yearbook ads and the prices that you chose. Explain how the prices you chose will help you meet the financial goal for the yearbook.

Project Extensions

Using Proportions Suppose you decide also to allow 3-section and 6-section ads, as shown. What prices should you set for these ads if price is proportional to area and the price of a 9-section ad is $210? Explain your answers.

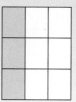
3 sections

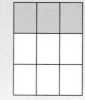
3 sections

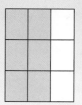
6 sections

6 sections

 Research CLASSZONE.COM Ad prices for newspapers and magazines are sometimes listed on rate cards. Use the Internet to find rate cards for several different newspapers or magazines. Are ad prices for sections of a page proportional to ad prices for a full page? Explain how you found your answer.

Career Most magazines and newspapers are at least partially funded by advertising sales. Find out more about careers in selling advertising space and careers in designing print ads.

Explore Find several yearbooks, magazines, or newspapers. How do these publications divide pages into sections for ads? Describe your findings.

Percents

How can you find the sale price of an item?

CHAPTER 7

INTERNET Preview

CLASSZONE.COM

- eEdition Plus Online
- eWorkbook Plus Online
- eTutorial Plus Online
- State Test Practice
- More Examples

MATH *In the* **Real World**

Shopping While shopping, you see a sign that says "All items 25% off original price." The number 25% is an example of a *percent*. In this chapter, you will use percents to find the prices of items on sale.

What do you think? Suppose you see a sign that says "Take $\frac{1}{3}$ off the price of every item in the store." You want to buy a hat whose original price is $18. What is the sale price of the hat?

Chapter Prerequisite Skills

Review Vocabulary
ratio, p. 269
proportion, p. 275
decimal, p. 770
fraction, p. 777

PREREQUISITE SKILLS QUIZ

Preparing for Success **To prepare for success in this chapter, test your knowledge of these concepts and skills. You may want to look at the pages referred to in blue for additional review.**

1. Vocabulary Write the ratio 4 to 12 in two other ways.

Write the fraction as a decimal or the decimal as a fraction. *(p. 219)*

2. $\dfrac{5}{8}$ **3.** $\dfrac{3}{25}$ **4.** 0.35   **5.** 0.175

Solve the proportion. *(pp. 275, 280)*

6. $\dfrac{3}{4} = \dfrac{y}{16}$ **7.** $\dfrac{30}{48} = \dfrac{10}{h}$ **8.** $\dfrac{7.5}{x} = \dfrac{5}{8}$ **9.** $\dfrac{r}{6} = \dfrac{10.5}{9}$

NOTETAKING STRATEGIES

Note *Worthy*

You will find a notetaking strategy at the beginning of each chapter. Look for additional notetaking and study strategies throughout the chapter.

CONCEPT GRID You can use a concept grid to take notes. A concept grid usually includes a definition, characteristics, examples, and nonexamples.

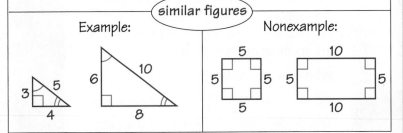

Definition:	Characteristics:
Two figures are similar if they have the same shape but not necessarily the same size.	Corresponding angles are congruent. The ratios of lengths of corresponding sides are equal.

similar figures

| Example: | Nonexample: |

In Lesson 7.7, making a concept grid can help you understand compound interest.

7.1

Percents *and* Fractions

BEFORE	Now	WHY?
You multiplied fractions and whole numbers.	You'll use a fraction to find the percent of a number.	So you can compare tennis players' serves, as in Ex. 7.

Vocabulary
percent, p. 329

Music In marching band competitions, each band is judged on its musical performance, marching, and visual effect. At many competitions, a marching band is rated on a 100 point scale. A band that earns 85 points has earned *85 percent* of the total possible points.

The word *percent* means "per hundred." A **percent** is a ratio whose denominator is 100. The symbol for percent is %.

Writing Percents

Words In the area model shown, 85 of the 100 squares are shaded. You can say that 85 percent of the squares are shaded.

Numbers $\dfrac{85}{100} = 85\%$ **Algebra** $\dfrac{p}{100} = p\%$

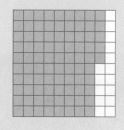

Example 1   *Writing Percents as Fractions, Fractions as Percents*

Write 29% and 45% as fractions in simplest form.

a. $29\% = \dfrac{29}{100}$

b. $45\% = \dfrac{45}{100} = \dfrac{9}{20}$

Write $\dfrac{7}{10}$ and $\dfrac{3}{5}$ as percents.

a. $\dfrac{7}{10} = \dfrac{7 \cdot 10}{10 \cdot 10} = \dfrac{70}{100} = 70\%$

b. $\dfrac{3}{5} = \dfrac{3 \cdot 20}{5 \cdot 20} = \dfrac{60}{100} = 60\%$

Review *Help*

For help with writing equivalent fractions, see p. 182.

 Checkpoint

Write the percent as a fraction in simplest form, or write the fraction as a percent.

1. 51%

2. 25%

3. $\dfrac{11}{20}$

4. $\dfrac{4}{25}$

Here are some common percent-fraction equivalents that may be useful to memorize.

Common Percents					
$10\% = \frac{1}{10}$	$20\% = \frac{1}{5}$	$25\% = \frac{1}{4}$	$30\% = \frac{3}{10}$	$40\% = \frac{2}{5}$	$50\% = \frac{1}{2}$
$60\% = \frac{3}{5}$	$70\% = \frac{7}{10}$	$75\% = \frac{3}{4}$	$80\% = \frac{4}{5}$	$90\% = \frac{9}{10}$	$100\% = 1$

Study *Strategy*

Probabilities can be written as percents between 0% (for an impossible event) and 100% (for an event that is certain to occur).

Example 2   *Writing a Probability as a Percent*

Prizes A radio station randomly selects 1 of 5 finalists for a prize. You are one of the finalists. What is the probability that you will win? Write your answer as a percent.

Solution

There are 5 possible outcomes, and 1 outcome is favorable.

$$P(\text{you win}) = \frac{1}{5} \qquad \text{Write probability as a fraction.}$$

$$= 20\% \qquad \text{Write fraction as a percent.}$$

Answer The probability that you will win is 20%.

Example 3   *Finding a Percent of a Number*

Tortoises A desert tortoise can go a year or more without drinking water. When it does drink, its body weight can increase by 40%. Suppose a desert tortoise weighs 15 pounds after a long period without water. How many pounds can the tortoise gain when it drinks?

Solution

To find 40% of 15 pounds, use the fact that $40\% = \frac{2}{5}$. Then multiply.

$$40\% \text{ of } 15 = \frac{2}{5} \cdot 15 \qquad \text{Write percent as a fraction.}$$

$$= \frac{30}{5} \qquad \text{Multiply.}$$

$$= 6 \qquad \text{Simplify.}$$

Answer The desert tortoise can gain 6 pounds when it drinks.

In the **Real World**

Tortoises A desert tortoise spends about 95% of its life in underground burrows. About what fraction of a desert tortoise's life is spent underground?

✔ *Checkpoint*

5. In Example 2, suppose that there are 10 finalists. What is the probability that you will win? Write your answer as a percent.

Find the percent of the number.

6. 25% of 36   **7.** 70% of 70   **8.** 50% of 14   **9.** 75% of 80

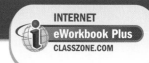
Guided Practice

Vocabulary Check

1. Copy and complete: A percent is a ratio whose denominator is ? .

2. Explain how you would rewrite $\frac{13}{25}$ as a percent.

Skill Check

Write the percent as a fraction in simplest form, or write the fraction as a percent.

3. 65%   **4.** 98%   **5.** $\frac{12}{25}$ **6.** $\frac{9}{10}$

Guided Problem Solving

7. Tennis In tennis, you can serve the ball a second time if your first serve is not successful. The table shows the first serves by you and your opponent in a match. How many more successful first serves did you have than did your opponent?

Player	Total first serves	Percent successful
You	152	75%
Your opponent	125	60%

1 Find the number of successful first serves you had.

2 Find the number of successful first serves your opponent had.

3 Find the difference of the numbers in Steps 1 and 2.

Practice and Problem Solving

Homework *Help*

Example	Exercises
1	8–27, 45
2	28–34
3	35–44

Online Resources
CLASSZONE.COM

• More Examples
• eTutorial Plus

Write the percent as a fraction.

8. 34%   **9.** 40%   **10.** 71%   **11.** 27%

12. 55%   **13.** 18%   **14.** 90%   **15.** 85%

Write the fraction as a percent.

16. $\frac{4}{5}$ **17.** $\frac{3}{25}$ **18.** $\frac{9}{20}$ **19.** $\frac{7}{10}$

20. $\frac{33}{50}$ **21.** $\frac{1}{4}$ **22.** $\frac{18}{25}$ **23.** $\frac{17}{20}$

24. Food You buy ice cream that contains 10% milk fat. What fraction of the ice cream is milk fat?

25. Currency The composition of a U.S. dollar bill is $\frac{3}{4}$ cotton and $\frac{1}{4}$ linen. What percent of a dollar bill is cotton?

26. Football A football player completes 19 of his 25 passes during the season. What percent of his passes did the player complete?

27. Art The bristles on a Chinese writing brush are 70% rabbit hair and 30% goat hair. What fraction of the bristles is goat hair?

A computer randomly generates an integer from 1 to 10. Find the probability of the given event. Write your answer as a percent.

28. $P(5)$ **29.** $P(4)$ **30.** P(odd number)

31. P(even number)   **32.** P(factor of 20)   **33.** P(prime number)

34. Tests A multiple choice question on a test has 4 answer choices. You guess at the answer. What is the probability that you will select the correct choice? Write your answer as a percent.

Find the percent of the number.

35. 75% of 12   **36.** 20% of 95   **37.** 30% of 50   **38.** 70% of 90

39. 50% of 94   **40.** 10% of 130   **41.** 40% of 175   **42.** 25% of 500

43. Plants Alfalfa plants can take up metals from the ground and store them in their roots and stems. In 2002, a scientist claimed that an alfalfa plant could produce 20% of its weight in gold by taking up tiny gold particles left behind from rock mining. How many pounds of gold could be produced from 3000 pounds of alfalfa plants?

44. Astronomy The International Space Station orbits Earth about every 90 minutes. About 40% of the time, Earth prevents the space station from receiving direct sunlight. About how many minutes per orbit does the space station *not* receive sunlight?

45. *Writing* Use the definition of percent to explain why 100% = 1.

Use a number line to order the numbers from least to greatest.

46. 89%, $\frac{4}{5}$, $\frac{7}{10}$, 0.83   **47.** 54%, $\frac{9}{20}$, 0.62, $\frac{16}{25}$ **48.** $\frac{9}{25}$, 17%, 0.22, $\frac{9}{50}$

Algebra Evaluate the expression when $k = 20$.

49. k% of 90   **50.** 40% of k **51.** $(80 - k)$% of 30

52. 25% of $(k + 8)$ **53.** $(k + 10)$% of 200   **54.** $(k - 10)$% of 350

55. Extended Problem Solving An 18th century Indian version of chess uses a 10 square by 10 square board. On the board shown, the dots represent your opponent's chess pieces at the start of the game.

    a. Illustrate Copy the board shown. Mark X's on your side of the board to represent your chess pieces in an arrangement that matches your opponent's.

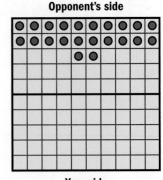
Opponent's side

Your side

    b. What percent of the squares are occupied at the start of a game?

    c. Explain During one game, 75% of the pieces are still on the board. Of these pieces, 14 belong to you. How many pieces belong to your opponent? Explain.

In the **Real World**

Chess A modern chess board is 8 squares by 8 squares. How many more squares does the board described in Exercise 55 have than a modern chess board?

56. Phone Numbers You forgot the last two digits of your friend's phone number. You know that the next-to-last digit is 4 or 5, and the last digit is an odd number. If you guess the phone number, what is the probability that you will be correct? Write your answer as a percent.

57. Estimation The circle graph shows the results of a class survey that asked 800 students where they make most of their music purchases.

a. Estimate how many students chose either record stores or other stores.

Music Purchases

- Record stores 45%
- Other stores 36%
- Music clubs 9%
- Internet 8%
- Other 2%

b. Estimate how many more students chose record stores than music clubs.

c. The class surveyed 100 other students and found that 9% of them make most of their purchases on the Internet. Estimate how many students in both surveys combined make most of their purchases on the Internet.

58. Challenge Suppose the length and width of rectangle A are each 40% of the length and width of rectangle B. Is the area of rectangle A 40% of the area of rectangle B? Justify your answer.

59. Critical Thinking Let x and y represent two different whole numbers.

a. Suppose you add 40% of x to 60% of y. Is this sum equal to 100% of the sum $x + y$? Justify your answer.

b. Suppose you find the average of 40% of x and 60% of y. Is this average equal to 50% of the sum $x + y$? Justify your answer.

Mixed Review

Find the product or quotient. (Lessons 5.4, 5.5)

60. $-8 \cdot 3\frac{3}{4}$ **61.** $-\frac{11}{25} \cdot \frac{10}{11}$ **62.** $\frac{5}{12} \div \left(-\frac{5}{6}\right)$ **63.** $3\frac{3}{14} \div \frac{3}{7}$

Use equivalent ratios to solve the proportion. (Lesson 6.2)

64. $\frac{a}{3} = \frac{14}{21}$ **65.** $\frac{b}{18} = \frac{5}{9}$ **66.** $\frac{11}{13} = \frac{x}{26}$ **67.** $\frac{5}{30} = \frac{y}{6}$

68. Groceries A grocery store charges $3 for 4 mangoes. How many mangoes can you buy with $6.75? (Lesson 6.3)

Standardized Test Practice

69. Multiple Choice The table shows how many of the 50 states entered the Union in each century. What percent of the states entered the Union after the 18th century?

Century	States
18th century	16
19th century	29
20th century	5

A. 16%   **B.** 29%

C. 34%   **D.** 68%

70. Short Response In a survey of 300 adults, 32% said they read the daily newspaper, and 56% said they read only the Sunday newspaper. Estimate how many more adults surveyed read only the Sunday newspaper than the daily newspaper. Explain your reasoning.

7.2 Using Percent Bar Models

Goal
Use a percent bar model to find the percent of a number.

Materials
- paper
- pencil

Investigate

Use a percent bar model to find 24% of 75.

1 Draw a percent bar model that has ten equal sections. Label the left side of the model from 0 to 75. Label the right side of the model from 0% to 100%. Shade the bar to the 24% mark. Let x represent the number that you need to find.

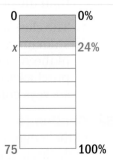

2 Write a proportion using the arrangement of the numbers in the percent bar model. Then solve the proportion to find 24% of 75.

$$\frac{x}{75} = \frac{24}{100}$$

$$75 \cdot \frac{x}{75} = 75 \cdot \frac{24}{100}$$

$$x = 18$$

Draw Conclusions

Use a percent bar model to find the percent of the number.

1. 18% of 30

2. 65% of 140

3. 36% of 225

4. 7% of 400

5. 22% of 600

6. 85% of 780

7. Critical Thinking Suppose that 40% of a number b is 28. You want to find b. Explain how you would use a percent bar model to illustrate the problem. Then write and solve a proportion to find b.

8. Critical Thinking You want to find what percent of 150 is 102. Draw a percent bar model that has ten equal sections. Explain how you would decide what part of the bar that you should shade. Then write and solve a proportion to find the percent.

Percents *and* Proportions

BEFORE	Now	WHY?
You found a percent of a number.	You'll use proportions to solve percent problems.	So you can find how much food adult cats eat daily, as in Ex. 16.

A percent bar model compares a *part* to a *base*. In the model shown, 35 is the base, and 14 is a part of the base. The percent bar model shows that 14 is 40% of 35 or, equivalently, that $\frac{14}{35} = \frac{40}{100}$.

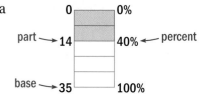

Solving Percent Problems

You can represent "*a* is *p* percent of *b*" using the proportion

$$\frac{a}{b} = \frac{p}{100}$$

where *a* is a part of the base *b* and *p*%, or $\frac{p}{100}$, is the percent.

Example 1   *Finding a Percent*

What percent of 7 is 4?

$\dfrac{a}{b} = \dfrac{p}{100}$	Write proportion.
$\dfrac{4}{7} = \dfrac{p}{100}$	Substitute 4 for *a* and 7 for *b*.
$100 \cdot \dfrac{4}{7} = 100 \cdot \dfrac{p}{100}$	Multiply each side by 100.
$57\dfrac{1}{7} = p$	Simplify.

Answer   4 is $57\frac{1}{7}$% of 7.

 Checkpoint

Use a proportion to answer the question.

  1. What percent of 72 is 54?   **2.** What percent of 60 is 25?

  3. What percent of 90 is 40?   **4.** What percent of 35 is 7?

Study *Strategy*

Reasonableness You can use common percents to check that an answer is reasonable. In Example 2, you know that 25% is close to 24%. Find 25% of 200.

$$25\% \text{ of } 200 = \frac{1}{4} \cdot 200$$
$$= 50$$

Because 50 is close to 48, the answer is reasonable.

Example 2	*Finding a Part of a Base*

What number is 24% of 200?

$$\frac{a}{b} = \frac{p}{100} \qquad \text{Write proportion.}$$

$$\frac{a}{200} = \frac{24}{100} \qquad \text{Substitute 200 for } b \text{ and 24 for } p.$$

$$200 \cdot \frac{a}{200} = 200 \cdot \frac{24}{100} \qquad \text{Multiply each side by 200.}$$

$$a = 48 \qquad \text{Simplify.}$$

Answer 48 is 24% of 200.

Example 3	*Finding a Base*

Heptathlon In a heptathlon, an athlete earns points in seven track-and-field events. Suppose an athlete earns 836 points in the 100 meter hurdles. This score makes up 16% of the total score. What is the total score?

Solution

In this situation, 836 is a part of the total score, which is the base.

$$\frac{a}{b} = \frac{p}{100} \qquad \text{Write proportion.}$$

$$\frac{836}{b} = \frac{16}{100} \qquad \text{Substitute 836 for } a \text{ and 16 for } p.$$

$$836 \cdot 100 = 16 \cdot b \qquad \text{Cross products property}$$

$$83,600 = 16b \qquad \text{Multiply.}$$

$$5225 = b \qquad \text{Divide each side by 16.}$$

Answer The athlete's total score is 5225 points.

✔ *Checkpoint*

Use a proportion to answer the question.

5. What number is 18% of 50? **6.** 105 is 84% of what number?

You may find it useful to group percent problems into three types.

Percent problem	Example	Proportion
Find a percent.	What percent of 48 is 12?	$\frac{12}{48} = \frac{p}{100}$
Find a part of a base.	What number is 15% of 80?	$\frac{a}{80} = \frac{15}{100}$
Find a base.	20 is 30% of what number?	$\frac{20}{b} = \frac{30}{100}$

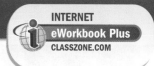
Guided Practice

Vocabulary Check

1. Choose the proportion you can use to represent this statement: 15 is 30% of 50.

   A. $\dfrac{30}{15} = \dfrac{50}{100}$ **B.** $\dfrac{15}{50} = \dfrac{30}{100}$ **C.** $\dfrac{30}{50} = \dfrac{15}{100}$

2. Tell whether the answer to the following question represents *the base*, *the part of the base*, or *the percent*: 30 is 85% of what number?

Skill Check   **Use a proportion to answer the question.**

3. What number is 65% of 120?   **4.** What percent of 24 is 4?

5. What percent of 30 is 27?   **6.** 18 is 45% of what number?

7. Error Analysis Describe and correct the error in finding what percent of 30 is 20.

$$\frac{a}{30} = \frac{20}{100}$$
$$100 \cdot a = 30 \cdot 20$$
$$100a = 600$$
$$a = 6$$

8. Soccer In the 2002 World Cup, 5 of the 32 soccer teams that competed were from South America. What percent of the teams were from South America?

Practice and Problem Solving

Homework *Help*

Example	Exercises
1	9–14, 18–20
2	9–16, 20
3	9–14, 17, 20

Online Resources
CLASSZONE.COM
• More Examples
• eTutorial Plus

Use a proportion to answer the question.

9. What percent of 56 is 14?   **10.** What percent of 125 is 98?

11. What number is 55% of 80?   **12.** What number is 30% of 130?

13. 11 is 22% of what number?   **14.** 48 is 75% of what number?

15. Basketball Of the 325 teams in NCAA Division 1 Women's Basketball, 4% are in the Mid-American Conference. How many teams are in the Mid-American Conference?

16. Cats An adult cat has a body mass of 3500 grams. It can eat up to 8% of its body mass in food each day. How many grams of food can the cat eat each day? Use estimation to justify that your answer is reasonable.

17. Paintings An artist's collection of paintings includes 22 portraits. The portraits make up 40% of the collection. How many paintings are in the collection?

18. Tanana River When a certain section of the ice breaks on the Tanana River in Nenana, Alaska, the townspeople consider spring to have started. During the period 1917–2001, the ice broke 34 times on or between May 4 and May 10. What percent of those 85 years were years in which the ice broke on or between May 4 and May 10?

19. Talent Show You are performing in a talent show. To decide who performs first, the names of all 15 participants are written on slips of paper and put in a hat. One name is drawn from the hat. What is the probability that you go first? Write your answer as a percent.

20. Solar Cars The 2001 American Solar Challenge was a race among solar-powered cars traveling from Chicago, Illinois, to Claremont, California.

   a. Three of the cars in the race weighed less than 600 pounds. These cars made up 10% of all the cars. How many cars were in the race?

   b. There were 16 three-wheeled cars in the race. What percent of the cars were three-wheeled?

   c. The course was 2247.39 miles long, and it was completed by 40% of the cars. How many cars completed the course?

21. *Writing* Write a real-world percent problem that can be solved by using the proportion $\frac{30}{x} = \frac{40}{100}$. Then find the value of x and solve the problem.

22. Extended Problem Solving You conduct a survey asking middle school students in which season they would prefer to hold their school trip. The bar graph shows the results of your survey.

   a. What percent of the students surveyed prefer summer? fall?

   b. Calculate Of the students who prefer spring, 75% are 8th graders. How many 8th graders prefer spring?

   c. Predict You are using the results of the survey to predict the preferences of all 780 students in the school. How many students do you predict would prefer a school trip in the spring? Explain your reasoning.

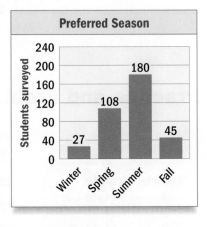

23. The table below shows several fractions whose percents may be useful to know. Use a proportion to find the equivalent percent for each fraction. Then copy and complete the table with the equivalent percents.

Fraction	$\frac{1}{8}$	$\frac{1}{3}$	$\frac{3}{8}$	$\frac{5}{8}$	$\frac{2}{3}$	$\frac{7}{8}$
Percent	?	?	?	?	?	?

Note *Worthy*

In your notes, you can create a table of percent-fraction equivalents like the one in Exercise 23. Include in your table other fractions whose percents may be useful to memorize.

24. Baseball A baseball player makes 152 hits in 570 times at bat in one season and 180 hits in 580 times at bat in the next season. For both seasons combined, what percent of the times at bat were hits?

25. Dogs In a dog agility competition, dogs are tested in their ability to get past obstacles. The table shows the number of dogs from each breed that competed in a dog agility competition.

a. What percent of the dogs that competed were spaniels? sheepdogs?

b. In the competition, 70% of the dogs that finished in the top half were sheepdogs. What percent of the sheepdogs finished in the top half?

Dog breed	Number that competed
Sheepdog	75
Spaniel	24
Terrier	14
Other	7

26. Algebra Solve for x in the following equation: $x\% = \dfrac{2x + 1}{300}$.

Use a proportion to answer the question in terms of y.

27. What number is 40% of $10y$?   **28.** What number is 75% of $8y$?

29. $3y$ is 60% of what number?   **30.** $11y$ is 25% of what number?

31. Challenge An art director has 75 photos to display in an art exhibit. Of these, 9 are color photos and 66 are black-and-white photos. The director wants to add more color photos so that they represent 25% of the photos at the exhibit. Write and solve a proportion to find the number of color photos to be added. Then find the total number of photos in the exhibit.

Mixed Review

Find the product. *(p. 775)*

32. 0.2×7 **33.** 0.75×1.3 **34.** 0.7×2.4 **35.** 0.003×0.5

36. Personal Finance You use an ATM to withdraw $20 from your checking account. The ATM receipt shows a balance of $168 after the withdrawal. Write and solve an equation to find the balance before the withdrawal. *(Lesson 2.5)*

Write the fraction or mixed number as a decimal. *(Lesson 5.1)*

37. $-\dfrac{1}{3}$ **38.** $\dfrac{7}{10}$ **39.** $-1\dfrac{3}{5}$ **40.** $\dfrac{11}{25}$

Standardized Test Practice

41. Multiple Choice Of the 32 teams in the National Football League, 4 teams are in the AFC East division. What percent of the teams are in the AFC East division?

A. 4%   **B.** 8%   **C.** $12\dfrac{1}{2}\%$ **D.** 28%

42. Multiple Choice A camel that weighs 1500 pounds can drink up to about 20% of its weight in water at one time. About how many pounds of water can a camel that weighs 1500 pounds drink at one time?

F. 10 pounds   **G.** 75 pounds   **H.** 300 pounds   **I.** 30,000 pounds

7.3

Percents *and* Decimals

BEFORE	Now	WHY?
You used fractions to solve percent problems.	You'll use decimals to solve percent problems.	So you can find the wind speed in a tornado, as in Ex. 45.

Review Vocabulary

percent, p. 329
decimal, p. 770

Pygmy Hippos The African pygmy hippo is the smallest species of hippopotamus. Suppose a common adult hippo weighs 5600 pounds, and an adult pygmy hippo's weight is 10.5% of the common adult hippo's weight. How much does the adult pygmy hippo weigh? You will find the answer in Example 4.

Common hippo

Pygmy hippo

Because $0.25 = \frac{25}{100}$ and $\frac{25}{100} = 25\%$, you can say that $0.25 = 25\%$.

This relationship suggests the following rules for writing decimals as percents and percents as decimals.

Percents and Decimals

- To write a decimal as a percent, move the decimal point two places to the right and write a percent sign.

- To write a percent as a decimal, move the decimal point two places to the left and remove the percent sign.

Study *Strategy*

Percents greater than 100% are written as numbers greater than 1. Percents less than 1% are written as numbers less than 0.01. To write such percents as decimals, follow the same steps as you would for percents between 1% and 100%.

Example 1 *Writing Decimals as Percents*

Write 0.62, 1, and 2.3 as percents.

  a. $0.62 = 0.62$
         $= 62\%$

  b. $1 = 1.00$
       $= 100\%$

  c. $2.3 = 2.30$
       $= 230\%$

Example 2 *Writing Percents as Decimals*

Write 75%, 0.4%, and 168% as decimals.

  a. $75\% = 75\%$
       $= 0.75$

  b. $0.4\% = 00.4\%$
        $= 0.004$

  c. $168\% = 168\%$
        $= 1.68$

 **Checkpoint**

Write the decimal as a percent or the percent as a decimal.

1. 0.461   **2.** 5   **3.** 1.9   **4.** 0.007

5. 27%   **6.** 184%   **7.** 3%   **8.** 0.55%

Fractions, Decimals, and Percents A fraction, a decimal, and a percent can all represent the same number. You can write a fraction as a percent by first writing the fraction as a decimal.

 Review *Help*

For help with writing fractions as decimals, see p. 219.

Example 3   *Writing Fractions as Percents*

Write $\frac{3}{8}$ and $\frac{5}{3}$ as percents.

a. $\frac{3}{8} = 0.375$ Write fraction as a decimal.

$= 37.5\%$ Write decimal as a percent.

b. $\frac{5}{3} = 1.666\ldots$ Write fraction as a decimal.

$= 166.\overline{6}\%$ Write decimal as a percent.

 Checkpoint

Write the fraction as a percent.

9. $\frac{7}{8}$ **10.** $\frac{5}{12}$ **11.** $\frac{11}{6}$ **12.** $\frac{5}{4}$

Example 4   *Finding a Percent of a Number*

Find the weight of the pygmy hippo described on page 340.

Solution

Find 10.5% of 5600.

10.5% of $5600 = 0.105 \cdot 5600$ Write percent as a decimal.

$= 588$ Multiply.

Answer The adult pygmy hippo weighs about 588 pounds.

✓ **Check** You can use estimation to check the reasonableness of the result. Because 10% of 5600 is 560, the answer is reasonable.

In the **Real World**

Pygmy Hippos Pygmy hippos weigh about 8 pounds at birth. How many times heavier than a newborn pygmy hippo is the adult pygmy hippo described in Example 4?

 Checkpoint

In Exercises 13–16, find the percent of the number.

13. 20% of 85   **14.** 3.8% of 45   **15.** 125% of 64   **16.** 0.5% of 600

17. In a survey of 1100 adults, 2% chose cooking as their favorite leisure activity. How many adults chose cooking?

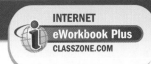
Guided Practice

Vocabulary Check

1. When you write a decimal as a percent, do you move the decimal point two places to the left or to the right?

2. Is 0.5 *less than*, *greater than*, or *equal to* 0.5%? Explain.

Skill Check **Write the decimal as a percent or the percent as a decimal.**

3. 0.13　　　4. 6.27　　　5. 5%　　　6. 0.98%

Write the fraction as a percent.

7. $\frac{1}{2}$　　　8. $\frac{2}{3}$　　　9. $\frac{7}{6}$　　　10. $\frac{11}{4}$

11. **Error Analysis** Describe and correct the error in writing 1.5 as a percent.

$$1.5 = 01.5$$
$$= 0.015\%$$

12. **Geography** The area of Earth's dry land is about 58 million square miles. The land area of North America is about 16% of Earth's land area. What is the approximate land area of North America?

Practice and Problem Solving

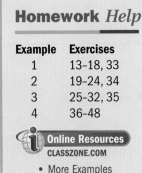

Homework *Help*

Example	Exercises
1	13–18, 33
2	19–24, 34
3	25–32, 35
4	36–48

Online Resources
CLASSZONE.COM
• More Examples
• eTutorial Plus

Write the decimal as a percent or the percent as a decimal.

13. 0.28　　　14. 0.1　　　15. 2　　　16. 5.46

17. 0.087　　　18. 0.00205　　　19. 8%　　　20. 19%

21. 108%　　　22. 104.2%　　　23. 0.302%　　　24. 0.051%

Write the fraction as a percent.

25. $\frac{3}{20}$　　　26. $\frac{1}{8}$　　　27. $\frac{2}{15}$　　　28. $\frac{1}{9}$

29. $\frac{7}{2}$　　　30. $\frac{9}{4}$　　　31. $\frac{4}{3}$　　　32. $\frac{6}{5}$

33. **Electricity** Wind power generates about 0.0015 of the world's electricity. What percent of the world's electricity does wind power generate?

34. **Water** About 0.3% of the water on Earth is usable by humans. Write 0.3% as a decimal.

35. **Music** Of a radio station's 40 most popular songs for the week, $\frac{5}{8}$ were sung by female soloists. What percent of the songs were sung by female soloists?

Find the percent of the number.

36. 12% of 150   **37.** 80% of 340   **38.** 18.2% of 90   **39.** 60.1% of 70

40. 225% of 80   **41.** 120% of 400   **42.** 0.4% of 260   **43.** 0.35% of 50

44. Raffle A total of 600 tickets were sold for a raffle. The probability that your friend will win the prize is 7%. How many of the raffle tickets did your friend buy?

45. Winds The winds on Neptune are the strongest on any planet in our solar system and can reach a speed of about 1500 miles per hour. The winds of a tornado near Bridge Creek, Oklahoma, in 1999 were about 21.2% as fast as the winds on Neptune. What was the wind speed in the tornado?

46. Internet Sales A company made $350 million in retail sales last year. About 0.9% of those sales were over the Internet. About how much money did the company make in sales over the Internet?

47. 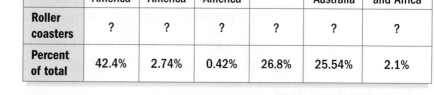 **Roller Coasters** There were 1429 operating roller coasters in the world in 2001. Copy the table. Then use a calculator to complete the table with the number of roller coasters in each region. Be sure to round answers to the nearest whole number.

Region	North America	South America	Central America	Europe	Asia and Australia	Middle East and Africa
Roller coasters	?	?	?	?	?	?
Percent of total	42.4%	2.74%	0.42%	26.8%	25.54%	2.1%

48. Number Sense Find 5% of 185. Use the result to find 15% of 185.

Use a number line to order the numbers from least to greatest.

49. 150%, 2, $\frac{5}{3}$, 100%, $\frac{3}{4}$ **50.** 0.45, 42%, $\frac{2}{5}$, 4%, 0.5

Algebra **Evaluate the expression when $k = 10$.**

51. k% of 67   **52.** 25% of k **53.** 120% of k **54.** k% of 400

55. 7.9% of $3k$ **56.** 0.8% of $2k$ **57.** $(k - 9)$% of 9   **58.** $\left(\frac{k}{4}\right)$% of 20

59. Ships In 1694, the English ship *Sussex* sank in the Mediterranean Sea while on its way to Spain. In 2002, a U.S. salvage company and Great Britain agreed to share any money made from the sale of gold and silver coins recovered from the wreckage of the ship.

  a. The company will get 80% of the first $45 million of the sales. If sales total $45 million, how much money will the company get?

  b. The company will get 50% of any sales between $45 million and $500 million. If sales total $500 million, how much money will the company get?

  c. The company will get 40% of any sales above $500 million. If sales total $650 million, how much money will the company get?

In the **Real World**

Ships The *Sussex* may have resembled the 17th century ship shown above. The *Sussex* was about 154 feet long. If a car is 15.5 feet long, about how many car lengths equal the length of the *Sussex*?

60. Extended Problem Solving The circle graph shows the results of a survey asking 500 students their main reason for using the Internet.

   a. How many students chose either games or chat rooms?

   b. Compare How many more students chose e-mail than news and research?

   c. Apply Suppose 300 other students were surveyed, and 14% of them chose games. What percent of all 800 students chose games?

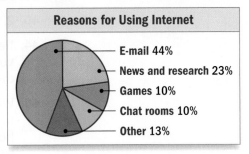

Reasons for Using Internet

- E-mail 44%
- News and research 23%
- Games 10%
- Chat rooms 10%
- Other 13%

61. Challenge Suppose x is 200% of y. What percent of x is y?

62. Geometry The area of square A is 400 square centimeters. The side length of square B is 65% of the side length of square A. Is the area of square B 65% of the area of square A? Explain your reasoning.

Mixed Review

Algebra Basics Solve the equation. *(Lesson 2.7)*

63. $0.3 = 5x$ **64.** $8 = 3.5 + x$ **65.** $7.6 = x - 8.3$ **66.** $1.2 = \frac{x}{6}$

67. The odds in favor of your winning a prize are 3 to 7. What is the probability that you will win the prize? *(Lesson 6.7)*

Use a proportion to answer the question. *(Lesson 7.2)*

68. What number is 10% of 60?   **69.** 93 is 124% of what number?

Standardized Test Practice

70. Multiple Choice You made 82.5% of your 160 attempted free throws in a basketball season. How many free throws did you make?

   A. 28   **B.** 78   **C.** 132   **D.** 140

71. Short Response In a survey of 3000 music buyers, 5% of them preferred cassettes and 89% preferred CDs. How many more music buyers preferred CDs than cassettes? Explain your reasoning.

Brain GAME

Percents in the Squares

Describe the pattern. Then draw the grid that represents the fifth figure.

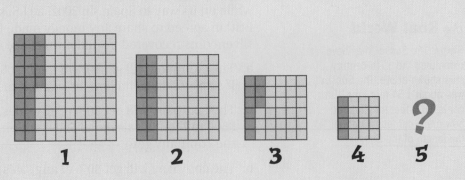

1   2   3   4   5

The Percent Equation

BEFORE　　　　　**Now**　　　　　　　　　**WHY?**

You used proportions to solve percent problems.　You'll use equations to solve percent problems.　So you can analyze the results of an election, as in Ex. 29.

Review Vocabulary
percent, p. 329

Astronomy On June 14, 2002, the distance between Earth and the moon was about 375,000 kilometers. On that day, a traveling asteroid missed Earth by about 32% of that distance. How far away from Earth was the asteroid at that time?

You have used the proportion $\frac{a}{b} = \frac{p}{100}$ to solve percent problems. When you solve this proportion for a and write $\frac{p}{100}$ as $p\%$, you get the equation $a = p\% \cdot b$.

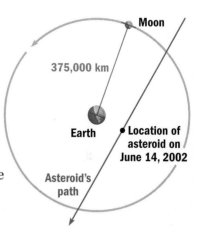

The Percent Equation

You can represent "a is p percent of b" using the equation

$$a = p\% \cdot b$$

where a is a part of the base b and $p\%$ is the percent.

Reading *Algebra*

Certain words can represent mathematical symbols. In the statement "a is $p\%$ of b," the word *is* corresponds to the equal sign, $=$, and the word *of* corresponds to the multiplication symbol, $\cdot$.

Example 1　　　*Finding a Part of a Base*

To find how far away from Earth the asteroid was, as described above, use the percent equation.

$a = p\% \cdot b$	**Write percent equation.**
$\ = 32\% \cdot 375{,}000$	**Substitute 32 for p and 375,000 for b.**
$\ = 0.32 \cdot 375{,}000$	**Write percent as a decimal.**
$\ = 120{,}000$	**Multiply.**

Answer The asteroid was about 120,000 kilometers away from Earth.

✔ *Checkpoint*

Use the percent equation to answer the question.

1. What number is 16% of 75?　　　**2.** What number is 89% of 110?

Example 2 Finding a Commission

Commission A car salesperson earns a 6.5% commission on every car sold. The salesperson sells a car for $21,800. What is the commission?

Solution

$a = p\% \cdot b$	Write percent equation.
$= 6.5\% \cdot 21,800$	Substitute 6.5 for p and 21,800 for b.
$= 0.065 \cdot 21,800$	Write percent as a decimal.
$= 1417$	Multiply.

Answer The salesperson's commission is $1417.

✔ **Checkpoint**

3. In Example 2, find the commission if a car is sold for $23,000.

Example 3 Finding a Percent

What percent of 25 is 60?

$a = p\% \cdot b$	Write percent equation.
$60 = p\% \cdot 25$	Substitute 60 for a and 25 for b.
$2.4 = p\%$	Divide each side by 25.
$240\% = p\%$	Write decimal as a percent.

Answer 60 is 240% of 25.

In the **Real World**

Movies In 2000, a person who went to a movie theater in the United States spent an average of $6.92. The average ticket price was $5.39. To the nearest whole percent, what percent of the average amount spent at a movie theater was for a movie ticket?

Example 4 Finding a Base

Movies Your friend paid $9 for a movie ticket. This amount was 72% of the total amount your friend spent at the theater. How much money did your friend spend?

Solution

$a = p\% \cdot b$	Write percent equation.
$9 = 72\% \cdot b$	Substitute 9 for a and 72 for p.
$9 = 0.72 \cdot b$	Write percent as a decimal.
$12.5 = b$	Divide each side by 0.72.

Answer Your friend spent $12.50 at the theater.

✔ **Checkpoint**

Use the percent equation to answer the question.

4. What percent of 48 is 45?   5. 27 is 7.5% of what number?

Note *Worthy*

In your notes, you should include examples of percent problems and their solutions. You can use these notes to help you decide which method to use when solving a percent problem.

SUMMARY **Methods for Solving a Percent Problem**

To find the percent of a number:

- Write the percent as a fraction.

  Example:
  $$20\% \text{ of } 35 = \frac{1}{5} \cdot 35 = 7$$

- Write the percent as a decimal.

  Example:
  $$5\% \text{ of } 16 = 0.05 \cdot 16 = 0.8$$

To find the percent $p\%$, the base b, or a part a of the base:

- Use the proportion
  $$\frac{a}{b} = \frac{p}{100}.$$

  Example:

  21 is 35% of what number?

  $$\frac{21}{b} = \frac{35}{100}$$

  $$60 = b$$

- Use the percent equation
  $$a = p\% \cdot b.$$

  Example:

  What percent of 250 is 40?

  $$40 = p\% \cdot 250$$

  $$16\% = p\%$$

7.4 Exercises

More Practice, p. 809

INTERNET
eWorkbook Plus
CLASSZONE.COM

Guided Practice

Vocabulary Check

1. Identify the percent, the base, and the part of the base in the following statement: 32 is 40% of 80.

2. Tell whether the answer to the following question represents *the base, the part of the base,* or *the percent*: What number is 20% of 65?

Skill Check **Use the percent equation to answer the question.**

3. What number is 60% of 25?

4. What percent of 25 is 24?

5. 18 is 36% of what number?

6. What percent of 48 is 36?

Guided Problem Solving

7. Income You earn a weekly salary of $200 plus a 3% commission on the total value of the sales made in the week. This week, your sales total $2000. What are your total earnings for the week?

(1) Identify the percent, the base, and the part of the base.

(2) Write and solve a percent equation to find the commission.

(3) Add the commission to the weekly salary to find the total earnings.

Practice and Problem Solving

Homework *Help*

Example	Exercises
1	8–19
2	20
3	8–17, 22
4	8–17, 21

Online Resources
CLASSZONE.COM

• More Examples
• eTutorial Plus

Use the percent equation to answer the question.

8. What number is 20% of 45?

9. What number is 10% of 56?

10. What percent of 500 is 25?

11. What percent of 200 is 1?

12. 9 is 0.03% of what number?

13. 10.5 is 30% of what number?

14. 90 is 120% of what number?

15. What percent of 90 is 72?

16. What percent of 80 is 212?

17. What number is 150% of 96?

18. Music A music collector has 1200 CDs, and 65% of them were produced after 1990. How many of the CDs were produced after 1990?

19. Community Service Your class surveyed 560 students and asked what kind of community service activity they prefer. Of the students surveyed, 25% chose recycling. How many students chose recycling?

20. Televisions A salesperson earns a 4% commission on the sales of televisions. If the salesperson's television sales total $7000, how much is the commission?

21. Survey A school newspaper says that 3 students, or 6% of the students surveyed, can wiggle their ears. How many students were surveyed?

22. Bake Sale At a club bake sale, cookies cost $.40 each and cupcakes cost $.65 each. The club sells 65 cookies and 60 cupcakes.

   a. How much money was made from selling cookies? cupcakes?

   b. What percent of the money made came from sales of cookies?

   c. Critical Thinking What percent of the baked goods sold were cookies? Why is this percent not the same as the percent you found in part (b)?

Use the percent equation to answer the question when $k = 20$.

23. What is $(k - 15)$% of 90?

24. What percent of 70 is $(k + 36)$?

25. $(2k)$ is 8% of what number?

26. What is $(3k)$% of 130?

27. *Writing* Would you change the percent to *a fraction* or to *a decimal* in order to find 75% of 120? 31% of 120? Explain your choices.

28. **Sports** The table shows a breakdown of the seats in a football stadium at Houston, Texas. Use a calculator to answer the following questions.

   a. About what percent of the seats are either main level seats or middle level seats?

   b. Suppose that 75% of the upper level seats and 50% of the middle level seats are occupied. How many seats in these two sections together are occupied?

Type of seat	Seats
Main level seats	25,739
Middle level seats	14,446
Upper level seats	24,968
Seats in suites	4,185

Football stadium at
Houston, Texas

29. 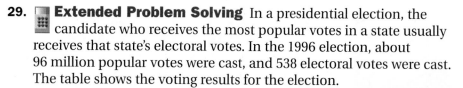 **Extended Problem Solving** In a presidential election, the candidate who receives the most popular votes in a state usually receives that state's electoral votes. In the 1996 election, about 96 million popular votes were cast, and 538 electoral votes were cast. The table shows the voting results for the election.

a. Compare For which candidate, Clinton or Dole, was the percent of popular votes greater than the percent of electoral votes?

b. Interpret Was this election closer with respect to popular votes or to electoral votes? Explain.

Candidate	Electoral votes	Popular votes (estimated)
Clinton	379	47 million
Dole	159	39 million
Other	0	10 million

30. Computers A salesperson earns a 4% commission on every computer sold. The salesperson wants to earn $1000 in commissions in the next 4 days. What is the average amount of computer sales that the salesperson needs to make per day to reach the goal?

31. Art Programs In New York City's Percent for Art Program, money is set aside for creating artwork at public building sites. The program requires that 1% of the first $20,000,000 of the cost of a building project and 0.5% of the remaining cost be spent on the artwork.

a. How much money must be spent on artwork if a project is expected to cost $30,000,000?

b. For each project, no more than $400,000 can be spent on artwork. The maximum amount that can be spent on artwork per year on all projects in the city is $1,500,000. Suppose that in one year the city has a project that costs $50,000,000 and another project that costs $62,000,000. What percent of the yearly maximum amount for artwork is used by the two projects?

32. Challenge The base b of a triangle is 60% of the height h. Write a formula for the area of the triangle in terms of h only.

In the **Real World**

Art Programs The artwork shown above was financed by New York City's Percent for Art Program. Titled *Multiple Choice*, it shows five benches that spell out the words ALWAYS, NEVER, OFTEN, SELDOM, and SOMETIMES. About what percent of the 31 letters used for the benches are E's?

Mixed Review

Find the difference. *(p. 774)*

33. $892.1 - 420.5$ **34.** $73.98 - 5.16$ **35.** $18.9 - 6.72$

Solve the equation. Check your solution. *(Lesson 2.6)*

36. $6x = 12$ **37.** $7x = -42$ **38.** $-9x = -36$

Write the fraction as a percent. *(Lesson 7.3)*

39. $\frac{1}{8}$ **40.** $\frac{11}{20}$ **41.** $\frac{12}{9}$

Standardized Test Practice

42. Multiple Choice In a class of 35 students, 28 take the bus to school. What percent of the students take the bus to school?

A. 7%   **B.** 63%   **C.** 80%   **D.** 125%

43. Short Response There are 20 marbles in a bag, and 35% of them are blue. You put 6 more blue marbles in the bag. What percent of the marbles in the bag are now blue? Explain how you got your answer.

Write the fraction as a percent.

1. $\frac{17}{25}$ **2.** $\frac{1}{5}$ **3.** $\frac{5}{6}$ **4.** $\frac{11}{16}$

Write the decimal as a percent.

5. 0.87   **6.** 0.728   **7.** 2   **8.** 0.0061

Find the percent of the number.

9. 75% of 64   **10.** 20% of 18   **11.** 30% of 300   **12.** 25% of 980

13. 35% of 90   **14.** 22.5% of 200   **15.** 140% of 500   **16.** 0.6% of 600

17. Flowers A bouquet of 40 flowers is made up of roses, carnations, and daisies. The bouquet is 45% roses and 15% carnations. How many of the flowers are roses? carnations?

Use a proportion or the percent equation to answer the question.

18. What number is 95% of 80?   **19.** What percent of 40 is 4?

20. What percent of 400 is 190?   **21.** 6 is 7.5% of what number?

22. Furniture A furniture salesperson earns a 4.5% commission on every piece of furniture sold. The salesperson sells a sofa for $1000 and a chair for $200. What commission does the salesperson earn?

Brain GAME

The Greatest Sum

Fill in the blue boxes with the numbers shown. Use each number only once. Find the percent of the number in parts (a), (b), and (c). Then add the results. What is the greatest sum that you can make?

75
40
35
100
28
64

a ? % of ? = ? → ?

b ? % of ? = ? → ?

c ? % of ? = ? → +?

———
?

Concept
Activity

7.5 Modeling Percent of Change

Goal
Model the percent of change in a quantity.

Materials
• graph paper
• colored pencils

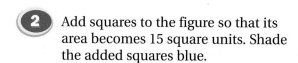
Investigate

A figure has an area of 10 square units. You increase its area to 15 square units. By what percent does the area of the figure change?

1 Let each square on your graph paper have an area of 1 square unit. Draw a figure that has an area of 10 square units, as shown at the right. Shade all of the squares red.

2 Add squares to the figure so that its area becomes 15 square units. Shade the added squares blue.

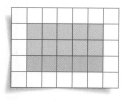

3 Find the ratio of the added area to the original area. Express the result as a percent. This percent is called the *percent of change.*

$$\frac{\text{Added area}}{\text{Original area}} = \frac{5 \text{ square units}}{10 \text{ square units}}$$
$$= 50\%$$

Draw Conclusions

Use a model to find the percent of change in the area of the figure.

1. Original area: 5 square units
New area: 7 square units

2. Original area: 4 square units
New area: 5 square units

3. Original area: 3 square units
New area: 6 square units

4. Original area: 5 square units
New area: 12 square units

5. Critical Thinking A figure has an area of 16 square units, and you increase its area to 20 square units. What percent of the original area is the new area? How is this percent related to the percent of change in the area?

Percent *of* Change

BEFORE	Now	WHY?
You found a percent of a number.	You'll find a percent of change in a quantity.	So you can analyze data about wetlands, as in Ex. 22.

Vocabulary

percent of change, p. 352
percent of increase, p. 352
percent of decrease, p. 352

Balloons The International Balloon Fiesta takes place every year in Albuquerque, New Mexico. In 1999, 903 balloons participated. In 2000, 1019 balloons participated. By about what percent did the number of balloons increase from 1999 to 2000?

A **percent of change** indicates how much a quantity increases or decreases with respect to the original amount. If the new amount is greater than the original amount, the percent of change is called a **percent of increase**. If the new amount is less than the original amount, the percent of change is called a **percent of decrease**.

Percent of Change

The percent of change is the ratio of the amount of increase or decrease to the original amount.

$$\text{Percent of change, } p\% = \frac{\text{Amount of increase or decrease}}{\text{Original amount}}$$

Example 1   Finding a Percent of Increase

To answer the question stated above, find the percent of increase in the number of balloons from 1999 to 2000.

$p\% = \dfrac{\text{Amount of increase}}{\text{Original amount}}$ **Write formula for percent of increase.**

$= \dfrac{1019 - 903}{903}$ **Substitute.**

$= \dfrac{116}{903}$ **Subtract.**

$\approx 0.128 = 12.8\%$ **Divide. Then write decimal as a percent.**

Answer The number of balloons increased by about 12.8%.

✔ *Checkpoint*

Find the percent of increase.

1. Original: 20
New: 25

2. Original: 150
New: 189

3. Original: 55
New: 143

Study *Strategy*

Reasonableness In Example 2, a decrease from 512 to 320 is about the same as a decrease from 500 to 300. Because

$$\frac{500-300}{500} = \frac{200}{500} = 40\%,$$

37.5% is a reasonable answer.

Example 2   *Finding a Percent of Decrease*

Find the percent of decrease from 512 to 320.

$p\% = \dfrac{\text{Amount of decrease}}{\text{Original amount}}$ Write formula for percent of decrease.

$= \dfrac{512 - 320}{512}$ Substitute.

$= \dfrac{192}{512}$ Subtract.

$= \dfrac{3}{8} = 37.5\%$ Simplify fraction. Then write as a percent.

Answer The percent of decrease is 37.5%.

 Checkpoint

Find the percent of decrease.

4. Original: 20
New: 15

5. Original: 75
New: 35

6. Original: 102
New: 51

Finding a New Amount If you know the original amount and the percent of change, you can find the new amount. First multiply the percent of change by the original amount to find the amount of change. Then increase or decrease the original amount by the amount of change.

Athlete in a motocross competition

Example 3   *Using a Percent of Increase*

Action Sports There were about 198,000 spectators at an action sports event in 1995. The number of spectators increased by about 12% from 1995 to 2002. About how many spectators were there in 2002?

Solution

To find the number of spectators in 2002, you need to increase the number of spectators in 1995 by 12%.

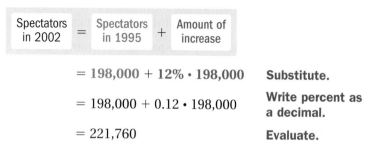

$= 198{,}000 + 12\% \cdot 198{,}000$ Substitute.

$= 198{,}000 + 0.12 \cdot 198{,}000$ Write percent as a decimal.

$= 221{,}760$ Evaluate.

Answer There were about 221,760 spectators in 2002.

 Checkpoint

Find the new amount.

7. Increase 45 by 20%.

8. Decrease 85 by 28%.

Another Way In Example 3, you can find the new amount by evaluating $100\% \cdot 198{,}000 + 12\% \cdot 198{,}000$, or $198{,}000 \cdot (100\% + 12\%)$. This result suggests another way to find a new amount.

- For a $p\%$ increase, multiply the original amount by $(100\% + p\%)$.
- For a $p\%$ decrease, multiply the original amount by $(100\% - p\%)$.

Example 4 — Finding a New Amount

Music In 1983, the average price of an audio CD was $21.50. By 2000, the average price had decreased by 34.8%. What was the average price of a CD in 2000?

Solution

Price in 2000 = **Price in 1983** $\cdot$ $(100\% - p\%)$	
$= 21.5 \cdot (100\% - 34.8\%)$	Substitute.
$= 21.5 \cdot 65.2\%$	Subtract percents.
$= 21.5 \cdot 0.652$	Write percent as a decimal.
$= 14.018$	Multiply.

Answer The average price of a CD in 2000 was about $14.02.

7.5 Exercises

More Practice, p. 809

INTERNET
eWorkbook Plus
CLASSZONE.COM

Guided Practice

Vocabulary Check

1. Is the percent of change from 79 to 56 *a percent of increase* or *a percent of decrease*?

2. A number is increased by 30%. Explain how you can find the new amount without first calculating the amount of increase.

Skill Check Identify the percent of change as an *increase* or a *decrease*. Then find the percent of change.

3. Original: 30
   New: 45

4. Original: 65
   New: 117

5. Original: 28
   New: 7

Guided Problem Solving

6. **Reptiles** In 1981, there were 25 endangered and threatened species of reptiles in the U.S. In 2001, there were 36 species. By what percent did the number of these reptile species change from 1981 to 2001?

   1 Tell whether the amount of change is *an increase* or *a decrease*.

   2 Find the amount of change from 1981 to 2001.

   3 Divide the amount of change by the original amount. Write the quotient as a percent.

Practice and Problem Solving

Homework *Help*

Example	Exercises
1	7–14
2	7–13, 15
3	16–19, 21
4	16–20

Online Resources
CLASSZONE.COM
• More Examples
• eTutorial Plus

Identify the percent of change as an *increase* or a *decrease*. Then find the percent of change.

7. Original: 28
New: 35

8. Original: 45
New: 72

9. Original: 70
New: 42

10. Original: 40
New: 9

11. Original: 140
New: 189

12. Original: 350
New: 196

13. Error Analysis Describe and correct the error in finding the percent of change from 90 to 50.

$$p\% = \frac{90 - 50}{50}$$
$$= \frac{40}{50} = 0.8 = 80\%$$

14. Hot Dogs In 1991, the price of a hot dog at a Texas baseball stadium was $1.25. In 2001, the price of a hot dog at the stadium was $2.25. By what percent did the price change from 1991 to 2001?

15. Lakes Lake Chad in Africa had a surface area of about 10,000 square miles in 1963. Because of climate changes and increased water usage by humans, the surface area decreased to about 850 square miles in 2001. By what percent did the surface area change from 1963 to 2001?

Find the new amount.

16. Increase 25 by 24%.

17. Increase 120 by 75%.

18. Decrease 35 by 60%.

19. Decrease 72 by 65%.

20. Computers In 1992, one gigabyte of information stored in computers cost $3000. In 2002, one gigabyte of stored information cost 99.9% less. How much did one gigabyte of stored information cost in 2002?

21. Auctions A sweater is being sold at an online auction. The minimum bid is $9. At the end of the auction, the sweater is sold for 75% above the minimum bid. What is the selling price of the sweater?

22. Wetlands A wetland is a region where water is usually present near or on the soil. The states in the table below had the greatest acreage of wetlands in the United States in the 1980s. The table shows the surface area of wetlands in these states in the 1780s and in the 1980s.

a. Compare In which state was the percent of change in the area of wetlands from the 1780s to the 1980s the least? the greatest?

b. Analyze For the four states combined, by about what percent did the area of wetlands change from the 1780s to the 1980s?

Area of Wetlands (millions of acres)		
State	**1780s**	**1980s**
Alaska	170.2	170.0
Florida	20.3	11.0
Louisiana	16.2	8.8
Minnesota	15.1	8.7

In the **Real World**

Wetlands The wetland shown above is located in Ocean City, Maryland. The land that makes up the United States had about 391 million acres of wetlands in the 1780s and about 274 million acres in the 1980s. By about what percent did the area of wetlands in the United States change from the 1780s to the 1980s?

23. *Writing* Can you increase an amount by more than 100%? Explain.

24. Investing An investor buys 500 shares of a stock at a price of $24 per share. Three years later the value of each share has increased by 15%. What is the total value of the 500 shares of the stock?

25. ▣ **Extended Problem Solving** The bar graph shows the number of pairs of footwear that were manufactured in the U.S. for 5 years. You may want to use a calculator to answer the following questions.

a. By about what percent did the number of pairs of footwear change from 1996 to 2000?

b. Compare In which year did the number of pairs of footwear decrease the most from the previous year? What was the approximate percent of change?

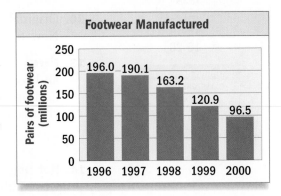

c. Interpret and Apply Can you conclude from the graph that footwear manufacturers have been making less money every year from 1996 to 2000? Explain.

26. Challenge The number of people between the ages of 2 and 18 who accessed streaming media on the Internet in November 1999 increased by 65% to about 7 million in November 2000. About how many people in this age group accessed streaming media in November 1999?

27. Critical Thinking Suppose an original amount decreases by 75%. By what percent must the new amount increase in order to return to the original amount? Justify your answer.

Mixed Review

Find the sum or difference. *(p. 774)*

28. $5.98 + 3.72$ **29.** $9 + 4.55$ **30.** $3.4 - 1.9$ **31.** $8.04 - 2.6$

Algebra Basics Solve the equation. Check your solution. *(Lesson 3.1)*

32. $9 = 5n + 4$ **33.** $6y + 1 = 19$ **34.** $14 = 4w - 2$ **35.** $9x - 7 = 20$

Use the percent equation to answer the question. *(Lesson 7.4)*

36. What number is 60% of 135? **37.** What percent of 120 is 78?

38. What percent of 96 is 84? **39.** 36 is 48% of what number?

Standardized Test Practice

40. Multiple Choice A homebuilder orders 10% more floor tiles than the original estimate of 170 tiles in case some tiles break while they are being installed. How many tiles does the homebuilder order?

A. 153 tiles **B.** 180 tiles **C.** 187 tiles **D.** 1700 tiles

41. Multiple Choice There were about 23,000 movie screens in the U.S. in 1990. The number of screens increased to about 34,500 by 2001. By what percent did the number of screens change from 1990 to 2001?

F. 25% **G.** 33% **H.** 50% **I.** 250%

7.6

Percent Applications

BEFORE	Now	WHY?
You found percents of change.	You'll find markups, discounts, sales tax, and tips.	So you can find the cost of in-line skates, as in Ex. 25.

Vocabulary
markup, p. 357
discount, p. 358

Jewelry A street vendor buys bracelets from a manufacturer for $7 each. The vendor marks up the price by 150%. What is the retail price?

A retailer buys items from manufacturers at *wholesale prices*. The retailer then sells those items to customers at *retail prices*. An increase from the wholesale price of an item to the retail price is a **markup**. The markup is calculated using a percent of the wholesale price.

Example 1 *Finding a Retail Price*

Find the retail price of a bracelet, as described above.

Solution

Method 1 Add the markup to the wholesale price.

Retail price	= **Wholesale price + Markup**	
	$= 7 + 150\% \cdot 7$	**Substitute.**
	$= 7 + 1.5 \cdot 7$	**Write 150% as a decimal.**
	$= 7 + 10.5$	**Multiply.**
	$= 17.5$	**Add.**

Method 2 Multiply the wholesale price by (100% + Markup percent).

Retail price	= **Wholesale price · (100% + Markup percent)**	
	$= 7 \cdot (100\% + 150\%)$	**Substitute.**
	$= 7 \cdot 250\%$	**Add percents.**
	$= 7 \cdot 2.5$	**Write 250% as a decimal.**
	$= 17.5$	**Multiply.**

Answer The retail price of a bracelet is $17.50.

✔ *Checkpoint*

1. In Example 1, what is the retail price of a bracelet if the markup percent is 120%?

Discounts A decrease from the original price of an item to the sale price is a **discount**. The discount is calculated using a percent of the original price.

Example 2 *Finding a Sale Price*

Electronics You buy an electronic organizer that is on sale for 15% off the original price of $25. What is the sale price?

Solution

Method 1 Subtract the discount from the original price.

Sale price = **Original price − Discount**

$$= 25 - 15\% \cdot 25 \qquad \text{Substitute.}$$
$$= 25 - 0.15 \cdot 25 \qquad \text{Write 15\% as a decimal.}$$
$$= 25 - 3.75 \qquad \text{Multiply.}$$
$$= 21.25 \qquad \text{Subtract.}$$

Method 2 Multiply the original price by (100% − Discount percent).

Sale price = **Original price · (100% − Discount percent)**

$$= 25 \cdot (100\% - 15\%) \qquad \text{Substitute.}$$
$$= 25 \cdot 85\% \qquad \text{Subtract percents.}$$
$$= 25 \cdot 0.85 \qquad \text{Write 85\% as a decimal.}$$
$$= 21.25 \qquad \text{Multiply.}$$

Answer The sale price of the electronic organizer is $21.25.

Watch *Out*

The tip at a restaurant is based on the food bill only. Do not include the sales tax when finding a tip.

Example 3 *Using Sales Tax and Tips*

Restaurants The bill for your restaurant meal is $22. You leave a 15% tip. The sales tax is 6%. What is the total cost of your meal?

Solution

Sales tax and tips are calculated using a percent of the purchase price. These amounts are then added to the purchase price.

Total = **Food bill + Sales tax + Tip**

$$= 22 + 6\% \cdot 22 + 15\% \cdot 22 \qquad \text{Substitute.}$$
$$= 22 + 0.06 \cdot 22 + 0.15 \cdot 22 \qquad \text{Write 6\% and 15\% as decimals.}$$
$$= 22 + 1.32 + 3.3 \qquad \text{Multiply.}$$
$$= 26.62 \qquad \text{Add.}$$

Answer The total cost of the meal is $26.62.

✔ Checkpoint

2. A pair of jeans that originally costs $42 is 25% off. Find the sale price.

3. In Example 3, find the total cost of the meal if the sales tax is 5%.

Study Strategy

Another Way In Example 4, you can use the verbal model

$$\text{Retail price} = \text{Wholesale price} + \text{Markup}$$

to find the wholesale price. When you substitute variables and values, you get the equation $35 = x + 0.8x$, where x is the wholesale price.

Example 4 *Finding an Original Amount*

Lamps A furniture store marks up the wholesale price of a desk lamp by 80%. The retail price is $35. What is the wholesale price?

Solution

Let x represent the wholesale price.

Retail price = Wholesale price · (100% + Markup percent)

$35 = x \cdot (100\% + 80\%)$	Substitute.
$35 = x \cdot 180\%$	Add percents.
$35 = x \cdot 1.8$	Write 180% as a decimal.
$19.44 \approx x$	Divide each side by 1.8.

Answer The wholesale price of the lamp is about $19.44.

 Checkpoint

4. A store marks up the wholesale price of a printer by 80%. The retail price is $120. What is the wholesale price of the printer?

7.6 Exercises

More Practice, p. 809

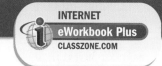

INTERNET
eWorkbook Plus
CLASSZONE.COM

Guided Practice

Vocabulary Check

1. Copy and complete: The retail price of an item for sale is the sum of the wholesale price and the ? .

2. Describe two methods for finding the sale price of an item if you know the original price and the discount percent.

Skill Check **In Exercises 3–6, use the given information to find the new amount.**

3. Wholesale price: $13
Markup percent: 110%

4. Original price: $60
Discount percent: 20%

5. Food bill: $15
Sales tax: 5%

6. Taxi fare: $22
Tip: 10%

Guided Problem Solving

7. Headsets When you use a coupon for 15% off the original price of a headset, you pay $27. What is the original price of the headset?

1) Identify the discount price and the discount percent.

2) Let x represent the original price. Write an equation that you can use to find the original price.

3) Solve the equation to find the original price of the headset.

Practice and Problem Solving

Homework *Help*

Example	Exercises
1	8–12
2	8–11, 13
3	14–18
4	19–23

Online Resources
CLASSZONE.COM

- More Examples
- eTutorial Plus

In Exercises 8–11, use the given information to find the new price.

8. Wholesale price: $34
Markup percent: 125%

9. Wholesale price: $125
Markup percent: 50%

10. Original price: $37
Discount percent: 25%

11. Original price: $54
Discount percent: 40%

12. Outdoor Speakers A music store buys a set of outdoor speakers for $90. The store marks up the wholesale price by 110%. What is the retail price of the speakers?

13. Zoo Trips For a child, the regular admission price to a zoo is $13. With a special pass, the admission price is discounted 20%. What is the admission price when the pass is used?

In Exercises 14–17, use the given information to find the total cost.

14. Original price: $42
Sales tax: 5%

15. Original price: $78
Sales tax: 6%

16. Food bill: $25
Sales tax: 6%
Tip: 15%

17. Food bill: $18
Sales tax: 5%
Tip: 20%

18. Walking Dogs A dog owner pays you $20 plus a 10% tip for walking a dog. What is the total amount of money that the dog owner pays you?

In Exercises 19–22, use the given information to find the original price.

19. Retail price: $50
Markup percent: 90%

20. Retail price: $24
Markup percent: 115%

21. Sale price: $150
Discount percent: 25%

22. Sale price: $210
Discount percent: 30%

23. Bicycles A store marks up the wholesale price of a bicycle by 120%. The retail price is $215. What is the wholesale price of the bicycle?

24. Laptops A laptop computer is on sale for 10% off the original price of $1500. When it doesn't sell, the laptop goes on sale for 15% off the sale price. What is the new sale price of the laptop?

25. In-line Skates A sports store is having a sale on in-line skates. You want to buy a pair of in-line skates that originally costs $135. The sales tax is 5.5%, and it will be applied to the sale price of the skates. What is the total cost of the skates?

SALE! 20% OFF every pair of in-line skates

26. Critical Thinking Which situation results in a greater final amount, an 80% markup of the wholesale price followed by a 30% discount of the retail price, or a 30% markup of the wholesale price followed by an 80% discount of the retail price? Justify your answer.

27. **Extended Problem Solving** The pizzas you order for home delivery cost $19. The sales tax is 4.9%, and you plan to give a 15% tip.

   a. **Estimate** Estimate the amount of the sales tax.

   b. **Estimate** Use mental math to estimate a 15% tip. Explain the method of estimation you use.

   c. **Interpret** Estimate the total cost of the order. Is your estimate a *high estimate* or a *low estimate* of the total cost? Explain.

   d. Find the exact total cost of the order. How close was your estimate?

28. **Challenge** A store marks up the wholesale price of an item by 60%. A month later the store puts the item on sale. If the store doesn't want to lose money on the item, what is the maximum discount percent the store can use?

Mixed Review

Give the place and value of the red digit. Then round the number to that place. *(p. 770)*

29. 93.21 **30.** 341.073 **31.** 1595.962 **32.** 17,024.981

Evaluate the expression when *x* = 5, *y* = 7, and *z* = 10. *(Lesson 1.3)*

33. *xyz* **34.** *x*(3*z* + *y*) **35.** *x*(5 + *yz*) **36.** *xz* − *xy*

Write the percent as a decimal. *(Lesson 7.3)*

37. 45% **38.** 8.6% **39.** 102% **40.** 0.4%

Standardized Test Practice

41. **Extended Response** Your bill for a meal at a diner is $11. The sales tax is 6%, and you plan to give a 15% tip.

   a. What is the total cost of the meal?

   b. If you have $14, what is the maximum amount you can give for a tip and still cover the food bill and sales tax? About what percent of the food bill would this tip be? Explain your thinking.

Brain GAME

Going $hopping

You have $500 to spend on items from the list shown. Spend as much of the money as you can using the following conditions:

• Buy no more than 1 of each item.

• Use a coupon for 15% off the original prices of your purchases.

• Add a sales tax of 5% of the sale prices of your purchases.

Which items did you buy, and how much money did you spend?

Hiking backpack . . $47
Digital camera $179
DVD player $90
Skateboard $79
Video game console . . $197
Electric guitar . . . $125
Bicycle $130
Television $110
Stereo system . . . $250
Music keyboard . $149
Telescope $50

Simple *and* Compound Interest

Vocabulary

interest, p. 362
principal, p. 362
simple interest, p. 362
annual interest rate,
  p. 362
balance, p. 363
compound interest,
  p. 363

Bonds People buy bonds as a way to earn money. If a $1500 bond earns 4% *simple interest* per year on its purchase price, how much will it earn in interest after 2 years?

The amount earned or paid for the use of money is called **interest** . The amount of money deposited or borrowed is the **principal** . Interest that is earned or paid only on the principal is called **simple interest** . The percent of the principal earned or paid per year is the **annual interest rate** .

For example, if you deposit $3000 into an account that earns simple interest, at an annual rate of 4.5%, then after one year the interest yielded would be $3000(0.045) = $135. The interest is only earned on the principal $3000, so another $135 would be earned in the second year. During the first three years, the total interest earned would be $3000(0.045) + $3000(0.045) + $3000(0.045) = $3000(0.045)(3) = $405. This suggests a formula for finding the amount of simple interest earned over time.

Simple Interest Formula

Simple interest I is given by the formula $I = Prt$ where P is the principal, r is the annual interest rate (written as a decimal), and t is the time in years.

Example 1   *Finding Simple Interest*

Find the interest earned after 2 years for the bond described above.

Solution

$$I = Prt$$ Write simple interest formula.

$$= (1500)(0.04)(2)$$ Substitute 1500 for *P*, 0.04 for *r*, and 2 for *t*.

$$= 120$$ Multiply.

Answer The bond will earn $120 in interest after 2 years.

✔ *Checkpoint*

1. A $1000 bond earns 6% simple annual interest. What is the interest earned after 4 years?

Balance When an account earns interest, the interest is added to the money in the account. The **balance** A of an account that earns simple annual interest is the sum of the principal P and the interest Prt.

$$A = P + Prt \quad \text{or} \quad A = P(1 + rt)$$

Example 2   *Finding an Interest Rate*

Summer Job You get a summer job at a bakery. Suppose you save $1400 of your pay and deposit it into an account that earns simple annual interest. After 9 months, the balance is $1421. Find the annual interest rate.

Solution

Because t in the formula $A = P(1 + rt)$ is the time in years, write 9 months as $\frac{9}{12}$, or $\frac{3}{4}$ year. Then solve for r after substituting values for A, P, and t in $A = P(1 + rt)$.

$A = P(1 + rt)$	**Write formula for finding balance.**
$1421 = 1400\left[1 + r\left(\dfrac{3}{4}\right)\right]$	**Substitute.**
$1421 = 1400 + 1050r$	**Distributive property**
$21 = 1050r$	**Subtract 1400 from each side.**
$0.02 = r$	**Divide each side by 1050.**

Answer The annual interest rate is 2%.

 Checkpoint

Find the unknown quantity for an account that earns simple annual interest.

2. $A = \underline{\ ?\ }$, $P = \$1000$,   **3.** $A = \$1424.50$, $P = \underline{\ ?\ }$,
     $r = 2.5\%$, $t = 2$ years $r = 3.5\%$, $t = 6$ months

Compound Interest **Compound interest** is interest that is earned on both the principal and any interest that has been earned previously. Suppose you deposit $50 into a savings account that earns 2% interest compounded annually. The table below shows the balance of your account after each of 3 years.

Reading *Algebra*

When you read the table, notice that the balances at the end of years 2 and 3 are found by adding exponents using the product of powers property.

Year	Principal at start of year	Balance at end of year
1	50	$50(1 + 0.02) = 50(1 + 0.02)^1$
2	$50(1 + 0.02)^1$	$50(1 + 0.02)^1 \cdot (1 + 0.02) = 50(1 + 0.02)^2$
3	$50(1 + 0.02)^2$	$50(1 + 0.02)^2 \cdot (1 + 0.02) = 50(1 + 0.02)^3$

The table above suggests a formula, shown on the next page, for finding the balance of an account that earns interest compounded annually.

Note *Worthy*

In your notes, you can make a concept grid that includes a definition, characteristics, an example, and a nonexample of compound interest. Your concept grid should have the formula for calculating compound interest.

Compound Interest Formula

When an account earns interest compounded annually, the balance A is given by the formula

$$A = P(1 + r)^t$$

where P is the principal, r is the annual interest rate (written as a decimal), and t is the time in years.

Example 3   *Calculating Compound Interest*

You deposit $1500 into an account that earns 2.4% interest compounded annually. Find the balance after 6 years.

Solution

$$A = P(1 + r)^t \qquad \text{Write formula.}$$

$$= 1500(1 + 0.024)^6 \qquad \text{Substitute.}$$

$$\approx 1729.38 \qquad \text{Use a calculator.}$$

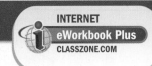

1500(1+.024)^6
1729.382257

Answer The balance of the account after 6 years is about $1729.38.

7.7   Exercises

More Practice, p. 809

Guided Practice

Vocabulary Check

1. In the simple interest formula $I = Prt$, what does P represent?

2. How is compound interest different from simple interest?

Skill Check **For an account that earns simple annual interest, find the interest and the balance of the account.**

3. $P = \$500$, $r = 7\%$, $t = 4$ years

4. $P = \$2500$, $r = 3\%$, $t = 9$ months

Find the unknown quantity for an account that earns simple annual interest.

5. $A = \$563$, $P = \$500$, $r = \underline{?}$, $t = 7$ years

6. $A = \$1670$, $P = \$1600$, $r = 3.5\%$, $t = \underline{?}$

7. Savings Account You deposit $700 into a savings account that earns 2% interest compounded annually. Find the balance of the account after 4 years. Round your answer to the nearest cent.

Practice and Problem Solving

Homework *Help*

Example	Exercises
1	8–13, 17
2	8–16
3	18–21

Online Resources
CLASSZONE.COM

- More Examples
- eTutorial Plus

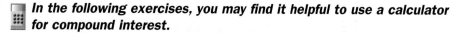 **In the following exercises, you may find it helpful to use a calculator for compound interest.**

For an account that earns simple annual interest, find the interest and the balance of the account.

8. $P = \$1250$, $r = 4\%$, $t = 10$ years   **9.** $P = \$325$, $r = 7\%$, $t = 8$ years

10. $P = \$600$, $r = 2.7\%$, $t = 4.5$ years **11.** $P = \$3200$, $r = 3.5\%$, $t = 3.5$ years

12. $P = \$100$, $r = 8\%$, $t = 6$ months **13.** $P = \$495$, $r = 5\%$, $t = 21$ months

14. Loan You loan your brother $300 and charge him 2% simple annual interest. He promises to repay you one year later. How much will your brother have to pay you?

15. The table shows three accounts that earn simple annual interest. Copy and complete the table by finding the unknown quantity.

Balance	Principal	Interest rate	Time
$5,000	$4,000	5%	?
$11,160	?	8%	36 months
$3,207	$3,000	?	18 months

16. Suppose you deposit $800 into an account that earns simple annual interest. After 2 years, the account balance is $900. Find the annual interest rate.

17. Error Analysis A $200 bond earns 5.5% simple annual interest. Describe and correct the error in finding the total interest earned after 6 months.

$$I = Prt$$
$$= (200)(0.055)(6)$$
$$= 66$$

For an account that earns interest compounded annually, find the balance of the account. Round your answer to the nearest cent.

18. $P = \$800$, $r = 5\%$, $t = 3$ years   **19.** $P = \$2200$, $r = 7\%$, $t = 8$ years

20. $P = \$1750$, $r = 2.3\%$, $t = 4$ years **21.** $P = \$680$, $r = 6.2\%$, $t = 10$ years

22. Bonds A certain bond pays simple annual interest directly to the investor every 6 months. Suppose an investor purchases this bond for $5000 at a 4.5% annual interest rate. What is the total amount of interest paid after 6 months? 18 months? 30 months?

23. Compare The accounts below earn interest compounded annually. Which account will have the greater balance in the given time?

Account A
Principal: $150
Interest rate: 3.25%
Time: 20 years

Account B
Principal: $150
Interest rate: 6.5%
Time: 10 years

24. *Writing* Does the amount of interest earned each year *increase*, *decrease*, or *stay the same* in a simple interest account? in a compound interest account? Explain your answers.

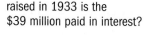

In the **Real World**

Bonds To pay for the 1933 construction of the Golden Gate Bridge, the state of California raised $35 million by selling bonds. The state had paid about $39 million in interest by the time the last of the bonds were repaid in 1971. What percent of the $35 million raised in 1933 is the $39 million paid in interest?

25. Extended Problem Solving You deposit $1000 into an account that earns 5% simple annual interest, and your friend deposits $1000 into an account that earns 5% interest compounded annually.

a. Calculate Copy and complete the table.

b. Graph Make a scatter plot of the data. Show the time in years on the *x*-axis and the account balance on the *y*-axis. Plot points representing the simple interest account balance in blue and the compound interest account balance in red.

Years	Simple interest account balance	Compound interest account balance
1	?	?
2	?	?
5	?	?
10	?	?
20	?	?

c. Compare Describe how the graph of the simple interest balance is different from the graph of the compound interest balance.

26. You deposit $1400 into an account that earns 4% interest compounded annually. You check the balance of the account after 5 years. By about what percent did the balance of the account change over those 5 years?

27. Critical Thinking How long will it take you to double your principal when you deposit it into an account that earns 10% simple annual interest? Explain how you found your answer.

28. Challenge At the start of every year, you deposit $3000 into an account that earns 7% interest compounded annually.

a. What is the balance at the end of the second year? third year?

b. Will you have enough money at the end of the fifth year to buy a car that costs $18,000? Explain your reasoning.

Mixed Review

Solve the equation. Check your solution. *(Lesson 3.3)*

29. $5x + 9 = 2x + 6$

30. $-5y - 13 = 7 - 15y$

Find the least common multiple of the numbers. *(Lesson 4.4)*

31. 3, 7 **32.** 9, 45 **33.** 12, 18 **34.** 40, 50

35. Video Game You buy a video game that is on sale for 15% off the original price of $35. Find the sale price. *(Lesson 7.6)*

Standardized Test Practice

36. Multiple Choice A $1200 bond earns 8.5% simple annual interest. What is the interest earned after 15 months?

A. $15.30 **B.** $127.50 **C.** $1275 **D.** $1530

37. Multiple Choice You deposit $3500 into an account that earns 10% interest compounded annually. What is the balance after 2 years?

F. $700 **G.** $4200 **H.** $4235 **I.** $7000

7.7 Computing Compound Interest

Goal Use a calculator to compute compound interest.

In many investment accounts, the interest is compounded several times a year. The balance A of an account that earns interest compounded n times a year is given by the formula

$$A = P\left(1 + \frac{r}{n}\right)^{nt}$$

where P is the principal, r is the annual interest rate (written as a decimal), and t is the time in years.

Example

You deposit $1000 into an account that earns 6% interest compounded semiannually. What is the balance after 4 years?

When interest is compounded semiannually, or twice a year, $n = 2$.

① Use the compound interest formula given above.

$$A = P\left(1 + \frac{r}{n}\right)^{nt}$$ **Write compound interest formula.**

$$= 1000\left(1 + \frac{0.06}{2}\right)^{2 \cdot 4}$$ **Substitute.**

② Enter the expression $1000\left(1 + \frac{0.06}{2}\right)^{2 \cdot 4}$ into your calculator.

Tech *Help*

In Step 2 of the example, you can simplify the expression to $1000(1.03)^8$ before you enter it into your calculator.

Keystrokes

1000 [( ] **1** [+] **.06** [÷] **2** [ )]
[^] [( ] **2** [×] **4** [ )] [=]

```
1000(1+.06÷2)→
        1266.770081
```

Answer The balance of the account after 4 years is about $1266.77.

Draw Conclusions

For an account that earns compound interest, find the balance of the account when interest is compounded as specified.

1. $P = \$200$, $r = 5\%$, $t = 9$ years; compounded semiannually

2. $P = \$3000$, $r = 6.2\%$, $t = 7$ years; compounded quarterly

3. $P = \$500$, $r = 4\%$, $t = 8$ years; compounded monthly

4. Critical Thinking In the example above, would the account have the greatest balance if the interest were compounded annually, semiannually, quarterly, or monthly? Justify your answer.

Chapter Review

Vocabulary Review

percent, p. 329
percent of change, p. 352
percent of increase, p. 352

percent of decrease, p. 352
markup, p. 357
discount, p. 358

interest, p. 362
principal, p. 362
simple interest, p. 362

annual interest rate, p. 362
balance, p. 363
compound interest, p. 363

Copy and complete the statement.

1. A(n) ? is a ratio whose denominator is 100.

2. A(n) ? is an increase from the wholesale price of an item to the retail price.

3. Is the percent of change from 85 to 34 a *percent of increase* or a *percent of decrease*?

4. You open an account with $500. After 1 year, the account has $510. Identify the principal, interest earned, and balance.

7.1 Percents and Fractions

Examples on pp. 329–330

▶ *Goal*

Use fractions to find the percent of a number.

Example Write 44% as a fraction and $\frac{4}{5}$ as a percent.

a. $44\% = \frac{44}{100} = \frac{11}{25}$

b. $\frac{4}{5} = \frac{4 \cdot 20}{5 \cdot 20} = \frac{80}{100} = 80\%$

Example Find 75% of 32.

75% of $32 = \frac{3}{4} \cdot 32$ Write percent as a fraction.

$= \frac{96}{4}$ Multiply.

$= 24$ Simplify.

✔ **Write the percent as a fraction.**

5. 53% **6.** 85% **7.** 60% **8.** 28%

Write the fraction as a percent.

9. $\frac{31}{100}$ **10.** $\frac{7}{20}$ **11.** $\frac{31}{50}$ **12.** $\frac{24}{25}$

Find the percent of the number.

13. 25% of 76 **14.** 60% of 50 **15.** 20% of 25 **16.** 90% of 70

7.2 Percents and Proportions

Examples on
pp. 335–336

▶ **Goal**

Use proportions to solve percent problems.

Example **117 is 65% of what number?**

$$\frac{a}{b} = \frac{p}{100}$$ Write proportion.

$$\frac{117}{b} = \frac{65}{100}$$ Substitute 117 for a and 65 for p.

$117 \cdot 100 = 65 \cdot b$ Cross products property

$11{,}700 = 65b$ Multiply.

$180 = b$ Divide each side by 65.

✔ **Use a proportion to answer the question.**

17. 36 is 24% of what number?   **18.** What number is 92% of 75?

19. What percent of 85 is 34?   **20.** 51 is 60% of what number?

21. What number is 22% of 150?   **22.** What percent of 120 is 108?

7.3 Percents and Decimals

Examples on
pp. 340–341

▶ **Goal**

Use decimals to find the percent of a number.

Example **Write 0.6 and $\frac{5}{8}$ as percents.**

a. $0.6 = 0.60 = 60\%$

b. $\frac{5}{8} = 0.625 = 62.5\%$

Example **Find 21.5% of 80.**

21.5% of $80 = 0.215 \cdot 80$ Write percent as a decimal.

$= 17.2$ Multiply.

✔ **Write the decimal as a percent.**

23. 0.589   **24.** 1.3   **25.** 0.48   **26.** 3

Write the fraction as a percent.

27. $\frac{3}{8}$ **28.** $\frac{9}{16}$ **29.** $\frac{2}{3}$ **30.** $\frac{6}{5}$

Find the percent of the number.

31. 45% of 75   **32.** 30.2% of 130   **33.** 105% of 450   **34.** 0.8% of 675

35. Shopping Last year you spent $210 on clothes. You spent 37.5% of this amount on school clothes. How much money did you spend last year on school clothes?

7.4 The Percent Equation

Examples on pp. 345–347

▶ *Goal*

Use an equation to solve percent problems.

Example What percent of 70 is 31.5?

$$a = p\% \cdot b \qquad \text{Write percent equation.}$$

$$31.5 = p\% \cdot 70 \qquad \text{Substitute 31.5 for } a \text{ and 70 for } b.$$

$$0.45 = p\% \qquad \text{Divide each side by 70.}$$

$$45\% = p\% \qquad \text{Write decimal as a percent.}$$

✔ **Use the percent equation to answer the question.**

36. What number is 40% of 26? **37.** What percent of 130 is 104?

38. What percent of 80 is 72? **39.** 2.56 is 8% of what number?

7.5 Percent of Change

Examples on pp. 352–354

▶ *Goal*

Solve problems involving percent of change.

Example Find the percent of decrease from 55 to 33.

$$p\% = \frac{\text{Amount of decrease}}{\text{Original amount}} \qquad \text{Write formula for percent of decrease.}$$

$$= \frac{55 - 33}{55} \qquad \text{Substitute.}$$

$$= \frac{22}{55} = 40\% \qquad \text{Subtract. Then write as a percent.}$$

Example Find the new amount when you increase 90 by 24%.

$$\text{New amount} = \text{Original amount} \cdot (100\% + p\%)$$

$$= 90 \cdot (100\% + 24\%) \qquad \text{Substitute.}$$

$$= 90 \cdot 124\% \qquad \text{Add percents.}$$

$$= 90 \cdot 1.24 = 111.6 \qquad \text{Write as a decimal. Multiply.}$$

✔ **Identify the percent of change as an *increase* or a *decrease*. Then find the percent of change.**

40. Original: 50 **41.** Original: 40 **42.** Original: 25 **43.** Original: 96
New: 90   New: 42   New: 24   New: 36

Find the new amount.

44. Increase 38 by 10%. **45.** Decrease 670 by 42%.

7.6 Percent Applications

Examples on pp. 357–359

▶ **Goal**

Find markups, discounts, sales tax, and tips.

Example You buy a cell phone that is 20% off the original price of $129. Find the sale price.

Sale price = **Original price** · (100% − **Discount percent**)

$$= \mathbf{129} \cdot (\mathbf{100\%} - \mathbf{20\%}) \quad \text{Substitute.}$$
$$= 129 \cdot 80\% \quad \text{Subtract percents.}$$
$$= 129 \cdot 0.8 \quad \text{Write 80\% as a decimal.}$$
$$= 103.2 \quad \text{Multiply. The sale price is \$103.20.}$$

✔ **Use the given information to find the new price.**

46. Wholesale price: $95
Markup percent: 120%

47. Original price: $330
Discount percent: 15%

7.7 Simple and Compound Interest

Examples on pp. 362–364

▶ **Goal**

Calculate interest earned and account balances.

Example Suppose you deposit $400 into an account that earns 5% simple annual interest. Find the balance of the account after 3 years.

$$A = P(1 + rt) \quad \text{Write formula for finding balance.}$$
$$= 400(1 + 0.05 \cdot 3) \quad \text{Substitute 400 for } P\text{, 0.05 for } r\text{, and 3 for } t.$$
$$= 460 \quad \text{Evaluate. The balance is \$460.}$$

Example You deposit $500 into an account that earns 4.5% interest compounded annually. Find the balance of the account after 6 years.

$$A = P(1 + r)^t \quad \text{Write formula for finding balance.}$$
$$= 500(1 + 0.045)^6 \quad \text{Substitute 500 for } P\text{, 0.045 for } r\text{, and 6 for } t.$$
$$\approx 651.13 \quad \text{Evaluate. The balance is about \$651.13.}$$

✔ **48.** Suppose you deposit $900 into an account that earns 4% simple annual interest. Find the balance of the account after 6 months.

49. You deposit $6000 into an account that earns 3.8% interest compounded annually. Find the balance of the account after 7 years.

Chapter Test

Write the percent as a fraction or the fraction as a percent.

1. 33% **2.** 65% **3.** $\dfrac{6}{25}$ **4.** $\dfrac{7}{50}$

Write the percent as a decimal or the decimal as a percent.

5. 68% **6.** 42.5% **7.** 0.9 **8.** 1.47

Find the percent of the number.

9. 75% of 68 **10.** 40% of 180 **11.** 27.5% of 300 **12.** 0.6% of 980

13. Baseball A baseball team won 55% of its 160 games during a season. How many games did the team win during the season?

Use a proportion or the percent equation to answer the question.

14. What number is 24% of 95? **15.** What number is 78% of 370?

16. What percent of 90 is 60? **17.** What percent of 70 is 31.5?

18. 4.5 is 0.9% of what number? **19.** 80 is 125% of what number?

20. Stamps Your friend has 480 stamps in a collection. Of these, 156 stamps depict historical events. What percent of the stamps in the collection depict historical events?

Identify the percent of change as an *increase* or a *decrease*. Then find the percent of change.

21. Original: 30
New: 21

22. Original: 50
New: 55

23. Original: 128
New: 176

24. Original: 380
New: 323

25. Teen Spending In 2000, about $155 billion was spent by teenagers in the United States. In 2001, the amount spent by teenagers increased by about 11%. About how much money did teenagers spend in 2001?

Use the given information to find the new amount.

26. Wholesale price: $400
Markup percent: 110%

27. Original price: $650
Discount percent: 20%

28. Food bill: $30
Sales tax: 6.5%

29. Bonds A $500 bond earns 6% simple annual interest. Find the total interest earned after 5 years.

30. Savings Account You deposit $1800 into a savings account that earns 2% interest compounded annually. Find the balance after 2 years.

Chapter Standardized Test

Test-Taking Strategy If you are having trouble with a question, skip it and return to it after you have answered the other questions on the test.

1. What is 45% as a fraction?

   A. $\frac{1}{45}$ **B.** $\frac{9}{20}$ **C.** $\frac{9}{10}$ **D.** $\frac{20}{9}$

2. What number is 40% of 20?

   F. 0.8   **G.** 8   **H.** 80   **I.** 800

3. What is $\frac{19}{50}$ as a percent?

   A. 19%   **B.** 31%   **C.** 38%   **D.** 260%

4. What percent of 140 is 56?

   F. 40%   **G.** 56%   **H.** 84%   **I.** 250%

5. In a survey of 380 people, 25% said that they enjoy reading before going to sleep. How many of the people surveyed enjoy reading before going to sleep?

   A. 25 people   **B.** 76 people

   C. 95 people   **D.** 355 people

6. Which situation represents the greatest percent of increase?

   F. Original: 60   **G.** Original: 900
   New: 75   New: 1000

   H. Original: 140   **I.** Original: 30
   New: 200   New: 60

7. What is the new amount when you increase 40 by 25%?

   A. 50   **B.** 65   **C.** 70   **D.** 100

8. A hat costs $28 after a 30% discount is applied. What was the hat's original price?

   F. $8.40   **G.** $36.40   **H.** $40.00   **I.** $58.00

9. The food bill for a meal at a restaurant is $12. The sales tax is 6.5%, and you leave a 15% tip. What is the total cost of the meal?

   A. $12.22   **B.** $12.96   **C.** $14.15   **D.** $14.58

10. A retail store buys a DVD player from a manufacturer for $140. The store then marks up the price by 115%. What is the retail price of the DVD player?

   F. $161   **G.** $255   **H.** $301   **I.** $1610

11. An $800 bond earns 4% simple annual interest. How much will the bond earn in interest after 6 years?

   A. $16   **B.** $32   **C.** $192   **D.** $1920

12. Short Response A backpack is on sale for 15% off the original price of $40. Another backpack is on sale for 40% off the original price of $55. Which backpack costs less after the discounts are applied? How much less? Explain how you got your answers.

13. Extended Response Suppose you deposit $500 into an account that earns 5% simple annual interest, and your friend deposits $350 into an account that earns 5.5% interest compounded annually.

   a. Find the balance of each account after 10 years.

   b. For each account, find the total interest earned after 10 years.

   c. Which account balance will have the greater amount of change after 10 years? Will this account balance also have the greater percent of change after 10 years? Explain your reasoning.

Strategies for Answering
Short Response Questions

Problem A CD player is on sale at a store for 25% off the retail price of $120. If you buy the CD player at the store, you pay a 5% sales tax on the sale price. An identical CD player is on sale at an Internet site for 30% off the retail price of $120. If you buy the CD player online, you pay a $20 shipping cost. Which is less, the total cost at the store or the total cost online?

Full credit solution

The steps of the solution are clearly written.

The total cost at the store is the sum of the sale price and a 5% sales tax on the sale price.

Sale price = Retail price − Discount
$$= 120 - 25\% \cdot 120 = 120 - 0.25 \cdot 120 = 90$$

The correct calculations are performed to find the total cost at the store and the total cost online.

Total cost at store = Sale price + Sales tax
$$= 90 + 5\% \cdot 90 = 90 + 0.05 \cdot 90 = 94.50$$

The total cost online is the sum of the sale price and the shipping cost.

Sale price = Retail price − Discount
$$= 120 - 30\% \cdot 120 = 120 - 0.3 \cdot 120 = 84$$

Total cost online = Sale price + Shipping cost
$$= 84 + 20 = 104$$

The question asked is answered correctly.

The total cost at the store, $94.50, is less than the total cost online, $104.

Partial credit solution

The total cost at the store and the total cost online are correct.

Total cost at store = $90 + $4.50 = $94.50
Total cost online = $84 + $20 = $104

There are no explanations to support the student's calculations.

Because $94.50 is less than $104, the total cost at the store is less than the total cost online.

Partial credit solution

The sales tax should be calculated using a percent of the sale price, not of the original price. ----------

Sale price at store = $120 - 0.25 \cdot 120 = 90$
Sales tax = $0.05 \cdot 120 = 6$

Total cost at store = $90 + 6 = 96$

Sale price online = $120 - 0.3 \cdot 120 = 84$
Shipping cost = 20

The total cost online is correct. ------ Total cost online = $84 + 20 = 104$

The total cost is less at the store than online.

No credit solution

The student wrongly interpreted a 25% discount as a $25 discount and a 5% sales tax as a $5 sales tax. -----

Total cost at store = Retail price − Discount + Sales tax
= $120 - 25 + 5 = 100$

Total cost online = Retail price − Discount + Shipping
= $120 - 30 + 20 = 110$

The total cost at the store and ------ The CD player costs $100 at the store and $110 online.
the total cost online are incorrect, and the question isn't answered.

Checkpoint

Score each solution to the short response question below as *full credit*, *partial credit*, or *no credit*. Explain your reasoning.

Problem The speed of light is about 3×10^8 meters per second in space. In 2 hours, how many meters does light travel? Write your answer in scientific notation.

Watch *Out*

When solving a problem that involves measurements, convert between units if necessary.

1. $(3 \times 10^8) \div 2 = 1.5 \times 10^8$. In 2 h, light travels 1.5×10^8 m.

2. Because $\dfrac{60 \text{ sec}}{1 \text{ min}} \times \dfrac{60 \text{ min}}{1 \text{ h}} \times 2 \text{ h} = 7200 \text{ sec}$, there are 7200 seconds in 2 hours. In 2 hours, light travels $7200 \times (3 \times 10^8) = 21{,}600 \times 10^8 = 2.16 \times 10^{12}$ meters.

3. Because 60 sec = 1 min and 60 min = 1 h, there are 3600 seconds in 1 hour. So, light travels $3600 \times (3 \times 10^8) = 1.08 \times 10^{12}$ meters.

Short Response

1. You are arranging 48 tables for a science fair. You want each row to have the same number of tables. You can have at most 6 tables per row and at most 20 rows. How many different arrangements are possible?

2. The table shows the mean distance of each planet from the Sun. Write the mean distances in standard notation. Then list the planets in order from the least to the greatest mean distance from the Sun.

Planet	Distance from Sun (km)
Earth	1.496×10^8
Jupiter	7.784×10^8
Mars	2.279×10^8
Mercury	5.79×10^7
Neptune	4.4982×10^9
Saturn	1.4267×10^9
Uranus	2.8709×10^9
Venus	1.082×10^8

3. A recipe calls for $\frac{2}{3}$ cup of milk, $\frac{1}{2}$ cup of sugar, and $2\frac{1}{4}$ cups of flour. You need to reduce the recipe by half. How much of each ingredient do you need?

4. A model train is $5\frac{1}{4}$ inches long. The scale used for the model is 1 inch : 160 inches. What is the length of the actual train?

5. A store sells hot dogs in packages of 10 and hot dog buns in packages of 6. You want to buy an equal number of hot dogs and hot dog buns. What is the least number of packages of hot dogs and hot dog buns you can buy?

6. For 5 days a week, you walk from home to school and back home. It takes you 14 minutes to walk each way. How many hours per week do you spend walking from home to school and back home? Write your answer as a mixed number.

7. You are ordering dinner at a restaurant. For the pasta, you can choose spaghetti, ziti, or shells. For a pasta topping, you can choose meatballs, veal, chicken, or eggplant. For the sauce, you can choose tomato sauce or cheese sauce. How many dinner combinations are possible?

8. You enlarge a 4 inch by 6 inch photo so that the shorter side is 8.5 inches long. What is the length of the longer side?

9. The original price of a hat is $28. You can buy it online for $17, or you can buy it at the store and use a coupon for a 30% discount. Does the hat cost less if you buy it online or at the store?

10. The circle graph shows the results of a survey asking 800 students what they prefer to receive as a gift. Of the students surveyed, how many more chose clothes than sports equipment?

Gift Preferences

- Clothes 37%
- Sports equipment 29%
- Toys 18%
- Gift certificates 10%
- Other 6%

11. The odds in favor of your winning a raffle are 1 to 49. The odds in favor of your friend's winning are 3 to 140. Who has the greater chance of winning the raffle, you or your friend? Explain your reasoning.

Multiple Choice

12. What is the prime factorization of 620?

A. $2 \cdot 3^2 \cdot 5 \cdot 7$ **B.** $2 \cdot 5 \cdot 61$

C. $2^2 \cdot 5 \cdot 31$ **D.** $2^7 \cdot 5$

13. What is the greatest common factor of $15x^3y^5$ and $6xy^2$?

F. $30x^3y^5$ **G.** $3xy^2$ **H.** $3x^3y^5$ **I.** $30xy^2$

14. Suppose you deposit $400 into an account that earns 3% simple annual interest. What is the account balance after 9 months?

A. $9 **B.** $108 **C.** $409 **D.** $508

15. Given $\triangle ABC \sim \triangle DEF$, what is the length of $\overline{DE}$?

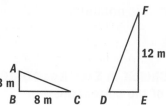

F. 2 m **G.** 4.5 m **H.** 24 m **I.** 32 m

16. You toss a coin 15 times, and the coin lands heads up 9 times. What is the experimental probability that the coin lands heads up?

A. 0.4 **B.** 0.5 **C.** 0.6 **D.** 0.9

17. What is the solution of the equation $1.6x - 5.2 = 9.28$?

F. 1.48 **G.** 2.55 **H.** 9.05 **I.** 11

18. Simplify the expression $\frac{4r^3}{5} \cdot \frac{15r^2}{14}$.

A. $\frac{6r^5}{7}$ **B.** $\frac{6r^6}{7}$ **C.** $\frac{64r^5}{75}$ **D.** $\frac{64r^6}{75}$

19. What is the percent of change from 76 to 190?

F. 60% **G.** 114% **H.** 150% **I.** 350%

20. A map has a scale of 1 cm : 150 m. If a map distance is 2.5 centimeters, what is the actual distance?

A. 151.5 meters **B.** 225 meters

C. 300 meters **D.** 375 meters

Extended Response

21. The table shows the population of Washington, D.C., every 10 years from 1950 to 2000.

a. Make a data display that shows the population for those years.

b. In which year did the population decrease the most from 10 years earlier, and what was the approximate percent of change?

c. Can you conclude from the table that the population of Washington, D.C., has decreased every year since 1950? Explain your reasoning.

Year	Population
1950	802,000
1960	764,000
1970	757,000
1980	638,000
1990	607,000
2000	572,000

22. A store sells granola bars in boxes of 8 and 20. A box of 8 bars costs $3.12, and a box of 20 bars costs $7.00.

a. List all the possible ways that you can buy exactly 80 granola bars.

b. How should you buy exactly 80 granola bars if you want to spend the least amount of money? Explain your reasoning.

Chapter 4

Multiple Choice In Exercises 1–7, choose the letter of the correct answer.

1. Which expression is equivalent to $x \cdot x \cdot y \cdot y \cdot y$? *(Lesson 4.1)*

   A. $6xy$ **B.** $x^2 y^3$ **C.** $2xy^3$ **D.** $3x^2 y$

2. What is the greatest common factor of $6mn$ and $27m^3$? *(Lesson 4.2)*

   F. $3m$ **G.** $3m^3 n$ **H.** $6m$ **I.** $54m^3 n$

3. Which expression is equivalent to $\dfrac{18a^6}{3a^2}$? *(Lesson 4.3)*

   A. $6a^3$ **B.** $6a^4$ **C.** $15a^3$ **D.** $15a^4$

4. What is the LCM of 32 and 48? *(Lesson 4.4)*

   F. 6   **G.** 48   **H.** 96   **I.** 144

5. Which expression is equivalent to $-2x^2 \cdot 3x^3 y$? *(Lesson 4.5)*

   A. $-6x^5 y$ **B.** $-6x^2 y$ **C.** $-6x^6 y$ **D.** x^2

6. Which list of numbers is ordered from least to greatest? *(Lesson 4.6)*

   F. $3^{-2}, 5^0, 2^{-3}, -7$ **G.** $2^{-3}, 3^{-2}, -7, 5^0$

   H. $-7, 3^{-2}, 5^0, 2^{-3}$ **I.** $-7, 3^{-2}, 2^{-3}, 5^0$

7. Which number is equivalent to 8×10^{-3}? *(Lesson 4.7)*

   A. 8000   **B.** 800   **C.** 0.08   **D.** 0.008

8. **Short Response** You are arranging 60 pictures on a poster board. The board can fit up to 4 rows of pictures, and each row can have up to 20 pictures. You want each row to have the same number of pictures. How many different ways can you arrange the pictures? *(Lesson 4.1)*

9. **Extended Response** The table shows the typical lengths of four species of roundworm. *(Lesson 4.7)*

Roundworm	Length (m)
Monochus	3.4×10^{-3}
Cephalobus	6×10^{-4}
Placentonema gigantissima	7.9×10^0
Syphacia peromysci	9.1×10^{-4}

   a. Order the lengths from least to greatest.

   b. How many meters less is the length of the shortest roundworm than the length of the next shortest roundworm? Write your answer in standard form and in scientific notation.

Chapter 5

Multiple Choice In Exercises 10–16, choose the letter of the correct answer.

10. Which fraction is equivalent to 0.8? *(Lesson 5.1)*

    A. $\dfrac{9}{10}$ **B.** $\dfrac{8}{9}$ **C.** $\dfrac{6}{7}$ **D.** $\dfrac{4}{5}$

11. Your pants have a length of 30 inches. A tailor cuts off $2\dfrac{1}{3}$ inches from the length so that the pants fit you. How long are the pants now? *(Lesson 5.2)*

    F. $27\dfrac{1}{3}$ inches   **G.** $27\dfrac{2}{3}$ inches

    H. $28\dfrac{1}{3}$ inches   **I.** $28\dfrac{2}{3}$ inches

12. Simplify the expression $\dfrac{a}{3} + \dfrac{3a}{4}$. *(Lesson 5.3)*

    A. $\dfrac{4a}{7}$ **B.** $\dfrac{13a}{12}$ **C.** $\dfrac{a}{3}$ **D.** $\dfrac{7a}{12}$

13. Simplify the expression $\frac{6r}{5} \cdot \frac{15r}{2}$. *(Lesson 5.4)*

F. $9r$ **G.** $9r^2$ **H.** $\frac{4r}{25}$ **I.** $\frac{4r^2}{25}$

14. Find the quotient $\frac{3}{4} \div 1\frac{7}{8}$. *(Lesson 5.5)*

A. $\frac{1}{3}$ **B.** $\frac{2}{5}$ **C.** $\frac{2}{3}$ **D.** $1\frac{1}{14}$

15. Your friend buys a skateboard that is on sale for one third off the original price. Your friend spent $36 less than the original price. What was the original price of the skateboard? *(Lesson 5.6)*

F. $12 **G.** $72 **H.** $108 **I.** $144

16. Which number is *not* a solution of the inequality $-\frac{3}{4}x - \frac{1}{4} \le 3$? *(Lesson 5.7)*

A. $-4\frac{2}{3}$ **B.** $-3\frac{1}{3}$ **C.** $3\frac{1}{3}$ **D.** $4\frac{2}{3}$

17. Short Response You agree to donate $.10 for every $\frac{1}{4}$ mile that your friend runs in a race for charity. If your friend runs 15 miles, how much money will you donate? Explain your reasoning. *(Lesson 5.6)*

18. Extended Response You have $1275.25 to buy stock in a company. Your stockbroker charges a brokerage fee of $12.75 for each transaction. Each share is currently worth $25.75. *(Lesson 5.7)*

a. How many shares can you buy in one transaction?

b. You save $800 to buy more stock. Each share is now worth $31.49. How many shares can you buy in one transaction of $800?

c. Suppose that the shares in parts (a) and (b) are now worth $28.36 each. What is the total value of the shares? Explain your reasoning.

Chapter 6

Multiple Choice In Exercises 19–25, choose the letter of the correct answer.

19. Which rate is equivalent to $\frac{40 \text{ m}}{1 \text{ sec}}$? *(Lesson 6.1)*

A. $\frac{2.4 \text{ km}}{1 \text{ h}}$ **B.** $\frac{24 \text{ km}}{1 \text{ h}}$

C. $\frac{144 \text{ km}}{1 \text{ h}}$ **D.** $\frac{1440 \text{ km}}{1 \text{ h}}$

20. You can buy 3 pens for $2. How much money will you spend if you buy 15 pens? *(Lesson 6.2)*

F. $10 **G.** $15 **H.** $30 **I.** $60

21. What is the solution of the proportion $\frac{8}{y} = \frac{5}{7}$? *(Lesson 6.3)*

A. 5.4 **B.** 5.7 **C.** 6 **D.** 11.2

22. Given $\triangle ABC \sim \triangle DEF$, which statement is *not* necessarily true? *(Lesson 6.4)*

F. $\angle A \cong \angle D$ **G.** $\overline{AC} \cong \overline{DF}$

H. $\frac{AB}{DE} = \frac{AC}{DF}$ **I.** $\frac{AB}{DE} = \frac{BC}{EF}$

23. Rectangle $ABCD$ is similar to rectangle $EFGH$. What is the length of $\overline{EF}$? *(Lesson 6.5)*

A. 6.3 **B.** 7.5 **C.** 9 **D.** 9.6

24. An airplane is 38.75 feet tall. A model of the airplane is 7.75 inches tall. What is the scale used for the model? *(Lesson 6.6)*

F. 1 in. : 0.2 ft **G.** 1 in. : 5 ft

H. 5 in. : 1 ft **I.** 7 in. : 38 ft

25. You roll a number cube. What are the odds in favor of rolling a number less than 3? *(Lesson 6.7)*

A. 1 to 3   **B.** 1 to 2   **C.** 3 to 7   **D.** 3 to 5

26. Short Response You can do 45 sit-ups in a minute. Your friend can do 40 sit-ups in a minute. At these rates, how many more sit-ups can you do than your friend in 4.5 minutes? Explain your steps. *(Lesson 6.1)*

27. Extended Response Six numbers are written on slips of paper and placed in one of two hats, as shown. You randomly choose a number from each hat. *(Lesson 6.8)*

First hat

Second hat

a. Use a tree diagram to list all the possible outcomes of choosing two numbers.

b. What is the probability that the sum of the two numbers you choose is even?

c. The number 3 is written on a slip of paper and placed in the first hat. Does the probability of choosing two numbers whose sum is even *increase*, *decrease*, or *stay the same*? Explain.

Chapter 7

Multiple Choice In Exercises 28–34, choose the letter of the correct answer.

28. What is 40% of 2100? *(Lesson 7.1)*

A. 84   **B.** 525   **C.** 840   **D.** 2060

29. 6 is what percent of 16? *(Lesson 7.2)*

F. $2\frac{2}{3}\%$ **G.** $37\frac{1}{2}\%$ **H.** 96%   **I.** 267%

30. What is 3.4% of 8700? *(Lesson 7.3)*

A. 29.58   **B.** 295.8   **C.** 2958   **D.** 29,580

31. 27 is 18% of what number? *(Lesson 7.4)*

F. 4.86   **G.** 45   **H.** 48.6   **I.** 150

32. What is the new amount when 70 is increased by 30%? *(Lesson 7.5)*

A. 73   **B.** 91   **C.** 100   **D.** 2100

33. You are ordering pizzas for home delivery. The pizzas cost $18. The sales tax is 6%, and you plan to give a 15% tip. What is the total cost of the order? *(Lesson 7.6)*

F. $18.21   **G.** $20.10   **H.** $21.78   **I.** $37.80

34. You deposit $1000 into an account that earns 10% interest compounded annually. What is the balance of the account after 2 years? *(Lesson 7.7)*

A. $1200   **B.** $1210   **C.** $1800   **D.** $3528

35. Short Response A computer is on sale for 25% off the original price of $800. You must pay a sales tax of 6.5% of the sale price. How much money do you spend for the computer? Explain your steps. *(Lesson 7.6)*

36. Extended Response Suppose you deposit $500 into an account that earns 3% simple annual interest, and your friend deposits $400 into an account that earns 5% simple annual interest. *(Lesson 7.7)*

a. Copy and complete the table.

Years	Your account balance	Your friend's account balance
1	?	?
3	?	?
5	?	?
10	?	?

b. After how many years will the balance in your friend's account equal the balance in your account? Explain your reasoning.

Functions, Geometry, *and* Measurement

Chapter 8 **Linear Functions**

- Represent and interpret relations and functions.
- Write and graph linear equations in two variables.
- Write and graph linear systems and linear inequalities.

Chapter 9 **Real Numbers and Right Triangles**

- Use square roots and the Pythagorean theorem to solve problems.
- Identify rational and irrational numbers.
- Use special right triangles and trigonometric ratios to solve problems.

Chapter 10 **Measurement, Area, and Volume**

- Find angle measures and side lengths of triangles and quadrilaterals.
- Find the areas of parallelograms, trapezoids, and circles.
- Find the surface areas and volumes of prisms, cylinders, pyramids, and cones.

From Chapter 10, p. 544
What is the surface area of a pyramid?

Linear Functions

BEFORE

In previous chapters you've . . .

• Located points in a coordinate plane

• Written and solved equations and inequalities

Now

In Chapter 8 you'll study . . .

• Representing relations and functions

• Finding and interpreting slopes of lines

• Writing and graphing linear equations in two variables

• Graphing and solving systems of linear equations

• Graphing linear inequalities in two variables

WHY?

So you can solve real-world problems about . . .

• hurricanes, p. 389

• transportation, p. 401

• horseback riding, p. 409

• robotics, p. 416

• marathons, p. 424

• rivers, p. 430

• video, p. 440

How can you use math to describe the steepness of a bike trail?

CHAPTER 8
INTERNET Preview
CLASSZONE.COM

- eEdition Plus Online
- eWorkbook Plus Online
- eTutorial Plus Online
- State Test Practice
- More Examples

MATH *In the **Real World***

Bike Trails The steepness of a bike trail, such as the Slickrock Trail in Utah, can be described by the ratio of the change in elevation to the horizontal distance traveled. In this chapter, you will use *slope* to compare the vertical change to the horizontal change between two points on a line in a coordinate plane.

What do you think? Suppose one bike trail rises 15 feet over a horizontal distance of 100 feet. Another trail rises 5 feet over a horizontal distance of 40 feet. Which trail do you think is steeper? Why?

Chapter Prerequisite Skills

PREREQUISITE SKILLS QUIZ

Review Vocabulary
equation, p. 85
solving an equation, p. 86
inequality, p. 138

Preparing for Success **To prepare for success in this chapter, test your knowledge of these concepts and skills. You may want to look at the pages referred to in blue for additional review.**

1. **Vocabulary** Describe the difference between an equation and an inequality.

2. **School Trip** You are saving money for a school trip. You have saved $156. This is $62 less than the trip costs. How much money does the trip cost? *(p. 91)*

Solve the equation. Check your solution. *(p. 125)*

3. $4(7 - 2t) = 4$

4. $-18 = 3(w - 1)$

5. $11y + 9 - 5y = -15$

6. $29 + 4(f + 2) = -7$

Write an inequality represented by the graph. *(p. 138)*

7.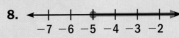
   $-3 \; -2 \; -1 \quad 0 \quad 1 \quad 2 \quad 3$

8.
   $-7 \; -6 \; -5 \; -4 \; -3 \; -2$

Solve the inequality. Graph your solution. *(pp. 138, 144)*

9. $x + 14 < 25$

10. $-5y \le 150$

11. $\dfrac{n}{3} \ge 11$

12. $m - 6 > 21$

NOTETAKING STRATEGIES

Note *Worthy*

You will find a notetaking strategy at the beginning of each chapter. Look for additional notetaking and study strategies throughout the chapter.

USING COLOR You may find it helpful to use color to identify important pieces of information and show how they are related to each other.

$5x + 6 + 9x + 2$

$= 5x + 6 + 9x + 2$ Use color to identify like terms.

$= 5x + 9x + 6 + 2$ Group like terms.

$= 14x + 8$ Combine like terms.

In Lesson 8.4, you can use color when finding slopes of lines.

8.1

Relations *and* Functions

Vocabulary

relation, p. 385
domain, p. 385
range, p. 385
input, p. 385
output, p. 385
function, p. 386
vertical line test, p. 387

BEFORE	Now	WHY?
You graphed ordered pairs.	You'll use graphs to represent relations and functions.	So you can show the growth of a bird over time, as in Ex. 26.

Alligators The table below shows the ages and lengths of five alligators.

Age (years), x	2	4	5	5	7
Length (in.), y	32	59	65	69	96

You can represent the relationship between age and length using the ordered pairs (x, y):

(2, 32), (4, 59), (5, 65), (5, 69), (7, 96)

The ordered pairs form a *relation*. A **relation** is a pairing of numbers in one set, called the **domain**, with numbers in another set, called the **range**. Each number in the domain is an **input**. Each number in the range is an **output**. For a relation represented by ordered pairs, the inputs are the x-coordinates and the outputs are the y-coordinates.

Example 1   *Identifying the Domain and Range*

a. Identify the domain and range of the relation given above.

b. Identify the domain and range of the relation represented by the table below, which shows one alligator's length at different ages.

Age (years), x	1	2	3	4	5
Length (in.), y	23	36	47	61	73

Solution

a. The domain of the relation is the set of all inputs, or x-coordinates. The range is the set of all outputs, or y-coordinates.

Domain: 2, 4, 5, 7   **Range:** 32, 59, 65, 69, 96

b. The relation consists of the ordered pairs (1, 23), (2, 36), (3, 47), (4, 61), and (5, 73). The domain and range are shown below.

Domain: 1, 2, 3, 4, 5   **Range:** 23, 36, 47, 61, 73

Study *Strategy*

When you specify a domain or range, you should list each repeated value only once. In part (a) of Example 1, for instance, the domain is 2, 4, 5, 7, not 2, 4, 5, 5, 7.

 *Checkpoint*

Identify the domain and range of the relation.

1. (0, 1), (2, 4), (3, 7), (5, 4)   **2.** $(-1, 2), (-3, -1), (6, 0), (-1, 4)$

Representing Relations In addition to using ordered pairs or a table to represent a relation, you can also use a graph or a *mapping diagram*.

Example 2   *Representing a Relation*

Represent the relation (−1, 1), (2, 0), (3, 1), (3, 2), (4, 5) as indicated.

a. A graph

b. A mapping diagram

Solution

a. Graph the ordered pairs as points in a coordinate plane.

b. List the inputs and the outputs in order. Draw arrows from the inputs to their outputs.

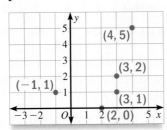

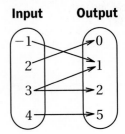

Functions A relation is a **function** if for each input there is *exactly one* output. In this case, the output *is a function of* the input.

Example 3   *Identifying Functions*

Tell whether the relation is a function.

a. The relation at the top of page 385, consisting of the ordered pairs (age, length) for five different alligators:

(2, 32), (4, 59), (5, 65), (5, 69), (7, 96)

b. The relation in part (b) of Example 1, consisting of the ordered pairs (age, length) for one alligator at different times:

(1, 23), (2, 36), (3, 47), (4, 61), (5, 73)

Solution

a. The relation *is not* a function because the input 5 is paired with two outputs, 65 and 69. This makes sense, as two alligators of the same age do not necessarily have the same length.

b. The relation *is* a function because every input is paired with exactly one output. This makes sense, as a single alligator can have only one length at a given point in time.

In the Real World

Alligators A newborn alligator is about 8 to 10 inches long. If the alligator is well fed, it will grow roughly 1 foot per year until it reaches a length of about 11 feet. What is the approximate length, in inches, of a 6-year-old alligator?

✔ *Checkpoint*

Represent the relation as a graph and as a mapping diagram. Then tell whether the relation is a function. Explain your reasoning.

3. (0, 3), (1, 2), (2, −1), (4, 4), (5, 4)   **4.** (−2, −1), (0, 2), (2, 3), (−2, −4)

Vertical Line Test When a relation is represented by a graph, you can use the *vertical line test* to tell whether the relation is a function. The **vertical line test** says that if you can find a vertical line passing through more than one point of the graph, then the relation *is not* a function. Otherwise, the relation *is* a function.

Study *Strategy*

In part (b) of Example 4, notice why the vertical line test works. Because the vertical line at $x = 3$ intersects the graph twice, the input 3 must be paired with two outputs, 1 and -2. So, the graph does not represent a function.

Example 4	*Using the Vertical Line Test*

a. In the graph below, no vertical line passes through more than one point. So, the relation represented by the graph *is* a function.

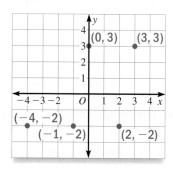

b. In the graph below, the vertical line shown passes through two points. So, the relation represented by the graph *is not* a function.

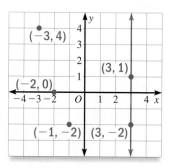

8.1 Exercises

More Practice, p. 810

Guided Practice

Vocabulary Check

1. Copy and complete: A relation is a(n) _?_ if for each input there is exactly one output.

2. Draw a mapping diagram that represents a relation with domain $-1, 0, 2$ and range 1, 4. Is only one answer possible? Explain.

Skill Check **Identify the domain and range of the relation.**

3. $(0, 0), (1, 2), (2, 4), (3, 6), (4, 8)$ **4.** $(2, 5), (-5, 2), (1, 5), (2, -3), (7, 5)$

Represent the relation as a graph and as a mapping diagram. Then tell whether the relation is a function. Explain your reasoning.

5. $(1, 2), (1, 5), (2, 4), (3, 3), (4, 1)$ **6.** $(-4, 2), (2, 3), (4, 8), (0, 3), (-2, 2)$

7. Error Analysis Describe and correct the error in the given statement.

> The relation $(1, -5), (2, -5), (3, 6), (4, 11)$ is not a function because the inputs 1 and 2 are both paired with the output -5.

Practice and Problem Solving

Homework *Help*

Example	Exercises
1	8-11, 21, 24
2	13-16, 21
3	13-17, 21
4	18-20, 22, 24

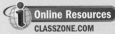

Online Resources
CLASSZONE.COM

• More Examples
• eTutorial Plus

Identify the domain and range of the relation.

8. $(-2, 5), (-1, 2), (0, 4), (1, -9)$

9. $(7, 3), (7, 6), (7, 9), (3, 3), (3, 6)$

10.

x	4	2	−3	4	−4
y	0	−1	0	−1	0

11.

x	1.5	1.5	2.8	2.8	6.5
y	4.3	6.5	4.3	3.9	0.2

12. Copy and complete using *always*, *sometimes*, or *never*: A relation is _?_ a function.

Represent the relation as a graph and as a mapping diagram. Then tell whether the relation is a function. Explain your reasoning.

13. $(1, 2), (2, 1), (3, 0), (3, 4), (4, 3)$

14. $(0, 4), (2, 0), (6, -4), (-4, 2), (8, 0)$

15.

x	−2	−1	0	1	2
y	−3	−3	−3	−3	−3

16.

x	0	−5	−10	5	−10
y	15	−10	−5	−15	20

17. Height The height of a person is measured every year from the age of 1 year to the age of 50 years.

    a. Do the ordered pairs (age, height) represent a function? Explain.

    b. Critical Thinking Would you expect the ordered pairs (height, age) to represent a function? Why or why not?

Tell whether the relation represented by the graph is a function.

18.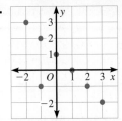

19.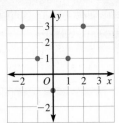

20.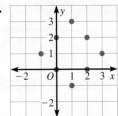

21. Basketball The table shows the numbers of games played and points scored by each starting player on the New Jersey Nets basketball team during the team's 2001–2002 regular season.

Player	Games played, x	Points scored, y
Todd MacCulloch	62	604
Kenyon Martin	73	1086
Keith Van Horn	81	1199
Kerry Kittles	82	1102
Jason Kidd	82	1208

    a. Identify the domain and range of the relation given by the ordered pairs (x, y).

    b. Draw a mapping diagram for the relation.

    c. Is the relation a function? Explain.

22. Hurricanes In 1995, a total of 32 regular weather advisories were issued during the storm that became Hurricane Opal. The graph shows the wind speed inside Opal at the time of each advisory.

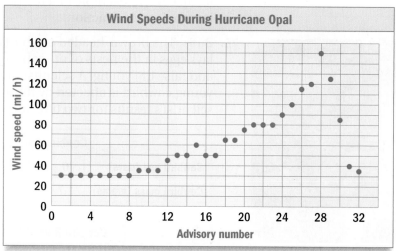

Wind Speeds During Hurricane Opal

Computer-enhanced satellite image of a hurricane

a. Is wind speed a function of advisory number? Explain.

b. Estimation An ocean storm is considered a hurricane if its wind speed is at least 74 miles per hour. For which advisories did Opal qualify as a hurricane?

23. *Writing* Suppose a relation is represented as a set of ordered pairs and as a mapping diagram. Which representation more clearly shows whether or not the relation is a function? Explain.

24. Extended Problem Solving A skydiver uses an altimeter to track altitude so that he or she knows when to open the parachute. The altimeter determines altitude by measuring changes in atmospheric pressure. The graph below shows how pressure varies with altitude as a skydiver falls from 12,000 feet to ground level. (The elevation of the ground is assumed to be 0 feet with respect to sea level.)

Reading *Algebra*

In the graph for Exercise 24, the symbol ⌇ on the vertical axis indicates a break in the scale. The interval between the first two tick marks represents 1200 lb/ft², while the interval between other consecutive tick marks represents only 200 lb/ft².

a. As a skydiver falls, does the atmospheric pressure increase or decrease? Does the reading on the skydiver's altimeter increase or decrease?

b. *Writing* Describe the domain and range of the relation represented by the graph.

c. Is the relation a function? Explain.

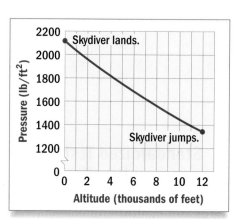

d. Interpret and Apply Some altimeters can sound an alarm warning a skydiver to open the parachute when the altitude falls to a certain level. If the alarm is set to go off at an altitude of 3000 feet, approximately what atmospheric pressure will trigger the alarm?

Lesson 8.1 Relations and Functions **389**

25. **Challenge** To form the *inverse* of a relation represented by a set of ordered pairs, you switch the coordinates of each ordered pair. For example, the inverse of the relation (1, 2), (3, 4), (5, 6) is (2, 1), (4, 3), (6, 5). Give an example of a relation that is a function, but whose inverse is *not* a function.

26. **Birds** The brown-headed cowbird does not raise its own offspring. It lays eggs in the nests of other bird species, which then hatch the eggs and raise the young. A scientist investigated whether the growth of a young cowbird is affected by the species of bird that raises it. The scientist's results for two bird species are shown below.

Nest with three wood thrush eggs and one cowbird egg

Cowbird Raised by Red-Eyed Vireo								
Cowbird age (days)	0	2	4	6	8	10	12	14
Cowbird mass (grams)	1.7	4.5	10.7	20.0	28.3	33.0	35.0	35.7

Cowbird Raised by Blue-Gray Gnatcatcher								
Cowbird age (days)	0	2	4	6	8	10	12	14
Cowbird mass (grams)	2.2	5.2	10.1	15.5	19.3	21.2	22.0	22.3

a. For each table, draw a graph for the relation given by the ordered pairs (age, mass). Draw both graphs in the same coordinate plane, and use a different color for each graph.

b. **Interpret** Compare the graphs from part (a). How is a cowbird's growth when raised by a red-eyed vireo like its growth when raised by a blue-gray gnatcatcher? How is its growth different?

Mixed Review

Evaluate the expression when $x = -5$ and $y = -7$. *(Lessons 1.5–1.7)*

27. $x + y$ 28. $y - x + 10$ 29. $2x^2y$ 30. $3x - 4y$

Tell whether the given value of the variable is a solution of the equation. *(Lesson 2.4)*

31. $x + 11 = 3; x = -8$

32. $-17 - a = -23; a = -6$

33. $-6m = -84; m = 13$

34. $\frac{-144}{u} = 12; u = -12$

For an account that earns simple annual interest, find the interest and the balance of the account. *(Lesson 7.7)*

35. $P = \$850, r = 3\%, t = 6$ years

36. $P = \$4200, r = 5\%, t = 7.5$ years

Standardized Test Practice

37. **Extended Response** The table shows the amount charged for standard ground shipping by an online electronics store.

a. Is shipping cost a function of merchandise cost? Explain.

b. Is merchandise cost a function of shipping cost? Explain.

Total cost of merchandise	Shipping cost
$.01–$25.00	$5.95
$25.01–$50.00	$7.95
$50.01–$75.00	$9.95
$75.01–$100.00	$11.95
Over $100.00	$13.95

8.2

Linear Equations *in* Two Variables

Vocabulary

equation in two variables, p. 391
solution of an equation in two variables, p. 391
graph of an equation in two variables, p. 392
linear equation, p. 392
function form, p. 393

BEFORE	*Now*	**WHY?**
You solved equations in one variable.	You'll find solutions of equations in two variables.	So you can find the speed of a platypus, as in Ex. 41.

Volcanoes The Hawaiian volcano Mauna Loa has erupted many times. In 1859, lava from the volcano traveled 32 miles to the Pacific Ocean at an average speed of 4 miles per hour. In Example 2, you'll see how to use an *equation in two variables* to describe the flow of the lava toward the ocean.

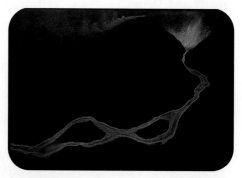

An example of an **equation in two variables** is $2x - y = 5$. A **solution** of an equation in x and y is an ordered pair (x, y) that produces a true statement when the values of x and y are substituted into the equation.

Example 1 | *Checking Solutions*

Tell whether the ordered pair is a solution of $2x - y = 5$.

  a. $(1, -3)$ **b.** $(4, 7)$

Solution

a. $2x - y = 5$ Write original equation.

     $2(1) - (-3) \stackrel{?}{=} 5$ Substitute 1 for x and -3 for y.

              $5 = 5$ ✓   Simplify.

Answer $(1, -3)$ is a solution of $2x - y = 5$.

b. $2x - y = 5$ Write original equation.

    $2(4) - 7 \stackrel{?}{=} 5$ Substitute 4 for x and 7 for y.

         $1 \neq 5$ Simplify.

Answer $(4, 7)$ is not a solution of $2x - y = 5$.

 Checkpoint

Tell whether the ordered pair is a solution of $3x + 2y = -8$.

  1. $(0, 4)$ **2.** $(-2, -1)$ **3.** $(4, -12)$ **4.** $(10, -19)$

Example 2 *Finding Solutions*

For the 1859 Mauna Loa eruption described on page 391, the lava's distance d (in miles) from the ocean t hours after it left the volcano can be approximated by the equation $d = 32 - 4t$.

  a. Make a table of solutions for the equation.

  b. How long did it take the lava to reach the ocean?

Solution

  a. Substitute values of t into the equation $d = 32 - 4t$, and find values of d. The table shows that the following ordered pairs are solutions of the equation:

t	Substitution	d
0	$d = 32 - 4(0)$	32
1	$d = 32 - 4(1)$	28
2	$d = 32 - 4(2)$	24

    (0, 32), (1, 28), (2, 24)

  b. Find the value of t when $d = 0$.

$0 = 32 - 4t$	Substitute 0 for d in the equation $d = 32 - 4t$.
$-32 = -4t$	Subtract 32 from each side.
$8 = t$	Divide each side by -4.

  Answer It took the lava about 8 hours to reach the ocean.

In the **Real World**

Volcanoes The temperature of lava from a Hawaiian volcano is about 1160°C. You can use the equation $F = 1.8C + 32$ to convert a Celsius temperature C to a Fahrenheit temperature F. What is the lava's temperature in degrees Fahrenheit?

Graphs The **graph** of an equation in two variables is the set of points in a coordinate plane that represent all the solutions of the equation. An equation whose graph is a line is called a **linear equation**.

Example 3 *Graphing a Linear Equation*

Graph $y = 2x - 1$.

  ① Make a table of solutions.

x	-2	-1	0	1	2
y	-5	-3	-1	1	3

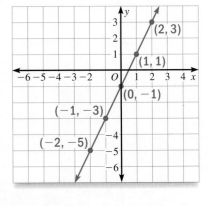

  ② List the solutions as ordered pairs.

    $(-2, -5)$, $(-1, -3)$, $(0, -1)$, $(1, 1)$, $(2, 3)$

  ③ Graph the ordered pairs, and note that the points lie on a line. Draw the line, which is the graph of $y = 2x - 1$.

Study *Strategy*

In Example 3, *every* point on the line shown represents a solution of $y = 2x - 1$, not just the points from the table. For instance, you can verify that the point (0.5, 0) on the line is a solution:

$$y = 2x - 1$$
$$0 \overset{?}{=} 2(0.5) - 1$$
$$0 = 0 ✓$$

✔ *Checkpoint*

Graph the equation.

  5. $y = 2x$ **6.** $y = -x + 3$ **7.** $y = 3x - 4$ **8.** $y = \frac{1}{2}x + 1$

Horizontal and Vertical Lines The graph of the equation $y = b$ is the horizontal line through $(0, b)$. The graph of the equation $x = a$ is the vertical line through $(a, 0)$.

Study *Strategy*

In Example 4, notice that the graph of $y = 3$ consists of all points with a y-coordinate of 3. Similarly, the graph of $x = -2$ consists of all points with an x-coordinate of -2.

Example 4 | *Graphing Horizontal and Vertical Lines*

Graph $y = 3$ and $x = -2$.

a. The graph of the equation $y = 3$ is the horizontal line through $(0, 3)$.

b. The graph of the equation $x = -2$ is the vertical line through $(-2, 0)$.

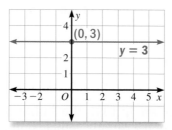
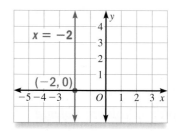

Equations as Functions In Examples 3 and 4, the vertical line test shows that $y = 2x - 1$ and $y = 3$ are functions, while $x = -2$ is not a function. In general, a linear equation is a function *unless* its graph is a vertical line. An equation that is solved for y is in **function form**. You may find it helpful to write an equation in function form before graphing it.

Not function form: $3x + y = 7$ | **Function form:** $y = -3x + 7$

Example 5 | *Writing an Equation in Function Form*

Write $x + 2y = 6$ in function form. Then graph the equation.

To write the equation in function form, solve for y.

$x + 2y = 6$ | Write original equation.

$2y = -x + 6$ | Subtract x from each side.

$y = -\dfrac{1}{2}x + 3$ | Multiply each side by $\dfrac{1}{2}$.

Study *Strategy*

In the table for Example 5, only even x-values are used so that all the y-values are integers. This makes the ordered pairs (x, y) easy to graph. Be sure to choose convenient x-values when you graph an equation that involves a fraction.

To graph the equation, use its function form to make a table of solutions. Graph the ordered pairs (x, y) from the table, and draw a line through the points.

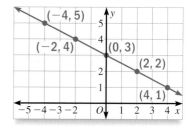

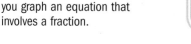

x	-4	-2	0	2	4
y	5	4	3	2	1

✔ **Checkpoint**

9. Graph $y = -1$ and $x = 4$. Tell whether each equation is a function.

10. Write $2x - 3y = 3$ in function form. Then graph the equation.

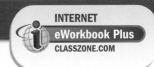

Guided Practice

Vocabulary Check

1. Copy and complete: An equation whose graph is a line is called a(n) ? .

2. Is the equation $x = 4y + 3$ in function form? Explain.

Skill Check

Tell whether the ordered pair is a solution of $y = 5x - 7$.

3. $(2, 3)$ 4. $(0, -6)$ 5. $(4, 14)$ 6. $(-3, -22)$

Graph the equation.

7. $y = x - 4$ 8. $x = -1$ 9. $y = 2$ 10. $3x + 2y = -2$

Guided Problem Solving

11. **Spacecraft** In 1997, the Pathfinder spacecraft landed on Mars. It contained a robotic vehicle named Sojourner that could roam up to 500 meters from the lander. The distance d (in meters) that Sojourner could travel in t hours is given by $d = 24t$. How long would it take Sojourner to reach its maximum distance from the lander?

    1 Copy and complete the table using the given equation.

t	0	5	10	15	20	25	30
d	?	?	?	?	?	?	?

    2 Use your completed table to graph $d = 24t$.

    3 Find the point on the graph whose d-coordinate is 500, and estimate the t-coordinate of this point. How much time would it take Sojourner to reach its maximum distance from the lander?

Practice and Problem Solving

Homework *Help*

Example	Exercises
1	12-15, 35-38
2	32-34, 39, 40
3	16-23
4	16-23
5	24-31

Tell whether the ordered pair is a solution of the equation.

12. $y = x - 3$; $(1, -4)$ 13. $y = -4x + 9$; $(3, -3)$

14. $x - 2y = 8$; $(-6, -7)$ 15. $3x - 5y = -1$; $(9, 5)$

Graph the equation. Tell whether the equation is a function.

16. $y = -x$ 17. $y = 2x - 3$ 18. $y = 1$ 19. $x = -4$

20. $y = \frac{3}{2}x + 1$ 21. $y = -5$ 22. $x = 3$ 23. $y = -5x + 2$

Write the equation in function form. Then graph the equation.

24. $y - x = -1$ 25. $2x + y = 1$ 26. $3x - y = 5$ 27. $8x + 2y = -4$

28. $x - 3y = -9$ 29. $3x + 4y = 0$ 30. $5x - 2y = 6$ 31. $2x + 3y = 12$

32. Converting Weights The formula $y = 2000x$ converts a weight x in tons to a weight y in pounds. The largest known blue whale weighed 195 tons. Find the weight of the whale in pounds.

33. Converting Units of Capacity The formula $y = 0.001x$ converts a capacity x in milliliters to a capacity y in liters. A juice can has a capacity of 355 milliliters. Find the capacity of the can in liters.

34. Converting Areas The formula $y \approx 2.59x$ converts an area x in square miles to an approximate area y in square kilometers. The state of Iowa has an area of 56,276 square miles. Find this area in square kilometers. Round your answer to the nearest thousand square kilometers.

Find the value of a that makes the ordered pair a solution of the equation.

35. $y = 2x + 5;\ (-1, a)$

36. $y = -3x - 1;\ (a, 5)$

37. $4x - 7y = 19;\ (-4, a)$

38. $6x + 5y = 21;\ (a + 2, -3)$

39. Extended Problem Solving The fork length of a shark is the distance from the tip of the shark's snout to the fork of its tail, as shown.

The table lists equations giving the fork length f as a function of the total length t for three species of sharks, where both f and t are measured in centimeters.

Species	Equation
Bigeye thresher	$f = 0.560t + 17.7$
Scalloped hammerhead	$f = 0.776t - 0.313$
White shark	$f = 0.944t - 5.74$

a. To the nearest centimeter, approximate the fork length of each given species of shark if the shark's total length is 250 centimeters.

b. Interpret For each species of shark, what percent of the total length does the fork length represent if the shark is 250 centimeters long? Round your answers to the nearest percent.

c. *Writing* Which species of shark do you think has the longest tail relative to its body size? Explain your reasoning.

40. Volcanoes The Hawaiian-Emperor chain of volcanoes is shown at the left. The age a (in millions of years) of a volcano in the chain can be approximated by $a = 0.0129d - 2.25$, where d is the volcano's distance (in kilometers) from Kilauea, measured along the chain.

a. Suiko is 4794 kilometers from Kilauea, measured along the chain. Approximate the age of Suiko to the nearest tenth of a million years.

b. Midway is about 27.7 million years old. Approximate Midway's distance along the chain from Kilauea to the nearest ten kilometers.

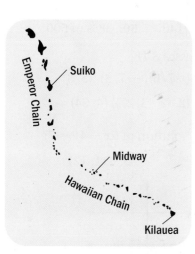

Some of the volcanoes on the map are extinct, and some are underwater.

41. Platypuses The platypus is an animal with a broad flat tail, webbed feet, and a snout like a duck's bill. Although a platypus spends much of its time in the water, it can also walk on land. The diagram below shows one complete stride of a walking platypus.

The stride frequency f is the number of strides per second the platypus takes. It can be approximated by the equation $f = 2.13s + 1.19$, where s is the speed of the platypus in meters per second.

a. Solve the given equation for s to obtain an equation that gives speed as a function of stride frequency.

b. Apply Use the equation from part (a) to approximate the speed of a platypus that takes 3 strides per second. Round your answer to the nearest tenth of a meter per second.

42. Challenge In this exercise, you will investigate the graph of $y = x^2$.

a. Copy and complete the table of solutions for $y = x^2$.

x	−3	−2	−1	0	1	2	3
y	?	?	?	?	?	?	?

b. Graph $y = x^2$ by plotting the points from the table and drawing a smooth curve that passes through all the points.

c. Is $y = x^2$ a linear equation? Is $y = x^2$ a function? Explain.

Mixed Review   Solve the equation. Check your solution. *(Lesson 3.1)*

43. $2x + 5 = -7$ **44.** $5c - 8 = 27$ **45.** $4 - 3w = 16$ **46.** $\dfrac{n}{6} + 2 = 9$

Find the percent of the number. *(Lesson 7.1)*

47. 25% of 12   **48.** 90% of 80   **49.** 75% of 140   **50.** 38% of 500

Identify the domain and range of the relation. *(Lesson 8.1)*

51. $(-2, 1)$, $(0, 2)$, $(2, 3)$, $(4, 4)$ **52.** $(5, 0)$, $(-7, 8)$, $(-7, 3)$, $(5, 3)$

53. $(6, 4)$, $(6, -2)$, $(6, 9)$, $(6, 1)$ **54.** $(1, 1)$, $(2, 8)$, $(3, 27)$, $(4, 64)$

Standardized Test Practice   **55. Multiple Choice** Which ordered pair is *not* a solution of $5x - 4y = 7$?

A. $(-9, -13)$ **B.** $(-5, -9)$ **C.** $(7, 7)$ **D.** $(11, 12)$

56. Multiple Choice The graph of which equation is shown?

F. $x = -2$ **G.** $y = -2$

H. $x = 2$ **I.** $y = 2$

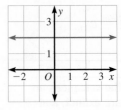

8.2 Graphing Linear Equations

Goal Use a graphing calculator to graph linear equations.

Example

Use a graphing calculator to solve the following problem.

A pool charges $6 for a summer membership, plus $1.25 per visit. The equation $C = 6 + 1.25v$ gives your cost C if you visit v times. How many times can you visit if you have $30 to spend on swimming?

1 Rewrite the equation using x and y.

$C = 6 + 1.25v$ **Write original equation.**

$y = 6 + 1.25x$ **Substitute x for v and y for C.**

2 Enter the equation.

Keystrokes   `Y=` 6 `+` 1.25 `x`

3 Press `WINDOW` to set the borders of the graph. Set the cursor increment to 1 unit: $\Delta X = 1$.

Press `GRAPH` to graph the equation. Press `TRACE` and move the cursor along the graph using `◄` and `►`.

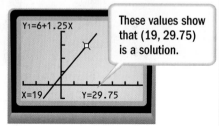

```
WINDOW
Xmin=-30
Xmax=64
ΔX=1
Xscl=10
Ymin=-10
Ymax=40
Yscl=10
```

ΔX is the increment between *x*-values when you trace.

Y₁=6+1.25X

X=19   Y=29.75

These values show that (19, 29.75) is a solution.

Answer The graph shows that you can visit 19 times for $29.75.

Tech *Help*

If the cursor moves out of view as you trace, press `ENTER` to redraw the screen with the cursor in the center.

Online Resources
CLASSZONE.COM

• Keystroke Help

Draw Conclusions

Use a graphing calculator to graph the equation. Find the unknown value in the ordered pair. (Use $\Delta X = 0.1$.)

1. $y = 5 - x$; $(1.8, \underline{\ ?\ })$

2. $y = x - 5$; $(\underline{\ ?\ }, -2.2)$

3. $y = -2.5x + 6$; $(3.2, \underline{\ ?\ })$

4. $y = -0.5x + 4$; $(\underline{\ ?\ }, 5.2)$

5. Video Games A video game store has a $15 membership fee and rents games for $3.25 each. Use a graphing calculator to graph $C = 15 + 3.25g$, which gives your cost C if you rent g games. How many games can you rent if you have $45 to spend?

Using Intercepts

BEFORE	*Now*	WHY?
You graphed using tables of solutions.	You'll use *x*- and *y*-intercepts to graph linear equations.	So you can find how much food to buy for a barbecue, as in Ex. 9.

Vocabulary

x-intercept, p. 398
y-intercept, p. 398

You can graph a linear equation quickly by recognizing that only two points are needed to draw a line. It is often convenient to choose points where the line crosses the axes.

The *x*-coordinate of a point where a graph crosses the *x*-axis is an **x-intercept**. The *y*-coordinate of a point where a graph crosses the *y*-axis is a **y-intercept**. The graph shown has an *x*-intercept of −6 and a *y*-intercept of 4.

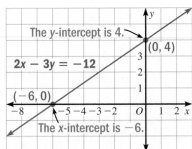

The *y*-intercept is 4.
(0, 4)
$2x - 3y = -12$
(−6, 0)
The *x*-intercept is −6.

Finding Intercepts

To find the *x*-intercept of a line, substitute 0 for *y* in the line's equation and solve for *x*.

To find the *y*-intercept of a line, substitute 0 for *x* in the line's equation and solve for *y*.

Example 1 *Finding Intercepts of a Graph*

Find the intercepts of the graph of $3x - 2y = 6$.

To find the *x*-intercept, let $y = 0$ and solve for *x*.

$3x - 2y = 6$	Write original equation.
$3x - 2(0) = 6$	Substitute 0 for *y*.
$3x = 6$	Simplify.
$x = 2$	Divide each side by 3.

To find the *y*-intercept, let $x = 0$ and solve for *y*.

$3x - 2y = 6$	Write original equation.
$3(0) - 2y = 6$	Substitute 0 for *x*.
$-2y = 6$	Simplify.
$y = -3$	Divide each side by −2.

Answer The *x*-intercept is 2, and the *y*-intercept is −3.

!

Watch *Out*

The intercepts of a graph are numbers, not ordered pairs. In Example 1, for instance, the *x*-intercept is 2, not (2, 0). Similarly, the *y*-intercept is −3, not (0, −3).

Example 2 Using Intercepts to Graph a Linear Equation

Graph the equation $3x - 2y = 6$ from Example 1.

The x-intercept is 2, so plot the point $(2, 0)$. The y-intercept is -3, so plot the point $(0, -3)$.

Draw a line through the two points.

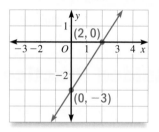

✔ Checkpoint

Find the intercepts of the equation's graph. Then graph the equation.

1. $x - 2y = -2$ **2.** $4x + 3y = 12$ **3.** $y = -2x - 8$

Example 3 Writing and Graphing an Equation

Canoeing You are canoeing along a 12 mile stretch of river. You travel 4 miles per hour when paddling and 2 miles per hour when drifting. Write and graph an equation describing your possible paddling and drifting times for the trip. Give three possible combinations of paddling and drifting times.

Solution

1 To write an equation, let x be the paddling time and let y be the drifting time (both in hours). First write a verbal model.

Paddling distance		Drifting distance		
Paddling rate	Paddling time	Drifting rate	Drifting time	Total distance

$$\text{Paddling rate} \cdot \text{Paddling time} + \text{Drifting rate} \cdot \text{Drifting time} = \text{Total distance}$$

Then use the verbal model to write the equation.

$$4x + 2y = 12$$

2 To graph the equation, find and use the intercepts.

Find x-intercept:
$$4x + 2y = 12$$
$$4x + 2(0) = 12$$
$$4x = 12$$
$$x = 3$$

Find y-intercept:
$$4x + 2y = 12$$
$$4(0) + 2y = 12$$
$$2y = 12$$
$$y = 6$$

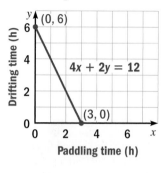

3 Three points on the graph are $(0, 6)$, $(2, 2)$, and $(3, 0)$. So, you can either not paddle at all and drift for 6 hours, or paddle for 2 hours and drift for 2 hours, or paddle for 3 hours and not drift at all.

Study *Strategy*

In Example 3, the graph lies entirely in the first quadrant because the paddling time x and the drifting time y must be nonnegative.

Guided Practice

Vocabulary Check

1. Copy and complete: For the line that passes through the points $(0, -7)$ and $(3, 0)$, the ? is -7 and the ? is 3.

2. Describe how you can find the x- and y-intercepts of a line by using the line's equation.

Skill Check **Identify the x-intercept and the y-intercept of the line.**

3.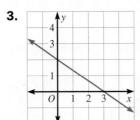

4.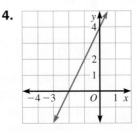

5.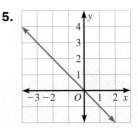

Draw the line with the given intercepts.

6. x-intercept: 4
   y-intercept: 5

7. x-intercept: -6
   y-intercept: 3

8. x-intercept: -1
   y-intercept: -2

9. **Shopping** You are in charge of buying food for a barbecue. You have budgeted \$30 for ground beef and chicken. Ground beef costs \$3 per pound, and chicken costs \$5 per pound. Write an equation describing the possible amounts of ground beef and chicken that you can buy. Use intercepts to graph the equation.

Practice and Problem Solving

Homework *Help*

Example	Exercises
1	10–18, 21–26
2	10–18, 21–26
3	19, 20, 29, 30

Online Resources
CLASSZONE.COM
• More Examples
• eTutorial Plus

Find the intercepts of the equation's graph. Then graph the equation.

10. $5x + y = 5$

11. $x - 2y = 4$

12. $3x - 2y = -6$

13. $4x + 5y = -20$

14. $4x + 3y = 24$

15. $2x - 3y = -18$

16. $y = 2x - 4$

17. $y = -x + 7$

18. $y = 3x + 9$

19. **Animal Nutrition** Your beagle is allowed to eat 800 Calories of food each day. You buy canned food containing 40 Calories per ounce and dry food containing 100 Calories per ounce.

   a. Write an equation describing the possible amounts of canned and dry food that you can feed your beagle each day.

   b. Use intercepts to graph the equation from part (a).

   c. **Apply** Give three possible combinations of canned and dry food that you can feed your beagle each day.

20. Transportation At the start of a trip, you fill up your car's fuel tank with gas. After you drive for x hours, the amount y (in gallons) of gas remaining is given by the equation $y = 18 - 2x$.

   a. Find the x-intercept and the y-intercept of the given equation's graph. Use the intercepts to graph the equation.

   b. Interpret What real-life quantities do the x- and y-intercepts represent in this situation?

   c. After how many hours of driving do you have only $\frac{1}{4}$ tank of gas left?

Find the intercepts of the equation's graph. Then graph the equation.

21. $1.9x - 1.9y = 3.8$ **22.** $2.1x + 3.5y = 10.5$ **23.** $y = 1.5x + 6$

24. $y = -\frac{2}{7}x - 2$ **25.** $\frac{1}{2}x + \frac{1}{4}y = \frac{3}{2}$ **26.** $y = \frac{7}{3}x - \frac{7}{2}$

27. Critical Thinking Write an equation of a line that has no x-intercept and an equation of a line that has no y-intercept. Describe the graph of each equation.

28. Visual Thinking For a certain line, the x-intercept is negative and the y-intercept is positive. Does the line slant *upward* or *downward* from left to right? Sketch a graph to justify your answer.

29. Extended Problem Solving At a flight school, pilots-in-training can rent single-engine airplanes for $60 per hour and twin-engine airplanes for $180 per hour. The flight school's goal is to take in $9000 in rental fees each month.

   a. Write an equation describing the number of hours per month each type of plane should be rented if the flight school is to meet its goal.

   b. Use intercepts to graph the equation from part (a).

   c. Estimation During one month, the twin-engine planes are rented for 30 hours. Use your graph to estimate how many hours the single-engine planes must be rented if the flight school is to meet its goal.

   d. Reasonableness Check your answer to part (c) by writing and solving an equation.

30. Geometry The rectangle shown has a perimeter of 16 inches.

   a. Write an equation describing the possible values of x and y.

   b. Use intercepts to graph the equation from part (a).

   c. Give three pairs of whole-number values of x and y that could represent side lengths of the rectangle.

   d. Critical Thinking Does either the x-intercept or the y-intercept represent a possible side length of the rectangle? Explain.

31. Number Sense Consider the equation $4x + 6y = c$. Find three values of c for which both the x-intercept and the y-intercept are integers. How are your values of c related to the coefficients of x and y in the given equation?

In the **Real World**

   Pilot's License To get a private pilot's license, a pilot-in-training must have 40 hours of flight time in a single-engine plane. What is the total cost of this much flight time at the flight school in Exercise 29?

32. Fitness You use a combination of running and walking to complete a race d miles long. Your running speed is r miles per hour and your walking speed is w miles per hour. Let x be your running time and let y be your walking time (both in hours). Then $rx + wy = d$.

  a. The table below shows equations of the form $rx + wy = d$. In each column, one of the values r, w, or d increases while the other two values stay the same. Draw a coordinate plane for each column, and graph the equations in the column on that plane.

r increases.	w increases.	d increases.
$3x + 2y = 18$	$9x + 2y = 18$	$6x + 2y = 12$
$6x + 2y = 18$	$9x + 3y = 18$	$6x + 2y = 18$
$9x + 2y = 18$	$9x + 6y = 18$	$6x + 2y = 24$

  b. What happens to the graph of $rx + wy = d$ when running speed increases while walking speed and racing distance stay the same?

  c. What happens to the graph of $rx + wy = d$ when walking speed increases while running speed and racing distance stay the same?

  d. What happens to the graph of $rx + wy = d$ when racing distance increases while running speed and walking speed stay the same?

33. Challenge For the graph of $y = ax + b$ where $a \neq 0$, show that the x-intercept is $-\dfrac{b}{a}$ and the y-intercept is b. Use these results to find the intercepts of the graph of $y = 3x + 12$.

Mixed Review

Evaluate the expression. *(Lessons 1.6, 1.7)*

34. $\dfrac{8 - (-1)}{4 - 1}$ **35.** $\dfrac{-3 - (-5)}{6 - 8}$ **36.** $\dfrac{4 - 24}{9 - 5}$ **37.** $\dfrac{-7 - 11}{-12 - (-3)}$

Identify the percent of change as an *increase* or *decrease*. Then find the percent of change. *(Lesson 7.5)*

38. Original: 40   **39.** Original: 60   **40.** Original: 78   **41.** Original: 250
New: 52   New: 111   New: 39   New: 195

Tell whether the ordered pair is a solution of the equation. *(Lesson 8.2)*

42. $y = -2x + 7$; $(8, -9)$ **43.** $y = 10x - 4$; $(0, 10)$

44. $5x + y = 15$; $(-6, 15)$ **45.** $3x - 8y = 12$; $(-4, -3)$

Standardized Test Practice

46. Multiple Choice What is the x-intercept of the graph of $y = 4x + 32$?

  A. -32 **B.** -8 **C.** 8 **D.** 32

47. Multiple Choice What is the y-intercept of the graph of $5x + 2y = 30$?

  F. -15 **G.** -6 **H.** 6 **I.** 15

48. Short Response A car wash charges \$8 for a basic wash and \$12 for a deluxe wash that includes a wax. On a certain day, sales at the car wash total \$960. Write and graph an equation describing the possible numbers of basic and deluxe washes that could have been done. Give three possible combinations of basic and deluxe washes.

8.4 Investigating Slope

Goal
Use slope to describe the steepness of a ramp.

Materials
- 5 books
- 2 rulers

A ramp's steepness is described by its *slope*, the ratio of the vertical rise to the horizontal run.

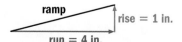

ramp
rise = 1 in.
run = 4 in.

$$\text{slope} = \frac{\text{rise}}{\text{run}} = \frac{1}{4}$$

Investigate

Use slope to describe the steepness of a ramp.

1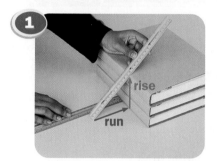

rise
run

Make a stack of books. Use one ruler as a ramp. Using the other ruler, measure and record the rise and the run of the ramp. Calculate and record the slope of the ramp.

2

Create ramps with the same rise but three different runs by moving the lower end of the ruler. Measure and record rise and the run of each ramp. Calculate and record each slope.

3

Create ramps with the same run but three different rises. Keep the lower end of the ruler in one spot. Add or subtract books to change the rise. Record the rise, the run, and the slope of each ramp.

Draw Conclusions

1. *Writing* If one ramp is steeper than a second ramp, what is true about the slopes of the two ramps?

2. **Describe** What is the relationship between the rise and the run of a ramp when the slope is 1? Explain.

3. **Critical Thinking** What happens to the slope of a ramp when the rise increases and the run stays the same?

Rise	Run	Slope
3 in.	4 in.	$\frac{3}{4}$

The Slope *of a* Line

BEFORE	Now	WHY?
You graphed lines in a coordinate plane.	You'll find and interpret slopes of lines.	So you can compare animal speeds, as in Ex. 17.

Vocabulary

slope, p. 404
rise, p. 404
run, p. 404

Wakeboarding How steep is a wakeboard ramp like the one shown? To find out, you can calculate the ramp's *slope*. The **slope** of a line is the ratio of the line's vertical change, called the **rise**, to its horizontal change, called the **run**.

Example 1 *Finding Slope*

A wakeboard ramp has a rise of 6 feet and a run of 10 feet. Find its slope.

$$\text{slope} = \frac{\text{rise}}{\text{run}} = \frac{6}{10} = \frac{3}{5}$$

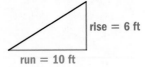

rise = 6 ft

run = 10 ft

Answer The wakeboard ramp has a slope of $\frac{3}{5}$.

To determine the slope of a line in a coordinate plane, you can find the ratio of the vertical change between two points on the line and the horizontal change between the points.

Note *Worthy*

You may find it helpful to use colors when you include examples in your notebook. In the notebook shown, notice how colors are used to associate the rise and run in the slope formula with the rise and run in the graph.

Slope of a Line

Given two points on a nonvertical line, you can find the slope m of the line using this formula:

$$m = \frac{\text{rise}}{\text{run}}$$

$$= \frac{\text{difference of } y\text{-coordinates}}{\text{difference of } x\text{-coordinates}}$$

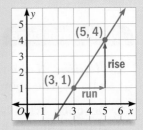

Example $m = \dfrac{4 - 1}{5 - 3} = \dfrac{3}{2}$

Comparing Slopes You can use the diagrams below to compare the slopes of different lines. Imagine that you are walking *to the right*.

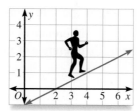

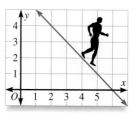

Positive slope
If the line rises,
the slope is *positive*.

Negative slope
If the line falls,
the slope is *negative*.

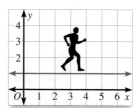

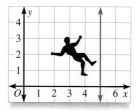

Zero slope
If the line is horizontal,
the slope is *zero*.

Undefined slope
If the line is vertical,
the slope is *undefined*.

Watch *Out*

When you calculate a slope, be sure to use the *x*- and *y*-coordinates of the two points in the same order. In part (a) of Example 2, for instance, the following expression for the slope would be incorrect:

$$m = \frac{5 - 2}{1 - 4} \quad ✗$$

Example 2 *Finding Positive and Negative Slope*

Find the slope of the line shown.

a. $m = \dfrac{\text{rise}}{\text{run}} = \dfrac{\text{difference of } y\text{-coordinates}}{\text{difference of } x\text{-coordinates}}$

$$= \frac{5 - 2}{4 - 1}$$

$$= \frac{3}{3} = 1$$

Answer The slope is 1.

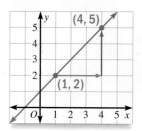

b. $m = \dfrac{\text{rise}}{\text{run}} = \dfrac{\text{difference of } y\text{-coordinates}}{\text{difference of } x\text{-coordinates}}$

$$= \frac{-3 - 1}{3 - 0}$$

$$= \frac{-4}{3} = -\frac{4}{3}$$

Answer The slope is $-\dfrac{4}{3}$.

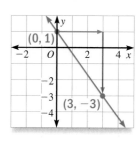

✔ *Checkpoint*

Find the slope of the line through the given points.

1. $(1, 2), (4, 7)$ **2.** $(-2, 5), (6, 1)$ **3.** $(0, 0), (3, -9)$ **4.** $(5, 0), (7, 8)$

Example 3 · Zero and Undefined Slope

Find the slope of the line shown.

a. $m = \dfrac{\text{rise}}{\text{run}} = \dfrac{\text{difference of } y\text{-coordinates}}{\text{difference of } x\text{-coordinates}}$

$= \dfrac{3-3}{4-1}$

$= \dfrac{0}{3} = 0$

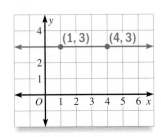

Answer The slope is 0.

b. $m = \dfrac{\text{rise}}{\text{run}} = \dfrac{\text{difference of } y\text{-coordinates}}{\text{difference of } x\text{-coordinates}}$

$= \dfrac{3-(-1)}{2-2}$

$= \dfrac{4}{0}$ **Division by zero is undefined.**

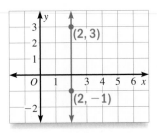

Answer The slope is undefined.

✔ Checkpoint

Find the slope of the line through the given points. Tell whether the slope is *positive*, *negative*, *zero*, or *undefined*.

5. $(2, 3), (4, 5)$ **6.** $(6, 3), (6, -1)$ **7.** $(-7, 4), (5, 4)$ **8.** $(1, 5), (4, 1)$

Example 4 · Interpreting Slope as a Rate of Change

The graph shows the distance traveled by a wakeboarder as a function of time. The slope of the line gives the wakeboarder's speed, which is the *rate of change* in distance traveled with respect to time. Find the wakeboarder's speed.

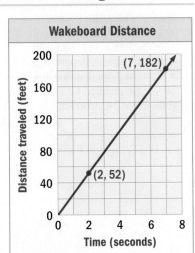

Wakeboard Distance

Solution

Use the points $(2, 52)$ and $(7, 182)$ to find the slope of the line.

$m = \dfrac{\text{difference of } y\text{-coordinates}}{\text{difference of } x\text{-coordinates}}$

$= \dfrac{182 \text{ ft} - 52 \text{ ft}}{7 \text{ sec} - 2 \text{ sec}}$

$= \dfrac{130 \text{ ft}}{5 \text{ sec}}$

$= 26 \text{ ft/sec}$

Answer The wakeboarder's speed is 26 feet per second.

In the **Real World**

Wakeboarding Experts recommend that wakeboarders travel at speeds from 16 to 19 miles per hour. Is the speed of the wakeboarder in Example 4 within this interval? Explain.

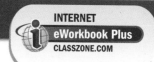
Guided Practice

Vocabulary Check

1. Copy and complete: The vertical change between two points on a line is called the _?_, and the horizontal change is called the _?_.

2. Why is the slope of a vertical line undefined?

Skill Check

3. **Error Analysis** Describe and correct the error in calculating the slope of the line through the points (5, 4) and (0, 2).

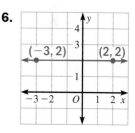

$$m = \frac{2-4}{5-0} = -\frac{2}{5}$$

Tell whether the slope of the line is *positive, negative, zero,* or *undefined.* Then find the slope.

4.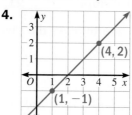

5.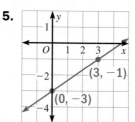

6.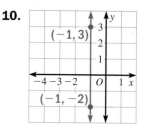

7. *Writing* A wakeboard ramp has a rise of 5 feet and a run of 12 feet. Find the slope of the ramp. Compare this slope with the slope of the ramp in Example 1.

Practice and Problem Solving

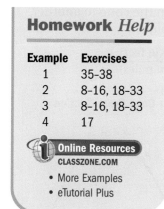

Homework *Help*

Example	Exercises
1	35–38
2	8–16, 18–33
3	8–16, 18–33
4	17

Online Resources
CLASSZONE.COM

• More Examples
• eTutorial Plus

Tell whether the slope of the line is *positive, negative, zero,* or *undefined.* Then find the slope.

8.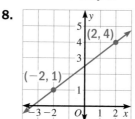

9.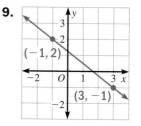

10.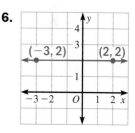

Find the coordinates of two points on the line with the given equation. Then use the points to find the slope of the line.

11. $y = 2x + 4$

12. $y = -1$

13. $y = \frac{3}{2}x - 5$

14. $x + 2y = 6$

15. $4x - 3y = 12$

16. $x = 3$

17. Extended Problem Solving The graph shows the distance run by a cheetah as a function of time.

a. Find the slope of the line.

b. **Interpret** What information about the cheetah can you obtain from the slope?

c. **Compare and Contrast** A gazelle's top speed is about 22 meters per second. Suppose you made a graph showing the distance run by a gazelle as a function of time. How would the graph for the gazelle compare with the graph for the cheetah? Explain your thinking.

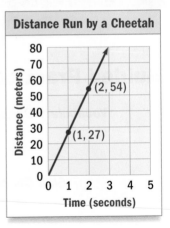

Distance Run by a Cheetah

Points shown: (1, 27), (2, 54)
x-axis: Time (seconds), 0 to 5
y-axis: Distance (meters), 0 to 80

Sketch an example of the type of line described.

18. A line with zero slope

19. A line with undefined slope

20. A line with positive slope

21. A line with negative slope

Find the slope of the line through the given points.

22. $(3, 3)$, $(5, 7)$

23. $(6, 1)$, $(4, 3)$

24. $(7, 3)$, $(7, 2)$

25. $(-3, -5)$, $(6, -11)$

26. $(4, 1)$, $(12, 8)$

27. $(5, -7)$, $(0, -7)$

28. $(-1, 0)$, $(0, -5)$

29. $(3, -2)$, $(-8, -2)$

30. $(-2, -6)$, $(-2, 6)$

31. $(-8, -8)$, $(-2, -6)$

32. $(65, 87)$, $(82, 16)$

33. $(-10, 10)$, $(-10, 0)$

34. *Writing* Describe the difference between a line with zero slope and a line with undefined slope.

35. Wheelchair Ramp You are building a wheelchair ramp that leads to a doorway 22 inches above the ground. The slope of the ramp must be $\frac{1}{12}$. Find the length of ground (in feet) that the ramp covers.

36. Cinder Cones A cinder cone is a type of volcano. To describe the steepness of a cinder cone from one point on the cone to another, you can find the *gradient* between the two points.

$$\text{Gradient} = \frac{\text{Change in elevation (in feet)}}{\text{Horizontal change (in miles)}}$$

The island shown above is a cinder cone in Crater Lake National Park, Oregon.

The graph shows a cross section of a cinder cone. Use the information in the graph to find the gradient between the given points on the cinder cone. Include units in your answers.

a. *A* and *B*

b. *B* and *C*

c. *A* and *C*

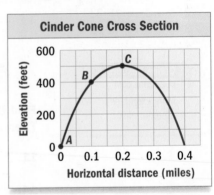

Cinder Cone Cross Section

x-axis: Horizontal distance (miles), 0 to 0.4
y-axis: Elevation (feet), 0 to 600
Points: A, B, C

37. Roads The *grade* of a road is its slope written as a percent. A warning sign must be posted if a section of road has a grade of at least 8% and is more than 750 feet long.

    a. Interpret and Apply A road rises 63 feet over a horizontal distance of 840 feet. Should a warning sign be posted? Explain your thinking.

    b. Critical Thinking The grade of a section of road that stretches over a horizontal distance of 1000 feet is 9%. How many feet does the road rise over that distance?

38. Horseback Riding A riding instructor takes students on mountain trails. The instructor wants to avoid steep trails. On the steepest part of trail A, the path rises 15 feet over a horizontal distance of 50 feet. On the steepest part of trail B, the path rises 30 feet over a horizontal distance of 75 feet. Which trail should the instructor take? Explain.

39. Logical Reasoning Choose three different pairs of points on the given line, and find the slope of the line using each pair. What conclusion can you draw from your results?

a. 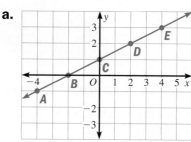   **b.**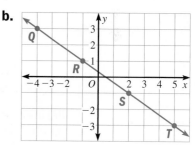

40. Challenge Without graphing, choose a point P so that the slope of the line through $(-1, 1)$ and P is $\frac{1}{9}$.

Mixed Review

Solve the equation. Check your solution. *(Lessons 2.5, 2.6)*

41. $x + 7 = -5$ **42.** $x - 3 = 21$ **43.** $-3y = 33$ **44.** $\frac{m}{-5} = 10$

Find the greatest common factor of the numbers. *(Lesson 4.2)*

45. 15, 48   **46.** 64, 56   **47.** 105, 125   **48.** 121, 132

Find the intercepts of the equation's graph. Then graph the equation. *(Lesson 8.3)*

49. $2x - y = 2$ **50.** $9x + 2y = 18$ **51.** $3x + 4y = -24$

Standardized Test Practice

52. Multiple Choice What is the slope of the line that passes through the points $(-1, -14)$ and $(5, 4)$?

    A. -3 **B.** $-\frac{1}{3}$ **C.** $\frac{1}{3}$ **D.** 3

53. Multiple Choice The slope of a line through the point $(0, 0)$ is 2. Which point is also on the line?

    F. $(-4, 2)$ **G.** $(2, 4)$ **H.** $(-2, 4)$ **I.** $(2, -4)$

Parallel, Perpendicular, and Skew Lines

Parallel Lines

Two lines are **parallel lines** if they lie in the same plane and do not intersect. The symbol ∥ is used to state that two lines are parallel. Triangles (▶) are used in a diagram to indicate that lines are parallel. In the diagram below, lines t and v are parallel.

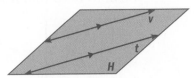

Example Name one pair of parallel lines that lie in plane P.

Because lines a and c are marked as being parallel, you know that $a \parallel c$.

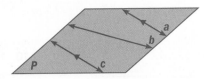

Perpendicular Lines

Two lines are **perpendicular lines** if they intersect to form a right angle. The symbol ⊥ is used to state that two lines are perpendicular. In the diagram, lines m and n are perpendicular.

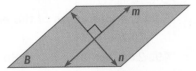

Example Name two lines that are perpendicular to line f.

Because lines g and j intersect line f at right angles, you know that $g \perp f$ and $j \perp f$.

Skew Lines

Two lines are **skew lines** if they do not lie in the same plane and do not intersect. In the diagram, lines r and s are skew lines.

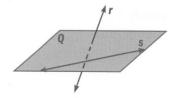

Example **Name two lines that are skew.**

Lines u and w are skew. Note that lines u and v are not skew because they intersect.

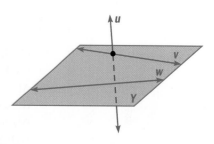

✓ Checkpoint

▶ **Test** your knowledge of parallel, perpendicular, and skew lines by solving these problems.

Tell whether the lines are *parallel* or *perpendicular*.

1. Lines a and b

2. Lines a and c

3. Lines d and b

4. Lines c and d

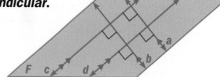

Tell whether the lines are skew. Explain.

5. Lines k and m

6. Lines k and j

7. Lines j and m

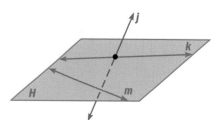

In Exercises 8–10, use the radio shown. The radio has the shape of a box with rectangular sides. Consider the antenna and each edge of the radio as part of a line.

8. Name three lines perpendicular to $\overleftrightarrow{GE}$.

9. Name two lines parallel to $\overleftrightarrow{AC}$.

10. Name two lines that are skew to $\overleftrightarrow{CD}$.

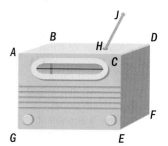

Slope-Intercept Form

BEFORE	Now	WHY?
You used intercepts to graph linear equations.	You'll graph linear equations in slope-intercept form.	So you can find how long it will take to knit a scarf, as in Ex. 9.

Vocabulary

slope-intercept form, p. 412

The graph of $y = 2x + 3$ is shown. You can see that the line's y-intercept is 3, and the line's slope m is 2:

$$m = \frac{\text{rise}}{\text{run}} = \frac{2}{1} = 2$$

Notice that the slope is equal to the coefficient of x in the equation $y = 2x + 3$. Also notice that the y-intercept is equal to the constant term in the equation. These results are always true for an equation written in *slope-intercept form*.

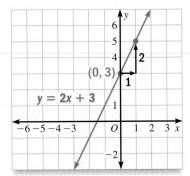

Slope-Intercept Form

Words A linear equation of the form $y = mx + b$ is said to be in **slope-intercept form**. The slope is m and the y-intercept is b.

Algebra $y = mx + b$ **Numbers** $y = 2x + 3$

Example 1   *Identifying the Slope and y-Intercept*

Identify the slope and *y*-intercept of the line with the given equation.

a. $y = x - 4$ **b.** $3x + 5y = 10$

Solution

a. Write the equation $y = x - 4$ as $y = 1x + (-4)$.

   Answer The line has a slope of 1 and a y-intercept of -4.

b. Write the equation $3x + 5y = 10$ in slope-intercept form by solving for y.

$3x + 5y = 10$	**Write original equation.**
$5y = -3x + 10$	**Subtract 3x from each side.**
$y = -\frac{3}{5}x + 2$	**Multiply each side by $\frac{1}{5}$.**

   Answer The line has a slope of $-\frac{3}{5}$ and a y-intercept of 2.

Reading *Algebra*

Recall that you wrote linear equations in function form in Lesson 8.2. In part (b) of Example 1, notice that writing $3x + 5y = 10$ in slope-intercept form is equivalent to writing the equation in function form.

Example 2	*Graphing an Equation in Slope-Intercept Form*

Graph the equation $y = -\frac{2}{3}x + 4$.

1 The *y*-intercept is 4, so plot the point (0, 4).

2 The slope is $-\frac{2}{3} = \frac{-2}{3}$.

Starting at (0, 4), plot another point by moving right 3 units and down 2 units.

3 Draw a line through the two points.

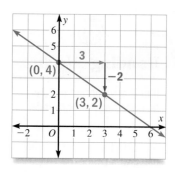

✔ *Checkpoint*

Identify the slope and *y*-intercept of the line with the given equation. Use the slope and *y*-intercept to graph the equation.

1. $y = -x + 1$ **2.** $3x - 2y = 6$ **3.** $y = 4x$

Real-Life Situations In a real-life problem involving a linear equation, the *y*-intercept is often an initial value, and the slope is a rate of change.

Example 3	*Using Slope and y-Intercept in Real Life*

Earth Science The temperature at Earth's surface averages about 20°C. In the crust below the surface, the temperature rises by about 25°C per kilometer of depth.

a. Write an equation that approximates the temperature below Earth's surface as a function of depth.

b. Underground bacteria exist that can survive temperatures of up to 110°C. Find the maximum depth at which these bacteria can live.

Solution

a. Let *x* be the depth (in kilometers) below Earth's surface, and let *y* be the temperature (in degrees Celsius) at that depth. Write a verbal model. Then use the verbal model to write an equation.

Temperature below surface	=	Temperature at surface	+	Rate of change in temperature	·	Depth below surface

$$y = 20 + 25x$$

b. Graph $y = 20 + 25x$ on a graphing calculator. Trace along the graph until the cursor is on a point where $y \approx 110$. For this point, $x \approx 3.6$. So, the maximum depth at which the bacteria can live is about 3.6 kilometers.

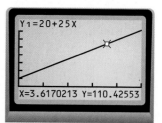

Scientists use airtight enclosures like the one shown to preserve bacteria found in Earth's crust.

Parallel and Perpendicular Lines There is an important relationship between the slopes of two nonvertical lines that are parallel and between the slopes of two nonvertical lines that are perpendicular.

Slopes of Parallel and Perpendicular Lines

Two nonvertical parallel lines have the same slope. For example, the parallel lines a and b below both have a slope of 2.

Two nonvertical perpendicular lines, such as lines a and c below, have slopes that are negative reciprocals of each other.

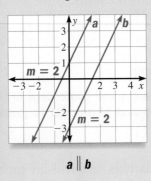

$a \parallel b$

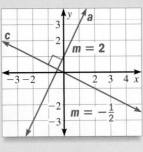

$a \perp c$

Example 4 *Finding Slopes of Parallel and Perpendicular Lines*

Find the slope of a line that has the given relationship to the line with equation $4x + 3y = -18$.

   a. Parallel to the line   **b.** Perpendicular to the line

Solution

  a. First write the given equation in slope-intercept form.

$4x + 3y = -18$	**Write original equation.**
$3y = -4x - 18$	**Subtract 4x from each side.**
$y = -\dfrac{4}{3}x - 6$	**Multiply each side by $\dfrac{1}{3}$.**

The slope of the given line is $-\dfrac{4}{3}$. Because parallel lines have the same slope, the slope of a parallel line is also $-\dfrac{4}{3}$.

  b. From part (a), the slope of the given line is $-\dfrac{4}{3}$. The slope of a perpendicular line is the negative reciprocal of $-\dfrac{4}{3}$, or $\dfrac{3}{4}$.

✓ *Checkpoint*

For the line with the given equation, find the slope of a parallel line and the slope of a perpendicular line.

    4. $y = -3x$ **5.** $y = 4x + 10$ **6.** $2x - 5y = 15$

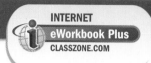
Guided Practice

Vocabulary Check

1. Copy and complete: An equation of the form $y = mx + b$ is written in __?__ form.

2. Without graphing, tell whether the lines with equations $y = 7x - 1$ and $y = 7x + 3$ are *parallel*, *perpendicular*, or *neither*. Explain.

Skill Check

Identify the slope and *y*-intercept of the line with the given equation. Use the slope and *y*-intercept to graph the equation.

3. $y = 2x$

4. $y = -3x + 4$

5. $x - 2y = 2$

For the line with the given equation, find the slope of a parallel line and the slope of a perpendicular line.

6. $y = x$

7. $y = -6x + 9$

8. $3x + 2y = 16$

Guided Problem Solving

9. Knitting You and a friend are knitting a scarf that will be 72 inches long. Your friend knits the first 24 inches and then gives you the scarf to finish. You expect to knit at a rate of 8 inches per day. After how many days will you finish the scarf?

① Use the verbal model to write an equation giving the length y of the scarf (in inches) after you have been knitting for x days.

Length of scarf	=	Length knitted by your friend	+	Knitting rate	·	Knitting time

② Identify the slope and *y*-intercept of the line with the equation from Step 1. Then graph the equation.

③ Use the graph to estimate how long you will take to finish the scarf.

Practice and Problem Solving

Homework *Help*

Example   Exercises
1   10–12, 14–19
2   10–12, 14–19
3   20, 21, 31
4   13, 22–31

Online Resources
CLASSZONE.COM
• More Examples
• eTutorial Plus

Match the equation with its graph.

10. $y = x + 2$

11. $y = -x + 2$

12. $y = x - 2$

A.

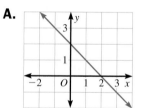

B.

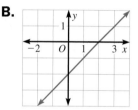

C.

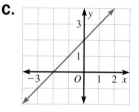

13. Critical Thinking Give the equations of three lines that are parallel to the line with equation $y = 3x + 2$.

Identify the slope and *y*-intercept of the line with the given equation. Use the slope and *y*-intercept to graph the equation.

14. $y = -2x + 3$ **15.** $y = \frac{1}{4}x + 1$ **16.** $y = -2$

17. $3x + y = -1$ **18.** $2x - 3y = 0$ **19.** $5x - 2y = -4$

20. Robotics In 2002, a robot explored a tunnel 210 feet long inside the Great Pyramid in Egypt. The robot could travel about 10 feet per minute. Write and graph an equation giving the distance *y* (in feet) that the robot could travel in *x* minutes. Use the graph to estimate how quickly the robot could reach the end of the tunnel.

21. Paramotoring A paramotor is a parachute propelled by a fan-like motor. Suppose that *x* minutes after beginning a descent, a paramotorist has an altitude *y* (in feet) given by $y = 2000 - 250x$.

     a. Graph the given equation on a graphing calculator. Use the *trace* feature to find how long it takes the paramotorist to reach the ground.

     b. Interpret Identify the slope and *y*-intercept of the graph. What real-life quantities do the slope and *y*-intercept represent?

For the line with the given equation, find the slope of a parallel line and the slope of a perpendicular line.

22. $y = 8x + 5$ **23.** $y = -x - 9$ **24.** $y = -7x + 4$

25. $4x - 5y = 30$ **26.** $11x + 6y = 18$ **27.** $x = 3y - 7$

Find the slope of a line parallel to the given line and the slope of a line perpendicular to the given line.

28. 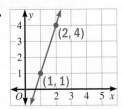   **29.** 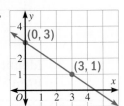   **30.**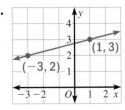

31. Extended Problem Solving Two farmers each harvest 50 acres of corn per day from their fields. The area of one farmer's field is 1000 acres, and the area of the other farmer's field is 600 acres.

     a. Write an equation giving the unharvested area *y* of the larger field (in acres) after *x* days.

     b. Write an equation giving the unharvested area *y* of the smaller field (in acres) after *x* days.

     c. Graph the equations from parts (a) and (b) in the same coordinate plane. Identify the slope and *y*-intercept of each graph.

     d. Compare What is the geometric relationship between the graphs from part (c)? How do you know?

     e. Interpret and Apply How long does it take to harvest the corn in the larger field? in the smaller field?

Paramotor

32. Walk-a-thon You are participating in a walk-a-thon. Donors can pledge a certain amount of money for each mile that you walk, or a fixed amount that doesn't depend on how far you walk, or both. The table gives the amounts pledged by four donors on your street.

Donor	Amount per mile	Fixed amount	Equation
Janette	None	$35	?
Ben	$2	$20	?
Salil	$5	None	?
Mary	$3	$15	?

a. Copy the table. For each person, write an equation giving the amount of money y the person will donate if you walk x miles.

b. Write an equation giving the *total* amount of money y you will raise from the donors on your street if you walk x miles.

c. *Writing* Consider the equations from part (a) and the equation from part (b). Which equation has the graph with the greatest slope? Explain why this is so.

33. Challenge Complete the following steps to show that the slope of the line $y = mx + b$ is m.

a. Show that two points on the graph of $y = mx + b$ are $(0, b)$ and $(1, m + b)$. (*Hint*: Find y when $x = 0$ and when $x = 1$.)

b. For the points $(0, b)$ and $(1, m + b)$, what is the difference of the second y-coordinate and the first y-coordinate? What is the difference of the second x-coordinate and the first x-coordinate?

c. Use your results from part (b) to write an expression for the slope of the line $y = mx + b$. Show that the slope is equal to m.

Mixed Review

Solve the equation. Check your solution. *(Lesson 3.2)*

34. $2(x - 4) = 16$

35. $-20 = 4(7 - 3z)$

36. $-6 + 5a + 13 = -8$

37. $14c + 33 - 10c = 5$

Use the percent equation to answer the question. *(Lesson 7.4)*

38. What number is 20% of 50?

39. What number is 125% of 80?

40. 45 is 75% of what number?

41. What percent of 140 is 56?

Find the slope of the line through the given points. *(Lesson 8.4)*

42. $(0, 0), (2, 8)$ **43.** $(1, 5), (4, -1)$ **44.** $(2, 6), (5, 4)$ **45.** $(-3, 7), (1, 17)$

Standardized Test Practice

46. Multiple Choice Which equation's graph has the greatest slope?

A. $y = 3x$ **B.** $y = x + 12$ **C.** $y = 5x - 1$ **D.** $y = 8x + 4$

47. Short Response You buy a prepaid phone card that has 500 minutes of calling time. You use about 25 minutes of calling time per week. Write and graph an equation that approximates your remaining calling time y (in minutes) after x weeks.

Mid-Chapter Quiz

Represent the relation as a graph and as a mapping diagram. Then tell whether the relation is a function. Explain your reasoning.

1. $(2, 1), (2, 2), (2, 3), (2, 4)$

2. $(8, -1), (6, 0), (4, 0), (2, -1)$

Graph the equation. Tell whether the equation is a function.

3. $y = -x + 7$ **4.** $x = 5$ **5.** $y = -1$ **6.** $x + 4y = 32$

Find the intercepts of the equation's graph. Then graph the equation.

7. $6x + 3y = 12$ **8.** $4x - y = 8$ **9.** $y = 2x - 6$ **10.** $-5x + 2y = 10$

Find the slope of the line through the given points.

11. $(1, 2), (2, 8)$ **12.** $(0, 4), (4, 4)$ **13.** $(-6, 10), (1, 2)$ **14.** $(-1, 2), (-1, 6)$

15. Drama Club The drama club pays a registration fee of $50 to take part in a festival of one-act plays and $40 for each play the club enters. Write and graph an equation giving the total cost y (in dollars) of entering x plays.

GAME   *Quarter Count*

The U.S. Mint began issuing special state quarters in 1999. Using a coordinate plane, follow the steps below to find out how many states had quarters issued each year. For each step after the first, start at the point in the plane where you ended in the previous step. All segments you draw should be 4 units long.

① Start at $(2, 4)$ and draw a segment that has a slope of 0 and an endpoint in Quadrant II.

② Draw a segment on the line $x = -2$ with an endpoint on the x-axis.

③ Draw a segment on the line $y = 0$ that has a positive x-coordinate.

④ Draw a segment that has an undefined slope and an endpoint in Quadrant IV.

⑤ Draw a segment on the line $y = -4$ that has an endpoint in Quadrant III.

Writing Linear Equations

BEFORE	Now	WHY?
You graphed linear equations.	You'll write linear equations.	So you can describe the area of glaciers, as in Ex. 26.

Vocabulary

best-fitting line, p. 421

Bamboo Bamboo is one of the fastest-growing plants on Earth. It can grow up to 4 feet in one day! In Example 4, you'll see how to write a linear equation that describes the growth of a bamboo plant.

You can write a linear equation in slope-intercept form, $y = mx + b$, if you know the slope m and the y-intercept b of the equation's graph.

Example 1   *Writing an Equation Given the Slope and y-Intercept*

Write an equation of the line with a slope of 3 and a *y*-intercept of −7.

$y = mx + b$	Write general slope-intercept equation.
$y = 3x + (-7)$	Substitute 3 for m and −7 for b.
$y = 3x - 7$	Simplify.

Example 2   *Writing an Equation of a Graph*

Write an equation of the line shown.

1 Find the slope m using the labeled points.

$$m = \frac{2-3}{4-0} = \frac{-1}{4} = -\frac{1}{4}$$

2 Find the y-intercept b. The line crosses the y-axis at (0, 3), so $b = 3$.

3 Write an equation of the form $y = mx + b$.

$$y = -\frac{1}{4}x + 3$$

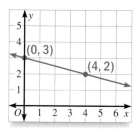

✔ **Checkpoint**

1. Write an equation of the line with a slope of 1 and a y-intercept of 5.

2. Write an equation of the line through the points $(-2, 6)$ and $(0, -4)$.

a. Write an equation of the line that is parallel to the line $y = 4x - 8$ and passes through the point $(0, 2)$.

b. Write an equation of the line that is perpendicular to the line $y = -5x + 1$ and passes through the point $(0, -9)$.

Solution

a. The slope of the given line is 4, so the slope of the parallel line is also 4. The parallel line passes through $(0, 2)$, so its y-intercept is 2.

Answer An equation of the line is $y = 4x + 2$.

b. Because the slope of the given line is -5, the slope of the perpendicular line is the negative reciprocal of -5, or $\frac{1}{5}$. The perpendicular line passes through $(0, -9)$, so its y-intercept is -9.

Answer An equation of the line is $y = \frac{1}{5}x + (-9)$, or $y = \frac{1}{5}x - 9$.

Example 4   *Writing an Equation from a Table*

The table shows a bamboo plant's growth over 8 hours. Show that the table represents a linear function. Write an equation for the function.

Time (h), x	0	2	4	6	8
Height (in.), y	6	10	14	18	22

Solution

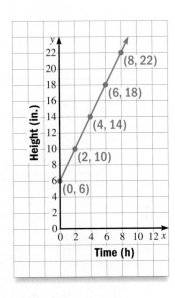

1 Make a scatter plot. The points lie on a nonvertical line, so the table represents a linear function.

2 Find the slope m using any two points on the line, such as $(0, 6)$ and $(2, 10)$.

$$m = \frac{10 - 6}{2 - 0} = \frac{4}{2} = 2$$

3 Find the y-intercept b. The line intersects the y-axis at $(0, 6)$, so $b = 6$.

4 Write the equation $y = mx + b$.

$$y = 2x + 6$$

In the **Real World**

Bamboo Bamboo is a rapidly renewable building material compared to trees such as oak. Bamboo takes about 5 years to grow, while oak takes about 120 years. How many bamboo forests can be grown and harvested in the time it takes to grow one oak forest?

✓ *Checkpoint*

3. Which representation of a function more clearly shows whether or not the function is linear: a table of values or a graph? Explain.

Best-Fitting Lines In Example 4, the points in the scatter plot lie *exactly* on a line. Often, however, there is no single line that passes through all the points in a data set. In such cases, you can find the **best-fitting line**, which is the line that lies as close as possible to the data points.

The following example uses a graphical method to approximate the equation of a best-fitting line. In the activity on page 425, you'll use a graphing calculator to find a better approximation of this line.

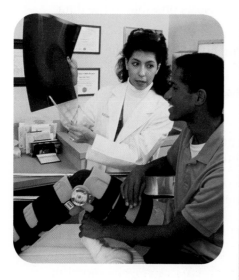

| **Example 5** | *Approximating a Best-Fitting Line* |

Medicine The table shows the number of female physicians in the United States for the years 1992–1999.

Years since 1992, x	0	1	2	3	4	5	6	7
Female physicians (in thousands), y	110	117	125	140	148	158	168	177

a. Approximate the equation of the best-fitting line for the data.

b. Predict the number of female physicians in 2005.

Solution

a. *First*, make a scatter plot of the data pairs.

Next, draw the line that appears to best fit the data points. There should be about the same number of points above the line as below it. The line does not have to pass through any of the data points.

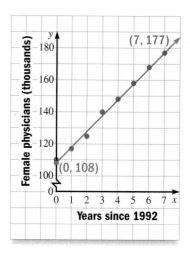

Finally, write an equation of the line. To find the slope, estimate the coordinates of two points on the line, such as $(0, 108)$ and $(7, 177)$.

$$m = \frac{177 - 108}{7 - 0} = \frac{69}{7} \approx 9.86$$

The line intersects the y-axis at $(0, 108)$, so the y-intercept is 108.

Answer An approximate equation of the best-fitting line is $y = 9.86x + 108$.

b. Note that $2005 - 1992 = 13$, so 2005 is 13 years after 1992. Calculate y when $x = 13$ using the equation from part (a).

$y = 9.86x + 108$ **Write equation of best-fitting line.**

$y = 9.86(13) + 108$ **Substitute 13 for x.**

$y \approx 236$ **Simplify.**

Answer In 2005, there will be about 236,000 female physicians in the United States.

Watch *Out*

In the table for Example 5, each year's number y of female physicians is given in thousands. So in part (b), a y-value of 236 means that the number of female physicians in 2005 will be about 236 *thousand*, not 236.

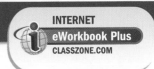
Guided Practice

Vocabulary Check

1. Copy and complete: The line that lies as close as possible to the data points in a scatter plot is called the ? .

2. Describe the steps you would use to write an equation of the line through the points $(-2, 3)$ and $(0, 9)$.

Skill Check **Write an equation of the line through the given points.**

3. $(0, 8), (1, 9)$ **4.** $(-2, 13), (0, 1)$ **5.** $(0, -5), (3, -3)$

6. Write an equation of the line that is perpendicular to the line $y = 2x - 11$ and passes through the point $(0, -7)$.

Guided Problem Solving

7. Clams The table shows the dimensions of seven butter clams. What is the approximate length of a butter clam that is 85 millimeters wide?

Width (mm), *x*	13	21	30	39	50	60	71
Length (mm), *y*	17	28	40	52	62	77	91

1 Make a scatter plot of the data pairs. Draw the line that appears to best fit the data points.

2 Write an equation of your line.

3 Use your equation to predict, to the nearest millimeter, the length of a butter clam that is 85 millimeters wide.

Practice and Problem Solving

Homework *Help*

Example	Exercises
1	8–11
2	12–17
3	18–23
4	24, 25, 32
5	26, 33

Online Resources
CLASSZONE.COM

• More Examples
• eTutorial Plus

Write an equation of the line with the given slope and *y*-intercept.

8. slope $= -3$; *y*-intercept $= 5$ **9.** slope $= 4$; *y*-intercept $= 10$

10. slope $= 13$; *y*-intercept $= -8$ **11.** slope $= -1$; *y*-intercept $= -20$

Write an equation of the line.

12.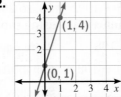

13.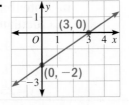

14.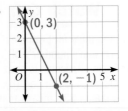

Write an equation of the line through the given points.

15. $(0, 9), (3, 15)$ **16.** $(0, -6), (8, -16)$ **17.** $(-2, -11), (0, -11)$

Write an equation of the line that is parallel to the given line and passes through the given point.

18. $y = 2x + 1$; $(0, 4)$ **19.** $y = -x - 3$; $(0, 7)$ **20.** $y = -8x + 9$; $(0, -2)$

Write an equation of the line that is perpendicular to the given line and passes through the given point.

21. $y = 3x + 4$; $(0, 6)$ **22.** $y = x - 7$; $(0, -5)$ **23.** $y = -\frac{1}{4}x + 3$; $(0, 1)$

Show that the table represents a linear function. Then write an equation for the function.

24.

x	−2	−1	0	1	2
y	−5	−2	1	4	7

25.

x	0	2	4	6	8
y	−3	−2	−1	0	1

26. Extended Problem Solving Since 1912, scientists have created five maps of the glaciers on top of Mount Kilimanjaro in Africa. The maps indicate that the glaciers are shrinking, as shown by the table.

Map number	1	2	3	4	5
Year map was made	1912	1953	1976	1989	2000
Area of glaciers (km²)	12.1	6.7	4.2	3.3	2.2

a. Graph Let x be the number of years since 1912. Let y be the area of the glaciers (in square kilometers). Make a scatter plot of the data pairs (x, y). Draw the line that appears to best fit the data points.

b. Represent Write an equation of your line.

c. Predict Estimate the year when the glaciers will disappear.

Glacier on Mount Kilimanjaro

Two variables x and y show *direct variation* if $y = kx$ for some nonzero number k. In Exercises 27–30, write a direct variation equation that has the given ordered pair as a solution.

Example *Writing a Direct Variation Equation*

Write a direct variation equation that has (4, 20) as a solution.

$y = kx$ Write general equation for direct variation.

$20 = k(4)$ Substitute 4 for x and 20 for y.

$5 = k$ Divide each side by 4.

Answer A direct variation equation is $y = 5x$.

27. $(5, 15)$ **28.** $(-3, 21)$ **29.** $(-8, -4)$ **30.** $(12, -16)$

31. Sales Lisa and John work in different department stores. Lisa earns a salary of $18,000 per year plus a 2% commission on her sales. John receives no salary but earns a 6% commission on his sales. For each person, tell whether annual sales and annual earnings show direct variation. Justify your answers mathematically.

32. Physics The table below gives the length of a spring when different masses are suspended from it.

Mass (g), x	0	50	100	150	200
Length (mm), y	80	110	140	170	200

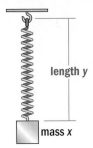

length y

mass x

a. Show that the table represents a linear function.

b. Write an equation for the function.

33. Marathons The table below shows the men's winning times in the Boston Marathon for every tenth year from 1900 to 2000. In the table, x represents the number of years since 1900, and y represents the corresponding winning time (to the nearest minute).

x	0	10	20	30	40	50	60	70	80	90	100
y	160	149	150	155	148	153	141	131	132	128	130

a. Make a scatter plot of the data pairs (x, y). Draw the line that appears to best fit the data points.

b. Write an equation of your line.

c. Predict Use your equation to predict, to the nearest minute, the men's winning time in the Boston Marathon for the year 2010.

d. *Writing* Do you think your equation will accurately predict winning times far into the future? Explain your reasoning.

Elijah Lagat, winner of the men's Boston Marathon in 2000

34. Challenge Write an equation of the line through $(2, -1)$ and $(6, 5)$. Describe the method you used to determine the equation.

Mixed Review

Solve the equation. Check your solution. *(Lesson 3.3)*

35. $8x - 5 = 5x + 7$

36. $-7y + 4 = -y + 22$

37. $4(m - 4) = 2m$

38. $6(1 - n) = -6n + 1$

Write the fraction as a percent. *(Lesson 7.3)*

39. $\dfrac{7}{10}$　　　**40.** $\dfrac{3}{8}$　　　**41.** $\dfrac{5}{2}$　　　**42.** $\dfrac{9}{5}$

Identify the slope and *y*-intercept of the line with the given equation. Use the slope and *y*-intercept to graph the equation. *(Lesson 8.5)*

43. $y = 3x - 2$　　**44.** $y = -x + 5$　　**45.** $3x + 2y = 0$　　**46.** $x - 2y = -2$

Standardized Test Practice

47. Multiple Choice What is an equation of the line through the points $(0, 8)$ and $(2, 0)$?

A. $y = 4x + 2$　　**B.** $y = 4x + 8$　　**C.** $y = -4x + 2$　　**D.** $y = -4x + 8$

48. Multiple Choice What is an equation of the line that is parallel to the line $y = 5x + 3$ and passes through the point $(0, -1)$?

F. $y = 5x - 1$　　**G.** $y = -5x - 1$　　**H.** $y = \dfrac{1}{5}x - 1$　　**I.** $y = -\dfrac{1}{5}x - 1$

8.6 Finding Best-Fitting Lines

Goal Use a graphing calculator to find the best-fitting line for a scatter plot.

Example

Use a graphing calculator to make a scatter plot of the female physician data on page 421 and find the best-fitting line.

1 Press [LIST] and enter the data into two lists, L1 and L2. Use the arrow keys to navigate.

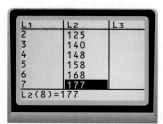

2 Press [2nd] **[PLOT]**, select Plot1, turn it from Off to On, and select the scatter plot icon. Then press [GRAPH].

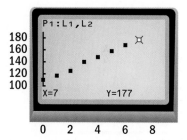

3 Press [2nd] **[STAT]**, select CALC, and select LinReg(ax+b). Then press [ENTER].

4 The best-fitting line has slope a and y-intercept b. Enter the equation of the line and graph it.

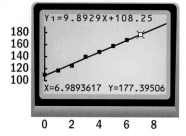

Tech *Help*

Press [ZOOM] and select ZoomStat to set a viewing window that will show all points in the scatter plot.

Press [TRACE] to move among the data points in the scatter plot or along the best-fitting line.

Draw Conclusions

1. **Predict** Use the best-fitting line from the example above to predict the number of female physicians in 2005.

2. **Dentistry** The table shows the average amount each person in the U.S. spent on dental services for the years 1992–1999. Use a graphing calculator to find the best-fitting line for the data.

Years since 1992, x	0	1	2	3	4	5	6	7
Amount (dollars), y	140	148	156	166	173	184	193	202

Function Notation

BEFORE   **Now**   **WHY?**

You wrote equations in   You'll use function notation.   So you can find the mass of a
function form.   squid, as in Ex. 28.

Vocabulary

function notation,
  p. 426

Science In 2001, a scientific balloon
like the one shown was launched near
McMurdo Station in Antarctica. In
Example 4, you'll see how *function
notation* can be used to describe the
balloon's altitude as a function of time.

When you use an equation to
represent a function, it is often
convenient to give the function a
name, such as *f* or *g*. For instance, the
function $y = x + 2$ can be written in
function notation as follows:

$$f(x) = x + 2$$

Watch *Out*

Don't confuse the parentheses
in $f(x)$ with parentheses used
to indicate multiplication. The
symbol $f(x)$ does *not* mean
"*f* times *x*."

The symbol $f(x)$, which replaces *y*, is read "*f* of *x*" and represents the
value of the function *f* at *x*. For instance, $f(3)$ is the value of *f* when $x = 3$.

Example 1   *Working with Function Notation*

Let $f(x) = -3x + 8$. Find $f(x)$ when $x = 5$, and find x when
$f(x) = -22$.

a. $f(x) = -3x + 8$ Write function.

   $f(5) = -3(5) + 8$ Substitute 5 for *x*.

   $\quad\quad = -7$ Simplify.

Answer When $x = 5$, $f(x) = -7$.

b. $f(x) = -3x + 8$ Write function.

   $-22 = -3x + 8$ Substitute −22 for $f(x)$.

   $-30 = -3x$ Subtract 8 from each side.

   $10 = x$ Divide each side by −3.

Answer When $f(x) = -22$, $x = 10$.

 Checkpoint

Let $g(x) = 4x - 5$. Find the indicated value.

1. $g(x)$ when $x = 2$ **2.** $g(-10)$ **3.** x when $g(x) = 19$

Graphing Functions To graph a function written in function notation, you may find it helpful to first rewrite the function in terms of x and y.

Example 2   Graphing a Function

Graph the function $f(x) = \frac{3}{4}x + 1$.

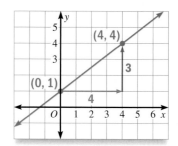

1) Rewrite the function as $y = \frac{3}{4}x + 1$.

2) The y-intercept is 1, so plot the point $(0, 1)$.

3) The slope is $\frac{3}{4}$. Starting at $(0, 1)$, plot another point by moving right 4 units and up 3 units.

4) Draw a line through the two points.

✔ **Checkpoint**

Graph the function.

4. $f(x) = 2x - 4$ **5.** $g(x) = -\frac{3}{2}x + 3$ **6.** $h(x) = -1$

If $f(c) = d$ for a function f, then you can conclude that the graph of f passes through the point (c, d).

Example 3   Writing a Function

Write a linear function g given that $g(0) = 9$ and $g(3) = -6$.

1) Find the slope m of the function's graph. From the values of $g(0)$ and $g(3)$, you know that the graph of g passes through the points $(0, 9)$ and $(3, -6)$. Use these points to calculate the slope.

$$m = \frac{-6 - 9}{3 - 0} = \frac{-15}{3} = -5$$

2) Find the y-intercept b of the function's graph. The graph passes through $(0, 9)$, so $b = 9$.

3) Write an equation of the form $g(x) = mx + b$.

$$g(x) = -5x + 9$$

Study *Strategy*

Reasonableness You can check the answer to Example 3 by verifying that the function g gives the desired values for $g(0)$ and $g(3)$:

$g(0) = -5(0) + 9 = 9$ ✓
$g(3) = -5(3) + 9 = -6$ ✓

✔ **Checkpoint**

Write a linear function that satisfies the given conditions.

7. $f(0) = 1, f(2) = 9$ **8.** $f(0) = -7, f(6) = 5$

9. $g(-6) = 16, g(0) = -5$ **10.** $r(-7) = 3, r(0) = 3$

Example 4 | *Using Function Notation in Real Life*

After the balloon described on page 426 was launched, it rose at a rate of about 500 feet per minute to a final altitude of 120,000 feet.

a. Use function notation to write an equation giving the altitude of the balloon as a function of time.

b. How long did it take the balloon to reach its final altitude?

Solution

a. Let t be the elapsed time (in minutes) since the balloon was launched, and let $a(t)$ be the altitude (in feet) at that time. Write a verbal model. Then use the verbal model to write an equation.

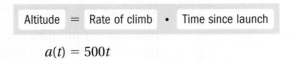

$$a(t) = 500t$$

b. Find the value of t for which $a(t) = 120{,}000$.

$a(t) = 500t$	Write function for altitude.
$120{,}000 = 500t$	Substitute 120,000 for $a(t)$.
$240 = t$	Divide each side by 500.

Answer It took the balloon about 240 minutes (or about 4 hours) to reach its final altitude.

8.7 Exercises

More Practice, p. 810

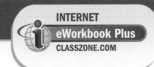

INTERNET
eWorkbook Plus
CLASSZONE.COM

Guided Practice

Vocabulary Check

1. Write the equation $y = 4x - 3$ using function notation.

2. Suppose f is a linear function with $f(2) = 5$ and $f(6) = -1$. Describe how you can find the slope of the graph of f.

Skill Check

Let $f(x) = 7x + 4$. Find the indicated value.

3. $f(x)$ when $x = -8$ **4.** $f(3)$ **5.** x when $f(x) = 67$

Graph the function.

6. $f(x) = -x + 3$ **7.** $g(x) = 3x - 5$ **8.** $h(x) = 2x$

9. Write a linear function f given that $f(-4) = 12$ and $f(0) = 8$.

10. Cable TV The average monthly cost of basic cable TV was $9.73 in 1985 and has increased by about $1.35 each year since then. Let t be the number of years since 1985. Use function notation to write an equation giving the monthly cost of basic cable TV as a function of t.

Practice and Problem Solving

Homework *Help*

Example	Exercises
1	11–16
2	17–22
3	24–27
4	28–30

Online Resources
CLASSZONE.COM
- More Examples
- eTutorial Plus

Let $f(x) = -3x + 1$ and $g(x) = 10x - 4$. Find the indicated value.

11. $f(x)$ when $x = -1$ 　　**12.** $g(x)$ when $x = 5$ 　　**13.** x when $f(x) = -17$

14. x when $g(x) = 31$ 　　**15.** $f(-20)$ 　　**16.** $f(4) + g(-3)$

Match the function with its graph.

17. $f(x) = 2x - 1$ 　　**18.** $g(x) = x - 1$ 　　**19.** $h(x) = 2x + 1$

A. 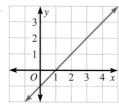 　　**B.** 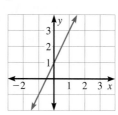 　　**C.**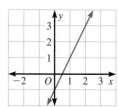

Graph the function.

20. $f(x) = -2x$ 　　**21.** $g(x) = 4x - 4$ 　　**22.** $h(x) = -\frac{2}{3}x + 5$

23. Critical Thinking Write a linear function g whose graph passes through the origin and is parallel to the graph of $f(x) = -8x - 2$.

Write a linear function that satisfies the given conditions.

24. $f(0) = 4, f(1) = 7$ 　　　　　**25.** $g(-2) = 10, g(0) = 0$

26. $h(0) = 13, h(3) = 1$ 　　　　　**27.** $r(-9) = -7, r(0) = -1$

28. Squid An arrow squid has a beak used for eating. Given the length b (in millimeters) of an arrow squid's lower beak, you can approximate the squid's mass (in grams) using the function $m(b) = 236b - 513$.

  a. The beak of an arrow squid washes ashore on a beach, where it is found and measured by a biologist. The lower beak has a length of 5 millimeters. Approximate the mass of the squid.

  b. To the nearest tenth of a millimeter, about how long is the lower beak of an arrow squid with a mass of 1100 grams?

Arrow squid

29. Extended Problem Solving You make and sell birdhouses. Your fixed costs for your tools and workspace are $3000. The cost of wood and other materials needed to make a birdhouse is $10. You sell each birdhouse for $50. Let x represent the number of birdhouses you make and sell.

  a. Write a function for your total costs, $c(x)$.

  b. Write a function for your income, $i(x)$.

  c. Analyze Your profit is the difference of your income and total costs. Write a function for your profit, $p(x)$.

  d. What is your profit when you make and sell 100 birdhouses?

  e. Interpret and Apply You are said to "break even" when your profit is $0. How many birdhouses do you need to make and sell in order to break even?

30. Rivers Surveyors measured the speed of the current below a dam on the Columbia River in Washington. Based on their data, the speed (in feet per second) can be approximated by $s(d) = -0.117d + 1.68$, where d is the depth (in feet) below the river's surface.

a. Graph the given function on a graphing calculator. Remember to replace d with x and $s(d)$ with y.

b. *Writing* Describe what happens to the speed of the current as you go deeper below the river's surface.

c. Apply Approximate the speed of the current at a depth of 9 feet.

31. Challenge The first four rectangles in a pattern are shown below.

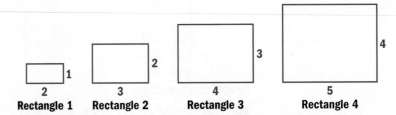

| Rectangle 1 | Rectangle 2 | Rectangle 3 | Rectangle 4 |

a. For the nth rectangle in the pattern, what are the dimensions in terms of n?

b. Write a function for the area $A(n)$ of the nth rectangle.

c. Write a function for the perimeter $P(n)$ of the nth rectangle.

d. Find the area and the perimeter of the 50th rectangle in the pattern.

Mixed Review

Simplify. *(Lesson 4.5)*

32. $x^3 \cdot x^5$ **33.** $2n^7 \cdot 5n^4$ **34.** $\dfrac{a^{12}}{a^8}$ **35.** $\dfrac{30c^9}{12c^2}$

Write the percent as a fraction in simplest form. *(Lesson 7.1)*

36. 40%   **37.** 64%   **38.** 99%   **39.** 150%

Write an equation of the line that is perpendicular to the given line and passes through the given point. *(Lesson 8.6)*

40. $y = 6x + 10$; $(0, -4)$ **41.** $y = -\dfrac{5}{9}x - 1$; $(0, 3)$

Standardized Test Practice

42. Multiple Choice Let $f(x) = -7x - 11$. What is the value of $f(-4)$?

A. -39 **B.** -22 **C.** 0 **D.** 17

43. Multiple Choice Suppose g is a linear function with $g(-3) = 28$ and $g(0) = 4$. What is the slope of the graph of g?

F. -8 **G.** $-\dfrac{1}{8}$ **H.** $\dfrac{1}{8}$ **I.** 8

44. Short Response For Oregon counties with population p, the function $w(p) = 0.878p - 4764$ approximates the amount of solid waste (in tons) that was disposed of during 1998. The population of Marion County, Oregon, was 271,750 in 1998. To the nearest thousand tons, about how much solid waste was disposed of in Marion County during 1998?

8.8

Systems *of* Linear Equations

You graphed linear equations.

You'll graph and solve systems of linear equations.

So you can decide which of two printers to buy, as in Ex. 25.

Vocabulary
system of linear equations, p. 431
solution of a linear system, p. 431

Internet Some providers of high-speed Internet service offer a choice of two plans. With plan A, you buy the modem and pay a monthly fee for Internet service. With plan B, the modem is free, but you pay a higher monthly fee than for plan A.

When is plan A a better deal than plan B? In Example 4, you'll see how to answer this question by solving a *system of linear equations*.

A **system of linear equations**, or simply a *linear system*, consists of two or more linear equations with the same variables. Below is an example.

$$y = 2x - 4 \qquad \text{Equation 1}$$
$$y = -3x + 1 \qquad \text{Equation 2}$$

A **solution of a linear system** in two variables is an ordered pair that is a solution of each equation in the system. A linear system has a solution at each point where the graphs of the equations in the system intersect.

Example 1 | *Solving a System of Linear Equations*

Solve the linear system: $y = 2x - 4$ Equation 1
                             $y = -3x + 1$ Equation 2

1) Graph the equations.

2) Identify the apparent intersection point, $(1, -2)$.

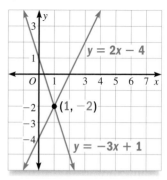

3) Verify that $(1, -2)$ is the solution of the system by substituting 1 for x and -2 for y in each equation.

Equation 1	**Equation 2**
$y = 2x - 4$	$y = -3x + 1$
$-2 \stackrel{?}{=} 2(1) - 4$	$-2 \stackrel{?}{=} -3(1) + 1$
$-2 = -2 \checkmark$	$-2 = -2 \checkmark$

Answer The solution is $(1, -2)$.

Numbers of Solutions As you saw in Example 1, when the graphs of two linear equations have exactly one point of intersection, the related system has exactly one solution. It is also possible for a linear system to have no solution or infinitely many solutions.

Example 2   *Solving a Linear System with No Solution*

Solve the linear system: $y = -2x + 1$ Equation 1
$y = -2x + 5$ Equation 2

Graph the equations. The graphs appear to be parallel lines. You can confirm that the lines are parallel by observing from their equations that they have the same slope, -2, but different y-intercepts, 1 and 5.

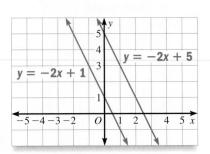

Answer Because parallel lines do not intersect, the linear system has no solution.

Example 3   *Solving a Linear System with Many Solutions*

Solve the linear system: $2x - y = -3$ Equation 1
$-4x + 2y = 6$ Equation 2

Write each equation in slope-intercept form.

Equation 1	**Equation 2**
$2x - y = -3$	$-4x + 2y = 6$
$-y = -2x - 3$	$2y = 4x + 6$
$y = 2x + 3$	$y = 2x + 3$

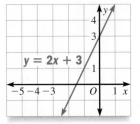

The slope-intercept forms of equations 1 and 2 are identical, so the graphs of the equations are the same line (shown at the right).

Answer Because the graphs have infinitely many points of intersection, the system has infinitely many solutions. Any point on the line $y = 2x + 3$ represents a solution.

✔ *Checkpoint*

Solve the linear system by graphing.

1. $y = 4x + 2$
$y = x + 2$

2. $x - y = -3$
$-4x + 4y = 12$

3. $-3x + y = -1$
$y = 3x + 4$

4. Critical Thinking If the graphs of two linear equations have different slopes, how many solutions does the related system have? Give a verbal and a graphical justification for your answer.

Note *Worthy*

In your notebook, draw diagrams showing the possible ways in which the graphs of two equations in a linear system can intersect. For each diagram, indicate the number of solutions the system has.

Example 4 **Writing and Solving a Linear System**

A company offers two plans for high-speed Internet service, as described on page 431.

> **Plan A:** You pay $200 for the modem and $30 per month for service.
>
> **Plan B:** The modem is free and you pay $40 per month for service.

a. After how many months are the total costs of the plans the same?

b. When is plan A a better deal? When is plan B a better deal?

Solution

a. Let y be the cost of each plan after x months. Write a linear system.

> **Plan A:** $y = 200 + 30x$
>
> **Plan B:** $y = 40x$

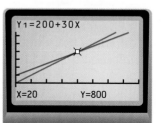

Use a graphing calculator to graph the equations. Trace along one of the graphs until the cursor is on the point of intersection. This point is (20, 800).

Answer The total costs of the plans are the same after 20 months, when each plan costs $800.

b. The graph for plan A lies below the graph for plan B when $x > 20$, so plan A costs less if you have service for more than 20 months.

The graph for plan B lies below the graph for plan A when $x < 20$, so plan B costs less if you have service for less than 20 months.

Tech *Help*

In Example 4, you can get a closer look at the point where the graphs intersect by using the calculator's *zoom* feature to zoom in on the intersection point.

8.8 Exercises

More Practice, p. 810

INTERNET
eWorkbook Plus
CLASSZONE.COM

Guided Practice

Vocabulary Check

1. What is a solution of a system of linear equations in two variables?

2. If the graphs of the two equations in a system are parallel lines, what can you say about the solution(s) of the system?

Skill Check **Solve the linear system by graphing.**

3. $y = 3x - 8$
$y = 2x - 5$

4. $x + y = 3$
$x - y = -5$

5. $y = -4x + 1$
$y = 5 - 4x$

6. Shoes One wall of a shoe store is used to display court shoes and running shoes. There is enough room on the wall for 120 styles of shoes. Based on past sales, the store manager wants to display twice as many running shoes as court shoes. Write and solve a linear system to find the number of each type of shoe to display.

Practice and Problem Solving

Homework *Help*

Example	Exercises
1	7–21
2	13–21
3	13–21
4	22, 23, 25

Online Resources
CLASSZONE.COM

• More Examples
• eTutorial Plus

Tell whether the ordered pair is a solution of the linear system.

7. $(0, -2)$;
$$3x - 2y = 4$$
$$-2x - y = -2$$

8. $(4, 2)$;
$$y = -5x + 22$$
$$y = 8x - 30$$

9. $(-24, -10)$;
$$x - 4y = 16$$
$$-2x + 6y = -12$$

Use the graph to identify the solution of the related linear system.

10.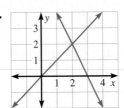

11.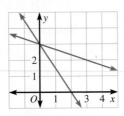

12.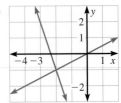

Solve the linear system by graphing.

13. $y = -3x + 2$
$y = x - 2$

14. $y = 2x - 1$
$y = 4x - 5$

15. $2x + 4y = 8$
$3x + 6y = 12$

16. $2x + y = -8$
$-x + y = 4$

17. $y = 5x - 3$
$y = 5x + 2$

18. $x + y = -7$
$y = x + 3$

19. $x - 3y = -6$
$2x + 3y = -3$

20. $3x + 2y = 8$
$4y = 16 - 6x$

21. $4x + y = 5$
$3x + 5y = 25$

22. Vacation Rentals A business rents in-line skates and bicycles to tourists on vacation. A pair of skates rents for $15 per day. A bicycle rents for $20 per day. On a certain day, the owner of the business has 25 rentals and takes in $450. Using the verbal model below, write and solve a system of equations to find the number of each item rented.

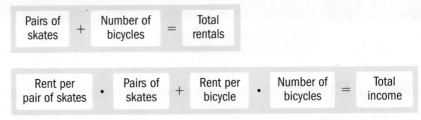

23. Advertising You own a business that advertises in a local newspaper and over the radio. A newspaper ad costs $600. A radio ad costs $300. You have a monthly advertising budget of $24,000 and want to run 50 ads each month. Write and solve a system of equations to find how many newspaper ads and radio ads you should run each month.

24. Geometry The graphs of the three equations below form a triangle. Find the coordinates of the triangle's vertices.

$$2x - y = 4$$
$$2x + 3y = 12$$
$$10x + 3y = -12$$

25. **Extended Problem Solving** You are trying to decide whether to buy an inkjet printer for $100 or a laser printer for $400. The operating costs are estimated to be $.15 per page for the inkjet printer and $.03 per page for the laser printer.

   a. Write a system of equations describing the total cost of buying and operating each printer.

   b. Use a graphing calculator to solve the system of equations. After how many pages are the total costs of the printers equal?

   c. **Interpret** When does the inkjet printer have the lower total cost? When does the laser printer have the lower total cost?

   d. **Apply** You plan to own the printer you buy for 3 years. Which printer offers the lower total cost if you print an average of 2 pages per day? if you print an average of 4 pages per day? Explain.

Tech *Help*

In Exercise 25, you may need to adjust the calculator's viewing window to see the intersection point for the graph of the system of equations.

Visual Thinking **In Exercises 26–28, find values of m and b for which the system below has the given number of solutions. Justify your answers.**

$$y = 3x - 2$$
$$y = mx + b$$

26. Exactly one   27. None   28. Infinitely many

29. **Challenge** You are designing a reflecting pool for a park. The design specifications say that the area of the pool should be 450 square feet. You want the pool to be rectangular and have a length that is twice the width. Let l be the pool's length, and let w be its width.

   a. Write a system of two equations for this situation. Each equation should be solved for l.

   b. Enter the equations from part (a) into a graphing calculator. Use the *table* feature to make a table of solutions for each equation. What ordered pair (w, l) has positive coordinates and satisfies both equations? What should the dimensions of the reflecting pool be?

Mixed Review

Solve the inequality. Graph your solution. *(Lessons 3.4, 3.5)*

30. $x + 4 > 9$ 31. $y - 5 \leq 2$ 32. $-3t \geq 12$ 33. $\dfrac{n}{2} < 6$

Write the number in scientific notation. *(Lesson 4.7)*

34. 1200   35. 309,000   36. 0.0005   37. 0.00000748

Write a linear function that satisfies the given conditions. *(Lesson 8.7)*

38. $f(0) = 8, f(3) = 10$ 39. $h(-4) = -7, h(0) = -27$

Standardized Test Practice

40. **Multiple Choice** Which ordered pair is the solution of the linear system $y = 2x + 16$ and $y = -x + 1$?

   A. $(0, 16)$ **B.** $(2, -1)$ **C.** $(-5, 6)$ **D.** $(-8, 9)$

41. **Multiple Choice** Which ordered pair is *not* a solution of the linear system $x - 3y = -12$ and $-3x + 9y = 36$?

   F. $(-3, 2)$ **G.** $(0, 4)$ **H.** $(3, 5)$ **I.** $(6, 6)$

Graphs *of* Linear Inequalities

BEFORE	Now	WHY?
You solved inequalities in one variable.	You'll graph inequalities in two variables.	So you can find how many kites to make from paper, as in Ex. 34.

Vocabulary

linear inequality in two
  variables, p. 436
solution of a linear
  inequality in two
  variables, p. 436
graph of a linear
  inequality in two
  variables, p. 436
half-plane, p. 436

Pottery How many bowls and vases can you make from a fixed amount of clay? In Example 4, you'll see how a *linear inequality* can be used to answer this question.

A **linear inequality** in two variables, such as $2x - 3y < 6$, is the result of replacing the equal sign in a linear equation with $<$, $\le$, $>$, or $\ge$.

An ordered pair (x, y) is a **solution of a linear inequality** if substituting the values of x and y into the inequality produces a true statement.

Example 1   *Checking Solutions of a Linear Inequality*

Tell whether the ordered pair is a solution of $2x - 3y < 6$.

  a. $(0, 1)$ **b.** $(4, -2)$

Solution

a. Substitute 0 for x and 1 for y.   **b.** Substitute 4 for x and -2 for y.

$$2x - 3y < 6$$
$$2(0) - 3(1) \overset{?}{<} 6$$
$$-3 < 6 \checkmark$$

$(0, 1)$ is a solution.

$$2x - 3y < 6$$
$$2(4) - 3(-2) \overset{?}{<} 6$$
$$14 \not< 6$$

$(4, -2)$ is not a solution.

Graphs The **graph of a linear inequality** in two variables is the set of points in a coordinate plane that represent all the inequality's solutions.

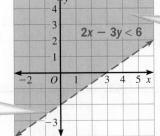

Reading *Algebra*

In the graph shown, a dashed boundary line is used to indicate that points on the line are *not* solutions of $2x - 3y < 6$. A solid boundary line would indicate that points on the line *are* solutions.

All solutions of $2x - 3y < 6$ lie on one side of the *boundary line* $2x - 3y = 6$.

The boundary line divides the plane into two **half-planes**. The shaded half-plane is the graph of $2x - 3y < 6$.

Graphing Linear Inequalities

1. Find the equation of the boundary line by replacing the inequality symbol with =. Graph this equation. Use a dashed line for < or >. Use a solid line for ≤ or ≥.

2. Test a point in one of the half-planes to determine whether it is a solution of the inequality.

3. If the test point is a solution, shade the half-plane that contains the point. If not, shade the other half-plane.

Example 2 *Graphing a Linear Inequality*

Graph $y \geq 2x + 4$.

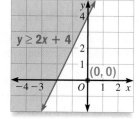

① Draw the boundary line $y = 2x + 4$. The inequality symbol is ≥, so use a solid line.

② Test the point $(0, 0)$ in the inequality.

$$y \geq 2x + 4$$
$$0 \overset{?}{\geq} 2(0) + 4$$
$$0 \ngeq 4$$

③ Because $(0, 0)$ is not a solution, shade the half-plane that does *not* contain $(0, 0)$.

Study *Strategy*

You can use any point not on the boundary line as a test point. Using (0, 0) is convenient because it is easy to evaluate expressions when 0 is substituted for each variable.

Example 3 *Graphing Inequalities with One Variable*

Graph $x < 3$ and $y \geq -2$ in a coordinate plane.

a. Graph $x = 3$ using a dashed line. Use $(0, 0)$ as a test point.

$$x < 3$$
$$0 < 3 \checkmark$$

Shade the half-plane that contains $(0, 0)$.

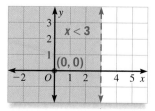

b. Graph $y = -2$ using a solid line. Use $(0, 0)$ as a test point.

$$y \geq -2$$
$$0 \geq -2 \checkmark$$

Shade the half-plane that contains $(0, 0)$.

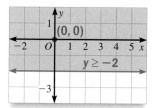

✔ *Checkpoint*

Graph the inequality in a coordinate plane.

1. $x + 2y > 6$ **2.** $x \geq -1$ **3.** $y < 3$

Example 4   *Writing and Graphing a Linear Inequality*

You have 100 pounds of clay to use for making bowls and vases. You need 5 pounds of clay for each bowl and 2 pounds for each vase.

a. Write an inequality describing the possible numbers of bowls and vases that you can make.

b. Graph the inequality from part (a).

c. Give three possible combinations of bowls and vases that you can make.

Solution

a. Let x be the number of bowls you make. Let y be the number of vases you make. Write a verbal model. Then use the verbal model to write an inequality.

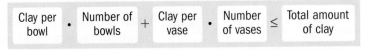

| Clay per bowl | $\cdot$ | Number of bowls | $+$ | Clay per vase | $\cdot$ | Number of vases | $\leq$ | Total amount of clay |

$$5x + 2y \leq 100$$

b. To graph the inequality, first draw the boundary line $5x + 2y = 100$. Use a solid line because the inequality symbol is $\leq$.

Test the point $(0, 0)$ in the inequality.

$$5x + 2y \leq 100$$
$$5(0) + 2(0) \overset{?}{\leq} 100$$
$$0 \leq 100 \checkmark$$

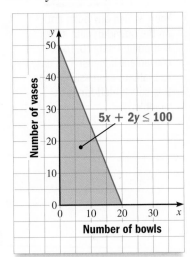

Because $(0, 0)$ is a solution, all solutions of $5x + 2y \leq 100$ lie in the half-plane containing $(0, 0)$. Shade the portion of this half-plane that lies in the first quadrant, as the numbers of bowls and vases made must be nonnegative.

c. Choose three points on the graph with whole-number coordinates, such as $(5, 20)$, $(10, 10)$, and $(20, 0)$. You can make 5 bowls and 20 vases, or 10 bowls and 10 vases, or 20 bowls and no vases.

In the **Real World**

Pottery In the year 2000, there were 904 companies in the United States that manufactured pottery products. These companies employed 20,054 people. What was the mean number of employees per company?

✔ *Checkpoint*

4. It is recommended that you get at least 60 milligrams of vitamin C each day. One fluid ounce of orange juice contains about 15 milligrams of vitamin C, and one fluid ounce of grapefruit juice contains about 12 milligrams. Write and graph an inequality describing the possible amounts of orange juice and grapefruit juice you can drink to meet your daily requirement for vitamin C.

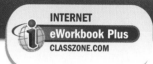

Guided Practice

Vocabulary Check

1. Copy and complete: The graph of a linear inequality in two variables is called a(n) _?_.

2. When graphing a linear inequality in two variables, explain how to determine which side of the boundary line to shade.

Skill Check **Tell whether the ordered pair is a solution of $4x + y > -1$.**

3. $(-2, 5)$ **4.** $(0, 0)$ **5.** $(4, -4)$ **6.** $(-1, 3)$

Graph the inequality in a coordinate plane.

7. $y < 3x + 1$ **8.** $4x - 5y \le 20$ **9.** $x > -2$ **10.** $y \ge 1$

Guided Problem Solving

11. Movies You have a gift certificate for $40 to use at a movie theater. Matinees cost $5 and evening shows cost $8. What are some possible combinations of matinees and evening shows that you can see?

1 Write an inequality for this situation.

2 Graph the inequality from Step 1.

3 Give three possible combinations of matinees and evening shows that you can see.

Practice and Problem Solving

Homework *Help*

Example	Exercises
1	16–19
2	12, 13, 20–27
3	28–31
4	32–34

Online Resources
CLASSZONE.COM
• More Examples
• eTutorial Plus

Error Analysis **Describe and correct the error in the graph of the given inequality.**

12. $y > x - 1$

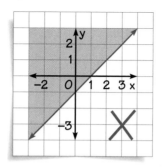

13. $y \le 2x + 2$

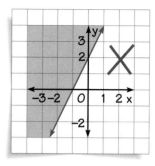

14. Critical Thinking When graphing the inequality $y \ge 2x$, can you use $(0, 0)$ as a test point to determine which side of the boundary line to shade? Explain.

15. Logical Reasoning Find an ordered pair that is a solution of $y \le x + 5$ but is *not* a solution of $y < x + 5$.

Tell whether the ordered pair is a solution of the inequality.

16. $y \geq -7x + 9$; $(1, 4)$

17. $y < 10x - 1$; $(-1, -11)$

18. $x \leq 6$; $(8, -9)$

19. $5x - 8y \geq 2$; $(0, -3)$

Graph the inequality in a coordinate plane.

20. $y < x + 4$

21. $y > -3x$

22. $y \geq \frac{2}{3}x - 5$

23. $y \leq -2x - 3$

24. $x + y \geq -2$

25. $-x + 2y \leq 6$

26. $3x - 2y > 2$

27. $4x + 3y < -12$

28. $y > -3$

29. $x \geq 1$

30. $x < -4$

31. $y \leq -1$

32. Entertainment At a county fair, you buy 20 tickets that you can use for carnival rides and other attractions. Some rides require 1 ticket while others require 2 tickets.

  a. Write an inequality describing the possible numbers of 1-ticket rides and 2-ticket rides that you can go on.

  b. Graph the inequality from part (a).

  c. Interpret and Apply Give three possible combinations of 1-ticket rides and 2-ticket rides that you can go on.

33. Video A widescreen format for a movie or TV show is one in which the image's height x and width y satisfy the inequality $y > \frac{4}{3}x$.

  a. Graph the given inequality.

  b. *Writing* Suppose the height of a widescreen image is 18 inches. Describe the possible widths of the image.

34. Extended Problem Solving You have 48 square feet of paper to use for making kites. You want to make the two types of kites shown below. Assume that the amount of paper needed for each kite is the area of the kite.

Kite A

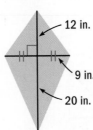

- 12 in.
- 9 in.
- 20 in.

Kite B

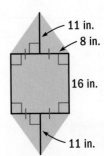

- 11 in.
- 8 in.
- 16 in.
- 11 in.

  a. Calculate Find the area of kite A and the area of kite B in square inches. Then convert the areas to square feet.

  b. Graph Write and graph an inequality describing how many of kite A and kite B you can make.

  c. Analyze What property is shared by points that represent solutions where you use up all your paper? What property is shared by points that represent solutions where you have paper left over?

$$y < x + 3$$
$$y \geq -2x - 3$$

35. Tell whether each ordered pair is a solution of the system.

    a. $(0, -4)$ **b.** $(1, 3)$ **c.** $(-2, 1)$

36. Graph the inequalities in the system. Draw both graphs in the same coordinate plane, and use a different color for each graph.

37. *Writing* Describe the region of the plane that contains the solutions of the system.

Mixed Review

Write the product using an exponent. *(Lesson 1.2)*

38. $8 \cdot 8 \cdot 8 \cdot 8 \cdot 8$ **39.** $(1.2)(1.2)(1.2)$ **40.** $x \cdot x \cdot x \cdot x \cdot x \cdot x \cdot x$

Write the expression using only positive exponents. *(Lesson 4.6)*

41. $5x^{-2}$ **42.** $2a^{-3}b^8$ **43.** $9m^{-5}n^{-4}$

Solve the linear system by graphing. *(Lesson 8.8)*

44. $y = 2x - 3$ **45.** $y = -3x - 6$ **46.** $x + y = -2$

     $y = x + 1$ $y = 2x + 4$ $2x + y = 0$

Standardized Test Practice

47. Multiple Choice Which ordered pair is *not* a solution of $y \geq -9x + 1$?

    A. $(1, -5)$ **B.** $(2, 1)$ **C.** $(-1, 10)$ **D.** $(-3, -1)$

48. Multiple Choice Which inequality has no solutions in the first quadrant of a coordinate plane?

    F. $x < 1$ **G.** $y \leq -2x + 6$ **H.** $x + y \leq 5$ **I.** $-3x - y > 6$

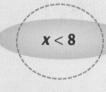

Brain GAME

Right to the Point

A list of ordered pairs is shown below.

  $(-3, -6)$ $(4, -4)$ $(-6, 9)$ $(2, -3)$ $(5, 2)$

Only one of the ordered pairs is a solution of *all* of the following inequalities. Which ordered pair is it?

$x < 8$

$y \geq -5$

$3x - y \leq 9$

$y > -2x - 4$

$x + y < 3$

Chapter Review

Vocabulary Review

relation, p. 385
domain, p. 385
range, p. 385
input, p. 385
output, p. 385
function, p. 386
vertical line test, p. 387
equation in two variables,
  p. 391

solution of an equation in
  two variables, p. 391
graph of an equation in two
  variables, p. 392
linear equation, p. 392
function form, p. 393
x-intercept, p. 398
y-intercept, p. 398
slope, p. 404

rise, p. 404
run, p. 404
slope-intercept form, p. 412
best-fitting line, p. 421
function notation, p. 426
system of linear equations,
  p. 431
solution of a linear system,
  p. 431

linear inequality in two
  variables, p. 436
solution of a linear inequality
  in two variables, p. 436
graph of a linear inequality
  in two variables, p. 436
half-plane, p. 436

1. What is the difference between the domain and the range of a relation?

2. Write a linear equation in slope-intercept form. Identify the slope and *y*-intercept.

3. How are the rise and run between two points on a line related to the line's slope?

4. Write the equation $y = -5x + 2$ using function notation.

8.1 Relations and Functions

Examples on pp. 385–387

▶ *Goal*

Use graphs and mapping diagrams to represent relations.

Example Represent the relation $(-2, -2)$, $(-1, 3)$, $(0, 4)$, $(3, 0)$ as a graph and as a mapping diagram.

a. Graph the ordered pairs as points in a coordinate plane.

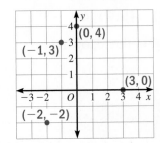

b. List the inputs and the outputs in order. Draw arrows from the inputs to their outputs.

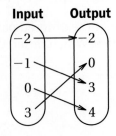

✔ **Represent the relation as a graph and as a mapping diagram.**

5. $(-5, 6)$, $(-4, 3)$, $(0, 0)$, $(4, -3)$

6. $(7, -2)$, $(6, 5)$, $(2, 3)$, $(2, -8)$, $(3, 0)$

8.2 Linear Equations in Two Variables

Examples on pp. 391–393

▶ **Goal**

Find solutions of linear equations in two variables.

Example Tell whether $(-4, -6)$ or $(2, 8)$ is a solution of $-3x + y = 6$.

a.

$$-3x + y = 6 \qquad \text{Write original equation.}$$

$$-3(-4) + (-6) \stackrel{?}{=} 6 \qquad \text{Substitute } -4 \text{ for } x \text{ and } -6 \text{ for } y.$$

$$6 = 6 \checkmark \qquad \text{Simplify.}$$

Answer $(-4, -6)$ is a solution of $-3x + y = 6$.

b.

$$-3x + y = 6 \qquad \text{Write original equation.}$$

$$-3(2) + 8 \stackrel{?}{=} 6 \qquad \text{Substitute 2 for } x \text{ and 8 for } y.$$

$$2 \neq 6 \qquad \text{Simplify.}$$

Answer $(2, 8)$ is not a solution of $-3x + y = 6$.

✔ **Tell whether the ordered pair is a solution of the equation.**

7. $y = -8x - 2$; $(-1, 6)$ **8.** $14x + 2y = -22$; $(-2, -3)$

8.3 Using Intercepts

Examples on pp. 398–399

▶ **Goal**

Find the intercepts of the graph of an equation.

Example Find the intercepts of the graph of $9x + 3y = 27$.

To find the x-intercept, let $y = 0$ and solve for x.

$$9x + 3y = 27 \qquad \text{Write original equation.}$$

$$9x + 3(0) = 27 \qquad \text{Substitute 0 for } y.$$

$$9x = 27 \qquad \text{Simplify.}$$

$$x = 3 \qquad \text{Divide each side by 9.}$$

To find the y-intercept, let $x = 0$ and solve for y.

$$9x + 3y = 27 \qquad \text{Write original equation.}$$

$$9(0) + 3y = 27 \qquad \text{Substitute 0 for } x.$$

$$3y = 27 \qquad \text{Simplify.}$$

$$y = 9 \qquad \text{Divide each side by 3.}$$

Answer The x-intercept is 3, and the y-intercept is 9.

✔ **Find the intercepts of the equation's graph.**

9. $3x - 12y = 24$ **10.** $y = 2x - 10$ **11.** $20x + 4y = -20$

8.4 The Slope of a Line

Examples on pp. 404–406

▶ **Goal**

Find the slope of a line.

Example Find the slope of the line through the points $(-3, 6)$ and $(-1, 2)$.

$$m = \frac{\text{rise}}{\text{run}} = \frac{\text{difference of } y\text{-coordinates}}{\text{difference of } x\text{-coordinates}}$$

$$= \frac{2 - 6}{-1 - (-3)} = \frac{-4}{2} = -2$$

✔ **Find the slope of the line through the given points.**

12. $(4, -7), (-2, -10)$ **13.** $(6, 9), (-3, 9)$ **14.** $(3, 4), (7, -12)$

8.5 Slope-Intercept Form

Examples on pp. 412–414

▶ **Goal**

Find the slope and y-intercept of a line.

Example Identify the slope and y-intercept of the line $24x + 4y = 80$.

$24x + 4y = 80$ Write original equation.

$4y = -24x + 80$ Subtract $24x$ from each side.

$y = -6x + 20$ Multiply each side by $\frac{1}{4}$.

Answer The line has a slope of -6 and a y-intercept of 20.

✔ **Identify the slope and y-intercept of the line with the given equation.**

15. $y = -3x + 2$ **16.** $2x + 3y = -6$ **17.** $-36x + 9y = 18$

8.6 Writing Linear Equations

Examples on pp. 419–421

▶ **Goal**

Write an equation of a line parallel to a given line.

Example Write an equation of the line that is parallel to the line $y = -3x + 4$ and passes through $(0, 7)$.

Because the slope of the given line is -3, the slope of the parallel line is also -3. The parallel line passes through $(0, 7)$, so its y-intercept is 7.

Answer An equation of the line is $y = -3x + 7$.

✔ **Write an equation of the line that is parallel to the given line and passes through the given point.**

18. $y = 3x - 8; (0, 2)$ **19.** $y = -x; (0, -6)$ **20.** $y = -9x + 1; (0, 5)$

8.7 Function Notation

Examples on
pp. 426–428

▶ **Goal**

Use function
notation.

Example Let $f(x) = 4x - 5$. Find $f(x)$ when $x = -3$.

$$f(x) = 4x - 5 \qquad \text{Write function.}$$

$$f(-3) = 4(-3) - 5 = -17 \qquad \text{Substitute } -3 \text{ for } x \text{ and simplify.}$$

✔ Let $g(x) = -2x + 6$. Find the indicated value.

21. $g(x)$ when $x = 4$ **22.** x when $g(x) = 14$ **23.** $g(-2)$

8.8 Systems of Linear Equations

Examples on
pp. 431–433

▶ **Goal**

Solve linear systems
in two variables by
graphing.

Example Solve the linear system: $y = -x + 4$
                           $y = 2x + 1$

① Graph the equations.

② Identify the apparent intersection point, $(1, 3)$.

③ Verify that $(1, 3)$ is the solution of the system by substituting 1 for x and 3 for y in each equation.

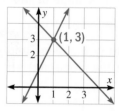

✔ Solve the linear system by graphing.

24. $y = -2x - 12$ **25.** $y = -2x + 5$ **26.** $2x + y = 1$
      $y = x - 3$ $y = 4x - 1$ $4x - 2y = 22$

8.9 Graphs of Linear Inequalities

Examples on
pp. 436–438

▶ **Goal**

Graph linear
inequalities in
two variables.

Example Graph $y > x - 3$.

① Graph the boundary line $y = x - 3$. Use a dashed line.

② Use $(0, 0)$ as a test point.

$$y > x - 3$$
$$0 > 0 - 3 = -3 ✔$$

③ Shade the half-plane that contains $(0, 0)$.

✔ Graph the inequality in a coordinate plane.

27. $y \leq 2x + 3$ **28.** $y \geq -4$ **29.** $3x + y > -6$

Chapter Test

Represent the relation as a graph and as a mapping diagram. Then tell whether the relation is a function. Explain your reasoning.

1. $(0, -2), (0, -1), (0, 0), (0, 1), (0, 2)$

2. $(3, 5), (6, 7) (9, 9), (8, 1)$

Tell whether each ordered pair is a solution of the equation.

3. $y = 7 - 2x; (5, 1), (6, -5), (2, 3)$

4. $y = -3x - 4; (-1, -1), (0, -4), (10, 34)$

Find the intercepts of the equation's graph. Then graph the equation.

5. $x + y = 4$

6. $4x - 3y = 24$

7. $y = \frac{5}{2}x - 10$

8. $y = 3x + 6$

Find the slope of the line through the given points.

9. $(8, -3), (10, 7)$

10. $(4, 2), (0, 3)$

11. $(-2, 0), (-2, 5)$

12. $(4, 7), (10, 7)$

Identify the slope and y-intercept of the line with the given equation. Use the slope and y-intercept to graph the equation.

13. $y = \frac{4}{3}x - 7$

14. $y = 5x + 1$

15. $-6x + y = -2$

16. $6x - 5y = 10$

17. Televisions The table shows the number of televisions sold each month at a retail store.

  a. Make a scatter plot of the data pairs. Draw the line that appears to best fit the data points.

  b. Write an equation of your line in slope-intercept form.

  c. Predict the number of televisions sold at the store during the 7th month.

Month, x	Televisions, y
1	360
2	375
3	380
4	389
5	402

Write a linear function that satisfies the given conditions.

18. $f(0) = 3, f(4) = 9$

19. $g(0) = -6, g(15) = -9$

20. $h(-4) = -5, h(0) = 10$

Solve the linear system by graphing.

21. $x + 5y = -10$
$x + 5y = 5$

22. $3x - y = -7$
$-3x + y = 7$

23. $2x - y = 5$
$x + 2y = -10$

Graph the inequality in a coordinate plane.

24. $x < 7$

25. $y \le 3x - 5$

26. $x + 2y > 6$

Chapter Standardized Test

Test-Taking Strategy You should use your answer sheet only for writing answers, but you can use your test booklet to write notes or draw sketches.

1. What is the domain of the relation $(8, 2)$, $(6, 4)$, $(4, 2)$, $(2, 4)$?

   A. 2, 4   **B.** 2, 4, 6, 8

   C. 6, 8   **D.** 2, 4, 8

2. Which equation is *not* a function?

   F. $x + y = 5$ **G.** $2x - y = 3$

   H. $x = 4$ **I.** $y = -1$

3. What is the x-intercept of the graph of $y = \frac{1}{4}x - 6$?

   A. -6 **B.** $\frac{1}{4}$ **C.** 6   **D.** 24

4. What is the slope of the line through the points $(2, 2)$ and $(4, 6)$?

   F. $\frac{1}{2}$ **G.** $\frac{3}{4}$ **H.** $\frac{4}{3}$ **I.** 2

5. What is the y-intercept of the graph of $-x + 4y = -24$?

   A. -6 **B.** 4   **C.** 6   **D.** 24

6. What is the slope of the line with equation $-x + 4y = -24$?

   F. -6 **G.** $\frac{1}{4}$ **H.** 6   **I.** 24

7. What is the slope of a line perpendicular to the line with equation $y = 4x - 5$?

   A. -4 **B.** $-\frac{1}{4}$ **C.** $\frac{1}{5}$ **D.** 5

8. Given that $f(x) = -2x + 1$, what is $f(5)$?

   F. -11 **G.** -9 **H.** -2 **I.** 2

9. How many solutions does the system of equations $4x + 2y = 6$ and $y = -2x + 6$ have?

   A. 0   **B.** 1

   C. 2   **D.** Infinitely many

10. What is the solution of the system of equations $3x + y = -11$ and $y = 2x + 9$?

    F. $(1, -4)$ **G.** $(-1, 4)$

    H. $(4, -1)$ **I.** $(-4, 1)$

11. The graph of which inequality is shown?

    A. $y < \frac{3}{2}x - 1$

    B. $2x + \frac{1}{3}y \geq -2$

    C. $3x + 2y > -2$

    D. $3x + 2y < -2$

    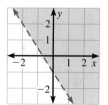

12. **Short Response** For which value of a are the lines $y = ax + 6$ and $x + 2y = 4$ parallel? For which value of a are the lines $y = ax + 6$ and $x + 2y = 4$ perpendicular? Explain.

13. **Extended Response** You have a $100 gift card to a store that rents movies and video games. The rental fee for a movie is $4, and the rental fee for a video game is $5.

    a. Write an equation describing the possible numbers of movies and video games you can rent.

    b. Use intercepts to graph the equation from part (a).

    c. Give three possible combinations of movies and video games you can rent.

Solving *the* Problem

Problems with No Solution or Many Solutions

Not all problems have a single solution. Instead, a problem may have no solution or many solutions.

Problem At your class picnic, you volunteer to grill hot dogs. The hot dogs come in packages of 8, and the hot dog buns come in packages of 6. After everyone is finished eating, you have an open package of hot dogs that contains 2 hot dogs and an open package of hot dog buns that contains 4 buns. How many hot dogs were eaten?

1 Write an equation.

Let x be the number of complete packages of hot dogs used. The total number d of hot dogs eaten is the sum of the 8x hot dogs in the complete packages used and the $8 - 2 = 6$ hot dogs used in the last package.

$$d = 8x + 6$$

Let y be the number of complete packages of buns used. The total number b of buns eaten is the sum of the 6y buns in the complete packages used and the $6 - 4 = 2$ buns used in the last package.

$$b = 6y + 2$$

Assume that the same number of buns and hot dogs were eaten. Then you can write an equation giving y as a function of x.

$$b = d$$
$$6y + 2 = 8x + 6$$
$$6y = 8x + 4$$
$$y = \frac{8}{6}x + \frac{4}{6}$$
$$y = \frac{4}{3}x + \frac{2}{3}$$

The possible numbers of complete hot dog and bun packages used are given by the solutions (x, y) of $y = \frac{4}{3}x + \frac{2}{3}$, where x and y are whole numbers.

2 Make a graph.

Graph $y = \frac{4}{3}x + \frac{2}{3}$. Label the points on the graph that have whole-number coordinates.

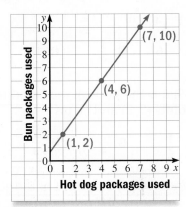

3 Solve the problem.

Make a table of values for $d = 8x + 6$ using the x-coordinates of the labeled points on the graph.

x	Substitution	d
1	$d = 8(1) + 6$	14
4	$d = 8(4) + 6$	38
7	$d = 8(7) + 6$	62

Answer Some possible numbers of hot dogs eaten are 14, 38, and 62.

Problem Solving Practice

Solve the given problem. If the problem has no solution, say so and explain why.

1. **Number Sense** Write three expressions such that each expression is equal to 1 and contains four 4's (but no other numbers). The following is an example:

$$\frac{4 + 4}{4 + 4}$$

2. **Refrigerators** Refrigerator A has a price of $600 and costs $35 per year in electricity to operate. Refrigerator B has a price of $800 and costs $40 per year in electricity to operate. After how many years are the total costs of the two refrigerators the same?

3. **Coins** Your uncle gives you and your sister a jar of coins from around the world. You divide them equally and have 1 coin left over. Then your mother tells you to share the coins with your cousin as well. After you divide the coins equally among the three of you, there are no coins left over. How many coins were in the jar?

4. **Magic Squares** A 3-by-3 *magic square* contains 9 consecutive integers arranged so that the sum of the numbers in each row, column, or diagonal is the same. Below is a 3-by-3 magic square that uses the integers 1 through 9. Make a 3-by-3 magic square that uses a different set of consecutive integers.

4	9	2
3	5	7
8	1	6

5. **Baking** You have 12 cups of fresh pumpkin to use for baking. You need $1\frac{1}{2}$ cups to make a pumpkin pie and 1 cup to make a loaf of pumpkin bread. Find three possible combinations of pies and loaves of bread you can make that use up all the pumpkin.

6. **Class Picnic** You are in charge of grilling hamburgers at your class picnic. The hamburger patties come in packages of 12, and the hamburger buns come in packages of 8. After everyone is finished eating, you have an open package of hamburger patties that contains 5 patties and an open package of hamburger buns that contains 5 buns. How many hamburgers were eaten?

7. **Swimming Pool** A municipal swimming pool is rectangular and covers an area of 15,000 square feet. What are the length and the width of the pool?

8. **Checkerboard** A standard checkerboard has 32 red squares and 32 black squares. Shown below is a checkerboard with two black squares removed from its upper left and lower right corners. Can you cover this checkerboard with dominoes, where each domino covers two adjacent squares in the same row or column? Explain.

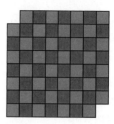

9. **Logical Reasoning** Find two consecutive integers that have the given property.

   a. The sum of the integers is 20.

   b. The product of the integers is 20.

Real Numbers *and* Right Triangles

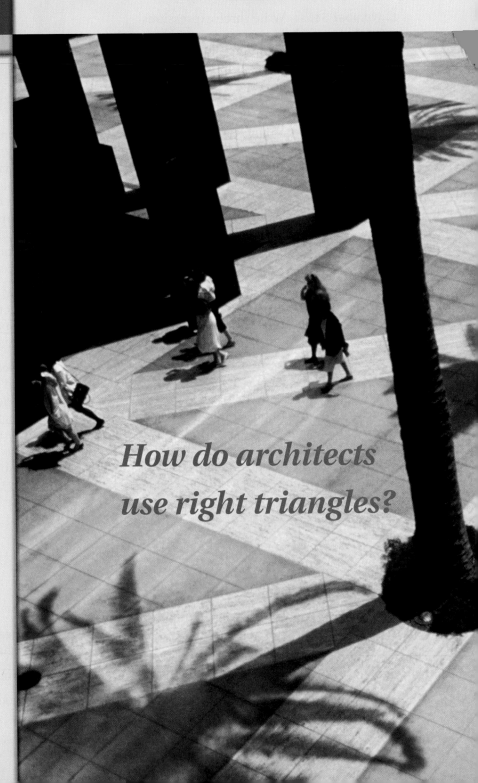

How do architects use right triangles?

CHAPTER 9
INTERNET Preview
CLASSZONE.COM

- **eEdition Plus Online**
- **eWorkbook Plus Online**
- **eTutorial Plus Online**
- **State Test Practice**
- **More Examples**

MATH *In the* **Real World**

Courtyard Each of the triangles in this courtyard in Los Angeles, California, is a right triangle. In this chapter, you will use special relationships among the side lengths of right triangles to solve problems about architecture.

What do you think? To create triangles like those in the photo, draw a square on graph paper. Then draw a diagonal of the square. Do the two triangles appear to be congruent? Explain.

Chapter Prerequisite Skills

PREREQUISITE SKILLS QUIZ

Preparing for Success **To prepare for success in this chapter, test your knowledge of these concepts and skills. You may want to look at the pages referred to in blue for additional review.**

1. **Vocabulary** Is the number -3 a rational number? an integer? a whole number?

2. Order the numbers $-\dfrac{17}{9}$, -2, $\dfrac{16}{3}$, and -3.7 from least to greatest. *(p. 219)*

Tell whether the ratio is in simplest form. If it is not, write it in simplest form. *(p. 269)*

3. 3 to 6

4. $\dfrac{34}{51}$

5. $\dfrac{23}{3}$

6. $76 : 38$

7. **Shadows** A student who is 5 feet tall is standing next to a fence post. The student casts a shadow 15 feet long. The fence post casts a shadow 18 feet long. How tall is the fence post? *(p. 293)*

Find the slope of the line through the given points. *(p. 404)*

8. $(-2, -8)$, $(7, 3)$

9. $(4, 5)$, $(4, 2)$

10. $(-5, 3)$, $(-10, 13)$

NOTETAKING STRATEGIES

Note *Worthy*

You will find a notetaking strategy at the beginning of each chapter. Look for additional notetaking and study strategies throughout the chapter.

USING A CONCEPT MAP When you learn new concepts that are related to each other, you may find it helpful to organize the ideas in a concept map.

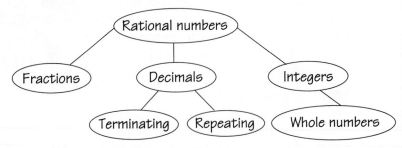

In Lesson 9.6, you can use a concept map to help you organize your notes on triangles.

9.1

Square Roots

BEFORE	Now	WHY?
You found squares of numbers.	You'll find and approximate square roots of numbers.	So you can find a person's running speed, as in Ex. 59.

Vocabulary

square root, p. 453
perfect square, p. 454
radical expression, p. 454

Human Chess In September of every even-numbered year, people in Marostica, Italy, play an unusual chess game. Each chess piece is portrayed by a person. The people portraying the knights are even on horseback!

The chessboard is a square with an area of 324 square meters. What is the length of each side of the board? To answer this question, you need to find the *square root* of 324.

A **square root** of a number n is a number m such that $m^2 = n$. Every positive number has two square roots. One square root is positive and the other is negative. The radical sign, $\sqrt{}$, represents a nonnegative square root. The symbol $\pm$, read "plus or minus," refers to both square roots of a positive number. For example:

$\sqrt{100} = 10$ **Positive square root of 100**

$-\sqrt{100} = -10$ **Negative square root of 100**

$\pm\sqrt{100} = \pm10$ **Positive or negative square root of 100**

Zero has only one square root, itself.

Study *Strategy*

In Example 1, it doesn't make sense to find the negative square root of 324, because length cannot be negative.

Example 1   *Finding a Square Root*

The chessboard described above is a square with an area of 324 square meters, so the length of each side of the chessboard is the positive square root of 324.

$\sqrt{324} = 18$ because $18^2 = 324$.

Answer The length of each side of the chessboard is 18 meters.

 Checkpoint

Find the square roots of the number.

1. 16   **2.** 64   **3.** 144   **4.** 256

Approximating Square Roots A **perfect square** is a number that is the square of an integer. For example, 1, 4, and 9 are perfect squares.

$$1 = 1^2, 4 = 2^2, \text{ and } 9 = 3^2$$

You can use perfect squares to approximate a square root of a number.

Note *Worthy*

You may find it helpful to make a list of the first 20 perfect squares and their square roots in your notebook and memorize them. You can find a table of squares and square roots on p. 822.

Example 2 *Approximating a Square Root*

Approximate $\sqrt{51}$ to the nearest integer.

The perfect square closest to, but less than, 51 is 49. The perfect square closest to, but greater than, 51 is 64. So, 51 is between 49 and 64. This statement can be expressed by the *compound inequality* $49 < 51 < 64$.

$49 < 51 < 64$	Identify perfect squares closest to **51**.
$\sqrt{49} < \sqrt{51} < \sqrt{64}$	Take positive square root of each number.
$7 < \sqrt{51} < 8$	Evaluate square root of each perfect square.

Answer Because 51 is closer to 49 than to 64, $\sqrt{51}$ is closer to 7 than to 8. So, to the nearest integer, $\sqrt{51} \approx 7$.

 *Checkpoint*

5. Approximate $\sqrt{125}$ to the nearest whole number.

Tech *Help*

When you enter a square root on the calculator, you should also enter a right parenthesis to close the left parenthesis that the calculator enters. Although the calculator shows 8 digits for the decimal part of the square root in Example 3, the decimal actually continues without end.

Example 3 *Using a Calculator*

Use a calculator to approximate $\sqrt{515}$. Round to the nearest tenth.

Keystrokes

[2nd] [√] **515** [ )] [=]

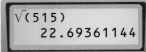
$$\sqrt{(515)}$$
$$22.69361144$$

Answer

$\sqrt{515} \approx 22.7$

Radical Expressions A **radical expression** is an expression that involves a radical sign. The horizontal bar in a radical sign is a grouping symbol. When you evaluate a radical expression, evaluate the expression inside the radical symbol before finding the square root.

Example 4 *Evaluating a Radical Expression*

Evaluate $2\sqrt{a + b^2}$ when $a = 11$ and $b = 5$.

$2\sqrt{a + b^2} = 2\sqrt{11 + 5^2}$	Substitute 11 for a and 5 for b.
$= 2\sqrt{36}$	Evaluate expression inside radical symbol.
$= 2 \cdot 6 = 12$	Evaluate square root. Multiply.

 **Checkpoint**

Evaluate the expression when $a = 12$ and $b = 4$.

6. $\sqrt{a + b}$ **7.** $\sqrt{b^2 - a}$ **8.** $3\sqrt{ab + 1}$

Example 5 | *Solving an Equation Using Square Roots*

Physics An amusement park ride includes a free fall drop of 272 feet. You can use the equation $d = 16t^2$ to determine the time t in seconds that it takes a dropped object to fall a distance of d feet. How long does the free fall part of the ride take?

Solution

$d = 16t^2$	Write original equation.
$272 = 16t^2$	Substitute 272 for d.
$17 = t^2$	Divide each side by 16.
$\pm\sqrt{17} = t$	Use definition of square root.
$\pm 4.1 \approx t$	Use a calculator to approximate square root.

Answer Because only the positive solution makes sense in this situation, the free fall part of the ride takes about 4.1 seconds.

9.1 Exercises

More Practice, p. 811

INTERNET
eWorkbook Plus
CLASSZONE.COM

Guided Practice

Vocabulary Check   **1.** Describe and give an example of a perfect square.

2. You know that one square root of a number x is -9. What is the other square root? What is the value of x?

Skill Check   **Find the square roots of the number.**

3. 4   **4.** 36   **5.** 121   **6.** 225

Approximate the square root to the nearest integer.

7. $\sqrt{10}$ **8.** $-\sqrt{84}$ **9.** $\sqrt{151}$ **10.** $-\sqrt{200}$

Solve the equation.

11. $a^2 = 9$ **12.** $n^2 = 25$ **13.** $361 = x^2$ **14.** $400 = y^2$

Guided Problem Solving   **15. Eiffel Tower** The base of the Eiffel Tower is a square with an area of 15,625 square feet. What is the length of a side of the base?

1) Write an equation that relates base area A and side length s.

2) Substitute 15,625 for A in the equation in Step 1 and solve for s.

Practice and Problem Solving

Homework *Help*

Example	Exercises
1	16–24
2	25–32, 54–57
3	33–40
4	41–44
5	45–53, 58–59

Online Resources
CLASSZONE.COM

- More Examples
- eTutorial Plus

In the following exercises, you may find it helpful to use a calculator for approximating square roots.

Find the square roots of the number.

16. 25　　　　**17.** 169　　　　**18.** 81　　　　**19.** 289

20. 1024　　　**21.** 484　　　　**22.** 1600　　　**23.** 900

24. Geometry The area of a square is 49 square feet. Find the side length.

Approximate the square root to the nearest integer.

25. $\sqrt{38}$　　　**26.** $-\sqrt{120}$　　**27.** $-\sqrt{148}$　　**28.** $\sqrt{17}$

29. $-\sqrt{78}$　　**30.** $\sqrt{250}$　　**31.** $\sqrt{15.3}$　　**32.** $-\sqrt{7.4}$

Use a calculator to approximate the square root. Round to the nearest tenth.

33. $\sqrt{3}$　　　**34.** $-\sqrt{10}$　　**35.** $\sqrt{86}$　　　**36.** $\sqrt{110}$

37. $-\sqrt{33}$　　**38.** $\sqrt{1325}$　　**39.** $\sqrt{19.5}$　　**40.** $\sqrt{6.92}$

Evaluate the expression when $a = 48$ and $b = 12$.

41. $\sqrt{a - b}$　　**42.** $\sqrt{a + b + 4}$　　**43.** $-3\sqrt{ab}$　　**44.** $\sqrt{b^2 - (a + 15)}$

Solve the equation. Round to the nearest tenth if necessary.

45. $x^2 = 49$　　**46.** $y^2 = 676$　　**47.** $441 = t^2$　　**48.** $n^2 = 576$

49. $20 = m^2$　　**50.** $c^2 = 125$　　**51.** $5y^2 = 110$　　**52.** $200 = 16t^2$

53. Critical Thinking Write an equation that has exactly two solutions, 1.5 and −1.5.

In Exercises 54–57, match the number with a point on the number line.

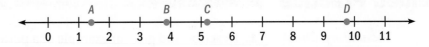

54. $\sqrt{15}$　　　　**55.** $\sqrt{2}$　　　　**56.** $\sqrt{95}$　　　　**57.** $\sqrt{27}$

58. Photography You can use the following rule of thumb when photographing fireworks: The f-stop, a number that describes the size of the opening of the camera lens, should be the number closest to the square root of the film speed. You have a camera with f-stop numbers 2.8, 4, 5.6, 8, 11, 16, and 22. Which f-stop should you use to photograph fireworks if you are using a film speed of 64? of 100?

59. Running You can use the formula $l = 0.0625s^2$ to approximate the maximum running speed s (in meters per second) that a person with leg length l (in meters) can sustain. Find the maximum running speed for a person with a leg length of 0.64 meter.

Solve the equation. Round to the nearest hundredth if necessary.

60. $15 = 2h^2 - 3$　　**61.** $162 = 0.5t^2$　　**62.** $1400 = 10z^2 + 2$

63. $3x^2 + 5 = 30$　　**64.** $1.5n^2 + 7 = 20$　　**65.** $2a^2 + 1 = 98$

Fireworks near the Space Needle in Seattle, Washington

66. Consider the function $y = \sqrt{x}$.

a. Make a table of ordered pairs (x, y) for $x = 0, 1, 4, 9, 16,$ and 25.

b. Plot the ordered pairs from part (a) on a coordinate plane.

c. *Writing* Is $y = \sqrt{x}$ a linear function? Explain.

67. Extended Problem Solving A *tsunami* is an ocean wave that moves very fast in deep water, but slows as it reaches shallow water. As the wave slows, it rises to great heights, often causing enormous destruction on land. A tsunami's speed s (in feet per second) and the depth d of the water (in feet) are related by the equation $s^2 = 32d$. Suppose an earthquake at sea produces a tsunami in water 15,000 feet deep.

a. Calculate Find the original speed of the wave to the nearest mile per hour.

b. Apply The wave enters a harbor 45 feet deep. Find the change in the wave's speed from the original speed. Give your answer to the nearest mile per hour.

In the **Real World**

Tsunamis An earthquake occurred off the coast of Chile in 1960, generating a tsunami. The tsunami reached Japan, about 10,000 miles away, 22 hours later. To the nearest mile per hour, how fast did the tsunami travel?

68. The *cube root* of a number n is the number m such that $m^3 = n$. For example, because $2^3 = 8$, the cube root of 8 is 2. You write this as $\sqrt[3]{8} = 2$. The table shows some whole numbers and their cube roots.

a	$\sqrt[3]{a}$
0	0
1	1
8	2
27	3
64	4

a. Use the table to approximate each cube root to the nearest integer: $\sqrt[3]{3}, \sqrt[3]{55}, \sqrt[3]{22}$.

b. Critical Thinking Do negative numbers have cube roots? Explain.

c. Solve the equation $x^3 = 125$.

69. Challenge Solve $(x - 2)^2 + 1 = 37$. Describe the steps you use.

Mixed Review

Write the prime factorization of the number. *(Lesson 4.1)*

70. 45   **71.** 98   **72.** 484   **73.** 700

Write the fraction in simplest form. *(Lesson 4.3)*

74. $\dfrac{21}{48}$ **75.** $\dfrac{13}{52}$ **76.** $\dfrac{30}{125}$ **77.** $\dfrac{30}{162}$

Use the percent equation to answer the question. *(Lesson 7.4)*

78. What percent of 240 is 42?   **79.** What number is 80% of 60?

80. 7 is 3.5% of what number?   **81.** What percent of 20 is 1.3?

Standardized Test Practice

82. Multiple Choice What is $\sqrt{500}$ to the nearest integer?

A. 20   **B.** 21   **C.** 22   **D.** 23

83. Multiple Choice What is the value of the expression $\sqrt{mn^2}$ when $m = 4$ and $n = 5$?

F. 10   **G.** 20   **H.** 80   **I.** 100

9.2 Simplifying Square Roots

BEFORE　　　　　Now　　　　　WHY?

You found square roots.　You'll simplify radical expressions.　So you can find the distance to the horizon, as in Ex. 27.

Vocabulary

simplest form of a radical expression, p. 458

Compare the following pair of products:

$$\sqrt{4} \cdot \sqrt{16} = 2 \cdot 4 = 8 \qquad\qquad \sqrt{4 \cdot 16} = \sqrt{64} = 8$$

Notice that $\sqrt{4} \cdot \sqrt{16} = \sqrt{4 \cdot 16}$. This result suggests the product property of square roots.

Product Property of Square Roots

Algebra

$\sqrt{ab} = \sqrt{a} \cdot \sqrt{b}$, where $a \geq 0$ and $b \geq 0$

Numbers

$\sqrt{9 \cdot 7} = \sqrt{9} \cdot \sqrt{7} = 3\sqrt{7}$

You can use the product property of square roots to simplify radical expressions. A radical expression is in **simplest form** when:

- No factor of the expression under the radical sign has any perfect square factor other than 1.

- There are no fractions under the radical sign, and no radical sign in the denominator of any fraction.

In this book, all variables in radical expressions represent nonnegative numbers.

Example 1　*Simplifying a Radical Expression*

$$\sqrt{180} = \sqrt{36 \cdot 5} \qquad \text{Factor using greatest perfect square factor.}$$
$$= \sqrt{36} \cdot \sqrt{5} \qquad \text{Product property of square roots}$$
$$= 6\sqrt{5} \qquad\qquad \text{Simplify.}$$

Reading *Algebra*

The final variable expression in Example 2 is written as $2s\sqrt{6}$ rather than as $2\sqrt{6}s$ to make it clear than the variable is *not* under the radical sign.

Example 2　*Simplifying a Variable Expression*

$$\sqrt{24s^2} = \sqrt{4 \cdot 6 \cdot s^2} \qquad \text{Factor using greatest perfect square factor.}$$
$$= \sqrt{4} \cdot \sqrt{6} \cdot \sqrt{s^2} \qquad \text{Product property of square roots}$$
$$= 2 \cdot \sqrt{6} \cdot s \qquad\qquad \text{Simplify.}$$
$$= 2s\sqrt{6} \qquad\qquad\quad \text{Commutative property}$$

Quotients Notice that $\sqrt{\dfrac{100}{4}} = \sqrt{25} = 5$, and $\dfrac{\sqrt{100}}{\sqrt{4}} = \dfrac{10}{2} = 5$. This result suggests the quotient property of square roots, which you can also use to simplify radical expressions.

Quotient Property of Square Roots

Algebra

$$\sqrt{\dfrac{a}{b}} = \dfrac{\sqrt{a}}{\sqrt{b}}, \text{ where } a \geq 0 \text{ and } b > 0$$

Numbers

$$\sqrt{\dfrac{11}{4}} = \dfrac{\sqrt{11}}{\sqrt{4}} = \dfrac{\sqrt{11}}{2}$$

Example 3 *Simplifying a Radical Expression*

$$\sqrt{\dfrac{13}{36}} = \dfrac{\sqrt{13}}{\sqrt{36}} \qquad \text{Quotient property of square roots}$$

$$= \dfrac{\sqrt{13}}{6} \qquad \text{Simplify.}$$

✔ *Checkpoint*

Simplify the expression.

1. $\sqrt{63}$ **2.** $\sqrt{54t^2}$ **3.** $\sqrt{\dfrac{15}{16}}$ **4.** $\sqrt{\dfrac{32}{n^2}}$

Example 4 *Using Radical Expressions*

Accident Investigation After a car accident, a police officer measures the length l (in feet) of a car's skid marks. The expression $\sqrt{27l}$ gives the car's speed in miles per hour at the time the brakes were applied.

a. Write the expression in simplest form.

b. The skid marks are 125 feet long. Use the simplified expression to approximate the car's speed when the brakes were applied.

Solution

a. $\sqrt{27l} = \sqrt{9 \cdot 3 \cdot l}$ Factor using greatest perfect square factor.

$\qquad = \sqrt{9} \cdot \sqrt{3l}$ Product property of square roots

$\qquad = 3\sqrt{3l}$ Simplify.

Answer In simplest form, $\sqrt{27l} = 3\sqrt{3l}$.

b. $3\sqrt{3l} = 3\sqrt{3 \cdot 125}$ Substitute 125 for l.

$\qquad = 3\sqrt{375}$ Multiply.

$\qquad \approx 58$ Approximate using a calculator.

Answer The car's speed was about 58 miles per hour.

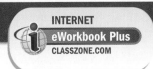
Guided Practice

Vocabulary Check

1. Tell whether the expression $3\sqrt{5}$ is in simplest form. Explain.

2. Explain how to use the product property of square roots to simplify the expression $\sqrt{700}$.

Skill Check   **In Exercises 3–6, simplify the expression.**

3. $\sqrt{12}$ 4. $\sqrt{48}$ 5. $\sqrt{\dfrac{81}{4}}$ 6. $\sqrt{\dfrac{7}{25}}$

7. A square has an area of 300 square units. Find the length of a side of the square as a radical expression in simplest form.

8. **Error Analysis** Describe and correct the error in writing $\sqrt{72}$ in simplest form.

$$\sqrt{72} = \sqrt{4 \cdot 18}$$
$$= \sqrt{4} \cdot \sqrt{18} = 2\sqrt{18}$$

Practice and Problem Solving

Homework *Help*

Example	Exercises
1	9–14
2	13–14, 23–26
3	15–20, 23–26
4	21–22

Online Resources
CLASSZONE.COM

• More Examples
• eTutorial Plus

In the following exercises, you may find it helpful to use a calculator for approximating square roots.

Simplify the expression.

9. $\sqrt{98}$ 10. $\sqrt{250}$ 11. $\sqrt{288}$ 12. $\sqrt{243}$

13. $\sqrt{300x}$ 14. $\sqrt{63b^2}$ 15. $\sqrt{\dfrac{11}{36}}$ 16. $\sqrt{\dfrac{35}{144}}$

17. $\sqrt{\dfrac{80}{81}}$ 18. $\sqrt{\dfrac{105}{121}}$ 19. $\sqrt{\dfrac{z}{64}}$ 20. $\sqrt{\dfrac{28f^2}{9}}$

21. **Dropped Object** You can use the expression $\sqrt{\dfrac{h}{16}}$ to find the time in seconds that it takes an object dropped from a height of h feet to hit the ground. You drop an object from a height of 63 feet. Write an expression in simplest form for the time it takes the object to hit the ground. Then approximate the time to the nearest second.

22. **Walking Speed** Your maximum walking speed in inches per second can be approximated using the expression $\sqrt{384l}$, where l is your leg length in inches. Suppose your leg length is 28 inches. Write an expression in simplest form for your maximum walking speed. Then approximate the speed to the nearest inch per second.

Simplify the expression.

23. $\sqrt{75x^2y}$ 24. $\sqrt{\dfrac{500n}{4y^2}}$ 25. $\sqrt{7200m^2n^2}$ 26. $\sqrt{\dfrac{5b^2}{125}}$

27. Extended Problem Solving The visual horizon is the distance you can see before your line of sight is blocked by Earth's surface. If you are in a boat on the ocean, the visual horizon in nautical miles can be approximated by the expression $\sqrt{4h}$, where h is the vertical distance in meters from your eye to the water's surface. Suppose your boat is approaching a lighthouse from which your friend is observing you.

a. Calculate Your eyes are 4 meters above the water's surface. Your friend's eyes are 52 meters above the water's surface. Find your visual horizon and your friend's visual horizon in simplest form.

b. Critical Thinking You will be able to see the lighthouse when your distance from it is the sum of your visual horizon and your friend's. Use the diagram to explain why this is true.

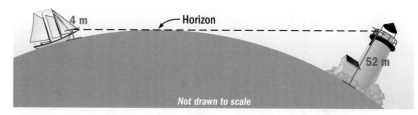

Not drawn to scale

c. Interpret and Apply Find the value of each expression in part (a) to the nearest nautical mile. Use the results to determine how far you will be from the lighthouse when you first see it.

28. *Writing* Describe how you could use the prime factorization of 450 to write $\sqrt{450}$ in simplest form.

Write the expression in simplest form.

29. $\sqrt{y^3}$ **30.** $\sqrt{n^5}$ **31.** $\sqrt{a^8}$ **32.** $\sqrt{n^9}$

33. Challenge Predict the next three numbers in the pattern:

$\sqrt{2},\ 2,\ \sqrt{6},\ 2\sqrt{2},\ \sqrt{10},\ 2\sqrt{3},\ \sqrt{14},\ 4,\ \ldots.$

Mixed Review

Evaluate the expression when $x = 6$, $y = 10$, and $z = 12$. *(Lesson 1.3)*

34. $x^2 + y^2$ **35.** $x^2 + z^2$ **36.** $z^2 - x^2$ **37.** $y^2 - x^2$

Write the fraction in simplest form. *(Lesson 4.3)*

38. $\dfrac{28x}{x^2}$ **39.** $\dfrac{6y^3}{9y^2}$ **40.** $\dfrac{21n}{6n^3}$ **41.** $\dfrac{8cd}{40c^2}$

Approximate the square root to the nearest integer. *(Lesson 9.1)*

42. $\sqrt{27}$ **43.** $\sqrt{47}$ **44.** $\sqrt{79}$ **45.** $\sqrt{103}$

Standardized Test Practice

46. Multiple Choice Which expression is *not* equivalent to $\sqrt{48}$?

A. $\sqrt{3 \cdot 16}$ **B.** $16\sqrt{3}$ **C.** $\sqrt{4^2 \cdot 3}$ **D.** $4\sqrt{3}$

47. Multiple Choice Which expression represents $\sqrt{\dfrac{9x}{y^2}}$ in simplest form?

F. $\dfrac{3x}{y}$ **G.** $\dfrac{\sqrt{3x}}{y}$ **H.** $\dfrac{\sqrt{9x}}{y}$ **I.** $\dfrac{3\sqrt{x}}{y}$

Triangles

▶ **Review** these topics in preparation for solving problems that involve triangles in Lessons 9.3, 9.6–9.8, and 10.1.

Sum of Angle Measures in a Triangle

The sum of the angle measures in any triangle is 180°, as the diagram below suggests. You can use this fact to find unknown measures in triangles.

Example Find the value of x.

$90° + 48° + x° = 180°$ **Sum of angle measures is 180°.**

$138 + x = 180$ **Add.**

$x = 42$ **Subtract 138 from each side.**

Answer The value of x is 42.

Classifying Triangles by Angle Measures

Triangles can be classified by the measures of their angles.

Acute triangle	Right triangle	Obtuse triangle	Equiangular triangle
3 acute angles	1 right angle	1 obtuse angle	3 congruent angles

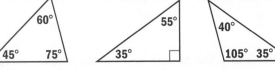

Example Classify the triangle by its angle measures.

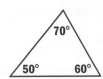

The triangle has 3 acute angles, so it is an acute triangle.

Classifying Triangles by Side Lengths

Triangles can be classified by the lengths of their sides.

Equilateral triangle
3 congruent sides

Isosceles triangle
At least 2 congruent sides

Scalene triangle
No congruent sides

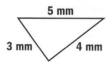

An equilateral triangle is isosceles and is also equiangular.

Example Classify the triangle by its side lengths.

The triangle has two congruent sides, so it is an isosceles triangle.

✔ Checkpoint

▶ **Test** your knowledge of triangles by solving these problems.

Find the value of x.

1.

45°

x°

2.

33° x°

27°

3.

x°

40°   55°

4. **Pennants** The angles at the wide end of the pennant have measures of 80° and 75°. Find the measure of the angle at the narrow end of the pennant.

GO EAGLES!

Classify the triangle by its angle measures.

5.

82°

60°   38°

6.

110°

10°

60°

7.

30°

60°

Classify the triangle by its side lengths.

8.

4 cm   8 cm

10 cm

9.

6 in.

6 in.

6 in.

10.

15 m

9 m   9 m

9.3 Investigating Right Triangles

Goal
Investigate how the lengths of the sides of a right triangle are related.

Materials
• graph paper
• pencil
• scissors
• tape

Investigate

Use graph paper to see how the lengths of the sides of a right triangle are related.

1 Draw a right triangle so that the sides that form the right angle have lengths of 3 units and 4 units. Draw a square on each side of the triangle.

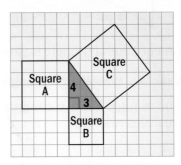

2 Cut out square A and square B. Arrange them side by side as shown.

3 Draw two copies of the right triangle in Step 1 on the squares as shown.

4 Cut along the longest side of the right triangles. Then reposition and tape the pieces as shown.

5 Position the square from Step 4 on the longest side of the triangle in Step 1. What do you notice?

Draw Conclusions

1. **Compare** How is the square formed in Step 4 related to square C in Step 1? What is the area of each square? How do you know?

2. *Writing* What is the length of a side of the square in Step 4? Explain.

3. **Critical Thinking** Write an equation that relates the areas of the squares in Step 1 in terms of their side lengths.

The Pythagorean Theorem

BEFORE ⟩ *Now* WHY?

You used square roots.

You'll use the Pythagorean theorem to solve problems.

So you can find the length of a side of a TV screen, as in Ex. 19.

Vocabulary

hypotenuse, p. 465
leg, p. 465
Pythagorean theorem,
  p. 465

Bridges The William H. Harsha Bridge is a cable-stayed bridge that spans the Ohio River between Maysville, Kentucky, and Aberdeen, Ohio. About how long is the cable shown in red?

In a right triangle, the **hypotenuse** is the side opposite the right angle. The **legs** are the sides that form the right angle. The lengths of the legs and the length of the hypotenuse of a right triangle are related by the **Pythagorean theorem**.

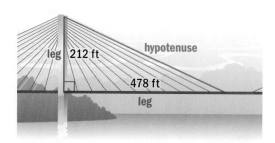

leg 212 ft

hypotenuse

478 ft

leg

Pythagorean Theorem

Words For any right triangle, the sum of the squares of the lengths of the legs equals the square of the length of the hypotenuse.

Algebra $a^2 + b^2 = c^2$

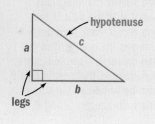

hypotenuse

a

c

b

legs

Example 1 *Finding the Length of a Hypotenuse*

To find the length (to the nearest foot) of the cable shown above, use the right triangle formed by the tower, the bridge surface, and the cable.

$$a^2 + b^2 = c^2 \quad \text{Pythagorean theorem}$$

$$212^2 + 478^2 = c^2 \quad \text{Substitute 212 for } a \text{ and 478 for } b.$$

$$44{,}944 + 228{,}484 = c^2 \quad \text{Evaluate powers.}$$

$$273{,}428 = c^2 \quad \text{Add.}$$

$$\sqrt{273{,}428} = c \quad \text{Take positive square root of each side.}$$

$$523 \approx c \quad \text{Use a calculator. Round to nearest whole number.}$$

Answer The length of the cable is about 523 feet.

Example 2 Finding the Length of a Leg

Find the unknown length a in simplest form.

$$a^2 + b^2 = c^2 \qquad \text{Pythagorean theorem}$$
$$a^2 + 10^2 = 12^2 \qquad \text{Substitute.}$$
$$a^2 + 100 = 144 \qquad \text{Evaluate powers.}$$
$$a^2 = 44 \qquad \text{Subtract 100 from each side.}$$
$$a = \sqrt{44} \qquad \text{Take positive square root of each side.}$$
$$a = 2\sqrt{11} \qquad \text{Simplify.}$$

Answer The unknown length a is $2\sqrt{11}$ units.

✔ Checkpoint

Find the unknown length. Write your answer in simplest form.

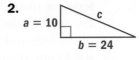

1. $c = 25$, $a = 20$, b

2. $a = 10$, $b = 24$, c

3. $b = 12$, a, $c = 14$

Reading *Algebra*

The converse of the theorem "If two integers are odd, then the sum of the integers is even" is "If the sum of two integers is even, then the two integers are odd." Notice that the converse is *not* true since, for example, the even integer 8 can be written as the sum of the even integers 2 and 6.

Converse of the Pythagorean Theorem The Pythagorean theorem can be written in "if-then" form.

Theorem: If **a triangle is a right triangle**, then $a^2 + b^2 = c^2$.

If you reverse the two parts of the statement, the new statement is called the *converse* of the Pythagorean theorem.

Converse: If $a^2 + b^2 = c^2$, then **the triangle is a right triangle**.

Although not all converses of true statements are true, the converse of the Pythagorean theorem is true. You can use it to determine whether a triangle is a right triangle.

Study *Strategy*

When determining whether three given lengths a, b, and c satisfy the equation $a^2 + b^2 = c^2$, always let c be the greatest length.

Example 3 Identifying Right Triangles

Determine whether the triangle with the given side lengths is a right triangle.

a. $a = 3$, $b = 5$, $c = 7$

b. $a = 15$, $b = 8$, $c = 17$

Solution

a. $a^2 + b^2 = c^2$
$$3^2 + 5^2 \stackrel{?}{=} 7^2$$
$$9 + 25 \stackrel{?}{=} 49$$
$$34 \neq 49$$

Answer Not a right triangle

b. $a^2 + b^2 = c^2$
$$15^2 + 8^2 \stackrel{?}{=} 17^2$$
$$225 + 64 \stackrel{?}{=} 289$$
$$289 = 289 \checkmark$$

Answer A right triangle

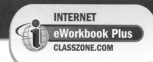

Guided Practice

Vocabulary Check

1. Copy and complete: The side opposite the right angle of a right triangle is called the _?_ .

2. The lengths of the sides of a triangle are 6, 8, and 10. Explain how you can determine whether the triangle is a right triangle.

Skill Check **In Exercises 3–5, find the unknown length.**

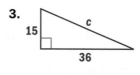

3.

15, c, 36

4.

25, a, 7

5.

9, b, 15

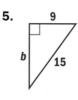

Guided Problem Solving

6. **Ladders** A ladder that is 15 feet long is placed against a wall. The bottom of the ladder is 5 feet from the wall. To the nearest foot, how far up the wall does the ladder reach?

① Copy the diagram. Label the known lengths. Label the unknown length *x*.

② Use the Pythagorean theorem to write an equation you can use to find the value of *x*.

③ Solve the equation in Step 2 for *x*.

④ Round your answer from Step 3 to the nearest whole number.

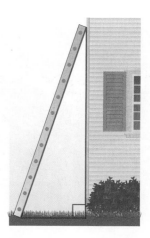

Practice and Problem Solving

Homework *Help*

Example **Exercises**
1   7–9, 20, 22–24,
         29–30
2   10–12, 19,
         25–28
3   13–18, 20–21

Online Resources
CLASSZONE.COM

• More Examples
• eTutorial Plus

Find the unknown length. Write your answer in simplest form.

7.

20, c, 21

8.

5, 12, c

9.

5, c, 5, 3

10.

a, 51, 45

11.

30, 32, a

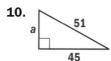

12.

b, 27, 40

Determine whether the triangle with the given side lengths is a right triangle.

13. 2, 3, 4   **14.** 12, 35, 37   **15.** 5, 12, 13

16. 8, 16, 18   **17.** 11, 60, 61   **18.** 8, 9, 12

19. Television Screen A television screen is a rectangle, and its size is indicated by the length of a diagonal. A 42 inch television screen is about 21 inches high. How wide is the screen to the nearest inch?

20. Carpentry To determine whether the corner of a shelf is actually a right angle, a carpenter uses a ruler and a pencil to make a mark at 3 inches along one side of the shelf and at 4 inches along the other. The carpenter takes a measurement and is satisfied that the corner is a right angle. What distance did the carpenter measure? Why does the carpenter's method work?

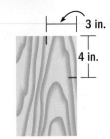

21. Pythagorean Triples A *Pythagorean triple* is a set of three positive integers a, b, and c such that $a^2 + b^2 = c^2$. That is, the integers a, b, and c are a Pythagorean triple if a triangle with side lengths a, b, and c is a right triangle. You can generate a Pythagorean triple by substituting an integer greater than 1 into each of these expressions: $2n$, $n^2 - 1$, and $n^2 + 1$. For example, the integers 3, 4, and 5 form a Pythagorean triple that is generated by the given expressions when $n = 2$.

a. Choose an integer value of n greater than 2 and substitute the given value into each of the given expressions.

b. Verify that the numbers you generated form a Pythagorean triple.

The lengths of the legs of a right triangle are given. Tell whether you would use *mental math*, *paper and pencil*, or a *calculator* to find the length of the hypotenuse. Explain your answers.

22. $a = 87$, $b = 136$ **23.** $a = 1$, $b = 2$ **24.** $a = 15$, $b = 20$

The lengths of two sides of a right triangle are given. Find the length of the third side.

25. $a = 28$, $c = 53$ **26.** $a = 48$, $c = 73$ **27.** $b = 24$, $c = 26$

28. $b = 77$, $c = 85$ **29.** $a = 84$, $b = 80$ **30.** $a = 48$, $b = 189$

31. Synchronized Swimming At the beginning of a performance, two synchronized swimmers start at opposite corners of a rectangular pool that is 50 meters long and 25 meters wide. They swim toward each other along a diagonal and meet halfway. To the nearest tenth of a meter, how far from their starting points do the swimmers meet?

32. *Writing* One leg of a right triangle has a length of 32 units. The hypotenuse has a length of 68 units. Describe how you would go about finding the area of the triangle.

In the **Real World**

Synchronized Swimming In a pool that meets minimum standards for an Olympic synchronized swimming competition, the bottom of the pool has a sloped surface over which the depth decreases from 3 meters to 2.5 meters. If the horizontal distance over which the depth changes is 8 meters, how long is the sloped edge of the bottom to the nearest tenth of a meter?

33. Soccer In a college soccer league, the smallest field allowed is a rectangle 65 yards wide and 110 yards long. The largest field allowed is a rectangle 80 yards wide and 120 yards long. To the nearest yard, how much longer is the diagonal of the largest field than the diagonal of the smallest field?

34. Extended Problem Solving You plan to support a young tree by attaching three wires to the tree. Your plan is to attach one end of each wire to the tree at a point 1.2 meters above the ground, and the other end of each wire to a stake in the ground at a point 0.5 meter from the tree.

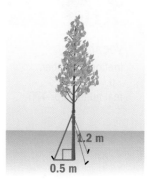

a. Calculate Find the total amount of wire you need. Include an extra 10 centimeters of wire at each attachment point.

b. Interpret and Apply You have only 4.2 meters of wire and plan to attach each wire 0.5 meter out from the tree, allowing extra wire as described in part (a). To the nearest tenth of a meter, how far up the tree can you attach each wire? Explain.

Challenge Find each unknown length in simplest form. In Exercise 36, use the fact that the edges of a cube meet at right angles.

35.

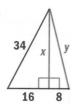

36.

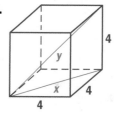

Mixed Review   Write the decimal as a fraction or mixed number. *(Lesson 5.1)*

37. 0.16   **38.** −0.45   **39.** 1.075   **40.** −3.875

41. Tree House You are building a tree house. In a scale drawing of the tree house, the length of one wall is 6 inches. The length of the actual wall is 5 feet. Find the scale of the drawing. *(Lesson 6.6)*

42. Eating Out At a restaurant, you choose a first course, a main dish, and a vegetable for dinner. You can choose fruit cup or soup for the first course. For the main course, you can choose steak, chicken, fish, or lasagna. For a vegetable, you can choose beans, broccoli, or carrots. Find the number of possible meals you can choose. *(Lesson 6.8)*

Standardized Test Practice   **43. Multiple Choice** Which lengths are *not* side lengths of a right triangle?

   A. 9, 12, 15   **B.** 13, 84, 85   **C.** 8, 14, 18   **D.** 24, 70, 74

44. Short Response A ship travels 7 miles due north, then 20 miles due east. The ship then sails directly back to its starting point. Explain how you would find the total distance of the trip. Then find the distance to the nearest mile.

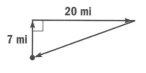

Real Numbers

BEFORE	Now	WHY?
You ordered rational numbers.	You'll compare and order real numbers.	So you can compare the periods of two pendulums, as in Ex. 34.

Vocabulary

irrational number, p. 470
real number, p. 470

In Lesson 5.1, you learned that a rational number is a number that can be written as a quotient of two integers. All rational numbers have decimal forms that terminate or repeat.

An **irrational number** is a number that cannot be written as a quotient of two integers. The decimal form of an irrational number neither terminates nor repeats. For example, in the irrational number below, the pattern of ones separated by an increasing number of zeros continues without end. The decimal neither terminates nor repeats.

$$0.1010010001000010000010000001\ldots$$

The **real numbers** consist of all rational and irrational numbers. The Venn diagram shows the relationships among the real numbers.

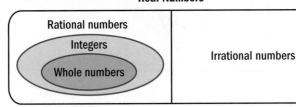

Real Numbers

Rational numbers
Integers
Whole numbers
Irrational numbers

Study *Strategy*

Notice in part (c) of Example 1 that $\sqrt{19}$ is irrational. The square root of any whole number that is not a perfect square is irrational.

Example 1   *Classifying Real Numbers*

Number	Decimal Form	Decimal Type	Type
a. $\frac{5}{8}$	$\frac{5}{8} = 0.625$	Terminating	Rational
b. $\frac{5}{6}$	$\frac{5}{6} = 0.83333\ldots = 0.8\overline{3}$	Repeating	Rational
c. $\sqrt{19}$	$\sqrt{19} = 4.35889894\ldots$	Nonterminating, nonrepeating	Irrational

 Checkpoint

Tell whether the number is *rational* or *irrational*.

1. $\frac{2}{3}$ **2.** $\sqrt{100}$ **3.** $\sqrt{6}$ **4.** $\sqrt{\frac{16}{25}}$

5. Critical Thinking Consider the positive square roots of the whole numbers from 1 to 10. What percent of these numbers are irrational?

Review *Help*

For help with using a compass, see p. 794.

Graphing Irrational Numbers You can graph an irrational number on a number line. For instance, to graph $\sqrt{2}$, draw a right triangle with one leg on the number line and each leg with a length of 1 unit, as shown. By the Pythagorean theorem, the length of the hypotenuse is $\sqrt{1^2 + 1^2} = \sqrt{2}$.

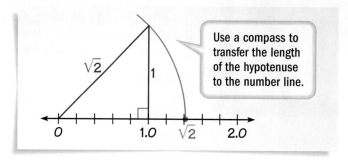

Use a compass to transfer the length of the hypotenuse to the number line.

Notice that the graph of $\sqrt{2}$ is close to the graph of 1.4. So, $\sqrt{2} \approx 1.4$, which agrees with the decimal form of $\sqrt{2}$, which is 1.41421356. . . .

Example 2 *Comparing Real Numbers*

Copy and complete $\sqrt{2}$? $\dfrac{9}{5}$ using <, >, or =.

$\sqrt{2}$ is to the left of $\dfrac{9}{5}$.

Answer $\sqrt{2} < \dfrac{9}{5}$

Example 3 *Ordering Real Numbers*

Study *Strategy*

Another Way You can compare and order real numbers by using a calculator to find decimal forms of the numbers, then comparing and ordering the decimals.

Use a number line to order the numbers $\dfrac{4}{3}$, -2.8, $\sqrt{3}$, and $-\sqrt{5}$ from least to greatest.

Graph the numbers on a number line and read them from left to right.

Answer From least to greatest, the numbers are -2.8, $-\sqrt{5}$, $\dfrac{4}{3}$, and $\sqrt{3}$.

✔ *Checkpoint*

Copy and complete the statement using <, >, or =.

6. $\sqrt{7}$? $\dfrac{8}{3}$ **7.** $-\dfrac{3}{2}$? $-\sqrt{2}$ **8.** $-3\sqrt{2}$? -4.2 **9.** $\dfrac{15}{4}$? $\sqrt{15}$

Use a number line to order the numbers from least to greatest.

10. 2.9, $\sqrt{10}$, $\dfrac{7}{3}$, $2\sqrt{2}$ **11.** $-\dfrac{16}{3}$, $-\sqrt{22}$, $-3\sqrt{2}$, -4.6

Example 4 | *Using Irrational Numbers*

Landmark Buildings Your class is visiting historical landmarks in Chicago. Outside the Washington Block, you break up into two groups. Group A walks about 800 meters east and 200 meters south to the Chicago Building. Group B walks about 600 meters south and 200 meters east to the Rookery Building. To the nearest 10 meters, how much farther is group A from the Washington Block than group B is?

Solution

Draw a diagram. Then use the Pythagorean theorem to find each distance from the Washington Block.

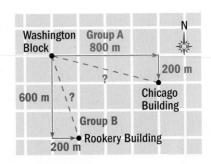

Group A: $\sqrt{800^2 + 200^2} = \sqrt{680{,}000}$
≈ 825

Group B: $\sqrt{600^2 + 200^2} = \sqrt{400{,}000}$
≈ 632

Difference in distances: $825 - 632 = 193$

Answer To the nearest 10 meters, group A is about 190 meters farther from the Washington Block than group B is.

9.4 Exercises

More Practice, p. 811

INTERNET
eWorkbook Plus
CLASSZONE.COM

Guided Practice

Vocabulary Check

1. Explain what an irrational number is. Give an example.

2. Where would the number $7.\overline{52}$ appear in the Venn diagram on page 470? Explain your thinking.

Skill Check **Tell whether the number is *rational* or *irrational*.**

3. $\dfrac{2}{7}$ 4. $\sqrt{49}$ 5. $-\sqrt{71}$ 6. $8.\overline{34}$

Copy and complete the statement using <, >, or =.

7. $-\sqrt{7} \;\underline{?}\; -2$ 8. $\sqrt{11} \;\underline{?}\; \sqrt{9}$ 9. $\sqrt{16} \;\underline{?}\; \dfrac{8}{3}$ 10. $\dfrac{5}{3} \;\underline{?}\; \sqrt{2}$

11. **Fences** A wire fence with wooden posts and rails has the dimensions shown. Each section of fence has a diagonal support brace as shown. Is the exact length of the brace a *rational* or an *irrational* number of feet?

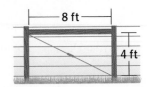

Practice and Problem Solving

Homework *Help*

Example	Exercises
1	12–19, 28–32
2	20–23
3	24–27
4	33–35

Online Resources
CLASSZONE.COM

• More Examples
• eTutorial Plus

Tell whether the number is *rational* or *irrational*.

12. $\dfrac{3}{4}$
13. $\sqrt{8}$
14. $-\sqrt{81}$
15. $\dfrac{\sqrt{16}}{5}$

16. $\sqrt{\dfrac{16}{5}}$
17. $-\sqrt{14.4}$
18. $17.\overline{65}$
19. $\sqrt{10.1}$

Copy and complete the statement using <, >, or =.

20. $\dfrac{5}{2}$? $\sqrt{6.25}$
21. $4\sqrt{3}$? $\dfrac{27}{4}$
22. $\sqrt{32}$? 5.6
23. $\sqrt{0.5}$? 0.5

Use a number line to order the numbers from least to greatest.

24. $3.5,\ 2\sqrt{3},\ \sqrt{13},\ \dfrac{19}{5},\ 3\dfrac{1}{4},\ \sqrt{8}$

25. $\sqrt{4},\ -\sqrt{5},\ 0,\ \dfrac{9}{5},\ -2,\ \sqrt{3}$

26. $\dfrac{17}{2},\ 8.6,\ \sqrt{64},\ 3\sqrt{6},\ 7\dfrac{3}{4},\ \sqrt{50}$

27. $-4,\ -\sqrt{18},\ -\sqrt{\dfrac{67}{4}},\ -\dfrac{25}{6}$

Copy and complete the statement using *always*, *sometimes*, or *never*. Explain your reasoning.

28. A negative integer is ? a whole number.

29. A square root of a positive number is ? an irrational number.

30. A real number is ? a rational number.

31. A whole number is ? an irrational number.

32. *Writing* The area of a square is 7 square meters. Is the perimeter of the square a *rational* or an *irrational* number of meters? Explain.

33. **Geometry** A rectangle is twice as long as it is wide, and it has an area of 20 square meters.

    a. Let w represent the width of the rectangle. Write a variable expression in terms of w for the length of the rectangle.

    b. Use the formula for the area of a rectangle to write an equation for the area of the given rectangle.

    c. Find the width of the rectangle to the nearest tenth of a meter.

    d. Find the length of the rectangle to the nearest tenth of a meter.

34. **Pendulums** The period of a pendulum is the time that it takes the pendulum to swing from one side to the other and back. A pendulum's period P (in seconds) and its length l (in feet) are related by the equation $P = 1.1\sqrt{l}$.

The giant pendulum in the Science Museum of Virginia in Richmond is about 96 feet long. The giant pendulum in the New Detroit Science Center in Detroit is 40 feet long. How much longer, to the nearest second, is the period of the pendulum in Richmond than the period of the pendulum in Detroit?

Pendulum in the Museum of Science in Boston, Massachusetts

35. Sailing The maximum speed at which a boat can travel is called its hull speed. The hull speed h (in nautical miles per hour) of some boats is given by the equation $h = \sqrt{1.8l}$, where l is the length in feet of the boat at the water line. One boat is 40 feet long at the water line. A second boat is 60 feet long at the water line. Which boat has a faster hull speed? How much faster? Give your answer to the nearest nautical mile per hour.

Name an irrational number between the given rational numbers.

36. 1 and 2   **37.** -4 and -3 **38.** 15 and $15\frac{1}{2}$ **39.** -10.1 and -10

40. Error Analysis Your friend says that $\sqrt{2}$ is rational because $\sqrt{2}$ can be written as the fraction $\dfrac{2\sqrt{2}}{2}$. Explain your friend's error.

41. Critical Thinking Is the product of two irrational numbers *always*, *sometimes*, or *never* irrational? Give examples to support your answer.

42. Extended Problem Solving Use the following method to draw the *Wheel of Theodorus*. The first three triangles in the wheel are shown.

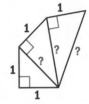

    a. Draw a Diagram Start near the center of a large sheet of paper. Draw a right triangle with legs 1 unit long. Draw the next right triangle using the hypotenuse of the previous triangle as one leg, and a length of 1 unit for the second leg. Repeat this process to draw at least six triangles.

    b. Calculate Beginning with the first triangle you drew, find the length of the hypotenuse of each triangle in simplest form. Label the length of each hypotenuse on your drawing.

    c. Critical Thinking Make a list of the hypotenuse lengths in your drawing. Describe the numbers in the list.

43. Challenge Show how to graph $\sqrt{34}$ on a number line using a right triangle. Explain your method.

This quilt is entitled *Wheel of Theodorus*.

Mixed Review   **Evaluate the expression when $a = 1.5$.** *(Lesson 1.2)*

44. a^2 **45.** a^3 **46.** a^4

Find the slope of the line through the given points. *(Lesson 8.4)*

47. $(-5, 2), (4, 3)$ **48.** $(3, 7), (-1, -5)$ **49.** $(-6, 2), (4, 8)$

Evaluate the expression when $a = 26$ and $b = 10$. *(Lesson 9.1)*

50. $\sqrt{a - b}$ **51.** $\sqrt{a + b}$ **52.** $\sqrt{b^2 - (a + 10)}$

Standardized Test Practice   **53. Extended Response** You are building four corner shelves, each in the shape of a right triangle. Each leg of each triangle is 14 inches long. You plan to cover the longest edge of each shelf with a strip of decorative trim that can be purchased only by the foot.

    a. Explain how to estimate the number of feet of trim you need to purchase for all four shelves.

    b. Find the exact amount of trim you need to use for all the shelves.

Mid-Chapter Quiz

Find the square roots of the number.

1. 1   **2.** 36   **3.** 169   **4.** 196

5. NASA Scientists at NASA drop objects from tall towers to study weightlessness. An object is dropped from a tower that is 24.1 meters high. Use the equation $d = 4.9t^2$ where d is the distance in meters that an object falls in t seconds to find (to the nearest tenth of a second) the time it takes the object to reach the ground.

Simplify the expression.

6. $\sqrt{108}$ **7.** $\sqrt{\dfrac{9}{49}}$ **8.** $\sqrt{\dfrac{200}{x^2}}$ **9.** $\sqrt{12b^2d}$

Find the unknown length. Write your answer in simplest form.

10.

11.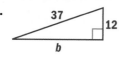

12.

13.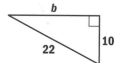

Tell whether the number is *rational* or *irrational*.

14. $\dfrac{7}{3}$ **15.** $\sqrt{12}$ **16.** $-\sqrt{64}$ **17.** $\dfrac{\sqrt{9}}{2}$

Brain GAME

★★★ **Presidential Proof** ★★★

What U.S. President came up with a proof of the Pythagorean theorem? The pair of numbers associated with each letter are the lengths of the legs of a right triangle. Find the length of the hypotenuse of the triangle. Match the corresponding letter to one of the lengths shown below. Some letters will not be used.

R: $\sqrt{7}$, 11   **N:** 7, $\sqrt{11}$ **I:** $\sqrt{19}$, 9

E: 10, 24   **D:** 2, 3   **F:** 5, 12

O: 1, 2   **A:** 2, $\sqrt{3}$ **T:** 5, 8

S: $\sqrt{10}$, $\sqrt{12}$ **L:** 15, 20   **G:** 3, 4

| ? | ? | ? | ? | ? | ? | ? | ? |

5    $\sqrt{7}$ $8\sqrt{2}$ 13   10   26   25 $\sqrt{13}$

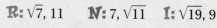

Vocabulary

midpoint, p. 478

BEFORE	Now	WHY?
You used the Pythagorean theorem.	You'll use the distance, midpoint, and slope formulas.	So you can compare points of interest on a map, as in Ex. 39.

To find the distance between points A and B, draw a right triangle as shown. Points A and C lie on a horizontal line. The distance between points A and C is the absolute value of the difference of their x-coordinates. Points B and C lie on a vertical line. The distance between points B and C is the absolute value of the difference of their y-coordinates.

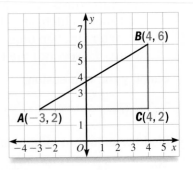

Then the lengths of the legs of $\triangle ABC$ are:

$$AC = |4 - (-3)| = |7| = 7$$
$$BC = |6 - 2| = |4| = 4$$

Because AB is the length of the hypotenuse of the triangle, use the Pythagorean theorem to find AB.

$(AB)^2 = (AC)^2 + (BC)^2$	**Pythagorean theorem**
$AB = \sqrt{(AC)^2 + (BC)^2}$	**Take positive square root of each side.**
$= \sqrt{7^2 + 4^2}$	**Substitute 7 for AC and 4 for BC.**
$= \sqrt{65}$	**Simplify.**

The example above suggests the following formula for finding the distance between any two points in a plane.

Reading *Algebra*

The ordered pairs (x_1, y_1) and (x_2, y_2) are read as "x sub one, y sub one" and "x sub two, y sub two," respectively. The subscripts 1 and 2 are used to distinguish the two x-coordinates and the two y-coordinates.

The Distance Formula

Words The distance between two points in a coordinate plane is equal to the square root of the sum of the horizontal change squared and the vertical change squared.

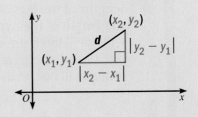

Algebra $d = \sqrt{(x_2 - x_1)^2 + (y_2 - y_1)^2}$

Study *Strategy*

Because the distance formula involves squaring the difference in the *x*-coordinates and the difference in the *y*-coordinates, you don't need to find the absolute value of either difference before squaring.

Example 1	*Finding the Distance Between Two Points*

Find the distance between the points *M*(6, 3) and *N*(5, 7).

$$d = \sqrt{(x_2 - x_1)^2 + (y_2 - y_1)^2}$$ **Distance formula**

$$= \sqrt{(5 - 6)^2 + (7 - 3)^2}$$ **Substitute 5 for x_2, 6 for x_1, 7 for y_2, and 3 for y_1.**

$$= \sqrt{(-1)^2 + 4^2}$$ **Subtract.**

$$= \sqrt{1 + 16}$$ **Evaluate powers.**

$$= \sqrt{17}$$ **Add.**

Answer The distance between the points *M*(6, 3) and *N*(5, 7) is $\sqrt{17}$ units.

✔ *Checkpoint*

Find the distance between the points.

1. (11, −2), (7, −5) **2.** (−1, 3), (5, −2) **3.** (0, −1), (10, −5)

Example 2	*Using the Distance Formula*

Bird Watching A bird watcher uses a grid to photograph and record the locations of birds feeding on the ground. The grid is made of fishing net with strands that are 1 foot apart. In the grid shown, each point represents the location of a bird. How far apart are the birds at points *A* and *B*?

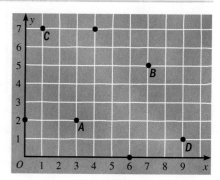

Solution

The coordinates of point *A* are (3, 2). The coordinates of point *B* are (7, 5).

$$d = \sqrt{(x_2 - x_1)^2 + (y_2 - y_1)^2}$$ **Distance formula**

$$= \sqrt{(7 - 3)^2 + (5 - 2)^2}$$ **Substitute 7 for x_2, 3 for x_1, 5 for y_2, and 2 for y_1.**

$$= \sqrt{4^2 + 3^2}$$ **Subtract.**

$$= \sqrt{16 + 9}$$ **Evaluate powers.**

$$= \sqrt{25}$$ **Add.**

$$= 5$$ **Simplify.**

Answer The birds at points *A* and *B* are 5 feet apart.

✔ *Checkpoint*

4. In Example 2, how far apart are the birds at points *C* and *D*?

Midpoint The **midpoint** of a segment is the point on the segment that is equally distant from the endpoints.

The Midpoint Formula

Words The coordinates of the midpoint of a segment are the average of the endpoints' *x*-coordinates and the average of the endpoints' *y*-coordinates.

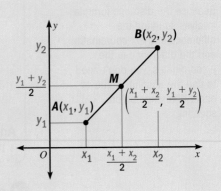

Algebra $M = \left(\dfrac{x_1 + x_2}{2}, \dfrac{y_1 + y_2}{2} \right)$

Example 3 — *Finding a Midpoint*

Find the midpoint *M* of the segment with endpoints (3, 8) and (−9, −4).

$$M = \left(\frac{x_1 + x_2}{2}, \frac{y_1 + y_2}{2} \right)$$ **Midpoint formula**

$$= \left(\frac{3 + (-9)}{2}, \frac{8 + (-4)}{2} \right)$$ **Substitute 3 for x_1, −9 for x_2, 8 for y_1, and −4 for y_2.**

$$= (-3, 2)$$ **Simplify.**

Review *Help*

For help with slope, see p. 404.

Slope If points $A(x_1, y_1)$ and $B(x_2, y_2)$ do not lie on a vertical line, you can use coordinate notation to write a formula for the slope of the line through *A* and *B*.

$$\text{slope} = \frac{\text{difference of } y\text{-coordinates}}{\text{difference of } x\text{-coordinates}} = \frac{y_2 - y_1}{x_2 - x_1}$$

Example 4 — *Finding Slope*

Find the slope of the line through (3, 7) and (8, −3).

$$\text{slope} = \frac{y_2 - y_1}{x_2 - x_1}$$ **Slope formula**

$$= \frac{-3 - 7}{8 - 3}$$ **Substitute −3 for y_2, 7 for y_1, 8 for x_2, and 3 for x_1.**

$$= \frac{-10}{5} = -2$$ **Simplify.**

✔ *Checkpoint*

5. Find the midpoint *M* of the segment with endpoints (−7, 1) and (5, 11).

6. Find the slope of the line through (2, 7) and (−3, 5).

Guided Practice

Vocabulary Check

1. Copy and complete: To find the length of a segment in a coordinate plane, you can use the ? formula.

2. Point M is the midpoint of $\overline{AB}$. How are AM and MB related?

Skill Check

In Exercises 3–5, use the coordinate grid shown.

3. Find the length of $\overline{PQ}$.

4. Find the midpoint of $\overline{PQ}$.

5. Find the slope of the line though P and Q.

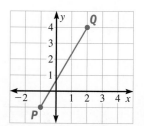

6. Error Analysis Describe and correct the error in finding the midpoint of the segment with endpoints (1, 8) and (7, 2).

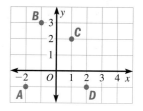

$$M = \left(\frac{7-1}{2}, \frac{2-8}{2}\right) = (3, -3)$$

Practice and Problem Solving

Homework *Help*

Example	Exercises
1	7–18, 39–42
2	39–40, 42
3	19–22, 27–32, 39–40, 42
4	23–26, 33–38

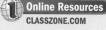

Online Resources
CLASSZONE.COM

• More Examples
• eTutorial Plus

Find the distance between the points. Write your answer in simplest form.

7. A and B **8.** B and C

9. C and D **10.** A and C

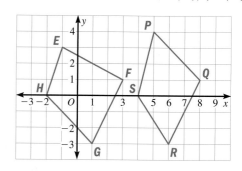

Find the distance between the points. Write your answer in simplest form.

11. (1, 3), (5, 8)   **12.** (−9, 0), (0, 7)   **13.** (12, 8), (0, 2)   **14.** (−4, 2), (5, −1)

15. (1.5, 4), (3, 6)   **16.** (−8, 6), (1, 7)   **17.** (1, 5), (−2, 2)   **18.** (1.2, 2), (8.7, 6)

Find the midpoint of the segment.

19. $\overline{EF}$ **20.** $\overline{FG}$

21. $\overline{GH}$ **22.** $\overline{EH}$

Find the slope of the line through the given points.

23. P and Q **24.** Q and R

25. R and S **26.** P and S

Find the midpoint of the segment with the given endpoints.

27. $(8, -6), (2, 12)$ **28.** $(-10, 7), (4, 5)$ **29.** $(6, -1), (9, 5)$

30. $(3.8, 4), (6, 0.2)$ **31.** $(3, -2), (5\frac{1}{2}, 7)$ **32.** $(17.4, 9.1), (3, 1.3)$

Find the slope of the line through the given points.

33. $(1, 2), (5, 6)$ **34.** $(4, 3), (-2, 8)$ **35.** $(6, 1), (0, -7)$

36. $(-4.2, 4), (8.6, 7.2)$ **37.** $(7\frac{3}{4}, -1), (6\frac{1}{4}, -5)$ **38.** $(-1.5, 0), (-6, 9)$

39. Maps A grid is superimposed on the map of a town to locate points of interest, as shown.

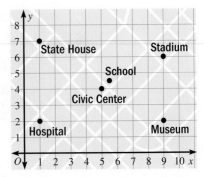

 a. Show that the Civic Center is halfway between the hospital and the stadium.

 b. **Compare** Which buildings are farther apart, the Civic Center and the stadium or the hospital and the State House?

40. Geometry Find the midpoint of the segment with endpoints $(-6, 8)$ and $(-2, 4)$. Use the distance formula to verify that the midpoint you found is equally distant from the endpoints.

41. Critical Thinking Does it matter which point you call (x_1, y_1) and which point you call (x_2, y_2) when you use the distance formula to find the distance between two points? Explain.

42. Geometry The points $P(0, 0)$, $Q(6, 0)$, and $R(6, 6)$ are the vertices of a right triangle in a coordinate plane.

 a. Draw the triangle in a coordinate plane.

 b. Find the coordinates of the midpoint M of the hypotenuse of $\triangle PQR$.

 c. **Analyze** Show that M is equally distant from P, Q, and R.

Tell which segment is longer.

43. $\overline{AB}$ has endpoints $A(-1, -2)$ and $B(6, 1)$. $\overline{PQ}$ has endpoints $P(1, 1)$ and $Q(6, 7)$.

44. $\overline{MN}$ has endpoints $M(-3, 2)$ and $N(5, 0)$. $\overline{JK}$ has endpoints $J(-3, 1)$ and $K(3, -5)$.

For $\overline{AB}$ with midpoint M, determine the coordinates of point B.

45. $A(0, 6); M = (-4, 3)$ **46.** $A(15, 25); M = (6.5, 16.5)$

47. $A(7, 6); M = (12, 9)$ **48.** $A(-2, 2); M = \left(1, 1\frac{1}{2}\right)$

49. Geometry Three points A, B, and C are on the same line if the slopes of the following three lines are equal: the line through points A and B, the line through points A and C, and the line through points B and C. Are the points $(-3, 9)$, $(1, 1)$, and $(4, -4)$ on the same line? Explain.

Plot the points _G_, _H_, and _J_ in a coordinate plane and draw triangle _GHJ_. Determine whether the triangle is a right triangle.

50. $G(2, 3)$, $H(5, 7)$, $J(8, 3)$

51. $G(2, 5)$, $H(5, 9)$, $J(10, -3)$

52. Extended Problem Solving An urban forester uses a grid to record information about trees in a city park. Each unit on the grid represents 10 meters.

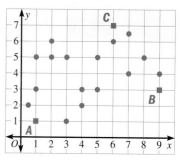

   a. Compare Which tree is farther from the tree at point _A_, the tree at point _B_ or the tree at point _C_? How much farther (to the nearest meter) is it from the tree at point _A_?

   b. Apply The trees at points _A_, _B_, and _C_ are to be cut down. Two trees will be planted, one at the midpoint of the segment with endpoints _A_ and _B_, the other at the midpoint of the segment with endpoints _B_ and _C_. To the nearest meter, how far apart will the new trees be?

53. Geometry The _center_ of a circle is equally distant from all points on the circle. Consider a circle with center _C_ and a segment that has endpoints $A(-2, -1)$ and $B(6, 5)$ on the circle. The segment passes through point _C_. Find the coordinates of point _C_.

54. Challenge Plot the point $A(1, 3)$ in a coordinate plane. Find and plot at least 6 points that are 5 units from _A_. Explain how you found the points.

Mixed Review

55. Sewing You are making curtains. The fabric costs $2.49 per yard. You have $15. Do you have enough money to buy 5 yards of fabric? _(Lesson 6.1)_

Write the decimal as a percent. _(Lesson 7.3)_

56. 0.206

57. 1.31

58. 0.004

Copy and complete the statement using <, >, or =. _(Lesson 9.4)_

59. $\sqrt{15} \underline{\ ?\ } \frac{11}{3}$

60. $\sqrt{\frac{1}{2}} \underline{\ ?\ } -\frac{5}{7}$

61. $7.25 \underline{\ ?\ } 3\sqrt{6}$

Standardized Test Practice

62. Multiple Choice What is the distance between points _A_ and _B_?

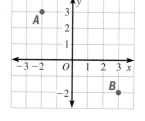

   A. $\sqrt{17}$ units

   B. 5 units

   C. $\sqrt{41}$ units

   D. $5\sqrt{2}$ units

63. Short Response Let _M_ be the midpoint of the segment with endpoints $A(1, 2)$ and $B(9, 6)$. Use the distance formula to show that $AB = 2 \cdot AM$ and $AB = 2 \cdot MB$.

9.6 Investigating Special Right Triangles

Goal
Investigate the relationships among sides lengths of special right triangles.

Materials
• graph paper
• metric ruler
• protractor

In this activity, you will investigate two special right triangles. One is a 45°-45°-90° triangle. The legs of such a triangle are congruent.

Another special right triangle is a 30°-60°-90° triangle. The hypotenuse of a 30°-60°-90° triangle is twice as long as the shorter leg.

Investigate

Use the Pythagorean theorem to establish relationships among the side lengths of special right triangles.

1 Draw 3 different 45°-45°-90° triangles using the leg lengths given in the table. Find the length (in centimeters) of the hypotenuse for each triangle. Write your answers in simplest form.

Length of leg	Length of hypotenuse
1 cm	?
2 cm	?
3 cm	?

2 Draw 3 different 30°-60°-90° triangles using the side lengths given in the table. Find the length (in centimeters) of the longer leg for each triangle. Write your answers in simplest form.

Length of hypotenuse	Length of shorter leg	Length of longer leg
2 cm	1 cm	?
4 cm	2 cm	?
6 cm	3 cm	?

Draw Conclusions

1. **Critical Thinking** Identify any pattern you see in the table for Step 1. Use the pattern to find the length of the hypotenuse of a 45°-45°-90° triangle with legs that are each n units long.

2. *Writing* Describe the relationship between the length of the longer leg of a 30°-60°-90° triangle and the length of the shorter leg.

Special Right Triangles

Review Vocabulary

hypotenuse, p. 465
leg, p. 465

A diagonal of a square divides it into two 45°-45°-90° triangles. In such a triangle, the lengths of the legs are equal. Let a represent the length of each leg, and let c represent the length of the hypotenuse. By the Pythagorean theorem, $c^2 = a^2 + a^2 = 2a^2$, so $c = \sqrt{2a^2} = a\sqrt{2}$.

45°-45°-90° Triangle

Words In a 45°-45°-90° triangle, the length of the hypotenuse is the product of the length of a leg and $\sqrt{2}$.

Algebra hypotenuse = leg · $\sqrt{2}$
= $a\sqrt{2}$

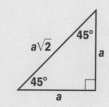

Example 1 *Using a 45°-45°-90° Triangle*

Gymnastics The mat used for floor exercises at a gymnastics competition is a square with a side length of 12 meters. A gymnast starts at one corner of the mat and does a tumbling routine along the diagonal to the opposite corner. To the nearest meter, how long is the gymnast's path?

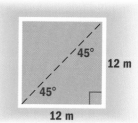

Solution

The diagonal divides the mat into two 45°-45°-90° triangles. The diagonal is the hypotenuse of each of the triangles.

hypotenuse = leg · $\sqrt{2}$ **Rule for 45°-45°-90° triangle**
= 12 · $\sqrt{2}$ **Substitute.**
≈ 17   **Use a calculator.**

Answer The gymnast's path is about 17 meters long.

30°-60°-90° Triangle You can divide an equilateral triangle in half as shown to make two 30°-60°-90° triangles. In the diagram, the equilateral triangle has side lengths of $2a$. Each right triangle has a hypotenuse of length $2a$ and a shorter leg of length a. Let b be the length of the longer leg. By the Pythagorean theorem, $(2a)^2 = a^2 + b^2$. Then $b^2 = 4a^2 - a^2 = 3a^2$, so $b = \sqrt{3a^2} = a\sqrt{3}$.

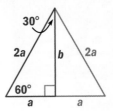

Study *Strategy*

In a 30°-60°-90° triangle, the shorter leg is opposite the 30° angle, and the longer leg is opposite the 60° angle.

30°-60°-90° Triangle

Words In a 30°-60°-90° triangle, the length of the hypotenuse is twice the length of the shorter leg. The length of the longer leg is the product of the length of the shorter leg and $\sqrt{3}$.

Algebra hypotenuse = 2 · shorter leg = $2a$

longer leg = shorter leg · $\sqrt{3}$ = $a\sqrt{3}$

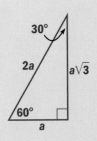

Example 2 *Using a 30°-60°-90° Triangle*

Find the length *x* of the hypotenuse and the length *y* of the longer leg of the triangle.

The triangle is a 30°-60°-90° triangle. The length of the shorter leg is 8 units.

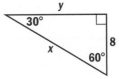

a. hypotenuse = 2 · shorter leg

$x = 2 \cdot 8$

$= 16$

Answer The length x of the hypotenuse is 16 units.

b. longer leg = shorter leg · $\sqrt{3}$

$y = 8\sqrt{3}$

Answer The length y of the longer leg is $8\sqrt{3}$ units.

 Checkpoint

Find the unknown lengths. Write your answer in simplest form.

1.

2.

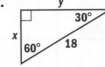

3.

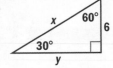

Example 3   *Using a Special Right Triangle*

Architecture The base of the Massachusetts Institute of Technology's Building 66, an engineering laboratory, is approximately a 30°-60°-90° triangle. The length of the hypotenuse of the triangle is about 294 feet. Find, to the nearest foot, the lengths of the legs of the triangle.

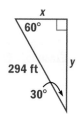

Solution

You need to find the length of the shorter leg first.

1 Find the length x of the shorter leg.

hypotenuse = 2 · shorter leg	Rule for 30°-60°-90° triangle
$294 = 2x$	Substitute.
$147 = x$	Divide each side by 2.

2 Find the length y of the longer leg.

longer leg = shorter leg · $\sqrt{3}$	Rule for 30°-60°-90° triangle
$y = 147\sqrt{3}$	Substitute.
≈ 255	Use a calculator.

Answer The length of the shorter leg of the triangle is 147 feet. The length of the longer leg is about 255 feet.

9.6   Exercises

More Practice, p. 811

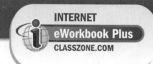

INTERNET
eWorkbook Plus
CLASSZONE.COM

Guided Practice

Vocabulary Check   **1.** Each leg of a 45°-45°-90° triangle has a length of 15 units. What is the length of the hypotenuse?

2. How is the length of the longer leg of a 30°-60°-90° triangle related to the length of the shorter leg?

Skill Check   **Find the unknown length. Write your answer in simplest form.**

3.

4.

5.

6. Graphic Arts A graphic artist's tools include a 30°-60°-90° triangle. The hypotenuse of the triangle has a length of 10 inches. To the nearest inch, how long are the legs of the triangle?

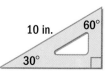

Practice and Problem Solving

Homework *Help*

Example	Exercises
1	7–9, 14, 16–18
2	10–12, 16–18
3	13, 15

Online Resources
CLASSZONE.COM
• More Examples
• eTutorial Plus

Find the unknown lengths. Write your answers in simplest form.

7.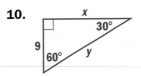

8.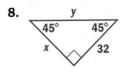

9.

10.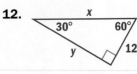

11.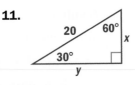

12.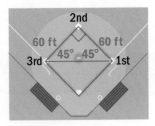

13. Speakers You connect a stereo system to your television set. The directions say that the speakers should be in line with your television and 12 feet apart as shown.

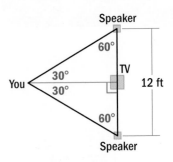

  a. Find the distance between you and the television set to the nearest foot.

  b. Find the distance between you and each speaker to the nearest foot.

14. *Writing* Explain why any two 45°-45°-90° triangles are similar.

15. Softball The bases on a softball field form a square with a side length of 60 feet. You throw a softball from first base to third base. How far do you throw the softball? Round your answer to the nearest foot.

Find the unknown lengths. Write your answers in simplest form.

16.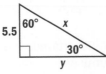

17.

18.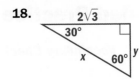

19. Extended Problem Solving There is a park in your town that is a square with a side length of 800 feet. You plan to walk from one corner of the square to the opposite corner.

  a. Compare To the nearest foot, how much shorter is the distance from one corner to the opposite corner along the diagonal than the distance along two sides of the square?

  b. You walk at a rate of 3 miles per hour. Find your rate in feet per second.

  c. Interpret To the nearest second, how much time would you save by walking along the diagonal rather than walking along two sides of the square?

20. Wrenches You must choose the right size wrench to tighten a nut. Each edge of the nut has a length of $\frac{1}{4}$ inch. You should choose a wrench size that is close to the distance across the nut from one edge to the opposite edge. Which wrench size should you use, $\frac{3}{8}$ inch, $\frac{7}{16}$ inch, or $\frac{1}{2}$ inch?

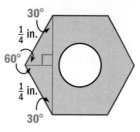

21. Challenge Find the value of x. Give your answer as a radical in simplest form.

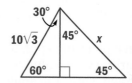

Mixed Review **Solve the proportion.** *(Lesson 6.2)*

22. $\dfrac{w}{7} = \dfrac{36}{42}$ **23.** $\dfrac{x}{10} = \dfrac{35}{50}$ **24.** $\dfrac{3}{4} = \dfrac{y}{52}$ **25.** $\dfrac{7}{12} = \dfrac{z}{105}$

26. Submarines A sailor on a submarine uses a periscope to view the surface of the ocean. The periscope's height h (in feet) above the surface and the distance d (in miles) that the sailor can see are related by the formula $h = \dfrac{d^2}{1.4}$. Suppose the periscope is at a height of 3 feet. To the nearest mile, how far can the sailor see? *(Lesson 9.1)*

Find the midpoint of the segment with the given endpoints. *(Lesson 9.5)*

27. $(-3, 4), (-1, 6)$ **28.** $(8, -3), (-2, 7)$ **29.** $(4, -1.1), (-2.4, -1.7)$

Standardized Test Practice

30. Multiple Choice What is the value of x?

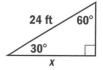

A. $\dfrac{12}{\sqrt{3}}$ ft **B.** 12 ft

C. $12\sqrt{3}$ ft **D.** $24\sqrt{3}$ ft

31. Multiple Choice Each leg of a 45°-45°-90° triangle has a length of 15 units. What is the length of the hypotenuse?

F. 7.5 units **G.** $\dfrac{15}{\sqrt{2}}$ units **H.** 15 units **I.** $15\sqrt{2}$ units

32. Short Response Explain how to find the area of the equilateral triangle shown.

9.7 Ratios of Leg Lengths of Similar Right Triangles

Goal
Compare the ratios of the leg lengths of similar right triangles.

Materials
• metric ruler
• protractor
• colored pencils

Investigate

Describe a relationship between the ratios of the leg lengths of similar right triangles.

1 On a piece of paper, draw a 35° angle, starting with a blue horizontal ray as shown. Label the angle *A*.

2 At intervals of 1 centimeter along the horizontal ray, draw vertical red segments to form at least four right triangles as shown. In each triangle, the leg shown in red is *opposite* ∠*A*. The leg shown in blue is *adjacent* to ∠*A*.

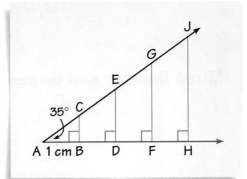

3 Copy and complete the table. For each triangle, measure (to the nearest tenth of a centimeter) the length of the leg opposite ∠*A*. Then calculate (to the nearest tenth)

the ratio $\dfrac{\text{length of opposite leg}}{\text{length of adjacent leg}}$.

Triangle	Leg opposite ∠A	Leg adjacent to ∠A	opposite/adjacent
△ABC	BC = ?	1 cm	?
△ADE	DE = ?	2 cm	?
△AFG	FG = ?	3 cm	?
△AHJ	HJ = ?	4 cm	?

Draw Conclusions

1. **Critical Thinking** What do you notice about the ratios of the leg lengths in the fourth column of your table?

2. *Writing* Use your results to answer the following question: For an acute angle of a right triangle, does the ratio $\dfrac{\text{opposite}}{\text{adjacent}}$ depend on the size of the triangle, on the measure of the angle, or on both? Explain.

The Tangent Ratio

BEFORE	Now	WHY?
You found side lengths of special right triangles.	You'll use tangent to find side lengths of right triangles.	So you can find the distance across a pond, as in Ex. 23.

Vocabulary

trigonometric ratio, p. 489
tangent, p. 489

Lunar Formations Scientists can use the measure of the angle at which the sun's rays strike the moon's surface to determine the height or depth of a lunar formation. In Example 3, you will see how you can use a *trigonometric ratio* to estimate the depth of a lunar crater.

A **trigonometric ratio** is a ratio of the lengths of two sides of a right triangle. One basic trigonometric ratio is *tangent*, abbreviated *tan*.

The Tangent Ratio

The **tangent** of an acute angle of a right triangle is the ratio of the length of the side opposite the angle to the length of the side adjacent to the angle.

$$\tan A = \frac{\text{side opposite } \angle A}{\text{side adjacent to } \angle A} = \frac{a}{b}$$

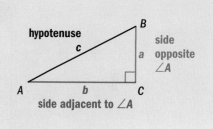

As the activity on page 488 suggests, the value of the tangent of an acute angle of a right triangle depends only on the measure of the angle, not on the size of the triangle.

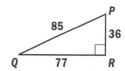

Reading *Geometry*

The leg *adjacent* to an acute angle of a right triangle is also a side of the angle. The leg *opposite* the angle is not a side of the angle.

Example 1 *Finding a Tangent Ratio*

For △PQR, find the tangent of ∠P.

$$\tan P = \frac{\text{opposite}}{\text{adjacent}} = \frac{77}{36}$$

✔ *Checkpoint*

1. For △PQR in Example 1, find tan Q.

Tangents of Angles You can use a calculator or the table of trigonometric ratios on page 823 to find tangents of angles. In this book, trigonometric ratios are rounded to four decimal places.

Tech *Help*

When using a calculator to find a trigonometric ratio, make sure the calculator is in degree mode. You do not need to enter a degree symbol, but you should enter a right parenthesis to close the left parenthesis that the calculator enters. Round the result to four decimal places if necessary.

Example 2   *Using a Calculator*

a. tan 18°

Keystrokes

2nd [TRIG] ◄ ◄
= 18) =

```
tan(18)
        0.324919696
```

Answer

tan 18° ≈ 0.3249

b. tan 45°

Keystrokes

2nd [TRIG] ◄ ◄
= 45) =

```
tan(45)
              1
```

Answer

tan 45° = 1

✔ *Checkpoint*

2. Use a calculator to approximate tan 10° and tan 75° to four decimal places.

Example 3   *Using a Tangent Ratio*

When the sun's rays strike the moon's surface at an angle of 6°, the edge of a lunar crater casts a shadow that has a length of about 4700 meters. What is the depth d (in meters) of the crater to the nearest 10 meters?

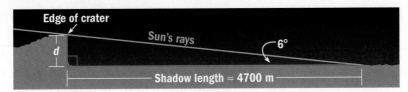

Edge of crater
Sun's rays
6°
d
Shadow length ≈ 4700 m

Solution

Use the tangent ratio. In the diagram, the length of the leg opposite the 6° angle is d. The length of the adjacent leg is about 4700 m.

$\tan 6° = \dfrac{\text{opposite}}{\text{adjacent}}$ **Definition of tangent ratio**

$\tan 6° = \dfrac{d}{4700}$ **Substitute.**

$0.1051 \approx \dfrac{d}{4700}$ **Use a calculator to approximate tan 6°.**

$494 \approx d$ **Multiply each side by 4700.**

Answer The depth of the crater is about 490 meters.

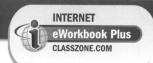
Guided Practice

Vocabulary Check   **In Exercises 1 and 2, use △ABC shown.**

1. a. Identify the leg opposite ∠A.

   b. Identify the leg adjacent to ∠A.

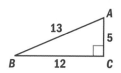

2. Which angle of △ABC has a tangent of $\frac{12}{5}$?

Skill Check   **Find tan A.**

3. 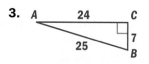   **4.** 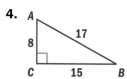   **5.**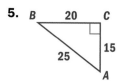

6. 🖩 **Roofs** Use a calculator to find, to the nearest foot, the height *h* of the roof shown in the diagram.

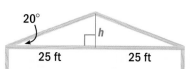

Practice and Problem Solving

Homework *Help*

Example	Exercises
1	7–9
2	10–17
3	18–23

🛈 **Online Resources**
CLASSZONE.COM

• More Examples
• eTutorial Plus

🖩 *In the following exercises, you may find it helpful to use a calculator for approximating tangent values.*

Find the tangent of each acute angle. Write your answers as fractions in simplest form.

7. 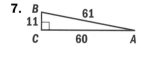   **8.**   **9.**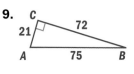

Approximate the tangent value to four decimal places.

10. tan 52°   **11.** tan 66°   **12.** tan 9°   **13.** tan 15°

14. tan 30°   **15.** tan 33°   **16.** tan 70°   **17.** tan 89°

Find the value of *x*. Round to the nearest tenth.

18. 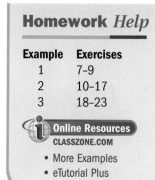   **19.**   **20.**
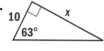

21. Forestry A forester stands 50 meters from the trunk of a tree and uses an instrument called a clinometer to measure the angle of elevation from eye level to the top of the tree. The distance from the forester's eye level to the ground is 1.5 meters.

Not drawn to scale

  a. Let d represent the distance from the forester's eye level to the top of the tree. Write an expression for the height of the tree in terms of d.

  b. Find d to the nearest tenth of a meter.

  c. Find the height of the tree to the nearest tenth of a meter.

22. Writing Draw a 45°-45°-90° triangle. Explain how you know what the tangent of each acute angle is without measuring the sides of the triangle.

23. Swimming You plan to swim across a pond from point C to point A along $\overline{AC}$. To approximate the distance across the pond, you start at point C and pace off 50 feet at a right angle to $\overline{AC}$ as shown, stopping at point B. You estimate that the measure of $\angle B$ is about 70°. To the nearest foot, how far do you have to swim?

Find the area of the triangle. Round your answer to the nearest tenth.

24.
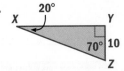

25.
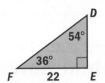

26.

27. Writing Draw $\triangle JKL$ with a right angle at L. Describe the relationship between $\tan J$ and $\tan K$. Use your drawing to justify your reasoning.

28. World's Largest Coffeepot A water tower in Stanton, Iowa, is the world's largest coffeepot. From a point on the ground 50 feet from the center of the tower's base, the angle of elevation to the top of the coffeepot is about 68.2°. The angle of elevation to the bottom of the coffeepot is about 60.7°.

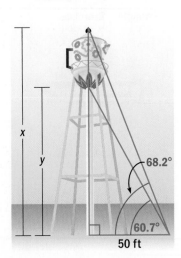

  a. Calculate Find the distance x between the top of the coffeepot and the ground, and find the distance y between the bottom of the coffeepot and the ground. Give each distance to the nearest foot.

  b. Apply About how tall is the coffeepot?

In the **Real World**

World's Largest Coffeepot
The water tower in the photo has a capacity of 40,000 gallons. How many 8 ounce cups of coffee would the tower hold?

29. Extended Problem Solving You can estimate the size of a fireworks star. As shown, let AC be the distance across the star, let d be the distance in feet from your eye to the star, and let $x°$ be the measure of the angle determined by point A, your eye, and point C.

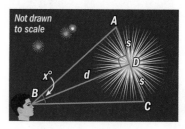
Not drawn to scale

a. Explain You see the light from the explosion almost instantly, but its sound travels at about 1100 feet per second. Suppose you count n seconds from the time you see the explosion until you hear it. Find d when $n = 4$. Explain your reasoning.

b. Critical Thinking In the diagram, $\triangle ABD \cong \triangle CBD$. How you can use one of the triangles to find s if you know the values of x and d?

c. Interpret and Apply Suppose $x = 5$. Use your answer from part (a) to estimate the distance across the fireworks star to the nearest foot.

30. Challenge Find the value of x to the nearest tenth of a centimeter.

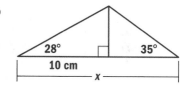

Mixed Review

31. You pay $1.17 for 3 cans of cat food. How much would you pay for 8 cans? *(Lesson 6.1)*

In Exercises 32–35, simplify the expression. *(Lesson 9.2)*

32. $\sqrt{25x^2}$ **33.** $\sqrt{36b}$ **34.** $\sqrt{18a^2b}$ **35.** $\sqrt{162f^2g^2}$

36. Find the distance between the points $(-9, 1)$ and $(6, 9)$. *(Lesson 9.5)*

Standardized Test Practice

37. Multiple Choice In $\triangle XYZ$, which ratio is equal to $\tan Y$?

   A. $\dfrac{x}{y}$ **B.** $\dfrac{y}{x}$ **C.** $\dfrac{x}{z}$ **D.** $\dfrac{y}{z}$

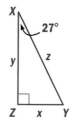

38. Multiple Choice In $\triangle XYZ$, let $y = 10$. Given that $\tan 27° \approx 0.5095$, what is the approximate value of x?

   F. 0.05   **G.** 5   **H.** 10.5   **I.** 20

Brain GAME

To a "T"

List the angle measures so that the tangents of the angles are in order from least to greatest. Write the letters for the first 6 angles in your list.

60°	80°	11°	71°	31°	52°	23°	45°	68°
E	N	T	R	A	O	P	T	G

What begins with T, ends with T, and has T in it?

Unscramble the letters to answer the riddle.

The Sine *and* Cosine Ratios

BEFORE ▸ *Now* **WHY?**

You used tangent to find triangle side lengths.

You'll use sine and cosine to find triangle side lengths.

So you can determine how to position a ladder, as in Ex. 22.

Vocabulary
sine, p. 494
cosine, p. 494

Ancient Sundial The structure shown is a sundial, built on a sunken platform in Jaipur, India, in the eighteenth century. The part of the structure above ground level is a right triangle. Its hypotenuse has a length of about 164 feet and makes an angle of 27° with the horizontal. About how far above ground level is the top of the triangle? In Example 4, you will see how to use a *sine* ratio to answer this question. Sine, abbreviated sin, *cosine*, abbreviated cos, and tangent are the three basic trigonometric ratios.

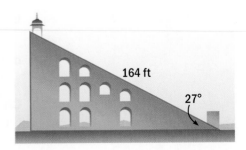

164 ft

27°

The Sine and Cosine Ratios

The **sine** of an acute angle of a right triangle is the ratio of the length of the side opposite the angle to the length of the hypotenuse.

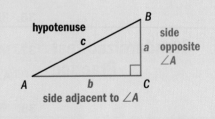

$$\sin A = \frac{\text{side opposite } \angle A}{\text{hypotenuse}} = \frac{a}{c}$$

The **cosine** of an acute angle of a right triangle is the ratio of the length of the angle's adjacent side to the length of the hypotenuse.

$$\cos A = \frac{\text{side adjacent to } \angle A}{\text{hypotenuse}} = \frac{b}{c}$$

Example 1 *Finding Sine and Cosine Ratios*

For △*JKL*, find the sine and cosine of ∠*L*.

$$\sin L = \frac{\text{opposite}}{\text{hypotenuse}} = \frac{8}{17}$$

$$\cos L = \frac{\text{adjacent}}{\text{hypotenuse}} = \frac{15}{17}$$

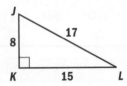

Example 2 · *Using a Calculator*

a. $\sin 38°$

Keystrokes

[2nd] [TRIG] [=]
38 [ )] [=]

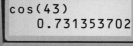

sin(38)
      0.615661475

Answer

$\sin 38° \approx 0.6157$

b. $\cos 43°$

Keystrokes

[2nd] [TRIG] [▶] [▶]
[=] 43 [ )] [=]

cos(43)
      0.731353702

Answer

$\cos 43° \approx 0.7314$

✔ Checkpoint

1. Use a calculator to approximate $\sin 74°$ and $\cos 12°$ to four decimal places.

Example 3 · *Using a Cosine Ratio*

In $\triangle DEF$ shown, $\overline{DE}$ is adjacent to $\angle D$. You know the length of the hypotenuse. To find the value of x, use $\cos D$.

$\cos D = \dfrac{\text{adjacent}}{\text{hypotenuse}}$ **Definition of cosine ratio**

$\cos 41° = \dfrac{x}{16}$ **Substitute.**

$0.7547 \approx \dfrac{x}{16}$ **Use a calculator to approximate $\cos 41°$.**

$12.1 \approx x$ **Multiply each side by 16.**

Example 4 · *Using a Sine Ratio*

To find the height above ground level of the top of the triangle on page 494, find the length of the side opposite the 27° angle. Because you know the length of the hypotenuse, use $\sin 27°$.

$\sin 27° = \dfrac{\text{opposite}}{\text{hypotenuse}}$ **Definition of sine ratio**

$\sin 27° = \dfrac{x}{164}$ **Substitute.**

$0.4540 \approx \dfrac{x}{164}$ **Use a calculator to approximate $\sin 27°$.**

$74.456 \approx x$ **Multiply each side by 164.**

Answer The top of the triangle is about 74 feet above ground level.

In the **Real World**

Ancient Sundial The sunken platform on which the ancient sundial described on page 494 stands is a rectangle approximately 134 feet wide and 146 feet long. What is the area of the platform?

SUMMARY **Right Triangle Relationships**

Pythagorean theorem	45°-45°-90° triangle	30°-60°-90° triangle

$$a^2 + b^2 = c^2$$

Trigonometric ratios

$$\tan A = \frac{a}{b} \qquad \sin A = \frac{a}{c} \qquad \cos A = \frac{b}{c}$$

9.8 Exercises

More Practice, p. 811

More Practice, p. 811

INTERNET
eWorkbook Plus
CLASSZONE.COM

Guided Practice

Vocabulary Check   **In Exercises 1 and 2, use** △*DEF*.

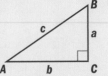

1. Which ratio is equal to sin *F*?

  A. $\frac{3}{5}$ **B.** $\frac{3}{4}$ **C.** $\frac{4}{5}$

2. Which side lengths do you need to know to find sin *D*?

Skill Check   **3.** Write the sine and cosine ratio for each acute angle of △*JKL*.

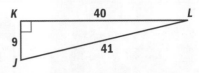

Guided Problem Solving   **4. Radio Tower** A support wire 225 feet long is fastened to the top of a radio tower. The wire makes an angle of 70° with the ground. How tall is the tower to the nearest foot?

  1 Determine which trigonometric ratio you can use to find the height *h* of the tower. Write an equation you can use to find *h*.

  2 Use a calculator to find the height of the tower to the nearest foot.

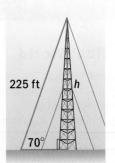

Practice and Problem Solving

Homework *Help*

Example	Exercises
1	5–7
2	8–15
3	16–25
4	16–25

Online Resources
CLASSZONE.COM

• More Examples
• eTutorial Plus

In the following exercises, you may find it helpful to use a calculator for approximating sine and cosine values.

Find the sine and cosine of each acute angle. Write your answers as fractions in simplest form.

5.

6.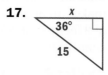

7.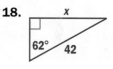

Approximate the sine or cosine value to four decimal places.

8. sin 60°   **9.** cos 22°   **10.** cos 34°   **11.** sin 72°

12. cos 15°   **13.** sin 65°   **14.** sin 23°   **15.** cos 1°

Find the value of *x* to the nearest tenth.

16.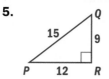

17.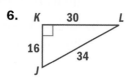

18.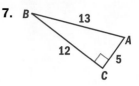

19.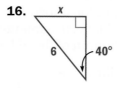

20.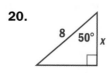

21.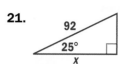

22. Ladders You set a 24 foot ladder against a building. For safety reasons, the angle that the ladder makes with the ground should be about 75°. To the nearest foot, how far from the building should you place the bottom of the ladder?

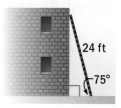

24 ft
75°

23. *Writing* Draw △*DEF* with a right angle at *E*. Use your drawing to describe the relationship between the sine of one acute angle of a right triangle and the cosine of the other acute angle.

24. Pyramids A diagram of a cross section of the pyramid of Amenemhet III at Hawara, Egypt, is shown. Find the height *h* of the pyramid to the nearest meter.

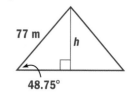

77 m   *h*   48.75°

25. Ramps An access ramp that is 4 meters long makes an angle of 4.8° with the ground, as shown. What horizontal distance *d* does the ramp cover? Round your answer to the nearest tenth of a meter.

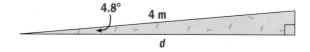

4.8°   4 m   *d*

26. Extended Problem Solving You are wearing a parachute and being pulled through the air by a tow line attached to a boat. The tow line is 600 feet long and makes an angle of 30° with the horizontal.

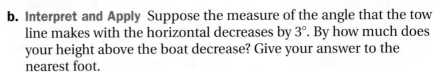

a. **Calculate** What is your height x (in feet) above the boat?

b. **Interpret and Apply** Suppose the measure of the angle that the tow line makes with the horizontal decreases by 3°. By how much does your height above the boat decrease? Give your answer to the nearest foot.

27. Critical Thinking In $\triangle ABC$, the measure of $\angle B$ is about 37°. Describe four methods you could use to find the value of b.

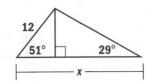

28. Chairlift A chairlift at a ski resort has a vertical climb of 440 feet and makes an angle of 11° with the horizontal. The chairlift travels at a rate of 9 feet per second. To the nearest minute, how long does it take the chairlift to go from the bottom of the hill to the top?

29. Challenge Find the value of x to the nearest tenth.

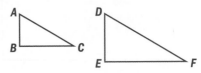

Bicyclists using a chairlift in summer

Mixed Review

Determine whether the triangle with the given side lengths is a right triangle. *(Lesson 9.3)*

30. 2.5, 6, 6.5   **31.** 10, 12, 16   **32.** 20, 22, 30

33. In the figure, $\triangle ABC \sim \triangle DEF$. Name the corresponding parts of the figures. *(Lesson 6.4)*

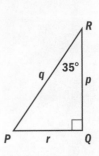

Tell whether the number is *rational* or *irrational*. *(Lesson 9.4)*

34. $\sqrt{900}$ **35.** $\sqrt{32}$ **36.** $\sqrt{8.5}$ **37.** $\sqrt{169}$

Standardized Test Practice

In Exercises 38 and 39, use $\triangle PQR$.

38. Multiple Choice Which ratio is equal to sin P?

A. $\dfrac{p}{r}$ **B.** $\dfrac{r}{q}$ **C.** $\dfrac{p}{q}$ **D.** $\dfrac{q}{p}$

39. Multiple Choice If $q = 45$, which equation can you use to find r?

F. $\sin 35° = \dfrac{r}{45}$ **G.** $\sin 35° = \dfrac{45}{r}$

H. $\cos 35° = \dfrac{r}{45}$ **I.** $\cos 35° = \dfrac{45}{r}$

9.8 Inverse Sine, Cosine, and Tangent

Goal Use a calculator to find angles using inverse trigonometric functions.

For right triangles, the sine, cosine, and tangent are functions that accept angle measures as inputs and give ratios of side lengths as outputs. The *inverse* sine, cosine, and tangent functions (written as $\sin^{-1}$, $\cos^{-1}$, and $\tan^{-1}$) accept ratios of side lengths as inputs and give angle measures as outputs. For instance:

$$\text{If } \sin x° = \frac{a}{b}, \text{ then } \sin^{-1}\left(\frac{a}{b}\right) = x°.$$

Example

A moving truck has a loading ramp that is 10 feet long. The deck of the truck is 3 feet above the ground. Use a calculator to find the angle the ramp makes with the ground.

When the loading ramp is extended from the back of the truck, a right triangle is formed.

$$\sin A = \frac{\text{opposite}}{\text{hypotenuse}} = \frac{3}{10}$$

$$m\angle A = \sin^{-1}\left(\frac{3}{10}\right)$$

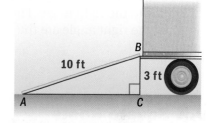

Keystrokes

[2nd] [TRIG] [▶] [=] 3 [/] 10

[)] [=]

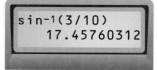

```
sin-1(3/10)
        17.45760312
```

Answer The ramp makes an angle of about 17.5° with the ground.

Tech *Help*

You use [/] to enter a ratio as a fraction, but you can also use [÷] to enter the ratio as a decimal.

Draw Conclusions

Use a calculator to evaluate the expression. Round to the nearest tenth of a degree.

1. $\sin^{-1}\left(\frac{3}{5}\right)$
2. $\sin^{-1}\left(\frac{1}{2}\right)$
3. $\cos^{-1}\left(\frac{12}{13}\right)$

4. $\cos^{-1}\left(\frac{2}{3}\right)$
5. $\tan^{-1}\left(\frac{4}{3}\right)$
6. $\tan^{-1}\left(\frac{1}{10}\right)$

7. **Moving Truck** The deck of another moving truck is only 2 feet above the ground. If a ramp is 10 feet long, what angle does it make with the ground?

Chapter Review

Vocabulary Review

square root, p. 453

perfect square, p. 454

radical expression, p. 454

simplest form of a radical
expression, p. 458

hypotenuse, p. 465

leg, p. 465

Pythagorean theorem, p. 465

irrational number, p. 470

real number, p. 470

midpoint, p. 478

trigonometric ratio, p. 489

tangent, p. 489

sine, p. 494

cosine, p. 494

In Exercises 1 and 2, copy and complete the statement.

1. A(n) _?_ of a number n is a number m such that $m^2 = n$.

2. In a right triangle, the _?_ is the side opposite the right angle. The sides that form the right angle are the _?_ .

3. What is the midpoint of a segment?

4. For $\triangle DEF$ below, write $\sin D$, $\cos D$, and $\tan D$ in terms of d, e, and f.

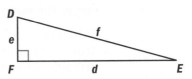

9.1 Square Roots

Examples on
pp. 453–455

▶ *Goal*

Find and approximate square roots.

Example Find the square roots of 2500.

You know that $50^2 = 2500$ and $(-50)^2 = 2500$. Therefore, the square roots of 2500 are 50 and -50.

Example Approximate $\sqrt{78}$ to the nearest integer.

$64 < 78 < 81$	Identify perfect squares closest to 78.
$\sqrt{64} < \sqrt{78} < \sqrt{81}$	Take positive square root of each number.
$8 < \sqrt{78} < 9$	Evaluate square root of each perfect square.

Answer Because 78 is closer to 81 than 64, $\sqrt{78}$ is closer to 9 than to 8. So, to the nearest integer, $\sqrt{78} \approx 9$.

✔ 5. Find the square roots of 625 and the square roots of 8100.

Approximate the square root to the nearest integer.

6. $\sqrt{18}$　　　　7. $-\sqrt{28}$　　　　8. $-\sqrt{39}$　　　　9. $\sqrt{60}$

9.2 Simplifying Square Roots

Examples on pp. 458–459

▶ **Goal**

Simplify radical expressions.

Example Simplify $\sqrt{112}$ and $\sqrt{\dfrac{33b}{25}}$.

a. $\sqrt{112} = \sqrt{16 \cdot 7}$ Factor using greatest perfect square factor.

$\quad\quad = \sqrt{16} \cdot \sqrt{7}$ Product property of square roots

$\quad\quad = 4\sqrt{7}$ Simplify.

b. $\sqrt{\dfrac{33b}{25}} = \dfrac{\sqrt{33b}}{\sqrt{25}}$ Quotient property of square roots

$\quad\quad = \dfrac{\sqrt{33b}}{5}$ Simplify.

✔ **Simplify the expression.**

10. $\sqrt{350}$ **11.** $\sqrt{72}$ **12.** $\sqrt{\dfrac{48}{49}}$ **13.** $\sqrt{\dfrac{29a}{100}}$

14. $\sqrt{\dfrac{8}{n^2}}$ **15.** $\sqrt{18z^2}$ **16.** $\sqrt{75m}$ **17.** $\sqrt{\dfrac{2a^2}{49}}$

9.3 The Pythagorean Theorem

Examples on pp. 465–466

▶ **Goal**

Use the Pythagorean theorem to find unknown side lengths of right triangles.

Example Find the unknown length c in simplest form.

$a^2 + b^2 = c^2$ Pythagorean theorem

$8^2 + 14^2 = c^2$ Substitute 8 for a and 14 for b.

$64 + 196 = c^2$ Evaluate powers.

$260 = c^2$ Add.

$\sqrt{260} = c$ Take positive square root of each side.

$2\sqrt{65} = c$ Simplify.

Answer The length c of the hypotenuse of the triangle is $2\sqrt{65}$ units.

✔ **Find the unknown length. Write your answer in simplest form.**

18.   **19.**   **20.**

21. Find the length x of the diagonal of the rectangle. Write your answer in simplest form.

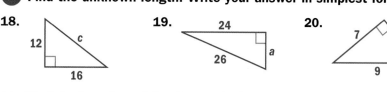

9.4 Real Numbers

Examples on pp. 470–472

▶ *Goal*

Compare and order real numbers.

Example Use a number line to order the numbers -2.5, $\sqrt{6}$, $\frac{17}{8}$, 1.8, and $-\sqrt{2}$ from least to greatest.

Graph the numbers on a number line and read them from left to right.

From least to greatest, the numbers are -2.5, $-\sqrt{2}$, 1.8, $\frac{17}{8}$, and $\sqrt{6}$.

✔ **Copy and complete the statement using <, >, or =.**

22. $\sqrt{10}$ _?_ 2.1   **23.** $\sqrt{15}$ _?_ $2\frac{1}{3}$ **24.** $\sqrt{1.44}$ _?_ 1.2   **25.** $5\frac{1}{2}$ _?_ $\sqrt{48}$

Use a number line to order the numbers from least to greatest.

26. $\sqrt{30}$, -3.5, $\frac{17}{5}$, $-\sqrt{12}$ **27.** $\frac{19}{6}$, $-\sqrt{18}$, $\sqrt{20}$, -5.01

9.5 The Distance and Midpoint Formulas

Examples on pp. 476–478

▶ *Goal*

Use the distance and midpoint formulas.

Example Given points $A(-5, 6)$ and $B(3, 8)$, find the distance d between the points, and find the midpoint M of $\overline{AB}$.

a. $d = \sqrt{(x_2 - x_1)^2 + (y_2 - y_1)^2}$ Distance formula

$ = \sqrt{(3 - (-5))^2 + (8 - 6)^2}$ Substitute 3 for x_2, -5 for x_1, 8 for y_2, and 6 for y_1.

$ = \sqrt{(8)^2 + (2)^2}$ Subtract.

$ = \sqrt{64 + 4}$ Evaluate powers.

$ = \sqrt{68}$ Add.

$ = 2\sqrt{17}$ Simplify.

b. $M = \left(\dfrac{x_1 + x_2}{2}, \dfrac{y_1 + y_2}{2}\right)$ Midpoint formula

$ = \left(\dfrac{-5 + 3}{2}, \dfrac{6 + 8}{2}\right)$ Substitute -5 for x_1, 3 for x_2, 6 for y_1, and 8 for y_2.

$ = (-1, 7)$ Simplify.

✔ **28.** Find the distance between points $A(9, 10)$ and $B(6, 6)$, and find the midpoint M of $\overline{AB}$.

9.6 Special Right Triangles

Examples on pp. 483–485

▶ **Goal**

Find unknown side lengths in special right triangles.

Example Find the value of x.

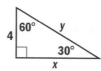

The triangle is a 45°-45°-90° triangle. The value of x, which is the length of the hypotenuse, is the product of the length of a leg and $\sqrt{2}$.

$$x = \text{leg} \cdot \sqrt{2} = 6\sqrt{2}$$

✔ **Find the values of x and y. Write your answers in simplest form.**

29.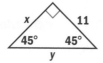

30.

31.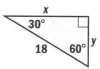

9.7 The Tangent Ratio

Examples on pp. 489–490

▶ **Goal**

Use the tangent ratio to find an unknown length in a right triangle.

Example Find the value of m. Round to the nearest tenth.

$\tan 20° = \dfrac{m}{48}$ **Definition of tangent ratio**

$0.3640 \approx \dfrac{m}{48}$ **Use a calculator to approximate tan 20°.**

$17.5 \approx m$ **Multiply each side by 48. Round.**

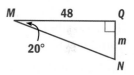

✔ **32.** In $\triangle PQR$ with right angle at R, $\angle P$ has a measure of 72°. The leg adjacent to $\angle P$ has a length of 8 units. Find the length of the leg opposite $\angle P$ to the nearest tenth.

9.8 The Sine and Cosine Ratios

Examples on pp. 494–495

▶ **Goal**

Use the sine and cosine ratios to find unknown lengths in a right triangle.

Example Find the value of a. Round to the nearest tenth.

$\sin 40° = \dfrac{a}{15}$ **Definition of sine ratio**

$0.6428 \approx \dfrac{a}{15}$ **Use a calculator to approximate sin 40°.**

$9.6 \approx a$ **Multiply each side by 15. Round.**

✔ **33.** Find the value of b in $\triangle ABC$. Round to the nearest tenth.

Chapter Test

Solve the equation. Round to the nearest tenth if necessary.

1. $x^2 = 25$ **2.** $225 = t^2$ **3.** $216 = 2z^2$ **4.** $3y^2 = 147$

Simplify the expression.

5. $\sqrt{162}$ **6.** $\sqrt{\dfrac{20}{121}}$ **7.** $\sqrt{\dfrac{x}{400}}$ **8.** $\sqrt{50a^2}$

Determine whether the triangle with the given side lengths is a right triangle.

9. 4, 5, 6 **10.** 15, 36, 39 **11.** 24, 45, 51 **12.** 5, 13, 15

Find the unknown length. Write your answer in simplest form.

13.

14.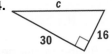

15.

16.

17. Use a number line to order the numbers $2\sqrt{5}$, 4.5, $\sqrt{19}$, $\dfrac{19}{4}$, and $3\sqrt{2}$ from least to greatest.

18. Find the midpoint M of the segment with endpoints $A(-2, 3)$ and $B(4, 6)$.

19. Find the distance between the points $P(-6, -2)$ and $Q(-2, 1)$.

20. Lightning Protection Many boats have a lightning protection system that includes a mast or other metal pole extending above the vessel. The pole and all the larger metal parts of the boat are connected to form a path along which electricity can be conducted to the water. The system forms a "cone of protection" extending 60° around the tip of the pole. How far does the cone extend from the mast at water level (distance DC in the diagram)? Give your answer to the nearest foot.

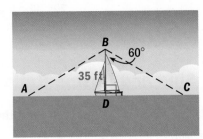

Use △ABC to complete Exercises 21 and 22.

21. Find the value of a to the nearest tenth.

22. Find the value of c to the nearest tenth.

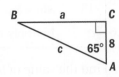

Chapter Standardized Test

Test-Taking Strategy Make sure that you are answering the question that is asked. Some questions have several steps.

---

1. Evaluate $\sqrt{x + y}$ when $x = 16$ and $y = 9$.

   A. $\sqrt{7}$ **B.** 5   **C.** 7   **D.** 25

2. Which expression is the simplest form of $\sqrt{\dfrac{320}{x^2}}$?

   F. $\dfrac{\sqrt{320}}{x}$ **G.** $\dfrac{4\sqrt{20}}{x}$ **H.** $\dfrac{8\sqrt{5}}{x}$ **I.** $8\sqrt{\dfrac{5}{x^2}}$

3. In 432 B.C., part of the Greek city of Olynthus was divided into rectangular city blocks measuring 120 feet by 300 feet. To the nearest foot, what is the diagonal distance across each city block?

   A. 275 feet   **B.** 323 feet

   C. 420 feet   **D.** 104,400 feet

4. Which number is irrational?

   F. $-\sqrt{49}$ **G.** $\sqrt{\dfrac{16}{2}}$ **H.** $\dfrac{\sqrt{25}}{6}$ **I.** $\sqrt{\dfrac{8}{2}}$

5. What is the distance between the points $(-8, 8)$ and $(4, 6)$?

   A. 12   **B.** $2\sqrt{37}$ **C.** $4\sqrt{53}$ **D.** $4\sqrt{85}$

6. What is the midpoint of the segment with endpoints $(-8, 8)$ and $(4, 6)$?

   F. $(-2, 7)$ **G.** $(-1, 6)$ **H.** $(0, 5)$ **I.** $(6, -1)$

7. The length of a leg in a 45°-45°-90° triangle is 13 yards. What is the length of the hypotenuse?

   A. 6.5 yards   **B.** 13 yards

   C. $13\sqrt{2}$ yards   **D.** $13\sqrt{3}$ yards

8. Find the value of r in $\triangle PQR$. Round to the nearest tenth.

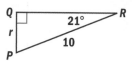

   F. 3.6   **G.** 3.8   **H.** 9.3   **I.** 9.6

9. Find the value of b in $\triangle ABC$. Round to the nearest tenth.

   A. 7.2   **B.** 9.6

   C. 11.2   **D.** 11.4

10. **Short Response** Plot the points $D(7, 3)$, $E(4, 7)$, $F(-4, 1)$, and $G(-1, -3)$ in a coordinate plane. Connect the points to form a rectangle. Explain how to find the perimeter and the area of the rectangle. Then find the perimeter and the area.

11. **Extended Response** You are in a high-rise building and look out a window. You see another building 100 feet away. The angle formed by the top of the building, your eye, and the horizontal is 65°. The angle formed by the horizontal, your eye, and the bottom of the building is 55°.

   a. Find the value of a to the nearest foot.

   b. Find the value of b to the nearest foot.

   c. How tall is the building you see?

   d. Explain how you decided which trigonometric ratio(s) to use to solve parts (a) and (b).

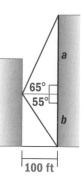

Designing a Ramp

Goal
Design a ramp for your school auditorium.

Key Skill
Using the Pythagorean theorem

Materials
• calculator
• measuring tape

An actor dashes through the audience and up onto the stage. Band members walk down a ramp and surround the audience with music. Exciting stage entrances and exits can be made on a ramp that connects the stage and the seating area. To design a ramp for your school's auditorium, you must first choose its dimensions and its slope.

Investigate

1. Measure the distance (in inches) between the floor of the auditorium and the stage. This distance is a.

2. Choose a point on the floor of the auditorium where the ramp can end. The distance from this point to the base of the stage should be greater than or equal to $3a$. Call this distance b.

3. Measure the distance b. Then choose two other points for the ramp's end and measure the distances from these points to the base of the stage. You will use these three values of b to design 3 different ramps.

4. Use the Pythagorean theorem to find the length of the walkway for each ramp design. Round to the nearest inch.

5. Find the slope of each ramp design.

6. Suppose the ramp must be 4 feet wide. What is the area of the walkway for each ramp design?

Consider and Decide

Choose the best ramp design for your auditorium. Consider the following:

- Which ramp is the steepest? Which is the least steep? Which ramp will be easiest to walk up or down? Why?

- Plywood is sold in sheets that are 4 feet by 8 feet. Which ramp design requires the fewest sheets of plywood?

Present Your Design

Make a scale drawing of the ramp design that works best for your auditorium. Include all the dimensions of the ramp and its slope. Explain why you chose this design.

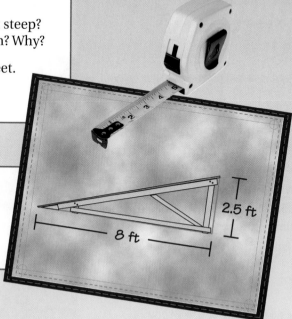

Project Extensions

Using Trigonometry Suppose the measure of the angle formed by the ramp and the floor of the auditorium must be less than 15°. What should the length of the ramp be? Show your work.

Explore Measure the rise and run of a ramp at your school or another building. What are the length of the walkway and the slope of the ramp? What is the purpose of the ramp? Compare the dimensions of this ramp with the dimensions of the one that you designed.

Career Many people are involved in the production of a play, including set designers, costume designers, and lighting designers. Find out more about one of these careers. Present your findings.

Research CLASSZONE.COM Use the Internet to learn about other uses of ramps, such as for skateboards, bikes, or wheelchairs. How are these ramps constructed? What slopes are commonly used for each type of ramp? Present your research.

Measurement, Area, *and* Volume

How does the size of a drum affect its sound?

CHAPTER 10
INTERNET Preview
CLASSZONE.COM

- eEdition Plus Online
- eWorkbook Plus Online
- eTutorial Plus Online
- State Test Practice
- More Examples

M A T H *In the* **Real World**

Drums When you strike a drum, it vibrates, producing sound. One reason a large drum sounds lower in pitch than a small drum is that the large drum vibrates more slowly. In this chapter, you will find the surface area and volume of objects like drums.

What do you think? The drums in the photo are cylinders. What shape do the top and bottom of a cylinder have? If you were to cut a cylinder's curved side straight down from top to bottom and flatten it, what shape would you see?

Chapter Prerequisite Skills

PREREQUISITE SKILLS QUIZ

Review Vocabulary

scale drawing, p. 300
scale, p. 300
hypotenuse, p. 465
leg, p. 465
Pythagorean theorem, p. 465

Preparing for Success **To prepare for success in this chapter, test your knowledge of these concepts and skills. You may want to look at the pages referred to in blue for additional review.**

1. Vocabulary Draw a right triangle. Label the hypotenuse and legs.

Solve the equation. *(p. 120)*

2. $15 = 2x - 7$ **3.** $8 - 3n = 50$ **4.** $-9 - 4y = 19$ **5.** $78 = 2p + 12$

Solve the proportion. *(pp. 275, 280)*

6. $\dfrac{a}{16} = \dfrac{5}{4}$ **7.** $\dfrac{90}{15} = \dfrac{t}{34}$ **8.** $\dfrac{3}{7} = \dfrac{31}{z}$ **9.** $\dfrac{2}{74} = \dfrac{96}{m}$

10. Architecture A scale drawing of a rectangular wall is 8 inches long and 14 inches high. The drawing has a scale of 1 inch : 3 feet. Find the wall's dimensions. *(p. 300)*

11. Determine whether a triangle with side lengths 20, 37.5, and 42.5 is a right triangle. *(p. 465)*

NOTETAKING STRATEGIES

MAIN IDEA WEB When you learn a new concept, you may want to make a web of details surrounding the concept in your notebook.

$$\tan A = \frac{\text{side opposite } \angle A}{\text{side adjacent to } \angle A} = \frac{a}{b}$$

Main Idea: A trigonometric ratio is a ratio of the lengths of two sides of a right triangle.

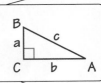

$$\sin A = \frac{\text{side opposite } \angle A}{\text{hypotenuse}} = \frac{a}{c}$$

$$\cos A = \frac{\text{side adjacent to } \angle A}{\text{hypotenuse}} = \frac{b}{c}$$

A main idea web will help you in Lesson 10.8.

10.1

Triangles

Review Vocabulary

acute triangle, p. 462
right triangle, p. 462
obtuse triangle, p. 462
equiangular triangle, p. 462
equilateral triangle, p. 463
isosceles triangle, p. 463
scalene triangle, p. 463

Construction Homes are often built with sloped roofs so that they can shed rain. Such roofs are built using a series of triangular roof trusses. The trusses may include braces that help the roof bear weight, such as the weight of snow.

Recall that you can classify a triangle by its angle measures or by its side lengths. When classified by angle measures, triangles are acute, right, obtuse, or equiangular. When classified by side lengths, triangles are equilateral, isosceles, or scalene.

Review *Help*

For help with classifying triangles, see pp. 462–463.

| **Example 1** | *Classifying a Triangle by Angle Measures* |

In the diagram, $m\angle DBE = 64°$ and $m\angle BDE = m\angle BED$. Find $m\angle BDE$ and $m\angle BED$. Then classify $\triangle BDE$ by its angle measures.

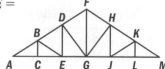

Solution

Let $x°$ represent $m\angle BDE$ and $m\angle BED$.

$m\angle BDE + m\angle BED + m\angle DBE = 180°$	**Sum of angle measures is 180°.**
$x° + x° + 64° = 180°$	**Substitute values.**
$2x + 64 = 180$	**Combine like terms.**
$2x = 116$	**Subtract 64 from each side.**
$x = 58$	**Divide each side by 2.**

Answer $m\angle BDE = m\angle BED = 58°$. Because $\angle BDE$, $\angle DBE$, and $\angle BED$ are acute angles, $\triangle BDE$ is an acute triangle.

✔ *Checkpoint*

1. Use the diagram in Example 1. Given that $m\angle EDG = 38°$ and the measure of $\angle DEG$ is 38° more than $m\angle DGE$, find $m\angle DGE$ and $m\angle DEG$. Then classify $\triangle DEG$ by its angle measures.

Example 2 Finding Unknown Side Lengths

The perimeter of a scalene triangle is 65 centimeters. The length of the first side is twice the length of the second side. The length of the third side is 20 centimeters. Find the lengths of the other two sides.

Solution

Draw the triangle. Let x and $2x$ represent the unknown side lengths. Write an equation for the perimeter P. Then solve for x.

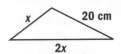

$P = 2x + x + 20$	**Formula for perimeter**
$65 = 2x + x + 20$	**Substitute 65 for P.**
$65 = 3x + 20$	**Combine like terms.**
$45 = 3x$	**Subtract 20 from each side.**
$15 = x$	**Divide each side by 3.**

Answer The length of the second side is 15 centimeters, and the length of the first side is $2(15) = 30$ centimeters.

✔ Checkpoint

2. The perimeter of an equilateral triangle is 42 meters. Find the length of each side.

Study *Strategy*

For a triangle whose angles measure 50°, 60°, and 70°, you can say that the ratio of the angle measures is 50 : 60 : 70, or 5 : 6 : 7. Therefore, if you know that the ratio of the angle measures is 5 : 6 : 7, you can say that the angle measures are 5x°, 6x°, and 7x° for some value of x.

Example 3 Finding Angle Measures Using a Ratio

The ratio of the angle measures of a triangle is 1 : 3 : 5. Find the angle measures. Then classify the triangle by its angle measures.

Solution

① Let $x°$, $3x°$, and $5x°$ represent the angle measures. Write an equation for the sum of the angle measures.

$x° + 3x° + 5x° = 180°$	**Sum of angle measures is 180°.**
$9x = 180$	**Combine like terms.**
$x = 20$	**Divide each side by 9.**

② Substitute 20 for x in the expression for each angle measure.

$$(20)° = 20° \qquad (3 \cdot 20)° = 60° \qquad (5 \cdot 20)° = 100°$$

Answer The angle measures of the triangle are 20°, 60°, and 100°. So, the triangle is an obtuse triangle.

✔ Checkpoint

3. The ratio of the angle measures of a triangle is 3 : 5 : 12. Find the angle measures. Then classify the triangle by its angle measures.

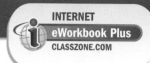
Guided Practice

Vocabulary Check   **1.** The ratio of the angle measures of a triangle is $1:1:1$. Find the angle measures. Then classify the triangle by its angle measures.

Skill Check   **Find the value of x. Then classify the triangle by its angle measures.**

2.

3.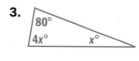

4.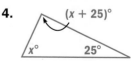

5. The perimeter of an isosceles triangle is 14 meters. The length of one side is 4 meters. The lengths of the other two sides are equal. Find the lengths of the other two sides.

6. The ratio of the angle measures in a triangle is $6:5:4$. Find the angle measures. Then classify the triangle by its angle measures.

7. Error Analysis Describe and correct the error in finding the value of x for the triangle shown below.

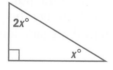

$$x° + 2x° = 180°$$
$$3x = 180$$
$$x = 60$$

Practice and Problem Solving

Find the value of x. Then classify the triangle by its angle measures.

Homework *Help*

Example	Exercises
1	8–13
2	15–18
3	19–21

Online Resources
CLASSZONE.COM
• More Examples
• eTutorial Plus

8.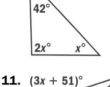

9.

10.

11.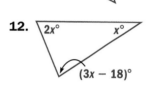

12.

13.

14. *Writing* Explain why the sum of the measures of the acute angles of a right triangle is 90°.

Find the unknown side length of the triangle given the perimeter *P*. Then classify the triangle by its side lengths.

15. *P* = 49 in.

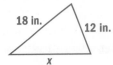
18 in. 12 in.
x

16. *P* = 22.5 yd

6.3 yd

17. *P* = 84.3 cm

18. The perimeter of a triangle is 29 millimeters. The length of the first side is twice the length of the second side. The length of the third side is 5 more than the length of the second side. Find the side lengths of the triangle. Then classify the triangle by its side lengths.

19. **Window** The perimeter of a triangular window is 141 inches. The ratio of the side lengths of the window is 11 : 18 : 18. Draw and label a diagram of the window. What are the side lengths of the window? Classify the window by its side lengths.

20. The ratio of the angle measures of a triangle is 7 : 16 : 22. Find the angle measures. Then classify the triangle by its angle measures.

21. The ratio of the side lengths of a triangle is 7 : 24 : 25. The perimeter of the triangle is 392 inches.

   a. Find the side lengths. Then classify the triangle by its side lengths.

   b. **Analyze** Is the triangle a right triangle? How do you know?

22. **Coordinate Geometry** Plot the points *A*(6, 3), *B*(−3, 9), and *C*(−3, −3) in a coordinate plane. Connect the points to form a triangle. Use the distance formula to find the side lengths. Then classify the triangle by its side lengths.

23. **Extended Problem Solving** You are building a set of nested tables. The surfaces of the tables will be 45°-45°-90° triangles.

   a. **Visual Thinking** Each of the two congruent edges of the surface of the smallest table has a length of 24 inches. Make and label a scale drawing of the surface of the smallest table.

   b. **Calculate** The ratio of an edge length of the surface of the smallest table to a corresponding edge length of the largest table is 1 : 2. Find the length of each of the two congruent edges of the surface of the largest table.

   c. **Calculate** The ratio of an edge length of the surface of the middle-sized table to a corresponding edge length of the surface of the smallest table is 3 : 2. Find the length of each of the two congruent edges of the surface of the middle-sized table.

   d. For each table surface, find the length of the third edge to the nearest inch. Make and label scale drawings of the surfaces of the two larger tables.

24. Winged Box Kite The design for a winged box kite uses four triangular pieces of cloth. To cut out one of these pieces, you fold a piece of cloth in half and pin a pattern on the cloth, as shown. You cut along $\overline{AB}$ and $\overline{BC}$. Then you remove the pattern and unfold the cloth.

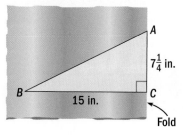

a. How many square inches of cloth do you need for each unfolded triangle? Round your answer to the nearest square inch.

b. Apply You need to attach wooden dowels to the congruent shorter sides of each of the 4 unfolded triangles. You can buy dowels that are 50 inches long. How many do you need to buy? Explain.

In the **Real World**

Winged Box Kite Using lightweight materials makes a kite easier to fly. Suppose you are choosing between two types of wooden dowels, each 50 inches long. The dowel made of balsa wood weighs 0.003 ounce per inch. The dowel made of pine weighs 0.017 ounce per inch. How much less does the dowel made of balsa wood weigh than the dowel made of pine?

25. Critical Thinking The perimeter of an isosceles triangle is 17 centimeters. The length of one side is 5 centimeters. Your friend claims that there is not enough information to find the other two side lengths of the triangle. Is your friend correct? Explain your reasoning. Include diagrams in your answer.

26. Triangle Inequality The triangle inequality theorem states that the sum of the lengths of any two sides of a triangle is greater than the length of the third side. Using this theorem, determine if the given side lengths form a triangle. Explain your reasoning.

    a. 4, 5, 10   **b.** 4, 5, 9   **c.** 4, 5, 7

27. Challenge The triangle shown is an equilateral triangle. Make 6 copies of the triangle. Put the 6 equilateral triangles together so that they all share a vertex and do not overlap. The figure formed is a *regular hexagon*. Find the sum of the measures of the angles of the regular hexagon. Explain your reasoning.

28. *Writing* Is it possible to have a triangle whose angle measures are in the ratio 3 : 4 : 5 and whose side lengths are in the same ratio? Explain.

Mixed Review

Write the sine and cosine ratios for both acute angles of the triangle. *(Lesson 9.8)*

29.

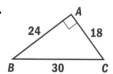

30.

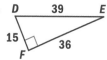

Standardized Test Practice

31. Multiple Choice The ratio of the side lengths of a triangle is 3 : 3 : 4. Classify the triangle by its side lengths.

    A. Scalene   **B.** Equilateral   **C.** Isosceles   **D.** Acute

32. Multiple Choice The ratio of the angle measures of a triangle is 1 : 2 : 3. Classify the triangle by its angle measures.

    F. Acute   **G.** Obtuse   **H.** Right   **I.** Equiangular

Polygons *and* Quadrilaterals

BEFORE	▶ *Now*	WHY?
You classified triangles.	You'll classify polygons and quadrilaterals.	So you can find the length of a side of a clock face, as in Ex. 21.

Vocabulary

polygon, p. 516
regular polygon,
  p. 516
convex, p. 516
concave, p. 516
pentagon, p. 516
hexagon, p. 516
heptagon, p. 516
octagon, p. 516
trapezoid, p. 517
parallelogram, p. 517
rhombus, p. 517
diagonal of a polygon,
  p. 518

A **polygon** is a closed plane figure whose sides are segments that intersect only at their endpoints. In a **regular polygon**, all the sides have the same length and all the angles have the same measure.

Polygons	Regular polygons	Not polygons

A polygon is **convex** if any two interior points can be connected with a segment that lies completely within the polygon. A polygon that is not convex is called **concave**.

convex concave

Reading *Geometry*

The name *n*-gon refers to a polygon that has *n* sides. For example, a 15-gon is a polygon that has 15 sides.

You already know that a 3-sided polygon is a triangle and a 4-sided polygon is a quadrilateral. Below are names of other polygons.

Polygons	Pentagon	Hexagon	Heptagon	Octagon	*n*-gon
Number of sides	5	6	7	8	*n*

Example 1 Identifying and Classifying Polygons

Tell whether the figure is a polygon. If it is a polygon, classify it and tell whether it is *convex* or *concave*. If not, explain why.

a.

The keyhole is not a polygon because the top part of the keyhole is round.

b.

The stop sign is an 8-sided polygon. So it is an octagon. It is convex and regular.

 **Checkpoint**

Tell whether the figure is a polygon. If it is a polygon, classify it and tell whether it is *convex* or *concave*. If not, explain why.

1.

2.

3.

Quadrilaterals Some quadrilaterals have special names based on whether they have parallel or congruent sides and whether they have right angles.

Quadrilaterals	Diagram
Trapezoid A **trapezoid** is a quadrilateral with exactly 1 pair of parallel sides.	
Parallelogram A **parallelogram** is a quadrilateral with both pairs of opposite sides parallel.	
Rhombus A **rhombus** is a parallelogram with 4 congruent sides.	
Rectangle A *rectangle* is a parallelogram with 4 right angles.	
Square A *square* is a parallelogram with 4 right angles and 4 congruent sides.	

Review *Help*

For help with identifying parallel lines, see pp. 410–411.

Watch *Out*

You cannot conclude that the quadrilateral in part (a) of Example 2 is a rectangle because no information is given about its angles.

Example 2   *Classifying Quadrilaterals*

Classify the quadrilateral.

a.

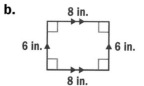

2.5 m, 4 m, 4 m, 2.5 m

The quadrilateral is a parallelogram because both pairs of opposite sides are parallel.

b.

8 in., 6 in., 6 in., 8 in.

The quadrilateral is a parallelogram with 4 right angles. So, it is a rectangle.

Segments that connect adjacent vertices of a polygon are the *sides* of the polygon. These segments are *not* considered to be diagonals.

Angle Measures in Quadrilaterals A **diagonal of a polygon** is a segment that joins two vertices that are not adjacent. You can use a diagonal of a quadrilateral to show that the sum of the angle measures in a quadrilateral is 360°.

1 Draw diagonal $\overline{FH}$, which divides quadrilateral *FGHI* into two triangles.

2 The sum of the angle measures in each triangle is 180°.

3 The sum of the angle measures in a quadrilateral is 180° + 180° = 360°.

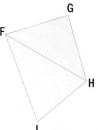

Example 3 *Finding an Unknown Angle Measure*

Find the value of x.

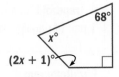

$$x° + (2x + 1)° + 90° + 68° = 360°$$ **Sum of angle measures in quadrilateral is 360°.**

$$3x + 159 = 360$$ **Combine like terms.**

$$3x = 201$$ **Subtract 159 from each side.**

$$x = 67$$ **Divide each side by 3.**

10.2 Exercises

More Practice, p. 812

INTERNET
eWorkbook Plus
CLASSZONE.COM

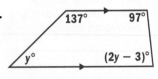

Guided Practice

Vocabulary Check   **1.** How are a trapezoid and a parallelogram different from each other?

Skill Check   **Tell whether the figure is a polygon. If it is a polygon, classify it and tell whether it is *convex* or *concave*. If not, explain why.**

2.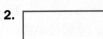

3.

4.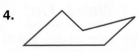

In Exercises 5 and 6, use the quadrilateral shown.

5. Classify the quadrilateral.

6. Find the value of *y*.

Practice and Problem Solving

Homework *Help*

Example	Exercises
1	7–9
2	11–17
3	18–20

Online Resources
CLASSZONE.COM
• More Examples
• eTutorial Plus

Tell whether the figure is a polygon. If it is a polygon, classify it and tell whether it is *convex* or *concave*. If not, explain why.

7.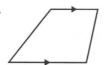

8.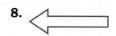

9.

10. Error Analysis Describe and correct the error in solving the following problem.

A quadrilateral has 4 congruent sides, and the opposite sides of the quadrilateral are parallel. Sketch and classify the quadrilateral.

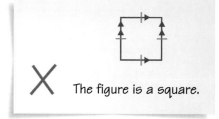

The figure is a square.

Classify the quadrilateral.

11.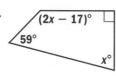

12.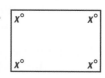

13.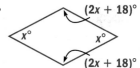

Copy and complete the statement using *always*, *sometimes*, or *never*.

14. A square is ? a rectangle.

15. A square is ? a rhombus.

16. A rhombus is ? a square.

17. A trapezoid is ? a parallelogram.

Find the value of *x*.

18. $(2x - 17)°$ $59°$ $x°$

19. $x°$ $x°$ $x°$ $x°$

20. $(2x + 18)°$ $x°$ $x°$ $(2x + 18)°$

21. Extended Problem Solving The Allen-Bradley Clock Tower in Milwaukee, Wisconsin, has four faces. Each face is a regular octagon. The perimeter of one octagonal face is approximately 133 feet.

  a. Calculate Find the length of one side of one of the octagonal faces.

  b. Visual Thinking Your friend says that you can find the area of one of the clocks by dividing one of the octagons into 8 congruent triangles. Sketch a regular octagon and show how to divide it into 8 congruent triangles.

  c. Critical Thinking What additional information would you need in part (b) to find the area of the clock face? Assume that you had this information. What would your next steps be?

22. For the trapezoid shown, the ratio $m\angle A : m\angle C$ is $2 : 1$. Write and solve an equation to find the value of *x*.

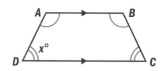

Allen-Bradley Clock Tower

23. In mathematics, a *kite* is a special type of quadrilateral. Two pairs of sides are congruent, but opposite sides are not congruent. Exactly one pair of opposite angles are congruent. In kite *ABCD* shown, the measure of ∠*A* is twice the measure of ∠*C*, and ∠*B* has a measure of 114°. Find the measures of ∠*A*, ∠*C*, and ∠*D*.

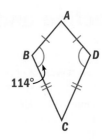

24. **Challenge** Use the figure shown to find *m*∠*WXY* and *m*∠*XYZ*. Explain your reasoning.

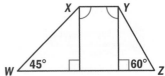

Mixed Review

Solve the linear system by graphing. *(Lesson 8.8)*

25. $y = x - 5$
$y = 2x + 1$

26. $y = -3x + 7$
$y = 3x + 4$

27. $x + y = 6$
$2x - 8y = -11$

28. Find the midpoint of the segment with endpoints $(-7, 5)$ and $(4, -20)$. *(Lesson 9.5)*

29. The ratio of the angle measures of a triangle is $2 : 3 : 7$. Find the angle measures. Then classify the triangle by its angle measures. *(Lesson 10.1)*

Standardized Test Practice

30. **Extended Response** The top of the picnic table shown has the shape of a regular polygon.

a. Sketch and classify the polygon. Is it convex or concave?

b. Draw a single segment that divides the polygon in your sketch into two trapezoids.

c. Find the sum of the measures of the angles of the polygon.

Brain GAME

Toothpick Task

Move exactly two toothpicks in the figure at the right to make 4 congruent squares instead of 5. Each toothpick must be used as a side of a square.

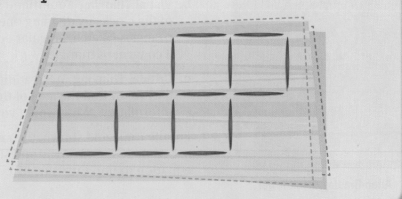

10.3

Areas *of* Parallelograms *and* Trapezoids

Vocabulary

base of a
parallelogram, p. 521
height of a
parallelogram, p. 521
bases of a trapezoid,
p. 522
height of a trapezoid,
p. 522

BEFORE	Now	WHY?
You classified polygons.	You'll find the areas of parallelograms and trapezoids.	So you can compare the areas of two parking lots, as in Ex. 26.

The **base of a parallelogram** is the length of any one of its sides. The **height of a parallelogram** is the perpendicular distance between the side whose length is the base and the opposite side. The diagrams below show how to change a parallelogram into a rectangle with the same base, height, and area as the parallelogram.

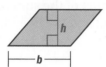      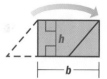

1) Start with any parallelogram.

2) Cut to form a right triangle and a trapezoid.

3) Move the triangle to form a rectangle.

Notice that the area of the rectangle above is the product of the base b and the height h. The diagram suggests the formula below.

Area of a Parallelogram

Words The area A of a parallelogram is the product of the base b and the height h.

Algebra $A = bh$

Numbers $A = 8 \cdot 6 = 48 \text{ m}^2$

Example 1   Finding the Area of a Parallelogram

The base of a parallelogram is 5 inches. The height is twice the base. Find the area of the parallelogram.

1) Find the height.

$h = 2b$
$= 2(5)$
$= 10 \text{ in.}$

2) Find the area.

$A = bh$
$= 5(10)$
$= 50 \text{ in.}^2$

Answer The parallelogram has an area of 50 square inches.

Trapezoids The **bases of a trapezoid** are the lengths of its parallel sides. The **height of a trapezoid** is the perpendicular distance between the sides whose lengths are the bases. The diagram below shows how two congruent trapezoids with height h and bases b_1 and b_2 can be put together to form a parallelogram with base $b_1 + b_2$ and height h.

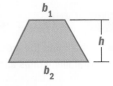

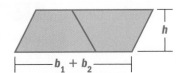

Notice the area of the parallelogram is twice the area of either trapezoid. This result suggests the formula below.

Area of a Trapezoid

Words The area A of a trapezoid is one half of the product of the sum of the bases, b_1 and b_2, and the height, h.

$b_1 = 5$ cm

$h = 4$ cm

$b_2 = 7$ cm

Algebra $A = \frac{1}{2}(b_1 + b_2)h$

Numbers $A = \frac{1}{2}(5 + 7)4 = 24$ cm^2

Example 2   *Finding the Area of a Trapezoid*

Quilts The diagram shows one of the trapezoids in a quilt design. Find the area of the trapezoid.

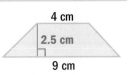

4 cm

2.5 cm

9 cm

Solution

$A = \frac{1}{2}(b_1 + b_2)h$ Write formula for area of a trapezoid.

$= \frac{1}{2}(4 + 9)2.5$ Substitute 4 for b_1, 9 for b_2, and 2.5 for h.

$= 16.25$ Simplify.

Answer The trapezoid has an area of 16.25 square centimeters.

✔ *Checkpoint*

Find the area of the parallelogram or trapezoid.

1.

5 ft

6 ft

2.   3 m

8.5 m

9 m

3.   22 in.

16 in.

13 in.

Example 3 — Finding an Unknown Length

The height of a trapezoid is 6 meters. One of its bases is 8 meters. The area of the trapezoid is 54 square meters. Find the other base.

$A = \frac{1}{2}(b_1 + b_2)h$ Write formula for area of a trapezoid.

$54 = \frac{1}{2}(8 + b_2)6$ Substitute 54 for A, 8 for b_1, and 6 for h.

$54 = 3(8 + b_2)$ Multiply.

$54 = 24 + 3b_2$ Distributive property

$30 = 3b_2$ Subtract 24 from each side.

$10 = b_2$ Divide each side by 3.

Answer The other base is 10 meters.

Study *Strategy*

Another Way You can divide the desktop in Example 4 in other ways. For instance, you can have an 8 ft by 3 ft rectangle and a trapezoid with bases 4 ft and 6 ft and height 3 ft.

Example 4 — Using Area of Trapezoids

Desk You are building an L-shaped desk for your room. The dimensions of the desktop are shown. Find the area of the desktop.

Solution

1 Divide the desktop into two trapezoids, A and B, as shown.

2 Find the sum of the areas of trapezoids A and B.

Area of trapezoid A $= \frac{1}{2}(b_1 + b_2)h$ Formula for area of a trapezoid

$= \frac{1}{2}(5 + 8)3 = \frac{39}{2} = 19\frac{1}{2}$ Substitute. Then simplify.

Area of trapezoid B $= \frac{1}{2}(b_1 + b_2)h$ Formula for area of a trapezoid

$= \frac{1}{2}(4 + 9)3 = \frac{39}{2} = 19\frac{1}{2}$ Substitute. Then simplify.

3 Add the areas.

Area of trapezoid A + Area of trapezoid B $= 19\frac{1}{2} + 19\frac{1}{2} = 39$

Answer The total area of the desktop is 39 square feet.

✔ Checkpoint

4. One base of a trapezoid is 9 feet, and the height is 4 feet. The area of the trapezoid is 28 square feet. Find the other base.

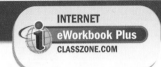

Guided Practice

Vocabulary Check

1. Sketch a trapezoid and label its bases and height. State the formula for finding its area.

2. The height of a parallelogram is 22 inches. The base is one half of the height. Find the area of the parallelogram.

Skill Check **Find the area of the trapezoid.**

3.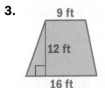
9 ft
12 ft
16 ft

4.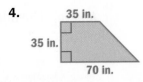
35 in.
35 in.
70 in.

5.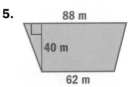
88 m
40 m
62 m

Find the unknown base or height of the parallelogram.

6. $A = 40$ in.^{2}, $b = 25$ in., $h = $?   **7.** $A = 300$ m^2, $b = $?, $h = 20$ m

Find the unknown base or height of the trapezoid.

8. $A = 12$ ft^2, $b_1 = 2$ ft, $b_2 = $?, $h = 3$ ft

9. $A = 240$ m^2, $b_1 = 16$ m, $b_2 = 8$ m, $h = $?

10. Track Uniform You are sewing a red stripe on the front of a track uniform. As shown, the stripe is a parallelogram. What is the area of the stripe?

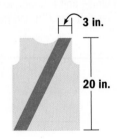
3 in.
20 in.

Practice and Problem Solving

Homework *Help*

Example	Exercises
1	11–13, 17
2	14–16, 18
3	19–24
4	25, 26

Online Resources
CLASSZONE.COM
• More Examples
• eTutorial Plus

Find the area of the parallelogram.

11.
5 in.
14 in.

12.
8 yd
9.5 yd

13.
8.3 mm
11.5 mm

Find the area of the trapezoid.

14.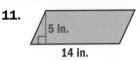
14 ft
12 ft
18 ft

15.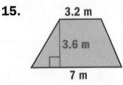
3.2 m
3.6 m
7 m

16.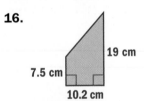
19 cm
7.5 cm
10.2 cm

17. The base of a parallelogram is 10 meters. The height is one fourth of the base. Find the area of the parallelogram.

18. The height of a trapezoid is 2 feet. One of the bases is three times the height, and the other base is four times the height. Find the area of the trapezoid.

Find the unknown measure of the parallelogram.

19. $A = 2025$ m^2 **20.** $A = 71.5$ in.^{2} **21.** $A = 1$ yd^2

45 m

b

h

6.5 in.

b

0.75 yd

Find the unknown measure of the trapezoid.

22. $A = 192.5$ cm^2 **23.** $A = 1800$ ft^2 **24.** $A = 16.555$ mm^2

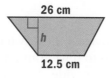
26 cm

h

12.5 cm

50 ft

48 ft

b_1

2.1 mm

4.3 mm

b_2

25. Aircraft Wings A wing of each aircraft described has the shape of a trapezoid. Find the area of the wing.

   a. An F-18 wing has bases of 6 feet and 15 feet and height of 13 feet.

   b. A Boeing 747 wing has bases of 13.3 feet and 54.3 feet and height of 81.3 feet.

26. Parking Lot Two parking lots each have space for 5 cars, as shown in the diagrams below.

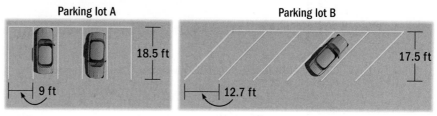

Parking lot A

18.5 ft

9 ft

Parking lot B

17.5 ft

12.7 ft

   a. Find the base of each figure formed by the 5 parking spaces.

   b. Find the area of each figure formed by the 5 parking spaces.

   c. Compare Which parking lot covers less area to park 5 cars?

Coordinate Geometry In Exercises 27 and 28, plot the points in a coordinate plane. Connect the points so that they form a polygon. Identify the polygon and find its area.

27. $(-2, -3), (-2, 0), (2, 3), (2, -4)$ **28.** $(-1, 3), (4, 3), (2, -1), (-3, -1)$

29. *Writing* What happens to the area of a trapezoid if you double its height? if you double both its bases? if you double the height and both bases?

Find the area of the figure.

30.
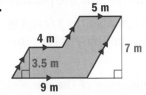

31.
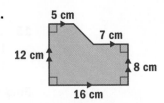

32. Summer Camp This summer at camp, you can stay in room A or room B with one roommate. Which room will give you and your roommate more space?

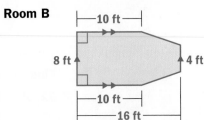

33. Picture Frame You have a 4 inch by 6 inch picture that you want to have framed. You want the frame to be 2 inches wide. A wooden frame can be made from four trapezoids, as shown. Find the areas of the bottom and side trapezoids. Then find the ratio of the area of the bottom trapezoid to the area of the side trapezoid.

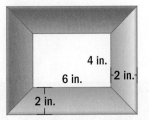

34. Challenge You form a rhombus by putting two equilateral triangles with side length $2n$ together, as shown. Write an expression for the area of the rhombus in terms of n. Explain your reasoning.

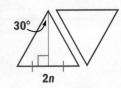

Mixed Review For an account that earns interest compounded annually, find the balance of the account. Round to the nearest cent. *(Lesson 7.7)*

35. $P = \$1200$, $r = 5\%$, $t = 3$ years

36. $P = \$8550$, $r = 3.5\%$, $t = 20$ years

Approximate the square root to the nearest integer. *(Lesson 9.1)*

37. $\sqrt{40}$ **38.** $\sqrt{587}$ **39.** $\sqrt{10.2}$ **40.** $\sqrt{0.725}$

41. Find the value of x in the quadrilateral shown. *(Lesson 10.2)*

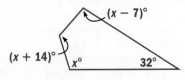

Standardized Test Practice

42. Multiple Choice The height of a parallelogram is 13.5 feet. The base is four times the height. What is the area of the parallelogram?

A. 45.5625 ft^2 **B.** 54 ft^2 **C.** 182.25 ft^2 **D.** 729 ft^2

43. Short Response Is it possible for two parallelograms to have the same area but not be congruent? Explain why or why not.

10.4 Investigating Circles

Goal

Compare the circumferences and the diameters of circles.

Materials

• compass
• metric ruler
• paper and pencil
• string

The *diameter* of a circle is the distance across the circle through its center. The *circumference* of a circle is the distance around the circle.

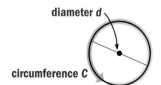

diameter *d*

circumference *C*

Investigate

Find the ratio of circumference to diameter of a circle.

1 Draw a circle of any size using a compass.

2 Lay a string around the circle. Mark the point where the string completes the circle. Straighten the string, and measure its length with a ruler.

The circumference is about 9.4 centimeters.

3 Measure the diameter of the circle with a ruler. Make sure the ruler goes through the center of the circle.

4 Write the ratio of the circumference to the diameter for the circle. Write the ratio as a decimal.

$$\frac{\text{circumference}}{\text{diameter}} \approx \frac{9.4}{3} \approx 3.13$$

The diameter is 3 centimeters.

Draw Conclusions

1. Conjecture Repeat Steps 1–4 of the activity for two circles of different diameters. What do you notice about the ratios in Step 4?

Predict the circumference of a circle with the given diameter *d*.

2. $d = 4$ feet   **3.** $d = 2$ meters   **4.** $d = 0.75$ inch   **5.** $d = 12$ feet

Circumference *and* Area *of a* Circle

Vocabulary
circle, p. 528
center, p. 528
radius, p. 528
diameter, p. 528
circumference, p. 528

BEFORE	Now	WHY?
You found perimeters and areas of polygons.	You'll find the circumferences and areas of circles.	So you can find the diameter of a circular floor, as in Ex. 28.

A **circle** consists of all points in a plane that are the same distance from a fixed point called the **center**. The distance between the center and any point on the circle is the **radius**. The distance across the circle through the center is the **diameter**.

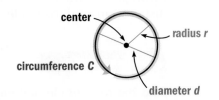

The **circumference** of a circle is the distance around the circle. For any circle, the ratio of its circumference to its diameter is an irrational number that is approximately equal to 3.14 or $\frac{22}{7}$. The Greek letter π (pi) is used to represent this ratio.

Circumference of a Circle

Words The circumference C of a circle is the product of π and the diameter d, or twice the product of π and the radius r.

Algebra $C = \pi d$ $C = 2\pi r$

UNITED STATES

MEXICO

Gulf of Mexico

Pacific Ocean

Example 1 Finding the Circumference of a Circle

Meteor Crater Scientists have identified the faint outline of part of an ancient meteor crater on the coast of Mexico. The rest of the approximately circular crater lies underwater. The crater's diameter is about 170 kilometers. Approximate the distance around the crater to the nearest kilometer.

Solution

$$C = \pi d \qquad \text{Write formula for circumference of a circle.}$$
$$\approx 3.14(170) \qquad \text{Substitute 3.14 for } \pi \text{ and 170 for } d.$$
$$= 533.8 \qquad \text{Multiply.}$$

Answer The distance around the crater is about 534 kilometers.

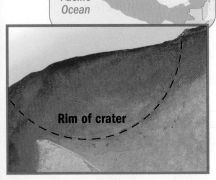
Rim of crater

Example 2 — Finding the Radius of a Circle

The circumference of a circle is 70 inches. Find the radius of the circle to the nearest inch.

$C = 2\pi r$	Write formula for circumference of a circle.
$70 \approx 2(3.14)r$	Substitute 70 for C and 3.14 for π.
$70 \approx 6.28r$	Multiply.
$11.1 \approx r$	Divide each side by 6.28. Use a calculator.

Answer The radius of the circle is about 11 inches.

Study Strategy

When the radius or diameter of a circle is divisible by 7, use $\frac{22}{7}$ to approximate π.

Otherwise, use 3.14 to approximate π.

✔ **Checkpoint**

1. The diameter of a circle is 28 feet. Find the circumference of the circle to the nearest foot.

2. The circumference of a circle is 186 centimeters. Find the radius of the circle to the nearest centimeter.

Area of a Circle

Words The area A of a circle is the product of π and the square of the radius r.

Algebra $A = \pi r^2$

Example 3 — Finding the Area of a Circle

Find the area of the circle to the nearest square foot.

① Find the radius.

$$r = \frac{d}{2} = \frac{26}{2} = 13$$

26 ft

② Find the area.

$A = \pi r^2$	Write formula for area of a circle.
$\approx 3.14(13)^2$	Substitute 3.14 for π and 13 for r.
≈ 530.7	Simplify.

Answer The area of the circle is about 531 square feet.

✔ **Checkpoint**

3. The diameter of a circle is 14 inches. Find the area of the circle to the nearest square inch.

4. **Critical Thinking** One circle has a diameter of 12 centimeters. Another circle has a radius of 7 centimeters. Which circle has a greater area? Explain your reasoning.

Example 4 — Finding the Radius of a Circle

The area of a circle is 72 square millimeters. Find the radius of the circle to the nearest millimeter.

$A = \pi r^2$ Write formula for area of a circle.

$72 \approx (3.14)r^2$ Substitute 72 for A and 3.14 for π.

$22.9 \approx r^2$ Divide each side by 3.14.

$\sqrt{22.9} \approx r$ Take positive square root of each side.

$4.8 \approx r$ Use a calculator to approximate square root.

Answer To the nearest millimeter, the radius is 5 millimeters.

✔ Checkpoint

Find the unknown measure. Round to the nearest whole number.

5. $A = 1567$ in.^{2}
$r = \underline{\ ?\ }$

6. $A = 59$ ft^2
$d = \underline{\ ?\ }$

7. $A = 197$ cm^2
$d = \underline{\ ?\ }$

8. Critical Thinking How is finding the diameter of a circle when given its area different from finding the radius when given its area?

Example 5 — Finding the Area of a Figure

Norman Windows A Norman window from Congress Hall in Philadelphia consists of a rectangle and a half circle, as shown. Find the area of the window to the nearest square foot.

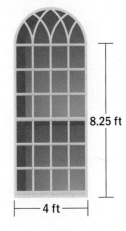

8.25 ft

4 ft

Solution

1 Find the area of the rectangle.

$A = lw = 8.25(4) = 33$

2 For the window shown, the radius of the half circle is half the width of the window, or 2 feet.

$A = \frac{1}{2}\pi r^2$ Write formula for area of a half circle.

$\approx \frac{1}{2}(3.14)(2)^2$ Substitute 3.14 for π and 2 for r.

$= 6.28$ Simplify.

3 Find the total area.

Total area $\approx 33 + 6.28 = 39.28$

Answer The area of the Norman window is about 39 square feet.

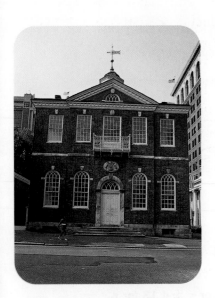

In the **Real World**

Norman Windows
Philadelphia was the capital of the United States from 1790 to 1800. During that time, the United States Congress met in Congress Hall. Congress Hall has 19 Norman windows of the same size. To the nearest square foot, what is the total area of the 19 windows?

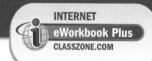
Guided Practice

Vocabulary Check

1. The diameter of a circle is 5 centimeters. What is the radius?

2. Copy and complete: The ratio of the _?_ of a circle to its diameter is equal to π.

Skill Check

3. Find the circumference and area of the circle shown. Use $\frac{22}{7}$ for π. Round your answers to the nearest whole number.

14 cm

4. The circumference of a circle is 22 meters. Find the radius of the circle to the nearest tenth of a meter.

5. The area of a circle is 87 square feet. Find the diameter of the circle to the nearest foot.

Guided Problem Solving

6. Wrestling Use the diagram of the square wrestling mat shown. The circle is the part of the mat used for competition. What is the area of the part that is *not* used for competition?

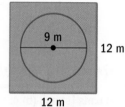

9 m

12 m

12 m

① Find the area of the entire mat.

② Find the area of the circle used for competition to the nearest square meter.

③ Subtract the area of the circle from the area of the mat.

Practice and Problem Solving

Homework *Help*

Example	Exercises
1	7–12
2	13–15
3	17–22, 26, 27
4	23–25, 28
5	30

Online Resources
CLASSZONE.COM

• More Examples
• eTutorial Plus

Find the circumference of the circle. Use 3.14 or $\frac{22}{7}$ for π. Round to the nearest whole number.

7.

18 in.

8.

22 m

9.

42 cm

10.

70 yd

11.

32 mm

12.

44 ft

For a circle with the given circumference C, find the radius and diameter of the circle. Round to the nearest whole number.

13. $C = 37$ m

14. $C = 25$ cm

15. $C = 51$ in.

16. **Error Analysis** Describe and correct the error in finding the approximate area of a circle with a diameter of 20 feet.

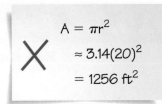

$$A = \pi r^2$$
$$\approx 3.14(20)^2$$
$$= 1256 \text{ ft}^2$$

Find the area of the circle. Use 3.14 or $\frac{22}{7}$ for π. Round to the nearest whole number.

17.   8 in.

18.   14 ft

19.   28 cm

20.   46 mm

21.   33 m

22.   52 yd

For a circle with the given area A, find the radius and diameter of the circle. Round to the nearest whole number.

23. $A = 254 \text{ m}^2$ 24. $A = 615 \text{ cm}^2$ 25. $A = 1109 \text{ in.}^2$

Reading *Algebra*

In parts (a) and (b) of Exercise 26, expressing an answer in terms of π means *not* substituting an approximation for π. For instance, a circle with a radius of 2 units has an area of 4π square units when the area is expressed in terms of π.

26. **Extended Problem Solving** A signal from a walkie-talkie can be received up to 1 mile away. A signal from a CB radio can be received up to 5 miles away.

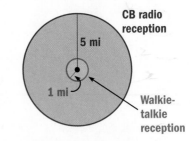
CB radio reception
5 mi
1 mi
Walkie-talkie reception

a. **Calculate** Over how great an area can a walkie-talkie transmit a signal? Express your answer in terms of π.

b. **Calculate** Over how great an area can a CB radio transmit a signal? Express your answer in terms of π.

c. **Compare** Write a ratio to compare the area of CB radio reception to the area of walkie-talkie reception.

27. **Round Barn** The Ryan barn in Annawan Township, Illinois, is a round barn built in 1910. The floor has a diameter of 85 feet. What is the area of the floor to the nearest square foot?

28. **Pantheon** The circular floor in the Pantheon in Rome has an area of about 1473 square meters. What is the diameter of the floor to the nearest tenth of a meter?

29. **Centrifuge Training** Astronauts train for space flight in a centrifuge, which consists of a rotating arm with a cab at the outer end of the arm. The arm, which has a length of 58 feet, is revolved about the center of the centrifuge. An astronaut sits in the cab, which is then rotated 50 times per minute. To the nearest hundred feet, how far does the astronaut travel in one minute?

30. Draw a rectangle that is 6 units by 5 units on graph paper. Use a compass to draw a half circle with a radius of 3 units on a longer side of the rectangle. Find the area of the figure to the nearest whole number.

31. Predict You double the radius of a circle. Predict what will happen to the circle's circumference and what will happen to its area. Test your prediction for a few circles. Use a different radius for each circle. Then predict how doubling a circle's diameter will affect its circumference and area. Test your prediction for a few circles with different diameters.

32. In the diagram, the diameter of the large circle is 18 meters. All four small circles are the same size. Find the area of one small circle and the area of the large circle in terms of π. Then find the ratio of the area of a small circle to the area of the large circle.

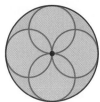

33. Challenge An air traffic control radar screen is a circle with a diameter of 24 inches.

   a. What is the area of the screen to the nearest square inch?

   b. The radar screen is set to have a scale of 6 inches : 25 nautical miles. To the nearest square nautical mile, what is the area of the circular region covered by the radar?

34. *Writing* A half circle is drawn on each side of a right triangle as shown. What is the relationship among the areas of the 3 half circles? Explain your reasoning.

Mixed Review

Evaluate the expression. *(Lesson 1.3)*

35. $64 \div 16 + 6 \div 2$ **36.** $3 \cdot 14 + 8$ **37.** $7 \cdot 5 + 3 \cdot 9 \cdot 5$

Find the slope of the line through the given points. *(Lesson 8.4)*

38. $(6, 1), (3, 4)$ **39.** $(-5, -3), (-5, 6)$ **40.** $(3, -6), (-1, -6)$

Find the area of the parallelogram or trapezoid. *(Lesson 10.3)*

41.

42.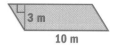

43.

Standardized Test Practice

44. Multiple Choice The diameter of a circle is 22 meters. What is the approximate area?

   A. 35 m^2 **B.** 69 m^2 **C.** 380 m^2 **D.** 1520 m^2

45. Short Response The base of the sundial shown is a square with a circle inside it. To the nearest square inch, what is the area of the part of the base that is *not* within the circle? Explain your answer.

Mid-Chapter Quiz

1. Find the value of x for the triangle shown. Then classify the triangle by its angles.

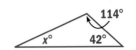

2. The perimeter of an equilateral triangle is 219 feet. Find the lengths of the sides.

Tell whether the figure is a polygon. If it is a polygon, classify it and tell whether it is *convex* or *concave*. If not, explain why.

3.

4.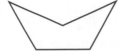

5.

Find the area of the parallelogram, trapezoid, or circle to the nearest square unit. Use 3.14 or $\frac{22}{7}$ for π.

6.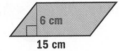
6 cm
15 cm

7.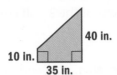
40 in.
10 in.
35 in.

8.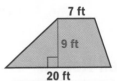
7 ft
9 ft
20 ft

9.
21 m

10.
8 mm
10 mm

11.
3 in.

Brain GAME

Farmland Feud

Three farmers inherit farmland that is divided into six fields. In the drawing, the green fields are trapezoids, the yellow fields are parallelograms, and the blue field is a rectangle. The farmers want to divide up the fields so that each farmer has the same area of land. They don't want to change the shape of any field. How can they distribute the fields fairly?

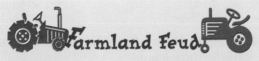
50 yd | 30 yd | 60 yd
30 yd A B C
30 yd | 90 yd | 60 yd
50 yd | 50 yd | 80 yd
30 yd D E F
50 yd | 90 yd | 80 yd

Solids

▶ **Review** this topic in preparation for solving problems that involve solids in Lessons 10.5–10.8.

Classifying Solids

A **solid** is a three-dimensional figure that encloses a part of space. The polygons that form the sides of a solid are called **faces**.

Four Types of Solids

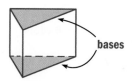
bases

A **prism** is a solid formed by polygons. Prisms have two congruent bases that lie in parallel planes. The other faces are rectangles.

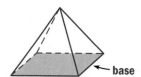
base

A **pyramid** is a solid formed by polygons. The base can be any polygon, and the other faces are triangles.

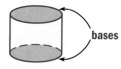
bases

A **cylinder** is a solid with two congruent circular bases that lie in parallel planes.

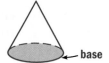
base

A **cone** is a solid with one circular base.

Example Classify the solid as a *prism*, *pyramid*, *cylinder*, or *cone*.

a.

b.

c.

Solution

a. The soup can has two congruent circular bases. It is a cylinder.

b. All sides of the gift box are rectangles. Any two opposite sides can be considered bases. The gift box is a rectangular prism.

c. The ice cream novelty has one circular base. It is a cone.

Continued

Counting Faces, Edges, and Vertices

The faces of a prism or a pyramid meet in segments called **edges**. Edges meet at points called **vertices**. (The singular form of *vertices* is *vertex*.)

Example **Count the number of faces, edges, and vertices in a triangular pyramid.**

| 4 faces | 6 edges | 4 vertices |

Sketching a Solid

You can sketch a solid so that it appears to be three-dimensional.

Example **Sketch a triangular prism.**

1 Sketch two congruent triangles.

2 Use segments to connect corresponding vertices.

3 Make any "hidden" lines dashed.

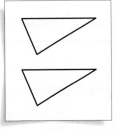 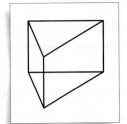 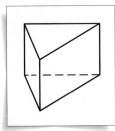

▶ **Test** your knowledge of solids by solving these problems.

✔ *Checkpoint*

Classify each solid as a *prism*, *pyramid*, *cylinder*, or *cone*. If the solid is a prism or a pyramid, count the number of faces, edges, and vertices.

1.

2.

3.

Sketch the solid.

4. Rectangular prism   5. Square pyramid   6. Cone

Concept *Activity*

10.5 Nets and Surface Area

Goal
Use the net of a rectangular prism to find the prism's surface area.

Materials
• cereal box
• ruler
• scissors

The *surface area* of a solid is the sum of the areas of all of its surfaces.

Investigate

Find the surface area of a cereal box.

 1 Cut along the edges of the box until you can flatten it as shown below. The resulting shape is called a *net*. Measure the length of each edge of the net using a ruler.

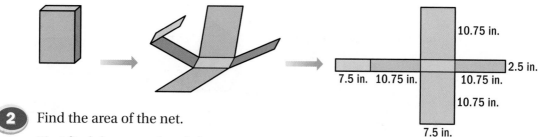

10.75 in.

2.5 in.

7.5 in.   10.75 in.   10.75 in.

10.75 in.

7.5 in.

2 Find the area of the net.

First find the area of each face.

Area of front or back: $(7.5)(10.75) = 80.625$ in.^{2}
Area of top or bottom: $(7.5)(2.5) = 18.75$ in.^{2}
Area of each side: $(2.5)(10.75) = 26.875$ in.^{2}

Then find the sum of the areas of the faces.

$$80.625 + 80.625 + 18.75 + 18.75 + 26.875 + 26.875 = 252.5 \text{ in.}^2$$

The surface area of the cereal box shown is 252.5 square inches.

Draw Conclusions

1. **Critical Thinking** How can you find the surface area of a box without making a net? Explain.

2. *Writing* Describe the net of the cylindrical oatmeal container shown. Make a sketch of the net. Find the surface area of the container and explain your reasoning.

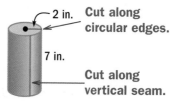

2 in. Cut along circular edges.

7 in.

Cut along vertical seam.

Surface Areas of Prisms *and* Cylinders

Vocabulary

surface area, p. 538
net, p. 538
lateral face of a prism, p. 539
lateral area of a prism, p. 539
lateral surface of a cylinder, p. 540
lateral area of a cylinder, p. 540

BEFORE   *Now*   **WHY?**

You found the areas of triangles and rectangles.

You'll find the surface areas of prisms and cylinders.

So you can find the area you need to paint, as in Ex. 14.

Pizza Box The **surface area** of a solid is the sum of the areas of its faces. The pizza box shown has the shape of a rectangular prism. What is its surface area?

In Example 1, a *net* is used to find the surface area of the pizza box. A **net** is a two-dimensional representation of a solid. The surface area of a solid is equal to the area of its net.

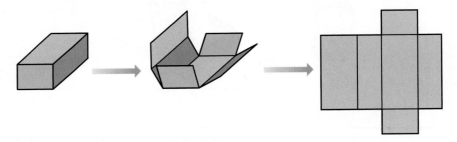

Example 1   *Using a Net to Find Surface Area*

The net at the right represents the pizza box shown above. (Any flaps or foldovers to hold the box together have been ignored.) Use the net to find the surface area of the pizza box.

Solution

① Find the area of each face.

    Area of top or bottom: $16 \cdot 16 = 256$ in.^{2}

    Area of each side: $16 \cdot 2 = 32$ in.^{2}

② Find the sum of the areas of the faces.

    $256 + 256 + 32 + 32 + 32 + 32 = 640$ in.^{2}

Answer The surface area of the pizza box is 640 square inches.

Surface Areas of Prisms The **lateral faces** of a prism are the faces that are not bases. The **lateral area** of a prism is the sum of the areas of the lateral faces. The surface area of a prism is the sum of the areas of the bases and the lateral area. In the diagram, *P* is the base perimeter.

Surface area	=	2 · Base area	+	Lateral area
	=	2*B*	+	*Ph*

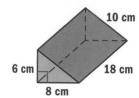

Surface Area of a Prism

Words The surface area S of a prism is the sum of twice the base area B and the product of the base perimeter P and the height h.

Algebra $S = 2B + Ph$

Numbers $S = 2(6 \cdot 4) + [2(6) + 2(4)]10 = 248$ square units

$h = 10$
$w = 4$
$l = 6$

Example 2 *Using a Formula to Find Surface Area*

Find the surface area of the prism.

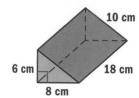
10 cm
6 cm
18 cm
8 cm

The bases of the prism are right triangles.

$S = 2B + Ph$ Write formula for surface area.

$= 2\left(\dfrac{1}{2} \cdot 6 \cdot 8\right) + (6 + 8 + 10)(18)$ Substitute.

$= 480$ Simplify.

Answer The surface area of the prism is 480 square centimeters.

✓ *Checkpoint*

Find the surface area of the prism.

1.
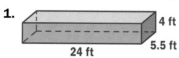
4 ft
5.5 ft
24 ft

2.
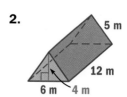
5 m
12 m
6 m   4 m

Surface Areas of Cylinders The curved surface of a cylinder is called the **lateral surface** . The **lateral area** of a cylinder is the area of the lateral suface. The surface area of a cylinder is the sum of the areas of the bases and the product of the base circumference and the height. In the diagram below, *C* represents the base circumference.

Surface area	=	2 • Base area	+	Lateral area
	=	2*B*	+	*Ch*

Surface Area of a Cylinder

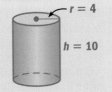

Words The surface area *S* of a cylinder is the sum of twice the base area *B* and the product of the base circumference *C* and the height *h*.

Algebra $S = 2B + Ch = 2\pi r^2 + 2\pi rh$

Numbers $S = 2\pi(4)^2 + 2\pi(4)(10) \approx 352$ square units

Example 3   *Using a Formula to Find Surface Area*

Racquetball Find the surface area of the container of racquetballs. Round to the nearest square inch.

Solution

The radius is one half of the diameter, so *r* = 1.25 inches.

$S = 2\pi r^2 + 2\pi rh$ Write formula for surface area of a cylinder.

$= 2\pi(1.25)^2 + 2\pi(1.25)(5)$ Substitute.

$= 15.625\pi$ Simplify.

≈ 49.1 Evaluate. Use a calculator.

Answer The surface area of the container of racquetballs is about 49 square inches.

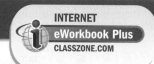
Guided Practice

Vocabulary Check

1. What formula would you use to find the surface area of a triangular prism?

2. How do you find the area of the bases of a cylinder? How do you find the lateral area of a cylinder?

Skill Check **Draw a net for the solid. Then find the surface area.**

3.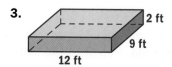
2 ft
9 ft
12 ft

4.
8 in.
11 in.

5. **Error Analysis** Describe and correct the error in finding the surface area of the prism.

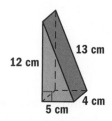
13 cm
12 cm
4 cm
5 cm

$S = 2B + Ph$
$= 2(5 \cdot 4) + (5 + 12 + 13)(4)$
$= 160$ square centimeters

Practice and Problem Solving

Homework *Help*

Example **Exercises**
1   6–9, 14
2   6–9, 14
3   10–12, 13

Online Resources
CLASSZONE.COM
• More Examples
• eTutorial Plus

Draw a net for the solid. Then find the surface area. Round to the nearest whole number.

6.
5 m
5 m
5 m

7.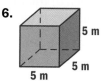
6 yd
20 yd
8 yd

8.
20 ft
12 ft
18 ft
16 ft

9.
4 m
5 m
5 m
4 m
6 m

10.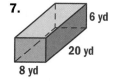
15 cm
4 cm

11.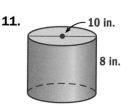
10 in.
8 in.

12. **Cans** A can of vegetables is in the shape of a cylinder. The diameter of the can is 7 centimeters, and the height is 11 centimeters. Find the surface area of the can. Round to the nearest square centimeter.

13. Marimba Pipes Find the lateral area of the marimba pipe. Round to the nearest square inch.

14. Painting You are going to paint the platforms shown below for your school's theater production. All sides of each platform must be painted yellow. What total area must the paint cover?

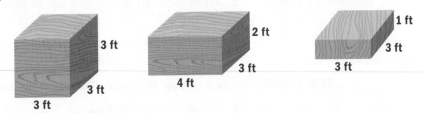

In the **Real World**

Marimbas The rectangular keys of a marimba are always made of rosewood. The dimensions of the longest key are $20\frac{1}{4}$ in. by $3\frac{1}{4}$ in. The dimensions of the shortest key are $7\frac{5}{8}$ in. by $1\frac{5}{8}$ in. What is the ratio of the area of the longest key to the area of the shortest key?

The solids shown are composed of prisms and half cylinders. Find the surface area of the solid. Round to the nearest whole number.

15.

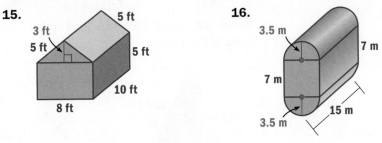

16.

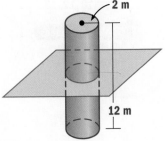

17. Critical Thinking A cylinder has a radius of r inches and a height of h inches. Suppose the radius and height of the cylinder are both doubled.

    a. How does the area of the base of the new cylinder compare with the area of the base of the original cylinder? Explain.

    b. How does the circumference of the new cylinder compare with the circumference of the original cylinder? Explain.

    c. How does the surface area of the new cylinder compare with the surface area of the original cylinder? Explain.

18. Visual Thinking When a plane intersects a solid, the intersection of the plane and the solid forms a *cross section*.

    a. A plane intersects a cylinder parallel to the bases of the cylinder, as shown. What shape does the cross section have? To the nearest square meter, what is the area of the cross section?

    b. Another plane intersects the cylinder perpendicular to the bases and passes through the centers of the bases. What shape does the cross section have? What is the area of the cross section?

Snowboarder on a mailbox slider

19. Mailbox Sliders Some snowboarding parks have a feature shaped like an elongated mailbox and called a mailbox slider. Snowboarders use their boards to jump onto the mailbox slider and slide along its top surface. A mailbox slider is composed of a half cylinder and a rectangular prism. Find the surface area of the mailbox slider shown. Round your answer to the nearest square inch.

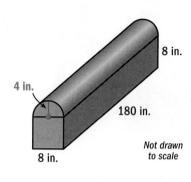

8 in.

4 in.

180 in.

8 in.

Not drawn to scale

20. Measurement Find an object that is shaped like a cylinder. Measure its radius and height, then find its surface area. Describe the procedure you used.

21. The diameter of a base of a cylinder is twice the height of the cylinder.

   a. Write a formula in terms of h for the surface area of the cylinder.

   b. The surface area of the cylinder is 64π square units. Find the radius and height of the cylinder.

22. Challenge Draw a cylinder and label the radius r and the height h. Assume a plane slices the cylinder in half by passing through the center of each base. Write a formula for the surface area of a half cylinder, including the region where the plane intersects the cylinder.

Mixed Review
23. The perimeter of a triangle is 37 feet. The length of the first side is 4 more than the length of the second side. The length of the third side is equal to the length of the second side. Find the length of each side. Then classify the triangle by its side lengths. *(Lesson 10.1)*

Find the area of the parallelogram or trapezoid. *(Lesson 10.3)*

24.
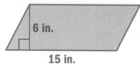

6 in.

15 in.

25.
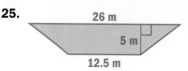

26 m

5 m

12.5 m

Find the circumference of the circle given the diameter *d* or the radius *r*. Use 3.14 or $\frac{22}{7}$ for π. Round to the nearest whole number. *(Lesson 10.4)*

26. $d = 30$ m   **27.** $d = 84$ in.   **28.** $r = 78$ ft   **29.** $r = 102$ cm

Standardized Test Practice
30. Multiple Choice What is the approximate surface area of the cylinder shown?

2 yd

4.4 yd

   A. 35 yd^2 **B.** 57 yd^2

   C. 68 yd^2 **D.** 80 yd^2

31. Short Response The length of a base of a rectangular prism is twice the width of the base. The height of the prism is 3 times the width of a base. The surface area is 792 square centimeters. What are the dimensions of the prism?

10.6 Surface Areas *of* Pyramids *and* Cones

Vocabulary

height of a pyramid, p. 544

regular pyramid, p. 544

slant height of a pyramid, p. 544

height of a cone, p. 546

slant height of a cone, p. 546

BEFORE	Now	WHY?
You found surface areas of prisms and cylinders.	You'll find the surface areas of pyramids and cones.	So you can find the surface area of an ant lion cone, as in Ex. 20.

Recall that the base of a pyramid is a polygon, and the lateral faces of the pyramid are triangles with a common vertex. The **height of a pyramid** is the perpendicular distance between the base and this common vertex.

In this lesson, all pyramids are *regular pyramids*. In a **regular pyramid**, the base is a regular polygon and all of the lateral faces of the pyramid are congruent isosceles triangles. The **slant height of a pyramid** is the height of any of these triangular lateral faces.

In this lesson, the variable *h* represents the height of the pyramid, and the variable *l* represents the slant height.

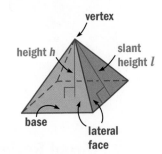

The Pyramid at California State University, Long Beach

Example 1 Finding the Slant Height of a Pyramid

Architecture The Pyramid at California State University, Long Beach, has a height of 192 feet. The base of the pyramid is a square with a side length of 345 feet. What is the slant height of the pyramid to the nearest foot?

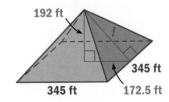

Solution

Notice that the slant height l of the pyramid is the hypotenuse of a right triangle. The length of one leg of this triangle is 192 feet. The length of the other leg is $\frac{345}{2} = 172.5$ feet. Use the Pythagorean theorem to find the slant height.

$$192^2 + (172.5)^2 = l^2 \qquad \text{Pythagorean theorem}$$
$$66{,}620.25 = l^2 \qquad \text{Simplify. Use a calculator.}$$
$$\sqrt{66{,}620.25} = l \qquad \text{Take positive square root of each side.}$$
$$258.1 \approx l \qquad \text{Approximate using a calculator.}$$

Answer The slant height of the Pyramid is about 258 feet.

Surface Areas of Regular Pyramids You can use a net of a pyramid with a square base to find a formula for its surface area. Let l be the slant height of the pyramid, and let s be the side length of the square base. The lateral area of the pyramid is the sum of the areas of the 4 triangular faces. In the diagram below, the area of 1 triangular face is $\frac{1}{2}sl$, and P is the perimeter of the square base.

Surface area	=	Base area	+	Lateral area
	=	B	+	$4\left(\frac{1}{2}sl\right)$
	=	B	+	$\frac{1}{2}(4sl)$
	=	B	+	$\frac{1}{2}Pl$

Surface Area of a Regular Pyramid

Words The surface area S of a regular pyramid is the sum of the base area B and one half of the product of the base perimeter P and the slant height l.

Algebra $S = B + \frac{1}{2}Pl$

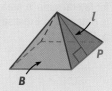

Example 2 *Finding the Surface Area of a Regular Pyramid*

Find the surface area of the regular pyramid.

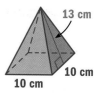

1 Find the perimeter and area of the base.

$P = 4(10) = 40$ cm

$B = 10^2 = 100$ cm^2

2 Find the surface area.

$S = B + \frac{1}{2}Pl$ — Write formula for surface area of a pyramid.

$= 100 + \frac{1}{2}(40)(13)$ — Substitute 100 for B, 40 for P, and 13 for l.

$= 360$ — Simplify.

Answer The surface area of the pyramid is 360 square centimeters.

Surface Areas of Cones The point on a cone directly above the center of its base is called the *vertex* of the cone. The distance between the vertex and center of the base is the **height of the cone**. The **slant height of the cone** is the distance between the vertex and any point on the edge of the base. To find the surface area of a cone, you need to know the radius r of the circular base and the slant height l.

Surface area	=	Base area	+	Lateral area
	=	B	+	$\pi r l$

$$= \quad A = \pi r^2 \quad + $$

slant height l

vertex

B

r

$A = \pi r l$

l

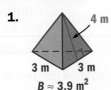

Surface Area of a Cone

Words The surface area S of a cone is the sum of the base area B and the product of π, the base radius r, and the slant height l.

Algebra $S = B + \pi r l = \pi r^2 + \pi r l$

l

r

Example 3   *Finding the Surface Area of a Cone*

Find the surface area of the cone. Round to the nearest square inch.

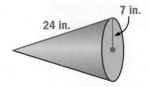

7 in.

24 in.

$$S = \pi r^2 + \pi r l \qquad \text{Write formula for surface area of a cone.}$$
$$= \pi(7)^2 + \pi(7)(24) \qquad \text{Substitute 7 for } r \text{ and 24 for } l.$$
$$= 217\pi \approx 681.7 \qquad \text{Simplify. Then evaluate using a calculator.}$$

Answer The surface area of the cone is about 682 square inches.

✔ *Checkpoint*

Find the surface area of the pyramid or cone. Round to the nearest whole number.

1.

4 m

3 m   3 m

$B \approx 3.9 \text{ m}^2$

2.

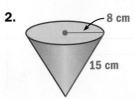

8 cm

15 cm

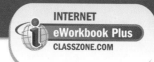
Guided Practice

Vocabulary Check

1. Explain the difference between the height and the slant height of a pyramid.

2. What part of the formula $S = \pi r^2 + \pi r l$ gives you the base area of a cone? Which part gives you the lateral area?

Skill Check **Find the surface area of the pyramid or cone. Round to the nearest whole number.**

3.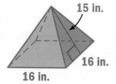
15 in.
16 in.
16 in.

4.
5 ft
4 ft   4 ft
$B \approx 6.9\ ft^2$

5.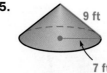
9 ft
7 ft

Guided Problem Solving

6. What is the surface area of the cone? Round to the nearest square centimeter.

① Find the slant height of the cone.

② Find the surface area of the cone to the nearest square centimeter.

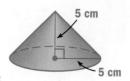
5 cm
5 cm

Practice and Problem Solving

Homework *Help*

Example	Exercises
1	7–9
2	10, 12, 14–16, 21
3	9, 11, 17–19, 22, 23

Online Resources
CLASSZONE.COM
• More Examples
• eTutorial Plus

Find the slant height of the pyramid or cone. Round to the nearest whole number.

7.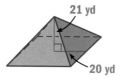
21 yd
20 yd

8.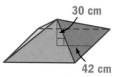
30 cm
42 cm

9.
36 m
15 m

Use the net to sketch the solid and find its surface area. Round to the nearest whole number.

10.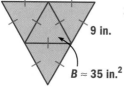
9 in.
$B \approx 35\ in.^2$

11.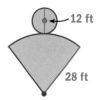
12 ft
28 ft

12.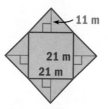
11 m
21 m
21 m

13. *Writing* Which is greater, a pyramid's height or its slant height? Explain your reasoning.

Find the surface area of the regular pyramid.

14.

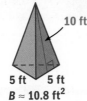

10 ft

5 ft 5 ft
$B \approx 10.8 \text{ ft}^2$

15.

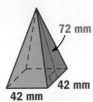

72 mm

42 mm

42 mm

16.

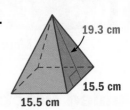

19.3 cm

15.5 cm

15.5 cm

Find the surface area of the cone. Round to the nearest whole number.

17.

8.5 m

3.25 m

18.

12 ft

18 ft

19.

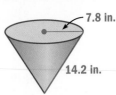

7.8 in.

14.2 in.

20. Ant Lions Ant lions are insects that dig cone-shaped pits that they use to trap ants for food. Find the surface area of the sloping walls of an ant lion pit. Round to the nearest square inch. (*Hint:* You need to find lateral area.)

2 in.

2 in.

Ant lion

Find the surface area of the pyramid or cone. Round to the nearest whole number.

21.

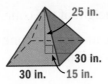

25 in.

30 in.

30 in. 15 in.

22.

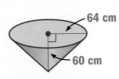

64 cm

60 cm

23.

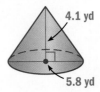

4.1 yd

5.8 yd

Spheres In Exercises 24–27, use the following information to find the surface area of the specified objects. Round to the nearest square unit.

A *sphere* is a solid formed by all points in space that are the same distance from a fixed point (the center). The formula for the surface area of a sphere is $S = 4\pi r^2$, where r is the radius.

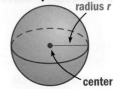

radius *r*

center

24. The radius of a spherical soap bubble is 0.5 inch.

25. The diameter of Europa, one of Jupiter's moons, is about 1950 miles.

26. The diameter of a table tennis ball is 40 millimeters.

27. The diameter of a large exercise ball is 2.5 feet.

28. Pyramid The unusual building shown in the photo includes a square pyramid turned upside down. The side length of the base of the pyramid is 74 feet, and the height of the pyramid is 48 feet. What is the surface area of the pyramid?

29. Critical Thinking The side length of the base of a square pyramid is 8 feet. The diameter of the base of a cone is 8 feet. The height of both solids is 3 feet. Sketch both solids. Which one has the greater surface area?

30. Visual Thinking You can cut the lateral surface of a cone into congruent wedges. You can rearrange these wedges to form a figure that resembles a parallelogram as shown. The more wedges you cut, the more closely the shape will resemble a parallelogram.

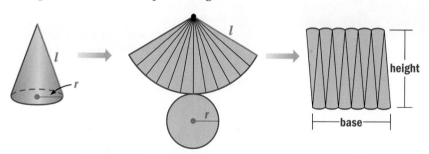

a. Write expressions for the height and the base of the parallelogram in terms of r and l.

b. Use the expressions from part (a) to write a formula for the area of the parallelogram in terms of r and l. How is this formula related to the formula for the surface area of a cone?

The solids shown are composed of cones, cylinders, and pyramids. Find the surface area of the solid. Round to the nearest whole number.

31.

6.5 m

5 m

7 m

32.

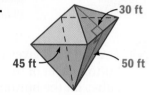

30 ft

45 ft

50 ft

33. Challenge The surface area of a cone is 90π square inches. The base radius of the cone is 5 inches. Find the slant height of the cone.

Mixed Review

Simplify the expression *(Lesson 9.2)*

34. $\sqrt{48}$ **35.** $\sqrt{288}$ **36.** $\sqrt{\dfrac{40}{9}}$ **37.** $\sqrt{\dfrac{24}{121}}$

38. Find the unknown side lengths of the triangle. Give exact answers. *(Lesson 9.6)*

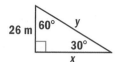

26 m 60° y 30° x

39. The base radius of a cylinder is 5 centimeters, and the height is 12 centimeters. Find the surface area of the cylinder. Round your answer to the nearest square centimeter. *(Lesson 10.5)*

Standardized Test Practice

40. Multiple Choice What is the approximate surface area of a cone that has a height of 14.5 meters and base diameter of 10 meters?

A. 140 m² **B.** 306 m² **C.** 319 m² **D.** 795 m²

41. Short Response Two pyramids have congruent bases. The slant height of the first pyramid is one third of the slant height of the second pyramid. Is the surface area of the first pyramid one third of the surface area of the second pyramid? Explain your reasoning.

10.7 Building and Sketching Solids

Goal
Build, sketch, and find the volume of solids using unit cubes and dot paper.

Materials
- unit cubes
- dot paper

In this activity, you will build or draw solids given the top, side, and front views. Assume that there are no missing blocks in views that are not shown.

Investigate

Use the three views of a solid to build the solid using unit cubes. Find the volume of the solid.

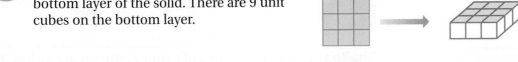

① The top view gives information about the bottom layer of the solid. There are 9 unit cubes on the bottom layer.

Top

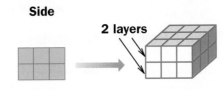

② The side view shows that there are two layers in the solid.

Side

2 layers

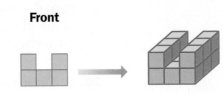

③ The front view shows you how to form the two layers of cubes. The middle row of cubes is missing from the top layer. The volume of the solid is 15 cubic units.

Front

Draw Conclusions

1. Use the three views of a solid to build the solid using unit cubes. Which solid has a greater volume?

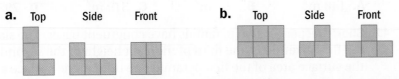

   a. Top   Side   Front   b. Top   Side   Front

Use the three views of a solid to draw the solid using dot paper. Find the volume of the solid.

Top   Side   Front

1 On dot paper, draw a set of three axes that form 120° angles.

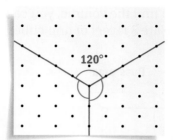

2 Draw a unit cube where the three axes intersect.

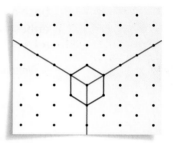

3 Draw the cubes you can see from the front.

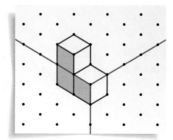

4 Draw the cubes you can see from the side.

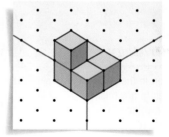

5 Check that the top view matches what you have drawn. The solid has a volume of 5 cubic units.

Draw Conclusions

2. Use the three views of each solid to draw the solids using dot paper. Which solid has a greater volume?

a. Top   Side   Front

b. Top   Side   Front

10.7

Volumes *of* **Prisms** *and* Cylinders

Review Vocabulary
volume, p. 789

BEFORE	*Now*	WHY?
You found surface areas of prisms and cylinders.	You'll find the volumes of prisms and cylinders.	So you can compare the volumes of two suitcases, as in Ex. 14.

Recall that the volume of a solid is the amount of space the solid occupies. Volume is measured in cubic units. For the prism below, the base area is 8 square units. To find the volume, you can imagine unit cubes filling the prism. There are 3 layers of unit cubes, so the volume is $8 \cdot 3 = 24$ cubic units.

Volume of a prism = Base area × Height

Study *Strategy*

The formula given in the notebook applies to any prism. When finding the volume of a rectangular prism, you can substitute lw for B. So, the formula $V = Bh$ becomes $V = lwh$.

Volume of a Prism

Words The volume V of a prism is the product of the base area B and the height h.

Algebra $V = Bh$

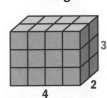

Example 1 *Finding the Volume of a Prism*

Find the volume of the prism shown.

The bases of the prism are triangles, so use the formula for the area of a triangle to find B.

$$V = Bh \qquad \text{Write formula for volume of a prism.}$$

$$= \frac{1}{2}(8)(6)(13) \qquad \text{Substitute values.}$$

$$= 312 \qquad \text{Multiply.}$$

Answer The volume of the prism is 312 cubic centimeters.

Cylinders The formula for the volume of a cylinder is like the formula for the volume of a prism.

Volume of a cylinder = **Base area** × **Height**

Volume of a Cylinder

Words The volume V of a cylinder is the product of the base area B and the height h.

Algebra $V = Bh = \pi r^2 h$

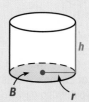

Example 2 *Finding the Volume of a Cylinder*

Swimming Pool Find the capacity (in gallons) of the swimming pool shown. Round to the nearest whole number. (Use the fact that $1 \text{ ft}^3 \approx 7.481$ gal.)

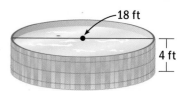

Solution

1 The radius is one half of the diameter. So, $r = 9$.

$V = \pi r^2 h$ **Write formula for volume of a cylinder.**

$= \pi(9)^2(4)$ **Substitute 9 for r and 4 for h.**

$= 324\pi$ **Simplify.**

2 Use a conversion factor that converts cubic feet to gallons.

$324\pi \text{ ft}^3 \cdot \dfrac{7.481 \text{ gal}}{1 \text{ ft}^3} \approx 7614.7$ gal **Evaluate. Use a calculator.**

Answer The capacity of the swimming pool is about 7615 gallons.

✔ *Checkpoint*

Find the volume of the prism or cylinder.

1.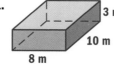

3 m, 10 m, 8 m

2.

4 yd, 9 yd, 6 yd

3.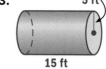

5 ft, 15 ft

4. **Critical Thinking** Which solid has a greater volume, a prism with bases that are squares with side length 8 units and a height of 11 units or a cylinder with a diameter of 11 units and a height of 8 units? Which solid has the greater surface area?

| Example 3 | Finding the Volume of a Solid |

The solid shown is composed of a rectangular prism and two half cylinders. Find the volume of the solid. Round to the nearest cubic foot.

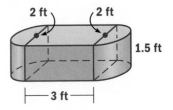

Solution

① Find the area of a base. Each end of a base is a half circle with a radius of 1 foot. Together, the ends form a complete circle.

B = Area of rectangle + Area of circle

$\quad = lw + \pi r^2$ Use formulas for area of a rectangle and area of a circle.

$\quad = 3(2) + \pi(1)^2$ Substitute 3 for *l*, 2 for *w*, and 1 for *r*.

$\quad = 6 + \pi$ Simplify. Leave in terms of π.

② $V = Bh$ Write formula for volume of a prism.

$\quad = (6 + \pi)1.5$ Substitute $6 + \pi$ for B and 1.5 for h.

$\quad = 9 + 1.5\pi$ Use distributive property.

$\quad \approx 13.71$ Evaluate. Use a calculator.

Answer The volume of the solid shown is about 14 cubic feet.

Study Strategy

Notice that the base area is left in terms of π in Step 1 of the solution of Example 3. This is done to avoid rounding twice, once when calculating B and again when calculating V. When possible, you should avoid rounding until the *end* of a calculation.

10.7 Exercises

More Practice, p. 812

INTERNET
eWorkbook Plus
CLASSZONE.COM

Guided Practice

Vocabulary Check
1. Copy and complete: The volume of a solid is measured in _?_ units.

2. Explain how to find the volume of any prism.

Skill Check   **Find the volume of the prism or cylinder. Round to the nearest whole number.**

3. 4 cm / 3 cm / 10 cm

4. 5 in. / 6 in.

5. 8 ft / 9 ft

6. **Error Analysis** Explain why the following calculation would not give the correct volume for the prism: $V = Bh = 6 \cdot 9 \cdot 10$.

6 in. / 10 in. / 9 in.

Practice and Problem Solving

Homework *Help*

Example	Exercises
1	7-9, 13-14
2	10-12, 15
3	19-20

Online Resources
CLASSZONE.COM
• More Examples
• eTutorial Plus

Find the volume of the prism or cylinder. Round to the nearest whole number.

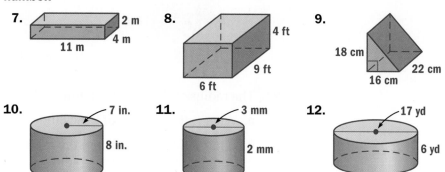

7. 11 m, 4 m, 2 m

8. 6 ft, 9 ft, 4 ft

9. 18 cm, 16 cm, 22 cm

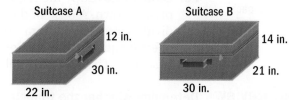

10. 7 in., 8 in.

11. 3 mm, 2 mm

12. 17 yd, 6 yd

13. **Mailing** You are mailing a gift box that is 17 inches by 14 inches by 10 inches. You want to put it in a larger box and surround it with foam packing. The larger box is 20 inches by 17 inches by 13 inches. How many cubic inches of foam packing do you need?

14. **Suitcases** Tell which suitcase holds more.

Suitcase A — 12 in., 30 in., 22 in.

Suitcase B — 14 in., 21 in., 30 in.

15. **Candles** The red candle costs $7.05, the blue candle costs $7.80, and the green candle costs $10.55.

3 in., 6 in.

3 in., 9 in.

4 in., 4 in.

a. How much wax is used in each candle? Round to the nearest cubic inch.

b. Find the ratio of the cost of a candle to the volume of wax used in the candle.

c. **Interpret and Apply** Which candle is the best buy? Explain.

Find the unknown dimension. Round to the nearest whole number.

16. $V = 210 \text{ cm}^3$

5 cm, 14 cm, h

17. $V = 301 \text{ in.}^3$

d, 6 in.

18. $V = 254 \text{ m}^3$

9 m, h

The solids shown are composed of prisms, cylinders, and half cylinders. Find the volume of the solid. Round to the nearest whole number.

19.

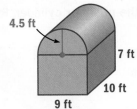

4.5 ft

7 ft

10 ft

9 ft

20.

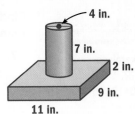

4 in.

7 in.

2 in.

9 in.

11 in.

21. The radius of a cylinder is 3 units, and the height is 4 units.

    a. What is the volume of the cylinder?

    b. What is the volume when the radius is doubled? when the height is doubled? when both the radius and height are doubled?

    c. **Compare** For each cylinder in part (b), compare its volume to the volume of the cylinder in part (a). What do you notice in each case?

22. **Salsa** You made 10 quarts of salsa. You are putting the salsa in jars with a diameter of 3 inches and a height of 5.5 inches. How many full jars of salsa will you have? (Use the fact that 1 in.^{3} ≈ 0.017 qt.)

Review *Help*
───────────

For help with units of capacity, see p. 791.

23. **Challenge** Copy the regular hexagonal prism shown. A base of the prism can be divided into 6 equilateral triangles. The height of each equilateral triangle is $2\sqrt{3}$. Find the base area. Then find the volume of the prism.

12

4

Mixed Review

Determine whether the triangle with the given side lengths is a right triangle. *(Lesson 9.3)*

24. 8, 11, 14   **25.** 8, 15, 17   **26.** 2, 4.8, 5.2

27. For $\triangle ABC$, find tan A and tan B. *(Lesson 9.7)*

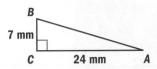

B

7 mm

C

24 mm

A

Find the surface area of the pyramid or cone. Round to the nearest whole number. *(Lesson 10.6)*

28.

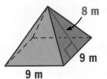

8 m

9 m

9 m

29.

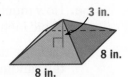

3 in.

8 in.

8 in.

30.

9 in.

4 in.

Standardized Test Practice

31. **Multiple Choice** What is the volume of a rectangular prism with a length of 16 inches, a height of 4 inches, and a width of 12 inches?

    A. 48 in.^{3} **B.** 768 in.^{3} **C.** 1810 in.^{3} **D.** 2413 in.^{3}

32. **Multiple Choice** What is the approximate volume of a cylinder with a diameter of 18 meters and a height of 3 meters?

    F. 54 m^3 **G.** 243 m^3 **H.** 763 m^3 **I.** 3054 m^3

10.7 Surface Area and Volume

Goal Use a spreadsheet to compare the surface areas and volumes of solids.

Example

Efficient packaging uses the least amount of material for the greatest volume. Compare the ratios of volume to surface area of the rectangular prisms below. Which prism is a more efficient package?

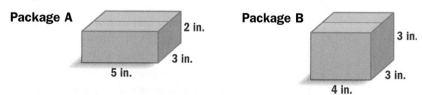

Package A — 5 in., 3 in., 2 in. Package B — 4 in., 3 in., 3 in.

Use a spreadsheet to compare the ratios of volume to surface area. The prism with the greater ratio is the more efficient package.

1 Label columns for length, width, height, surface area, volume, and ratio in row 1. Enter the dimensions of package A and the formulas for surface area, volume, and ratio in row 2 as shown.

	A	B	C	D	E	F
1	*l*	*w*	*h*	Surface area	Volume	Ratio
2	5	3	2	=2*A2*B2+2*A2*C2+2*B2*C2	=A2*B2*C2	=E2/D2

2 Enter the dimensions of package B in row 3. Use the *Fill down* feature to calculate the surface area, volume, and ratio of the second prism.

	A	B	C	D	E	F
1	*l*	*w*	*h*	Surface area	Volume	Ratio
2	5	3	2	62	30	0.48
3	4	3	3	66	36	0.55

Because 0.55 > 0.48, package B is more efficient than package A.

Draw Conclusions

1. **Compare** Find the ratio of volume to surface area for a cube that is 5 inches long, 5 inches wide, and 5 inches high. Is the cube more efficient or less efficient than the packages in the example above?

2. **Critical Thinking** A product is packaged in cylinders. Package A has a radius of 2 inches and a height of 6 inches. Package B has a radius of 3 inches and a height of 4 inches. Which package is more efficient?

10.8 Volumes *of* Pyramids *and* Cones

Review Vocabulary
volume, p. 789

BEFORE	*Now*	WHY?
You found the volumes of prisms and cylinders.	You'll find the volumes of pyramids and cones.	So you can find the volume of a composter, as in Ex. 15.

Consider a prism and a pyramid that have the same base area and the same height. If you completely fill the pyramid with sand and pour the sand into the prism, you'll find that the sand fills one third of the prism. You can conclude that the volume of the pyramid is one third of the volume of the prism. The same relationship holds for a cylinder and a cone with the same base area and the same height.

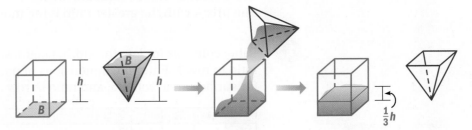

Study *Strategy*

Unlike the formula for the surface area of a pyramid, the formula for the volume of a pyramid can also be used for pyramids whose bases are not regular.

Volume of a Pyramid or a Cone

Words The volume V of a pyramid or a cone is one third of the product of the base area B and the height h.

Algebra $V = \frac{1}{3}Bh$

Example 1 *Finding the Volume of a Pyramid*

The base of a pyramid is a square. The side length of the square is 24 feet. The height of the pyramid is 9 feet. Find the volume of the pyramid.

$V = \frac{1}{3}Bh$ Write formula for volume of a pyramid.

$= \frac{1}{3}(24^2)(9)$ Substitute 24^2 for B and 9 for h.

$= 1728$ Simplify.

Answer The volume of the pyramid is 1728 cubic feet.

Example 2 *Finding the Volume of a Cone*

Find the volume of the cone shown.
Round to the nearest cubic millimeter.

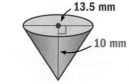

The radius is one half of the diameter,
so $r = 6.75$.

$$V = \frac{1}{3}\pi r^2 h \qquad \text{Write formula for volume of a cone.}$$

$$= \frac{1}{3}\pi(6.75)^2(10) \qquad \text{Substitute 6.75 for } r \text{ and 10 for } h.$$

$$\approx 477.1 \qquad \text{Evaluate. Use a calculator.}$$

Answer The volume of the cone is about 477 cubic millimeters.

In the **Real World**

Silos Suppose you have planted 360 acres of corn on your family farm and expect to produce about 140 bushels of shelled corn per acre. A bushel is a unit of volume equal to about 1.25 cubic feet. How many silos, each the size of the one in Example 3, would it take to store your entire crop?

Example 3 *Finding the Volume of a Solid*

Silos The grain silo shown is composed of a cylinder and a cone. Find the volume of the silo to the nearest cubic foot.

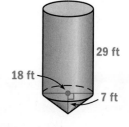

Solution

1 Find the volume of the cylindrical section. The radius is one half of the diameter, so $r = 9$.

$$V = \pi r^2 h \qquad \text{Write formula for volume of a cylinder.}$$

$$= \pi(9)^2(29) = 2349\pi \qquad \text{Substitute values. Then simplify.}$$

2 Find the volume of the conical section.

$$V = \frac{1}{3}\pi r^2 h \qquad \text{Write formula for volume of a cone.}$$

$$= \frac{1}{3}\pi(9)^2(7) = 189\pi \qquad \begin{array}{l}\text{Substitute 9 for } r \text{ and 7 for } h.\\ \text{Then simplify.}\end{array}$$

3 Find the sum of the volumes.

$$2349\pi + 189\pi = 2538\pi \approx 7973.4$$

Answer The volume of the silo is about 7973 cubic feet.

✔ *Checkpoint*

Find the volume of the pyramid or cone. Round to the nearest whole number.

1. 10 cm   14 cm   14 cm

2. 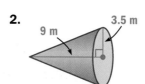 9 m   3.5 m

3. 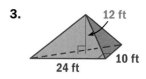 12 ft   24 ft   10 ft

Lesson 10.8 Volumes of Pyramids and Cones   **559**

SUMMARY   Surface Areas and Volumes of Solids

Prism	Cylinder
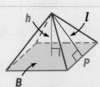 **Surface Area** $S = 2B + Ph$ **Volume** $V = Bh$	**Surface Area** $S = 2\pi r^2 + 2\pi rh$ **Volume** $V = \pi r^2 h$
Pyramid	**Cone**
Surface Area $S = B + \frac{1}{2}Pl$ **Volume** $V = \frac{1}{3}Bh$	**Surface Area** $S = \pi r^2 + \pi rl$ **Volume** $V = \frac{1}{3}\pi r^2 h$

Note *Worthy*

Use a main idea web like the one on p. 510 to summarize the concepts of surface area and volume in your notes.

10.8 Exercises

More Practice, p. 812

INTERNET
eWorkbook Plus
CLASSZONE.COM

Guided Practice

Vocabulary Check

1. What formula can you use to find the volume of a pyramid?

2. How is the formula for the volume of a cone related to the formula for the volume of a cylinder?

Skill Check   **Find the volume of the pyramid or cone. Round to the nearest whole number.**

3.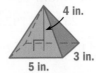
4 in.
3 in.
5 in.

4.
8 in.
15 in.

5. Error Analysis Describe and correct the error in finding the volume of the solid shown.

7 cm   8 cm

$$V = \frac{1}{3}Bh$$

$$\times \quad = \frac{1}{3}\pi(8)^2(7)$$

$$\approx 469 \text{ cm}^3$$

Practice and Problem Solving

Homework *Help*

Example	Exercises
1	6–8
2	9–12, 16
3	13–15

Online Resources
CLASSZONE.COM

• More Examples
• eTutorial Plus

Find the volume of the pyramid or cone. Round to the nearest whole number.

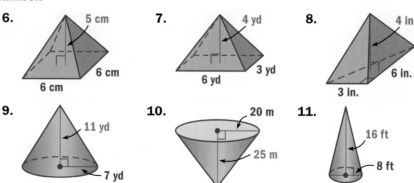

6. 5 cm, 6 cm, 6 cm

7. 4 yd, 3 yd, 6 yd

8. 4 in., 6 in., 3 in.

9. 11 yd, 7 yd

10. 20 m, 25 m

11. 16 ft, 8 ft

12. The diameter of a cone-shaped paper cup is 8 centimeters, and the height is 10 centimeters. The radius of another cone-shaped paper cup is 3 centimeters, and the height is 11 centimeters.

   a. **Predict** Which cup do you predict will hold more water? Explain your prediction.

   b. **Compare** Find the volume of each paper cup to the nearest tenth of a cubic centimeter. Which cup holds more water?

The solid in Exercise 13 is composed of a cylinder and a cone. The solid in Exercise 14 is a cube with a cone-shaped hole in it. Find the volume of the solid. Round your answer to the nearest whole number.

13.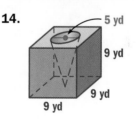

8 cm   6 cm

14. 5 yd, 9 yd, 9 yd, 9 yd

15. **Extended Problem Solving** The composter shown turns biodegradable materials like leaves and grass into fertilizer.

   a. Find the volume of the cylindrical portion of the composter in terms of π.

   b. Find the volume of the top cone and the volume of the bottom cone in terms of π.

   c. **Apply** Find the total volume of the composter to the nearest cubic inch.

   d. *Writing* When assembling the composter, you can adjust the height and the radius. Which has the greater effect on the volume of the composter, changing the *height* or changing the *radius*? Explain.

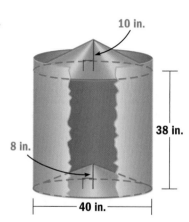

10 in.

38 in.

8 in.

40 in.

16. 🖩 **Compare** The radius of cone A is 3 inches, and its height is 7 inches. The radius of cone B is 4 inches, and its height is 6 inches. Create a spreadsheet to compare the volumes and surface areas of the cones. Which cone has a greater ratio of volume to surface area?

17. Paperweight A solid crystal paperweight is in the shape of a cube that has an edge length of 6 centimeters. A triangular pyramid is cut from one corner of the cube. The base area of the pyramid is about 7.64 square centimeters, and the height of the pyramid is about 1.7 centimeters. Find the volume of the paperweight to the nearest hundredth of a cubic centimeter.

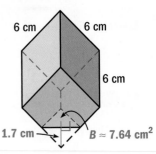

Find the unknown dimension of the pyramid or cone. Round to the nearest whole number.

18. $V = 12.4\pi$ ft³

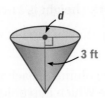

19. $V = 1452$ mm³

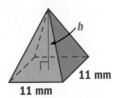

20. Funnel Most funnels consist of a cone whose tip is removed. The cone is then attached to a narrow cylinder. In the diagram below, the small cone inside the cylinder shows the portion of the large cone that has been cut off.

a. Find the volume of the large cone and the volume of the small cone to the nearest hundredth of a cubic inch.

b. Calculate the difference between the volume of the large cone and the volume of the small cone.

c. Find the volume of the cylinder to the nearest hundredth of a cubic inch.

d. Use your results from part (b) and part (c) to find the total volume of the funnel to the nearest tenth of a cubic inch.

Review *Help*

For help with spheres, see p. 548.

🖩 **Spheres** In Exercises 21–23, find the volume *V* of the spherical object using the formula $V = \frac{4}{3}\pi r^3$, where *r* is the radius. Round to the nearest cubic unit.

21. The diameter of a pearl is 8.3 millimeters.

22. The radius of a women's basketball is 4.5 inches.

23. The diameter of an inflatable beach ball is 3 feet.

24. Challenge Find the volume of the cone shown. Round to the nearest hundredth of a cubic meter.

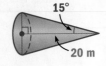

Mixed Review

25. Given that $\triangle ABC \sim \triangle ADE$, find DE. *(Lesson 6.5)*

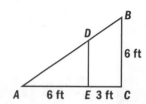

Algebra Basics **Identify the slope and *y*-intercept of the line.** *(Lesson 8.5)*

26. $y = -5x + 2$ **27.** $y = \dfrac{3}{2}x - 1$ **28.** $y = 13$ **29.** $2y = 9$

30. What is the volume of the cylinder shown? Round to the nearest cubic inch. *(Lesson 10.7)*

31. What is the volume of a rectangular prism with a length of 8 inches, a width of 4 inches, and a height of 4 inches? *(Lesson 10.7)*

Standardized Test Practice

32. Multiple Choice A cone has a height of 3 feet. The radius of the base is 4 feet. What is the approximate volume of the cone?

A. 12.6 ft^3 **B.** 37.7 ft^3 **C.** 50.3 ft^3 **D.** 150.8 ft^3

33. Multiple Choice The base area of a triangular pyramid is 12 square centimeters. The height of the pyramid is 5 centimeters. What is the volume of the pyramid?

F. 20 cm^3 **G.** 30 cm^3 **H.** 60 cm^3 **I.** 120 cm^3

34. Short Response A marble monument is in the shape of a square pyramid. The side length of the base is 5 feet. The height of the pyramid is 5 feet. Find the volume of the pyramid. Use the fact that 1 cubic foot of marble weighs about 170 pounds. To the nearest pound, how much does the monument weigh? Explain your reasoning.

Thinking About Sculptures

Each sculpture below is a prism, a cylinder, a cone, or a pyramid. Find the volume of each sculpture in terms of *a* and *b*. Then compare the coefficients of the five volume expressions to order the volumes from least to greatest. The letters associated with the sculptures will spell out the last name of the artist who created a famous statue called *The Thinker*.

N

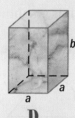

D

I

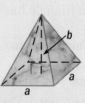

R

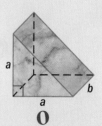

O

Vocabulary Review

polygon, p. 516
regular polygon, p. 516
convex, concave p. 516
polygons: pentagon, hexagon,
  heptagon, octagon, p. 516
quadrilaterals: trapezoid,
  parallelogram, rhombus,
  p. 517

diagonal of a polygon, p. 518
base, height of a
  parallelogram, p. 521
bases, height of a trapezoid,
  p. 522
circles: center, radius,
  diameter, p. 528
circumference, p. 528

surface area, p. 538
net, p. 538
lateral face of a prism,
  p. 539
lateral area of a prism,
  p. 539
lateral surface of a cylinder,
  p. 540

lateral area of a cylinder,
  p. 540
height, slant height of a
  pyramid, p. 544
regular pyramid, p. 544
height, slant height of a
  cone, p. 546

1. When finding the area of a trapezoid, what lengths do you need to know?

2. Describe convex and concave polygons. Tell how they are alike and how they are different.

3. Describe how to find the surface area of a prism using a net.

4. Tell how the slant height of a cone is different from the height of the cone.

10.1 Triangles

Examples on
pp. 511–512

▶ *Goal*

Find unknown angle measures and classify triangles.

Example **Find the value of *y*. Then classify the triangle by its angle measures.**

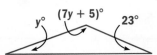

$$23° + (7y + 5)° + y° = 180°$$ Sum of angle measures is 180°.

$$8y + 28 = 180$$ Combine like terms.

$$8y = 152$$ Subtract 28 from each side.

$$y = 19$$ Divide each side by 8.

$$7y + 5 = 7(19) + 5 = 138$$ Find unknown angle measure.

The triangle has 1 obtuse angle, so it is an obtuse triangle.

✔ **Find the value of *y*. Then classify the triangle by its angle measures.**

5.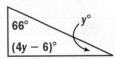

6.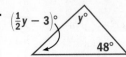

7.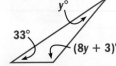

10.2 Polygons and Quadrilaterals

Examples on pp. 516–518

▶ **Goal**

Classify polygons and quadrilaterals.

Example Tell whether the figure is a polygon. If it is, classify it. If not, explain why.

The figure is a 6-sided polygon. So, it is a hexagon. It is convex and regular.

✔ Tell whether the figure is a polygon. If it is, classify it. If not, explain why.

8.   9.   10.

10.3 Areas of Parallelograms and Trapezoids

Examples on pp. 521–523

▶ **Goal**

Find the areas of parallelograms and trapezoids.

Example Find the area of the trapezoid.

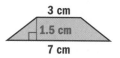

$$A = \frac{1}{2}(b_1 + b_2)h \qquad \text{Write formula for area of a trapezoid.}$$

$$= \frac{1}{2}(3 + 7)(1.5) \qquad \text{Substitute 3 for } b_1, \text{ 7 for } b_2, \text{ and 1.5 for } h.$$

$$= 7.5 \text{ cm}^2 \qquad \text{Simplify.}$$

✔ Find the area of the parallelogram or trapezoid.

11. 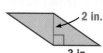   12. 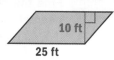   13.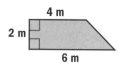

 3 in.   25 ft   6 m

10.4 Circumference and Area of a Circle

Examples on pp. 528–530

▶ **Goal**

Find circumferences and areas of circles.

Example Find the area of the circle to the nearest square inch. Use 3.14 for π.

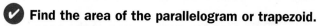

$$A = \pi r^2 \qquad \text{Write the area of a circle.}$$

$$\approx 3.14(9)^2 \qquad \text{Substitute 3.14 for } \pi \text{ and 9 for } r.$$

$$\approx 254 \text{ in.}^2 \qquad \text{Simplify.}$$

✔ 14. The diameter of a circle is 16 inches. Find the circumference and area of the circle. Round your answers to the nearest whole number.

10.5 Surface Areas of Prisms and Cylinders

Examples on pp. 538–540

▶ **Goal**

Find the surface areas of prisms and cylinders.

Example Find the surface area of the prism.

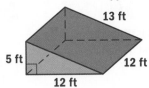

The bases of the prism are right triangles.

$S = 2B + Ph$ Write formula for surface area of a prism.

$= 2\left(\frac{1}{2} \cdot 5 \cdot 12\right) + (5 + 12 + 13)(12)$ Substitute values.

$= 420 \text{ ft}^2$ Simplify.

✔ Find the surface area of the prism or cylinder to the nearest square inch.

15.

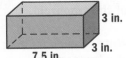

3 in.
3 in.
7.5 in.

16.

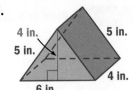

4 in.
5 in.
5 in.
4 in.
6 in.

17.

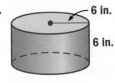

6 in.
6 in.

10.6 Surface Areas of Pyramids and Cones

Examples on pp. 544–546

▶ **Goal**

Find the surface areas of pyramids and cones.

Example Find the surface area of the cone to the nearest square meter.

$S = \pi r^2 + \pi r l$ Write formula for surface area of a cone.

$= \pi (9)^2 + \pi (9)(41)$ Substitute 9 for r and 41 for l.

$\approx 1414 \text{ m}^2$ Evaluate. Use a calculator.

41 m
9 m

✔ Find the surface area of the regular pyramid or cone to the nearest square foot.

18.

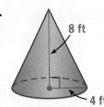

8 ft
4 ft

19.

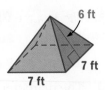

6 ft
7 ft
7 ft

20.

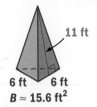

11 ft
6 ft   6 ft
$B \approx 15.6 \text{ ft}^2$

10.7 Volumes of Prisms and Cylinders

Examples on
pp. 552–554

▶ **Goal**

Find the volumes of prisms and cylinders.

Example Find the volume of the cylinder to the nearest cubic centimeter.

The radius is one half of the diameter, so $r = 10$.

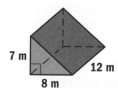
20 cm
24 cm

$V = \pi r^2 h$ Write formula for volume of a cylinder.

$= \pi(10)^2(24)$ Substitute 10 for r and 24 for h.

$= 2400\pi$ Simplify.

≈ 7539.8 Evaluate. Use a calculator.

The volume of the cylinder is about 7540 cubic centimeters.

✔ **Find the volume of the prism or cylinder. Round to the nearest whole number.**

21.

3 in.
8 in.

22.

6 cm
12 cm
6 cm

23.

7 m
8 m
12 m

10.8 Volumes of Pyramids and Cones

Examples on
pp. 558–559

▶ **Goal**

Find the volumes of pyramids and cones.

Example Find the volume of the pyramid.

$V = \frac{1}{3}Bh$ Write formula for volume of a pyramid.

$= \frac{1}{3}(5^2)(3)$ Substitute 5^2 for B (because the base is a square) and 3 for h.

$= 25$ Simplify.

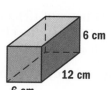
3 m
5 m
5 m

The volume of the pyramid is 25 cubic meters.

✔ **Find the volume of the pyramid or cone. Round to the nearest whole number.**

24.

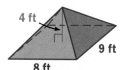
4 ft
9 ft
8 ft

25.

14 cm
8 cm

26.

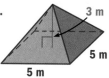
6 in.
17 in.

1. The perimeter of a triangle is 53 inches. The length of one side is 15 inches. The other two sides are congruent. Find their lengths.

2. The ratio of the angle measures of a triangle is $1:3:8$. Find the angle measures. Then classify the triangle by its angle measures.

3. Tell whether the figure shown is a polygon. If it is, classify it. If not, explain why.

Find the area of the parallelogram or trapezoid.

4.
20 m
12 m
10 m

5.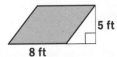
5 ft
8 ft

6.
4 m
8 m
14 m

7. **Rug** A circular rug has a diameter of 15 feet. Find the area of the rug to the nearest square foot. Then find the circumference of the rug to the nearest foot. Use 3.14 for π.

Find the surface area of the pyramid, cylinder, or cone. Round to the nearest whole number.

8.
8 mm
18 mm

9.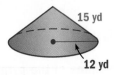
15 yd
12 yd

10.
12 ft
10 ft
10 ft

11. **Doorstop** You are decorating a doorstop to use for your bedroom door. The doorstop is a triangular prism. In order to buy paint for the doorstop, you need to know its surface area. What is the surface area of the doorstop?

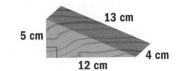
13 cm
5 cm
4 cm
12 cm

Find the volume of the prism, pyramid, or cone. Round to the nearest whole number.

12.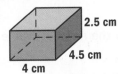
2.5 cm
4.5 cm
4 cm

13.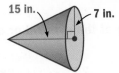
15 in.
7 in.

14.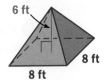
6 ft
8 ft
8 ft

15. **Container** You use a plastic container to hold pasta salad for your lunch. The container is a cylinder with a diameter of 5 inches and a height of 3 inches. Find its volume to the nearest cubic inch.

Chapter Standardized Test

Test-Taking Strategy If you finish the test and have time, look over your work and check as many of your answers as possible.

1. The perimeter of a triangle is 20 feet. The length of a side is 4 feet. The lengths of the other two sides are equal. What are the lengths of the other two sides?

   A. 4 ft   **B.** 8 ft   **C.** 10 ft   **D.** 16 ft

2. What is the value of x in the quadrilateral shown?

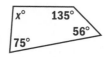

   F. 11   **G.** 94

   H. 105   **I.** 285

3. The height of a parallelogram is 20 meters. The base is one fifth of the height. What is the area of the parallelogram?

   A. 4 m^2 **B.** 40 m^2 **C.** 80 m^2 **D.** 100 m^2

4. What is the approximate circumference of the circle?

   F. 6 ft   **G.** 12 ft

   H. 24 ft   **I.** 48 ft

5. The area of a circle is 64 square inches. What is its approximate diameter?

   A. 5 in.   **B.** 9 in.   **C.** 10 in.   **D.** 20 in.

6. What is the surface area of the rectangular prism?

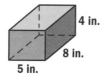

   F. 92 in.^2 **G.** 104 in.^2

   H. 160 in.^2 **I.** 184 in.^2

7. What is the volume of the prism in Exercise 6?

   A. 92 in.^3 **B.** 104 in.^3

   C. 160 in.^3 **D.** 184 in.^3

8. The height of a cylinder is 10 inches, and the diameter of the base is 6 inches. What is the approximate volume of the cylinder?

   F. 117 in.^3 **G.** 283 in.^3

   H. 360 in.^3 **I.** 1130 in.^3

9. What is the approximate volume of the cone?

   A. 9.42 mm^3

   B. 18.84 mm^3

   C. 28.26 mm^3

   D. 56.52 mm^3

10. **Short Response** A base of a trapezoid is 16 feet, and the height is 3 feet. The area of the trapezoid is 36 square feet. Find the length of the other base.

11. **Extended Response** The lampshade shown below can be described as part of a cone.

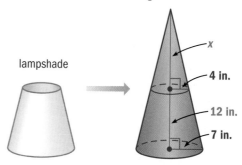

lampshade

   a. The right triangles shown with the cone are similar. Find the value of x. Explain how you found your answer.

   b. Find the lateral areas of the large and small cones to the nearest square inch.

   c. Find the lateral area of the lampshade.

Building Test-Taking Skills

Strategies for Answering
Context-Based Multiple Choice Questions

Some of the information you need to solve a context-based multiple choice question may appear in a table, a diagram, or a graph.

Problem 1 Tim and Karen leave school at different times but agree to meet each other at the theater. Tim takes the path in blue, while Karen takes the path in red. How much farther does Tim walk than Karen?

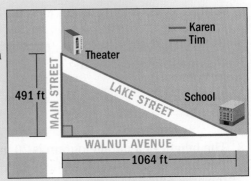

A. 108 ft   **B.** 383 ft

C. 681 ft   **D.** 1172 ft

Read the problem carefully. Decide what information you are given and how you can use it to solve the problem. ------

Solution

1) You know that Lake Street, Walnut Avenue, and Main Street form a right triangle. You know Tim walks 1064 feet on Walnut Avenue, and he walks 491 feet on Main Street.

The path that Tim walks and the path that Karen walks form a right triangle. You can use the Pythagorean theorem to find the distance that Karen walks.

2) Let a represent the distance Tim walks on Walnut Avenue. Let b represent the distance Tim walks on Main Street. Let c represent the distance Karen walks on Lake Street.

$$a^2 + b^2 = c^2 \quad \text{Pythagorean theorem}$$
$$1064^2 + 491^2 = c^2 \quad \text{Substitute for } a \text{ and } b.$$
$$1{,}373{,}177 = c^2 \quad \text{Simplify.}$$
$$1172 \approx c \quad \text{Take positive square root of each side.}$$

Subtract to find how much farther Tim walks than Karen.

3) $\underset{\text{Tim walks}}{\text{Distance}} - \underset{\text{Karen walks}}{\text{Distance}} \approx (1064 + 491) - 1172 = 383$

Tim walks about 383 feet farther than Karen.

The correct answer is B.

Problem 2 The graph of which equation is perpendicular to the line shown?

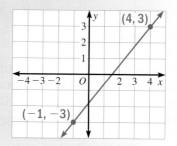

F. $6x + y = -7$

G. $y = \dfrac{6}{5}x + 4$

H. $5x + 6y = 24$

I. $6x - 5y = -15$

Solution

Use the given points to find the slope of the line. ----->

1) Use the graph to find the slope of the line.

$$m = \frac{rise}{run} = \frac{difference\ of\ y\text{-}coordinates}{difference\ of\ x\text{-}coordinates} = \frac{3 - (-3)}{4 - (-1)} = \frac{6}{5}$$

Find the slope of a line perpendicular to the given line. ----->

2) A line perpendicular to the line shown would have a slope that is the negative reciprocal of the slope found in Step 1. The negative reciprocal of $\dfrac{6}{5}$ is $-\dfrac{5}{6}$.

Eliminate answer choices that have the incorrect slope. ----->

3) Find the answer choice with a slope of $-\dfrac{5}{6}$ by writing each equation in slope-intercept form.

F. $6x + y = -7 \quad \longrightarrow \quad y = -6x - 7$ ✗

G. $y = \dfrac{6}{5}x + 4$ ✗

H. $5x + 6y = 24 \quad \longrightarrow \quad y = -\dfrac{5}{6}x + 4$ ✓

The equation $5x + 6y = 24$ has a slope of $-\dfrac{5}{6}$.

The correct answer is H.

Checkpoint

Watch *Out*

Be sure that you know what question you are asked to answer. Some answers may be intended to distract you.

1. What is the surface area of the prism shown?

A. 190 cm^2 **B.** 305 cm^2

C. 330 cm^2 **D.** 350 cm^2

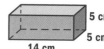

2. What is the volume of the prism in Exercise 1?

F. 190 cm^3 **G.** 305 cm^3 **H.** 330 cm^3 **I.** 350 cm^3

Multiple Choice

1. The table shows the numbers of British pounds that several tourists received when they exchanged their U.S. dollars. Which linear equation represents the data in the table?

Dollars, x	25	75	90	130
Pounds, y	15	45	54	78

A. $y = \frac{3}{5}x - 15$ **B.** $y = -\frac{5}{3}x$

C. $y = \frac{3}{5}x$ **D.** $y = \frac{5}{3}x$

2. The graph of which equation is shown?

F. $y = -\frac{3}{2}x + 3$

G. $y = -\frac{2}{3}x + 2$

H. $y = \frac{3}{2}x - 3$

I. $y = \frac{2}{3}x + 3$

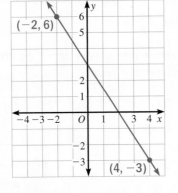

3. What is the distance between points C and D?

A. $2\sqrt{2}$

B. 4

C. 10

D. 14

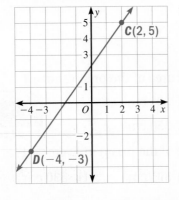

4. What is the midpoint of $\overline{CD}$ in Exercise 3?

F. $(-2, -4)$ **G.** $(-1, 1)$

H. $(-1, -1)$ **I.** $(2, 4)$

5. What is the value of x?

A. 5 in. **B.** 25 in.

C. 88.5 in. **D.** 625 in.

6. The bases of a baseball diamond form a square. What is the distance between second base and home plate?

F. $\sqrt{19}$ ft

G. $6\sqrt{5}$ ft

H. $90\sqrt{2}$ ft

I. $90\sqrt{3}$ ft

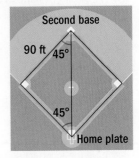

7. What is the approximate circumference of the circular pizza stone shown?

A. 57 in. **B.** 113 in.

C. 254 in. **D.** 1018 in.

8. What is the approximate area of the pizza stone in Exercise 7?

F. 57 in.^{2} **G.** 113 in.^{2}

H. 254 in.^{2} **I.** 1018 in.^{2}

9. The tent shown has the shape of a triangular prism. What is the surface area of the tent?

A. 28 ft^2 **B.** 140 ft^2

C. 136 ft^2 **D.** 160 ft^2

Short Response

10. As a fundraiser, your class sells packages of wrapping paper for $5 and boxes of greeting cards for $2. Total sales from the fundraiser are $1546. Write an equation describing the possible numbers of packages of wrapping paper and boxes of greeting cards that could have been sold. Then give three possible combinations of packages of wrapping paper and boxes of greeting cards that could have been sold.

11. A stained glass light fixture is in the shape of a square pyramid. Describe how you would find the area of the 4 triangular faces of the pyramid. Then find the combined area of these faces.

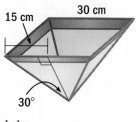

15 cm   30 cm   30°

12. Plot the points $A(-2, 1)$, $B(-5, -3)$, $C(5, -3)$, and $D(2, 1)$ in a coordinate plane. Connect the points to form a trapezoid. Explain how you would find the perimeter and area of the trapezoid. Then find the perimeter and area.

13. Graph the linear inequality $y \leq 2x + 3$. Name three ordered pairs that are solutions of the inequality.

14. An enter sign is composed of a triangle, a rectangle, and two congruent parallelograms. Find the area of the sign.

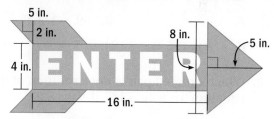

5 in.   2 in.   8 in.   5 in.   4 in.   16 in.

Extended Response

15. a. Write an equation of the line shown.

b. Write an equation of a line that is parallel to the line shown and passes through the point $(-7, -6)$.

c. Write an equation of a line that is perpendicular to the line shown and passes through the point $(-3, 4)$.

d. Write an equation of a line that is perpendicular to the line shown and passes through the point $(5, -2)$.

e. Graph the lines in parts (a)–(d) in the same coordinate plane. Identify the polygon formed. Explain your reasoning.

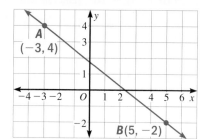

$A(-3, 4)$ $B(5, -2)$

16. The diagram shows an escalator in the Louisville International Airport in Kentucky.

a. What is the measure of $\angle A$?

b. Use the sine ratio to find the length of $\overline{AC}$.

c. Use the cosine ratio to find the length of $\overline{BC}$.

d. Use the tangent ratio to verify the lengths of $\overline{AC}$ and $\overline{BC}$.

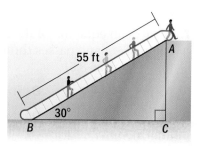

55 ft   A   30°   B   C

Chapter 8

Multiple Choice In Exercises 1–9, choose the letter of the correct answer.

1. What is the domain of the relation $(-9, 4)$, $(-3, -2)$, $(3, 7)$, $(8, 5)$? *(Lesson 8.1)*

   A. 3, 8   **B.** $-9, -3, 3, 8$

   C. 4, -2, 7, 5   **D.** 7, 5

2. What is the range of the relation in Exercise 1? *(Lesson 8.1)*

   F. 3, 8   **G.** $-9, -3, 3, 8$

   H. 4, -2, 7, 5   **I.** 7, 5

3. Which ordered pair is *not* a solution of the equation $3x + 4y = 14$? *(Lesson 8.2)*

   A. $(-10, 11)$ **B.** $(2, 2)$

   C. $(6, 8)$ **D.** $(10, -4)$

4. What is the y-intercept of the graph of $-6x - 3y = 18$? *(Lesson 8.3)*

   F. -6 **G.** -3 **H.** 3   **I.** 6

5. What is the x-intercept of the graph of the equation in Exercise 4? *(Lesson 8.3)*

   A. -6 **B.** -3 **C.** 3   **D.** 6

6. What is the slope of the line through the points $(6, -4)$ and $(9, 3)$? *(Lesson 8.4)*

   F. $-\dfrac{7}{3}$ **G.** $-\dfrac{3}{7}$ **H.** $\dfrac{3}{7}$ **I.** $\dfrac{7}{3}$

7. What is an equation of the line that has a slope of -4 and passes through the point $(0, 7)$? *(Lesson 8.6)*

   A. $y = -4x - 7$ **B.** $y = -4x + 7$

   C. $y = 7x - 4$ **D.** $y = 7x + 4$

8. Which ordered pair is a solution of the linear system $x + 4y = 18$ and $-3x + 2y = 16$? *(Lesson 8.8)*

   F. $(-2, -5)$ **G.** $(-2, 5)$

   H. $(2, 5)$ **I.** $(2, -5)$

9. The graph of which inequality is shown? *(Lesson 8.9)*

   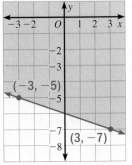

   A. $y > -3x - 6$

   B. $3x - y < 6$

   C. $x + 3y \geq -18$

   D. $y \leq -\dfrac{1}{3}x - 6$

10. **Short Response** Find the slope of a line perpendicular to the line $-5x + 2y = 16$. Then find an equation of a line that is perpendicular to the line $-5x + 2y = 16$ and passes through the point $(5, 7)$. *(Lesson 8.5)*

11. **Extended Response** A computer repair shop charges a flat rate of $50 plus $35 per hour spent repairing each computer. *(Lesson 8.7)*

    a. Let h be the number of hours spent repairing a computer. Use function notation to write an equation that gives the total charges for repairing a computer as a function of h. Graph the function.

    b. How much will the repair shop charge if the shop does 2.5 hours of work?

    c. The repair shop charges $172.50 to repair a computer. How many hours did the shop work on the computer?

Chapter 9

Multiple Choice In Exercises 12–22, choose the letter of the correct answer.

12. What is the value of $\sqrt{y^2 - z}$ when $y = -6$ and $z = 3$? *(Lesson 9.1)*

A. $\sqrt{15}$ **B.** $\sqrt{33}$ **C.** 15 **D.** 33

13. Which expression is *not* equivalent to $\sqrt{32}$? *(Lesson 9.2)*

F. $4\sqrt{2}$ **G.** $\sqrt{2 \cdot 4^2}$ **H.** $16\sqrt{2}$ **I.** $\sqrt{2 \cdot 16}$

14. The length of the hypotenuse of a right triangle is 32.5 centimeters, and the length of one leg is 12.5 centimeters. What is the length of the other leg? *(Lesson 9.3)*

A. 25 cm **B.** 30 cm **C.** 35 cm **D.** 900 cm

15. Which list of numbers is in order from least to greatest? *(Lesson 9.4)*

F. $-2.4, -\sqrt{6}, \sqrt{5}, \frac{7}{3}$ **G.** $-2.4, -\sqrt{6}, \frac{7}{3}, \sqrt{5}$

H. $-\sqrt{6}, -2.4, \sqrt{5}, \frac{7}{3}$ **I.** $-\sqrt{6}, -2.4, \frac{7}{3}, \sqrt{5}$

16. What is the midpoint of the segment with endpoints $(-3, 4)$ and $(6, -2)$? *(Lesson 9.5)*

A. $(1\frac{1}{2}, 1)$ **B.** $(-1\frac{1}{2}, 1)$

C. $(4\frac{1}{2}, 3)$ **D.** $(-4\frac{1}{2}, 3)$

17. The length of each leg of a 45°-45°-90° triangle is 7 meters. What is the length of the hypotenuse? *(Lesson 9.6)*

F. 2.6 m **G.** 4.9 m **H.** 7 m **I.** $7\sqrt{2}$ m

18. The length of the hypotenuse of a 30°-60°-90° triangle is 11 inches. What is the length of the shorter leg? *(Lesson 9.6)*

A. 5.5 in. **B.** $\frac{11\sqrt{3}}{2}$ in.

C. $11\sqrt{3}$ in. **D.** 22 in.

19. Which ratio is equal to tan A? *(Lesson 9.7)*

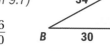

F. $\frac{16}{34}$ **G.** $\frac{16}{30}$

H. $\frac{30}{34}$ **I.** $\frac{30}{16}$

20. Which ratio is equal to tan B for the triangle in Exercise 19? *(Lesson 9.7)*

A. $\frac{16}{34}$ **B.** $\frac{16}{30}$ **C.** $\frac{30}{34}$ **D.** $\frac{30}{16}$

21. Which ratio is equal to sin B for the triangle in Exercise 19? *(Lesson 9.8)*

F. $\frac{16}{34}$ **G.** $\frac{16}{30}$ **H.** $\frac{30}{34}$ **I.** $\frac{30}{16}$

22. Which ratio is equal to sin A for the triangle in Exercise 19? *(Lesson 9.8)*

A. $\frac{16}{34}$ **B.** $\frac{16}{30}$ **C.** $\frac{30}{34}$ **D.** $\frac{30}{16}$

23. **Short Response** The time t (in seconds) that it takes a dropped object to fall a distance d (in feet) is given by the formula $d = 16t^2$. Two balls are dropped from the tops of two buildings. The heights of the two buildings are 150 feet and 600 feet. How much longer does it take the ball dropped from the taller building to hit the ground? Show your work. *(Lesson 9.2)*

24. **Extended Response** The vertices of an isosceles triangle are $P(6, 5)$, $Q(-4, 3)$, and $R(2, -1)$. *(Lessons 9.3, 9.5)*

a. Graph the triangle.

b. Find the lengths of $\overline{PQ}$, $\overline{QR}$, and $\overline{RP}$.

c. Find the midpoint M of $\overline{PQ}$.

d. Find the distance between points M and R.

e. Use the converse of the Pythagorean theorem to show that $\triangle MQR$ and $\triangle PMR$ are right triangles.

Chapter 10

Multiple Choice In Exercises 25–32, choose the letter of the correct answer.

25. What is the value of x? *(Lesson 10.1)*

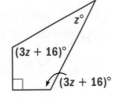

   A. 10.5   **B.** 21

   C. 24   **D.** 42

26. Classify the triangle in Exercise 25 by its angle measures. *(Lesson 10.1)*

   F. Acute   **G.** Isosceles

   H. Obtuse   **I.** Right

27. What is the value of z? *(Lesson 10.2)*

   A. 34   **B.** 90

   C. 118   **D.** 208

28. Your garden is in the shape of a parallelogram. The height of the parallelogram is 18 feet. The base is $1\frac{1}{2}$ times the height. What is the area of the garden? *(Lesson 10.3)*

   F. 18 ft^2 **G.** 40.5 ft^2

   H. 216 ft^2 **I.** 486 ft^2

29. The area of a circle is 94.2 square centimeters. What is the approximate radius of the circle? *(Lesson 10.4)*

   A. 3.9 cm **B.** 5.5 cm **C.** 15 cm **D.** 30 cm

30. A box has the shape of a rectangular prism that is 15 centimeters long, 4.5 centimeters wide, and 22 centimeters high. What is the surface area of the prism? *(Lesson 10.5)*

   F. 41.5 cm   **G.** 496.5 cm^2

   H. 993 cm^2 **I.** 1485 cm^3

31. What is the surface area of the square pyramid shown? *(Lesson 10.6)*

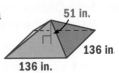

   A. 23,256 in.^{2} **B.** 32,368 in.^{2}

   C. 41,616 in.^{2} **D.** 314,432 in.^{2}

32. A mailbox is composed of a prism and a half cylinder. What is the approximate volume of the mailbox? *(Lessons 10.7, 10.8)*

   F. 1148 in.^{3}

   G. 1778 in.^{3}

   H. 2036 in.^{3}

   I. 2746 in.^{3}

33. **Short Response** The area of a trapezoid is 225 square meters. The height of the trapezoid is 25 meters. One of the bases is twice the other base. Do you have enough information to find each of the bases? If so, find the bases. If not, explain why not. *(Lesson 10.3)*

34. **Extended Response** A cylindrical display tank at an aquarium has a cylindrical viewing chamber inside it. Water fills the space between the two glass cylinders, as shown. *(Lesson 10.7)*

   a. What is the volume of the water in the tank to the nearest cubic inch?

   b. How many gallons of water are needed to fill the tank? Use the fact that 1 cubic inch of water is approximately equal to 0.00433 gallon.

Data Analysis, Polynomials, *and* Transformations

Chapter 11 Data Analysis and Probability

- Make and interpret data displays.
- Conduct surveys and analyze survey results.
- Calculate probabilities of events.

Chapter 12 Polynomials and Nonlinear Functions

- Add, subtract, and multiply polynomials.
- Evaluate powers of products, quotients, and powers.
- Graph quadratic and exponential functions.

Chapter 13 Angle Relationships and Transformations

- Identify special pairs of angles and find their measures.
- Find the measures of interior and exterior angles of polygons.
- Translate, reflect, rotate, and dilate geometric figures.

From Chapter 12, p. 651
What is the height of the volleyball?

CHAPTER

11

Data Analysis *and* Probability

BEFORE

In previous chapters you've . . .

- Found experimental and theoretical probabilities
- Used the counting principle

Now

In Chapter 11 you'll study . . .

- Making histograms and box-and-whisker plots
- Choosing appropriate displays for data
- Collecting and interpreting data
- Finding permutations and combinations
- Finding probabilities of disjoint and overlapping events
- Finding probabilities of dependent and independent events

WHY?

So you can solve real-world problems about . . .

- canaries, p. 585
- energy, p. 599
- snapping turtles, p. 604
- elections, p. 612
- Hawaii, p. 618
- pizza, p. 624
- field hockey, p. 639

What types of dogs do people prefer as pets?

578

CHAPTER 11
INTERNET Preview
CLASSZONE.COM

- eEdition Plus Online
- eWorkbook Plus Online
- eTutorial Plus Online
- State Test Practice
- More Examples

MATH *In the* **Real World**

Pets In 2002, the top three types of dogs registered with the American Kennel Club were Labrador retrievers, golden retrievers, and German shepherds. In this chapter, you will collect and interpret data, such as information about pets.

What do you think? In 2002, there were 154,616 Labrador retrievers, 56,124 golden retrievers, and 46,963 German shepherds registered with the American Kennel Club. Make a bar graph of the data.

Chapter Prerequisite Skills

PREREQUISITE SKILLS QUIZ

Review Vocabulary

reciprocal, p. 243
outcomes, p. 306
event, p. 306
favorable outcomes, p. 306
probability, p. 306
odds in favor, p. 308
odds against, p. 308
tree diagram, p. 313
counting principle, p. 314

Preparing for Success **To prepare for success in this chapter, test your knowledge of these concepts and skills. You may want to look at the pages referred to in blue for additional review.**

1. **Vocabulary** Copy and complete: The _?_ of an event is never greater than 1 and never less than 0.

2. **Vocabulary** Give an example of an event involving a number cube.

Find the sum or difference. *(p. 225)*

3. $\dfrac{15}{16} + \dfrac{3}{16}$ 4. $-\dfrac{5}{7} + \dfrac{2}{7}$ 5. $-\dfrac{4}{5} - \dfrac{2}{5}$ 6. $\dfrac{8}{9} - \dfrac{1}{9}$

7. **Lunch Special** A restaurant's lunch special includes a sandwich, a side order, and a drink. The restaurant's menu has 5 different sandwiches, 3 different side orders, and 4 different drinks. How many different combinations of the lunch special are possible? *(p. 313)*

Write the fraction as a percent. *(p. 329)*

8. $\dfrac{3}{20}$ 9. $\dfrac{5}{4}$ 10. $\dfrac{5}{8}$ 11. $\dfrac{1}{500}$

NOTETAKING STRATEGIES

Note *Worthy*

You will find a notetaking strategy at the beginning of each chapter. Look for additional notetaking and study strategies throughout the chapter.

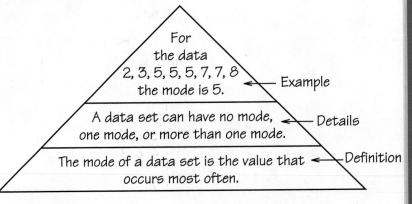

WORD TRIANGLE When you learn a new vocabulary word or formula, write it in your notes with details and examples in a word triangle like the one shown.

For the data
2, 3, 5, 5, 5, 7, 7, 8
the mode is 5. ← Example

A data set can have no mode, one mode, or more than one mode. ← Details

The mode of a data set is the value that occurs most often. ← Definition

In Lesson 11.6, you can use a word triangle to take notes about permutations.

Stem-and-Leaf Plots *and* Histograms

Vocabulary

stem-and-leaf plot, p. 581

frequency, p. 582

frequency table, p. 582

histogram, p. 583

BEFORE	Now	WHY?
You found the median of a data set.	You'll make stem-and-leaf plots and histograms.	So you can compare marathon times, as in Ex. 16.

Track The distances (in centimeters) of 11 jumps from the final round of a women's long jump competition are listed below. How can you display the data to show the distribution of the distances?

669, 702, 644, 701, 684, 686,

676, 673, 688, 670, 662

A **stem-and-leaf plot** is a data display that organizes data based on their digits. Each data value is separated into a *stem* (the leading digits) and a *leaf* (the last digit).

Example 1 *Making a Stem-and-Leaf Plot*

You can use a stem-and-leaf plot to display the distances listed above.

① The least data value is 644 and the greatest is 702. Let the **stems** be the hundreds' and tens' digits of the data values (from 64 to 70). Let the **leaves** be the ones' digits.

② Write the stems first. Then record each distance by writing its ones' digit on the same line as its corresponding stem.

③ Make an ordered plot. Give it a key and a title.

Reading *Algebra*

Each stem in a stem-and-leaf plot determines an interval. For the stem-and-leaf plot in Example 1, for instance, the stem 64 determines the interval 640–649. There is only one data value, 644, that falls in this interval.

Women's Long Jump

Unordered Plot	Ordered Plot
64 | 4	64 | 4
65 |	65 |
66 | 9 2	66 | 2 9
67 | 6 3 0	67 | 0 3 6
68 | 4 6 8	68 | 4 6 8
69 |	69 |
70 | 2 1	70 | 1 2
Key: 64 | 4 = 644 cm	Key: 64 | 4 = 644 cm

> In an ordered stem-and-leaf plot, list the leaves for each stem in order from least to greatest.

> A stem-and-leaf plot's key tells what numbers the stems and leaves represent.

Review *Help*

For help with finding the mean, median, mode, or range of a data set, see p. 39.

Data Distributions A stem-and-leaf plot shows how data are distributed. From a stem-and-leaf plot you can draw conclusions about the data. For example, you can see if data values are grouped together or tell whether most of the data are above or below the mean.

Example 2   *Interpreting Stem-and-Leaf Plots*

Sneakers The stem-and-leaf plots show the prices (in dollars) of pairs of sneakers at two shoe stores. What can you conclude about the prices at the two stores?

Solution

- Store A has a median price of $49. Store B has a median price of $43.

- Store B has more sneakers priced under $50 than Store A.

- More than half of the sneakers at Store B have prices in the $30–$39 and $40–$49 intervals. The sneaker prices at Store A are more evenly distributed over all intervals.

Store A

```
3 | 0 2 5 6 9
4 | 1 1 5 5 9
5 | 0 3 4 5 8
6 | 0 0 2 5
```

Store B

```
3 | 0 0 5 5 9
4 | 0 0 2 3 3 5 5 5
5 | 4 4 5 8
6 | 5 9
```

Key: 3|0 = $30

Frequency Tables A stem-and-leaf plot shows the *frequency* of each interval in the display. The **frequency** of an interval is the number of data values in that interval. A **frequency table** is another type of display that groups data into intervals to show frequencies.

Study *Strategy*

To choose the interval size for a frequency table, divide the range of the data by the number of intervals you want the table to have. Use the quotient as an approximate interval size.

Example 3   *Making a Frequency Table*

Hurricanes In the United States, hurricane season starts June 1 and lasts about 26 weeks. Meteorologists record the number of weeks into the season each hurricane occurs. The number of weeks into the hurricane season in which Atlantic hurricanes occurred from 1997 to 2000 are listed below. Make a frequency table of the data.

6, 7, 14, 12, 13, 14, 16, 16, 17, 17, 19, 21, 26, 12, 12,

13, 15, 15, 20, 20, 24, 10, 12, 15, 16, 17, 17, 18, 20

Solution

1) Choose intervals of equal size for the data.

2) Use a tally mark to record the interval in which each data value falls.

3) Write the frequency for each interval by counting the number of tally marks for the interval.

Weeks	Tally	Frequency
6–8	||	2
9–11			1
12–14	ЖН |||	8
15–17	ЖН ЖН	10
18–20	ЖН	5
21–23			1
24–26	||	2

Histograms A **histogram** displays data from a frequency table. A histogram has one bar for each interval. The length of a bar indicates the frequency of the interval. There is no space between bars because there are no gaps between intervals. Because the intervals of a histogram have equal size, the bars have equal width.

Example 4   *Making a Histogram*

Make a histogram using the frequency table in Example 3.

1. Show the intervals from the frequency table on the horizontal axis, and show the frequencies on the vertical axis.

2. Draw a bar to represent the frequency for each interval.

3. Give the histogram a title.

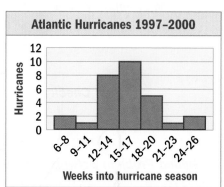

Example 5   *Interpreting a Histogram*

Internet The histogram shows the number of minutes that 100 students spent on the Internet in one day. Make several conclusions about the data.

Solution

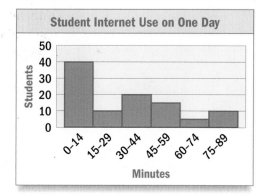

- Almost half of the students spent less than 15 minutes on the Internet.

- Of the students who spent more than 15 minutes on the Internet, the majority spent from 30 to 59 minutes on the Internet.

- Few of the students spent 60 minutes or more on the Internet.

✔ Checkpoint

1. Your bowling scores in your last 15 games are as follows: 125, 158, 143, 177, 135, 117, 101, 158, 160, 144, 199, 129, 122, 131, 116.

   a. Make a frequency table and histogram for your bowling scores.

   b. Interpret the histogram. What scores do you usually bowl? Are your scores distributed evenly over all intervals? How unusual is it for you to bowl a game over 150?

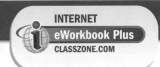
Guided Practice

Vocabulary Check

1. You want to make a stem-and-leaf plot of the data values 90, 93, 85, 86, and 74. What numbers would you use as the stems?

2. How can you tell which interval on a histogram has the greatest frequency?

Skill Check

Make an ordered stem-and-leaf plot of the data.

3. 27, 56, 40, 29, 44, 40, 60, 58, 62, 21, 56, 31, 33, 46, 41

4. 12, 50, 72, 67, 33, 98, 44, 16, 91, 47, 42, 53, 33, 11, 60, 77, 35, 79

Guided Problem Solving

5. Earthquakes For the period 1980–1998, the table below shows the number of earthquakes with magnitudes greater than 7.0 on the Richter scale. In 1999 there were 11 earthquakes greater than 7.0 on the Richter scale. How did 1999 compare with the preceding years?

1 Make a frequency table of the data.

2 Use your frequency table to make a histogram.

3 Into which interval does the number of earthquakes in 1999 fall? How does the frequency of this interval compare with the frequencies of the other intervals?

High-Magnitude Earthquakes Per Year
18, 14, 10, 15, 8, 15, 6, 11, 8, 7, 13, 10, 23, 16, 15, 25, 22, 20, 16

Practice and Problem Solving

Homework *Help*

Example	Exercises
1	6–9, 14
2	14, 16
3	10–13, 21
4	10–13, 18, 19, 21
5	15, 21

Online Resources
CLASSZONE.COM
• More Examples
• eTutorial Plus

Make an ordered stem-and-leaf plot of the data.

6. 350, 314, 378, 391, 395, 300, 357, 309, 312, 343, 389, 350, 306, 387, 381

7. 62, 77, 50, 6, 44, 61, 70, 9, 62, 71, 65, 41, 54, 63, 58, 64, 70

8. 3.23, 3.01, 2.68, 3.16, 2.88, 3.11, 2.55, 3.19, 2.56, 3.21, 2.66, 3.50, 2.66

9. 13.5, 15.7, 15.0, 12.6, 14.2, 15.1, 18.0, 13.9, 15.2, 14.1, 12.5, 12.1, 13.4

Use the data to make a frequency table and a histogram.

10. 9, 15, 2, 4, 9, 11, 10, 1, 18, 4, 9, 2, 8, 7, 4, 11, 10, 9, 16, 5

11. 137, 182, 145, 109, 118, 200, 120, 136, 191, 133, 122, 184, 127, 140

12. 1300, 2800, 9100, 7600, 3100, 2200, 1300, 2500, 4200, 1800, 1100, 6000

13. 66, 78, 91, 42, 45, 88, 69, 73, 76, 80, 50, 63, 57, 54, 71, 66

14. Canaries The weights (in grams) of 13 canaries at a pet shop are as follows: 15, 17, 9, 22, 19, 21, 20, 25, 11, 12, 9, 20, 17.

    a. Make an ordered stem-and-leaf plot of the data.

    b. Find the median and the range of the data.

    c. Compare Another canary weighs 18 grams. How does this canary compare with the others?

15. Extended Problem Solving The histogram shows the average number of vacation days that working citizens in 30 major cities in Europe and North America have each year.

    a. What interval has the greatest frequency?

    b. Interpret In what percent of the cities surveyed do working citizens have fewer than 20 vacation days per year?

    c. Critical Thinking Citizens of Shanghai, China, average 16 vacation days per year. How does Shanghai compare with the data given for North America and Europe? Explain.

16. Marathon The stem-and-leaf plot shows the times (in minutes) for 30 men who completed the 2002 Boston Marathon using a wheelchair.

    a. What was the fastest time?

    b. Find the median of the times.

    c. What percent of the participants finished the race in less than 2 hours?

    d. The fastest female wheelchair time in the marathon was 1 hour 46 minutes. How does this time compare with the times of the 30 male participants?

Wheelchair Marathon Times

```
 8 | 3 6
 9 | 0 3 3 5 6
10 | 0 0 1 3 3 3 3 3 3 3 6 9
11 | 1 2 3 9 9
12 | 1 2 4 9 9
13 | 3
```

Key: 8 | 3 = 83 minutes

17. Critical Thinking A stem-and-leaf plot has a stem of 4 and a leaf of 6, but the plot has no key. Give two possible values that the stem and leaf could represent. Explain your thinking.

Make a histogram from the stem-and-leaf plot. Do not use the same intervals in your histogram as are used in the stem-and-leaf plot.

18.
```
36 | 4
37 | 0 0 5
38 | 2 2 3 7 7 7 8 9
39 | 0 1 4 6 7
```

Key: 36 | 4 = 364

19.
```
 9 | 1 3 5 7 8 8 9
10 | 2 2 2 2 3 7 7 8 9
11 | 3 5 7
12 | 1 2 5 6 6 7 8 8 8 8
```

Key: 9 | 1 = 9.1

Javelin throw

20. *Writing* Compare stem-and-leaf plots and histograms. How are they alike? What advantages do stem-and-leaf plots have over histograms? What advantages do histograms have over stem-and-leaf plots?

21. Javelin The results of the top ten distances (in meters) for men and women in a javelin competition are listed below.

Men: 87.00, 92.80, 85.52, 89.95, 86.46, 83.64, 91.31, 81.80, 80.56, 82.82

Women: 63.11, 61.01, 65.78, 58.45, 69.53, 61.60, 62.08, 64.69, 61.94, 60.91

a. Make frequency tables for both the men's and women's distances.

b. Use the frequency tables you made in part (a) to make histograms for the two sets of data.

c. Analyze What conclusions can you make from the distributions of the data?

22. Challenge The histogram shows the results of a survey that asked 40 students at one school how many pets they owned. Use the histogram to find the experimental probability that a student at the school has 2 or more pets.

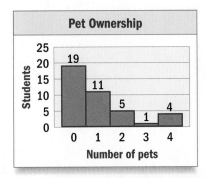

Mixed Review

23. Sweater You buy a sweater that is on sale for 15% off the original price of $40. What is the sale price of the sweater? *(Lesson 7.6)*

Find the slope of the line through the given points. *(Lesson 8.4)*

24. (4, 2), (3, 8)   **25.** (−3, −5), (−6, 7)   **26.** (3, −6), (−2, 2)

Find the midpoint of the segment with the given endpoints. *(Lesson 9.5)*

27. (2, 6), (−10, −2)   **28.** (−16, −5), (5, 5)   **29.** (−3, 4), (4, −2)

Standardized Test Practice

30. Extended Response A theater group handed out cards at its last performance to gather information about the ages of people who attend the group's performances. The histogram shows the results of the survey.

a. What percent of people who attended the show were under 30 years old? Round your answer to the nearest percent.

b. In which age group does the median age fall? Explain.

c. The theater group advertises its performances on the radio. Should the group advertise on a station that younger adults like or one that older adults like? Explain.

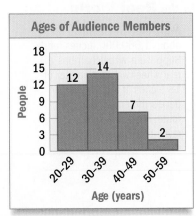

11.1 Making a Histogram

Goal Use a graphing calculator to make a histogram.

Example

Use a graphing calculator to make a histogram of the following data.

The average precipitation (in inches) for each month in Juneau, Alaska, is given below.

4.54, 3.75, 3.28, 2.77, 3.42, 3.15, 4.16, 5.32, 6.73, 7.84, 4.91, 4.44

1 Press LIST . Enter the data into list L1.

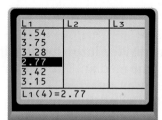

2 Press 2nd [PLOT]. Select Plot1 and choose the histogram from the menu. Set the value for Xlist to L1.

Tech *Help*

You do not need to change the value of ΔX in the WINDOW settings.

Online Resources
CLASSZONE.COM

• Keystroke Help

3 Press WINDOW . Set Xmin and Xmax to include all the data values. Use Xscl to set the width of the bars. Set Ymin and Ymax so that the tops and bottoms of the bars can be viewed.

4 Press GRAPH to graph the data. Press TRACE and the left and right arrow keys to move from bar to bar and examine the histogram.

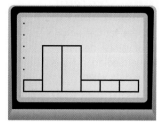

Draw Conclusions

1. Use a graphing calculator to make a histogram of the following test scores: 67, 68, 75, 73, 82, 96, 71, 73, 89, 84, 82, 91, 85, 88, 94.

2. **Analyze** Interpret the histogram in the example above. Are the data bunched together or spread out? Would you say that the average monthly precipitation is less than or greater than 5 inches? Explain.

Box-and-Whisker Plots

BEFORE | *Now* | WHY?

You made stem-and-leaf plots and histograms. | You'll make and interpret box-and-whisker plots. | So you can compare clothing prices, as in Ex. 12.

Vocabulary

box-and-whisker plot, p. 588
lower quartile, p. 588
upper quartile, p. 588
lower extreme, p. 588
upper extreme, p. 588
interquartile range, p. 590

Agriculture A farmer recorded the number of oranges that an orange tree produced for each of the last 9 years. The data are given below.

572, 452, 457, 460, 360, 407, 380, 458, 264

A useful way to display the data is with a *box-and-whisker plot*. A **box-and-whisker plot** is a data display that organizes data values into four groups.

Ordered data are divided into a lower half and an upper half by the median. The median of the lower half is the **lower quartile**. The median of the upper half is the **upper quartile**. The **lower extreme** is the least data value, and the **upper extreme** is the greatest data value.

Example 1   *Making a Box-and-Whisker Plot*

Study *Strategy*

When a data set has an odd number of values, do not include the median in either half of the data when determining the quartiles.

To display the data given above in a box-and-whisker plot, first order the data to find the median, the quartiles, and the extremes.

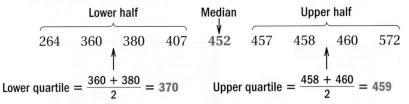

| | Lower half | | | | Median | Upper half | | | |
| 264 | 360 | 380 | 407 | | **452** | 457 | 458 | 460 | 572 |

Lower quartile $= \dfrac{360 + 380}{2} = 370$ Upper quartile $= \dfrac{458 + 460}{2} = 459$

Plot the median, the quartiles, and the extremes below a number line.

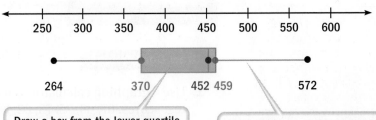

Draw a box from the lower quartile to the upper quartile. Then draw a vertical line through the median.

Draw a horizontal line (a "whisker") from the box to each of the extremes.

Interpreting a Box-and-Whisker Plot A box-and-whisker plot separates data into four sections: the two parts of the box and two whiskers. All four sections contain approximately the same number of data values.

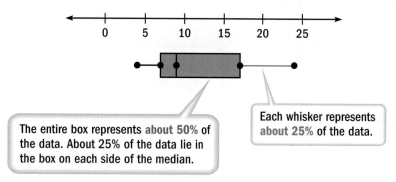

The entire box represents **about 50%** of the data. About 25% of the data lie in the box on each side of the median.

Each whisker represents **about 25%** of the data.

The lengths of sections tell you how spread out the data are. For instance, the data in Example 1 are more spread out between the lower quartile and the median than they are between the median and the upper quartile.

Example 2 · *Interpreting a Box-and-Whisker Plot*

State Parks The box-and-whisker plot below displays the number of visitors (in millions) to the state parks in each of the 50 states in 2000.

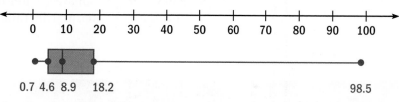

0.7 4.6 8.9   18.2   98.5

a. About how many states had fewer than 18.2 million visitors to their state parks?

b. West Virginia had 8.0 million visitors to its state parks. How does West Virginia compare with the rest of the states?

Solution

a. The upper quartile is 18.2. Each whisker and each part of the box represents about 25% of the states. So, about 75% of the 50 states, or 37 states, had fewer than 18.2 million visitors.

b. West Virginia's number of visitors is greater than the lower quartile (8.0 > 4.6), so West Virginia had more visitors than about 25% of the states. West Virginia's number of visitors is also less than the median (8.0 < 8.9), so West Virginia had fewer visitors than about 50% of the states.

✔ *Checkpoint*

1. The prices (in dollars) of several CD players are as follows: 35, 65, 90, 30, 120, 100, 80, 49, 60, 30, 55, 72, 108. Make a box-and-whisker plot of the data. Is the $72 CD player more expensive than 50% of the CD players? Explain.

In the **Real World**

State Parks Approximately 750 million people visit state parks in the United States each year, with the state of California having the most visitors. Based on the data in Example 2, about what percent of the total visitors to U.S. state parks visit California state parks?

Study *Strategy*

A data set may contain values that are much greater or much less than the other values. Because these values affect the range but not the interquartile range of the data set, the interquartile range is sometimes a more representative measure of how spread out the data are.

Interquartile Range The range of a set of data is the difference of the greatest and least values. The **interquartile range** of a data set is the difference of the upper quartile and the lower quartile.

Example 3   *Comparing Box-and-Whisker Plots*

Weather The box-and-whisker plots below show the average monthly temperatures for Boston and Seattle. What conclusions can you make?

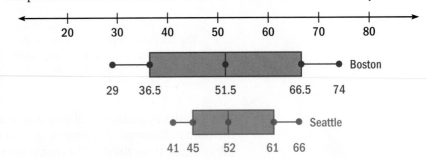

Solution

• Boston and Seattle have nearly identical median temperatures.

• Boston's temperatures are much more spread out than Seattle's. Both Boston's range (74 − 29 = 45) and Boston's interquartile range (66.5 − 36.5 = 30) are greater than Seattle's range (66 − 41 = 25) and Seattle's interquartile range (61 − 45 = 16), respectively.

11.2   Exercises

More Practice, p. 813

INTERNET
eWorkbook Plus
CLASSZONE.COM

Guided Practice

Vocabulary Check

1. Which value is the upper extreme for the data 12, 6, 23, 10?

2. Explain how to determine the interquartile range for a data set.

Skill Check   **Make a box-and-whisker plot of the data.**

3. 14, 6, 13, 17, 1, 12, 9, 18

4. 7, 19, 6, 12, 5, 17, 6, 13

Guided Problem Solving

5. Archery On 6 different days, two archers record the number of bull's-eyes they score out of 10 tries. Which archer is more consistent?

  1) Make a box-and-whisker plot for each archer.

  2) Find the range and interquartile range for each archer.

  3) For which archer is the range of the scores less?

Day	1	2	3	4	5	6
Archer 1	3	5	8	4	9	1
Archer 2	4	7	6	5	8	6

Practice and Problem Solving

Homework *Help*

Example	Exercises
1	6–9, 11, 12
2	11
3	9, 10, 12

Online Resources
CLASSZONE.COM
• More Examples
• eTutorial Plus

In Exercises 6–8, make a box-and-whisker plot of the data.

6. Students' heights (in inches): 50, 61, 55, 54, 53, 60, 65, 66, 57, 68

7. Sweater prices (in dollars): 15, 20, 19, 18, 17, 26, 22, 25, 20, 23, 18

8. Number of CDs in collections: 25, 32, 16, 40, 68, 52, 45, 95, 60, 41

9. **Test Scores** The data below are a class's test scores for two tests.

   Test 1: 50, 93, 81, 75, 70, 66, 68, 59, 60, 58, 71, 62, 84, 88, 65, 85

   Test 2: 65, 73, 84, 92, 87, 83, 80, 77, 67, 74, 75, 81, 90, 88, 78, 85

   a. Make a box-and-whisker plot for each data set. Draw both box-and-whisker plots using the same number line.

   b. Compare the range and the interquartile range for the two tests.

   c. **Interpret** On test 1 you scored 71. On test 2 you scored 74. On which test did you do better compared with the rest of the class? Explain.

10. **Baseball** The box-and-whisker plots below show the ages of the players on the New York Yankees and the Texas Rangers baseball teams during the 2002 season.

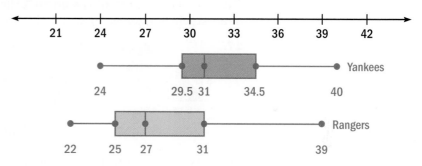

   a. **Compare** Compare the median, range, and interquartile range for the two teams.

   b. **Analyze** About what percent of the Yankees are less than 31 years old? About what percent of the Rangers are less than 31 years old?

   c. *Writing* Which team would you say is the "older" team? Explain.

11. **Extended Problem Solving** An *outlier* is a data value whose distance from the upper or lower quartile is more than 1.5 times the interquartile range.

   a. Make a box-and-whisker plot for the following data: 109, 113, 119, 121, 124, 125, 128, 134, 134, 136, 198.

   b. **Calculate** Determine if there are any outliers in the data set.

   c. Make a box-and-whisker plot for the data, excluding any outliers.

   d. *Writing* Explain how removing an outlier changes the appearance of the box-and-whisker plot. What conclusion can you make from the plot in part (c) that you would not make from the plot in part (a)?

The Ballpark at Arlington, Texas

12. Clothing Prices The table lists the prices of a set of comparable items of women's and men's clothing in 9 different cities.

a. Make box-and-whisker plots for the women's and men's data.

b. How do the prices in Houston compare with the rest of the cities for both women's and men's clothing? Explain your reasoning.

c. **Interpret** Would you say women's clothing prices or men's clothing prices vary more in the cities in the survey? Explain your reasoning.

City	Women's	Men's
New York	$690	$1190
Los Angeles	$450	$620
Chicago	$590	$1100
Houston	$440	$900
Paris	$430	$700
London	$350	$660
Toronto	$310	$850
Tokyo	$760	$1050
Mexico City	$380	$620

13. Challenge Write a set of data values for which the extremes, quartiles, and median are all equally spaced. Explain how you chose the values.

Mixed Review

Graph the inequality in a coordinate plane. *(Lesson 8.9)*

14. $y < -2x + 3$ **15.** $y > 3x - 5$ **16.** $y > 0.5x + 1.5$

Find the surface area of the prism, cylinder, or pyramid. Round to the nearest whole number. *(Lessons 10.5, 10.6)*

17.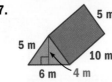

18.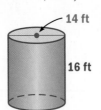

19.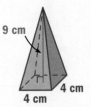

20. Make a stem-and-leaf plot of the following data: 8, 11, 23, 24, 13, 35, 14, 11, 16, 17, 18, 9, 16, 17, 15, 21, 25, 20, 21, 37, 22. *(Lesson 11.1)*

Standardized Test Practice

In Exercises 21–23, use the box-and-whisker plot below.

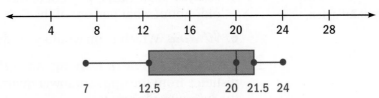

21. Multiple Choice What is the interquartile range of the data in the box-and-whisker plot?

A. 9   **B.** 12.5   **C.** 20   **D.** 21.5

22. Multiple Choice About what percent of data values are less than 21?

F. 12.5%   **G.** 25%   **H.** 50%   **I.** 75%

23. Short Response The data set consisted of 12 whole numbers. How many of the numbers are less than 12.5? Explain.

11.2 Making a Box-and-Whisker Plot

Goal Use a graphing calculator to make a box-and-whisker plot.

Use a graphing calculator to make a box-and-whisker plot of the following data.

In the 2002–2003 season, the roster for the NBA's Boston Celtics listed 13 players, and the roster for the Houston Rockets listed 14 players. The heights (in inches) of the players are given below.

Celtics: 83, 84, 74, 79, 81, 74, 81, 82, 78, 86, 81, 80, 74

Rockets: 74, 83, 84, 75, 82, 79, 76, 75, 89, 81, 81, 80, 80, 81

1 Press **LIST**. Enter the data into two lists, L1 and L2.

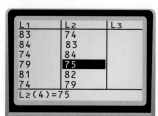

2 Press **2nd** [**PLOT**]. Select Plot1 and choose the box-and-whisker plot from the menu. Set the value for Xlist to L1.

3 Press **2nd** [**PLOT**]. Select Plot2 and choose the box-and-whisker plot from the menu. Set the value for Xlist to L2.

4 To graph the plots, press **ZOOM** **7**. Press **TRACE** and the left and right arrow keys to examine the plots.

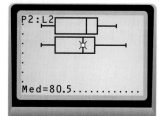

Tech *Help*

You do not need to set the values on the WINDOW screen. **ZOOM** **7** will set these automatically.

Online Resources
CLASSZONE.COM

• Keystroke Help

Draw Conclusions

1. Use a graphing calculator to make a box-and-whisker plot of the following data: 8, 11, 12, 7, 11, 14, 13, 4, 11, 9, 9, 17.

2. **Analyze** Compare the median heights of the two teams in the example above. Also compare the ranges of the heights of the two teams. What conclusions can you make?

Making Data Displays

Making a Bar Graph

In a **bar graph**, the lengths of the bars are used to represent and compare data. The bars can be vertical or horizontal. To make a bar graph, first choose a scale. Then draw and label the graph.

Example **Make a bar graph of the data in the table.**

Households with Computers in 2001	
State	**Percent**
Alaska	68.7%
Texas	67.7%
Georgia	63.1%
Florida	52.4%

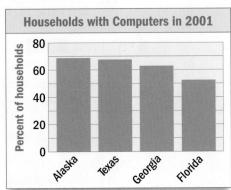

Making a Line Graph

In a **line graph**, points that represent data values are connected using segments. Line graphs often show a change in data over time. To make a line graph, first choose scales for the horizontal and vertical axes. Then plot the data and connect consecutive points with segments. Label the graph.

Example **Make a line graph of the data in the table.**

Public Schools with Internet Access	
Year	**Percent**
1996	65%
1997	78%
1998	89%
1999	95%
2000	98%
2001	99%

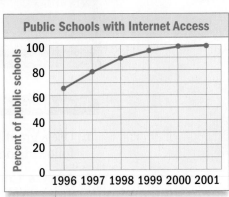

Making a Circle Graph

A **circle graph** displays data as sections of a circle. The entire circle represents all the data. To make a circle graph, first find the angle measure for each section by finding the product of the percent for that section and 360°, the number of degrees in a circle. Then use a compass to draw a circle. Finally, use a protractor to measure and draw an angle for each section.

Example **Make a circle graph of the data in the table.**

Percent of Internet Users by Age	
Age	**Percent**
18–34	39%
35–54	47%
55 and over	14%

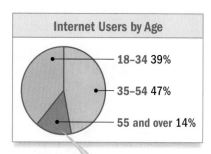

Internet Users by Age

18–34 39%

35–54 47%

55 and over 14%

The angle measure for this section is $0.14 \times 360° \approx 50°$.

The angle for this section measures 50°.

✓ Checkpoint

▶ **Test** your knowledge of bar graphs, line graphs, and circle graphs by solving these problems.

1. Make a bar graph showing the percent of people surveyed who enjoy each kind of entertainment.

Activities People Choose for Entertainment			
Activity	Movies	Sporting events	Amusement park
Percent	66%	41%	57%

2. Make a line graph showing the percent of single women who worked in the U.S. from 1970 to 2000.

U.S. Single Women Who Work				
Year	1970	1980	1990	2000
Percent	53%	62%	66%	69%

3. Make a circle graph showing the percent of U.S. curbside recycling programs in 2000 that existed in each region.

U.S. Curbside Recycling Programs by Region in 2000				
Region	Northeast	South	Midwest	West
Percent	37.41%	15.43%	38.74%	8.42%

4. Explain why you cannot use a circle graph to display the data in Exercise 1.

11.3

Using Data Displays

BEFORE	*Now*	WHY?
You interpreted data displays.	You'll choose appropriate displays for data sets.	So you can interpret data about winter sports, as in Ex. 16.

Vocabulary
categorical data,
 p. 596
numerical data, p. 596

Data that consist of names, labels, or other nonnumerical values, such as types of animals or colors of hair, are **categorical data**. Data that consist of numbers, such as weights of animals or lengths of hair, are **numerical data**. When you choose a data display, one factor you should consider is whether the data are categorical or numerical.

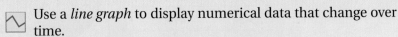

SUMMARY Choosing Appropriate Data Displays

Use a *line graph* to display numerical data that change over time.

Use a *scatter plot* to see trends in paired numerical data.

Use a *bar graph* to compare categorical data.

Use a *circle graph* to represent categorical data as parts of a whole.

Use a *stem-and-leaf plot* to organize numerical data based on their digits.

Use a *histogram* to compare the frequencies of numerical data that fall in equal intervals.

Use a *box-and-whisker plot* to organize numerical data into four groups of approximately equal size.

Note *Worthy*

You may want to include an example of each type of data display in your notes.

Example 1   *Choosing an Appropriate Data Display*

The table shows the results of a survey that asked students to name their favorite type of movie. Which display(s) can you use to display the data?

Solution

The responses to the survey consist of movie types, which are categorical data. Notice that the sum of the percents is 100%. So, the best choice is to use a circle graph. A bar graph could also be used.

Favorite Type of Movie	
Type	**Percent**
Drama	17%
Comedy	44%
Action	28%
Sci-Fi	9%
Other	2%

Example 2 — Comparing Data Displays

Test Scores A teacher uses a histogram and a box-and-whisker plot to display the test scores of the students in a math class. What are the advantages of each display?

a.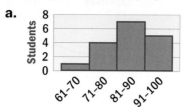

b.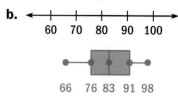

Solution

a. Using the histogram, the teacher can quickly compare the number of students in each of the intervals. For example, the teacher can see that 7 students scored from 81 to 90, while only 4 students scored from 71 to 80.

b. Using the box-and-whisker plot, the teacher can easily divide the scores into low, low-middle, high-middle, and high groups of approximately equal size. For example, the teacher can conclude that about 25% of the class scored 91 or better, and that about 50% of the class scored from 76 to 91.

✔ Checkpoint

1. In Example 2, the teacher wants to display the test scores so that the display shows all the individual scores. What type of display should the teacher use?

Review *Help*

For help with reading line graphs, see p. 782.

Misleading Data Displays The way a data display is drawn can lead people to make incorrect conclusions. Three examples of potentially misleading data displays are shown below.

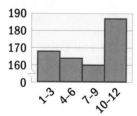

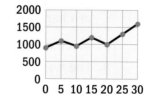

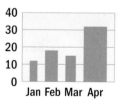

Broken Vertical Axis

The broken vertical axis exaggerates the differences in the bar lengths.

Large Increments

The large increments on the vertical axis minimize the changes in the data.

Different Widths

The different bar widths suggest a comparison of areas, not lengths.

✔ Checkpoint

2. The rightmost bar of the histogram above appears to be twice as long as any of the other bars. Is the frequency of the 10–12 interval twice as great as the frequency of any other interval? Explain.

Example 3 | *Identifying Misleading Data Displays*

Business The line graphs display a company's expenses and profits for each year from 2000 to 2003. What is misleading about each display?

a.

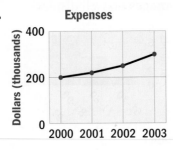

Expenses

b.

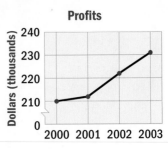

Profits

Solution

a. The increments on the vertical axis are too large. It appears that the company's expenses have increased only slightly from 2000 to 2003, when they have actually increased by 50%.

b. The vertical axis is broken. It appears that profits have risen dramatically from 2000 to 2003, when they have risen only 10%.

11.3 Exercises

More Practice, p. 813

INTERNET
eWorkbook Plus
CLASSZONE.COM

Guided Practice

Vocabulary Check

1. Name two data displays that can be used with categorical data.

2. How could it be potentially misleading to use bars with different widths in a bar graph?

Skill Check

Tell which data display(s) you could use to display the data. Explain why.

3. The responses to a survey question with a choice of yes, no, or maybe

4. The heights (in meters) of different palm trees

Guided Problem Solving

5. Bikes The bar graph shows the number of bikes shipped in the U.S. over four years. Is the graph potentially misleading?

1) Compare the lengths of the bars for 1997 and 2000. About how many times longer is the bar for 2000 than the bar for 1997?

2) How many times more bikes were shipped in 2000 than 1997?

3) Do you think the bar graph is misleading? Explain.

Practice and Problem Solving

Homework *Help*

Example	Exercises
1	6-12
2	13, 15
3	14, 16, 17

Online Resources
CLASSZONE.COM
• More Examples
• eTutorial Plus

In Exercises 6–8, tell whether the data are *numerical* or *categorical*. Then tell which data display(s) you would use to display the data. Explain your reasoning.

6. **Bald Eagles** A study was done to find the wingspans (in centimeters) of captured bald eagles.

7. **Hockey** A coach recorded the number of goals scored by each member of a hockey team.

8. **Energy** A study determined the amount of energy that was produced by different means, such as electric, solar, wind, and natural gas.

In Exercises 9–12, tell which data display(s) allow you to identify the specified information.

9. The median of the data set

10. The greatest value of the data set

11. The mode of the data set

12. The frequency of an interval

13. **Critical Thinking** What information can you get from a box-and-whisker plot that you cannot get from a histogram? What information can you get from a histogram that you cannot get from a box-and-whisker plot? Explain.

14. **Exercising** Twenty people were asked to state the number of hours per week that they exercise. The frequency table shows the results.

   a. Is the frequency table misleading? Explain.

   b. **Interpret** What conclusions can you make from the frequency table?

Exercise Per Week (hours)		
Interval	Tally	Frequency
0–2 hours	II	2
2–4 hours	IIII	5
4–8 hours	IIII I	6
8–16 hours	IIII II	7

15. **Club** A club president records the ages of the members in a club and wants to group the data in intervals of 2 years. Should the president use a stem-and-leaf plot or a histogram? Explain.

16. **Extended Problem Solving** The table shows the number of visitors (in millions) to ski areas in the United States in 10 different years.

   a. **Interpret** Make a line graph using every 5th year, starting with 1980. What trend does the graph show?

   b. **Interpret** Make a new line graph using all the years given in the table. What trend does it show?

   c. **Critical Thinking** Which line graph represents the data more accurately, the one in part (a) or the one in part (b)? Explain.

U.S. Skier/Snowboarder Visits			
Year	Visitors	Year	Visitors
1978	50.2	1990	46.7
1980	39.7	1993	54.6
1983	50.6	1995	54.0
1985	51.9	1998	52.1
1988	53.3	2000	57.3

In the **Real World**

Winter Sports In 1978, the Rocky Mountains had 15.8 million skiers and snowboarders. In 2000, the Rocky Mountains had 19.3 million skiers and snowboarders. Did the Rocky Mountains or the entire U.S. have a greater percent of increase in the number of skiers and snowboarders from 1978 to 2000?

17. Critical Thinking The circle graph shows the results of a survey that asked students what their favorite beach activity is. In what way is this graph misleading? Explain.

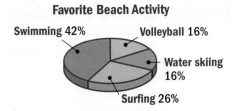

Favorite Beach Activity

Swimming 42%
Volleyball 16%
Water skiing 16%
Surfing 26%

18. Challenge Find and copy a data display from a newspaper or magazine.

    a. Are the data in the display numerical or categorical?

    b. *Writing* Do you think the display is potentially misleading? Explain.

Mixed Review

Find the sum or difference. *(Lessons 5.2, 5.3)*

19. $\frac{3}{7} + \left(-\frac{2}{7}\right)$ **20.** $-\frac{7}{18} - \frac{5}{18}$ **21.** $\frac{4}{5} - \frac{7}{15}$ **22.** $-\frac{3}{4} + \frac{1}{12}$

23. Geometry A trapezoid has an area of 140 square centimeters and bases of 15 centimeters and 20 centimeters. What is the height of the trapezoid? *(Lesson 10.3)*

24. Make a box-and-whisker plot of the following data: 255, 287, 299, 224, 200, 360, 231, 388, 318, 364, 381. *(Lesson 11.2)*

Standardized Test Practice

25. Multiple Choice Which would be an appropriate display for the data?

    A. Line graph   **B.** Circle graph

    C. Scatter plot   **D.** Histogram

Candidate	Percent of vote
A	43%
B	28%
C	29%

26. Short Response A meteorologist has measured the amount of precipitation each month in a certain area. The meteorologist wants to use a data display that shows patterns in monthly precipitation changes. What type of display should the meteorologist use? Explain.

Brain GAME

Double Data

Two of the displays shown represent the same data. Which one doesn't?

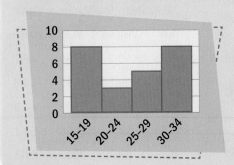

1 | 5 5 5 7 7 8
2 | 0 2 2 3 5 6 6 8 9
3 | 0 0 1 1 2 2 3 3 4

Key: 1 | 5 = 15

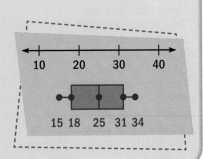

11.4

Collecting Data

Vocabulary

population, p. 601
sample, p. 601
samples: random, systematic, stratified, convenience, self-selected, p. 601
biased sample, p. 602
biased question, p. 603

One way to collect data about a group is to conduct a survey. The entire group that you want information about is called a **population**. It is usually difficult to survey every member of a population. Instead, you can survey a **sample**, which is a part of the population. Five sampling methods are described below.

Sampling Methods

In a **random sample**, every member of the population has an equal chance of being selected.

In a **systematic sample**, a rule is used to select members of the population.

In a **stratified sample**, the population is divided into distinct groups. Members are selected from each group.

In a **convenience sample**, only members of the population who are easily accessible are selected.

In a **self-selected sample**, members of the population can select themselves by volunteering.

Example 1   Identifying Populations and Sampling Methods

For each survey, describe the population and the sampling method.

a. A school newspaper reporter asks every fifth student entering a school building whether a new gymnasium should be built.

b. A manager at a television station randomly telephones 75 residents under 30 years old and 75 residents 30 years old and over to determine the station's most watched programs.

Solution

a. The population consists of all the students at the school. Because the reporter uses the rule "interview every fifth person," the sample is a systematic sample.

b. The population consists of the television station's entire viewing audience. Because the manager divides the population into two groups and chooses members from each group, the sample is a stratified sample.

Samples When conducting a survey, you want a sample that is *representative* of the population. A sample that is not representative is a **biased sample** .

The sampling method can affect how representative a sample is. The most reliable way to have a representative sample is to use random sampling. However, non-random sampling is often used because it usually takes less time, money, and effort to perform.

Example 2 — *Identifying Potentially Biased Samples*

Government A city council wants residents to help choose a new building project. Residents can choose one of the three ideas listed at the right.

Because the council cannot survey every resident, it decides to survey a sample. Tell whether the survey method could result in a biased sample. Explain.

a. Survey the city council members and their families.

b. Survey parents at the city's recreation center.

c. Survey shoppers at the local mall.

Which project should the city undertake this year?

☐ Build a new library.

☐ Build a new city hall.

☐ Build a new park.

Solution

a. This method could result in a biased sample because the city council members and their families have an interest in city government. They may favor building a new city hall.

b. This method could result in a biased sample because the parents at the recreation center have an interest in recreation. They may favor building a new park.

c. This method is less likely to result in a biased sample because a wide range of people will be surveyed. This method is not a true random sample because people who are not at the mall have no chance of being selected. As a result, the sample may be biased.

✔ *Checkpoint*

1. The manager of an apartment building wants to know if noise is a problem in the building. The manager asks one person on each floor if the person thinks noise is a problem.

   a. Describe the survey's population and sampling method.

   b. Do you think the survey could result in a biased sample? Explain.

   c. Describe another sampling method the manager could use. Could this method result in a biased sample? Explain.

Biased Questions Questions that encourage particular responses are **biased questions** . When creating a survey, you should phrase questions to avoid bias.

Example 3 *Identifying Potentially Biased Questions*

Tell whether the question is potentially biased. Explain your answer. If the question is biased, rewrite it so that it is not.

a. Don't you agree that planting more shade trees will make our beautiful downtown area even better?

b. Are you willing to pay higher taxes so that the city can build a new stadium, even though we already have a stadium?

Solution

a. This question is biased because it suggests that planting shade trees is a good thing to do. An unbiased question is "Are you in favor of the plan to plant new shade trees in the downtown area?"

b. This question is biased because it suggests that another stadium is not necessary and will be expensive. An unbiased question is "Do you support the plan to build a new stadium?"

11.4 Exercises

More Practice, p. 813

Guided Practice

Vocabulary Check

1. Copy and complete: A sample in which every member of the population has an equal chance of being selected is a(n) ? .

2. Give an example of a non-random sampling method.

Skill Check

3. You ask the first 30 people coming out of a movie theater what type of movie they prefer. Is your sample likely to represent the population of all moviegoers? Explain.

Guided Problem Solving

4. Camping A survey was conducted to find the percent of Americans who enjoy camping. The surveyor randomly selected 20 individuals from each of the 50 states and asked, "Do you enjoy, greatly enjoy, or not enjoy camping in the woods, where the air is fresh and clean?" How much should you trust the results of this survey?

1) Identify the sampling method and population.

2) Do you think the sample chosen was representative of the population? Explain.

3) Do you think the question is biased? If so, explain how it would affect the results of the survey.

Practice and Problem Solving

Homework *Help*

Example	Exercises
1	5–11
2	9–11
3	12–14

Online Resources
CLASSZONE.COM
- More Examples
- eTutorial Plus

A school newspaper is conducting a survey to predict who will win the next school election. Tell whether the sampling method is *random*, *systematic*, *stratified*, *convenience*, or *self-selected*.

5. Set up a booth where students can come to give their opinions.

6. Get the ID numbers of every student in the school and have a computer randomly choose which students will be surveyed.

7. Interview every third student as students leave the school.

8. Interview 20 students from each grade.

In Exercises 9 and 10, describe the population and tell what type of sampling method is used. Then tell whether the sample is likely to represent the population. Explain your answer.

9. A writer for a magazine wants to determine the most popular flavor of ice cream among residents in a town. The writer asks each customer at several local ice cream shops what their favorite flavor of ice cream is.

10. A researcher wants to know the opinions that people in a state have about filling out surveys. The researcher asks the first 30 people who volunteer to take a survey, "Do you think surveys are a useful tool for gathering information?"

11. **Museum** The director of a museum wants to know which exhibits museum visitors enjoy the most. The director places the questionnaire shown near the exit for people to fill out as they leave the museum.

   a. Describe the population and the sampling method.

   b. **Critical Thinking** Is the questionnaire likely to represent the population? Explain why or why not.

Which exhibits did you see today?

Which exhibit was your favorite?

Which exhibit was your least favorite?

In Exercises 12–14, tell whether the question is potentially biased. Explain your answer. If the question is biased, rewrite it so that it is not.

12. Do you still support the school football team, even though the team is having its worst season in 10 years?

13. How many times per week do you eat cereal?

14. Don't you think that cats are better pets than dogs?

15. **Snapping Turtles** Two scientists are attempting to gather data in order to find the average weight of snapping turtles. The first scientist weighs all of the snapping turtles that live in a certain pond. The second scientist weighs a number of snapping turtles from several ponds. Which sample do you think will give a more accurate estimate of the average weight of snapping turtles? Explain.

16. Photography Club You want to find out if the students in your school would be interested in joining a new photography club.

   a. *Writing* Describe a method for choosing a representative sample of the student population.

   b. Write an unbiased question that you could ask to find out if students are interested in joining the club.

17. Pine Trees Scientists conducted a study to determine the average height of pine trees in a large forest. They did so by measuring 200 trees from the forest. Tell whether the following statements, if true, would lower your confidence in the results of the study. Explain your answers.

   a. The scientists chose the trees in their sample randomly.

   b. The scientists selected trees only from the western portion of the forest.

   c. Some of the trees measured in the study were much taller than others.

   d. The scientists measured only a small fraction of the total number of pine trees in the forest they studied.

18. Challenge Find the results of a survey in a newspaper or magazine. Identify the population and the sampling method used and tell whether any of the questions asked are likely to be biased. How much confidence do you have in the results of the survey? Explain.

Mixed Review

Solve the equation. Check your solution. *(Lesson 3.3)*

19. $5x - 12 = 2x + 6$ **20.** $10 - 3x = -x - 8$ **21.** $4x + 7 = 6 - 3(x + 1)$

A map has a scale of 1 centimeter : 25 kilometers. Use the given map distance to find the actual distance. *(Lesson 6.6)*

22. 11 cm   **23.** 6 cm   **24.** 5 mm

25. Find the value of x to the nearest tenth.
(Lesson 9.8)

Standardized Test Practice

26. Multiple Choice Which question is *not* biased?

   A. Don't you think that renovating the old town hall would be a mistake?

   B. Do you support the governor's proposal to reduce state taxes?

   C. Are you willing to deal with heavy increases in traffic where you live just so another mall can be built?

   D. Do you think we should elect a new mayor in the next election, or re-elect the leader who has served this town for so many years?

27. Short Response You ask 10 students in your math class a survey question. Which population is better represented by the responses you get, the 30 students in your math class or the 1000 students in your school? Explain.

11.4 Searching for Data

Goal Use an Internet search engine to find data. Use a spreadsheet to make data displays.

Example 1

Use an Internet search engine to find the record of wins, losses, ties, and overtime losses of a National Hockey League (NHL) team.

1 Choose a search engine. Type keywords that cover the topic you would like to search. Then select Search.

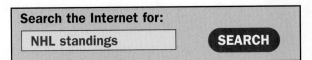

Search the Internet for:

NHL standings   **SEARCH**

Tech *Help*

When searching for data on the Internet, if the first keywords you try do not give you the results you want, try other keywords.

Online Resources
CLASSZONE.COM

• Keystroke Help

2 Of the results the search engine finds, choose a website that is likely to have the information you need.

3 Select a team. Enter the data in the first two columns of a spreadsheet, as shown for the Philadelphia Flyers' 2001–2002 record.

	A	B
1	Result of game	Number
2	Win	42
3	Loss	27
4	Tie	10
5	Overtime loss	3

Draw Conclusions

Use the Internet and spreadsheet software to complete the following exercises.

1. Search the Internet for the record of wins, losses, ties, and overtime losses for two NHL teams. Enter the data into a spreadsheet.

2. **Analyze** Compare the records of the two teams. Which team has the better record? Explain.

3. **Compare** Find the records of wins, losses, and ties for two Major League Soccer (MLS) teams. Use the phrase "MLS standings" to search for the data. Then enter the data into a spreadsheet. Use the spreadsheet to compare the team records.

Example 2

Use a spreadsheet to display the data from Example 1.

Each cell on a spreadsheet is labeled using a letter to indicate the column and a number to indicate the row. Highlight the data in cells A2:B5. The expression A2:B5 refers to the rectangular array of cells with A2 and B5 at the corners.

Tech *Help*

The spreadsheet sets the scale for the bar graph automatically.

Online Resources
CLASSZONE.COM
• Keystroke Help

1 Use the *insert* menu to insert a graph. Select a vertical bar graph, or column chart, as the type of graph. Then choose options for your graph, such as a title and labels for the horizontal and vertical axes.

2 To change other features of your graph after it has been created, double click on the part of the graph that you wish to change and adjust the formatting.

3 To obtain a different data display, such as a circle graph, repeat Steps 1 and 2, but this time select a circle graph.

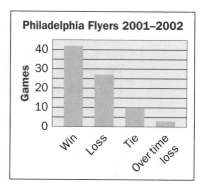

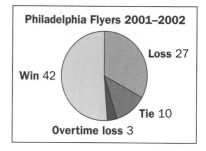

Draw Conclusions

Use spreadsheet software to complete the following exercises.

4. Use the data from Exercise 1 on page 606 to make a bar graph and a circle graph for each team.

5. **Analyze** Use the circle graphs from Exercise 4 to compare the records of the two teams. Which team has a greater percent of games won?

6. **Compare** Use the data from Exercise 3 on page 606 to make a circle graph and a bar graph for each team. Which team has the better record? Explain.

11.5 Investigating Random Samples

Goal
Determine how well a random sample represents a population.

Materials
- 50 slips of paper
- container
- pencil

Investigate

Use slips of paper to see how well a random sample represents the population from which it was taken.

1 The results of an election in which 50 people voted are given in the table. Use slips of paper to represent the votes cast in the election. Write A on 25 slips of paper, B on 15 slips, and C on 10 slips. Put the slips in a container.

Candidate	Number of votes	Percent of population's votes
A	25	50%
B	15	30%
C	10	20%
Total	50	100%

2 To see how well a sample represents the population of voters in an election, randomly select 10 slips of paper from the container. Copy and complete the table at the right using your sample.

Candidate	Number of votes	Percent of sample's votes
A	?	?
B	?	?
C	?	?
Total	10	100%

3 Replace the 10 slips of paper and repeat Step 2 three more times. Make a new table for each new sample.

Draw Conclusions

1. **Compare** For each sample, compare each candidate's percent of the sample's votes with the candidate's percent of the population's votes. Are the values the same for any candidate? How well does each sample represent the population? Explain your thinking.

2. **Critical Thinking** Find the mean of the results for each candidate from the random samples drawn by the entire class. How well do the means of these samples represent the population?

LESSON 11.5

Interpreting Data

Vocabulary

margin of error, p. 610

Television Television networks rely on surveys to determine how many people watch their programs. In a survey of 5000 randomly selected American households, 780 of the households watched a certain program. Of all American households, how many watched the program?

You can use a sample to make a prediction about a population. If $p\%$ of a sample gives a particular response and the sample is representative of the population, then:

$$\text{Predicted number of people in population giving the response} = p\% \cdot \text{Number of people in population}$$

Example 1   *Making a Population Prediction*

There are about 105 million households in the United States. To estimate the number of households that watched the program described above, follow these steps:

1) Find the percent of households in the sample that watched the program.

$$\frac{780}{5000} = 0.156 = 15.6\%$$

2) Find 15.6% of the total number of households in the United States.

$$15.6\% \cdot 105 \text{ million households} \approx 16.4 \text{ million households}$$

Answer About 16.4 million households in the United States watched the program.

✔ *Checkpoint*

1. In a survey of 5000 randomly selected American households, 460 households watched a certain program. Of all American households, about how many watched the program?

Watch *Out*

A margin of error accounts only for errors due to the nature of random sampling. It does not account for errors that result from biased questions or biased sampling.

Margin of Error When a survey samples only a portion of a population, different surveys of the same population may have different results. For example, one survey might find that 32% of the population uses a cell phone. Another might find that 36% does. The actual percent might be 33%.

Due to such variation, a survey should include a *margin of error*. The **margin of error** of a random sample defines an interval centered on the sample percent in which the population percent is most likely to lie. For example, a sample percent of 32% with a margin of error of ±5% means that the population percent is most likely between 27% and 37%.

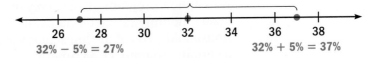

The population percent most likely lies between 27% and 37%.

$32\% - 5\% = 27\%$ $32\% + 5\% = 37\%$

Example 2   *Interpreting a Margin of Error*

Election A survey of a random sample of voters predicts that candidate A will receive 52% of the votes and that candidate B will receive 48% of the votes. The margin of error is ±3%. Can you predict who will win the election?

Solution

Use the margin of error to find intervals in which each candidate's actual percent is most likely to lie.

Candidate A: $52\% - 3\% = 49\%$ $52\% + 3\% = 55\%$

Candidate B: $48\% - 3\% = 45\%$ $48\% + 3\% = 51\%$

Using the margin of error, you can conclude that candidate A is likely to receive between 49% and 55% of the votes. Candidate B is likely to receive between 45% and 51% of the votes.

Answer Because the intervals overlap for the two candidates, you cannot predict which candidate will win the election.

SUMMARY   **Summary of Data Analysis**

When reading the results of a survey, consider the following.

- Identify the population and the sampling method.
- Determine whether the sample represents the population.
- Determine whether the survey questions are biased.
- Identify the margin of error.
- Determine whether any data displays are potentially misleading.
- Decide if the conclusions are supported by the data.

Example 3 | *Interpreting a Newspaper Survey*

Tell what conclusions you can make from the following newspaper article.

Sample is not truly random. Not everyone participates in phone surveys.

Snakes Are Americans' Number One Fear!

Recently, researchers surveyed about 1000 Americans by telephone and asked them if they were "very afraid," "somewhat afraid," or "not afraid" of a number of things. From the results shown below, only one conclusion is possible: Americans fear snakes more than anything else!

Question is not biased, but respondents may have different interpretations of what "very afraid" means.

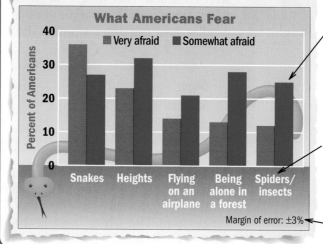

What Americans Fear

Percent of Americans

■ Very afraid ■ Somewhat afraid

Snakes | Heights | Flying on an airplane | Being alone in a forest | Spiders/ insects

Margin of error: ±3%

Bar graph doesn't appear misleading. There is no break in the frequency axis, and all the bars have the same width.

List of fearful things is limited. Something not on this list might be the number one fear.

Margin of error is given.

11.5 Exercises

More Practice, p. 813

Guided Practice

Vocabulary Check

1. Explain what is meant by a margin of error for a survey.

2. List several things to check when you read the results of a survey.

Skill Check

3. **Dog Food** A survey of 200 randomly selected dog owners finds that 130 dog owners prefer brand A dog food. Predict how many owners in a town of 1500 dog owners prefer brand A dog food.

Guided Problem Solving

4. **Polls** A newspaper surveys a random sample of 200 voters with a margin of error of ±7%. Of these voters, 88 plan to vote for candidate A, and 112 plan to vote for candidate B. Can you predict the winner?

   1 Find the percent of voters who plan to vote for each candidate.

   2 Find the interval in which the percent of votes for each candidate is most likely to lie.

   3 Does the survey tell you who will win the election? Explain.

Practice and Problem Solving

Homework *Help*

Example	Exercises
1	5, 6, 8, 12
2	7, 13
3	9

Online Resources
CLASSZONE.COM
- More Examples
- eTutorial Plus

5. **DVD Player** A survey finds that 35 families in a random sample of 200 families in a town own a DVD player. The town has 6000 families. Predict how many families in the town own a DVD player.

6. **Favorite Subject** You interview a random sample of 100 students in a school. Thirty students say that math is their favorite subject. There are 1200 students in the school. Predict how many students in the school would say that math is their favorite subject.

7. **Election** Four surveys based on random samples of registered voters were conducted before a local election. The results are shown in the table, along with the margin of error for each survey. For each election, predict a winner or tell whether the election is too close to call.

Position	Leading candidate	Trailing candidate	Margin of error
Mayor	56%	44%	±3.5%
Treasurer	53%	47%	±4%
Sheriff	55%	45%	±4%
Controller	54%	46%	±6%

8. **Petition** A school's student council has said that it would change the school's colors if 600 students sign a petition. You interview a random sample of 50 students. You find that 37 students say they would sign the petition. The school has 900 students. Do you think enough students will sign the petition? Justify your reasoning.

9. **Pet Survey** Review the newspaper article below, which summarizes the results of a survey. How much trust do you have in the survey? Do you think the conclusions in the article are valid? Explain.

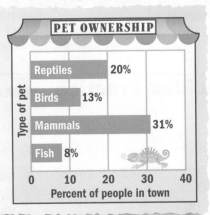

Reptiles and Birds Becoming Common Pets!

A recent survey of 200 people at the local mall found that more people in town own reptiles or birds than own traditional mammals, such as cats and dogs. The survey was conducted by Reba's Reptiles, a store in the local mall that sells unusual pets.

PET OWNERSHIP

Type of pet:
- Reptiles: 20%
- Birds: 13%
- Mammals: 31%
- Fish: 8%

Percent of people in town

10. **Critical Thinking** A survey claims that a population percent is very likely to be between 35% and 45%. What is the margin of error for the survey? What percent did the survey obtain from its sample?

11. **Critical Thinking** Suppose there are 20 students in your math class. Four of the students have the flu. Can you use this information to predict how many people in your town have the flu? Explain why or why not.

12. **Extended Problem Solving** A nationwide survey of a random sample of teenagers asked whether or not they play the saxophone.

   a. **Predict** The survey concluded that 4% of teenagers play the saxophone. Use this information to predict how many students in a school with 1000 teenage students play the saxophone.

   b. **Predict** Suppose 2 of the 29 people in a math class play the saxophone. Use this information to predict how many of the 1000 students in the school play the saxophone.

   c. *Writing* Do you think the prediction from part (a) or the prediction from part (b) is more accurate? Explain your answer.

13. **Part-time Jobs** A school has 1200 students. A survey of a random sample of 250 students found that 65 students have part-time jobs. The survey has a margin of error of ±6%. Find the interval in which the total number of students who have part-time jobs is likely to lie.

14. **Hair Color** A town has 5000 residents. A survey finds that 81 residents out of a random sample of 625 residents have red hair. The margin of error for the survey is ±4%. Find the interval in which the total number of residents with red hair is most likely to lie.

15. **Challenge** When a random sample of size n is taken from a large population, the sample has a margin of error of about $\pm \frac{100}{\sqrt{n}}$%.

   a. How many people need to be surveyed for a sample to have a margin of error of about ±3%? Round to the nearest whole number.

   b. To have a margin of error of ±2%, should you increase or decrease the sample size in part (a)? Explain.

Mixed Review

Simplify. *(Lesson 4.5)*

16. $\frac{2x^2 \cdot 34x}{17x}$ 17. $\frac{3m^4 \cdot 16m^2}{6m^2}$ 18. $\frac{5a \cdot 2a}{a^2}$ 19. $\frac{15c \cdot 4c}{6c^2}$

Solve the proportion. *(Lesson 6.3)*

20. $\frac{12}{x} = \frac{4}{10}$ 21. $\frac{400}{525} = \frac{90}{y}$ 22. $\frac{16}{z} = \frac{20}{30}$ 23. $\frac{15}{24} = \frac{10}{w}$

24. **Survey** A researcher interviews 75 men and 75 women in a town. Describe the sampling method used by the researcher. *(Lesson 11.4)*

Standardized Test Practice

25. **Multiple Choice** A survey with a margin of error of ±2% finds that history is the favorite subject of 39% of a random sample of students. In which interval is the population percent most likely to lie?

   A. Between 36% and 42%   **B.** Between 37% and 41%

   C. Between 37% and 39%   **D.** Between 39% and 41%

26. **Multiple Choice** A school has 800 students. A survey of a random sample of 80 students finds that 48 students enjoy swimming. Predict the total number of students in the school who enjoy swimming.

   F. 48   **G.** 384   **H.** 480   **I.** 3840

1. **Temperature** Make a frequency table and a histogram of the following low temperatures (in degrees Fahrenheit) that were recorded over a 10 day period in Chicago, Illinois: 28, 14, 8, 26, 18, 15, 30, 31, 30, 28.

2. **CD Prices** Make a box-and-whisker plot of the following prices (in dollars) of CDs you bought: 9, 16, 17, 13, 14, 12, 9, 11, 14, 16, 13, 11.

In Exercises 3 and 4, tell whether the data are *numerical* or *categorical*. Then tell which data display(s) you would use to display the data. Explain your reasoning.

3. The number of games won by each team in a softball league

4. The ways people travel to school, such as car, bus, and walking

In Exercises 5 and 6, describe the population and tell what type of sampling method is used. Then tell whether the sampling method is likely to represent the population. Explain your answer.

5. A writer for the school newspaper wants to find out students' favorite lunch. She asks 20 students who work on the newspaper to name their favorite lunch.

6. The director at an amusement park wants to determine which rides visitors enjoy the most. The director asks every tenth person who leaves the park to list his or her three favorite rides.

7. **Cell Phones** A survey found that 35 families out of a random sample of 150 families in a town own at least one cell phone. The town has 7500 families. How many families would you predict own at least one cell phone?

Brain GAME **Musical Chairs**

In a survey about music, 30 people liked rock, 31 people liked hip-hop, and 32 people liked pop. Of the people who liked rock, 6 also liked hip-hop, and 10 also liked pop. Of the people who liked pop, 12 also liked hip-hop. Five people liked all three types of music, and 5 people didn't like any of the three.

How many people were surveyed?

11.6

Permutations

BEFORE	*Now*	WHY?
You used the counting principle.	You'll use permutations to count possibilities.	So you can count possible TV lineups, as in Ex. 26.

Vocabulary

permutation, p. 615
n factorial, p. 615

A **permutation** is an arrangement of objects in which order is important. For example, the six permutations of the letters A, B, and C are shown.

ABC   ACB   BAC   BCA   CAB   CBA

You can use the counting principle to count permutations. Each time you choose a letter to make a permutation of the letters A, B, and C, the number of remaining letters that can be chosen decreases by 1.

$$\begin{array}{c} \text{Number of} \\ \text{permutations} \end{array} = \begin{array}{c} \text{Choices for} \\ \text{first letter} \end{array} \cdot \begin{array}{c} \text{Choices for} \\ \text{second letter} \end{array} \cdot \begin{array}{c} \text{Choices for} \\ \text{third letter} \end{array}$$

$$= 3 \cdot 2 \cdot 1$$

$$= 6$$

The expression $3 \cdot 2 \cdot 1$ can be written as 3!, which is read as "3 *factorial*." For any positive integer n, the product of the integers from 1 to n is called ***n* factorial** and is written $n!$

$$n! = n \cdot (n - 1) \cdot (n - 2) \cdot \ldots \cdot 1$$

The value of 0! is defined to be 1.

Note *Worthy*

You can make a word triangle, like the one on page 580, to take notes about factorials.

Example 1   *Counting Permutations*

Posters You have four posters to hang in your room. You want to put one poster on each wall. How many ways can you arrange the posters?

Solution

You have 4 choices for the first wall, 3 for the second wall, 2 for the third wall, and 1 for the fourth wall. So, the number of ways you can arrange the posters is 4!.

$$4! = 4 \cdot 3 \cdot 2 \cdot 1 = 24$$

Answer There are 24 ways you can arrange the posters.

 **Checkpoint**

Evaluate the factorial.

1. 2!   **2.** 5!   **3.** 6!   **4.** 7!

Suppose in Example 1 you had 7 posters and wanted to choose 1 poster for each wall. As in Example 1, you can use the counting principle to count the number of possible arrangements of the posters.

Number of permutations	=	Choices for first wall	·	Choices for second wall	·	Choices for third wall	·	Choices for fourth wall

$$= 7 \cdot 6 \cdot 5 \cdot 4$$

$$= 840$$

This situation is an example of finding the number of permutations of 7 objects taken 4 at a time. Notice that $7 \cdot 6 \cdot 5 \cdot 4$ can be written as $\dfrac{7 \cdot 6 \cdot 5 \cdot 4 \cdot 3 \cdot 2 \cdot 1}{3 \cdot 2 \cdot 1} = \dfrac{7!}{3!}$. This example suggests the following rule.

Reading *Algebra*

$_nP_r$ is read "permutations of n choose r."

Permutations

Algebra The number of permutations of n objects taken r at a time can be written as $_nP_r$, where $_nP_r = \dfrac{n!}{(n-r)!}$.

Numbers $_5P_3 = \dfrac{5!}{(5-3)!} = \dfrac{5!}{2!} = \dfrac{5 \cdot 4 \cdot 3 \cdot \overset{1}{\cancel{2}} \cdot 1}{\underset{1}{\cancel{2}} \cdot 1} = 60$

Example 2   Counting Permutations

Science Fair Judges at a science fair are awarding prizes to the first-, second-, and third-place finishers. The science fair has 10 contestants. How many different ways can the first-, second-, and third-place prizes be awarded?

Solution

To find the number of ways that prizes can be awarded, find $_{10}P_3$.

$$_{10}P_3 = \dfrac{10!}{(10-3)!} \qquad \text{Use permutations formula.}$$

$$= \dfrac{10!}{7!} \qquad \text{Subtract.}$$

$$= \dfrac{10 \cdot 9 \cdot 8 \cdot \overset{1}{\cancel{7}} \cdot \overset{1}{\cancel{6}} \cdot \overset{1}{\cancel{5}} \cdot \overset{1}{\cancel{4}} \cdot \overset{1}{\cancel{3}} \cdot \overset{1}{\cancel{2}} \cdot 1}{\underset{1}{\cancel{7}} \cdot \underset{1}{\cancel{6}} \cdot \underset{1}{\cancel{5}} \cdot \underset{1}{\cancel{4}} \cdot \underset{1}{\cancel{3}} \cdot \underset{1}{\cancel{2}} \cdot 1} \qquad \begin{array}{l}\text{Expand factorials.}\\ \text{Divide out common factors.}\end{array}$$

$$= 10 \cdot 9 \cdot 8 = 720 \qquad \text{Multiply.}$$

Answer There are 720 ways the prizes can be awarded.

 Checkpoint

Find the number of permutations.

5. $_6P_2$ **6.** $_8P_3$ **7.** $_5P_5$ **8.** $_{70}P_2$

Tech *Help*

To evaluate a factorial or use permutation notation with your calculator, press PRB and choose from the list of commands.

Using a Calculator You may want to use a calculator to find factorials and permutations that involve multiplying large numbers. Many calculators have commands that allow you to evaluate factorials and use the permutation notation $_nP_r$. The solutions to Examples 1 and 2 are shown.

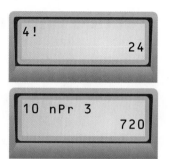

Example 3   *Finding a Probability Using Permutations*

Garage Door Your garage has a keypad that can be used to open the garage door. The code has five digits. You remember that the five digits are 1, 3, 5, 7, and 9, but you cannot remember the sequence. What is the probability that you open the garage on the first try?

Solution

Each possible code is a permutation of the digits 1, 3, 5, 7, and 9. The number of permutations of the five digits is 5!.

$$5! = 5 \cdot 4 \cdot 3 \cdot 2 \cdot 1 = 120$$

Only one of the possible permutations is correct, so the probability of opening the garage door on the first try is $\frac{1}{120}$.

11.6   Exercises

More Practice, p. 813

INTERNET
eWorkbook Plus
CLASSZONE.COM

Guided Practice

Vocabulary Check   **1.** Write and evaluate an expression for 6 factorial.

2. List all the permutations of the letters A, B, C, and D.

Skill Check   **Find the number of permutations.**

3. $_5P_3$ **4.** $_4P_1$ **5.** $_2P_2$ **6.** $_6P_0$

7. Books You have 6 books, but there is enough space on your bookshelf for only 4 of them. How many different arrangements of the books are possible on your bookshelf?

8. Lock The combination for a lock consists of the numbers 4, 22, and 8. You don't remember the order in which the three numbers are to be entered. Find the probability that you open the lock on the first try.

9. Error Analysis Describe and correct the error in finding the number of permutations of 4 objects taken 3 at a time.

$$\frac{4!}{3!} = 4$$

Practice and Problem Solving

Homework *Help*

Example	Exercises
1	10–17, 30
2	18–27, 29, 40
3	28, 31, 38

Online Resources
CLASSZONE.COM
• More Examples
• eTutorial Plus

Evaluate the factorial.

10. 3! **11.** 0! **12.** 1! **13.** 10!

14. 8! **15.** 11! **16.** 9! **17.** 12!

Find the number of permutations.

18. $_5P_4$ **19.** $_9P_1$ **20.** $_7P_2$ **21.** $_8P_5$

22. $_6P_6$ **23.** $_{11}P_0$ **24.** $_{25}P_2$ **25.** $_{18}P_6$

26. TV Lineups A TV network has 15 comedy shows that it plans to air. It wants to choose 4 of them for a special Monday night lineup. How many different possible lineups are there for Monday night?

27. Shirts You have 8 shirts and plan to wear a different one each day from Monday through Friday. How many possible arrangements of shirts are possible for those 5 days?

28. Password Sonia created a password for her computer by rearranging the letters of her name. You know how she created the password, but you do not know what the password is. What is the probability that you will guess the password on the first try?

29. **Restaurant** A restaurant has 12 identical tables. One evening, the restaurant accepts reservations for 6 of the tables. How many choices does the restaurant have for seating the 6 groups?

30. Hawaii You are visiting Hawaii and plan to stay for 3 days. You want to go to the beach, see Mauna Loa, and shop in Honolulu. How many ways can you arrange your schedule for the 3 days so that you do 1 activity each day?

31. Waiter A waiter takes lunch orders for 5 people, but quickly forgets which person ordered which meal. If the waiter randomly chooses a person to give each meal to, what is the probability that the waiter will serve the correct meal to each person?

32. *Writing* You have 5 objects. Are there more ways to arrange 4 of the objects or more ways to arrange 5 of the objects? Explain.

Write the expression using factorials.

33. $30 \cdot 29$ **34.** $20 \cdot 19 \cdot 18 \cdot 17$

35. $12 \cdot 11 \cdot 10 \cdot 9 \cdot 8 \cdot 7 \cdot 6$ **36.** 60

37. Critical Thinking For each of the following situations, tell how you found your answer. Then tell whether the situation involves permutations.

a. How many 3-digit numbers can you make using each of the digits 1, 2, and 3 exactly once?

b. How many 3-digit numbers can you make using only the digits 1, 2, or 3 if you are able to use each digit more than once?

38. Anagrams An anagram is a rearrangement of the letters in a word to form another word. For example, an anagram of STOP is POST.

a. How many arrangements of the letters R, A, and T are there?

b. What is the probability that a random arrangement of the letters in the word RAT will be an anagram of RAT?

39. Seating At a party, 2 men and 2 women are to be seated on one side of a table so that no man is sitting next to another man and no woman is sitting next to another woman.

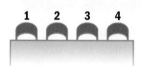

a. How many possible seating arrangements are there if a man sits in the first seat?

b. How many possible seating arrangements are there if a woman sits in the first seat?

c. How many possible seating arrangements are there altogether?

40. *Writing* Find $_5P_1$, $_5P_2$, $_5P_3$, $_5P_4$, and $_5P_5$. What pattern do you notice? Explain why this pattern occurs.

41. Critical Thinking How many times greater is $n!$ than $(n - 1)!$? Explain.

42. Critical Thinking Explain why $_nP_r = n!$ when $n = r$.

43. Challenge The letters of the word BALL are written on cards and placed in a hat. The two cards with L on them are identical.

a. Three cards are randomly drawn from the hat, one at a time. Write all the different permutations of 3 letters that could result.

b. Is your answer to part (a) greater than or less than $_4P_3$? Explain.

Mixed Review

44. You roll two number cubes. Find the probability that you roll two even numbers. *(Lesson 6.8)*

Find the unknown length. Write your answer in simplest form. *(Lesson 9.3)*

45.
20 m, c, 48 m

46.
b, 10 in., 6 in.

47.
a, 2 ft, 5 ft

48. Family Reunion Make a stem-and-leaf plot of the following ages of people at a family reunion: 46, 66, 3, 5, 18, 49, 28, 2, 21, 44, 9, 13, 17, 8, 52, 25, 39, 68, 73, 37, 5, 15. *(Lesson 11.1)*

Standardized Test Practice

49. Multiple Choice You have 12 CDs and choose 4 of them to play one afternoon. Which expression gives the number of possible orders for playing the 4 CDs?

A. $\dfrac{4!}{12!}$ **B.** $\dfrac{8!}{12!}$ **C.** $\dfrac{12!}{8!}$ **D.** $\dfrac{12!}{4!}$

50. Multiple Choice Eight horses are running in a race. In how many ways can the horses finish in first, second, and third place?

F. 6   **G.** 336   **H.** 6720   **I.** 40,320

Combinations

BEFORE	Now	WHY?
You used permutations to count possibilities.	You'll use combinations to count possibilities.	So you can count possible yearbook designs, as in Ex. 9.

Vocabulary

combination, p. 620

Basketball A basketball league has 5 teams. Two of the teams are chosen to play one another. How many different possible matchups are there?

In Lesson 11.6, you learned that a permutation is an arrangement in which order is important. A **combination** is a selection of objects where the order in which the objects are chosen is not important. In the problem above, suppose team A and team B are the two teams selected to play one another. It does not matter if team A is chosen first or if team B is chosen first. The same game will be played.

Example 1 *Listing Combinations*

List and count the different possible matchups of the basketball teams described above.

Solution

Use the letters A, B, C, D, and E to represent the five teams. List all possible matchups. Then cross out any duplicates that represent the same matchup.

AB	AC	AD	AE
B̶A̶	BC	BD	BE
C̶A̶	C̶B̶	CD	CE
D̶A̶	D̶B̶	D̶C̶	(DE)
E̶A̶	E̶B̶	E̶C̶	(E̶D̶)

> DE and ED are duplicates, because they represent the same matchup.

Answer There are 10 different matchups.

✔ *Checkpoint*

1. You want to buy 4 different CDs. You can afford to buy only 3 of them. How many combinations of CDs can you buy?

Study *Strategy*

For every combination of 2 teams, there are 2!, or 2, permutations of the chosen teams. So, $_5P_2 = 2! \cdot {_5C_2}$, or $_5C_2 = \dfrac{_5P_2}{2!}$.

Relating Combinations and Permutations Before matchups are crossed out, the list in Example 1 shows the permutations of 5 teams chosen 2 at a time, or $_5P_2$. After the duplicate matchups are crossed out, the list shows the number of combinations of 5 teams chosen 2 at a time. This is written as $_5C_2$. Notice that in this situation $_5C_2 = \dfrac{_5P_2}{2!}$, which suggests the following result.

Combinations

Words To find the number of combinations of n objects taken r at a time, divide the number of permutations of n objects taken r at a time by $r!$.

Numbers $_9C_5 = \dfrac{_9P_5}{5!}$ **Algebra** $_nC_r = \dfrac{_nP_r}{r!}$

Example 2   *Counting Combinations*

Book Reports You need to write 4 book reports for your English class. Your teacher gives the class a list of 7 books from which to choose. How many different groups of 4 books can you choose from the list?

Solution

The order in which you choose the books is not important. So, to find the number of different ways to choose 4 books from 7, find $_7C_4$.

$$_7C_4 = \dfrac{_7P_4}{4!}$$ Use combinations formula.

$$= \dfrac{7 \cdot 6 \cdot 5 \cdot 4}{4 \cdot 3 \cdot 2 \cdot 1}$$ Write $_7P_4$ and 4! as products.

$$= \dfrac{7 \cdot \cancel{6}^{1} \cdot 5 \cdot \cancel{4}^{1}}{\cancel{4} \cdot \cancel{3} \cdot \cancel{2} \cdot 1}$$ Divide out common factors.

$$= 35$$ Simplify.

Answer There are 35 different combinations of books.

 Checkpoint

Find the number of combinations.

   2. $_6C_3$ **3.** $_8C_5$ **4.** $_{10}C_2$ **5.** $_4C_4$

Using a Calculator Many calculators can evaluate combinations. The solution for Example 2 is shown. You may find it helpful to use a calculator when evaluating combinations that involve large numbers.

You can determine whether a problem requires permutations or combinations by deciding if order is important.

Example 3 *Choosing Between Permutations and Combinations*

Tell whether the possibilities can be counted using *permutations* or *combinations*.

a. There are 30 dogs in a dog show. Blue ribbons are awarded to the top 3 dogs. How many different groups of dogs can receive blue ribbons?

b. There are 30 runners in a cross country race. How many different groups of runners can finish first, second, and third?

Solution

a. The order in which the 3 blue ribbons are awarded does not matter. So, the possibilities can be counted using combinations.

b. Because the runners can finish first, second, or third, order is important. So, the possibilities can be counted using permutations.

Example 4 *Finding a Probability Using Combinations*

Marbles You have 10 marbles in a bag. Each marble is a different color, including red, blue, and green. You draw 3 marbles at random. Find the probability that you draw a red, a blue, and a green marble.

Solution

The order in which the marbles are drawn is not important. Find $_{10}C_3$.

$$_{10}C_3 = \frac{_{10}P_3}{3!}$$ **Use combinations formula.**

$$= \frac{10 \cdot 9 \cdot 8}{3 \cdot 2 \cdot 1}$$ **Write $_{10}P_3$ and 3! as products.**

$$= \frac{10 \cdot \overset{3}{\cancel{9}} \cdot \overset{4}{\cancel{8}}}{\underset{1}{\cancel{3}} \cdot \underset{1}{\cancel{2}} \cdot 1}$$ **Divide out common factors.**

$$= 120$$ **Simplify.**

Answer There are 120 different combinations of 3 marbles you can draw. Only one of the combinations includes a red, a blue, and a green marble. So, the probability is $\frac{1}{120}$.

✔ **Checkpoint**

6. You are choosing 10 of 30 friends to invite to a party. Can you count the possibilities using *permutations* or *combinations*?

7. You have 12 marbles in a bag. Each marble is a different color, including red and blue. You draw 2 marbles at random. What is the probability that you draw a red marble and a blue marble?

INTERNET
eWorkbook Plus
CLASSZONE.COM

Guided Practice

Vocabulary Check

1. Copy and complete: You can write the number of combinations of 12 objects taken 3 at a time as ___?___.

2. Explain when to use a permutation and when to use a combination when choosing r objects from n objects.

Skill Check **Find the number of combinations.**

3. $_2C_1$ **4.** $_5C_4$ **5.** $_3C_3$ **6.** $_6C_4$

7. Track and Field A gym coach selects a team of 4 athletes from 14 athletes to represent the school at a track and field meet. Tell whether the number of teams the coach can select can be counted using permutations or combinations. Then find the number of teams.

Guided Problem Solving

8. Concert A radio station takes the names of the first 20 listeners who call in after hearing a certain song. The station will randomly select 3 of the callers to win tickets to a concert. If 3 friends are among the first 20 callers, what is the probability that the 3 friends will win tickets?

(1) How many possible combinations of 3 callers can be selected to win tickets?

(2) How many possible combinations of 3 ticket winners include all 3 of the friends?

(3) Find the probability that the 3 friends win tickets.

Practice and Problem Solving

Homework *Help*

Example	Exercises
1	9, 10
2	11–22
3	23–26, 28
4	27, 31

Online Resources
CLASSZONE.COM
• More Examples
• eTutorial Plus

9. Yearbook The school yearbook photographer took one photo of the school during each of the 4 seasons and wants to choose 3 of the photos for the cover. How many sets of 3 photos are there? Make a list of all the possible combinations.

10. Club Meetings A club is scheduling a week of meetings to plan for its annual fundraiser. The club wants to meet on 3 of the evenings next week, from Monday through Friday. How many different schedules can the club choose? Make a list of all the possible combinations.

Find the number of combinations.

11. $_3C_2$ **12.** $_4C_1$ **13.** $_7C_3$ **14.** $_6C_5$

15. $_4C_3$ **16.** $_9C_8$ **17.** $_8C_3$ **18.** $_{11}C_7$

19. $_{12}C_3$ **20.** $_{15}C_6$ **21.** $_7C_7$ **22.** $_{10}C_0$

In Exercises 23–25, tell whether the possibilities can be counted using *permutations* or *combinations*. Then answer the question.

23. A survey asks people to rank basketball, baseball, tennis, soccer, and football according to how much they enjoy watching each sport. How many possible responses are there?

24. A history test lists the names of 5 presidents, and each student is to choose two of them to compare in an essay. How many different pairings are possible?

25. A subway car has 8 empty seats. At one stop, 5 people enter the car and no one gets off. How many ways can the 5 people arrange themselves in the 8 empty seats if each person takes one seat?

26. Talent Show At an upcoming talent show, you plan to play 3 songs on the piano. There are 6 songs you know well enough to perform.

  a. How many different groups of 3 songs can you choose to play?

  b. Once you have chosen 3 songs, in how many ways can you play them at the talent show?

27. Chocolates A box of chocolates contains 10 pieces of chocolate, and 4 of the pieces have cream in the center. Suppose you randomly select 4 pieces of chocolate. Find the probability that you select all 4 of the pieces that have cream in the center.

28. Tiles A designer is making a sample design that will use 3 different kinds of tiles. The designer has 9 different kinds of tiles from which to choose.

  a. How many possible combinations of tiles can the designer choose?

  b. The designer will create a sample design by placing 3 tiles side by side. How many different sample designs can the designer make from the 3 chosen tiles?

29. *Writing* Explain why $_5C_4 = {}_5C_1$. Find another example of two different combinations that are equal.

30. Critical Thinking Which is greater, $_4C_2$ or $_4P_2$? Explain why.

31. Raffle In a raffle, 2 of 50 tickets are randomly selected to be the winning tickets.

  a. You have 2 raffle tickets. Find the probability that you are holding both winning tickets.

  b. Does buying twice as many tickets double the probability that you are holding both winning tickets? Explain.

32. Pizza You and your friends are choosing toppings for a pizza. There are 4 meat toppings and 6 vegetable toppings from which to choose.

  a. How many pizzas having 1 meat topping and 2 different vegetable toppings can you choose?

  b. How many pizzas having 2 different meat toppings and 1 vegetable topping can you choose?

  c. How many pizzas having 3 different toppings can you choose?

Review *Help*

To review the strategy *break into parts*, see p. 802.

33. Break into Parts How many ways can you choose three of the numbers 3, 4, 6, 8, and 9 so that at least one of the numbers is greater than 6? Explain.

34. Critical Thinking You have 100 different coins. Are there more combinations of 99 of the coins than there are of 100 coins? Explain.

35. Challenge The numbers 1 through 5 are written on separate slips of paper and placed in a hat, and 3 of the slips are drawn randomly. What is the probability that one of the slips that are drawn shows a 4?

Mixed Review

36. Roads There are 3 roads from town A to town B. There are 4 roads from town B to town C. How many different ways are there to get from town A to town B to town C? *(Lesson 6.8)*

In Exercises 37 and 38, make a box-and-whisker plot of the data. *(Lesson 11.2)*

37. Basketball game scores: 98, 104, 93, 96, 122, 106, 102, 107

38. Temperatures (in degrees Fahrenheit): 30, 35, 38, 28, 41, 30, 40, 37, 40, 36, 38

39. Movies You rent 6 movies. In how many different ways can you watch all 6 of the movies? *(Lesson 11.6)*

Standardized Test Practice

40. Multiple Choice What is the value of $_8C_4$?

A. 56   **B.** 70   **C.** 1680   **D.** 40,296

41. Multiple Choice Two cars are available for 7 students to take to a high school football game. Car A holds 4 students, and car B holds 3 students. How many different groups of 3 students can be formed to ride in car B?

F. 4   **G.** 24   **H.** 35   **I.** 210

Brain GAME

Playoff Series

In many playoff series, the team that wins a majority of the games is the winner. In a best-of-five series, the first team to win 3 games is the winner of the series. One way to win a best-of-five series is to win the first 3 games. Another way is to lose the first 2 games, then win the next 3.

How many different ways are there to win a best-of-three series? a best-of-five series? a best-of-seven series?

11.8 Counting with Venn Diagrams

Goal
Count outcomes using Venn diagrams.

Materials
• paper
• pencil

Investigate

Use a Venn diagram to count the number of students in your math class who participate in two activities.

1 Copy the Venn diagram shown. Ask the members of your math class if they play a musical instrument, play on a school sports team, do both, or do neither. Write their names in the appropriate part of the Venn diagram.

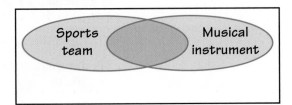

2 Copy and complete the frequency table. When determining the frequency for a category, be sure to include all the students in your math class who are in the category.

Description	Number of students
Play a musical instrument	?
Play on a school sports team	?
Play a musical instrument *and* play on a school sports team	?
Play a musical instrument *or* play on a school sports team	?
Do *not* play an instrument and do *not* play on a school sports team	?

Draw Conclusions

1. Critical Thinking Your friend uses the following verbal model to find the number of students in your class who play on a school sports team *or* play a musical instrument.

$$\boxed{\text{Number of students who play on a school sports team}} + \boxed{\text{Number of students who play a musical instrument}} = \boxed{\text{Number of students who play on a school sports team } or \text{ play a musical instrument}}$$

Do you agree with your friend's reasoning? Explain why or why not. If not, correct the left side of the verbal model.

2. Probability A student from your class is chosen at random. Find the probability of each event. Explain how you found the probability.

a. Choosing a student who plays a musical instrument

b. Choosing a student who plays a musical instrument *and* plays on a school sports team

11.8

Probabilities *of* Disjoint *and* Overlapping Events

Vocabulary

disjoint events, p. 627
mutually exclusive
  events, p. 627
overlapping events,
  p. 627
complementary
  events, p. 630

BEFORE	Now	WHY?
You found the probability of an event.	You'll find the probability that event A *or* event B occurs.	So you can analyze data about blood types, as in Ex. 23.

In this lesson, you will find the probability that an event A *or* an event B occurs. To find the probability, first determine whether the events are *disjoint* or *overlapping*. **Disjoint events**, or **mutually exclusive events**, are events that have no outcomes in common. **Overlapping events** are events that have one or more outcomes in common.

For example, suppose you roll a number cube. The Venn diagrams below illustrate examples of disjoint events and overlapping events.

Review *Help*

For help with using Venn diagrams, see p. 784.

Disjoint Events

Event A: Roll a 2.

Event B: Roll an odd number.

Overlapping Events

Event A: Roll an even number.

Event B: Roll a prime number.

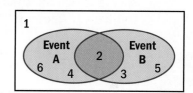

Example 1   *Identifying Disjoint and Overlapping Events*

Tell whether the events are *disjoint* or *overlapping*.

  a. Roll a number cube.

    Event A: Roll a number less than 4.

    Event B: Roll a 5.

  b. Randomly select a student.

    Event A: Select a 7th grader.

    Event B: Select a boy.

Solution

  a. The outcomes for event A are 1, 2, and 3. The outcome for event B is 5. There are no outcomes in common.

    Answer The events are disjoint.

  b. Because some 7th graders are boys, the events have outcomes in common.

    Answer The events are overlapping.

✔ **Checkpoint**

1. Suppose you choose a book to read. Are the events "choosing a hard cover book" and "choosing a fiction book" disjoint or overlapping?

Probability of Disjoint Events The Venn diagram shows two disjoint events that involve rolling a number cube.

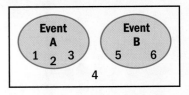

Event A: Roll a number less than 4.

Event B: Roll a number greater than 4.

There are 6 possible outcomes. There are 5 favorable outcomes for the event A *or* B. So, $P(A \text{ or } B) = \frac{5}{6}$. You can also find $P(A \text{ or } B)$ by finding the sum of the probability of event A and the probability of event B.

$$P(A \text{ or } B) = P(A) + P(B) = \frac{3}{6} + \frac{2}{6} = \frac{5}{6}$$

This result suggests the following rule.

Probability of Disjoint Events

Words For two disjoint events, the probability that either of the events occurs is the sum of the probabilities of the events.

Algebra If A and B are disjoint events, then
$P(A \text{ or } B) = P(A) + P(B)$.

Example 2   *Finding the Probability of Disjoint Events*

Raffle Fifty tickets are sold for a raffle. You buy 2 tickets, and your friend buys 3 tickets. One ticket is randomly chosen as the winning ticket. What is the probability that you or your friend wins the raffle?

Solution

The events are disjoint because you and your friend cannot both win.

Event A: You win the raffle.

Event B: Your friend wins the raffle.

$P(A \text{ or } B) = P(A) + P(B)$ **Probability of disjoint events**

$= \frac{2}{50} + \frac{3}{50}$ **Substitute probabilities.**

$= \frac{5}{50} = \frac{1}{10}$ **Add. Then simplify.**

Answer The probability that you or your friend wins the raffle is $\frac{1}{10}$.

✔ *Checkpoint*

2. In an election, candidate A received 35% of the vote, candidate B received 22% of the vote, and candidate C received 43% of the vote. If you randomly select a person from all who voted, what is the probability that the person voted for either candidate A *or* candidate B?

Probability of Overlapping Events The Venn diagram shows two overlapping events that involve rolling a number cube.

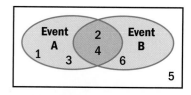

Event A: Roll a number less than 5.

Event B: Roll an even number.

There are 6 possible outcomes. There are 5 favorable outcomes for the event A *or* B. So, $P(A \text{ or } B) = \frac{5}{6}$. There are 2 favorable outcomes for the event A *and* B. So, $P(A \text{ and } B) = \frac{2}{6}$. These outcomes are counted twice when you find the sum of $P(A)$ and $P(B)$. In order to find $P(A \text{ or } B)$ using the sum of $P(A)$ and $P(B)$, you must subtract $P(A \text{ and } B)$ *once*.

$$P(A \text{ or } B) = P(A) + P(B) - P(A \text{ and } B) = \frac{4}{6} + \frac{3}{6} - \frac{2}{6} = \frac{5}{6}$$

Probability of Overlapping Events

Words For two overlapping events, the probability that either of the events occurs is the sum of the probabilities of the events minus the probability of both events.

Algebra If A and B are overlapping events, then $P(A \text{ or } B) = P(A) + P(B) - P(A \text{ and } B)$.

Example 3 *Finding the Probability of Overlapping Events*

You roll two number cubes, one red and one blue. What is the probability that you roll a 4 on at least one of the number cubes?

Solution

The table lists all the possible outcomes of rolling the two number cubes.

Event A: The red number cube shows 4.

Event B: The blue number cube shows 4.

1, 1	2, 1	3, 1	4, 1	5, 1	6, 1
1, 2	2, 2	3, 2	4, 2	5, 2	6, 2
1, 3	2, 3	3, 3	4, 3	5, 3	6, 3
1, 4	2, 4	3, 4	4, 4	5, 4	6, 4
1, 5	2, 5	3, 5	4, 5	5, 5	6, 5
1, 6	2, 6	3, 6	4, 6	5, 6	6, 6

$P(B) = \frac{6}{36}$ $P(A) = \frac{6}{36}$ $P(A \text{ and } B) = \frac{1}{36}$

$$P(A \text{ or } B) = P(A) + P(B) - P(A \text{ and } B) \qquad \text{Probability of overlapping events}$$

$$= \frac{6}{36} + \frac{6}{36} - \frac{1}{36} \qquad \text{Substitute probabilities.}$$

$$= \frac{11}{36} \qquad \text{Simplify.}$$

Answer The probability that you roll a 4 is $\frac{11}{36}$.

Review *Help*

In Example 2, a table is used to display all the possible outcomes. For help with making tables, see p. 799.

Complementary Events Two events are **complementary events** if they are disjoint events and one event or the other must occur. The sum of the probabilities of complementary events is always 1. If you know the probability of an event A, then the probability of the complementary event, *not* A, is given by the following rule.

$$P(\text{not } A) = 1 - P(A)$$

Example 4 | *Finding the Probability of Complementary Events*

Weather The forecast claims that there is a 40% probability of snow tomorrow. What is the probability that it will *not* snow tomorrow?

Solution

The events snow and no snow are complementary events because one or the other must occur.

$P(\text{no snow}) = 1 - P(\text{snow})$ **Probability of complementary events**

$\phantom{P(\text{no snow})} = 1 - 0.4$ **Substitute 40%, or 0.4, for $P(\text{snow})$.**

$\phantom{P(\text{no snow})} = 0.6$ **Subtract.**

Answer The probability that it will not snow tomorrow is 0.6, or 60%.

11.8 Exercises

More Practice, p. 813

INTERNET
eWorkbook Plus
CLASSZONE.COM

Guided Practice

Vocabulary Check
1. Explain what it means for two events to be disjoint.

2. What is the complement of rolling an odd number on a number cube?

Skill Check
You roll a number cube. Tell whether the events are *disjoint* or *overlapping*. Then find *P(A or B)*.

3. **Event A:** Roll an even number.
   Event B: Roll a 3.

4. **Event A:** Roll a number less than 2.
   Event B: Roll an odd number.

5. **Event A:** Roll a multiple of 3.
   Event B: Roll a 5.

6. **Event A:** Roll an odd number.
   Event B: Roll a 1.

Guided Problem Solving
7. **Marbles** A bag contains 3 red marbles, 4 black marbles, 4 blue marbles, and 3 yellow marbles. You randomly draw a marble from the bag. What is the probability that you draw a red or a blue marble?

   1 Are the events disjoint or overlapping?

   2 Find the probability that you draw a red marble.

   3 Find the probability that you draw a blue marble.

   4 Find the probability that you draw a red or a blue marble.

Practice and Problem Solving

Homework *Help*

Example	Exercises
1	8-11,
2	8-15, 23
3	8-11, 16-18, 24
4	19-23, 25

Online Resources
CLASSZONE.COM

• More Examples
• eTutorial Plus

The spinner is divided into equal parts. For the specified events A and B, tell whether the events are *disjoint* or *overlapping*. Then find P(A or B).

8. **Event A:** Stops on an even number.
   Event B: Stops on green.

9. **Event A:** Stops on an odd number.
   Event B: Stops on a multiple of 3.

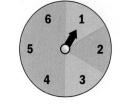

10. **Event A:** Stops on red.
    Event B: Stops on blue.

11. **Event A:** Stops on blue.
    Event B: Stops on a multiple of 3.

Events A and B are disjoint. Find P(A or B).

12. $P(A) = \frac{4}{25}$, $P(B) = \frac{17}{25}$

13. $P(A) = \frac{7}{15}$, $P(B) = \frac{2}{15}$

14. $P(A) = \frac{7}{20}$, $P(B) = \frac{3}{20}$

15. $P(A) = \frac{13}{50}$, $P(B) = \frac{22}{50}$

Events A and B are overlapping. Find P(A or B).

16. $P(A) = \frac{7}{10}$, $P(B) = \frac{3}{10}$, $P(A \text{ and } B) = \frac{1}{10}$

17. $P(A) = \frac{13}{25}$, $P(B) = \frac{8}{25}$, $P(A \text{ and } B) = \frac{3}{25}$

18. $P(A) = \frac{1}{6}$, $P(B) = \frac{1}{9}$, $P(A \text{ and } B) = \frac{3}{36}$

Given P(A), find P(not A).

19. $P(A) = 45\%$ 20. $P(A) = 82\%$ 21. $P(A) = \frac{11}{23}$ 22. $P(A) = \frac{16}{33}$

23. **Blood Types** A city surveyed its population to find the blood types of its residents. Each resident has only one type of blood. The results of the survey are given in the circle graph.

   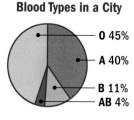

   Blood Types in a City

   O 45%
   A 40%
   B 11%
   AB 4%

   a. Individuals with type A blood can accept type A or type O blood in a blood transfusion. Find the probability that blood from a randomly selected resident will be either type A or type O.

   b. Individuals with type B blood can accept type B or type O blood in a blood transfusion. Find the probability that blood from a randomly selected resident will be either type B or type O.

   c. What is the probability that a randomly selected resident does not have type O blood?

   d. What is the probability that a randomly selected resident does not have type A or type B blood?

24. Pets A survey found that in a city, 19% of the population owned dogs, 14% of the population owned cats, and 6% of the population owned both a cat and a dog. Find the probability that a randomly chosen member of the population owns a cat or a dog.

25. Speech You and your friend are among 12 students who will give speeches in front of the class. The teacher will randomly choose one of the 12 students to give the first speech. Each student has an equal probability of being chosen. Find the probability that *neither* you *nor* your friend will be chosen to give the first speech.

26. *Writing* The probability that a coin shows heads when you flip it is 0.5. Explain why, when you flip two coins at the same time, the probability that at least one coin shows heads is *not* $0.5 + 0.5 = 1.0$.

27. Critical Thinking You know that $P(A \text{ and } B) = 0$. What can you conclude about event A and event B? Explain.

28. Critical Thinking You roll a number cube. What is the probability that the number cube shows a number that is not even *or* that is not a multiple of 3?

29. Challenge The numbers 1 through 20 are written on separate slips of paper and placed in a hat. One of the slips is randomly drawn.

   a. Draw a Venn diagram that shows the possible outcomes for three events: the number drawn is less than 5, the number drawn is prime, and the number drawn is a multiple of 3.

   b. Find the probability that the number drawn is less than 5 *or* a prime number *or* a multiple of 3.

   c. Write a general rule for finding $P(A \text{ or } B \text{ or } C)$ for overlapping events A, B, and C.

Mixed Review

Find the product. *(Lesson 5.4)*

30. $-\dfrac{4}{7} \cdot \dfrac{5}{9}$ **31.** $-\dfrac{5}{8} \cdot \left(-\dfrac{3}{4}\right)$ **32.** $-\dfrac{9}{10} \cdot \dfrac{5}{12}$ **33.** $\dfrac{13}{18} \cdot \left(-\dfrac{15}{48}\right)$

34. Map A cartographer is creating a map of 5 states. Each state is to be a different color. The cartographer will use red, green, blue, brown, and yellow. How many different ways can the cartographer color the map? *(Lesson 11.6)*

Find the number of combinations. *(Lesson 11.7)*

35. $_{11}C_5$ **36.** $_9C_4$ **37.** $_{10}C_6$ **38.** $_{15}C_8$

Standardized Test Practice

39. Multiple Choice A meteorologist forecasts that there is a 30% probability of rain tomorrow. What is the probability that it will *not* rain tomorrow?

    A. 30%   **B.** 60%   **C.** 70%   **D.** 100%

40. Short Response The numbers 1 through 10 are written on separate slips of paper and placed in a hat. One of the slips is randomly drawn. Find the probability that the slip shows a number that is *neither* odd *nor* greater than 5. Explain your reasoning.

11.9 Performing a Simulation

Goal
Use a simulation to find an experimental probability.

Materials
- number cube
- paper
- pencil

A *simulation* is an experiment that you can use to represent a real-world situation and make predictions.

Investigate

Each box of a brand of cereal contains 1 of 6 different prizes. Use a simulation to predict the number of boxes you must buy before you have all 6 prizes.

1 Assume that the probability that a box contains a particular prize is $\frac{1}{6}$. Because there are 6 equally likely outcomes for each box you buy, you can use each of the 6 numbers on a number cube to represent one of the 6 prizes.

2 Roll the number cube one time for each box of cereal you buy. Record the results of the rolls in a table like the one shown.

Roll	1	2	3	4	5	6	· · ·
Prize number	?	?	?	?	?	?	· · ·

3 Keep rolling until you have rolled all six numbers at least once. Circle the first occurrence of each number. How many rolls did it take before you rolled all 6 numbers?

4 Repeat the simulation 4 more times. Based on your 5 simulations, what is the average (mean) number of boxes you have to buy before you have all 6 prizes? Round to the nearest whole number.

Draw Conclusions

1. **Critical Thinking** Another brand of cereal is offering 1 of 3 different prizes in each box. Assume that the probability that a box contains a particular prize is $\frac{1}{3}$. You want to collect all 3 prizes. Explain how you could use a number cube simulation to determine how many boxes, on average, you have to buy before you have all 3 prizes.

2. *Writing* Compare performing the simulation above to carrying out an experiment that involves buying actual cereal boxes. What are the advantages of the simulation?

Independent *and* Dependent Events

BEFORE	*Now*	WHY?
You found *P*(A or B).	You'll find the probability that event A *and* event B occur.	So you can predict field hockey goals, as in Ex. 16.

Jelly Beans A jar of jelly beans contains 50 red jelly beans, 45 yellow jelly beans, and 30 green jelly beans. You reach into the jar and randomly select a jelly bean, then select another without putting the first jelly bean back. What is the probability that you draw two red jelly beans? Example 3 shows how to find this probability.

To find the probability that one event *and* another event occur, first decide if the events are *independent* or *dependent*. Two events are **independent events** if the occurrence of one event does *not* affect the probability of the occurrence of the other event. Two events are **dependent events** if the occurrence of one event *does* affect the probability of the occurrence of the other event.

Example 1   *Identifying Independent and Dependent Events*

Tell whether the events are *independent* or *dependent*.

a. You toss a coin and it shows heads. You toss the coin again and it shows tails.

b. You randomly draw a name from a hat. Then, without putting the first name back, you randomly draw a second name.

Solution

a. The result of the first coin toss does not affect the result of the second coin toss. So, the events are independent.

b. Because you do not replace the first name, there is one fewer name in the hat for the second draw. This affects the results of the second draw. So, the events are dependent.

✔ *Checkpoint*

Tell whether the events are *independent* or *dependent*.

1. You roll a 5 on a number cube, then you roll a 6.

2. You randomly draw a marble from a bag. Then you put it back in the bag and randomly draw another marble from the bag.

Independent Events You roll a number cube and toss a coin. These events are independent because rolling the number cube does not affect the result of the coin toss. From the table, you can see that there are 12 possible outcomes. The probability of rolling an odd number *and* getting heads is $\frac{3}{12}$, or $\frac{1}{4}$.

You can also find the probability of rolling an odd number and getting heads by multiplying.

Possible Outcomes	
1, H	1, T
2, H	2, T
3, H	3, T
4, H	4, T
5, H	5, T
6, H	6, T

$$P(\text{odd number and heads}) = P(\text{odd number}) \cdot P(\text{heads})$$

$$= \frac{3}{6} \cdot \frac{1}{2} = \frac{3}{12} = \frac{1}{4}$$

This result suggests the following rule.

Study *Strategy*

You can extend the formula for the probability of independent events to include more than two events. For example, the probability that independent events A, B, and C occur is the product $P(A) \cdot P(B) \cdot P(C)$.

Probability of Independent Events

Words For two independent events, the probability that both events occur is the product of the probabilities of the events.

Algebra If A and B are independent events, then $P(A \text{ and } B) = P(A) \cdot P(B)$.

Example 2 *Finding the Probability of Independent Events*

Passwords A computer randomly generates 4-digit passwords. Each digit can be used more than once. What is the probability that the first two digits in your password are both 1?

Solution

Each digit can be used more than once, so generating a digit and generating another digit are independent events. Because there are 10 digits, the probability of randomly generating a 1 is $\frac{1}{10}$.

$$P(1 \text{ and } 1) = P(1) \cdot P(1) \qquad \text{Probability of independent events}$$

$$= \frac{1}{10} \cdot \frac{1}{10} \qquad \text{Substitute probabilities.}$$

$$= \frac{1}{100} \qquad \text{Multiply.}$$

Answer The probability that the first two digits are both 1 is $\frac{1}{100}$.

✓ *Checkpoint*

3. Refer to Example 2. What is the probability that all four digits are 1?

4. **Critical Thinking** In Example 2, if each digit can be used only once, are the events still independent? Explain.

Dependent Events A bag contains 5 red marbles and 5 blue marbles. You randomly draw a marble, then you randomly draw a second marble without replacing the first marble. Because you don't replace the first marble, the probability that the second marble is a certain color is affected by the color of the first marble that you draw. These two events are dependent.

The probability that you draw a blue marble after drawing a red marble is written as P(blue given red). You can find the probability of drawing a red marble and then drawing a blue marble as shown.

$$P(\text{red}) = \frac{5}{10} = \frac{1}{2} \qquad P(\text{blue given red}) = \frac{5}{9}$$

$$P(\text{red and then blue}) = P(\text{red}) \cdot P(\text{blue given red}) = \frac{1}{2} \cdot \frac{5}{9} = \frac{5}{18}$$

Probability of Dependent Events

Words For two dependent events, the probability that both events occur is the product of the probability that the first event occurs and the probability that the second event occurs given that the first event has occurred.

Algebra If A and B are dependent events, then $P(\text{A and B}) = P(\text{A}) \cdot P(\text{B given A})$.

Example 3 *Finding the Probability of Dependent Events*

Find the probability that both the first and second jelly bean drawn from the jar described on page 634 are red.

Solution

Because you don't replace the first jelly bean, the events are dependent. So, $P(\text{red and then red}) = P(\text{red}) \cdot P(\text{red given red})$.

$$P(\text{red}) = \frac{50}{125}$$
There are 50 red jelly beans and 125 total jelly beans.

$$P(\text{red given red}) = \frac{49}{124}$$
There are 49 red jelly beans remaining and 124 total jelly beans remaining.

$$P(\text{red and then red}) = \frac{50}{125} \cdot \frac{49}{124}$$
Substitute probabilities.

$$= \frac{2{,}450}{15{,}500} \approx 0.16$$
Multiply. Write as a decimal.

Answer The probability that you draw two red jelly beans is about 16%.

Guided Practice

Vocabulary Check

1. Tell what it means for two events to be independent.

2. Give an example of dependent events.

Skill Check — **Tell whether the events are *independent* or *dependent*.**

3. **Event A:** You roll an odd number on a number cube.
Event B: You roll the number cube again and roll an even number.

4. **Event A:** You choose a member of a baseball team to be the pitcher.
Event B: You choose a different member of the team to be the catcher.

Guided Problem Solving

5. **Raffle** You and your friend each purchased a ticket in a raffle in which 30 tickets were sold. The owner of the first ticket drawn wins the grand prize and is removed from the drawing. The owner of the second ticket drawn wins the runner-up prize. What is the probability that you win the grand prize and your friend wins the runner-up prize?

1 Decide whether your winning the grand prize and your friend's winning the runner-up prize are independent or dependent events.

2 What is the probability that you win the grand prize?

3 If you win the grand prize, what is the probability that your friend wins the runner-up prize?

4 Find the probability that you win the grand prize and your friend wins the runner-up prize.

Practice and Problem Solving

Homework *Help*

Example	Exercises
1	6–8, 10
2	12, 14, 16, 17
3	9, 11, 13

Online Resources
CLASSZONE.COM
• More Examples
• eTutorial Plus

In Exercises 6–8, tell whether the events are *independent* or *dependent*.

6. A teacher is randomly assigning you, your friend, and 4 other students to 6 different seats.
Event A: You are assigned the first seat.
Event B: Your friend is assigned the second seat.

7. A computer randomly chooses a digit from 1 to 100. A digit can be chosen more than once.
Event A: The digit is prime.
Event B: The digit is odd.

8. You randomly choose a utensil from a drawer with 12 spoons, 8 forks, and 6 knives. Without replacing the first item, you draw another.
Event A: You draw a spoon first.
Event B: You draw a fork second.

9. **Art Class** An art class consists of 8 boys and 10 girls. The teacher randomly chooses 3 students to present their work. Find the probability that all 3 of the students chosen are girls.

10. **CD Player** A CD player has two settings, random and shuffle. The shuffle setting plays all the songs on the CD only once in random order. The random setting selects songs randomly from the CD, but does not keep track of which songs have already been played.

    a. You play a CD using the random setting. Are the selections of the first two songs that are played independent or dependent events?

    b. You play a CD that has 11 songs using the random setting. Find the probability that the CD player plays song 3 first and then song 5.

    c. You play a CD using the shuffle setting. Are the selections of the first two songs that are played independent or dependent events?

    d. You play a CD with 11 songs using the shuffle setting. Find the probability that the CD player plays song 3 first and then song 5.

11. **Candy** A gumball machine has 21 red gumballs, 24 yellow gumballs, and 15 blue gumballs. The gumballs are randomly mixed.

    a. What is the probability that the gumball machine dispenses 2 red gumballs in a row?

    b. What is the probability that the gumball machine dispenses a red gumball, then a yellow gumball?

    c. What is the probability that the gumball machine dispenses a red gumball, then a blue gumball?

12. **Seeds** A package of daisy seeds claims that the probability that each seed in the package sprouts under optimal conditions is 55%. Suppose you plant two daisy seeds under optimal conditions.

    a. What is the probability that both seeds sprout?

    b. What is the probability that neither of the seeds sprouts?

13. **Socks** A drawer contains 4 blue socks, 6 gray socks, and 8 black socks. You randomly choose one sock, then another from the drawer.

    a. Find the probability that you choose 2 blue socks.

    b. Find the probability that you choose 2 gray socks.

    c. Find the probability that you choose 2 black socks.

    d. Find the probability that you choose 2 socks that match.

14. **Batteries** A company has determined that 1% of the batteries it sells are defective. You recently bought 2 batteries from the company. What is the probability that they are both defective?

15. *Writing* A bag contains 20 red marbles and 20 blue marbles. You randomly draw a marble from the bag, then randomly draw another marble. Do you have a greater probability of drawing 2 red marbles if you replace the first marble after you draw it, or if you do not replace the first marble? Explain.

In the **Real World**

Seeds A package of seeds must be labeled according to state regulations. A package of snapdragon seeds claims that the probability that a seed sprouts under optimal conditions is 55%. Suppose you plant 35 snapdragon seeds. How many seeds do you expect will sprout?

16. Extended Problem Solving Suppose that a field hockey player scores a goal in 17% of her goal attempts. Assume that each attempt is independent of the previous one.

    a. Calculate Find the probability that the player will score on her next two attempts.

    b. Calculate Find the probability that the player will score on her next three attempts.

    c. *Writing* Do you think it is reasonable to assume that each attempt is independent of the previous one? Explain your answer.

17. Contest The probability of winning $1000 in a contest is advertised to be 1 in 10^5. The probability that one entry wins is independent of whether or not the other entries win. What is the probability that two friends who enter the contest both win $1000?

18. Challenge Write a general rule for the probability that a coin shows heads each time when it is flipped n times in a row.

19. Fishing You are fishing in a small pond that is stocked with 10 rainbow trout and 20 brook trout. There are no other types of fish in the pond. You keep any rainbow trout that you catch. You throw any brook trout back into the pond as soon as you catch them.

    a. Suppose you catch exactly 2 fish. Make a list of all the possible arrangements of 2 fish that you could catch.

    b. Suppose each fish has an equal chance of being caught. Find the probability of each arrangement in part (a). Round your answers to the nearest percent.

    c. Find the probability that at least one of the two fish you catch is a rainbow trout. Explain how you found your answer.

Mixed Review

Simplify the expression. *(Lesson 2.3)*

20. $7x + 3 - 2x$ **21.** $-3 + 4s^2 + 1 - 7s^2$ **22.** $2a^2 + 6a + 3a + 11a^2$

23. Term Project A group of 5 students is to be chosen from a class of 20 students to work on a term project. How many different groups of students can be chosen from the class? *(Lesson 11.7)*

24. Sports A soccer goalie has a save percentage of 95%. What is the probability that the goalie will *not* make the next save? *(Lesson 11.8)*

Standardized Test Practice

25. Multiple Choice If a digit can be used more than once, what is the probability that the last two digits of a randomly generated 5-digit number are both 4?

    A. $\frac{1}{100}$ **B.** $\frac{1}{90}$ **C.** $\frac{1}{81}$ **D.** $\frac{1}{10}$

26. Short Response Events A and B are dependent events. The probability that event A occurs is 20%. The probability that events A and B both occur is 8%. What is the probability that event B occurs given that event A occurs? Explain how you found your answer.

Chapter Review

Vocabulary Review

stem-and-leaf plot, p. 581
frequency, p. 582
frequency table, p. 582
histogram, p. 583
box-and-whisker plot, p. 588
lower quartile, p. 588
upper quartile, p. 588

lower extreme, p. 588
upper extreme, p. 588
interquartile range, p. 590
categorical data, p. 596
numerical data, p. 596
population, p. 601
sample, p. 601

samples: random, systematic,
    stratified, convenience,
    self-selected, p. 601
biased sample, p. 602
biased question, p. 603
margin of error, p. 610
permutation, p. 615

n factorial, p. 615
combination, p. 620
events: disjoint, mutually
    exclusive, overlapping,
    p. 627
complementary events, p. 630
independent events, p. 634
dependent events, p. 634

Copy and complete the statement.

1. The _?_ of a random sample provides an interval around a sample percent in which the population percent most likely occurs.

2. Two events are _?_ if the occurrence of one event does *not* affect the probability of the occurrence of the other event.

11.1 Stem-and-Leaf Plots and Histograms

Examples on
pp. 581–583

▶ *Goal*

Make stem-and-leaf plots and histograms.

Example Make a stem-and-leaf plot and a histogram of the following ages (in years) of customers in a store.

27, 11, 39, 21, 45, 23, 42, 28, 30, 16, 31, 42, 35, 38, 17, 40, 35, 31

Ages of Customers

```
1 | 1 6 7
2 | 1 3 7 8
3 | 0 1 1 5 5 8 9
4 | 0 2 2 5
```

Key: 3 | 8 = 38 years

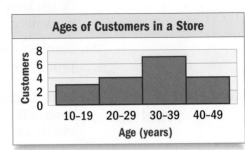

Ages of Customers in a Store

3. Make a stem-and-leaf plot and a histogram of the following amounts (in dollars) spent on purchases in a store: 16, 15, 35, 10, 16, 34, 45, 33, 32, 36, 12, 44, 48, 32, 34.

4. Make a histogram of the following heights (in inches) of students in a club: 59, 60, 62, 72, 70, 67, 71, 61, 62, 63, 68, 67, 66, 61.

11.2 Box-and-Whisker Plots

Examples on
pp. 588–590

▶ **Goal**

Make box-and-whisker plots.

Example Make a box-and-whisker plot of the following costs (in dollars) of 11 different computer desks.

98.85, 88.64, 109.97, 95.99, 129.75, 100.50, 87.95, 99.99, 110.54, 105.61, 96.84

Order the data to find the median, the quartiles, and the extremes.

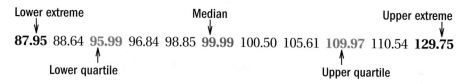

Draw a box-and-whisker plot using these values.

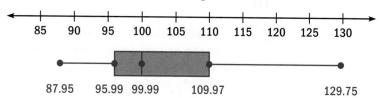

✔ **5.** Make a box-and-whisker plot of the following ages (in years) of people performing in a play: 15, 12, 11, 16, 10, 14, 13, 12.

11.3 Using Data Displays

Examples on
pp. 596–598

▶ **Goal**

Choose appropriate displays for data sets.

Example The data below are the numbers of points scored by a girls' high school basketball team in the last 15 games. What data display(s) can you use to display the data?

49, 84, 65, 71, 53, 54, 52, 64, 66, 63, 61, 70, 81, 78, 55

You can use a stem-and-leaf plot to display the data in numerical order. You can use a histogram to compare the numbers of scores that fall into intervals of equal size. You can also use a box-and-whisker plot to show the data divided into four groups of approximately equal size.

✔ **6.** The table shows the average yearly food cost (in dollars) in the United States. What data display(s) can you use to display the data? Explain your reasoning.

Year	1994	1995	1996	1997	1998	1999	2000
Cost (dollars)	4411	4505	4698	4801	4810	5031	5158

11.4 Collecting Data

Examples on pp. 601–603

▶ *Goal*

Identify populations and sampling methods.

Example A website operator posts the question "Should the background color on this page be blue?" on a website along with a link to a page where anyone can post a reply. Describe the population and tell what type of sampling method is used.

The population consists of all visitors to the website. Because visitors have the choice of answering or not, the sample is self-selected.

 7. The manager of a pizza parlor asks the first 10 customers if they would like a new topping added to the menu. Describe the population and tell what type of sampling method is used.

11.5 Interpreting Data

Examples on pp. 609–611

▶ *Goal*

Make conclusions about populations using surveys.

Example A school has 1000 students. A survey asks 375 students chosen at random to name their favorite color. Thirty say their favorite color is blue. Use this result to predict how many students at the school would say blue is their favorite color.

1 Find the sample percent: $\frac{30}{375} = 0.08 = 8\%$

2 Find 8% of 1000: 8% • 1000 students = 80 students

8. In a survey of a random sample of 400 students at the school in the example above, 70 students said they prefer to exercise before school. Predict how many students at the school would prefer to exercise before school.

11.6 Permutations

Examples on pp. 615–617

▶ *Goal*

Use permutations to count possibilities.

Example Find $_7P_3$.

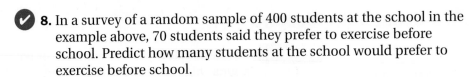

$_7P_3 = \frac{7!}{(7-3)!} = \frac{7!}{4!}$ Use permutations formula. Subtract.

$= \frac{7 \cdot 6 \cdot 5 \cdot \cancel{4} \cdot \cancel{3} \cdot \cancel{2} \cdot 1}{\cancel{4} \cdot \cancel{3} \cdot \cancel{2} \cdot 1}$ Expand factorials. Divide out common factors.

$= 7 \cdot 6 \cdot 5 = 210$ Multiply.

✔ **Find the number of permutations.**

9. $_9P_2$ **10.** $_{11}P_3$ **11.** $_8P_6$ **12.** $_{36}P_2$

11.7 Combinations

Examples on pp. 620–622

▶ **Goal**

Use combinations to count possibilities.

Example Find $_{12}C_4$.

$$_{12}C_4 = \frac{_{12}P_4}{4!} = \frac{12 \cdot 11 \cdot 10 \cdot 9}{4 \cdot 3 \cdot 2 \cdot 1}$$

Use combinations formula.
Write $_{12}P_4$ and 4! as products.

$$= \frac{\overset{1}{\cancel{12}} \cdot 11 \cdot \overset{5}{\cancel{10}} \cdot 9}{\underset{1}{\cancel{4}} \cdot \underset{1}{\cancel{3}} \cdot \underset{1}{\cancel{2}} \cdot 1} = 495$$

Divide out common factors.
Multiply.

✔ **13.** Find $_5C_2$ and $_{12}C_5$.

11.8 Probabilities of Disjoint and Overlapping Events

Examples on pp. 627–630

▶ **Goal**

Find probabilities of disjoint and overlapping events.

Example You roll a number cube. What is the probability that you roll a multiple of 3 (event A) or an even number (event B)?

$$P(A) = \frac{2}{6} \qquad P(B) = \frac{3}{6} \qquad P(A \text{ and } B) = \frac{1}{6}$$

$P(A \text{ or } B) = P(A) + P(B) - P(A \text{ and } B)$ **Probability of overlapping events**

$$= \frac{2}{6} + \frac{3}{6} - \frac{1}{6} = \frac{4}{6} = \frac{2}{3}$$ **Substitute probabilities. Simplify.**

✔ **14.** You roll two number cubes. What is the probability that you roll a number less than 3 on at least one number cube?

11.9 Independent and Dependent Events

Examples on pp. 634–636

▶ **Goal**

Find probabilities of independent and dependent events.

Example A bag has 5 green, 6 red, and 9 blue marbles. You randomly draw one marble, then you randomly draw a second without replacing the first. What is the probability that you draw a red and then a green marble?

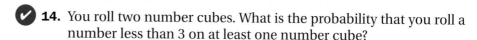

$P(\text{red}) = \frac{6}{20}$ $P(\text{green given red}) = \frac{5}{19}$ ← 5 green marbles still in bag
← 19 marbles left after 1 is drawn

$P(\text{red and green}) = P(\text{red}) \cdot P(\text{green given red})$

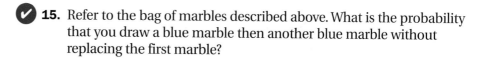

$$= \frac{6}{20} \cdot \frac{5}{19} = \frac{3}{38} \approx 0.079$$ **Substitute probabilities. Multiply.**

✔ **15.** Refer to the bag of marbles described above. What is the probability that you draw a blue marble then another blue marble without replacing the first marble?

In Exercises 1 and 2, make a stem-and-leaf plot and a histogram of the data.

1. Grade point averages: 3.2, 2.5, 3.9, 3.0, 3.2, 2.4, 3.2, 3.5, 3.8, 1.8, 3.9, 2.8

2. Video game scores: 542, 529, 564, 531, 566, 538, 562, 540, 522, 548, 531

3. **DVDs** Make a box-and-whisker plot of the following prices (in dollars) of some DVDs:
   10.99, 12.99, 15.99, 10.99, 26.99, 14.99, 19.99, 19.99, 9.99, 21.99, 20.99

4. Give two examples of categorical data. Which data display(s) can be used to display categorical data?

In Exercises 5 and 6, tell whether the question is potentially biased. Explain your answer. If the question is biased, rewrite it so that it is not.

5. Would you prefer to take a long, difficult essay test or a quick, simple multiple choice test?

6. Which team do you think will win the race?

7. **Surveys** The U.S. population is about 290 million. In a survey of a random sample of 2000 Americans, 600 said that they enjoy watching plays. Predict about how many Americans enjoy watching plays.

Evaluate.

8. $4!$

9. $6!$

10. $_5P_2$

11. $_8P_4$

12. $_9P_4$

13. $_3C_1$

14. $_6C_6$

15. $_5C_0$

In Exercises 16 and 17, tell whether the possibilities can be counted using *permutations* or *combinations*. Then answer the question.

16. You and five friends are posing for a photograph. In how many ways can you pose in a line for the photograph?

17. You are setting up a display for a store. There are 12 different types of sweaters. In how many ways can you display 4 different types of sweaters?

18. **Projects** The 25 students in your class will present projects. Your teacher randomly selects a student to give the first presentation. Find the probability that you are *not* selected first.

19. **Jobs** Of the 400 students at a school, 35% have part-time jobs. Find the probability that two students selected at random have part-time jobs.

Chapter Standardized Test

Test-Taking Strategy To check an answer, solve the problem using a method different from the one you originally used. Then compare your answers.

1. Which statement about the stem-and-leaf plot shown is *not* true?

  A. The greatest data value is 79.

  B. The range is 28.

  C. The median is 67.

  D. The mode is 77.

$$
\begin{array}{c|ccccc}
5 & 1 & 6 & 7 & & \\
6 & 0 & 2 & 5 & & \\
7 & 4 & 6 & 7 & 7 & 9 \\
\end{array}
$$
Key: $5\,|\,1 = 51$

2. Which of the following could produce a misleading histogram?

  F. There is no space between bars.

  G. Intervals are of equal size.

  H. Vertical axis is broken.

  I. Bar heights are different.

3. Your teacher asks every third student if he or she would rather have homework or a quiz. What is this method of sampling called?

  A. Convenience   **B.** Self-selected

  C. Stratified   **D.** Systematic

4. A town's population is 3400. In a random sample of 400 townspeople, 24 said they are in favor of a new tax. Predict how many townspeople would be in favor of the tax.

  F. 9   **G.** 17   **H.** 142   **I.** 204

5. Which expression is equivalent to $_{20}P_{14}$?

  A. $\dfrac{14!}{20!}$ **B.** $\dfrac{6!}{20!}$ **C.** $\dfrac{20!}{6!}$ **D.** $\dfrac{20!}{14!}$

6. A club has 10 members. How many different combinations of 4 members can be chosen?

  F. 40   **G.** 210   **H.** 5040   **I.** 151,200

7. You roll a number cube. What is the probability that you roll a 3 *or* a 5?

  A. $\dfrac{1}{36}$ **B.** $\dfrac{1}{12}$ **C.** $\dfrac{1}{6}$ **D.** $\dfrac{1}{3}$

8. Your friend made 12 vanilla, 12 chocolate, and 16 strawberry cupcakes. You randomly choose a cupcake for yourself, then you randomly choose one for a friend. Find the probability that you choose 2 vanilla ones.

  F. $\dfrac{11}{130}$ **G.** $\dfrac{9}{100}$ **H.** $\dfrac{227}{390}$ **I.** $\dfrac{3}{5}$

9. **Short Response** The data in the histogram are for the year 2001. Make at least three conclusions about the data.

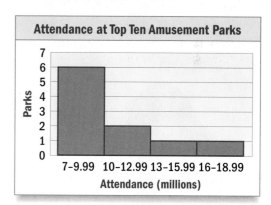

Attendance at Top Ten Amusement Parks

10. **Extended Response** The data below are the 60 meter dash times (in seconds) of two runners on 6 different days.

  Rachel: 9.82, 10.35, 9.75, 9.91, 10.04, 9.87
  Vivian: 9.79, 10.24, 10.08, 9.73, 9.81, 9.85

  a. Make a box-and-whisker plot of each set of data.

  b. Compare the medians and ranges for the two runners.

  c. Which runner is faster? Explain.

Conducting a Survey

Goal
Decide whether students in your school are in favor of a longer or shorter lunch period.

Key Skill
Collecting data

Materials
• calculator

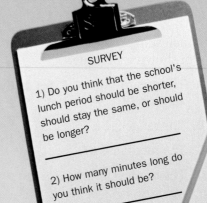

SURVEY

1) Do you think that the school's lunch period should be shorter, should stay the same, or should be longer?

_____

2) How many minutes long do you think it should be?

_____

Do you think students at your school want a longer lunch period, even if this means extending the school day? If so, how much longer? Do you think students at your school want a shorter lunch period if it means a shortened school day? If so, how much shorter?

To answer these questions, you will work in a group. Instead of asking every student in the school, your group will survey a sample of students at your school. Then you will analyze the results and create data displays to decide what the answers to these questions are.

Investigate

1 Create a survey by writing unbiased questions about the length of the lunch period. Include some questions that have "yes" or "no" answers. Include other questions that have numerical answers. For example, you could ask, "By how many minutes would you want to extend the lunch period?"

2 Decide how to choose a sample of students at your school.

3 Decide which group members will conduct the survey. Then ask the students in your sample the questions in your survey.

Consider and Decide

Analyze the data that you collected. Consider the following:

- Do you have a clear answer to the questions asked in your survey, or are your data inconclusive? Explain. How could you improve your questions?

- Which type of data displays are most appropriate for your data? Make data displays for your data.

- Do students in your school want a longer lunch period or a shorter lunch period? How do your data support your answer?

Present Your Results

Make a poster that shows your survey results. Include your survey questions, your data displays, and your conclusions. Explain how you decided what length of lunch period students at your school prefer.

Project Extensions

Using Proportions Use the results of your survey to estimate the total number of students at your school who want a longer lunch period.

Writing Write an article for your school newspaper or website about how students feel about the length of the lunch period. Include your survey results and data displays.

Research CLASSZONE.COM Use the Internet to find a report of the results of a public opinion poll. Investigate how the poll was conducted and what the poll questions were. Do you think that the report accurately reflects the poll results? Present your research.

Career Many people conduct or analyze surveys as part of their jobs, including population analysts, market researchers, and public opinion pollsters. Find out more about one of these careers.

How can you use math to describe the path of a stream of water in a fountain?

CHAPTER 12

INTERNET Preview
CLASSZONE.COM

- eEdition Plus Online
- eWorkbook Plus Online
- eTutorial Plus Online
- State Test Practice
- More Examples

M A T H *In the* **Real World**

Fountains Gravity pulls down on the drops of water in the stream from a fountain, causing them to fall back to the fountain's basin. In this chapter, you will use *quadratic functions* to describe the motion of objects affected by gravity.

What do you think? The equation $y = x^2$ is a quadratic function. Make a table of values for this function. Use the table to write and graph at least seven ordered pairs. Can you connect the points with a straight line? Explain.

Chapter Prerequisite Skills

PREREQUISITE SKILLS QUIZ

Review Vocabulary

monomial, p. 174
function, p. 386
graph of an equation in
   two variables, p. 392
function form, p. 393

Preparing for Success **To prepare for success in this chapter, test your knowledge of these concepts and skills. You may want to look at the pages referred to in blue for additional review.**

1. Vocabulary When is a relation a function?

Simplify. *(p. 194)*

2. $6^8 \cdot 6^5$ **3.** $a^4 \cdot a^{11}$ **4.** $\dfrac{7^9}{7^7}$ **5.** $\dfrac{3z \cdot 8z^{12}}{6z^6}$

Write the expression using only positive exponents. *(p. 199)*

6. 7^{-4} **7.** 120^{-2} **8.** $5x^{-6}$ **9.** $m^{-3}n^5$

Graph the equation. *(p. 391)*

10. $y = x + 5$ **11.** $y = -3x - 6$ **12.** $y = -\dfrac{1}{2}x$ **13.** $y = \dfrac{1}{4}x - 2$

NOTETAKING STRATEGIES

Note *Worthy*

You will find a notetaking strategy at the beginning of each chapter. Look for additional notetaking and study strategies throughout the chapter.

TAKING NOTES IN CLASS Leave space after examples that your teacher writes on the board. Use the space to write down any questions asked by you or other students. Record the teacher's answer.

Example: Graph y ≤ −x + 3.

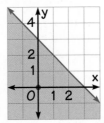

Step 1: Graph y = −x + 3. Use a solid line.

Step 2: Shade the appropriate half-plane.

Question: Do I shade above or below the line?

Answer: To determine which half-plane to shade, test the coordinates of a point in the inequality.

In Lesson 12.7, write down any questions you have about exponential functions, as well as your teacher's answers.

12.1

Polynomials

BEFORE	Now	WHY?
You simplified expressions.	You'll classify and write polynomials in standard form.	So you can find the braking distance of a train, as in Ex. 59.

Vocabulary
polynomial, p. 651
term, p. 651
binomial, p. 651
trinomial, p. 651
degree of a term, p. 652
degree of a polynomial, p. 652
standard form, p. 652

Volleyball A volleyball is hit upward from a height of 1.2 meters. You can use the expression $-4.9t^2 + 8.1t + 1.2$ to find the height (in meters) of the volleyball t seconds after it is hit. What is the height of the volleyball after 1 second? In Example 4, you'll see how to answer this question by evaluating the expression.

Recall that expressions such as $-4.9t^2$, $8.1t$, and 1.2 are called monomials. A **polynomial** is a sum of monomials. Each monomial in a polynomial is called a **term**. A polynomial like $3x^2 + (-5x) + (-2)$ is usually written as $3x^2 - 5x - 2$. Some polynomials can be classified by the number of their terms.

Monomial (1 term)	Binomial (2 terms)	Trinomial (3 terms)
$-3xyz$	$5x + 1$	$-4b^2 + 6b - 3$
8	$-p^3 - 2p^2$	$2 + 11t - 7t^3$

Example 1   *Identifying and Classifying Polynomials*

Tell whether the expression is a polynomial. If it is a polynomial, list its terms and classify it.

a. $7m^{-2} + 4$　　　　**b.** $-b$　　　　**c.** $3x^2 + 8xy - 1$

Solution

a. This expression is not a polynomial. The variable m has an exponent that is not a whole number.

b. This expression is a polynomial. The only term is $-b$. Because it has one term, it is a monomial.

c. This expression is a polynomial. The terms are $3x^2$, $8xy$, and -1. Because it has three terms, it is a trinomial.

Study *Strategy*

To identify the terms of the expression in part (c) of Example 1, write the expression $3x^2 + 8xy - 1$ as $3x^2 + 8xy + (-1)$.

 Checkpoint

Tell whether the expression is a polynomial. If it is a polynomial, list its terms and classify it.

1. $6x^4 - 5x^3$　　　**2.** $m^3 - m^{-1} - 1$　　　**3.** $-3a + 7ab^2 + 2$

Degree The **degree of a term** is the sum of the exponents of its variables. The **degree of a polynomial** is the greatest degree of its terms. The degree of a nonzero constant is 0. The constant 0 has no degree.

Example 2 | Finding the Degree of a Polynomial

Find the degree of the polynomial.

a. Polynomial: $5x^3 + 8x - 9$

Degree of term: 3   1   0

The greatest degree of the terms is 3. So, the degree of $5x^3 + 8x - 9$ is 3.

b. Polynomial: $p - p^3q^2 + q^4$

Degree of term: 1 $3 + 2 = 5$ 4

The greatest degree of the terms is 5. So, the degree of $p - p^3q^2 + q^4$ is 5.

✓ Checkpoint

Find the degree of the polynomial.

4. $8x^4 - x + 1$ **5.** $2 + 6z^3 - 5z$ **6.** $-y^4 + y^5 - 8$

7. $a^2 - b^3$ **8.** $7cd + 4c^2d^2$ **9.** $mn^3 - 3n^4$

Standard Form To simplify a polynomial, combine like terms. Remember that like terms are terms with identical variable parts, such as $8ab^2$ and $3ab^2$. A polynomial is written in **standard form** if it is simplified and the terms are arranged so the degree of each term decreases or stays the same from left to right.

Example 3 | Writing a Polynomial in Standard Form

Write $-m^2 + 5 + 2(4m + m^2)$ as a polynomial in standard form.

$-m^2 + 5 + 2(4m + m^2)$

$= -m^2 + 5 + 8m + 2m^2$ Distributive property

$= -1m^2 + 5 + 8m + 2m^2$ Write $-m^2$ as $-1m^2$.

$= -1m^2 + 2m^2 + 5 + 8m$ Group like terms.

$= m^2 + 5 + 8m$ Combine like terms.

$= m^2 + 8m + 5$ Standard form

✓ Checkpoint

Write the expression as a polynomial in standard form.

10. $3x - 4x^2 + 8$ **11.** $7t^3 + 2 + t^3 - 5$ **12.** $9y^2 + 8y^4 - y^2$

13. $4a - 5(a^3 + a) - 3$ **14.** $3(4b + b^2) - b^2$ **15.** $c^2 + 8c^3 - 2(c - 5)$

Example 4   *Evaluating a Polynomial*

Find the height of the volleyball 1 second after it is hit, as described on page 651.

Solution

Evaluate the polynomial $-4.9t^2 + 8.1t + 1.2$ when $t = 1$.

$$-4.9t^2 + 8.1t + 1.2 = -4.9(1)^2 + 8.1(1) + 1.2 \qquad \text{Substitute 1 for } t.$$
$$= -4.9(1) + 8.1(1) + 1.2 \qquad \text{Evaluate power.}$$
$$= -4.9 + 8.1 + 1.2 \qquad \text{Multiply.}$$
$$= 4.4 \qquad \text{Add.}$$

Answer The volleyball's height after 1 second is 4.4 meters.

 Checkpoint

Evaluate the polynomial when $x = 3$ and $y = -2$.

16. $x^2 - 4x + 4$ **17.** $2y^2 + 5y - 1$ **18.** $x + 3y$

19. $xy - 7x - 2$ **20.** $-2x^2 + y^3 + 1$ **21.** $x^2y^2 + xy$

12.1   Exercises

More Practice, p. 814

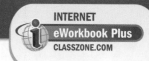

INTERNET
eWorkbook Plus
CLASSZONE.COM

Guided Practice

Vocabulary Check   **1.** Copy and complete: The polynomial $4x^2 + 3x + 5$ has a(n) <u>?</u> of 2.

     2. Give an example of a polynomial of degree 3 that is written in standard form.

Skill Check   **Tell whether the expression is a polynomial. If it is a polynomial, list its terms and classify it.**

     3. $5x^3$ **4.** $2a + 9$ **5.** $p^3 + p^2 + 3p^{-1}$

     Find the degree of the polynomial.

     6. $-6x^2 + x - 5$ **7.** $10 - y$ **8.** $b^3 - 7b^2 + b$

     Write the expression as a polynomial in standard form.

     9. $2x + 7 + 5 + 4x$ **10.** $4g^2 + 9 - g^2 + 3g$ **11.** $3z + 8 + 6z - z^2 + z$

     12. $a^2 - 1 - 3(6a + 7)$ **13.** $5(x^2 + 2x) - 3x^2$ **14.** $11y + 2(7 - 3y^2) + 9$

     Evaluate the polynomial when $x = 4$.

     15. $5x - 3$ **16.** $2x^2 + x - 7$ **17.** $x^3 + x^2 - 6x - 8$

     18. Error Analysis Your friend says that the degree of the polynomial $x^2 + xy^2$ is 2. Describe and correct your friend's error.

Practice and Problem Solving

Homework *Help*

Example	Exercises
1	19–24
2	25–30, 32
3	31, 33–38, 47–49
4	39–46

Online Resources
CLASSZONE.COM

• More Examples
• eTutorial Plus

Tell whether the expression is a polynomial. If it is a polynomial, list its terms and classify it.

19. $8a^2$

20. $3b^{-1} + 6b$

21. $3c^3 - 2c^2 - 7$

22. $\dfrac{x}{y} + 29$

23. $\dfrac{x^2 + 2}{x}$

24. $\dfrac{x^2}{7} - 4x - 3$

Find the degree of the polynomial.

25. $4m^2 + 5m - 2$

26. 7

27. $-2x^3 - 6x^2 + 3x - 4$

28. $x^2 + 3x^4 - 7$

29. $-3n + 5$

30. $24a^3 + 24a^5$

31. *Writing* Is the polynomial $3x^2 + 5x^2y + 7$ written in standard form? Explain your reasoning.

32. Critical Thinking Give an example of a term that has degree 6 but that contains no variable with an exponent greater than 2. Explain your answer.

Write the expression as a polynomial in standard form.

33. $9x + 4 - 2 - 3x$

34. $-7x^2 - 3 - 3x^2$

35. $8 + 5y + 5 - y - 6$

36. $-3y^2 - y - 8(2y^2 + 7)$

37. $10z^2 + 3(z^2 - 6z) - 4z$

38. $2z^2 + 4(1 - 5z) + 11$

39. Golf The height (in feet) of a golf ball t seconds after it is hit is given by the polynomial $-16t^2 + 100t$. What is the height of the golf ball 3 seconds after it is hit? 5 seconds after it is hit?

Evaluate the polynomial when $a = 2$.

40. $5a^2 + 3a + 1$

41. $a^4 + 7a^2$

42. $a^2 - 2a^2 - 6$

43. $-9a^2 + a^2 - 20$

44. $3a^3 - 10a + 1$

45. $-a^2 + 2a + 7$

46. Alternative-Fueled Vehicles For the period 1993–2001, the number (in thousands) of alternative-fueled vehicles in the United States can be approximated by the polynomial $2.1t^2 + 4.6t + 320$, where t is the number of years since 1993.

    a. What is the degree of the polynomial?

    b. Evaluate the polynomial when $t = 0$ to find the approximate number (in thousands) of alternative-fueled vehicles in 1993.

    c. Evaluate the polynomial when $t = 8$ to find the approximate number (in thousands) of alternative-fueled vehicles in 2001.

Write a polynomial expression for the perimeter of the figure. Give your answer in standard form.

47.

$3x + 1$

48.

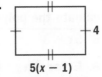

$5(x - 1)$

49.

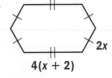

$4(x + 2)$

Find the degree of the polynomial.

50. $a + b + c + d$ **51.** $25abc$ **52.** $ab + cd + ac$

53. $ab + a^2b^2$ **54.** $-a^2b^3c^2 + 5$ **55.** $a^3 - a^2b^2 + b^2$

Evaluate the polynomial when $x = -1$ and $y = 2$.

56. $4x^2 + 3y^3$ **57.** $x^4 - x^2y$ **58.** $-2x^2 + x^2y^3$

59. Extended Problem Solving The polynomials below give the approximate braking distance (in feet) needed to stop a car or train. In each polynomial, v is the vehicle's speed in miles per hour and r is the reaction time (in seconds) of the car's driver or the train's engineer. For the questions below, use $r = 0.5$ second.

Car: $1.47vr + 0.05v^2$ **Train:** $1.47vr + 0.5v^2$

   a. Calculate What is the braking distance (to the nearest foot) of a car traveling 30 miles per hour? 55 miles per hour?

   b. Calculate What is the braking distance (to the nearest foot) of a train traveling 80 miles per hour? 125 miles per hour?

   c. Compare How much greater is the braking distance of a train than the braking distance of a car if both vehicles are traveling at 55 miles per hour?

Find the degree of the polynomial. Write your answer in terms of n.

60. $x^n + x^{n-1} + x^{n-2}$ **61.** $x^ny^4 + 5x^3y^n$ **62.** $6x^ny^n + x^2y^{2n}$

63. Challenge If possible, give an example of the polynomial described. If it is not possible to give an example, explain why not.

   a. A simplified binomial of degree 0

   b. A simplified trinomial of degree 1

Mixed Review   **State the opposite of the number.** *(Lesson 1.4)*

64. -12 **65.** 27 **66.** 61 **67.** -135

Find the area of the parallelogram or trapezoid. *(Lesson 10.3)*

68.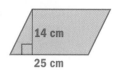

14 cm

25 cm

69.

7 m

9 m

11 m

70. Each letter in the word POLYNOMIAL is written on a separate card and placed in a stack. You randomly select a card from the stack. Then you randomly select a second card without putting the first card back. Find the probability of selecting O, then M. *(Lesson 11.9)*

Standardized Test Practice

71. Multiple Choice Which expression is *not* a polynomial?

   A. $-12b$ **B.** $x^2 + x^{-1}$ **C.** $y^2 - 2y + 7$ **D.** -50

72. Multiple Choice What is the degree of $x^2 - x^3 + 4$?

   F. 1   **G.** 2   **H.** 3   **I.** 4

12.2 Modeling Polynomial Addition

Goal
Model polynomial addition using algebra tiles.

Materials
• algebra tiles

You can use algebra tiles to model polynomials.

1   −1

x $-x$

x^2 $-x^2$

Each of these x-by-x square tiles has an area of x^2 square units.

Investigate

Find the sum of $2x^2 + 3x - 4$ and $x^2 + 2x + 5$ using algebra tiles.

1 Use algebra tiles to model $2x^2 + 3x - 4$ and $x^2 + 2x + 5$.

$2x^2$ $+$ $3x$ $-$ 4 $x^2 + 2x +$ 5

2 To add the polynomials, combine like terms. Group the x^2-tiles, the x-tiles, and the 1-tiles.

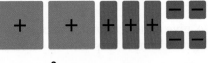

3 A tile and its opposite form a *zero pair*. Remove the zero pairs. The sum is $3x^2 + 5x + 1$.

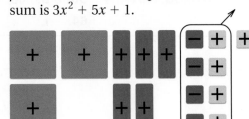

Draw Conclusions

Use algebra tiles to find the sum.

1. $(x^2 + 5x + 2) + (3x^2 + x + 2)$ **2.** $(x^2 - x + 5) + (-3x^2 + x + 5)$

3. Critical Thinking You can also use algebra tiles to model polynomial subtraction. Use algebra tiles to find the difference of $2x^2 + 5x + 2$ and $x^2 + 3x + 1$. Include drawings of the tiles to illustrate your steps.

Adding *and* Subtracting Polynomials

Review Vocabulary
opposite, p. 23
like terms, p. 78

BEFORE	*Now*	WHY?
You classified and simplified polynomials.	You'll add and subtract polynomials.	So you can compare spending on newspaper ads, as in Ex. 39.

Money You are saving for a trip to Costa Rica. You deposit $500 into a bank account that earns interest compounded annually. One year later, you deposit an additional $600 into the account. Let r be the annual interest rate. What is the balance A of the account 2 years after the initial deposit? In Example 2, you will see how to solve this problem by adding polynomials.

You add polynomials by combining like terms. One way to add polynomials is to align like terms in columns. If one of the polynomials is missing a term, you can either leave a space in that term's column, or write the term with a coefficient of 0.

Example 1 — Adding Polynomials Vertically

Find the sum.

a. $(-8x^3 + 4x^2 + x + 1) + (3x^3 - 2x^2 + 7)$

b. $(2x^4 + 6x^3 - 5x^2 + x - 7) + (x^3 - 3x^2 + 2x + 1)$

Solution

a.
$$\begin{array}{r} -8x^3 + 4x^2 + x + 1 \\ +\quad 3x^3 - 2x^2 \quad\ \ + 7 \\ \hline -5x^3 + 2x^2 + x + 8 \end{array}$$
Arrange like terms in columns.
Add like terms.

b.
$$\begin{array}{r} 2x^4 + 6x^3 - 5x^2 +\ \ x - 7 \\ +\qquad\quad x^3 - 3x^2 + 2x + 1 \\ \hline 2x^4 + 7x^3 - 8x^2 + 3x - 6 \end{array}$$
Arrange like terms in columns.
Add like terms.

✔ *Checkpoint*

Find the sum using a vertical format.

1. $(5p^2 + 3p - 7) + (2p^2 - 8p + 4)$ **2.** $(-4z + 7) + (3z^2 - 3z - 8)$

3. $(4x^2 - 6x + 3) + (8x + 1)$ **4.** $(-w^3 + w + 2) + (w^2 - 5)$

Example 2   *Adding Polynomials Horizontally*

For the savings account described on page 657, the balance from the first deposit is given by the polynomial $500 + 1000r + 500r^2$. After 1 year, the balance from the second deposit is given by $600 + 600r$. In both polynomials, r is expressed as a decimal.

a. Find the balance A in terms of r after 2 years.

b. Find the balance after 2 years when $r = 0.02$.

Solution

a. To find the total balance A, add the balances from each deposit.

$$A = (500 + 1000r + 500r^2) + (600 + 600r) \qquad \text{Add balances.}$$

$$= 500 + 600 + 1000r + 600r + 500r^2 \qquad \text{Group like terms.}$$

$$= 1100 + 1600r + 500r^2 \qquad \text{Combine like terms.}$$

Answer After 2 years, the balance is $1100 + 1600r + 500r^2$.

b. Evaluate the polynomial when $r = 0.02$.

$$1100 + 1600r + 500r^2 \qquad \text{Write polynomial.}$$

$$= 1100 + 1600(0.02) + 500(0.02)^2 \qquad \text{Substitute 0.02 for } r.$$

$$= 1100 + 1600(0.02) + 500(0.0004) \qquad \text{Evaluate power.}$$

$$= 1100 + 32 + 0.2 \qquad \text{Multiply.}$$

$$= 1132.2 \qquad \text{Add.}$$

Answer The balance after 2 years when $r = 0.02$ is \$1132.20.

In the **Real World**

Money The unit of currency in Costa Rica is the *colon.* One dollar is worth about 385 *colones.* What is the approximate value in dollars of 50,000 colones?

✔ Checkpoint

Find the sum using a horizontal format.

5. $(2x^2 + x + 10) + (3x^2 - 7x - 2)$ **6.** $(-5y^3 + 6y^2 - 2y) + (2y^3 - y)$

Subtracting Polynomials You can subtract a polynomial by adding its opposite. To find the opposite of a polynomial, multiply each of its terms by -1. You can subtract polynomials vertically or horizontally.

Example 3   *Subtracting Polynomials Vertically*

Find the difference $(6x^2 + 4x - 7) - (2x^2 - x + 8)$.

$$\begin{array}{r} 6x^2 + 4x - 7 \\ -(2x^2 - x + 8) \end{array} \qquad\longrightarrow\qquad \begin{array}{r} 6x^2 + 4x - 7 \\ + (-2x^2 + x - 8) \\ \hline 4x^2 + 5x - 15 \end{array} \qquad \begin{array}{l} \text{Write opposite.} \\ \text{Add like terms.} \end{array}$$

✔ Checkpoint

Find the difference using a vertical format.

7. $(6x^2 + 4x + 7) - (5x^2 + x - 9)$ **8.** $(14b^2 - 12b) - (9b^2 - 5b + 1)$

Example 4 | *Subtracting Polynomials Horizontally*

Find the difference $(x^2 + 4x - 9) - (4x^2 - 5x + 11)$.

$$(x^2 + 4x - 9) - (4x^2 - 5x + 11)$$ Write difference.

$$= x^2 + 4x - 9 + (-4x^2 + 5x - 11)$$ Write opposite of second polynomial.

$$= x^2 - 4x^2 + 4x + 5x - 9 - 11$$ Group like terms.

$$= -3x^2 + 9x - 20$$ Combine like terms.

✔ **Checkpoint**

Find the difference using a horizontal format.

9. $(10y^2 - y + 6) - (7y^2 + 3y - 5)$ **10.** $(c^2 + 4c - 13) - (8c^2 - 2c + 7)$

11. $(3t^3 + 7t) - (3t^3 + 2t^2 - t + 4)$ **12.** $(5n^3 - n + 2) - (n^3 - 6n^2 - 9)$

12.2 Exercises

More Practice, p. 814

INTERNET
eWorkbook Plus
CLASSZONE.COM

Guided Practice

Vocabulary Check

1. Copy and complete: To add polynomials, you combine ？.

2. Finding the difference of $x^2 - 4x + 1$ and $x^2 - x + 3$ is the same as finding the sum of what two polynomials?

Skill Check **Find the sum using a vertical format.**

3. $(x + 4) + (2x + 7)$ **4.** $(z^2 + 3z + 9) + (-2z^2 + 5)$

Find the sum using a horizontal format.

5. $(3a^2 + 1) + (a^2 - 5)$ **6.** $(9a - 7) + (a^2 - 2a + 8)$

Find the difference using a vertical format.

7. $(10z - 1) - (z + 4)$ **8.** $(x^2 + 7x - 3) - (x^2 + 1)$

Find the difference using a horizontal format.

9. $(b^2 + 9) - (3b^2 + b + 2)$ **10.** $(5b^2 + 6b + 7) - (b^2 + 4b - 6)$

11. Error Analysis Describe and correct the error in finding the difference of $x^2 + 3x - 1$ and $x^2 + x + 2$.

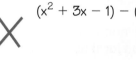

$$(x^2 + 3x - 1) - (x^2 + x + 2) = x^2 + 3x - 1 - x^2 + x + 2$$
$$= x^2 - x^2 + 3x + x - 1 + 2$$
$$= 4x + 1$$

Practice and Problem Solving

Homework *Help*

Example	Exercises
1	12–19, 29–32
2	12–19, 29–32, 39
3	20–27, 28, 33–36
4	20–27, 28, 33–36

Online Resources
CLASSZONE.COM

• More Examples
• eTutorial Plus

Find the sum.

12. $(x^2 + x + 15) + (x^2 + x + 6)$ **13.** $(-x^2 - 9x) + (x^2 + 3x - 8)$

14. $(y^2 - 2y + 1) + (4y^3 - y - 5)$ **15.** $(y^4 - 5y^2) + (y^4 + 2y^2 - 9)$

16. $(-12z^2 - z + 3) + (2z^2 + 6z - 1)$ **17.** $(-4z^3 + 6z - 8) + (z^2 - 3z + 5)$

18. $(13m^3 + 12m) + (4m^2 - 8m + 5)$ **19.** $(3m^2 + 1) + (m^2 - 4m)$

Find the difference.

20. $(5a + 2) - (3a^2 + 1)$ **21.** $(8a^2 + 7a + 2) - (5a^2 + 4)$

22. $(4b^2 + 3b + 5) - (6b^2 + 7)$ **23.** $(b^3 - 5b^2 + b) - (-2b^3 - b^2 - b)$

24. $(4c^3 - 7c - 2) - (c^2 + 6c - 5)$ **25.** $(c^2 - c + 6) - (-3c^3 + c - 6)$

26. $(8d^4 + 5) - (7d^4 - 1)$ **27.** $(d^2 + 5d + 2) - (3d^2 + d + 2)$

28. Extended Problem Solving You want to cut 12 circles from a rectangular sheet of leather that measures $6r$ inches by $10r$ inches. Each circle has a radius of r inches.

  a. Write a polynomial expression for the area of the rectangular sheet.

  b. Analyze Write a polynomial expression for the combined area of the 12 circles. Use 3.14 for π.

  c. Apply What area of the rectangular sheet is unused?

  d. Visual Thinking Could you cut *more* than 12 circles from the rectangular sheet? Draw a diagram and explain your answer.

A machine cuts circles of leather.

Find the sum or difference.

29. $(13x - 4y) + (2x + 5y)$ **30.** $(-2r + 3s + 17t) + (15r - 7t)$

31. $(3cd + 2) + (-9cd - 4)$ **32.** $(8a^2b - 7a) + (2a^2b - 9b)$

33. $(m - 8n) - (-3m + 9n)$ **34.** $(6a + 7b) - (11a + 5b + 14c)$

35. $(2rs + 4r - 3s) - (13rs + 2r)$ **36.** $(2x^2 + 7y^2) - (x^2 - y^2 - 18)$

37. Critical Thinking What polynomial do you add to $x^2 + 5x + 1$ to get a sum of $4x^2 - 3$?

38. *Writing* Suppose two polynomials have the same degree. Will their sum have this degree also? Give an example to support your answer.

39. Newspaper Advertising The polynomials below approximate the amounts (in millions of dollars) spent on advertising in national and local newspapers for each year during the period 1990–2000. In each polynomial, x represents the number of years since 1990.

    National: $59x^2 - 262x + 3888$

    Local: $-33x^3 + 611x^2 - 1433x + 28{,}060$

Write a polynomial that gives the *combined* amount spent each year on national and local newspaper advertising.

40. Challenge The solid shown is composed of two cylinders. Write a polynomial expression for the entire surface area of the solid. Give your answer in standard form.

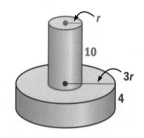

Mixed Review

Use the distributive property to write an equivalent variable expression. *(Lesson 2.2)*

41. $7(3 + a)$ **42.** $-3(z - 14)$ **43.** $(-3t + 15)4$ **44.** $(8 - w)(-2)$

Find the product. Write your answer using exponents. *(Lesson 4.5)*

45. $3^4 \cdot 3^2$ **46.** $11^2 \cdot 11^5$ **47.** $m^4 \cdot m^9$ **48.** $3b^6 \cdot 5b^2$

Tell whether the expression is a polynomial. *(Lesson 12.1)*

49. $y^5 - y^3 + y - 8$ **50.** $4y^{-2} + 2y^{-1} - 1$

Standardized Test Practice

51. Multiple Choice What is the sum of $(4x^2 + 5x - 8)$ and $(3x^2 - 6x + 1)$?

    A. $7x^2 + x - 7$ **B.** $7x^2 - x - 7$ **C.** $7x^2 + x + 7$ **D.** $7x^2 - x + 7$

52. Multiple Choice Which expression is equivalent to $3x^2 + 4x - 1$?

    F. $(x^2 + 3x - 1) - (2x^2 + x)$ **G.** $(3x^2 - 8) + (4x^2 + 7)$

    H. $(2x^2 + 4x + 1) - (-x^2 + 2)$ **I.** $(2x^2 + 4x + 1) + (-x^2 + 2)$

Pu**zz**ling Polynomials

Four of the sums below equal four of the differences. Match the sums and the differences that are equal. Then unscramble the corresponding letters to answer the riddle. Do not use the letters of sums or differences without a match.

What has keys that don't open locks, has space but no rooms, and you can enter but not go into?

A $(-9x^4 - 3x^3 - 7x) + (8x^4 - 5x^2 + 6x + 4)$ **D** $(2x^3 + 9x - 8) - (5x^3 + 4x - 6)$

N $(3x^2 - 7x + 1) + (2x^3 + 4x^2 + 3x)$ **S** $(2x^3 - 8x^2 - 5) - (-15x^2 - 3x + 6)$

R $(5x^4 + 3x^2 + 5) + (-5x^4 - 5x^2 - 2x + 7)$ **I** $(-11x^3 + 2x^2 - 4x) - (7x^4 - 2x^3 - x)$

B $(4x^3 - 3x^2 - 5x - 1) + (x^3 - 2x - 4)$ **Y** $(7x^3 - 2x^2 + x) - (7x^3 + 3x - 12)$

T $(-8x^3 + 4x^2 - 5x) + (-7x^4 - x^3 + 2x)$ **E** $(-x^3 - 5x^2 - 3) - (x^4 + 2x^3 + x - 7)$

K $(x^2 + 5x - 4) + (-3x^3 - x^2 + 2)$ **O** $(x^2 - 7x - 12) - (-5x^3 + 4x^2 - 7)$

Multiplying Monomials *and* Polynomials

BEFORE	*Now*	WHY?
You added and subtracted polynomials.	You'll multiply polynomials and monomials.	So you can write a polynomial for the area of a rug, as in Ex. 35.

Horse Corral You are enclosing a rectangular horse corral that will be connected to a barn as shown. You have 200 feet of fencing. Let l represent the length of the corral. What is a polynomial expression in terms of l that represents the area of the corral?

To find the area of the corral, you need to find the product of a monomial and a binomial.

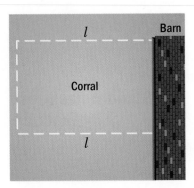

Example 1   *Multiplying a Monomial and a Binomial*

To find a polynomial expression in terms of l for the corral's area as described above, follow the steps below.

1 You are enclosing only three sides of the corral, so you can write the equation $F = 2l + w$, where F is the total length of the fencing and w is the width of the corral. Solve this equation for w after substituting 200 for F.

$F = 2l + w$	**Write equation.**
$200 = 2l + w$	**Substitute 200 for F.**
$200 - 2l = w$	**Subtract 2l from each side.**

2 Find the area in terms of l.

$A = lw$	**Formula for area of a rectangle**
$= l(200 - 2l)$	**Substitute $200 - 2l$ for w.**
$= l(200) - l(2l)$	**Distributive property**
$= 200l - 2l^2$	**Product of powers property**

Answer The area can be represented by the polynomial $200l - 2l^2$.

 Checkpoint

Find the product.

1. $3x(5x + 6)$ **2.** $(-7z + 1)2z$ **3.** $(t - 4)(-5t^2)$ **4.** $a^2(a^2 - 7a)$

Example 2   *Multiplying a Monomial and a Trinomial*

Find the product.

a. $(x^3 - 3x + 7)2x^3$ **b.** $-ab(2ab - a + 4b)$

Solution

a. $(x^3 - 3x + 7)2x^3$ Write product.

$= x^3(2x^3) - 3x(2x^3) + 7(2x^3)$ Distributive property

$= 2x^6 - 6x^4 + 14x^3$ Product of powers property

b. $-ab(2ab - a + 4b)$ Write product.

$= (-ab)2ab - (-ab)a + (-ab)4b$ Distributive property

$= -2a^2b^2 + a^2b - 4ab^2$ Product of powers property

✔ **Checkpoint**

Find the product.

5. $3x(4x^2 - x + 2)$ **6.** $(w^2 + w - 3)(-7w)$ **7.** $-8y(2y^2 + 3y - 5)$

8. $x^2(xy + x - 8y)$ **9.** $(ab + 3b^2 - b)a^2$ **10.** $2cd(d^2 - 7cd - 1)$

Dividing by a Monomial To divide a polynomial by a monomial, divide each term in the polynomial by the monomial, then use the quotient of powers property.

Example 3   *Dividing a Polynomial by a Monomial*

Find the quotient $\dfrac{6x^6 - 10x^4 + 2x^2}{-2x^2}$.

$\dfrac{6x^6 - 10x^4 + 2x^2}{-2x^2} = \dfrac{6x^6}{-2x^2} + \dfrac{-10x^4}{-2x^2} + \dfrac{2x^2}{-2x^2}$ Rewrite quotient.

$= \dfrac{-3x^6}{x^2} + \dfrac{5x^4}{x^2} + \dfrac{-x^2}{x^2}$ Divide numerators and denominators by −2.

$= -3x^{6-2} + 5x^{4-2} - x^{2-2}$ Quotient of powers property

$= -3x^4 + 5x^2 - x^0$ Simplify exponents.

$= -3x^4 + 5x^2 - 1$ Definition of zero exponent

✔ **Checkpoint**

Find the quotient.

11. $\dfrac{9x^2 - 15x + 6}{-3}$ **12.** $\dfrac{35x^3 + 5x^2 - 25x}{5x}$ **13.** $\dfrac{2x^4 + 8x^3 - 6x^2}{-2x^2}$

Review *Help*

To review the product of powers property, see p. 194.

Review *Help*

To review the quotient of powers property, see p. 195.

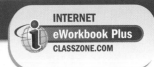
Guided Practice

Vocabulary Check

1. Copy and complete: To find the product of x and $y + 3$, use the _?_ property.

2. Describe how to use the product of powers property when finding the product of y^3 and $y^2 + 7y - 3$.

Skill Check **Find the product.**

3. $-2x(3x^2 + x)$

4. $(6y - 1)4y^2$

5. $(8z + 3)z^2$

6. $-3a^2(3a^2 + a + 2)$

7. $10b(3b^2 + 7b + 4)$

8. $(d^2 + 9d - 2)(-7d)$

Guided Problem Solving

9. **Rabbits** You have 50 feet of wire fencing that you want to use to make a rectangular pen for rabbits. Let l be the length of the pen. What is a polynomial expression in terms of l for the area of the pen?

   (1) Write the formula for the perimeter of a rectangle. Substitute 50 for the perimeter.

   (2) Solve the equation from Step 1 for w to obtain a polynomial expression in terms of l for the width.

   (3) Multiply the expression from Step 2 by l to obtain a polynomial expression in terms of l for the area of the pen.

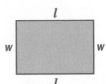

l

w w

l

Perimeter = 50 ft

Practice and Problem Solving

Find the product.

Homework *Help*

Example	Exercises
1	10–15, 28, 33, 35
2	16–21, 29–32, 34, 36–44
3	22–27, 29–32

Online Resources
CLASSZONE.COM

• More Examples
• eTutorial Plus

10. $(3g + 10)12g$

11. $5x(x^2 - 2x)$

12. $-8t^2(4 + t^2)$

13. $(4f^2 - 1)3f$

14. $-4n^2(n^2 + 2n)$

15. $-g^2(g^2 - 6g)$

16. $2(3x^2 + x + 2)$

17. $5d^2(d^2 - 7d + 1)$

18. $-r(-r^2 + 2r - 1)$

19. $-7y(3y^2 + 4y - 2)$

20. $(m^3 + 9m^2 + 1)3m^2$

21. $(w^3 - 6w^2 + w)6w$

Find the quotient.

22. $\dfrac{24p^2 + 16p}{-4p}$

23. $\dfrac{-10z^2 - 25z}{5z}$

24. $\dfrac{-6h^4 + h^3 + 10h^2}{2h^2}$

25. $\dfrac{11m^8 - m^6 - 2m^4}{m^2}$

26. $\dfrac{2t^6 + t^4 - 3t^3}{-t^2}$

27. $\dfrac{-3n^3 + n^2 - 2n}{-2n}$

28. **Geometry** A rectangle has a length that is 3 units more than twice the width w. Sketch the rectangle. Write a polynomial expression in terms of w for the area of the rectangle. Give your answer in standard form.

In Exercises 29–32, match the product or quotient with the equivalent polynomial.

29. $-3x(2x^2 - x - 7)$

30. $\dfrac{-12x^2 + 6x^3 - 42x^4}{-2x^2}$

31. $(-7 + x + 2x^2)3x^2$

32. $\dfrac{-21x + 3x^2 - 6x^3}{-x}$

A. $21 - 3x + 6x^2$

B. $21x + 3x^2 - 6x^3$

C. $21x^2 - 3x + 6$

D. $-21x^2 + 3x^3 + 6x^4$

33. Geometry Write a polynomial expression for the area of the figure. Give your answer in standard form.

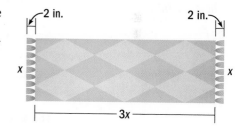

34. *Writing* Your friend says that the product of x^2 and $x^3 + 5x^2 + 1$ is $x^6 + 5x^4 + x^2$. Do you agree with your friend? If not, explain your reasoning.

35. Rugs The length of a rug is three times the width. There are 2 inches of fringe on each end of the rug, as shown. Write a polynomial expression for the area of the rug, including the fringe. Give your answer in standard form.

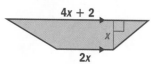

Find the product.

36. $a(3a + 4b - c)$

37. $(9m + n - 4)2n$

38. $(g + 11h + gh)(-4g)$

39. $(5x + 6y + 8)xy$

40. $-2x(x + xy + 3y)$

41. $-3n^2(m + n^2 + 2)$

42. $(5rs - 2r - s^2)(-rs)$

43. $-5c(-c^2 + 7d^2 - d)$

44. $(2ab - a^2 + 4b)ab$

45. Extended Problem Solving You are designing a poster for a student government election. The poster includes text and an enlarged photo. The original photo was 10 inches long and 8 inches wide. The dimensions of the enlarged photo are x times the dimensions of the original photo. As shown, you want space for 5 inches of text at the top and bottom of the poster, along the shorter sides of the photo.

a. Write polynomial expressions in terms of x for the length and width of the poster.

b. Apply Write a polynomial expression in terms of x for the area of the poster. What is the area of the poster when $x = 5$?

c. Compare Compare the area of the poster when $x = 10$ to the area of the poster when $x = 5$.

46. Reflecting Pool The rectangular Reflecting Pool near the Washington Monument in Washington, D.C., has a length that is 50 feet more than 15 times the width. The pool has a depth that is $\frac{1}{50}$ of the width. Let w represent the width of the pool.

a. Write polynomial expressions in terms of w for the length and depth of the pool. Write a polynomial expression in terms of w for the volume of the pool. Give your answers in standard form.

b. The depth of the pool is 3 feet. What is the volume of the pool?

47. Geometry To form the figure shown, start with a rectangle measuring a units by b units, and remove a square measuring x units on a side. Use the figure to complete the following.

a. Find a polynomial expression for the area of the shaded figure by adding the areas of rectangle 1 and rectangle 2.

b. Find a polynomial expression for the area of the shaded figure by subtracting the area of the square from the area of the rectangle that includes the shaded figure and the square.

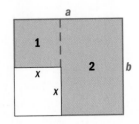

c. **Critical Thinking** Show that the polynomial expressions from parts (a) and (b) are equivalent.

48. Challenge You are finding the product of a monomial and a binomial. How is the degree of the product related to the degree of the monomial and the degree of the binomial? Give examples and explain your reasoning.

Mixed Review

Identify the domain and range of the relation. *(Lesson 8.1)*

49. $(5, 0), (0, 5), (3, 3), (-4, -4)$

50. $(2, 7), (3, 8), (2, 8), (3, 7), (4, 9)$

51. $(9, 9), (7, -8), (6, 10), (8, -8)$

52. $(0, 2), (5, 7), (8, 10), (0, -2)$

53. Skateboard Ramp A skateboard ramp is 12 feet long. The ramp makes an angle of 30° with the ground. Find the distance d along the bottom of the ramp. Round to the nearest tenth of a foot. *(Lesson 9.6)*

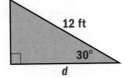

Find the sum or difference. *(Lesson 12.2)*

54. $(7x^3 - 2x^2 + x) + (-2x^2 - 1)$

55. $(-2x^2 + 5x + 4) - (x^2 + 7x - 6)$

Standardized Test Practice

56. Extended Response You have 24 feet of fencing that you want to use to make a rectangular dog pen. Let l represent the length of the pen.

a. Draw a diagram of the pen.

b. Write a polynomial for the width in terms of l. Write a polynomial for the area in terms of l.

c. What is the area of the pen if $l = 4$? if $l = 10$?

12.4 Modeling Binomial Multiplication

Goal
Model binomial multiplication using algebra tiles.

Materials
• algebra tiles

Investigate

Find the product (3x + 1)(x + 4) using algebra tiles.

 1 Represent each binomial using algebra tiles. Arrange the first binomial vertically and the second binomial horizontally, as shown.

 2 The binomials define a rectangular region with length $(3x + 1)$ units and width $(x + 4)$ units. Fill in the region with the appropriate tiles.

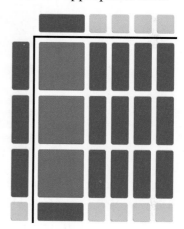

 3 The tiles covering the rectangular region represent $3x^2 + 13x + 4$. This expression is the product of the binomials.

Draw Conclusions

Use algebra tiles to find the product. Draw your model.

1. $(x + 3)(x + 3)$ **2.** $(2x + 1)(x + 3)$ **3.** $(5x + 1)(x + 2)$

4. $(3x + 4)(2x + 1)$ **5.** $(4x + 2)(3x + 1)$ **6.** $(x + 5)(6x + 2)$

7. *Writing* Describe how you can use algebra tiles to find the product $2x(x + 3)$. Do you get the same result using the distributive property, as in Lesson 12.3? Explain.

8. **Critical Thinking** You can also use the distributive property to multiply binomials. Describe how you could use the distributive property to find the product $(3x + 1)(x + 4)$. Begin by distributing $x + 4$ to each term of $3x + 1$.

12.4 Multiplying Binomials

BEFORE	Now	WHY?
You multiplied monomials and polynomials.	You'll multiply binomials.	So you can find the area of a garden and walkway, as in Ex. 32.

Review Vocabulary

binomial, p. 651

In the activity on page 667, you learned how to model binomial multiplication using algebra tiles. You can also use a table to multiply two binomials. The model and table below show the product $(x + 4)(2x + 3)$. Notice how using a table is similar to using algebra tiles.

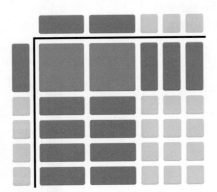

Terms of the first binomial

Terms of the second binomial

	2x	**3**
x	$2x^2$	$3x$
4	$8x$	12

Multiply terms to fill in the table. For example, $4 \cdot 2x = 8x$.

From the table, you can see that $(x + 4)(2x + 3)$ is $2x^2 + 3x + 8x + 12$, or $2x^2 + 11x + 12$.

Example 1 *Multiplying Binomials Using a Table*

Find the product $(-2x + 5)(3x - 1)$.

Write any subtractions in the binomials as additions.

$$(-2x + 5)(3x - 1) = (-2x + 5)[3x + (-1)]$$

First binomial ⟶ Second binomial

	$3x$	-1
$-2x$	$-6x^2$	$2x$
5	$15x$	-5

The product is $-6x^2 + 2x + 15x - 5$, or $-6x^2 + 17x - 5$.

✔ Checkpoint

Use a table to find the product.

1. $(4x + 1)(2x + 3)$ **2.** $(-m + 2)(5m + 2)$ **3.** $(2a - 3)(5a - 6)$

4. $(-n + 7)(11n + 1)$ **5.** $(6s - 9)(-2s + 5)$ **6.** $(-6b - 4)(-b + 3)$

Distributive Property Another way to multiply binomials is to use the distributive property.

Example 2   *Using the Distributive Property*

Photograph You are enlarging a photo that is 7 inches long and 5 inches wide. The length and width of the enlargement are x times the length and width of the original photo. The enlargement will have a 2 inch mat. Write a polynomial expression for the combined area of the enlargement and mat.

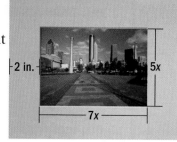

Solution

The total length of the enlargement and mat is $(7x + 4)$ inches. The total width is $(5x + 4)$ inches. To find the area, multiply.

$$(7x + 4)(5x + 4) = 7x(5x + 4) + 4(5x + 4) \quad \textbf{Distribute } 5x + 4.$$
$$= 35x^2 + 28x + 20x + 16 \quad \textbf{Distribute } 7x \textbf{ and } 4.$$
$$= 35x^2 + 48x + 16 \quad \textbf{Combine like terms.}$$

Answer The area is $(35x^2 + 48x + 16)$ square inches.

FOIL Method Notice that using the distributive property to multiply binomials produces four products that are then added. These four products are the products of the *first* terms, the *outer* terms, the *inner* terms, and the *last* terms of the binomials. You can use the shorthand **FOIL** to remind you of the words **F**irst, **O**uter, **I**nner, and **L**ast.

$$\overbrace{(2x + 5)(6x + 1)} = 12x^2 + 2x + 30x + 5$$

First   Outer   Inner   Last

Note *Worthy*

In this lesson you have learned three methods for multiplying binomials. Record and compare these methods in your notebook.

Example 3   *Using the FOIL Method*

Find the product $(4x + 3)(5x - 2)$.

$$\begin{array}{cccc} \text{First} & + \textbf{O}\text{uter} & + \text{Inner} & + \text{Last} \\ (4x)(5x) & + (4x)(-2) & + (3)(5x) & + (3)(-2) \\ 20x^2 & + (-8x) & + 15x & + (-6) \end{array}$$ **Write products of terms.**

Multiply.

$$20x^2 + 7x - 6 \quad \textbf{Combine like terms.}$$

✔ *Checkpoint*

Find the product.

7. $(x + 5)(x - 9)$ **8.** $(8k - 1)(-3k - 5)$ **9.** $(-z + 6)(10z + 2)$

10. $(b + 4)(b + 9)$ **11.** $(m - 3)(m - 2)$ **12.** $(5t - 1)(2t + 7)$

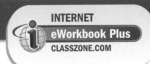

Guided Practice

Vocabulary Check

1. What does each letter in FOIL represent?

2. Describe how you can use the distributive property to find the product of two binomials.

Skill Check **Use a table to find the product.**

3. $(a + 2)(4a + 3)$ 4. $(3b - 7)(3b + 2)$ 5. $(-4c + 5)(2c - 4)$

Use the distributive property to find the product.

6. $(2x + 1)(3x + 8)$ 7. $(8y + 2)(y - 2)$ 8. $(-5z - 3)(4z + 6)$

Use the FOIL method to find the product.

9. $(a + 7)(3a + 1)$ 10. $(-2b + 5)(3b + 6)$ 11. $(10c - 4)(5c - 1)$

12. **Error Analysis** Describe and correct the error in finding the product $(x - 3)(4x + 2)$.

$$(x - 3)(4x + 2) = x(4x + 2) + (-3)(4x + 2)$$
$$= 4x^2 + 2x - 12x + 6$$
$$= 4x^2 - 10x + 6$$

Practice and Problem Solving

Homework *Help*

Example	Exercises
1	13-30, 32-41
2	13-27, 32-41
3	13-27, 32-41

Online Resources
CLASSZONE.COM
• More Examples
• eTutorial Plus

Find the product.

13. $(x + 4)(3x + 1)$ 14. $(5a + 2)(2a + 3)$ 15. $(4t - 8)(3t + 2)$

16. $(b + 12)(b - 10)$ 17. $(7p - 4)(6p - 2)$ 18. $(9n - 6)(2n - 5)$

19. $(-3w + 8)(8w + 1)$ 20. $(10s - 4)^2$ 21. $(-4m + 7)^2$

22. $(-8r + 9)(-3r - 2)$ 23. $(11v - 6)(-v - 6)$ 24. $(-2y - 11)(-12y - 3)$

Geometry **Write a polynomial expression for the area of the figure. Give your answer in standard form.**

25.
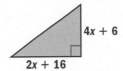
$4x + 6$
$2x + 16$

26.
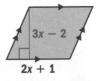
$3x - 2$
$2x + 1$

27.

$2x + 5$
$x + 10$
$4x - 1$

Mental Math Copy and complete the table.

28.

	$-5x$	2
x	$-5x^2$	$?$
-1	$?$	-2

29.

	$?$	4
$-3x$	$-6x^2$	$-12x$
7	$14x$	$?$

30.

	$2x$	$?$
$?$	$8x^2$	$20x$
-3	$-6x$	-15

31. *Writing* How is finding the product of two binomials like finding the product of a monomial and a polynomial? How is it different?

32. Garden The length of a rectangular garden is three times the width. A stone walkway 4 feet wide surrounds the garden. Write a polynomial expression for the area of the garden and walkway. Give your answer in standard form.

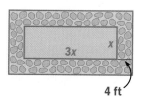

Find the product.

33. $(-x + 1.2)(2x + 5)$ **34.** $(4t + 0.6)(t - 1)$ **35.** $(5g - 4)(0.2g + 3.5)$

36. $\left(\frac{1}{2}k - 6\right)\left(k - \frac{4}{7}\right)$ **37.** $\left(12h + \frac{3}{8}\right)\left(3h + \frac{5}{4}\right)$ **38.** $\left(\frac{4}{3}u - 8\right)\left(\frac{9}{2}u - 1\right)$

39. $(11a - b)(2a + 8b)$ **40.** $(7c + 2d)(-c + d)$ **41.** $(-3x + 2y)(4x - y)$

42. Webpages You are designing a webpage. At the top is a banner ad that is 1.5 inches high. On the left side is an index that is 2 inches wide. The width and height of the page depend on the user's browser. Use the diagram to find a polynomial expression for the area of the webpage, excluding the banner ad and index. Give your answer in standard form.

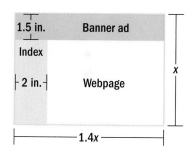

43. Mozzarella For the period 1990–1999, the amount of mozzarella (in pounds) consumed each year by a typical person in the U.S. can be approximated by the first polynomial below. For the same period, the U.S. population (in millions) can be approximated by the second polynomial below. In both polynomials, x represents the number of years since 1990.

Mozzarella consumption: $0.2x + 7$ **U.S. population:** $2.6x + 250$

a. Write a polynomial, in terms of x, that approximates the *total* amount of mozzarella (in millions of pounds) consumed in the U.S.

b. Evaluate the polynomial from part (a) when $x = 0$ to find the approximate total consumption of mozzarella in the U.S. in 1990.

c. Evaluate the polynomial from part (a) when $x = 9$ to find the approximate total consumption of mozzarella in the U.S. in 1999. Round your answer to the nearest million pounds.

44. Geometry The figure shown is composed of a triangle and a rectangle. Write a polynomial expression for the area of the figure. Give your answer in standard form.

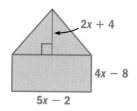

45. Critical Thinking You want to find the product of three binomials. Which method would you use—algebra tiles, a table, the distributive property, or the FOIL method? Explain your reasoning.

46. Write polynomial expressions for the surface area and volume of the rectangular prism shown. Give your answers in standard form.

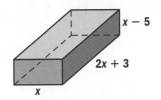

47. Extended Problem Solving You want to make a box with no lid for storing small items. You have an 11 inch by 7 inch piece of stiff cardboard. You cut out squares of side length x inches from each corner. Then you fold the sides up and tape them together as shown.

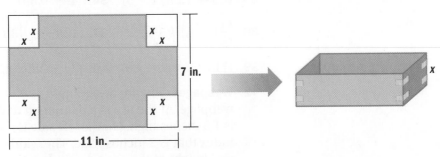

   a. Analyze Write polynomials for the length, width, and height of the box. Write inequalities to describe the possible values of x.

   b. Write a polynomial in standard form for the volume of the box.

   c. ▦ **Apply** Use the *table* feature on a graphing calculator to find the value of x, to the nearest tenth of an inch, that gives the greatest volume.

48. Challenge Find the products below. What pattern do you notice? Make and test a conjecture based on your observations.

$$(x + 1)(x - 1) \qquad (x + 2)(x - 2) \qquad (x + 3)(x - 3) \qquad (x + 4)(x - 4)$$

Mixed Review

Find the product. Write your answer using only positive exponents. *(Lesson 4.6)*

49. $(5^{-4})(5^7)$ **50.** $(11^{-2})(11^{-4})$ **51.** $(x^{-12})(x^5)$ **52.** $(m^{-9})(m^{-4})$

Approximate the square root to the nearest integer. *(Lesson 9.1)*

53. $-\sqrt{10}$ **54.** $\sqrt{68}$ **55.** $\sqrt{145}$ **56.** $-\sqrt{232}$

Find the product. *(Lesson 12.3)*

57. $7x(3x - 4)$ **58.** $12z(5z + 1)$ **59.** $4s^2(-s - 10)$ **60.** $-2y^2(7y^2 + 8y)$

Standardized Test Practice

61. Multiple Choice A rectangular painting is twice as long as it is wide. The painting has a 3 inch wide frame. Let x represent the painting's width. Which product gives the area of the painting and frame?

   A. $(2x)(x)$ **B.** $(2x + 3)(x + 3)$

   C. $(2x + 3)(x + 6)$ **D.** $(2x + 6)(x + 6)$

62. Multiple Choice Which product equals $6x^2 - 7x + 2$?

   F. $(6x + 1)(x - 7)$ **G.** $(-6x + 1)(-x + 7)$

   H. $(2x - 1)(3x + 2)$ **I.** $(-2x + 1)(-3x + 2)$

Mid-Chapter Quiz

Find the degree of the polynomial.

1. $5x^3 - x + 2$

2. $-1 + 3z^4 - 7z$

3. $5y^3 - 3xy + 7x^2$

Write the expression as a polynomial in standard form.

4. $y + 2y^2 - 9 + 5y$

5. $-14 + 5b^2 - 7b(b + 1)$

6. $3k^2(2 - k) + 18k^4$

Find the sum or difference.

7. $(8x^2 + 3x) + (7x^2 - 15x)$

8. $(-x^3 + 5x) + (3x^2 - 7x)$

9. $(x^3 - x^2 + 7x) - (2x^3 + x + 1)$

10. Photography You have a photograph that is 5 inches long and 3 inches wide. You want to surround the photo with a mat that will be x inches wide on all sides, as shown.

    a. Write a polynomial expression for the total width of the photo and the mat.

    b. Write a polynomial expression for the total length of the photo and the mat.

    c. Write a polynomial expression for the combined area of the photo and mat.

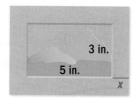

3 in.

5 in.

x

Find the product.

11. $(3b + 4)(b - 7)$

12. $(9p - 1)^2$

13. $(n - 8)(3n - 5)$

Brain GAME

Missing Monomials

Find the missing terms in the equations below. Locate these terms in the table. Then unscramble the letters below the terms to answer the following riddle.

How many letters are there in the alphabet?

$(2a + 5)(3a - 8) = 6a^2 + \underline{\ ?\ } - 40$ $(b - 6)(2b + \underline{\ ?\ }) = 2b^2 - 8b - 24$

$(4c + \underline{\ ?\ })(\underline{\ ?\ } - 1) = 4c^2 - 7c + 3$ $(3d + 7)(\underline{\ ?\ } + \underline{\ ?\ }) = 12d^2 + 34d + 14$

Term	$-a$	b	c	$-d$	$2a$	$3b$	$-2c$	$4d$	-8	-3	1	2	4
Letter	E	D	L	R	T	W	I	E	H	E	O	V	N

Other Rules *of* Exponents

BEFORE	*Now*	WHY?
You simplified products and quotients of powers.	You'll simplify powers of products and quotients.	So you can find the area of a transistor, as in Ex. 11.

Review Vocabulary

power, p. 10
exponent, p. 10

Notice what happens when you raise a product or a quotient to a power.

$$(ab)^3 = (ab)(ab)(ab)$$
$$= (a \cdot a \cdot a)(b \cdot b \cdot b)$$
$$= a^3 b^3$$

$$\left(\frac{a}{b}\right)^3 = \left(\frac{a}{b}\right)\left(\frac{a}{b}\right)\left(\frac{a}{b}\right)$$
$$= \frac{a \cdot a \cdot a}{b \cdot b \cdot b}$$
$$= \frac{a^3}{b^3}$$

Rules of Exponents

Power of a Product Property

Words To find the power of a product, find the power of each factor and multiply.

Algebra $(ab)^m = a^m b^m$ **Numbers** $(3 \cdot 4)^2 = 3^2 \cdot 4^2$

Power of a Quotient Property

Words To find the power of a quotient, find the power of the numerator and the power of the denominator and divide.

Algebra $\left(\frac{a}{b}\right)^m = \frac{a^m}{b^m}$, where $b \neq 0$ **Numbers** $\left(\frac{4}{7}\right)^5 = \frac{4^5}{7^5}$

Example 1   *Finding Powers of Products*

a. $(2x)^3 = 2^3 \cdot x^3$ **Power of a product property**
$\qquad = 8x^3$ **Evaluate power.**

b. $(-5y)^2 = (-5)^2 \cdot y^2$ **Power of a product property**
$\qquad\quad = 25y^2$ **Evaluate power.**

 Checkpoint

Simplify the expression.

1. $(4y)^3$ **2.** $(3x)^4$ **3.** $(-5m)^3$ **4.** $(-7b)^2$

Example 2 *Finding Powers of Quotients*

Simplify the expression.

a. $\left(\dfrac{m}{n}\right)^7 = \dfrac{m^7}{n^7}$ Power of a quotient property

b. $\left(\dfrac{-3}{k}\right)^5 = \dfrac{(-3)^5}{k^5}$ Power of a quotient property

          $= \dfrac{-243}{k^5}$ Evaluate power.

 Checkpoint

Simplify the expression.

5. $\left(\dfrac{a}{6}\right)^2$ **6.** $\left(\dfrac{b}{c}\right)^3$ **7.** $\left(\dfrac{x}{-9}\right)^2$ **8.** $\left(\dfrac{-2}{n}\right)^5$

Power of a Power Property Another rule of exponents is the power of a power property. The example below suggests the general rule.

$$(a^2)^4 = (a^2)(a^2)(a^2)(a^2)$$
$$= (a \cdot a)(a \cdot a)(a \cdot a)(a \cdot a)$$
$$= a^8$$

Rules of Exponents

Power of a Power Property

Words To find the power of a power, multiply the exponents.

Algebra $(a^m)^n = a^{mn}$ **Numbers** $(7^2)^3 = 7^{2 \times 3} = 7^6$

Watch *Out*

When you multiply exponents to apply the power of a power property, don't forget to consider the signs of the exponents.

Example 3 *Finding a Power of a Power*

Simplify the expression. Use positive exponents.

a. $(10^3)^3 = 10^9$ Power of a power property

b. $(p^{-4})^5 = p^{-20}$ Power of a power property

          $= \dfrac{1}{p^{20}}$ Definition of negative exponent

Checkpoint

Simplify the expression. Write your answer using positive exponents.

9. $(2^3)^4$ **10.** $(5^2)^{-2}$ **11.** $(k^6)^3$ **12.** $(a^{-2})^5$

13. $(4^{-1})^3$ **14.** $(3^{-4})^2$ **15.** $(b^7)^4$ **16.** $(x^{-3})^{-2}$

Example 4   Using Properties of Exponents

World's Tiniest Book The square pages of the world's tiniest book are about 2.5×10^{-3} meter on each side. What is the approximate area of one page of this book?

Solution

To find the area of one page, use the formula for the area of a square.

$A = s^2$	Formula for area of a square
$= (2.5 \times 10^{-3})^2$	Substitute 2.5×10^{-3} for s.
$= (2.5)^2 \times (10^{-3})^2$	Power of a product property
$= (2.5)^2 \times 10^{-6}$	Power of a power property
$= 6.25 \times 10^{-6}$	Evaluate power.

Answer Each page has an area of about 6.25×10^{-6} square meter.

 Checkpoint

Simplify the expression. Write your answer in scientific notation.

17. $(3.1 \times 10^8)^2$ **18.** $(2.1 \times 10^{-5})^2$ **19.** $(1.7 \times 10^{-9})^3$ **20.** $(4.5 \times 10^7)^3$

12.5 Exercises

More Practice, p. 814

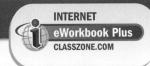

INTERNET
eWorkbook Plus
CLASSZONE.COM

Guided Practice

Vocabulary Check   **1.** Describe the power of a quotient property and give an example.

2. Tell what property or properties of exponents you could use to simplify the expression.

   a. $(x^3)^4$ **b.** $(mn)^5$ **c.** $\left(\dfrac{p}{q}\right)^3$ **d.** $(a^2b)^6$

Skill Check   **Simplify the expression. Write your answer using positive exponents.**

   3. $(-6x)^3$ **4.** $(5y)^4$ **5.** $\left(\dfrac{n}{-7}\right)^2$ **6.** $\left(\dfrac{2}{m}\right)^5$

   7. $(7^{-1})^{-6}$ **8.** $(3^2)^{-5}$ **9.** $(y^3)^2$ **10.** $(a^{-1})^4$

11. Computers Some transistors used in computers are squares with a side length of 1.3×10^{-7} meter. What is the area of one of these transistors?

12. Error Analysis Describe and correct the error in simplifying $(3x)^4$.

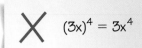

Practice and Problem Solving

Homework *Help*

Example	Exercises
1	13–20, 36–39
2	21–24, 40–43
3	25–28, 36–43
4	29–35

Online Resources
CLASSZONE.COM
• More Examples
• eTutorial Plus

Simplify the expression. Write your answer using positive exponents.

13. $(yz)^6$ **14.** $(pr)^7$ **15.** $(3t)^4$ **16.** $(5c)^2$

17. $(-3y)^8$ **18.** $(-7x)^3$ **19.** $(ab)^3$ **20.** $(pq)^8$

21. $\left(\dfrac{p}{10}\right)^5$ **22.** $\left(\dfrac{w}{12}\right)^2$ **23.** $\left(\dfrac{-3}{x}\right)^4$ **24.** $\left(\dfrac{m}{-2}\right)^6$

25. $(5^2)^4$ **26.** $(4^{-3})^2$ **27.** $(a^4)^{-2}$ **28.** $(x^{-1})^{-6}$

Simplify the expression. Write your answer in scientific notation. Round the decimal part of your answer to the nearest hundredth.

29. $(1.8 \times 10^6)^3$ **30.** $(2.4 \times 10^{-8})^2$ **31.** $(2.2 \times 10^{12})^2$

32. $(6.1 \times 10^2)^5$ **33.** $(3.5 \times 10^{-10})^3$ **34.** $(9.6 \times 10^{-1})^4$

35. Hoag's Object Hoag's Object is a galaxy composed of a blue ring around a yellow center. The diameter of the blue ring is about 1.2×10^5 light-years. Find the area of the circle formed by the blue ring. Use 3.14 for π. Write your answer in scientific notation, rounding the decimal part to the nearest hundredth.

Simplify the expression. Write your answer using positive exponents.

36. $(ab^2)^3$ **37.** $(x^2y)^4$ **38.** $(m^2n)^5$ **39.** $(d^3e^4)^2$

40. $\left(\dfrac{x^5}{y^4}\right)^6$ **41.** $\left(\dfrac{w^3}{v^5}\right)^5$ **42.** $\left(\dfrac{p^3}{t^2}\right)^2$ **43.** $\left(\dfrac{-r}{s^4}\right)^3$

Hoag's Object

In Exercises 44–49, copy and complete the statement.

Example *Converting Units For Area or Volume*

Copy and complete: $3 \text{ ft}^3 = \underline{\ ?\ } \text{ in.}^3$

Cube the conversion factor for converting feet to inches.

$3 \text{ ft}^3 = 3 \text{ ft}^3 \times \left(\dfrac{12 \text{ in.}}{1 \text{ ft}}\right)^3$ **Multiply by cube of conversion factor.**

$= 3 \text{ ft}^3 \times \dfrac{(12 \text{ in.})^3}{(1 \text{ ft})^3}$ **Power of a quotient property**

$= 3 \text{ ft}^3 \times \dfrac{1728 \text{ in.}^3}{1 \text{ ft}^3}$ **Evaluate powers. Divide out common unit.**

$= 5184 \text{ in.}^3$ **Simplify.**

44. $5 \text{ ft}^2 = \underline{\ ?\ } \text{ in.}^2$ **45.** $45 \text{ m}^2 = \underline{\ ?\ } \text{ km}^2$ **46.** $1 \text{ yd}^2 = \underline{\ ?\ } \text{ ft}^2$

47. $6 \text{ m}^3 = \underline{\ ?\ } \text{ cm}^3$ **48.** $3 \text{ mm}^3 = \underline{\ ?\ } \text{ cm}^3$ **49.** $2 \text{ mi}^2 = \underline{\ ?\ } \text{ ft}^2$

50. *Writing* Compare the power of a product property from this lesson with the product of powers property on page 194. Write an expression to which *both* properties can be applied, then apply the properties.

51. Extended Problem Solving The pistons in a hydraulic system are cylinders containing fluid. When one piston is pushed down, another piston is pushed up by an equal volume of fluid. Use the information in the diagram to answer the following questions.

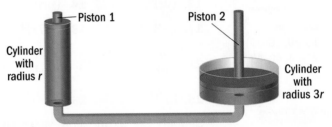

a. Piston 1 is pushed down 7 inches. What volume of fluid is displaced from piston 1? Use 3.14 for π.

b. Interpret and Apply How many inches will the volume you calculated in part (a) push up piston 2? Explain.

c. Critical Thinking Suppose piston 2 is pushed down a distance d (in inches). How far (in terms of d) is piston 1 pushed up?

52. Challenge Scientists have developed microscopic spheres called nanospheres that circulate in the bloodstream and deliver medicine for several hours. A nanosphere's radius can be as small as 4.5×10^{-8} m. The formula for the volume of a sphere is $V = \frac{4}{3}\pi r^3$. Use this formula to find the volume of a nanosphere. Use 3.14 for π. Write your answer in scientific notation, rounding the decimal part to the nearest hundredth.

This hydraulic crane is being used to assemble a sculpture.

Mixed Review

Algebra Basics Graph the equation. Tell whether the equation is a function. (Lesson 8.2)

53. $y = -\frac{1}{3}x + 6$ **54.** $y = 4x - 3$ **55.** $x = 30$ **56.** $24x + 4y = 16$

Algebra Basics Graph the inequality in a coordinate plane. (Lesson 8.9)

57. $y > 2x - 7$ **58.** $y \geq -\frac{5}{6}x - 3$ **59.** $8x + 48 \leq 12y$ **60.** $-8x + 3y < 21$

Write a polynomial expression for the area of the rectangle, triangle, or parallelogram. Give your answer in standard form. (Lesson 12.4)

61. 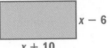 **62.** **63.**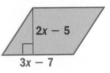

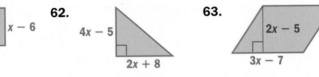

Standardized Test Practice

64. Multiple Choice Which expression is equivalent to $\left(\dfrac{-4}{x^2}\right)^3$?

A. $\dfrac{64}{x^6}$ **B.** $\dfrac{-64}{x^6}$ **C.** $\dfrac{64}{x^3}$ **D.** $\dfrac{-64}{x^3}$

65. Multiple Choice Which expression is equivalent to $-a^8 b^6$?

F. $-(a^4 b^3)^2$ **G.** $(-a^4 b^3)^2$ **H.** $(-a)^8 (b^3)^2$ **I.** $-(a^4)(b^3)^2$

12.6

Quadratic Functions

Vocabulary

quadratic function, p. 679
parabola, p. 680
nonlinear function, p. 680
minimum value, p. 681
maximum value, p. 681

Acrobats An acrobat is launched into the air from a teeterboard. The acrobat's height from the ground (in feet) is given by the function

$$h = -16t^2 + 33t + 3,$$

where t is the time in seconds after the launch. What is the greatest height that the acrobat reaches? You will see how to answer this question in Example 4.

The function $h = -16t^2 + 33t + 3$ is a *quadratic function*. A **quadratic function** is an equation in two variables that can be written in the form $y = ax^2 + bx + c$, where a, b, and c are constants and $a \neq 0$.

Example 1 — Evaluating a Quadratic Function

To make a table of values for the quadratic function $y = 2x^2 + 3x + 1$, substitute several values of x into the equation. Then simplify to find the corresponding values for y.

x	Substitution	y
-2	$y = 2(-2)^2 + 3(-2) + 1$ $= 8 + (-6) + 1$ $= 3$	3
-1	$y = 2(-1)^2 + 3(-1) + 1$	0
0	$y = 2(0)^2 + 3(0) + 1$	1
1	$y = 2(1)^2 + 3(1) + 1$	6
2	$y = 2(2)^2 + 3(2) + 1$	15

For $x = -2$, the process of substituting and simplifying is shown.

For $x = -1, 0, 1,$ and 2, only the substitution is shown.

 Checkpoint

Make a table of values for the given function.

1. $y = -x^2 + 2x + 1$ **2.** $y = x^2 - 4x + 7$ **3.** $y = 3x^2 + 6x - 9$

Graphing Quadratic Functions The graph of a quadratic function is a U-shaped curve called a **parabola**. A quadratic function is an example of a *nonlinear function*. A **nonlinear function** is any function whose graph is not a line.

Example 2   *Graphing a Quadratic Function*

Graph the function $y = \frac{1}{2}x^2 + 1$.

1. Make a table of values. Choose several x-values and find the corresponding y-values.

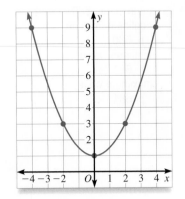

x	-4	-2	0	2	4
y	9	3	1	3	9

2. Use the table to make a list of ordered pairs.

   $(-4, 9)$, $(-2, 3)$, $(0, 1)$, $(2, 3)$, $(4, 9)$

3. Graph the ordered pairs. Then draw a smooth curve through the points.

✔ *Checkpoint*

Make a table of values for the given function. Then graph the function.

4. $y = 2x^2 + 5$ **5.** $y = x^2 - 8x - 2$ **6.** $y = x^2 + 4x$

Example 3   *Graphing a Quadratic Function*

Graph the function $y = -x^2 + 2x - 1$.

1. Make a table of values. Choose several x-values and find the corresponding y-values.

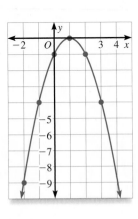

x	-2	-1	0	1	2	3
y	-9	-4	-1	0	-1	-4

2. Use the table to make a list of ordered pairs.

   $(-2, -9)$, $(-1, -4)$, $(0, -1)$, $(1, 0)$, $(2, -1)$, $(3, -4)$

3. Graph the ordered pairs. Then draw a smooth curve through the points.

Make a table of values for the given function. Then graph the function.

7. $y = -x^2 - 3$　　　　**8.** $y = -2x^2 + 4x$　　　　**9.** $y = -x^2 + 6x + 1$

Maximum and Minimum Values In the quadratic function $y = ax^2 + bx + c$, the value of a indicates whether the graph opens upward or downward.

When $a > 0$, as in Example 2, the graph of the function opens upward. In this case, the function has a **minimum value**, which is the y-coordinate of the lowest point on the graph.

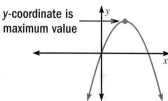

y-coordinate is minimum value

When $a < 0$, as in Example 3, the graph of the function opens downward. In this case, the function has a **maximum value**, which is the y-coordinate of the highest point on the graph.

y-coordinate is maximum value

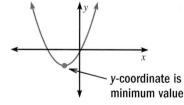

Study *Strategy*

The function in Example 2 has a minimum value of 1 at $x = 0$. The function in Example 3 has a maximum value of 0 at $x = 1$.

Example 4　　*Using a Calculator to Find a Maximum Value*

Find the greatest height reached by the acrobat described on page 679.

Solution

Use a graphing calculator to graph $h = -16t^2 + 33t + 3$. Set the viewing window so that you can see the highest point on the graph. Using the calculator's *trace* feature, you can determine that the highest point on the graph is about (1.02, 20.01). So, the maximum value is about 20.

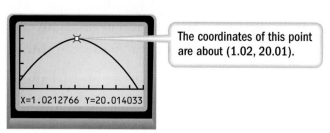

The coordinates of this point are about (1.02, 20.01).

X=1.0212766　Y=20.014033

Answer The greatest height reached by the acrobat is about 20 feet.

● **Checkpoint**

Tell whether the function has a *maximum* or *minimum* value.

10. $y = 4.5x^2 - 9x$　　　**11.** $y = x^2 - 17$　　　**12.** $y = -3x^2 - 6x + 3$

 **Tell whether the function has a *maximum* or *minimum* value. Then graph the function using a graphing calculator and approximate the maximum or minimum value.**

13. $y = -x^2 + 6x + 5$　　**14.** $y = -x^2 + 9x + 1$　　**15.** $y = 5x^2 - 10x + 13$

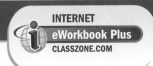

Guided Practice

Vocabulary Check

1. Describe the shape of the graph of a quadratic function.

2. Copy and complete: The graph of a quadratic function with a maximum value opens ? .

Skill Check **Make a table of values for the given function.**

3. $y = -x^2 + 17$ 4. $y = -4x^2 - 5$ 5. $y = 3x^2 + 12x$

Make a table of values for the given function. Then graph the function.

6. $y = -x^2$ 7. $y = x^2 + 1$ 8. $y = -2x^2 - 1$

Tell whether the function has a *maximum* or *minimum* value.

9. $y = -14x^2 + 9x$ 10. $y = 3x^2 - 17$ 11. $y = -6x^2 - 6x + 5$

Guided Problem Solving

12. **Rainbow Trout** The lengths and masses of rainbow trout taken from the Spokane River in Washington are related by the quadratic function $y = 0.90x^2 - 26.5x + 290$, where x is the length (in centimeters) of a rainbow trout and y is its mass (in grams). What is the approximate length of a rainbow trout with a mass of 600 grams?

① Use a graphing calculator to graph the function.

② Use trace to find the approximate x-value when $y = 600$.

Practice and Problem Solving

Homework *Help*

Example	Exercises
1	13-21
2	22-30
3	22-30
4	31-36, 38-43

Online Resources
CLASSZONE.COM

- More Examples
- eTutorial Plus

Make a table of values for the given function.

13. $y = -x^2 - 6x$ 14. $y = 3x^2 + 4$ 15. $y = 5x^2 - 20x$

16. $y = \frac{1}{4}x^2 - 2x$ 17. $y = x^2 - 4x + 5$ 18. $y = -x^2 + 6x + 4$

19. $y = \frac{1}{2}x^2 + x + 4$ 20. $y = 4x^2 + 8x - 3$ 21. $y = -\frac{1}{2}x^2 + 4x - 6$

Matching Match the function with its graph.

22. 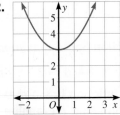   23. 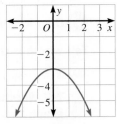   24.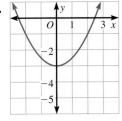

A. $y = \frac{1}{2}x^2 - 3$ **B.** $y = \frac{1}{2}x^2 + 3$ **C.** $y = -\frac{1}{2}x^2 - 3$

Make a table of values for the given function. Then graph the function.

25. $y = -x^2 + 5$ **26.** $y = \frac{1}{2}x^2 + 2x$ **27.** $y = x^2 + 9$

28. $y = \frac{1}{2}x^2 - 3x + 2$ **29.** $y = \frac{1}{6}x^2 - 3x$ **30.** $y = \frac{1}{4}x^2 + \frac{1}{2}x$

Tell whether the function has a *maximum* or *minimum* value.

31. $y = -20x^2 - 9x$ **32.** $y = 5x^2 - 20x + 3$ **33.** $y = 2x^2 - 4x + 5$

34. $y = -x^2 + 9x + 2$ **35.** $y = -x^2 - 9x + 17$ **36.** $y = 3.5x^2 - 1.5x - 2$

37. Wind and Waves For certain bodies of water, the height of the waves and the speed of the wind can be related by the quadratic function $h = 0.007s^2 + 0.15s - 0.15$, where s is the wind speed in meters per second and h is the wave height in meters. Use the graph below to answer the following questions.

a. The ideal wave height for sailing is between 3 meters and 7 meters. What wind speeds correspond to these wave heights?

b. Wave heights greater than 11 meters are considered dangerous when sailing. What wind speeds correspond to wave heights greater than 11 meters?

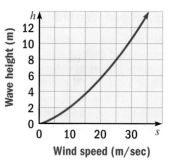

Wind speed (m/sec)

Tell whether the function has a *maximum* or *minimum* value. Then graph the function using a graphing calculator and approximate the maximum or minimum value.

38. $y = -x^2 + 11x + 5$ **39.** $y = -8x^2 + 9x + 1$ **40.** $y = 5x^2 - 9x + 13$

41. $y = -16x^2 + 192x$ **42.** $y = x^2 - 25x - 100$ **43.** $y = 3x^2 + x - 42$

44. *Writing* Graph the functions $y = x^2$, $y = x^2 - 1$, and $y = x^2 + 1$ in the same coordinate plane. Describe how the graphs are related. Predict what the graph of $y = x^2 - 2$ looks like. Then test your prediction.

45. Critical Thinking Describe how to find the y-intercept of the graph of a quadratic function *without* graphing the function.

46. Geometry Recall that the formula for the volume V of a cylinder is $V = \pi r^2 h$, where r is the radius and h is the height. Use 3.14 for π.

a. A cylinder has a fixed height of 4 units. The radius can vary. Write a formula for the volume of this cylinder as a function of its radius. Make a table of values for zero and whole number values of r. Graph the function.

b. A cylinder has a fixed radius of 3 units. The height can vary. Write a formula for the volume of this cylinder as a function of its height. Make a table of values for zero and whole number values of h. Graph the function.

c. Compare Compare the functions from parts (a) and (b). Which of the functions is linear and which is nonlinear?

47. **Extended Problem Solving** For the period 1990–1999, the amount of bottled water consumed annually by a typical person in the United States can be approximated by $y = 0.1x^2 + 0.1x + 7.9$, where y is the amount of water (in gallons) and x is the number of years since 1990.

    a. Use a graphing calculator to graph the function.

    b. **Analyze** What was the first year that a typical person in the United States consumed more than 9 gallons of bottled water annually?

    c. **Interpret and Apply** In which year did annual bottled water consumption increase the most from the previous year? Explain how you can use the graph to answer this question.

48. **Cubic Functions** A *cubic function* is an equation in two variables that can be written in the form $y = ax^3 + bx^2 + cx + d$, where a, b, c, and d are constants and $a \neq 0$.

In the **Real World**

Water Some nutritionists recommend drinking eight 8 ounce glasses of water each day. If you drank 64 ounces of water each day, about how much water would you drink in a year? in 50 years?

    a. Use a graphing calculator to graph the functions $y = x^3$, $y = -x^3$, and $y = 2x^3$.

    b. **Compare** Describe the shapes of the graphs. How are the graphs alike? How are they different?

49. **Challenge** Consider the functions $y = -4x + 3$ and $y = -2x^2 + 6x + 4$.

    a. For each function, make a table of values for $x = 0, 1, 2, 3, 4, 5, 6$. Then graph each function.

    b. For each function, find the slope between each consecutive pair of points you plotted in part (a).

    c. **Interpret** What can you say about the slopes you calculated for the linear function? What can you say about the slopes you calculated for the quadratic function?

Mixed Review **Write the expression using only positive exponents.** *(Lesson 4.6)*

50. 7^{-3} **51.** $5b^{-7}$ **52.** $m^{-9}n^2$

Graph the function. *(Lesson 8.7)*

53. $f(x) = 4x + 3$ **54.** $f(x) = -0.5x + 9$ **55.** $g(x) = -x - 10$

Simplify. Write your answer using positive exponents. *(Lesson 12.5)*

56. $(-3y)^3$ **57.** $\left(\dfrac{5}{n}\right)^2$ **58.** $(m^8)^{-11}$

Standardized Test Practice **59.** **Multiple Choice** At what point does the minimum value of the function $y = 3x^2 - 8$ occur?

    A. $(0, 8)$ **B.** $(0, -8)$ **C.** $(8, 0)$ **D.** $(-8, 0)$

60. **Short Response** Scientists have studied how protein consumption affects the growth of pigs. The average growth of the pigs can be approximated by $y = -1.9x^2 + 1.7x + 0.3$, where y is the average daily growth in kilograms and x is the daily protein consumption in kilograms. Use a graphing calculator to approximate the maximum daily growth and the daily protein consumption needed to achieve that growth.

12.6 Graphing Quadratic Functions

Goal Use a graphing calculator to investigate the graph of $y = ax^2$.

Investigate

Use a graphing calculator to compare the graph of $y = x^2$ with the graph of $y = \frac{1}{2}x^2$.

1 Enter the functions to be graphed. (Note: Your calculator will not show any colors. Red is used here to distinguish the two functions.)

Keystrokes

2 Graph the functions using the calculator's standard window.

Keystrokes

ZOOM 6

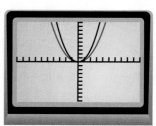

3 Compare and contrast the graphs.

Both parabolas open up, and both pass through the origin. But the graph of $y = \frac{1}{2}x^2$ is wider than the graph of $y = x^2$.

Draw Conclusions

Compare the graph of $y = x^2$ with the graph of the given function.

1. $y = 4x^2$ **2.** $y = -3x^2$

3. $y = -0.5x^2$ **4.** $y = 0.2x^2$

5. Analyze How does the value of a affect the shape of the graph of the equation $y = ax^2$? In your answer, discuss both positive and negative values of a.

12.7

Exponential Growth *and* Decay

BEFORE	Now	WHY?
You graphed quadratic functions.	You'll graph exponential functions.	So you can calculate rounds in a tournament, as in Ex. 32.

Vocabulary

exponential function,
  p. 686
exponential growth,
  p. 687
exponential decay,
  p. 687

Muskoxen In 1937, there were 39 muskoxen on Nunivak Island, Alaska. For the period 1937–1948, the muskox population on the island can be approximated by

$$P = 39(1.1)^t,$$

where *t* is the number of years since 1937. After how many years did the muskox population on Nunivak Island double? Example 4 shows how to use a graphing calculator to answer this question.

The function $P = 39(1.1)^t$ is an example of an *exponential function*. An **exponential function** is an equation in two variables that can be written in the form $y = ab^x$, where $a \neq 0$, $b > 0$, and $b \neq 1$.

Example 1 *Graphing an Exponential Function*

Graph the exponential function $y = 4(2)^x$.

Study *Strategy*

Exponential functions are nonlinear functions because their graphs are not lines.

1 Make a table of values. Choose several *x*-values and find the corresponding *y*-values.

x	−3	−2	−1	0	1	2
y	$\frac{1}{2}$	1	2	4	8	16

2 Use the table to make a list of ordered pairs.

$$\left(-3, \frac{1}{2}\right), (-2, 1), (-1, 2), (0, 4),$$

$$(1, 8), (2, 16)$$

3 Graph the ordered pairs. Draw a smooth curve through the points as shown.

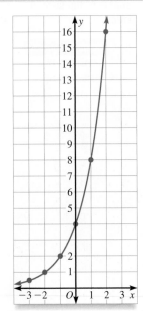

Example 2 Graphing an Exponential Function

Graph the exponential function $y = \left(\dfrac{1}{3}\right)^x$.

1 Rewrite the function. Because $\left(\dfrac{1}{3}\right)^x = (3^{-1})^x = 3^{-x}$, the given function is equivalent to the function $y = 3^{-x}$.

2 Make a table of values. Choose x-values and find the corresponding y-values.

x	-2	-1	0	1	2
y	9	3	1	$\dfrac{1}{3}$	$\dfrac{1}{9}$

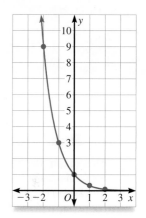

3 Make a list of ordered pairs.

$(-2, 9),\ (-1, 3),\ (0, 1),\ \left(1, \dfrac{1}{3}\right),\ \left(2, \dfrac{1}{9}\right)$

4 Graph the ordered pairs. Draw a smooth curve through the points as shown.

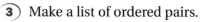

Reading Algebra

The expression 3^{-x} means "3 raised to the opposite of x." When evaluating $y = 3^{-x}$ in Step 2 of Example 2, don't forget to take the opposite of x. For instance, when $x = -2$, $y = 3^{-(-2)} = 3^2 = 9$.

✔ **Checkpoint**

Make a table of values for the given function. Then graph the function.

1. $y = 3^x$ **2.** $y = 5^x$ **3.** $y = \left(\dfrac{1}{4}\right)^x$ **4.** $y = 4\left(\dfrac{1}{2}\right)^x$

Growth and Decay A quantity that increases shows **exponential growth** if it can be described by an exponential function of the form $y = ab^x$, where $a > 0$ and $b > 1$. A quantity that decreases shows **exponential decay** if it can be described by an exponential function of the form $y = ab^x$, where $a > 0$ and $0 < b < 1$.

Example 3 Solving Problems Involving Exponential Decay

Cars The value of a car decreases over time. Suppose your parents buy a car for $10,000. The car's value t years after purchase can be approximated by the function $V = 10,000(0.9)^t$. After how many years will the value of the car be less than $7000?

Solution

Make a table of values for the function.

t	0	1	2	3	4
V	10,000	9,000	8,100	7,290	6,561

Notice that when $t = 4$, $V < 7000$.

Answer After four years the car will be worth less than $7000.

Note Worthy

When taking notes on Example 3, be sure to leave space to write down questions asked by you or other students. Record your teacher's answers.

Example 4 Solving Problems Involving Exponential Growth

Find when the muskox population described on page 686 doubled.

Solution

Use a graphing calculator to graph the exponential function $P = 39(1.1)^t$. To estimate the value of t when $P = 2 \cdot 39 = 78$, use the calculator's *trace* feature. You can determine that when $P = 78$, $t \approx 7.3$.

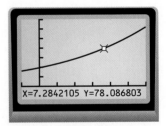

X=7.2842105 Y=78.086803

Answer The muskox population doubled after about 7.3 years.

✔ *Checkpoint*

In the **Real World**

Muskoxen The mass of a typical muskox is about 300 kilograms. What is the approximate mass of a herd of 78 muskoxen?

5. The function $A = 2500(1.05)^t$ gives the balance (in dollars) of a savings account t years after it is opened. Tell whether this function is an example of exponential growth or decay. Explain your answer.

SUMMARY **Linear and Nonlinear Functions**

Linear Functions

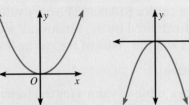

$y = mx + b$
$m > 0$

$y = mx + b$
$m < 0$

$y = b$
$m = 0$

Nonlinear Functions

Quadratic Functions   **Exponential Functions**

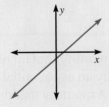 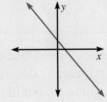   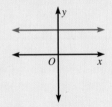 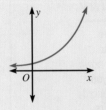

$y = ax^2 + bx + c$ $y = ax^2 + bx + c$
$a > 0$ $a < 0$

$y = ab^x$ $y = ab^x$
$a > 0, b > 1$ $a > 0, 0 < b < 1$

Exponential   **Exponential**
growth   **decay**

688 **Chapter 12** Polynomials and Nonlinear Functions

12.7 Exercises

More Practice, p. 814

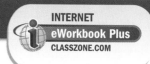

Guided Practice

Vocabulary Check

1. Tell whether the function $y = 5(0.5)^x$ is an example of *exponential growth* or *exponential decay*.

2. Give an example of an exponential function whose graph rises from left to right.

Skill Check **Make a table of values for the given function. Then graph the function.**

3. $y = 4^x$ **4.** $y = 5(2)^x$ **5.** $y = 3\left(\frac{1}{2}\right)^x$ **6.** $y = 2\left(\frac{1}{3}\right)^x$

Guided Problem Solving

7. Paper Cutting You have a 10 centimeter by 10 centimeter piece of paper. You cut the paper in half repeatedly. After each cut you discard one half. After how many cuts is the area of the remaining paper less than 6 square centimeters?

1 Copy and complete the table.

Number of cuts	0	1	2	3	4	5
Area (in square centimeters)	100	50	?	?	?	?

2 After how many cuts is the area of the paper less than 6 square centimeters?

Practice and Problem Solving

Homework *Help*

Example	Exercises
1	8–23, 29–31
2	8–23, 29–31
3	32
4	24–27, 34

Online Resources
CLASSZONE.COM
• More Examples
• eTutorial Plus

Make a table of values for the given function.

8. $y = 5(4)^x$ **9.** $y = 2(3)^x$ **10.** $y = 12(2)^x$ **11.** $y = \frac{1}{2}(6)^x$

12. $y = 2\left(\frac{1}{2}\right)^x$ **13.** $y = 9\left(\frac{1}{3}\right)^x$ **14.** $y = 3\left(\frac{1}{4}\right)^x$ **15.** $y = 10\left(\frac{1}{2}\right)^x$

Graph the function.

16. $y = 2(3)^x$ **17.** $y = 3(6)^x$ **18.** $y = 6^x$ **19.** $y = 3(5)^x$

20. $y = 2\left(\frac{1}{2}\right)^x$ **21.** $y = 3\left(\frac{1}{3}\right)^x$ **22.** $y = 8\left(\frac{1}{4}\right)^x$ **23.** $y = 3\left(\frac{1}{2}\right)^x$

Use a graphing calculator to graph the function. Then tell whether the function is an example of *exponential growth* or *exponential decay*.

24. $y = (0.2)^x$ **25.** $y = 6(0.4)^x$ **26.** $y = (3.5)^x$ **27.** $y = 4(1.5)^x$

28. *Writing* Compare the graphs of the functions $y = 8(2)^x$ and $y = 8\left(\frac{1}{2}\right)^x$.

Match the function with its graph.

29. $y = \frac{1}{4}(3)^x$

30. $y = 3\left(\frac{1}{4}\right)^x$

31. $y = \frac{1}{3}(4)^x$

A.

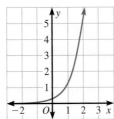

B.

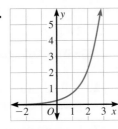

C.

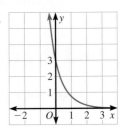

32. Extended Problem Solving A citywide youth tennis tournament has 128 players at the start. After each round, half the players are eliminated. The number of players remaining at the end of each round is given by the function $y = 128\left(\frac{1}{2}\right)^x$ where x is the number of rounds played.

   a. Make a table of values for the function.

   b. Analyze After how many rounds do only 2 players remain? After how many rounds does only 1 player remain?

   c. Critical Thinking Suppose the tournament started with 512 players instead of 128. After how many rounds would only 1 player remain?

33. **Predict** Consider the functions $y = 2(3)^x$ and $y = 3(2)^x$. Suppose you were to graph each function and find the value of x when $y = 100$. Predict which function would have a lesser x-value. Explain your prediction. Then use a graphing calculator to check your prediction.

34. Compound Interest Recall that the balance A of an account earning interest compounded annually is given by the equation $A = P(1 + r)^t$, where P is the principal, r is the annual interest rate (expressed as a decimal), and t is the number of years.

   a. Critical Thinking For any given values of P and r, is the equation $A = P(1 + r)^t$ an example of exponential growth or exponential decay? Explain your answer.

   b. You deposit $500 into an account earning 5% interest compounded annually. Write a function that gives the balance after t years.

   c. Use a graphing calculator to graph the function from part (b). After how many years will the balance be greater than $700?

Review *Help*

For help with compound interest, see p. 364.

35. Medicine You take 500 milligrams of aspirin. The amount of aspirin (in milligrams) in your bloodstream after t hours is given by the function $y = 500(0.8)^t$.

   a. Critical Thinking Is this function an example of exponential growth or exponential decay? Explain your answer.

   b. Use a graphing calculator to graph the function. How much aspirin is left in your bloodstream after 24 hours?

   c. Interpret and Apply When will the amount of aspirin in your bloodstream be less than 132 milligrams? less than 22 milligrams?

36. **Challenge** A pair of sneakers costs $45. The price of the sneakers will be reduced by 20% at the end of each week until the sneakers are sold.

    a. Write an exponential function that gives the cost of the sneakers after t weeks.

    b. Make a table of values and graph the function from part (a).

    c. After how many weeks will the sneakers cost less than $20?

Mixed Review

Find the sine and cosine of each acute angle. Write your answers as fractions in simplest form. *(Lesson 9.8)*

37.

38.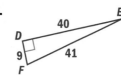

39.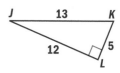

Find the number of combinations. *(Lesson 11.7)*

40. $_9C_4$ 41. $_8C_7$ 42. $_6C_4$ 43. $_5C_5$

Make a table of values for the given function. *(Lesson 12.6)*

44. $y = -x^2 + 4$ 45. $y = 2x^2 + 1$ 46. $y = x^2 - 5$ 47. $y = 3x^2 - 9$

Standardized Test Practice

48. **Multiple Choice** For the function $y = 2(5)^x$, what is the value of y when $x = 4$?

    A. $\dfrac{1}{1250}$ **B.** $\dfrac{1}{625}$ **C.** 1250 **D.** 3125

49. **Multiple Choice** Which function is an example of exponential decay?

    F. $y = 0.5(3)^x$ **G.** $y = 3(0.5)^x$ **H.** $y = 0.2(2)^x$ **I.** $y = 3(5)^x$

50. **Short Response** You deposit $1200 into an account that earns 7% interest compounded annually. The balance A after t years is given by the function $A = 1200(1.07)^t$. Use a calculator to make a table of values for the function. After how many years will the balance be greater than $1700?

Payday Puzzle

You are hired for a job that lasts 20 days. You have a choice of how you will be paid. You can either be paid $300 per day or $.01 on the first day, $.02 on the second day, $.04 on the third day, and so on, with the amount you're paid doubling each day. Which offer should you accept? Explain your reasoning.

12.8

Sequences

BEFORE	Now	WHY?
You wrote rules for and graphed functions.	You'll extend and graph sequences.	So you can find the height of a bouncing ball, as in Ex. 31.

Vocabulary

sequence, p. 692
term, p. 692
arithmetic sequence, p. 692
common difference, p. 692
geometric sequence, p. 692
common ratio, p. 692

A **sequence** is an ordered list of numbers. Each number in a sequence is called a **term**. One type of sequence is an *arithmetic sequence*. In an **arithmetic sequence**, the difference between consecutive terms is constant. This difference is called the **common difference**.

Position number:	1	2	3	4	5 . . .
Term:	4	7	10	13	16 . . .

$$7 - 4 = 3 \quad 10 - 7 = 3 \quad 13 - 10 = 3 \quad 16 - 13 = 3$$

The common difference is 3.

Example 1 *Extending Arithmetic Sequences*

Find the common difference for the arithmetic sequence. Then find the next three terms.

a. 12, 17, 22, 27, 32, . . .   **b.** 5, 3, 1, −1, −3, . . .

Solution

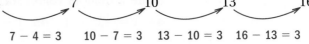

a. 12, 17, 22, 27, 32, . . .
   $+5 \quad +5 \quad +5 \quad +5$

The common difference is 5. The next three terms in the sequence are 37, 42, and 47.

b. 5, 3, 1, −1, −3, . . .
   $-2 \quad -2 \quad -2 \quad -2$

The common difference is −2. The next three terms in the sequence are −5, −7, and −9.

Watch *Out*

In part (b) of Example 1, each term is 2 *less* than the previous term, so the common difference is −2, not 2.

Geometric Sequences Another type of sequence is a *geometric sequence*. In a **geometric sequence**, the ratio of any term to the previous term is constant. This ratio is called the **common ratio**.

Position number:	1	2	3	4	5 . . .
Term:	3	6	12	24	48 . . .

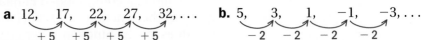

$$\frac{6}{3} = 2 \quad\quad \frac{12}{6} = 2 \quad\quad \frac{24}{12} = 2 \quad\quad \frac{48}{24} = 2$$

The common ratio is 2.

Study *Strategy*

In Example 2, notice that the common ratio is the number you can multiply one term by to get the next term in the sequence.

Example 2 *Extending Geometric Sequences*

Find the common ratio for the geometric sequence. Then find the next three terms.

a. 2, 6, 18, 54, . . .

b. 160, 80, 40, 20, . . .

Solution

a. 2,   6,   18,   54, . . .

       $\times 3$ $\times 3$ $\times 3$

The common ratio is 3. The next three terms in the sequence are 162, 486, and 1458.

b. 160,   80,   40,   20, . . .
       $\times \frac{1}{2}$ $\times \frac{1}{2}$ $\times \frac{1}{2}$

The common ratio is $\frac{1}{2}$. The next three terms in the sequence are 10, 5, and 2.5.

✔ *Checkpoint*

Tell whether the sequence is *arithmetic* or *geometric*. Then find the common difference or common ratio, and write the next three terms.

1. $-4, 2, 8, 14, \ldots$ **2.** $3, -4, -11, -18, \ldots$ **3.** $100, 10, 1, 0.1, \ldots$

Example 3 *Using Sequences*

Mountain Bike You start saving for a $360 mountain bike in January when you receive $200 in cash for your birthday. In February and each month after, you save $20 from doing chores. After how many months of saving will you have enough for the bike?

Solution

① Use a table to write a sequence for your savings after each month.

Month number	1	2	3	4	. . .
Savings	200	200 + 20(1)	200 + 20(2)	200 + 20(3)	. . .
Sequence	200	220	240	260	. . .

② Notice that the sequence is arithmetic. Your savings from chores is the product of $20 and 1 less than the month number. Your total savings is the sum of $200 and your savings from chores.

     Savings after n months $= 200 + 20(n - 1)$

③ Write and solve an equation to find how many months will pass before you have the $360 you need for the mountain bike.

     $360 = 200 + 20(n - 1)$ **Write equation.**

     $160 = 20(n - 1)$ **Subtract 200 from each side.**

      $8 = n - 1$ **Divide each side by 20.**

      $9 = n$ **Add 1 to each side.**

Answer You will have saved enough for the bike after 9 months.

Graphing Sequences To graph a sequence, let the position numbers of the terms in the sequence be the x-coordinates and let the terms be the y-coordinates. Each term corresponds to a point on the graph.

Example 4 *Graphing an Arithmetic Sequence*

Graph the arithmetic sequence 5, 10, 15, 20, 25, ...

Write the sequence as a table of values.

Position number, x	1	2	3	4	5
Term, y	5	10	15	20	25

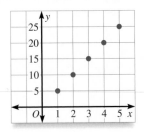

Then plot the points (1, 5), (2, 10), (3, 15), (4, 20), (5, 25), ...

Example 5 *Graphing a Geometric Sequence*

Fractal Tree To construct what is known as a *fractal tree*, begin with a single segment (the trunk) and add two shorter segments to form the first pair of branches, as shown in Step 1. Then continue adding pairs of shorter branches to each existing branch.

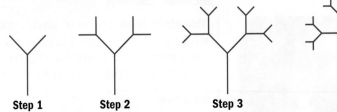

Step 1   Step 2   Step 3   Step 4

Write and graph a sequence for the number of new branches at each step of constructing the fractal tree.

Solution

The sequence 2, 4, 8, 16, . . . gives the number of new branches at each step. Because each term is 2 times the previous term, the sequence is geometric.

To graph the sequence, write the sequence as a table of values.

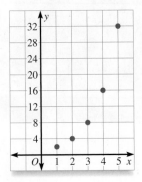

Position number, x	1	2	3	4	5
Term, y	2	4	8	16	32

Then plot the points (1, 2), (2, 4), (3, 8), (4, 16), (5, 32), ...

✔ **Checkpoint**

Write the next three terms of the sequence. Then graph the sequence.

4. 1, 2, 4, 8, . . .   **5.** 16, 13, 10, 7, . . .   **6.** 11, 17, 23, 29, . . .

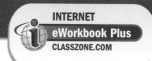

Guided Practice

Vocabulary Check

1. Copy and complete: In a geometric sequence, the ratio of any term to the previous term is the __?__.

2. Tell whether the following sequence is *arithmetic* or *geometric*: $-4, 8, 20, 32, \ldots$.

Skill Check

Find the common difference for the arithmetic sequence. Then write the next three terms.

3. $3, 8, 13, 18, \ldots$ 4. $14, 12, 10, 8, \ldots$ 5. $-16, -8, 0, 8, \ldots$

Find the common ratio for the geometric sequence. Then write the next three terms.

6. $1, 5, 25, 125, \ldots$ 7. $-2, -6, -18, \ldots$ 8. $96, 48, 24, 12, \ldots$

9. **Error Analysis** Describe and correct the error in graphing the sequence $3, 5, 7, 9, \ldots$.

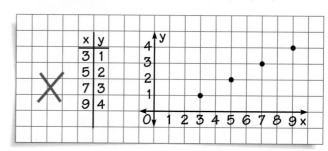

Practice and Problem Solving

Homework *Help*

Example	Exercises
1	10–21
2	10–21
3	29–37
4	22–27
5	22–27

Online Resources
CLASSZONE.COM
• More Examples
• eTutorial Plus

Tell whether the sequence is *arithmetic* or *geometric*. Then find the common difference or the common ratio, and write the next three terms.

10. $15, 11, 7, 3, \ldots$ 11. $-2, 4, -8, 16, \ldots$ 12. $-7, -1, 5, 11, \ldots$

13. $4, 19, 34, 49, \ldots$ 14. $1024, 256, 64, \ldots$ 15. $\frac{1}{2}, 2, 8, 32, \ldots$

16. $52, 61, 70, 79, \ldots$ 17. $500, 100, 20, 4, \ldots$ 18. $1, -2, 4, -8, \ldots$

19. $18, 36, 54, 72, \ldots$ 20. $16, 24, 36, 54, \ldots$ 21. $243, 162, 108, 72, \ldots$

Tell whether the sequence is *arithmetic* or *geometric*. Write the next three terms of the sequence. Then graph the sequence.

22. $16, 8, 4, 2, \ldots$ 23. $-18, -4, 10, \ldots$ 24. $-2, -5, -8, -11, \ldots$

25. $15, 25, 35, 45, \ldots$ 26. $20, 10, 5, 2.5, \ldots$ 27. $4, 12, 36, 108, \ldots$

28. *Writing* The first two terms of a sequence are 3 and 6. Can you tell whether this sequence is arithmetic or geometric? To justify your answer, give examples of sequences that begin with these two terms.

29. Extended Problem Solving A supermarket stores shopping carts by nesting them. Each shopping cart is 36 inches long. The first cart contributes its entire length to the line. Each additional cart adds 9 inches to the line. Consider the sequence that gives the length of a line of carts, starting with 1 cart, then 2 carts, then 3 carts, and so on.

  a. Write the first 6 terms of the sequence. Is the sequence arithmetic or geometric?

  b. Analyze Write a variable expression for the length of a line of n carts.

  c. Apply The supermarket has a space that is 240 inches long to store the carts. How many nested carts can fit in this space?

30. Sierpinski Triangle To create the *Sierpinski triangle*, begin with a shaded triangle. Replace the middle of the shaded triangle with a smaller white triangle, as shown. Then, for every shaded triangle that is formed, replace its middle with a smaller white triangle.

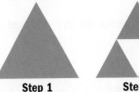

Step 1	Step 2	Step 3	Step 4
1 shaded triangle	3 shaded triangles	9 shaded triangles	27 shaded triangles

  a. Consider the sequence for the number of shaded triangles at each step. Write the first 6 terms of the sequence. Is the sequence arithmetic or geometric?

  b. Analyze Write a variable expression for the number of shaded triangles at the nth step.

  c. Use a calculator to find the number of shaded triangles at the 15th step.

31. Bounce Height When you drop a ball, the height to which the ball rises, called its bounce height, decreases on each successive bounce. For a certain ball, the bounce height of each bounce is 40% of the previous bounce height. You drop the ball from a height of 30 feet.

  a. Consider the sequence that gives the bounce height at each bounce. Is this sequence arithmetic or geometric?

  b. Use a calculator to find the first 7 terms of this sequence. After how many bounces is the bounce height less than 0.25 foot?

Write the next three terms of the arithmetic sequence. Then write a variable expression for the nth term and evaluate it for $n = 12$.

32. 52, 41, 30, 19, . . .   **33.** $-3, -1.5, 0, 1.5, . . .$ **34.** 7, 23, 39, 55, . . .

Write the next three terms of the geometric sequence. Then write a variable expression for the nth term and evaluate it for $n = 9$.

35. 1, 11, 121, 1331, . . .   **36.** 800, 80, 8, 0.8, . . .   **37.** 128, 64, 32, 16, . . .

38. Critical Thinking The first term of an arithmetic sequence is 15. The fourth term is 39. What is the second term of this sequence? Explain.

39. Fibonacci Sequence The *Fibonacci sequence* is a sequence in which each term is the sum of the two terms before it. The sequence begins as shown.

1,	1,	2,	3,	5,	8,	13,	...
first term	second term	$1 + 1$	$1 + 2$	$2 + 3$	$3 + 5$	$5 + 8$	

a. Is the Fibonacci sequence arithmetic, geometric, or neither? Explain.

b. Write the next 5 terms of the Fibonnaci sequence.

c. Graph the sequence. Is the graph linear?

40. Challenge Consider the figures made of toothpicks below.

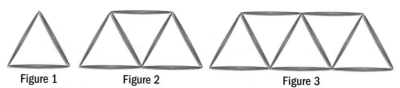

Figure 1   Figure 2   Figure 3

a. Draw the next three figures in the pattern.

b. Analyze How is the number of triangles in each figure related to the figure number? Write a sequence that gives the number of triangles in each figure.

c. Analyze How is the number of toothpicks in each figure related to the figure number? Write a formula for the sequence that gives the number of toothpicks in each figure.

d. Apply Suppose you have 100 toothpicks. What is the greatest number of triangles you can construct using the given pattern?

The number of clockwise and counterclockwise spirals formed by a pine cone's scales are numbers in the Fibonacci sequence. This pine cone has 8 clockwise spirals and 13 counterclockwise spirals.

Mixed Review

41. The perimeter of an isosceles triangle is 16 meters. The length of a side is 4 meters. The lengths of the other two sides are equal. Find the lengths of the other two sides. *(Lesson 10.1)*

Find the degree of the polynomial. *(Lesson 12.1)*

42. $5x^6 - 8x + 2$ **43.** $12 - 9t^2 - 4t$ **44.** $-c^3 + c^3d + dc^2$

Graph the function. *(Lesson 12.7)*

45. $y = 2^x$ **46.** $y = 1.5(3)^x$ **47.** $y = 10(0.25)^x$

Standardized Test Practice

48. Multiple Choice What is the next term in the sequence 12, 8, 4, 0, ... ?

A. 2   **B.** 1   **C.** 0   **D.** -4

49. Multiple Choice The cost of a taxicab ride is $1.50 for the first quarter-mile and $.25 for each additional quarter-mile. Which sequence gives the cost of a taxicab ride, starting with a ride that is 1 quarter-mile, then 2 quarter-miles, then 3 quarter-miles, and so on?

F. 0.25, 1.75, 3.25, 4.75, ...   **G.** 0.25, 1.50, 2.75, 4.25, ...

H. 1.50, 1.75, 2.00, 2.25, ...   **I.** 1.75, 2.00, 2.25, 2.50, ...

Chapter Review

Vocabulary Review

polynomial, p. 651
term of a polynomial, p. 651
binomial, p. 651
trinomial, p. 651
degree of a term, p. 652
degree of a polynomial, p. 652

standard form, p. 652
quadratic function, p. 679
parabola, p. 680
nonlinear function, p. 680
minimum value of a function,
  p. 681

maximum value of a function,
  p. 681
exponential function, p. 686
exponential growth, p. 687
exponential decay, p. 687
sequence, p. 692

term of a sequence, p. 692
arithmetic sequence, p. 692
common difference, p. 692
geometric sequence, p. 692
common ratio, p. 692

Copy and complete.

1. A(n) ? is any function whose graph is not a line.

2. The graph of a quadratic function is a U-shaped curve called a(n) ?.

3. In a(n) ?, the difference between consecutive terms is constant.

4. In a(n) ?, the ratio of any term to the previous term is constant.

5. Describe how to find the degree of a polynomial.

6. Give an example of a trinomial in standard form.

7. Describe the graph of a quadratic function that has a maximum value.

8. Describe the graph of a function that shows exponential decay.

12.1 Polynomials

Examples on pp. 651–653

▶ *Goal*

Identify polynomials and write them in standard form.

Example Write $-5x - 4x^2 + 3(2x^2 + 3x)$ as a polynomial in standard form.

$$-5x - 4x^2 + 3(2x^2 + 3x)$$

$= -5x - 4x^2 + 6x^2 + 9x$	**Distributive property**
$= -5x + 9x + (-4x^2) + 6x^2$	**Group like terms.**
$= 4x + 2x^2$	**Combine like terms.**
$= 2x^2 + 4x$	**Standard form**

✔ **Write the expression as a polynomial in standard form.**

9. $3x - 7 + 2x^2 - 3$

10. $10x + 4x^3 - 9 + 7x - 3x^3$

11. $-6x - 5 + 4(2x^2 + x + 3)$

12. $15x^2 - 4x + 6(3 - 8x^2 - 2x)$

12.2 Adding and Subtracting Polynomials

Examples on pp. 657–659

▶ **Goal**

Add and subtract polynomials.

Example Find the difference $(y^2 - 6y + 3) - (5y^2 + 8y)$.

$$(y^2 - 6y + 3) - (5y^2 + 8y)$$ Write difference.

$$= y^2 - 6y + 3 + (-5y^2 - 8y)$$ Write opposite of second polynomial.

$$= y^2 - 5y^2 - 6y - 8y + 3$$ Group like terms.

$$= -4y^2 - 14y + 3$$ Combine like terms.

✔ **Find the sum or difference.**

13. $(m^2 + 2m - 3) - (5m + 7)$ **14.** $(8d^2 + 4d + 4) + (9d - 15)$

15. $(4a^3 - 6a^2 + 3) + (7a^2 + a + 7)$ **16.** $(6y^3 - 4y + 1) - (7y^3 + 2y^2 - 3)$

12.3 Multiplying Monomials and Polynomials

Examples on pp. 662–663

▶ **Goal**

Multiply a monomial and a polynomial.

Example Find the product $x(5x^2 + 3x + 2)$.

$$x(5x^2 + 3x + 2) = x(5x^2) + x(3x) + x(2)$$ Distributive property

$$= 5x^3 + 3x^2 + 2x$$ Product of powers property

✔ **Find the product.**

17. $-7z(z^3 - 6z)$ **18.** $(-c^2 + 3)4c^2$ **19.** $(p^2 + 8p + 3)(-9p)$

20. $6a^2(a^2 - 4a + 1)$ **21.** $-5n^2(5 - 3n)$ **22.** $(6s^2 - 7)8s$

12.4 Multiplying Binomials

Examples on pp. 668–669

▶ **Goal**

Multiply binomials.

Example Find the product $(5x + 4)(2x - 7)$.

First	+	Outer	+	Inner	+	Last	
$5x \cdot 2x$	+	$5x(-7)$	+	$4 \cdot 2x$	+	$4(-7)$	Write products of terms.
$10x^2$	+	$(-35x)$	+	$8x$	+	(-28)	Multiply.
		$10x^2 - 27x - 28$					Combine like terms.

✔ **Find the product.**

23. $(b + 7)(b + 2)$ **24.** $(x + 3)(x + 9)$ **25.** $(z - 5)(z - 4)$

26. $(y - 8)(y + 11)$ **27.** $(3c + 1)(c - 6)$ **28.** $(8a + 7)(2a + 9)$

12.5 Other Rules of Exponents

Examples on pp. 674–676

▶ *Goal*

Simplify powers of products and quotients.

Example Simplify the expressions $(3y)^3$, $\left(\dfrac{7}{k}\right)^2$, and $(-2m^4)^3$.

a. $(3y)^3 = 3^3 \cdot y^3$ **Power of a product property**

      $= 27y^3$ **Evaluate power.**

b. $\left(\dfrac{7}{k}\right)^2 = \dfrac{7^2}{k^2}$ **Power of a quotient property**

      $= \dfrac{49}{k^2}$ **Evaluate power.**

c. $(-2m^4)^3 = (-2)^3 \cdot (m^4)^3$ **Power of a product property**

      $= (-2)^3 \cdot m^{12}$ **Power of a power property**

      $= -8m^{12}$ **Evaluate power.**

✔ **Simplify the expression. Write your answer using positive exponents.**

29. $(yz)^6$ **30.** $(h^7)^{-2}$ **31.** $\left(\dfrac{x}{2}\right)^4$ **32.** $\left(\dfrac{w}{-9}\right)^3$

33. $(5k)^4$ **34.** $(abc)^3$ **35.** $(z^{-3})^{-4}$ **36.** $(3b^2)^7$

12.6 Quadratic Functions

Examples on pp. 679–681

▶ *Goal*

Graph quadratic functions.

Example Graph the function $y = x^2 - 2x - 1$.

① Make a table of values. Choose several x-values and find the corresponding y-values.

x	-1	0	1	2	3
y	2	-1	-2	-1	2

② Use the table to make a list of ordered pairs.

$(-1, 2)$, $(0, -1)$, $(1, -2)$, $(2, -1)$, $(3, 2)$

③ Graph the ordered pairs. Then draw a smooth curve through the points.

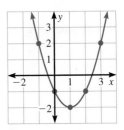

✔ **Make a table of values for the given function. Then graph the function.**

37. $y = 2x^2 + 9$ **38.** $y = -x^2 - 4$ **39.** $y = -2x^2 + 4x + 1$

12.7 Exponential Growth and Decay

Examples on pp. 686–688

▶ *Goal*

Solve problems involving exponential growth.

Example This year 10,000 people attended a benefit concert. The concert's organizers want to make it an annual event. They predict the attendance *A* in *t* years using the function $A = 10,000(1.05)^t$. When will the attendance exceed 12,000?

Make a table of values for the function.

t	0	1	2	3	4
A	10,000	10,500	11,025	11,576	12,155

From the table, you can see that when $t = 4$, $A > 12,000$.

Answer The attendance at the benefit concert will exceed 12,000 after 4 years.

✔ **40.** You deposit $450 into an account earning 4% interest compounded annually. The balance *A* of the account is given by the function $A = 450(1.04)^t$, where *t* is the number of years after the deposit. After how many years will the account have a balance greater than $500?

12.8 Sequences

Examples on pp. 692–694

▶ *Goal*

Extend sequences.

Example Tell whether the sequence is *arithmetic* or *geometric*. Then find the common difference or common ratio, and write the next three terms.

a. 6, 10, 14, 18, . . .

Each term after the first is 4 more than the previous term. So, the sequence is arithmetic. The common difference is 4. The next three terms in the sequence are 22, 26, and 30.

b. 13, 65, 325, 1625, . . .

Each term after the first is 5 times the previous term. So, the sequence is geometric. The common ratio is 5. The next three terms in the sequence are 8125, 40,625, and 203,125.

✔ Tell whether the sequence is *arithmetic* or *geometric*. Then find the common difference or common ratio, and write the next three terms.

41. −1, 4, 9, 14, . . .   **42.** 448, 112, 28, 7, . . .   **43.** 3, 21, 147, 1029, . . .

Chapter Test

Find the degree of the polynomial.

1. $-4h$ **2.** 0 **3.** $x - 3x^2y^3 - 2y^4$ **4.** $9z^2$

5. Write the expression $-9 + 5y^2 + y(2 - 3y)$ as a polynomial in standard form.

Find the sum or difference.

6. $(7x^2 - 3x + 4) + (-3x^2 + 3x + 2)$

7. $(4x^3 + 10x) + (5x^2 - 3x + 1)$

8. $(6d^2 + 1) - (-7 + 11d^2)$

9. $(2y^2 - y + 7) - (-8y^2 + y - 15)$

Find the product.

10. $3m(m^4 - 2m^2)$ **11.** $(b^2 + 4)2b$ **12.** $(x + 9)(2x + 5)$ **13.** $(3h - 8)(2h - 5)$

Simplify the expression. Write your answer using positive exponents.

14. $(-ab)^5$ **15.** $(3m^4)^2$ **16.** $\left(\dfrac{15}{t}\right)^2$ **17.** $\left(\dfrac{7}{c}\right)^3$

Make a table of values for the given function. Then graph the function.

18. $y = x^2 - 1$ **19.** $y = 2x^2 + 3$ **20.** $y = -x^2 + 4$ **21.** $y = -3x^2 - 7$

22. **Baseball** You are throwing a baseball up in the air. The baseball's height (in feet) is given by the function $h = -16t^2 + 40t + 4$, where t is the time in seconds after the ball leaves your hand. Use a graphing calculator to graph the function. Then find the greatest height the baseball reaches.

Graph the function.

23. $y = 4^x$ **24.** $y = 3(4)^x$ **25.** $y = 5\left(\dfrac{1}{4}\right)^x$ **26.** $y = (0.3)^x$

Tell whether the sequence is *arithmetic* or *geometric*. Then find the common difference or the common ratio, and write the next three terms.

27. $3, -9, 27, -81, \ldots$ **28.** $12, 36, 108, 324, \ldots$ **29.** $65, 50, 35, 20, \ldots$ **30.** $17, 28, 39, 50, \ldots$

31. **Plants** You run a business that takes care of people's plants while they are out of town. You charge $5 for the first day and $4 for each additional day that you water plants.

    a. Write the first 6 terms of the sequence. Is the sequence *arithmetic* or *geometric*?

    b. Write a variable expression for how much you are paid for n days.

Chapter Standardized Test

Test-Taking Strategy Before you take a test, know what topics the test will cover and what types of questions will be asked.

1. Which of the following is a trinomial?

   A. $9x^3$
   B. $3x^4 - 4x$
   C. $x^5 - x^2 + 1$
   D. $x^3 - x^2 - x + 9$

2. What is the degree of the polynomial $9 - 3x + 4y - x^2$?

   F. 1
   G. 2
   H. 3
   I. 4

3. Find the sum $(4z^2 - 5z) + (2z^3 - z^2 + 3z)$.

   A. $6z^3 - 6z$
   B. $2z^3 + 3z^2 - 8z$
   C. $6z^3 - z^2 - 2z$
   D. $2z^3 + 3z^2 - 2z$

4. You are painting a rectangular tabletop. The length of the tabletop is 6 inches less than 3 times the width. Let w represent the width. Which expression represents the area you are painting?

   F. $3w^2 - 6w$
   G. $6w - 3w^2$
   H. $8w - 12$
   I. $4w - 6$

5. Find the product $(3x + 4)(x - 9)$.

   A. $3x^2 - 23x + 36$
   B. $3x^2 - 23x - 36$
   C. $3x^2 - 31x + 36$
   D. $3x^2 - 31x - 36$

6. A square painting has sides of length s inches. The frame for the painting is 5 inches wide all around. Which expression represents the combined area (in square inches) of the painting and the frame?

   F. $s^2 + 25$
   G. $s^2 + 10s + 25$
   H. $s^2 + 15s + 50$
   I. $s^2 + 20s + 100$

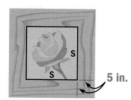

7. Which expression is equivalent to $\left(\dfrac{3a^{-3}}{4b}\right)^2$?

   A. $\dfrac{3}{4ab^2}$
   B. $\dfrac{3}{4a^6b^2}$
   C. $\dfrac{9}{16ab^2}$
   D. $\dfrac{9}{16a^6b^2}$

8. Which function has a minimum value?

   F. $y = -4x^2 + 3$
   G. $y = -4x^2 - 3$
   H. $y = -4x^2$
   I. $y = 4x^2 + 3$

9. What is the common ratio of the geometric sequence $54, -18, 6, -2, \ldots$?

   A. -3
   B. 3
   C. $-\dfrac{1}{3}$
   D. $\dfrac{1}{3}$

10. What is the next term in the sequence $-3, -6, -9, -12, \ldots$?

    F. -15
    G. -3
    H. 3
    I. 15

11. **Short Response** Describe how to determine if the exponential function $y = ab^x$ shows exponential growth or decay.

12. **Extended Response** Use the trapezoid.

    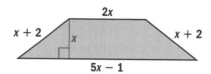

    a. Write a polynomial expression in standard form for the perimeter of the figure.

    b. Write a polynomial expression in standard form for the area of the figure.

    c. Are the degrees of the polynomials in parts (a) and (b) the same or different? Explain.

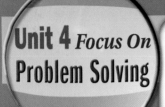
Looking Back

Generalizing and Extending a Solution

Once you solve a problem, you may be able to generalize or extend the solution to solve other problems.

Problem In a soccer tournament, each team plays every other team exactly once. Find the number of games played if there are 4 teams and if there are n teams. Then extend the solutions of these problems to find a formula for the number of diagonals of an n-gon.

1 Solve a specific problem.

For the specific case where there are 4 teams, represent the teams as 4 points on a circle. When one team plays another team, let the game be represented by a segment connecting the teams. Draw a segment from each team to every other team. From any of the 4 teams, there are 3 possible segments that you can draw. So, the total number of segments is $4 \cdot 3 = 12$.

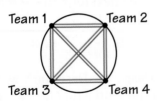

However, the procedure described above causes each pair of teams to be connected twice even though they play each other only once. Therefore, the number of games played is just half the number of segments.

$$\frac{\text{Games played}}{\text{among 4 teams}} = \frac{12}{2} = 6$$

You can represent the games played using 6 segments (rather than 12), as shown below.

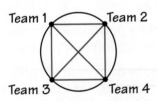

2 Generalize the solution.

To find the number of games played when there are n teams, generalize the solution in Step 1. Represent the teams as n points on a circle, and draw a segment from each team to every other team. The number of segments drawn is $n(n - 1) = n^2 - n$. The number of games played is half the number of segments.

$$\frac{\text{Games played}}{\text{among n teams}} = \frac{n^2 - n}{2} = \frac{1}{2}n^2 - \frac{1}{2}n$$

3 Extend the solution.

You can extend the solutions in Steps 1 and 2 to find a formula for the number of diagonals $d(n)$ of an n-gon. First look at the second diagram in Step 1. The segments connecting the 4 points on the circle form a 4-gon and the diagonals of the 4-gon. Therefore:

$$d(4) = \frac{\text{Number of ways to}}{\text{connect 4 points}} - \frac{\text{Number of}}{\text{sides of 4-gon}}$$

You can generalize this result to the case where there are n points connected by segments.

$$d(n) = \frac{\text{Number of ways to}}{\text{connect n points}} - \frac{\text{Number of}}{\text{sides of n-gon}}$$

Now use the result in Step 2 and the fact that an n-gon has n sides to find a formula for $d(n)$.

$$d(n) = \left(\frac{1}{2}n^2 - \frac{1}{2}n\right) - n = \frac{1}{2}n^2 - \frac{3}{2}n$$

Problem Solving Practice

1. **Geometry** A circle inside a square just touches each side, as shown.

   a. Copy and complete the table. What do you notice about the ratios?

Value of r	1	2	3	4
Area of circle	?	?	?	?
Area of square	?	?	?	?
Ratio of circle's area to square's area	?	?	?	?

   b. Generalize your results from part (a) by first writing expressions in terms of r for the area of the circle and the area of the square. Then write and simplify an expression for the ratio of the circle's area to the square's area. Compare your answer with the results from part (a).

2. **Video Games** Of the video game consoles made by a company, 2% are defective. What is the probability that a console is not defective? that neither of 2 consoles is defective? that there are no defective consoles in a shipment of n consoles?

3. **Finance** You invest $500 from a summer job in shares of a company's stock.

   a. Suppose the value of your shares increases by 10% the first year and then decreases by 10% the second year. What is the value of your shares after 2 years? Did you have an overall gain or loss?

   b. Consider a more general case in which the value of your shares has a percent of increase p the first year and a percent of decrease p the second year (where p is written as a decimal). Write a polynomial in terms of p for the value of your shares after 2 years. Did you have an overall gain or loss? Explain.

4. **Soccer** You need 4 teams to hold an elimination soccer tournament with 2 rounds, as shown below.

   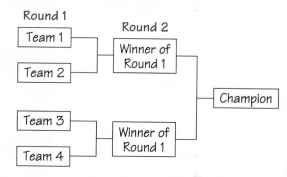

   a. How many teams do you need for an elimination tournament with 3 rounds?

   b. Write a formula for the number of teams $t(n)$ that you need for an elimination tournament with n rounds.

   c. A men's tournament and a women's tournament each have n rounds. Write and simplify an expression for the total number of teams in both tournaments.

5. **Patterns** Consider the following sequence:

   $$\frac{1}{2}, \left(\frac{1}{2}\right)^2, \left(\frac{1}{2}\right)^3, \left(\frac{1}{2}\right)^4, \ldots$$

   Let $S(n)$ represent the sum of the first n terms in the sequence.

   a. Find $S(1)$, $S(2)$, $S(3)$, and $S(4)$. Write your answers as fractions in simplest form.

   b. Based on the pattern from part (a), write a formula for $S(n)$ in terms of n.

Angle Relationships *and* **Transformations**

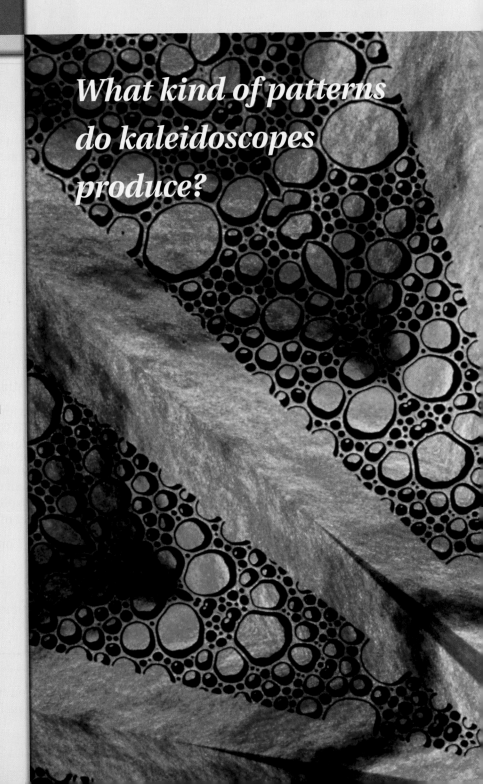

What kind of patterns do kaleidoscopes produce?

CHAPTER 13

INTERNET Preview
CLASSZONE.COM

• eEdition Plus Online
• eWorkbook Plus Online
• eTutorial Plus Online
• State Test Practice
• More Examples

MATH *In the* **Real World**

Kaleidoscopes Each of the images on this page was produced by a kaleidoscope, an instrument that uses mirrors to create a pattern with rotational symmetry. In this chapter, you will identify figures that have rotational symmetry.

What do you think? Lay the edge of a small mirror through the center of the image shown in the circular inset photograph. Hold the mirror perpendicular to the image. What do you notice? What happens if you turn the mirror so that it lies along a different diameter of the circle?

Chapter Prerequisite Skills

PREREQUISITE SKILLS QUIZ

Review Vocabulary

quadrilateral, p. 286
scale, p. 300
triangle, p. 785
acute angle, p. 793
right angle, p. 793
obtuse angle, p. 793
straight angle, p. 793

Preparing for Success To prepare for success in this chapter, test your knowledge of these concepts and skills. You may want to look at the pages referred to in blue for additional review.

Vocabulary Classify the angle with the given measure as *acute*, *right*, *obtuse*, or *straight*. (p. 793)

1. $74°$ **2.** $180°$ **3.** $90°$ **4.** $31°$

A map has a scale of **1 inch : 24 miles.** Use the map distance to find the actual distance. (p. 300)

5. 3 inches   **6.** 8 inches   **7.** 2.5 inches   **8.** $\frac{1}{4}$ inch

Find the value of x or y. (pp. 511, 516)

9.
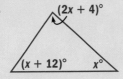

10.
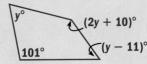

NOTETAKING STRATEGIES

Note *Worthy*

You will find a notetaking strategy at the beginning of each chapter. Look for additional notetaking and study strategies throughout the chapter.

SUMMARIZING MATERIAL In your notes, you should write a summary of key ideas that are related to one another. Include examples in your summary.

Ways to Represent a Function

Equation: $y = 2x + 1$

Table:

x	−2	−1	0	1	2
y	−3	−1	1	3	5

Graph:

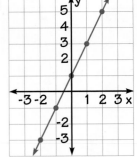

In Lesson 13.7, you can summarize key ideas about transformations in a coordinate plane.

13.1

Angle Relationships

BEFORE	*Now*	WHY?
You classified angles and triangles.	You'll classify special pairs of angles.	So you can find the height of a sculpture, as in Ex. 32.

Vocabulary

complementary
angles, p. 709
supplementary angles,
p. 709
vertical angles, p. 710

Two angles are **complementary angles** if the sum of their measures is 90°. Two angles are **supplementary angles** if the sum of their measures is 180°.

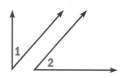

Complementary angles

$m\angle 1 = 42°, m\angle 2 = 48°$
$m\angle 1 + m\angle 2 = 90°$

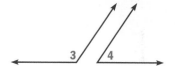

Supplementary angles

$m\angle 3 = 125°, m\angle 4 = 55°$
$m\angle 3 + m\angle 4 = 180°$

Adjacent angles that form a right angle are complementary. Adjacent angles that form a straight angle are supplementary. In the diagram at the right, $\angle BEC$ and $\angle CED$ are complementary angles, and $\angle AEC$ and $\angle CED$ are supplementary angles.

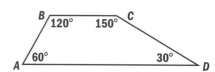

 Review *Help*

For help with classifying angles, see p. 793.

Example 1   *Identifying Complementary, Supplementary Angles*

In quadrilateral *ABCD*, identify all pairs of complementary angles and supplementary angles.

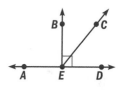

Solution

a. Because $m\angle A + m\angle D = 60° + 30° = 90°$, $\angle A$ and $\angle D$ are complementary angles.

b. Because $m\angle A + m\angle B = 60° + 120° = 180°$, $\angle A$ and $\angle B$ are supplementary angles.

Because $m\angle C + m\angle D = 150° + 30° = 180°$, $\angle C$ and $\angle D$ are supplementary angles.

✔ *Checkpoint*

Tell whether the angles are *complementary*, *supplementary*, or *neither*.

1. $m\angle 1 = 63°$
$m\angle 2 = 27°$

2. $m\angle 3 = 146°$
$m\angle 4 = 44°$

3. $m\angle 5 = 95°$
$m\angle 6 = 85°$

Example 2 · Finding an Angle Measure

Stage Monitors Stage monitors are speakers that performers use so that they can clearly hear the sounds they make on a stage. For the stage monitor shown, $\angle 1$ and $\angle 2$ are complementary angles, and $m\angle 1 = 35°$. Find $m\angle 2$.

Solution

$m\angle 1 + m\angle 2 = 90°$	Definition of complementary angles
$35° + m\angle 2 = 90°$	Substitute 35° for $m\angle 1$.
$m\angle 2 = 55°$	Subtract 35° from each side.

Vertical Angles When two lines intersect at one point, the angles that are opposite each other are **vertical angles**. Vertical angles have the same measure, as you will see in Exercise 31.

Vertical angles
$\angle 1$ and $\angle 3$
$\angle 2$ and $\angle 4$

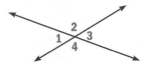

Example 3 · Using Supplementary and Vertical Angles

Television Trays For the television tray shown, $m\angle 1 = 110°$. Find $m\angle 2$, $m\angle 3$, and $m\angle 4$.

Solution

a.
$m\angle 1 + m\angle 2 = 180°$	$\angle 1$ and $\angle 2$ are supplementary.
$110° + m\angle 2 = 180°$	Substitute 110° for $m\angle 1$.
$m\angle 2 = 70°$	Subtract 110° from each side.

b.
$m\angle 3 = m\angle 1$	Vertical angles have same measure.
$m\angle 3 = 110°$	Substitute 110° for $m\angle 1$.

c.
$m\angle 4 = m\angle 2$	Vertical angles have same measure.
$m\angle 4 = 70°$	Substitute 70° for $m\angle 2$.

✔ Checkpoint

4. $\angle 1$ and $\angle 2$ are supplementary angles, and $m\angle 1 = 118°$. Find $m\angle 2$.

5. $\angle 3$ and $\angle 4$ are complementary angles, and $m\angle 3 = 24°$. Find $m\angle 4$.

6. In Example 3, suppose that $m\angle 1 = 135°$. Find $m\angle 2$, $m\angle 3$, and $m\angle 4$.

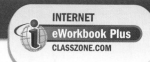

Guided Practice

Vocabulary Check   **1.** Copy and complete: The sum of the measures of two ? angles is 90°.

2. What can you say about the measures of two vertical angles?

Skill Check   **Tell whether the angles are *complementary*, *supplementary*, or *neither*.**

3. $m\angle 1 = 10°$
$m\angle 2 = 70°$

4. $m\angle 3 = 108°$
$m\angle 4 = 72°$

5. $m\angle 5 = 58°$
$m\angle 6 = 32°$

In Exercises 6 and 7, use the given information to find $m\angle 2$.

6. $\angle 1$ and $\angle 2$ are complementary angles, and $m\angle 1 = 45°$.

7. $\angle 1$ and $\angle 2$ are supplementary angles, and $m\angle 1 = 160°$.

Guided Problem Solving   **8.** In the diagram shown, $m\angle 1 = 35°$ and $m\angle 3 = 110°$. What is $m\angle 5$?

1 Tell how $\angle 1$ and $\angle 2$ are related. Then find $m\angle 2$.

2 Tell how $\angle 3$ and $\angle 4$ are related. Then find $m\angle 4$.

3 Use what you know about the sum of the measures of the angles of a triangle to find $m\angle 5$.

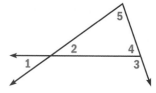

Practice and Problem Solving

Homework *Help*

Example	Exercises
1	9–16
2	17, 22–24
3	18–21, 24–25

Online Resources
CLASSZONE.COM
• More Examples
• eTutorial Plus

Use the diagram shown. Identify all pairs of the specified angles.

9. Complementary angles

10. Supplementary angles

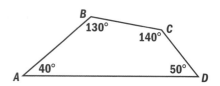

Tell whether the angles are *complementary*, *supplementary*, or *neither*.

11. $m\angle 1 = 22°$
$m\angle 2 = 58°$

12. $m\angle 3 = 98°$
$m\angle 4 = 82°$

13. $m\angle 5 = 37°$
$m\angle 6 = 53°$

14. $m\angle 1 = 71°$
$m\angle 2 = 19°$

15. $m\angle 3 = 64°$
$m\angle 4 = 116°$

16. $m\angle 5 = 98°$
$m\angle 6 = 72°$

Find $m\angle 1$.

17.

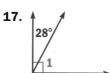

18.

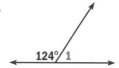

19.

20. Geography The intersection of the borders of Utah, Colorado, New Mexico, and Arizona is called Four Corners. On the map, $m\angle 1 = 90°$. Find $m\angle 2$, $m\angle 3$, and $m\angle 4$.

Use the given information to find $m\angle 2$.

21. $\angle 1$ and $\angle 2$ are vertical angles, and $m\angle 1 = 140°$.

22. $\angle 1$ and $\angle 2$ are supplementary angles, and $m\angle 1 = 137°$.

23. $\angle 1$ and $\angle 2$ are complementary angles, and $m\angle 1 = 81°$.

24. Architecture As shown in the diagram, the two structures of the *Puerta de Europa* (Door of Europe) in Madrid, Spain, lean toward each other at an angle of 15° from the vertical.

a. In the diagram, $\angle 1$ and the angle that measures 15° are complementary angles. Find $m\angle 1$.

b. Tell whether $\angle 1$ and $\angle 2$ are *complementary* or *supplementary* angles. Then use your answer to part (a) to find $m\angle 2$.

25. *Writing* When two lines intersect at one point, how many pairs of vertical angles are formed? Explain your answer.

Algebra Find the value of x in the figure. Then find the unknown angle measures.

26.

27.

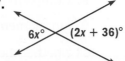

28.

Critical Thinking In Exercises 29 and 30, tell whether a triangle exists for the given description. If so, classify the triangle by its angles. If not, explain why not.

29. Two of the angles are complementary.

30. Two of the angles are supplementary.

31. In the diagram, use only what you know about supplementary angles to write expressions for $m\angle 1$, $m\angle 2$, and $m\angle 3$ in terms of x. Then use the expressions to show that the vertical angles have equal measures.

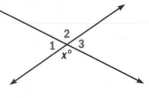

In the **Real World**

Geography The Four Corners Monument is the only place in the United States where you can stand in four states at one time. How many pairs of supplementary angles are formed by the borders of the four states?

Clothespin
by Claes Oldenburg

32. Sculptures The diagram shows the sculpture *Clothespin* casting a shadow. In the diagram, ∠2 is the angle of the sun above the horizon.

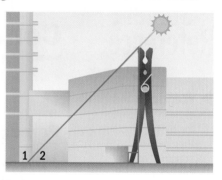

a. 🖩 At a certain time of the day, $m\angle 1 = 148°$, and the shadow has a length of 72 feet. Use a calculator to find the height of the sculpture. Round to the nearest tenth.

b. At a certain time of the day, $m\angle 1 = 135°$. How is the length of the shadow related to the height of the sculpture? Explain your reasoning.

33. Critical Thinking Let ∠1 and ∠2 be vertical angles. What are their measures if they are complementary angles? supplementary angles?

34. Geometry Use the diagram shown.

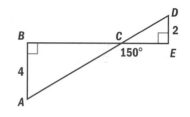

a. For △*ABC* and △*DEC*, find the measure of each angle and the length of each side.

b. **Compare** How are △*ABC* and △*DEC* related? Explain your reasoning.

35. Challenge Let ∠1 and ∠2 be complementary angles, and let ∠2 and ∠3 be supplementary angles. If $m\angle 1 = x°$ and $m\angle 2 = 2x°$, find x. Then find $m\angle 1$, $m\angle 2$, and $m\angle 3$.

Mixed Review **Use a compass and a straightedge to draw a segment whose length is the sum of the lengths of the given segments.** *(p. 794)*

36. ————

37. ————

38. ————

————

————

————

Solve the equation. Check your solution. *(Lesson 3.1)*

39. $5x - 12 = 38$ **40.** $10 - 3x = 37$ **41.** $4x + 7 = -113$

Tell whether the sequence is *arithmetic* or *geometric*. *(Lesson 12.8)*

42. 1, 5, 25, 125, . . .   **43.** 3, 11, 19, 27, . . .   **44.** 80, 40, 20, 10, . . .

Standardized Test Practice **45. Multiple Choice** If ∠1 and ∠2 are complementary angles, what could their measures be?

A. $m\angle 1 = 36°$
$m\angle 2 = 24°$

B. $m\angle 1 = 52°$
$m\angle 2 = 38°$

C. $m\angle 1 = 61°$
$m\angle 2 = 61°$

D. $m\angle 1 = 89°$
$m\angle 2 = 91°$

46. Multiple Choice In the diagram shown, $m\angle 3 = 72°$. What is $m\angle 4$?

F. 18°   **G.** 36°

H. 108°   **I.** 144°

Constructions

▶ **Review** this topic in preparation for solving problems that involve constructions in Lesson 13.2. For a review of using a compass and a straightedge, see p. 794.

Perpendicular Bisectors

A **perpendicular bisector** of $\overline{AB}$ is a line, ray, or segment that is perpendicular to $\overline{AB}$ at its midpoint.

Example **Use a compass and a straightedge to construct a perpendicular bisector of a segment.**

1) Draw $\overline{KL}$. Using a compass setting greater than half the length of $\overline{KL}$, draw an arc with center K. Using the same compass setting, draw an arc with center L.

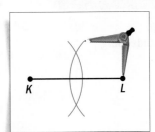

2) Label M and N as shown. Then draw $\overleftrightarrow{MN}$, the perpendicular bisector of $\overline{KL}$.

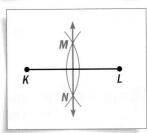

Copying an Angle

Example **Use a compass and a straightedge to copy an angle.**

1) Draw $\angle E$ and a ray with endpoint H. Then draw an arc with center E. Label F and G as shown. Using the same compass setting, draw an arc with center H. Label J as shown.

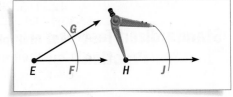

2) Draw an arc with center F that intersects G. Using the same compass setting, draw an arc with center J. Label K as shown. Then draw $\overrightarrow{HK}$.

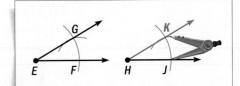

Angle Bisectors

An **angle bisector** is a ray that divides an angle into two adjacent, congruent angles.

Example Use a compass and a straightedge to construct the bisector of an angle.

1) Draw ∠P. Then draw an arc with center P. Label Q and R as shown.

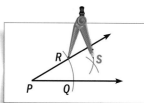

2) Draw an arc with center Q. Then, using the same compass setting, draw an arc with center R. Label S as shown.

3) Draw $\overrightarrow{PS}$, the bisector of ∠RPQ.

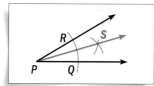

✔ Checkpoint

▶ Test your knowledge of constructions by solving these problems.

Draw two segments like the ones shown. Then use a compass and a straightedge to perform the construction.

1. Copy $\overline{AB}$. Then construct the perpendicular bisector of $\overline{AB}$.

2. Copy $\overline{CD}$. Then construct the perpendicular bisector of $\overline{CD}$.

3. Construct a segment whose length is $\frac{1}{4}$ of the length of $\overline{CD}$. Describe the steps you take.

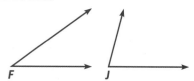

In Exercises 4–6, draw two angles like the ones shown. Then use a compass and a straightedge to perform the construction.

4. Copy ∠F and ∠J. Then construct the bisectors of ∠F and ∠J.

5. Construct an angle whose measure is twice the measure of ∠J.

6. Construct an angle whose measure is the sum of the measures of ∠F and ∠J. Then construct the bisector of that angle.

7. **Apply** Construct a 45° angle using what you know about constructing perpendicular bisectors and angle bisectors. Describe the steps you take.

13.2

Angles *and* Parallel Lines

BEFORE	Now	WHY?
You classified special pairs of angles.	You'll identify angles when a transversal intersects lines.	So you can analyze the shape of a chair, as in Ex. 16.

Vocabulary

transversal, p. 716
corresponding angles, p. 716
alternate interior angles, p. 716
alternate exterior angles, p. 716

A line that intersects two or more lines at different points is a **transversal** . When a transversal intersects two lines, several pairs of angles are formed. Two angles that occupy corresponding positions are **corresponding angles** . Two angles that lie between the two lines on opposite sides of the transversal are **alternate interior angles** . Two angles that lie outside the two lines on opposite sides of the transversal are **alternate exterior angles** .

Corresponding angles
∠1 and ∠5, ∠2 and ∠6,
∠3 and ∠7, ∠4 and ∠8

Alternate interior angles
∠3 and ∠6, ∠4 and ∠5

Alternate exterior angles
∠1 and ∠8, ∠2 and ∠7

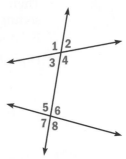

John Hancock Center

Example 1   Identifying Angles

Skyscrapers In the diagram of the John Hancock Center in Chicago, line *t* is a transversal. Tell whether the angles are corresponding, alternate interior, or alternate exterior angles.

a. ∠1 and ∠8

b. ∠2 and ∠6

c. ∠4 and ∠5

Solution

a. ∠1 and ∠8 are alternate exterior angles.

b. ∠2 and ∠6 are corresponding angles.

c. ∠4 and ∠5 are alternate interior angles.

✔ *Checkpoint*

In Example 1, tell whether the angles are *corresponding*, *alternate interior*, or *alternate exterior* angles.

1. ∠2 and ∠7   **2.** ∠3 and ∠6   **3.** ∠4 and ∠8

Transversals and Parallel Lines When a transversal intersects two parallel lines, certain pairs of angles that are formed have equal measures.

Angles and Parallel Lines

In the diagram, transversal *t* intersects parallel lines *m* and *n*.

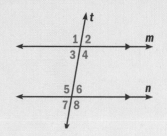

Corresponding angles

$m\angle 1 = m\angle 5$ $m\angle 2 = m\angle 6$
$m\angle 3 = m\angle 7$ $m\angle 4 = m\angle 8$

Alternate interior angles

$m\angle 3 = m\angle 6$ $m\angle 4 = m\angle 5$

Alternate exterior angles

$m\angle 1 = m\angle 8$ $m\angle 2 = m\angle 7$

Example 2   *Finding Angle Measures*

In the diagram, transversal *t* intersects parallel lines *m* and *n*. If $m\angle 1 = 75°$, find the measures of the other numbered angles.

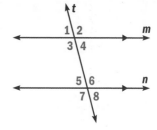

Solution

$m\angle 5 = 75°$, because ∠1 and ∠5 are corresponding angles.

$m\angle 4 = 75°$, because ∠4 and ∠5 are alternate interior angles.

$m\angle 8 = 75°$, because ∠1 and ∠8 are alternate exterior angles.

$m\angle 2 = 105°$, because ∠1 and ∠2 are supplementary angles.

$m\angle 6 = 105°$, because ∠2 and ∠6 are corresponding angles.

$m\angle 3 = 105°$, because ∠3 and ∠6 are alternate interior angles.

$m\angle 7 = 105°$, because ∠2 and ∠7 are alternate exterior angles.

✔ *Checkpoint*

Find the measures of the numbered angles in the diagram.

4.

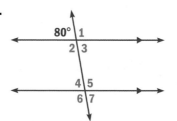

5.

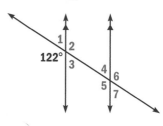

6. Critical Thinking In Example 2, if you know only $m\angle 6$, can you find the measures of the other numbered angles? Explain.

Corresponding Angles If a transversal intersects two lines so that the corresponding angles have the same measure, then the lines are parallel.

Example 3 *Finding the Value of a Variable*

Find the value of *x* that makes lines *m* and *n* parallel.

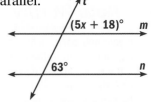

Solution

The labeled angles in the diagram are corresponding angles. Lines *m* and *n* are parallel when the measures are equal.

$(5x + 18)° = 63°$ **Set measures equal.**

$5x = 45$ **Subtract 18 from each side.**

$x = 9$ **Divide each side by 5.**

13.2 Exercises

More Practice, p. 815

INTERNET
eWorkbook Plus
CLASSZONE.COM

Guided Practice

Vocabulary Check

1. Draw two lines and a transversal intersecting both lines. Then number the angles and identify both pairs of alternate interior angles.

2. A transversal intersects lines *m* and *n*. If the corresponding angles are congruent, what can you conclude about lines *m* and *n*?

Skill Check

In Exercises 3–6, tell whether the angles in the diagram are *corresponding*, *alternate interior*, or *alternate exterior* angles.

3. ∠2 and ∠6

4. ∠4 and ∠8

5. ∠3 and ∠6

6. ∠2 and ∠7

7. If $m\angle 1 = 65°$, find the measures of the other numbered angles in the diagram.

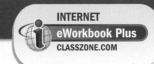

Guided Problem Solving

8. Use the diagram. For lines *m* and *n* to be parallel, what must the value of *x* be?

  1 Tell whether the labeled angles are *corresponding*, *alternate interior*, or *alternate exterior* angles.

  2 Write an equation that relates the angle measures.

  3 Solve the equation for *x*.

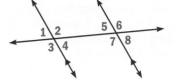

Practice and Problem Solving

Homework *Help*

Example	Exercises
1	9–12, 15–16
2	13–16
3	17–18

Online Resources
CLASSZONE.COM

• More Examples
• eTutorial Plus

In Exercises 9–12, tell whether the angles in the diagram are *corresponding*, *alternate interior*, or *alternate exterior* angles.

9. ∠1 and ∠8   **10.** ∠4 and ∠5

11. ∠1 and ∠5   **12.** ∠3 and ∠7

13. Which angles have the same measure as ∠1 in the diagram?

14. If $m\angle 1 = 43°$, find the measures of the other numbered angles in the diagram.

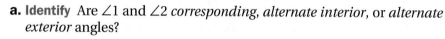

15. Extended Problem Solving In the bicycle frame shown, ∠1 is called the head angle, and ∠2 is called the seat angle. Lines *m* and *n* are parallel.

a. Identify Are ∠1 and ∠2 *corresponding, alternate interior,* or *alternate exterior* angles?

b. Explain Do ∠1 and ∠2 have the same measure? Explain.

c. Calculate Find $m\angle 1$ and $m\angle 2$. Explain how you got your answers.

16. Chairs The diagram shown is a side view of a chair designed in the 1930s. In the diagram, $m\angle 1 = 95°$ and $m\angle 3 = 45°$. Tell whether the statement is *true* or *false*. Explain your reasoning.

a. ∠2 and ∠3 are corresponding angles.

b. ∠2 and ∠3 have equal measures.

c. ∠2 and ∠3 are complementary angles.

d. The sum of the measures of ∠1, ∠2, and ∠3 is 180°.

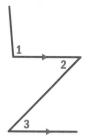

Algebra Find the value of *x* that makes lines *m* and *n* parallel.

17.

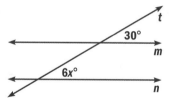

18.

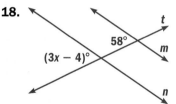

In the **Real World**

Chairs The chair shown is called a zig-zag chair. In 1934, Gerrit Rietveld built a zig-zag chair that was 74 centimeters high, 45 centimeters long, and 37.5 centimeters wide. If the chair is enclosed in a box with these dimensions, what is the volume of the box?

Geometry Find the measures of the numbered angles in the diagram.

19.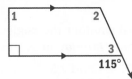

20.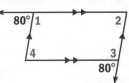

21. Visual Thinking A transversal intersects two parallel lines, forming alternate interior angles $\angle 1$ and $\angle 2$ and vertical angles $\angle 1$ and $\angle 3$. Illustrate the situation. How are $m\angle 2$ and $m\angle 3$ related? Explain.

22. *Writing* The drawing is a Hering illusion, in which intersecting transversals make two parallel lines appear to be curved. Describe a way you can use a protractor to verify that the two lines are parallel.

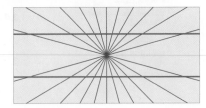

23. Construction Draw a line *t* using a straightedge. Then use a compass and a straightedge to construct two lines *m* and *n* that are perpendicular to *t* at two different points. How are *m* and *n* related? Explain your reasoning.

24. Challenge Use the diagram.

   a. Write expressions for $m\angle 1$, $m\angle 2$, and $m\angle 3$ in terms of *x* and *y*. Explain your reasoning.

   b. Use the expressions you wrote in part (a) to show that the sum of the measures of the angles in $\triangle ABC$ is 180°.

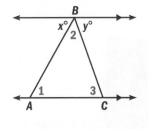

Review *Help*

For help with using a protractor, see p. 792.

Mixed Review   Solve the equation by first clearing the fractions. *(Lesson 5.7)*

25. $\frac{1}{2}x + \frac{3}{4} = \frac{5}{6}$ **26.** $\frac{7}{10}x - \frac{1}{5} = \frac{3}{8}$ **27.** $-\frac{1}{12} = \frac{1}{2}x - \frac{4}{9}$

28. A quadrilateral has angle measures of $(2x + 1)°$, $(x - 3)°$, 100°, and $(3x - 2)°$. Find the value of *x*. *(Lesson 10.2)*

Tell whether the angles are *complementary*, *supplementary*, or *neither*. *(Lesson 13.1)*

29. $m\angle 1 = 140°$ **30.** $m\angle 3 = 118°$ **31.** $m\angle 5 = 24°$
    $m\angle 2 = 40°$ $m\angle 4 = 72°$ $m\angle 6 = 66°$

Standardized Test Practice   In Exercises 32 and 33, use the diagram.

32. Multiple Choice What is $m\angle 6$?

   A. 30°   **B.** 60°

   C. 90°   **D.** 120°

33. Short Response Which numbered angles have the same measure as $\angle 1$? Explain your reasoning.

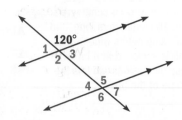

Concept Activity

13.3 Finding Sums of Angle Measures

Goal
Find the sum of the measures of the angles of a convex polygon.

Materials
- paper
- pencil

Investigate

Find the sum of the measures of the angles of a convex polygon.

1 Draw a convex polygon. Then draw all the diagonals from one vertex of the polygon.

2 Multiply the number of triangles formed in Step 1 by 180°. The product is the sum of the measures of the angles of the polygon.

$3 \cdot 180° = 540°$

3 Copy and complete the table.

Convex polygon	Quadrilateral	Pentagon	Hexagon	Heptagon	Octagon
Sides	?	5	?	?	?
Triangles formed	?	3	?	?	?
Sum of angle measures	?	$3 \cdot 180° = 540°$	?	?	?

Draw Conclusions

1. **Critical Thinking** In Step 2, why do you multiply the number of triangles formed by 180°?

2. **Compare** How is the number of triangles formed by drawing diagonals from one vertex related to the number of sides of a convex polygon? How many triangles would be formed using a convex polygon with n sides?

3. **Analyze** Write a formula for the sum of the measures of the angles of a convex polygon with n sides.

4. **Apply** Use the formula you wrote in Exercise 3 to find the sum of the measures of the angles of a convex polygon with 9 sides.

Angles *and* Polygons

BEFORE | Now | WHY?

You found angle measures of triangles. | You'll find measures of interior and exterior angles. | So you can analyze a street map, as in Ex. 22.

Vocabulary

interior angle, p. 722
exterior angle, p. 723

Tambourines The frame of the tambourine shown is a regular heptagon. What is the measure of each angle of the heptagon? You will find the answer in Example 2.

An **interior angle** of a polygon is an angle inside the polygon. In the activity on page 721, you used triangles to find the sum of the measures of the interior angles of a convex polygon. You can find the measure of an interior angle of a regular polygon by dividing the sum of the measures of the interior angles by the number of sides.

Review *Help*

For help with convex polygons and regular polygons, see p. 516.

> ### Measures of Interior Angles of a Convex Polygon
>
> The sum of the measures of the interior angles of a convex n-gon is given by the formula $(n - 2) \cdot 180°$.
>
> The measure of an interior angle of a regular n-gon is given by the formula $\dfrac{(n - 2) \cdot 180°}{n}$.

Example 1   *Finding the Sum of a Polygon's Interior Angles*

Find the sum of the measures of the interior angles of the polygon.

a.

b.

Solution

a. For a convex pentagon, $n = 5$.

$$(n - 2) \cdot 180° = (5 - 2) \cdot 180°$$
$$= 3 \cdot 180°$$
$$= 540°$$

b. For a convex octagon, $n = 8$.

$$(n - 2) \cdot 180° = (8 - 2) \cdot 180°$$
$$= 6 \cdot 180°$$
$$= 1080°$$

Watch *Out*

The formula $\dfrac{(n-2) \cdot 180°}{n}$ is valid only for a regular polygon. You cannot use this formula to find the measure of an interior angle of a convex polygon that is not regular.

Example 2 — *Finding the Measure of an Interior Angle*

Find the measure of an interior angle of the frame of the tambourine shown on page 722.

Solution

Because the tambourine is a regular heptagon, $n = 7$.

$$\begin{aligned}
\text{Measure of an interior angle} &= \frac{(n-2) \cdot 180°}{n} && \text{Write formula.}\\[2mm]
&= \frac{(7-2) \cdot 180°}{7} && \text{Substitute 7 for } n.\\[2mm]
&\approx 128.6° && \text{Evaluate. Use a calculator.}
\end{aligned}$$

Answer The measure of an interior angle of the frame of the tambourine is about 128.6°.

✔ *Checkpoint*

1. Find the sum of the measures of the interior angles of a convex 10-gon.

2. Find the measure of an interior angle of a regular 12-gon.

Exterior Angles When you extend a side of a polygon, the angle that is adjacent to the interior angle is an **exterior angle**. In the diagram, $\angle 1$ and $\angle 2$ are exterior angles. An interior angle and an exterior angle at the same vertex form a straight angle.

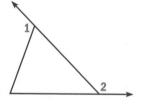

Example 3 — *Finding the Measure of an Exterior Angle*

Find $m\angle 1$ in the diagram.

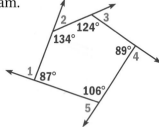

Solution

The angle that measures 87° forms a straight angle with $\angle 1$, which is the exterior angle at the same vertex.

$$\begin{aligned}
m\angle 1 + 87° &= 180° && \text{Angles are supplementary.}\\
m\angle 1 &= 93° && \text{Subtract 87° from each side.}
\end{aligned}$$

✔ *Checkpoint*

3. In Example 3, find $m\angle 2$, $m\angle 3$, $m\angle 4$, and $m\angle 5$.

Example 4   *An Exterior Angle Measure of a Regular Polygon*

Teapots The diagram shows a teapot in the shape of a regular hexagon. Find $m\angle 2$.

Solution

The measure of an interior angle of a regular hexagon is $\dfrac{(6-2)\cdot 180°}{6}$.

$$m\angle 1 + m\angle 2 = 180° \qquad \text{Angles are supplementary.}$$

$$\frac{(6-2)\cdot 180°}{6} + m\angle 2 = 180° \qquad \text{Substitute formula for } m\angle 1.$$

$$120° + m\angle 2 = 180° \qquad \text{Simplify.}$$

$$m\angle 2 = 60° \qquad \text{Subtract } 120° \text{ from each side.}$$

Sum of Exterior Angle Measures Each vertex of a convex polygon has two exterior angles. If you draw one exterior angle at each vertex, then the sum of the measures of these angles is 360°. The calculations below show that this is true for a triangle.

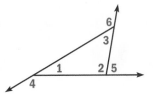

$$m\angle 4 + m\angle 5 + m\angle 6 = (180° - m\angle 1) + (180° - m\angle 2) + (180° - m\angle 3)$$

$$= (180° + 180° + 180°) - (m\angle 1 + m\angle 2 + m\angle 3)$$

$$= 540° - 180° = 360°$$

Example 5   *Using the Sum of Measures of Exterior Angles*

Find the unknown angle measure in the diagram.

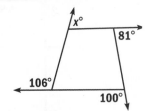

Solution

$$x° + 81° + 100° + 106° = 360° \qquad \text{Sum of measures of exterior angles of convex polygon is } 360°.$$

$$x + 287 = 360 \qquad \text{Add.}$$

$$x = 73 \qquad \text{Subtract } 287 \text{ from each side.}$$

Answer The angle measure is 73°.

✔ *Checkpoint*

4. Find the measure of an exterior angle of a regular pentagon.

5. Four exterior angles of a convex pentagon have measures 14°, 87°, 56°, and 30°. Find the measure of the fifth exterior angle.

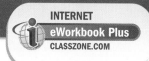
Guided Practice

Vocabulary Check   **1.** Draw a convex polygon that has exactly 8 interior angles.

2. Draw a quadrilateral and show one exterior angle at each vertex.

Skill Check   **In Exercises 3–6, match the description with the correct value.**

3. Sum of measures of interior angles of a convex heptagon   **A.** 360°

4. Measure of an interior angle of a regular hexagon   **B.** 45°

5. Measure of an exterior angle of a regular octagon   **C.** 900°

6. Sum of measures of exterior angles of a convex 12-gon   **D.** 120°

Guided Problem Solving   **7.** In the diagram shown, what is $m\angle 2$?

① Find the sum of the measures of the interior angles of the polygon.

② Find $m\angle 1$.

③ Subtract your answer to Step 2 from 180°.

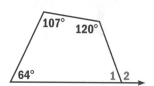

Practice and Problem Solving

Homework *Help*

Example	Exercises
1	8–11
2	12–17, 22–23
3	18, 22
4	12–17, 21
5	19–20

Online Resources
CLASSZONE.COM
• More Examples
• eTutorial Plus

Find the sum of the measures of the interior angles of the polygon.

8.   **9.**   **10.**

      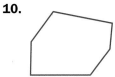

11. *Writing* Is the formula for the sum of the interior angles of a polygon valid for a triangle? Explain your reasoning.

In Exercises 12–17, find the measure of an interior angle and the measure of an exterior angle for the regular polygon.

12. Triangle   **13.** Quadrilateral   **14.** Octagon

15. Pentagon   **16.** 10-gon   **17.** 15-gon

18. For the triangle shown, what is the measure of an exterior angle at vertex A? at vertex B? at vertex C?

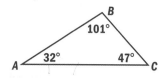

In Exercises 19 and 20, find the unknown angle measure.

19.

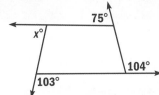

20.

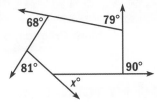

21. *Writing* Suppose you know only the number of sides of a regular polygon. Describe the steps you would take to find the measure of an exterior angle of the polygon.

22. **Cotati Hub** The map shows a section of Cotati, California. This area is called the Cotati Hub. It is made up of six streets that form a regular hexagon.

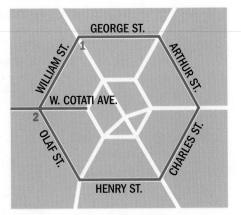

   a. William Street and George Street form ∠1. Find $m∠1$.

   b. West Cotati Avenue bisects the interior angle formed by William Street and Olaf Street. Find $m∠2$.

23. **Critical Thinking** Suppose you know only the sum of the measures of the interior angles of a pentagon. Can you always find the measure of one of the interior angles? Explain your reasoning.

Algebra Find the values of *x* and *y*.

24.

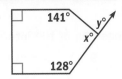

25.

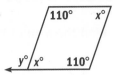

26.

27. **Extended Problem Solving** The table shows the relationship between *x*, the number of sides of a regular polygon, and *y*, the measure of an interior angle.

x	3	4	5	6	7	8	9	10
y	60°	?	?	?	?	?	?	?

   a. **Graph** Copy and complete the table. Round to the nearest tenth, if necessary. Then plot the ordered pairs (*x*, *y*) in a coordinate plane.

   b. **Analyze** As the number of sides increases, does the change in the measure of an interior angle *increase*, *decrease*, or *stay the same*?

   c. **Decide** Your friend says that *y* = 148° when *x* = 11. Based on the numbers in the table, do you agree? Explain your reasoning.

28. For which regular polygon is the ratio of an exterior angle measure to an interior angle measure 1 to 1? 2 to 1? 2 to 3?

29. Baseball In baseball, home plate is in the shape of a pentagon, as shown. Find the value of x.

30. Interpret Generate a sequence by evaluating the expression $180 \cdot (n - 2)$ for $n = 3, 4, 5, 6,$ and 7. Then tell whether the sequence is *arithmetic* or *geometric*.

31. Critical Thinking Draw a convex polygon and show two exterior angles at each vertex. Why do the two exterior angles at one vertex of the polygon have the same measure?

32. The measures of the exterior angles of a triangle are $5x°$, $(x + 47)°$, and $(6x - 35)°$. Classify the triangle by its angles. Explain your reasoning.

In Exercises 33–35, the sum of the measures of the interior angles of a convex polygon is given. Classify the polygon.

33. $1620°$　　　　　**34.** $2160°$　　　　　**35.** $2700°$

36. Challenge Let $w°$, $x°$, $y°$, and $z°$ represent the measures of the interior angles of a quadrilateral. Show that the sum of the exterior angles, one exterior angle at each vertex, is $360°$.

Mixed Review

Find the sum. *(Lesson 1.5)*

37. $8 + (-3)$　　　**38.** $-17 + 8$　　　**39.** $-9 + (-5)$　　　**40.** $-10 + (-12)$

Graph the equation. Tell whether the equation is a function. *(Lesson 8.2)*

41. $y = 3x + 2$　　　**42.** $y = -3$　　　**43.** $y = x - 4$　　　**44.** $x = 6$

Find the value of x that makes lines m and n parallel. *(Lesson 13.2)*

45.

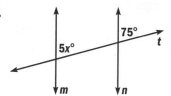

46.

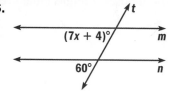

Standardized Test Practice

47. Multiple Choice The base of a gazebo is in the shape of a hexagon. What is the sum of the measures of the interior angles of the base?

A. $360°$　　　**B.** $540°$　　　**C.** $720°$　　　**D.** $900°$

48. Multiple Choice The shape of a traffic sign usually indicates the sign's meaning. The shape of a stop sign is always a regular octagon. What is the measure of an interior angle of a stop sign?

F. $90°$　　　**G.** $108°$　　　**H.** $135°$　　　**I.** $144°$

49. Short Response The 20 cent Euro coin has 7 indentations. If you connect the indentations with segments, you obtain a regular polygon, as shown. What is the measure of an exterior angle of the polygon? Explain your reasoning.

Mid-Chapter Quiz

Tell whether the angles are *complementary*, *supplementary*, or *neither*.

1. $m\angle 1 = 54°$
$m\angle 2 = 126°$

2. $m\angle 3 = 18°$
$m\angle 4 = 18°$

3. $m\angle 5 = 37°$
$m\angle 6 = 53°$

Find $m\angle 1$.

4.

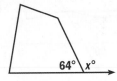

5.

6.

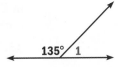

In Exercises 7–10, tell whether the angles in the diagram are *corresponding*, *alternate interior*, or *alternate exterior* angles.

7. $\angle 1$ and $\angle 8$

8. $\angle 3$ and $\angle 6$

9. $\angle 2$ and $\angle 7$

10. $\angle 2$ and $\angle 6$

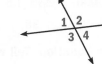

11. If $m\angle 6 = 112°$, find the measures of the other numbered angles in the diagram.

12. Find the measure of an interior angle of a regular pentagon.

Find the unknown angle measure in the diagram.

13.

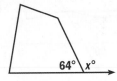

14.

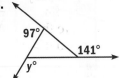

15.

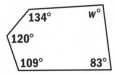

A Perfect Fit

In the figure shown, point X is the common vertex of an equilateral triangle, two squares, and a fourth regular polygon. Two of the sides of the fourth polygon are $\overline{XZ}$ and $\overline{XY}$. How many sides does the fourth polygon have? Explain your reasoning.

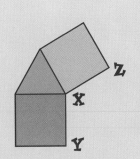

Translations

BEFORE	*Now*	WHY?
You plotted points in a coordinate plane.	You'll translate figures in a coordinate plane.	So you can create a design for a blanket, as in Ex. 12.

Vocabulary

transformation, p. 729
image, p. 729
translation, p. 729
tessellation, p. 730

Snow Tubing Snow tubing involves sliding down a snow-covered hill on an inflated tube. As you will see in Example 1, you can use a *translation* to describe a change in the position of a person sliding down a hill.

A **transformation** is a change made to the location or to the size of a figure. The new figure formed by a transformation is called an **image**. In this book, the original figure is blue, and the image is red. *Prime notation* is used to identify the image of point *A*. You read *A′* as "*A* prime."

A **translation** is a transformation in which each point of a figure moves the same distance in the same direction. In a translation, a figure and its image are congruent.

Example 1 Describing a Translation

For the diagram shown, describe the translation in words.

Solution

Think of moving horizontally and vertically from a point on the original figure to the corresponding point on the new figure. For instance, you move 200 feet to the right and 40 feet down from *A*(0, 100) to reach *A′*(200, 60).

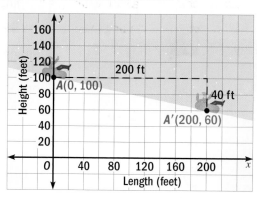

✔ **Checkpoint**

Describe the translation in words.

1.
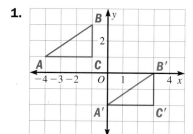

2.
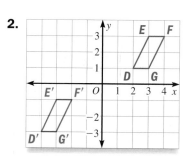

Reading *Algebra*

In the translation $(x, y) \rightarrow (x + 4, y - 1)$, the expression $y - 1$ can be written as $y + (-1)$ to indicate that each point (x, y) of a figure moves 1 unit down.

Coordinate Notation You can describe a translation of each point (x, y) of a figure using the coordinate notation

$$(x, y) \rightarrow (x + a, y + b)$$

where a indicates how many units a point moves horizontally, and b indicates how many units a point moves vertically. Move the point (x, y) to the right if a is positive and to the left if a is negative. Move the point up if b is positive and down if b is negative.

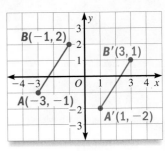

$$(x, y) \rightarrow (x + 4, y - 1)$$

Example 2 *Translating a Figure*

Draw $\triangle ABC$ with vertices $A(3, -4)$, $B(3, 0)$, and $C(5, 2)$. Then find the coordinates of the vertices of the image after the translation $(x, y) \rightarrow (x - 6, y + 2)$, and draw the image.

Solution

First draw $\triangle ABC$. Then, to translate $\triangle ABC$, subtract 6 from the x-coordinate and add 2 to the y-coordinate of each vertex.

Original	**Image**
(x, y)	$\rightarrow (x - 6, y + 2)$
$A(3, -4)$	$\rightarrow A'(-3, -2)$
$B(3, 0)$	$\rightarrow B'(-3, 2)$
$C(5, 2)$	$\rightarrow C'(-1, 4)$

Finally, draw $\triangle A'B'C'$, as shown. Notice that each point on $\triangle ABC$ moves 6 units to the left and 2 units up.

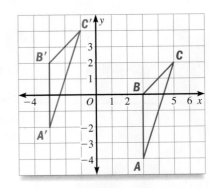

✔ Checkpoint

3. Draw quadrilateral $JKLM$ with vertices $J(-5, 0)$, $K(-2, 0)$, $L(3, -4)$, and $M(-2, -4)$. Then find the coordinates of the vertices of the image after the translation $(x, y) \rightarrow (x + 7, y + 4)$, and draw the image.

4. **Compare** Describe how the translations $(x, y) \rightarrow (x + 3, y + 2)$ and $(x, y) \rightarrow (x - 3, y + 2)$ are different.

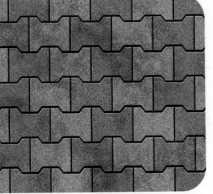

In the **Real World**

Tessellations You can see various tessellations on buildings, sidewalks, and other structures that have tiling patterns. In the tessellation above, is the polygon used a regular polygon? Is the polygon *concave* or *convex*?

Tessellations A **tessellation** is a covering of a plane with a repeating pattern of one or more shapes. A tessellation has no gaps or overlaps. One way to create a tessellation is to translate a shape, as illustrated using a parallelogram.

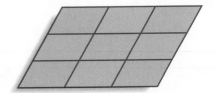

Example 3	*Creating Tessellations*

Tell whether you can create a tessellation using only translations of the given polygon. If you can, create a tessellation. If not, explain why not.

a.   30° 150°

b.

Solution

a. You can translate the rhombus to create a tessellation. Notice in the design that there are no gaps or overlaps.

b. You can't translate a regular pentagon to create a tessellation. As shown below, there will be gaps or overlaps.

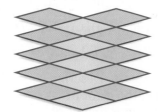

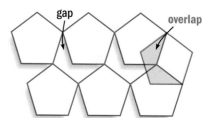

Study *Strategy*

Notice in part (a) of Example 3 that the two 30° angles and the two 150° angles at each vertex in the tessellation have a total measure of 360°.

13.4 Exercises

More Practice, p. 815

INTERNET
eWorkbook Plus
CLASSZONE.COM

Guided Practice

Vocabulary Check

1. Copy and complete: The figure formed by a translation of a figure is the ? of the figure.

2. Describe the translation $(x, y) \to (x + 3, y - 7)$ in words.

Skill Check **Describe the translation in words.**

3.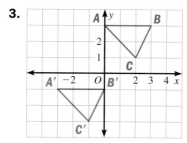

4.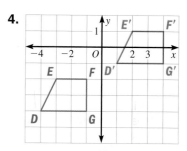

5. Draw $\triangle DEF$ with vertices $D(-1, -6)$, $E(-2, 4)$, and $F(3, -2)$. Then find the coordinates of the vertices of the image after the translation $(x, y) \to (x - 2, y - 1)$, and draw the image.

Practice and Problem Solving

Homework *Help*

Example	Exercises
1	6–7, 16
2	8–12, 16
3	13–15

Online Resources
CLASSZONE.COM

• More Examples
• eTutorial Plus

Describe the translation in words.

6.
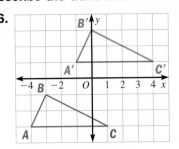

7.
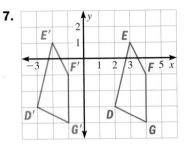

The vertices of a polygon are given. Draw the polygon. Then find the coordinates of the vertices of the image after the specified translation, and draw the image.

8. $P(-5, 4)$, $Q(1, 4)$, $R(1, 1)$; $(x, y) \rightarrow (x + 1, y - 6)$

9. $A(-2, -1)$, $B(-3, 4)$, $C(-1, 3)$, $D(-1, -1)$; $(x, y) \rightarrow (x - 4, y - 2)$

10. $J(-3, 2)$, $K(-2, 1)$, $L(1, 1)$, $M(1, -2)$, $N(0, -4)$; $(x, y) \rightarrow (x - 3, y)$

11. Error Analysis Describe and correct the error in finding the coordinates of the endpoints of the image of $\overline{AB}$ after the translation $(x, y) \rightarrow (x + 3, y - 4)$.

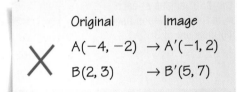

12. Blankets You can create designs for a blanket using translations.

    a. Use coordinate notation to describe the translation from figure 1 to figure 2.

    b. Use coordinate notation to describe the translation from figure 2 to figure 3.

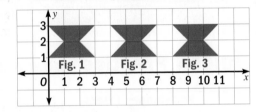

    c. Use your answers to parts (a) and (b) to draw figure 4.

Tell whether you can create a tessellation using only translations of the given polygon. If you can, create a tessellation. If not, explain why not.

13.

14.

15.

16. Draw $\triangle ABC$ with vertices $A(-4, 1)$, $B(1, 2)$, and $C(1, -3)$. Let $\triangle A'B'C'$ be the image of $\triangle ABC$, and let $\triangle A''B''C''$ be the image of $\triangle A'B'C'$.

    a. Draw $\triangle A'B'C'$ using the translation $(x, y) \rightarrow (x + 2, y - 5)$.

    b. Draw $\triangle A''B''C''$ using the translation $(x, y) \rightarrow (x - 4, y - 3)$.

    c. How could you move $\triangle ABC$ to $\triangle A''B''C''$ using only one translation?

17. Tessellations A polygon that tessellates can be altered to create other tessellations, as illustrated below with a parallelogram. Use this approach to create a tessellation by altering a rhombus.

1 Cut a piece from a polygon that tessellates and translate it to any part of the opposite side.

2 Translate the new figure repeatedly to create a tessellation.

 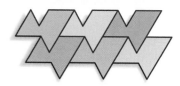

18. Writing You translate a figure using $(x, y) \rightarrow (x - 3, y + 5)$. Use coordinate notation to describe the translation from the image to the original figure. Explain your reasoning.

19. Critical Thinking You translate a figure using $(x, y) \rightarrow (x - 3, y - 4)$. You then translate its image using $(x, y) \rightarrow (x + 2, y - 6)$. If you switch the order of the translations, is the final image the same? Justify your answer with an example.

20. Escalators Use the diagram of the escalator shown.

a. ▣ Find the horizontal distance h and the vertical distance v. Round to the nearest tenth, if necessary.

b. Assume that the escalator moves down. Describe the translation from the top of the escalator to the bottom of the escalator in feet.

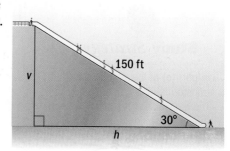

21. Challenge Given points $A(-6, -4)$ and $B(5, 5)$, use coordinate notation to describe a translation from A to the midpoint of $\overline{AB}$.

Mixed Review

Find the product. *(Lesson 1.7)*

22. $-8 \cdot (-3)$ **23.** $-12 \cdot 5$ **24.** $9 \cdot (-4)$

Find the distance between the points. *(Lesson 9.5)*

25. $(3, -2), (3, 2)$ **26.** $(5, 9), (-2, 4)$ **27.** $(3, -1), (-2, -5)$

28. Find the measure of an interior angle of a regular 9-gon. *(Lesson 13.3)*

Standardized Test Practice

In Exercises 29 and 30, $\triangle ABC$ has vertices $A(1, 2)$, $B(5, 3)$, and $C(4, 1)$. Let $\triangle A'B'C'$ be the image of $\triangle ABC$ after the translation $(x, y) \rightarrow (x - 3, y + 2)$.

29. Multiple Choice What are the coordinates of B'?

     A. $(-3, 2)$ **B.** $(-2, 4)$ **C.** $(-1, 3)$ **D.** $(2, 5)$

30. Multiple Choice In which quadrant does A' lie?

     F. Quadrant I   **G.** Quadrant II   **H.** Quadrant III   **I.** Quadrant IV

13.5 Reflections *and* Symmetry

BEFORE	*Now*	WHY?
You translated figures in a coordinate plane.	You'll reflect figures and identify lines of symmetry.	So you can analyze the symmetry of flags, as in Example 3.

Vocabulary

reflection, p. 734
line of reflection, p. 734
line symmetry, p. 735
line of symmetry, p. 735

Birds In the photo, a bird is reflected in a pool of water to produce a mirror image. A **reflection** is a transformation in which a figure is reflected, or flipped, in a line, called the **line of reflection**. In the photo, the red line is a line of reflection.

Study *Strategy*

In part (c) of Example 1, the transformation is a translation. The reflection of the figure in the *x*-axis would appear as shown below:

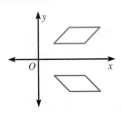

Example 1 **Identifying Reflections**

Tell whether the transformation is a reflection. If so, identify the line of reflection.

a. 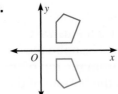 **b.** 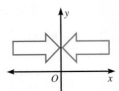 **c.**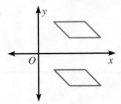

Solution

a. Reflection in *x*-axis **b.** Reflection in *y*-axis **c.** Not a reflection

Coordinate Notation You can use coordinate notation to describe the images of figures after reflections in the axes of a coordinate plane.

Reflection in the *x*-axis

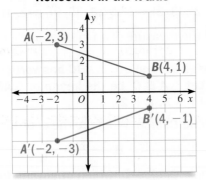

Multiply the *y*-coordinate by −1.
$(x, y) \rightarrow (x, -y)$

Reflection in the *y*-axis

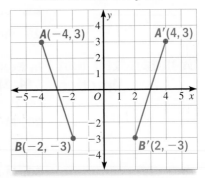

Multiply the *x*-coordinate by −1.
$(x, y) \rightarrow (-x, y)$

Study *Strategy*

In a reflection, a point and its image are the same distance from the line of reflection. Notice that in Example 2, B and B' are both 3 units from the y-axis, which is the line of reflection.

Example 2 | **Reflecting a Triangle**

Draw $\triangle ABC$ with vertices $A(1, -1)$, $B(3, 2)$, and $C(4, -3)$. Then find the coordinates of the vertices of the image after a reflection in the y-axis, and draw the image.

Solution

First draw $\triangle ABC$. Then, to reflect $\triangle ABC$ in the y-axis, multiply the x-coordinate of each vertex by -1.

Original		Image
(x, y)	$\rightarrow$	$(-x, y)$
$A(1, -1)$	$\rightarrow$	$A'(-1, -1)$
$B(3, 2)$	$\rightarrow$	$B'(-3, 2)$
$C(4, -3)$	$\rightarrow$	$C'(-4, -3)$

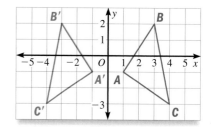

Finally, draw $\triangle A'B'C'$, as shown.

✔ *Checkpoint*

1. Draw $\triangle ABC$ with vertices $A(-1, 3)$, $B(2, 4)$, and $C(4, 1)$. Then find the coordinates of the vertices of the image of $\triangle ABC$ after a reflection in the x-axis, and draw the image.

Line Symmetry A figure has **line symmetry** if a line, called the **line of symmetry**, divides the figure into two parts that are reflections of each other in the line. A figure may have more than one line of symmetry.

Example 3 | **Identifying Lines of Symmetry**

Flags Tell how many lines of symmetry the flag has.

a. 1 line of symmetry

b. No lines of symmetry

c. 2 lines of symmetry

Colorado

Puerto Rico

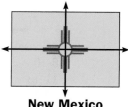

New Mexico

✔ *Checkpoint*

Tell how many lines of symmetry the figure has.

2.

3.

4.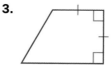

More Practice, p. 815

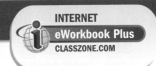

Guided Practice

Vocabulary Check

1. A figure lies in the first quadrant of a coordinate plane. It is reflected in the *x*-axis. In which quadrant does the image of the figure lie?

2. How many lines of symmetry does a 3 inch by 4 inch rectangle have?

Skill Check **Tell whether the transformation is a reflection. If so, identify the line of reflection.**

3.

4.

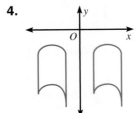

5.

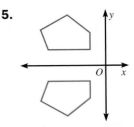

6. Draw △*ABC* with vertices *A*(−5, −1), *B*(−4, 3), and *C*(0, 2). Then find the coordinates of the vertices of the image after a reflection in the *y*-axis, and draw the image.

7. **Error Analysis** Describe and correct the error in finding the coordinates of the endpoints of the image of $\overline{AB}$ after a reflection in the *x*-axis.

Original	Image
A(−2, 1) → A′(2, 1)
B(3, 6) → B′(−3, 6)

✗

Practice and Problem Solving

Tell whether the transformation is a reflection. If so, identify the line of reflection.

Homework *Help*

Example	Exercises
1	8–10
2	11–13
3	14–17

Online Resources
CLASSZONE.COM

• More Examples
• eTutorial Plus

8.

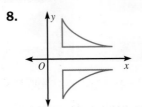

9.

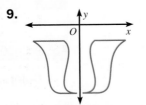

10.

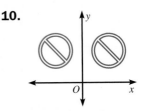

The vertices of a polygon are given. Draw the polygon. Then find the coordinates of the vertices of the image after the specified reflection, and draw the image.

11. *A*(1, −2), *B*(3, −1), *C*(4, −4); reflection in the *x*-axis

12. *D*(1, 7), *E*(6, 8), *F*(5, 4), *G*(2, 2); reflection in the *y*-axis

13. *J*(−6, 4), *K*(−4, 7), *L*(−3, 8), *M*(0, 5), *N*(−1, 2); reflection in the *y*-axis

Tell how many lines of symmetry the figure has.

14.

15.

16.

17. **Extended Problem Solving** The table shows several regular polygons.

Regular polygon	Quadrilateral	Pentagon	Hexagon	Octagon
Drawing of regular polygon				
Lines of symmetry	4	?	?	?

a. Copy and complete the table by drawing the lines of symmetry that each polygon has and recording the number of lines of symmetry.

b. **Analyze** How is the number of sides of a regular polygon related to the number of lines of symmetry?

c. **Predict** Predict the number of lines of symmetry that a regular 28-gon has.

Draw the polygon shown. Then find the coordinates of the vertices of the final image after the specified transformations, and draw the final image.

18. Reflect the polygon in the x-axis, then translate the image using $(x, y) \rightarrow (x + 2, y + 4)$.

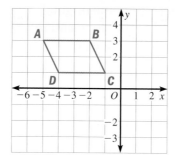

19. Reflect the polygon in the y-axis, then translate the image using $(x, y) \rightarrow (x + 5, y - 1)$.

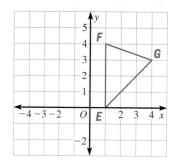

20. Let $\triangle ABC$ have vertices $A(-5, 4)$, $B(-1, 3)$, and $C(-2, 1)$, and let $\triangle DEF$ have vertices $D(0, -4)$, $E(3, -1)$, and $F(6, -6)$.

a. Reflect $\triangle ABC$ in the y-axis, then reflect its image in the x-axis. What are the coordinates of the vertices of the final image?

b. Reflect $\triangle DEF$ in the x-axis, then reflect its image in the y-axis. What are the coordinates of the vertices of the final image?

c. **Critical Thinking** Use coordinate notation to describe how a reflection of a figure in one axis followed by a reflection of its image in the other axis can be performed in one step.

21. In the diagram, △*ABC* is reflected in the line *x* = 3. Draw the image of △*ABC* after the specified reflection.

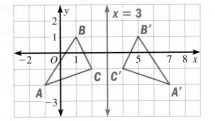

    a. Reflection in the line *x* = 5

    b. Reflection in the line *y* = −4

22. **Tessellations** You can use reflections and translations of a parallelogram to create a tessellation, as shown below. Use this approach to create a tessellation using an equilateral triangle.

    1⟩ Draw any parallelogram and reflect it in one side.

    2⟩ Translate the new figure repeatedly to create a tessellation.

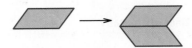

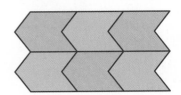

23. *Writing* How are a line of reflection and a line of symmetry alike? How are they different?

24. **Challenge** Use the line shown.

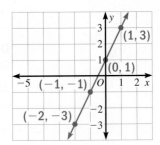

    a. What is an equation of the line?

    b. Draw the image of the line after a reflection in the *y*-axis. Then find an equation of the image.

    c. **Compare** How are the slope and the *y*-intercept of the original line related to the slope and the *y*-intercept of the image?

Mixed Review

State the absolute value and the opposite of the number. *(Lesson 1.4)*

25. 71   **26.** −45   **27.** −100   **28.** 265

Find the least common multiple of the numbers. *(Lesson 4.4)*

29. 6, 11   **30.** 8, 12   **31.** 5, 9, 10   **32.** 4, 12, 15

33. Draw △*JKL* with vertices *J*(0, 0), *K*(3, 0), and *L*(3, −5). Then find the coordinates of the vertices of the image after the translation $(x, y) \rightarrow (x - 6, y - 2)$, and draw the image. *(Lesson 13.4)*

Standardized Test Practice

34. **Multiple Choice** Each leg of a right triangle has a length of 3 inches. How many lines of symmetry does the triangle have?

    A. 1 line   **B.** 2 lines   **C.** 3 lines   **D.** 6 lines

35. **Short Response** Draw $\overline{AB}$ with endpoints *A*(3, 1) and *B*(2, 3). Explain how you would find the coordinates of the endpoints of the image of $\overline{AB}$ after a reflection in the *x*-axis, and draw the image.

13.5 Reflecting in a Line

Goal Use a graphing calculator to perform a reflection in the line $y = x$.

Example

Reflect the points $A(2, -3)$, $B(3, 1)$, and $C(5, 4)$ in the line $y = x$.

1 Enter the equation $y = x$.

Keystrokes [Y=] [X]

2 Use the *list* feature to enter the coordinates of points A, B, and C. Press [LIST] and enter the x-coordinates in the column for L1 and the y-coordinates in the column for L2, as shown in the first screen. Then use the *plot* feature to plot the points. Press [2nd] **[PLOT]** and select Plot1. Then enter the settings shown in the second screen.

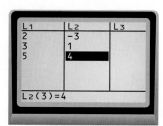

3 To reflect in the line $y = x$, you need to switch the coordinates of each point. Press [2nd] **[PLOT]** and select Plot2. Then enter the settings shown in the first screen below, making sure that you switch the places of L1 and L2. Press [ZOOM] **7** then [ZOOM] **5** to display the reflection in the line $y = x$, as shown in the second screen below.

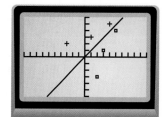

Tech *Help*

When you use
[ZOOM] **7**, all of the
points are displayed on
the screen. When you
use [ZOOM] **5**, the
line $y = x$ makes a 45°
angle with the x- and
y-axes on the screen.

Draw Conclusions

1. Reflect the points $D(-1, 4)$, $E(-5, -2)$, and $F(-3, 0)$ in the line $y = x$. Then use the *trace* feature to find the coordinates of D', E', and F'.

2. Interpret Use coordinate notation to describe a reflection in the line $y = x$.

13.6 Rotating a Segment

Goal
Rotate a segment through a given
angle about the origin.

Materials
• grid paper
• protractor
• compass

**Given $\overline{AB}$ with endpoints $A(1, 2)$ and $B(3, 1)$, draw the image of $\overline{AB}$ after
a 90° clockwise rotation about the origin. (*Clockwise* refers to the
direction that the hands on a clock turn.)**

1 Draw $\overline{AB}$. Then draw $\overline{OA}$ connecting
the origin to point A.

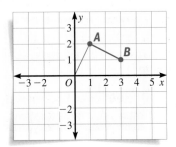

2 Use a protractor to draw a ray from
the origin so that the ray creates
an angle of 90° clockwise with $\overline{OA}$.

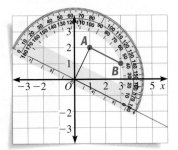

3 Use a compass to copy $\overline{OA}$ on the ray
by drawing an arc from A to the ray.
Label the point of intersection A'.

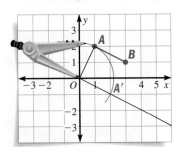

4 Repeat Steps 1–3 for point B. The
endpoints of the image, $\overline{A'B'}$, are
$A'(2, -1)$ and $B'(1, -3)$.

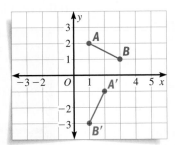

Draw Conclusions

**Draw $\overline{AB}$ with the given endpoints. Then draw the image of $\overline{AB}$ after a
90° clockwise rotation about the origin.**

1. $A(-3, 1)$, $B(-2, 3)$ **2.** $A(4, -1)$, $B(3, -4)$ **3.** $A(-3, -1)$, $B(-2, -4)$

4. Interpret Based on your results from Exercises 1–3, use coordinate
notation to describe a 90° clockwise rotation about the origin.

13.6

Rotations *and* Symmetry

BEFORE	*Now*	WHY?
You translated and reflected figures.	You'll rotate figures and identify rotational symmetry.	So you can describe how a CD tray rotates, as in Ex. 17.

Vocabulary

rotation, p. 741
center of rotation, p. 741
angle of rotation, p. 741
rotational symmetry, p. 743

Family Crests A family crest is a design that symbolizes a family's heritage. An example of a family crest for a Japanese family is shown. In Example 4, you will look at the *rotational symmetry* of the design.

A **rotation** is a transformation in which a figure is turned about a fixed point, called the **center of rotation**. The **angle of rotation** is formed by rays drawn from the center of rotation through corresponding points on an original figure and its image. The direction of rotation can be *clockwise* or *counterclockwise*. In a rotation, a figure and its image are congruent.

Reading *Geometry*

Clockwise refers to the direction that the hands on a clock turn. *Counterclockwise* refers to the opposite of the direction that the hands on a clock turn.

45° clockwise rotation

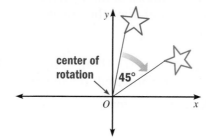

120° counterclockwise rotation

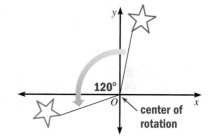

Example 1 *Identifying Rotations*

Tell whether the transformation is a rotation about the origin. If so, give the angle and direction of rotation.

a. 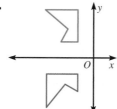 **b.** 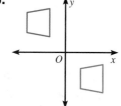 **c.**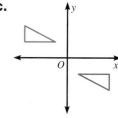

Solution

a. 90° clockwise rotation

b. Not a rotation

c. 180° rotation in either direction

90° Rotations In this book, all rotations in the coordinate plane are centered at the origin. You can use coordinate notation to describe a 90° rotation of a figure about the origin.

90° clockwise rotation

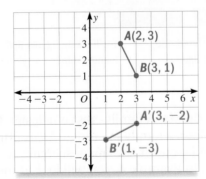

90° counterclockwise rotation

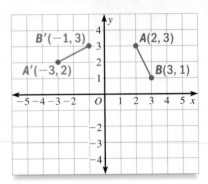

Switch the coordinates, then multiply the new *y*-coordinate by −1.
$(x, y) \rightarrow (y, -x)$

Switch the coordinates, then multiply the new *x*-coordinate by −1.
$(x, y) \rightarrow (-y, x)$

Example 2 *Rotating a Triangle*

Draw $\triangle ABC$ with vertices $A(-3, 4)$, $B(-2, 3)$, and $C(-2, 1)$. Then find the coordinates of the vertices of the image after a 90° clockwise rotation, and draw the image.

Solution

First draw $\triangle ABC$. Then, to rotate $\triangle ABC$ 90° clockwise, switch the coordinates and multiply the new *y*-coordinate by −1.

Original	Image
(x, y)	$\rightarrow (y, -x)$
$A(-3, 4)$	$\rightarrow A'(4, 3)$
$B(-2, 3)$	$\rightarrow B'(3, 2)$
$C(-2, 1)$	$\rightarrow C'(1, 2)$

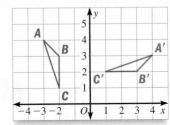

Finally, draw $\triangle A'B'C'$, as shown.

✔ **Checkpoint**

1. In Example 2, find the coordinates of the vertices of the image of $\triangle A'B'C'$ after a 90° clockwise rotation, and draw the image $\triangle A''B''C''$. How are the coordinates of the vertices of $\triangle A''B''C''$ related to those of $\triangle ABC$?

2. In Example 2, find the coordinates of the vertices of the image of $\triangle ABC$ after a 90° counterclockwise rotation, and draw the image.

3. **Critical Thinking** A figure lies in the third quadrant of a coordinate plane. In what quadrant does the image lie after a 90° clockwise rotation? after a 90° counterclockwise rotation?

180° Rotations To rotate a point 180° about the origin, multiply each coordinate by −1. The image is the same whether you rotate the figure clockwise or counterclockwise.

$$(x, y) \rightarrow (-x, -y)$$

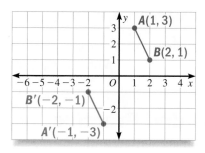

Example 3 | *Rotating a Triangle*

Draw △*MNP* with vertices *M*(1, −2), *N*(4, −1), and *P*(2, −3). Then find the coordinates of the vertices of the image after a 180° rotation, and draw the image.

Solution

First draw △*MNP*. Then, to rotate △*MNP* 180°, multiply the coordinates by −1.

Original		Image
(x, y)	$\rightarrow$	$(-x, -y)$
$M(1, -2)$	$\rightarrow$	$M'(-1, 2)$
$N(4, -1)$	$\rightarrow$	$N'(-4, 1)$
$P(2, -3)$	$\rightarrow$	$P'(-2, 3)$

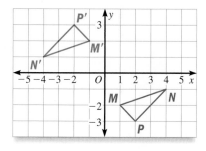

Finally, draw △*M'N'P'*, as shown.

✔ *Checkpoint*

4. Draw △*DEF* with vertices *D*(−6, −1), *E*(0, −2), and *F*(−5, −4). Then find the coordinates of the vertices of the image after a 180° rotation, and draw the image.

Rotational Symmetry A figure has **rotational symmetry** if a rotation of 180° or less clockwise (or counterclockwise) about its center produces an image that fits exactly on the original figure.

Example 4 | *Identifying Rotational Symmetry*

The family crest shown on page 741 has rotational symmetry for a 90° or 180° clockwise (or counterclockwise) rotation.

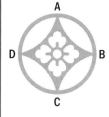

Original

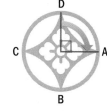

90° clockwise

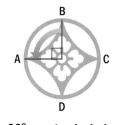

90° counterclockwise

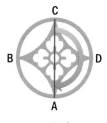

180°

Guided Practice

Vocabulary Check

1. How are rotational symmetry and line symmetry different?

2. Use coordinate notation to describe a 90° counterclockwise rotation.

Skill Check

Tell whether the transformation is a rotation about the origin. If so, give the angle and direction of rotation.

3. 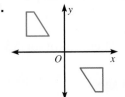   **4.** 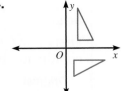   **5.**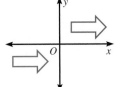

6. Draw △*ABC* with vertices *A*(3, 2), *B*(5, 1), and *C*(6, 4). Then find the coordinates of the vertices of the image after a 90° clockwise rotation, and draw the image.

7. Error Analysis Describe and correct the error in finding the coordinates of the vertices of the image of △*ABC* after a 90° clockwise rotation.

> Original   Image
>
> $A(3, -5) \rightarrow A'(5, 3)$
>
> $B(2, -4) \rightarrow B'(4, 2)$
>
> ✗ $C(4, -1) \rightarrow C'(1, 4)$

Practice and Problem Solving

Homework *Help*

Example	Exercises
1	8–10
2	11–12, 18
3	13, 18
4	14–17, 19

Online Resources
CLASSZONE.COM
- More Examples
- eTutorial Plus

Tell whether the transformation is a rotation about the origin. If so, give the angle and direction of rotation.

8. 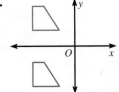   **9.** 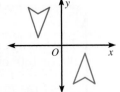   **10.**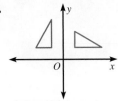

The vertices of a polygon are given. Draw the polygon. Then find the coordinates of the vertices of the image under the specified rotation, and draw the image.

11. *A*(1, 3), *B*(5, 6), *C*(5, 3); 90° counterclockwise rotation

12. *P*(−6, 2), *Q*(−3, 4), *R*(−1, 3), *S*(−5, 0); 90° clockwise rotation

13. *J*(2, −1), *K*(4, −1), *L*(4, −5), *M*(3, −6), *N*(2, −5); 180° rotation

Tell whether the figure has rotational symmetry. If so, give each angle and direction of rotation that produce rotational symmetry.

14.

15.

16.

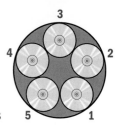

17. **CD Player** Your CD player can hold five compact discs on a rotating tray like the one shown.

   a. Does the tray have rotational symmetry? Explain.

   b. The tray can move only clockwise. A CD in position 1 is currently playing. How many degrees must the tray rotate to play a CD in position 3?

18. Draw △*JKL* with vertices *J*(−6, −5), *K*(−4, −3), and *L*(−2, −3).

   a. You rotate △*JKL* 90° clockwise, then you rotate its image 180°. Find the coordinates of the final image. Then draw the image.

   b. **Critical Thinking** Use coordinate notation to describe how to rotate △*JKL* to the final image in part (a) using one rotation.

19. **Extended Problem Solving** The table shows the first four regular polygons that have an even number of sides.

Regular polygon	Quadrilateral	Hexagon	Octagon	10-gon
Sides	4	?	?	?
Angles of rotation (in either direction)	90°, 180°	?	?	?

   a. Copy and complete the table by finding the number of sides of each regular polygon and the angles of rotation that produce rotational symmetry.

   b. **Compare** How is the number of sides related to the number of angles of rotation?

   c. **Predict** Add a column in the table for a regular 16-gon.

Draw the polygon shown. Then find the coordinates of the vertices of the final image after the specified transformations, and draw the final image.

20. Rotate the polygon 180°, then reflect the image in the *y*-axis.

21. Rotate the polygon 90° clockwise, then reflect the image in the *x*-axis.

22. Rotate the polygon 90° counterclockwise, then translate the image using $(x, y) \rightarrow (x + 3, y + 4)$.

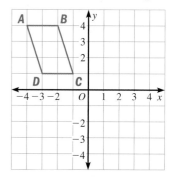

23. **Tessellations** You can rotate and translate a quadrilateral to create a tessellation, as shown. Use this approach to create a tessellation using a different quadrilateral.

① Draw any quadrilateral and rotate it 180° about the midpoint of one of its sides.

② Translate the new figure repeatedly to form a tessellation.

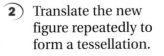

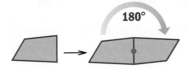

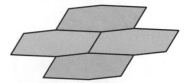

24. **Challenge** A triangle is rotated 90° clockwise about the origin, then its image is translated using $(x, y) \rightarrow (x + 3, y - 1)$. The coordinates of the vertices of the final image are $(1, -4)$, $(3, -2)$, and $(6, -5)$. Find the coordinates of the vertices of the original triangle.

Mixed Review **A map has a scale of 1 inch : 50 miles. Use the given map distance to find the actual distance.** *(Lesson 6.6)*

25. 1.5 inches   **26.** 3 inches   **27.** 6 inches   **28.** 8.5 inches

29. Draw $\triangle PQR$ with vertices $P(-5, -4)$, $Q(-3, 0)$, and $R(-1, -3)$. Then find the coordinates of the vertices of the image after a reflection in the y-axis, and draw the image. *(Lesson 13.5)*

Standardized Test Practice **30.** **Extended Response** $\triangle ABC$ has vertices $A(-6, 2)$, $B(-2, 5)$, and $C(-4, 1)$.

a. Find the coordinates of the vertices of the image of $\triangle ABC$ after a 90° clockwise rotation about the origin, and draw the image $\triangle A'B'C'$. Then find the coordinates of the vertices of the image of $\triangle A'B'C'$ after a reflection in the x-axis, and draw the image $\triangle A''B''C''$.

b. If you switch the order of the transformations, is the image $\triangle A''B''C''$ the same? Justify your answer.

Brain GAME   Treasure Hunt

You are located at the point (3, 4) in a coordinate plane. You need to find your way to a treasure chest. Starting at (3, 4), move from one image point to the next by following the order of the transformations listed. The final image point is the location of the treasure chest.

1. Rotate 180°.
2. Reflect in the y-axis.
3. Translate 5 units to the left and 4 units up.
4. Reflect in the x-axis.
5. Rotate 90° clockwise.

Dilations

BEFORE	Now	WHY?
You translated, reflected, and rotated figures.	You'll dilate figures in a coordinate plane.	So you can create an illusion of a moving object, as in Ex. 11.

Vocabulary

dilation, p. 747
center of dilation, p. 747
scale factor, p. 747

A **dilation** is a transformation in which a figure stretches or shrinks with respect to a fixed point, called the **center of dilation**. In this book, the origin of a coordinate plane is the center of dilation. In a dilation, a figure and its image are similar.

The **scale factor** of a dilation is the ratio of a side length of the image to the corresponding side length of the original figure. In the diagram, $\overline{A'B'}$ is the image of $\overline{AB}$ after a dilation.

Because $\frac{A'B'}{AB} = 2$, the scale factor is 2.

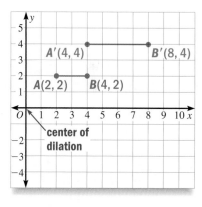

You can describe a dilation with respect to the origin using the notation

$$(x, y) \rightarrow (kx, ky)$$

where k is the scale factor.

Example 1   Dilating a Quadrilateral

Draw quadrilateral $ABCD$ with vertices $A(-1, 2)$, $B(3, 1)$, $C(2, -1)$, and $D(-1, -1)$. Then find the coordinates of the vertices of the image after a dilation having a scale factor of 3, and draw the image.

Solution

First draw quadrilateral $ABCD$. Then, to dilate $ABCD$, multiply the x- and y-coordinates of each vertex by 3.

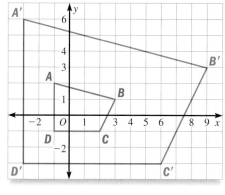

Original		Image
(x, y)	$\rightarrow$	$(3x, 3y)$
$A(-1, 2)$	$\rightarrow$	$A'(-3, 6)$
$B(3, 1)$	$\rightarrow$	$B'(9, 3)$
$C(2, -1)$	$\rightarrow$	$C'(6, -3)$
$D(-1, -1)$	$\rightarrow$	$D'(-3, -3)$

Finally, draw quadrilateral $A'B'C'D'$, as shown.

Study *Strategy*

Notice in Example 1 that when $k > 1$, the new figure is an enlargement of the original figure. As you will see in Example 2, when $k < 1$, the new figure is a reduction of the original figure.

Example 2 | *Using a Scale Factor Less than 1*

Draw $\triangle PQR$ with vertices $P(4, 4)$, $Q(8, 0)$, and $R(6, -2)$. Then find the coordinates of the vertices of the image after a dilation having a scale factor of 0.5, and draw the image.

Solution

Draw $\triangle PQR$. Then, to dilate $\triangle PQR$, multiply the x- and the y-coordinates of each vertex by 0.5.

Original	Image
(x, y)	$\rightarrow (0.5x, 0.5y)$
$P(4, 4)$	$\rightarrow P'(2, 2)$
$Q(8, 0)$	$\rightarrow Q'(4, 0)$
$R(6, -2)$	$\rightarrow R'(3, -1)$

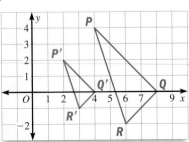

Finally, draw $\triangle P'Q'R'$, as shown.

✔ **Checkpoint**

Draw $\triangle ABC$ with vertices $A(4, 0)$, $B(4, 4)$, and $C(-4, 0)$. Then find the coordinates of the vertices of the image after a dilation having the given scale factor, and draw the image.

1. $k = 4$ **2.** $k = \dfrac{1}{4}$

Example 3 | *Finding a Scale Factor*

Computer Graphics An artist uses a computer program to enlarge a design, as shown. What is the scale factor of the dilation?

Solution

The width of the original design is $5 - 2 = 3$ units. The width of the image is $12.5 - 5 = 7.5$ units. So, the scale factor is $\dfrac{7.5 \text{ units}}{3 \text{ units}}$, or 2.5.

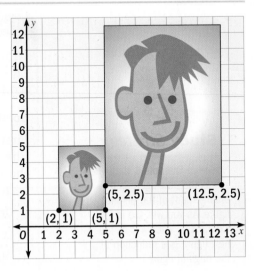

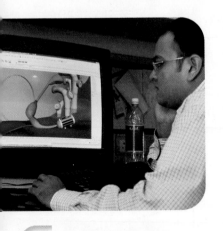

In the **Real World**

Computer Graphics
Computer graphics designers may create pictures called bit graphics. A 4 bit graphic can have $2^4 = 16$ colors, and an 8 bit graphic can have $2^8 = 256$ colors. How many colors can a 16 bit graphic have?

✔ **Checkpoint**

3. Given $\overline{AB}$ with endpoints $A(0.5, 1)$ and $B(1.5, 1)$, let $\overline{A'B'}$ with endpoints $A'(3, 6)$ and $B'(9, 6)$ be the image of $\overline{AB}$ after a dilation. Find the scale factor.

Note *Worthy*

For each transformation that you studied in this chapter, you should include an example in your notebook along with a summary of the characteristics of the transformation.

SUMMARY **Transformations in a Coordinate Plane**

Translations

In a translation, each point of a figure is moved the same distance in the same direction.

$(x, y) \rightarrow (x + a, y + b)$

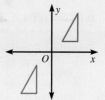

Reflections

In a reflection, a figure is flipped over a line.

Reflection in x-axis: $(x, y) \rightarrow (x, -y)$
Reflection in y-axis (shown): $(x, y) \rightarrow (-x, y)$

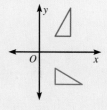

Rotations

In the rotations below, a figure is turned about the origin through a given angle and direction.

90° clockwise rotation (shown): $(x, y) \rightarrow (y, -x)$
90° counterclockwise rotation: $(x, y) \rightarrow (-y, x)$
180° rotation: $(x, y) \rightarrow (-x, -y)$

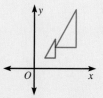

Dilations

In the dilation below, a figure stretches or shrinks with respect to the origin.

$(x, y) \rightarrow (kx, ky)$, where k is the scale factor

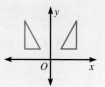

13.7 Exercises

More Practice, p. 815

INTERNET
eWorkbook Plus
CLASSZONE.COM

Guided Practice

Vocabulary Check

1. Copy and complete: In a translation, a figure and its image are congruent. In a dilation, a figure and its image are _?_ .

2. Let $P(2, 3)$ be a point on a figure. The figure is dilated by a scale factor of 4. What are the coordinates of P'?

Skill Check

3. Draw $\triangle ABC$ with vertices $A(-2, 0)$, $B(1, 1)$, and $C(2, -1)$. Then find the coordinates of the vertices of the image after a dilation having a scale factor of 3, and draw the image.

4. Given $\overline{AB}$ with endpoints $A(-2, 3)$ and $B(-2, -4)$, let $\overline{A'B'}$ with endpoints $A'(-5, 7.5)$ and $B'(-5, -10)$ be the image of $\overline{AB}$ after a dilation. What is the scale factor of the dilation?

Practice and Problem Solving

Homework *Help*

Example	Exercises
1	5-6, 11-12
2	7-8, 12
3	9-10

Online Resources
CLASSZONE.COM

• More Examples
• eTutorial Plus

The vertices of a polygon are given. Draw the polygon. Then find the coordinates of the vertices of the image after a dilation having the given scale factor, and draw the image.

5. $A(-1, 2)$, $B(3, 1)$, $C(1, -4)$; $k = 2$

6. $X(-1, 2)$, $Y(2, 1)$, $Z(-1, -3)$; $k = 3$

7. $P(-6, 2)$, $Q(2, 2)$, $R(2, 0)$, $S(-6, 0)$; $k = 0.5$

8. $E(-8, 4)$, $F(4, 4)$, $G(0, -4)$, $H(-4, -4)$; $k = \dfrac{1}{4}$

Find the scale factor of the dilation.

9.

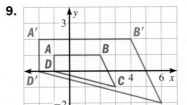

10.

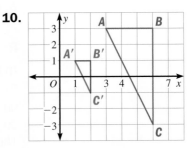

11. Illusions You can use dilations to create the illusion of an object moving toward you.

   a. Draw rectangle $ABCD$ with vertices $A(-2, -1,)$, $B(-1, -1)$, $C(-1, -1.5)$, and $D(-2, -1.5)$.

   b. On the same coordinate plane, draw the images of rectangle $ABCD$ using the following scale factors: 2, 4, 8.

12. *Writing* Is an image *smaller than*, *larger than*, or *congruent to* the original figure when the scale factor is 3? 0.5? 1? Explain.

13. Draw $\triangle ABC$ with vertices $A(-2, 4)$, $B(4, 0)$, and $C(2, -4)$.

   a. You dilate $\triangle ABC$ using a scale factor of 0.25. You then dilate its image using a scale factor of 2. Find the coordinates of the vertices of the final image, and draw the image.

   b. Use the scale factors given in part (a) to find the scale factor you could use to dilate $\triangle ABC$ to the final image in one step.

   c. Critical Thinking Do you get the same final image if you switch the order of the dilations in part (a)? Explain your reasoning.

14. Nesting Dolls The figure is the front view of one of the dolls in a set of nesting dolls. Draw the outline of the figure. Then, on the same coordinate plane, draw the images of the outline after dilations having the following scale factors: $\dfrac{1}{2}$, $1\dfrac{1}{2}$, 2.

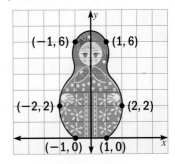

In Exercises 15 and 16, △DEF has vertices D(−2, −4), E(6, 2), and F(0, 4). Draw △DEF. Then find the coordinates of the vertices of the final image after the specified transformations, and draw the final image.

15. Dilate △DEF using a scale factor of 2, then translate its image using $(x, y) \rightarrow (x − 2, y + 3)$.

16. Dilate △DEF using a scale factor of 0.5, then rotate its image 180°.

17. Challenge A triangle is dilated using a scale factor of 2, then its image is reflected in the y-axis. The figure shown is the final image. Find the coordinates of the vertices of the original triangle, and draw the original triangle.

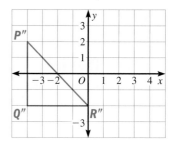

18. Extended Problem Solving Draw △ABC with vertices A(0, −3), B(3, 1), and C(3, −3).

  a. Calculate Find the perimeter and the area of △ABC.

  b. Find the coordinates of the vertices of the image of △ABC after a dilation having a scale factor of 3, and draw the image. Then find the perimeter and the area of the image.

  c. Compare How is the scale factor related to the ratios

$$\frac{\text{Perimeter of image of } \triangle ABC}{\text{Perimeter of } \triangle ABC} \text{ and } \frac{\text{Area of image of } \triangle ABC}{\text{Area of } \triangle ABC}?$$

Mixed Review

Find the number of permutations or combinations. *(Lessons 11.6, 11.7)*

19. $_4P_2$ **20.** $_8P_5$ **21.** $_9C_9$ **22.** $_{25}C_3$

Write the expression as a polynomial in standard form. *(Lesson 12.1)*

23. $4t + 1 − 6t + t^4 − 4$ **24.** $2(b − 6b^2) − 9b$

25. Draw △DEF with vertices D(4, 3), E(6, 2), and F(5, 1). Then find the coordinates of the vertices of the image after a 90° counterclockwise rotation about the origin, and draw the image. *(Lesson 13.6)*

Standardized Test Practice

26. Multiple Choice Let P(2, 4) be a point on a figure, and let P′ be the corresponding point on the image. The figure is dilated by a scale factor of 4. What are the coordinates of P′?

  A. $(−2, 0)$ **B.** $\left(\frac{1}{2}, 1\right)$ **C.** $(6, 8)$ **D.** $(8, 16)$

27. Multiple Choice In the diagram, quadrilateral A′B′C′D′ is the image of quadrilateral ABCD after a dilation. What is the scale factor?

  F. $\frac{1}{4}$ **G.** $\frac{1}{2}$

  H. 2   **I.** 3

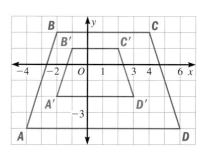

Chapter Review

Vocabulary Review

complementary angles,
  p. 709
supplementary angles,
  p. 709
vertical angles, p. 710
transversal, p. 716
corresponding angles, p. 716

alternate interior angles,
  p. 716
alternate exterior angles,
  p. 716
interior angle, p. 722
exterior angle, p. 723
transformation, p. 729
image, p. 729

translation, p. 729
tessellation, p. 730
reflection, p. 734
line of reflection, p. 734
line symmetry, p. 735
line of symmetry, p. 735
rotation, p. 741

center of rotation, p. 741
angle of rotation, p. 741
rotational symmetry, p. 743
dilation, p. 747
center of dilation, p. 747
scale factor, p. 747

1. What is the sum of the measures of two complementary angles? two supplementary angles?

2. How can you tell whether a figure has line symmetry? rotational symmetry?

3. Let $P(x, y)$ be a point on a figure. What are the coordinates of P' when the figure is reflected in the x-axis? rotated 180°? dilated using a scale factor of 2?

4. How are the measures of two vertical angles related?

Copy and complete the statement.

5. When a transversal intersects two lines, the angles that lie between the two lines on opposites sides of the transversal are _?_ .

6. A(n) _?_ angle of a polygon is an angle that lies inside the polygon.

13.1 Angle Relationships

Examples on pp. 709–710

▶ *Goal*

Identify and find measures of complementary, supplementary, and vertical angles.

Example ∠1 and ∠2 are supplementary angles, and $m∠1 = 46°$. Find $m∠2$.

$m∠1 + m∠2 = 180°$	**Definition of supplementary angles**
$46° + m∠2 = 180°$	**Substitute 46° for $m∠1$.**
$m∠2 = 134°$	**Subtract 46° from each side.**

✔ **Use the given information to find $m∠2$.**

7. ∠1 and ∠2 are complementary angles, and $m∠1 = 76°$.

8. ∠1 and ∠2 are vertical angles, and $m∠1 = 84°$.

9. ∠1 and ∠2 are supplementary angles, and $m∠1 = 121°$.

13.2 Angles and Parallel Lines

Examples on
pp. 716–718

▶ *Goal*

Identify angles formed when a transversal intersects two lines.

Example Tell whether ∠1 and ∠8 in the diagram are *corresponding, alternate interior,* or *alternate exterior* angles.

Because ∠1 and ∠8 lie outside lines *m* and *n* on opposite sides of the transversal *t*, they are alternate exterior angles.

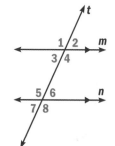

Example In the diagram, lines *m* and *n* are parallel, and *m*∠1 = 115°. Find *m*∠8.

Because ∠1 and ∠8 are alternate exterior angles, they have the same measure when formed by parallel lines. So, *m*∠8 = 115°.

✔ **Tell whether the angles in the diagram above are *corresponding, alternate interior,* or *alternate exterior* angles.**

10. ∠2 and ∠6   **11.** ∠3 and ∠6   **12.** ∠2 and ∠7   **13.** ∠4 and ∠5

In the diagram above, lines *m* and *n* are parallel, and *m*∠1 = 115°. Find the specified angle measure.

14. *m*∠2   **15.** *m*∠4   **16.** *m*∠5   **17.** *m*∠7

13.3 Angles and Polygons

Examples on
pp. 722–724

▶ *Goal*

Find measures of interior and exterior angles of convex polygons.

Example Find the measures of an interior angle and an exterior angle of a regular pentagon.

a. The measure of an interior angle of a regular pentagon is
$\frac{(5 - 2) \cdot 180°}{5} = 108°$.

b. An interior angle and an exterior angle at the same vertex form a straight angle. Because the measure of an interior angle of a regular pentagon is 108°, the measure of an exterior angle is 180° − 108° = 72°.

✔ **Find the measures of an interior angle and an exterior angle of the regular polygon. Round to the nearest tenth, if necessary.**

18. Heptagon   **19.** Octagon   **20.** 10-gon   **21.** 13-gon

22. The measures of a triangle's exterior angles, one at each vertex, are 97°, 102°, and *y*°. Find the value of *y*.

13.4 Translations

Examples on
pp. 729–731

▶ **Goal**

Translate figures in
a coordinate plane.

Example Draw △*ABC* with vertices *A*(−4, 1), *B*(−2, 3), and
C(−1, 1). Then find the coordinates of the vertices of the
image after the translation (*x*, *y*) → (*x* + 5, *y* − 2), and draw
the image.

First draw △*ABC*. Then, to translate △*ABC*, add 5 to the *x*-coordinate and
subtract 2 from the *y*-coordinate of each vertex.

Original		**Image**
(*x*, *y*)	→	(*x* + 5, *y* − 2)
A(−4, 1)	→	*A*′(1, −1)
B(−2, 3)	→	*B*′(3, 1)
C(−1, 1)	→	*C*′(4, −1)

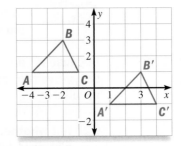

Finally, draw △*A*′*B*′*C*′, as shown.

✔ **23.** Draw △*ABC* given above. Then find the coordinates of the vertices
of the image after the translation (*x*, *y*) → (*x* − 3, *y* − 4), and draw
the image.

13.5 Reflections and Symmetry

Examples on
pp. 734–735

▶ **Goal**

Reflect figures in a
coordinate plane.

Example Draw △*DEF* with vertices *D*(1, 3), *E*(3, 2), and
F(2, −1). Then find the coordinates of the vertices of the
image after a reflection in the *y*-axis, and draw the image.

First draw △*DEF*. Then, to reflect △*DEF* in the *y*-axis, multiply the
x-coordinate of each vertex by −1.

Original		**Image**
(*x*, *y*)	→	(−*x*, *y*)
D(1, 3)	→	*D*′(−1, 3)
E(3, 2)	→	*E*′(−3, 2)
F(2, −1)	→	*F*′(−2, −1)

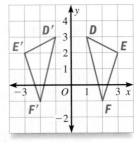

Finally, draw △*D*′*E*′*F*′, as shown.

✔ Draw △*LMN* with vertices *L*(−3, −1), *M*(−2, −2), and *N*(−4, −3).
Then find the coordinates of the vertices of the image after the
specified reflection, and draw the image.

24. Reflection in the *x*-axis   **25.** Reflection in the *y*-axis

13.6 Rotations and Symmetry

Examples on pp. 741–743

▶ *Goal*

Rotate figures in a coordinate plane.

Example Draw △*PQR* with vertices *P*(1, 2), *Q*(2, 3), and *R*(3, 1). Then find the coordinates of the vertices of the image after a 90° counterclockwise rotation, and draw the image.

First draw △*PQR*. Then, to rotate △*PQR* 90° counterclockwise, switch the coordinates and multiply the new *x*-coordinate of each vertex by −1.

Original		Image
(x, y)	→	$(-y, x)$
$P(1, 2)$	→	$P'(-2, 1)$
$Q(2, 3)$	→	$Q'(-3, 2)$
$R(3, 1)$	→	$R'(-1, 3)$

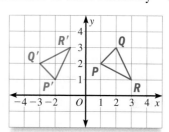

Finally, draw △*P'Q'R'*, as shown.

✔ **Draw △*PQR* given above. Then find the coordinates of the vertices of the image after the specified rotation, and draw the image.**

26. 90° clockwise rotation **27.** 180° rotation

13.7 Dilations

Examples on pp. 747–749

▶ *Goal*

Dilate figures in a coordinate plane.

Example Draw △*STU* with vertices *S*(−2, −1), *T*(0, 1), and *U*(1, −1). Then find the coordinates of the vertices of the image after a dilation having a scale factor of 2, and draw the image.

First draw △*STU*. Then, to dilate △*STU*, multiply the coordinates of each vertex by 2.

Original		Image
(x, y)	→	$(2x, 2y)$
$S(-2, -1)$	→	$S'(-4, -2)$
$T(0, 1)$	→	$T'(0, 2)$
$U(1, -1)$	→	$U'(2, -2)$

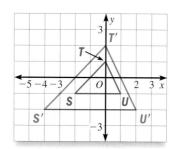

Finally, draw △*S'T'U'*, as shown.

✔ **Draw △*FGH* with vertices *F*(−4, −2), *G*(0, 2), and *H*(4, 2). Then find the coordinates of the vertices of the image after a dilation having the given scale factor *k*, and draw the image.**

28. $k = 3$ **29.** $k = 0.5$

Use the given information to find $m\angle 2$.

1. $\angle 1$ and $\angle 2$ are supplementary angles, and $m\angle 1 = 64°$.

2. $\angle 1$ and $\angle 2$ are vertical angles, and $m\angle 1 = 81°$.

3. $\angle 1$ and $\angle 2$ are complementary angles, and $m\angle 1 = 77°$.

In Exercises 4–7, tell whether the angles in the diagram are *corresponding*, *alternate interior*, or *alternate exterior* angles.

4. $\angle 1$ and $\angle 5$ **5.** $\angle 2$ and $\angle 7$

6. $\angle 4$ and $\angle 5$ **7.** $\angle 4$ and $\angle 8$

8. If $m\angle 3 = 128°$, find the measures of the other numbered angles in the diagram.

9. Find the measure of an interior angle of a regular hexagon.

10. Find the measure of an exterior angle of a regular 9-gon.

Find the unknown angle measure in the diagram.

11.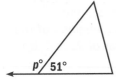

12.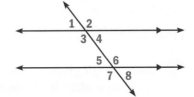

13.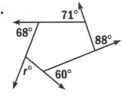

Draw the polygon and any lines of symmetry. If the polygon has rotational symmetry, give each angle and direction of rotation that produce rotational symmetry.

14. 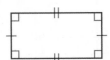   **15.**    **16.**

Draw $\triangle ABC$ with vertices $A(-3, 4)$, $B(-2, 5)$, and $C(-1, 3)$. Then find the coordinates of the vertices of the image after the specified transformation, and draw the image.

17. $(x, y) \rightarrow (x + 4, y - 7)$ **18.** Reflection in the *x*-axis

19. 90° counterclockwise rotation   **20.** Dilation having a scale factor of 2

Chapter Standardized Test

Test-Taking Strategy Think positively when you take a test. A positive attitude can help you stay focused on the questions.

1. In the diagram, $m\angle 1 = 73°$. What is $m\angle 2$?

  A. 17°   **B.** 73°

  C. 107°   **D.** 146°

2. If $\angle 3$ and $\angle 4$ are supplementary angles, what could their measures be?

  F. $m\angle 3 = 110°$ **G.** $m\angle 3 = 97°$
  $\quad m\angle 4 = 110°$ $\quad m\angle 4 = 83°$

  H. $m\angle 3 = 57°$ **I.** $m\angle 3 = 82°$
  $\quad m\angle 4 = 33°$ $\quad m\angle 4 = 41°$

In Exercises 3 and 4, use the diagram.

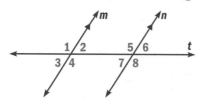

3. Which angles are alternate exterior angles?

  A. $\angle 1$ and $\angle 4$ **B.** $\angle 3$ and $\angle 6$

  C. $\angle 2$ and $\angle 7$ **D.** $\angle 1$ and $\angle 5$

4. Transversal t intersects parallel lines m and n. If $m\angle 2 = 57°$, what is $m\angle 7$?

  F. 33°   **G.** 57°   **H.** 114°   **I.** 123°

5. What is the sum of the measures of the interior angles of a convex octagon?

  A. 135°   **B.** 360°   **C.** 720°   **D.** 1080°

6. What is the measure of an exterior angle of a regular pentagon?

  F. 72°   **G.** 108°   **H.** 120°   **I.** 540°

In Exercises 7–9, use the diagram.

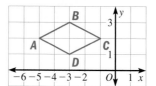

7. What are the coordinates of C' after the translation $(x, y) \rightarrow (x + 2, y - 1)$?

  A. $(1, 1)$ **B.** $(1, 3)$ **C.** $(0, 0)$ **D.** $(0, 4)$

8. How many lines of symmetry does quadrilateral $ABCD$ have?

  F. 1   **G.** 2   **H.** 4   **I.** 8

9. The coordinates of D' are $(-9, 3)$ after a dilation. What is the scale factor?

  A. 0.25   **B.** 0.5   **C.** 2   **D.** 3

10. Short Response The measures of a pentagon's exterior angles, one exterior angle at each vertex, are 67°, 102°, 131°, 28°, and $2x°$. Find the value of x. Explain your reasoning.

11. Extended Response $\triangle ABC$ has vertices $A(3, 2)$, $B(3, 4)$, and $C(6, 2)$.

  a. Find the coordinates of the vertices of the image of $\triangle ABC$ after a reflection in the y-axis, and draw the image $\triangle A'B'C'$.

  b. Find the coordinates of the vertices of the image of $\triangle A'B'C'$ after a 180° rotation about the origin, and draw the image $\triangle A''B''C''$.

  c. How can you move $\triangle ABC$ to $\triangle A''B''C''$ using one transformation? Explain your reasoning.

Strategies for Answering
Extended Response Questions

Problem You spend $240 for a lawn mower to start a lawn mowing business. You charge $15 per lawn. For each lawn you mow, you spend about $2 on gas.

a. Write a polynomial you can use to calculate your profit.

b. Complete the table and draw a graph showing how your profit changes as the number of lawns mowed increases.

Lawns	20	30	40	50	60
Profit	?	?	?	?	?

c. If you mow 60 lawns, will your profit be twice as much as if you mow 30 lawns? Explain.

Full credit solution

a. Your profit is the amount you earn minus the amount you spend. You earn $15 for every lawn and spend $2 for every lawn. Your start-up cost was $240.

Let x represent the number of lawns you mow.

The polynomial is correct.

$$\text{Profit} = 15x - (2x + 240)$$
$$= 13x - 240$$

The table and the graph are correct and reflect an understanding of the problem.

b.

Lawns	Profit
20	$20
30	$150
40	$280
50	$410
60	$540

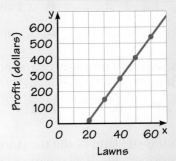

The answer is correct.

The reasoning behind the answer is explained clearly. Extra information is included to support the reasoning.

c. Your profit from mowing 60 lawns is more than twice your profit from mowing 30 lawns. In fact, if you mow 60 lawns you will earn more than three times as much as you earn from mowing 30 lawns. You would earn twice as much for 60 lawns as for 30 lawns if your profit per lawn were constant. Because your start-up cost of $240 is the same regardless of how many lawns you mow, your profit per lawn increases as you mow more lawns.

Partial credit solution

The polynomial is correct. ----

a. Polynomial:
$15x - (2x + 240) = 13x - 240$

b.

Lawns	Profit
20	$20
30	$150
40	$280
50	$410
60	$540

The table and the graph are ---- correct and reflect an understanding of the problem.

The answer is incorrect. ----

c. Because $540 is less than twice $280, you will earn less than twice as much mowing 60 lawns than mowing 30 lawns.

No credit solution

The polynomial is incorrect. ----

a. Profit = 15x

b.

Lawns	20	30	40	50	60
Profit	$300	$450	$600	$750	$900

The table is incorrect, and there is no graph. ----

The answer is based on ---- the incorrect table.

c. You will earn twice as much because $900 is twice $450.

Checkpoint

1. A student's answer to the problem on page 758 is given below. Score the answer as *full credit, partial credit,* or *no credit.* Explain your choice. If you choose *partial credit* or *no credit,* explain how you would change the answer to earn a score of *full credit.*

Watch *Out*

Scoring is often based on how clearly you explain your reasoning.

a. Polynomial:
$15x - (2x + 240) = 13x - 240$

b.

Lawns	Profit
20	$20
30	$150
40	$280
50	$410
60	$540

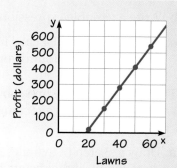

c. You will earn $390 more mowing 60 lawns than mowing 30 lawns.

Extended Response

1. You are in a class of 15 students. The teacher randomly selects students to work in groups on their unit projects. Your group will include yourself and 4 other students.

   a. How many different groups of 5 students can your teacher choose that include you?

   b. Your friend is also in the class. How many different groups of 5 students can your teacher choose that include you and your friend?

   c. Is it likely that you and your friend will be in the same group? Use probability to explain your answer.

2. The box-and-whisker plots show the numbers of points that the players on two basketball teams scored during a game. Each team has 12 players. Use the box-and-whisker plots to justify your answers to the following questions.

   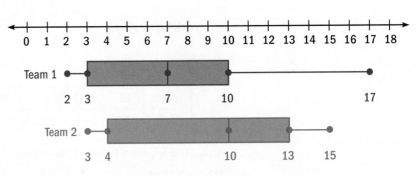

   a. Which team had more players who scored fewer than 10 points? Explain.

   b. Which team do you think won the game? Explain.

3. You are stacking cans for a store display. The top level has 1 can. Each level below the top has 2 more cans than the level above it.

   a. Consider the sequence for the number of cans at each level. Write the first 6 terms of this sequence.

   b. Write a variable expression for the number of cans at the nth level.

   c. Suppose you use 64 cans in your display. How many levels are there? Explain how you found your answer.

4. Tiles identical to the one shown will be used to create a mosaic. Two tiles will be used to form a rectangle. The rectangle will be tessellated to create the mosaic.

   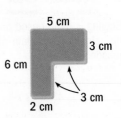

   a. Draw a sketch of two tiles positioned to form a rectangle. Give the dimensions of the rectangle.

   b. The mosaic must fit into a rectangular space that is 28 inches long and 18 inches wide. How many tiles fit into the space? Explain.

Multiple Choice

5. A scientist records the lengths of the tails of 45 spider monkeys. Which of the following should *not* be used to display the data?

  A. A histogram

  B. A stem-and-leaf plot

  C. A line graph

  D. A box-and-whisker plot

6. What is the value of $_9C_5$?

  F. 4   **G.** 126   **H.** 252   **I.** 15,120

7. Find the product $(3x - 4)(x + 2)$.

  A. $3x^2 + 2x - 8$ **B.** $3x^2 - 2x + 8$

  C. $3x^2 - 10x - 8$ **D.** $3x^2 - 10x + 8$

8. What is the degree of the polynomial $x^3 - 6x^3y$?

  F. 3   **G.** 4   **H.** 5   **I.** 6

9. What is the measure of $\angle 1$?

  A. 35°   **B.** 90°

  C. 125°   **D.** 180°

10. What type of transformation is shown?

  F. Translation

  G. Dilation

  H. Reflection

  I. Rotation

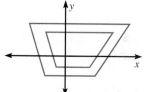

Short Response

11. Draw $\overline{AB}$ with endpoints $A(2, 3)$ and $B(6, 1)$. Find the coordinates of the endpoints of the image after a 90° clockwise rotation, and explain your steps. Then draw the image $\overline{A'B'}$.

12. A game uses tiles with a letter of the alphabet printed on each of them. A player has 7 tiles, each with a different letter. How many arrangements using all 7 tiles are possible? How many arrangements using 5 of the 7 tiles are possible?

13. For each labeled angle, tell whether the angle is complementary, supplementary, or congruent to $\angle 3$. Suppose the measure of $\angle 3$ is 124°. Find the measures of the other angles.

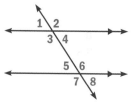

14. A proposition on a voting ballot needs two thirds of the votes to pass. A survey of a random sample of voters finds that 69% of the voters plan to vote for the proposition. The survey's margin of error is ±3%. Can you conclude that the proposition will pass? Explain.

15. A rectangle is 2 inches longer than it is wide. Write polynomial expressions for the length and width of the rectangle's image after dilation by a scale factor of 11. Then write a polynomial expression for the area of the rectangle's image. Write the expressions in standard form.

16. The polygon shown was created by removing a square from the corner of a larger square. Write polynomial expressions for the area and the perimeter of the polygon. Then find the area and perimeter of the polygon if $x = 5$.

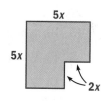

Chapter 11

Multiple Choice In Exercises 1–7, choose the letter of the correct answer.

1. What is the lower quartile of the data below? *(Lesson 11.2)*

   15, 22, 18, 14, 19, 22, 30, 28, 11, 25, 33

   A. 11   **B.** 15   **C.** 22   **D.** 28

2. Which of the following *cannot* be used to display numerical data? *(Lesson 11.3)*

   F. Histogram

   G. Line graph

   H. Bar graph

   I. Box-and-whisker plot

3. You want to gather information from students at your school. You hand out a survey to students during the lunch period and record the responses that are returned to you. What method of sampling is this? *(Lesson 11.4)*

   A. Random   **B.** Systematic

   C. Stratified   **D.** Self-selected

4. A survey found that 28% of a random sample of adults floss regularly. The survey's margin of error was ±4%. In which interval is the actual percent of adults who floss most likely to lie? *(Lesson 11.5)*

   F. Between 24% and 28%

   G. Between 28% and 32%

   H. Between 26% and 30%

   I. Between 24% and 32%

5. How many 4-digit numbers include each of the digits 2, 3, 4, and 5? *(Lesson 11.6)*

   A. 4   **B.** 14   **C.** 24   **D.** 120

6. You are at a bakery and want to buy 6 different kinds of doughnuts. The bakery sells 10 different kinds of doughnuts. How many combinations are possible? *(Lesson 11.7)*

   F. 90   **G.** 210   **H.** 720   **I.** 151,200

7. A game show contestant is trying to guess the last two digits in the price of a car. No digit in the price of the car is used more than once. What is the probability that the contestant correctly guesses the last two digits in the price of the car? *(Lesson 11.9)*

   $$\boxed{\$}\ \boxed{1}\ \boxed{4}\ \boxed{7}\ \boxed{?}\ \boxed{?}$$

   A. $\frac{1}{90}$ **B.** $\frac{1}{56}$ **C.** $\frac{1}{49}$ **D.** $\frac{1}{42}$

8. **Short Response** A game involves rolling two number cubes to move around a board. In order to win the game on your next turn, you need to roll a 6 on one of the number cubes. What is the probability that you roll a 6 on at least one number cube? Explain your reasoning. *(Lesson 11.8)*

9. **Extended Response** The stem-and-leaf plot shows the masses (in kilograms) of 21 bowling balls in a bowling alley. *(Lesson 11.1)*

3	5 6 6 6 7	Key: 3 $\mid$ 5 = 3.5 kg
4	4 5 5 6	
5	0 4 4 5 5 5 5 8 8 9 9 9	

   a. What is the median mass?

   b. You randomly choose a ball. Do you think the ball's mass will be greater than 4.0 kg? Explain using probability.

   c. Your friend has her own bowling ball with a mass of 5.3 kg. How does this mass compare with the masses of balls in the bowling alley? Explain.

Chapter 12

Multiple Choice In Exercises 10–20, choose the letter of the correct answer.

10. Write $8x - 5 - 3(2x^2 - 4x + 1)$ as a polynomial in standard form. *(Lesson 12.1)*

   A. $-6x^2 - 4x - 8$ **B.** $-6x^2 + 20x - 8$

   C. $6x^2 + 4x - 8$ **D.** $-6x^2 + 4x - 8$

11. Find the difference. *(Lesson 12.2)*

$$(2x^3 + 7x^2 - x) - (3x^3 - 5x^2 + x)$$

   F. $-x^3 + 12x^2$ **G.** $-x^3 + 2x^2$

   H. $-x^3 + 12x^2 - 2x$ **I.** $-x^3 + 2x^2 - 2x$

12. Which polynomial expression represents the perimeter of the rectangle? *(Lesson 12.2)*

3x

5x − 4

   A. $15x^2 - 12x$ **B.** $10x - 8$

   C. $16x - 8$ **D.** $8x - 4$

13. Find the product. *(Lesson 12.3)*

$$(p^4 + 6p^3 - p + 7)(2p^2)$$

   F. $2p^6 + 12p^5 - 12p^2$

   G. $2p^6 + 12p^5 + 2p^3 + 14p^2$

   H. $2p^8 + 12p^6 - 2p^3 + 14p^2$

   I. $2p^6 + 12p^5 - 2p^3 + 14p^2$

14. Find the product $(6y + 5)(5y - 6)$. *(Lesson 12.4)*

   A. $30y^2 - 11y - 30$ **B.** $30y^2 + 11y - 30$

   C. $30y^2 - 30$ **D.** $30y^2 - 11y + 30$

15. Which expression represents the area of the circle? *(Lesson 12.5)*

8x

   F. $64\pi x$ **G.** $64\pi x^2$

   H. $8\pi x$ **I.** $8\pi x^2$

16. Simplify $(a^2 b)^4$. *(Lesson 12.5)*

   A. $a^6 b$ **B.** $a^8 b^4$ **C.** $a^2 b^4$ **D.** $a^6 b^4$

17. Simplify $(2 \times 10^3)^3$. *(Lesson 12.5)*

   F. 2×10^5 **G.** 2×10^6

   H. 8×10^6 **I.** 8×10^9

18. The graph of which equation is shown? *(Lesson 12.6)*

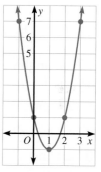

   A. $y = -2x^2 - 4x + 1$

   B. $y = 2x^2 + 4x + 1$

   C. $y = 2x^2 - 4x - 1$

   D. $y = 2x^2 - 4x + 1$

19. What is the next term in the sequence $1600, 400, 100, 25, \ldots$? *(Lesson 12.8)*

   F. 4 **G.** 6.25 **H.** 9 **I.** 16

20. What is the next term in the sequence $-9, -3, 3, 9, \ldots$? *(Lesson 12.8)*

   A. 3 **B.** 12 **C.** 15 **D.** 27

21. **Short Response** Simplify the expression $\dfrac{8x^3 - 24x^2 + 20x}{4x}$. Explain your steps. *(Lesson 12.3)*

22. **Extended Response** You purchase a new snowmobile. The value V (in dollars) of the snowmobile after t years is given by the function $V = 8900(0.75)^t$. *(Lesson 12.7)*

   a. Does this function model exponential growth or exponential decay? Explain.

   b. Graph the function.

   c. After how many years will the value of the snowmobile be less than \$5000? Explain your reasoning.

Cumulative Practice continued

Chapter 13

Multiple Choice In Exercises 23–29, choose the letter of the correct answer.

23. Given that $\angle 3$ and $\angle 4$ are complementary angles and $m\angle 3 = 82°$, find $m\angle 4$. *(Lesson 13.1)*

   A. $8°$ **B.** $18°$ **C.** $98°$ **D.** $118°$

24. Which angles are congruent? *(Lesson 13.2)*

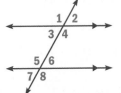

   F. $\angle 1$ and $\angle 3$

   G. $\angle 2$ and $\angle 6$

   H. $\angle 3$ and $\angle 5$

   I. $\angle 4$ and $\angle 7$

25. Each angle in a regular octagon measures $(6x + 3)°$. What is the value of x? *(Lesson 13.3)*

   A. 7   **B.** 22   **C.** 29.5   **D.** 239.5

26. Which transformation is shown in the graph? *(Lessons 13.4–13.7)*

   F. Reflection in the x-axis

   G. Dilation using a scale factor of $\frac{1}{2}$

   H. Translation of 1 unit to the right and 2 units down

   I. $90°$ clockwise rotation

27. How many lines of symmetry does the figure have? *(Lesson 13.5)*

   A. 1   **B.** 2

   C. 3   **D.** 4

28. A segment with endpoints $A(3, -3)$ and $B(3, -4)$ is rotated $90°$ clockwise. Find the coordinates of the image of B. *(Lesson 13.6)*

   F. $B'(4, 3)$ **G.** $B'(3, 4)$

   H. $B'(-4, -3)$ **I.** $B'(-3, -4)$

29. $\triangle ABC$ has vertices $A(-4, 8)$, $B(0, 2)$, and $C(4, 0)$. Find the coordinates of the vertices of the image after dilation by a scale factor of $\frac{1}{4}$. *(Lesson 13.7)*

   A. $A'(-1, 8)$, $B'(0, 2)$, $C'(1, 0)$

   B. $A'(-4, -2)$, $B'\left(0, \frac{1}{2}\right)$, $C'(4, 0)$

   C. $A'(-1, 2)$, $B'\left(0, \frac{1}{2}\right)$, $C'(1, 0)$

   D. $A'(-16, -32)$, $B'(0, 8)$, $C'(16, 0)$

30. **Short Response** Find the value of x in the diagram. Explain how you found your answer. *(Lesson 13.3)*

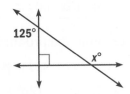

31. **Extended Response** The vertices of rectangle $ABCD$ have the coordinates shown. *(Lessons 13.5, 13.6)*

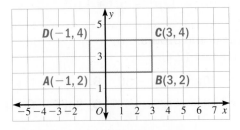

   a. Rotate rectangle $ABCD$ $180°$.

   b. Reflect rectangle $ABCD$ in the x-axis.

   c. Compare the two images of rectangle $ABCD$ from parts (a) and (b). How are they alike, and how are they different?

Integers, Equations, and Inequalities

Evaluate the expression when $x = 2$, $y = 3$, and $z = 5$.

1. $x + z$

2. $0.6z - x$

3. $(y + z)^2 - 3$

4. $\dfrac{x + 4y}{7}$

Find the sum, difference, product, or quotient.

5. $-23 + 16$

6. $-36 + (-40)$

7. $29 - (-17)$

8. $-61 - 42$

9. $12(-5)$

10. $-15(-7)$

11. $\dfrac{-99}{-11}$

12. $\dfrac{144}{-6}$

State the absolute value and the opposite of the number.

13. 8

14. -15

15. -10

16. 24

Plot the point in a coordinate plane. Describe the location of the point.

17. $A(-5, -8)$

18. $B(-6, 1)$

19. $C(0, -3)$

20. $D(4, -2)$

Identify the property that the statement illustrates.

21. $(ab) \cdot 1 = ab$

22. $x + 0 = x$

23. $m + n = n + m$

24. $rst = rts$

Evaluate the expression using the distributive property and mental math.

25. $4(93)$

26. $9(104)$

27. $7(8.3)$

28. $6(5.9)$

Simplify the expression.

29. $21 + x - 14 + 9x$

30. $4a + 2a + 3a$

31. $-4(4m - 2) + 3$

32. $6(7n - 4) + 2n$

Write the verbal sentence as an equation. Then tell whether 6 is a solution of the equation.

33. The sum of x and 13 is 7.

34. The product of -11 and z is -66.

Solve the equation. Check your solution.

35. $x - 12 = 20$

36. $\dfrac{x}{-6} = -8$

37. $7x = -63$

38. $4.2 + x = 9.9$

39. $5x + 3 = -22$

40. $-9x - 4 = 32$

41. $5(x + 4) = 60$

42. $102 = 6(5 - 3x)$

Solve the inequality. Graph and check your solution.

43. $x - 7 \le 19$

44. $-2x < -16$

45. $4 + 3x > -17$

46. $6x - 8 \ge 7x$

▶ Rational Numbers and Proportions

Find the greatest common factor and the least common multiple of the monomials.

47. $4x, 6x$

48. $15x^2, 9x$

49. $20xy^2, 5y$

50. $7x^2y^3, 5x^3y^4$

Find the product or quotient. Write your answer using only positive exponents.

51. $k^7 \cdot k^3$

52. $\dfrac{q^5}{q^2}$

53. $r^{-8} \cdot r^6$

54. $\dfrac{s^{-6}}{s^{-3}}$

Find the sum, difference, product, or quotient.

55. $-\dfrac{4}{9} + \dfrac{5}{9}$

56. $-6\dfrac{2}{3} - 4\dfrac{7}{8}$

57. $-2\dfrac{1}{3} \cdot \left(3\dfrac{3}{5}\right)$

58. $-1\dfrac{2}{5} \div \left(-8\dfrac{3}{10}\right)$

Solve the equation or inequality by first clearing the fractions or the decimals.

59. $\dfrac{4}{9}x - 2 > \dfrac{2}{3}$

60. $-\dfrac{2}{7}x - \dfrac{2}{3} \le \dfrac{1}{7}$

61. $1.6x - 2.8 = 5.2$

62. $2.5x + 2.79 = 10.21$

Solve the proportion.

63. $\dfrac{8}{120} = \dfrac{2}{y}$

64. $\dfrac{99}{w} = \dfrac{9}{14}$

65. $\dfrac{6}{21} = \dfrac{8}{z}$

66. $\dfrac{1.4}{x} = \dfrac{11.2}{72}$

Given $ABCD \sim EFGH$, find the indicated measure.

67. $m\angle A$

68. $m\angle D$

69. GH

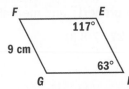

70. Each letter in the word ALGEBRA is written on a separate slip of paper and placed in a hat. A letter is chosen at random from the hat. What is the probability that the chosen letter is a consonant?

Use a proportion or the percent equation to answer the question.

71. What percent of 200 is 24?

72. 11.4 is 9.5% of what number?

Identify the percent of change as an *increase* or a *decrease*. Then find the percent of change.

73. Original: 60
New: 75

74. Original: 95
New: 76

75. Original: 32
New: 20

76. Original: 44
New: 55

77. A dress shirt is on sale for 20% off the original price of $32. What is the sale price of the dress shirt?

Graph the equation. Then tell whether the equation is a function.

78. $y = 3x$ **79.** $y = 5x + 15$ **80.** $y = -4$ **81.** $y = 3$

82. $x = 6$ **83.** $x = -7$ **84.** $9x + 3y = 27$ **85.** $4x + 5y = 18$

Write an equation of the line through the given points.

86. $(0, 5), (6, 12)$ **87.** $(-4, -8), (0, 2)$ **88.** $(3, -7), (0, 11)$ **89.** $(0, 1), (10, -2)$

Let $f(x) = -3x + 5$ and $g(x) = 4x - 2$. Find the indicated value.

90. $f(4)$ **91.** $g(-10)$ **92.** $f(5) + g(-12)$ **93.** x when $g(x) = 16$

Graph the inequality in a coordinate plane.

94. $y < 5$ **95.** $x \geq -2$ **96.** $2x + 5y \leq 20$ **97.** $y > 2x + 1$

Simplify the expression.

98. $\sqrt{60}$ **99.** $\sqrt{\dfrac{14}{64}}$ **100.** $\sqrt{40m^2}$ **101.** $\sqrt{\dfrac{25b^2}{36}}$

Determine whether the triangle with the given side lengths is a right triangle.

102. $6, 8, 10$ **103.** $5, 12, 15$ **104.** $10, 24, 26$ **105.** $2, 3, 4$

Find the midpoint of the segment with the given endpoints. Then find the distance between the points. Write your answer in simplest form.

106. $(4, 7), (0, 5)$ **107.** $(8, 15), (-6, -9)$ **108.** $(9, -2), (5, -12)$ **109.** $(-4, 10), (-7, 1)$

110. Each leg of a 45°-45°-90° triangle has a length of 12 meters. Find the length of the hypotenuse. Write your answer in simplest form.

111. In $\triangle ABC$ with right angle at C, $m\angle A = 49°$ and $AB = 25$. Find BC to the nearest tenth.

The angle measures of a polygon are given. Find the value of x.

112. Triangle: $3x°, (2x + 4)°, 46°$ **113.** Quadrilateral: $15°, 8x°, 4x°, (x + 7)°$

Find the area of the figure with the given dimensions. Use 3.14 for π. Round to the nearest whole number.

114. Circle: $r = 23$ in.   **115.** Trapezoid: $h = 6$ in., $b_1 = 26$ in., $b_2 = 16$ in.

Find the surface area and the volume of the solid with the given dimensions. Round to the nearest whole number.

116. Cylinder: $r = 9$ ft, $h = 12$ ft   **117.** Cone: $r = 8$ ft, $h = 15$ ft

▶ Data Analysis, Polynomials, and Transformations

Make an ordered stem-and-leaf plot, a histogram, and a box-and-whisker plot of the data.

118. 18, 28, 8, 20, 12, 36, 28, 4, 16, 24

119. 71, 53, 67, 74, 50, 68, 51, 63, 79, 60

Evaluate.

120. $_8P_3$

121. $_{16}C_{10}$

122. $_{20}C_{20}$

123. $5!$

124. A computer randomly generates whole numbers from 1 to 20. Find the probability that the computer generates a 12 or a multiple of 3.

125. A box has 3 red pencils and 5 blue pencils. You randomly choose two pencils. Find the probability that both pencils are blue.

Find the sum, difference, or product.

126. $(2x^2 + x + 9) + (3x^2 - 4x - 5)$

127. $(9x^2 + 2x) - (-5x^2 - 6x)$

128. $(-8x - 3)(-7x + 2)$

129. $3x(12x^5 + 16x^3)$

Simplify the expression. Write your answer using positive exponents.

130. $(xy)^8$

131. $(-2x^3)^4$

132. $(x^5)^{-6}$

133. $(y^{-2})^{-7}$

Make a table of values for the given function. Then graph the function.

134. $y = x^2 + 3$

135. $y = 2x^2 - 4x$

136. $y = 5^x$

137. $y = 3(4)^x$

Tell whether the sequence is *arithmetic* or *geometric*. Then find the common difference or the common ratio, and write the next three terms.

138. 182, 168, 154, 140, . . .

139. 1.7, 5.1, 15.3, 45.9, . . .

Tell whether the angles are *complementary*, *supplementary*, or *neither*.

140. $m\angle 1 = 54°$, $m\angle 2 = 36°$

141. $m\angle 3 = 82°$, $m\angle 4 = 98°$

Tell whether the angles in the diagram are *vertical*, *corresponding*, *alternate interior*, or *alternate exterior* angles.

142. $\angle 1$ and $\angle 8$

143. $\angle 3$ and $\angle 7$

144. $\angle 4$ and $\angle 5$

145. $\angle 5$ and $\angle 8$

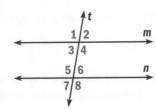

146. Find the measure of an exterior angle of a regular 12-gon.

Draw △ABC with vertices A(−1, 2), B(−2, 3), and C(−3, 1). Then find the coordinates of the vertices of the image after the specified transformation, and draw the image.

147. $(x, y) \rightarrow (x - 3, y + 6)$ **148.** Reflection in the *y*-axis **149.** 90° clockwise rotation

Contents of Student Resources

Skills Review Handbook

Place Value and Rounding

The **whole numbers** are the numbers 0, 1, 2, 3, ... A **digit** is any of the numbers 0, 1, 2, 3, 4, 5, 6, 7, 8, or 9. **Decimals** are numbers such as 8.56, 234.12, and 6.985, in which the digits in the ones' place and the tenths' place are separated by a decimal point. The value of each digit in a number depends on the position, or place, of the digit within the number. In the number 813,794.0562, the value of **6** is 6 × 0.001, or 0.006, because 6 is in the thousandths' place.

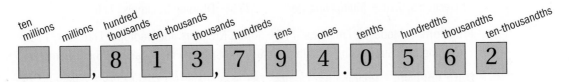

Example Give the place and value of the red digit in 19.786**2**.

Answer The 2 is in the ten-thousandths' place. Its value is 2 × 0.0001, or 0.0002.

To **round** a number means to approximate it to a given place. When rounding, look at the digit to the right of the given place. If the digit to the right is less than 5, round down by replacing all digits to the right with zeros. If the digit to the right is 5 or greater, round up by adding one to the given digit and replacing all digits to the right with zeros.

Example Round 88.1**7**3 to the place of the red digit.

Because 7 is in the hundredths' place, round 88.173 to the nearest hundredth. The digit to the right, in the thousandths' place, is 3. Because 3 < 5, replace the 3 with a 0.

Answer Rounded to the nearest hundredth, 88.173 is 88.170, or 88.17.

✔ Practice

Give the place and value of the red digit. Then round the number to that place.

1. 56.7**5**
2. 19.3**6**
3. 912.7**5**6
4. 539.5**2**
5. 6528.98**3**
6. 7251.0**4**1
7. 40,192.0**7**1
8. 504.03**8**
9. 10,064.6**5**5
10. 357.0**8**15
11. 112.3**4**97
12. 46,312.7**4**6
13. 482,6**1**5.8
14. 54.3**8**52
15. **9**172.043
16. 12,099.518**6**

Estimating Sums and Differences

A **sum** is the result of adding two or more numbers. A **difference** is the result of subtracting two numbers. One strategy you can use to estimate a sum or difference is to round to the place of the *leading digit.* The leading digit of a whole number is the leftmost digit.

Example Estimate the sum 42,143 + 18,672 + 21,047.

Each number has five digits. The leading digit is in the ten thousands' place. Round each number to the nearest ten thousand.

$$42{,}143 + 18{,}672 + 21{,}047 \approx 40{,}000 + 20{,}000 + 20{,}000$$

The symbol ≈ means "is approximately equal to."

$$= 80{,}000$$

Answer The sum 42,143 + 18,672 + 21,047 is *about* 80,000.

Example Estimate the difference 812,236 − 587,429.

Each number has six digits. The leading digit is in the hundred thousands' place. Round each number to the nearest hundred thousand.

$$812{,}236 - 587{,}429 \approx 800{,}000 - 600{,}000$$

$$= 200{,}000$$

Answer The difference 812,236 − 587,429 is *about* 200,000.

For a more accurate estimate of a sum or difference, you can round each number to a place to the right of the leading digit. For instance, in the first example above, you might round to the nearest thousand.

$$42{,}143 + 18{,}672 + 21{,}047 \approx 42{,}000 + 19{,}000 + 21{,}000 = 82{,}000$$

 Practice

Estimate the sum or difference by rounding each number to the place of its leading digit.

1. 1704 + 8233

2. 23,867 + 11,999

3. 48,119 + 13,974

4. 462,311 + 109,878

5. 5284 + 2916 + 4238

6. 51,098 + 14,235 + 38,794

7. 7641 − 3244

8. 24,109 − 12,344

9. 45,098 − 24,672

10. 89,405 − 43,288

11. 436,966 − 178,056

12. 687,005 − 119,684

13. 219,477 − 105,819

14. 868,212 − 514,709

Estimating Products and Quotients

A **product** is the result of multiplying two or more numbers. Each number multiplied is a **factor** of the product. A **quotient** is the result of dividing a number by a nonzero number. The number being divided is the **dividend**, and the number it is being divided by is the **divisor**. One way to estimate a product or a quotient is to find a low estimate and a high estimate using *compatible numbers*. Compatible numbers are numbers that make a calculation easier.

Skills Review Handbook

Example Find a low and high estimate for the product 783 × 48.

1 For a low estimate, round both factors *down*.

$$\begin{array}{r} 700 \\ \times\ 40 \\ \hline 28{,}000 \end{array}$$

When rounding down, replace all digits after the first with zeros.

2 For a high estimate, round both factors *up*.

$$\begin{array}{r} 800 \\ \times\ 50 \\ \hline 40{,}000 \end{array}$$

When rounding up, increase the first digit by 1, and replace all digits after the first with zeros.

Answer The product 783 × 48 is between 28,000 and 40,000.

Example Find a low and high estimate for the quotient 556,772 ÷ 861.

When the divisor has more than one digit, round it as described below.

1 For a *low* estimate, round the divisor, 861, *up* and replace the dividend, 556,772, with a number that is divisible by 900 and is *less* than 556,772.

$$900\overline{)540{,}000} \quad\to\quad 600$$

2 For a *high* estimate, round the divisor, 861, *down* and replace the dividend, 556,772, with a number that is divisible by 800 and is *greater* than 556,772.

$$800\overline{)560{,}000} \quad\to\quad 700$$

Answer The quotient 556,772 ÷ 861 is between 600 and 700.

✔ Practice

Find a low and high estimate for the product or quotient.

1. 787 × 63 **2.** 97 × 314 **3.** 925 × 492 **4.** 206 × 475

5. 955 ÷ 29 **6.** 724 ÷ 87 **7.** 432 ÷ 76 **8.** 3195 ÷ 58

9. 293 × 51 **10.** 7615 × 32 **11.** 47 × 673 **12.** 312 × 4918

13. 4792 ÷ 17 **14.** 21,246 ÷ 419 **15.** 25,421 ÷ 42 **16.** 44,521 ÷ 66

Comparing and Ordering Decimals

A **number line** is a line whose points are associated with numbers. You can use a number line to compare and order decimals. First graph the numbers on a number line. Then read the numbers in order as they appear from left to right. Remember that the symbol < means *is less than* and the symbol > means *is greater than*.

Example Copy and complete the statement using <, >, or =.

a. 0.543 _?_ 0.54

b. 1.12 _?_ 1.21

Solution

a.

0.543 is to the right of 0.54, so 0.543 is greater than 0.54.

Answer 0.543 > 0.54

b.

1.12 is to the left of 1.21, so 1.12 is less than 1.21.

Answer 1.12 < 1.21

Example Order the numbers 5.1, 5.2, 5.05, 5, 5.12, and 5.15 from least to greatest.

Graph all the numbers on the same number line.

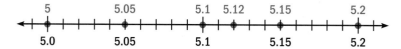

Answer From least to greatest, the numbers are 5, 5.05, 5.1, 5.12, 5.15, and 5.2.

✔ Practice

Copy and complete the statement using <, >, or =.

1. 0.3 _?_ 0.28

2. 0.57 _?_ 0.6

3. 0.19 _?_ 0.190

4. 4.5 _?_ 4.51

5. 67.2 _?_ 66.9

6. 1.03 _?_ 1.30

Order the numbers from least to greatest.

7. 1.3, 1.29, 2.19, 1.9

8. 5.4, 4.55, 5.45, 4.44

9. 0.52, 0.55, 0.49, 0.5

10. 1.0, 0.97, 1.02, 0.99

11. 6.21, 6.19, 6.32, 6.3

12. 8.9, 9.02, 9.1, 8.69

Adding and Subtracting Decimals

Use a vertical format to add or subtract decimals. Begin by lining up the decimal points. Write zeros as placeholders if necessary. Then add or subtract as you would with whole numbers. Be sure to place the decimal point in the answer.

Example Find the sum 0.283 + 0.54.

1 Line up the decimal points and write zero as a placeholder. Add the thousandths.

$$
\begin{array}{r}
0.283 \\
+ \ 0.540 \\
\hline
3
\end{array}
$$

2 Add the hundredths. Regroup 12 hundredths as 1 tenth and 2 hundredths.

$$
\begin{array}{r}
\overset{1}{} \\
0.283 \\
+ \ 0.540 \\
\hline
23
\end{array}
$$

3 Add the tenths. Place the decimal point in the answer.

$$
\begin{array}{r}
\overset{1}{} \\
0.283 \\
+ \ 0.540 \\
\hline
0.823
\end{array}
$$

Answer $0.283 + 0.54 = 0.823$

Example Find the difference 20 − 2.8.

1 Start with the tenths. There are no tenths in 20 from which to subtract 8 tenths.

$$
\begin{array}{r}
20.0 \\
- \ 2.8 \\
\hline
\end{array}
$$

2 Move to the ones. There are no ones in 20, so regroup 1 ten as 9 ones and 10 tenths.

$$
\begin{array}{r}
9 \\
1\ \cancel{10}\ 10 \\
2\cancel{0}.0 \\
- \ 2.8 \\
\hline
\end{array}
$$

3 Subtract. Place the decimal point in the answer.

$$
\begin{array}{r}
9 \\
1\ \cancel{10}\ 10 \\
2\cancel{0}.0 \\
- \ 2.8 \\
\hline
17.2
\end{array}
$$

Answer $20 - 2.8 = 17.2$

✓ **Check** Because addition and subtraction are inverse operations, you can check your answer by adding: $17.2 + 2.8 = 20$.

✔ Practice

Find the sum or difference.

1. $4.1 + 2.3$

2. $0.37 + 0.55$

3. $8.7 - 4.5$

4. $2.6 - 0.9$

5. $1.34 + 0.9$

6. $6.78 + 4.99$

7. $41.39 - 23.17$

8. $67.38 - 37.46$

9. $84.34 + 67.23$

10. $28.4 + 3.7$

11. $0.67 - 0.43$

12. $4.956 - 1.234$

13. $3.596 + 5.618$

14. $8.95 + 3.476$

15. $3.7 - 2.95$

16. $8.267 - 6.52$

Multiplying Decimals

To multiply decimals, multiply as you would whole numbers, then place the decimal point in the product. The number of decimal places in the product is equal to the sum of the number of decimal places in the factors.

Example Find the product 4.94 × 0.45.

$$
\begin{array}{r}
4.94 \\
\times\, 0.45 \\
\hline
2470 \\
1976 \\
\hline
2.2230
\end{array}
$$

2 decimal places
+ 2 decimal places

4 decimal places

After you place the decimal point, you can drop the zero at the end of the product.

Answer $4.94 \times 0.45 = 2.223$

You may need to write zeros as placeholders so that the answer has the correct number of decimal places.

Example Find the product 3.6 × 0.023.

$$
\begin{array}{r}
3.6 \\
\times\, 0.023 \\
\hline
108 \\
72 \\
\hline
0.0828
\end{array}
$$

1 decimal place
+ 3 decimal places

4 decimal places

Write a zero before the 8 as a placeholder so that the number has four decimal places.

Answer $3.6 \times 0.023 = 0.0828$

✔ Practice

Find the product.

1. 2.4×5.9 **2.** 1.2×2.3 **3.** 2.5×6.4 **4.** 2.53×0.8

5. 1.45×0.7 **6.** 1.4×0.35 **7.** 0.72×0.06 **8.** 0.91×0.6

9. 15.2×0.004 **10.** 13.4×0.65 **11.** 8.52×3.5 **12.** 0.05×0.03

13. 5.25×1.18 **14.** 7.2×0.053 **15.** 3.06×4.28 **16.** 4.33×0.019

Dividing Decimals

To divide decimals, multiply both the divisor and the dividend by a power of 10 that will make the divisor a whole number. Then line up the decimal point in the quotient with the decimal point in the dividend.

Example Find the quotient 7.848 ÷ 0.24.

$$0.24\overline{)7.848}$$

To multiply the divisor and dividend by 100, move both decimal points 2 places to the right.

$$
\begin{array}{r}
32.7 \\
24\overline{)784.8} \\
72 \\
\hline
64 \\
48 \\
\hline
168 \\
168 \\
\hline
0
\end{array}
$$

Divide as you would with whole numbers. Place the decimal point in the quotient directly above the decimal point in the dividend.

Answer 7.848 ÷ 0.24 = 32.7

You may need to write additional zeros in a dividend to continue dividing. The zeros do not change the value of the dividend.

Example Find the quotient 7 ÷ 1.4.

$$1.4\overline{)7.0}$$

To multiply the divisor and dividend by 10, move both decimal points 1 place to the right. Write a zero as a placeholder.

$$
\begin{array}{r}
5 \\
14\overline{)70} \\
70 \\
\hline
0
\end{array}
$$

Divide as you would with whole numbers.

Answer 7 ÷ 1.4 = 5

Practice

Find the quotient.

1. 1.2 ÷ 0.3   **2.** 2.6 ÷ 0.2   **3.** 1.25 ÷ 0.25   **4.** 8.84 ÷ 3.4

5. 51.3 ÷ 2.7   **6.** 1.44 ÷ 3.6   **7.** 4.41 ÷ 2.1   **8.** 2.52 ÷ 0.7

9. 4.95 ÷ 5.5   **10.** 43.25 ÷ 2.5   **11.** 70.59 ÷ 54.3   **12.** 160.72 ÷ 32.8

13. 87.92 ÷ 6.28   **14.** 206.08 ÷ 2.3   **15.** 628.2 ÷ 34.9   **16.** 1.593 ÷ 5.9

17. 6.7 ÷ 0.05   **18.** 36.75 ÷ 2.45   **19.** 289.25 ÷ 12.5   **20.** 332.88 ÷ 36.5

Modeling Fractions

A **fraction** is a number of the form $\frac{a}{b}$ $(b \neq 0)$, where a is called the **numerator** and b is called the **denominator.** The number $2\frac{1}{4}$ is a *mixed number.* A **mixed number** is the sum of a whole number and a fraction.

Example Write a fraction to represent the shaded part of the region.

The region is divided into 16 equal parts. Of those, 9 parts are shaded.

Answer The fraction that represents the shaded part of the region is $\frac{9}{16}$.

Example Write a mixed number to represent the shaded region.

Each circle is divided into 6 equal parts. Three whole circles are shaded, and five parts of the fourth circle are shaded.

Answer The mixed number that represents the shaded region is $3\frac{5}{6}$.

✔ Practice

Write a fraction to represent the shaded part of the set or region.

1.

2.

3.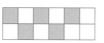

4.

5.

6.

Write a mixed number to represent the shaded region.

7.

8.

9.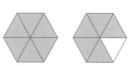

10.

11.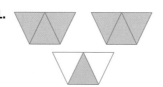

12.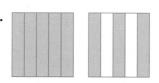

Mixed Numbers and Improper Fractions

Recall that a mixed number is the sum of a whole number and a fraction. An **improper fraction**, such as $\frac{21}{8}$, is any fraction in which the numerator is greater than or equal to the denominator.

Example Write $2\frac{5}{8}$ as an improper fraction.

$$2\frac{5}{8} = 2 + \frac{5}{8} \qquad \text{Definition of mixed number}$$

$$= \frac{16}{8} + \frac{5}{8} \qquad \text{1 whole} = \frac{8}{8}, \text{ so 2 wholes} = \frac{2 \times 8}{8}, \text{ or } \frac{16}{8}.$$

$$= \frac{21}{8} \qquad \text{Add.}$$

Answer The mixed number $2\frac{5}{8}$ is equivalent to the improper fraction $\frac{21}{8}$.

Example Write $\frac{19}{6}$ as a mixed number.

$$\begin{array}{r} 3\,\text{R}1 \\ 6\overline{)19} \\ 18 \\ \hline 1 \end{array} \qquad \text{Divide 19 by 6.}$$

$$3 + \frac{1}{6} = 3\frac{1}{6} \qquad \text{Write the remainder as a fraction, } \frac{\text{remainder}}{\text{divisor}}.$$

Answer The improper fraction $\frac{19}{6}$ is equivalent to the mixed number $3\frac{1}{6}$.

✔ Practice

Write the mixed number as an improper fraction.

1. $1\frac{9}{10}$ **2.** $1\frac{3}{5}$ **3.** $9\frac{1}{6}$ **4.** $5\frac{1}{9}$ **5.** $3\frac{4}{7}$

6. $4\frac{2}{5}$ **7.** $2\frac{3}{8}$ **8.** $8\frac{1}{2}$ **9.** $6\frac{2}{3}$ **10.** $4\frac{3}{11}$

11. $7\frac{3}{4}$ **12.** $4\frac{7}{13}$ **13.** $8\frac{11}{20}$ **14.** $12\frac{13}{15}$ **15.** $15\frac{7}{9}$

Write the improper fraction as a mixed number.

16. $\frac{14}{5}$ **17.** $\frac{11}{2}$ **18.** $\frac{22}{3}$ **19.** $\frac{29}{9}$ **20.** $\frac{53}{10}$

21. $\frac{37}{6}$ **22.** $\frac{43}{4}$ **23.** $\frac{31}{8}$ **24.** $\frac{57}{7}$ **25.** $\frac{115}{12}$

Adding and Subtracting Fractions

To add fractions with a common denominator, write the sum of the numerators over the denominator.

Numbers: $\dfrac{3}{9} + \dfrac{4}{9} = \dfrac{3+4}{9} = \dfrac{7}{9}$ **Model:**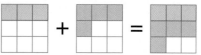

Example Find the sum $\dfrac{7}{8} + \dfrac{4}{8}$.

$\dfrac{7}{8} + \dfrac{4}{8} = \dfrac{7+4}{8}$ **Write sum of numerators over common denominator.**

$= \dfrac{11}{8}$ **Add.**

$= 1\dfrac{3}{8}$ **Write improper fraction as a mixed number.**

To subtract fractions with a common denominator, write the difference of the numerators over the denominator.

Numbers: $\dfrac{4}{5} - \dfrac{1}{5} = \dfrac{4-1}{5} = \dfrac{3}{5}$ **Model:**

Example Find the difference $\dfrac{7}{20} - \dfrac{4}{20}$.

$\dfrac{7}{20} - \dfrac{4}{20} = \dfrac{7-4}{20}$ **Write difference of numerators over common denominator.**

$= \dfrac{3}{20}$ **Subtract.**

✔ Practice

Find the sum or difference.

1. $\dfrac{2}{5} + \dfrac{2}{5}$ **2.** $\dfrac{7}{15} + \dfrac{6}{15}$ **3.** $\dfrac{4}{7} - \dfrac{1}{7}$ **4.** $\dfrac{8}{9} - \dfrac{4}{9}$ **5.** $\dfrac{6}{11} - \dfrac{5}{11}$

6. $\dfrac{8}{13} - \dfrac{3}{13}$ **7.** $\dfrac{9}{14} + \dfrac{4}{14}$ **8.** $\dfrac{3}{20} + \dfrac{8}{20}$ **9.** $\dfrac{5}{6} - \dfrac{4}{6}$ **10.** $\dfrac{11}{12} - \dfrac{6}{12}$

11. $\dfrac{19}{20} - \dfrac{6}{20}$ **12.** $\dfrac{22}{27} - \dfrac{5}{27}$ **13.** $\dfrac{12}{13} + \dfrac{9}{13}$ **14.** $\dfrac{9}{10} + \dfrac{8}{10}$ **15.** $\dfrac{26}{18} - \dfrac{7}{18}$

16. $\dfrac{17}{16} + \dfrac{15}{16}$ **17.** $\dfrac{5}{6} + \dfrac{1}{6}$ **18.** $\dfrac{7}{8} + \dfrac{6}{8}$ **19.** $\dfrac{2}{3} + \dfrac{2}{3}$ **20.** $\dfrac{19}{21} - \dfrac{6}{21}$

Multiplying Fractions and Whole Numbers

Multiplying a fraction by a whole number can be thought of as repeated addition.

Numbers: $5 \times \frac{3}{4} = \frac{3}{4} + \frac{3}{4} + \frac{3}{4} + \frac{3}{4} + \frac{3}{4}$ **Model:**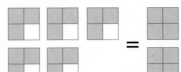

$$= \frac{15}{4} = 3\frac{3}{4}$$

The above example suggests the following rule: To multiply a fraction by a whole number, multiply the numerator of the fraction by the whole number and write the product over the denominator of the fraction. Simplify if possible.

Example Find the product $18 \times \frac{5}{6}$.

$18 \times \frac{5}{6} = \frac{18 \times 5}{6}$ **Write product of whole number and numerator over denominator.**

$= \frac{90}{6}$ **Multiply.**

$= 15$ **Write improper fraction as whole number.**

Example Find the product $\frac{2}{3} \times 14$.

$\frac{2}{3} \times 14 = \frac{2 \times 14}{3}$ **Write product of whole number and numerator over denominator.**

$= \frac{28}{3}$ **Multiply.**

$= 9\frac{1}{3}$ **Write improper fraction as mixed number.**

✔ Practice

Find the product.

1. $6 \times \frac{1}{2}$ **2.** $10 \times \frac{4}{5}$ **3.** $16 \times \frac{7}{8}$ **4.** $\frac{9}{10} \times 20$

5. $\frac{3}{7} \times 24$ **6.** $24 \times \frac{1}{5}$ **7.** $20 \times \frac{3}{5}$ **8.** $\frac{5}{8} \times 16$

9. $\frac{1}{4} \times 9$ **10.** $\frac{1}{5} \times 21$ **11.** $12 \times \frac{5}{7}$ **12.** $\frac{5}{11} \times 24$

13. $\frac{5}{9} \times 27$ **14.** $\frac{3}{8} \times 15$ **15.** $\frac{3}{4} \times 12$ **16.** $\frac{5}{6} \times 7$

Reading Bar Graphs

Data are numbers or facts. A *bar graph* is one way to display data. A **bar graph** uses bars to show how quantities in categories compare.

Example The bar graph below shows the results of a survey of students who perform community service. More students serve in which location than in any other location? Fewer students serve in which location than in any other location?

Solution

The longest bar on the graph represents the 14 students who serve in a hospital. So, more students serve in a hospital than in any other location.

The shortest bar on the graph represents the 5 students who serve in a library. So, fewer students serve in a library than in any other location.

✔ *Practice*

In Exercises 1–3, use the bar graph above to answer the question.

1. How many of the students serve in a food pantry?

2. Students serve in equal numbers in which two locations?

3. How many more students serve in a hospital than in an animal shelter?

In Exercises 4–7, use the bar graph, which shows the results of a survey on favorite breakfast foods.

4. Which food was chosen by the greatest number of people?

5. Which two foods were chosen by the same number of people?

6. How many more people chose eggs than chose pancakes?

7. Which foods were chosen by fewer than 12 people?

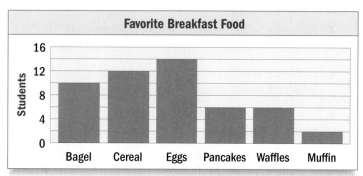

Reading Line Graphs

You can use a *line graph* to display data. A **line graph** uses segments to show how a quantity changes over time.

Example Students recorded the outdoor temperature every hour from 10 A.M. until 4 P.M. on one day. The line graph below shows the results. Between which two hours did the greatest increase in temperature occur? What was the amount of that increase?

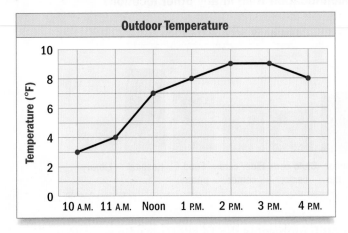

Outdoor Temperature

Solution
The steepest segment in the line graph is from 11 A.M. to noon. The temperature was 4°F at 11 A.M. and 7°F at noon, an increase of 3°F.

✔ Practice

In Exercises 1–3, use the line graph above to answer the question.

1. What was the temperature at 1 P.M.?

2. At what time was the temperature 3°F?

3. Between which two hours did the temperature decrease? What was the amount of that decrease?

In Exercises 4–7, use the line graph, which shows the height (in millimeters) of a bean plant as it grew over six days.

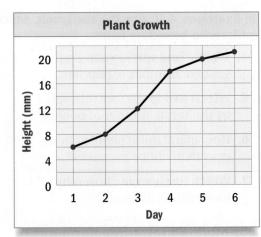

Plant Growth

4. Between which two days was the increase in height the greatest? What was that increase?

5. Between which two days was the increase in height 4 millimeters?

6. On which day was the height of the bean plant 21 millimeters?

7. What was the total increase in the height of the plant over the six days?

Reading Circle Graphs

A **circle graph** displays data as sections of a circle. The entire circle represents all of the data. The sections of the graph may be labeled using the actual data or the data expressed as fractions, decimals, or percents. When expressed as fractions, decimals, or percents, the data have a sum of 1.

Example The circle graph below shows the results of a survey that asked 100 people how their homes are heated. How many more homes are heated by natural gas than by electricity?

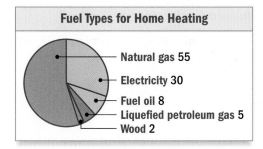

Fuel Types for Home Heating

- Natural gas 55
- Electricity 30
- Fuel oil 8
- Liquefied petroleum gas 5
- Wood 2

Solution

The graph shows that 55 homes are heated by natural gas and 30 homes are heated by electricity. Because $55 - 30 = 25$, there are 25 more homes that are heated by natural gas than by electricity.

✓ Practice

In Exercises 1–4, use the circle graph above to answer the question.

1. How many homes are heated by liquefied petroleum gas?

2. How many homes are heated by either fuel oil or electricity?

3. How many homes are heated using a source *other* than fuel oil, electricity, or natural gas?

4. How does the number of homes heated by natural gas compare with the total number of homes heated by all other sources in the graph?

In Exercises 5–8, use the circle graph, which shows the results of a survey that asked 100 people who do not work at home how long their travel time to work is.

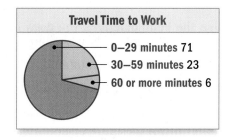

Travel Time to Work

- 0–29 minutes 71
- 30–59 minutes 23
- 60 or more minutes 6

5. How many people have a travel time of 60 or more minutes?

6. How many people have a travel time of 30 or more minutes?

7. How many people have a travel time of less than 30 minutes?

8. How many people have a travel time of less than 1 hour?

Venn Diagrams and Logical Reasoning

A **Venn diagram** uses shapes to show how sets are related. A **counterexample** is an example that shows that a statement is false. You need only a single counterexample to show that a statement is false.

> **Example** **Draw and use a Venn diagram.**
>
> **a.** Draw a Venn diagram of the whole numbers less than 10 where set A consists of factors of 18 and set B consists of even numbers.
>
> **b.** Is the following statement *true* or *false*? Explain.
> *No even whole number less than 10 is a factor of 18.*
>
> **c.** Is the following statement *always, sometimes,* or *never* true? Explain.
> *A whole-number factor of 18 that is less than 10 is even.*
>
> **Solution**
>
> **a.**
>
>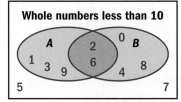
>
> **b.** False. A counterexample is 2, which is even and a factor of 18.
>
> **c.** Sometimes. It is true that 2 and 6 are whole-number factors of 18 that are less than 10 and are even, but 1, 3, and 9 are whole-number factors of 18 that are less than 10 and are odd.

✔ Practice

Draw a Venn diagram of the sets described.

1. Of the whole numbers less than 10, set A consists of factors of 12 and set B consists of even numbers.

2. Of the whole numbers less than 10, set A consists of factors of 20 and set B consists of numbers greater than 5.

Use the Venn diagrams you drew in Exercises 1 and 2 to answer the question. Explain your reasoning.

3. Are the following statements *true* or *false*?

   a. *A whole-number factor of 20 that is less than 10 is also greater than 5.*

   b. *There are exactly three even whole numbers less than 10 that are factors of 12.*

4. Is the following statement *always, sometimes,* or *never* true? Explain.
   An even whole number less than 10 is a factor of 12.

Basic Geometric Figures

A **triangle** is a geometric figure having 3 sides and 3 angles.

A **rectangle** has 4 sides and 4 right angles. Opposite sides have the same length.

A **square** is a rectangle with all four sides the same length.

The point where two sides of a figure meet is called a **vertex** (plural: **vertices**). The distance around a figure is called its **perimeter**. If a figure has straight sides, its perimeter is the sum of the lengths of the sides.

Example Find the perimeter.

The perimeter is 7 ft + 4 ft + 7 ft + 4 ft = 22 ft.

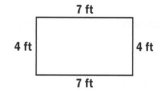

Example Draw and label a square with a side length of 2 cm. Then find its perimeter.

Draw a horizontal side 2 cm long.
Then draw the two vertical sides 2 cm long.
Finally, draw the second horizontal side 2 cm long.

The perimeter is 2 cm + 2 cm + 2 cm + 2 cm = 8 cm.

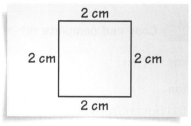

✔ Practice

Find the perimeter.

1.

2.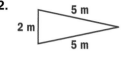

3.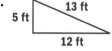

4.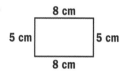

Draw and label the figure described. Then find its perimeter.

5. A square with sides 3 cm long

6. A square with sides 2 in. long

7. A rectangle with a length of 4 in. and a width of 1 in.

8. A rectangle with a length of 5 cm and a width of 2 cm

Units of Length

Two commonly used systems for measuring length are the U.S. customary system and the metric system. The tables below show equivalent lengths in each system.

Equivalent U.S. Customary Lengths
1 mile (mi) = 5280 feet (ft)
1 yard (yd) = 3 feet (ft)
1 foot (ft) = 12 inches (in.)

Equivalent Metric Lengths
1 kilometer (km) = 1000 meters (m)
1 meter (m) = 100 centimeters (cm)
1 meter (m) = 1000 millimeters (mm)

Each length equivalent can be used to form a **conversion factor** that is equal to 1. Here are some examples:

$$\frac{1 \text{ km}}{1000 \text{ m}} = 1 \qquad \frac{1000 \text{ m}}{1 \text{ km}} = 1 \qquad \frac{1 \text{ mi}}{5280 \text{ ft}} = 1 \qquad \frac{5280 \text{ ft}}{1 \text{ mi}} = 1$$

The choice of conversion factors depends on **unit analysis**.

- To convert kilometers to meters, multiply by $\frac{1000 \text{ m}}{1 \text{ km}}$ because

$$\cancel{\text{km}} \times \frac{\text{m}}{\cancel{\text{km}}} = \text{m}.$$

- To convert feet to miles, multiply by $\frac{1 \text{ mi}}{5280 \text{ ft}}$ because

$$\cancel{\text{ft}} \times \frac{\text{mi}}{\cancel{\text{ft}}} = \text{mi}.$$

Example **Copy and complete the statement.**

a. 6 km = $\underline{\ ?\ }$ m

b. 108 inches = $\underline{\ ?\ }$ yards

Solution

a. To convert from kilometers to meters, multiply by $\frac{1000 \text{ m}}{1 \text{ km}}$.

$$6 \ \cancel{\text{km}} \times \frac{1000 \text{ m}}{1 \ \cancel{\text{km}}} = 6000 \text{ m}$$

b. To convert from inches to yards, multiply by $\frac{1 \text{ yd}}{3 \ \cancel{\text{ft}}} \times \frac{1 \ \cancel{\text{ft}}}{12 \text{ in.}} = \frac{1 \text{ yd}}{36 \text{ in.}}$.

$$\overset{3}{\cancel{108 \text{ in.}}} \times \frac{1 \text{ yd}}{\underset{1}{\cancel{36 \text{ in.}}}} = 3 \text{ yd}$$

✔ Practice

Copy and complete.

1. 6000 cm = $\underline{\ ?\ }$ m

2. 4830 mm = $\underline{\ ?\ }$ m

3. 0.9 km = $\underline{\ ?\ }$ cm

4. 6 ft = $\underline{\ ?\ }$ in.

5. 21 ft = $\underline{\ ?\ }$ yd

6. 63,360 in. = $\underline{\ ?\ }$ mi

Using a Ruler

An **inch ruler** has markings for inches, halves of an inch, fourths of an inch, eighths of an inch, and sixteenths of an inch. As the lengths get shorter, so do the markings.

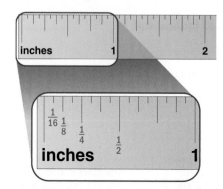 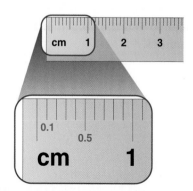

A **centimeter ruler** has markings for centimeters, halves of centimeters, and tenths of a centimeter (also called *millimeters*). Like an inch ruler, as the lengths get shorter, so do the markings.

Example Use a ruler to draw a segment with the given length.

a. $2\frac{3}{16}$ inches

b. 5.4 centimeters

Solution

a.

inches   1   2

Start at the leftmost mark on the ruler.

Draw a segment so that the other end is at the third $\frac{1}{16}$ in. mark after 2 in.

b.

cm   1   2   3   4   5   6

Start at the leftmost mark on the ruler.

Draw a segment so that the other end is at the fourth 0.1 cm mark after 5 cm.

✔ Practice

Use a ruler to draw a segment with the given length.

1. $\frac{3}{4}$ inch

2. $2\frac{1}{8}$ inches

3. $3\frac{1}{2}$ inches

4. $\frac{13}{16}$ inch

5. $\frac{7}{8}$ inch

6. $\frac{5}{16}$ inch

7. $1\frac{1}{4}$ inches

8. $4\frac{1}{16}$ inches

9. 3.5 centimeters

10. 6.5 centimeters

11. 3.7 centimeters

12. 4.9 centimeters

13. 1.3 centimeters

14. 2.6 centimeters

15. 5.1 centimeters

16. 4.2 centimeters

Measuring Lengths

You can use an inch ruler or a centimeter ruler to measure lengths of segments.

Example Use a ruler to find the length of the segment in inches and in centimeters.

a. Measure in inches.

b. Measure in centimeters.

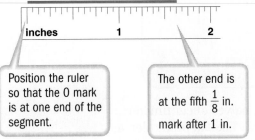

Position the ruler so that the 0 mark is at one end of the segment.

The other end is at the fifth $\frac{1}{8}$ in. mark after 1 in.

Position the ruler so that the 0 mark is at one end of the segment.

The other end is at the first 0.1 cm mark after 4 cm.

Answer The segment is $1\frac{5}{8}$ in. long.

Answer The segment is 4.1 cm long.

Sometimes you want to measure a length to a specified degree of accuracy.

Example Measure the segment shown to the nearest 0.5 cm.

To measure the segment to the nearest 0.5 cm, locate the two 0.5 cm marks that are nearest to the end of the segment and choose the closer one.

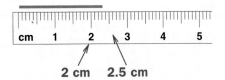

2 cm   2.5 cm

The end of the segment is closer to 2.5 cm.

Answer To the nearest 0.5 cm, the segment is 2.5 cm long.

✔ Practice

Use a ruler to find the length of the segment in inches and in centimeters.

1. ——————————

2. ——————

Find the length of the segment to the specified degree of accuracy.

3. To the nearest $\frac{1}{4}$ inch

4. To the nearest centimeter

Units of Area and Volume

Area is the number of unit squares that are needed to cover a figure.

Unit square

1 unit

1 unit

Volume is the number of unit cubes needed to fill a solid.

Unit cube

1 unit

1 unit

1 unit

The area A of a square is given by the formula $A = s^2$, where s is the length of a side.

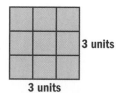

3 units

3 units

Area $= 3^2 = 9$ square units

The volume V of a cube is given by the formula $V = s^3$, where s is the length of an edge.

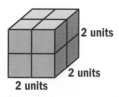

2 units

2 units

2 units

Volume $= 2^3 = 8$ cubic units

Example Find the area of the square and the volume of the cube.

a.

6 in.

6 in.

b.

8 m

8 m

8 m

Solution

a. $A = 6^2 = 36$ in.^{2}

The area is 36 square inches.

b. $V = 8^3 = 512$ m^3

The volume is 512 cubic meters.

✔ Practice

Find the area of the square.

1.

4 mi

4 mi

2.

18 mm

18 mm

3.

1.4 cm

1.4 cm

4.

7 in.

7 in.

Find the volume of the cube.

5.

11 ft

11 ft

11 ft

6.

20 km

20 km

20 km

7.

5 cm

5 cm

5 cm

8.

4.5 yd

4.5 yd

4.5 yd

Units of Weight and Mass

Tables of equivalent weights and masses in the U.S. customary system and the metric system are shown below.

Equivalent U.S. Customary Weights
1 ton (ton) = 2000 pounds (lb)
1 pound (lb) = 16 ounces (oz)

Equivalent Metric Masses
1 kilogram (kg) = 1000 grams (g)
1 gram (g) = 1000 milligrams (mg)

Example Copy and complete the statement using <, >, or =.

a. 8 kg _?_ 7900 g

b. 93 oz _?_ 6 lb

Solution

a. $8 \text{ kg} \times \dfrac{1000 \text{ g}}{1 \text{ kg}} = 8000 \text{ g}$

Answer So, 8 kg > 7900 g.

b. $6 \text{ lb} \times \dfrac{16 \text{ oz}}{1 \text{ lb}} = 96 \text{ oz}$

Answer So, 93 oz < 6 lb.

Example Find the weight or mass of the object.

a.

b.

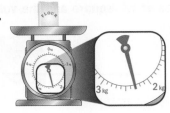

Solution

a. Each pound is divided into sixteenths, so the weight of the squashes is $3\dfrac{12}{16}$, or $3\dfrac{3}{4}$ pounds.

b. Each kilogram is divided into tenths, so the mass of the flour is 2.3 kilograms.

✔ Practice

Copy and complete the statement using <, >, or =.

1. 2.5 tons _?_ 4900 lb

2. 0.62 kg _?_ 622 g

3. 9400 mg _?_ 9.4 g

4. 30 lb _?_ 470 oz

5. 19,217 oz _?_ 0.6 ton

6. 1.8 kg _?_ 1,790,000 mg

Find the weight or mass of the object.

7.

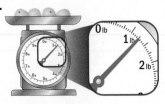

8.

9.

Units of Capacity

Equivalent U.S. Customary Capacities
1 cup (c) = 8 fluid ounces (fl oz)
1 pint (pt) = 2 cups (c)
1 quart (qt) = 2 pints (pt)
1 gallon (gal) = 4 quarts (qt)

Equivalent Metric Capacities
1 kiloliter (kL) = 1000 liters (L)
1 liter (L) = 1000 milliliters (mL)

Example Copy and complete the statement using <, >, or =.

a. 9400 mL _?_ 9.6 L

b. 6 gal _?_ 46 pt

Solution

a. $9400 \text{ mL} \times \dfrac{1 \text{ L}}{1000 \text{ mL}} = 9.4 \text{ L}$

Answer So, 9400 mL < 9.6 L.

b. $6 \text{ gal} \times \dfrac{4 \text{ qt}}{1 \text{ gal}} \times \dfrac{2 \text{ pt}}{1 \text{ qt}} = 48 \text{ pt}$

Answer So, 6 gal > 46 pt.

Example Find the amount of liquid in the measuring cup.

a.

b.

Solution

a. Each cup is divided into fourths, so the liquid is at the $2\frac{3}{4}$ cups level.

b. Each 100 milliliters is divided into fourths, so the liquid is at the 250 milliliters level.

✔ Practice

Copy and complete the statement using <, >, or =.

1. 3 kL _?_ 3010 L

2. 32 fl oz _?_ 1 qt

3. 40 qt _?_ 168 c

4. 1 gal _?_ 128 fl oz

5. 34 pt _?_ 4 gal

6. 34,710 mL _?_ 0.035 kL

Find the amount of liquid in the measuring cup.

7.

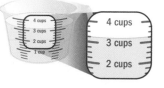

8.

9.

Using a Protractor

A **protractor** is a tool that you can use to draw and measure angles. A unit of measure for angles is the **degree** (°).

Example Find the measure of the angle.

1. Place the protractor on the angle so the protractor's center point is on the point where the two rays meet. Line up one ray with the 0° line. Notice that the ray passes through the 0° mark on the *outer scale*.

2. Read where the other ray crosses the outer scale of the protractor. The measure of ∠*ABC* is 143°. You can write this as *m*∠*ABC* = 143°.

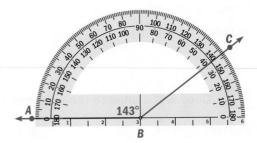

Example Use a protractor to draw an angle that has a measure of 73°.

1. Draw and label a ray.

2. Place the center of the protractor at the endpoint of the ray. Line up the ray with the 0° line. Notice that the ray passes through the 0° mark on the *inner scale*. Draw and label a point at the 73° mark on the inner scale.

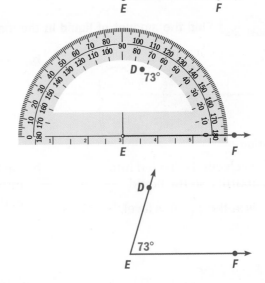

3. Remove the protractor and draw $\overrightarrow{ED}$ to complete the angle.

✔ Practice

Use a protractor to measure the angle.

1.    2. 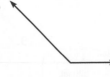   3. 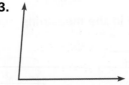   4.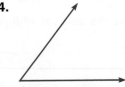

Use a protractor to draw an angle that has the given measure.

5. 55°   6. 168°   7. 90°   8. 77°

Classifying Angles

Classifying Angles	
An **acute angle** has a measure less than 90°: $m\angle ABC < 90°$. 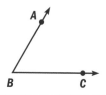	A **right angle** has a measure of exactly 90°: $m\angle ABC = 90°$. 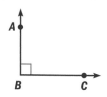
An **obtuse angle** has a measure between 90° and 180°: $m\angle ABC > 90°$ and $m\angle ABC < 180°$. 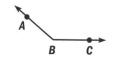	A **straight angle** has a measure of exactly 180°: $m\angle ABC = 180°$.

Example Find the measure of the given angle. Then classify the angle as *acute, right, obtuse,* or *straight.*

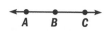

a. $m\angle AFC$

b. $m\angle BFD$

Solution

a. $m\angle AFC = m\angle AFB + m\angle BFC$

$= 25° + 65°$

$= 90°$

Answer $m\angle AFC = 90°$, so $\angle AFC$ is a right angle.

b. $m\angle BFD = m\angle BFC + m\angle CFD$

$= 65° + 12°$

$= 87°$

Answer $m\angle BFD = 87°$, so $\angle BFD$ is an acute angle.

✔ Practice

Find the measure of the angle. Then classify the angle as *acute, right, obtuse,* or *straight.*

1. $m\angle QWS$

2. $m\angle RWU$

3. $m\angle TWV$

4. $m\angle QWT$

5. $m\angle SWV$

6. $m\angle RWT$

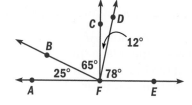

Using a Compass

A **compass** is an instrument used to draw circles. A **straightedge** is any object that can be used to draw a segment.

Example Use a compass to draw a circle with radius 1 cm.

Recall that the *radius* of a circle is the distance between the center of the circle and any point on the circle.

Use a centimeter ruler to open the compass so that the distance between the point and the pencil is 1 cm.

Place the point on a piece of paper and rotate the pencil around the point to draw the circle.

1 cm

Example Use a straightedge and a compass to draw a segment whose length is the sum of the lengths of $\overline{AB}$ and $\overline{CD}$.

A ——————————— B C —————— D

Solution

Use a straightedge to draw a segment longer than both given segments.

Open your compass to measure $\overline{AB}$. Using this compass setting, place the point at the left end of your segment and make a mark that crosses your segment.

Then open your compass to measure $\overline{CD}$. Using this compass setting, place the point at the first mark you made on your segment and make another mark that crosses your segment.

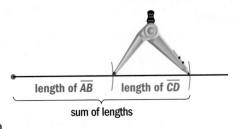

length of $\overline{AB}$ length of $\overline{CD}$

sum of lengths

✔ Practice

Use a compass to draw a circle with the given radius.

1. 1 inch   **2.** 3 cm   **3.** 2 inches   **4.** 2 cm   **5.** 1.7 cm

6. Use a straightedge and a compass to draw a segment whose length is the *sum* of the lengths of the two given segments.

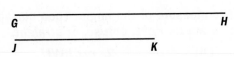

G ——————————————— H

J ——————— K

7. Use a straightedge and a compass to draw a segment whose length is the *difference* of the lengths of the two given segments in Exercise 6.

Skills Review Handbook

Draw a Diagram

When a problem to be solved is not illustrated, you may find it helpful to draw a diagram that summarizes the information you are given.

> **Example** **Draw a diagram to solve the following problem.**
>
> You are using a word processing program to write a science report. You plan to print the report on paper that is 8.5 inches wide. The left and right margins are each 1 inch wide. On one page of your report, you plan to include a table that is as wide as possible and has 3 columns of equal width. How wide should you make each column?
>
> **Solution**
>
> Draw a diagram of the sheet of paper with the table.

8.5 in.

1 in. — Column 1 | Column 2 | Column 3 — 1 in.

> To find the width of the entire table, subtract the widths of the left and right margins from the width of the paper.
>
> Width of table $= 8.5 - 1 - 1 = 6.5$ in.
>
> Then divide the width of the table by 3 to find the width of each column.
>
> Width of each column $= \dfrac{6.5}{3} \approx 2.17$ in.
>
> **Answer** You should make each column about 2.17 inches wide.

✔ Practice

Use the strategy *draw a diagram* to solve the problem.

1. **Paintings** You are hanging 3 paintings on a wall that is 22 feet long. The width of each painting is 2 feet. You want to position the paintings so that the gaps between paintings and between a painting and an end of the wall have the same width. How wide should each gap be?

2. **Travel** Your town is laid out as a grid. Starting at your home, you walk north 6 blocks to buy some snacks at a store. You then walk east 3 blocks to meet a friend, and finally south 2 blocks to a park. What is the shortest distance (in blocks) back to your home?

3. **Garden** A square garden has sides that are 25 feet long. A path around the garden is 3 feet wide. What is the area of the path?

Look for a Pattern

You can solve some problems by looking for, identifying, and extending a pattern.

> **Example** The table shows the cost of a large pizza at a restaurant for different numbers of toppings. What is the cost of a large pizza with 7 toppings?
>
> | Number of toppings | 0 | 1 | 2 | 3 | 4 | 5 |
> |---|---|---|---|---|---|---|
> | Cost of large pizza | $9.00 | $9.75 | $10.50 | $11.25 | $12.00 | $12.75 |
>
> ### Solution
>
> Look for a pattern in the costs as the number of toppings increases. Notice that each additional topping increases the cost by $.75.
>
> | Number of toppings | 0 | 1 | 2 | 3 | 4 | 5 |
> |---|---|---|---|---|---|---|
> | Cost of large pizza | $9.00 | $9.75 | $10.50 | $11.25 | $12.00 | $12.75 |
>
> + $.75   + $.75   + $.75   + $.75   + $.75
>
> Because a 7-topping pizza has 2 more toppings than a 5-topping pizza, you can find the cost of a 7-topping pizza by adding 2($.75) to the cost of a 5-topping pizza.
>
> Cost of 7-topping pizza = $12.75 + 2($.75) = $14.25
>
> **Answer** A large pizza with 7 toppings costs $14.25.

✔ Practice

Use the strategy *look for a pattern* to solve the problem.

1. **Buses** The table shows part of a bus schedule for a stop near your home. Based on the pattern, when does the 9th bus make a stop?

Bus number	1	2	3	4	5	6
Time of bus stop	5:45	6:10	6:35	7:00	7:25	7:50

2. **Logical Reasoning** Find the next number in the list below. Explain your reasoning.

   1, 2, 4, 7, 11, 16, 22, _?_

3. **Stacking Cans** A grocery store clerk stacks cans in the shape of a pyramid. The top 3 layers of cans are shown from above. If the pyramid has 8 layers, how many cans are in the pyramid?

   Top layer   **Layer 2**   **Layer 3**

Guess, Check, and Revise

An effective way to solve certain problems is to make a reasonable guess of the answer and then check whether the guess is correct. If the guess is not correct, you can revise the guess and try again.

> **Example** You are saving money for a new bike that costs $275. You already have $80. You can save $15 a week. How long will it take you to save enough money for the bike?
>
> **Solution**
>
> **Guess:** Try 10 weeks.
>
> **Check:** After 10 weeks, you will have saved $80 + 10($15) = $230, which is less than the cost of the bike.
>
> **Revise:** Try saving for more weeks.
>
> **Guess:** Try 14 weeks.
>
> **Check:** After 14 weeks, you will have saved $80 + 14($15) = $290, which is greater than the cost of the bike.
>
> **Revise:** Try saving for fewer weeks.
>
> **Guess:** Try 13 weeks.
>
> **Check:** After 13 weeks, you will have saved $80 + 13($15) = $275, which is equal to the cost of the bike.
>
> **Answer** It will take you 13 weeks to save enough money for the bike.

✔ Practice

Use the strategy *guess, check, and revise* to solve the problem.

1. **Loan** You are paying back a $132 loan that your parents made to you. You have already repaid $20 and plan to pay back $7 a week from now on. How long will it take you to repay the loan?

2. **Number Sense** The sum of three consecutive integers is 129. What are the integers?

3. **Trees** A tree farm sold 17 spruce trees for $940. Some of the trees were white spruce, which cost $50 each. The rest were blue spruce, which cost $65 each. How many of each type of tree were sold?

4. **Fans** A store sells small fans for $12 each and large fans for $35 each. If the store sells 14 fans for $375, how many of each type of fan are sold?

5. **Classroom** The floor of a classroom is a square with an area of 676 square feet. What is the length of a side of the floor?

6. **Geometry** The volume of a cube is 29,791 cubic centimeters. What is the length of an edge of the cube?

Act It Out

Sometimes you may wish to "act out" a problem using the actual objects described in the problem or other items that represent those objects. The process of acting out the problem may lead you to the solution.

Example Ben and Paul buy a box of 42 baseball cards at a garage sale. Ben pays twice as much of the cost as Paul, so they agree that Ben should get twice as many of the cards. How many cards should each person get?

Solution

Use 42 pieces of paper to represent the 42 baseball cards. Divide the pieces into two groups, one for Ben and one for Paul. For every 2 pieces of paper you give to Ben, give 1 piece to Paul.

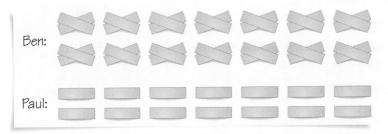

Answer Because Ben has 28 pieces of paper and Paul has 14 pieces, Ben should get 28 baseball cards and Paul should get 14 baseball cards.

✔ Practice

Use the strategy *act it out* to solve the problem.

1. **Computers** Rosa and Kim buy a package of 25 blank CDs to use for backing up their computer files. Rosa has more files to back up, so they agree that she should get 3 CDs for every 2 CDs Kim gets. How many CDs should each person get?

2. **Class Project** Gail, Carlos, and Tonya have a package of 50 sheets of construction paper to use for a class project. Gail takes 6 sheets, Carlos takes twice as many sheets as Gail, and Tonya takes one quarter of the remaining sheets. How many sheets of paper are left?

3. **Seating** Ann, Bill, Carrie, Devon, Ellie, and Fred are sitting at the table shown. Ellie is sitting in seat 3. Ann is sitting across from Ellie. Carrie is sitting between Ann and Fred. Devon is sitting across from Carrie. In which seat is Bill sitting?

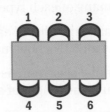

Make a List or Table

Sometimes a problem asks you to generate and record a large amount of information. For such problems, it can be helpful to organize the information using a list or a table.

Example At a mall, you want to visit the book store, the pet store, the record store, and the shoe store. In how many orders can you visit these stores?

Solution

Let B represent the book store, P represent the pet store, R represent the record store, and S represent the shoe store. Each arrangement of the letters B, P, R, and S represents an order in which you can visit the stores. You want to find all possible arrangements of the letters.

First list the arrangements that begin with the letter **B**.

   BPRS   **B**PSR   **B**RPS   **B**RSP   **B**SPR   **B**SRP

Similarly, list the arrangements that begin with **P**, **R**, and **S**.

   PBRS   **P**BSR   **P**RBS   **P**RSB   **P**SBR   **P**SRB

   RBPS   **R**BSP   **R**PBS   **R**PSB   **R**SBP   **R**SPB

   SBPR   **S**BRP   **S**PBR   **S**PRB   **S**RBP   **S**RPB

Count the arrangements of the letters. There are 24 arrangements.

Answer There are 24 orders in which you can visit the stores.

✓ Practice

Use the strategy *make a list or table* to solve the problem.

1. **Table Tennis** Aaron, Lori, Mary, and Carlos are playing table tennis at a community center. Each person plays every other person exactly once. How many table tennis matches are played?

2. **Cafeteria** On Mondays, a school cafeteria offers 2 main courses (spaghetti and ham), 3 side dishes (salad, corn, and green beans), and 2 desserts (pie and cake). You can choose 1 main course, 1 side dish, and 1 dessert for your lunch. How many lunches are possible?

3. **Air Conditioning** The cost of electricity needed to operate a certain air conditioner is $.25 an hour. Copy and complete the table below. How many hours can you run the air conditioner each month if you want to spend at most $35 a month in electricity?

Hours of operation	20	40	60	80	100	120	140	160	180
Cost of electricity	?	?	?	?	?	?	?	?	?

Solve a Simpler or Related Problem

If a problem seems too difficult, try solving a similar problem that has simpler conditions. Doing so may lead to a solution of the original problem.

Example A *diameter* of a circle is a segment that passes through the center of the circle and has endpoints on the circle. If you draw 10 diameters of a circle, how many sections are produced?

Solution

Begin with a simpler task. Find the number of sections produced when you draw 1, 2, or 3 diameters of a circle. Look for a pattern in the results.

1 diameter
2 sections

2 diameters
4 sections

3 diameters
6 sections

In each case, the number of sections is twice the number of diameters.

Answer Based on the pattern, if you draw 10 diameters of a circle, 20 sections are produced.

✔ Practice

Use the strategy *solve a simpler or related problem* to solve the problem.

1. **Restaurant** A restaurant has 12 square tables that seat one person on each side. For a private party, the tables are joined together in a row to form one long table. How many people can be seated at the party?

2. **Geometry** The first four figures in a pattern are shown below. Consider the problem of finding the number of squares of different sizes in each figure, where all the sides of each square are segments in the figure. For instance, there is 1 square (a 1×1 square) in the first figure. There are 5 squares (four 1×1 squares and one 2×2 square) in the second figure. Predict the number of squares in the 10th figure of the pattern.

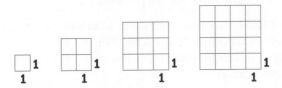

3. **Logical Reasoning** Consider the list of numbers such that the first number is 1 and each number after the first is twice the number before it: 1, 2, 4, 8, 16, ... What is the 15th number in the list? What is the sum of the first 15 numbers?

Work Backward

A problem may involve a series of actions where the final result of the actions is known and you need to determine the beginning conditions. It may be helpful to work backward.

Example At the end of a day, you have $19 in your wallet. You remember spending $14 on dinner, collecting $23 owed you from a friend, and spending $11 on a T-shirt. How much money did you have at the beginning of the day?

Solution

Work backward from the final amount of money in your wallet, $19. Use the following steps.

1 Add back the $14 spent on dinner to the final amount in your wallet.

$19 + $14 = $33

2 Subtract away the $23 your friend paid you from the result in Step 1.

$33 − $23 = $10

3 Add back the $11 spent on a T-shirt to the result in Step 2.

$10 + $11 = $21

Answer You had $21 at the beginning of the day.

✔ Practice

Use the strategy *work backward* to solve the problem.

1. **Scheduling** On Saturday, you need to be at soccer practice at 3:00 P.M. It takes 25 minutes to walk to the soccer field. Before you leave, you need to mow your lawn, which takes 1 hour 15 minutes. By what time should you start mowing if you are to get to soccer practice on time?

2. **Finance** The table shows the changes in the price of a share of stock during a certain week. At the end of the week, the price is $23.52. What was the price at the beginning of the week?

Day of week	Monday	Tuesday	Wednesday	Thursday	Friday
Change in price	Down $.18	Up $.41	Up $1.09	Down $.37	Down $.03

3. **Books** You borrow a book from the library to read during your vacation. On the first day of vacation, you read one quarter of the book. On the second day, you read half of the remaining pages. On the third day, you finish the last 120 pages of the book. How many pages does the book have?

Break into Parts

Sometimes a problem cannot be solved in one step. Instead, you need to break the problem into smaller parts in order to find the solution.

Example Two baseball teams, the Hawks and the Tigers, are playing a best-of-five playoff series. For this type of series, the first team to win three games wins the series. In how many ways can the Hawks win the series?

Solution

Let W represent a game that the Hawks win, and let L represent a game that they lose. Break the problem into three cases.

Case 1: The Hawks win the series in 3 games.

In this case, there is only 1 possible sequence of wins and losses:

WWW

Case 2: The Hawks win the series in 4 games.

In this case, the Hawks must have 3 wins and 1 loss, and the last game must be a win. There are 3 possible sequences of wins and losses:

LWWW   WLWW   WWLW

Case 3: The Hawks win the series in 5 games.

In this case, the Hawks must have 3 wins and 2 losses, and the last game must be a win. There are 6 possible sequences of wins and losses:

LLWWW   LWLWW   LWWLW   WLLWW   WLWLW   WWLLW

Answer The number of ways in which the Hawks can win the series is the sum of the results from the three cases: $1 + 3 + 6 = 10$ ways.

✔ Practice

Use the strategy _break into parts_ to solve the problem.

1. **Volleyball** The varsity and junior varsity volleyball teams at a high school are playing a best-of-three series during practice. For this type of series, the first team to win two games wins the series. In how many ways can the varsity team win the series?

2. **Cell Phone** The base cost of a cell phone plan is $55.25 a month, which includes 600 minutes of calling time. You were billed $72.40 last month for using 649 minutes. What is the per-minute cost of exceeding the calling time included in the base cost?

3. **Omelets** A diner offers the following ingredients in its omelets: ham, cheese, onion, and mushrooms. How many different omelets with at least 2 ingredients are possible?

Extra Practice

Chapter 1

1.1 Evaluate the expression when $x = 9$, $y = 3$, and $z = 12$.

1. $17 - x$ **2.** $8y$ **3.** $z - y$ **4.** $\dfrac{z}{y}$

1.2 Write the power in words and as a repeated multiplication. Then evaluate the power.

5. 1^8 **6.** 11^3 **7.** 5^3 **8.** $(1.3)^2$

1.3 Evaluate the expression.

9. $9 \cdot 6 - 5 \cdot 8$ **10.** $\dfrac{49 - 11}{12 + 7}$ **11.** $6(14 + 4^2)$ **12.** $72 \div [(15 - 9) \cdot 2]$

1.4 Graph the integers on a number line. Then write the integers in order from least to greatest.

13. $-7, 0, -3, 9, 4$ **14.** $-1, -13, -10, 2, 5$ **15.** $-67, -19, -34, -51$

1.4 State the absolute value and the opposite of the number.

16. -98 **17.** 43 **18.** 15 **19.** -3

1.5 Find the sum.

20. $15 + (-18)$ **21.** $-17 + 56$ **22.** $-42 + (-31)$ **23.** $-28 + 16 + 34$

1.6 Find the difference.

24. $6 - 13$ **25.** $14 - (-9)$ **26.** $-8 - 15$ **27.** $-3 - (-22)$

1.7 Find the product or quotient.

28. $11(-6)$ **29.** $-4(-9)$ **30.** $\dfrac{-420}{-6}$ **31.** $-45 \div 15$

1.8 Give the coordinates of the point.

32. A **33.** B

34. C **35.** D

36. E **37.** F

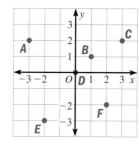

1.8 Plot the point in a coordinate plane. Describe the location of the point.

38. $M(0, -4)$ **39.** $N(5, 6)$ **40.** $P(-3, 2)$ **41.** $Q(-2, -4)$

Chapter 2

2.1 **Evaluate the expression. Justify each of your steps.**

1. $(17 + 9) + 3$ **2.** $(5.63)(2.45)(0)$ **3.** $0 + 8 \cdot 1$ **4.** $2(-18)(5)$

2.1 **Evaluate the expression when $x = -7$ and $y = 5$.**

5. $8xy$ **6.** $27 + 3y^2 + x$ **7.** $35 + 4x + y$ **8.** $12xy^2$

2.1 **Simplify the expression.**

9. $-4(11m)$ **10.** $(3a)(17)$ **11.** $b + (-14) + 35$ **12.** $8 + c + (-5)$

2.1 **Identify the property that the statement illustrates.**

13. $-5a + 0 = -5a$ **14.** $4^4 + 21 = 21 + 4^4$ **15.** $(3 \cdot 5) \cdot 6 = 3 \cdot (5 \cdot 6)$

2.2 **Use the distributive property to evaluate the expression.**

16. $4(8 - 13)$ **17.** $(6 + 12)3$ **18.** $-9(3 + 10)$ **19.** $(-5 - 2)(-6)$

2.2 **Use the distributive property to write an equivalent variable expression.**

20. $7(m - 5)$ **21.** $-3(5a + 3)$ **22.** $(15 + 4b)(-2)$ **23.** $(2 - 3z)6$

2.3 **Simplify the expression.**

24. $d + 7d$ **25.** $-5y + 8y - 2y$ **26.** $6x - (x - 1)$ **27.** $2(c + 4) + 3c$

28. $4m - 6m - 7m$ **29.** $-3b + 11b$ **30.** $-3(r + 2) - 3r$ **31.** $-p + 3(p - 5)$

2.4 **Solve the equation using mental math.**

32. $3 + x = 19$ **33.** $n - 9 = -4$ **34.** $32 = -8u$ **35.** $5 = \dfrac{55}{g}$

Solve the equation. Check your solution.

2.5 **36.** $y + 8 = 17$ **37.** $r - 13 = -5$ **38.** $18 = p - 4$ **39.** $-15 = 7 + u$

40. $742 + b = 534$ **41.** $157 = c + 48$ **42.** $173 = x - 23$ **43.** $j - 15 = -47$

2.6 **44.** $-15z = 0$ **45.** $-78 = 3g$ **46.** $17 = -t$ **47.** $-13w = -91$

48. $\dfrac{k}{14} = 5$ **49.** $\dfrac{s}{-9} = 16$ **50.** $-20 = \dfrac{x}{-17}$ **51.** $-7 = \dfrac{r}{50}$

2.7 **Perform the indicated operation.**

52. $6.3 + (-11.9)$ **53.** $-9.8 - 1.34$ **54.** $13.16 \div (-2.35)$ **55.** $3.7(-4.9)$

2.7 **Solve the equation. Check your solution.**

56. $-9.5 = \dfrac{u}{-2.72}$ **57.** $g + 4.6 = 19.3$ **58.** $-0.32b = 2.08$ **59.** $-12.3 = h - 5.47$

Chapter 3

Solve the equation. Check your solution.

3.1
1. $6m + 11 = 83$
2. $39 = 15a + 24$
3. $23 = 19k - 34$
4. $59 - 4n = 91$
5. $\dfrac{x}{8} + 12 = -5$
6. $5 = \dfrac{c}{-4} + 7$
7. $\dfrac{b}{3} - 13 = 14$
8. $-8 = -14 - \dfrac{d}{9}$

3.2
9. $11a + 9 - 3a = -7$
10. $4r + 41 + 5r = 104$
11. $32 = 8(p + 3)$
12. $42 = -7(j - 4)$
13. $6(7 - 4y) = 18$
14. $-3(2s + 5) = 15$
15. $17 + 5(t + 1) = 37$
16. $7h - 4(h - 3) = 33$
17. $49 = -6b + 9 + 2b$

3.3
18. $14k + 55 = 11k + 94$
19. $-4m - 7 = 8 - 9m$
20. $23f - 41 = 54f + 21$
21. $16z - 18 = 4 + 5z$
22. $d + 3 = 2(9 - d)$
23. $4(7c + 2) = 28c$
24. $6(x + 8) = 5x + 4$
25. $12n + 6 = 3(4n + 2)$
26. $18r - 7 = 3 + 8r$

3.3 Write the verbal sentence as an equation. Then solve the equation.

27. Ten plus 7 times a number is equal to 6 less than 5 times the number.

28. Eleven minus 4 times a number is equal to 6 plus the number.

3.4 Write an inequality represented by the graph.

29.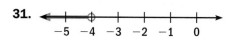

30.

31.

32.

Solve the inequality. Graph your solution.

3.4
33. $a + 3 < 10$
34. $u + 7 \geq 5$
35. $-5 \leq p - 2$
36. $41 > g + 45$
37. $19 \geq b - 29$
38. $7.9 < n - 5$
39. $k + 3.7 > 4$
40. $s + 4.2 \leq 7.8$

3.5
41. $\dfrac{b}{8} \leq 13$
42. $\dfrac{a}{-5} < 9$
43. $\dfrac{x}{4} \geq -2$
44. $\dfrac{d}{7} > 3$
45. $-5d > 40$
46. $7w \geq 84$
47. $-12 < 3t$
48. $-4z \leq -16$

3.5 Write the verbal sentence as an inequality. Then solve the inequality.

49. Three times a number is at most 18.
50. Nine times a number is greater than 36.
51. A number divided by -2 is less than 10.
52. A number divided by 5 is at least 20.

3.6 Solve the inequality. Graph your solution.

53. $3w + 8 > 17$
54. $8n - 21 \leq -5$
55. $43 < 31 - 2z$
56. $9 + 5d \geq 44$
57. $8 + \dfrac{c}{11} \leq 10$
58. $\dfrac{s}{4} - 9 > -15$
59. $-6r + 3 > 9 - 7r$
60. $3y - 7 \geq -32 + 8y$

Chapter 4

4.1 Tell whether the number is *prime* or *composite*.

1. 93   **2.** 76   **3.** 23   **4.** 53

4.1 Write the prime factorization of the number.

5. 72   **6.** 47   **7.** 96   **8.** 400

4.2 Find the greatest common factor of the numbers. Then tell whether the numbers are relatively prime.

9. 51, 63   **10.** 21, 44   **11.** 32, 110   **12.** 56, 136

4.2 Find the greatest common factor of the monomials.

13. $48y^2, 52y$ **14.** $16p, 68p$ **15.** $12s, 118s^4$ **16.** $3x, 9x^2, 12x^3$

4.3 Write the fraction in simplest form.

17. $\dfrac{15}{80}$ **18.** $\dfrac{8}{84}$ **19.** $\dfrac{28}{44}$ **20.** $\dfrac{38}{95}$

21. $\dfrac{14m^2}{21m^3}$ **22.** $\dfrac{36r}{6r^2s}$ **23.** $\dfrac{38abc}{4c^2}$ **24.** $\dfrac{50x^4}{12x}$

4.4 Find the least common multiple of the numbers.

25. 10, 15   **26.** 21, 28   **27.** 32, 60   **28.** 18, 45

4.4 Find the least common multiple of the monomials.

29. $5c, 18c^2$ **30.** $4s^3, 36s^2$ **31.** $10n^2p, 16np$ **32.** $57z^4, 39z^2$

4.5 Find the product or quotient. Write your answer using exponents.

33. $6^5 \cdot 6^9$ **34.** $12^3 \cdot 12^4 \cdot 12^2$ **35.** $\dfrac{4^{11}}{4^5}$ **36.** $\dfrac{3^8}{3}$

4.5 Simplify.

37. $4c^3 \cdot 5c^2$ **38.** $7d^5 \cdot d^2$ **39.** $\dfrac{6a^6}{a^3}$ **40.** $\dfrac{15r^7}{12r^4}$

4.6 Write the expression using only positive exponents.

41. 18^{-4} **42.** 7^{-8} **43.** s^3t^0 **44.** $5w^{-2}$

4.7 Write the number in scientific notation.

45. 16,000,000   **46.** 3,120,000,000   **47.** 0.00004   **48.** 0.0000078

4.7 Write the number in standard form.

49. 8.23×10^8 **50.** 4.367×10^5 **51.** 2.1×10^{-3} **52.** 7.893×10^{-7}

Chapter 5

5.1 Show that the number is rational by writing it as a quotient of two integers.

1. -4 **2.** 0.58 **3.** $3\frac{5}{16}$ **4.** 70

5.1 Write the fraction or mixed number as a decimal.

5. $\frac{3}{5}$ **6.** $-\frac{14}{9}$ **7.** $-6\frac{13}{25}$ **8.** $2\frac{5}{12}$

5.1 Write the decimal as a fraction or mixed number.

9. 0.34 **10.** -3.78 **11.** 9.27 **12.** $0.\overline{5}$

Find the sum or difference.

5.2 **13.** $-\frac{4}{11} + \frac{9}{11}$ **14.** $\frac{7}{18} - \frac{17}{18}$ **15.** $-4\frac{7}{15} - 2\frac{11}{15}$ **16.** $-9\frac{1}{3} + 1\frac{2}{3}$

5.3 **17.** $-\frac{3}{4} - \frac{2}{7}$ **18.** $\frac{7}{8} + \left(-\frac{3}{16}\right)$ **19.** $-3\frac{1}{6} + 6\frac{5}{22}$ **20.** $5\frac{2}{9} - 7\frac{8}{15}$

5.3 Simplify the expression.

21. $\frac{w}{12} + \frac{w}{15}$ **22.** $\frac{x}{21} - \frac{x}{3}$ **23.** $-\frac{5z}{14} + \frac{9z}{28}$ **24.** $\frac{2y}{25} - \frac{3y}{10}$

5.4 Find the product.

25. $\frac{3}{7} \cdot \frac{5}{18}$ **26.** $\frac{9}{10}\left(-\frac{5}{21}\right)$ **27.** $-24 \cdot \left(-\frac{7}{16}\right)$ **28.** $-3\frac{1}{3} \cdot 5\frac{13}{20}$

5.5 Find the quotient.

29. $\frac{5}{16} \div \frac{35}{48}$ **30.** $-\frac{11}{12} \div \frac{3}{8}$ **31.** $-7\frac{49}{54} \div 5\frac{5}{6}$ **32.** $-22 \div \left(-\frac{4}{11}\right)$

5.6 Solve the equation. Check your solution.

33. $\frac{6}{7}a = 18$ **34.** $\frac{5}{14}c = -\frac{1}{2}$ **35.** $\frac{2}{7}x - 5 = 17$ **36.** $\frac{4}{9} = \frac{1}{3}x - \frac{5}{9}$

5.7 Solve the equation by first clearing the fractions or the decimals.

37. $\frac{1}{4}x + \frac{1}{6} = -\frac{5}{12}$ **38.** $\frac{4}{7} = \frac{1}{8}x - 3$ **39.** $6.8x + 5.3 = 7$ **40.** $27.62 = 3.4x - 5.7$

5.7 Solve the inequality.

41. $-\frac{4}{5}p + 15 > \frac{3}{5}$ **42.** $\frac{1}{9}m - 2 \geq \frac{2}{3}$ **43.** $\frac{3}{4}z - \frac{3}{8} \leq \frac{1}{4}$ **44.** $\frac{1}{2} + \frac{4}{11}y < \frac{19}{22}$

Chapter 6

6.1   **Find the unit rate.**

1. $\dfrac{\$13.92}{8 \text{ gallons}}$ **2.** $\dfrac{58 \text{ mi}}{4 \text{ h}}$ **3.** $\dfrac{15 \text{ L}}{5 \text{ days}}$ **4.** $\dfrac{\$87.50}{5 \text{ tickets}}$

6.1   **Write the equivalent rate.**

5. $\dfrac{50 \text{ mi}}{1 \text{ h}} = \dfrac{? \text{ ft}}{1 \text{ h}}$ **6.** $\dfrac{\$58}{1 \text{ day}} = \dfrac{? \text{ dollars}}{1 \text{ week}}$ **7.** $\dfrac{440 \text{ ft}}{1 \text{ min}} = \dfrac{? \text{ ft}}{1 \text{ h}}$ **8.** $\dfrac{70 \text{ m}}{30 \text{ sec}} = \dfrac{? \text{ m}}{1 \text{ min}}$

Solve the proportion.

6.2   **9.** $\dfrac{4}{5} = \dfrac{x}{20}$ **10.** $\dfrac{5}{12} = \dfrac{a}{84}$ **11.** $\dfrac{z}{15} = \dfrac{12}{45}$ **12.** $\dfrac{c}{8} = \dfrac{28}{32}$

13. $\dfrac{8}{13} = \dfrac{w}{52}$ **14.** $\dfrac{3}{7} = \dfrac{d}{42}$ **15.** $\dfrac{b}{6} = \dfrac{75}{90}$ **16.** $\dfrac{n}{9} = \dfrac{56}{72}$

6.3   **17.** $\dfrac{12}{18} = \dfrac{2}{p}$ **18.** $\dfrac{24}{y} = \dfrac{21}{35}$ **19.** $\dfrac{36}{g} = \dfrac{27}{63}$ **20.** $\dfrac{3.8}{95} = \dfrac{5.7}{s}$

6.4   **In Exercises 21 and 22, the figures are similar. Find the ratio of the lengths of corresponding sides of figure A to figure B.**

21.

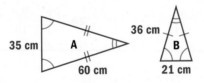

22.

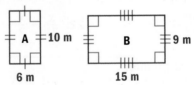

6.5   **23.** Given $LMNP \sim QRST$, find ST.   **24.** Given $\triangle ABC \sim \triangle DEF$, find DF.

 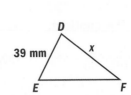

6.6   **A map has a scale of 1 inch : 25 miles. Use the given map distance to find the actual distance.**

25. 2 inches   **26.** 5 inches   **27.** 0.5 inch   **28.** 6.5 inches

6.7   **In Exercises 29–32, suppose you roll a number cube. Find the probability of the event.**

29. A multiple of 3   **30.** A multiple of 4   **31.** A factor of 6   **32.** An even number

6.8   **33.** You are working on a page for the yearbook and can choose one of 5 action photos, one of 3 group photos, and one of 6 individual photos. How many different groups of 3 photos can you choose?

Chapter 7

7.1 Write the percent as a fraction or the fraction as a percent.

1. 43%
2. 15%
3. $\frac{13}{20}$
4. $\frac{8}{25}$

7.1 Find the percent of the number.

5. 40% of 300
6. 25% of 28
7. 75% of 76
8. 90% of 430

7.2 Use a proportion to answer the question.

9. What percent of 140 is 28?
10. 15 is 60% of what number?

11. What number is 45% of 180?
12. What percent of 136 is 850?

7.3 Write the decimal as a percent or the percent as a decimal.

13. 0.045
14. 1.34
15. 7%
16. 0.25%

7.3 Write the fraction as a percent.

17. $\frac{7}{12}$
18. $\frac{13}{15}$
19. $\frac{15}{8}$
20. $\frac{11}{6}$

7.4 Use the percent equation to answer the question.

21. What number is 52% of 625?
22. What percent of 72 is 252?

23. 117 is 45% of what number?
24. What number is 0.5% of 3400?

7.5 Identify the percent of change as an *increase* or a *decrease*. Then find the percent of change.

25. Original: 40
New: 62
26. Original: 650
New: 806
27. Original: 92
New: 23
28. Original: 248
New: 217

7.6 Use the given information to find the new price.

29. Wholesale price: $130
Markup percent: 80%
30. Wholesale price: $14
Markup percent: 120%
31. Original price: $24
Discount percent: 30%

7.6 In Exercises 32–34, use the given information to find the total cost.

32. Original price: $90
Sales tax: 6%
33. Original price: $65
Sales tax: 5%
34. Original price: $34
Sales tax: 4%

7.7 **35.** A $400 bond earns 2% simple annual interest. After how many years will it earn $72 in interest?

7.7 **36.** You deposit $600 into a savings account that earns 3% interest compounded annually. Find the balance of the account after 5 years. Round your answer to the nearest cent.

Chapter 8

Represent the relation as a graph and as a mapping diagram. Then tell whether the relation is a function. Explain your reasoning.

1. $(3, 4), (-2, 5), (4, 3), (6, 4), (-3, -4)$

2. $(5, 6), (1, -3), (4, -2), (1, 4), (-2, -4)$

8.2 Graph the equation. Tell whether the equation is a function.

3. $y = -4x$ **4.** $y = 3$ **5.** $x = -2$ **6.** $y = 2x + 3$

8.3 Find the intercepts of the equation's graph. Then graph the equation.

7. $x - 2y = 10$ **8.** $2x + 6y = 12$ **9.** $3x + 5y = -15$ **10.** $y = -3x - 6$

8.4 Find the coordinates of two points on the line with the given equation. Then use the points to find the slope of the line.

11. $y = -4$ **12.** $y = \frac{1}{2}x + 7$ **13.** $x - 3y = 9$ **14.** $x = 6$

8.4 Find the slope of the line through the given points.

15. $(-1, 4), (3, 1)$ **16.** $(0, 8), (-2, -3)$ **17.** $(5, 6), (9, 10)$ **18.** $(4, -5), (7, -5)$

8.5 Identify the slope and *y*-intercept of the line with the given equation. Use the slope and *y*-intercept to graph the equation.

19. $y = 4x - 1$ **20.** $y = -\frac{2}{3}x + 4$ **21.** $10x - 2y = 4$ **22.** $x + 7y = 21$

23. $y = \frac{1}{4}x + 2$ **24.** $y = -2x - 3$ **25.** $2x + 5y = 15$ **26.** $3x - 4y = 4$

8.6 Write an equation of the line that is parallel to the given line and passes through the given point.

27. $y = -4x + 3; (0, -2)$ **28.** $y = -\frac{4}{5}x - 2; (0, 3)$

29. $y = \frac{7}{3}x - 6; (0, -1)$ **30.** $y = x + 4; (0, -5)$

8.7 Graph the function.

31. $f(x) = 6x$ **32.** $g(x) = 3x - 2$ **33.** $h(x) = \frac{1}{4}x + 5$ **34.** $r(x) = -4x - 7$

8.8 Solve the linear system by graphing.

35. $y = -4x + 3$ **36.** $y = 5x - 2$ **37.** $2x - 3y = 12$ **38.** $5x + 4y = 20$
$\ y = x - 7$ $\ y = -2x + 5$ $\ x - y = 3$ $\ y = 3x + 5$

8.9 Graph the inequality in a coordinate plane.

39. $y \geq 2x - 2$ **40.** $x - 2y > -14$ **41.** $x < -1$ **42.** $y \leq 2$

Chapter 9

9.1 **Find the square roots of the number.**

1. 49   **2.** 2500   **3.** 324   **4.** 441

9.1 **Solve the equation.**

5. $x^2 = 121$ **6.** $3y^2 = 75$ **7.** $2a^2 = 72$ **8.** $6c^2 = 486$

9.2 **Simplify the expression.**

9. $\sqrt{162}$ **10.** $\sqrt{\dfrac{12}{25}}$ **11.** $\sqrt{\dfrac{32a^2}{81}}$ **12.** $\sqrt{54x}$

9.3 **Find the unknown length. Write your answer in simplest form.**

13. 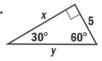   **14.**   **15.**   **16.**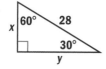

9.4 **Use a number line to order the numbers from least to greatest.**

17. $\sqrt{30}, 5.8, \dfrac{46}{9}, 2\sqrt{7}$ **18.** $\dfrac{4}{5}, -1.5, -\sqrt{2}, 0$

19. $-\sqrt{36}, -6.9, -3\sqrt{5}, -\dfrac{19}{3}$ **20.** $3\sqrt{5}, 7.2, \dfrac{22}{3}, \sqrt{47}$

9.5 **Find the midpoint of the segment with the given endpoints. Then find the distance between the points. Write your answer in simplest form.**

21. $(4, 2), (6, 10)$ **22.** $(-3, 5), (4, 9)$ **23.** $(0, -4), (-2, 11)$ **24.** $(-1, -2), (6, -8)$

9.6 **Find the unknown lengths. Write your answers in simplest form.**

25.   **26.** 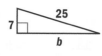   **27.**   **28.**

Find the value of x. Round to the nearest tenth.

9.7   **29.** 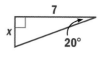   **30.**   **31.** 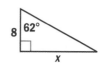   **32.**

9.8   **33.**   **34.**   **35.**   **36.**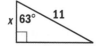

Chapter 10

10.1 Find the value of *x*. Then classify the triangle by its angle measures.

1.
$(2x + 11)°$
$94°$
$x°$

2.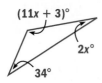
$(11x + 3)°$
$2x°$
$34°$

3.
$90°$
$x°$
$(x + 20)°$

4.
$2x°$
$40°$
$3x°$

10.2 Find the value of *x*.

5.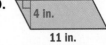
$138°$ $x°$
$x°$
$(3x + 12)°$

6.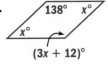
$x°$ $127°$
$x°$
$(2x + 21)°$

7.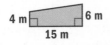
$(x - 58)°$ $61°$
$x°$ $x°$

8.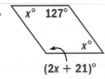
$(x - 2)°$
$x°$
$80°$ $(2x + 14)°$

10.3 Find the area of the parallelogram or trapezoid.

9.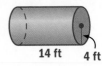
4 in.
11 in.

10.
4 m   6 m
15 m

11.
24 ft
5 ft
12 ft

12.
9 cm   6 cm

10.4 For a circle with the given radius *r* or diameter *d*, find the area and circumference of the circle. Round to the nearest whole number.

13. $r = 31$ in.   **14.** $r = 3$ m   **15.** $d = 28$ cm   **16.** $d = 16$ yd

10.5 Draw a net for the prism or cylinder. Then find the surface area. Round to the nearest whole number.

17.
14 ft   4 ft

18.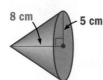
3 m
16 m
8 m

19.
6 cm
8 cm
11 cm

20.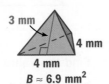
7 in.
6 in.

10.6 Find the surface area of the regular pyramid or cone. Round to the nearest whole number.

21.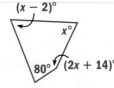
17 yd
12 yd
12 yd

22.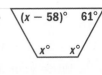
8 cm   5 cm

23.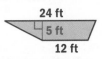
10 ft
22 ft

24.
3 mm
4 mm
4 mm
$B \approx 6.9$ mm^2

Find the volume of the solid. Round to the nearest whole number.

10.7 **25.** A cylinder with a radius of 4 cm and a height of 5 cm

26. A rectangular prism with a height of 4 ft, a width of 9 ft, and a length of 11 ft

10.8 **27.** A square pyramid with a base side length of 6 yd and a height of 8 yd

28. A cone with a radius of 7 in. and a height of 10 in.

Chapter 11

11.1 **1.** Make a stem-and-leaf plot and a histogram of the following numbers of participants in twelve community service days sponsored by a school.

35, 42, 21, 31, 42, 23, 12, 34, 36, 40, 25, 22

11.2 **2.** Make a box-and-whisker plot of the following monthly average high temperatures (in degrees Fahrenheit) for Atlanta, Georgia.

53, 57, 65, 73, 80, 87, 89, 88, 82, 73, 63, 55

11.3 **Tell whether the data are *numerical* or *categorical*. Then tell which data display(s) you would use to display the data. Explain your reasoning.**

3. A teacher recorded the test score of each student in a class.

4. A student recorded the colors of the shirts of students in her class.

11.4 **In Exercises 5 and 6, tell whether the question is potentially biased. Explain your answer. If the question is biased, rewrite it so that it is not.**

5. Don't you think that having a school dance is a good idea?

6. How many times a week do you exercise?

11.5 **7.** A town's population is 12,500. In a random sample of 300 townspeople, 204 said they support the building of a new movie theater. Predict the number of townspeople who would support the building of a new movie theater.

11.6 **Evaluate the factorial.**

8. $13!$ **9.** $0!$ **10.** $7!$ **11.** $2!$

11.6 **Find the number of permutations.**

12. $_4P_4$ **13.** $_{13}P_2$ **14.** $_{20}P_3$ **15.** $_8P_1$

11.7 **Find the number of combinations.**

16. $_7C_4$ **17.** $_{12}C_8$ **18.** $_{15}C_1$ **19.** $_3C_3$

11.8 **In Exercises 20 and 21, events A and B are overlapping. Find $P(A$ or $B)$.**

20. $P(A) = \frac{7}{30}$, $P(B) = \frac{11}{30}$, $P(A$ and $B) = \frac{1}{10}$ **21.** $P(A) = \frac{2}{5}$, $P(B) = \frac{1}{5}$, $P(A$ and $B) = \frac{1}{20}$

11.9 **22.** A bag contains 5 red marbles, 11 blue marbles, and 6 yellow marbles. You randomly draw a marble from the bag. Then you randomly draw another marble without replacing the first marble. Find the probability of drawing a blue marble, then a red marble.

Chapter 12

12.1 Write the expression as a polynomial in standard form.

1. $7x - 3 - 10x + 9$

2. $-2z^2 + 4 - 5z^2$

3. $4y^2 - 2y - 3(y^2 - 6)$

4. $5a^2 + 2(2 - 3a^2) + 7$

12.2 Find the sum or difference.

5. $(x^2 - 4x + 7) + (-2x^2 + 7x + 9)$

6. $(4c^3 - 6c - 1) + (-5c^2 + 3c - 9)$

7. $(3w^3 + 4w^2 + 8) - (5w^3 - 4w - 6)$

8. $(6s^2 - 8s - 3) - (s^3 + 2s^2 + 7s - 4)$

9. $(6g^4 - 7g^2) + (4g^3 - 3g^2 + 2)$

10. $(8n^2 - 5) + (n^2 - 3n)$

11. $(5d^3 + 2) - (4d^3 - 5)$

12. $(4f^2 - 7f + 11) - (9f^2 - 13)$

12.3 Find the product.

13. $(8f + 9)4f$

14. $-6p^2(p^3 - 5)$

15. $-2t(t^2 - 3t + 10)$

16. $(y^3 + 2y^2 - 3)5y$

12.3 Find the quotient.

17. $\dfrac{18n^2 - 21n}{-3n}$

18. $\dfrac{8r^4 + 2r^3 - 12r^2}{2r}$

19. $\dfrac{5z^6 - z^5 - 3z^4}{z^2}$

20. $\dfrac{-6w^6 + 4w^4 + 2w^2}{-2w^2}$

12.4 Find the product.

21. $(x - 4)(3x + 2)$

22. $(4z - 2)(2z - 1)$

23. $(5a + 3)^2$

24. $(-2c - 7)(3c - 8)$

12.5 Simplify the expression. Write your answer using positive exponents.

25. $(-3g)^3$

26. $\left(\dfrac{5}{a}\right)^4$

27. $(6^{-5})^4$

28. $(b^8)^{-3}$

12.5 Simplify the expression. Write your answer in scientific notation. Round the decimal part of your answer to the nearest hundredth.

29. $(4.5 \times 10^{-7})^3$

30. $(8.7 \times 10^3)^5$

31. $(1.4 \times 10^4)^2$

32. $(6.3 \times 10^{-6})^4$

12.6 Make a table of values for the given function. Then graph the function.

33. $y = 3x^2 + 4$

34. $y = -2x^2 - 3$

35. $y = -\dfrac{1}{2}x^2 + 5$

36. $y = \dfrac{3}{4}x^2 - 1$

12.7 Graph the function.

37. $y = 4(3)^x$

38. $y = 6\left(\dfrac{1}{3}\right)^x$

39. $y = 2\left(\dfrac{1}{4}\right)^x$

40. $y = 10(4)^x$

12.8 Tell whether the sequence is *arithmetic* or *geometric*. Then find the common difference or the common ratio, and write the next three terms.

41. $-9, -5, -1, 3, \ldots$

42. $-3, 6, -12, 24, \ldots$

43. $224, 112, 56, 28, \ldots$

44. $289, 252, 215, 178, \ldots$

Chapter 13

13.1 Tell whether the angles are *complementary*, *supplementary*, or *neither*.

1. $m\angle 1 = 42°$
$m\angle 2 = 48°$

2. $m\angle 1 = 138°$
$m\angle 2 = 52°$

3. $m\angle 1 = 123°$
$m\angle 2 = 57°$

4. $m\angle 1 = 31°$
$m\angle 2 = 59°$

13.2 Tell whether the angles in the diagram are *corresponding*, *alternate interior*, or *alternate exterior* angles.

5. $\angle 2$ and $\angle 6$

6. $\angle 4$ and $\angle 5$

7. $\angle 1$ and $\angle 8$

8. $\angle 3$ and $\angle 7$

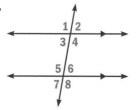

13.3 Find the measure of an interior angle and the measure of an exterior angle for the regular polygon. Round to the nearest tenth, if necessary.

9. Heptagon　　　**10.** Hexagon　　　**11.** 12-gon　　　**12.** 9-gon

13.4 The vertices of a polygon are given. Draw the polygon. Then find the coordinates of the vertices of the image after the specified translation, and draw the image.

13. $A(-2, -1), B(-3, 2), C(-1, 4); (x, y) \rightarrow (x + 4, y - 3)$

14. $P(1, -2), Q(-1, 1), R(2, 2), S(4, -2); (x, y) \rightarrow (x - 3, y - 1)$

13.5 The vertices of a polygon are given. Draw the polygon. Then find the coordinates of the vertices of the image after the specified reflection, and draw the image.

15. $A(-3, -1), B(2, -2), C(-1, -4)$; reflection in the x-axis

16. $P(1, 4), Q(4, 3), R(4, 0), S(1, 1)$; reflection in the y-axis

13.6 Tell whether the transformation is a rotation about the origin. If so, give the angle and direction of rotation.

17.

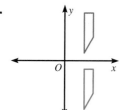

18.

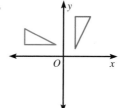

19.

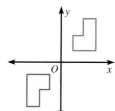

13.7 The vertices of a polygon are given. Draw the polygon. Then find the coordinates of the vertices of the image after a dilation having the given scale factor, and draw the image.

20. $R(-3, 0), S(6, 3), T(3, -3); k = \dfrac{1}{3}$

21. $A(-2, 2), B(1, 3), C(1, -1), D(-2, -1); k = 2$

Table of Symbols

Symbol	Meaning	Page
$3 \cdot x$ $3x$ $3(x)$	3 times x	5
$\dfrac{n}{2}$	n divided by 2	6
$\ldots$	continues on	9
4^3	4 to the third power, or $4 \cdot 4 \cdot 4$	10
$(\ )$	parentheses— a grouping symbol	17
$[\ ]$	brackets—a grouping symbol	17
-3	negative 3	22
$\lvert a \rvert$	absolute value of a number a	23
$-a$	the opposite of a number a	23
(x, y)	ordered pair	47
$=$	equals, is equal to	85
$\overset{?}{=}$	is equal to?	85
$\neq$	is not equal to	85
$<$	is less than	138
$>$	is greater than	138
$\geq$	is greater than or equal to	138
$\leq$	is less than or equal to	138
$1.1\overline{6}$	repeating decimal 1.16666...	220
$a:b, \dfrac{a}{b}$	ratio of a to b	269
$\overleftrightarrow{AB}$	line AB	285
$\overline{AB}$	line segment AB, or segment AB	285
AB	length of segment AB	285

Symbol	Meaning	Page
$\overrightarrow{AB}$	ray AB	285
$\angle ABC, \angle B$	angle ABC, angle with vertex B	285
$m\angle B$	measure of angle B	285
$\triangle ABC$	triangle with vertices A, B, and C	286
$\cong$	is congruent to	286
$\sim$	is similar to	288
$\%$	percent	329
$\parallel$	is parallel to	410
$\longleftrightarrow \longleftrightarrow$	parallel lines	410
$\perp$	is perpendicular to	410
$f(x)$	the value of the function f at x	426
$\sqrt{a}$	the positive square root of a number a where $a \geq 0$	453
$\pm$	plus or minus	453
$\sqrt[3]{a}$	the cube root of a number a	457
π	pi—a number approximately equal to 3.14	528
$3!$	3 factorial, or $3 \cdot 2 \cdot 1$	615
$_8P_3$	permutations of 8 objects taken 3 at a time	616
$_5C_2$	combinations of 5 objects taken 2 at a time	621
A'	the image of point A	729
$\approx$	is approximately equal to	771
$\llcorner$	right angle	793

Table of Measures

TIME

60 seconds (sec) = 1 minute (min)
60 minutes = 1 hour (h)
24 hours = 1 day (d)
7 days = 1 week (wk)
4 weeks (approx.) = 1 month

$\left.\begin{array}{r}365 \text{ days} \\ 52 \text{ weeks (approx.)} \\ 12 \text{ months}\end{array}\right\}$ = 1 year

10 years = 1 decade
100 years = 1 century

METRIC

Length

10 millimeters (mm) = 1 centimeter (cm)

$\left.\begin{array}{r}100 \text{ cm} \\ 1000 \text{ mm}\end{array}\right\}$ = 1 meter (m)

1000 m = 1 kilometer (km)

Area

100 square millimeters = 1 square centimeter
(mm^2) (cm^2)
$10{,}000 \text{ cm}^2 = 1$ square meter (m^2)
$10{,}000 \text{ m}^2 = 1$ hectare (ha)

Volume

1000 cubic millimeters = 1 cubic centimeter
(mm^3) (cm^3)
$1{,}000{,}000 \text{ cm}^3 = 1$ cubic meter (m^3)

Liquid Capacity

$\left.\begin{array}{r}1000 \text{ milliliters (mL)} \\ 1000 \text{ cubic centimeters } (\text{cm}^3)\end{array}\right\}$ = 1 liter (L)

1000 L = 1 kiloliter (kL)

Mass

1000 milligrams (mg) = 1 gram (g)
1000 g = 1 kilogram (kg)
1000 kg = 1 metric ton (t)

Temperature   Degrees Celsius (°C)

0°C = freezing point of water
37°C = normal body temperature
100°C = boiling point of water

UNITED STATES CUSTOMARY

Length

12 inches (in.) = 1 foot (ft)

$\left.\begin{array}{r}36 \text{ in.} \\ 3 \text{ ft}\end{array}\right\}$ = 1 yard (yd)

$\left.\begin{array}{r}5280 \text{ ft} \\ 1760 \text{ yd}\end{array}\right\}$ = 1 mile (mi)

Area

144 square inches $(\text{in.}^2) = 1$ square foot (ft^2)
$9 \text{ ft}^2 = 1$ square yard (yd^2)

$\left.\begin{array}{r}43{,}560 \text{ ft}^2 \\ 4840 \text{ yd}^2\end{array}\right\}$ = 1 acre (A)

Volume

1728 cubic inches $(\text{in.}^3) = 1$ cubic foot (ft^3)
$27 \text{ ft}^3 = 1$ cubic yard (yd^3)

Liquid Capacity

8 fluid ounces (fl oz) = 1 cup (c)
2 c = 1 pint (pt)
2 pt = 1 quart (qt)
4 qt = 1 gallon (gal)

Weight

16 ounces (oz) = 1 pound (lb)
2000 lb = 1 ton

Temperature   Degrees Fahrenheit (°F)

32°F = freezing point of water
98.6°F = normal body temperature
212°F = boiling point of water

Table of Measures

Table of Formulas

Geometric Formulas

Rectangle (p. 69)

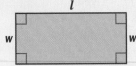

Area
$A = lw$

Perimeter
$P = 2l + 2w$

Square (p. 69)

Area
$A = s^2$

Perimeter
$P = 4s$

Triangle (p. 70)

Area
$A = \frac{1}{2}bh$

Pythagorean Theorem (p. 465)

In a right triangle, $a^2 + b^2 = c^2$ where a and b are the lengths of the legs and c is the length of the hypotenuse.

Parallelogram (p. 521)

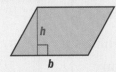

Area
$A = bh$

Trapezoid (p. 522)

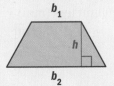

Area
$A = \frac{1}{2}(b_1 + b_2)h$

Circle (pp. 528, 529)

Circumference
$C = \pi d$ or
$C = 2\pi r$

Area
$A = \pi r^2$

Prism (pp. 539, 552)

Surface Area
$S = 2B + Ph$

Volume
$V = Bh$

Cylinder (pp. 540, 553)

Surface Area
$S = 2\pi r^2 + 2\pi rh$

Volume
$V = \pi r^2 h$

Pyramid (pp. 545, 558)

Surface Area
$S = B + \frac{1}{2}Pl$

Volume
$V = \frac{1}{3}Bh$

Cone (pp. 546, 558)

Surface Area
$S = \pi r^2 + \pi rl$

Volume
$V = \frac{1}{3}Bh$
$= \frac{1}{3}\pi r^2 h$

Sphere (pp. 548, 562)

Surface Area
$S = 4\pi r^2$

Volume
$V = \frac{4}{3}\pi r^3$

Table of Formulas

Other Formulas

Distance traveled (p. 77)	$d = rt$ where d is distance, r is rate, and t is time
Probability of an event (p. 306)	The probability of an event when all the outcomes are equally likely is: $P(\text{event}) = \dfrac{\text{Number of favorable outcomes}}{\text{Number of possible outcomes}}$
Experimental probability (p. 307)	The experimental probability of an event is: $P(\text{event}) = \dfrac{\text{Number of successes}}{\text{Number of trials}}$
Simple interest (p. 362)	$I = Prt$ where I is simple interest, P is the principal, r is the annual interest rate (written as a decimal), and t is the time in years
Compound interest (p. 364)	$A = P(1 + r)^t$ where A is the balance, P is the principal, r is the annual interest rate (written as a decimal), and t is the time in years
Distance formula (p. 476)	The distance d between two points (x_1, y_1) and (x_2, y_2) is given by $d = \sqrt{(x_2 - x_1)^2 + (y_2 - y_1)^2}$.
Midpoint formula (p. 478)	The coordinates of the midpoint M of a segment with endpoints $A(x_1, y_1)$ and $B(x_2, y_2)$ are given by $M = \left(\dfrac{x_1 + x_2}{2}, \dfrac{y_1 + y_2}{2} \right).$
Slope formula (p. 478)	If points $A(x_1, y_1)$ and $B(x_2, y_2)$ do not lie on a vertical line, then the slope of $\overleftrightarrow{AB}$ is $\dfrac{y_2 - y_1}{x_2 - x_1}$.
Permutations (p. 616)	The number of permutations of n objects taken r at a time can be written as ${}_nP_r$ where ${}_nP_r = \dfrac{n!}{(n - r)!}$.
Combinations (p. 621)	The number of combinations of n objects taken r at a time can be written as ${}_nC_r$ where ${}_nC_r = \dfrac{{}_nP_r}{r!}$.
Probability of disjoint or overlapping events (pp. 628, 629)	If A and B are disjoint events, then $P(A \text{ or } B) = P(A) + P(B)$. If A and B are overlapping events, then $P(A \text{ or } B) = P(A) + P(B) - P(A \text{ and } B)$.
Probability of independent or dependent events (pp. 635, 636)	If A and B are independent events, then $P(A \text{ and } B) = P(A) \cdot P(B)$. If A and B are dependent events, then $P(A \text{ and } B) = P(A) \cdot P(B \text{ given } A)$.

Table of Formulas

Table of Properties

Properties of Addition and Multiplication

Inverse Properties (pp. 30, 247) The sum of a number and its additive inverse, or opposite, is 0. The product of a nonzero number and its multiplicative inverse, or reciprocal, is 1.	$a + (-a) = 0$ $\dfrac{a}{b} \cdot \dfrac{b}{a} = 1 \ (a \neq 0, b \neq 0)$
Commutative Properties (p. 63) In a sum, you can add the numbers in any order. In a product, you can multiply the numbers in any order.	$a + b = b + a$ $ab = ba$
Associative Properties (p. 63) Changing the grouping of the numbers in a sum does not change the sum. Changing the grouping of the numbers in a product does not change the product.	$(a + b) + c = a + (b + c)$ $(ab)c = a(bc)$
Identity Properties (p. 64) The sum of a number and the additive identity, 0, is the number. The product of a number and the multiplicative identity, 1, is the number.	$a + 0 = a$ $a \cdot 1 = a$
Distributive Property (p. 71) You can multiply a number and a sum by multiplying each term of the sum by the number and then adding these products. The same property applies to subtraction.	$a(b + c) = ab + ac$ $a(b - c) = ab - ac$

Properties of Equality

Subtraction Property of Equality (p. 91) Subtracting the same number from each side of an equation produces an equivalent equation.	If $x + a = b$, then $x + a - a = b - a$, or $x = b - a$.
Addition Property of Equality (p. 92) Adding the same number to each side of an equation produces an equivalent equation.	If $x - a = b$, then $x - a + a = b + a$, or $x = b + a$.
Division Property of Equality (p. 97) Dividing each side of an equation by the same nonzero number produces an equivalent equation.	If $ax = b$ and $a \neq 0$, then $\dfrac{ax}{a} = \dfrac{b}{a}$, or $x = \dfrac{b}{a}$.
Multiplication Property of Equality (p. 98) Multiplying each side of an equation by the same nonzero number produces an equivalent equation.	If $\dfrac{x}{a} = b$ and $a \neq 0$, then $a \cdot \dfrac{x}{a} = a \cdot b$, or $x = ab$.

Table of Properties

Properties of Inequality

Addition and Subtraction Properties of Inequality (p. 139) Adding or subtracting the same number on each side of an inequality produces an equivalent inequality.	If $a < b$, then $a + c < b + c$ and $a - c < b - c$. If $a > b$, then $a + c > b + c$ and $a - c > b - c$.
Multiplication and Division Properties of Inequality (pp. 144, 145) Multiplying or dividing each side of an inequality by a *positive* number produces an equivalent inequality. Multiplying or dividing each side of an inequality by a *negative* number and *reversing the direction of the inequality symbol* produces an equivalent inequality.	If $a < b$ and $c > 0$, then $ac < bc$ and $\dfrac{a}{c} < \dfrac{b}{c}$. If $a < b$ and $c < 0$, then $ac > bc$ and $\dfrac{a}{c} > \dfrac{b}{c}$.

Properties of Exponents

Product of Powers Property (p. 194) To multiply powers with the same base, add their exponents.	$a^m \cdot a^n = a^{m + n}$
Quotient of Powers Property (p. 195) To divide powers with the same nonzero base, subtract the denominator's exponent from the numerator's exponent.	$\dfrac{a^m}{a^n} = a^{m - n}, a \neq 0$
Power of a Product Property (p. 674) To find the power of a product, find the power of each factor and multiply.	$(ab)^m = a^m b^m$
Power of a Quotient Property (p. 674) To find the power of a quotient, find the power of the numerator and the power of the denominator and divide.	$\left(\dfrac{a}{b}\right)^m = \dfrac{a^m}{b^m}, b \neq 0$
Power of a Power Property (p. 675) To find the power of a power, multiply the exponents.	$(a^m)^n = a^{mn}$

Other Properties

Cross Products Property (p. 281) The cross products of a proportion are equal.	If $\dfrac{a}{b} = \dfrac{c}{d}$ $(b, d \neq 0)$, then $ad = bc$.
Product Property of Square Roots (p. 458) The square root of a product is equal to the product of the square roots of the factors.	$\sqrt{ab} = \sqrt{a} \cdot \sqrt{b}, a \geq 0$ and $b \geq 0$
Quotient Properties of Square Roots (p. 459) The square root of a quotient is equal to the quotient of the square root of the numerator and the square root of the denominator.	$\sqrt{\dfrac{a}{b}} = \dfrac{\sqrt{a}}{\sqrt{b}}, a \geq 0$ and $b > 0$

Table of Squares and Square Roots

No.	Square	Sq. Root	No.	Square	Sq. Root	No.	Square	Sq. Root
1	1	1.000	51	2601	7.141	101	10,201	10.050
2	4	1.414	52	2704	7.211	102	10,404	10.100
3	9	1.732	53	2809	7.280	103	10,609	10.149
4	16	2.000	54	2916	7.348	104	10,816	10.198
5	25	2.236	55	3025	7.416	105	11,025	10.247
6	36	2.449	56	3136	7.483	106	11,236	10.296
7	49	2.646	57	3249	7.550	107	11,449	10.344
8	64	2.828	58	3364	7.616	108	11,664	10.392
9	81	3.000	59	3481	7.681	109	11,881	10.440
10	100	3.162	60	3600	7.746	110	12,100	10.488
11	121	3.317	61	3721	7.810	111	12,321	10.536
12	144	3.464	62	3844	7.874	112	12,544	10.583
13	169	3.606	63	3969	7.937	113	12,769	10.630
14	196	3.742	64	4096	8.000	114	12,996	10.677
15	225	3.873	65	4225	8.062	115	13,225	10.724
16	256	4.000	66	4356	8.124	116	13,456	10.770
17	289	4.123	67	4489	8.185	117	13,689	10.817
18	324	4.243	68	4624	8.246	118	13,924	10.863
19	361	4.359	69	4761	8.307	119	14,161	10.909
20	400	4.472	70	4900	8.367	120	14,400	10.954
21	441	4.583	71	5041	8.426	121	14,641	11.000
22	484	4.690	72	5184	8.485	122	14,884	11.045
23	529	4.796	73	5329	8.544	123	15,129	11.091
24	576	4.899	74	5476	8.602	124	15,376	11.136
25	625	5.000	75	5625	8.660	125	15,625	11.180
26	676	5.099	76	5776	8.718	126	15,876	11.225
27	729	5.196	77	5929	8.775	127	16,129	11.269
28	784	5.292	78	6084	8.832	128	16,384	11.314
29	841	5.385	79	6241	8.888	129	16,641	11.358
30	900	5.477	80	6400	8.944	130	16,900	11.402
31	961	5.568	81	6561	9.000	131	17,161	11.446
32	1024	5.657	82	6724	9.055	132	17,424	11.489
33	1089	5.745	83	6889	9.110	133	17,689	11.533
34	1156	5.831	84	7056	9.165	134	17,956	11.576
35	1225	5.916	85	7225	9.220	135	18,225	11.619
36	1296	6.000	86	7396	9.274	136	18,496	11.662
37	1369	6.083	87	7569	9.327	137	18,769	11.705
38	1444	6.164	88	7744	9.381	138	19,044	11.747
39	1521	6.245	89	7921	9.434	139	19,321	11.790
40	1600	6.325	90	8100	9.487	140	19,600	11.832
41	1681	6.403	91	8281	9.539	141	19,881	11.874
42	1764	6.481	92	8464	9.592	142	20,164	11.916
43	1849	6.557	93	8649	9.644	143	20,449	11.958
44	1936	6.633	94	8836	9.695	144	20,736	12.000
45	2025	6.708	95	9025	9.747	145	21,025	12.042
46	2116	6.782	96	9216	9.798	146	21,316	12.083
47	2209	6.856	97	9409	9.849	147	21,609	12.124
48	2304	6.928	98	9604	9.899	148	21,904	12.166
49	2401	7.000	99	9801	9.950	149	22,201	12.207
50	2500	7.071	100	10,000	10.000	150	22,500	12.247

Squares and Square Roots

Table of Trigonometric Ratios

Angle	Sine	Cosine	Tangent
1°	.0175	.9998	.0175
2°	.0349	.9994	.0349
3°	.0523	.9986	.0524
4°	.0698	.9976	.0699
5°	.0872	.9962	.0875
6°	.1045	.9945	.1051
7°	.1219	.9925	.1228
8°	.1392	.9903	.1405
9°	.1564	.9877	.1584
10°	.1736	.9848	.1763
11°	.1908	.9816	.1944
12°	.2079	.9781	.2126
13°	.2250	.9744	.2309
14°	.2419	.9703	.2493
15°	.2588	.9659	.2679
16°	.2756	.9613	.2867
17°	.2924	.9563	.3057
18°	.3090	.9511	.3249
19°	.3256	.9455	.3443
20°	.3420	.9397	.3640
21°	.3584	.9336	.3839
22°	.3746	.9272	.4040
23°	.3907	.9205	.4245
24°	.4067	.9135	.4452
25°	.4226	.9063	.4663
26°	.4384	.8988	.4877
27°	.4540	.8910	.5095
28°	.4695	.8829	.5317
29°	.4848	.8746	.5543
30°	.5000	.8660	.5774
31°	.5150	.8572	.6009
32°	.5299	.8480	.6249
33°	.5446	.8387	.6494
34°	.5592	.8290	.6745
35°	.5736	.8192	.7002
36°	.5878	.8090	.7265
37°	.6018	.7986	.7536
38°	.6157	.7880	.7813
39°	.6293	.7771	.8098
40°	.6428	.7660	.8391
41°	.6561	.7547	.8693
42°	.6691	.7431	.9004
43°	.6820	.7314	.9325
44°	.6947	.7193	.9657
45°	.7071	.7071	1.0000

Angle	Sine	Cosine	Tangent
46°	.7193	.6947	1.0355
47°	.7314	.6820	1.0724
48°	.7431	.6691	1.1106
49°	.7547	.6561	1.1504
50°	.7660	.6428	1.1918
51°	.7771	.6293	1.2349
52°	.7880	.6157	1.2799
53°	.7986	.6018	1.3270
54°	.8090	.5878	1.3764
55°	.8192	.5736	1.4281
56°	.8290	.5592	1.4826
57°	.8387	.5446	1.5399
58°	.8480	.5299	1.6003
59°	.8572	.5150	1.6643
60°	.8660	.5000	1.7321
61°	.8746	.4848	1.8040
62°	.8829	.4695	1.8807
63°	.8910	.4540	1.9626
64°	.8988	.4384	2.0503
65°	.9063	.4226	2.1445
66°	.9135	.4067	2.2460
67°	.9205	.3907	2.3559
68°	.9272	.3746	2.4751
69°	.9336	.3584	2.6051
70°	.9397	.3420	2.7475
71°	.9455	.3256	2.9042
72°	.9511	.3090	3.0777
73°	.9563	.2924	3.2709
74°	.9613	.2756	3.4874
75°	.9659	.2588	3.7321
76°	.9703	.2419	4.0108
77°	.9744	.2250	4.3315
78°	.9781	.2079	4.7046
79°	.9816	.1908	5.1446
80°	.9848	.1736	5.6713
81°	.9877	.1564	6.3138
82°	.9903	.1392	7.1154
83°	.9925	.1219	8.1443
84°	.9945	.1045	9.5144
85°	.9962	.0872	11.4301
86°	.9976	.0698	14.3007
87°	.9986	.0523	19.0811
88°	.9994	.0349	28.6363
89°	.9998	.0175	57.2900

Trigonometric Ratios

Absolute Value Equations

GOAL Solve absolute value equations.

Recall that the *absolute value* of a number a, written $|a|$, is the distance between a and 0 on a number line. An **absolute value equation** is an equation that involves the absolute value of a variable or variable expression. For example, $|x| = 6$ and $|x - 3| = 7$ are absolute value equations. You can solve an absolute value equation using mental math or using algebra.

Example 1 *Using Mental Math*

Use mental math to solve $|x| = 6$.

Ask yourself, "What number(s) are 6 units from the origin?" The number line shows that both -6 and 6 are 6 units from the origin.

Answer The solutions are 6 and -6.

Example 2 *Solving an Absolute Value Equation*

Solve $|x - 3| = 7$.

Because $|x - 3| = 7$, the expression $x - 3$ can be equal to 7 or -7.

$$|x - 3| = 7$$

$x - 3 = 7$ *or* $x - 3 = -7$		**Expression can equal 7 or -7.**
$x = 10$ *or* $x = -4$		**Add 3 to each side.**

Answer The solutions are 10 and -4.

✓Check Use substitution to check the solutions.

$|x - 3| = 7$	$|x - 3| = 7$	**Write original equation.**
$|10 - 3| \stackrel{?}{=} 7$	$|-4 - 3| \stackrel{?}{=} 7$	**Substitute for x.**
$|7| \stackrel{?}{=} 7$	$|-7| \stackrel{?}{=} 7$	**Subtract.**
$7 = 7$✓	$7 = 7$✓	**Simplify. The solution checks.**

Example 3 **An Equation with No Solution**

Solve $|2x| = -6$.

The absolute value of a real number cannot be negative because a number's distance from 0 on a number line cannot be negative. So, this absolute value equation has no solution.

Isolating Expressions Sometimes you must first isolate the absolute value expression on one side of the equation before solving.

Example 4 **Isolating an Expression First**

Solve $|4x - 8| + 3 = 23$.

1 Isolate the absolute value expression on one side of the equation.

$$|4x - 8| + 3 = 23 \qquad \text{Write original equation.}$$
$$|4x - 8| = 20 \qquad \text{Subtract 3 from each side.}$$

2 Solve the revised equation from Step 1.

$$|4x - 8| = 20$$

$$4x - 8 = 20 \quad or \quad 4x - 8 = -20 \qquad \text{Expression can equal 20 or } -20.$$
$$4x = 28 \quad or \qquad 4x = -12 \qquad \text{Add 8 to each side.}$$
$$x = 7 \quad or \qquad x = -3 \qquad \text{Divide each side by 4.}$$

Answer The solutions are 7 and -3. To check the solutions, use substitution.

Practice

Solve the equation, if possible.

1. $|x| = 4$ 　　　　　　　**2.** $|x| = 18$ 　　　　　　　**3.** $|2x| = 50$

4. $|3x| = -27$ 　　　　　**5.** $|x + 6| = 20$ 　　　　**6.** $|x + 5| = 11$

7. $|x - 4| = 6$ 　　　　　**8.** $|4x - 2| = 22$ 　　　**9.** $|2x + 7| = 17$

10. $|2x - 4| - 8 = 10$ 　**11.** $|5 - 4x| - 3 = 4$ 　**12.** $|3 - 2x| + 9 = 11$

13. $|6 + x| + 2 = 19$ 　　**14.** $-|x + 5| = -15$ 　**15.** $-|3x + 1| = 15$

16. Manufacturing A machine is supposed to fill bottles with 12 fluid ounces of water. A bottle is rejected when the actual volume differs from the desired volume by more than 0.5 fluid ounce. The maximum and minimum acceptable volumes are the solutions of $|x - 12| = 0.5$. What are the maximum and minimum acceptable volumes?

Proportion Applications

GOAL Use proportions to read maps and convert international currencies.

A **scale drawing** is a diagram of a place or object in which the dimensions are proportional to the actual dimensions of the place or object. The **scale** of a scale drawing is a ratio that tells how the drawing's dimensions and the actual dimensions are related.

Example 1 *Use the Scale of a Map*

Use a metric ruler and the map to estimate the distance between Cleveland and Columbus.

Solution

From the map's scale, 1 centimeter represents 85 kilometers. On the map, the distance between Cleveland and Columbus is 2.4 centimeters. Write and solve a proportion to find the actual distance x between the cities.

1 cm : 85 km

$$\frac{1}{85} = \frac{2.4}{x} \quad \longleftarrow \text{ centimeters} \\ \longleftarrow \text{ kilometers}$$

$1 \cdot x = 85 \cdot 2.4$ **Cross multiply.**

$x = 204$ **Simplify.**

Answer The actual distance between Cleveland and Columbus is about 204 kilometers.

Example 2 *Convert Currency*

Suppose the exchange rate for purchasing Chinese renminbi using American dollars is $1.00 (US) to ¥8.00. How many renminbi can the Smith family buy with $485.00?

Write and solve a proportion.

$$\frac{1}{8} = \frac{485}{x} \quad \longleftarrow \text{ dollars} \\ \longleftarrow \text{ renminbi}$$

$1 \cdot x = 8 \cdot 485$ **Cross multiply.**

$x = 3880$ **Simplify.**

Answer The Smiths can buy ¥3880 with $485.

Appendix 2

Practice

The map of the hiking trail has a scale of 1 inch to 3.2 miles. Use a ruler to approximate the actual distance between the two locations.

1. Meadow View and Lookout Point

2. Lookout Point and Whispering Pines

3. Whispering Pines and Blueberry Hill

4. Meadow View and Blueberry Hill

Using the scale 1 cm : 48 km, predict the distance in centimeters *on the map* for the given actual distance.

5. 24 kilometers

6. 168 kilometers

7. 72 kilometers

Convert the indicated sum of money into US dollars or foreign currency, as indicated, using the given exchange rate.

8. How many Australian dollars (A$) can you buy with $550 (US) at the exchange rate of $1.00 (US) to A$1.34?

9. How many New Zealand dollars (NZ$) can you buy with $2250 (US) at the exchange rate of $1.00 (US) to NZ$1.50?

10. How many US dollars can you buy with $1350 (Argentine pesos) at the exchange rate of $1.00 (peso) to $0.33 (US)?

11. How many US dollars can Peter buy with R2500 (South African rands) at the exchange rate of R1.00 to $0.16 (US)?

12. How many Israeli new sheqels (₪) can Anna buy with $2500 (US) at the exchange rate of $1.00 to ₪4.70?

13. How many US dollars can you buy with Bds$1200 (Barbados dollars) at the exchange rate of Bds$1.00 to $0.51 (US)?

Answer the questions about unit prices.

14. Francesca pays $3.88 for 4 ounces of cinnamon. How much does the cinnamon cost per ounce?

15. Nani buys 7 pounds of oats for $6.51. What is the price per pound?

16. You buy $2\frac{1}{2}$ pounds of granola for $6.35. What is the price per pound?

17. A quart of organic milk costs $1.79. What is the price per gallon?

18. Michael pays $11.67 for 3 pints of ice cream. Daniel pays $19.35 for 5 pints of ice cream. Who pays less per pint of ice cream, Michael or Daniel? How much less per pint does he pay?

Using Small *and* Large Percents

GOAL Calculate with very small (< 1%) and very large (> 100%) percents.

Example 1 *Finding a Percent of a Number*

a. Find 0.4% of 350.

$$0.4\% \text{ of } 350 = 0.004 \cdot 350 \qquad \text{Write percent as decimal.}$$
$$= 1.4 \qquad \text{Multiply.}$$

b. Find 0.01% of 800.

$$0.01\% \text{ of } 800 = 0.0001 \cdot 8000 \qquad \text{Write percent as decimal.}$$
$$= 0.08 \qquad \text{Multiply.}$$

c. Find 150% of 29.

$$150\% \text{ of } 29 = 1.5 \cdot 29 \qquad \text{Write percent as decimal.}$$
$$= 43.5 \qquad \text{Multiply.}$$

d. Find 2800% of 1.1.

$$2800\% \text{ of } 1.1 = 28 \cdot 1.1 \qquad \text{Write percent as decimal.}$$
$$= 30.8 \qquad \text{Multiply.}$$

Notice that 0.4% of 350 is less than 1% of 350 (1.4 < 3.5). Also notice that 150% of 29 is greater than 29.

Example 2 *Finding a Real World Percent*

A zookeeper is recording the growth of a snake at the zoo. The snake was 550 centimeters long when it was previously measured. A new measurement shows that the snake has grown 2.75 centimeters longer. What is the percent of increase?

Solution

a.

$$\frac{a}{b} = \frac{p}{100} \qquad \text{Use } \frac{a}{b} = \frac{p}{100} \text{ to represent that } a \text{ is } p \text{ percent of } b.$$

$$\frac{2.75}{550} = \frac{p}{100} \qquad \text{Substitute 2.75 for } a \text{ and 550 for } p.$$

$$100 \cdot 2.75 = 550 \cdot p \qquad \text{Use cross products property.}$$

$$p = 0.5 \qquad \text{Solve for } p.$$

Answer The snake has grown 0.5%.

Example 3 *Finding a Real World Base*

Your family paid $900 for a new television. This amount is 180% of the total amount that your friend's family paid for their new television. How much did your friend's family spend on their new television?

Solution

$a = p\% \cdot b$ Use $a = p\% \cdot b$ to represent that a is p percent of b.

$900 = 180\% \cdot b$ Substitute **900** for a and **180** for p.

$900 = 1.8 \cdot b$ Write percent as a decimal.

$500 = b$ Divide each side by **1.8**.

Answer Your friend's family paid $500 for their new television.

Practice

Find the percent of the number.

1. 115% of 194

2. 0.08% of 410,000

3. 0.4% of 900

4. 775% of 76

5. 0.7% of 680,000

6. 355% of 22

Copy and complete each statement using <, >, or =.

7. 150% of 7 _?_ 0.5% of 2100

8. 180% of 45 _?_ 200% of 40

9. 0.25% of 800 _?_ 0.5% of 500

10. 0.1% of 1100 _?_ 105% of 1

11. 0.9% of 300 _?_ 0.7% of 400

12. 145% of 40 _?_ 400% of 14.5

Use a percent equation to answer the question.

13. 621 is what percent of 460?

14. 138 is 1150% of what number?

15. 4 is 0.8% of what number?

16. 18 is what percent of 4500?

17. 1961 is what percent of 925?

18. 189 is 135% of what number?

19. 11 is 0.02% of what number?

20. 9 is what percent of 1200?

21. 476 is what percent of 280?

22. 30 is 0.6% of what number?

23. Bamboo A bamboo cane was 36 cm long when it was previously measured. A new measurement shows that the cane has grown 171 cm longer. What is the percent of increase?

24. Budget In one year, a small company paid $850 for office supplies. This amount is 0.2% of the company's total operating expenses for the year. What were the company's total operating expenses for the year?

25. Hurricane A hurricane's top wind speed was 125 miles per hour when it was previously measured. A new measurement shows that the hurricane's top wind speed has increased by 1 mile per hour. What is the percent of increase?

26. Park Visits A park had 6080 visitors in May. This amount is 1520% of the number of visitors it had in January. How many visitors did the park have in January?

Operations with Square Roots

GOAL Perform operations with expressions containing square roots.

In Lesson 9.1, you learned that every positive number has two square roots, one positive and one negative. As with any other real number, the real square roots of a number can be plotted on a number line, as shown below.

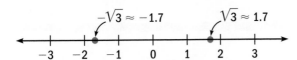

Square roots can also be represented as lengths on a number line. You can use square roots represented as lengths to evaluate sums and differences involving square roots.

Example 1   *Representing Square Roots on a Number Line*

Use a number line to approximate the sum or difference.

  a. $3 + \sqrt{7}$ **b.** $\sqrt{21} - 5$

Solution

  a.

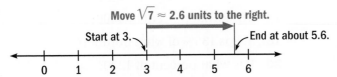

    Answer The final position is about 5.6. So, $3 + \sqrt{7} \approx 5.6$.

  b.

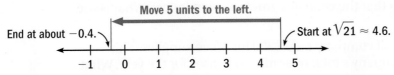

    Answer The final position is about -0.4. So, $\sqrt{21} - 5 \approx -0.4$.

Products of Radical Expressions In Lesson 9.2, you used the product property of square roots to simplify radical expressions. This property can also be used to multiply radical expressions, as shown in Example 2.

Example 2 — Multiplying Radical Expressions

a. $\sqrt{15} \cdot \sqrt{6} = \sqrt{15 \cdot 6}$ **Product property of square roots**

$\phantom{\sqrt{15} \cdot \sqrt{6}} = \sqrt{90}$ **Multiply.**

$\phantom{\sqrt{15} \cdot \sqrt{6}} = \sqrt{9} \cdot \sqrt{10}$ **Product property of square roots**

$\phantom{\sqrt{15} \cdot \sqrt{6}} = 3\sqrt{10}$ **Simplify.**

b. $\sqrt{2x} \cdot \sqrt{8x^3} = \sqrt{2x \cdot 8x^3}$ **Product property of square roots**

$\phantom{\sqrt{2x} \cdot \sqrt{8x^3}} = \sqrt{16x^4}$ **Multiply.**

$\phantom{\sqrt{2x} \cdot \sqrt{8x^3}} = \sqrt{16} \cdot \sqrt{x^4}$ **Product property of square roots**

$\phantom{\sqrt{2x} \cdot \sqrt{8x^3}} = 4x^2$ **Simplify.**

Quotients of Radical Expressions When you divide two radical expressions, you must rewrite the resulting quotient so that no radical appears in the denominator. Eliminating a radical in a denominator is called **rationalizing the denominator**. In general, you can rationalize the denominator of an expression of the form $\dfrac{\sqrt{a}}{\sqrt{b}}$ by multiplying the numerator and denominator by $\sqrt{b}$.

$$\frac{\sqrt{a}}{\sqrt{b}} = \frac{\sqrt{a}}{\sqrt{b}} \cdot \frac{\sqrt{b}}{\sqrt{b}}$$

$$= \frac{\sqrt{ab}}{\sqrt{b^2}}$$

$$= \frac{\sqrt{ab}}{b}$$

Example 3 — Dividing Radical Expressions

a. $\dfrac{\sqrt{7}}{\sqrt{2}} = \dfrac{\sqrt{7}}{\sqrt{2}} \cdot \dfrac{\sqrt{2}}{\sqrt{2}}$ **Multiply numerator and denominator by $\sqrt{2}$.**

$\phantom{\dfrac{\sqrt{7}}{\sqrt{2}}} = \dfrac{\sqrt{14}}{2}$ **Multiply fractions.**

b. $\dfrac{\sqrt{12}}{\sqrt{t}} = \dfrac{\sqrt{12}}{\sqrt{t}} \cdot \dfrac{\sqrt{t}}{\sqrt{t}}$ **Multiply numerator and denominator by $\sqrt{t}$.**

$\phantom{\dfrac{\sqrt{12}}{\sqrt{t}}} = \dfrac{\sqrt{12t}}{t}$ **Multiply fractions.**

$\phantom{\dfrac{\sqrt{12}}{\sqrt{t}}} = \dfrac{\sqrt{4} \cdot \sqrt{3t}}{t}$ **Product property of square roots**

$\phantom{\dfrac{\sqrt{12}}{\sqrt{t}}} = \dfrac{2\sqrt{3t}}{t}$ **Simplify.**

Sums and Differences of Radical Expressions You can use the distributive property to add or subtract two square root expressions provided each expression has the same *radicand*. The **radicand** is the expression beneath the radical symbol.

Example 4   *Adding or Subtracting Radical Expressions*

Simplify the expression, if possible.

  a. $7\sqrt{3} + 4\sqrt{3}$ **b.** $2\sqrt{5y} - 8\sqrt{5y}$ **c.** $8\sqrt{6t} + 9\sqrt{t}$

Solution

  a. $7\sqrt{3} + 4\sqrt{3} = (7 + 4)\sqrt{3}$ **Distributive property**

                  $= 11\sqrt{3}$ **Simplify.**

  b. $2\sqrt{5y} - 8\sqrt{5y} = (2 - 8)\sqrt{5y}$ **Distributive property**

                   $= -6\sqrt{5y}$ **Simplify.**

  c. The radicands $\sqrt{6t}$ and $\sqrt{t}$ are not alike. The expression $8\sqrt{6t} + 9\sqrt{t}$ is already in simplest form.

Practice

Graph the number on a number line.

  1. $\sqrt{11}$ **2.** $\sqrt{6}$ **3.** $\sqrt{20}$

  4. $\sqrt{45}$ **5.** $\sqrt{3}$ **6.** $\sqrt{8}$

Use a number line to approximate the sum or difference.

  7. $2 + \sqrt{5}$ **8.** $-8 + \sqrt{45}$ **9.** $-1 - \sqrt{11}$

  10. $9 - \sqrt{2}$ **11.** $\sqrt{18} + 3$ **12.** $\sqrt{24} - 7$

Simplify the expression, if possible.

  13. $\sqrt{14} \cdot \sqrt{30}$ **14.** $\sqrt{7n} \cdot \sqrt{11n}$ **15.** $\sqrt{10r^3} \cdot \sqrt{15r^2}$

  16. $\dfrac{\sqrt{13}}{\sqrt{5}}$ **17.** $\dfrac{\sqrt{21}}{\sqrt{3}}$ **18.** $\dfrac{\sqrt{18}}{\sqrt{2x}}$

  19. $3\sqrt{7} + 6\sqrt{7}$ **20.** $8\sqrt{y} + 4\sqrt{2y}$ **21.** $\sqrt{b} + 5\sqrt{b}$

  22. $5\sqrt{17} - 2\sqrt{17}$ **23.** $4\sqrt{m} - \sqrt{m}$ **24.** $3\sqrt{5s} - 7\sqrt{5s}$

  25. $9\sqrt{3} - 8\sqrt{6}$ **26.** $\sqrt{27} + 6\sqrt{3}$ **27.** $8\sqrt{2} \cdot \sqrt{8x}$

  28. $\dfrac{\sqrt{5}}{2} \cdot \dfrac{10}{\sqrt{2}}$ **29.** $\dfrac{\sqrt{3} + 4\sqrt{3}}{\sqrt{7}}$ **30.** $\sqrt{28}\left(3\sqrt{2} - 9\sqrt{2}\right)$

Appendix 5   Use after Lesson 9.3

Vocabulary
truth value, p. 834
truth table, p. 834

Symbolic Notation *and* Truth Tables

GOAL   Use symbolic notation to represent logical statements.

Conditional statements can be written using *symbolic notation*, where letters are used to represent statements. An arrow ($\rightarrow$), read "implies," connects the hypothesis and conclusion. To write the negation of a statement p you write the symbol for negation ($\sim$) before the letter. So, "not p" is written $\sim p$.

Symbolic Notation

Let p be "the angle is a right angle" and let q be "the measure of the angle is 90°."

Conditional   If p, then q. $p \rightarrow q$

Example: If an angle is a right angle, then its measure is 90°.

Converse   If q, then p. $q \rightarrow p$

Example: If the measure of an angle is 90°, then the angle is a right angle.

Inverse   If not p, then not q. $\sim p \rightarrow \sim q$

Example: If an angle is not a right angle, then its measure is not 90°.

Contrapositive   If not q, then not p. $\sim q \rightarrow \sim p$

If the measure of an angle is not 90°, then the angle is not a right angle.

Biconditional p if and only if q $p \leftrightarrow q$

Example: An angle is a right angle if and only if its measure is 90°.

Example 1   *Use Symbolic Notation*

Let p be "the car is running" and let q be "the key is in the ignition."

a. Write the conditional statement $p \rightarrow q$ in words.

b. Write the converse $q \rightarrow p$ in words.

c. Write the inverse $\sim p \rightarrow \sim q$ in words.

d. Write the contrapositive $\sim q \rightarrow \sim p$ in words.

Solution

a. Conditional: If the car is running, then the key is in the ignition.

b. Converse: If the key is in the ignition, then the car is running.

c. Inverse: If the car is not running, then the key is not in the ignition.

d. Contrapositive: If the key is not in the ignition, then the car is not running.

Truth tables The **truth value** of a statement is either true (T) or false (F). You can determine the conditions under which a conditional statement is true by using a **truth table**. The truth table at the right shows the truth values for hypothesis p and conclusion q. The conditional $p \to q$ is only false when a true hypothesis produces a false conclusion.

Conditional		
p	q	$p \to q$
T	T	T
T	F	F
F	T	T
F	F	T

Example 2   Make a truth table

Use the truth table above to make a truth table for the inverse of a conditional statement $p \to q$.

Solution

Inverse				
p	q	$\sim p$	$\sim q$	$\sim p \to \sim q$
T	T	F	F	T
T	F	F	T	T
F	T	T	F	F
F	F	T	T	T

Practice

1. **Writing** *Describe* how to use symbolic notation to represent the contrapositive of a conditional statement.

Writing Statements Use p and q to write the symbolic statement in words.

   p: Polygon *ABCDE* is equiangular and equilateral.

   q: Polygon *ABCDE* is a regular polygon.

2. $p \to q$ 3. $\sim p$ 4. $\sim q \to \sim p$ 5. $p \leftrightarrow q$

6. **Law of Syllogism** The *Law of Syllogism* states that if $p \to q$ and $q \to r$, then $p \to r$. Use the statements p, q, and r below to write a series of conditionals that would satisfy the Law of Syllogism. How could you write your reasoning using symbolic notation?

   p: $x + 5 = 12$ q: $x = 7$ r: $3x = 21$

7. **Writing** Is the truth value of a statement always true (T)? *Explain.*

8. **Truth Table** Use the truth table at the top of this page to make a truth table for the converse of a conditional statement $p \to q$.

9. **Truth Table** Use the truth table at the top of this page to make a truth table for the contrapositive of a conditional statement $p \to q$.

Appendix 6   Use after Lesson 11.3

Vocabulary
Venn diagram, p. 835
intersection, p. 835
union, p. 835

Using Venn Diagrams

GOAL   Sort data using Venn diagrams.

A **Venn diagram** groups items within circles to show the relations among them. An **intersection** consists of all items belonging to each of two or more circles. A **union** consists of all items belonging to any of two or more circles.

Example 1   *Sort Data with a Venn Diagram*

Tina, Marvin, Juan, and Cho excel at music. Juan, Cho, and Bea excel at sports. Show these facts in a Venn diagram.

Solution

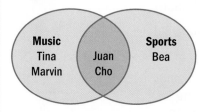

Tina and Marvin excel only at music.

Bea excels only at sports.

Juan and Cho excel at both. This is the intersection.

All five excel at one or at both. This is the union.

Example 2   *Sort Data with a Venn Diagram*

Each person in your group at the Grand Canyon chooses at least one of the following activities: a mule ride, a ranger-led walk, and a conservation film. Of the 75 people in the group, 18 choose all three, 15 choose only the ride, 12 only the walk, 9 only the film, and 5 both the ride and the walk. The total number who choose the mule ride is 48. How many choose the walk and the film?

Solution

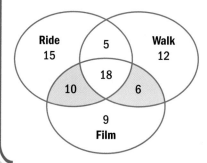

Number who choose the ride and the film = $48 - (15 + 5 + 18) = $ **10**
Number who choose the walk and the film = $75 - (48 + 12 + 9) = $ **6**

Practice

Create a Venn diagram to show the information presented using the two categories given.

1. Baseball, lacrosse, and soccer are all sports that are played with a *ball*. Baseball, lacrosse, and hockey are all played with a *stick*.

2. According to scientists, apples, oranges, and tomatoes are *fruits*. According to cooks, tomatoes, carrots and broccoli are *vegetables*.

3. The states of California, Arizona, Colorado, Texas, and Louisiana are all *west* of the Mississippi River. Louisiana, Georgia, and New York are *east* of it. The Mississippi River flows through the southern part of Louisiana, effectively dividing the state into two parts.

4. *French* is an official language of France, Senegal (in West Africa), and Canada. English is an official language of Canada, Australia, New Zealand, and the United Kingdom.

5. Mike and Steve won 12 tickets to a basketball game. They each made a list of the people they would like to invite.

   Mike's list: Mike, Steve, Mr. Marlin, Jacob, Sarah, Lauren, David, William

   Steve's list: Mike, Steve, Mr. Hopkins, William, Sarah, Ryan, Austin, Morgan

Use a Venn diagram to solve the problem.

6. In a class of 24 students, 8 are studying only French, 10 are studying only Spanish, and 5 are studying both French and Spanish. How many students are not studying either language?

7. Dora made necklaces of red, blue, and yellow beads. Fourteen contain only red beads, 16 contain only blue beads, and 12 contain only yellow beads. Six necklaces contain only blue and yellow beads, and 2 contain only yellow and red beads. Five contain beads of all three colors. If Dora made 30 necklaces that contained blue beads, how many contained blue and red beads?

8. **Error Analysis** Thirty-two families live on Oak Lane. Half of the families own a dog. Eight families own a cat, and three own both a dog and a cat. A student says that $\frac{3}{4}$ of the families own a dog or a cat. Describe and correct the error in the student's reasoning.

9. T-shirts, sweatshirts, and hats are being sold at the school store. In one month, 26 students buy T-shirts, and 20 students buy hats. Two students buy all three items, and 3 buy T-shirts and hats, but not sweatshirts. Seventeen buy just T-shirts and 10 buy just hats. How many students buy exactly two of the three items?

10. There are 30 students in Mr. Wu's homeroom class. Eighteen of them are taking an art course. Nine are taking just a painting class, 4 are taking just a sculpture class, and 2 are taking both painting and sculpture. What percent of the students in the homeroom class are taking an art course different from painting or sculpture?

Vocabulary
relation, p. 385
function, p. 386
vertical line test,
p. 387

Linear *and* Nonlinear Relations *and* Functions

GOAL Identify linear and nonlinear relations and functions.

Linear Relations You can decide whether a relation is linear by inspecting its graph. A relation is linear if all of its points lie on the same line.

Example 1 | *Identifying Linear and Nonlinear Relations*

Tell whether the relation is *linear* or *nonlinear*.

a.

x	−2	−1	0	1	2
y	−4	−2	0	2	4

b. Input   Output

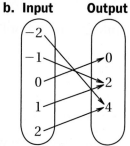

Solution

a. Represent the relation using a graph by plotting the ordered pairs from the table, as shown.

All of the points lie on the line $y = 2x$, so the relation is linear.

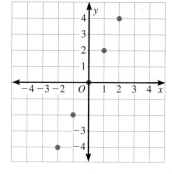

b. Represent the relation using a graph by plotting the ordered pairs from the mapping diagram, as shown.

The points do not all lie on the same line, so the relation is nonlinear.

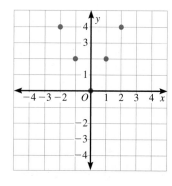

Identifying Functions Recall from Lesson 8.1 that you can use the vertical line test to tell whether a relation represented by a graph is a function.

Example 2   *Identifying Linear and Nonlinear Functions*

Tell whether the relation represented by the graph is a function. If so, decide whether it is a linear function or a nonlinear function.

a. 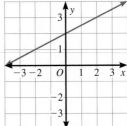   **b.** 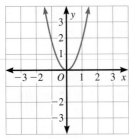   **c.**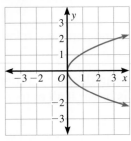

Solution

a. The graph passes the vertical line test and is linear. So, the relation is a linear function.

b. The graph passes the vertical line test and is nonlinear. So, the relation is a nonlinear function.

c. The graph does not pass the vertical line test, so the relation is not a function.

Recognizing Linear Equations A linear equation in two variables is an equation that can be written in the form $ax + by = c$ where a and b are not both zero. The exponent of each variable in a linear equation is one.

Example 3   *Identifying Linear and Nonlinear Equations*

Tell whether the equation is *linear* or *nonlinear*.

a. $y = x + 2$ **b.** $y = x^2 + 2x + 2$ **c.** $xy = 1$

Solution

a. Subtracting x from each side of the equation yields $-x + y = 2$. So, the equation can be written in the form $ax + by = c$, and therefore $y = x + 2$ is a linear equation.

b. The equation has an x^2-term and therefore cannot be written in the form $ax + by = c$. So, $y = x^2 + 2x + 2$ is a nonlinear equation.

c. The exponent of each variable is one, but the equation cannot be written in the form $ax + by = c$. So, $xy = 1$ is a nonlinear equation.

Checking Because the graph of a linear equation is a line, you can check the answers in Example 3 by graphing each equation using a calculator or by making and graphing a table of values.

Practice

Tell whether the relation is *linear* or *nonlinear*.

1.

x	−1	0	1	2	3
y	−8	−2	4	10	16

2.

x	−3	−1	0	1	3
y	−10	−4	−1	4	10

3. Input   Output

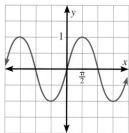

4. Input   Output

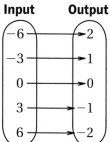

Tell whether the relation represented by the graph is a function.
If so, decide whether it is a linear function or a nonlinear function.

5.

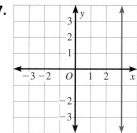

6.

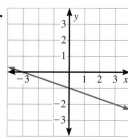

7.

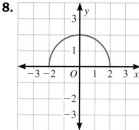

8.

Tell whether the equation is *linear* or *nonlinear*.

9. $y = 5x^2 - x + 9$

10. $y = 3x - 2$

11. $y - x = 4$

12. $y - x = x^2 + 9$

13. $y = \frac{1}{2}x + 8$

14. $y = \frac{5}{x}$

15. $3y - x = 1$

16. $-4x + y = 5x^4 + 2$

17. $xy - 2x = 8$

18. Hot Air Balloon The altitude h (in feet) of a hot air balloon after t minutes in flight is shown in the table. Is h a linear function of t? Explain.

t	0	1	2	3	4
h	250	270	290	310	330

Glossary

	Example
a	
absolute value (p. 23) The absolute value of a number a is its distance from 0 on a number line. The absolute value of a number a is written as $\lvert a \rvert$.	$\lvert 3 \rvert = 3 \quad \lvert -5 \rvert = 5 \quad \lvert 0 \rvert = 0$
additive identity (p. 64) The number 0 is the additive identity, because the sum of any number and 0 is the number.	$-3 + 0 = -3$ $a + 0 = a$
additive inverse (p. 30) The additive inverse of a number a is its opposite, $-a$. The sum of a number and its additive inverse is 0.	The additive inverse of 5 is -5, so $5 + (-5) = 0$.
alternate exterior angles (p. 716) When a transversal intersects two lines, two angles that lie outside the two lines on opposite sides of the transversal.	*See* transversal.
alternate interior angles (p. 716) When a transversal intersects two lines, two angles that lie between the two lines on opposite sides of the transversal.	*See* transversal.
angle of rotation (p. 741) In a rotation, the angle formed by two rays drawn from the center of rotation through corresponding points on the original figure and its image.	*See* rotation.
annual interest rate (p. 362) The percent of the principal earned or paid per year.	*See* simple interest *and* compound interest.
arithmetic sequence (p. 692) A sequence in which the difference between consecutive terms is constant.	1, 5, 9, 13, 17, . . . is an arithmetic sequence with a common difference of 4.
b	
balance of an account (p. 363) The sum of the principal and all interest earned.	*See* simple interest *and* compound interest.
base of a parallelogram (p. 521) The length of any side of the parallelogram.	*See* parallelogram.
base of a power (p. 10) The number or expression that is used as a factor in a repeated multiplication.	In the power 2^7, the base is 2.
bases of a trapezoid (p. 522) The lengths of the parallel sides of the trapezoid.	*See* trapezoid.

	Example
best-fitting line (p. 421) The line that lies as close as possible to the points of a scatter plot.	The best-fitting line for the scatter plot is shown in red.
biased question (p. 603) A question that encourages a particular response.	"Don't you think it would be better if the school built a new gymnasium?" is a biased question.
biased sample (p. 602) A sample that is not representative of a population.	The members of a school's basketball team are a biased sample for a survey about support for building a new gymnasium.
binomial (p. 651) A polynomial with two terms.	$a^2 + 5a$ and $9 - y$ are binomials.
box-and-whisker plot (p. 588) A data display that organizes data values into four groups using the lower extreme, lower quartile, median, upper quartile, and upper extreme.	

C

categorical data (p. 596) Data that consist of names, labels, or other nonnumerical values.	A list of eye colors is a set of categorical data.
center of a circle (p. 528) The point inside the circle that is the same distance from all points on the circle.	*See* circle.
center of dilation (p. 747) The point with respect to which a figure stretches or shrinks when the figure undergoes a dilation.	*See* dilation.
center of rotation (p. 741) The point about which a figure is turned when the figure undergoes a rotation.	*See* rotation.
circle (p. 528) All points in a plane that are the same distance, called the radius, from a fixed point, called the center.	

	Example
circumference of a circle (p. 528) The distance around the circle.	*See* circle.
coefficient (p. 78) The number part of a term with a variable.	The coefficient of $-7x$ is -7.
combination (p. 620) A selection of objects where the order in which the objects are chosen is not important.	There are 3 combinations of 2 letters chosen from the letters A, H, T: AH AT HT
common difference (p. 692) The difference between consecutive terms of an arithmetic sequence.	*See* arithmetic sequence.
common factor (p. 177) A whole number that is a factor of two or more nonzero whole numbers.	The common factors of 12 and 20 are 1, 2, and 4.
common multiple (p. 187) A whole number that is a multiple of two or more nonzero whole numbers.	The common multiples of 6 and 9 are 18, 36, 54, ...
common ratio (p. 692) The ratio of any term of a geometric sequence to the previous term of the sequence.	*See* geometric sequence.
complementary angles (p. 709) Two angles whose measures have a sum of 90°.	 32° 58°
complementary events (p. 630) Two disjoint events such that one event or the other must occur.	When you roll a number cube, the events "roll an odd number" and "roll an even number" are complementary events.
composite number (p. 173) A whole number greater than 1 that has more than two whole number factors.	6 is a composite number, because its whole number factors are 1, 2, 3, and 6.
compound interest (p. 363) Interest that is earned on both the principal and any interest that has been earned previously. The balance A of an account that earns interest compounded annually is $A = P(1 + r)^t$, where P is the principal, r is the annual interest rate (written as a decimal), and t is the time in years.	You deposit \$1000 into an account that earns 3% interest compounded annually. After 5 years, your account balance is $A = P(1 + r)^t = 1000(1 + 0.03)^5 \approx \$1159.27$.
concave (p. 516) A polygon is concave if a segment joining any two interior points does not lie completely within the polygon.	*See* convex.

	Example

congruent figures (p. 290) Figures that have the same shape and the same size. Corresponding angles and corresponding sides of congruent figures are congruent.

$\triangle ABC \cong \triangle DEF$

constant term (p. 78) A term that has a number but no variable.

In the expression $8a + 4$, the term 4 is a constant term.

convenience sample (p. 601) A sample in which only members of a population who are easily accessible are selected.

You can select a convenience sample of your school's student population by choosing only students who are in your classes.

convex (p. 516) A polygon is convex if a segment joining any two interior points lies completely within the polygon. A polygon that is not convex is called *concave*.

Convex   Concave

coordinate plane (p. 47) A coordinate system formed by the intersection of a horizontal number line called the *x*-axis and a vertical number line called the *y*-axis.

corresponding angles (p. 716) Two angles that occupy corresponding positions when a transversal intersects two lines.

See transversal.

corresponding parts (p. 288) A pair of sides or angles that have the same relative position in two figures.

$\angle A$ and $\angle D$ are corresponding angles. $\overline{AC}$ and $\overline{DF}$ are corresponding sides.

cosine (p. 494) For a right triangle, the cosine of an acute angle A (cos A) is the ratio of the length of the side adjacent to $\angle A$ to the length of the hypotenuse.

See trigonometric ratio.

	Example
counting principle (p. 314) If one event can occur in m ways, and for each of these ways a second event can occur in n ways, then the number of ways that the two events can occur together is $m \cdot n$.	You have 3 shirts and 4 pairs of pants. The total number of shirt-and-pants combinations that you can choose from is $3 \cdot 4 = 12$.
cross product (p. 280) The product of the numerator of one ratio and the denominator of another ratio. The cross products of a proportion are equal.	The cross products of the proportion $\frac{2}{3} = \frac{8}{12}$ are $2 \cdot 12 = 24$ and $3 \cdot 8 = 24$.

d

	Example
degree of a polynomial (p. 652) The greatest degree of the terms of the polynomial.	In the polynomial $a^2 + 4a^2b + 5$, the degree of the term a^2 is 2, the degree of the term $4a^2b$ is 3, and the degree of the term 5 is 0. The degree of the polynomial is 3, the greatest degree of the terms.
degree of a term (p. 652) The sum of the exponents of the variables in the term. The degree of a nonzero constant is 0.	*See* degree of a polynomial.
dependent events (p. 634) Two events such that the occurrence of one event affects the probability of the occurrence of the other event.	A bag contains 4 red marbles and 5 green marbles. You randomly choose a marble, do not replace it, then randomly choose a second marble. The events "first marble is red" and "second marble is red" are dependent events.
diagonal of a polygon (p. 518) A segment that joins two vertices of the polygon that are not adjacent.	
diameter of a circle (p. 528) The distance across the circle through the center.	*See* circle.
dilation (p. 747) A transformation in which a figure stretches or shrinks with respect to a fixed point, called the center of dilation.	$\triangle ABC$ is dilated with respect to the origin using a scale factor of 3.

	Example
discount (p. 358) The decrease from the original price of an item to the sale price.	The original price of a sweater is $32.99, but the store sells it for $25.99. The discount is $7.00.
disjoint events (p. 627) Events that have no outcomes in common; also called mutually exclusive events.	When you roll a number cube, the events "roll a 3" and "roll an even number" are disjoint events.
domain of a relation (p. 385) The set of all possible inputs for the relation.	*See* relation.

e

equation (p. 85) A mathematical sentence formed by placing an equal sign, =, between two expressions.	$3x - 2 = 12 + 10x$ is an equation.
equation in two variables (p. 391) An equation that contains two different variables.	$3x - 4y = 2$ is an equation in two variables.
equivalent equations (p. 91) Equivalent equations have the same solution.	$5y - 2 = 8$ and $5y = 10$ are equivalent equations, because the solution of both equations is 2.
equivalent fractions (p. 182) Two fractions that represent the same number.	$\frac{4}{8}$ and $\frac{10}{20}$ are equivalent fractions that both represent $\frac{1}{2}$.
equivalent inequalities (p. 139) Inequalities that have the same solution.	$3y + 7 > 25$ and $3y > 18$ are equivalent inequalities, because the solution of both inequalities is all numbers greater than 6.
equivalent numerical expressions (p. 71) Numerical expressions that have the same value.	$5(10 - 6)$ and $5(10) - 5(6)$ are equivalent numerical expressions, because they each have the value 20.
equivalent ratios (p. 270) Two or more ratios that have the same value.	$\frac{3}{4}, \frac{9}{12}$, and $\frac{15}{20}$ are equivalent ratios, because they each have the value 0.75.
equivalent variable expressions (p. 72) Variable expressions that have the same value for all values of the variable(s).	$5(x + 1) + x$ and $6x + 5$ are equivalent variable expressions.

	Example
evaluate a variable expression (p. 5) To find the value of the variable expression by substituting a number for each variable, and then finding the value of the resulting numerical expression.	The value of $2y - 5$ when $y = 3$ is $2(3) - 5 = 1$.
event (p. 306) An outcome or a collection of outcomes.	An event for rolling a number cube is "roll an even number."
experimental probability (p. 307) A probability based on repeated trials of an experiment. The experimental probability of an event is the ratio of the number of successes (favorable outcomes for the event) to the number of trials.	A basketball player has made 30 out of 36 attempted free throws this season. The experimental probability that she will make a free throw is $\frac{30}{36} = \frac{5}{6}$, or about 0.83.
exponent (p. 10) A number or expression that shows how many times a base is used as a factor in a repeated multiplication.	In the power 2^7, the exponent is 7.
exponential decay (p. 687) A quantity that decreases shows exponential decay if it can be described by an exponential function of the form $y = ab^x$, where $a > 0$ and $0 < b < 1$.	The function $y = \left(\frac{1}{3}\right)^x$ shows exponential decay. *See* exponential function.
exponential function (p. 686) An equation in two variables that can be written in the form $y = ab^x$, where $a \neq 0$, $b > 0$, and $b \neq 1$.	$y = 3(2)^x$ and $y = \left(\frac{1}{3}\right)^x$ are exponential functions.
exponential growth (p. 687) A quantity that increases shows exponential growth if it can be described by an exponential function of the form $y = ab^x$, where $a > 0$ and $b > 1$.	The function $y = 3(2)^x$ shows exponential growth. *See* exponential function.
exterior angle of a polygon (p. 723) An angle adjacent to an interior angle of the polygon, formed by extending one side of the polygon.	*See* interior angle of a polygon.

Glossary

	Example
factor tree (p. 173) A diagram that can be used to write the prime factorization of a number.	$$\begin{array}{c} 28 \\ 4 \quad \cdot \quad 7 \\ 2 \cdot 2 \cdot 7 \end{array}$$
favorable outcomes (p. 306) Outcomes that correspond to a specified event.	When you roll a number cube, the favorable outcomes for the event "roll an even number" are 2, 4, and 6.
frequency (p. 582) The number of data values in an interval.	*See* frequency table *and* histogram.
frequency table (p. 582) A data display that groups data into intervals.	<table><tr><th>Interval</th><th>Tally</th><th>Frequency</th></tr><tr><td>0–9</td><td>‖</td><td>2</td></tr><tr><td>10–19</td><td></td><td>0</td></tr><tr><td>20–29</td><td>‖‖</td><td>4</td></tr></table>
function (p. 386) A relation with the property that for each input there is *exactly one* output.	The relation (1, 0), (2, 1), (3, 0), (4, 1), (5, 0) is a function, because each input is paired with exactly one output. The relation (1, 0), (2, 0), (2, 1), (3, 0), (3, 1), (3, 2) is not a function, because the inputs 2 and 3 are each paired with more than one output.
function form of an equation (p. 393) An equation in x and y is in function form if it is solved for y.	The equation $y - 2x = 8$ can be written in function form as $y = 2x + 8$.
function notation (p. 426) The use of the symbol $f(x)$, instead of y, in an equation to represent the output of the function f for the input x. The symbol $f(x)$ is read "f of x."	The function $y = 3x - 5$ can be written in function notation as $f(x) = 3x - 5$.
g	
geometric sequence (p. 692) A sequence in which the ratio of any term to the previous term is constant.	1, 2, 4, 8, 16, . . . is a geometric sequence with a common ratio of 2.

	Example
graph of a linear inequality in two variables (p. 436) The set of points in a coordinate plane that represent all the solutions of the inequality.	 The graph of $y \geq x + 3$ is the shaded half-plane.
graph of an equation in two variables (p. 392) The set of points in a coordinate plane that represent all the solutions of the equation.	
greatest common factor (GCF) (p. 177) The greatest whole number that is a common factor of two or more nonzero whole numbers.	The GCF of 30 and 54 is 6. The GCF of 30, 60, and 75 is 15.

h

half-plane (p. 436) All points on one side of a line in a coordinate plane.	*See* graph of a linear inequality in two variables.
height of a cone (p. 546) The distance between the vertex and the center of the base.	
height of a parallelogram (p. 521) The perpendicular distance between the side whose length is the base and the opposite side.	*See* parallelogram.
height of a pyramid (p. 544) The perpendicular distance between the base and the vertex.	*See* regular pyramid.
height of a trapezoid (p. 522) The perpendicular distance between the sides whose lengths are the bases.	*See* trapezoid.
heptagon (p. 516) A polygon with 7 sides.	

	Example
hexagon (p. 516) A polygon with 6 sides.	
histogram (p. 583) A data display showing data from a frequency table.	 **Library Visitors on a Saturday**
hypotenuse (p. 465) The side of a right triangle that is opposite the right angle.	

ℹ

image (p. 729) The new figure formed by a transformation. The image of point A is written A'.	*See* translation, reflection, rotation, *and* dilation.
independent events (p. 634) Two events such that the occurrence of one event does not affect the probability of the occurrence of the other event.	You roll a number cube twice. The events "roll a 3 first" and "then roll a 4" are independent events.
inequality (p. 138) A mathematical statement formed by placing an inequality symbol between two expressions.	$4 > -7$ and $5x - 3 \le 2$ are inequalities.
input (p. 385) A number in the domain of a relation.	*See* relation.
integers (p. 22) The numbers . . . , -3, -2, -1, 0, 1, 2, 3, . . . consisting of the negative integers, zero, and the positive integers.	-9 and 23 are integers. -9.25 and $23\frac{1}{2}$ are *not* integers.
interest (p. 362) The amount earned or paid for the use of money.	*See* simple interest *and* compound interest.
interior angle of a polygon (p. 722) An angle inside the polygon.	 $\angle 1$ is an interior angle of $\triangle ABC$. $\angle 2$ is an exterior angle of $\triangle ABC$.

	Example
interquartile range (p. 590) The difference of the upper quartile and the lower quartile of a data set.	*See* box-and-whisker plot.
inverse operations (p. 91) Two operations that undo each other.	Addition and subtraction are inverse operations. Multiplication and division are inverse operations.
irrational number (p. 470) A number that cannot be written as a quotient of two integers. The decimal form of an irrational number neither terminates nor repeats.	$\sqrt{3}$, π, and 0.202002000. . . are irrational numbers.

I

lateral area of a cylinder (p. 540) The area of the curved surface of the cylinder.	Lateral area $= (2 \cdot \pi \cdot 2)(5)$ $= 20\pi$ $\approx 62.8 \text{ m}^2$
lateral area of a prism (p. 539) The sum of the areas of the lateral faces of the prism.	Lateral area $= 2(3) + 2(4) + 2(5)$ $= 24 \text{ in.}^2$
lateral faces of a prism (p. 539) The faces of the prism that are not bases.	*See* lateral area of a prism.
lateral surface of a cylinder (p. 540) The curved surface of the cylinder.	*See* lateral area of a cylinder.

	Example
least common denominator (LCD) (p. 188) The least common multiple of the denominators of two or more fractions.	The LCD of $\frac{3}{4}$ and $\frac{5}{6}$ is 12, the LCM of 4 and 6.
least common multiple (LCM) (p. 187) The least number that is a common multiple of two or more numbers.	The LCM of 6 and 10 is 30. The LCM of 4, 5, and 6 is 60.
legs of a right triangle (p. 465) The two sides of a right triangle that form the right angle.	*See* hypotenuse.
like terms (p. 78) Terms that have identical variable parts. Two or more constant terms are also like terms.	In the expression $x + 5 - 7x + 1$, x and $-7x$ are like terms, and 5 and 1 are like terms.
linear equation in two variables (p. 392) An equation whose graph is a line.	*See* graph of an equation in two variables.
linear inequality in two variables (p. 436) An inequality that is the result of replacing the equal sign in a linear equation in two variables with $<$, $\leq$, $>$, or $\geq$.	$3x - 7y < -1$ and $y \geq x + 4$ are linear inequalities in two variables.
line of reflection (p. 734) The line in which a figure is flipped when the figure undergoes a reflection.	*See* reflection.
line of symmetry (p. 735) A line that divides a figure into two parts that are reflections of each other in the line.	*See* line symmetry.
line symmetry (p. 735) A figure has line symmetry if a line, called the line of symmetry, divides the figure into two parts that are reflections of each other in the line.	A square has 4 lines of symmetry.
lower extreme (p. 588) The least value in a data set.	*See* box-and-whisker plot.
lower quartile (p. 588) The median of the lower half of an ordered data set.	*See* box-and-whisker plot.

m

margin of error (p. 610) The margin of error of a random sample defines an interval centered on a sample percent in which a population percent is most likely to lie.	A prediction that you will get 58% of the votes in an election, with a margin of error of $\pm4\%$, means that your percent of the votes is most likely to lie between 54% and 62%.

	Example
markup (p. 357) The increase from the wholesale price of an item to the retail price.	The wholesale price of a gallon of milk is \$2.30, but the store sells it for \$3.19. The markup is \$.89.
maximum value of a function (p. 681) The y-coordinate of the highest point on the graph of the function. A quadratic function $y = ax^2 + bx + c$ has a maximum value when $a < 0$.	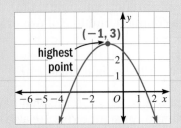 The maximum value of $y = -\frac{1}{2}x^2 - x + \frac{5}{2}$ is 3.
midpoint of a segment (p. 478) The point on the segment that is equally distant from the endpoints.	 M is the midpoint of $\overline{AB}$.
minimum value of a function (p. 681) The y-coordinate of the lowest point on the graph of the function. A quadratic function $y = ax^2 + bx + c$ has a minimum value when $a > 0$.	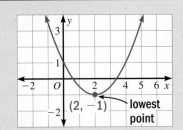 The minimum value of $y = \frac{1}{2}x^2 - 2x + 1$ is -1.
monomial (p. 174) A number, a variable, or the product of a number and one or more variables raised to whole number powers.	$8xy$, $5a^3$, n^2m, p, and 12 are all monomials.
multiple (p. 187) The product of a number and any nonzero whole number.	The multiples of 7 are 7, 14, 21, 28, ...
multiplicative identity (p. 64) The number 1 is the multiplicative identity, because the product of any number and 1 is the number.	$5 \cdot 1 = 5$ $a \cdot 1 = a$
multiplicative inverse (p. 247) The multiplicative inverse of a nonzero number $\frac{a}{b}$, where $a \neq 0$ and $b \neq 0$, is its reciprocal $\frac{b}{a}$. The product of a number and its multiplicative inverse is 1.	The multiplicative inverse of $\frac{5}{3}$ is $\frac{3}{5}$, so $\frac{5}{3} \cdot \frac{3}{5} = 1$.

	Example
mutually exclusive events (p. 627) Events that have no outcomes in common; also called disjoint events.	*See* disjoint events.

n

negative integers (p. 22) The integers that are less than 0.	$-1, -2, -3, -4, \ldots$
net (p. 538) A two-dimensional representation of a solid. The surface area of a solid is equal to the area of its net.	*See* lateral area of a cylinder *and* lateral area of a prism.
n factorial (p. 615) For any positive integer n, the product of the integers from 1 to n is called n factorial and is written $n!$.	$5! = 5 \cdot 4 \cdot 3 \cdot 2 \cdot 1 = 120$
nonlinear function (p. 680) A function whose graph is not a line.	A quadratic function is a nonlinear function. *See* parabola.
numerical data (p. 596) Data that consist of numbers.	A list of heights is a set of numerical data.
numerical expression (p. 5) An expression that consists of numbers and operations.	$5(2) + 7$ is a numerical expression.

o

octagon (p. 516) A polygon with 8 sides.	
odds against (p. 308) When all outcomes are equally likely, the ratio of the number of unfavorable outcomes to the number of favorable outcomes is called the odds against an event.	When you randomly choose an integer from 1 to 10, the odds against choosing an integer divisible by 3 are $\frac{7}{3}$, or 7 to 3.
odds in favor (p. 308) When all outcomes are equally likely, the ratio of the number of favorable outcomes to the number of unfavorable outcomes is called the odds in favor of an event.	When you randomly choose an integer from 1 to 10, the odds in favor of choosing an integer divisible by 3 are $\frac{3}{7}$, or 3 to 7.
opposites (p. 23) Two numbers that have the same absolute value but different signs.	-4 and 4 are opposites.

Glossary

ordered pair (p. 47) A pair of numbers (x, y) that can be used to represent a point in a coordinate plane. The first number is the x-coordinate, and the second number is the y-coordinate.

order of operations (p. 16) A set of rules for evaluating an expression involving more than one operation.

To evaluate $5 - 2^2$, evaluate the power before subtracting:

$$5 - 2^2 = 5 - 4 = 1$$

origin (p. 47) The point $(0, 0)$ where the x-axis and the y-axis meet in a coordinate plane.

See coordinate plane.

outcomes (p. 306) The possible results of an experiment.

When you toss a coin, the outcomes are heads and tails.

output (p. 385) A number in the range of a relation.

See relation.

overlapping events (p. 627) Events that have one or more outcomes in common.

When you roll a number cube, the events "roll a 3" and "roll an odd number" are overlapping events.

p

parabola (p. 680) A U-shaped curve that is the graph of a quadratic function.

The graph of $y = x^2 - 2x - 3$ is a parabola.

parallelogram (p. 517) A quadrilateral with both pairs of opposite sides parallel.

pentagon (p. 516) A polygon with 5 sides.

percent (p. 329) A ratio whose denominator is 100. The symbol for percent is %.

$$\frac{7}{25} = \frac{7 \cdot 4}{25 \cdot 4} = \frac{28}{100} = 28\%$$

	Example
percent of change (p. 352) A percent that indicates how much a quantity increases or decreases with respect to the original amount. Percent of change, $p\% = \dfrac{\text{Amount of increase or decrease}}{\text{Original amount}}$	The percent of change $p\%$ from 12 to 20 is: $p\% = \dfrac{20 - 12}{12} = \dfrac{8}{12} \approx 0.667 = 66.7\%$
percent of decrease (p. 352) The percent of change in a quantity when the new amount is less than the original amount.	*See* percent of change.
percent of increase (p. 352) The percent of change in a quantity when the new amount is greater than the original amount.	*See* percent of change.
perfect square (p. 454) A number that is the square of an integer.	36 is a perfect square, because $36 = 6^2$.
permutation (p. 615) An arrangement of objects in which order is important.	There are 6 permutations of the 3 letters A, H, T: AHT ATH THA TAH HTA HAT
polygon (p. 516) A closed plane figure whose sides are segments that intersect only at their endpoints.	**Polygons** **Not polygons**
polynomial (p. 651) A sum of monomials.	*See* monomial, binomial, *and* trinomial.
population (p. 601) An entire group about which information is gathered.	If a biologist wants to determine the average age of the elephants in a wildlife refuge, the population consists of every elephant in the refuge.
positive integers (p. 22) The integers that are greater than 0.	1, 2, 3, 4, . . .
power (p. 10) The result of a repeated multiplication of the same factor. A power can be expressed using a base and an exponent.	64 is a power, because $64 = 4 \cdot 4 \cdot 4$, or $64 = 4^3$.
prime factorization (p. 173) A whole number written as the product of prime factors.	The prime factorization of 60 is $2 \cdot 2 \cdot 3 \cdot 5 = 2^2 \cdot 3 \cdot 5$.

	Example
prime number (p. 173) A whole number greater than 1 that has exactly two whole number factors, 1 and itself.	7 is a prime number, because its only whole number factors are 1 and 7.
principal (p. 362) An amount of money that is deposited or borrowed.	*See* simple interest *and* compound interest.
probability (p. 306) A number from 0 to 1 that measures the likelihood that an event will occur.	*See* experimental probability *and* theoretical probability.
proportion (p. 275) An equation that states that two ratios are equal.	$\frac{2}{7} = \frac{10}{35}$ and $\frac{x}{20} = \frac{4}{5}$ are proportions.
Pythagorean theorem (p. 465) For any right triangle, the sum of the squares of the lengths a and b of the legs equals the square of the length c of the hypotenuse: $a^2 + b^2 = c^2$.	$a = 5$, $b = 12$, $c = 13$ $5^2 + 12^2 = 13^2$

q

quadrant (p. 47) One of the four regions that a coordinate plane is divided into by the x-axis and the y-axis.	*See* coordinate plane.
quadratic function (p. 679) An equation in two variables that can be written in the form $y = ax^2 + bx + c$, where a, b, and c are constants and $a \neq 0$.	$y = 3x^2 + 5x - 7$ is a quadratic function.

r

radical expression (p. 454) An expression that involves a radical sign, $\sqrt{\ }$.	$3\sqrt{4a + b}$ is a radical expression.
radius of a circle (p. 528) The distance between the center and any point on the circle.	*See* circle.
random sample (p. 601) A sample in which every member of a population has an equal chance of being selected.	You can select a random sample of your school's student population by having a computer randomly choose 100 student identification numbers.
range of a relation (p. 385) The set of all possible outputs for the relation.	*See* relation.

Glossary

	Example
ratio (p. 269) A comparison of two numbers using division. The ratio of a to b (where $b \neq 0$) can be written as a to b, as $a:b$, or as $\frac{a}{b}$.	The ratio of 4 to 5 can be written as 4 to 5, as $4:5$, or as $\frac{4}{5}$.
rational number (p. 219) A number that can be written as a quotient of two integers.	$-\frac{1}{2} = \frac{-1}{2}$, $0 = \frac{0}{1}$, $0.45 = \frac{9}{20}$, $8\frac{3}{4} = \frac{35}{4}$, and $10 = \frac{10}{1}$ are all rational numbers.
real numbers (p. 470) The set of all rational numbers and irrational numbers.	-5, 0, $\frac{2}{3}$, π, 4.37, and 19 are all real numbers.
reciprocals (p. 243) Two nonzero numbers whose product is 1.	5 and $\frac{1}{5}$ are reciprocals.
reflection (p. 734) A transformation in which a figure is reflected, or flipped, in a line, called the line of reflection.	 Reflection in the x-axis
regular polygon (p. 516) A polygon whose sides all have the same length and whose angles all have the same measure.	
regular pyramid (p. 544) A pyramid whose base is a regular polygon and whose lateral faces are all congruent isosceles triangles.	 The base is a regular polygon.
relation (p. 385) A pairing of numbers in one set (the domain, or set of possible inputs) with numbers in another set (the range, or set of possible outputs). For a relation represented by ordered pairs (x, y), the inputs are the x-coordinates, and the outputs are the y-coordinates.	The set of ordered pairs $(1, 0)$, $(2, 1)$, $(3, 0)$, $(4, 1)$, $(5, 0)$ is a relation. The domain of the relation is the set of inputs: 1, 2, 3, 4, 5. The range of the relation is the set of outputs: 0, 1.

	Example
relatively prime numbers (p. 178) Two or more nonzero whole numbers whose greatest common factor is 1.	10 and 21 are relatively prime because their GCF is 1.
repeating decimal (p. 219) A decimal that has a digit or block of digits that repeats without end. A repeating decimal can be written as a quotient of integers $\frac{a}{b}$, where $b \neq 0$.	0.3333... and $6.\overline{15}$ are repeating decimals. $0.3333... = \frac{1}{3}$ $6.\overline{15} = 6\frac{15}{99} = 6\frac{5}{33}$
rhombus (p. 517) A parallelogram with 4 congruent sides.	
rise (p. 404) The vertical change between two points on a line.	*See* slope.
rotation (p. 741) A transformation in which a figure is turned through a given angle, called the angle of rotation, and in a given direction about a fixed point, called the center of rotation.	 45° clockwise rotation about the origin
rotational symmetry (p. 743) A figure has rotational symmetry if a rotation of 180° or less clockwise (or counterclockwise) about its center produces an image that fits exactly on the original figure.	 A square has 180° rotational symmetry. A square also has 90° clockwise (or counterclockwise) rotational symmetry.
run (p. 404) The horizontal change between two points on a line.	*See* slope.

S

	Example
sample (p. 601) A part of a population.	To predict the results of an election, a survey is given to a sample of voters.
scale (p. 300) A ratio that gives the relationship between the dimensions of a scale drawing or a scale model and the actual dimensions of the object.	The scale 1 cm : 100 m means that 1 centimeter in the scale drawing represents an actual distance of 100 meters.
scale drawing (p. 300) A two-dimensional drawing that is similar to the object it represents.	A map is a scale drawing of the land area it shows.
scale factor (p. 747) For a dilation, the ratio of a side length of the image to the corresponding side length of the original figure.	*See* dilation.
scale model (p. 300) A three-dimensional model that is similar to the object it represents.	A globe is a scale model of Earth.
scatter plot (p. 48) A graph in a coordinate plane that displays paired data. Each data pair is plotted as a point.	*See* best-fitting line.
scientific notation (p. 204) A number is written in scientific notation if it has the form $c \times 10^n$ where $1 \le c < 10$ and n is an integer.	In scientific notation, 253,000 is written as 2.53×10^5, and 0.00047 is written as 4.7×10^{-4}.
self-selected sample (p. 601) A sample in which members of a population can select themselves by volunteering.	You put a survey questionnaire in the mailbox of each teacher at your school. The group of all teachers who answer the questionnaire is a self-selected sample of the school's teacher population.
sequence (p. 692) An ordered list of numbers.	1, 5, 9, 13, 17, . . .
similar figures (p. 288) Figures that have the same shape but not necessarily the same size. Corresponding angles of similar figures are congruent, and the ratios of the lengths of corresponding sides are equal. The symbol ~ indicates that two figures are similar.	$\triangle LMN \sim \triangle PQR$

Glossary

	Example
simple interest (p. 362) Interest that is earned or paid only on the principal. Simple interest I is the product of the principal P, the annual interest rate r (written as a decimal), and the time t in years: $I = Prt$ The balance A of an account that earns simple annual interest is $A = P + Prt$, or $A = P(1 + rt)$.	You deposit \$500 into a savings account that earns 2.5% simple annual interest. After 3 years, the interest earned is $I = Prt = (500)(0.025)(3) = \$37.50$, and your account balance is $\$500 + \$37.50 = \$537.50$.
simplest form of a fraction (p. 183) A fraction is in simplest form when its numerator and denominator are relatively prime.	The simplest form of the fraction $\frac{8}{12}$ is $\frac{2}{3}$.
simplest form of a radical expression (p. 458) A radical expression is in simplest form when (1) no factor of the expression under the radical sign is a perfect square other than 1, and (2) there are no fractions under the radical sign and no radical sign in the denominator of any fraction.	In simplest form, $\sqrt{72}$ is written as $6\sqrt{2}$.
sine (p. 494) For a right triangle, the sine of an acute angle A (sin A) is the ratio of the length of the side opposite $\angle A$ to the length of the hypotenuse.	*See* trigonometric ratio.
slant height of a cone (p. 546) The distance between the vertex and any point on the edge of the base.	*See* height of a cone.
slant height of a pyramid (p. 544) The height of a triangular lateral face of the pyramid.	*See* regular pyramid.
slope (p. 404) The slope of a nonvertical line is the ratio of the rise (vertical change) to the run (horizontal change) between any two points on the line.	 The slope of the line shown is: slope $= \dfrac{\text{rise}}{\text{run}} = \dfrac{-2}{5} = -\dfrac{2}{5}$
slope-intercept form (p. 412) The form of a linear equation $y = mx + b$ where m is the slope and b is the y-intercept.	$y = 3x + 7$ is in slope-intercept form. The slope is 3 and the y-intercept is 7.
solution of a linear inequality in two variables (p. 436) An ordered pair that produces a true statement when the coordinates of the ordered pair are substituted for the variables in the inequality.	$(0, 1)$ is a solution of the linear inequality $3x - 7y < -1$, because $3(0) - 7(1) < -1$.

	Example
solution of a linear system (p. 431) An ordered pair that is a solution of each equation in the system. A solution of a linear system occurs at an intersection point of the graphs of the equations in the system.	$(-1, 3)$ is the solution of this linear system: $$y = -2x + 1$$ $$y = 3x + 6$$
solution of an equation (p. 85) A number that produces a true statement when it is substituted for the variable in the equation.	The solution of the equation $8 - a = 10$ is -2, because $8 - (-2) = 10$.
solution of an equation in two variables (p. 391) An ordered pair that produces a true statement when the coordinates of the ordered pair are substituted for the variables in the equation.	$(2, 1)$ is a solution of the equation $3x - 4y = 2$, because $3(2) - 4(1) = 2$.
solution of an inequality (p. 138) The set of all numbers that produce true statements when substituted for the variable in the inequality.	The solution of the inequality $4n < 36$ is $n < 9$, because any number less than 9, when substituted for n, makes $4n < 36$ a true statement.
solving an equation (p. 86) Finding all the solutions of the equation.	To solve the equation $3x = 15$, find the number that can be multiplied by 3 to equal 15. Because $3(5) = 15$, the solution of $3x = 15$ is 5.
square root (p. 453) A square root of a number n is a number m such that $m^2 = n$. The radical sign, $\sqrt{\ }$, represents a nonnegative square root.	The square roots of 25 are 5 and -5, because $5^2 = 25$ and $(-5)^2 = 25$. So, $\sqrt{25} = 5$ and $-\sqrt{25} = -5$.
standard form of a polynomial (p. 652) A polynomial is written in standard form if all like terms are combined and the terms are arranged so that the degree of each term decreases or stays the same from left to right.	The expression $3(x^2 + 5) - x^2 - 3$ can be written as $2x^2 + 12$, a polynomial in standard form.
stem-and-leaf plot (p. 581) A display that organizes data based on their digits.	**stems** **leaves** 10 | 8 11 | 2 2 5 12 | 1 3 Key: 10 | 8 = 108
stratified sample (p. 601) A sample in which a population is divided into distinct groups. Members are selected from each group.	You can select a stratified sample of your school's student population by choosing 20 students from each grade level.

	Example

supplementary angles (p. 709) Two angles whose measures have a sum of 180°.

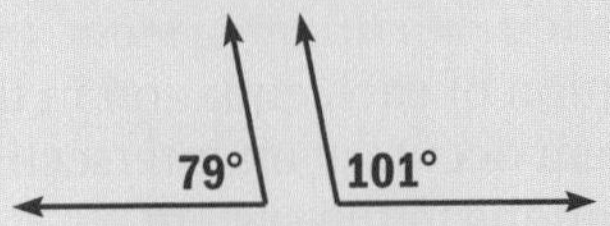

79° 101°

---

surface area of a solid (p. 538) The sum of the areas of the solid's faces.

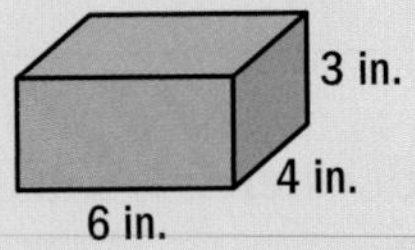

3 in.
4 in.
6 in.

Surface area
$$= 2(6)(4) + 2(6)(3) + 2(4)(3)$$
$$= 108 \text{ in.}^2$$

---

systematic sample (p. 601) A sample in which a rule is used to select members of a population.

You can select a systematic sample of your school's student population by giving a questionnaire to every tenth student on an alphabetical list of all students at the school.

---

system of linear equations (p. 431) Two or more linear equations with the same variables; also called a linear system.

The two equations shown below form a linear system:

$$y = -2x + 1$$
$$y = 3x + 6$$

---

t

tangent (p. 489) For a right triangle, the tangent of an acute angle A (tan A) is the ratio of the length of the side opposite $\angle A$ to the length of the side adjacent to $\angle A$.

See trigonometric ratio.

---

terminating decimal (p. 219) A decimal that has a final digit. A terminating decimal can be written as a quotient of integers $\frac{a}{b}$, where $b \neq 0$.

0.8 and 2.307 are terminating decimals.

$$0.8 = \frac{8}{10} = \frac{4}{5}$$

$$2.307 = 2\frac{307}{1000} = \frac{2307}{1000}$$

---

terms of an expression (p. 78) The parts of an expression that are added together.

The terms of the expression $5x + (-2x) + 1$ are $5x$, $-2x$, and 1.

---

terms of a polynomial (p. 651) The monomials that are added together in the polynomial.

The terms of the polynomial $x^2 + 5x - 1$ are x^2, $5x$, and -1.

---

terms of a sequence (p. 692) The numbers in the sequence.

The fourth term of the sequence 1, 5, 9, 13, 17, . . . is 13.

	Example
tessellation (p. 730) A covering of a plane with a repeating pattern of one or more shapes, with no gaps or overlaps.	
theoretical probability (p. 307) When all outcomes are equally likely, the theoretical probability of an event is the ratio of the number of favorable outcomes to the number of possible outcomes.	A bag of 40 marbles contains 8 blue marbles. The theoretical probability of randomly choosing a blue marble from the bag is $\frac{8}{40} = \frac{1}{5}$, or 0.2.
transformation (p. 729) A change made to the location or to the size of a figure, resulting in a new figure, called the image.	*See* translation, reflection, rotation, *and* dilation.
translation (p. 729) A transformation in which each point of a figure moves the same distance in the same direction.	$\triangle ABC$ is translated 4 units to the right.
transversal (p. 716) A line that intersects two or more lines at different points.	Line t is a transversal. $\angle 1$ and $\angle 3$ are corresponding angles. $\angle 2$ and $\angle 3$ are alternate interior angles. $\angle 1$ and $\angle 4$ are alternate exterior angles.
trapezoid (p. 517) A quadrilateral with exactly one pair of parallel sides.	base b_1 height h base b_2

	Example

tree diagram (p. 313) A diagram that uses branching to list all possible choices or outcomes.

Possibilities:
HH   HT   TH   TT

---

trigonometric ratio (p. 489) A ratio of the lengths of two sides of a right triangle. For an acute angle A of a right triangle, three trigonometric ratios are defined: sine of $\angle A$ (sin A), cosine of $\angle A$ (cos A), and tangent of $\angle A$ (tan A).

$$\sin A = \frac{a}{c} \qquad \cos A = \frac{b}{c} \qquad \tan A = \frac{a}{b}$$

---

trinomial (p. 651) A polynomial with three terms.

$a^2 + 5a + 6$ is a trinomial.

---

u

upper extreme (p. 588) The greatest value in a data set.

See box-and-whisker plot.

---

upper quartile (p. 588) The median of the upper half of an ordered data set.

See box-and-whisker plot.

---

v

variable (p. 5) A letter that is used to represent one or more numbers.

In the expression $n + 3$, the letter n is the variable.

---

variable expression (p. 5) An expression that consists of numbers, variables, and operations.

$x - 7$, $\frac{2a}{b}$, and $2t + 3r - 3$ are all variable expressions.

---

verbal model (p. 6) An expression that describes a problem using words as labels and using math symbols to relate the words.

$$\text{Distance} \atop \text{traveled} = {\text{Rate} \atop \text{of travel}} \cdot {\text{Time} \atop \text{traveled}}$$

---

vertical angles (p. 710) A pair of opposite angles formed when two lines intersect at one point.

$\angle 1$ and $\angle 3$ are vertical angles.
$\angle 2$ and $\angle 4$ are vertical angles.

	Example

vertical line test (p. 387) For a relation represented by a graph, if any vertical line passes through more than one point of the graph, then the relation is not a function. If no vertical line passes through more than one point of the graph, then the relation is a function.

The graph is not a function, because a vertical line passes through two points.

X

x-axis (p. 47) The horizontal number line in a coordinate plane.

See coordinate plane.

x-coordinate (p. 47) The first number in an ordered pair representing a point in a coordinate plane.

The *x*-coordinate of the ordered pair $(5, -3)$ is 5.

x-intercept (p. 398) The *x*-coordinate of a point where a graph crosses the *x*-axis.

y

y-axis (p. 47) The vertical number line in a coordinate plane.

See coordinate plane.

y-coordinate (p. 47) The second number in an ordered pair representing a point in a coordinate plane.

The *y*-coordinate of the ordered pair $(5, -3)$ is -3.

y-intercept (p. 398) The *y*-coordinate of a point where a graph crosses the *y*-axis.

See x-intercept.

Glosario

	Ejemplo
a	
absolute value / valor absoluto (p. 23) El valor absoluto de un número a es la distancia entre a y 0 en una recta numérica. El símbolo $\lvert a \rvert$ representa el valor absoluto de a.	$\lvert 3 \rvert = 3 \quad \lvert -5 \rvert = 5 \quad \lvert 0 \rvert = 0$
additive identity / identidad aditiva (p. 64) El número 0 es la identidad aditiva ya que la suma de cualquier número y 0 es ese número.	$-3 + 0 = -3$ $a + 0 = a$
additive inverse / inverso aditivo (p. 30) El inverso aditivo de un número a es su opuesto, $-a$. La suma de un número y su inverso aditivo es 0.	El inverso aditivo de 5 es -5, entonces $5 + (-5) = 0$.
alternate exterior angles / ángulos externos alternos (p. 716) Dos ángulos formados por dos rectas y una transversal y que se encuentran en el exterior de las dos rectas en lados opuestos de la transversal.	*Ver* transversal / transversal.
alternate interior angles / ángulos internos alternos (p. 716) Dos ángulos formados por dos rectas y una transversal y que se encuentran entre las dos rectas en lados opuestos de la transversal.	*Ver* transversal / transversal.
angle of rotation / ángulo de rotación (p. 741) En una rotación, el ángulo formado por dos semirrectas trazadas desde el centro de rotación a través de los puntos correspondientes en la figura original y su imagen.	*Ver* rotation / rotación.
annual interest rate / tasa de interés anual (p. 362) El porcentaje del capital ganado o pagado por año.	*Ver* simple interest / interés simple e compound interest / interés compuesto.
arithmetic sequence / progresión aritmética (p. 692) Progresión en la que la diferencia entre los términos consecutivos es constante.	1, 5, 9, 13, 17, . . . es una progresión aritmética en la que la diferencia entre los términos consecutivos es 4.
b	
balance of an account / saldo de una cuenta (p. 363) La suma del capital y todo interés ganado.	*Ver* simple interest / interés simple e compound interest / interés compuesto.
base of a parallelogram / base de un paralelogramo (p. 521) La longitud de cualquier lado del paralelogramo puede usarse como la base.	*Ver* parallelogram / paralelogramo.

	Ejemplo
base of a power / base de una potencia (p. 10) El número o la expresión que se usa como factor en la multiplicación repetida.	En la potencia 2^7, la base es 2.
bases of a trapezoid / bases de un trapecio (p. 522) Las longitudes de los lados paralelos del trapecio.	*Ver* trapezoid / trapecio.
best-fitting line / mejor recta de regresión (p. 421) La recta que está situada lo más cerca posible de los puntos de un diagrama de dispersión.	Se muestra en rojo la mejor recta de regresión del diagrama de dispersión.
biased question / pregunta capciosa (p. 603) Pregunta que impulsa a dar una respuesta determinada.	"¿No crees que sería mejor si la escuela construyera un gimnasio nuevo?" es una pregunta capciosa.
biased sample / muestra sesgada (p. 602) Muestra que no es representativa de la población.	Los miembros del equipo de baloncesto de una escuela formarían una muestra sesgada si participaran en una encuesta sobre si quieren que se construya un nuevo gimnasio.
binomial / binomio (p. 651) Polinomio con dos términos.	$a^2 + 5a$ y $9 - y$ son binomios.
box-and-whisker plot / gráfica de frecuencias acumuladas (p. 588) Presentación de datos que organiza los valores de los datos en cuatro grupos usando el extremo inferior, el cuartil inferior, la mediana, el cuartil superior y el extremo superior.	
C	
categorical data / datos categóricos (p. 596) Datos que consisten de nombres, etiquetas u otros valores no numéricos.	Una lista de colores de ojos es un conjunto de datos categóricos.
center of a circle / centro de un círculo (p. 528) El punto en el interior del círculo que está a la misma distancia de todos los puntos del círculo.	*Ver* circle / círculo.

Glosario

	Ejemplo
center of dilation / centro de dilatación (p. 747) El punto en torno al cual una figura se amplía o se reduce cuando la figura experimenta una dilatación.	*Ver* dilation / dilatación.
center of rotation / centro de rotación (p. 741) El punto alrededor del cual gira una figura cuando se la hace rotar.	*Ver* rotation / rotación.
circle / círculo (p. 528) El conjunto de todos los puntos de un plano que son equidistantes de un punto dado, llamado centro del círculo.	
circumference of a circle / circunferencia de un círculo (p. 528) La distancia por el contorno de un círculo.	*Ver* circle / círculo.
coefficient / coeficiente (p. 78) La parte numérica de un término con una variable.	El coeficiente de $-7x$ es -7.
combination / combinación (p. 620) Selección de objetos en la cual el orden en que se eligen los objetos no es importante.	Existen 3 combinaciones de 2 letras tomadas de las letras A, H, T: 　　AH　　AT　　HT
common difference / diferencia común (p. 692) La diferencia constante entre los términos consecutivos de una progresión aritmética.	*Ver* arithmetic sequence / progresión aritmética.
common factor / factor común (p. 177) Un número natural que es factor de dos o más números naturales distintos de cero.	Los factores comunes de 12 y 20 son 1, 2 y 4.
common multiple / múltiplo común (p. 187) Un número natural que es múltiplo de dos o más números naturales distintos de cero.	Los múltiplos comunes de 6 y 9 son 18, 36, 54, ...
common ratio / razón común (p. 692) La razón entre cualquier término de una progresión geométrica y el término anterior de la progresión.	*Ver* geometric sequence / progresión geométrica.
complementary angles / ángulos complementarios (p. 709) Dos ángulos cuyas medidas suman 90°.	

	Ejemplo
complementary events / sucesos complementarios (p. 630) Dos sucesos disjuntos de modo que debe ocurrir un suceso o el otro.	Cuando lanzas un dado de números, los sucesos "obtener un número impar" y "obtener un número par" son sucesos complementarios.
composite number / número compuesto (p. 173) Un número natural mayor que 1 que tiene factores distintos a sí mismo y a 1.	6 es un número compuesto porque sus factores son 1, 2, 3 y 6.
compound interest / interés compuesto (p. 363) Interés obtenido tanto sobre la inversión inicial como sobre el interés conseguido anteriormente. El saldo A de una cuenta que obtiene interés compuesto anual es $A = P(1 + r)^t$, donde P es el capital, r es la tasa de interés anual (expresada como decimal) y t es el tiempo en años.	Depositas \$1000 en una cuenta al 3% anual de interés compuesto. Después de 5 años, el saldo de la cuenta es $A = P(1 + r)^t = 1000(1 + 0.03)^5 \approx \$1159.27$.
concave / cóncavo (p. 516) Un polígono es cóncavo si un segmento que une dos puntos interiores cualesquiera no está situado completamente dentro del polígono.	*Ver* convex / convexo.
congruent figures / figuras congruentes (p. 290) Figuras que tienen la misma forma y el mismo tamaño. Los ángulos correspondientes y los lados correspondientes de las figuras congruentes son congruentes.	$\triangle ABC \cong \triangle DEF$
constant term / término constante (p. 78) Término que tiene una parte numérica sin variable.	En la expresión $8a + 4$, el término constante es 4.
convenience sample / muestra de conveniencia (p. 601) Muestra en la que se selecciona sólo a los miembros de una población fácilmente accesibles.	Para seleccionar una muestra de conveniencia de la población de estudiantes de una escuela, puedes escoger sólo a los estudiantes que están en tus clases.
convex / convexo (p. 516) Un polígono es convexo si un segmento que une dos puntos interiores cualesquiera está situado completamente dentro del polígono. Un polígono que no es convexo se conoce como *cóncavo*.	Convexo Cóncavo

	Ejemplo

coordinate plane / plano de coordenadas (p. 47) Un plano dividido en cuatro cuadrantes por una recta numérica horizontal llamada eje x y una recta numérica vertical llamada eje y.

corresponding angles / ángulos correspondientes (p. 716) Dos ángulos formados por dos rectas y una transversal y que ocupan posiciones correspondientes.

Ver transversal / transversal.

corresponding parts / partes correspondientes (p. 288) Un par de lados o ángulos que tienen la misma posición relativa en dos figuras.

$\angle A$ y $\angle D$ son ángulos correspondientes. $\overline{AC}$ y $\overline{DF}$ son lados correspondientes.

cosine / coseno (p. 494) En un triángulo rectángulo, el coseno de un ángulo agudo A (cos A) es la razón entre la longitud del lado adyacente a $\angle A$ y la longitud del hipotenusa.

See trigonometric ratio / razón trigonométrica.

counting principle / principio de conteo (p. 314) Si un suceso puede ocurrir de m maneras, y para cada una de estas maneras un segundo suceso puede ocurrir de n maneras, entonces el número de maneras en que los dos sucesos pueden ocurrir juntos es $m \cdot n$.

Tienes 3 camisas y 4 pares de pantalones. El número total de combinaciones de camisas-pantalones que puedes elegir es $3 \cdot 4 = 12$.

cross product / producto cruzado (p. 280) En una proporción, un producto cruzado es el producto del numerador de una de las razones y el denominador de la otra razón. Los productos cruzados de una proporción son iguales.

Los productos cruzados de la proporción $\frac{2}{3} = \frac{8}{12}$ son $2 \cdot 12 = 24$ y $3 \cdot 8 = 24$.

	Ejemplo
degree of a polynomial / grado de un polinomio (p. 652) El mayor grado de los términos del polinomio.	En el polinomio $a^2 + 4a^2b + 5$, el grado del término a^2 es 2, el grado del término $4a^2b$ es 3 y el grado del término 5 es 0. El grado del polinomio es 3, el grado mayor de los términos.
degree of a term / grado de un término (p. 652) La suma de los exponentes de las variables de un término. El grado de una constante distinta de cero es 0.	*Ver* degree of a polynomial / grado de un polinomio.
dependent events / sucesos dependientes (p. 634) Dos sucesos tales que la ocurrencia de uno de ellos afecta a la ocurrencia del otro.	Una bolsa contiene 4 canicas rojas y 5 verdes. Saca al azar una canica y no la reemplaces; luego saca al azar otra canica. Los sucesos "la primera canica es roja" y "la segunda canica es roja" son sucesos dependientes.
diagonal of a polygon / diagonal de un polígono (p. 518) Segmento que une dos vértices no consecutivos de un polígono.	
diameter of a circle / diámetro de un círculo (p. 528) La distancia que atraviesa el círculo por el centro.	*Ver* circle / círculo.
dilation / dilatación (p. 747) Transformación por la cual una figura se amplía o reduce en torno a un punto fijo, llamado el centro de dilatación.	$\triangle ABC$ se dilata con respecto al origen usando un factor de escala de 3.
discount / descuento (p. 358) Una cantidad restada del precio habitual de un artículo para obtener el precio de oferta.	El precio original de un abrigo es $32.99, pero la tienda lo vende a $25.99. El descuento es $7.00.
disjoint events / sucesos disjuntos (p. 627) Sucesos que no tienen ningún en común; también se llaman sucesos mutuamente excluyentes.	Al lanzar un dado, los sucesos "obtener un número par" y "obtener un 3" son sucesos disjuntos.

	Ejemplo
domain of a relation / dominio de una relación (p. 385) El conjunto de todos los valores de entrada posibles para la relación.	*Ver* relation / relación.

e

equation / ecuación (p. 85) Un enunciado matemático que se forma colocando un signo de igualdad = entre dos expresiones.	$3x - 2 = 12 + 10x$ es una ecuación.
equation in two variables / ecuación con dos variables (p. 391) Ecuación que tiene dos variables diferentes.	$3x - 4y = 2$ es una ecuación con dos variables.
equivalent equations / ecuaciones equivalentes (p. 91) Ecuaciones que tienen la misma solución o soluciones.	$5y - 2 = 8$ y $5y = 10$ son ecuaciones equivalentes.
equivalent fractions / fracciones equivalentes (p. 182) Fracciones que representan el mismo número.	$\frac{4}{8}$ y $\frac{10}{20}$ son fracciones equivalentes porque ambas representan $\frac{1}{2}$.
equivalent inequalities / desigualdades equivalentes (p. 139) Desigualdades con las mismas soluciones.	$3y + 7 > 25$ y $3y > 18$ son desigualdades equivalentes ya que las soluciones de ambas son todos los números mayores que 6.
equivalent numerical expressions / expresiones numéricas equivalentes (p. 71) Expresiones numéricas que tienen el mismo valor.	$5(10 - 6)$ y $5(10) - 5(6)$ son expresiones numéricas equivalentes porque cada una tiene un valor de 20.
equivalent ratios / razones equivalentes (p. 270) Dos o más razones que tienen el mismo valor.	$\frac{3}{4}$, $\frac{9}{12}$ y $\frac{15}{20}$ son razones equivalentes porque cada una tiene un valor de 0.75.
equivalent variable expressions / expresiones variables equivalentes (p. 72) Expresiones variables que tienen el mismo valor para todos los valores de la/s variable/s.	$5(x + 1) + x$ y $6x + 5$ son expresiones variables equivalentes.
evaluate a variable expression / evaluar una expresión variable (p. 5) Hallar el valor de una expresión variable sustituyendo cada variable por un número y luego hallando el valor de la expresión numérica resultante.	El valor de $2y - 5$ cuando $y = 3$ es $2(3) - 5 = 1$.
event / suceso (p. 306) Caso o colección de casos.	Cuando lanzas un dado, "salir número par" es un suceso.

	Ejemplo
experimental probability / probabilidad experimental (p. 307) Una probabilidad basada en el número de ensayos de un experimento. La probabilidad experimental de un suceso es la razón entre el número de sucesos (resultados favorables de un suceso) y el número de ensayos.	Una jugadora de basquetbol ha encestado 30 de los 36 tiros libres que lanzó esta temporada. La probabilidad experimental de que enceste un tiro libre es $\frac{30}{36} = \frac{5}{6}$, o aproximadamente 0.83.
exponent / exponente (p. 10) Número o expresión que indica cuántas veces se usa la base como factor en una multiplicación repetida.	En la potencia 2^7, el exponente es 7.
exponential decay / decrecimiento exponencial (p. 687) Una cantidad que disminuye muestra decrecimiento exponencial si puede describirse como una función exponencial de la forma $y = ab^x$, donde $a > 0$ y $0 < b < 1$.	La función $y = \left(\frac{1}{3}\right)^x$ muestra decrecimiento exponencial. *Ver* exponential function / función exponencial.
exponential function / función exponencial (p. 686) Ecuación con dos variables de la forma $y = ab^x$, donde $a \neq 0$, $b > 0$ y $b \neq 1$.	$y = 3(2)^x$ e $y = \left(\frac{1}{3}\right)^x$ son funciones exponenciales.
exponential growth / crecimiento exponencial (p. 687) Una cantidad que aumenta muestra crecimiento exponencial si puede describirse como una función exponencial de la forma $y = ab^x$, donde $a > 0$ y $b > 1$.	La función $y = 3(2)^x$ muestra crecimiento exponencial. *Ver* exponential function / función exponencial.
exterior angle of a polygon / ángulo externo de un polígono (p. 723) Un ángulo adyacente a un ángulo interno del polígono, que se forma extendiendo un lado del polígono.	*Ver* interior angle of a polygon / ángulo interno de un polígono.
f	
factor tree / árbol de factores (p. 173) Un diagrama que puede usarse para escribir la descomposición de un número en factores primos.	28 / 4 · 7 \\ 2 · 2 · 7

	Ejemplo
favorable outcomes / casos favorables (p. 306) Resultados que corresponden a un suceso específico.	Cuando lanzas un dado de números, los resultados favorables del suceso "obtener un número par" son 2, 4 y 6.
frequency / frecuencia (p. 582) La frecuencia de un intervalo es el número de datos de valores que hay en ese intervalo.	*Ver* frequency table / tabla de frecuencias *e* histogram / histograma.
frequency table / tabla de frecuencias (p. 582) Presentación de datos en la que se agrupan los datos en intervalos iguales.	<table><thead><tr><th>Intervalo</th><th>Marca</th><th>Frecuencia</th></tr></thead><tbody><tr><td>0–9</td><td>||</td><td>2</td></tr><tr><td>10–19</td><td></td><td>0</td></tr><tr><td>20–29</td><td>||||</td><td>4</td></tr></tbody></table>
function / función (p. 386) Una relación con la propiedad de que para cada entrada existe *exactamente una* salida.	La relación $(1, 0)$, $(2, 1)$, $(3, 0)$, $(4, 1)$, $(5, 0)$ es una función porque a cada entrada le corresponde exactamente una salida. La relación $(1, 0)$, $(2, 0)$, $(2, 1)$, $(3, 0)$, $(3, 1)$, $(3, 2)$ no es una función porque a las entradas 2 y 3 les corresponde más de una salida.
function form of an equation / forma de función de una ecuación (p. 393) Una ecuación con x e y está en forma de función si resuelve la y.	La ecuación $y - 2x = 8$ puede escribirse en forma de función como $y = 2x + 8$.
function notation / notación de función (p. 426) El uso del símbolo $f(x)$, en lugar de y, en una ecuación para representar la salida de una función f para la entrada x. El símbolo $f(x)$ se lee "f de x."	La función $y = 3x - 5$ puede escribirse como notación de función como $f(x) = 3x - 5$.

g

geometric sequence / progresión geométrica (p. 692) Progresión en la que la razón entre cualquier término y el término anterior es constante.	La progresión $1, 2, 4, 8, 16, \ldots$ es una progresión geométrica cuya razón común es 2.
graph of a linear inequality in two variables / gráfica de una desigualdad lineal con dos variables (p. 436) El conjunto de todos los puntos de un plano de coordenadas que representan las soluciones de la desigualdad.	La gráfica de $y \geq x + 3$ es el semiplano sombreado.

	Ejemplo
graph of an equation in two variables / gráfica de una ecuación con dos variables (p. 392) El conjunto de puntos de un plano de coordenadas que representa todas las soluciones de la ecuación.	$y = -x + 1$
greatest common factor (GCF) / máximo común divisor (MCD) (p. 177) El mayor de los factores comunes de dos o más números naturales distintos de cero.	El MCD de 30 y 54 es 6. El MCD de 30, 60 y 75 es 15.

h

	Ejemplo
half-plane / semiplano (p. 436) En un plano de coordenadas, la región situada a cada lado de una recta límite.	*Ver* graph of a linear inequality in two variables / gráfica de una desigualdad lineal con dos variables.
height of a cone / altura de un cono (p. 546) La distancia entre el vértice y el centro de la base.	vértice apotema lateral *l* altura *h* radio *r*
height of a parallelogram / altura de un paralelogramo (p. 521) La distancia perpendicular entre las bases de un paralelogramo.	*Ver* parallelogram / paralelogramo.
height of a pyramid / altura de una pirámide (p. 544) La distancia perpendicular entre la base y el vértice.	*Ver* regular pyramid / pirámide regular.
height of a trapezoid / altura de un trapecio (p. 522) La distancia perpendicular entre las bases de un trapecio.	*Ver* trapezoid / trapecio.
heptagon / heptágono (p. 516) Un polígono con 7 lados.	
hexagon / hexágono (p. 516) Polígono con 6 lados.	

histogram / histograma (p. 583) Presentación de datos de una tabla de frecuencias.

Visitas a la biblioteca en día sábado

Edad (años)

hypotenuse / hipotenusa (p. 465) El lado de un triángulo rectángulo opuesto al ángulo recto.

image / imagen (p. 729) La nueva figura que resulta tras una transformación. La imagen del punto A se escribe A'.

Ver translation / traslación, reflection / reflexión, rotation / rotación *y* dilation / dilatación.

independent events / sucesos independientes (p. 634) Dos sucesos tales que la ocurrencia de uno de ellos no afecta a la ocurrencia del otro.

Lanzas un cubo numerado dos veces. Los sucesos "salir primero el 3" y "salir después el 4" son sucesos independientes.

inequality / desigualdad (p. 138) Enunciado matemático formado mediante signo de desigualdad entre dos expresiones entre dos expresiones.

$4 > -7$ y $5x - 3 \leq 2$ son desigualdades.

input / entrada (p. 385) Número del dominio de una relación.

Ver relation / relación.

integers / números enteros (p. 22) Los números . . . , -3, -2, -1, 0, 1, 2, 3, . . . que constan de los números enteros negativos, cero y los números enteros positivos.

-9 y 23 son números enteros.

-9.25 y $23\frac{1}{2}$ *no* son números enteros.

interest / interés (p. 362) La cantidad obtenida o pagada por el uso de dinero.

Ver simple interest / interés simple *e* compound interest / interés compuesto.

interior angle of a polygon / ángulo interno de un polígono (p. 722) Ángulo que se encuentra dentro del polígono.

$\angle 1$ es una ángulo interno de $\triangle ABC$.
$\angle 2$ es una ángulo externo de $\triangle ABC$.

Glosario

interquartile range / rango intercuartílico (p. 590) La diferencia entre el cuartil superior y el cuartil inferior de un conjunto de datos.	*Ver* box-and-whisker plot / gráfica de frecuencias acumuladas.
inverse operations / operaciones inversas (p. 91) Dos operaciones que se anulan entre sí.	La suma y la resta son operaciones inversas. La multiplicación y la división también son operaciones inversas.
irrational number / número irracional (p. 470) Número que no puede escribirse como cociente de dos números enteros. La forma decimal de un número irracional no termina ni se repite.	$\sqrt{3}$, π, y 0.202002000. . . son números irracionales.

I

lateral area of a cylinder / área lateral de un cilindro (p. 540) El área de la superficie curvada del cilindro.	 Área lateral $= (2 \cdot \pi \cdot 2)(5)$ $= 20\pi$ $\approx 62.8 \text{ m}^2$
lateral area of a prism / área lateral de un prisma (p. 539) La suma de las áreas de las caras laterales del prisma.	 Área lateral $= 2(3) + 2(4) + 2(5)$ $= 24 \text{ pulg}^2$
lateral faces of a prism / caras laterales de un prisma (p. 539) Las caras de un prisma que no son las bases.	*Ver* lateral area of a prism / área lateral de un prisma.
lateral surface of a cylinder / superficie lateral de un cilindro (p. 540) La superficie curvada del cilindro.	*Ver* lateral area of a cylinder / área lateral de un cilindro.

	Ejemplo
least common denominator (LCD) / mínimo común denominador (m.c.d.) (p. 188) El múltiplo común menor de los denominadores de dos o más fracciones.	El m.c.d. de $\frac{3}{4}$ y $\frac{5}{6}$ es 12, el m.c.m. de 4 y 6.
least common multiple (LCM) / mínimo común múltiplo (m.c.m.) (p. 187) El menor de los números que es un múltiplo común de dos o más números.	El m.c.m. de 6 y 10 es 30. El m.c.m. de 4, 5 y 6 es 60.
legs of a right triangle / catetos de un triángulo rectángulo (p. 465) En un triángulo rectángulo, los lados adyacentes al ángulo recto.	*Ver* hypotenuse / hipotenusa.
like terms / términos semejantes (p. 78) Términos que tienen las mismas variables. Los términos constantes también son términos semejantes.	En la expresión $x + 5 - 7x + 1$, x y $-7x$ son términos semejantes, y 5 y 1 también son términos semejantes.
linear equation in two variables / ecuación lineal con dos variables (p. 392) Una ecuación cuya gráfica es una recta.	*Ver* graph of an equation in two variables / gráfica de una ecuación con dos variables.
linear inequality in two variables / desigualdad lineal con dos variables (p. 436) Desigualdad que resulta de reemplazar el signo igual en una ecuación lineal con dos variables con $<$, $\leq$, $>$ o $\geq$.	$3x - 7y < -1$ e $y \geq x + 4$ son desigualdades lineales con dos variables.
line of reflection / línea de reflexión (p. 734) La recta sobre la que se voltea una figura cuando dicha figura se refleja.	*Ver* reflection / reflexión.
line of symmetry / línea de simetría (p. 735) Una línea que divide una figura en dos partes que son imágenes reflejas de sí mismas sobre la línea.	*Ver* line symmetry / simetría lineal.
line symmetry / simetría lineal (p. 735) Una figura tiene simetría lineal si puede dividirse por una línea, llamada línea de simetría, en dos partes que son imágenes reflejas entre sí.	Un cuadrado tiene 4 líneas de simetría.
lower extreme / extremo inferior (p. 588) El menor valor en un conjunto de datos.	*Ver* box-and-whisker plot / gráfica de frecuencias acumuladas.
lower quartile / cuartil inferior (p. 588) La mediana de la mitad inferior de un conjunto de datos.	*Ver* box-and-whisker plot / gráfica de frecuencias acumuladas.

	Ejemplo
m	
margin of error / margen de error (p. 610) El margen de error indica un límite acerca de cuánto se preve que diferirían las respuestas obtenidas en una muestra de las obtenidas en la población.	Si una predicción indica que obtendrás el 58% de votos en una elección, con un margen de error del 64%, esto significa que es muy probable que el porcentaje de los votos que obtengas esté entre el 54% y el 62%.
markup / margen de ganancia (p. 357) El aumento del precio mayorista de un artículo sobre el precio de venta.	El precio mayorista de un galón de leche es $2.30, pero la tienda lo vende a $3.19. El margen de ganancia es $.89.
maximum value of a function / valor máximo de una función (p. 681) La coordenada y del punto más alto en la gráfica de la función. Una función cuadrática $y = ax^2 + bx + c$ tiene un valor máximo cuando $a < 0$.	 El valor máximo de $y = -\frac{1}{2}x^2 - x + \frac{5}{2}$ es 3.
midpoint of a segment / punto medio de un segmento (p. 478) El punto del segmento que es equidistante de los extremos.	 M es el punto medio de $\overline{AB}$.
minimum value of a function / valor mínimo de una función (p. 681) La coordenada y del punto más bajo en la gráfica de la función. Una función cuadrática $y = ax^2 + bx + c$ tiene un valor mínimo cuando $a > 0$.	 El valor mínimo de $y = \frac{1}{2}x^2 - 2x + 1$ es -1.
monomial / monomio (p. 174) Un número, una variable o el producto de un número y una o más variables que tienen exponentes expresados por números naturales.	$8xy$, $5a^3$, n^2m, p y 12 son monomios.
multiple / múltiplo (p. 187) Un múltiplo de un número natural es el producto de ese número y cualquier número natural distinto de cero.	Los múltiplos de 7 son 7, 14, 21, 28, ...

	Ejemplo
multiplicative identity / identidad multiplicativa (p. 64) El número 1 es la identidad multiplicativa ya que el producto de cualquier número y 1 es ese número.	$5 \cdot 1 = 5$ $a \cdot 1 = a$
multiplicative inverse / inverso multiplicativo (p. 247) El inverso multiplicativo de un número distinto de cero $\frac{a}{b}$, donde $a \neq 0$ y $b \neq 0$, es su recíproco $\frac{b}{a}$. El producto de un número y su inverso multiplicativo es 1.	El inverso multiplicativo de $\frac{5}{3}$ es $\frac{3}{5}$, entonces $\frac{5}{3} \cdot \frac{3}{5} = 1$.
mutually exclusive events / sucesos mutuamente excluyentes (p. 627) Sucesos que no tienen ningún caso en común.	*Ver* disjoint events / sucesos disjuntos.

n

negative integers / números enteros negativos (p. 22) Los números enteros menores que 0.	$-1, -2, -3, -4, \ldots$
net / patrón (p. 538) La representación bidimensional de un sólido. El área de la superficie de un sólido es igual al área de su patrón.	*Ver* lateral area of a cylinder / área lateral de un cilindro *y* lateral area of a prism / área lateral de un prisma.
n factorial / factorial n (p. 615) Para cualquier número entero positivo *n*, el producto de los números enteros de 1 a *n* se denomina factorial *n* y se escribe *n*!.	$5! = 5 \cdot 4 \cdot 3 \cdot 2 \cdot 1 = 120$
nonlinear function / función no lineal (p. 680) Una función cuya gráfica no es una recta.	Una función cuadrática es una función no lineal. *Ver* parabola / parábola.
numerical data / datos numéricos (p. 596) Datos que consisten de números.	Una lista de alturas es un conjunto de datos numéricos.
numerical expression / expresión numérica (p. 5) Expresión formada por números y operaciones.	$5(2) + 7$ es una expresión numérica.

o

octagon / octágono (p. 516) Polígono con ocho lados.	
odds against / probabilidad en contra (p. 308) Cuando todos los casos son igualmente posibles, la probabilidad en contra de que ocurra un suceso se define como la razón entre el número de casos desfavorables y el número de casos favorables.	Cuando eliges un número entero al azar de 1 a 10, las probabilidades en contra de que elijas un número entero divisible por 3 son $\frac{7}{3}$ ó 7 a 3.

	Ejemplo
odds in favor / probabilidad a favor (p. 308) Cuando todos los casos son igualmente posibles, la probabilidad a favor de que ocurra un suceso se define como la razón entre el número de casos favorables y el número de casos desfavorables.	Cuando eliges un número entero al azar de 1 a 10, las probabilidades a favor de que elijas un número entero divisible por 3 son $\frac{3}{7}$ ó 3 a 7.
opposites / opuestos (p. 23) Dos números que tienen el mismo valor absoluto pero distinto signo.	-4 y 4 son opuestos.
ordered pair / par ordenado (p. 47) Un par de números (x, y) que pueden usarse para representar un punto en un plano de coordenadas. El primer número es la coordenada x, y el segundo número es la coordenada y.	
order of operations / orden de operaciones (p. 16) Un conjunto de reglas para evaluar una expresión que incluye más de una operación.	Para evaluar $5 - 2^2$, evalúa la potencia y después resta: $$5 - 2^2 = 5 - 4 = 1$$
origin / origen (p. 47) El punto $(0, 0)$ donde el eje x y el eje y se encuentran en un plano de coordenadas.	*Ver* coordinate plane / plano de coordenadas.
outcomes / casos (p. 306) Resultados posibles de un experimento.	Cuando lanzas una moneda, los casos son cara y cruz.
output / salida (p. 385) Número que pertenece al rango de una relación.	*Ver* relation / relación.
overlapping events / sucesos superpuestos (p. 627) Sucesos que tienen uno o más casos en común.	Al lanzar un dado, los sucesos "obtener un número menor que 3" y "obtener un número par" son sucesos superpuestos.

p

parabola / parábola (p. 680) La gráfica en forma de U de una función cuadrática.	La gráfica de $y = x^2 - 2x - 3$ es una parábola.

	Ejemplo
parallelogram / paralelogramo (p. 517) Cuadrilátero que tiene ambos pares de lados opuestos paralelos.	
pentagon / pentágono (p. 516) Polígono con cinco lados.	
percent / porcentaje (p. 329) Una razón cuyo denominador es 100. El símbolo de porcentaje es %.	$\dfrac{7}{25} = \dfrac{7 \cdot 4}{25 \cdot 4} = \dfrac{28}{100} = 28\%$
percent of change / porcentaje de cambio (p. 352) Porcentaje que indica cuánto aumenta o disminuye una cantidad con respecto a la cantidad original. Porcentaje de cambio, $p\% = \dfrac{\text{Cantidad de aumento o disminución}}{\text{Cantidad original}}$	El porcentaje de cambio, $p\%$, de 12 a 20 es: $p\% = \dfrac{20 - 12}{12} = \dfrac{8}{12} \approx 0.667 = 66.7\%$
percent of decrease / porcentaje de disminución (p. 352) El porcentaje de cambio de una cantidad cuando la nueva cantidad es menor que la cantidad original.	*Ver* percent of change / porcentaje de cambio.
percent of increase / porcentaje de aumento (p. 352) El porcentaje de cambio de una cantidad cuando la nueva cantidad es mayor que la cantidad original.	*Ver* percent of change / porcentaje de cambio.
perfect square / cuadrado perfecto (p. 454) Número que es el cuadrado de un número entero.	36 es un cuadrado perfecto ya que $36 = 6^2$.
permutation / permutación (p. 615) Disposición de objetos en la que el orden es importante.	Existen 6 permutaciones de las 3 letras A, H, T: AHT ATH THA TAH HTA HAT
polygon / polígono (p. 516) Figura plana cerrada cuyos lados son segmentos que se cortan solamente en sus extremos.	Son polígonos No son polígonos
polynomial / polinomio (p. 651) Suma de monomios.	*Ver* monomial / monomio, binomial / binomio y trinomial / trinomio.

	Ejemplo
population / población (p. 601) El grupo entero sobre el que se desea información.	Una revista invita a sus lectores a enviar por correo las respuestas a un cuestionario sobre la calidad de la revista. La población está formada por todos los lectores de la revista.
positive integers / números enteros positivos (p. 22) Los números enteros mayores que 0.	1, 2, 3, 4, . . .
power / potencia (p. 10) Un producto que se obtiene mediante la multiplicación repetida por el mismo número o expresión. Una potencia se compone de una base y un exponente.	64 es una potencia porque $64 = 4 \cdot 4 \cdot 4$, o $64 = 4^3$.
prime factorization / descomposición en factores primos (p. 173) Número natural escrito como producto de factores primos.	La descomposición en factores primos de 60 es $2 \cdot 2 \cdot 3 \cdot 5 = 2^2 \cdot 3 \cdot 5$.
prime number / número primo (p. 173) Número natural mayor que 1 cuyos únicos factores son 1 y él mismo.	7 es un número primo, porque sus únicos factores son 1 y el mismo número 7.
principal / capital (p. 362) Una cantidad de dinero que se deposita o se pide prestado.	*Ver* simple interest / interés simple *e* compound interest / interés compuesto.
probability / probabilidad (p. 306) Número comprendido entre 0 y 1 que mide la posibilidad de que ocurra un suceso.	*Ver* experimental probability / probabilidad experimental *y* theoretical probability / probabilidad teórica.
proportion / proporción (p. 275) Ecuación que establece que dos razones son iguales.	$\frac{2}{7} = \frac{10}{35}$ y $\frac{x}{20} = \frac{4}{5}$ son proporciones.
Pythagorean theorem / teorema de Pitágoras (p. 465) Para cualquier triángulo rectángulo, la suma de los cuadrados de las longitudes a y b de los catetos es igual al cuadrado de la longitud c de la hipotenusa: $a^2 + b^2 = c^2$.	$a = 5$, $c = 13$, $b = 12$ $5^2 + 12^2 = 13^2$
q	
quadrant / cuadrante (p. 47) Una de las cuatro regiones en las que se divide un plano de coordenadas por el eje x y el eje y.	*Ver* coordinate plane / plano de coordenadas.
quadratic function / función cuadrática (p. 679) Ecuación con dos variables que puede escribirse en la forma $y = ax^2 + bx + c$, donde a, b y c son constantes y $a \neq 0$.	$y = 3x^2 + 5x - 7$ es una función cuadrática.

r

	Ejemplo
radical expression / expresión radical (p. 454) Una expresión que involucra un símbolo radical, $\sqrt{\ }$.	$3\sqrt{4a + b}$ es una expresión radical.
radius of a circle / radio de un círculo (p. 528) La distancia desde el centro a cualquier punto del círculo.	*Ver* circle / círculo.
random sample / muestra aleatoria (p. 601) Muestra en la que cada miembro de la población tiene igual probabilidad de ser seleccionado.	Para seleccionar una muestra aleatoria de la población de estudiantes de una escuela, puedes usar la computadora para elegir al azar 100 números de identificación estudiantil.
range of a relation / rango de una relación (p. 385) El conjunto de todas las salidas posibles de una relación.	*Ver* relation / relación.
ratio / razón (p. 269) Comparación entre dos números usando la división. La razón de a a b (donde $b \neq 0$) puede escribirse como a a b, como $a : b$, o como $\frac{a}{b}$.	La razón de 4 a 5 puede escribirse si 4 a 5, si $4 : 5$, ó si $\frac{4}{5}$.
rational number / número racional (p. 219) Número que puede escribirse como el cociente de dos números enteros.	$-\frac{1}{2} = \frac{-1}{2}$, $0 = \frac{0}{1}$, $0.45 = \frac{9}{20}$, $8\frac{3}{4} = \frac{35}{4}$ y $10 = \frac{10}{1}$ son todos números racionales.
real numbers / números reales (p. 470) El conjunto de todos los números racionales e irracionales.	-5, 0, $\frac{2}{3}$, π, 4.37 y 19 son números reales.
reciprocals / recíprocos (p. 243) Dos números cuyo producto es 1.	5 y $\frac{1}{5}$ son recíprocos.
reflection / reflexión (p. 734) Una transformación que refleja una figura en una línea, llamada línea de reflexión, y crea una imagen espejo de la figura.	línea de reflexíon Reflexión sobre el eje x
regular polygon / polígono regular (p. 516) Un polígono cuyos lados tienen igual longitud y cuyos ángulos miden lo mismo.	

	Ejemplo
regular pyramid / pirámide regular (p. 544) Pirámide cuya base es un polígono regular y cuyas caras laterales son todos triángulos isósceles congruentes.	La base es un polígono regular.
relation / relación (p. 385) Correspondencia entre los números de un conjunto (el dominio, o conjunto de entradas posibles) y los números de otro conjunto (el rango, o conjunto de salidas posibles). En una relación representada por pares ordenados (x, y), las entradas son las coordenadas x y las salidas son las coordenadas y.	El conjunto de pares ordenados $(1, 0)$, $(2, 1)$, $(3, 0)$, $(4, 1)$, $(5, 0)$ es una relación. El dominio de la relación es el conjunto de entradas: 1, 2, 3, 4, 5. El rango de la relación es el conjunto de salidas: 0, 1.
relatively prime numbers / números primos relativos (p. 178) Dos o más números enteros positivos distintos de cero cuyo máximo común divisor es 1.	10 y 21 son números primos relativos porque su M.C.D. es 1.
repeating decimal / decimal periódico (p. 219) Un decimal que tiene un dígito o varios dígitos que se repiten indefinidamente. Un decimal periódico puede escribirse como un cociente de números enteros $\frac{a}{b}$, en el que $b \neq 0$.	$0.3333\ldots$ y $6.\overline{15}$ son decimales periódicos. $0.3333\ldots = \frac{1}{3}$ $6.\overline{15} = 6\frac{15}{99} = 6\frac{5}{33}$
rhombus / rombo (p. 517) Paralelogramo que tiene los cuatro lados congruentes.	
rise / distancia vertical (p. 404) El cambio vertical entre dos puntos de una recta.	*Ver* slope / pendiente.
rotation / rotación (p. 741) Una transformación que rota una figura por un ángulo dado, llamado ángulo de rotación, y en una dirección dada alrededor de un punto fijo, llamado centro de rotación; también se conoce como giro.	45° de rotación sobre el origen.

	Ejemplo

rotational symmetry / simetría rotacional (p. 743) Una figura tiene simetría rotacional si al girar 180° o menos en sentido de las agujas del reloj (o en contrario) sobre su centro da como resultado una imagen que se corresponde exactamente con la figura original.

90°
180°

Un cuadrado tiene simetría rotacional de 180°.

Un cuadrado también tiene simetría rotacional al girar 90° en sentido de las agujas del reloj (o en sentido contrario).

run / distancia horizontal (p. 404) El cambio horizontal entre dos puntos de una recta.

Ver slope / pendiente.

S

sample / muestra (p. 601) Una parte de una población.

Para predecir los resultados de una elección, se realiza una encuesta a una muestra de votantes.

scale / escala (p. 300) Razón que relaciona las dimensiones de un dibujo a escala o un modelo a escala con las dimensiones reales.

La escala 1 pulg : 12 pies en un diagrama de planta significa que 1 pulgada en el diagrama de planta representa una distancia real de 12 pies.

scale drawing / dibujo a escala (p. 300) Dibujo bidimensional que es similar al objeto que representa.

Un mapa es un dibujo a escala de la superficie terrestre que muestra.

scale factor / factor de escala (p. 747) En una dilatación, la razón entre una longitud de lado de la imagen y la longitud de lado correspondiente de la figura original.

Ver dilation / dilatación.

scale model / modelo a escala (p. 300) Modelo tridimensional que es similar al objeto que representa.

Un globo terráqueo es un modelo a escala de la Tierra.

scatter plot / diagrama de dispersión (p. 48) Gráfica en un plano de coordenadas que muestra pares de datos. Cada par de datos está graficado como un punto.

Ver best-fitting line / mejor recta de regresión.

scientific notation / notación científica (p. 204) Un número está escrito en notación científica cuando tiene la forma $c \times 10^n$ donde $1 \leq c < 10$ y n es un número entero.

En notación científica, 253,000 se escribe 2.53×10^5, y 0.00047 se escribe 4.7×10^{-4}.

	Ejemplo
self-selected sample / muestra autoseleccionada (p. 601) Muestra en la que los miembros de la población se seleccionan a sí mismos ofreciéndose a participar.	Para obtener una muestra autoseleccionada de la población de estudiantes de una escuela, puedes pedir a los estudiantes que hagan la encuesta que la depositen en un recipiente de recogida.
sequence / progresión (p. 692) Una lista ordenada de números.	1, 5, 9, 13, 17, . . .
similar figures / figuras semejantes (p. 288) Figuras que tienen la misma forma pero no necesariamente el mismo tamaño. Los ángulos correspondientes de las figuras semejantes son congruentes, y las razones de las longitudes de los lados correspondientes son iguales. El símbolo ~ indica que dos figuras son semejantes.	$\triangle LMN \sim \triangle PQR$
simple interest / interés simple (p. 362) Interés obtenido o pagado sólo sobre el capital. El interés simple I es el producto del capital P, la tasa de interés anual r (escrito como decimal), y el tiempo t en años: $I = Prt$ El saldo A de una cuenta que gana interés simple anual es $A = P + Prt$, or $A = P(1 + rt)$.	Depositas \$500 en una caja de ahorro que da un 2.5% de interés simple anual. Después de 3 años, el interés obtenido es $I = Prt = (500)(0.025)(3) = \$37.50$, y el saldo de tu cuenta es $\$500 + \$37.50 = \$537.50$.
simplest form of a fraction / mínima expresión de una fracción (p. 183) Una fracción está en su mínima expresión si el numerador y el denominador son números primos relativos.	La mínima expresión de la fracción $\frac{8}{12}$ es $\frac{2}{3}$.
simplest form of a radical expression / forma simplificada de una expresión radical (p. 458) Una expresión radical está en forma simplificada cuando (1) ningún factor de la expresión bajo el signo radical es un cuadrado perfecto excepto 1, y (2) no hay fracciones debajo del signo radical ni ningún signo radical en el denominador de ninguna fracción.	En forma simplificada, $\sqrt{72}$ se escribe como $6\sqrt{2}$.
sine / seno (p. 494) El seno de un ángulo agudo A de un triángulo rectángulo (sin A) es la razón entre el cateto opuesto $\angle A$ y la hipotenusa.	*Ver* trigonometric ratio / razón trigonométrica.
slant height of a cone / apotema lateral de un cono (p. 546) La distancia entre el vértice y cualquier punto de la arista de la base.	*Ver* height of a cone / altura de un cono.

	Ejemplo

slant height of a pyramid / apotema lateral de una pirámide (p. 544) La altura de una cara lateral triangular de la pirámide.

Ver regular pyramid / pirámide regular.

slope / pendiente (p. 404) La pendiente de una recta no vertical es la razón entre la distancia vertical (cambio vertical) y la distancia horizontal (cambio horizontal) entre dos puntos cualesquiera sobre la recta.

La pendiente de la recta anterior es:

$$\text{pendiente} = \frac{\text{distancia vertical}}{\text{distancia horizontal}} = \frac{-2}{5} = -\frac{2}{5}$$

slope-intercept form / forma de pendiente e intersección (p. 412) La forma de una ecuación lineal $y = mx + b$ donde m representa la pendiente y b representa la intersección con el eje y.

$y = 3x + 7$ está en la forma de pendiente e intersección. La pendiente es 3 y el punto de intersección de y es 7.

solution of a linear inequality in two variables / solución de una desigualdad lineal con dos variables (p. 436) Un par ordenado que produce un enunciado verdadero cuando las coordenadas del par ordenado se sustituyen con las variables de las desigualdad.

$(0, 1)$ es una solución de la desigualdad lineal $3x - 7y < -1$, porque $3(0) - 7(1) < -1$.

solution of a linear system / solución de un sistema lineal (p. 431) Un par ordenado que es la solución de cada ecuación en un sistema. Una solución de un sistema lineal se da en un punto de intersección de las gráficas de la ecuaciones del sistema.

$(-1, 3)$ es la solución de este sistema lineal:

$y = -2x + 1$
$y = 3x + 6$

solution of an equation / solución de una ecuación (p. 85) Un número que, cuando sustituye la variable en la ecuación, hace la ecuación verdadera.

La solución de la ecuación $8 - a = 10$ es -2, ya que $8 - (-2) = 10$.

solution of an equation in two variables / solución de una ecuación con dos variables (p. 391) Par ordenado (x, y) que produce una expresión verdadera al sustituir x e y por sus valores en la ecuación.

$(2, 1)$ es una solución de $3x - 4y = 2$, ya que $3(2) - 4(1) = 2$.

solution of an inequality / solución de una desigualdad (p. 138) El conjunto de todos los números que, cuando sustituyen la variable en la desigualdad, hacen que la desigualdad sea verdadera.

La solución de la desigualdad $4n < 36$ es $n < 9$, porque cualquier número menor de 9, cuando se reemplaza por n, hace que $4n < 36$, sea un enunciado verdadero.

	Ejemplo
solving an equation / resolver una ecuación (p. 86) Hallar todas las soluciones de la ecuación.	Para resolver la ecuación $3x = 15$, halla el número que puede multiplicarse por 3 para obtener 15. Como $3(5) = 15$, la solución de $3x = 15$ es 5.
square root / raíz cuadrada (p. 453) La raíz cuadrada de un número n es un número m de modo que $m^2 = n$. El signo radical, $\sqrt{\ }$, representa una raíz cuadrada no negativa.	Las raíces cuadradas de 25 son 5 y -5, ya que $5^2 = 25$ y $(-5)^2 = 25$. Así pues, $\sqrt{25} = 5$ y $-\sqrt{25} = -5$.
standard form of a polynomial / forma usual de un polinomio (p. 652) Un polinomio está escrito en forma usual si todos los términos similares están combinados y los términos están ordenados de modo que el grado de cada término disminuye o permanece igual de izquierda a derecha.	La expresión $3(x^2 + 5) - x^2 - 3$ puede escribirse $2x^2 + 12$, a un polinomio en forma usual.
stem-and-leaf plot / tabla arborescente (p. 581) Presentación de datos que organiza los datos basándose en sus dígitos.	**raíces hojas** 10 | 8 11 | 2 2 5 12 | 1 3 Solución: 10|8 = 108
stratified sample / muestra estratificada (p. 601) Muestra en la que la población está dividida en grupos diferenciados. Los miembros se seleccionan entre los miembros de cada grupo.	Puedes seleccionar una muestra estratificada de la población de estudiantes de tu escuela escogiendo 20 estudiantes de cada grado.
supplementary angles / ángulos suplementarios (p. 709) Dos ángulos cuyas medidas suman 180°.	$79°$ $101°$
surface area of a solid / área de la superficie de un sólido (p. 538) La suma de las áreas de las caras de un sólido.	3 pulg, 4 pulg, 6 pulg Área de la superficie $= 2(6)(4) + 2(6)(3) + 2(4)(3)$ $= 108 \text{ pulg}^2$

Glosario

	Ejemplo
systematic sample / muestra sistemática (p. 601) Una muestra en la que se usa una regla para seleccionar a los miembros de una población.	Puedes seleccionar una muestra sistemática de la población de estudiantes de tu escuela dándole un cuestionario a cada décimo estudiante de una lista ordenada alfabéticamente de todos los estudiantes de la escuela.
system of linear equations / sistema de ecuaciones lineales (p. 431) Dos o más ecuaciones lineales con las mismas variables; llamado también sistema lineal.	Las siguientes ecuaciones forman un sistema de ecuaciones lineales: $y = -2x + 1$ $y = 3x + 6$

t

tangent / tangente (p. 489) En un triángulo rectángulo, la tangente de un ángulo agudo A ($\tan A$) es la razón entre la longitud del lado opuesto $\angle A$ y la longitud del lado adyacente a $\angle A$.	*Ver* trigonometric ratio / razón trigonométrica.
terminating decimal / decimal finito (p. 219) Un decimal que tiene un dígito final. Un decimal finito puede escribirse como un cociente de números enteros $\frac{a}{b}$, en el que $b \neq 0$.	0.8 y 2.307 son decimales finitos. $0.8 = \frac{8}{10} = \frac{4}{5}$ $2.307 = 2\frac{307}{1000} = \frac{2307}{1000}$
terms of an expression / términos de una expresión (p. 78) Las partes de una expresión que se suman.	Los términos de la expresión $5x + (-2x) + 1$ son $5x$, $-2x$ y 1.
terms of a polynomial / términos de un polinomio (p. 651) Los monomios que se suman en el polinomio.	Los términos del polinomio $x^2 + 5x - 1$ son x^2, $5x$ y -1.
terms of a sequence / términos de una progresión (p. 692) Los números de una progresión.	El cuarto término de la progresión 1, 5, 9, 13, 17, . . . es 13.
tessellation / teselado (p. 730) La cobertura de un plano con copias congruentes del mismo patrón de modo que no haya espacios de separación ni superposiciones.	
theoretical probability/probabilidad teórica (p. 307) Cuando todos los casos son igualmente probables, la probabilidad teórica de un suceso es la razón entre el número de casos favorables y el número de casos posibles.	Una bolsa de 40 canicas contiene 8 canicas azules. La probabilidad teórica de tomar al azar una canica azul de la bolsa es: $\frac{8}{40} = \frac{1}{5}$, o 0.2.

Glosario

	Ejemplo
transformation / transformación (p. 729) Cambio en la ubicación o el tamaño de una figura que da como resultado una nueva figura, que se llama imagen.	*Ver* translation / traslación, reflection / reflexión, rotation / rotación *y* dilation / dilatación.
translation / traslación (p. 729) Una transformación en la que se mueve cada punto de una figura la misma distancia en la misma dirección.	$\triangle ABC$ se traslada 4 unidades a la derecha.
transversal / transversal (p. 716) Recta que corta a dos o más rectas en distintos puntos.	La recta t es una transversal. $\angle 1$ y $\angle 3$ son ángulos correspondientes. $\angle 2$ y $\angle 3$ son ángulos internos alternos. $\angle 1$ y $\angle 4$ son ángulos externos alternos.
trapezoid / trapecio (p. 517) Cuadrilátero que tiene exactamente un par de lados paralelos.	
tree diagram / diagrama de árbol (p. 313) Un diagrama que usa ramas para enumerar todas las opciones o casos posibles.	Posibilidades: HH HT TH TT

	Ejemplo
trigonometric ratio / razón trigonométrica (p. 489) Una razón entre las longitudes de dos lados de un triángulo rectángulo. En un ángulo agudo A de un triángulo rectángulo, las razones se definen de esta manera: seno de $\angle A$ (sen A), coseno de $\angle A$ (cos A) y tangente de $\angle A$ (tan A).	$\operatorname{sen} A = \dfrac{a}{c} \quad \cos A = \dfrac{b}{c} \quad \tan A = \dfrac{a}{b}$
trinomial / trinomio (p. 651) Polinomio de tres términos.	$a^2 + 5a + 6$ es un trinomio.

u

upper extreme / extremo superior (p. 588) El valor mayor de un conjunto de datos.	*Ver* box-and-whisker plot / gráfica de frecuencias acumuladas.
upper quartile / cuartil superior (p. 588) La mediana de la mitad superior de un conjunto de datos ordenados.	*Ver* box-and-whisker plot / gráfica de frecuencias acumuladas.

v

variable / variable (p. 5) Letra que sirve para representar uno o más números.	En la expresión $n + 3$, la letra n es la variable.
variable expression / expresión variable (p. 5) Una expresión que consiste de números, variables y operaciones.	$x - 7$, $\dfrac{2a}{b}$ y $2t + 3r - 3$ son todas expresiones variables
verbal model / modelo verbal (p. 6) Un modelo verbal describe una situación de la vida real mediante palabras que la exponen y símbolos matemáticos que relacionan esas palabras.	$\underset{\text{(millas)}}{\text{Distancia}} = \underset{\text{(millas/hora)}}{\text{Velocidad}} \cdot \underset{\text{(horas)}}{\text{Tiempo}}$
vertical angles / ángulos opuestos por el vértice (p. 710) Par de ángulos opuestos que se forman cuando dos rectas se cortan en un punto.	$\angle 1$ y $\angle 3$ son ángulos opuestos. $\angle 2$ y $\angle 4$ son ángulos opuestos.

	Ejemplo

vertical line test / prueba de recta vertical (p. 387) En una relación representada por una gráfica, si cualquier recta vertical pasa por más de un punto de la gráfica, entonces la relación no es una función. Si ninguna recta vertical pasa por más de un punto de la gráfica, entonces la relación es una función.

La gráfica no es una función porque una recta vertical pasa por dos puntos.

---

x-axis / eje x (p. 47) La recta numérica horizontal en un plano de coordenadas.

Ver coordinate plane / plano de coordenadas.

---

x-coordinate / coordenada x (p. 47) El primer número en un par ordenado que representa un punto en un plano de coordenadas.

La coordenada x del par ordenado $(5, -3)$ es 5.

---

x-intercept / intercepto en x (p. 398) La coordenada x de un punto donde la gráfica corta al eje x.

---

y-axis / eje y (p. 47) La recta numérica vertical en un plano de coordenadas.

Ver coordinate plane / plano de coordenadas.

---

y-coordinate / coordenada y (p. 47) El segundo número en un par ordenado que representa un punto en un plano de coordenadas.

La coordenada y del par ordenado $(5, -3)$ es -3.

---

y-intercept / intercepto en y (p. 398) La coordenada y de un punto donde la gráfica corta al eje y.

Ver x-intercept / intercepto en x.

Index

exercises, 135, 148, 153, 176, 181, 203, 208, 251, 311, 332, 339, 343, 344, 356, 563, 678, 712, 719, 726

expressions
coefficients and, 78
constant terms and, 78
with exponents, 674–678
like terms and, 78
numerical, 5, 16–21, 71–75
polynomial, 651–661
using properties to simplify, 64–68
radical, 454–461, 501
terms of, 78
two-variable, 6–9, 52
variable, 5–9, 17–21, 52, 72–75, 78–83, 109, 458–461

formulas
area of a circle, 529
area of a parallelogram, 521
area of a square, 11, 69, 789
area of a trapezoid, 522
area of a triangle, 70, 73
circumference of a circle, 528
combinations, 621
compound interest, 363, 364, 367
distance, 77, 476, 502
midpoint, 478
percent of change, 351, 352
perimeter of a rectangle, 69
perimeter of a square, 69
perimeter of a triangle, 69
permutations, 616
probability of dependent events, 636
probability of disjoint events, 628
probability of independent events, 635
probability of overlapping events, 629
Pythagorean theorem, 465
simple interest, 362
sum of the measures of the interior angles of a convex *n*-gon, 722
surface area of a cone, 546
surface area of a cylinder, 540
surface area of a prism, 539
surface area of a regular pyramid, 545
surface area of a sphere, 548
volume of a cone, 558

volume of a cube, 11, 789
volume of a cylinder, 553
volume of a prism, 552
volume of a pyramid, 558

functions
cubic, 684
exponential, 686–691
graphing, 427–430, 680–685, 686–691
identifying, 386–390
linear, 426–430
quadratic, 679–685, 700
relations and, 385–390, 442

games, 107, 129, 137, 661, 673, 691

inequalities
compound, 142
equivalent, 139
with fractions, 254–257
graphing, 138–142, 436–441
linear, 436–441, 445
multi-step, 149–153, 157
in two variables, 436–441

monomials, 174–176, 178, 188–191, 662–666

order of operations, 16–21, 53, 454

polynomials, 651–655, 656–661, 662–666, 667–672, 699

properties
associative, 63–68
commutative, 63–68
cross products, 281
distributive, 71–75, 109
of equality, 91, 92, 97, 98
identity, 64–68
of inequality, 139, 143, 144, 145
inverse, 30, 247
power of a power, 675
power of a product, 674
power of a quotient, 674
of square roots, 458, 459

proportions, 275–279, 280–284, 319

Algebra tiles
modeling addition equations, 90
modeling binomial multiplication, 667
modeling equations with variables on both sides, 130
modeling multiplication equations, 96
modeling polynomial addition, 656

modeling two-step equations, 119

Algebraic expression, *See* Variable expression

Alternate exterior angles, 716–720, 753

Alternate interior angles, 716–720, 753

Alternative assessment, *See* Activities; Games; Problem solving, extended response questions; Problem solving, short response questions; Projects; Test-taking skills

Altitude, *See* Height

Analyze, exercises, 67, 123, 124, 153, 176, 180, 186, 223, 234, 240, 246, 305, 317, 355, 429, 440, 480, 514, 587, 591, 593, 606, 660, 672, 685, 690, 696, 697, 721, 726, 737

Angle(s), 285–286
acute, 793
alternate exterior, 716–720, 753
alternate interior, 716–720, 753
in circle graphs, 595
classifying, 793
classifying triangles by, 462, 511, 513–515, 564
complementary, 709, 711–713
congruent, 286, 290–292
constructions
bisecting, 715
copying, 714, 715
corresponding, 287, 288–292, 716–720, 753
drawing with a protractor, 792
of elevation, 492
exterior, 723
interior, 722
measures, 285–286
of corresponding angles, 287
in quadrilaterals, 518–520
ratio and, 512–515
in triangles, 462, 511, 513–515, 564
measuring with a protractor, 287, 482, 488, 595, 740, 792
obtuse, 793
and parallel lines, 717–720
right, 793
of rotation, 741–746
straight, 793
sums of measures
for exterior angles of a polygon, 724–727

493, 497, 505, 511–515, 525, 526, 527, 537, 542, 661, 671, 703, 795, 797

medicine, 421, 425, 631, 690

money, 165, 257, 292, 315, 317, 797, 801

mountain climbing, 94

music, 8, 120, 122, 128, 177, 180, 273, 315, 329, 342, 348, 354, 360, 486, 508–509, 542, 613, 614, 623, 626, 710, 722

nutrition, 67, 77, 400, 438, 684

Olympics, 13, 74

parties, 87, 129, 270, 619, 622, 800

photography, 128, 376, 456, 669, 673, 734

physics, 116–117, 256, 424, 455, 459, 460, 678, 696, 702

plants, 19, 101, 206, 293, 294, 295, 310, 332, 350, 419, 420, 481, 603, 605, 638, 702, 782, 797

politics, 190, 279, 349, 761

population, 93, 278, 377, 430

recreation, 15, 123, 159, 276, 283, 360, 416, 434, 474, 498, 553, 583, 589, 598, 603, 693, 762, 763, 799

recycling, 223, 348, 595

robotics, 271, 416

safety, 497

school, 163, 278, 317, 332, 384, 594, 597, 601, 604, 605, 621, 624, 626, 632, 637, 638, 644, 645, 760, 798, 799

shopping, 63, 133, 154, 158, 254, 256, 326–327, 369, 400, 799

skating, 150, 360

skiing, 77, 142

soccer, 149, 162, 192, 289, 337, 469, 639, 704, 705

space exploration, 7, 25, 77, 301, 394, 475, 532

stock market, 42, 43, 801

structures, 76, 147, 197, 300, 449, 455, 465, 469, 472, 491, 492, 496, 497, 519, 530, 532, 544, 548, 559, 573, 576, 662, 666, 710, 719, 727, 733

submersibles, 45

surveying, 67, 296

surveys, 348, 373, 376, 586, 596, 600, 601, 602, 603, 604, 605, 609–610, 611, 612, 613, 624, 644, 762, 781, 783

swimming, 15, 84, 222, 468, 492, 553

technology, 20, 27, 99, 100, 101, 164, 197, 203, 208, 316, 355, 360, 594, 612, 614, 617, 618, 635, 638, 748, 795, 798

temperature, 26, 36, 44, 59, 75, 138, 141, 161, 162, 164, 166, 392, 614, 625, 782

tennis, 67, 331

time, 38, 100, 265, 298, 376, 494, 495, 783, 796, 801

track and field, 60–61, 235, 236, 336, 456, 581, 586

trains, 81, 123, 141, 655

travel, 59, 110, 123, 124, 134, 159, 257, 278, 283, 319, 401, 469, 614, 618, 625, 657, 795

triathalon, 140

volleyball, 651, 653, 802

wakeboarding, 404, 406, 407

weather, 74, 234, 309, 389, 582, 583, 590, 600, 630, 632

winter sports, 160, 188, 543, 599

wrestling, 531

Approximation, *See also* Estimation
of angle cosines, 495–498, 503
of angle sines, 495–498, 503
of angle tangents, 490–493, 503
of best-fitting line, 421–425
of decimal values for real numbers, 471
of maximum value for a quadratic function, 681–684
of minimum value for a quadratic function, 681–684
for pi, 529, 540
rounding to a given place, 770
of square root, 454–457, 500
of surface area, 540–543, 544, 546–549
of volume, 554–556, 559–563

Arc notation, to show equal angle measures, 286

Area, *See also* Surface area
of a circle, 528–533, 534, 565
of a composite figure, 523, 526, 530
converting units for, 66, 677
of a cross section, 542
definition of, 789
exercises, 33
game, 534
of a half circle, 530
lateral, of a prism, 539, 541–543
of a parallelogram, 521, 524–526, 549, 565
modeling, 521

of a rectangle, 69–70, 73–75
of a square, 11, 69–70, 789
of a trapezoid, 522–526, 565
modeling, 522
of a triangle, 70, 73–75
units of, 789

Area models
to show addition of fractions, 230
to show area, 789
to show division of fractions, 242
to show fractions, 777
to show mixed numbers, 777
to show multiplication of fractions, 237
to show percent, 329
to show percent of change, 351

Arithmetic sequence, 692–697
common difference in, 692
graphing, 694–697

Arrangement
combinations, 620–625, 643
permutations, 615–619, 642

Aspect ratio, 270

Assessment
Assessing Progress, xxvi
Chapter Standardized Test, 57, 113, 159, 215, 263, 323, 373, 447, 505, 569, 645, 703, 757
Chapter Test, 56, 112, 158, 214, 262, 322, 372, 446, 504, 568, 644, 702, 756
End-of-Course Test, 765–768
Mid-Chapter Quiz, 27, 84, 137, 192, 236, 298, 350, 418, 475, 534, 614, 673, 728
Pre-Course Test, xxvii–xxviii
Prerequisite Skills Quiz, 4, 62, 118, 170, 218, 268, 328, 384, 452, 510, 580, 650, 708
scoring rubric
for extended response questions, 758
for short response questions, 374
Standardized Test Practice, 9, 13, 20, 26, 33, 38, 46, 51, 68, 75, 82, 89, 95, 101, 107, 124, 129, 135, 142, 148, 153, 176, 181, 186, 191, 198, 203, 208, 224, 229, 235, 241, 246, 251, 257, 274, 279, 284, 292, 297, 304, 311, 317, 333, 339, 344, 349, 356, 361, 366, 390, 396, 402, 409, 417, 424, 430, 435, 441, 457, 461, 469, 474, 481, 487, 493, 498, 515, 520, 526, 533,

Index

variable
    equivalent, 72–75
    evaluating, 5–9, 17–21, 52
    simplifying, 78–83, 109,
        458–461
    writing, 6–9, 80–82
Extended problem solving, *See*
    Problem solving
Extended response questions, *See*
    Problem solving
Exterior angle(s), 723
    of a polygon
        measure of, 723, 725–727
        sum of measures of, 724–727
Extra Practice, 803–815
Extremes, 588–592
    lower, 588
    upper, 588

f

Face, of a solid, 535
Factor(s), 172–176, 210
    conversion, 65–68
    definition of, 772
    greatest common, 177–181, 211
    powers and, 10–13
    prime, 173–176, 210
    writing, 172–176
Factor tree, prime factorization
    and, 173–176, 210
Factorial(s), 615
    on a calculator, 617
    permutations and, 615–619
Factoring
    monomials, 174–176
    numbers, 172–176
Favorable outcome, 306
Fibonacci sequence, 697
Find the error, *See* Error analysis
Flips, *See* Reflections
FOIL method, 669–672
Formula(s)
    area
        of a circle, 529
        of a parallelogram, 521
        of a rectangle, 69, 73
        of a square, 11, 69, 789
        of a trapezoid, 522
        of a triangle, 70, 73
    circumference, 528
    combinations, 621
    compound interest, 363, 364, 367
    definition of, 11

to describe a generalization, 704,
    800
distance, 77, 476, 502
midpoint, 478, 502
odds, 308
percent of change, 351, 352
perimeter
    of a rectangle, 69
    of a square, 69
    of a triangle, 69
permutations, 616
probability
    of dependent events, 636
    of disjoint events, 628
    of independent events, 635
    of overlapping events, 629
Pythagorean theorem, 465, 501
    involving a rate, 77
    simple interest, 362
    sum of the measures of the
        interior angles of a convex
        n-gon, 722
surface area
    of a cone, 546
    of a cylinder, 540
    of a prism, 539
    of a regular pyramid, 545
    of a sphere, 548
table of, 818–819
volume
    of a cone, 558
    of a cube, 11, 789
    of a cylinder, 553, 683
    of a prism, 552
    of a pyramid, 558
45°-45°-90° right triangle, 482, 483,
    485–487, 503
Fractal
    Sierpinski carpet, 304
    Sierpinski triangle, 696
    tree, 694
Fraction(s)
    adding
        game, 236
        like denominators, 225–229,
            259, 779
        modeling, 230, 779
        to simplify expressions,
            227–229, 233–235
        unlike denominators, 230–235,
            259
    clearing
        to solve equations, 253–257
        to solve inequalities, 255–257
    comparing, 188–191
        using decimals, 220, 222–224

definition, 777
denominator, 777
to describe probability, 305–311
dividing, 242–246, 260
    using reciprocals, 243–246
equations with, 247–253,
    255–257, 261
equivalent, 182–186, 211
    definition of, 182
games, 192, 236, 251
improper, 226–229, 232–235,
    238–241, 244–246, 778
modeling, 777
multiplying, 237–241, 260
    modeling, 237
    to simplify expressions,
        239–241
numerator, 777
ordering, 189–191
percent and, 329–333, 341–344,
    368
    common equivalents, 330
reciprocals and, 243–246
rewriting using positive
    exponents, 200–203
simplest form, 183–186
simplifying, 183–186
subtracting
    like denominators, 225–229,
        259, 779
    modeling, 230, 779
    to simplify expressions,
        227–229, 233–235
    unlike denominators, 230–235,
        259
writing as decimals, 220–224, 258
Frequency, meaning of, 582
Frequency distribution, *See*
    Histogram
Frequency table
    definition of, 582
    intervals for, 582
    making, 582, 584–586
Function(s), *See also* Linear
    equations
    cubic, 684
    definition of, 386
    graphing, 427–430, 680–685,
        686–691
    identifying, 386–390
    linear, 426–430, 837–839
    nonlinear, 680, 837–839
        exponential, 686–691
        game, 691
        quadratic, 679–685, 700
    relations and, 385–390, 442

multiplying, 41–46, 55
  mixed numbers and, 238, 240
negative, 22
opposite, 23–26
  modeling on a number line, 23
ordering, 22–26, 53
  on a number line, 22
positive, 22
subtracting, 34–38, 54
zero, 22

Intercept(s)
finding, 398–402
using to graph linear equations,
  398–402, 443
x-intercept, 398
y-intercept, 398

Interdisciplinary, *See* Applications

Interest
compound, 363–367, 371
simple, 362–366, 371

Interest rate, 362

Interior angle(s)
of a polygon, 722
of regular polygons, measures of,
  723–727
sum of the measures of, 721–722,
  725–727

Internet resources, *See also*
  Student help
eTutorial Plus, 7, 12, 19, 25, 32,
  36, 45, 49, 66, 74, 81, 87, 93,
  99, 105, 123, 127, 134, 141,
  146, 175, 179, 185, 190, 197,
  202, 207, 222, 228, 234, 240,
  245, 249, 256, 272, 278, 283,
  291, 295, 302, 309, 315, 331,
  337, 342, 348, 355, 360, 365,
  388, 394, 400, 407, 415, 422,
  429, 434, 439, 456, 460, 467,
  473, 479, 486, 491, 497, 513,
  519, 524, 531, 541, 547, 555,
  561, 584, 591, 599, 604, 612,
  618, 623, 631, 637, 654, 660,
  664, 670, 677, 682, 689, 695,
  711, 719, 725, 732, 736, 744,
  750
eWorkbook Plus, 7, 12, 18, 24, 31,
  36, 44, 49, 66, 73, 80, 87, 93,
  99, 105, 122, 127, 133, 140,
  146, 151, 174, 179, 184, 189,
  196, 201, 206, 222, 227, 233,
  239, 245, 249, 255, 272, 277,
  282, 290, 295, 302, 309, 315,
  331, 337, 342, 347, 354, 359,
  364, 387, 394, 400, 407, 415,
  422, 428, 433, 439, 455, 460,

467, 472, 479, 485, 491, 496,
  513, 518, 524, 531, 541, 547,
  554, 560, 584, 590, 598, 603,
  611, 617, 623, 630, 637, 653,
  659, 664, 670, 676, 682, 689,
  695, 711, 718, 725, 731, 736,
  744, 749
research, 115, 325, 507, 606–607,
  647

Interpret, exercises, 8, 26, 32, 50,
  68, 75, 88, 94, 119, 123, 147,
  152, 223, 240, 273, 349, 356,
  361, 389, 390, 395, 401, 408,
  416, 429, 435, 440, 461, 469,
  486, 493, 498, 555, 585, 591,
  592, 599, 678, 684, 690, 727,
  739, 740

Interquartile range, 590

Inverse
additive, 30
multiplicative, 247

Inverse cosine, 499

Inverse operations
addition and subtraction, 91–95
definition of, 91
multiplication and division,
  97–101

Inverse sine, 499

Inverse tangent, 499

Investigations, *See* Activities;
  Technology activities

Irrational number, 470–474
definition of, 470
graphing, 471

Irrelevant information,
  recognizing, 58–59

Isometric drawing, 551

Isosceles triangle, 463

Journal, *See* Notebook entries;
  Notetaking strategies; Note
  Worthy notes; Writing

Keystrokes, *See* Technology
  activities

Kite, quadrilateral, 520

Labs, *See* Activities; Technology
  activities

Lateral area, of a prism, 539,
  541–543

Lateral face
of a prism, 539
of a pyramid, 544

Lateral surface area
of a cone, 546
of a pyramid, 545

Leading digit, definition of, 771

**Least common denominator
  (LCD),** 188–191, 212
comparing fractions using,
  188–191, 212
ordering fractions using, 189–191
ordering mixed numbers using,
  189–191
rewriting variable expressions
  with, 191
solving equations using, 253,
  255–257

Least common multiple (LCM),
  187–191, 212
of monomials, 188–191

Leg(s)
adjacent to an angle, 488, 489
opposite an angle, 488, 489
of a right triangle, 465

Length, converting among units of,
  65, 66, 67, 786

Like terms, 78
combining, 79–83
  to add polynomials, 657–661
  to solve equations, 125–129,
    155

Likely event, 307

Line(s), 285–286
parallel, 410–411
  angles and, 717–720, 753
  slopes of, 414–417
  transversals and, 717–720
  writing equations of, 420–424
perpendicular, 410–411
  slopes of, 414–417
  writing equations of, 420–424
of reflection, 734
slope of, 404–409
of symmetry, 735–738

Line of best fit, *See* Best-fitting line

Line graph
choosing a data display, 596–600
interpreting, 160

in a plane, 410–411
slopes of, 414–417
transversals and, 717–720
writing equations of, 420–424
Parallelogram, 517–520
  area of, 521, 524–526, 549, 565
  base of, 521
  height of, 521
Parentheses
  order of operations and, 16–21
  solving equations with, 125–129,
    155

Patterns, *See also* Arithmetic
    sequence; Functions;
    Geometric sequence;
    Sequence
  in data, 582
  division, rational numbers, 242
  exercises, 13, 705
  exponents and, 193, 198, 199
  for finding prime numbers, 171
  finding to solve problems, 796
  multiplication, integer, 41
  percent, 344
  Sierpinski carpet, 304
  tessellation, 730–733, 738, 746
  visual, 20, 190
Pentagon, sum of angle measures
    of, 721
Per, meaning of, 270
Percent
  applications, 357–361, 371
    discount, 358–361
    markup, 357–361, 371
    sales tax, 358–361
  of change, 351–356, 370
    modeling, 351
  circle graphs and, 596, 600
  decimals and, 340–344, 369
  of decrease, 352–356
  equation, 345–349, 370
  fractions and, 329–333, 341–344,
    368
    common equivalents, 330
  games, 344, 350, 361
  greater than 100%, 828–829
  of increase, 352–356
  interest
    compound, 363–367, 371
    simple, 362–366, 371
  less than 1%, 828–829
  meaning of, 329
  modeling, 334, 335
  of a number, 330–334, 341–344
  probability and, 330, 332, 333
  problem types, 336, 347
  proportion and, 334–339, 369

Percent bar model, 334, 335
Perfect number, 176
Perfect square, 176, 454, 470
Perimeter, 69–70, 785
Permutations, 615–619, 642
  combinations and, 621, 622
  expressed as *n*-factorial, 615
  for finding probability, 617–619
  formula, 616
Perpendicular bisector,
    constructing, 714, 715
Perpendicular lines
  in a plane, 410–411
  slopes of, 414–417
  writing equations of, 420–424
Pi, 527, 528, 529, 540
  modeling, 527
Place value, 770
Plane, 285–286
  cross section, 542
Plot(s)
  box-and-whisker, 588–593, 641
  choosing a data display, 596–600
  scatter plot, 48–51
    best-fitting line and, 421–425
  stem-and-leaf, 581–582, 584–586,
    640
Point(s), 285–286
  in a coordinate plane
    distance between, 476–477,
      479–481
    plotting, 47–51, 55
Polygon(s), *See also* Area;
    Perimeter; specific polygons
  angle sums
    exterior angles, 724–727
    interior angles, 721–722,
      725–727
  classifying, 516–520, 565
  concave, 516–519
  convex, 516–519
  definition of, 516
  diagonal of, 518
  exterior angles of, 723
  game, 728
  interior angles of, 722
  regular, 516
    measure of an interior angle
      of, 723–727
Polyhedron, *See* Solids
Polynomial(s), *See also* Binomials;
    Monomials; Trinomials
  adding, 656–661, 699
    using models, 656
  classifying, 651, 653, 654
  dividing by monomials, 663–666
  evaluating, 654–655

finding the degree of, 652–655
  games, 661, 673
  identifying, 651, 653, 654
  multiplied by monomials,
    662–666, 699
  multiplying, 667–672, 699
    using models, 667
  standard form of, 652–655, 698
  subtracting, 658–661, 699
  terms of, 651
Population, definition of, 601
Positive decimal, 102
Positive integer, 22–26
Positive slope, 405
Positive square root, 453
Power(s)
  base, 10
  definition of, 10
  dividing, 193, 195–198
  exponents and, 10–13, 52–53
  game, 198
  multiplying, 193–198
  with negative exponents,
    199–203
  order of operations and, 16–21
  of powers, 675–678
  product of, 194–198
  of products, 674–678
  properties, 194–198, 674–678
    with negative exponents,
      200–203
  quotient of, 195–198
  of quotients, 674–678
  reading, 10
  scientific notation and, 204–209
  with zero as an exponent,
    199–203
Power of a power property, 675
Power of a product property, 674
Power of a quotient property, 674
Prediction
  best–fitting line, 421–425
  exercises, 171, 292, 305, 310, 338,
    423, 424, 425, 461, 533, 561,
    613, 737, 745
  from an experiment, 305
  using probability, 308–311
  from a survey, 609–613
Prerequisite skills, *See also* Skills
    Review Handbook; Student
    Reference
Prerequisite Skills Quiz, 4, 62, 118,
    170, 218, 268, 328, 384, 452,
    510, 580, 650, 708
Prime factorization, 173–176, 210
  factor trees, 173, 175

Projects

conducting a survey, 646–647

designing a ramp, 506–507

indirect measurement, 114–115

making a business decision, 324–325

Proof

of the cross products property, 281

definition of, 281

of the formula for the area of a parallelogram, 521

of the formula for the area of a trapezoid, 522

of the formula for the surface area of a cylinder, 540

of the formula for the surface area of a prism, 539

of the formula for the surface area of a regular pyramid, 545

of formulas for the intercepts of $y = ax + b$, 402

of the Pythagorean theorem, 464

of the relationships among the side lengths of special right triangles, 483, 484

that the slope of $y = mx + b$ is m, 417

that the sum of the angle measures in a triangle is 180°, 720

that the sum of the exterior angle measures for a quadrilateral is 360°, 727

Properties

associative

addition, 63–68

multiplication, 63–68

commutative

addition, 63–68

multiplication, 63–68

cross products, 281

distributive, 71–75, 109

of equality

addition, 92

division, 97

multiplication, 98

subtraction, 91

game, 84

identity

addition, 64–68

multiplication, 64–68

of inequality

addition, 139

division, 143, 145

multiplication, 143, 144

subtraction, 139

inverse

additive, 30

multiplicative, 247

power

with negative exponents, 200–203

of a power, 675

of a product, 674

product of, 194

of a quotient, 674

quotient of, 195

of similar figures, 288

of square roots

product property, 458

quotient property, 459

table of, 820–821

Proportion(s)

cross products and, 280–284, 319

currency exchange and, 826–827

definition of, 275

dilation and, 747–751

maps and, 826–827

methods for solving, 282

percent and, 334–339, 369

project, 324–325

scale drawing and, 299–304

setting up, 276

similarity and, 287–297

solving

using algebra, 276–279, 319

using cross products, 280–284, 319

using equivalent ratios, 275–279, 319

writing, 275–279, 280–284

Proportional reasoning

cross products, 280–284, 319

dilation, 747–751

equivalent fractions, 182–186, 211

equivalent rates, 271–274

equivalent ratios, 270–274

using fractions, 329–333, 341–344

indirect measurement, 293–297

odds, 308–311

using percent, 334–339

percent of change, 351–356

percent discount, 358–361

using the percent equation, 345–349

percent markup, 357–361

probability, 306–311

proportions, 275–284

representing pi, 527

scale drawing, 299–304

similar figures, 287–297

simple interest, 362–366, 371

translations, 729–733

unit analysis, 76–77

unit rates, 270–274

Protractor

how to use, 792

using, 287, 482, 488, 595, 740

Pyramid

base of, 535

definition of, 535, 544

faces, edges, and vertices of, 536

height of, 544

lateral faces of, 544

lateral surface area of, 545

net for, 545, 547

regular, 544

slant height of, 544, 547

surface area of, 545, 547–549, 566

volume of, 558–563, 567

Pythagorean theorem, 465–469, 501

converse of, 466–469

distance on the coordinate plane and, 476–477, 479–481

game, 475

indirect measurement and, 467, 468, 469

modeling, 464

project using, 506–507

Pythagorean triple, 468

q

Quadrant, 47

Quadratic function

definition of, 679

evaluating, 679, 681–684, 700

graphing, 680–685, 700

on a graphing calculator, 685

maximum value, 681

minimum value, 681

Quadrilateral(s), 286, 517–520

angle measures of, 518–520

classifying, 517–520

sum of angle measures of, 721

Quartile(s), 588–593

lower, 588

upper, 588

Quotient, definition of, 772

Quotient of powers property, 195

with negative exponents, 200–203

using, 195–198

Quotient property of square roots, 459

Radical expression, 454–461
meaning of, 454
operations with, 830–832
simplest form of, 458–461
Radius
of a circle, 528–533, 794
of a sphere, 548
Random number(s), generating on
a calculator, 312
Random sample, 601
as representative of a population,
608
Range, 40
interquartile, 590
output and, 385
of probabilities, 307
of a relation, 385
Rate(s)
of change, 406–409
definition of, 76, 270
equivalent, 271–274
formula, 77
interest, 362–367
ratio and, 270–274, 318
unit, 76–77, 270–274, 318
unit analysis and, 76–77
variable expressions and, 76–77
Ratio(s), *See also* Proportion; Rate
angle measures and, 512–515
aspect, 270
common, for a geometric
sequence, 692
comparing, 270–274
cosine, 494–498, 503
inverse, 499
definition of, 269
equivalent, 270–274
cross products and, 280–284
indirect measurement and,
293–297
odds and, 308–311
ordering, 270–274
pi, 527, 528
rates and, 270–274, 318
scale drawings and, 299–304
scale factor of a dilation, 747–751
similar figures and, 288–292,
293–297
simplest form, 269
sine, 494–498, 503
inverse, 499
slope, 404–409
tangent, 488–493, 503
inverse, 499

trigonometric, 489
writing, 269–274
Rational number(s), 219–224, *See
also* Fractions
concept map of, 452
definition of, 219
dividing, 242–246
equations with, 247–257, 261
ordering, 221, 223–224
real numbers and, 470–474
repeating decimal, 219–224
terminating decimal, 219–224
Ray, 285–286
Reading algebra, 6, 23, 48, 71, 80,
85, 91, 121, 139, 220, 254,
275, 300, 306, 308, 310, 345,
363, 389, 414, 436, 476, 492,
532, 616, 652, 687, 730
Reading geometry, 288, 489, 516,
518, 741
Reading mathematics
reading bar graphs, 781
reading box-and-whisker plots,
589–593
reading circle graphs, 783
reading coordinate notation,
730–733
reading histograms, 583–587
reading line graphs, 782
reading misleading data displays,
597–600
reading odds, 308
reading powers, 10
reading prime notation, 729
reading probability, 307, 308
reading stem-and-leaf plots, 582,
584–586
to solve problems, 14–15
translating verbal sentences,
85–89, 138–142
Real number(s), 470–474, 502
classifying, 470
comparing, 471–474
decimal form of, 470–474
definition of, 470
ordering, 471–474, 502
Venn diagram of, 470
Reasonableness
checking for, 413, 414, 427
eliminate unreasonable choices,
161
estimating to determine, 232,
336, 341, 353
exercises, 401

Reasoning, *See also* Conclusions;
Critical thinking; Decision
making; Error analysis;
Problem solving, extended
response questions;
Problem solving, short
response questions;
Problem solving strategies
analyze, exercises, 67, 123, 124,
153, 176, 180, 186, 223, 234,
240, 246, 305, 317, 355, 429,
440, 480, 514, 587, 591, 593,
606, 660, 672, 685, 690, 696,
697, 721, 726, 737
concept grid, 328, 364
concept map, 452
converse of a statement, 466
draw conclusions, exercises, 21,
83, 96, 119, 130, 136, 143,
171, 193, 209, 230, 242, 252,
287, 299, 305, 312, 334, 351,
367, 397, 403, 425, 464, 482,
488, 499, 527, 537, 550, 557,
587, 593, 606, 608, 626, 656,
685, 721, 739, 740
eliminate unreasonable choices,
161
exercises, 9, 67, 198, 409, 439,
449, 796, 800
making a generalization, 704–705
margin of error, 610
use number sense, 161
problem solving plan, 14–15,
58–59, 264–265, 448–449,
704–705
recognizing relevant, irrelevant,
and missing information,
58–59
tree diagram, 173–176, 313
unit analysis, 65–68, 76–77
Venn diagram, 219, 470, 626, 627,
628, 629, 784, 835–836
visual thinking, exercises, 401,
435, 514, 519, 542, 549, 660,
720
Reciprocals
definition of, 243
for dividing fractions, 243–246
negative, 414
Rectangle, 517–520
area of, 69–70, 73–75
definition of, 785
perimeter of, 69–70, 785
Rectangular coordinate system,
See Coordinate plane

Rounding, 770
    to estimate differences, 771
    to estimate products, 772
    to estimate quotients, 772
    to estimate sums, 771
Ruler
    drawing segments with, 787
    measuring segments with, 788
    using, 114, 287, 299, 403, 482,
        488, 527, 537, 787, 788
Run, slope and, 403, 404

S

Sales tax, percent, 358–361
Sample, 601–605
    biased, 602
    convenience, 601
    predicting from, 609–613
    random, 601
    representative, 602
    self-selected, 601
    stratified, 601
    systematic, 601
Sample space, 306, *See also*
    Probability
Sampling methods, 601–602
Scaffolding, *See* Problem solving
Scale
    for a drawing, 300
    graph
        bar, 594
        line, 594
        representing breaks, 389
    for a map, 826–827
    for a model, 300
Scale drawing, 299–304, 321, 826
    definition of, 299, 300
    making, 299
    proportion and, 299–304, 826
Scale factor, 747–751
Scale model, 300–304
Scalene triangle, 463
Scatter plot, 48–51
    best-fitting line and, 421–425
    choosing an appropriate data
        display, 596–600
    drawing on a graphing
        calculator, 425
Scientific notation, 204–209, 213
    using a calculator, 209
    comparing numbers in, 205–208
    dividing numbers in, 241
    multiplying numbers in, 206–209
    ordering numbers in, 205–208
    writing numbers in, 204–208

Scoring rubric
    for extended response questions,
        758
    for short response questions, 374
Segment(s), 285–286, 518
    congruent, 286
    constructing perpendicular, 714,
        715
    copying, 794
    rotating, 740
Self-selected sample, 601
Semicircle, *See* Half circle
Sequence, 692–697, *See also*
    Patterns
    arithmetic, 692–697, 701
    Fibonacci, 697
    geometric, 692–697, 701
    graphing, 694–697
    meaning of, 692
    terms of, 692
Short response questions, *See*
    Problem solving
Side(s)
    classifying triangles by, 463
    congruent, 286, 290–292
    corresponding, 287–292
    of a right triangle, 465, 488
        Pythagorean theorem and,
        465–469
    of a triangle, 286
Sierpinski carpet, 304
Sierpinski triangle, 696
Similar figures, 287–292, 320
    definition of, 287, 288
    game, 297
    indirect measurement and,
        293–297
    investigating, 287
    measurement and, 293–297, 320
    naming, 288
    properties of, 288
    scale drawing and, 299–304
Similar triangles
    indirect measurement and,
        293–297
    ratios of leg lengths of, 488
Similarity
    indirect measurement and,
        293–297
    measurement and, 293–297, 320
Simple event, *See* Event
Simple interest, 362–366, 371
Simplest form
    fraction, 183–186, 211
    ratio, 269
    variable expression, 184–186, 211

Simulation
    definition of, 633
    performing, 305, 310, 312, 608,
        633
Sine
    definition of, 494
    inverse, 499
Sine ratio, 494–498, 503
    on a calculator, 495
Skew lines, 410–411
Skills Review Handbook, 770–802
    data analysis
        logical reasoning, 784
        reading bar graphs, 781
        reading circle graphs, 783
        reading line graphs, 782
        Venn diagrams, 784
    decimals
        adding and subtracting, 774
        comparing and ordering, 773
        dividing, 776
        multiplying, 775
    estimating
        products and quotients, 772
        sums and differences, 771
    fractions
        adding and subtracting, 779
        modeling, 777
        multiplying, 780
    geometry, basic figures, 785
    measurement
        classifying angles, 793
        using a compass, 794
        measuring length, 788
        using a protractor, 792
        using a ruler, 787
        units of area, 789
        units of capacity, 791
        units of length, 786
        units of mass, 790
        units of volume, 789
        units of weight, 790
    mixed numbers, improper
        fractions and, 778
    place value, 770
    problem solving
        act it out, 798
        break into parts, 802
        draw a diagram, 795
        guess, check, and revise, 797
        look for a pattern, 796
        make a list or table, 799
        solve a simpler or related
        problem, 800
        work backward, 801
    rounding, 770

Index

Index

Credits

Cover

Bottom left © Jake Martin/Getty Images; *center right* Comstock.

Authors

Larson Meridian Creative Group; *Boswell* Robert C. Jenks/Jenks Studio; *Kanold* McDougal Littell/Houghton Mifflin Co.; *Stiff* Jerry Head Jr.

Photography and Illustration

vi © Julie Houck/Corbis; **vii** © Scott Sroka/National Geographic Image Collection; **viii** © Darryl Torckler/Getty Images; **ix** © Chaco Mohler/Mountain Stock/Sportschrome, Inc.; **x** © Esbin-Anderson/The Image Works; **xi** © Jeremy Woodhouse/Getty Images; **xii** © Jose Luis Pelaez, Inc./Corbis; **xiii** © Sport the Library/Sportschrome, Inc.; **xiv** © Paul A. Souders/Corbis; **xv** #14106 Winged Box Kite courtesy of goflyakite.com; **xvi** © Michael Newman/PhotoEdit; **xvii** © Gale Beery/Index Stock Imagery; **xviii** *Zig Zag Chair* (1995), Designed by Gerrit Rietveld. Philadelphia Museum of Art, purchased with the Fiske Kimball fund and with funds contributed by COLLAB: The Group for Modern and Contemporary Design at the Philadelphia Museum of Art (1995-65-1); **1** © Stephen Simpson/Getty Images; **2–3** © Alison Wright/The Image Works; **5** © Doc White/SeaPics.com, Inc.; **7** Franz Walther/Artville; **8** © Cleve Bryant/PhotoEdit; **9** *top left* © Duomo/Corbis; *top right* © Royalty-Free/Corbis; **11** © Xinhua/Sovfoto; **13** Courtesy of Midwest-Tropical; **15** © Francisco J. Rangel; **16** © Bill Morson; **19** *center left* © David Young-Wolff/PhotoEdit; *center right* © Bill Ross/Corbis; **20** Elizabeth Tustian; **22** © Charles W. Mann/Photo Researchers, Inc.; **25** *bottom left* © David L. Arnold/National Geographic Image Collection; *center right* NASA; **26** © Hugh Rose/AccentAlaska.com; **29** © Julie Houck/Corbis; **30** © Jeffrey L. Rotman/Corbis; **32** © Jeff Vinnick/Getty Images; **33** *top left* © Image Makers/Getty Images; *top right* Image based on illustration from Dr. Michael Studinger/Lamont-Doherty Earth Observatory of Columbia University; **35** © Stella Snead/www.bciusa.com; **37** © William Bacon/Photo Researchers, Inc.; © Antonio Luiz Hamdan/Getty Images; **42** Comstock; **43** © elektraVision/Index Stock Imagery; **45** © Ralph White/Corbis; **46** © Allsport Concepts/Getty Images; **48** © Eric Figge/Index Stock Imagery; **50** *top left* Courtesy of American Honda Motors, Inc; *bottom left* © Jim Sugar/Corbis; **51** Steve Pica/McDougal Littell/Houghton Mifflin Co.; **58** © PhotoDisc; **59** © David Young-Wolff/PhotoEdit; **60–61** © Omni Photo Communinications/Index Stock Imagery; **63** © Chuck Savage/Corbis; **65** © AFP/Getty Images; **67** © Tami Chappell/Reuters; **68** The Granger Collection, New York; **71** © Tom Stewart/Corbis; **72** *top left* © Javier Garcia-Guinea/Reuters; *top right* © Maurice Nimmo/Frank Lane Picture Agency/Corbis; **75** © Scott Sroka/National Geographic Image Collection; **77** © GK Hart/Vikki Hart/PhotoDisc; **78** © David Young-Wolff/PhotoEdit; **80** © Steve Chenn/Corbis; **82** © Ed Young/Corbis; **84** Steve Pica/McDougal Littell/Houghton Mifflin Co.; **85** © Royalty-Free/Corbis; **86** © Reed Saxon/AP Images; **88** © Anthony Bannister/Gallo Images/Corbis; **89** © Corbis; **91** © Joseph Sohm/Visions of America/Corbis; **92** © Kit Houghton/Corbis; **94** Stacy Allison; **95** © Macduff Everton/Corbis; **97, 98** Solar & Heliospheric Observatory (SOHO) (ESA and NASA); **99** © Royalty-Free/Corbis; **100** *top* © Stephen Simpson/Getty Images; *bottom* © Stephen Simpson/Getty Images; **101** © Siede Preis/PhotoDisc; **102** © Gary W. Carter/Corbis; **104** © Frank Cezus/Getty Images; **106** © Roger Ressmeyer/Corbis; **107** *top* © Mark Wagner/Getty Images; *bottom* Steve Pica/McDougal Littell/Houghton Mifflin Co.; **114** *center right* © Ron Chapple/Getty Images; *bottom* Ken O'Donoghue/McDougal Littell/Houghton Mifflin Co.; **115** *top* © Alison Wright/Corbis; *bottom* © Charles O'Rear/Corbis; **116–117** © Richard Cummins/viestiphoto.com; **120** © Michael Newman/PhotoEdit; **122** © EyeWire; **123** © Darryl Torckler/Getty Images; **124** © Robert W. Ginn/PhotoEdit; **125** *bottom left* © SW Productions/Getty Images; *top right* © Steve Cole/PhotoDisc; **128** Stockbyte; **131** © David Young-Wolff/Getty Images; **132** Ken O'Donoghue/McDougal Littell/Houghton Mifflin Co.; **134** © Royalty-Free/Corbis; **138** © Kevin Schafer/Getty Images; **140** © Frank Boxler/AP Images; **141** © Richard Cummins/Corbis; **142** © Richard Hamilton Smith/Corbis; **144** © Bill Brooks/Masterfile; **145** © Jeff Albertson/Corbis; **147** *top left* © Scott Markewitz/Getty Images; *bottom left* © Joe McDonald/Corbis; **148** Steve Pica/McDougal Littell/Houghton Mifflin Co.; **149** *top right* PhotoSpin; *center left* © Tracy Frankel/Getty Images; **150** © AP Images; **152** © Phil Hunt/Getty Images; **153** Jennifer Smith; **167** © AFP/Getty Images; **168–169** NASA; **172** *top right* © Jeff Greenberg/PhotoEdit; *bottom left all* Stockbyte; **175** © Bob Daemmrich/The Image Works; **176** © Mark A. Schneider/Photo Researchers, Inc.; **177** © Oscar C. Williams; **179** Ken O'Donoghue/McDougal Littell/Houghton Mifflin Co.; **180** Photo Courtesy of Robert Murray, The Mars Society; **181** Steve Pica/McDougal Littell/Houghton Mifflin Co.; **185** © Ryan McVay/Getty Images; **186** *top left* © Joel Sartore/National Geographic Image Collection; *top right* © Peter J. Bryant/BPS/Getty Images; **187** © David Zimmerman/Corbis; **188** © Chaco Mohler/Mountain Stock/Sportschrome, Inc.; **190** © Todd Powell/Index Stock Imagery; **194** Tom Bol Photography; **197** T.A. Rector (NRAO/AUI/NSF and NOAO/AURA/NSF) and M. Hanna (NOAO/AURA/NSF); **201** © Peter Weber/Getty Images; **202** © Lucent Technologies' Bell Labs/Science Photo Library/Photo Researchers, Inc.; **203** © Royalty-Free/Corbis; **204** *bottom left* © Ralph C. Eagle, Jr./Photo Researchers, Inc.; *top right* © Scott Bodell/Getty Images; **206** © W. P. Armstrong/Palomar College; **207** © K. H. Kjeldsen/Science Photo Library/Photo Researchers, Inc.; **208** *top left* © ThinkStock LLC/Index Stock Imagery; *center left* © Derek Berwin/Getty Images; **216–217** © Fred Bruemmer/DRK Photo; **220** © Eckart Pott/www.bciusa.com; **223** © Carl Schneider/Getty Images; **225** © Roy Corral/Corbis; **227** Ken O'Donoghue/McDougal Littell/Houghton Mifflin Co.; **228** © Syracuse newspapers/Gary Walts/The Image Works; **229** © Jane Burton/www.bciusa.com; **231** © William S. Kuta/Alamy; **232** © SW Productions/Getty Images; **234** © Suzanne L. Collins and Joseph T. Collins/Photo Researchers, Inc.; **238** © AP Images; **241** © Esbin-Anderson/The Image Works; **244** © Kim Steele/Getty Images; **246** Ken O'Donoghue/McDougal Littell/Houghton Mifflin Co.; **247** © Adam Hart-Davis/Science Photo Library/Photo Researchers, Inc.; **248** © Didier Givois/ImageState; **250** © Barry Winkler/Index Stock Imagery; **251** Steve Pica/McDougal Littell/Houghton Mifflin Co.; **254** © SW Production/Index Stock Imagery; **256** © Don Mason/Corbis; **257** © Mary Kate Denny/PhotoEdit; **264** © PhotoDisc; **265** © Paul T. McMahon; **266** *center* Digital Image © The Museum of Modern Art/Licensed by SCALA/Art Resource, NY; **266–267** Art Resource, NY; **269** © AP Images; **270** Mike Danzenbaker; **271** Courtesy of Sandia National Laboratories; **273** © Tom McHugh/Photo Researchers, Inc.; **275** © Jeremy Woodhouse/Getty Images; **276** © Don Romero/Index Stock Imagery; **278** © Royalty-Free/Corbis; **281** © Serge Krouglikoff/Getty Images; **283** © Charles O'Rear/Corbis; **284** © Chihuly Studio/Dale Chihuly, "Saffron and Red Tower," 2000. Rutherford, California. Photo: Mark McDonnell; **289** © Duomo/Corbis; **291** © Bob Daemmrich/Stock Boston, LLC; **292** © John Van Hasselt/Corbis Sygma; **293** © Darrell Gulin/Corbis; **294** © Gail Shumway/Getty Images; **296** © George H. H. Huey/Corbis; **297** Steve Pica/McDougal Littell/Houghton Mifflin Co.; **300** © Angelo Hornak/Corbis; **301** © Reuters/Corbis; **303** © Chris Minerva/Index Stock Imagery; **304** Laurie O'Keefe/McDougal Littell/Houghton Mifflin Co.; **305** Frank Siteman/McDougal Littell/Houghton Mifflin Co.; **307** SW Productions/Brand X; **308** © Tony Freeman/PhotoEdit; **313** *top right* © Jon Feingersh/Corbis; *center left* Comstock; **314** © Royalty-Free/Corbis; **316** © Ian Shaw/Getty Images; **317** Frank Siteman/McDougal Littell/Houghton Mifflin Co.; **324** © Tony Freeman/PhotoEdit; **325** © Kwame Zikomo/SuperStock; **326–327** © David Young-Wolff/PhotoEdit; **329** © Gary Conner/PhotoEdit; **330** © Kennan Ward/Corbis; **332** © Jose Luis Pelaez, Inc./Corbis; **336** © Jeff Greenberg/PhotoEdit;

Selected Answers

Chapter 1

1.1 Guided Practice (p. 7) 1. d **3.** 6   **5.** 8   **7.** 3   **9.** 1
11. Step 1: 16d; Step 2: 196; Step 3: 3136 sunrises

1.1 Practice and Problem Solving (pp. 7–9) 13. 9
15. 2   **17.** 4   **19.** 21   **21.** 12   **23.** 2   **25.** 4   **27.** 8
29. 14   **31.** 20   **33–37.** Sample answers are given.
33. $q - 1$ **35.** $n + 9.4$ **37.** $\frac{n}{41}$ **39.** \$32   **41.** 17.5
43. 52.5   **45.** 6   **47.** 1.4   **49.** $12x$ **51. a.** Row 3: 12,
188; Row 4: 16, 184   **b.** $4r$ **c.** $200 - 4r$ **d.** 50 rentals. *Sample answer:* Find the greatest value of r so
that $200 - 4r$ is not less than zero.   **53.** Yes; when
$a = 2$, the value of $2 + a$ is 4 and the value of $2a$
is 4.   **55.** The cost with a coupon is \$.50 less than
the cost of the item; $n - 0.50$.   **57.** 7.9   **59.** 5.2
61. 105.6   **63.** 7.6   **65.** 7.8, 7.98, 8.79, 8.9, 9.78, 9.87

1.2 Guided Practice (p. 12) 1. base: 13; exponent: 5
3. 12 squared; 12 • 12; 144   **5.** 1.2 cubed;
$(1.2)(1.2)(1.2)$; 1.728   **7.** 36   **9.** 1296   **11.** 2744 in.^{3}

1.2 Practice and Problem Solving (pp. 12–13)
13. 32^2 **15.** 6^5 **17.** $(5.6)^3$ **19.** z^3 **21.** 8 cubed; 8 •
8 • 8; 512   **23.** 10 to the sixth power; 10 • 10 • 10 •
10 • 10 • 10; 1,000,000   **25.** 9 cubed; 9 • 9 • 9; 729
27. 0.2 squared; $(0.2)(0.2)$; 0.04   **29. a.** Row 3: 4^3, 64;
Row 4: 4^4, 256   **b.** 262,144 e-mails   **c.** stage 10
31. 343; 0.064   **33.** 16,807; 0.01024   **35.** *Sample
answer:* If you use the base 1 as a factor any
number of times, the product is 1.   **37. a.** Row 3: 9;
Row 4: 16; Row 5: $1 + 3 + 5 + 7 + 9 = 25$; the sum
of the first n odd numbers equals n squared.
b. n^2 **c.** 10,000   **39.** 17.75   **41.** 0.5   **43.** 115 gold
medals   **45.** 185   **47.** 45

Student Reference (p. 15) 1. 9:00 A.M.   **3.** 24 orders

1.3 Guided Practice (p. 18) 1. *Sample answer:*
Fraction bar, parentheses, brackets   **3.** 3
5. 44   **7.** 10   **9.** $2(2697) + 3(29) + 4(2) + 5(1) =$
5494 people

1.3 Practice and Problem Solving (pp. 19–20) 11. 32
13. 20.7   **15.** 6   **17.** 122.5   **19.** 4   **21.** 8   **23.** 9.1
25. 7   **27.** 20   **29.** 5 • 72 + 4 • 48; 552 in.
31. \$119.93   **33.** 7   **35.** 4.3   **37. a.** 1,310,720 pixels
b. 1.3 megapixels   **c.** No; $\frac{1.3}{8 \cdot 10} \approx 0.016$,
$0.016 < 0.017$, so the print will not be clear.
41. <   **43.** 2^8; 256 colors

1.3 Technology Activity (p. 21) 1. 57   **3.** 9   **5.** 4
7. 2   **9.** 396.2652439; for the expression
$100 + 87 \div 328 + 296$, the calculator will first do
the division $87 \div 328$, then do the additions.

1.4 Guided Practice (p. 24) 1. 22.5   **3.** $-9, -5, -3,$
$0, 6, 12$ **5.** 9   **7.** 12   **9.** 33   **11.** -81 **13.** 4   **15.** 47
17. the top of Kilauea

1.4 Practice and Problem Solving (pp. 25–26)
19. >   **21.** <
23. (number line) $-8, -5, -4, 7, 15$
25. (number line) $-30, -25, -22, -16$
27. 7   **29.** 40   **31.** 42   **33.** 105   **35.** -9 **37.** 11
39. 67   **41.** -100 **43.** 8   **45.** 24   **47.** 40   **49.** 13
51. a. $-3, -8, -12, -37$
b. (number line)
c. Unnamed city, Bay of Bengal   **d.** closer to
53. a. increase   **b.** decrease   **c.** Wednesday;
Saturday   **d.** The high temperature consistently
rose from Sunday through Wednesday and
consistently fell from Wednesday through
Saturday.   **55.** 15   **57.** 11   **59.** 2   **61.** 7   **63.** 0
67. *Sample answer:* 500   **69.** between 42,000 and
56,000   **71.** between 12,000 and 20,000   **73.** 17

1.5 Guided Practice (p. 31) 1. absolute value
3. 2   **5.** 8   **7.** -12 **9.** -6 **11.** -12 **13.** The arrow
should start at -2 and go 5 units in the positive
direction; $-2 + 5 = 3$.

1.5 Practice and Problem Solving (pp. 32–33)
15. -16 **17.** -10 **19.** -14 **21.** 6   **23.** -9 **25.** -52
27. -26 **29.** -102 **31.** 5   **33.** 7   **35.** -24 **37.** -13

39. 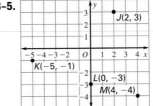*Sample answer:* The length of the arrow is the absolute value of the second number. The direction of the arrow is right if the second number is positive and left if the second number is negative.   **41.** $63
43. -1915 **45. a.** -3743 m   **b.** -4943 m   **47.** -24
49. 65 **51.** -17 **53.** -18 **55.** Even; the sum of two odd numbers is even.   **57.** $x \le 0$; if $x < 0$, then $|x|$ and x are opposites so their sum is 0; if $x = 0$, then $|x|$ and x are both 0 so their sum is 0.
61. $n + 14.5$ **63.** 4900 yd^2 **65.** $<$

1.6 Guided Practice (p. 36) **1.** $-15 - x$ **3.** -5
5. -13 **7.** -10 **9.** 13 **11.** Step 1: -110; Step 2: -90; Step 3: -20 ft

1.6 Practice and Problem Solving (pp. 36–38) **13.** 9
15. 12 **17.** 39 **19.** 52 **21.** -71 **23.** -52 **25.** 10
27. -10 **29.** -19 **31.** -10 **33.** $41°C$ **35.** $25°C$
37. 30 ft   **39.** -190 **41.** 235 **43.** -12 **45.** -16
47. solution B; $24°C$ lower   **49.** No; if $b = 0$, then $a + b = a - b$ and if $b < 0$, then $a + b < a - b$.
51. 6 **53.** -2 **55.** 6:40 A.M.   **57.** 30 **59.** 6 **61.** 29
63. -51

Student Reference (p. 40) **1.** 86; 86; no mode; 24
3. 0.6; 0.5; 0.5; 0.6   **5.** 183; 178; no mode; 104

1.7 Guided Practice (p. 44) **1.** The mean of a data set is the sum of the values divided by the number of values.   **3.** positive   **5.** negative   **7.** negative
9. positive   **11.** Step 1: -3; Step 2: $9(-3)$; -27; Step 3: $-5°C$

1.7 Practice and Problem Solving (pp. 45–46) **13.** 2
15. -132 **17.** -2 **19.** -360 **21.** 17 **23.** -120
25. *Sample answer:* The rules are alike in that if the two signs are alike the product or quotient is positive and if the two signs are different the product or quotient is negative. The rules are different for zero: for multiplication, if either factor is zero then the product is zero, but for division you have to check that the divisor is not zero.   **27. a.** $-20,000$ ft   **b.** 10 min   **29.** -1250
31. 5 **33.** -4 **35.** $<$ **37.** 67 ft   **39.** 4.5 **41.** -6.4

43. No; the product of an odd number of negative factors is negative, while the product of an even number of negative factors is positive, so $(-1)^n = -1$ is true for any odd positive integer. For example $(-1)^3 = -1$ but $(-1)^4 = 1$.   **45.** -21, -12, -5, 0, 13, 31 **47.** 24 **49.** -51

1.8 Guided Practice (p. 49) **1.** -12; 7
3–5. 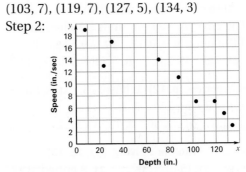   **3.** Quadrant I   **5.** y-axis

7. Step 1: $(8, 19)$, $(24, 13)$, $(31, 17)$, $(71, 14)$, $(88, 11)$, $(103, 7)$, $(119, 7)$, $(127, 5)$, $(134, 3)$
Step 2: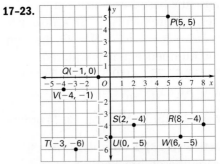

Step 3: The points generally fall from left to right. We can conclude that as the depth increases the speed tends to decrease.

1.8 Practice and Problem Solving (pp. 49–51)
9. $(0, 3)$ **11.** $(4, 0)$ **13.** $(3, -3)$ **15.** $(-3, -2)$
17–23.

17. Quadrant I   **19.** Quadrant IV   **21.** Quadrant III
23. Quadrant III   **25.** The first number refers to left/right and the second number refers to up/down; the point $(2, -8)$ is 2 units to the right of the origin and 8 units down.

27. a.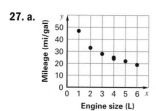

b. The points generally fall from left to right, so we can conclude that as the engine size increases the mileage tends to decrease.

29. a. $-5, -3, -1, 1, 3, 5, 7$ **b.** $(-3, -5), (-2, -3),$ $(-1, -1), (0, 1), (1, 3), (2, 5), (3, 7)$

c.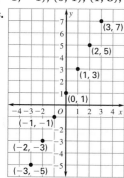

d. The points lie on a line.

31. *Sample answer:* $P(5, 0), Q(5, 5), R(0, 5);$ the distance from O to P is 5 units, the distance from P to Q is 5 units, the distance from Q to R is 5 units, and the distance from R to O is 5 units.
35. $20 - 2c$ **37.** never **39.** -45 **41.** 21

Chapter Review (pp. 52–55)

1.

Quadrant II	Quadrant I
y-axis →	origin
Quadrant III	Quadrant IV

x-axis

3. The opposite of a nonzero integer has the same absolute value but a different sign. The opposite of zero is zero.

5. 23 **7.** 5 **9.** 13.5 **11.** 8 **13.** 10,000 **15.** 156.25
17. 3125 **19.** 1.728 **21.** 121 **23.** 21
25. $-6, -4, -3, 2, 5, 6$
27. $18, -18$ **29.** $4, -4$ **31.** -6 **33.** 11 **35.** 17
37. -12 **39.** $17°F$ **41.** 0 **43.** 19 **45.** -9 **47.** 31
49. 108 **51.** -51 **53.** 5 **55.** -3 **57.** $(1, 2)$
59. $(-3, -3)$

61–63.
61. Quadrant II
63. Quadrant III

B(−2, 5), *C(0, 4)*, *D(−3, −1)*, *E(4, −2)*

Focus on Problem Solving (p. 59) **1.** $.98; $5.88
3. 5 c. *Sample answer:* You can find the information in a dictionary or almanac, or on the Internet.
5. yes **7.** Sun.: $-6°F$, Mon.: $+4°F$, Tues.: $-13°F$, Wed.: $-13°F$, Thu.: $+1°F$, Fri.: $-8°F$, Sat.: $0°F$; $-5°F$

Chapter 2

2.1 Guided Practice (p. 66)

1. associative property of addition
3. $(26 + 18) + 34$
$= (18 + 26) + 34$ [commutative property of addition]
$= 18 + (26 + 34)$ [associative property of addition]
$= 18 + 60$ [Add 26 and 34.]
$= 78$ [Add 18 and 60.]
5. $(3.45)(6.26)(0)$
$= [(3.45)(6.26)](0)$ [Use order of operations.]
$= 0$ [multiplication property of zero]
7. 220 **9.** $x + 17$ **11.** $y + 6$ **13.** commutative property of multiplication **15.** *Sample answer:* The conversion factor should be $\dfrac{1\ \text{pound}}{16\ \text{ounces}}$ so that the common factor of ounces can be divided out. This gives 80 ounces $= 80$ ounces $\cdot \dfrac{1\ \text{pound}}{16\ \text{ounces}} =$ 5 pounds.

2.1 Practice and Problem Solving (pp. 66–68)

17. $15(-9)(2)$
$= [15(-9)](2)$ [Use order of operations.]
$= [-9(15)](2)$ [commutative property of multiplication]
$= -9[(15)(2)]$ [associative property of multiplication]
$= -9(30)$ [Multiply 15 and 2.]
$= -270$ [Multiply -9 and 30.]
19. $45 + 29 + 55$
$= (45 + 29) + 55$ [Use order of operations.]
$= (29 + 45) + 55$ [commutative property of addition]
$= 29 + (45 + 55)$ [associative property of addition]
$= 29 + 100$ [Add 45 and 55.]
$= 129$ [Add 29 and 100.]
21. -8100 **23.** 56 **25.** $j - 6$ **27.** $130y$

29. commutative property of multiplication
31. identity property of multiplication   **33.** 7500 g
35. 3 ft^2 **37.** \$140   **39.** 312 yd^2
41. $1.25 + 1.38 + 0.75$
$= (1.25 + 1.38) + 0.75$ [Use order of operations.]
$= (1.38 + 1.25) + 0.75$ [commutative property
                                          of addition]
$= 1.38 + (1.25 + 0.75)$ [associative property of
                                          addition]
$= 1.38 + 2$ [Add 1.25 and 0.75.]
$= 3.38$ [Add 1.38 and 2.]
43. $4(20)(25)(-5)$
$= 4[(20)(25)](-5)$ [associative property of
                                    multiplication]
$= 4[(25)(20)](-5)$ [commutative property of
                                    multiplication]
$= [4(25)][(20)(-5)]$ [associative property of
                                     multiplication]
$= 100[(20)(-5)]$ [Multiply 4 and 25.]
$= 100(-100)$ [Multiply 20 and -5.]
$= -10,000$ [Multiply 100 and -100.]
45. -450 **47. a.** 19.5 m   **b.** 6.5 m   **49.** Row 1: 5, -5;
Row 2: 2, $\frac{1}{2}$; Row 3: 2, 10; Row 4: 4, 16; no. *Sample
answer:* The results of evaluating each expression
after attempting to apply a commutative or
associative property are different from those
before applying the property.   **51. a.** \$8   **b.** $80x$
c. \$2000   **53.** 81   **55.** 1000   **57.** 11   **59.** \$13.13
61–63.

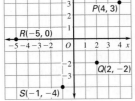

61. Quadrant IV
63. Quadrant III

Student Reference (p. 70) **1.** 36 ft   **3.** 73 in.
5. 600 cm^2 **7.** 268 ft, 4200 ft^2

2.2 Guided Practice (p. 73) **1.** distributive property
3. 288   **5.** 17.9   **7.** $2x - 12$ **9.** $20k + 45$
11. a. $15(20 + l)$ **b.** $300 + 15l$ **c.** $15(20 + l) =$
$15(20) + 15(l) = 300 + 15l$

2.2 Practice and Problem Solving (pp. 74–75) **13.** 30
15. 18.2   **17.** -81 **19.** 9   **21.** 763   **23.** -1980
25. 3.98   **27.** -36.18 **29.** $3y + 27$ **31.** $-7s - 140$

33. $-25q + 20$ **35.** $16n + 24$ **37.** 295 inches per
year $\approx$ 300 inches per year, so the total snowfall
will be about $5(300) = 1500$ inches; $5(295) =$
$5(300 - 5) = 5(300) - 5(5) = 1500 - 25 = 1475$
inches, which is close to the answer obtained
by estimation.   **39.** $(45a + 63)$ units^2 **41.** 65
43. 28   **45. a.** $W = 176,000 - 4400d$ **b.** 110,000 lb
c. 110 days   **47.** $5m - m^2$ **49.** $-3y^2 - 24y$ **51.** 11
53. -139 **55.** $-4°F$ **57.** commutative property of
addition   **59.** identity property of multiplication

Student Reference (p. 77) **1.** $\dfrac{17 \text{ m}}{1 \text{ sec}}$ **3.** $\dfrac{1.5 \text{ in.}}{1 \text{ h}}$
5. 150 lb   **7.** \$230   **9.** $15x$ Cal

2.3 Guided Practice (p. 80) **1.** constant terms
3. terms: $6x$, x, 2, 4; like terms: $6x$ and x, 2 and 4;
coefficients: 6, 1; constant terms: 2, 4; $7x + 6$
5. terms: $5n$, 1, $-n$, -8; like terms: $5n$ and $-n$,
1 and -8; coefficients: 5, -1; constant terms: 1,
-8; $4n - 7$ **7.** $-3r - 21$ **9.** *Sample answer:* The
distributive property was incorrectly applied. You
can rewrite $5a - (3a - 7)$ as $5a + (-1)(3a - 7)$.
Applying the distributive property gives
$5a + (-1)(3a) - (-1)(7) = 5a - 3a + 7 = 2a + 7$.

2.3 Practice and Problem Solving (pp. 81–82)
11. terms: $4y$, 23, $-y$, -6; like terms: $4y$ and $-y$, 23
and -6; coefficients: 4, -1; constant terms: 23, -6;
$3y + 17$ **13.** terms: $2b$, -8, $4b$, $-6b$; like terms: $2b$,
$4b$, and $-6b$; coefficients: 2, 4, -6; constant term:
-8; -8 **15.** terms: $8p$, $-5p$, 5, $-p$, -2; like terms:
$8p$, $-5p$, and $-p$; 5 and -2; coefficients: 8, -5,
and -1; constant terms: 5, -2; $2p + 3$ **17.** $7a$
19. $6x$ **21.** $21y$ **23.** $4k - 28$ **25.** $7n + 3$
27. $-4w + 17$ **29.** $7q + 13$ **31.** $14(45 - s) + 8s$,
$630 - 6s$ **33.** $x + (x + 5) + (2x + 1)$, $4x + 6$
35. $2(7y - 5) + 2(2y)$, $18y - 10$ **37. a.** $500x$;
$500(800 - x)$, or $400,000 - 500x$ **b.** $0.27(500x) +$
$0.10(400,000 - 500x)$, $85x + 40,000$ **c.** \$69,750
39. $x = 14$ **41.** $n - 3$ **43.** $\dfrac{n}{6}$ **45.** $-2x - 6$
47. $-6m + 30$ **49.** $24t - 56$ **51.** $-24w - 27$

2.3 Technology Activity (p. 83) **1.** $7x + 14$
3. $-5x - 4$ **5.** $8x - 15$

7. When $x = 0$, $2(x - 1) + x = 2(0 - 1) + 0 = 2(-1) = -2$ and $4x - 2 = 4(0) - 2 = 0 - 2 = -2$; no. *Sample answer:* Let Y1 $= 2(X - 1) + X$ and Y2 $= 4X - 2$. The pairs of values in each row of the table are not always the same, so the two expressions are not equivalent.

2.4 Guided Practice (p. 87) 1. solution **3.** $x + 10 = 15$; yes **5.** $-6x = 54$; no **7.** Step 1: $4x$; Step 2: 36 wedges; Step 3: $4x = 36$; Step 4: 9 quesadillas

2.4 Practice and Problem Solving (pp. 87–89)
9. $26 + y = 43$ **11.** $14m = 56$ **13.** yes **15.** no
21. 28 **23.** -5 **25.** 5 **27.** -13 **29.** 30 **31.** 231
33. about 134 million personal computers
35. a. $x + 9 + 8 + 5 + 9 = 35$, or $x + 31 = 35$
b. 4 cm **37.** *Sample answer:* An expression consists of numbers and/or variables and operations, but has no equal sign or inequality signs. An example is $24x - 7$. An equation uses an equal sign to show that an expression is equal to a number or another expression. An example is $24x - 7 = 17$.
39. a. $200 + 800x = 13,000$

b. *Sample:* 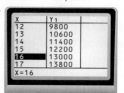 16; 16 sec

41. -8 **43.** -2 **45.** 985 **47.** $12c + 2$ **49.** $10x - 2$
51. -10

2.5 Guided Practice (p. 93) 1. inverse **3.** 6 **5.** 9
7. -9 **9.** The number 8 was subtracted from the left side of the equation, but added to the right side. It should have been subtracted from each side, giving $x + 8 - 8 = 10 - 8$, which simplifies to $x = 2$.

2.5 Practice and Problem Solving (pp. 93–95) 11. 5
13. -8 **15.** 11 **17.** -17 **19.** -29 **21.** 17 **23.** 23
25. -226 **27.** 45°C **29.** 3035 ft **31.** You can add -9 to each side of the equation. **33.** -18 **35.** 12
37. 4 **39.** 24 cm **41. a.** $190 = x + 45 + \frac{125}{5}$
b. 120 mg/dL **c.** borderline **43.** $39 = y + 5$
47. 0.3^2 **49.** t^6 **51.** 2401 **53.** 15.625 **55.** 27
57. -144 **59.** 7 **61.** 3

2.6 Guided Practice (p. 99) 1. division **3.** -3
5. 24 **7.** Step 1: $8x = 40$, 5 min; Step 2: $5x = 20$, 4 min; Step 3: 9 min

2.6 Practice and Problem Solving (pp. 99–101) 9. 13
11. -4 **13.** -24 **15.** -77 **17.** 19 **19.** 7 **21.** 289
23. -3348 **25.** 5 min **27.** 512 sec, or 8 min 32 sec; $37\frac{1}{3}$ sec; about 19.1 sec **29.** -5 **31.** 5 **33.** 104
35. a. $100x$ mi **b.** 0; 500; 1000; 1500; 2000; 2500

c-d.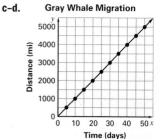

c. *Sample answer:* The points all lie on a straight line that passes through the origin. **d.** 50 days

e. Solving the equation $100x = 5000$ gives an answer of 50, so the answers are the same.
37. *Sample answer:* The Montoyas expect to average 50 miles per hour on their trip to the coast. If it is 400 miles to the coast, how long will the trip take? The solution is 8 hours. **41.** 12.81
43. 1.499 **45.** 60.0222 **47.** 2.4 **49.** -33 **51.** -2
53. 184 **55.** 9

2.7 Guided Practice (p. 105) 1. absolute value
3. -1.7 **5.** 3.32 **7.** 5.4 **9.** -41.18 **11.** Step 1: -0.61 m; Step 2: $x - 0.61 = 182.98$; Step 3: 183.59 m

2.7 Practice and Problem Solving (pp. 105–107)
13. 13.15 **15.** -12.6 **17.** 0.121 **19.** 79.794
21. -6.2 **23.** 2.8 **25.** -2.51 **27.** -6.1 **29.** 0.324
31. 0.75 **33.** -20.7 **35.** 64.792 **37.** 2.1 m^2
39. $-4.5x$ **41.** $2.4 - 7.4n$ **43.** 6.4 ft **45. a.** More money. *Sample answer:* Each year of deficit can be paired with a year in which the surplus was greater than the absolute value of the deficit: 1995 with 2000, 1996 with 1999, and 1997 with 1998.
b. \$136.7 billion surplus **c.** \$22.8 billion surplus
d. \$23.6 billion. *Sample answer:* The median and the mean are almost the same. **47. a.** Cessna Skyhawk: 141 mi/h; Boeing 747: 570 mi/h; Concorde: 1346 mi/h **b.** Cessna Skyhawk: 3.9 h; Boeing 747: 1.0 h; Concorde: 0.4 h

49. terms: $-3p$, 2, p, -4; like terms: $-3p$ and p, 2 and -4; coefficients: -3, 1; constant terms: 2, -4; $-2p - 2$ **51.** terms: 8, $2y$, -1, $-9y$, 3; like terms: 8, -1, and 3, $2y$ and $-9y$; coefficients: 2, -9; constant terms: 8, -1, 3; $10 - 7y$ **53.** 5 **55.** -152

Chapter Review (pp. 108–111) **1.** 0; 1
3. equivalent numerical expressions
5. $16 + 18 + 14$
$= (16 + 18) + 14$ [Use order of operations.]
$= (18 + 16) + 14$ [commutative property of addition]
$= 18 + (16 + 14)$ [associative property of addition]
$= 18 + 30$ [Add 16 and 14.]
$= 48$ [Add 18 and 30.]
7. $4.7 + 2.5 + 2.3$
$= (4.7 + 2.5) + 2.3$ [Use order of operations.]
$= (2.5 + 4.7) + 2.3$ [commutative property of addition]
$= 2.5 + (4.7 + 2.3)$ [associative property of addition]
$= 2.5 + 7$ [Add 4.7 and 2.3.]
$= 9.5$ [Add 2.5 and 7.]
9. $5(-3)(12)$
$= [5(-3)](12)$ [Use order of operations.]
$= [-3(5)](12)$ [commutative property of multiplication]
$= -3[(5)(12)]$ [associative property of multiplication]
$= -3(60)$ [Multiply 5 and 12.]
$= -180$ [Multiply -3 and 60.]
11. 318 **13.** 41.6 **15.** $-2x - 8$ **17.** $28a + 8$
19. terms: $4t$, $13t$, 2; like terms: $4t$ and $13t$; coefficients: 4, 13; constant term: 2 **21.** terms: 12, $-7k$, 9, $-k$; like terms: 12 and 9, $-7k$ and $-k$; coefficients: -7, -1; constant terms: 12, 9
23. $7u + 4$ **25.** 13 **27.** -9 **29.** 3 h **31.** -25
33. 93 **35.** -9 **37.** 32 **39.** 90 fliers **41.** 7.5
43. -2.8 **45.** -3.5 **47.** 8.3

Chapter 3

3.1 Guided Practice (p. 122) **1.** inverse **3.** 5 **5.** 1
7. Step 1: Cost for parts, Number of hours of labor; Step 2: $168 = 78 + 45h$; Step 3: 2 h

3.1 Practice and Problem Solving (pp. 123–124)
9. 3 **11.** 72 **13.** 48 **15.** -24 **17.** -55 **19.** -98

21. \$9 **23.** $5 - 2n = 7$; -1 **25.** $13 + 6n = 67$; 9
27. a. 12 flocks **b.** 2 pigs **c.** No. *Sample answer:* A heifer and two pigs cost $500 + 2 \cdot \$120 = \$740$. This leaves $\$755 - \$740 = \$15$, which is less than the \$20 cost of a flock of chicks. **29.** -3.2
31. 18.5 **33.** -4.68 **35. a.** $278 + 50m$; Column 2: \$328, \$378, \$428, \$478

b.

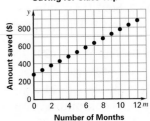

Saving for Class Trip

Sample answer: The points lie along a straight line; you can extend the scatter plot either by plotting more points as shown or by drawing a line through the plotted points and estimating what value along the horizontal axis corresponds to a value of \$850 on the vertical axis. **c.** $278 + 50m = 850$, 12 mo
d. *Sample answer:* The scatter plot gives a nice, visual picture of the relationship, and once it is plotted, it is easy to find the time and savings values that relate to each other, but it is time-consuming to make the plot. For finding a single value, it is very simple to solve the equation, and the equation has the advantage of giving an exact value, but it has the disadvantage of not providing a visual image of the relationship. **37.** $66z + 154$
39. $36 - 60y$ **41.** 11 **43.** -28

3.2 Guided Practice (p. 127) **1.** distributive property **3.** -1 **5.** 10 **7.** 3 **9.** Step 1: $2(10) + 2(x + 2) = 28$; Step 2: 2; Step 3: 4 units; Step 4: $2(10) + 2(x + 2) = 2(10) + 2(2 + 2) = 2(10) + 2(4) = 20 + 8 = 28$

3.2 Practice and Problem Solving (pp. 127–129)
11. 3 **13.** 12 **15.** 2 **17.** -3 **19.** 21 **21.** 5 people
23. 3 **25.** 34 **27.** -2 **29.** 2 **31.** 5 **33.** 11
35. 15 **37. a.** $29.50 = 19.50 + 0.25(m - 200)$
b. 240 **c.** 40 min

41–47.

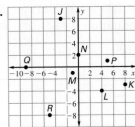

41. Quadrant IV
43. Quadrant III
45. Quadrant I
47. Quadrant III
49. $5b$
51. $5y - 1$
53. $-2x + 11$

3.3 Guided Practice (p. 133) 1. *Sample answer:* First I would get the variable on only one side of the equation by subtracting $2x$ from each side to obtain $6x + 5 = -7$. Then I would subtract 5 from each side to obtain $6x = -12$, and divide each side by 6 to obtain $x = -2$. **3.** 4 **5.** 9 **7.** 2 **9.** *Sample answer:* In going from the second to the third statement, the result of subtracting $4x$ from x should have been $-3x$, not $3x$, so the third statement should be $7 = -3x - 2$, followed by $7 + 2 = -3x - 2 + 2$, $9 = -3x$, and $-3 = x$.

3.3 Practice and Problem Solving (pp. 134–135)
11. 9 **13.** -12 **15.** no solution **17.** -4 **19.** all numbers **21.** all numbers **23.** $9 + 2n = 3n - 2$; 11 **25.** $4 - 7n = 12 - 3n$; -2 **27.** 16 times **29.** 288 **31. a.** $700 - 60x$ **b.** $400 + 60x$ **c.** $700 - 60x = 400 + 60x$, 2.5 h **d.** $3\frac{1}{3}$ h, or 3 h 20 min

33. *Sample answer:* Your brother and sister are saving money for a summer camp. Your brother begins with \$5, and saves \$11 each week. Your sister begins with \$23, and saves \$8 each week. Let x be the number of weeks the two of them have been saving. The solution is 6, and indicates after how many weeks your brother and sister will have saved the same amount. **35.** 7 **37.** 2 **39.** 21.78 **41.** -8.9 **45.** -21 **47.** 6 **49.** 5

3.3 Technology Activity (p. 136) 1. 4 **3.** 8 **5.** 1 **7.** $\frac{2}{5}$, or 0.4. *Sample answer:* If you change the value of ΔTbl to .1, you can see that the solution is $x = 0.4$.

3.4 Guided Practice (p. 140) 1. inequalities that have the same solution **3.** yes **5.** yes
7. $x > -5$;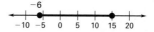
9. $x < -1$;
11. Step 1: $250 + h \geq 1000$;
　　Step 2: $h \geq 750$;
　　Step 3: The pilot must log at least 750 additional hours to become a pilot astronaut.

3.4 Practice and Problem Solving (pp. 141–142)
13. $s \leq 55$ **15.** $h \geq 48$ **17.** $x > -1$ **19.** $x \leq 6$
21. $x < 1$;

23. $-16 < y$, or $y > -16$;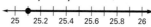
25. $-29 > g$, or $g < -29$;
27. $f \geq -9$;
29. $25.1 \leq p$, or $p \geq 25.1$;
31. $b \leq 0$;
33. $t \geq -411$;
35. $n < 51$;
37. $q \geq 10$;
39. No. *Sample answer:* There are infinitely many solutions—all points to the left or right of a given point, so you can only check sample points; no.
41.
43. $t \geq -6$, $t \leq 15$; $t \geq -6$ and $t \leq 15$;
45. 9.15 m **47.** $5 + 4n = 7n + 11$; -2

3.5 Guided Practice (p. 146) 1. division property of inequality
3. $v > 16$;
5. $u \geq 18$;
7. $a < -7$;
9. $r \geq 7$;
11. Step 1: $200 \cdot c \geq 500$; Step 2: $c \geq 2.5$, or $c \geq 2\frac{1}{2}$; Step 3: *Sample answer:* You must eat at least $2\frac{1}{2}$ cups of pasta at one meal to get the desired number of calories.

3.5 Practice and Problem Solving (pp. 146–148)
13. $b > 49$;
15. $y < -3$;
17. $d \geq -66$;
19. $w \leq 17$;
21. $h \geq -78$;

23. $q > -14$;

25. $m < -15$;

27. $n \le 15$;

29. more than 5 times   **31.** $\dfrac{n}{4} \le 8$; $n \le 32$

33. $7n > -35$; $n > -5$ **35.** $3n > -18$; $n > -6$

37. at least 15 pages

39. $b \le -4.6$;

41. $z < -24.48$;

43. $c \ge -11.2$;

45. less than 30 min   **47.** not more than $1.66/\text{ft}^2$

51. 12.5   **53.** 72.2

55. $x > 84$;

57. $x \le 59$;

3.6 Guided Practice (p. 151)   **1.** $5 + 2n < 20$; $n < 7.5$

3. $x > 0$;

5. $x > 40$;

7. $y \le 8$;

9. Step 1: $23v + 10v$, or $33v$; Step 2: $120 + 8v < 33v$; Step 3: $4.8 < v$, or $v > 4.8$. *Sample answer:* You must visit the park at least 5 times for the cost with the season pass to be less.

3.6 Practice and Problem Solving (pp. 151–153)

11. yes   **13.** no

15. $n \le -1$;

17. $m < 11$;

19. $b < 12$;

21. $x > 16$;

23. not more than 290 days

25. $b < 1$;

27. $y < 3$;

29. $s \le 16$;

31. at least 5 sets   **35.** $(1, 3)$ **37.** $(3, 0)$ **39.** $(-4, 4)$
41. $26a + 13$ **43.** $6a$ **45.** 3   **47.** $3n + 9 = 2n - 7$, -16

Chapter Review (pp. 154–157) **1.** solution of an inequality   **3.** equivalent   **5.** $2.45   **7.** 14   **9.** 3
11. no solution

13. $y < 12$;

15. $x \le 19$;

17. $-27 < a$, or $a > -27$;

19. $c \le 8$;

21. $12 < r$, or $r > 12$;

23. $h < -8$;

25. $m > -2$;

27. $6 \ge z$, or $z \le 6$;

29. $p \le 168$;

31. $q \le 1$;

33. $a \ge 2$;

Chapter 4

4.1 Guided Practice (p. 174) **1.** *Sample answer:* Write the number as the product of two whole number factors that are not equal to 1 or the number itself. Continue this process with any composite factors until only prime numbers remain. Write the original number as the product of the prime numbers that remain, using exponents for prime factors that repeat.
3. 1, 2, 4, 8, 16   **5.** 1, 29   **7.** composite   **9.** prime
11. $2 \cdot 5$ **13.** 5^2 **15.** *Sample answer:* The factor 4 is composite, and equals $2 \cdot 2$. The prime factorization is $60 = 2^2 \cdot 3 \cdot 5$.

4.1 Practice and Problem Solving (pp. 175–176)
17. 1, 53   **19.** 1, 3, 11, 33   **21.** 1, 2, 3, 4, 5, 6, 10, 12, 15, 20, 30, 60   **23.** 1, 2, 3, 4, 6, 8, 9, 12, 16, 18, 24, 36, 48, 72, 144   **25.** composite   **27.** prime
29. composite   **31.** composite   **33.** Row 2: 20; Row 3: 3, 4; Row 4: 3, 5; $2^2 \cdot 3^2 \cdot 5$ **35.** $2 \cdot 29$
37. $5 \cdot 17$ **39.** $2^5 \cdot 5$ **41.** $3 \cdot 5 \cdot 13$ **43.** $2 \cdot 3 \cdot 5 \cdot 7$
45. $3^2 \cdot 5^2$ **47.** *Sample answer:* $8x^3y^2$ is a monomial because it is the product only of a number and variables that are raised to whole number powers; $8x^3y^2 + 1$ is not a monomial because it is the sum of two monomials.

49. $19 \cdot m \cdot m \cdot m$ **51.** $3 \cdot 7 \cdot a \cdot b$ **53.** $5 \cdot 7 \cdot r \cdot s \cdot$ $s \cdot s \cdot s \cdot s$ **55.** $2 \cdot 2 \cdot 2 \cdot 5 \cdot m \cdot m \cdot n$ **57.** *Sample answer:* If 5 is the ones digit, then the number must be a multiple of 5. This is because, for example, $15 = 10 + 5 = 5(2 + 1)$, $25 = 20 + 5 = 5(4 + 1)$, and $35 = 30 + 5 = 5(6 + 1)$. **59.** 1, 5, 67, 335 **61.** 1, 3, 67, 201 **63.** 1, 2, 4, 13, 26, 52, w, $2w$, $4w$, $13w$, $26w$, $52w$ **65.** 1, 7, x, y, z, xy, xz, yz, xyz, $7x$, $7y$, $7z$, $7xy$, $7xz$, $7yz$, $7xyz$ **67.** 2^2, 3^2, 2^4, 5^2, $2^2 \cdot 3^2$, 2^6. *Sample answer:* All exponents in the prime factorization of a perfect square must be even. **69.** 1, 2, 3, 6, 9. *Sample answer:* 36, 54, and 72 have 18 as a factor, and also have 1, 2, 3, 6, and 9 as factors. **71.** -8 **73.** 32 **75.** 8 **77.** -63 **79.** $15 + n = 21 - n$; 3 **81.** $8 + n = -3n$; -2

4.2 Guided Practice (p. 179) **1.** *Sample answer:* It is a whole number that is a factor of both numbers. **3.** 7; not relatively prime **5.** 1; relatively prime **7.** $2c$ **9.** $5m$ **11.** Step 1: $225 = 3^2 \cdot 5^2$, $75 = 3 \cdot 5^2$, $120 = 2^3 \cdot 3 \cdot 5$; Step 2: 3 and 5; 15; Step 3: the greatest number of gift bags the owner can make, each with 15 pastel crayons, 5 paintbrushes, and 8 tubes of oil paint

4.2 Practice and Problem Solving (pp. 179–181)
13. 3 **15.** 12 **17.** 1 **19.** 120 **21.** 11; not relatively prime **23.** 1; relatively prime **25.** 1; relatively prime **27.** 28; not relatively prime **29.** m **31.** $2x$ **33.** 7 bouquets; 9 daisies, 8 lilies, 6 irises, 3 freesias **35.** relatively prime **37.** $2m^2n$ **39.** $4mn$ **41.** x **43.** $9wx$ **45.** s **47.** 15 cm **49. a.** 40 min **b.** 36 space-hours; 37 space-hours **c.** 7560 space-hours **51.** Sometimes. *Sample answer:* Let $a = 4$, $b = 5$, and $c = 8$. Then a and b are relatively prime and b and c are relatively prime, but a and c have common factors of 2 and 4, and therefore are not relatively prime. On the other hand, let $a = 2$, $b = 7$, and $c = 13$. Then a and b are relatively prime, b and c are relatively prime, and a and c are relatively prime. **53.** $\dfrac{7}{9}$ **55.** $\dfrac{6}{15}$ **57.** 18 **59.** 15 **61.** 5^3 **63.** $2^2 \cdot 13$

4.3 Guided Practice (p. 184) **1.** *Sample answer:* It means that the numerator and denominator have no whole number common factors other than 1.

3. *Sample answer:* $\dfrac{3}{4}, \dfrac{24}{32}$ **5.** *Sample answer:* $\dfrac{4}{7}, \dfrac{16}{28}$ **7.** $\dfrac{8}{19}$ **9.** $\dfrac{21a^2}{11}$ **11.** Step 1: 248 films; Step 2: $\dfrac{30}{248}$; Step 3: $\dfrac{15}{124}$

4.3 Practice and Problem Solving (pp. 185–186)
13–19. Sample answers are given. **13.** $\dfrac{1}{3}, \dfrac{10}{30}$ **15.** $\dfrac{6}{7}, \dfrac{36}{42}$ **17.** $\dfrac{1}{9}, \dfrac{6}{54}$ **19.** $\dfrac{10}{16}, \dfrac{15}{24}$ **21.** $\dfrac{5}{7}$ **23.** $\dfrac{4}{15}$ **25.** $\dfrac{4}{5}$ **27.** $\dfrac{12}{19}$ **29.** $\dfrac{1}{a}$ **31.** $\dfrac{9cd}{4}$ **33.** $\dfrac{3}{5w}$ **35.** $\dfrac{77x^2}{6}$ **37. a.** $\dfrac{3}{8}$ **b.** $\dfrac{1}{8}$ **39.** no **41.** $\dfrac{4}{5}, \dfrac{13}{15}$; no **43.** $\dfrac{3}{8}, \dfrac{5}{16}$; no **45.** $\dfrac{7}{9}, \dfrac{7}{9}$; yes **47.** *Sample answer:* Divide the numerator and denominator of each fraction by the GCF of their absolute values. For $\dfrac{-12}{27}$, divide the numerator and denominator by 3 to get $\dfrac{-4}{9}$ or $-\dfrac{4}{9}$. For $\dfrac{25}{-35}$, divide the numerator and denominator by 5 to get $\dfrac{5}{-7}$, or $-\dfrac{5}{7}$. For $\dfrac{-33}{-55}$, divide the numerator and denominator by 11 to get $\dfrac{-3}{-5}$, or $\dfrac{3}{5}$. **49.** 20 **51.** 5 **53. a.** $\dfrac{96}{216}; \dfrac{4}{9}$ **b.** $\dfrac{4}{3y}; \dfrac{4}{9}$ **c.** The results are the same. *Sample answer:* The second method; it is easier to simplify the expression before evaluating it because it is easier to identify common factors. Simplifying first also results in an expression that is much easier to evaluate than the original expression, and that can be easily evaluated for any value of y without having to consider the value of x. **d.** (a) $\dfrac{288}{864}; \dfrac{1}{3}$; (b) $\dfrac{4}{3y}; \dfrac{1}{3}$. *Sample answer:* The results supporting that the second method is easier are even stronger for the new values of x and y. **55.** 13 **57.** 18 **59.** identity property of multiplication **61.** $2x$ **63.** $5r$

4.4 Guided Practice (p. 189) **1.** *Sample answer:* The least common denominator of two or more fractions is the least common multiple of the denominators of the fractions. **3.** 12 **5.** 72 **7.** $3s^2$ **9.** $45m^2$ **11.** $\dfrac{3}{4}$ **13.** $\dfrac{2}{5}$

15. *Sample answer:* When you write the product you will compute to find the LCM, you use the power of each prime factor with the greatest exponent that it has in the given numbers. The power of 2 is 2^4, not 2^5; so the LCM is $2^4 \cdot 3 \cdot 5 = 240$.

4.4 Practice and Problem Solving (pp. 190–191)
17. 24 **19.** 30 **21.** 180 **23.** 462 **25.** 792 **27.** 240 **29.** $63w^2$ **31.** $42x^4$ **33.** $8n^3$ **35.** $33s^2$ **37.** No. *Sample answer:* You can multiply any common multiple that you can find by a whole number greater than 1 to find an even greater common multiple. **39.** $\frac{2}{7}$ **41.** $\frac{11}{15}$ **43.** $\frac{5}{12}$ **45.** $\frac{8}{21}$ **47.** $\frac{7}{6}, \frac{11}{9},$ $1\frac{1}{3}$ **49.** $\frac{1}{5}, \frac{3}{10}, \frac{8}{15}$ **51.** $\frac{4}{9}, \frac{7}{15}, \frac{3}{4}$ **53.** $\frac{43}{18}, \frac{12}{5}, 2\frac{5}{12}$ **55.** 25. *Sample answer:* The prime factorization of 12 is $2^2 \cdot 3$. The only additional factor needed is 5^2 to obtain the product $2^2 \cdot 3 \cdot 5^2$ for the LCM 300. Therefore, 5^2 or 25 is the least number that meets the requirements. **57.** $15x^3y^5$ **59.** $495g^4h^3$ **61.** $364ab^2c^3$ **63.** $120d^3ef^2$ **65.** $\frac{4x}{12}, \frac{3x}{12}$ **67.** $\frac{15x^2}{20xy^2},$ $\frac{8y}{20xy^2}$ **69.** *Sample answer:* $\frac{1}{4}$ **71.** 25 **73.** 625 **75.** $2^2 \cdot 7$ **77.** 3^4 **79.** 8 gift boxes

4.5 Guided Practice (p. 196) 1. add **3.** 4^{11} **5.** 6^8 **7.** 2^5 **9.** 3^3 **11.** m^7 **13.** x^6 **15.** The coefficients of each expression should have been multiplied to obtain $2x^5 \cdot 2x^4 = 2 \cdot 2 \cdot x^{5+4} = 4x^9$.

4.5 Practice and Problem Solving (pp. 197–198)
17. 9^5 **19.** 8^8 **21.** 8^6 **23.** 9^{10} **25.** b^{15} **27.** $8z^{11}$ **29.** $8r^6$ **31.** z^{14} **33.** $7y^3$ **35.** $\frac{2s^3}{3}$ **37.** $=$ **39.** $>$ **41.** The powers a^7 and b^7 do not have the same base. **43.** 2 **45.** 3 **47.** $4m^5n^7$ **49.** p^7q^4 **51.** $\frac{7m^4n^5}{3}$ **53.** $\frac{7c^4d^5}{6}$ **55.** $\frac{3a^3}{7}$ **57.** $4w^{10}$ **59. a.** 5^{m-n} **b.** *Sample answer:* $m = 4$ and $n = 3$ **c.** Yes. *Sample answer:* Any pair of integers m and n such that m is 1 more than n will result in a true equation. **61.** *Sample answer:* $2^1 \cdot 2^5, 2^2 \cdot 2^4,$ and $2^3 \cdot 2^3; \frac{2^7}{2^1}, \frac{2^8}{2^2},$ and $\frac{2^9}{2^3}$ **65.** 7 **67.** 112 **69.** x **71.** 25 **73.** $15x^2y^2$ **75.** $72x^2y^3$

4.6 Guided Practice (p. 201) 1. $\frac{1}{7^2}$ **3.** $\frac{1}{5^3}$ **5.** $\frac{4}{a^6}$ **7.** 3^{-3} **9.** $4x^{-3}$ **11.** 6^3 **13.** x^8 **15.** Step 1: $\frac{10^{-3}}{10^{-9}}$; Step 2: 10^6

4.6 Practice and Problem Solving (pp. 202–203)
17. 1 **19.** $\frac{1}{20^4}$ **21.** $\frac{18}{f}$ **23.** $\frac{c^3}{d}$ **25.** 19^{-1} **27.** 2^{-6} **29.** $4d^{-1}$ **31.** $9a^2b^{-6}$ **33.** $\frac{1}{5^4}$ **35.** 13^6 **37.** $\frac{15}{t^{11}}$ **39.** $\frac{1}{b^{14}}$ **41.** *Sample answer:* $6^2 = 6 \cdot 6 = 36$, but $6^{-2} = \frac{1}{6^2} = \frac{1}{36}$. **43.** $\frac{1}{2^3}$ **45.** $\frac{1}{16}$ **47.** $\frac{17}{a^4}$ **49.** $2w^8$ **51.** 0.011 **53.** 0.010 **55. a.** 10^{-9} m² **b.** 10^{-5} m² **57.** $\frac{d^6}{c^6}$ **59.** $\frac{1}{x^8y^6}$ **63.** 5 **65.** -48 **67.** 3^4 **69.** 2^5

4.7 Guided Practice (p. 206) 1. *Sample answer:* 4.7×10^{-4} **3.** 9.18×10^6 **5.** 7.23×10^5 **7.** 27,800,000 **9.** 0.0000415 **11.** 5×10^{-5} m

4.7 Practice and Problem Solving (pp. 207–208)
13. 4.62×10^7 **15.** 1.7×10^3 **17.** 1.04×10^5 **19.** 2.3×10^{-5} **21.** 1.06×10^{-5} **23.** 5,617,000 **25.** 0.0000000038 **27.** 0.0000006 **29.** 2,280,000,000 **31.** 3.721×10^9 people **33.** 3.34×10^{-10} sec **35.** 0.00003 m **37.** *Sample answer:* The friend did not compare powers of 10. Because $4 \times 10^3 = 4000$ and $2 \times 10^2 = 200$, 4×10^3 is actually 20 times greater than 2×10^2. **39.** 4.2×10^{-4} m, 2.8×10^{-4} m, 2×10^6 dust mites **41.** $<$ **43.** $>$ **45.** 5.4×10^{13} **47.** 5.95×10^{-8} **49.** 1.97×10^3; 8700; 3.98×10^4 **51.** 8.4×10^{-6}; 0.00009; 7.61×10^{-3} **53. a.** 2.07×10^4 plankton **b.** about 7.45×10^7 plankton **c.** about 1.12×10^9 plankton **d.** about 4.47×10^{-4} Cal **55.** $-17, -16, 11, 13$ **57.** $-119, -114, -98, 99$ **59.** 20.7 **61.** $x > 5$;
63. $x < -5$;

4.7 Technology Activity (p. 209) 1. 5.46796×10^7 **3.** 1.5×10^{28} kg

Chapter Review (pp. 210–213) 1. *Sample answer:* prime: 23, composite: 120 **3.** *Sample answer:* $\frac{2}{3}$ and $\frac{10}{15}$; they are equivalent because $\frac{10}{15}$ in simplest form is $\frac{10 \div 5}{15 \div 5} = \frac{2}{3}$. **5.** $3 \cdot 5^2$ **7.** $3 \cdot 43$

9. $2 \cdot 2 \cdot 3 \cdot 3 \cdot a \cdot a \cdot a \cdot a \cdot b \cdot b \cdot b$ **11.** $2 \cdot 2 \cdot 2 \cdot 3 \cdot 3 \cdot w \cdot w \cdot w \cdot w \cdot w \cdot w \cdot z$ **13.** 2   **15.** 4
17. $\frac{2}{9}$ **19.** $\frac{1}{4}$ **21.** $\frac{3a}{2b}$ **23.** $\frac{4}{x}$ **25.** $\frac{1}{12}$ **27.** $\frac{11}{36}$ **29.** the friend's team   **31.** 3^{12} **33.** 10^8 **35.** $8c^{11}$ **37.** y^9
39. 1   **41.** $\frac{15}{d^9}$ **43.** 6.7×10^7 **45.** 4.28×10^9 **47.** $<$

Chapter 5

5.1 Guided Practice (p. 222) 1. terminating decimal   **3.** terminating decimal   **5.** *Sample answer:* If you can write the number as a quotient of two integers, it is rational. Otherwise, it is not rational.   **7.** $\frac{-2}{1}$ or $\frac{2}{-1}$ **9.** $\frac{-4}{3}$ or $\frac{4}{-3}$ **11.** 1.8
13. -9.625 **15.** $\frac{81}{250}$ **17.** $2\frac{2}{3}$ **19.** Only the "78" repeats, so these are the only digits that should be under the bar: $5.07878\ldots = 5.0\overline{78}$.

5.1 Practice and Problem Solving (pp. 222–224)

21. $\frac{-29}{1}$ or $\frac{29}{-1}$ **23.** $\frac{-1}{8}$ or $\frac{1}{-8}$ **25.** $\frac{-17}{1}$ or $\frac{17}{-1}$
27. $\frac{87}{100}$ **29.** -0.875 **31.** $3.1\overline{6}$ **33.** $-1.\overline{18}$
35. -13.7 **37.** $\frac{63}{100}$ **39.** $2\frac{93}{1000}$ **41.** $\frac{19}{1000}$ **43.** $-1\frac{51}{500}$
45. a. Nov.: $\frac{8}{25}$, Dec.: $\frac{17}{45}$, Jan.: $\frac{7}{10}$, Feb.: $\frac{39}{55}$, Mar.: $\frac{107}{150}$
b. 0.32, $0.3\overline{7}$, 0.7, $0.70\overline{9}$, $0.71\overline{3}$; March   **c.** *Sample answer:* I think it increased recycling efforts. Before January 1, the portion of trash recycled was less than 0.4. After January 1, the portion recycled was at least 0.7.   **47.** sometimes   **49.** $\frac{8}{9}$ **51.** $-\frac{4}{9}$
53. $\frac{4}{33}$ **55.** $\frac{299}{333}$ **57.** $-2, 0.8, \frac{7}{8}, 1\frac{1}{3}, 2.1$ **59.** $-\frac{1}{5}$,
$-0.1, 0.21, 0.\overline{2}, 2.3, \frac{8}{3}$ **61. a.** Maria: 13 at bats, 5 hits; Laura: 13 at bats, 3 hits; Jenny: 12 at bats, 6 hits   **b.** Maria: 0.385; Laura: 0.231; Jenny: 0.500
c. *Sample answer:* I would rank Jenny first, followed by Maria, then Laura. I think that the higher a person's batting average is, the better the player is at hitting.   **63.** *Sample answer:* I do not see any repeating pattern of digits or any sign of termination; $0.\overline{0588235294117647}$; the calculator does not show enough decimal places for the repeating pattern to appear, since the pattern has 16 digits.   **67.** $-m - 9$ **69.** 180   **71.** 189

5.2 Guided Practice (p. 227) 1. numerators   **3.** $\frac{8}{9}$
5. $-\frac{1}{4}$ **7.** $-12\frac{1}{8}$ **9.** Step 1: $\frac{15}{4}, \frac{7}{4}$; Step 2: $5\frac{1}{2}$;
Step 3: No. *Sample answer:* Since $\frac{1}{2} = \frac{2}{4}, 5\frac{1}{2} > 5\frac{1}{4}$.

5.2 Practice and Problem Solving (pp. 228–229)

11. $1\frac{1}{19}$ **13.** $1\frac{2}{7}$ **15.** $-\frac{3}{13}$ **17.** $-1\frac{1}{17}$ **19.** -5 **21.** 3
23. $-6\frac{2}{9}$ **25.** $-9\frac{1}{7}$ **27.** $1\frac{1}{2}$ h   **29.** $\frac{3x}{4}$ **31.** $\frac{1}{p}$
33. $-\frac{n}{3}$ **35.** $-\frac{14}{9a}$ **37.** $2\frac{1}{2}$ in.   **39.** $\frac{1}{10}$ **41.** $1\frac{1}{5}$
43. $-2\frac{5}{14}$ **45.** *Sample answer:* $-\frac{1}{4}$ and $\frac{3}{4}$ **47.** $-\frac{6}{11}$
49. $2\frac{7}{9}$ **51.** $6\frac{2}{13}$ **55.** $3s$ **57.** $\frac{13m^2}{16}$ **59.** $18mn$
61. $12a^3b$

5.3 Guided Practice (p. 233) 1. 6   **3.** $-\frac{1}{8}$ **5.** $2\frac{2}{3}$
7. $\frac{7a}{30}$ **9.** $\frac{3a}{2}$ **11.** Step 1: $\frac{21}{2}, \frac{14}{3}$; Step 2: $\frac{63}{6}, \frac{28}{6}$;
Step 3: $\frac{35}{6}$; $5\frac{5}{6}$ lb

5.3 Practice and Problem Solving (pp. 234–235)

13. $\frac{1}{6}$ **15.** $-\frac{7}{18}$ **17.** $-\frac{9}{56}$ **19.** $-\frac{1}{55}$ **21.** $-1\frac{7}{36}$
23. $-\frac{13}{36}$ **25.** $7\frac{1}{8}$ **27.** $3\frac{23}{26}$ **29.** $5\frac{5}{6}$ **31.** $7\frac{13}{15}$
33. length: $4\frac{1}{8}$ in., perimeter: 13 in.   **35. a.** small: $\frac{3}{8}$ in., medium: $\frac{3}{8}$ in., large: $\frac{3}{8}$ in., extra large: $\frac{3}{8}$ in.
b. 3 medium, 2 large, 1 extra large   **c.** *Sample answer:* I would make it so that there are no missing measurements in the chart by making small from 21 to $21\frac{1}{2}$, medium from $21\frac{5}{8}$ to $22\frac{1}{4}$, large from $22\frac{3}{8}$ to 23, and extra large from $23\frac{1}{8}$ to 24.   **37.** $-\frac{2y}{35}$
39. $-\frac{83r}{88}$ **41.** $-\frac{x}{24}$ **43.** $\frac{13w}{36}$ **45.** $9\frac{1}{4}$ **47.** $\frac{7}{24}$
49. $-2\frac{13}{30}$ **51.** Yes; yes. *Sample answer:* Using 48, the equivalent fractions are $\frac{42}{48}$ and $\frac{20}{48}$, so the sum is $\frac{62}{48}$. Dividing out the common factor 2 from the numerator and denominator then gives $\frac{31}{24}$, or $1\frac{7}{24}$.

Using the LCD, 24, the equivalent fractions are $\frac{21}{24}$ and $\frac{10}{24}$, so the sum is $\frac{31}{24}$. So using the LCD, you do not have to perform the additional step of simplifying in this case. **53.** 6 **55.** 18 **57.** b^{11} **59.** d^{-2} **61.** 14 ft, $1\frac{1}{2}$ in.

5.4 Guided Practice (p. 239) 1. numerators, denominators **3.** $\frac{15}{32}$ **5.** $-6\frac{2}{3}$ **7.** *Sample answer:* The product of powers rule was applied incorrectly. To find the product $c^2 \cdot c^4$, you must add the exponents, not multiply them, so the result should be $\frac{4c^6}{35}$.

5.4 Practice and Problem Solving (pp. 240–241)
9. $-\frac{1}{8}$ **11.** $\frac{7}{16}$ **13.** -16 **15.** $18\frac{3}{4}$ **17.** $40\frac{5}{6}$ **19.** $8\frac{5}{23}$
21. a. $98\frac{7}{16}$ ft^2 **b.** Yes. *Sample answer:* Two coats will take enough paint for $2 \cdot 98\frac{7}{16} = 196\frac{7}{8}$ square feet, which is less than the 200 square feet the paint should cover. **23.** $\frac{3a^2}{55}$ **25.** $-\frac{44c^9}{9}$ **27.** $\frac{8x^2}{35}$
29. a. $\frac{3}{8} - \frac{3}{64}y$;

Time (*y*)	1	2	3
Tread depth (in.)	$\frac{21}{64}$	$\frac{9}{32}$	$\frac{15}{64}$

b.

Time (*y*)	1	2	3	4	5	6	7
Tread depth (in.)	$\frac{21}{64}$	$\frac{9}{32}$	$\frac{15}{64}$	$\frac{3}{16}$	$\frac{9}{64}$	$\frac{3}{32}$	$\frac{3}{64}$

Sample answer: Since $\frac{1}{16} = \frac{4}{64}$ and $\frac{3}{32} = \frac{6}{64}$, there is still sufficient tread left after 6 years but not after 7 years, so the tires should be replaced sometime after 6 years. **31.** 0 **33.** $2\frac{7}{8}$ **35.** $\frac{145}{363}$ **37.** 2.0×10^2
39. 2.0×10^{-4} **43.** 6 **45.** -3 **47.** 6.5
49. $b > -2$;

5.5 Guided Practice (p. 245) 1. *Sample answer:* Since $0.25 = \frac{1}{4}$, $0.25 \cdot 4 = \frac{1}{4} \cdot 4 = 1$. **3.** $\frac{1}{8}$ **5.** $\frac{4}{3}$
7. $\frac{320}{363}$ **9.** $-\frac{11}{36}$ **11.** $\frac{27}{182}$ **13.** $\frac{1}{65}$
15. *Sample answer:* $\frac{25}{4}$ should not have been multiplied by $\frac{1}{2}$, but by its reciprocal, which is 2, to obtain $\frac{25}{4} \cdot \frac{2}{1} = \frac{25}{2} = 12\frac{1}{2}$.

5.5 Practice and Problem Solving (pp. 245–246)
17. $-1\frac{7}{20}$ **19.** $1\frac{15}{19}$ **21.** $2\frac{20}{53}$ **23.** $-1\frac{13}{99}$ **25.** -99
27. $-\frac{8}{189}$ **29.** 6 lanes **31.** 2 **33.** $3\frac{11}{30}$ **35.** $2\frac{17}{39}$
39. 6 **41.** 7 **43.** $\frac{7}{15}$ **45.** $\frac{3}{8}$ **47.** $-\frac{2b}{11}$ **49.** $\frac{19d}{18}$

5.6 Guided Practice (p. 249) 1. the number's reciprocal **3.** -36 **5.** $-1\frac{2}{7}$ **7.** 16 **9.** Step 1: ant A: $10\frac{1}{2} = \frac{3}{4}t$; ant B: $11\frac{3}{8} = \frac{7}{8}t$; Step 2: ant A: $t = 14$ sec; ant B: $t = 13$ sec; Step 3: ant B

5.6 Practice and Problem Solving (pp. 249–251)
11. 54 **13.** -60 **15.** $-\frac{9}{10}$ **17.** $-\frac{8}{17}$ **19.** $1\frac{9}{10}w = 5$, $2\frac{12}{19}$ ft **21.** 54 **23.** -20 **25.** $3\frac{4}{5}$ **27.** $2\frac{2}{3}$ **29.** $2\frac{1}{3}$
31. $8\frac{6}{7}$ min **33.** $-\frac{2}{5}$
35. $y > 14$;

37. $z \geq -3$;

39. $\frac{5}{12}$ **41.** $-1\frac{1}{36}$

5.6 Technology Activity (p. 252) 1. 36 **3.** -91
5. 112 stitches

5.7 Guided Practice (p. 255) 1. LCD **3.** $-24\frac{1}{4}$ **5.** 3
7. -4 **9.** $x > 2\frac{11}{14}$ **11.** $x < 2\frac{3}{8}$

5.7 Practice and Problem Solving (pp. 256–257)
13. $\frac{1}{8}$ **15.** $\frac{19}{30}$ **17.** $1\frac{16}{17}$ **19.** $-\frac{7}{27}$ **21.** $-\frac{19}{70}$
23. 2.2 **25.** 1.25 **27.** -4 **29.** 1.2 **31.** 5 paychecks
33. $k \leq -68\frac{8}{9}$ **35.** $r > -\frac{5}{8}$ **37.** $d \geq 1\frac{1}{3}$
39. $8 + j - \frac{2}{3}j \leq 18$ or $8 + \frac{1}{3}j \leq 18$, not more than $30
41. 19.95°C **43.** 7 costumes **45.** $2.73 **47.** 120
49. -36 **51.** $\frac{44r}{45}$ **53.** $\frac{7t}{3}$ **55.** 10 h

Chapter Review (pp. 258–261) 1. *Sample answer:* -7
3. *Sample answer:* 18 **5.** *Sample answer:* $\frac{9}{16}$ and $\frac{16}{9}$
7. $0.\overline{63}$ **9.** -2.6 **11.** $-\frac{263}{25}$, -5.24, $5.\overline{3}$, $\frac{134}{25}$, $5\frac{9}{20}$
13. $-1\frac{2}{7}$ **15.** 15 **17.** $\frac{11}{42}$ **19.** $5\frac{7}{12}$ **21.** $-8\frac{32}{105}$

23. $-\dfrac{1}{12}$ **25.** -48 **27.** $\dfrac{4b^3}{7}$ **29.** $-\dfrac{3s^5}{5}$ **31.** $-1\dfrac{27}{29}$
33. $-2\dfrac{1}{2}$ **35.** $-\dfrac{16}{17}$ **37.** $-\dfrac{1}{4}$ **39.** $\dfrac{13}{28}$

Focus on Problem Solving (p. 265) 1. 4 h **3.** 3 h
5. about 26 min **7.** 1 h **9.** 3 h

Chapter 6

6.1 Guided Practice (p. 272) 1. *Sample answer:*
A unit rate is a ratio of two quantities that have
different units for which the denominator is 1
when expressed in fraction form; $\dfrac{\$5.20}{1\text{ lb}}$.
3. no; 4 to 3; $\dfrac{4}{3}$, $4:3$ **5.** no; $3:1$; $\dfrac{3}{1}$, 3 to 1 **7.** $1:7$,
2 to 9, $\dfrac{7}{28}$, $\dfrac{3}{10}$, 2 to 6 **9.** Step 1: decorator A:
125 roses, decorator B: 240 roses, decorator C:
240 roses; Step 2: decorator A: \$.96, decorator B:
\$.85, decorator C: \$.75; Step 3: decorator C

6.1 Practice and Problem Solving (pp. 272–274)
11. yes; $\dfrac{4}{5}$, 4 to 5 **13.** no; $\dfrac{25}{3}$; 25 to 3, $25:3$ **15.** no;
$3:1$; $\dfrac{3}{1}$, 3 to 1 **17.** no; 14 to 5; $\dfrac{14}{5}$, $14:5$ **19.** 18 to 6,
$\dfrac{53}{15}$, $\dfrac{15}{4}$, 19 to 5, $4:1$ **21.** $9:2$, $5:1$, $\dfrac{100}{19}$, $65:12$, $\dfrac{22}{4}$
23. $\dfrac{\$23}{1\text{ share}}$ **25.** $\dfrac{14\text{ mi}}{1\text{ h}}$ **27.** $\dfrac{8\frac{2}{3}\text{ points}}{1\text{ quarter}}$ **29.** $\dfrac{\frac{5}{8}\text{ win}}{1\text{ game}}$
31. 900 **33.** 2750 **35.** 0.375, or $\dfrac{3}{8}$ **37.** *Sample*
answer: About \$.75 per cookie; I rounded \$11.88
to \$12 and \$12 divided by 16 cookies is \$0.75.
39. a. 24 gal **b.** 600 mi **c.** \$.06 **d.** No. *Sample*
answer: At a rate of \$.06 per mile, gasoline for
350 miles will cost 350 mi $\cdot \dfrac{\$.06}{1\text{ mi}} = \$21$.
41. $\dfrac{1}{3}$ **43.** $\dfrac{1}{1}$ **45. a.** 12.5 mi/h **b.** 0.2 mi/min
c. 1101.1 ft/min **49.** $-\dfrac{2}{27}$ **51.** 55 stamps;
40 stamps **53.** $y \le -57$

6.2 Guided Practice (p. 277) 1. *Sample answer:*
$\dfrac{2}{3} = \dfrac{4}{6}$, or $\dfrac{2}{4} = \dfrac{3}{6}$ **3.** 25 **5.** 7 **7.** *Sample answer:* A
proportion must use comparable ratios. Because
the fraction on the left compares pencils to cost,
the fraction on the right must do likewise, so it
should be $\dfrac{30}{x}$, not $\dfrac{x}{30}$.

6.2 Practice and Problem Solving (pp. 278–279)
9. 25 **11.** 11 **13.** 70 **15.** 40 **17.** 5 **19.** 18 **21.** 5
23. 34 **25.** 15 erasers **27. a.** no **b.** *Sample answer:*
$\dfrac{24}{9} = \dfrac{x}{15}$, 40 goals **29.** *Sample answer:* $\dfrac{15}{18} = \dfrac{5}{6}$;
8 ways; there are 2 ways to arrange the proportion
with 15 as the numerator of the first fraction,
$\dfrac{15}{18} = \dfrac{5}{6}$ or $\dfrac{15}{5} = \dfrac{18}{6}$. 15 is 1 of 4 numbers that could
be the numerator of the first fraction, so there are
$4 \cdot 2$ or 8 ways to rearrange the 4 numbers.
31. a. $1:26$ **b.** 2 kg **33. a.** $\dfrac{1}{4}$ **b.** 5 red stripes
35. It decreases. **37.** $24m^2$ **39.** 1 **41.** $-\dfrac{3}{16}$ **43.** $\dfrac{11}{24}$
45. $z > 4\dfrac{8}{15}$ **47.** $x \le 1\dfrac{29}{35}$

6.3 Guided Practice (p. 282) 1. $3 \cdot 12$ and $4 \cdot 9$
3. yes **5.** yes **7.** 3 **9.** 2 **11.** Step 1: $\dfrac{\$.66}{12\text{ min}}$;
Step 2: $\dfrac{\$1.21}{m\text{ min}}$; Step 3: $\dfrac{\$.66}{12\text{ min}} = \dfrac{\$1.21}{m\text{ min}}$; 22 min

6.3 Practice and Problem Solving (pp. 283–284)
13. no **15.** no **17.** no **19.** yes **21.** 5 **23.** 25
25. 175 **27.** 28 **29.** 0.8 **31.** 3 **33. a.** \$20 **b.** 18 gal
35. a. 125 g **b.** 36 g **37.** 22 **39.** 6
41. *Sample answer:*

$\dfrac{a}{b} = \dfrac{c}{d}$ [Given]
$a \cdot d = b \cdot c$ [Form cross products.]
$\dfrac{ad}{ac} = \dfrac{bc}{ac}$ [Divide each side by ac.]
$\dfrac{d}{c} = \dfrac{b}{a}$ [Simplify.]

43. $\dfrac{3}{5}$. *Sample answer:* Forming cross products
gives $4a = 3b$ and $4c = 5b$. I noticed that because
$\dfrac{a}{c} = \dfrac{4a}{4c}$, I could substitute $3b$ for $4a$ and $5b$ for $4c$
and write $\dfrac{a}{c} = \dfrac{3b}{5b} = \dfrac{3}{5}$. **45–47.** Check students'
work. **49.** 5.001×10^6 **51.** 4 to 9 **53.** $\dfrac{7}{12}$

Student Reference (p. 286) 1. any three of $M, N, P,$
R, S **3.** plane Y and plane Z **5.** any one of $\overline{RS}$,
$\overline{MN}$, $\overline{NP}$ **7.** *Sample answer:* quadrilateral $DEFG$
9. $\angle D, \angle E, \angle F, \angle G$

6.4 Guided Practice (p. 290) **1.** Corresponding angles are congruent and corresponding sides are congruent. **3.** corresponding sides: $\overline{AB}$ and $\overline{DE}$, $\overline{BC}$ and $\overline{EF}$, $\overline{AC}$ and $\overline{DF}$; corresponding angles: $\angle A$ and $\angle D$, $\angle B$ and $\angle E$, $\angle C$ and $\angle F$ **5.** 90°

6.4 Practice and Problem Solving (pp. 291–292) **7.** corresponding angles: $\angle A$ and $\angle D$, $\angle B$ and $\angle E$, $\angle C$ and $\angle F$; corresponding sides: $\overline{AB}$ and $\overline{DE}$, $\overline{BC}$ and $\overline{EF}$, $\overline{AC}$ and $\overline{DF}$ **9.** $\frac{10}{13}$ **11.** $\frac{2}{3}$ **13.** 128°
15. 18 in. **17.** Sometimes. *Sample answer:* Corresponding angles of similar figures are congruent, but similar figures are congruent only if they are also the same size. **19.** Sometimes. *Sample answer:* All angles are congruent and have measures of 90°, but rectangles are congruent only if they have the same shape and same size.
21. a. Yes. *Sample answer:* The ratio of the lengths is $\frac{9.41}{6.14} \approx 1.53$, and the ratio of the widths is $\frac{4.00}{2.61} \approx 1.53$, so both ratios are greater than $1\frac{1}{2}$, or 1.5.
b. Yes. *Sample answer:* The ratio of the lengths is $\frac{4.00}{6.14} \approx 0.65$, and the ratio of the widths is $\frac{1.70}{2.61} \approx 0.65$, so both ratios are less than $\frac{3}{4}$, or 0.75. **c.** no
25. $\frac{5}{6}$ **27.** $\frac{2}{5xy^3}$ **29.** 6 h

6.5 Guided Practice (p. 295) **1.** $\overline{EH}$ **3.** 4 m
5. Step 1: *Sample answer:* $\frac{x}{74} = \frac{80}{26}$; Step 2: 228 in.

6.5 Practice and Problem Solving (pp. 295–297) **7.** 15 mm **9.** 12.5 yd **11.** 9 m **13.** 3.75 ft; 12.5 ft **15. a.** $DE = 10$ cm, $FG = 12.5$ cm **b.** $AE = 26$ cm, $AG = 32.5$ cm **19.** -27 **21.** $\frac{2}{5}$ **23.** $\frac{22}{20}, \frac{44}{33}$, 35 : 25, 15 to 9, 8 : 3

6.6 Guided Practice (p. 302) **1.** A two-dimensional drawing that is similar to the object it represents. **3.** 200 mi **5.** 1280 mi **7.** 1 : 1008 **9.** 1 : 1200 **11.** Step 1: 1 cm : 0.8 m; Step 2: 1 : 80; Step 3: *Sample answer:* $\frac{1}{80} = \frac{1.5}{l}$, $l = 120$ cm, or 1.2 m; $\frac{1}{80} = \frac{0.5}{w}$, $w = 40$ cm, or 0.4 m

6.6 Practice and Problem Solving (pp. 303–304) **13.** 55 km **15.** 185 km **17.** 7.5 km **19.** 45 km **21.** 30 in. **23.** $4\frac{2}{3}$ in. **25.** 0.5 in. **27.** $\frac{1}{6}$ in. **29.** 1 : 240 **31.** 1 : 360 **33.** 1 : 500,000 **35.** 1 : 340 **37.** 1 : 32 **39. a.** 126 in., or 10 ft 6 in. **b.** 84 in., or 7 ft **c.** 21 in. by $31\frac{1}{2}$ in. **41.** 20 ft **43.** 3 : 2 **45.** head: 2.5 mm, thorax: 3.25 mm, abdomen: 4.25 mm **47.** $17\frac{3}{11}$ **49.** $-15\frac{1}{2}$

6.7 Guided Practice (p. 309) **1.** experimental **3.** $\frac{1}{2}$ **5.** $\frac{2}{3}$

6.7 Practice and Problem Solving (pp. 309–311) **7.** $\frac{1}{4}$ **9.** 3 to 1 **11. a.** $\frac{2}{11}$ **b.** $\frac{5}{11}$ **c.** 6 to 5 **d.** *Sample answer:* RIVER **13.** 15 seeds
15. *Sample answer:* Write the probability as a ratio. For the odds in favor, write a ratio whose numerator is the numerator of the probability ratio, and whose denominator is the difference in the denominator and numerator of the probability ratio. The odds against are just the reciprocal of the odds in favor. **17.** $\frac{16}{143}$, or about 0.1119
19. a. about 400 times **b.** about 20,000 hits
21. $\frac{5}{6}$; $1 - \frac{1}{n}$. *Sample answer:* In a probability experiment, it is certain that a given event must either occur or not occur. The probability of something that is certain is 1. So, the sum of the probabilities of an event occurring and not occurring is 1. If the probability of an event is $\frac{1}{n}$, then $P(\text{not event}) + \frac{1}{n} = 1$, and $P(\text{not event}) = 1 - \frac{1}{n}$. **23.** -18 **25.** -252 **27.** $-2.7, -1.5, -\frac{3}{5}$, $1\frac{5}{9}, \frac{13}{5}$ **29.** 7 m

6.7 Technology Activity (p. 312) **Steps 1–3.** Check work. **1.** Check work. Note that there is a 43% chance that the experiment will require 4 or fewer trials and a 62% chance that it will require 5 or fewer trials. A typical mean might be between 4 and 5.

6.8 Guided Practice (p. 315)

1.

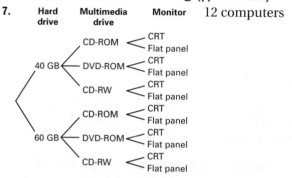

First flip / Second flip

heads — heads, tails
tails — heads, tails

3. 12 outfits **5.** 256 outfits

6.8 Practice and Problem Solving (pp. 315–317)

7.

Hard drive / Multimedia drive / Monitor   12 computers

40 GB — CD-ROM (CRT, Flat panel), DVD-ROM (CRT, Flat panel), CD-RW (CRT, Flat panel)
60 GB — CD-ROM (CRT, Flat panel), DVD-ROM (CRT, Flat panel), CD-RW (CRT, Flat panel)

9. a. 210 matchups **b.** 64 matchups **c.** No. *Sample answer:* Part b only considers possible matchups. The probability of two teams reaching the finals is not random, but depends at least partially on how good the teams are. **11.** 25 possible outcomes; $\frac{1}{25}$

13. 20 possible outcomes; $\frac{1}{5}$ **15.** $\frac{1}{4,569,760,000}$

17a.

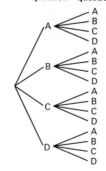

First question / Second question

A — A, B, C, D
B — A, B, C, D
C — A, B, C, D
D — A, B, C, D

b. $\frac{1}{16}$ **c.** 7 outcomes; $\frac{7}{16}$

19. a. 100,000 phone numbers **b.** 10,000 phone numbers **c.** 5 digits **21.** $-1\frac{1}{4}$ **23.** $\frac{25}{56}$ **25.** 20

27. 13.5

Chapter Review (pp. 318–321) **1.** *Sample answer:* You can write the ratios in simplest form or as decimals. If they have the same simplest form or decimal form, they are equivalent. Another way is to find the cross products of the ratios. If the cross products are equal, then the ratios form a proportion, and are equivalent. **3.** *Sample answer:* Congruent figures have the same size and shape. Similar figures have the same shape, but are not necessarily the same size. The lengths of corresponding sides of similar figures have the same ratio, but that ratio is not necessarily 1, as it is for congruent figures. **5.** *Sample answer:* The probability of an event is the ratio of the number of favorable outcomes to the number of possible outcomes, while the odds in favor of an event is the ratio of the number of favorable outcomes to the number of unfavorable outcomes. **7.** $\frac{55 \text{ mi}}{1 \text{ h}}$

9. $\frac{\frac{1}{4} \text{ lap}}{1 \text{ min}}$ or $\frac{0.25 \text{ lap}}{1 \text{ min}}$ **11.** \$8.50 per ticket **13.** 2

15. 5 **17.** *Sample answer:* $\frac{5}{6} = \frac{s}{24}$, 20 h **19.** 8.5

21. 14 **23.** $\frac{9}{5}$ **25.** 15 cm **27.** 21 yd **29.** 54 yd

31. $\frac{1}{4}$ **33.** $\frac{1}{8}$ **35.** 18 outfits

Chapter 7

7.1 Guided Practice (p. 331) **1.** 100 **3.** $\frac{13}{20}$ **5.** 48%

7. Step 1: 114 serves; Step 2: 75 serves; Step 3: 39 serves

7.1 Practice and Problem Solving (pp. 331–333)

9. $\frac{2}{5}$ **11.** $\frac{27}{100}$ **13.** $\frac{9}{50}$ **15.** $\frac{17}{20}$ **17.** 12% **19.** 70%

21. 25% **23.** 85% **25.** 75% **27.** $\frac{3}{10}$ **29.** 10%

31. 50% **33.** 40% **35.** 9 **37.** 15 **39.** 47 **41.** 70

43. 600 lb **45.** *Sample answer:* Because $p\% = \frac{p}{100}$, $100\% = \frac{100}{100}$. Simplifying $\frac{100}{100}$ gives 1, so $100\% = 1$.

47. $\frac{9}{20}$, 54%, 0.62, $\frac{16}{25}$ **49.** 18 **51.** 18 **53.** 60

55. a.

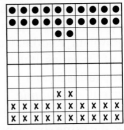

Opponent's side

Your side

b. 44%
c. 19 pieces. *Sample answer:* To start the game, there are 44 total pieces on the board. 75% of 44 is 33, so there are 33 pieces remaining. If 14 of these 33 belong to you, then $33 - 14$ or 19 pieces belong to the opponent. **57. a.** about 640 students **b.** about 320 students **c.** about 90 students **59. a.** No. *Sample answer:* 40% of x is $0.4x$, and 60% of y is $0.6y$, so their sum is $0.4x + 0.6y$, which is not the same as 100% of $x + y$, which is just $x + y$. **b.** No. *Sample answer:* The average of 40% of x and 60% of y is $\frac{1}{2}(0.4x + 0.6y)$, but 50%, or $\frac{1}{2}$, of the sum of x and y is $\frac{1}{2}(x + y)$. **61.** $-\frac{2}{5}$ **63.** $7\frac{1}{2}$ **65.** 10 **67.** 1

7.2 Guided Practice (p. 337) 3. 78 **5.** 90%
7. *Sample answer:* The proportion shown is to find part of a base, not a percent, which is what is being sought. The unknown is the percent, $p\%$, so the proportion should be $\frac{20}{30} = \frac{p}{100}$, which gives $100 \cdot \frac{20}{30} = 100 \cdot \frac{p}{100}$, and $p = 66\frac{2}{3}\%$.

7.2 Practice and Problem Solving (pp. 337–339)
9. 25% **11.** 44 **13.** 50 **15.** 13 teams

17. 55 paintings **19.** $6\frac{2}{3}\%$ **21.** *Sample answer:*
Biologists have tagged 40% of a herd of elk. If they have tagged 30 elk in the herd, what is the total number of elk in the herd? Solving the proportion gives $x = 75$, so there are 75 elk in the herd.
23. $12\frac{1}{2}\%$, $33\frac{1}{3}\%$, $37\frac{1}{2}\%$, $62\frac{1}{2}\%$, $66\frac{2}{3}\%$, $87\frac{1}{2}\%$

25. a. 20%; $62\frac{1}{2}\%$ **b.** 56% **27.** $4y$ **29.** $5y$ **33.** 0.975
35. 0.0015 **37.** $-0.\overline{3}$ **39.** -1.6

7.3 Guided Practice (p. 342) 1. to the right **3.** 13%
5. 0.05 **7.** 50% **9.** $116.\overline{6}\%$ **11.** The decimal point should have been moved two places to the right instead of to the left: $1.5 = 1.50 = 150\%$.

7.3 Practice and Problem Solving (pp. 342–344)
13. 28% **15.** 200% **17.** 8.7% **19.** 0.08 **21.** 1.08
23. 0.00302 **25.** 15% **27.** $13.\overline{3}\%$ **29.** 350%
31. $133.\overline{3}\%$ **33.** 0.15% **35.** 62.5% **37.** 272
39. 42.07 **41.** 480 **43.** 0.175 **45.** about 318 mi/h
47. 606, 39, 6, 383, 365, 30 **49.** $\frac{3}{4}$, 100%, 150%, $\frac{5}{3}$, 2
51. 6.7 **53.** 12 **55.** 2.37 **57.** 0.09 **59. a.** $36 million
b. $263.5 million **c.** $323.5 million **63.** 0.06
65. 15.9 **67.** $\frac{3}{10}$ **69.** 75

7.4 Guided Practice (p. 347) 1. percent: 40%, base: 80, part of the base: 32 **3.** 15 **5.** 50 **7.** Step 1: percent: 3%, base: $2000, part of the base: amount of commission; Step 2: $a = 3\% \cdot \$2000$, $60; Step 3: $260

7.4 Practice and Problem Solving (pp. 348–349)
9. 5.6 **11.** 0.5% **13.** 35 **15.** 80% **17.** 144
19. 140 students **21.** 50 students **23.** 4.5 **25.** 500
27. *Sample answer:* A fraction; a decimal; I would convert 75% to the fraction $\frac{3}{4}$ because 120 is evenly divisible by 4, but because 120 is not evenly divisible by 100, there is no clear advantage to changing 31% to a fraction. **29. a.** Dole
b. Popular votes. *Sample answer:* The difference in the popular votes was about $49.0\% - 40.6\%$, or about 8%, while the difference in the electoral votes was about $70.4\% - 29.6\%$, or about 41%.
31. a. $250,000 **b.** 50% **33.** 471.6 **35.** 12.18
37. -6 **39.** 12.5% **41.** $133.\overline{3}\%$

7.5 Guided Practice (p. 354) 1. a percent of decrease **3.** increase; 50% **5.** decrease; 75%

7.5 Practice and Problem Solving (pp. 355–356)
7. increase; 25% **9.** decrease; 40% **11.** increase; 35% **13.** In the formula for percent of change, the denominator is the original amount, not the new amount, so the denominator should be 90: $p = \frac{90 - 50}{90} = \frac{40}{90} = \frac{4}{9} = 44.\overline{4}\%$. **15.** 91.5% decrease
17. 210 **19.** 25.2 **21.** $15.75 **23.** Yes. *Sample answer:* A 100% increase represents only a doubling, so if a quantity is more than doubled, the increase is greater than 100%.

25. a. about 50.8% decrease **b.** 1999; about 25.9%
c. No. *Sample answer:* The graph does not indicate the amount that is made per pair of shoes. Also, it is possible that the decrease might be because the manufacturers are having the shoes made for them outside of the United States. **27.** 300%. *Sample answer:* A decrease of 75% is the same as $100\% - 75\% = 25\%$, or $\frac{1}{4}$, of the original amount. So to return to the original amount requires adding back $\frac{3}{4}$ of the original amount, and $\frac{3}{4}$ is 300% of $\frac{1}{4}$. **29.** 13.55 **31.** 5.44 **33.** 3 **35.** 3 **37.** 65% **39.** 75

7.6 Guided Practice (p. 359) **1.** markup **3.** $27.30
5. $15.75 **7.** Step 1: discount price: $27, discount percent: 15%; Step 2: $27 = x - 15\% \cdot x$, or $27 = x \cdot (100\% - 15\%)$; Step 3: about $31.76

7.6 Practice and Problem Solving (pp. 360–361)
9. $187.50 **11.** $32.40 **13.** $10.40 **15.** $82.68
17. $22.50 **19.** about $26.32 **21.** $200 **23.** about $97.73 **25.** $113.94 **27. a.** about $1 **b.** *Sample answer:* About $3; first I rounded the price up to $20. Then because 10% of $20 is $2, and 5% of $20 is half of 10% of $20, I estimated the tip as $2 + $1 = $3. **c.** *Sample answer:* About $24; a high estimate; I rounded the price up to $20 and the tax up to 5%, and also calculated the tip based on the $20 price, so I overestimated both the tax and the tip. **d.** $22.78. *Sample answer:* My estimate was $1.22 high. **29.** ones, 3; 93
31. tenths, 0.9; 1596.0 **33.** 350 **35.** 375 **37.** 0.45
39. 1.02

7.7 Guided Practice (p. 364) **1.** the principal, or the amount deposited or borrowed **3.** $140, $640
5. 1.8% **7.** $757.70

7.7 Practice and Problem Solving (pp. 365–366)
9. $182, $507 **11.** $392, $3592 **13.** $43.31, $538.31
15. Row 1: 5 y; Row 2: $9000; Row 3: 4.6%
17. In the formula, *t* represents the time in years. Because 6 months = 0.5 year, 0.5 should have been substituted for *t*: $I = Prt = (200)(0.055)(0.5) = 5.5$. The interest earned is $5.50. **19.** $3780.01
21. $1240.95 **23.** account A

25. a. Row 1: $1050, $1050; Row 2: $1100, $1102.50; Row 3: $1250, $1276.28; Row 4: $1500, $1628.89; Row 5: $2000, $2653.30
b.

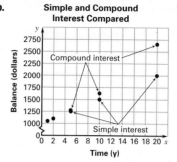

c. *Sample answer:* The points on the simple interest graph lie along a straight line, while the points on the compound interest graph lie on a curve that keeps rising more and more steeply.
27. 10 y. *Sample answer:* The account will double when the interest earned equals the principal. The interest earned is $P(0.1)t$, so I reasoned that this quantity will equal P when $0.1t = 1$, or when $t = 10$.
29. -1 **31.** 21 **33.** 36 **35.** $29.75

7.7 Technology Activity (p. 367) **1.** $311.93
3. $688.20

Chapter Review (pp. 368–371) **1.** percent
3. percent of decrease **5.** $\frac{53}{100}$ **7.** $\frac{3}{5}$ **9.** 31%
11. 62% **13.** 19 **15.** 5 **17.** 150 **19.** 40% **21.** 33
23. 58.9% **25.** 48% **27.** 37.5% **29.** $66.\overline{6}\%$
31. 33.75 **33.** 472.5 **35.** $78.75 **37.** 80% **39.** 32
41. 5% increase **43.** 62.5% decrease **45.** 388.6
47. $280.50 **49.** $7789.92

Chapter 8

8.1 Guided Practice (p. 387) **1.** function
3. domain: 0, 1, 2, 3, 4; range: 0, 2, 4, 6, 8
5.

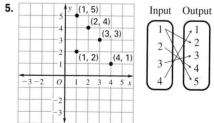

No; the input 1 is paired with two outputs, 2 and 5.

7. *Sample answer:* The relation is a function. A function can have two inputs paired with one output, as in this case, as long as it does not have two outputs paired with one input.

8.1 Practice and Problem Solving (pp. 388–390)

9. domain: 3, 7; range: 3, 6, 9 **11.** domain: 1.5, 2.8, 6.5; range: 0.2, 3.9, 4.3, 6.5

13.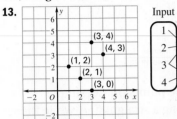

No; the input 3 is paired with two outputs, 0 and 4.

15.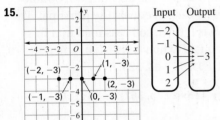

Yes; every input is paired with exactly one output.

17. a. Yes. *Sample answer:* A person can have only one height (output) for any given age (input).
b. No. *Sample answer:* A person can have more than one age (outputs) for a given height (input) because the height of an adult remains the same for many years. **19.** yes **21. a.** domain: 62, 73, 81, 82; range: 604, 1086, 1102, 1199, 1208

b. 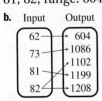 **c.** No; the input 82 is paired with two outputs, 1102 and 1208.

23. Mapping diagram. *Sample answer:* A mapping diagram allows you to just look at the mapping and see if there is an input that has more than one arrow going from it, whereas with ordered pairs, you need to compare *x* and *y* values. **27.** −12
29. −350 **31.** yes **33.** no **35.** $153, $1003

8.2 Guided Practice (p. 394) **1.** linear equation

3. yes **5.** no

7. 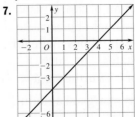 **9.**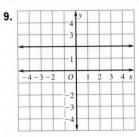

11. Step 1: 0, 120, 240, 360, 480, 600, 720;
Step 2: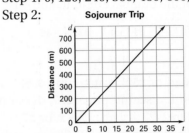

Step 3: about 21; about 21 h

8.2 Practice and Problem Solving (pp. 394–396)

13. yes **15.** no

17. 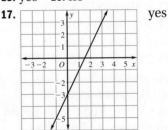 yes

19. 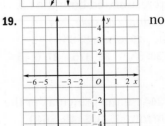 no

21. 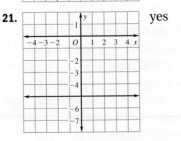 yes

23. 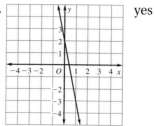 yes

25. $y = -2x + 1$;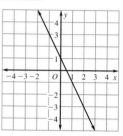

27. $y = -4x - 2$;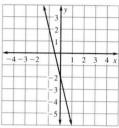

29. $y = -\frac{3}{4}x$;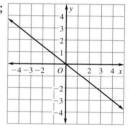

31. $y = -\frac{2}{3}x + 4$;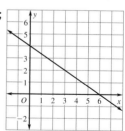

33. 0.355 L **35.** 3 **37.** -5 **39. a.** bigeye thresher: 158 cm, scalloped hammerhead: 194 cm, white shark: 230 cm **b.** bigeye thresher: 63%, scalloped hammerhead: 78%, white shark: 92% **c.** Bigeye thresher. *Sample answer:* The bigeye thresher has the shortest body relative to its total length, so it must have the longest tail relative to its body length.

41. a. $s = \dfrac{f - 1.19}{2.13}$, or $s \approx \dfrac{f}{2.13} - 0.56$
b. about 0.8 m/sec **43.** -6 **45.** -4 **47.** 3
49. 105 **51.** domain: $-2, 0, 2, 4$; range: 1, 2, 3, 4
53. domain: 6; range: $-2, 1, 4, 9$

8.2 Technology Activity (p. 397)

1. 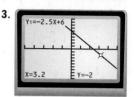 3.2

3.  -2

5. 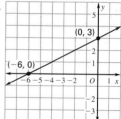 9 games

8.3 Guided Practice (p. 400)
1. y-intercept, x-intercept **3.** x-intercept: 3; y-intercept: 2
5. x-intercept: 0; y-intercept: 0

7.

9. Let x be the amount of ground beef and y be the amount of chicken (both in pounds). Then $3x + 5y = 30$.

8.3 Practice and Problem Solving (pp. 400–402)

11. x-intercept: 4; y-intercept: −2;

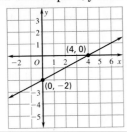

13. x-intercept: −5; y-intercept: −4;

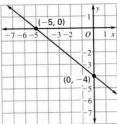

15. x-intercept: −9; y-intercept: 6;

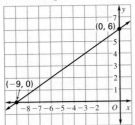

17. x-intercept: 7; y-intercept: 7;

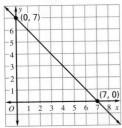

19. a. Let x be the amount of canned food and y be the amount of dry food (both in ounces). Then $40x + 100y = 800$. **b.**

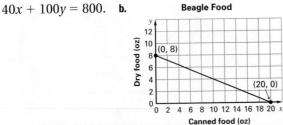

c. Sample answer: 0 oz canned and 8 oz dry, 10 oz canned and 4 oz dry, 20 oz canned and 0 oz dry

21. x-intercept: 2; y-intercept: −2;

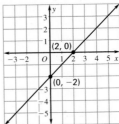

23. x-intercept: −4; y-intercept: 6;

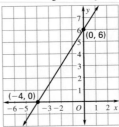

25. x-intercept: 3; y-intercept: 6;

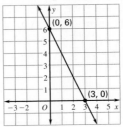

27. Sample answer: $y = 3$, $x = 4$; the graph of $y = 3$ is the horizontal line with y-intercept 3, and the graph of $x = 4$ is the vertical line with x-intercept 4.

29. a. Let x be the time the single-engine plane is rented and y be the time the twin-engine plane is rented (both in hours). Then $60x + 180y = 9000$.

b.

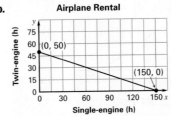

c. about 60 h   **d.** $60x + 180(30) = 9000$, $x = 60$ h

31. Sample answer: 12, 24, and 36; they are common multiples of the coefficients.   **35.** −1

37. 2   **39.** 85% increase   **41.** 22% decrease

43. no   **45.** yes

8.4 Guided Practice (p. 407) 1. rise, run
3. *Sample answer:* The x- and y-coordinates of the two points are not used in the same order. If you subtract the second x-coordinate from the first x-coordinate to obtain the denominator $5 - 0$, then you should subtract the second y-coordinate from the first y-coordinate to obtain the numerator $4 - 2$. So, $m = \frac{4 - 2}{5 - 0} = \frac{2}{5}$. **5.** positive; $\frac{2}{3}$ **7.** $\frac{5}{12}$.
Sample answer: $\frac{5}{12} = 0.41\overline{6}$ and $\frac{3}{5} = 0.6$, so the slope of the ramp in Example 1 is greater.

8.4 Practice and Problem Solving (pp. 407–409)
9. negative; $-\frac{3}{4}$ **11–15.** Sample coordinates are given. **11.** $(-2, 0)$ and $(0, 4)$; 2 **13.** $(0, -5)$ and $(4, 1)$; $\frac{3}{2}$ **15.** $(3, 0)$ and $(0, -4)$; $\frac{4}{3}$ **17. a.** 27 **b.** its speed in meters per second **c.** *Sample answer:* It would also start at the origin, but rise less steeply because the gazelle's speed of 22 meters per second is less than the cheetah's speed of 27 meters per second, and the speed is indicated by the slope.

19. **21.**

23. -1 **25.** $-\frac{2}{3}$ **27.** 0 **29.** 0 **31.** $\frac{1}{3}$ **33.** undefined
35. 22 ft **37. a.** No. *Sample answer:* The grade is $\frac{63}{840} = 0.075 = 7.5\%$, which is less than 8%.

b. 90 ft **39. a.** For any pair of points, the slope is $\frac{1}{2}$; the slope does not depend on which two different points are chosen. **b.** For any pair of points, the slope is $-\frac{2}{3}$; the slope does not depend on which two different points are chosen. **41.** -12 **43.** -11
45. 3 **47.** 5

49. x-intercept: 1; y-intercept: -2;

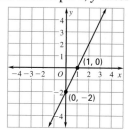

51. x-intercept: -8; y-intercept: -6;

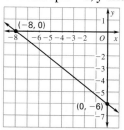

Student Reference (p. 411) 1. parallel
3. perpendicular **5.** No; they lie in the same plane. **7.** Yes; they do not lie in the same plane and do not intersect. **9.** *Sample answer:* $\overleftrightarrow{BD}$, $\overleftrightarrow{EG}$

8.5 Guided Practice (p. 415) 1. slope-intercept
3. slope: 2; y-intercept: 0;

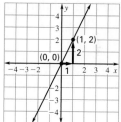

5. slope: $\frac{1}{2}$; y-intercept: -1;

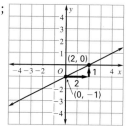

7. parallel: -6; perpendicular: $\frac{1}{6}$

9. Step 1: $y = 24 + 8x$;
Step 2: slope: 8; y-intercept: 24;

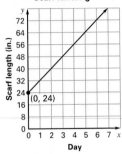

Scarf Knitting

Step 3: about 6 days

8.5 Practice and Problem Solving (pp. 415–417)

13. *Sample answer:* $y = 3x$, $y = 3x + 8$, $y = 3x - 1.1$

15. slope: $\frac{1}{4}$; y-intercept: 1;

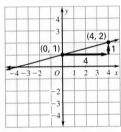

17. slope: -3; y-intercept: -1;

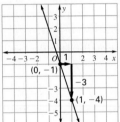

19. slope: $\frac{5}{2}$; y-intercept: 2;

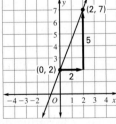

21. a.

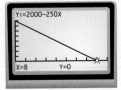

8 min

b. Slope: -250; y-intercept: 2000; the slope represents the rate of descent in feet per minute, and the y-intercept represents the beginning altitude in feet. **23.** parallel: -1; perpendicular: 1

25. parallel: $\frac{4}{5}$; perpendicular: $-\frac{5}{4}$ **27.** parallel: $\frac{1}{3}$; perpendicular: -3 **29.** parallel: $-\frac{2}{3}$; perpendicular: $\frac{3}{2}$ **31. a.** $y = 1000 - 50x$

b. $y = 600 - 50x$

c.

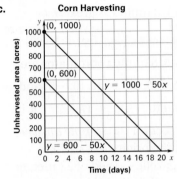

Corn Harvesting

For $y = 1000 - 50x$, the slope is -50 and the y-intercept is 1000. For $y = 600 - 50x$, the slope is -50 and the y-intercept is 600.

d. They are parallel; they have the same slope, -50, and different y-intercepts. **e.** 20 days; 12 days

35. 4 **37.** -7 **39.** 100 **41.** 40% **43.** -2 **45.** $\frac{5}{2}$

8.6 Guided Practice (p. 422) **1.** best-fitting line

3. $y = x + 8$ **5.** $y = \frac{2}{3}x - 5$

7. Step 1:

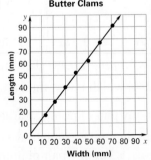

Butter Clams

Best-fitting lines may vary.

Step 2: *Sample answer:* Using (10, 14) and (60, 77): $y = 1.26x + 1.4$; Step 3: 109 mm

8.6 Practice and Problem Solving (pp. 422–424)

9. $y = 4x + 10$ **11.** $y = -x - 20$ **13.** $y = \frac{2}{3}x - 2$

15. $y = 2x + 9$ **17.** $y = -11$ **19.** $y = -x + 7$

21. $y = -\frac{1}{3}x + 6$ **23.** $y = 4x + 1$

25. 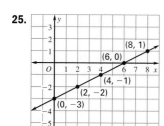 The points lie on a nonvertical line, so the table represents a linear function; $y = \frac{1}{2}x - 3$.

27. $y = 3x$ **29.** $y = \frac{1}{2}x$ **31.** Lisa: no; John: yes.

Sample answer: Let x represent annual sales and y represent annual earnings. Lisa's earnings would then be $y = 0.02x + 18{,}000$ which does not model the direct variation equation $y = kx$. John's earnings would be $y = 0.06x$ which does model the direct variation equation.

33. a. 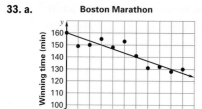 Best-fitting lines may vary.

b. *Sample answer:* Using $(0, 160)$ and $(90, 130)$: $y = -\frac{1}{3}x + 160$ **c.** about 123 min **d.** No. *Sample answer:* The equation predicts a winning time of 0 minutes eventually, which is impossible. I would expect the winning times eventually to level off and decrease very little, if any. **35.** 4 **37.** 8 **39.** 70% **41.** 250%

43. slope: 3; y-intercept: -2;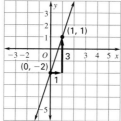

45. slope: $-\frac{3}{2}$; y-intercept: 0;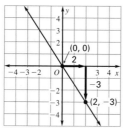

8.6 Technology Activity (p. 425)
1. about 237,000 physicians

8.7 Guided Practice (p. 428) **1.** $f(x) = 4x - 3$
3. -52 **5.** 9

7. 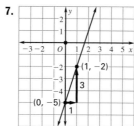 **9.** $f(x) = -x + 8$

8.7 Practice and Problem Solving (pp. 429–430)
11. 4 **13.** 6 **15.** 61

21.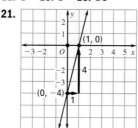
23. $g(x) = -8x$
25. $g(x) = -5x$
27. $r(x) = \frac{2}{3}x - 1$
29. a. $c(x) = 10x + 3000$
b. $i(x) = 50x$
c. $p(x) = 40x - 3000$
d. \$1000
e. 75 birdhouses

33. $10n^{11}$ **35.** $\frac{5c^7}{2}$ **37.** $\frac{16}{25}$ **39.** $\frac{3}{2}$ **41.** $y = \frac{9}{5}x + 3$

8.8 Guided Practice (p. 433) **1.** an ordered pair that is a solution of each equation in the system
3. $(3, 1)$ **5.** no solution

8.8 Practice and Problem Solving (pp. 434–435)
7. no **9.** yes **11.** $(0, 3)$ **13.** $(1, -1)$ **15.** infinitely many solutions—any point on the line $y = -\frac{1}{2}x + 2$ **17.** no solution **19.** $(-3, 1)$ **21.** $(0, 5)$

23. Let x be the number of newspaper ads and y be the number of radio ads; $x + y = 50$, $600x + 300y = 24{,}000$; 30 newspaper ads and 20 radio ads.
25. a. Let x be the number of pages and y be the total cost; inkjet: $y = 0.15x + 100$, laser: $y = 0.03x + 400$. **b.** 2500 pages **c.** when fewer than 2500 pages are printed; when more than 2500 pages are printed **d.** The inkjet printer; the laser printer. *Sample answer:* For 3 years, 2 pages per day is $2 \cdot 365 \cdot 3 = 2190$ pages, which is less than 2500, and 4 pages per day is $4 \cdot 365 \cdot 3 = 4380$ pages, which is more than 2500.

27. *Sample answer:* $m = 3$, $b = 5$; for there to be no solution, the lines should be parallel, which means that they must have the same slope but not be the same line.

31. $y \leq 7$;

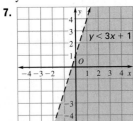

33. $n < 12$;

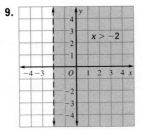

35. 3.09×10^{5} **37.** 7.48×10^{-6} **39.** $h(x) = -5x - 27$

8.9 Guided Practice (p. 439) **1.** half-plane **3.** no
5. yes

7.

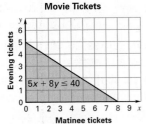

9.

11. Step 1: Let x be the number of matinee tickets and y be the number of evening tickets. Then $5x + 8y \leq 40$.

Step 2:

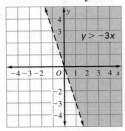

Movie Tickets

Step 3: *Sample answer:* 0 matinees and 5 evening shows, 3 matinees and 3 evening shows, 6 matinees and 1 evening show

8.9 Practice and Problem Solving (pp. 439–441)
13. The wrong half-plane is shaded. The half-plane to the right and below the boundary should be shaded. **15.** *Sample answer:* $(-2, 3)$, or any other point on the line $y = x + 5$ **17.** no **19.** yes

21.

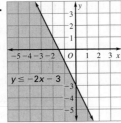

23.

25.

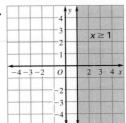

27.

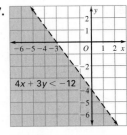

29.

31.

33. a. **Widescreen Format**

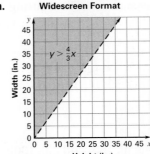

b. any width greater than 24 inches

39. 1.2^{3} **41.** $\dfrac{5}{x^{2}}$ **43.** $\dfrac{9}{m^{5}n^{4}}$ **45.** $(-2, 0)$

Chapter Review (pp. 442–445) **1.** *Sample answer:* In a relation, which pairs numbers in one set with numbers in another set, the domain consists of the inputs and the range consists of the outputs. In a relation represented by ordered pairs (x, y), the domain consists of the x-coordinates and the range consists of the y-coordinates. **3.** *Sample answer:* The slope is the ratio of the rise to the run.

5.

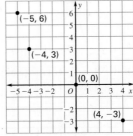

7. yes **9.** x-intercept: 8; y-intercept: -2
11. x-intercept: -1; y-intercept: -5 **13.** 0
15. slope: -3; y-intercept: 2 **17.** slope: 4; y-intercept: 2 **19.** $y = -x - 6$ **21.** -2

23. 10 **25.** (1, 3)

27. 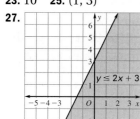 **29.**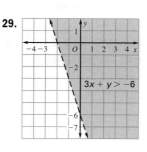

Focus on Problem Solving (p. 449) **1.** *Sample answer:* $\frac{4 \cdot 4}{4 \cdot 4}$, $\frac{4 \div 4}{4 \div 4}$, $4^4 \div 4^4$ **3.** Some possible numbers of coins are 9, 15, and 21. **5.** *Sample answer:* 6 pies and 3 loaves, 4 pies and 6 loaves, 2 pies and 9 loaves **7.** Some possible dimensions of the swimming pool are 150 feet by 100 feet, 125 feet by 120 feet, and 200 feet by 75 feet.
9. a. No solution. *Sample answer:* For any two consecutive integers, one is even and one is odd. So the sum of two consecutive integers must be odd, but 20 is even. **b.** 4 and 5, or -4 and -5

Chapter 9

9.1 Guided Practice (p. 455) **1.** *Sample answer:* A perfect square is the square of an integer. An example is 169, since $13^2 = 169$. **3.** ± 2 **5.** ± 11
7. 3 **9.** 12 **11.** ± 3 **13.** ± 19 **15.** Step 1: $A = s^2$; Step 2: $15{,}625 = s^2$, 125 ft

9.1 Practice and Problem Solving (pp. 456–457)
17. ± 13 **19.** ± 17 **21.** ± 22 **23.** ± 30 **25.** 6
27. -12 **29.** -9 **31.** 4 **33.** 1.7 **35.** 9.3 **37.** -5.7
39. 4.4 **41.** 6 **43.** -72 **45.** ± 7 **47.** ± 21
49. ± 4.5 **51.** ± 4.7 **53.** *Sample answer:* $x^2 = 2.25$
59. 3.2 m/sec **61.** ± 18 **63.** ± 2.89 **65.** ± 6.96
67. a. 472 mi/h **b.** 446 mi/h slower **71.** $2 \cdot 7^2$
73. $2^2 \cdot 5^2 \cdot 7$ **75.** $\frac{1}{4}$ **77.** $\frac{5}{27}$ **79.** 48 **81.** 6.5%

9.2 Guided Practice (p. 460) **1.** Yes. *Sample answer:* The only perfect square factor of 5 is 1, so it is in simplest form. **3.** $2\sqrt{3}$ **5.** $\frac{9}{2}$ **7.** $10\sqrt{3}$ units

9.2 Practice and Problem Solving (pp. 460–461)
9. $7\sqrt{2}$ **11.** $12\sqrt{2}$ **13.** $10\sqrt{3x}$ **15.** $\frac{\sqrt{11}}{6}$ **17.** $\frac{4\sqrt{5}}{9}$
19. $\frac{\sqrt{z}}{8}$ **21.** $\frac{3\sqrt{7}}{4}$; 2 sec **23.** $5x\sqrt{3y}$ **25.** $60mn\sqrt{2}$

27. a. yours: 4 nautical miles, your friend's: $4\sqrt{13}$ nautical miles **b.** *Sample answer:* For you and your friend on top of the lighthouse to see each other, you must first come close enough to be able to see to the same spot on the ocean. The first moment this happens is at the visual horizon both for you and your friend, so your distance from each other is the sum of your visual horizon and your friend's. **c.** 4, about 14; 18 nautical miles
29. $y\sqrt{y}$ **31.** a^4 **35.** 180 **37.** 64 **39.** $\frac{2y}{3}$ **41.** $\frac{d}{5c}$
43. 7 **45.** 10

Student Reference (p. 463) **1.** 45 **3.** 85 **5.** acute
7. right **9.** equilateral

9.3 Guided Practice (p. 467) **1.** hypotenuse **3.** 39
5. 12

9.3 Practice and Problem Solving (pp. 467–469)
7. 29 **9.** $\sqrt{34}$ **11.** $2\sqrt{31}$ **13.** no **15.** yes **17.** yes
19. 36 in. **21. a.** *Sample answer:* Let $n = 5$. Then $2n = 2(5) = 10$, $n^2 - 1 = 5^2 - 1 = 24$, and $n^2 + 1 = 5^2 + 1 = 26$. **b.** *Sample answer:* $10^2 + 24^2 = 100 + 576 = 676 = 26^2$ **23.** *Sample answer:* Mental math; the squares of 1 and 2 can be calculated quickly mentally. **25.** 45 **27.** 10 **29.** 116
31. 28.0 m **33.** 16 yd **37.** $\frac{4}{25}$ **39.** $1\frac{3}{40}$ **41.** 1 : 10

9.4 Guided Practice (p. 472) **1.** A number that cannot be written as the quotient of two integers. *Sample answer:* $\sqrt{11}$ **3.** rational **5.** irrational
7. $<$ **9.** $>$ **11.** irrational

9.4 Practice and Problem Solving (pp. 473–474)
13. irrational **15.** rational **17.** irrational
19. irrational **21.** $>$ **23.** $>$ **25.** $-\sqrt{5}$, -2, 0, $\sqrt{3}$, $\frac{9}{5}$, $\sqrt{4}$ **27.** $-\sqrt{18}$, $-\frac{25}{6}$, $-\sqrt{\frac{67}{4}}$, -4 **29.** Sometimes.
Sample answer: For example, $\sqrt{\frac{4}{9}} = \frac{2}{3}$ is rational, but $\sqrt{20}$ is irrational. **31.** Never. *Sample answer:* Any whole number can be written as the quotient of itself and 1, so a whole number is a rational number. **33. a.** $2w$ **b.** $20 = (2w)(w)$, or $20 = 2w^2$
c. 3.2 m **d.** 6.3 m **35.** the longer boat; 2 nautical miles per hour **37.** *Sample answer:* $-\sqrt{10}$

39. *Sample answer:* $-\sqrt{101}$ **41.** Sometimes. *Sample answer:* $\sqrt{2} \cdot \sqrt{2} = 2$, which is rational, but $\sqrt{2} \cdot \sqrt{3} = \sqrt{6}$, which is irrational. **45.** 3.375 **47.** $\frac{1}{9}$ **49.** $\frac{3}{5}$ **51.** 6

9.5 Guided Practice (p. 479)
1. distance **3.** $\sqrt{34}$ units **5.** $\frac{5}{3}$

9.5 Practice and Problem Solving (pp. 479–481)
7. $\sqrt{17}$ units **9.** $\sqrt{10}$ units **11.** $\sqrt{41}$ units **13.** $6\sqrt{5}$ units **15.** 2.5 units **17.** $3\sqrt{2}$ units **19.** $(1, 2)$ **21.** $\left(-\frac{1}{2}, -\frac{3}{2}\right)$ **23.** -1 **25.** $-\frac{3}{2}$ **27.** $(5, 3)$ **29.** $\left(7\frac{1}{2}, 2\right)$ **31.** $\left(4\frac{1}{4}, 2\frac{1}{2}\right)$ **33.** 1 **35.** $\frac{4}{3}$ **37.** $\frac{8}{3}$

39. a. The midpoint between the hospital and the stadium is $\left(\frac{1+9}{2}, \frac{2+6}{2}\right) = (5, 4)$, which matches the coordinates of the Civic Center. **b.** the hospital and the State House **41.** No. *Sample answer:* Since the differences between the x-coordinates and between the y-coordinates are squared in the distance formula, the results are the same. For example, $(2-3)^2 = (-1)^2 = 1$, and $(3-2)^2 = (1)^2 = 1$.

43. $\overline{PQ}$ **45.** $B(-8, 0)$ **47.** $B(17, 12)$
49. No. *Sample answer:* The line through $(-3, 9)$ and $(1, 1)$ has slope -2, the line through $(-3, 9)$ and $(4, -4)$ has slope $-\frac{13}{7}$, and the line through $(1, 1)$ and $(4, -4)$ has slope $-\frac{5}{3}$. Since the lines have different slopes, the three points do not lie on the same line.

51.

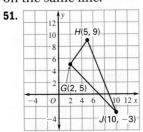

no **53.** $C(2, 2)$
55. yes
57. 131%
59. $>$
61. $<$

9.6 Guided Practice (p. 485)
1. $15\sqrt{2}$ units **3.** $6\sqrt{2}$
5. $5\sqrt{3}$

9.6 Practice and Problem Solving (pp. 486–487)
7. $x = 11$, $y = 11\sqrt{2}$ **9.** $x = 5$, $y = 5\sqrt{2}$ **11.** $x = 10$, $y = 10\sqrt{3}$ **13. a.** 10 ft **b.** 12 ft **15.** 85 ft **17.** $x = 10$, $y = 10$ **19. a.** 469 ft **b.** 4.4 ft/sec **c.** 107 sec, or 1 min 47 sec **23.** 7 **25.** 61.25 **27.** $(-2, 5)$ **29.** $(0.8, -1.4)$

9.7 Guided Practice (p. 491)
1. a. $\overline{BC}$ **b.** $\overline{AC}$
3. $\frac{7}{24}$ **5.** $\frac{4}{3}$

9.7 Practice and Problem Solving (pp. 491–493)
7. $\tan A = \frac{11}{60}$, $\tan B = \frac{60}{11}$ **9.** $\tan A = \frac{24}{7}$, $\tan B = \frac{7}{24}$ **11.** 2.2460 **13.** 0.2679 **15.** 0.6494 **17.** 57.2900 **19.** 19.6 **21. a.** $d + 1.5$ **b.** 64.0 m **c.** 65.5 m **23.** 137 ft **25.** 175.8 square units
27. *Sample:*

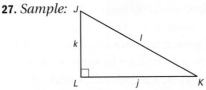

They are reciprocals. *Sample answer:* The side opposite each of the acute angles is the side adjacent to the other. From the drawing, $\tan J = \frac{j}{k}$ and $\tan K = \frac{k}{j}$, and $\frac{j}{k}$ and $\frac{k}{j}$ are reciprocals since $\frac{j}{k} \cdot \frac{k}{j} = 1$.

29. a. About 4400 ft. *Sample answer:* Since $d = rt$, $d = 1100 \cdot 4 = 4400$ feet. **b.** *Sample answer:* Use the fact that triangles ABD and CBD are right triangles with an acute angle with measure $\frac{x^\circ}{2}$ at your eye. Then you can use the tangent ratio: $\tan \frac{x^\circ}{2} = \frac{s}{d}$. **c.** 384 ft **31.** $3.12 **33.** $6\sqrt{b}$
35. $9fg\sqrt{2}$

9.8 Guided Practice (p. 496)
3. $\sin J = \frac{40}{41}$, $\cos J = \frac{9}{41}$, $\sin L = \frac{9}{41}$, $\cos L = \frac{40}{41}$

9.8 Practice and Problem Solving (pp. 497–498)
5. $\sin P = \frac{3}{5}$, $\cos P = \frac{4}{5}$, $\sin Q = \frac{4}{5}$, $\cos Q = \frac{3}{5}$
7. $\sin A = \frac{12}{13}$, $\cos A = \frac{5}{13}$, $\sin B = \frac{5}{13}$, $\cos B = \frac{12}{13}$
9. 0.9272 **11.** 0.9511 **13.** 0.9063 **15.** 0.9998 **17.** 12.1 **19.** 88.2 **21.** 83.4

23. *Sample:*

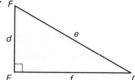

The side opposite each of the acute angles is the side adjacent to the other, so the sine of one acute angle is equal to the cosine of the other acute angle. From the drawing, $\sin D = \dfrac{d}{e} = \cos F$, and $\sin F = \dfrac{f}{e} = \cos D$.

25. 4.0 m   **27.** *Sample answer:* (1) Use the Pythagorean theorem to write the equation $28^2 + b^2 = 35^2$ and then solve to find that $b = 21$. (2) Use the tangent ratio to write the equation $\tan 37° = \dfrac{b}{28}$ and solve. (3) Use the sine ratio to write the equation $\sin 37° = \dfrac{b}{35}$ and solve. (4) Find $m\angle A$: $m\angle A = 90 - 37 = 53°$. Then use the cosine ratio to write the equation $\cos 53° = \dfrac{b}{35}$ and solve.

31. no   **33.** $\angle A$ and $\angle D$, $\angle B$ and $\angle E$, $\angle C$ and $\angle F$, $\overline{AB}$ and $\overline{DE}$, $\overline{BC}$ and $\overline{EF}$, $\overline{AC}$ and $\overline{DF}$

35. irrational   **37.** rational

9.8 Technology Activity (p. 499) 1. 36.9°   **3.** 22.6°
5. 53.1°   **7.** 11.5°

Chapter Review (pp. 500–503) 1. square root
3. the point on the segment that is equally distant from the endpoints   **5.** ± 25, ± 90 **7.** -5 **9.** 8
11. $6\sqrt{2}$ **13.** $\dfrac{\sqrt{29a}}{10}$ **15.** $3z\sqrt{2}$ **17.** $\dfrac{a\sqrt{2}}{7}$ **19.** 10
21. $\sqrt{58}$ **23.** $>$ **25.** $<$ **27.** -5.01, $-\sqrt{18}$, $\dfrac{19}{6}$, $\sqrt{20}$
29. $x = 11$, $y = 11\sqrt{2}$ **31.** $x = 9\sqrt{3}$, $y = 9$ **33.** 11.5

Chapter 10

10.1 Guided Practice (p. 513) 1. 60°, 60°, and 60°; acute   **3.** 20; acute   **5.** 5 m   **7.** *Sample answer:* The measure of the right angle was omitted. The correct equation and solution are $x° + 2x° + 90° = 180°$, $3x = 90$, and $x = 30$.

**10.1 Practice and Problem Solving (pp. 513–515)
9.** 15; acute   **11.** 23; obtuse   **13.** 63; acute
15. 19 in.; scalene   **17.** 28.1 cm; equilateral

19.

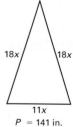

33 in., 54 in., and 54 in.; isosceles

21. a. 49 in., 168 in., 175 in.; scalene   **b.** Yes. *Sample answer:* By the converse of the Pythagorean theorem: $49^2 + 168^2 = 2401 + 28{,}224 = 30{,}625 = 175^2$.   **23. a.**

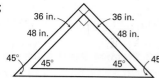

b. 48 in.   **c.** 36 in.
d. 34 in., 51 in., 68 in.;

25. Yes. *Sample answer:* There are two possibilities, as shown in the diagram, depending on whether 5 centimeters is the length of one of the congruent sides or the length of the other side.

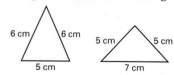

29. $\sin B = \dfrac{3}{5}$, $\sin C = \dfrac{4}{5}$, $\cos B = \dfrac{4}{5}$, $\cos C = \dfrac{3}{5}$

10.2 Guided Practice (p. 518) 1. *Sample answer:* A trapezoid has exactly one pair of parallel sides, while a parallelogram has two pairs of parallel sides.   **3.** No; it is a circle, which is curved.
5. trapezoid

**10.2 Practice and Problem Solving (pp. 519–520)
7.** yes; 16-gon, concave   **9.** No; the top of the figure is curved.   **11.** trapezoid   **13.** parallelogram
15. always   **17.** never   **19.** 90   **21. a.** about $16\dfrac{5}{8}$ ft, or 16 ft 7.5 in.   **b.**

c. *Sample answer:* You would need to know the height of each triangle. Then you could use the area formula for a triangle, $A = \frac{1}{2}bh$, to find the area of one of the triangles, and multiply the result by 8 to find the area of the octagon. **23.** $m\angle A = 88°$, $m\angle C = 44°$, $m\angle D = 114°$ **25.** $(-6, -11)$ **27.** $(3.7, 2.3)$ **29.** $30°, 45°, 105°$; obtuse

10.3 Guided Practice (p. 524)

1. *Sample:*

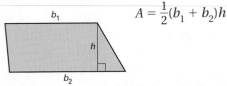

$$A = \frac{1}{2}(b_1 + b_2)h$$

3. 150 ft^2 **5.** 3000 m^2 **7.** 15 m **9.** 20 m

10.3 Practice and Problem Solving (pp. 524–526)

11. 70 in.^2 **13.** 95.45 mm^2 **15.** 18.36 m^2

17. 25 m^2 **19.** 45 m **21.** $1\frac{1}{3} \text{ yd}$ **23.** 25 ft

25. a. 136.5 ft^2 **b.** 2747.94 ft^2

27.

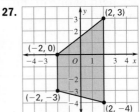

trapezoid, 20 square units

29. It doubles; it doubles; it quadruples.

31. 156 cm^2 **33.** 16 in.^2, 12 in.^2; $\frac{4}{3}$ **35.** 1389.15

37. 6 **39.** 3 **41.** 107

10.4 Guided Practice (p. 531) 1. 2.5 cm **3.** 88 cm, 616 cm^2 **5.** 11 ft

10.4 Practice and Problem Solving (pp. 531–533)

7. 113 in. **9.** 132 cm **11.** 100 mm **13.** 6 m, 12 m

15. 8 in., 16 in. **17.** 201 in.^2 **19.** 2464 cm^2

21. 855 m^2 **23.** 9 m, 18 m **25.** 19 in., 38 in.

27. 5672 ft^2 **29.** $18,200 \text{ ft}$ **31.** Doubling the radius will double the circumference and quadruple the area. *Sample answer:* For example, if the radius is 7, then the circumference is about 44 units and the area is about 154 square units. If the radius is 14, the circumference is about 88 units and the area is about 616 square units. Doubling the diameter will also double the circumference and quadruple the area.

For example, if the diameter is 2, then the circumference is about 6.28 units and the area is about 3.14 square units. If the diameter is 4, the circumference is about 12.56 units and the area is about 12.56 square units. **35.** 7 **37.** 170 **39.** undefined **41.** 35 cm^2 **43.** 37.5 in.^2

Student Reference (p. 536) 1. cone **3.** cylinder **5.** *Sample:*

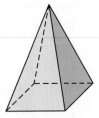

10.5 Guided Practice (p. 541) 1. $S = 2B + Ph$ **3.** *Sample answer:* 300 ft^2

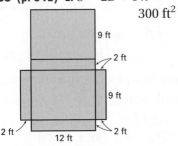

5. *Sample answer:* In this case, the base is not the surface on which the prism is resting, but a triangle with sides 5, 12, and 13: $S = 2B + Ph = 2(0.5 \cdot 5 \cdot 12) + (5 + 12 + 13)(4) = 180$ square centimeters.

10.5 Practice and Problem Solving (pp. 541–543)

7–11. Sample nets are given.

7. 656 yd^2

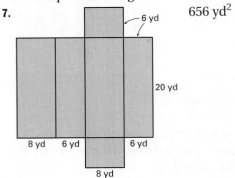

9. 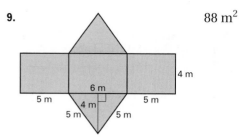 88 m²

11. 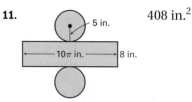 408 in.²

13. 126 in.² **15.** 384 ft² **17. a.** It is quadrupled. *Sample answer:* The area of a base of the original cylinder is πr^2, and of the new cylinder is $\pi(2r)^2 = 4\pi r^2$. **b.** It is doubled. *Sample answer:* The circumference of the original cylinder is $2\pi r$, and of the new cylinder is $2\pi(2r) = 4\pi r$. **c.** It is quadrupled. *Sample answer:* The surface area of the original cylinder is $2\pi r^2 + 2\pi rh$, and of the new cylinder is $2(4\pi r^2) + (4\pi r)(2h) = 4(2\pi r^2) + 4(2\pi rh) = 4(2\pi r^2 + 2\pi rh)$. **19.** 6760 in.²
21. a. $S = 4\pi h^2$ **b.** 4 units; 4 units **23.** 15 ft, 11 ft, 11 ft; isosceles **25.** 96.25 m² **27.** 264 in.
29. 641 cm

10.6 Guided Practice (p. 547) 1. *Sample answer:* The height is the perpendicular distance between the base and the vertex that is not on the base, while the slant height is the height of a lateral face. **3.** 736 in.² **5.** 352 ft²

10.6 Practice and Problem Solving (pp. 547–549)
7. 29 yd **9.** 39 m
11. 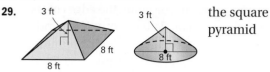 641 ft²

13. Slant height. *Sample answer:* A right triangle can be formed with the pyramid's height, slant height, and half the distance across the base. The pyramid's height would be a leg of the right triangle and the slant height would be the hypotenuse. Since the hypotenuse is always the longest side in a right triangle, the pyramid's slant height is greater than its height. **15.** 7812 mm²

17. 120 m² **19.** 539 in.² **21.** 2649 in.² **23.** 72 yd²
25. 11,945,906 mi² **27.** 20 ft²
29. the square pyramid

31. 220 m² **35.** $12\sqrt{2}$ **37.** $\dfrac{2\sqrt{6}}{11}$ **39.** 534 cm²

10.7 Guided Practice (p. 554) 1. cubic **3.** 120 cm³
5. 1810 ft³

10.7 Practice and Problem Solving (pp. 555–556)
7. 88 m³ **9.** 3168 cm³ **11.** 14 mm³ **13.** 2040 in.³
15. a. red: 42 in.³, blue: 64 in.³, green: 50 in.³
b. red: about \$.168/in.³, blue: about \$.122/in.³, green: \$.211/in.³ **c.** The blue candle. *Sample answer:* It has the lowest price per cubic inch of wax. **17.** 8 in. **19.** 948 ft³ **21. a.** 36π cubic units **b.** 144π cubic units, 72π cubic units, 288π cubic units **c.** *Sample answer:* Doubling the radius quadruples the volume. Doubling the height doubles the volume. Doubling both the radius and the height multiplies the volume by a factor of 8.
25. yes **27.** $\tan A = \dfrac{7}{24}$, $\tan B = \dfrac{24}{7}$ **29.** 144 in.²

10.7 Technology Activity (p. 557)
1. about 0.83; more efficient

10.8 Guided Practice (p. 560) 1. $V = \dfrac{1}{3}Bh$
3. 20 in.³ **5.** In finding the area of the base, the diameter was used instead of the radius. The correct result is $\dfrac{1}{3}\pi(4)^2(7) \approx 117$ cm³.

10.8 Practice and Problem Solving (pp. 561–563)
7. 24 yd³ **9.** 564 yd³ **11.** 268 ft³ **13.** 283 cm³
15. a. $15{,}200\pi$ in.³ **b.** top: $1333\dfrac{1}{3}\pi$ in.³, bottom: $1066\dfrac{2}{3}\pi$ in.³ **c.** 48,590 in.³ **d.** Radius. *Sample answer:* In the volume formulas for cylinders and cones, the radius is squared, but the height is not.
17. 211.67 cm³ **19.** 36 mm **21.** 299 mm³
23. 14 ft³ **25.** 4 ft **27.** slope: $\dfrac{3}{2}$, y-intercept: -1
29. slope: 0, y-intercept: $\dfrac{9}{2}$, or $4\dfrac{1}{2}$ **31.** 128 in.³

Chapter Review (pp. 564–567) 1. the lengths of the bases and the height **3.** *Sample answer:* Form a net by imagining cutting along the edges of the prism so that you can flatten it out. Then find the area of the polygons in the net, which represent the faces of the prism, and add the areas. **5.** 24; right **7.** 16; obtuse **9.** yes; square **11.** 6 in.^{2} **13.** 10 m^2 **15.** 108 in.^{2} **17.** 452 in.^{2} **19.** 133 ft^2 **21.** 226 in.^{3} **23.** 336 m^3 **25.** 938 cm^3

Chapter 11

11.1 Guided Practice (p. 584) 1. 7, 8, and 9

3.
```
2 | 1 7 9
3 | 1 3
4 | 0 0 1 4 6
5 | 6 6 8
6 | 0 2
```
Key: 2 | 1 = 21

5. Step 1: *Sample answer:*

Earthquakes	Tally	Frequency
5–8	IIII	4
9–12	III	3
13–16	JHT II	7
17–20	II	2
21–24	II	2
25–28	I	1

Step 2:

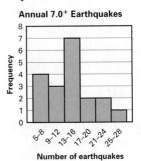

Step 3: *Sample answer:* 9–12; it is the third most frequent interval, after 13–16 and 5–8. Nearly two thirds of the annual numbers of earthquakes, however, are above the interval in which 11 lies.

11.1 Practice and Problem Solving (pp. 584–586)

7.
```
0 | 6 9
1 |
2 |
3 |
4 | 1 4
5 | 0 4 8
6 | 1 2 2 3 4 5
7 | 0 0 1 7
```
Key: 0 | 6 = 6

9.
```
12 | 1 5 6
13 | 4 5 9
14 | 1 2
15 | 0 1 2 7
16 |
17 |
18 | 0
```
Key: 12 | 1 = 12.1

11. *Sample answer:*

Interval	Tally	Frequency
101–120	III	3
121–140	JHT I	6
141–160	I	1
161–180		0
181–200	IIII	4

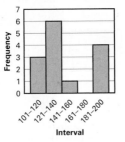

13. *Sample answer:*

Interval	Tally	Frequency
40–49	II	2
50–59	III	3
60–69	IIII	4
70–79	IIII	4
80–89	II	2
90–99	I	1

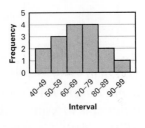

15. a. 25–29 **b.** $33\frac{1}{3}\%$ **c.** *Sample answer:* The vacation days in Shanghai are fewer than for most cities in North America and Europe. At least two thirds of the cities in Europe and North America have more vacation days. **17.** *Sample answer:* 4.6 and 46; in 4.6, the stem 4 represents the ones place and 6 represents the tenths place; in 46, the stem 4 represents the tens place and 6 represents the ones place.

19. *Sample:*

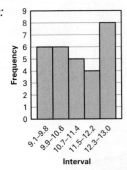

21. a. *Sample answer:*

Men's Javelin Throws		
Meters	Tally	Frequency
80.00–82.99	III	3
83.00–85.99	II	2
86.00–88.99	II	2
89.00–91.99	II	2
92.00–94.99	I	1

Women's Javelin Throws		
Meters	Tally	Frequency
58.00–60.99	II	2
61.00–63.99	JHT	5
64.00–66.99	II	2
67.00–69.99	I	1

b. *Sample:*

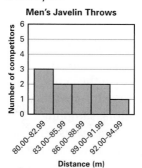

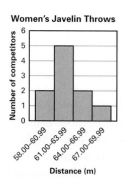

Men's Javelin Throws

Women's Javelin Throws

c. *Sample answer:* There is more variation in the distances for the men's throws than in the distances for the women's throws. All the distances for the men's throws are significantly greater than even the greatest distances for the women's throws. **23.** $34 **25.** -4 **27.** $(-4, 2)$ **29.** $(0.5, 1)$

11.1 Technology Activity (p. 587)

1. *Sample:*

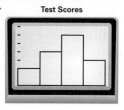

Test Scores

11.2 Guided Practice (p. 590) **1.** 23

3.

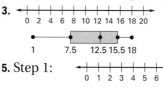

5. Step 1:

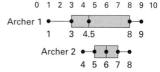

Step 2: Archer 1: 8, 5; Archer 2: 4, 2;
Step 3: Archer 2

11.2 Practice and Problem Solving (pp. 591–592)

7.

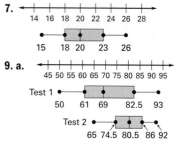

9. a.

b. *Sample answer:* On test 1, the range was 43, and the interquartile range was 21.5. These are considerably greater than the range of 27 and interquartile range of 11.5 for test 2. **c.** Test 1. *Sample answer:* On test 1, the score of 71 was above the median, but on test 2, the score of 74 was below the median.

11. a. **b.** 198

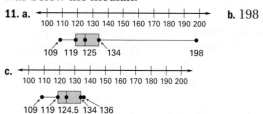

c.

d. *Sample answer:* Though it changes the appearance of the left whisker and the box very little, excluding the outlier greatly shortens the length of the right whisker; from the plot in part (c), you can conclude that all values other than the outlier that are above the upper quartile are very, very close to the upper quartile.

15. 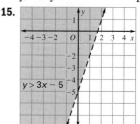 **17.** 184 m² **19.** 90 cm²

$y > 3x - 5$

11.2 Technology Activity (p. 593)

1.

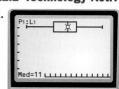

Student Reference (p. 595)

1.

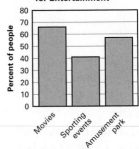

Activities People Choose
for Entertainment

3.

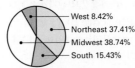

U.S. Curbside Recycling
Programs by Region

- West 8.42%
- Northeast 37.41%
- Midwest 38.74%
- South 15.43%

11.3 Guided Practice (p. 598)

1. bar graph, circle graph   **3.** Bar graph, circle graph. *Sample answer:* These are categorical data.   **5.** Step 1: about 4 times; Step 2: about 1.4 times more bikes; Step 3: Yes. *Sample answer:* The broken vertical axis exaggerates the differences in the bar heights.

11.3 Practice and Problem Solving (pp. 599–600)

7. Categorical. *Sample answer:* I would use a bar graph, because it would allow the most direct visual comparison between players' numbers of goals.   **9.** stem-and-leaf plot, box-and-whisker plot   **11.** stem-and-leaf plot   **13.** The extremes, range, and quartiles, and how they divide the data into four equal-sized groups; the frequency of occurrence in chosen equal intervals. *Sample answer:* A box-and-whisker plot divides data into intervals of sorts, the quartiles, but they are not equal. For a histogram, you can determine in what intervals the quartiles and extremes lie, but you cannot determine their exact values.   **15.** Histogram. *Sample answer:* There are no stems that correspond to 2-year intervals.   **17.** *Sample answer:* You might mistakenly conclude that volleyball is more popular than water skiing, though the numbers are the same. This is because the view at an angle makes the distance along the circle greater for the "Volleyball" section than for the "Water Skiing" section.   **19.** $\frac{1}{7}$ **21.** $\frac{1}{3}$ **23.** 8 cm

11.4 Guided Practice (p. 603)

1. random sample   **3.** No. *Sample answer:* Since the movies usually end at different times, it is possible that all the people you interview have gone to the same movie, so they may be inclined to like the same kind of movie.

11.4 Practice and Problem Solving (pp. 604–605)

5. self-selected   **7.** systematic   **9.** Population: residents of the town; sampling method: convenience sample; no. *Sample answer:* The customers of the ice cream shops are likely more enthusiastic about ice cream than the general population, and may have different preferences.   **11. a.** Population: museum visitors; sampling method: self-selected   **b.** No. *Sample answer:* The people who decide to fill out the survey are likely those with strong opinions, and as such may not represent the views of most museum visitors.   **13.** *Sample answer:* No; the question is straightforward and can be answered with a simple numerical fact.   **15.** *Sample answer:* The sample from several ponds; the turtles from a single pond are likely to be more genetically similar, and are all subject to the availability of food in just that single pond.   **17a–d.** Sample answers are given.   **17. a.** No; a random sample should be representative.   **b.** Yes; trees in one portion might be genetically more similar, as well as subject to local environmental influences.   **c.** Yes; if some trees were unusually tall, they would make the average height taller than might be "typical" for the forest.   **d.** No; it is the function of a sample to represent a larger population. If the sample is representative, and not biased in any way, the results should reflect those in the forest as a whole.   **19.** 6   **21.** $-\frac{4}{7}$ **23.** 150 km   **25.** 26.4

11.4 Technology Activity (p. 606)

1–6. Answers may vary.

11.5 Guided Practice (p. 611)

1. *Sample answer:* It is an amount added and subtracted to a sample percent to determine the upper and lower boundaries for an interval in which the population percent is most likely to lie.   **3.** about 975 dog owners

11.5 Practice and Problem Solving (pp. 612–613)
5. about 1050 families   **7.** mayor: leading candidate; treasurer: too close to call; sheriff: leading candidate; controller: too close to call
9. *Sample answer:* I do not trust the survey or the conclusions. First, the population is just those shoppers at one mall. Also, there is no information as to how the survey was carried out or what sampling method was used to ensure that the survey truly represents even those people at the mall. The survey is even more troublesome because the survey conductor has an interest in the popularity of unusual pets. Finally, no margin of error is given. It seems very likely the interval around the sample percent for mammals, 31%, may overlap the interval around the total sample percent for reptiles and birds, 33%.   **11.** No. *Sample answer:* The sample is not random, and represents only a few people of a certain age. Also, because all the students in the classroom are close together, they may be likely to transmit the flu among each other.   **13.** 240 students to 384 students   **17.** $8m^4$ **19.** 10   **21.** 118.125, or $118\frac{1}{8}$ **23.** 16

11.6 Guided Practice (p. 617)   **1.** 6! = 720   **3.** 60
5. 2   **7.** 360 arrangements   **9.** *Sample answer:* In this situation, $n = 4$ and $r = 3$. The formula is $_nP_r = \frac{n!}{(n-r)!}$, but the quantity shown is $\frac{n!}{r!}$. The correct solution is $\frac{4!}{(4-3)!} = 4! = 24$.

11.6 Practice and Problem Solving (pp. 618–619)
11. 1   **13.** 3,628,800   **15.** 39,916,800
17. 479,001,600   **19.** 9   **21.** 6720   **23.** 1
25. 13,366,080   **27.** 6720 arrangements
29. 665,280 choices   **31.** $\frac{1}{120}$ **33.** $\frac{30!}{28!}$ **35.** $\frac{12!}{5!}$
37. a. *Sample answer:* This is the number of permutations of 3 digits taken 3 at a time: $_3P_3 = 6$; yes.   **b.** *Sample answer:* For each of the 3 places, you have the same number of choices, 3. The number of 3-digit numbers is $3 \cdot 3 \cdot 3 = 27$; no.
39. a. 4 arrangements   **b.** 4 arrangements
c. 8 arrangements   **41.** n times. *Sample answer:*
$n! = n \cdot (n-1) \cdot (n-2) \cdot \ldots \cdot 1 = n \cdot [(n-1) \cdot (n-2) \cdot \ldots \cdot 1] = n \cdot (n-1)!$ **45.** 52 m   **47.** $\sqrt{21}$ ft

11.7 Guided Practice (p. 623)   **1.** $_{12}C_3$ **3.** 2   **5.** 1
7. combinations; 1001 teams

11.7 Practice and Problem Solving (pp. 623–625)
9. 4 sets; winter, spring, and summer; winter, spring, and fall; winter, summer, and fall; spring, summer, and fall   **11.** 3   **13.** 35   **15.** 4   **17.** 56
19. 220   **21.** 1   **23.** permutations; 120 responses
25. permutations; 6720 ways   **27.** $\frac{1}{210}$ **29.** *Sample answer:* If you choose 4 objects from a group of 5, then for each group of 4 objects chosen, there is 1 object not chosen. Likewise, each time you choose 1 object from 5, there is a group of 4 objects not chosen. Because each group has exactly 1 matching group, there are the same number in each group. Another example is $_7C_3 = {_7C_4} = 35$.
31. a. $\frac{1}{1225}$ **b.** No. *Sample answer:* It multiplies it by 6. If you have 4 of the tickets, then you have $_4C_2 = 6$ of the combinations of two tickets in your hand, so the probability that you are holding both winning tickets is $\frac{6}{1225}$.   **33.** 9 ways. *Sample answer:* If 8 is the only number greater than 6 that is chosen, then there are $_3C_2 = 3$ ways. If 9 is the only number greater than 6 that is chosen, then there are $_3C_2 = 3$ ways. If 8 and 9 are both chosen, then there are $_3C_1 = 3$ ways. There are $3 + 3 + 3 = 9$ ways total.
37.

39. 720 ways

11.8 Guided Practice (p. 630)   **1.** They have no outcomes in common.   **3.** disjoint; $\frac{2}{3}$
5. disjoint; $\frac{1}{2}$ **7.** Step 1: disjoint; Step 2: $\frac{3}{14}$; Step 3: $\frac{2}{7}$; Step 4: $\frac{1}{2}$

11.8 Practice and Problem Solving (pp. 631–632)
9. overlapping; $\frac{2}{3}$ **11.** overlapping; $\frac{1}{2}$ **13.** $\frac{3}{5}$
15. $\frac{7}{10}$ **17.** $\frac{18}{25}$ **19.** 55%   **21.** $\frac{12}{23}$ **23. a.** 85%   **b.** 56%
c. 55%   **d.** 49%   **25.** $\frac{5}{6}$

27. They are disjoint. *Sample answer:* $P(A \text{ and } B) = 0$ means that A and B will not happen at the same time, therefore events A and B are disjoint.
31. $\dfrac{15}{32}$ **33.** $-\dfrac{65}{288}$ **35.** 462   **37.** 210

11.9 Guided Practice (p. 637) 1. *Sample answer:* Whether or not one of the events occurs does not affect whether or not the other occurs.
3. independent   **5.** Step 1: dependent; Step 2: $\dfrac{1}{30}$; Step 3: $\dfrac{1}{29}$; Step 4: $\dfrac{1}{870}$

11.9 Practice and Problem Solving (pp. 637–639)
7. independent   **9.** $\dfrac{5}{34}$ **11. a.** $\dfrac{7}{59}$ **b.** $\dfrac{42}{295}$ **c.** $\dfrac{21}{236}$
13. a. $\dfrac{2}{51}$ **b.** $\dfrac{5}{51}$ **c.** $\dfrac{28}{153}$ **d.** $\dfrac{49}{153}$ **15.** If you do replace it. *Sample answer:* The probability if you replace the red marble is $\dfrac{1}{2} \cdot \dfrac{1}{2} = \dfrac{1}{4} = 0.25$, and the probability if you do not replace it is $\dfrac{1}{2} \cdot \dfrac{19}{39} = \dfrac{19}{78} \approx$ 0.244.   **17.** 1 in 10^{10}, or $\dfrac{1}{10{,}000{,}000{,}000}$ **19. a.** BR, RB, RR, BB   **b.** BR: $\dfrac{2}{9} \approx 22\%$, RB: $\dfrac{20}{87} \approx 23\%$, RR: $\dfrac{3}{29} \approx 10\%$, BB: $\dfrac{4}{9} \approx 44\%$ **c.** $\dfrac{5}{9} \approx 56\%$. *Sample answer:* Since the complement of catching at least one rainbow trout is catching no rainbow trout, I subtracted the probability for BB from 1.
21. $-3s^2 - 2$ **23.** 15,504 groups

Chapter Review (pp. 640–643) 1. margin of error
3. Amount of Purchase ($)   *Sample:*

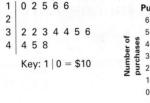

Key: 1 | 0 = $10

5.

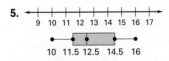

7. population: customers of a pizza parlor; sampling method: convenience sample   **9.** 72
11. 20,160   **13.** 10; 792   **15.** $\dfrac{18}{95}$

Chapter 12

12.1 Guided Practice (p. 653) 1. degree   **3.** yes; $5x^3$; monomial   **5.** no   **7.** 1   **9.** $6x + 12$
11. $-z^2 + 10z + 8$ **13.** $2x^2 + 10x$ **15.** 17   **17.** 48

12.1 Practice and Problem Solving (pp. 654–655)
19. yes; $8a^2$; monomial   **21.** yes; $3c^3$, $-2c^2$, and -7; trinomial   **23.** no   **25.** 2   **27.** 3   **29.** 1   **31.** No. *Sample answer:* In standard form, the degree of each term decreases or stays the same from left to right. The degree of the term $5x^2y$ is 3, so the polynomial in standard form is $5x^2y + 3x^2 + 7$.
33. $6x + 2$ **35.** $4y + 7$ **37.** $13z^2 - 22z$ **39.** 156 ft; 100 ft   **41.** 44   **43.** -52 **45.** 7   **47.** $3x + 15$
49. $16x + 16$ **51.** 3   **53.** 4   **55.** 4   **57.** -1
59. a. 67 ft; 192 ft   **b.** 3259 ft; 7904 ft   **c.** about 1361 ft   **61.** $n + 4$ **65.** -27 **67.** 135   **69.** 81 m^2

12.2 Guided Practice (p. 659) 1. like terms
3. $3x + 11$ **5.** $4a^2 - 4$ **7.** $9z - 5$ **9.** $-2b^2 - b + 7$
11. *Sample answer:* When subtracting the second polynomial, the opposite should have been found for each term, not just the first term. So, $(x^2 + 3x - 1) - (x^2 + x + 2) = x^2 + 3x - 1 - x^2 - x - 2 = x^2 - x^2 + 3x - x - 1 - 2 = 2x - 3$.

12.2 Practice and Problem Solving (pp. 660–661)
13. $-6x - 8$ **15.** $2y^4 - 3y^2 - 9$ **17.** $-4z^3 + z^2 + 3z - 3$ **19.** $4m^2 - 4m + 1$ **21.** $3a^2 + 7a - 2$
23. $3b^3 - 4b^2 + 2b$ **25.** $3c^3 + c^2 - 2c + 12$
27. $-2d^2 + 4d$ **29.** $15x + y$ **31.** $-6cd - 2$
33. $4m - 17n$ **35.** $-11rs + 2r - 3s$ **37.** $3x^2 - 5x - 4$ **39.** $-33x^3 + 670x^2 - 1695x + 31{,}948$
41. $21 + 7a$ **43.** $-12t + 60$ **45.** 3^6 **47.** m^{13} **49.** yes

12.3 Guided Practice (p. 664) 1. distributive
3. $-6x^3 - 2x^2$ **5.** $8z^3 + 3z^2$ **7.** $30b^3 + 70b^2 + 40b$
9. Step 1: $50 = 2l + 2w$; Step 2: $w = 25 - l$; Step 3: $25l - l^2$

12.3 Practice and Problem Solving (pp. 664–666)
11. $5x^3 - 10x^2$ **13.** $12f^3 - 3f$ **15.** $-g^4 + 6g^3$
17. $5d^4 - 35d^3 + 5d^2$ **19.** $-21y^3 - 28y^2 + 14y$
21. $6w^4 - 36w^3 + 6w^2$ **23.** $-2z - 5$
25. $11m^6 - m^4 - 2m^2$ **27.** $\dfrac{3n^2}{2} - \dfrac{n}{2} + 1$
33. $3x^2 + x$ **35.** $3x^2 + 4x$ **37.** $18mn + 2n^2 - 8n$
39. $5x^2y + 6xy^2 + 8xy$ **41.** $-3mn^2 - 3n^4 - 6n^2$

43. $5c^3 - 35cd^2 + 5cd$ **45. a.** length: $10x + 10$, width: $8x$ **b.** $80x^2 + 80x$; 2400 in.^{2} **c.** *Sample answer:* When $x = 10$, the area is 8800 in.^{2}, which is $3\frac{2}{3}$ times the area when $x = 5$.
47. a. $x(b - x) + b(a - x)$ **b.** $ab - x^2$ **c.** $x(b - x) + b(a - x) = xb - x^2 + ba - bx = bx - bx - x^2 + ab = ab - x^2$ **49.** domain:$-4, 0, 3, 5$; range: $-4, 0, 3, 5$ **51.** domain: 6, 7, 8, 9; range: $-8, 9, 10$ **53.** 10.4 ft **55.** $-3x^2 - 2x + 10$

12.4 Guided Practice (p. 670) 1. F: First, O: Outer, I: Inner, L: Last **3.** $4a^2 + 11a + 6$ **5.** $-8c^2 + 26c - 20$ **7.** $8y^2 - 14y - 4$ **9.** $3a^2 + 22a + 7$ **11.** $50c^2 - 30c + 4$

12.4 Practice and Problem Solving (pp. 670–672)
13. $3x^2 + 13x + 4$ **15.** $12t^2 - 16t - 16$ **17.** $42p^2 - 38p + 8$ **19.** $-24w^2 + 61w + 8$ **21.** $16m^2 - 56m + 49$ **23.** $-11v^2 - 60v + 36$ **25.** $4x^2 + 38x + 48$ **27.** $3x^2 + 32x + 20$ **29.** Above: $2x$, Row 2: 28
31. *Sample answer:* It is similar because you can use the distributive property. It is different because when you multiply two binomials you have to apply the distributive property twice instead of once and because you may also have to combine like terms to simplify the product.
33. $-2x^2 - 2.6x + 6$ **35.** $g^2 + 16.7g - 14$
37. $36h^2 + \frac{129}{8}h + \frac{15}{32}$ **39.** $22a^2 + 86ab - 8b^2$
41. $-12x^2 + 11xy - 2y^2$ **43. a.** $0.52x^2 + 68.2x + 1750$ **b.** 1750 million pounds **c.** 2406 million pounds **45.** The distributive property. *Sample answer:* First I would use the FOIL method to multiply two of the binomials, but then I would use the distributive property to multiply the result by the third binomial because the result will likely have too many terms for the FOIL method to work, and because algebra tiles and tables would be burdensome with the extra computation.
47. a. length: $11 - 2x$, width: $7 - 2x$, height: x; $x > 0$ and $x < 3.5$ **b.** $4x^3 - 36x^2 + 77x$ **c.** 1.4 in.
49. 5^3 **51.** $\frac{1}{x^7}$ **53.** -3 **55.** 12 **57.** $21x^2 - 28x$
59. $-4s^3 - 40s^2$

12.5 Guided Practice (p. 676) 1. *Sample answer:* The power of a quotient property states that the power of a quotient is the power of the numerator divided by the power of the denominator. For example, $\left(\dfrac{2x}{y}\right)^3 = \dfrac{(2x)^3}{y^3} = \dfrac{8x^3}{y^3}$. **3.** $-216x^3$ **5.** $\dfrac{n^2}{49}$
7. 7^6 **9.** y^6 **11.** 1.69×10^{-14} m^2

12.5 Practice and Problem Solving (pp. 677–678)
13. y^6z^6 **15.** $81t^4$ **17.** $6561y^8$ **19.** a^3b^3 **21.** $\dfrac{p^5}{100,000}$
23. $\dfrac{81}{x^4}$ **25.** 5^8 **27.** $\dfrac{1}{a^8}$ **29.** 5.83×10^{18} **31.** 4.84×10^{24} **33.** 4.29×10^{-29} **35.** 1.13×10^{10} square light-years **37.** x^8y^4 **39.** d^6e^8 **41.** $\dfrac{w^{15}}{v^{25}}$ **43.** $-\dfrac{r^3}{s^{12}}$
45. 0.000045 **47.** 6,000,000 **49.** 55,756,800
51. a. about $21.98r^2$ in.^{3} **b.** $\frac{7}{9}$ in. *Sample answer:* The volumes of oil in each cylinder must be equal. The volume in the cylinder with radius $3r$ is about $3.14(3r)^2h$, so $3.14(3r)^2h = 21.98r^2$. Solving for h gives $h = \frac{7}{9}$ inch. **c.** $9d$ in.

53.
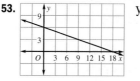
yes

55.
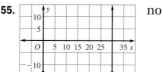
no

57.
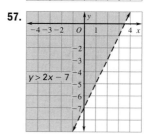

$y > 2x - 7$

59.
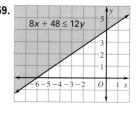

$8x + 48 \le 12y$

61. $x^2 + 4x - 60$ **63.** $6x^2 - 29x + 35$

12.6 Guided Practice (p. 682) 1. *Sample answer:* It is a U-shaped graph that opens upward if the coefficient of the x^2-term is positive and downward if the coefficient of the x^2-term is negative.
3. *Sample answer:*

x	−2	−1	0	1	2
y	13	16	17	16	13

5. *Sample answer:*

x	−4	−3	−2	−1	0
y	0	−9	−12	−9	0

7. Labeled points on the graph represent sample points for a table.

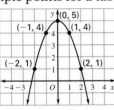

9. maximum   **11.** maximum

12.6 Practice and Problem Solving (pp. 682–684)

13–21. Sample tables are given.

13.

x	−5	−4	−3	−2	−1
y	5	8	9	8	5

15.

x	0	1	2	3	4
y	0	−15	−20	−15	0

17.

x	0	1	2	3	4
y	5	2	1	2	5

19.

x	−5	−3	−1	1	3
y	$11\frac{1}{2}$	$5\frac{1}{2}$	$3\frac{1}{2}$	$5\frac{1}{2}$	$11\frac{1}{2}$

21.

x	0	2	4	6	8
y	−6	0	2	0	−6

25–30. Labeled points on the graph represent sample points for a table.

25.

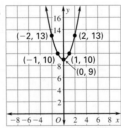

27.

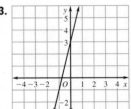

29.

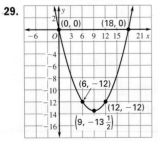

31. maximum   **33.** minimum   **35.** maximum

37. a. about 13 m/sec to 23 m/sec   **b.** above about 31 m/sec

39. maximum;

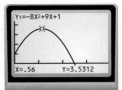

about 3.53

41. maximum;

576

43. minimum;

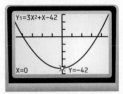

−42

45. *Sample answer:* Substitute $x = 0$ in the equation of the function and solve for y.

47. a.

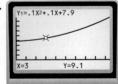

b. 1993
c. 1999. *Sample answer:* The graph gets steeper as the year increases, which means that the amount of increase in water consumption gets larger as the year increases.

51. $\dfrac{5}{b^7}$ **53.**

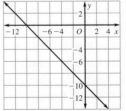

55.

57. $\dfrac{25}{n^2}$

12.6 Technology Activity (p. 685) **1–5.** Sample answers are given.   **1.** Both open up and pass through the origin, but the graph of $y = 4x^2$ is narrower than the graph of $y = x^2$.

3. Both pass through the origin, but the graph of $y = -0.5x^2$ opens downward and is wider than the graph of $y = x^2$. **5.** If a is positive, the graph opens upward. If a is negative, the graph opens downward. Also, the greater the absolute value of a, the narrower the graph.

12.7 Guided Practice (p. 689) 1. exponential decay
3. Labeled points on the graph represent sample points for a table.

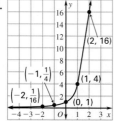

5. Labeled points on the graph represent sample points for a table.

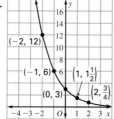

7. Step 1: 25, 12.5, 6.25, 3.125; Step 2: 5 cuts

12.7 Practice and Problem Solving (pp. 689–691)
9–15. Sample tables are given.

9.

x	−2	−1	0	1	2
y	$\frac{2}{9}$	$\frac{2}{3}$	2	6	18

11.

x	−2	−1	0	1	2
y	$\frac{1}{72}$	$\frac{1}{12}$	$\frac{1}{2}$	3	18

13.

x	−2	−1	0	1	2
y	81	27	9	3	1

15.

x	−2	−1	0	1	2
y	40	20	10	5	$\frac{5}{2}$

17.

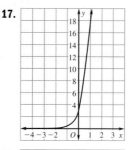

19.

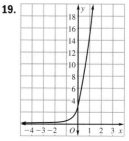

21.

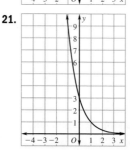

23.

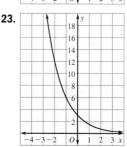

25.

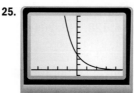

exponential decay

27.

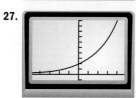

exponential growth

33. $y = 2(3)^x$. *Sample answer:* Since $y = 2(3)^x$ is increasing by powers of 3, it increases faster than $y = 3(2)^x$, which is increasing by powers of 2.
35. a. Exponential decay. *Sample answer:* It is of the form $y = ab^x$ where $a = 500$ and $b = 0.8$. Since $0 < b < 1$, the function represents exponential decay.
b.

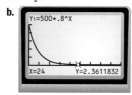

about 2.36 mg

c. after about 6 h; after about 14 h
37. $\sin A = \frac{4}{5}$, $\cos A = \frac{3}{5}$, $\sin B = \frac{3}{5}$, $\cos B = \frac{4}{5}$
39. $\sin J = \frac{5}{13}$, $\cos J = \frac{12}{13}$, $\sin K = \frac{12}{13}$, $\cos K = \frac{5}{13}$
41. 8 **43.** 1

45.

x	−2	−1	0	1	2
y	9	3	1	3	9

47.

x	−2	−1	0	1	2
y	3	−6	−9	−6	3

12.8 Guided Practice (p. 695) **1.** common ratio
3. 5; 23, 28, 33 **5.** 8; 16, 24, 32 **7.** 3; −54, −162,
−486 **9.** *Sample answer:* The coordinates in the
table are not in the correct columns. The first
term is 3, so 1 should go under the *x* and 3 under
the *y*. The second term is 5 so 2 goes under *x* and
5 under *y*, and so on. The points plotted should be
(1, 3), (2, 5), (3, 7), and (4, 9).

12.8 Practice and Problem Solving (pp. 695-697)
11. geometric; common ratio: −2; −32, 64, −128
13. arithmetic; common difference: 15; 64, 79, 94
15. geometric; common ratio: 4; 128, 512, 2048
17. geometric; common ratio: $\frac{1}{5}$; $\frac{4}{5}, \frac{4}{25}, \frac{4}{125}$
19. arithmetic; common difference: 18; 90, 108, 126
21. geometric; common ratio: $\frac{2}{3}$; 48, 32, $21\frac{1}{3}$
23. arithmetic; 24, 38, 52;

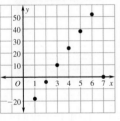

25. arithmetic; 55, 65, 75;

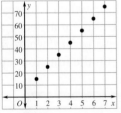

27. geometric; 324, 972, 2916;

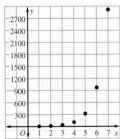

29. a. 36, 45, 54, 63, 72, 81; arithmetic **b.** $9n + 27$
c. 23 carts **31. a.** geometric **b.** 12, 4.8, 1.92, 0.768,
0.3072, 0.12288, 0.049152; after 6 bounces
33. 3, 4.5, 6; $-3 + 1.5(n - 1)$, or $1.5n - 4.5$; 13.5
35. 14,641; 161,051; 1,771,561; 11^{n-1}; 214,358,881
37. 8, 4, 2; $128\left(\frac{1}{2}\right)^{n-1}$; $\frac{1}{2}$ **39. a.** Neither. *Sample*
answer: The difference between consecutive
terms varies, as does the ratio between
consecutive terms. **b.** 21, 34, 55, 89, 144
c.

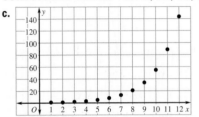

no

41. 6 m **43.** 2

45.

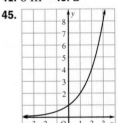

47.

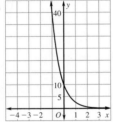

Chapter Review (pp. 698-701) **1.** nonlinear function
3. arithmetic sequence **5.** *Sample answer:* First
find the degree of each term by finding the sum
of the exponents of its variables. The degree of
the polynomial is the greatest degree of its terms.
7. *Sample answer:* It is a U-shaped curve that opens
downward. **9.** $2x^2 + 3x - 10$ **11.** $8x^2 - 2x + 7$
13. $m^2 - 3m - 10$ **15.** $4a^3 + a^2 + a + 10$
17. $-7z^4 + 42z^2$ **19.** $-9p^3 - 72p^2 - 27p$
21. $-25n^2 + 15n^3$ **23.** $b^2 + 9b + 14$
25. $z^2 - 9z + 20$ **27.** $3c^2 - 17c - 6$ **29.** y^6z^6
31. $\frac{x^4}{16}$ **33.** $625k^4$ **35.** z^{12}
37. Labeled points on the graph represent sample
points for a table.

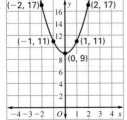

39. Labeled points on the graph represent sample points for a table.

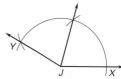

41. arithmetic; common difference: 5; 19, 24, 29
43. geometric; common ratio: 7; 7203; 50,421; 352,947

Focus on Problem Solving (p. 705) 1. a. Row 2: $\pi, 4\pi,$ $9\pi, 16\pi$; Row 3: 4, 16, 36, 64; Row 4: $\frac{\pi}{4}, \frac{\pi}{4}, \frac{\pi}{4}, \frac{\pi}{4}$; the ratios are the same.   **b.** Circle: πr^2; square: $(2r)^2 = 4r^2$; ratio: $\frac{\pi r^2}{4r^2} = \frac{\pi}{4}$; the results are the same.
3. a. \$495; loss   **b.** $500 - 500p^2$; loss. *Sample answer:* p^2 is positive, so $500p^2$ is positive. You are subtracting a positive number from 500, so the result is less than 500.   **5. a.** $S(1) = \frac{1}{2}$, $S(2) = \frac{3}{4}$, $S(3) = \frac{7}{8}$, $S(4) = \frac{15}{16}$ **b.** $S(n) = 1 - \left(\frac{1}{2}\right)^n$

Chapter 13

13.1 Guided Practice (p. 711) 1. complementary
3. neither   **5.** complementary   **7.** $20°$

13.1 Practice and Problem Solving (pp. 711–713)
9. $\angle A$ and $\angle D$ **11.** neither   **13.** complementary
15. supplementary   **17.** $62°$ **19.** $65°$ **21.** $140°$
23. $9°$ **25.** 2 pairs. *Sample answer:* Vertical angles are opposite each other, and meet only at one point. There are only two pairs of angles in this situation for which this is true. Any other pair of angles share a side.   **27.** 9; $54°$ and $54°$ **29.** yes; right   **31.** $m\angle 1 = 180° - x°$, $m\angle 2 = x°$, $m\angle 3 = 180° - x°$; $m\angle 1 = m\angle 3 = 180° - x°$, $m($angle labeled $x°) = m\angle 2 = x°$ **33.** $45°$; $90°$ **37.** Check students' work.   **39.** 10   **41.** -30 **43.** arithmetic

Student Reference (p. 715)
1–3. A ———— B
C ———————— D

1.
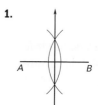
3.
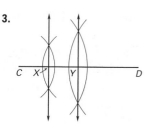

Sample answer: First I copied $\overline{CD}$ and constructed its perpendicular bisector to form two segments with lengths half that of $\overline{CD}$. Then I constructed the perpendicular bisector of one of these segments. The lengths of $\overline{CX}$ and $\overline{XY}$ are one fourth that of $\overline{CD}$.

5.

$\angle XJY$ has twice the measure of $\angle J$.

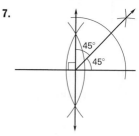

7.

Sample answer: First I drew a segment and constructed its perpendicular bisector, forming four right angles. Then I constructed the angle bisector of one of the right angles to create two $45°$ angles.

13.2 Guided Practice (p. 718)
1. *Sample:*

$\angle 4$ and $\angle 6$, $\angle 3$ and $\angle 5$

3. corresponding   **5.** alternate exterior
7. $m\angle 2 = 115°$, $m\angle 3 = 115°$, $m\angle 4 = 65°$, $m\angle 5 = 65°$, $m\angle 6 = 115°$, $m\angle 7 = 115°$, $m\angle 8 = 65°$

13.2 Practice and Problem Solving (pp. 719–720)

9. alternate exterior **11.** corresponding **13.** $\angle 4$, $\angle 5$, $\angle 8$ **15. a.** alternate interior **b.** Yes. *Sample answer:* Because m and n are parallel, alternate interior angles have the same measure. **c.** $m\angle 1 = m\angle 2 = 72°$. *Sample answer:* $\angle 2$ and the angle with measure 108° are supplementary, so $m\angle 2 = 180° - 108° = 72°$. Also, $m\angle 1 = m\angle 2$ as noted.
17. 5 **19.** $m\angle 1 = 90°$, $m\angle 2 = 115°$, $m\angle 3 = 65°$
21. *Sample:*

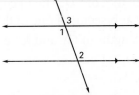

They are the same; they are the measures of corresponding angles formed by a transversal intersecting two parallel lines: $m\angle 1 = m\angle 2$, and $m\angle 1 = m\angle 3$, so $m\angle 2 = m\angle 3$.
23. *Sample:*

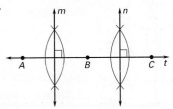

They are parallel. *Sample answer:* Line t is a transversal of lines m and n. Since m and n intersect t in right angles, the corresponding angles have the same measure, so m and n must be parallel. **25.** $\frac{1}{6}$ **27.** $\frac{13}{18}$ **29.** supplementary
31. complementary

13.3 Guided Practice (p. 725)

1. *Sample:*

7. Step 1: 360°; Step 2: 69°; Step 3: 111°

13.3 Practice and Problem Solving (pp. 725–727)

9. 900° **11.** Yes. *Sample answer:* For a triangle, $n = 3$, so $(n - 2) \cdot 180° = (3 - 2) \cdot 180° = 180°$, as expected. **13.** interior: 90°, exterior: 90°
15. interior: 108°, exterior: 72° **17.** interior: 156°, exterior: 24° **19.** 78°

21. *Sample answer:* First use the formula for the measure of an interior angle of a regular n-gon. Then use the fact that the sum of the measures of an interior angle and an exterior angle at each vertex is 180°. **23.** No. *Sample answer:* You can only apply the formula for the measure of an interior angle if the pentagon is regular.
25. $x = 70$, $y = 110$
27. a. 90°, 108°, 120°, 128.6°, 135°, 140°, 144°;

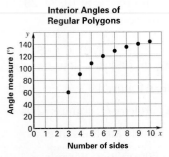

b. decrease
c. No. *Sample answer:* The numbers in the second row of the table are increasing by a smaller amount each time. The last increment was 4, so this increment will be less than 4, which would make $y < 148°$. **29.** 135
31. *Sample:*

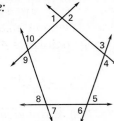

Sample answer: Each combines with the same interior angle to form a straight angle.

33. 11-gon **35.** 17-gon **37.** 5 **39.** -14
41.

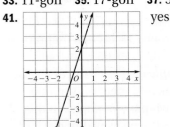

yes

43.

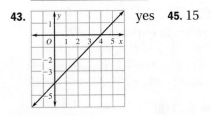

yes **45.** 15

13.4 Guided Practice (p. 731) **1.** image **3.** 3 units left and 4 units down

5.

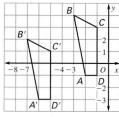

$D'(-3, -7), E'(-4, 3),$
$F'(1, -3)$

13.4 Practice and Problem Solving (pp. 732–733)

7. 5 units left   **9.** $A'(-6, -3), B'(-7, 2), C'(-5, 1),$
$D'(-5, -3);$

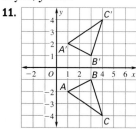

11. *Sample answer:* For the y-coordinates, the translation is $y - 4$, which means that 4 should be subtracted from the original y-coordinates instead of added. The correct image points are $A'(-1, -6)$ and $B'(5, -1)$.

13. Yes. *Sample:*   **15.** Yes. *Sample:*

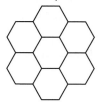

17. *Sample:*

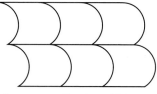

19. Yes. *Sample answer:* Begin with $(2, -7)$. Applying $(x, y) \rightarrow (x - 3, y - 4)$ gives $(-1, -11)$. Then applying $(x, y) \rightarrow (x + 2, y - 6)$ to $(-1, -11)$ gives $(1, -17)$. If instead you first apply $(x, y) \rightarrow (x + 2, y - 6)$ to $(2, -7)$, you get $(4, -13)$. Then applying $(x, y) \rightarrow (x - 3, y - 4)$ to $(4, -13)$ gives $(1, -17)$, which is the same result.   **23.** -60
25. 4 units   **27.** $\sqrt{41}$ units

3. yes; y-axis   **5.** yes; x-axis   **7.** *Sample answer:* For a reflection in the x-axis, the y-coordinate is multiplied by -1. The translation shown is a reflection in the y-axis, in which the x-coordinate is multiplied by -1. The correct image points are $A'(-2, -1)$ and $B'(3, -6)$.

13.5 Practice and Problem Solving (pp. 736–738)

9. yes; y-axis

11.

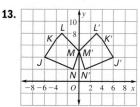

$A'(1, 2), B'(3, 1), C'(4, 4)$

13.

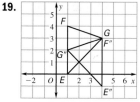

$J'(6, 4), K'(4, 7), L'(3, 8),$
$M'(0, 5), N'(1, 2)$

15. 2 lines of symmetry

17. a.

Row 2: 5, 6, 8

b. They are the same.   **c.** 28 lines of symmetry

19.

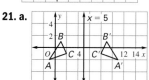

$E''(4, -1), F''(4, 3),$
$G''(1, 2)$

21. a.

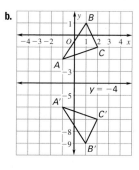

b.

23. *Sample answer:* They are alike in that both are lines of reflection. They are different in that a line of symmetry has the special property that it reflects a figure back onto itself so that the image and the original look exactly the same.

25. 71, −71 **27.** 100, 100 **29.** 66 **31.** 90

33.

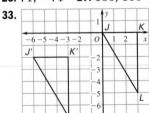

$J'(-6, -2)$,
$K'(-3, -2)$,
$L'(-3, -7)$

13.5 Technology Activity (p. 739) **1.** $D'(4, -1)$, $E'(-2, -5)$, $F'(0, -3)$

13.6 Guided Practice (p. 744) **1.** *Sample answer:* In line symmetry, the image that fits exactly on the original figure is formed by reflecting, or flipping, the figure in a line that passes through the center of the figure, while in rotational symmetry the image is formed by turning the original figure a certain angle measure around its center. **3.** yes; 180° in either direction **5.** no **7.** *Sample answer:* For a 90° clockwise rotation, the coordinate notation is $(x, y) \rightarrow (y, -x)$. The transformation shown is $(x, y) \rightarrow (-y, x)$, which represents a 90° *counterclockwise* rotation. The correct image points are $A'(-5, -3)$, $B'(-4, -2)$, and $C'(-1, -4)$.

13.6 Practice and Problem Solving (pp. 744–746)
9. yes; 180° in either direction

11.

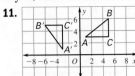

$A'(-3, 1)$, $B'(-6, 5)$, $C'(-3, 5)$

13.

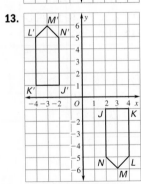

$J'(-2, 1)$, $K'(-4, 1)$, $L'(-4, 5)$, $M'(-3, 6)$, $N'(-2, 5)$

15. yes; 90° and 180° in either direction **17. a.** Yes. *Sample answer:* Each rotation of 72° will produce an image that fits the original. **b.** 144°
19. a. Row 1: 6, 8, 10; Row 2: 60°, 120°, 180°; 45°, 90°, 135°, 180°; 36°, 72°, 108°, 144°, 180° **b.** It is twice the number of angles of rotation. **c.** sides: 16; angles of rotation: 22.5°, 45°, 67.5°, 90°, 112.5°, 135°, 157.5°, 180°

21.

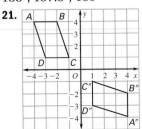

$A''(4, -4)$, $B''(4, -2)$, $C''(1, -1)$, $D''(1, -3)$

23. *Sample:*

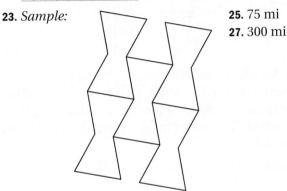

25. 75 mi
27. 300 mi

29.

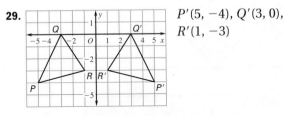

$P'(5, -4)$, $Q'(3, 0)$, $R'(1, -3)$

13.7 Guided Practice (p. 749) **1.** similar

3.

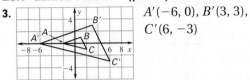

$A'(-6, 0)$, $B'(3, 3)$, $C'(6, -3)$

13.7 Practice and Problem Solving (pp. 750–751)

5.

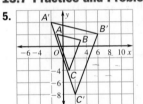

$A'(-2, 4)$, $B'(6, 2)$, $C'(2, -8)$

7. 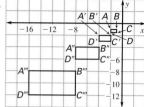 $P'(-3, 1), Q'(1, 1),$ $R'(1, 0), S'(-3, 0)$

9. 2   **11a–b.**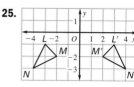

13. a. $A''(-1, 2), B''(2, 0), C''(1, -2);$

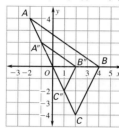 **b.** 0.5   **c.** Yes. *Sample answer:* Since dilating a figure just multiplies the coordinates by the scale factor, and multiplication is commutative, it does not matter in what order you apply multiple scale factors.

15. 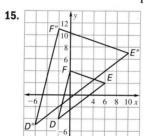 $D''(-6, -5), E''(10, 7),$ $F''(-2, 11)$

19. 12   **21.** 1   **23.** $t^4 - 2t - 3$

25. 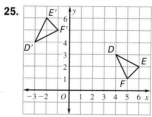 $D'(-3, 4), E'(-2, 6),$ $F'(-1, 5)$

Chapter Review (pp. 752–755) **1.** 90°; 180°
3. $P'(x, -y); P'(-x, -y); P'(2x, 2y)$ **5.** alternate interior angles   **7.** 14°   **9.** 59°   **11.** alternate interior   **13.** alternate interior   **15.** 115°   **17.** 65°
19. 135°, 45°   **21.** 152.3°, 27.7°

23. 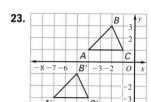 $A'(-7, -3), B'(-5, -1),$ $C'(-4, -3)$

25. 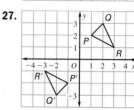 $L'(3, -1), M'(2, -2),$ $N'(4, -3)$

27. 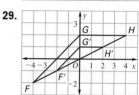 $P'(-1, -2), Q'(-2, -3),$ $R'(-3, -1)$

29. 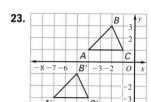 $F'(-2, -1), G'(0, 1),$ $H'(2, 1)$

Skills Review Handbook

Place Value and Rounding (p. 770) **1.** tens, 50; 60
3. hundreds, 900; 900   **5.** thousands, 6000; 7000
7. ten thousands, 40,000; 40,000   **9.** hundredths, 0.05; 10,064.66   **11.** thousandths, 0.009; 112.350
13. hundred thousands, 400,000; 500,000
15. hundreds, 100; 9200

Estimating Sums and Differences (p. 771)
1. 10,000   **3.** 60,000   **5.** 12,000   **7.** 5000   **9.** 30,000
11. 200,000   **13.** 100,000

Estimating Products and Quotients (p. 772)
1–15. Estimates may vary.   **1.** 42,000; 56,000
3. 360,000; 500,000   **5.** 30; 50   **7.** 5; 7   **9.** 10,000;
18,000   **11.** 24,000; 35,000   **13.** 200; 500
15. 500; 700

Comparing and Ordering Decimals (p. 773) **1.** >
3. =   **5.** >   **7.** 1.29, 1.3, 1.9, 2.19   **9.** 0.49, 0.5, 0.52, 0.55   **11.** 6.19, 6.21, 6.3, 6.32

Adding and Subtracting Decimals (p. 774) **1.** 6.4
3. 4.2   **5.** 2.24   **7.** 18.22   **9.** 151.57   **11.** 0.24
13. 9.214   **15.** 0.75

Multiplying Decimals (p. 775) **1.** 14.16 **3.** 16
5. 1.015 **7.** 0.0432 **9.** 0.0608 **11.** 29.82 **13.** 6.195
15. 13.0968

Dividing Decimals (p. 776) **1.** 4 **3.** 5 **5.** 19 **7.** 2.1
9. 0.9 **11.** 1.3 **13.** 14 **15.** 18 **17.** 134 **19.** 23.14

Modeling Fractions (p. 777) **1.** $\frac{1}{3}$ **3.** $\frac{3}{7}$ **5.** $\frac{5}{8}$ **7.** $2\frac{2}{5}$
9. $1\frac{5}{6}$ **11.** $2\frac{1}{3}$

Mixed Numbers and Improper Fractions (p. 778)
1. $\frac{19}{10}$ **3.** $\frac{55}{6}$ **5.** $\frac{25}{7}$ **7.** $\frac{19}{8}$ **9.** $\frac{20}{3}$ **11.** $\frac{31}{4}$ **13.** $\frac{171}{20}$
15. $\frac{142}{9}$ **17.** $5\frac{1}{2}$ **19.** $3\frac{2}{9}$ **21.** $6\frac{1}{6}$ **23.** $3\frac{7}{8}$ **25.** $9\frac{7}{12}$

Adding and Subtracting Fractions (p. 779) **1.** $\frac{4}{5}$ **3.** $\frac{3}{7}$
5. $\frac{1}{11}$ **7.** $\frac{13}{14}$ **9.** $\frac{1}{6}$ **11.** $\frac{13}{20}$ **13.** $1\frac{8}{13}$ **15.** $1\frac{1}{18}$ **17.** 1
19. $1\frac{1}{3}$

Multiplying Fractions and Whole Numbers (p. 780)
1. 3 **3.** 14 **5.** $10\frac{2}{7}$ **7.** 12 **9.** $2\frac{1}{4}$ **11.** $8\frac{4}{7}$ **13.** 15
15. 9

Reading Bar Graphs (p. 781) **1.** 10 students
3. 4 more students **5.** pancakes and waffles
7. bagel, pancakes, waffles, muffin

Reading Line Graphs (p. 782) **1.** 8°F **3.** between
3 P.M. and 4 P.M.; 1°F **5.** between days 2 and 3
7. 15 mm

Reading Circle Graphs (p. 783) **1.** 5 homes
3. 7 homes **5.** 6 people **7.** 71 people

Venn Diagrams and Logical Reasoning (p. 784)
1.
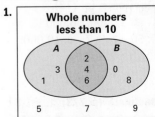

3. a. False. *Sample answer:* A counterexample is 2,
which is a factor of 20 that is less than 10 and is
less than 5. **b.** True. *Sample answer:* They are 2, 4,
and 6.

Basic Geometric Figures (p. 785) **1.** 16 in. **3.** 30 ft
5. Check students' drawings; 12 cm. **7.** Check
students' drawings; 10 in.

Units of Length (p. 786) **1.** 60 **3.** 90,000 **5.** 7

Using a Ruler (p. 787) **1–15.** Check students' work.

Measuring Lengths (p. 788) **1.** $2\frac{1}{8}$ in., 5.4 cm
3. $1\frac{1}{2}$ in.

Units of Area and Volume (p. 789) **1.** 16 mi^2
3. 1.96 cm^2 **5.** 1331 ft^3 **7.** 125 cm^3

Units of Weight and Mass (p. 790) **1.** > **3.** = **5.** >
7. $1\frac{1}{4}$ lb **9.** $2\frac{1}{2}$ lb

Units of Capacity (p. 791) **1.** < **3.** < **5.** > **7.** $3\frac{1}{4}$ c
9. $4\frac{1}{2}$ c

Using a Protractor (p. 792) **1.** 38° **3.** 84°
5.   **7.**
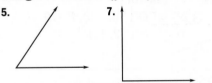

Classifying Angles (p. 793) **1.** 92°; obtuse **3.** 61°;
acute **5.** 126°; obtuse

Using a Compass (p. 794) **1–7.** Check students'
work.

Draw a Diagram (p. 795) **1.** 4 ft **3.** 336 ft^2

Look for a Pattern (p. 796) **1.** 9:05 **3.** 204 cans

Guess, Check, and Revise (p. 797) **1.** 16 weeks
3. 11 white spruce and 6 blue spruce **5.** 26 ft

Act It Out (p. 798) **1.** Rosa: 15 CDs, Kim: 10 CDs
3. seat 1

Make a List or Table (p. 799) **1.** 6 matches
3. Row 2: $5, $10, $15, $20, $25, $30, $35, $40, $45;
140 h or less

Solve a Simpler or Related Problem (p. 800)
1. 26 people **3.** 16,384; 32,767

Work Backward (p. 801) **1.** 1:20 P.M. **3.** 320 pages

Break into Parts (p. 802) **1.** 3 ways **3.** 11 omelets

Extra Practice

Chapter 1 (p. 803) **1.** 8 **3.** 9 **5.** 1 to the eighth power; $1 \cdot 1 \cdot 1 \cdot 1 \cdot 1 \cdot 1 \cdot 1 \cdot 1$; 1 **7.** 5 to the third power, or 5 cubed; $5 \cdot 5 \cdot 5$; 125 **9.** 14 **11.** 180

13.  $-7, -3, 0, 4, 9$

15. $-67, -51, -34, -19$

17. 43, -43 **19.** 3, 3 **21.** 39 **23.** 22 **25.** 23 **27.** 19 **29.** 36 **31.** -3 **33.** (1, 1) **35.** (0, 0) **37.** (2, -2)

39–41. **39.** Quadrant I **41.** Quadrant III

Chapter 2 (p. 804)

1. $(17 + 9) + 3$
$= (9 + 17) + 3$ [commutative property of addition]
$= 9 + (17 + 3)$ [associative property of addition]
$= 9 + 20$ [Add 17 and 3.]
$= 29$ [Add 9 and 20.]

3. $0 + 8 \cdot 1$
$= 0 + (8 \cdot 1)$ [Use order of operations.]
$= 0 + 8$ [identity property of multiplication]
$= 8$ [identity property of addition]

5. -280 **7.** 12 **9.** $-44m$ **11.** $b + 21$ **13.** identity property of addition **15.** associative property of multiplication **17.** 54 **19.** 42 **21.** $-15a - 9$ **23.** $12 - 18z$ **25.** y **27.** $5c + 8$ **29.** $8b$ **31.** $2p - 15$ **33.** 5 **35.** 11 **37.** 8 **39.** -22 **41.** 109 **43.** -32 **45.** -26 **47.** 7 **49.** -144 **51.** -350 **53.** -11.14 **55.** -18.13 **57.** 14.7 **59.** -6.83

Chapter 3 (p. 805) **1.** 12 **3.** 3 **5.** -136 **7.** 81 **9.** -2 **11.** 1 **13.** 1 **15.** 3 **17.** -10 **19.** 3 **21.** 2 **23.** no solution **25.** all real numbers **27.** $10 + 7x = 5x - 6$; -8 **29.** $x \geq -3$ **31.** $x < -4$

33. $a < 7$;

35. $p \geq -3$;

37. $b \leq 48$;

39. $k > 0.3$;

41. $b \leq 104$;

43. $x \geq -8$;

45. $d < -8$;

47. $t > -4$;

49. $3x \leq 18$; $x \leq 6$ **51.** $\dfrac{x}{-2} < 10$; $x > -20$

53. $w > 3$;

55. $z < -6$;

57. $c \leq 22$;

59. $r > 6$;

Chapter 4 (p. 806) **1.** composite **3.** prime **5.** $2^3 \cdot 3^2$ **7.** $2^5 \cdot 3$ **9.** 3; no **11.** 2; no **13.** $4y$ **15.** $2s$ **17.** $\dfrac{3}{16}$ **19.** $\dfrac{7}{11}$ **21.** $\dfrac{2}{3m}$ **23.** $\dfrac{19ab}{2c}$ **25.** 30 **27.** 480 **29.** $90c^2$ **31.** $80n^2p$ **33.** 6^{14} **35.** 4^6 **37.** $20c^5$ **39.** $6a^3$ **41.** $\dfrac{1}{18^4}$ **43.** s^3 **45.** 1.6×10^7 **47.** 4×10^{-5} **49.** 823,000,000 **51.** 0.0021

Chapter 5 (p. 807) **1.** *Sample answer:* $\dfrac{-4}{1}$ or $\dfrac{4}{-1}$ **3.** *Sample answer:* $\dfrac{53}{16}$ **5.** 0.6 **7.** -6.52 **9.** $\dfrac{17}{50}$ **11.** $9\dfrac{27}{100}$ **13.** $\dfrac{5}{11}$ **15.** $-7\dfrac{1}{5}$ **17.** $-1\dfrac{1}{28}$ **19.** $3\dfrac{2}{33}$ **21.** $\dfrac{3w}{20}$ **23.** $-\dfrac{z}{28}$ **25.** $\dfrac{5}{42}$ **27.** $10\dfrac{1}{2}$ **29.** $\dfrac{3}{7}$ **31.** $-1\dfrac{16}{45}$ **33.** 21 **35.** 77 **37.** $-2\dfrac{1}{3}$ **39.** 0.25 **41.** $p < 18$ **43.** $z \leq \dfrac{5}{6}$

Chapter 6 (p. 808) **1.** $\dfrac{\$1.74}{1 \text{ gal}}$ **3.** $\dfrac{3 \text{ L}}{1 \text{ day}}$ **5.** 264,000 **7.** 26,400 **9.** 16 **11.** 4 **13.** 32 **15.** 5 **17.** 3 **19.** 84 **21.** $\dfrac{5}{3}$ **23.** 22 in. **25.** 50 mi **27.** 12.5 mi **29.** $\dfrac{1}{3}$ **31.** $\dfrac{2}{3}$ **33.** 90 groups

Chapter 7 (p. 809) **1.** $\dfrac{43}{100}$ **3.** 65% **5.** 120 **7.** 57
9. 20% **11.** 81 **13.** 4.5% **15.** 0.07 **17.** 58.$\overline{3}$%
19. 187.5% **21.** 325 **23.** 260 **25.** increase; 55%
27. decrease; 75% **29.** $234 **31.** $16.80
33. $68.25 **35.** 9 y

Chapter 8 (p. 810)

1.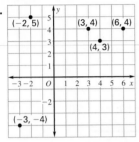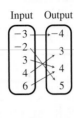

Yes; every input is paired with exactly one
output.

3. 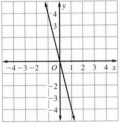 yes

5. 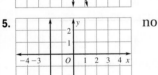 no

7. x-intercept: 10, y-intercept: -5;

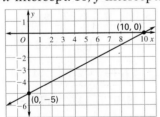

9. x-intercept: -5, y-intercept: -3;

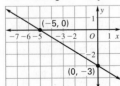

11. *Sample answer:* $(0, -4)$, $(5, -4)$; 0 **13.** *Sample*
answer: $(0, -3)$, $(3, -2)$; $\dfrac{1}{3}$ **15.** $-\dfrac{3}{4}$ **17.** 1

19. slope: 4, y-intercept: -1;

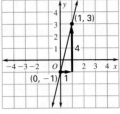

21. slope: 5, y-intercept: -2;

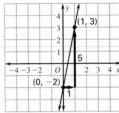

23. slope: $\dfrac{1}{4}$, y-intercept: 2;

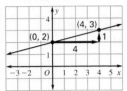

25. slope: $-\dfrac{2}{5}$, y-intercept: 3;

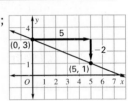

27. $y = -4x - 2$ **29.** $y = \dfrac{7}{3}x - 1$

31. 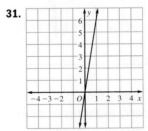 **33.**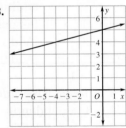

35. $(2, -5)$ **37.** $(-3, -6)$

39. 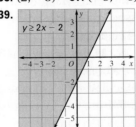 **41.**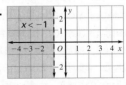

Chapter 9 (p. 811) **1.** ± 7 **3.** ± 18 **5.** ± 11 **7.** ± 6
9. $9\sqrt{2}$ **11.** $\dfrac{4a\sqrt{2}}{9}$ **13.** 40 **15.** $\sqrt{65}$

17. $\frac{46}{9}, 2\sqrt{7}, \sqrt{30}, 5.8$ **19.** $-6.9, -3\sqrt{5}, -\frac{19}{3}, -\sqrt{36}$
21. $(5, 6); 2\sqrt{17}$ units   **23.** $(-1, 3.5); \sqrt{229}$ units
25. $x = 5\sqrt{3}, y = 10$ **27.** $x = 3, y = 3\sqrt{2}$ **29.** 2.5
31. 15.0   **33.** 3.9   **35.** 15.5

Chapter 10 (p. 812) **1.** 25; obtuse   **3.** 35; right
5. 42   **7.** 119   **9.** 44 in.^{2} **11.** 90 ft^2 **13.** 3018 in.^{2},
195 in.   **15.** 616 cm^2, 88 cm
17. *Sample answer:*
452 ft^2

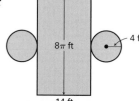

19. *Sample answer:*
312 cm^2

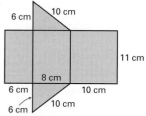

21. 552 yd^2 **23.** 894 ft^2 **25.** 251 cm^3 **27.** 96 yd^3

Chapter 11 (p. 813)

1.
```
1 | 2
2 | 1 2 3 5
3 | 1 4 5 6
4 | 0 2 2
   Key: 1 | 2 = 12
```

Sample:

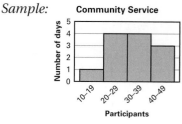

3. Numerical. *Sample answer:* If the data values are few, I might use a stem-and-leaf plot so that I can view all the values. If there are many data values, I might use a histogram, since I can divide the data into equal intervals by test score, or a box-and-whisker plot, since I can calculate the extremes and the quartiles for the data. Either of these displays would provide a convenient pictorial representation.   **5.** Yes. *Sample answer:* It suggests that a person should think that a school dance is a good thing. An alternative question is, "Do you think that a school dance should or should not be held?"   **7.** about 8500 townspeople

9. 1   **11.** 2   **13.** 156   **15.** 8   **17.** 495   **19.** 1   **21.** $\frac{11}{20}$

Chapter 12 (p. 814) **1.** $-3x + 6$ **3.** $y^2 - 2y + 18$
5. $-x^2 + 3x + 16$ **7.** $-2w^3 + 4w^2 + 4w + 14$
9. $6g^4 + 4g^3 - 10g^2 + 2$ **11.** $d^3 + 7$ **13.** $32f^2 + 36f$
15. $-2t^3 + 6t^2 - 20t$ **17.** $-6n + 7$ **19.** $5z^4 - z^3 - 3z^2$ **21.** $3x^2 - 10x - 8$ **23.** $25a^2 + 30a + 9$
25. $-27g^3$ **27.** $\frac{1}{6^{20}}$ **29.** 9.11×10^{-20} **31.** 1.96×10^8

33. *Sample answer:*

x	−2	−1	0	1	2
y	16	7	4	7	16

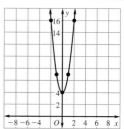

35. *Sample answer:*

x	−4	−2	0	2	4
y	−3	3	5	3	−3

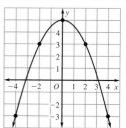

37.

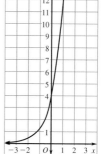

39.

41. arithmetic; common difference: 4; 7, 11, 15
43. geometric; common ratio: $\frac{1}{2}$; 14, 7, $3\frac{1}{2}$

Chapter 13 (p. 815) **1.** complementary
3. supplementary   **5.** corresponding   **7.** alternate exterior   **9.** interior: 128.6°, exterior: 51.4°
11. interior: 150°, exterior: 30°

13. $A'(2, -4)$, $B'(1, -1)$, $C'(3, 1)$;

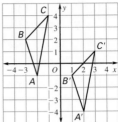

15. $A'(-3, 1)$, $B'(2, 2)$, $C'(-1, 4)$;

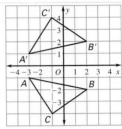

17. no   **19.** yes; 180° in either direction

21. $A'(-4, 4)$, $B'(2, 6)$, $C'(2, -2)$, $D'(-4, -2)$;

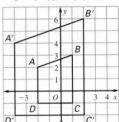